MW00999961

THE OXFORD HANDBOOK OF

EDGAR ALLAN POE

THE OXFORD HANDBOOK OF

EDGAR ALLAN POE

Edited by

J. GERALD KENNEDY

and

SCOTT PEEPLES

Editorial Assistant

CALEB DOAN

Oxford University Press is a department of the University of Oxford. It furthers the University's objective of excellence in research, scholarship, and education by publishing worldwide. Oxford is a registered trade mark of Oxford University Press in the UK and certain other countries.

Published in the United States of America by Oxford University Press
198 Madison Avenue, New York, NY 10016, United States of America.

© Oxford University Press 2019

All rights reserved. No part of this publication may be reproduced, stored in a retrieval system, or transmitted, in any form or by any means, without the prior permission in writing of Oxford University Press, or as expressly permitted by law, by license, or under terms agreed with the appropriate reproduction rights organization. Inquiries concerning reproduction outside the scope of the above should be sent to the Rights Department, Oxford University Press, at the address above.

You must not circulate this work in any other form
and you must impose this same condition on any acquirer.

Library of Congress Cataloging-in-Publication Data
Names: Kennedy, J. Gerald, editor. | Peeples, Scott, editor.
Title: The Oxford handbook of Edgar Allan Poe / edited by J. Gerald Kennedy and Scott Peeples.
Description: New York, NY : Oxford University Press, 2019. | Includes bibliographical references and index.
Identifiers: LCCN 2018019391 | ISBN 9780190641870 (hardcover: acid-free paper)
Subjects: LCSH: Poe, Edgar Allan, 1809–1849—Criticism and interpretation—Handbooks, manuals, etc.
Classification: LCC PS2638 .O94 2018 | DDC 818/.309—dc23
LC record available at https://lccn.loc.gov/2018019391

1 3 5 7 9 8 6 4 2

Printed by Sheridan Books, Inc., United States of America

Contents

Abbreviations of Poe's Works

H Poe, Edgar Allan. *The Complete Works of Edgar Allan Poe*. Edited by James A. Harrison. 17 vols. New York: AMS Press, [1902] 1965.

M Poe, Edgar Allan. *Collected Works of Edgar Allan Poe*. Edited by Thomas Ollive Mabbott. 3 vols. Cambridge MA: Belknap Press of Harvard University Press, 1969–1978.

P Poe, Edgar Allan. *Collected Writings of Edgar Allan Poe*. Edited by Burton R. Pollin. 5 vols. New York: Gordian Press, 1981–1997.

CL Poe, Edgar Allan. *The Collected Letters of Edgar Allan Poe*. Third edition. Edited by John Ward Ostrom; revised, corrected, and expanded by Burton R. Pollin and Jeffrey A. Savoye. 2 vols. New York: Gordian Press, 2008.

L1 Poe, Edgar Allan. *Eureka*. Edited by Stuart Levine and Susan F. Levine. Urbana: University of Illinois Press, 2004.

L2 Poe, Edgar Allan. *Critical Theory: The Major Documents*. Edited by Stuart Levine and Susan F. Levine. Urbana: University of Illinois Press, 2009.

ER Poe, Edgar Allan. *Essays and Reviews*. Edited by G. R. Thompson. New York: Library of America, 1984.

PL *The Poe Log: A Documentary Life of Edgar Allan Poe, 1809–1849*. Edited by Dwight Thomas and David K. Jackson, Boston: G. K. Hall, 1987.

Contributors

Branka Arsić is Charles and Lynn Zhang Professor of English and Comparative Literature at Columbia University. She is the author of *Bird Relics: Grief and Vitalism in Thoreau* (2016), which was awarded the MLA James Russell Lowell Prize for the most outstanding book of 2016. She has also written *On Leaving: A Reading in Emerson* (2010) and a book on Melville entitled *Passive Constitutions or 7½ Times Bartleby* (2007). She is now working on a volume on Poe, science, and vitalism.

Jacob Rama Berman is Associate Professor of English at Louisiana State University and the author of *American Arabesque: Arabs, Islam, and the Nineteenth Century Imaginary* (2012). His work has appeared in *American Literature, English Studies in Canada, J19*, and *ALH*, as well as the *Los Angeles Review of Books*.

Barbara Cantalupo is Professor of English at the Pennsylvania State University and editor of *The Edgar Allan Poe Review* and of Lehigh University Press's *Perspectives on Poe* series. Her monograph, *Poe and the Visual Arts* (2014), won the PSA's Patrick F. Quinn Award; her edited books include *Poe's Pervasive Influence* (2012), *Emma Wolf's Short Stories in the Smart Set* (2010), and *Emma Wolf's Other Things Being Equal* (2017). She is currently working with Lori Harrison-Kahan on a reissue of Emma Wolf's novel, *Heirs of Yesterday*, and with Richard Kopley on an edited collection from the 2015 Poe conference, *Influencing Poe*.

Lauren Coats is Associate Professor of English and Director of the Digital Scholarship Lab at Louisiana State University. She is completing a collaborative digital edition of *The Broadway Journal*, which Poe once edited and owned. She is founding editor of the digital *Archive Journal* and has published work in *J19* and *PMLA* and through Lehigh University Press Digital Scholarly Editions. She is completing a book manuscript on textual practices and genres for mapping North American spaces in the late eighteenth and early nineteenth centuries.

Michael C. Cohen is Associate Professor of English at UCLA. He is the author of *The Social Lives of Poems in Nineteenth-Century America* (2015), named a *Choice* Outstanding Academic Title for 2016, and coeditor of *The Poetry of Charles Brockden Brown* (forthcoming). He has published many essays on nineteenth-century poetry and edited a special issue of *Nineteenth-Century Literature* on the ballad and historical poetics.

Jonathan Elmer is Professor of English at Indiana University, where he is also Director of the College Arts and Humanities Institute. From 2015 to 2017, he was Artistic Director of the Chicago Humanities Festival. He is the author of two monographs: *Reading at the Social Limit: Affect, Mass Culture, and Edgar Allan Poe* (1995) and *On Lingering and Being Last: Race and Sovereignty in the New World* (2008).

William E. Engel is the Nick B. Williams Professor of Literature at Sewanee, The University of the South. He is the author of five books, including *Early Modern Poetics in Melville and Poe* (2013), and he coedited *The Memory Arts in Renaissance England: A Critical Anthology* (2016). He has served on the Executive Committee of the Poe Studies Association and the PSA's Gargano and Quinn Awards Committee and is on the Editorial Board of *Renaissance Quarterly.*

Emron Esplin is an Associate Professor of US literature and inter-American literary studies in the English Department at Brigham Young University. He is the editor, with Margarida Vale de Gato, of *Translated Poe* (2014) and the author of *Borges's Poe: The Influence and Reinvention of Edgar Allan Poe in Spanish America* (2016). With Jana Argersinger, he currently coedits *Poe Studies: History, Theory, Interpretation*. He received the 2013 James W. Gargano Award from the Poe Studies Association for his essay "Borges's Philosophy of Poe's Composition," published in *Comparative Literature Studies.*

Paul Gilmore, Administrative Dean of the Honors College at Rutgers University–New Brunswick, is the author of *The Genuine Article: Race, Mass Culture, and American Literary Manhood* (2001) and *Aesthetic Materialism: Electricity and American Romanticism* (2009). He has published articles in leading literary journals on subjects as varied as blackface minstrelsy, telegraphy, and early brain science.

Lesley Ginsberg is Professor of English at the University of Colorado, Colorado Springs. She has published articles in *American Literature, Studies in American Fiction*, and *The Nathaniel Hawthorne Review* and essays in *The Children's Table: Childhood Studies and the Humanities* (2012) and *Ecogothic in Nineteenth-Century American Literature* (2018). Other essays on Poe appear in *American Gothic: New Interventions in a National Narrative* (1998) and *Approaches to Teaching Poe's Prose and Poetry* (2008). She is coeditor of *Romantic Education in Nineteenth-Century American Literature: National and Transatlantic Contexts* (2014).

Paul Grimstad is the author of *Experience and Experimental Writing: Literary Pragmatism from Emerson to the Jameses* (2013). His essays and reviews have appeared in *Bookforum*, the *London Review of Books n+1*, the *New Republic*, the *New Yorker*, the *Paris Review*, and the *Times Literary Supplement* and *Raritan*, among other journals and magazines. He has taught literature at NYU, Yale, and Columbia universities.

John Gruesser is Senior Research Scholar at Sam Houston State University and Past President of the Poe Studies Association. He has authored five books, including *Race, Gender and Empire in American Detective Fiction* (2013), and edited five others, including *The Unruly Voice: Rediscovering Pauline Elizabeth Hopkins* (1996), *The Black Sleuth* by John E. Bruce (2002), *A Century of Detection: Twenty Great Mystery Stories 1841–1940* (2010), and (with Hanna Wallinger) *The Hindered Hand; Or, the Reign of the Repressionist* by Sutton E. Griggs (2017). His *Edgar Allan Poe and His Nineteenth-Century American Counterparts* will appear in 2019.

Alexander Hammond is Associate Professor Emeritus in the Department of English at Washington State University. An editor and coeditor of *Poe Studies* from 1975 through 2008, he has focused his scholarship on Edgar Allan Poe's literary career, especially his early fiction. An honorary member of the Poe Studies Association, he currently serves as consulting editor on *Poe Studies: History, Theory, Interpretation* and board member on the *Edgar Allan Poe Review*. He is doing research for a gathering of his essays and papers on Poe's Folio Club tales and working on a guide to WSU's Palmer C. Holt Poe Source Collection.

Paul Hurh is Associate Professor of English at the University of Arizona. He is the author of *American Terror: The Feeling of Thinking in Edwards, Poe, and Melville* (2015). His work focuses on questions of literary aesthetics, philosophy, and intellectual history, and his essays have appeared in *Poe Studies, Nineteenth-Century Literature, Style,* and *Novel.*

James M. Hutchisson is Professor of English at The Citadel and author of two literary biographies, *Poe* (2005) and *Ernest Hemingway: A New Life* (2016). He is also the editor of *Edgar Allan Poe: Beyond Gothicism* (2011) and author of a cultural history, *Renaissance in Charleston* (2003) as well as a scholarly study, *The Rise of Sinclair Lewis, 1920–1930* (1996). He has also edited *Conversations with Paul Auster* (2013) and published a cultural biography, *DuBose Heyward: A Charleston Gentleman and the World of* Porgy and Bess (2000).

Virginia Jackson is UCI Endowed Chair of Rhetoric and Critical Theory in the Departments of English and Comparative Literature at UC Irvine. She is the author of *Dickinson's Misery: A Theory of Lyric Reading* (2005), which won the Christian Gauss Prize and the MLA Prize for a First Book. She is the editor of *On Periodization: Selected Essays from the English Institute* (2010), and, with Yopie Prins, coeditor of *The Lyric Theory Reader: A Critical Anthology* (2014). Her next book, *Before Modernism: The Invention of American Poetry* is forthcoming.

Paul Christian Jones is the Sam and Susan Crowl Professor of English at Ohio University. He is the author of two books, *Unwelcome Voices: Subversive Fiction in the Antebellum South* (2005) and *Against the Gallows: Antebellum American Writers and the Movement to Abolish Capital Punishment* (2011), and numerous journal articles on nineteenth-century American literature. His current book project examines Poe's work through the lens of queer temporality.

J. Gerald Kennedy, volume coeditor, is Boyd Professor of English, Louisiana State University, and author of *Strange Nation: Literary Nationalism and Cultural Conflict* *in the Age of Poe* (2016) and *Poe, Death, and the Life of Writing* (1987). Kennedy also published *The Narrative of Arthur Gordon Pym and the Abyss of Interpretation* (1993). He later edited *The Historical Guide to Edgar Allan Poe* (2001) and the *Portable Edgar Allan Poe* (2006). With Liliane Weissberg, he coedited *Romancing the Shadow: Poe and Race* (2001), and with Jerome McGann, he coedited *Poe and the Remapping of Antebellum Print Culture* (2012).

Richard Kopley is Distinguished Professor of English, Emeritus, from Penn State DuBois. His books include *The Threads of The Scarlet Letter* (2003), *Edgar Allan Poe and the Dupin Mysteries* (2008), and the forthcoming *The Formal Center in Literature: Explorations from Poe to the Present*. His work-in-progress is a biography of Poe. He also publishes short stories and children's picture books.

Maurice S. Lee is Chair and Professor of English at Boston University, where his work focuses on nineteenth-century American literature. His essays on Poe have appeared in *American Literature*, *Poe and the Remapping Antebellum Culture* (2012) and *A Companion to Crime Fiction* (2012). Chapters on Poe also appear in his books *Slavery, Philosophy, and American Literature*, 1830–1860 (2005) and *Uncertain Chances: Science, Skepticism, and Belief in Nineteenth-Century America Literature* (2012).

Kent P. Ljungquist, Emeritus Professor of English at Worcester Polytechnic Institute, has written extensively on Poe's contributions to and reception in American magazines and newspapers. He is the author of *The Grand and the Fair: Poe's Landscape Aesthetics and Pictorial Techniques* (1985), coeditor of James Fenimore Cooper's *The Deerslayer* (1998), and editor of *Conversations with Stanley Kunitz* (2013). He has done bibliographical and critical work on Poe's contemporaries and has edited several reference works on American writers.

Stacey Margolis, Professor of English at the University of Utah, is author of *The Public Life of Privacy in Nineteenth-Century American Literature* (2005) and *Fictions of Mass Democracy in Nineteenth-Century America* (2015). She is coeditor (with Elizabeth Duquette) of *J19: the Journal of Nineteenth-Century Americanists*. Her current book project concerns contemporary fiction and intergenerational justice.

Bruce Mills is Professor of English at Kalamazoo College in Michigan. He is the author of *Poe, Fuller, and the Mesmeric Arts: Transition States in the American Renaissance* (2006), a book examining the impact of early notions of the unconscious and receptive states of mind on antebellum literary form and social reform. He is also the author of *Cultural Reformations: Lydia Maria Child and the Literature of Reform* (1994) and the editor of Child's *Letters from New York*.

Agnieszka Soltysik Monnet is Professor of American Literature and codirector of the MA Specialization Program in American Studies at the University of Lausanne. Her publications include *The Poetics and Politics of the American Gothic: Gender and Slavery in Nineteenth Century American Literature* (2010), *The Gothic in Contemporary Literature and Popular Culture* (2012), *War Gothic* (coedited with Steffen Hantke, 2016), and *Neoliberal Gothic: International Gothic in the Neoliberal Age* (coedited with Linnie Blake, 2017). She has also published articles on feminism and queer theory, war writing, horror, and melodrama, among many other topics.

Sean Moreland teaches in the English Department at the University of Ottawa. His essays on Gothic, horror, and weird fiction in its literary, cinematic, and sequential art guises have appeared in many collections and journals, and he blogs about related subjects. He edited the essay collections *The Lovecraftian Poe* (2017) and the forthcoming *New Directions in Supernatural Horror Literature: The Critical Legacy of H. P. Lovecraft* (2018). He is working on a monograph tentatively titled *Repulsive Influences: A Historical Poetics of Atomic Horror.*

Carl Ostrowski is Professor of English at Middle Tennessee State University. He is the author of *Literature and Criminal Justice in Antebellum America* (2016). He has published articles on Edgar Allan Poe, Walt Whitman, George Lippard, and other nineteenth-century American authors in various journals, including *ESQ, Modern Language Studies*, and *African American Literature.* He is editor of the forthcoming *Edgar Allan Poe: Tales, Poems, and Critical Writings.*

Scott Peeples, volume coeditor, is Professor of English at the College of Charleston and the author of *Edgar Allan Poe Revisited* (1998) and *The Afterlife of Edgar Allan Poe* (2004), which received the Patrick F. Quinn Award from the Poe Studies Association. He has published numerous articles on Poe and nineteenth-century American literature. Peeples coedited the journal *Poe Studies* from 2008 to 2013 and currently serves on the editorial board of the *Edgar Allan Poe Review.*

Leland S. Person is Nathaniel Ropes Professor of English at the University of Cincinnati. He is the author of *Aesthetic Headaches: Women and a Masculine Poetics in Poe, Melville, and Hawthorne* (1988), *Henry James and the Suspense of Masculinity* (2003), and *The Cambridge Introduction to Nathaniel Hawthorne* (2007). He edited the Norton Critical Edition of *The Scarlet Letter* (2017) and has served as president of the Hawthorne and James societies. He is also a former coeditor of *Poe Studies.*

Philip Edward Phillips is Professor of English and Associate Dean of the University Honors College at Middle Tennessee State University. His publications include articles in *Edgar Allan Poe in 20 Objects* (2016), *Edgar Allan Poe in Context* (2013), *Deciphering Poe: Subtexts, Contexts, Subversive Meanings* (2013), and *Approaches to Teaching Poe's Prose and Poetry* (2008). His edited collection, *Poe and Place,* is forthcoming from Palgrave Macmillan. He is a past president of the Poe Studies Association, a member of *The Edgar Allan Poe Review* editorial committee, and was program chair of the 2018 Kyoto conference.

W. Scott Poole is Professor of History at the College of Charleston. His 2016 biography of H. P. Lovecraft *In the Mountains of Madness* was a finalist for the Bram Stoker Award. His book *Wasteland: The Great War and the Origins of Modern Horror* will be published in 2018 along with a revised and expanded edition of his award-winning *Monsters in America*, which first appeared in 2011.

Stephen Rachman is Associate Professor in the Department of English, former Director of the American Studies Program, and Codirector of the Digital Humanities Literary Cognition Laboratory at Michigan State University. He is coauthor of the award-winning *Cholera, Chloroform, and the Science of Medicine: A Life of John Snow* (2003) and coeditor of *The American Face of Edgar Allan Poe* (1995). A past president of the Poe Studies Association, he is currently completing a study entitled *The Jingle Man: Edgar Allan Poe and the Problems of Culture.*

Valerie Rohy is Professor of English at the University of Vermont. She is the author of *Impossible Women: Lesbian Figures and American Literature* (2000), *Anachronism and Its Others: Sexuality, Race, Temporality* (2009), and *Lost Causes: Narrative, Etiology, and Queer Theory* (2015). She teaches and studies nineteenth- and twentieth-century American literature, queer theory, feminist theory, and psychoanalytic theory.

Kelly Ross is an Assistant Professor of English at Rider University. She specializes in early and nineteenth-century American literature with interests in twentieth-century American literature, detective fiction, poetry, African American literature, and American studies. Her article "Babo's Heterochronic Creativity," appeared in *Leviathan*, and she is currently completing a monograph on slavery and surveillance in antebellum literature.

John Carlos Rowe is USC Associates' Professor of the Humanities and Professor of English, American Studies and Ethnicity, and Comparative Literature at the University of Southern California. He is the author of nine books, more than 150 essays and reviews, and editor or co-editor of eleven books, including *Literary Culture and U.S. Imperialism: From the Revolution to World War II* (2000), *A Concise Companion to American Studies* (2010), *Afterlives of Modernism* (2011), and *The Cultural Politics of the New American Studies* (2012).

Laura Saltz is Associate Professor and Director of American Studies at Colby College. Her manuscript in progress, *Imponderables: Antebellum Science, Light, and Literature*, devotes a chapter to Poe. Her past work on Poe includes "'(Horrible to Relate!)': Recovering the Body of Marie Rogêt" in *The American Face of Edgar Allan Poe*, 1995) and "'Eyes which Behold': Poe's 'Domain of Arnheim' and the Science of Vision" in *The Edgar Allan Poe Review*, 2006, reprinted in *Edgar Allan Poe: Beyond Gothicism*, 2011. "Eyes which Behold" won the James M. Gargano Prize for the outstanding essay on Poe in 2006.

Matt Sandler directs the MA program in American Studies at the Center for the Study of Ethnicity and Race at Columbia University. His article, "'Negras Aguas': The Poe Tradition and the Limits of American Africanism" appeared in Comparative Literature, and he has published essays elsewhere on Byron, Whitman, and Dunbar. His book about the African American poets of the abolition movement is forthcoming from Verso.

Susan Elizabeth Sweeney is Monsignor Murray Professor of Arts and Humanities at the College of the Holy Cross. Her work on Poe includes a coedited volume, *Detecting Texts: The Metaphysical Detective Story from Poe to Postmodernism* (1999); a screenplay, *The Raven Woos the Dove*, about his courtship of Sarah Helen Whitman; and essays on visual culture, including "The Horror of Taking a Picture in Poe's 'Tell-Tale Heart.'" She served on the editorial board of the *Edgar Allan Poe Review* and as president of the Poe Studies Association. She also publishes on detective fiction, postmodernist narrative, and Vladimir Nabokov.

Sandra Tomc is Professor of English at the University of British Columbia, specializing in early nineteenth-century US literature and print culture. She is the author of *Industry and the Creative Mind: The Eccentric Writer in American Literature and Entertainment, 1790–1860* (2012). Her scholarly articles on Poe and the US publishing scene appear in *ELH, American Literature, Representations,* and *Nineteenth-Century Literature.* She is currently researching a book about unpaid work economies in the early nineteenth-century US magazine industry.

Alexandra Urakova works as a senior researcher at the A. M. Gorky Institute of World Literature of the Russian Academy of Sciences, Moscow, Russia. She is author of *The Poetics of the Body in the Short Fiction of Edgar Allan Poe* (2009, in Russian), editor of *Deciphering Poe: Subtexts, Contexts, Subversive Meanings* (2013), and coeditor of *Poe, Baudelaire, Dostoevsky: Splendors and Miseries of National Genius* (2017, in Russian). She has published on Poe in *Nineteenth-Century Literature, The Edgar Allan Poe Review, Poe Studies*, and numerous collections.

Margarida Vale de Gato is an Assistant Professor at the Universidade de Lisboa's School of Arts and Humanities and Coordinator of the American Studies Research Group in ULICES (Ulisboa Centre for English Studies). She completed her PhD in 2008 with a dissertation on the rewritings of Poe in late nineteenth-century Portuguese poetry and translated Poe's complete poetic works into Portuguese (2009). She guest-edited the Spring 2010 volume of *The Edgar Allan Poe Review* on the theme "Poe and Gothic Creativity." She coedited *Translated Poe* (2014), with Emron Esplin, and their current project is *Anthologizing Poe* (2019).

Ellen Weinauer is Dean of the Honors College and Associate Professor of English at the University of Southern Mississippi. She has published widely in American literature, especially on Gothic tropes and themes in such writers as Hawthorne, Melville, Douglass, and Elizabeth Stoddard. Her publications include "Race and the American Gothic" (*The Cambridge Companion to the American Gothic*, 2017), "Law and the Gothic in the Slaveholding South" (*The Palgrave Handbook of the Southern Gothic*, 2016), and "Poe, Southworth, and the Antebellum Wife" (*E.D.E.N. Southworth: Recovering a Nineteenth-Century Popular Novelist*, 2012).

Cindy Weinstein is Eli and Edythe Broad Professor of English at the California Institute of Technology. Her publications include *Time, Tense, and American Literature: When*

Is Now? (2015), the Norton Critical Edition of Melville's *Pierre, or the Ambiguities*, coedited with Robert S. Levine (2017), and an edited volume of essays, *A Question of Time: American Literature from Colonial Encounter to Contemporary Fiction* (forthcoming).

Jeffrey Andrew Weinstock is Professor of English at Central Michigan University and an associate editor for *The Journal of the Fantastic in the Arts*. He is an author or editor of twenty books, including the MLA *Approaches to Teaching Poe's Prose and Poetry* (with Anthony Magistrale) and *The Cambridge Companion to American Gothic*.

Edward Whitley is Associate Professor of English at Lehigh University. He is the author of *American Bards: Walt Whitman and Other Unlikely Candidates for National Poet* (2010) and, with Joanna Levin, coeditor of *Whitman Among the Bohemians* (2014). He has published essays on Poe's relationship with Whitman and the bohemians of antebellum New York City in the journals *Poe Studies* and *American Literary History*.

Christina Zwarg is Associate Professor of English at Haverford College. Author of *Feminist Conversations: Fuller, Emerson, and the Play of Reading*, she has published a wide variety of articles on nineteenth- and early twentieth-century authors and topics in *American Literature, Studies in Romanticism, Poe Studies, American Literary History, Criticism, Novel, Cultural Critique, Adaptation, Social Text*, and in several Norton Critical editions and anthologies. She is completing a book on trauma theory before Freud entitled *The Stunning Rehearsal: Traumatic Archives, Crisis, and the Black Reconstruction of Democracy*.

INTRODUCTION

The Unfolding Investigation of Edgar Poe

J. GERALD KENNEDY AND SCOTT PEEPLES

EDGAR Allan Poe remains the best-known, most widely recognized American author of the early nineteenth century. At his death in 1849, however, no one could have imagined his emergence as a figure of worldwide popularity. Only a handful of friends and relatives attended his funeral rites in Baltimore, and Rev. Rufus W. Griswold's notorious obituary portrayed Poe as a friendless lunatic, muttering curses as he lurched through city streets. After Poe's demise, a heated debate about his reputation and character unfolded in print, and early biographers of the 1880s and 1890s continued to wrestle with his complicated legacy. When American literature became an academic discipline in the 1920s, Poe still figured as a problematic talent in literary histories and biographical accounts. He seemed to Vernon L. Parrington far from the "main currents of American thought." Damning with homophobic innuendo, Paul Elmer More called Poe "the poet of unripe boys and unsound men." F. O. Matthiessen notoriously denied Poe a place in his account of a national literary resurgence.[1] But serious work by early scholars such as James Harrison, Mary E. Phillips, Margaret Alterton, Killis Campbell, and Thomas Ollive Mabbott helped to establish the study of Poe's life and work as a significant enterprise.[2]

The controversy that swirled around Poe and his place in American literature did not, however, immediately subside. Critical practices came and went, but Poe remained a vexing figure who defied reductive characterization. Part of his appeal has always inhered in his contradictory tendencies. Like the singular London stranger in "The Man of the Crowd," Poe's work reveals an enigmatic mix of multiple, paradoxical qualities. The old man in that 1840 tale excites impressions "of vast mental power, of caution, of penuriousness, of avarice, of coolness, of malice, of blood-thirstiness, of triumph, of merriment, of excessive terror, of intense—of extreme despair" (M 2: 511). With the possible exception of "avarice"—which may indeed form the satirical object of "Von Kempelen and His Discovery"—these passions at some point all infuse the life and works of Poe. As a cryptographer, he flaunted his "vast mental power," and while accusing Longfellow of plagiarism, he critically exercised "coolness" and "malice." Wracked by poverty, or "penuriousness," he was alternately discouraged or brazen. Of "terror," Poe was the master, and he surely knew "despair," though "merriment" also informs his many satires, burlesques, and parodies. "The Tell-Tale Heart" and "The Cask of Amontillado" attest to Poe's understanding of that most troubling attribute, "blood-thirstiness." Critics have rightly warned us not to confuse Poe with his fictional characters or to embrace naïve, autobiographical readings. But the old man's cryptic traits align so closely with Poe's intensities that they at least highlight the difficulty of gauging his dazzling yet uneven achievement. In a review of Charles Baudelaire, the French poet who idolized and translated Poe, Henry James fussed that "to take [Poe] with more than a certain degree of seriousness is to lack seriousness one's self."[3] Yet the burgeoning scholarship that emerged, ironically, from Griswold's multivolume Poe edition in the 1850s, had by the 1950s established Poe's lasting significance as a writer of poetry, tales, and literary criticism.[4] Controversies still persist, and the author's contradictions retain an addictive fascination, driving the collective project of Poe studies in new and productive directions in the twenty-first century.

The title of our *Handbook of Edgar Allan Poe* includes the middle name Allan and thus the formal moniker by which Poe has long been known. But this was not the identity Poe preferred. As a young man, he despised his foster father, the Richmond merchant John Allan, and throughout his literary career (initially launched in defiance of Allan), he signed himself Edgar A. Poe almost invariably. We considered a title using that version of his name, wishing to defamiliarize his persona slightly, the better to invite fresh thinking about Poe and to suggest the tantalizing elusiveness of the man himself. But in the end, the familiar formulation proved more practical. By "Poe" we wish to signify not the actual historical personage so much as the mind and imagination insinuated by the writing, the "author function" (in Foucault's formulation) who figures as a guarantor of quality.[5] Only a handful of our chapters explicitly concern Poe's life or the biographies devoted to him. And yet Poe himself is everywhere, implicated in diverse readings of his heterogeneous compositions. Close, prolonged study of the writing itself reveals not an invariant, absolute Poe but rather a complicated personality and a changing consciousness, a volatile sensibility affected by age, circumstance, and relentless productivity.

The mercurial aspect of Poe's temperament reveals itself in works written in close proximity. Though precise dates of composition defy authentication, we know that he completed his slapstick "The Man That Was Used Up" in 1839, just before (or after) he wrote "The Fall of the House of Usher." He penned a weird postmortem conversation of spirits, "The Colloquy of Monos and Una," in late spring of 1841, about the time he was composing the preposterous "Never Bet the Devil Your Head." Similarly, he wrote the satire "Some Words with a Mummy" in late 1845 on the brink of producing his signature poetic masterwork, "The Raven." The list might be greatly extended, because surprising juxtapositions abound. Poe liked to change direction, and just like Emerson, the Transcendentalist he loved to mock, he saw no virtue in foolish consistency. He was mainly a poet in the 1820s and then a "magazinist" and writer of tales in the 1830s and 1840s, though he still composed poems sporadically and interposed verses in a few fictional works. In "How to Write a Blackwood Article," he ridiculed the tale of sensation that he exploited for roughly fifteen years with consummate brilliance and effect (M 2: 334–362). In a famous letter to Philip Pendleton Cooke, he demystified and disparaged the tale of ratiocination he had introduced in "The Murders in the Rue Morgue" (CL 1: 594–597). Poe was a relentless experimentalist. And he was for many years a hard-working editor, who as a reviewer churned out scores of critiques under brutal deadlines, tackling works of astonishing diversity. In addition to novels, memoirs, and poetry, he reviewed books about flowers, medicine, travel, history, navigation, and religion. Poe was surely mocking his own writing career when he personified his tireless magazine tyro, Thingum Bob: "I leaned to the right. I leaned to the left. I sat forward. I sat backward. I sat upon end. . . . Through all, I—*wrote*. Through joy and through sorrow, I—*wrote*. Through hunger and through thirst, I—*wrote*" (M 3: 1145).

Poe's extreme, experimental edge helps to account for his appeal in our time. But how will Poe fare in the century that lies ahead? In what format will his writings be available to future readers? Electronic forms of communication, display, and data retrieval are rapidly displacing daily newspapers and magazines, perhaps auguring the eclipse of print media and the demise of the book. Even so, print forms persist as seemingly indispensable artifacts, complementing globally accessible electronic databases by providing a more stable, secure archive of human knowledge. This *Handbook* will appear in both a conventional hardback publication and as a fluid, online resource that can be updated, expanded, and revised periodically. In the brave new world of social media and instant messaging, the future of reading and writing seems uncertain, and much will depend on civic debate about the future aims of public education. New forms of visual and technological literacy now vie for attention, redefining the ongoing study of great works of literature, history, and philosophy. In some fashion or another, digital technology will alter the future of Poe studies, as we will suggest in closing.

Our collective enterprise unfolds in a context of uncertainty. The apotheosis of science, technology, engineering, and mathematics as essential disciplines has in recent decades reshaped higher education, somewhat displacing the arts, humanities, and social sciences from their traditional centrality. Will subsequent young scholars still choose disciplines that nurture cultural understanding and critical thinking, or will the lure of lucrative employment in business or technology diminish the cohort of aspiring humanities scholars? Government emphasis on productivity and profit is already imposing upon literary scholars new demands of public accountability. If economic prosperity becomes the new benchmark for cultural vitality, will anyone really need to read "Ligeia," let alone "Why the Little Frenchman Wears His Hand in a Sling"? One way to frame the objective of this volume is to assume the persistence of intellectual values from prior centuries and take for granted the continuing importance of literary study. From that perspective, Poe's stock is rising; as noted earlier, he now claims unprecedented prominence among his antebellum American contemporaries. Another approach, however, would recognize skepticism about humanistic education itself in a commercial, materialistic milieu. The assault on public entities that once nurtured the arts and humanities continues relentlessly. And so students of literature, the prospective scholars of coming decades, must understand—and be prepared to justify—the research they do and the subjects they care about.

A long view of the domain of Poe studies reveals many shifts in the focus of literary research over the past 150 years. Scholarly, critical, and theoretical work on Poe has tacitly embodied the compelling intellectual preoccupations of modern culture. Understanding the evolution of this scholarship places advanced students in a stronger position to articulate the stakes of future research and to identify projects that truly contribute to new understanding or knowledge. Perhaps because Poe was both a traditionalist and controversialist, mocking popular illusions as he defended learning and intellect, certain polarities in the critical debate about Poe have persisted. Biographical concerns have long formed one axis of controversy: in what way do the details of Poe's life contribute insight into his poetry and fiction, and what makes such inferences salient or legitimate? To what extent have psychoanalytic ideas usefully connected Poe's life experiences with poetic or fictional predicaments? Another axis of disagreement pertains to Poe's theological anguish: can his ideas about God, matter, spirit, and cosmology be reconciled with his expressions of despair, skepticism, and disbelief? This conundrum has long generated competing notions of "essential" works and personal convictions, making *Eureka* a litmus test of critical intention. A third axis of argument has cohered around Poe's implied social and political thinking, pondering the impact of raging issues in Jacksonian America—such as slavery and Indian removal but also scientific skepticism and notions of "progress"—on Poe's poetry and fiction. Challenging formalist disregard for context, sociohistorical readings have in recent decades teased out provocative cultural allusions and critiques. A fourth axis of dispute has problematized Poe's creativity in relation to his reading, privileging the impact of printed sources on his literary productivity at the expense of biographical and cultural influences. Sometimes locating an unmistakable creative impetus, scholars have at other times reduced composition to scavenging work. Across the past 175 years, research into Poe's life and work has eliminated many misconceptions and solved countless mysteries, but as our understanding of Poe has expanded, it has likewise become more complicated and nuanced, revealing an author who more than ever defies critical essentializing.

Poe courted public controversy throughout his career. He made his name writing vituperative reviews laden with sarcasm and personal insult, largely to entertain magazine readers. Later, he challenged readers to outwit him with cryptographs, published attention-getting hoaxes, publicly accused a beloved American poet of plagiarism while carrying on a public flirtation with another, and sparred with the Boston literary establishment as well as several of the New York literati. His enemies ridiculed his alcoholism and alleged mental derangement in print, and not long before his death, his former friend, James Russell Lowell, caricatured him as pompous and pedantic in a verse satire:

> There comes Poe with his Raven like Barnaby Rudge,
> Three fifths of him genius and two fifths sheer fudge,
> Who talks like a book of iambs and pentameters,
> In a way to make people of common sense damn meters,
> Who has written some things quite the best of their kind,
> But the heart somehow seems all squeezed out by the mind.[6]

All of which is to say that Rufus Griswold's inflammatory obituary and memoir, libelous as they were, did not arise from a vacuum. But Griswold's portrayal inflated Poe's infamy; moreover, it demanded responses, and the defensive tone of those responses still characterizes some writing about Poe—in biography, literary criticism, and popular culture—well into the twenty-first century. In *Edgar Poe and His Critics* (1860), Sarah Helen Whitman, to whom Poe had been briefly engaged, made her purpose clear from the outset: "Dr. Griswold's Memoir of Edgar Poe has been extensively read and circulated; its perverted facts and baseless assumptions have been adopted into every subsequent memoir and notice of the poet, and have been translated into many languages. For ten years this great wrong to the dead has passed unchallenged and unrebuked."[7] In fact, Poe had been defended repeatedly in the first decade after his death—notably by former employers George Rex Graham and N. P. Willis—and he would be championed, sometimes to the point of hagiography, by his earliest biographers, William F. Gill and John Henry Ingram. Magazine articles on Poe throughout the late nineteenth century fueled a debate that sometimes conflated personal character with literary achievement. The "Poe Bookshelf" at the invaluable Edgar Allan Poe Society of Baltimore website (eapoe.org) includes dozens of articles from 1850 to 1900: reminiscences by Poe's associates, neighbors, and brief acquaintances; conjectures about what made him tick; descriptions of his personality; and assessments of his character. In addition to disproving any claim that Poe was neglected or forgotten after his death, these articles demonstrate the partisan divide over Poe's personality, even among those who knew him personally. Provocatively, Poe's *Broadway Journal* coeditor C. F. Briggs, in an 1877 article defending Griswold's assessment, claimed that Poe never really cared what people thought of him personally, only that they admired his writing: "If he were alive to read the angry discussions that have been going on ever since his melancholy death respecting his morals and manners, he would laugh scornfully to think that anybody should deem it worthwhile to waste a word on a point which to him was a matter of perfect indifference."[8]

For many years, Poe's reputation among prominent American authors was similarly divided. Alongside Henry James's dismissal, Emerson belittled his poetry—at least according to William Dean Howells—referring to him as "the Jingle Man" in 1859; Mark Twain (in a 1909 letter to Howells) called Poe's prose "unreadable."[9] Among poets and fiction writers, Poe's most devoted admirers in the late nineteenth and early twentieth centuries tended not to be American or British but rather a phalanx of global enthusiasts. Poe's most influential nineteenth-century advocate and disciple was French poet Charles Baudelaire, who identified strongly with Poe and tirelessly translated his work, promoting it among the French avant garde. Spurred, perhaps, by French reverence for Poe, literary pundits such as Charles Leonard Moore would refer to "The American Rejection of Poe" (in the Chicago literary magazine *The Dial*), and Poe's nonelection to the Hall of Fame for Great Americans in the first two rounds of inductions—1900 and 1905—reinforced his partisans' sense that he was destined to be better appreciated abroad than in his home country.[10] It is relevant to note that when Parker Brothers popularized the card game "Authors" at the turn of the century, the deck paired great British authors (like Shakespeare) with such American writers as Cooper, Irving, Hawthorne, Longfellow, and Alcott—but not Poe.

In terms of public recognition, if not by literary veneration, reports of Poe's neglect in the United States were, however, greatly exaggerated. The collection of his works compiled by Griswold went through about thirty printings before its copyright expired in 1876, after which countless new editions appeared. Poe entered the Hall of Fame in 1910, one year after Baltimore, Charlottesville, and other cities celebrated the centennial of his birth. He had been honored with a prominent burial marker in Baltimore in 1875, a marble bust in the Metropolitan Museum of Art in 1885, and a bronze bust at the University of Virginia in 1899. In 1913 the State of New York established Poe Park in the Bronx and moved Poe's cottage there to preserve it and afford better public access. Commissioning Sir Moses Ezekiel to execute the work, Baltimore's Poe Memorial Association in 1921 dedicated an imposing statue of Poe (now located at the University of Baltimore).[11] Richmond's Poe Memorial Association, founded in 1906, established the Poe Shrine in 1922, which soon evolved into the Poe Museum, a site Gertrude Stein dutifully visited during her American tour of 1935.

As scholars established American literature as a field of academic study in the 1910s, Poe immediately became part of the national canon, even as some gatekeepers expressed doubts about his legitimacy. At the height of modernism, Aldous Huxley and Yvor Winters wrote essays disparaging Poe's poetry, while T. S. Eliot grudgingly conceded Poe's influence in a 1948 Library of Congress lecture on the symbolist movement: "one cannot be sure that one's writing has *not* been influenced by Mr. Poe."[12] Cleanth Brooks and Robert Penn Warren included Poe in their influential college literature textbooks *Understanding Poetry* and *Understanding Fiction*, but primarily for the negative examples he provided—for instance, unfavorably comparing Poe's use of place names in "Ulalume" to Hardy's in "Channel Firing" or Keats's in "Ode on a Grecian Urn." Of "The Fall of the House of Usher," they assert that "The horror is relatively meaningless—it is generated for its own sake."[13] Like Eliot, Brooks and Warren regarded Poe as unavoidable but not inherently valuable. Similarly ambivalent, F. O. Matthiessen (as noted earlier) left Poe out of his landmark 1941 study *American Renaissance* but then wrote the Poe chapter for Spiller and Thorp's influential *Literary History of the United States* in 1948, calling Poe "one of the very few great innovators in American literature."[14] Poe was included with less skepticism in the college American literature anthologies that began to appear after World War I, with typically over a dozen poems and four or five tales.[15]

Although high priests of New Criticism such as Brooks and Warren denigrated Poe, adept practitioners of close reading began to reveal the tension, irony, and psychological complexity in his best work, especially the tales. Earlier debates over Poe's character were channeled in the 1920s into Freudian readings of his work, in which Poe's own supposed neuroses and obsessions formed the real subject of inquiry. Without specifically mentioning Freud, D. H. Lawrence demonstrated the potential for psychoanalytic reading in the Poe chapter of his 1925 *Studies in Classic American Literature*, and from the 1920s to the 1970s, Freud remained a touchstone. But the heavyweight champion in the psychoanalytic division appeared in 1933, with Marie Bonaparte's *Edgar Poe: Étude psychanalytique*, translated into English fifteen years later. For more than 700 pages, Bonaparte offers a Freudian narrative of Poe's life followed by interpretations of his tales-as-dreams, drawing on archetypes and myths but ultimately leading back to Poe's personal obsessions and grief stemming from his mother's death. Although her aggressively Oedipal and often reductive readings would elicit skeptical and even dismissive reactions as the influence of psychoanalytic criticism waned, Bonaparte solidified Poe's close posthumous relationship with Freud while demonstrating the hermeneutical depth of the tales.[16]

The close readings that began to appear at mid-century—blending not only Freudian but also archetypal and mythological approaches, as well as perspectives from intellectual history—yielded insightful interpretations of Poe's fiction throughout the mid-twentieth century. Edward Davidson's *Poe: A Critical Study* (1957) offered an alternative to psychoanalysis as a means of synthesizing Poe's work, instead drawing on philosophy and aesthetics to posit Poe as an artist who destroys the material world and builds his own through the imaginative use of language.[17] Somewhat similar readings were developed at mid-century by the poets Allen Tate and Richard Wilbur. The latter's introduction to a mass-market paperback of Poe's poetry offered a trenchant analysis of Poe's *tales*—because Wilbur discerned in the fiction a "narrative basis" for the myth of creative destructiveness reflected in the poems.[18] Readings that teased out the subtleties of Poe's fiction, providing context from literary history while generally avoiding reductive psychoanalysis or biographical concerns, proliferated from the 1950s well into the 1970s: Patrick F. Quinn's *The French Face of Edgar Allan Poe* (1957), Harry Levin's *The Power of Blackness* (which grouped Poe with Hawthorne and Melville, 1958), and essays by Darrel Abel ("A Key to the House of Usher," 1949), Clark Griffith ("Poe's 'Ligeia' and the English Romantics," 1954), Joseph Patrick Roppolo ("Meaning and 'The Masque of the Red Death,'" 1963), James Gargano ("The Question of Poe's Narrators," 1963), James M. Cox ("Edgar Poe: Style as Pose," 1968), and David H. Hirsch ("The Pit and the Apocalypse," 1968) represent a wave of scholarship that attested to Poe's craftsmanship and to the resonance of his work.[19]

Indeed, throughout the middle decades of the last century, the field of Poe studies was established not only by critics such as those named earlier but also by path-clearing biographers and editors. While several significant lives of Poe had appeared since Ingram's in 1880, there was no truly coherent, comprehensive, and scrupulously factual biography until 1941, when Arthur Hobson Quinn produced his 800-page *Edgar Allan Poe: A Critical Biography.* Quinn dismantled Griswold-inspired myths without idealizing the author; his inclusion of many previously unpublished letters and careful documentation provided a bedrock of reliable information while situating Poe's literary accomplishments within the narrative of his life and career.[20] Thomas Ollive Mabbott devoted much of his long career to the editing of Poe's works; while he published various facsimile, scholarly, and popular editions from the 1920s to the 1950s, his ultimate project was a complete variorum edition of Poe. The first volume—*Complete Poems*—was published in 1969, months after Mabbott's death; the two *Tales and Sketches* volumes followed, completed by Eleanor D. Kewer and Maureen C. Mabbott, in 1978; and subsequent volumes of Poe's journalism, "imaginary voyages," and other writings were edited by Burton R. Pollin and published in the 1980s. Poe's letters were collected in 1948 by John Ward Ostrom; sixty years later, a revised and expanded edition of the letters was published under the editorial guidance of Pollin and Jeffrey A. Savoye. In the early 2000s, when the University of Illinois Press reprinted the three Mabbott volumes, they commissioned Stuart and Susan F. Levine to edit volumes of Poe's critical theory and *Eureka*. Collectively, then, the volumes by Mabbott, Pollin, Ostrom, Savoye, and the Levines comprise a motley but reliable standard edition of Poe's writing, though for some texts, scholars frequently refer to the Library of America edition of Poe's *Essays and Reviews* or James Harrison's 1902 *Complete Works of Edgar Allan Poe* (republished in 1965). Our *Handbook* index of scholarly sources and their abbreviations reflects the indispensability of these volumes.

Amid this proliferation of bibliographic and critical work in the 1960s, G. R. Thompson established the *Poe Newsletter* in 1968, inspired partly by a wish to promote collegial cooperation among scholars working on Poe. In the *Newsletter*'s first article, J. Albert Robbins lamented that while "there is no shortage of books and articles on Poe," the "flood of words . . . threaten[s] to drown, not buoy us."[21] The newsletter, renamed *Poe Studies* in 1971, helped to organize and encourage the ongoing scholarly discussion. Founded in 1972, the Poe Studies Association has maintained a network for scholars interested in Poe, sponsoring regular panels at the Modern Language Association and American Literature Association conferences, hosting its own international conferences since 1999, establishing awards for outstanding research on Poe, and promoting that research through its own publications—the *PSA Newsletter*, supplanted in 2000 by the biannual journal *The Edgar Allan Poe Review*. Other late-twentieth-century landmarks for Poe scholars include the publication of two biographical works that, half a century after Quinn, immediately became essential: Dwight Thomas and David K. Jackson's *The Poe Log: A Documentary Life of Edgar Allan Poe* (1987) and Kenneth Silverman's *Edgar A. Poe: Mournful and Never-ending Remembrance* (1991).[22] Since 1997, Jeffrey Savoye, on behalf of the Edgar Allan Poe Society of Baltimore, has made the Poe canon, along with many volumes of out-of-print material about Poe, accessible to the public on the Society's extensive website, an archive to be discussed further in our conclusion.

Alongside the mid-twentieth century's burgeoning academic Poe industry, popular culture embraced Poe—appropriating his name, reduplicating his dour image, and freely adapting his work—through the media of comics, popular fiction, and movies. Thomas Inge has chronicled the close relationship between Poe and comic books, which began in the 1940s with *Classic Comics* and *Classics Illustrated* and thrived over subsequent decades in *Chilling Tales, Creepy, Eerie, Scream, Nightmare*, and, more recently, in *Graphic Classics* and a spate of graphic novels.[23] Poe's movie career is much longer, more varied, and has had an enormous impact on his popular image. As early as 1909, Poe figured in a D. W. Griffith short in which he composes "The Raven" at his wife's deathbed. He would appear as a character in the romanticized biopics *The Raven* (1915) and *The Loves of Edgar Allan Poe* (1942), and as a character in a number of other films, ranging from Griffith's *The Avenging Conscience* (1915) to Fletcher Markle's *The Man with a Cloak* (1951) to James McTeigue's *The Raven* (2012). But he would be best known to moviegoers throughout the twentieth century as the inspiration for, first, a trio of Universal Studios horror films starring Bela Lugosi and/or Boris Karloff, and then a series of low-budget blockbusters directed by Roger Corman and starring Vincent Price. In his encyclopedic study *The Poe Cinema*, Don G. Smith surveys eighty-eight Poe-related films through 1992, and dozens more have appeared since then.[24] Poe adaptations and allusions abound on television, in popular music, in podcasts, in novels (especially mysteries), and his image—usually some variation on the "Ultima Thule" daguerreotype—appears on countless tote bags, t-shirts, lunchboxes, adhesive bandages, and tattoos, both temporary and permanent. For over a century, the pop-culture Poe industry—from shrines and statues to films and Internet memes—has helped support the academic Poe industry by attracting students, audiences to public lectures, and publishers.

At the same time, those two enterprises, popular and academic, often seemed to be built around different Poes, especially as more theoretically informed treatments of his work emerged in the 1970s. The epicenter for the deconstructive earthquake in Poe studies was Jacques Derrida's 1975 essay "Le facteur de la vérité" ("The Purveyor of Truth"), a critique of Jacques Lacan's 1956 "Seminar on 'The Purloined Letter.'" Seeking to deflate Lacan's claims at having located a psychoanalytic "truth," Derrida, much like Dupin, exposes his rival's blind spot, essentially the position of the story's narrator and its application in analysis; the story, for Derrida, becomes an allegory of interpretation and its deferral of meaning. Appropriately for such a discussion, Derrida's essay set off a chain reaction of commentary, some of which is collected in the 1988 volume *The Purloined Poe*.[25] If previous generations of critics had been determined to reveal or tease out unnoticed coherence, patterns, and meanings in Poe's work, critics influenced by Derrida, Roland Barthes, Paul de Man, and other poststructuralist theorists unraveled those coherences and patterns, emphasizing the textual self-referentiality of what Poe himself referred to (in "Al Aaraaf") as a "world of words." Indeed, with his literary gamesmanship, his hoaxes, his antididacticism, his travel narratives without destinations, his poems that foreground the imposition of meaning on a bird's croaking or a bell's ringing, Poe had much to offer theorists and critics exploring the instability and play of language. Jean Ricardou's essay on *Pym*, "Le Caractère singulier de cette eau" ("The Singular Character of the Water"), first published in 1967 (translated into English in 1976), was at the vanguard of poststructuralist readings of Poe. Innovative readings by Joseph N. Riddel (1979), John T. Irwin (1980), John Carlos Rowe (1982), Louis A. Renza (1985), J. Gerald Kennedy (1987), Michael J. S. Williams (1988), and Dennis Pahl (1989), among others, highlighted in various ways Poe's tendency to destabilize or challenge logocentrism.[26]

The list of white, male scholars just cited is fairly representative of Poe studies throughout the twentieth century. Colin (Joan) Dayan's essay "Amorous Bondage: Poe, Ladies, and Slaves" not only broke new ground in analyzing the race-and-gender-based power dynamics of Poe's fiction but called out the Poe studies establishment for having ignored or dismissed such concerns as late as the 1990s.[27] Until then, feminist readings of Poe—who famously declared the death of a beautiful woman "the most poetical topic in the world" in "The Philosophy of Composition"—had been scarce, with notable exceptions of Judith Fetterley's discussion of "Rue Morgue" in the collection *Gender and Reading* (1986), Cynthia Jordan's chapter on Poe in *Second Stories* (1989), and Leland S. Person's *Aesthetic Headaches* (1988). The mid-1990s saw more gender-based work on Poe—a special issue of *Poe Studies* on "Poe and Women" (1993), J. Gerald Kennedy's essay on gender dynamics in Poe's poetry and tales of dying women (1993), and essays by David Leverenz and Laura Saltz, along with Dayan's, in a section labeled "Imagining Gender" in Shawn Rosenheim and Stephen Rachman's collection *The American Face of Edgar Allan Poe* (1995).[28] That volume signaled a new direction in Poe studies: its title playing off Quinn's *French Face of Edgar Poe*, the volume opened fresh avenues of discussion not only of gender politics and violence but also Poe's place in antebellum literary and social culture generally. Jonathan Elmer's *Reading at the Social Limit: Affect, Mass Culture, and Edgar Allan Poe* (1995) and Terence Whalen's *Edgar Allan Poe and the Masses* (1999), while very different in approach, both lean on Marxist theory while situating Poe in relation to commercial print culture.[29] Meanwhile, one element of antebellum culture—slavery and the racist taxonomy that sustained it—drew increasing attention from Poe scholars in the 1990s, setting off skirmishes within the larger culture wars of that time. Questions hinging on Poe's editing a decidedly Southern journal, his use of stereotyped black characters and "darky" humor, and the coded allegory of race in *Pym*, as well as the tropes of killer orangutans and abused black cats, drove a rereading of the Poe canon, which acquired urgency when Toni Morrison, on the verge of winning the Nobel Prize in Literature, proclaimed in *Playing in the Dark* (1992) that "No American writer is more important to the concept of American Africanism than Poe."[30] This new emphasis sparked by Morrison and the New Historicism peaked with a volume edited by J. Gerald Kennedy and Liliane Weissberg, *Romancing the Shadow: Poe and Race* (2001).[31] The subject likewise figures in passing in some of the essays collected in Kennedy's *Historical Guide to Edgar Allan Poe* (2001).

While other trends and "turns" have had less sustained impact on Poe studies than the late-twentieth-century academic shockwaves of poststructuralist theory and New Historicism, in recent decades Poe scholarship has been informed by a variety of approaches, including media studies, object theory, animal studies, queer theory, and trauma studies. For example, Valerie Rohy's 2006 essay, "Ahistorical," offers a queer reading of "Ligeia" that challenges assumptions about how "history" is used in literary study. Colleen Glenney Boggs's *Animalia Americana* (2013) includes a chapter on the beasts of Poe's imagination. Jacob Rama Berman's *American Arabesque* (2012) in one chapter explores the implications of Poe's taste for arabesque designs. Matthew Taylor devotes a chapter in *Universes Without Us* (2013) to decoding Poe's "meta/physics." Notable essays on Poe have also appeared with remarkable regularity; many of them, including articles by Taylor, Emron Esplin, Jerome McGann, Maurice Lee, Laura Saltz, Cindy Weinstein, and Stephen Rachman, have garnered the James Gargano Award from the Poe Studies Association for best essay of the year.[32]

In the new millennium, books featuring Poe indicate his palpably expanding reputation. Scott Peeples assesses the author's contemporary cultural impact in *The Afterlife of Edgar Allan Poe* (2003). Poe's relation to female poets and salon culture informs Eliza Richards's *Gender and the Poetics of Reception in Poe's Circle* (2004), while another study, Meredith McGill's *American Literature and the Culture of Reprinting, 1837–1853* (2003) deals importantly with Poe and partly inspires the volume of essays by Kennedy and Jerome McGann, *Poe and the Remapping of Antebellum Print Culture* (2012). McGann's own *The Poet Edgar Allan Poe: Alien Angel* (2014) marks the first book on Poe's poetry in years, a revolutionary study emphasizing the modernist, performative excesses of the verse. Kennedy's *Strange Nation: Literary Nationalism and Cultural Conflict in the Age of Poe* (2016) frames the tangled story of antebellum nation-building with chapters unpacking Poe's critique of literary jingoism. Global perspectives inform *Translated Poe* (2014), edited by Emron Esplin and Margarida Vale de Gato, while Esplin's more recent book, *Borges's Poe: The Influence and Reinvention of Edgar Allan Poe in Latin America* (2016), offers a hemispheric sequel of sorts to John T. Irwin's *The Mystery to a Solution: Poe, Borges, and the Analytic Detective Story* (1994). Finally, the international influence of Poe's writing on painters and illustrators forms the subject of Barbara Cantalupo's *Poe and the Visual* Arts (2014).[33]

The future of Poe studies remains only roughly imaginable. Emerging models of literary and cultural analysis will generate innovative approaches to familiar texts, reconfirming the radical suggestiveness of Poe's writings. How these new interpretive paradigms will produce ground-breaking critical, historical, or theoretical readings of Poe cannot, however, be guessed. Traditional forms of scholarship will also surely continue apace. Recent interest in antebellum print culture has suggested a need for closer attention to the periodical contexts in which Poe's works first appeared. Beyond the biographies cited earlier, more full-length life studies will follow, incorporating additional pieces of information, making greater or lesser use of the poetry and fiction, and perhaps digging into cultural history to elaborate more fully Poe's relationship to print culture in Jacksonian America. Benjamin Fisher's *Poe in His Own Time: A Biographical Chronicle of His Life Drawn from Recollections, Interviews, and Memoirs by Family, Friends, and Associates* (2010), which collects anecdotes and observations, may suggest a few new lines of inquiry.[34] One area of Poe studies that still seems oddly neglected is bibliography. Yes, each volume of *American Literary Scholarship* includes, as part of a longer chapter, a review of Poe research for that year, and the *MLA Bibliography* annually lists all Poe books, essays, or articles for the previous year, sorted by work or topic. *Poe Studies* and *The Edgar Allan Poe Review* have both in the past included selective, occasional bibliographical features but provide no systematic tracking. Richard Kopley's annotated *Poe Oxford Bibliography Online* represents a valuable, annotated multiyear online resource, but the approach is selective, emphasizing books, and can be accessed only via university library subscriptions.[35] Nowhere can Poe scholars go online to consult a free, current, and historically inclusive bibliography of published Poe scholarship, from books to notes and queries, digitally indexed to be searchable by work, topic, genre, and so on. Digital technology makes such a site feasible, but in recent years, bibliography has perhaps become too professionally unfashionable to inspire the necessary effort. Such work needs to be done, however, for without scholarly due diligence, too many young author-critics will repeat arguments rolled out years ago.

However one envisions the future of Poe studies, digital technology will play a crucial role. As textbook publishers market electronic editions, readable on tablets or laptops, those e-texts must be edited and annotated with the same rigor as scholarly, print editions. Who wants to teach "The Fall of the House of Usher" from a faulty text rife with laughable errors? The digital format widens options for annotation, including the use of hyperlinks to famous illustrations of Poe's tales. Indeed, significant textual allusions can be linked to a wide array of online resources; the constraints of physical, print editions no longer apply. But electronic editing, which includes preparation of digital scholarly editions for the twenty-first century, represents only one basic application of new technology to produce materials for research and pedagogy.

As noted earlier, the best, most authoritative digital resource for Poe studies has for many years been the archive eapoe.org, which was created single-handedly by Jeffrey Savoye. By dint of unbelievable labor over two decades, he has compiled electronic versions of every printing of every Poe text, whether poetry, fiction, correspondence, reviews, essays, sketches, lecture, or miscellanea. He has moreover supplemented this material with digital versions of the standard scholarly editions, including the expanded edition of Poe letters he produced with Burton Pollin. The site also makes available other key research tools such as the *Poe Log*, an online version of the A. H. Quinn biography, a selection of Poe portraits (courtesy of Michael Deas), and a "Poe bookshelf" as well as a file of back issues of *Poe Studies*. Anyone who works on Poe in a serious way has already used eapoe.org many times. It is an indispensable resource and an extraordinary achievement for anyone—but almost incomprehensible as the creation of an independent scholar working without institutional support. All current Poe scholars owe a huge debt to Savoye.

But the reality is that eapoe.org in its present form is, in the long term, logistically unsustainable. Savoye has updated the coding behind his texts to XHTML and CSS, which ensures better browser compatibility than his old HTML files. But the updating is not yet complete and each text added to the archive (which now runs over 6,000 pages) requires the insertion of new links in extant files to which it relates. Comparing the scope of the prize-winning Edgar Allan Poe Society of Baltimore website with archives maintained at large universities by teams of graduate students, supported by hefty grants, and drawing on the resources of a university DH center highlights the monumentality of Savoye's accomplishment. And it also hints at the limitations against which he has struggled. Archives in academe typically enjoy renewable funding, abundant trained labor, and creative teams to develop interpretive tools. For some time, the Baltimore Poe archive has relied, sensibly and pragmatically, on the impressive capabilities of Google Search. But there are no interactive features, Savoye has a backlist of unfinished chores, and he acknowledges proofreading as likely a "perpetual task."

There is another stark, human reality. Eapoe.org exists online because Savoye maintains it. He pays an annual fee to keep it alive on a server maintained by a private hosting service. Unless or until a major benefactor steps forward, its survival will continue to depend entirely on his labor and longevity. He has provided copies of his material to the Mabbott Archive at the University of Iowa, but that library has no active Poe DH commitment to keep the archive online and updated. Rising Poe scholars with digital training need to be aware of eapoe.org and the critical importance of preserving it. Perhaps its long-term survival will have been assured when the *Oxford Handbook of Edgar Allan Poe* appears. But if not, scholars face the eventual loss of an extraordinary asset. The answer would seem to be a spin-off Poe site, built from Savoye's texts with his permission. It might then be possible to construct, under a different domain name, a sustainable archive that, on its home page, pays tribute to Savoye's groundbreaking work. A university setting seems most likely to offer the requisite logistical support and financial commitment. Establishing a mutually agreeable arrangement with the Edgar Allan Poe Society of Baltimore and Savoye (who plans to continue developing eapoe.org) would be a necessary first step. Assembling a team of content experts, librarians, archivists, designers, and IT specialists would then become essential.

By sensibly repurposing Savoye's texts rather than starting anew, a new Poe digital research site would likely take on a fresh look, advance the brand of the sponsoring university, and assume a different organizational architecture, perhaps introducing tools for crowdsourcing, data mining, topic modeling, or other digital strategies. One could also imagine an effort, with the cooperation of many libraries and special collections, to incorporate online page images of all extant Poe manuscripts and letters. Another possible initiative might generate a digital compilation of "Poe's Reading," collating and vetting book references in his reviews, tales, letters, and marginalia against extant evidence of actual perusal. The possibilities are intriguing, though the eapoe.org content figures to remain the essential core of any future Poe archive. Anyone eager to take on such challenges must also understand the hard reality that digital work is painfully slow and laborious under the best of circumstances. It demands a long-term commitment by a collaborative group motivated to inspire new and older forms of Poe research.

But digital technology also opens up exciting possibilities for smaller-scale Poe projects. One could curate a site on the Folio Club tales, for example, or reconstruct the social networks of print culture in the 1830s and 1840s, or map the journals in which Poe's work appeared, or focus on his bid to start a monthly magazine, or track the evolution of his critical vocabulary (via word frequency counts) from 1835 to 1849. Software programs can already identify and differentiate authorial styles based on usage algorithms; as Stefan Schöberlein has recently demonstrated, it now seems possible to say with much greater certainty, for example, that Nathaniel Beverley Tucker, not Poe, wrote the infamous 1836 *Messenger* review of Paulding's book about slavery.[36] The same stylistic analysis could be applied to the apocryphal writings ascribed to Poe or to anonymous squibs in the journals Poe helped to edit. Scholars today have at hand digital resources from Google Books, the Hathi Trust, and Archive.org, obviating much travel and archival excavation required of scholars a generation ago. Material for research on Poe the magazinist can be found through the ProQuest commercial database, American Periodicals Series, or at the open-source Cornell-Michigan Making of America archive. We can now look at more texts, even obscure volumes, faster than ever. Digital tools also exist for classroom use, including programs like the Harvard "Highbrow" deep-zoom widget that aggregates student responses to critical prompts ("What is the most frightening moment in this tale?") by tagging passages that can be displayed on a computer screen in summary form. Although the hard work of close reading, scholarly digging, and nimble critical thinking will remain at the heart of Poe studies, digital resources will form an important part of its future. We hope the essays in this volume help to prepare a new generation of students and scholars to pursue the elusive Edgar Poe and to contribute to an exciting, ongoing intellectual enterprise.

Notes

1. See Vernon Louis Parrington, *Main Currents of American Thought, vol. 2, The Romantic Revolution in America, 1800–1860* (New York: Harcourt, Brace, and Co., 1927), 57–59; Paul Elmer More, "A Note on Poe's Method," *Studies in Philology* 20, no. 3 (July 1923): 309; and F. O. Matthiesen, *American Renaissance: Art and Expression in the Age of Emerson and Whitman* (New York: Oxford University Press, 1941), xii.
2. Especially see Harrison, ed., *The Complete Works of Edgar Allan Poe* (H); Mary E. Phillips, *Edgar Allan Poe: The Man*, 2 vols. (Chicago: The John C. Winston Co., 1926); Margaret Alterton, *Origins of Poe's Critical Theory* (Iowa City: Iowa Humanistic Studies, 1925); Killis Campbell, *The Mind of Poe and Other Studies* (Cambridge, MA: Harvard University Press, 1933); and Mabbott, ed., *Collected Works of Edgar Allan Poe* (M).
3. Excerpt from James, "Baudelaire," in *The Recognition of Edgar Allan Poe*, ed. Eric W. Carlson (Ann Arbor: University of Michigan Press, 1966), 66.
4. Rufus W. Griswold, ed., *The Works of the Late Edgar Allan Poe*, 4 vols. (New York: J. S. Redfield, 1850–1856).
5. Foucault, "What Is an Author?," in *Textual Strategies: Perspectives in Post-Structuralist Criticism*, ed. Josué V. Harari (Ithaca, NY: Cornell University Press, 1979), 141–160.
6. James Russell Lowell, *Lowell's Complete Poems* (New York: Houghton, 1898), 142.
7. Sarah Helen Whitman, *Edgar Poe and His Critics* (New York: Rudd & Carleton, 1860), 1.
8. Charles F. Briggs, "The Personality of Poe," *The Independent* 29, no. 1414 (Dec. 13, 1877): 1.
9. William Dean Howells, *Literary Friends and Acquaintances: A Personal Retrospect of American Authorship*, ed. David F. Hiatt and Edwin H. Cady (Bloomington: Indiana University Press, 1968), 58; *Mark Twain—Howells Letters: The Correspondence of Samuel L. Clemens and William D. Howells*, ed. Henry Nash Smith and William M. Gibson, vol. 2, 1872–1910 (Cambridge, MA: Harvard University Press, 1960), 841.
10. Charles Leonard Moore, "The American Rejection of Poe," *The Dial* 47 (Jan. 1899): 40–42.

11. See Scott Peeples, *The Afterlife of Edgar Allan Poe* (Rochester, NY: Camden House, 2004), 16–17.
12. T. S. Eliot, "From Poe to Valéry," in *The Recognition of Edgar Allan Poe*, ed. Eric W. Carlson (Ann Arbor: University of Michigan Press), 205.
13. Cleanth Brooks and Robert Penn Warren, *Understanding Poetry*, rev. ed. (1938; New York: Henry Holt, 1950), 199; *Understanding Fiction* (Englewood Cliffs, NJ: Prentice Hall, 1946), 204–205.
14. Matthiessen, "Edgar Allan Poe," in *Literary History of the United States*, ed. Robert E. Spiller, Willard Thorp, Thomas H. Johnson, and Henry Seidel Canby (New York: The Macmillan Company, 1948), 1:342.
15. Joseph Csicsila, *Canons by Consensus: Critical Trends and American Literature Anthologies* (Tuscaloosa: University of Alabama Press, 2004), 36–38.
16. D. H. Lawrence, *Studies in Classic American Literature* (1925; repr., London: Penguin, 1977); Marie Bonaparte, *The Life and Works of Edgar Allan Poe: A Psychoanalytic Interpretation*, trans. John Rodker (London: Imago, 1949).
17. Edward H. Davidson, *Poe: A Critical Study* (Cambridge, MA: Harvard University Press, 1957).
18. Allen Tate, "The Angelic Imagination," in *The Recognition of Edgar Allan Poe*, ed. Eric W. Carlson (Ann Arbor: University of Michigan Press, 1966), 236–254; Richard Wilbur, Introduction to *Poe: Complete Poems* (New York: Dell, 1959), 7–39.
19. Patrick F. Quinn, *The French Face of Edgar Poe* (Carbondale: Southern Illinois University Press, 1957); Harry Levin, *The Power of Blackness* (New York: Knopf, 1958); Darrel Abel, "A Key to the House of Usher," *University of Toronto Quarterly* 18 (1949): 176–185; Clark Griffith, "Poe's 'Ligeia' and the English Romantics," *University of Toronto Quarterly* 24 (1954): 8–26; Joseph Patrick Roppolo, "Meaning and 'The Masque of the Red Death,'" *Tulane Studies in English* 13 (1963): 59–69; James W. Gargano, "The Question of Poe's Narrators," *College English* 25 (1963): 177–181; James M. Cox, "Edgar Poe: Style as Pose," *Virginia Quarterly Review* 44 (1968): 67–89; David H. Hirsch, "The Pit and the Apocalypse," *Sewanee Review* 76 (1968): 632–652.
20. Arthur Hobson Quinn, *Edgar Allan Poe: A Critical Biography* (1941; repr., Baltimore and London: Johns Hopkins University Press, 1998).
21. Robbins, "The State of Poe Studies," *Poe Newsletter* 1, no. 1 (April 1968): 1.
22. Kenneth Silverman, *Edgar A. Poe: Mournful and Never-ending Remembrance* (New York: HarperCollins, 1991).
23. M. Thomas Inge, "Comic Book and Graphic Novel Adaptations of the Works of Edgar Allan Poe: A Chronology," in *Adapting Poe: Re-Imaginings in Popular Culture*, edited by Dennis R. Perry and Carl H. Sederholm (New York: Palgrave Macmillan, 2012), 231–247; M. Thomas Inge, *The Incredible Mr. Poe: Comic Book Adaptations of the Works of Edgar Allan Poe, 1943–2007* (Richmond: Edgar Allan Poe Museum, 2003).
24. Don G. Smith, *The Poe Cinema: A Critical Filmography* (Jefferson, NC: McFarland, 1999).
25. John P. Muller and William J. Richardson, eds., *The Purloined Poe: Lacan, Derrida, and Psychoanalytic Reading* (Baltimore: Johns Hopkins University Press, 1988).
26. Jean Ricardou, "The Singular Character of the Water" ("Le Caractère Singulier de cette eau," 1967), trans. Frank Towne, *Poe Studies* 9 (1976): 1–6; Riddel's essay—"The 'Crypt' of Edgar Poe," *boundary 2* 7, no. 3 (Spring, 1979): 117–144—was included as a chapter in his book *Purloined Letters: Originality and Repetition in American Literature* (Baton Rouge: Louisiana State University Press, 1995), 121–148; John T. Irwin, *American*

Hieroglyphics: The Symbol of Egyptian Hieroglyphics in the American Renaissance (New Haven, CT: Yale University Press, 1980); John Carlos Rowe, *Through The Custom-House: Nineteenth-Century American Fiction and Modern Theory* (Baltimore: Johns Hopkins University Press, 1982); Louis A. Renza, "Poe's Secret Autobiography," in *The American Renaissance Reconsidered: Selected Papers from the English Institute, 1982–83*, ed. Walter Benn Michaels and Donald E. Pease (Baltimore: Johns Hopkins University Press, 1985), 58–89; J. Gerald Kennedy, *Poe, Death, and the Life of Writing* (New Haven, CT: Yale University Press, 1987); Michael J. S. Williams, *A World of Words: Language and Displacement in the Fiction of Edgar Allan Poe* (Durham, NC: Duke University Press, 1988); Dennis Pahl, *Architects of the Abyss: The Indeterminate Fictions of Poe, Hawthorne, and Melville* (Columbia: University of Missouri Press, 1989).

27. Joan Dayan, "Amorous Bondage: Poe, Ladies, and Slaves," in *The American Face of Edgar Allan Poe*, ed. Shawn Rosenheim and Stephen Rachman (Baltimore: Johns Hopkins University Press, 1995), 179–209.
28. Judith Fetterley, "Reading about Reading: 'A Jury of Her Peers,' 'The Murders in the Rue Morgue,' and 'The Yellow Wallpaper,'" in *Gender and Reading: Essays on Readers, Texts, and Contexts*, ed. Elizabeth A. Flynn and Patrocinio P. Schweickart (Baltimore: Johns Hopkins University Press, 1986), 147–164; Cynthia S. Jordan, *Second Stories: The Politics of Language, Form, and Gender in Early American Fiction* (Chapel Hill: University of North Carolina Press, 1989); Leland S. Person, *Aesthetic Headaches: Women and a Masculine Poetics in Poe, Melville, and Hawthorne* (Athens: University of Georgia Press, 1988); J. Gerald Kennedy, "Poe, 'Ligeia,' and the Problem of Dying Women," in *New Essays on Poe's Major Tales*, ed. Kenneth Silverman (Cambridge: Cambridge University Press, 1993), 113–129; David Leverenz, "Poe and Gentry Virginia," in *The American Face of Edgar Allan Poe*, 210–236; and Laura Saltz, "'(Horrible to Relate!)': Recovering the Body of Marie Roget," in *The American Face of Edgar Allan Poe*, 237–267.
29. Terence Whalen, *Edgar Allan Poe and the Masses: The Political Economy of Literature in Antebellum America* (Princeton, NJ: Princeton University Press, 1999); Jonathan Elmer, *Reading at the Social Limit: Affect, Mass Culture, and Edgar Allan Poe* (Stanford, CA: Stanford University Press, 1995).
30. Toni Morrison, *Playing in the Dark: Whiteness and the Literary Imagination* (New York: Vintage, 1992), 32.
31. J. Gerald Kennedy and Liliane Weissberg, *Romancing the Shadow: Poe and Race* (New York: Oxford University Press, 2001).
32. Rohy, "Ahistorical," *GLQ* 12, no. 12 (November 2006): 61–83; Colleen Glenney Boggs, "Animals and the Letter of the Law: Edgar Allan Poe," in *Animalia Americana: Animal Representations and Biopolitical Subjectivity* (New York: Columbia University Press, 2013), 109–132; Jacob Rama Berman, "Poe's Taste for the Arabesque," in *American Arabesque: Arabs and Islam in the 19th-Century Imaginary* (New York: New York University Press, 2012), 138–178; Matthew A. Taylor, *Universes Without Us: Posthuman Cosmologies in American Literature* (Minneapolis: University of Minnesota Press, 2013); Taylor, "Edgar Allan Poe's (Meta)Physics: A Pre-History of the Post-Human," *Nineteenth Century Literature* 62, no. 2 (Sept. 2007): 193–221; Emron Esplin, "Borges's Philosophy of Poe's Composition," *Comparative Literature Studies* 50, no. 3 (2013): 458–489; Jerome McGann, "'The Bells,' Performance, and the Politics of Poetry," *The Edgar Allan Poe Review* 15, no. 1 (2014): 47–58; Maurice S. Lee, "Absolute Poe: His System of Transcendental Racism," *American Literature* 75, no. 4 (2003): 751–781; Laura Saltz, "'Eyes Which

Behold': Poe's 'Domain of Arnheim' and the Science of Vision," *The Edgar Allan Poe Review* 7, no. 1 (2006): 4–30; Cindy Weinstein, "When Is Now? Poe's Aesthetics of Temporality," *Poe Studies* 41 (2008): 81–107; Stephen Rachman, "Poe's Drinking, Poe's Delirium: The Privacy of Imps," *The Edgar Allan Poe Review* 12, no. 2 (2011): 6–40.

33. Scott Peeples, *The Afterlife of Edgar Allan Poe* (Rochester, NY: Camden House, 2004); Eliza Richards, *Gender and the Poetics of Reception in Poe's Circle* (Cambridge: University of Cambridge Press, 2004); Meredith McGill, *American Literature and the Culture of Reprinting, 1837–1853* (Philadelphia: University of Pennsylvania Press, 2003); Kennedy and McGann, eds., *Poe and the Remapping of Antebellum Print Culture* (Baton Rouge: Louisiana State University Press, 2012); McGann, *The Poet Edgar Allan Poe: Alien Angel* (Cambridge, MA: Harvard University Press, 2014); Kennedy, *Strange Nation: Literary Nationalism and Cultural Conflict in the Age of Poe* (New York: Oxford University Press, 2016), Emron Esplin and Margarida Vale de Gato, eds., *Translated Poe* (Bethlehem, PA: Lehigh University Press, 2014); Esplin, *Borges's Poe: The Influence and Reinvention of Edgar Allan Poe in Spanish America* (Athens: University of Georgia Press, 2016); John T. Irwin, *The Mystery to a Solution: Poe, Borges, and the Analytic Detective Story* (Baltimore: Johns Hopkins University Press, 1994); Barbara Cantalupo, *Poe and the Visual Arts* (University Park: Pennsylvania State University Press, 2014).
34. Benjamin F. Fisher, ed., *Poe in His Own Time: A Biographical Chronicle of His Life Drawn from Recollections, Interviews, and Memoirs by Family, Friends, and Associates* (Iowa City: University of Iowa Press, 2010).
35. Richard Kopley, "Edgar Allan Poe," *Oxford Bibliographies*, published online August 2012, last modified October 2016, doi: http://dx.doi.org/10.1093/obo/9780199827251-0050.
36. Stefan Schöberlein, "Poe or Not Poe? A Stylometric Analysis of Edgar Allan Poe's Disputed Writings," *Digital Scholarship in the Humanities* 32, no. 3 (2017): 643–659, doi: https://doi.org/10.1093/llc/fqw019.

CHAPTER 1

AN ORPHAN'S LIFE: 1809-1831

JAMES M. HUTCHISSON

IN his 1829 poem "Alone," Edgar Allan Poe wrote, "From childhood's hour I have not been/As others were—," "And all I lov'd—*I* lov'd alone" (M 1: 146, lines 1–2, 8). Poe's early life was characterized by loss, perhaps the key element that pervaded much of what Poe wrote, especially his early poetry. This is not at all surprising, for Poe's early years were marked by the painful losses of many whom he held dear: his birth mother, Elizabeth Arnold Poe; his foster mother, Frances Allan; and a Richmond neighbor whom he regarded as a surrogate mother, Jane Stanard—the subject of his poem "To Helen." In his early years, Poe also lived through a series of traumas brought on first by the losses of the nurturing female figures in his life and then later exacerbated by his ostracism from his foster father, John Allan—and, by extension, from Richmond society. The sense of being unwanted accounted for the emotional tenor of his early verse. It would also send him on a restless, lifelong journey to find a family and a place where he would feel secure.

Edgar Allan Poe was born the second child of three to David and Eliza Poe in Boston on January 19, 1849. An older brother, William Henry Leonard Poe, had arrived two years earlier, and a younger sister named Rosalie, possibly from another father, came in December 1810. The Poes were itinerant actors. David Poe, Jr., had been born in Baltimore in 1784, the son of a merchant who had fought in the Revolutionary War and, rather zealously, had also contributed some forty thousand dollars of his own money toward the colonists' cause. In local circles Edgar's grandfather was revered as a great patriot. (Although holding the rank only of major as Deputy Quartermaster for a Baltimore regiment, he was given the courtesy title of "General" and thereafter became known as General Poe, something his grandson would later exaggerate for its ring of elevated social status.) David had been training to become a lawyer, but he had drifted into the theater instead. Obstinate and mercurial, he was given to fits of anger abetted by drink. As an actor, he was apparently not well regarded, and he took offense at the critics who skewered him in print, challenging more than one reviewer to a fistfight to settle the score. He was most likely an alcoholic, a genetic inheritance that was later handed down to his son, whose predisposition to drink—and his utter inability to "drink well"—became widely known among his friends and competitors. Edgar also inherited from his father a flair for melodrama and for indulging in theatrical bursts of pique, especially when he felt that the world was against him.[1]

In contrast to her husband, Poe's mother, Eliza, was a brilliant performer and highly talented actress. She had been born in England and brought to America in January 1796 by her parents, actors themselves, who came to the New World in search of steady work. Eliza got her start on the stage quite early, singing in the intermission between two plays one evening at the Federal Street Theater in Boston at age nine. Her performance was well received—a trend that would continue in her career as she grew older and took on more ambitious roles. Among the plays she appeared in were *Romeo and Juliet, Hamlet*, and numerous other Shakespeare dramas. By the time she was twenty-four years old, she had turned in almost three hundred performances. Eliza was also lauded as a singer. Eventually the newspapers bestowed on her the sobriquet "The Nightingale," as a testament to her mellifluous voice.

David Poe abandoned the family around the time that Rosalie was born. He was known to have been living in or around Baltimore shortly thereafter, but then he essentially fell out of sight, and today, the rest of his life—and death—is mostly a blank space in the documentary record. Biographers have placed the time of his death as early as October 1810, in Norfolk, or as late as January 1811, in Richmond. With her husband's departure, Eliza, a young mother with three children, was thrown back on her own resources and had to make a living for her growing family. She therefore toured up and down the eastern seaboard with an acting troupe, turning in her usual stellar performances, carrying her weight backstage, and pitching in to do all the usual yeoman's work that a member of a theatrical troupe at that time would be expected to do.[2] It was a hardscrabble existence.

While performing at the Richmond Theatre in November 1811, Eliza fell ill. She spiralled downward quickly—and foresaw her fate. Charitable society women in the city placed an announcement in the *Richmond Enquirer* on November 29, stating, "On this night, *Mrs. Poe*, lingering on the bed of disease and surrounded by her children, asks your assistance, and *asks it perhaps for the last time*" (PL: 13). Eliza passed away soon thereafter, on December 8, 1811. It is possible that Edgar was at her deathbed; if he was, it was a traumatic moment that would stay with him in memory for his entire life, for he seems to have replayed it his imagination over and over again in numerous scenes where fragile, beautiful, and generously loving women die and leave behind for those who loved them a tragic legacy of unvanquishable grief. Poe lived with what he would later name, in his famous essay "The Philosophy of Composition," a "mournful and never-ending remembrance" (ER: 25).

The newspaper announcement of Eliza's destitute circumstances had ended with the words, "The generosity of a Richmond Audience can need no other appeal" (PL: 13). Accordingly, the city's society families responded to the plight of the young children, now orphaned. Poe's brother Henry was sent to live with relatives in Baltimore, while his sister Rosalie was taken into the care of a prominent Richmond family, the Mackenzies.

And Poe went to live with John and Frances Allan, another family well known in local society. John and Frances had differing views of the young Poe. "Fanny," as Poe's foster mother was known, was much like Eliza—about the same age, with some of the same physical features, and possessed of a nurturing personality. Fanny too had been an orphan, raised by a guardian from the age of ten. Poe grew attached to Fanny very quickly when he became part of the Allan family. Fanny's husband, John, was another matter. A Scotsman by birth, John was all hard edges. Hawk-eyed, blunt-nosed, and plain speaking by nature, he lived by a bootstraps philosophy holding that life meant hard work, and he brooked no idleness. He was a merchant, and he saw the world in the same way he thought of his accounts—strictly in terms of profit and loss. (Poe lampooned the mercantile world in a later story, "The Business Man," whose central character, "Peter Proffitt," may have been modeled on John Allan.[3]) Allan never had any intention of taking in an orphaned son of an actor and only reluctantly went along with the idea because his wife had wanted it. Allan therefore saw Edgar as a drain on his resources, both of time and of money—red ink spilling over the pages of his family ledger. As Edgar grew into an adolescent and then a teenager, Allan's resentment of him would grow concomitantly, and the two would inevitably clash. Poe would eventually come to feel that he was not part of the Allan family—an adjunct member at best, an embarrassment at worst. He was never formally adopted by John Allan and, although he was baptized Edgar Allan Poe, in his adult life he nearly always signed himself "Edgar Poe" or "Edgar A. Poe."[4] The now-familiar "Allan" was foisted on him posthumously, and perhaps mean-spiritedly, by his literary executor and erstwhile friend, Rufus W. Griswold, who published a scabrous obituary about him that tarnished his reputation for decades.

To his credit, however, Allan provided a comfortable and privileged, although not opulent, life for Edgar during the author's childhood. Surviving are numerous bills for clothes and schooling, the purchase of a crib, and, from letters, reports of relief that the young boy had recovered from such illnesses as whooping cough and measles. Poe was privately educated, first by Clotilda Fisher, whom biographer Arthur Hobson Quinn speculated probably ran a local "dame's school," then by William Ewing;[5] he was outfitted with nice suits of clothes; and he accompanied his foster parents on trips to expensive resorts, such as the one in White Sulphur Springs, Virginia (PL: 17). Poe was probably attended by a black "mammie" and waited on by black slaves (although it has never been determined how many enslaved servants the Allans owned); he apparently developed a friendship with one, a servant named Armistead Gordon. According to Thomas Ollive Mabbott, Gordon regaled Poe (and frightened him dreadfully) with scary stories about the supernatural world.[6]

When Poe was six years old, in 1815, John Allan moved the family to central London as his firm, Ellis and Allan, was attempting to expand its import-export business. After a sea journey of thirty-some days, the family arrived in Scotland, where they first spent five weeks visiting Allan relations; they then traveled down to London, where they were to reside for the next five years. Here, Poe was exposed to London's cosmopolitan culture during a formative period in his life. At age seven, Edgar enrolled for schooling, boarding first at the school of the Misses Dubourg (the family of John Allan's young clerk, George), on Sloane Street in Chelsea, about three miles from the Allans' rented flat in Russell Square. The schoolmistresses took good care of their charge, notifying Allan that the boy was "well & happy."[7] Later, he was sent to a boarding school in nearby Stoke Newington, run by the Reverend Dr. John Bransby, who reappears as the schoolmaster in Poe's 1839 story "William Wilson." At Bransby's, Poe excelled in languages. He was not particularly well liked by his fellow students, however; no doubt they saw him as an upstart colonial—the memory of the War of 1812 still being fresh in the English mind, especially given the beating the British had suffered at the hands of the Americans.[8]

Moreover, Poe—in a foreign country at a young and impressionable age—did not see his foster family much at all, intensifying his feelings of separation and dislocation. Away at school, he was without parents; and assuming he came home on weekends, they were probably largely absent even then. Allan was preoccupied with making his business a success (which it was, after a somewhat plodding start). The person Poe was closest to in the family was Fanny, but she was not really available to him in any meaningful sense because she was so often shut up in her room due to frequent, or even chronic, illnesses. John Allan seems to have provided for Poe well, but biographer Kenneth Silverman makes the point that letters sent to the Allans in England from various Richmond friends usually asked to be remembered to Fanny and to her sister, Nancy (who had accompanied them), but never to Poe. It was as if his presence were known but did not bear mentioning.[9] Allan apparently did not want Poe to continue to be schooled in London. Several months after arriving in London and beginning his schooling there, Poe blanched at the plan Allan had to send him to Scotland for his education, no doubt feeling that it would put him at an even further level of removal from the family. That he was afraid and angry can be seen in an account later given by James Galt, a member of Allan's uncle's family, fifteen at the time and living in Scotland. Allan sent Edgar, just seven years old, back to Scotland in the company of Galt. Throughout the journey, Galt recalled, Edgar was recalcitrant and obstreperous, and at the school in Irvine, Scotland, where Allan wanted him to board, he refused to study and was frequently disobedient. Galt thought that if he had not kept close watch over the boy, he would have tried to travel back to London on his own.[10]

A financial panic hit the English banks in 1819, caused largely by a slump in the tobacco market, and Allan's business was nearly destroyed by it. He clung on for several months, just barely financially afloat, but eventually he reached the point where he could not pay his creditors the quarter of a million dollars he owed them, and he had to return with his family to Richmond, chastened—and perhaps privately feeling disgraced. Poe continued his schooling in Richmond, but he must have felt awkwardly uprooted and somewhat ill at ease, back among his countrymen after living abroad for five years. One month after the Allans returned to Richmond in August 1820, Poe entered the school of Joseph H. Clarke. Poe was not a particularly good student, by contemporary accounts, but he loved to read and write poetry. He was also a born performer (like his parents), adept at public speaking. Once, he won first place in an elocution contest, outstripping the talents of much older boys than he. Clarke found the boy "remarkable for self-respect" and "ambitious to excel," although "not conspicuously studious." Poe also displayed a flair for poetry. In 1820, Clarke recognized that what Poe was writing was truly imaginative and not merely "mechanical"; it was, to Clarke's mind, "genuine poetry" (PL: 47). When Clarke left Richmond in 1822, Poe's classmates elected him to write an ode to Clarke to commemorate his time there.

As a youth, Poe was likely not fully aware of the political culture and social attitudes that pervaded Richmond, but neither could he have been oblivious to them. Virginia was one of the first colonies to import slaves from Africa in the early days of the Atlantic slave trade. Richmond became the capital of the southern slave trade and benefited financially from it, bested only by New Orleans. Traders would come through Richmond looking to purchase slaves; the ones sold would be manacled and marched naked along the James River and taken to auction houses in the downtown areas of Shockoe Slip and in a sunken spot known as Shockoe Bottom.[11] Enslaved men and women were sold in public view—respectable citizens attended these auctions and at least tacitly seemed to approve of the way the slaves were handled. Prior to being auctioned, many slaves were held at a notorious jail owned by the slave trader Robert Lumpkin in Shockoe Bottom. The jail was also known as "the devil's half acre." (An archeological expedition in 2009 found the 80-by-160-foot complex buried under fourteen feet of earth—a raw, damp place where hundreds of slaves were confined and tortured.)[12]

Richmond was a fast-growing city bursting at the seams with a prosperity that came from the slave labor that produced coal, tobacco, and flour, and went directly into the pockets of a planter class of wealthy aristocrats. Even more important, the slave population was changing. It was restless and, in the eyes of white citizens, unstable. As J. Gerald Kennedy points out, "blacks possessed economic leverage" because tobacco processors paid money to slaves who boarded out, even giving them overtime pay in certain circumstances. Thus, slaves were seen in a new way throughout the city—with money, with time on their hands, and without having to remain within the borders of the plantation or home to which they belonged.[13] It was also a period where some of the first rumblings of turbulence were to be heard over the issue of slaveholders versus abolitionists, antagonisms that anticipated the later Virginia legislative debates over emancipation, which would come to the fore in 1831–1832. Fear of blacks by white society was exacerbated by the Southampton Insurrection of 1831, led by the slave Nat Turner.

Poe probably absorbed the social attitudes of his peers, but he did not always feel that he belonged in Richmond society. Most of his would-be peers were of the landed gentry—the planter class—while John Allan was a merchant. Poe certainly aspired to a higher class, and he affected an aristocratic air at a young age, but he actually had to promote himself in other ways. One was through scholarship—Poe eventually became a very good student, and he was quick to point out to others the degree of his erudition. Another was through athleticism. Friends later recalled that in 1824 or 1825—accounts vary—Poe astounded them by swimming six miles, mostly against the current, in the powerful James River on a hot June afternoon.[14] Although small of stature, Poe was strong and fit; he was a born competitor who was intent on besting his peers.

Despite being something of an outsider in Richmond society, Poe grew up in relatively pleasant circumstances. He had many friends, among them John Preston and

Matthew Sully, nephew of the portrait painter Thomas Sully. A prominent family in Richmond whom Poe saw much of was the Mackenzies, who had adopted Rosalie; she later attended a school run by one of the Mackenzie daughters, Jane, and, when Charles Mackenzie died, John Mackenzie, one of Poe's childhood playmates, became her legal guardian. In Richmond, Poe also continued to hold on to his Poe family ties. Remembering his grandfather David Poe, the young boy was excited when in August 1824 the Revolutionary War hero Lafayette began his triumphal tour of the United States. Poe took part in celebrations marking the general's visit to Richmond in October of that year as part of the Junior Morgan Riflemen (also known as the Junior Richmond Volunteers), whom Lafayette had selected as his guard detail. One friend recalled Poe walking, proud and erect, outside the state capitol while Lafayette held a grand reception inside (PL: 59).

Thomas H. Ellis, son of Allan's business partner Charles and his wife, Margaret Ellis, was probably his closest friend. Ellis later recalled that everything he knew about the outdoors—hunting, swimming, and other pastimes—he learned from Poe, whom he called a "leader among boys" and someone for whom his "admiration held no bounds." This was a circumstance that sometimes led him astray, as the two boys were wont to go off on dares and take risks that they shouldn't have. Ellis recalled that once Poe had to save him from drowning after his friend pushed him headlong into the falls and then realized that Ellis did not have the strength or skill to stay afloat (PL: 49).

In contrast to his own youthful robustness, Poe's foster mother, Fanny, seemed to grow progressively frailer and more sickly as the years went on. Her husband brusquely recorded that she was "never clear of complaint," and he grew annoyed at her absence from his side (PL: 58). Fanny spent many of her days in her darkened bedroom—light seeming to give her blinding headaches and nausea. Although Poe would sometimes be invited by her to come to her sickroom, he still felt shut off; Fanny seemed elusively distant from him. Like Eliza leaving him, this mother, too, was slipping away and seemingly withdrawing her love for him in the process.

Around this time, perhaps to compensate for Fanny's absence in his life, Poe struck up an unusually close friendship with a neighbor, Jane Stith Craig Stanard, the mother of Poe's friend Robert Stanard. With eerie coincidence once again, Jane, like Fanny, also resembled Poe's birth mother, Eliza. Like Eliza and Fanny, she too was frequently ill; eventually, she fell into a prolonged period of depression and full-blown mental illness, brought on by an unhappy marriage. She lived in this chaotic mental state for about a year before dying in 1824. When she passed, Poe was bereft. He frequently visited Jane's grave in Shockoe Hill Cemetery. He associated the loss of Jane imaginatively with the loss of his birth mother: both young and generously loving women who had been cheated of a happy existence. The traumatic effect of these losses on Poe cannot be underestimated.

Like Eliza and other nurturing figures in Poe's life, Jane Stanard remained in his memory. He called her "the first, purely ideal love of my soul" and she inspired one of his most beautiful poems, "To Helen." Poe's aunt, Maria Clemm, told Sarah Helen Whitman, one of Poe's later love interests, "When Eddie was unhappy at home (which was often the case), he went to her for sympathy, and she always consoled and comforted him. . . . He visited [at her home] for years."[15] In "To Helen" Jane Stanard became the ideal of feminine beauty, like the Helen who became a visionary classical ideal—perfect and unattainable:

> On desperate seas long wont to roam,
> Thy hyacinth hair, thy classic face,
> Thy naiad airs have brought me home
> To the glory that was Greece,
> And the grandeur that was Rome. (M 1: 166, lines 6–10)

The closing couplet of that stanza is among Poe's most memorable verses. It is also revealing of his views of women—as nurturing beings that he needed in order to assure himself that he was loved, and as alabaster-skinned beauties forever immortalized in memory, through art.

In 1825, the year after Jane Stanard died, Edgar became secretly engaged to Sarah Elmira Royster, the fifteen-year-old daughter of a neighbor. She too, however, turned out to be unattainable, since her father later forbade the marriage. Edgar was an orphan, with no financial resources of his own, and no immediate future in a "solid" line of work, like banking or a trade. Poe was beginning to feel as if he had no path forward in life. One of his early poems, "Song" (originally, "To ——"), shows a wistful longing for a loving wife: "Happiness around thee lay," the poet says, "The world all love before thee" (M 1: 66, lines 3–4). The poem, in fact, may have had its origins when Poe learned that he had lost Elmira to a rival suitor, Alexander Shelton. He was given the news in the most brutal way imaginable. Calling on her at her home one evening, he arrived to find an engagement party in progress. Poe had been unaware of recent developments.[16]

Poe found some consolation in his close relationship with his brother William Henry Leonard Poe, who had lived first with the Poe grandparents until General Poe died; the widowed grandmother then took Henry with her to live with the Clemm relations in Baltimore. Despite the physical distance between them, the brothers remained in touch, and Henry was able to visit Edgar in Richmond around the time of his ill-fated courtship of Elmira (PL: 63). Like his brother, Henry had a sometimes wild, whimsical temperament and a romanticized self-image. Soon after visiting Poe, Henry took to sea, perhaps as a merchantman (no record of him exists in the United States Navy). Henry seems to have visited the near East, parts of the Mediterranean, and possibly Russia. Poe later enhanced and embellished accounts of Henry's exploits as a wandering adventurer, even incorporating parts of them into his own biography in accounts that he provided to various newspapers and magazines later in his career. In 1827, Henry returned to Baltimore and worked for a while at a law office, where he developed an interest in writing poetry, often similar to Poe's early verse in their portrayals of doomed love and self-exile.[17] He died of tuberculosis, in 1831.

As a teenager in Richmond, Poe eventually grew rebellious and surly, behavior abetted by his feeling that he did not belong in the Allan family. This behavior did not sit well with John Allan, who would not abide disorder or lack of harmony in his house. A clash was inevitable, as the foster father provided for him faithfully, paying his tuition, shelling out money for clothes and "trimmings," yet receiving, he claimed, "not a Spark of affection" nor a "particle of gratitude" in return (PL: 61). When Allan thought about all he had done for the boy, Edgar's unresponsiveness galled him even more: "Had I done my duty as faithfully to my God as I have to Edgar," he would later write, "then, had Death come," it would hold "no terrors" for him.[18] In a letter to Poe's brother Henry, Allan inaugurated what would become a steady series of tirades about Edgar's behavior. Taking in hand a recent letter from Henry to Poe, Allan wrote on the pretext of apologizing for Poe's not writing back sooner. "He has had little else to do for me," Allan wrote, "he does nothing & seems quite miserable, surly & ill-tempered to all the Family. How we have acted to produce this is beyond my conception—why I have put up for so long with his conduct is a little less wonderful" (PL: 61).

Allan's dark mood was in part due to business losses. The collapse of the land and cotton booms had sent the country into a deep economic depression that lasted until 1824 and severely affected his firm. Yet a dramatic reversal of misfortune occurred in Allan's life in March 1825. Allan's uncle William Galt, said to be one of the richest men in Virginia, with several hundred acres of land and hundreds of slaves, died and left him a bequest of $750,000. (In today's currency, this would be nearly $20,000,000.) With his newfound wealth, Allan immediately acceded to the life of a moneyed gentleman. Within two months, he had purchased one of the most impressive houses in Richmond—Moldavia, an imposing stone mansion on a huge lot, once owned by a titan of the milling industry.

Despite his poor relationship with Allan, Poe succeeded in convincing his foster father to send him to the newly established University of Virginia in 1826, some seventy miles distant in Charlottesville. Poe did well there, excelling in languages, mathematics, and debate. He loved books and learning, music and art. He enrolled in courses in ancient and modern languages, earning high grades in the senior Latin and French classes. He also joined the Jefferson Society, a debating club, and became noted for his verbal facility. Poe's intellect was well above average. One classmate testified that Poe rarely had to prepare his lessons in advance and that his memory was so sharp that he required only a few minutes of study before class in order to give the best recitation in the group. Another fellow student noted Poe's artistic abilities, recalling that he would "with a piece of charcoal evince his versatile genius by sketching upon the walls of his dormitory, whimsical, fanciful and grotesque figures, with so much artistic skill, as to leave us in doubt whether Poe in future life would be Painter or Poet" (PL: 69). At the end of the first term, in December 1826, Poe was examined in his subjects by two former presidents of the United States: James Monroe and James Madison, who had succeeded Thomas Jefferson as rector, or head of school. In ancient and modern languages, Poe passed with highest honors.[19]

The so-called academical village, however, was not without its eccentricities. It had been shaped in the vision of its founder, Jefferson, and was unlike the more established universities in the north, such as Princeton and Harvard. For one thing, it had no religious affiliation (in keeping with Jefferson's humanistic views). For another, the students were largely self-governing, which is to say, essentially unsupervised—again, an extension of Jefferson's Enlightenment-derived principles of reason and common sense. As a result, the atmosphere there was often rowdy to the point of being violent. Duels were common; knives were brought out in drunken disputes at late-night card games and in drinking bouts. Drinking was rampant, and Poe's low tolerance for alcohol prompted one classmate to note that "One glass at a time was about all he could take."[20] Moreover, the violence extended beyond the students. One professor, for instance, was seen horsewhipping his wife in full view of the other campus residents.[21] What Poe may have made of such scenes, beyond being obviously shocked, we do not know; however, they may certainly have colored his vision of man as at times a perverse being, subject to the caprices of his baser instincts and even capable of animalistic behavior.

Poe's gambling got him into trouble and precipitated Allan's withdrawing him from the university after only one term of study there. Poe was apparently fond of card games but unsuccessful at them; he ran up huge debts and was forced to borrow money, most likely at exorbitant interest rates, from lenders in the town. Poe's defense was that Allan had sent him to the university without enough money. "I will boldly say that it was wholly and entirely your own mistaken parsimony that caused all the difficulties in which I was involved while at Charlottesville," he later wrote Allan. "The expenses of the institution at the lowest estimate were $350 per annum. You sent me there with $110" (CL 1: 59). Poe felt that he had to keep up appearances with his wealthy classmates, who brought with them servants, well-tailored clothes, and other gentlemanly trappings.

Who wronged whom in this phase of Poe's life can probably never be determined. Allan said that he had given Poe plenty of money to live on, but it also could be true that he had deliberately shortchanged him, expecting him to make do with little, as he himself had done before his inheritance. What resulted was an exchange of acrimonious letters, which grew more hateful and vitriolic in tone with each one written and received. Poe was forced to withdraw from school. He may then have gone to work for a while in Allan's counting room, where he was supposed to gain some practical skills like bookkeeping and writing business letters, but another confrontation was inevitable. About two months after Edgar's leaving Charlottesville, the strained relations between foster father and unwanted son snapped violently, and nearly two years of friction between them erupted into an ugly confrontation. Poe had been pursued at home for his debts at the university, and Allan refused to pay them. Incensed, Edgar moved out of Moldavia before leaving Richmond altogether. (He may have intended to take to sea, like his brother Henry, and might have convinced a friend, Ebenezer Burling, to go with him as far as Norfolk [PL: 78].) More letters were exchanged, with the most damning criticism coming from Edgar's pen: "You suffer me to be subjected to the whims & caprice, not only of your white family but the complete authority of the blacks" (CL 1: 11).

Poe's defensiveness would become a habitual reflex action, the beginning of a pattern in which he felt that people treated him shabbily, even persecuted him.

When Allan finally replied, it was with derision and a particularly hurtful slight on Edgar's recent academic training, for Allan said that this was what reading novels and other literary indulgences had taught the boy: "It is true I taught you to aspire, even to eminence in Public Life, but I never expected that Don Quixotte [*sic*], Gil Blas, Jo: Miller & such works were calculated to promote the end." "Eating the bread of idleness," the dour Allan called it (PL: 77). His gloomy, Calvinistic outlook on life would admit no such frivolities as literature.

Poe could not tolerate such an existence for very long, and soon thereafter, he fled—really, the first episode in a lifetime of nomadism and restless searching for a place where he could fit. He ran off to Boston—the place of his birth. The one memento of his mother that he had was a watercolor painting of Boston Harbor; on the reverse, Eliza had written, "For my little son Edgar, who should ever love Boston, the place of his birth, and where his mother found her *best*, and *most sympathetic friends*" (PL: 3). Having been hounded out of Allan's home and made to feel unwanted, Poe felt that he might come into a clearer vision of himself if he went to his birthplace. What he actually did there is not entirely known, but he may have worked for a while in a merchandise house (PL: 79). More important, during his time in Boston, Poe sought publication for his poetry. In June or July 1827, a local printer, Calvin F. S. Thomas, brought out Poe's first collection of verse. The title poem of the collection *Tamerlane and Other Poems*, which purportedly recounted the life of a fictional Turkish warrior, was heavily indebted to the poetry of George Gordon, Lord Byron, whom Poe slavishly idolized in his youth. Poe published the volume anonymously, identifying himself on the title page as "a Bostonian."

Poe next wound up in an unlikely place: he enlisted in the United States Army on May 26, 1827, under the name "Edgar A. Perry." Poe's decision to join the Army was unpredictable, and it may seem enigmatic. Yet given the overtolerant environment of the University of Virginia, Poe may have been seeking some kind of corrective to what he had self-diagnosed as a wayward life. And despite his dreamy manner and aversion to banal employment, he had also done well with orders and systems: he had trained as an athlete; he had memorized poetry with precision and conjugated verbs in modern languages expertly; he had even drilled as a youth with the local Richmond militia. The young Poe thrived when discipline and order were required.

Poe was stationed first at Fort Independence, at the mouth of Boston Harbor. Then, a few months later, his unit was transferred to Fort Moultrie on Sullivan's Island, a barrier island off the coast of South Carolina, where he was stationed until the end of 1828. (Later, he would set his prize-winning detective story "The Gold-Bug" there.) The Army then sent Poe back to Virginia, to Old Point Comfort on the Chesapeake Bay in Hampton. Poe excelled during his time in the military, attaining the rank of Sergeant-Major, the highest possible rank for a noncommissioned officer.

While Poe was at Fort Monroe, his foster mother, Fanny Allan, passed away at the age of forty-four. Poe was bereft, and he tried to get emergency leave to return to Richmond in time for the funeral, but when he arrived he found he had missed it by a day. Fanny was buried in Shockoe Hill cemetery, near Jane Stanard. Fanny's death, however, may have contributed to a temporary thawing of the icy relations between Poe and Allan. Both men mourned her loss. In the back of Poe's mind must also have been the assumption that when Allan died, at least part of his vast estate would come to Poe, although that would not turn out to be true. In the two men's finding common ground, a new prospect appeared on Poe's horizon: he decided that he wanted to go to West Point.

Allan acquiesced to Poe's request for help in applying to the Army academy and began working his connections to get Poe an appointment. It was a difficult task, for the paperwork required Poe—and also Allan—to prevaricate about Poe's parentage and about the stability of his upbringing. Allan, for example, had to attest to the youth's sterling character and strong sense of honor, qualities that Allan did not necessarily believe that Poe possessed. Poe also had to go to Washington, DC, to be interviewed by the Secretary of War, Major John Henry Eaton, an appointment that caused him considerable stress and anxiety, although he seems to have acquitted himself creditably in the meeting (PL: 94).

While waiting for word of whether he would be admitted to West Point, Poe occupied himself with more writing. This move, however, rekindled the fire of animosities that had been temporarily extinguished between Poe and Allan owing to the death of Fanny and Poe's choice of the military as a career. Poe unwisely asked Allan to put up a sum of money as a guarantee against sales of a book of poems that he wanted to publish. Allan, perhaps predictably, would not do so, and this made him revert to his earlier dim view of Poe's prospects in life and his generally sour outlook on writing as gainful employment. Another barrage of angry letters flew back and forth between the foundling and his foster father, and Poe thus found himself stranded in Washington, forbidden by Allan from returning to Moldavia.

However, Poe had family in Baltimore on his father's side: his aunt Maria Clemm, her young daughter Virginia, and his brother Henry, as well as some other Clemm relations. Poe importuned them to let him stay there while he waited to hear from West Point. While in Baltimore, Poe shopped around his second verse collection, the expanded and slightly emended version of his first book, now called *Al Aaraaf, Tamerlane, and Minor Poems*; it was brought out in a small edition by the Baltimore firm of Hatch and Dunning in December 1829. As with *Tamerlane*, a number of the poems in this volume are highly experimental, and their subjects range fairly widely across the poetic spectrum. The book, however, attracted only a handful of reviews—three favorable and two unfavorable—and it did not earn Poe what he wanted, to be seen as a new voice in American poetry (PL: 101, 103, 104). Today, however, the poems in this volume are seen as quite avant-garde for their time; they anticipate, as Derek Pollard has argued, both the European and American innovative poetics of the twentieth century, often by "teasing at the preferred reading" that expected conventions "are meant to authorize."[22] But at the time, few critics were interested in Poe's book.

In the spring of 1830, word arrived at last that Poe had been admitted to West Point. As he had at Joseph Clarke's academy and at the University of Virginia, Poe made friends easily and flourished academically. He was a particularly strong student in French and discovered a new interest in mathematics. Moreover, he became a model cadet, executing drills and formations with precision, discharging his military duties with efficiency and effectiveness, and gaining the trust and praise of his superiors at the academy.

In what came to be characteristic of Poe, however, in the space of a few short months, he decided again that the Army was not the place for him, and he started making inquiries about how to get out of his five-year contract. He began to disobey orders and neglect his duties. A general court-martial was thus convened in late January or early February 1831, and very quickly, Poe was expelled. A long letter to John Allan at the end of January of that year provides a summary of the entire history of their ill relations. Poe repeats the complaint that Allan has not given him a reasonable allowance, somewhat disingenuously citing his decision to leave because he cannot abide the stresses of his military duties without the consolation of a comfortable bank balance (CL 1: 58–62). Any hopes for a permanent reconciliation with Allan were now quashed. Allan had written on what would be the last of Poe's letters to him: "I do not think the Boy has one good quality. . . . I cannot believe a word he writes."[23] Poe left West Point on February 19, 1831.

Before he left, however, Poe managed to solicit from his fellow cadets the necessary funds for the private publication of a third book of poems, *Poems by Edgar A. Poe*, which was published by Elam Bliss in the spring of 1831. Poe dedicated the book to "The U.S. Corps of Cadets." Poe's well-defined ideas about the nature of poetry were articulated in a preface to the volume, entitled "Letter to Mr. B—-" (possibly Elam Bliss, the publisher of the book). Taking his cue from Coleridge in his *Biographia Literaria*, Poe averred that the goal of literature was not to mirror reality but instead to pursue Beauty in its highest and widest sense. As Poe put it, "A poem . . . is opposed to a work of science by having for its *immediate* object, pleasure, not truth" (ER: 11). This statement would serve as the cornerstone for much of what Poe would write in the coming years—both verse and prose—as he doggedly rejected the didactic in favor of the wholly imaginative.

Today, Poe's early poems provide a revealing portrait of the artist as a young man, for Tamerlane, the speaker in the lengthy title poem of the first book, is an orphanlike figure of uncertain parentage, with a "feigned name," solitary and wandering, abetted by an unquenchable thirst for power and control: "I was ambitious—have ye known/Its fiery passion? . . ./A cottager, I mark'd a throne/Of half the world, as all my own" (M 1: 33, lines 203–206). The Byronic verse ("Tamerlane" strikingly resembles Byron's "Turkish" poem, *The Giaour* [1813]) exudes a romantic pessimism borne of a disappointed childhood and the speaker's great passion and emotion. Byron's own Oriental romances were a clear influence on Poe, with their lyrical mood pictures and their representations of the Other. (Some have also read the blighted love in the poem as reflective of the doomed love affair of Poe and Elmira Royster [M 1: 22–25, 61–64].)

Byronic echoes can be heard throughout much of Poe's early verse. "Imitation," believed by most to be an early version of "A Dream Within a Dream," is an imitation of Byron: "A dark unfathom'd tide/Of interminable pride—/A mystery, and a dream,/Should my early life seem" (M 1: 75, lines 1–4). Poe opened another poem, untitled but later assigned the title "Stanzas" (by Stedman and Woodberry in their edition of Poe's works published in 1894), with a motto from Byron's *Island*, Canto I (M 1: 76–77). And there are numerous gestures toward the English poet in "The Lake": "In youth's spring it was my lot/To haunt of the wide world a spot/The which I could not love the less,/So lovely was the loneliness/Of a wild lake with black rock bound,/And the tall pines that tower'd around" (M 1: 84–85, lines 1–6).

Poe's poems also stress the power of the imagination. For example, "Fairyland" could be read as a template for orthodox Romanticism; that poem, as well as "A Dream," "The Valley of Unrest," and "Spirits of the Dead" are set in dreamlike, lyrical landscapes.[24] In "Sonnet—to Science," the speaker indicts reason and empiricism for destroying the beauty of the poetic imagination: "Hast thou not dragg'd Diana from her car,/And driv'n the Hamadryad from the wood . . . . The elfin from the green grass? and from me/The summer dream beneath the shrubbery?" (M 1: 91, lines 9–10, 13–14). Other themes include ideal love and supreme beauty, passion, and the nature of the afterlife. A black sense of foreboding almost overpowers the poem entitled "The Happiest Day." Poe writes, "Ev'n *then* I felt—that brightest hour/I would not live again:/For on its wing was dark alloy/And as it flutter'd—fell/An essence—powerful to destroy/A Soul that knew it well" (M 1: 82, lines 19–24). In "Dreams" we see an early reference to some kind of childhood trauma, a theme that echoes through later poems: "A chaos of deep passion from . . . birth" (M 1: 68, line 8). "Oh! that my young life were a lasting dream"; if even of "hopeless sorrow," it would be "better than the cold reality/Of waking life. . . . I *have been* happy, tho' in a dream" (M 1: 68, lines 1, 4, 5–6, 27). And the poems introduce some characteristics of Poe's fictive narrators as well, such as their lack of identity and vague origins. Emotional dislocation is a repeated theme, as is a woman who has once had emotional sway over the speaker's life.

In the spring of 1831, having left New York and with few options for where to go, Poe fetched up at the home of the Clemms in Baltimore, where he was reunited with his brother Henry and where he would become close to his cousin Virginia, whom he would later marry. Poe had endured his share of travails during this first part of his life—some beyond his control, some of his own making—and he had used them to dramatic effect in his writing. The three volumes of verse that Poe produced before 1831 are in fact an admirable achievement for a young, untested, and largely untutored poet. His sense of being isolated, his desperate search for a love that would not leave him, and his need to find a rooted identity that would prove him to be a success in the eyes of society all animate his writing to this point. The content of many of the verses in *Poems*, especially "Evening Star," "To Helen," "The Valley of Death," "Irene," and "The Doomed City," reveal Poe's intense preoccupation with death, dying, and the afterlife—unsurprising, since his early life had been marked by so much loss. Women are frequently the sole focus of these poems, and of many of his stories—idealized beauties like Jane Stanard of "To Helen." As much as the speaker of these poems is weary of his journeying and wants to return *home* (as Edgar wished he could return to the bosom of Eliza or, barring that, to Fanny Allan and Richmond), the wanderer is also forever melancholy, musing on the Hellenic beauty of the women he has lost and thus on the nature of death itself. This would, somewhat sadly, be the trajectory of much of Poe's poetic expressiveness in the years to come, a main theme of the short stories he would soon begin writing, and of much of the rest of his life.

NOTES

1. Kenneth Silverman, *Edgar A. Poe: Mournful and Never-Ending Remembrance* (New York: HarperCollins, 1991), 3–4.
2. Geddeth Smith, *The Brief Career of Eliza Poe* (Newark: University of Delaware Press, 1988), 27–28, passim.
3. See J. A. Leo Lemay, "Poe's "The Business Man": Its Contexts and Satire of Franklin's *Autobiography*," *Poe Studies* 15 (Dec. 1982): 29–37.
4. Silverman notes that Poe signed himself "Edgar Allan Poe" about three times in his adult life, in *Edgar A. Poe*, 126.
5. Arthur Hobson Quinn, *Edgar Allan Poe: A Critical Biography* (New York: Crowell, 1941), 60.
6. Mabbott, ed., *Selected Poetry and Prose of Edgar Allan Poe* (New York: Modern Library, 1951), xiv.
7. Quoted in Arthur Hobson Quinn, *Edgar Allan Poe: A Critical Biography*, 73.
8. Jeffrey Meyers, *Edgar Allan Poe: Life and Legacy* (New York: Putnam, 1992), 12.
9. Silverman, *Edgar A. Poe: Mournful and Never-Ending Remembrance*, 19.
10. Quinn, *Edgar Allan Poe: A Critical Biography*, 67–68.
11. Abigail Tucker, "Digging Up the Past at a Richmond Jail," *Smithsonian*, March 2009, http://www.smithsonianmag.com/history/digging-up-the-past-at-a-richmond-jail-50642859/.
12. Tucker, "Digging Up the Past."
13. Kennedy, "Trust No Man: Poe, Douglass, and the Culture of Slavery," in *Romancing the Shadow: Poe and Race*, ed. J. Gerald Kennedy and Liliane Weisberg (Oxford: Oxford University Press, 2001), 232.
14. See Quinn, *Edgar Allan Poe: A Critical Biography*, 82–83.
15. Quinn, *Edgar Allan Poe: A Critical Biography*, 86, 87.
16. Quinn, *Edgar Allan Poe: A Critical Biography*, 90.
17. Silverman, *Edgar A. Poe: Mournful and Never-Ending Remembrance*, 37.
18. Quinn, *Edgar Allan Poe: A Critical Biography*, 89.
19. Meyers, *Edgar Allan Poe: Life and Legacy*, 23.
20. Charles Kent, "Poe's Student Days at the University of Virginia," *Bookman* 44 (Jan. 1917): 37
21. Silverman, *Edgar A. Poe: Mournful and Never-Ending Remembrance*, 31–32.
22. Pollard, " 'Sonnet—To Science' and the Case for Poe's Avant-Garde Poetics," *Edgar Allan Poe Review* 17 (Autumn 2016): 105–115. Likewise, Peter Swirski, in *Between Literature and Science: Poe, Lem, and Explorations in Aesthetics, Cognitive Science, and Literary Knowledge* (Montreal: McGill-Queen's Press, 2000), notes Poe's championing of imagination and intuition in "To Science" while he at the same time sees "imagination-boggling marvels" in the processes exhibited by scientific inquiry itself (29).
23. Quinn, *Edgar Allan Poe: A Critical Biography*, 173.
24. Poe would later revise many of these poems for inclusion in later verse collections, sometimes dramatically; Russell Brickley shows how the second version of "Fairyland," which Poe rewrote for his third poetic volume, essentially turns orthodox Romanticism upside down, dismissing it through the speaker's caustic, sarcastic tone. See Brickley, "The Trouble with Fairyland: Two Versions of Poe's Sarcastic Sublime," *Edgar Allan Poe Review* 13 (Spring 2012): 18–40.

Bibliography

Allen, Hervey, and Thomas O. Mabbott. *Poe's Brother: The Poems of William Henry Leonard Poe*. New York: George H. Doran, 1926.

Bondurant, Agnes. *Poe's Richmond*. Richmond, VA: Garrett & Masie, 1942.

Hecker, William F. *Private Perry and Mr. Poe: The West Point Poems, 1831*. Baton Rouge: Louisiana State University Press, 2005.

Hutchisson, James M. *Poe*. Jackson: University Press of Mississippi, 2005.

Semter, Christopher. *Edgar Allan Poe's Richmond: The Raven in the River City*. Charleston, SC: History Press, 2012.

Silverman, Kenneth. *Edgar A. Poe: Mournful and Never-Ending Remembrance*. New York: HarperCollins, 1991.

Smith, Geddeth. *The Brief Career of Eliza Poe*. Newark: University of Delaware Press, 1988.

CHAPTER 2

A LIFE IN PRINT

1831–1849

SCOTT PEEPLES

> Mr. Poe is at once the most discriminating, philosophical, and fearless critic upon imaginative works who has written in America. It may be that we should qualify our remark a little and say that he might be, rather than that he always is, for he seems sometimes to mistake his phial of prussic-acid for his inkstand. . . . Had Mr. Poe had the control of a magazine of his own, in which to display his critical abilities, he would have been as autocratic, ere this, in America, as Professor Wilson has been in England; and his criticisms, we are sure, would have been far more profound and philosophical than those of the Scotsman. As it is, he has squared out blocks enough to build an enduring pyramid, but has left them lying carelessly and unclaimed in many different quarries.[1]
>
> —James Russell Lowell, 1845

THAT passage comes from an overview of Poe's life and career written by James Russell Lowell in late 1844 and published in *Graham's Magazine* just as "The Raven" was taking the country by storm in February 1845. Since Lowell consulted Poe on the article and told Poe that he wrote it "to please you rather than the public," it is safe to assume that the article represents Poe almost exactly as he wished to be known at what turned out to be the pinnacle of his career.[2] Interwoven with discussions of the state of American literature and the nature of genius, Lowell's assessment of Poe's career ensures that even the negatives were actually positives. Poe relished his reputation as a fearless "tomahawking" critic, and Lowell suggests that the remedy for Poe's overly caustic reviews would be to control his own magazine—which just happened to be the very project Poe was pursuing feverishly in the mid-1840s. Similarly, the complaint that Poe had left his "blocks" of criticism—and, by implication, poetry and fiction—lying carelessly across the literary landscape is essentially an advertisement for future collections of his work. Elsewhere Lowell praises Poe's early verse as "the most remarkable boyish poems that we have ever read"; describes Poe's unique "genius" as a combination of "vigorous yet minute analysis" and "a wonderful fecundity of imagination"; and highlights the variety of Poe's literary productions, a point Poe himself made more than once, fearing that as a fiction writer he would be pigeonholed as a "Germanic" Gothicist or, later, a writer of "ratiocinative" stories.[3]

Lowell's article was light on biography, but its presentation of Poe's life also smooths out some rough edges and omits some inconvenient truths. The orphaned "offspring of a romantic marriage," Poe was "adopted" by "a wealthy Virginian, whose barren marriage-bed seemed the warranty of a wealthy estate to the young poet." The word "adopted," not legally factual, emphasizes Poe's right to an inheritance, which Lowell later stresses in explaining his departure from West Point: "he obtained a dismissal on hearing of the birth of a son to his adopted father, by a second marriage, an event which cut off his expectations as an heir." As he did consistently, Poe suppressed his two-year enlistment in the US Army, substituting a more romantic reference to a "boyish attempt" to fight for Greek independence and having to be rescued from St. Petersburg by the American consul.[4] Lowell cites Poe's credentials as a magazine editor but of course makes no reference to his turbulent relationships with his employers Thomas W. White or William Burton. He also obligingly makes his thirty-six-year-old subject a bit younger: "Mr. Poe is still in the prime of life, being about thirty-two years of age."[5] Though this last alternative fact might seem inconsequential, it underscores Poe's desire to be seen not as a journeyman magazinist whose career was ready to be summed up but as a versatile author/editor whose best work lay ahead. Unfortunately, it would be hard to deny that most of his best work was in fact behind him by early 1845. And, tragically, he was old at thirty-six: his physical and mental health would fluctuate over the next four and a half years, and he would be dead at age forty.

I begin with Lowell's overview of Poe because it exposes the gap between the literary life Poe imagined for himself, tantalizingly close to reality—unjustly disinherited boy genius overcoming obstacles to play a leading role in the republic of letters—and the sadder, messier career described in this chapter. But it also underscores the extent to which Poe sought to shape an identity through print, and specifically through periodicals. Moreover, it suggests how much he was shaped *by* that medium—he worked antebellum print culture in bold, innovative ways, even as it worked him.

Following his expulsion from West Point and a brief stay in New York City, Poe returned to Baltimore in the spring of 1831, moving into the household overseen by his widowed aunt Maria Poe Clemm on Wilkes Street (now Eastern Avenue) in the Fells Point area. Penniless, Poe probably had no other option, though he did continue to write to John Allan, still hoping for some financial support if not reconciliation. But Allan was done with Poe, so Edgar made his home with "blood" relatives: Maria, his incapacitated grandmother Elizabeth Poe, his older brother Henry, his nine-year-old cousin Virginia, and possibly another cousin (Maria's thirteen-year-old son Henry). In Maria, whom he called "Muddy," and Virginia, or "Sissy," Poe found the family he would remain with for the rest of his life; and yet this period could hardly have been a happy one. The house was crowded and there was little income. Poe's brother died on August 1, 1831, probably of tuberculosis or cholera. Edgar probably contributed to the family coffers, but he seems not to have found regular employment. At one point in 1831, he was imprisoned for debt, or so he told his foster father in one of several begging letters (CL 1: 69). Allan waited about five weeks before sending money to Poe one last time.

Having attained little notice with his three slender volumes of poetry, Poe began experimenting with short fiction, imitating and in some cases parodying popular literary subgenres. He entered five stories in a contest run by the *Saturday Courier* of Philadelphia, for a $100 "premium"—the prize went to Delia S. Bacon's "Love's Martyr," but the *Courier* published Poe's entries, beginning with the Gothic tale "Metzengerstein" in January 1832. In a fitting welcome to what he would later call the "magazine prison-house," Poe gained exposure but no compensation. In 1833 he won a $50 premium sponsored by a Baltimore paper, the *Saturday Visiter*: he sent a packet of six stories collectively titled "The Tales of the Folio Club," out of which the prize committee chose "MS. Found in a Bottle." He had also submitted a poem for the *Visiter*'s $25 prize and was later told by members of the committee that had he not been the winner of the story contest, he would have received the prize for "The Coliseum" as well (CL 1: 96). One of the judges, novelist John Pendleton Kennedy, befriended Poe, loaned him money, and used his influence to try to advance Poe's career. Specifically, Kennedy recommended Poe's "Folio Club" collection—eleven tales with an opening comic sketch that introduced the fictionalized club members—to the Philadelphia firm Carey, Lea & Blanchard. Henry Carey told Kennedy he would publish Poe's book, even though he complained, "I do not expect to make anything." In the meantime, however, Carey encouraged Poe to sell individual stories to gift books and magazines; he then stalled and never followed through on publication.[6]

The Poe-Clemm family moved to a small house in sparsely developed West Baltimore in early 1833. In March 1834, John Allan died; as expected, he left nothing to Poe in his will. According to a later account by Poe's childhood friend Thomas Ellis, Poe had made an unannounced visit to the Allan mansion in Richmond about a month before his foster father's death, and an infirm Allan threatened him with a cane (PL: 137). Still impoverished, Poe continued to pursue a literary career, publishing "The Assignation" in the widely circulated *Godey's Lady's Book* in 1834 and finding a regular outlet for his fiction when Kennedy introduced him by letter to Thomas Willis White, who had just begun publishing the monthly *Southern Literary Messenger* in Richmond. White published stories by Poe in four consecutive issues in early 1835, while the two men corresponded about his plans for the magazine. Poe's talent as a fiction writer was developing rapidly, though White expressed mixed feelings about some of what Poe sent him. After publishing "Berenice" in March, White questioned Poe's cringe-inducing conclusion, in which the narrator reveals that he has extracted the teeth from his prematurely buried fiancée. Poe admitted that the story's subject "is by far too horrible" and said that he hesitated to submit it—but then proceeded to defend the strategy of publishing sensational fictions that test the limits of decency: "To be appreciated you must be *read*, and these things are invariably sought after with avidity. They are, if you will take notice, the articles which find their way into other periodicals, and into the papers, and in this manner, taking hold of the public mind they augment the reputation of the source where they originated" (CL 1: 84–85). White did not fully embrace this strategy, but he was impressed enough to offer Poe an editorial position with the magazine that summer.

Not long after moving to Richmond to work on the *Messenger*, Poe faced a personal crisis that led to one of the most significant decisions of his life. With the death of Poe's grandmother in July 1835, Maria Clemm lost access to the pension paid to her for David Poe, Sr.'s service during the American Revolution, a vital source of income. Meanwhile, Poe had fallen in love with his young cousin Virginia and apparently broached the subject of marriage. Edgar's second cousin Neilson Poe, married and living in Baltimore, offered to take in Virginia, a financial rescue but perhaps also a move to postpone a marriage he quite reasonably opposed, since Virginia had just turned thirteen. From Richmond, Poe wrote to Muddy, pouring his heart out and essentially giving mother and daughter an ultimatum:

> I have procured a sweet little house in a retired situation on [ch]urch hill . . . . I have been dreaming every day & night since of the rapture I should feel in [havi]ng my only friends—all I love on Earth with me there, [and] the pride I would take in making you both comfort[table] & in calling her my wife—But the dream is over[.] [Oh G]od have mercy on me. What have I *to live for*? Among strangers with *not one soul to love me.* (CL 1: 102–103)

He added a postscript to Virginia: "My love, my own sweetest Sissy, my darling little wifey, thi[nk w]ell before you break the heart of your cousin Eddy" (CL 1: 104). There is no getting around the strangeness of Poe's determination to marry his young cousin. While marriage between first cousins was not taboo in 1830s America, marriage between a twenty-six-year-old man and a thirteen-year-old girl was certainly unusual.[7] The precise sequence of events and their causes remain unclear: Poe's letter indicates that he had already discussed marriage, but had that discussion preceded his knowledge of Neilson's offer? To what extent was he pressing his suit to block Neilson, as opposed to having already set his heart on marrying Virginia regardless of her age?[8] In Poe's mind, was he clinging desperately to a sister ("Sissy") and mother ("Muddy") or to a wife and *her* mother? Almost certainly these relationships were not clearly delineated for Poe, as suggested by his phrase "my darling little wifey." Judging from his letter, and his life story generally, he knew only that he could not let them go. Edgar and Virginia may have married secretly in Baltimore in September 1835 (PL: 171); they were publicly married in Richmond, where Virginia and Muddy had relocated, on May 16 of the following year.

Meanwhile, the *Southern Literary Messenger* served as a springboard for Poe's career. With a mostly free editorial hand, he published his own fiction, including new tales such as "Morella" and the voyage-to-the-moon adventure "Hans Pfaall," as well as stories originally intended for the "Folio Club" volume; a number of poems from his three obscure collections; "Scenes from an Unpublished Drama" (also known as *Politian*); a lengthy exposé about a fake mechanical chess player; satirical analyses of famous writers' autographs; and a series of provocative book reviews that established him as the acid-penned critic described by Lowell a decade later. Poe's justification for the gore of

"Berenice" might have applied equally to the take-no-prisoners approach of his reviews; he was particularly eager to deflate reputations made by "puffing," the practice of indiscriminately praising works by writers in one's network or clique. Deploying overstatement and sarcasm, he sought to make literary reviews entertaining and comic, appealing to a mass audience, as Paul Huhr argues in another chapter of this volume. "Well!—here we have it! This is *the* book—*the* book par excellence—the book bepuffed, beplastered, and be-*Mirrored*": so begins Poe's review of *Norman Leslie* by Theodore S. Fay, an editor of the *New York Mirror* and thus a well-connected figure in the New York literary establishment. Poe goes on to mock the hype and the pretense of anonymity surrounding Fay's novel: "the book 'attributed to' Mr. Blank, and 'said to be from the pen' of Mr. Asterisk: the book which has been 'about to appear'—'in press'—'in progress'—'in preparation'—and 'forthcoming'. . . . For the sake of every thing puffed, puffing, and puffable, let us take a peep at its contents!" (ER: 540). Poe takes more than a peep, mocking the novel mercilessly as he summarizes its plot, pronouncing it "the most inestimable piece of balderdash with which the common sense of the good people of America was ever so openly or so villainously insulted" (ER: 546). He must have felt he had nothing to lose in taking on a literary coterie over 300 miles to the north, and everything to gain by calling attention to his own fearlessness and superior artistic sensibility.

Poe would later claim that under his editorial guidance the Messenger's circulation exploded from 700 to 5,500, but in fact the increase was much more modest, from about 1,300 to just over 1,800 in the year that Poe did most of the editorial work.[9] While both Poe and White benefited from their association, the relationship was strained almost from the beginning. It came to resemble Edgar's earlier tug of war with his foster father: he had returned to Richmond and been taken in (professionally, this time) by an older man to whom he needed to prove himself but against whom he inevitably rebelled. The more pious, conservative White might have reconciled himself to Poe's swashbuckling print persona, but he found it difficult managing Poe as an employee. Industrious as he was, Poe was also, by this time, a problem drinker. After a brief separation in late 1835—Poe either quit or was fired, and had returned to Baltimore—White offered him his old position on the condition that he stay sober: "Edgar, when you once again tread these streets, I have my fears that your resolve will fall through,—and that you would again sip the juice, even till it stole away your senses."[10] Just over a year later, he had either dismissed Poe or convinced him to resign. After publicly announcing Poe's departure, White confided to the novelist and jurist Nathaniel Beverley Tucker in terms that echo John Allan's exasperation: "Poe pesters me no little—he is trying every manoeuver to foist himself on some one at the North. . . . He is continually after me for money. I am as sick of his writings, as I am of him,—and am rather more than half inclined to send him up another dozen dollars in the morning, and along with it all his unpublished manuscripts" (PL: 242). For just over a year, Edgar had lived with his new family in the city he had called home with the Allans. He had quickly made a name for himself but had probably come to believe that greater success would require moving to one of the publishing centers of the Northeast. He departed with Virginia and Muddy for New York City in February 1837.

Early 1837 turned out to be a particularly bad time to lose—or leave—a steady job and move to a new city, particularly one where the effects of economic downturns were felt immediately. A financial panic struck soon after Poe's arrival, ushering in an almost decade-long recession; New York was the epicenter, as its banks suspended specie payments for paper currency in May. Early that year, Harper & Brothers had agreed to publish Poe's hastily written but fascinating novel *The Narrative of Arthur Gordon Pym*, the first installments of which had run in the *Messenger* in January and February, but the panic caused the Harpers to delay publication until the following summer. When *Pym* did appear, it received mixed reviews and sold poorly; though Poe's only novel would attract intense critical attention over a century after his death for its metafictional elements and veiled commentary on race and colonialism, Poe and his contemporaries gave it scant notice. He published little else while in New York: the story "Von Jung, the Mystific" (later renamed "Mystification"), a short, evocative fiction entitled "Siope" (later renamed "Silence.—A Fable"), and an unsigned book review. Prior to the Panic, Poe attended a publishers' dinner for booksellers and proposed a toast "to the *Monthlies* of Gotham" (PL: 244). Almost nothing else is known of Poe's first New York foray, but its short duration and documentary invisibility suggest that it was a difficult, unproductive year.

Poe, Virginia, and Maria had now lived in three different cities in as many years; their next stop was Philadelphia, sometime in early 1838, and their six years there would make it the longest stay in any city of Poe's adult life. Around the time of the move, he hit a creative streak that would continue throughout his years in the Quaker City. It began with "Ligeia," a complex psychological Gothic tale that also appears to satirize the genre, and the burlesque satire "The Psyche Zenobia" (a double story later titled "How to Write a Blackwood Article" and "A Predicament"), both of which appeared in the Baltimore *American Museum* in late 1838. The steady stream of fiction that followed includes the majority of Poe's best-known tales of mystery and terror: "The Fall of the House of Usher" (1839), "William Wilson" (1839), "The Man of the Crowd" (1840), "The Murders in the Rue Morgue" (1841), "The Oval Portrait" (1842), "The Masque of the Red Death" (1842), "The Mystery of Marie Roget" (1842–1843), "The Pit and the Pendulum" (1843), "The Tell-Tale Heart" (1843), "The Gold-Bug" (1843), and "The Black Cat" (1843). But during the same period, Poe published an equal number of stories in a wide range of generic and stylistic registers: the American social satires "The Man That Was Used Up" (1839) and "Peter Pendulum, the Business Man" (1840); the verbal slapstick of "The Devil in the Belfry" (1839), "Why the Little Frenchman Wears His Hand in a Sling" (1840), "Never Bet the Devil Your Head" (1841), and "The Spectacles" (1844); a pair of philosophical dialogues on the afterlife, "Conversation of Eiros and Charmion" (1839) and "The Colloquy of Monos and Una" (1841); a few descriptive landscape "sketches"; the sensation/adventure tale "A Descent into the Maelstrom" (1841); and the undying-love story "Eleonora" (1841). In Philadelphia, Poe wrote and/or published about half of the stories he would produce throughout his career. Moreover, five years after the disappointment of his ill-fated "Folio Club" concept, he finally saw a story collection into print. *Tales of the Grotesque and Arabesque* (1840) included all twenty-five of his previously published stories, along with a preface assuring readers that he was not attached to the predominant style of the volume: "Let us admit, for the moment, that the 'phantasy-pieces' now given *are* Germanic, or what not. . . . To morrow I may be anything but German, as yesterday I was everything else." But lest he be perceived as a trend chaser, Poe assures his readers that, "If in many of my productions terror has been the thesis, I maintain that terror is not of Germany, but of the soul" (M 2: 473). The collection received numerous laudatory reviews but—true to the prediction of its publisher, Lea & Blanchard---it failed to sell out even its modest print run of 750.

Meanwhile, Poe's career as an editor-critic continued to flourish. In May 1839, he was hired by William Burton, an English actor, to help edit *Burton's Gentleman's Magazine*. Before purchasing the magazine, Burton had contributed an unusually harsh review of Poe's *Narrative of Arthur Gordon Pym*; either Poe held his novel in such low regard that he was not offended—as he later claimed in a letter to Burton—or, more likely, he managed to swallow his pride out of dire need for steady work. Ironically, Burton would soon be cautioning his new assistant against "your uncalled for severity in criticism" (PL: 262). As he had with White and the *Messenger*, Poe provided not only severe literary criticism and other editorial copy but also clerical work and general guidance for a proprietor and nominal editor who was not well versed in the profession. And as with the *Messenger*, Poe's employment lasted only about a year, as he chafed under the yoke of a boss who knew and cared far less about the business of letters than he did. Poe disapproved of Burton's practice of announcing premiums to garner submissions and then cancelling the prizes on the pretext of not having received enough entries; Burton found Poe's job performance erratic. But the last straw seems to have been that Burton planned to sell the magazine without consulting Poe, while Poe was making his own plans to jump ship and start his own journal: both justified their actions by citing the other's supposed treachery (CL 1: 220).

But *Burton's*, again like the *Messenger*, had served Poe well, providing a platform for his critical pronouncements and an outlet for new fiction, notably "The Man That Was Used Up," "William Wilson," "The Fall of the House of Usher," and "The Man of the Crowd." As he had done with *Pym* for the *Messenger*, Poe began another adventure serial, *The Journal of Julius Rodman*, which also presented itself as an authentic account, in this case by "the First White Man that ever crossed the Western Wilderness, and passed the desert ridges of the Rocky Mountains" (P 1: 509). Poe apparently thought even less of *Rodman* than of *Pym*, because when he left the magazine with six installments in print, he did not bother to complete it. He had plagiarized portions of *Pym*, and he did so to a greater extent with *Rodman*, which borrows from several sources but most heavily from the journals of Lewis and Clark and Washington Irving's *Astoria*. Of course, Poe was ostensibly claiming *not* to have written "Rodman's" journal, and he tipped his hand by alluding to the works he cribbed; still, he exposed himself to charges of plagiarism at the very moment that he made the first of what would become a long series of unfair accusations of literary thievery against one of the most popular poets of his day, Henry Wadsworth Longfellow. Whether Poe's accusation against Longfellow was driven by jealousy and a slightly warped sense of injustice, or he was just test-marketing a public controversy, he was continuing a pattern of picking fights while styling himself a crusader for literary integrity.

Burton's was purchased in 1840 by the publishing entrepreneur George Rex Graham, who combined it with another Philadelphia monthly, *The Casket*, to found *Graham's Lady's and Gentleman's Magazine* and develop it into one of the most successful periodicals of the antebellum period. He hired Poe as an assistant editor at $800 a year, a modest salary but the best steady income Poe would ever have. Graham knew how to run a magazine and did not rely on his assistant to the extent that White and Burton had; thus, Poe had a more competent, understanding boss but less editorial control.[11] While with Graham, he continued to write groundbreaking stories and provocative criticism, raising his profile on the national literary scene. Throughout 1840 and 1841, he enhanced his reputation as an intellectual prodigy by challenging readers to stump him with coded texts or "ciphers." Though Poe largely controlled the terms of the running challenge (and, in biographer Kenneth Silverman's estimation, was actually a novice), he attracted readers with his cryptographic skill.[12]

That type of code-breaking acumen—or the appearance of it—lent itself to a new kind of fiction that Poe pioneered in the early 1840s. His series of detective tales began with what might be called a deliberate failure: the narrator of "The Man of the Crowd"—Poe's first story for *Graham's*—follows a stranger in whom he sees "the type and genius of deep crime" through the streets of London for an entire night before concluding that he is an insoluble mystery, a book "that does not permit itself to be read" (M 2: 506). But in his next published tale, "The Murders in the Rue Morgue," Poe introduced C. Auguste Dupin, an amateur sleuth capable of perceiving and correctly interpreting clues that baffle Paris's Prefect of Police. With these stories and the two additional Dupin tales, Poe was responding to a public fascination with cities whose rapid growth and constant change made them frightening and mysterious—London and Paris, but also, by implication, Philadelphia and New York—as well as the spirit of gamesmanship that would largely define the genre. Another tale from this period, "The Gold-Bug," substituted a buried-treasure hunt for crime solving, but with a similar emphasis on the protagonist's process of ratiocination. At the end of the story, the fictional cryptographer William Legrand uses his decoding skills to unearth a large fortune; Poe was less well rewarded for creating these tantalizing fictions, though "The Gold-Bug" did provide the biggest single payday of his career, a $100 prize from the *Dollar Newspaper*. Poe's renown was sufficient to gain him an interview with Charles Dickens, then the most famous writer in the English-speaking world, when "Boz" stopped in Philadelphia on his American tour in 1842.

Following the pattern of his previous editorial jobs, Poe left *Graham's* after a little over a year, in April 1842, though this time he parted on good terms with his employer. Both Poe and Graham believed he would soon be editing a journal of his own, a project Graham supported. As early as 1840, Poe had circulated a prospectus for a monthly literary magazine to be called "The Penn," later renaming it "The Stylus." To control his own quality magazine was Poe's career-long dream; not only did he lack control at Graham's, but, as he told his friend F. W. Thomas, he had become "disgust[ed] with the namby-pamby character of the Magazine—a character which it was impossible to eradicate—I allude to the contemptible pictures, fashion-plates, music and love tales" (CL 1: 333). Poe envisioned a more high-toned, literary, and implicitly "masculine" publication. But it didn't happen; Poe was unable to raise enough subscriptions, and he lacked private capital or credit. He had to rely on the sale of individual tales and other articles for his meager income. While working for Burton and Graham, Poe lived with Virginia and Muddy in what he referred to as a "small house," probably on Sixteenth Street near Locust Street, in the city's sparsely populated Western frontier.[13] They lived there for almost four years, leaving around the time Poe resigned from *Graham's*. Tragically, during their last few months in the "small house," Virginia suddenly began exhibiting the symptoms of tuberculosis. Poe later reported that she was singing when a blood vessel burst, causing her to cough up blood. Her illness cast a shadow over the family for the remainder of her life and beyond, as she would linger, often bedridden, for five more years.

Poe's successor at *Graham's* was Rufus W. Griswold, a twenty-seven-year-old editor who had recently worked for Horace Greeley's *New York Tribune* and who would soon become known as a leading anthologist of American writing. The year before he joined *Graham's*, he had edited *The Poets and Poetry of America*, which included three poems by Poe, a rather slight representation. According to Poe, Griswold bribed him to write a positive review of the book; Poe delivered a less than bribe-worthy product, complimenting but also insulting the volume's editor. It marked the beginning of a rivalry, sometimes masked in friendship, that would continue, infamously, even after Poe's death.

Probably seeking cheaper rent, but perhaps also a healthier environment for Virginia, the family relocated in mid-1842 to Philadelphia's northern suburbs, living for about seven months on Coates (now Fairmount) Street between the waterworks on the Schuylkill River and Eastern State Penitentiary, then moving across town to a house adjoining the larger home of a Quaker businessman, on Seventh Street just north of Spring Garden. As the relocations suggest, Poe's relatively stable life in Philadelphia had been rocked by Virginia's illness and his inability to replace steady employment with a magazine of his own. Having been mostly sober for a few years, he began drinking much more; he would later write of this period and the emotional turmoil accompanying Virginia's health, "I became insane, with long intervals of horrible sanity. During these fits of absolute unconsciousness I drank, God only knows how often or how much" (CL 2: 641). In the summer of 1842, he travelled to New York looking for work but became intoxicated, apparently for several days, and was eventually found in the woods near Jersey City, "wandering about like a crazy man," according to one source (PL: 371). A few months later, Poe's friend Frederick Thomas tried to help him land a Custom House appointment through a connection with Robert Tyler, son of President John Tyler. Hoping to secure the position, Poe traveled to Washington, DC, the following March, but he got drunk, embarrassed himself repeatedly, and lost out on the job.

By early 1844, Poe must have felt the need for a fresh start, for he moved with Virginia, followed by Muddy, back to New York in April. New York was, already, the nation's most populous city by far; it had also surpassed Boston and Philadelphia as a publishing mecca. Poe seems to have been buoyed by the promise of a fresh start after his arrival with Sissy, as he wrote Muddy a hopeful letter upon their arrival, detailing the lavish array of food at their boarding house and promising to send for her as soon as he can "scrape together enough money." "I feel in excellent spirits & have'nt drank a drop," he told her, "so that I hope so[on] to get out of trouble" (CL 1: 438). After Muddy's arrival, the trio found inexpensive lodging on a farm owned by Patrick and Mary Brennan, well north of the built city, near what is now Broadway and West 84th Street—almost certainly a move designed to keep Poe out of financial and alcoholic trouble in addition to providing fresher air for Virginia. While Poe now found himself at an inconvenient distance from the downtown publishing hub—he told Thomas he was "playing hermit in earnest"—he was nothing if not productive while living on the farm. He wrote a short series of journalistic observations of New York—"Doings of Gotham"—for a small-town Pennsylvania paper; he took another assistant editor job, writing filler for the weekly *New York Mirror*; and for the *Democratic Review* he wrote a series of "Marginalia"—brief, random observations pretending to be his own reading responses. Even before moving to the farm, Poe published a fake news item in the New York *Sun*, a detailed account of a three-day transatlantic balloon voyage. He published no fewer than eleven new stories in 1844 and wrote several that did not appear until the following year.

But Poe would achieve his greatest fame, both immediate and eternal, for a poem that he completed at the Brennan Farm and published in early 1845. Though as usual, he received small payment—probably ten or fifteen dollars—he became a celebrity overnight as "The Raven" went viral through reprinting and recitation.[14] " 'The Raven' has had a great 'run,' " he told F. W. Thomas, "but I wrote it for the express purpose of running [that is, being widely circulated]—just as I did the 'Gold-Bug,' you know. The bird beat the bug, though, all hollow" (CL 1: 505). Around this time, Poe was courted by, and allied himself with, the group of literary nationalists known as Young America. He supported their campaign for an international copyright law that would protect American authors, and even before moving to New York, he had begun setting more of his stories in the United States; yet he seems never to have fully embraced Young America's uncritical promotion of American authors and subjects.[15] Meanwhile, with his move to New York, Poe had revived his ambition to launch his own magazine. Lowell's biography, cited at the beginning of this chapter, was implicitly part of that campaign, in its promotion of Poe as an ambitious writer-critic in need of a professional home base. "The Raven" was also great publicity, and Poe saw the opportunity it presented—it would be easier to start a magazine if he were famous, and now he was.

Poe had also begun writing for a new weekly, *The Broadway Journal*, and after publishing "The Raven" he began editing it along with C. F. Briggs and Henry C. Watson. The *Journal* was not the high-quality monthly Poe had envisioned, but the editors and publisher, John Bisco, offered him a partnership—he would receive one-third of the profits—in contrast with the hired-hand status he had known previously, and Poe might have imagined that the *Journal* could gradually be remade in his own image. Then, over the course of a few months, Poe actually became the sole editor and proprietor, at least partly by his own machinations. "After a prodigious deal of manoeuvering," he wrote to Rufus Griswold, with whom he was now at least nominally on good terms, "I have succeeded in getting the 'Broadway Journal' entirely within my own control"; he then asked Griswold to lend him fifty dollars (CL 1: 529). He made the same appeal to his Baltimore mentor John P. Kennedy, claiming that he had "succeeded in getting rid, one by one, of all my associates in 'The Broadway Journal' " (PL: 582). Whether he conquered his rival editors, as he suggests, or his "associates" wisely abandoned a struggling publication and their headstrong, intemperate coeditor, the *Journal* did not rebound under Poe's control, and he was unable to raise enough funds or find enough waking hours in the day to even keep it afloat for long. In December, he transferred half his "interest and property" in the publication to Thomas H. Lane, who in turn paid off its debts. Within a month, though, the *Broadway Journal* ceased publication. Cornelia Wells Walter, writing in the Boston *Evening Transcript*, recalled that, upon assuming control of the *Journal*, Poe had printed a plea for subscribers—"may we not hope for the support of our friends?"—before taunting Poe in verse:

> To trust in friends is but so so,
> Especially when cash is low;
> The Broadway Journal's proved *"no go"*—
> *Friends* would not pay the pen of POE. (PL: 614)

Walter, a Bostonian editor, had reason to exult in Poe's failure. Throughout 1845, Poe had engaged in a relentless one-man campaign against Longfellow, reviving and expanding his earlier charge of plagiarism. Writing first in the *New York Mirror* and then in the *Broadway Journal*, he published a series of disquisitions on the subject, egged on by a mysterious foil named "Outis"; much of their debate is a serious discussion of the nature of influence, imitation, and plagiarism, the examples going beyond Longfellow and including "The Raven."[16] But Longfellow remained Poe's primary target, and in attacking Longfellow, a Harvard professor and beloved New England poet, Poe was attacking Boston. If that weren't enough, in October, having been invited—through Lowell's efforts—to deliver a new poem at the Boston Lyceum, Poe ignited another war of words. Finding himself unable to compose a new work, Poe read his long poetic fantasy "Al Aaraaf," first published in 1829 and temporarily renamed "The Messenger Star." Accounts of Poe's performance that evening vary, but he seems to have acquitted himself reasonably well and could have gone back to New York relieved either that no one noticed he was recycling an old poem or that no one cared. Instead, upon his return, Poe began boasting in the *Journal* of having "quizzed" the Bostonians by delivering an incomprehensible "juvenile poem," and claiming that the undiscriminating Lyceum audience loved it. An exchange with the Boston press, including Walter, ensued, Poe baiting the Bostonians with sharper insults: "We like Boston. We were born there—and perhaps it is just as well not to mention that we are heartily ashamed of the fact" (P 3: 298). Poe might have hoped that public interest in his literary battles would somehow boost the circulation of the *Broadway Journal*, while providing him with page-filling content. At the same time, the "Longfellow War" and "Lyceum Incident" might have been manifestations of real bitterness and the kind of self-destructive impulse he wrote into some of his best-known tales. Whatever drove this combative behavior, it was not helping his career.

Indeed, as he was antagonizing Bostonians, Poe was also squandering his cultural capital in New York. Early in 1845, he moved with Virginia and Muddy back to lower Manhattan, where the author of "The Raven" suddenly found himself a guest at literary salons, particularly the gatherings hosted by Anne Charlotte Lynch at her home near Washington Square. Initially, the salons suited Poe well, as they affirmed his place among the literati, allowed him to network, and generally did not include alcohol, removing a temptation that might lead to embarrassment. But embarrassment took another form. Through the salon circuit, Poe developed a relationship with the popular poet Frances Osgood. Though she was also married, Osgood seems to have admired Poe as much as he did her, and the two exchanged love poems in the pages of the *Broadway Journal.* It remains unclear whether or not they engaged in a sexual affair, but they certainly provided grist for the gossip mill. After another poet, Elizabeth Ellet, visited Poe's house and saw one of Osgood's private letters, she sent emissaries to retrieve it, in order to protect Osgood's reputation. Poe was taken aback by this visit and retorted that Ellet should be more concerned about her own letters to him. By the time this soap-opera episode had run its course, Poe had gotten into a fistfight with his sometime friend Thomas Dunn English after trying to get English to lend him a pistol to defend himself from Ellet's brother, who had threatened him. Moreover, he had alienated himself from Ellet, Lynch, and the polite society of New York generally.

Between the notoriety brought on by the Osgood-Ellet scandal, ongoing poverty, and Virginia's ever-precarious health, Poe had good reason to move the family from lower Manhattan again in the spring of 1846. They lived for a short time in rural Turtle Bay, near the East River, before settling in what would later become known as the Bronx, near recently founded Fordham University. In moving even farther north of the city than they had been on Brennan Farm, the family seemed to be fulfilling the wish expressed by Virginia in a valentine poem she had given Edgar earlier that year:

Give me a cottage for my home
And a rich old cypress vine,
Removed from the world with its sin and care
And the tattling of many tongues.
Love alone shall guide us when we are there—
Love shall heal my weakened lungs[.] (PL: 625)

The rural setting seems to have agreed with Poe, but his career had lost momentum, and he remained frustrated and distraught. As a fiction writer, he seemed nearly spent: in the three-year period beginning in February 1846, he published only two stories, though both are significant and likely reflect his preoccupations: revenge in "The Cask of Amontillado," and escape in "The Domain of Arnheim," a fantasy of landscaping a private earthly paradise.

While he had physically distanced himself from the literary and publishing hub of Nassau and Fulton Streets, Poe was still determined to play the role of tastemaker and maverick critic. In May 1846 he began a series for *Godey's Lady's Book* entitled "The Literati of New York City." Each of the six installments included several verbal sketches of individual writers, commenting on their appearance, personal reputation, and quality of their work. Poe's assessments ranged from laudatory to innocuous to petty and cruel. One insulted writer, the same Thomas Dunn English with whom Poe had recently brawled, struck back, publishing a withering attack on Poe's character in the *New York Mirror*. In addition to exposing some embarrassing episodes from Poe's past, English accused Poe of obtaining funds from him (to support the *Broadway Journal*) under false pretenses and of committing forgery. After firing back a long reply in print, Poe sued the *Mirror* for libel and was eventually awarded $225.06. But the damage to his reputation was done, and Poe became, to a considerable extent, an object of pity and scorn among the literati he had set out to appraise.

On January 30, 1847, Virginia Clemm Poe died in the family's cottage in Fordham. Anxiety over her illness and long decline had already taken its toll on Poe, and his grief was profound. Aside from a midsummer trip to Washington and Philadelphia, he stayed close to home for the remainder of the year; he occasionally saw visitors and developed one particularly close friendship, with Marie Louise Shew, who had volunteered to nurse Virginia in her last days while helping to support the family. He published little, the most notable exception being "Ulalume: A Ballad," one of his most original and beguiling poems, which appeared in the *American Review* in December. Tellingly, it depicts a mourner's confused state of mind as he unwittingly retraces his steps to his beloved's tomb. But Poe's major writing project in the year following Virginia's death was *Eureka*, a speculative treatise subtitled both "A Prose Poem" and "An Essay on the Material and Spiritual Universe." Poe posited that the universe originated through something much like a big bang, and argued that having expanded to its limit, the universe contracts, then expands again: "a novel Universe swelling into existence, and then subsiding into nothingness, at every throb of the Heart Divine" (L1: 103). Published in mid-1848 by G. P. Putnam, the 143-page cosmology did not sell well, but Poe continued to regard it as his crowning achievement; a year after its publication, he would tell Maria Clemm, "I have no desire to live since I have done 'Eureka.' I could accomplish nothing more" (CL 2: 820).

In early 1848, Poe declared himself sober and in good health (CL 2: 648), and he renewed his campaign to establish his own quality magazine. He gave a public lecture on "The Universe" in February, "The Poets and Poetry of America" in July, and "The Poetic Principle" in December. And he began seeking a new wife. Throughout the second half of the year, he ardently pursued the poet Sarah Helen Whitman, traveling to her residence in Providence, Rhode Island, several times to press his suit. At the same time, he developed an intense quasi-romantic relationship with Nancy Richmond, whom he called "Annie," a married woman living in Lowell, Massachusetts. Poe wrote of his longing to live with her, even as he was expressing similar devotion to Helen Whitman. Knowing that Mrs. Richmond's marriage limited him to a platonic relationship, he confided with her about his pursuit of Helen. At one point, his conflicted feelings and frustration drove him to attempt suicide by taking an overdose of laudanum, opium diluted in alcohol. According to his own account, he swallowed an ounce of the drug and wrote to Annie, asking her to meet him in Boston, where he would take another ounce and die in her arms—but he became too incapacitated to post the letter. Poe was clearly no longer the sober, healthy man he had claimed to be at the beginning of the year. Meanwhile, Helen Whitman received warnings about his character and his drinking problem, but she was equally drawn to him and at one point agreed to an engagement, contingent upon his staying sober. Had Poe been able to keep that pledge, they probably would have married, despite her family's expressed disapproval—but one evening in late December, Poe attended a gathering at the Whitman home slightly under the influence, and the next day Helen broke off the engagement.

Poe had lately put more energy into romantic endeavors than his career, but he managed a professional comeback of sorts in 1849; after a long fiction-writing drought, he published five new stories, including the futuristic satire "Mellonta Tauta" and the unsettling tale of a court jester's revenge, "Hop-Frog." Either Poe was now unable to place his tales in higher-echelon publications or he sought only quick payment for his work, because he sent what turned out to be his last four tales, as well as his new poems "For Annie," "To My Mother," and "Eldorado," to a cheap Boston weekly, *The Flag of Our Union*. He sent a few poems, including then-unsold "Annabel Lee," to Rufus Griswold, who was assembling a new edition of his *Poets and Poetry of America* (M 1: 475). Meanwhile, he revived his "Marginalia" series for the *Southern Literary Messenger* and added a similar series called "Fifty Suggestions" in *Graham's*, though for many entries he merely warmed over previously published nuggets of wisdom and ephemera, either his or someone else's.[17]

Poe's prospects got a more significant boost when a wealthy young publisher from Illinois, Edward Horton Norton Patterson, contacted him about partnering on a magazine. They began negotiating informally, and Patterson sent Poe travel money so that he could lecture and solicit subscriptions outside of New York. At the end of June, Poe left Fordham for Philadelphia, where he spent two calamitous weeks, at times inebriated, possibly ill, briefly jailed, and suffering from paranoid delusions. In mid-July, he continued on to Richmond, where he spent the rest of the summer. While in Richmond, Poe tried to fulfill his mission, making the rounds of Richmond society, lecturing, and reciting "The Raven." He also renewed his pursuit of a new wife, courting the now-widowed Elmira Royster Shelton, to whom he had been secretly engaged when they were teenagers. On September 27, Poe left Richmond, with plans to stop in Philadelphia for a $100 freelance editing job before continuing to New York; whether he and Mrs. Shelton had definite wedding plans or not, it seems likely that he intended to return to Richmond with Maria Clemm. When Mrs. Shelton saw Poe the night of September 26, he was "very sad, and complained of being quite sick" and feverish (PL: 843); she was surprised to discover the next day that he had left on a steamship for Baltimore, the first leg of the journey, as planned.

Poe made it to Baltimore, but no further. Five days later, a printer named Joseph Walker discovered him in a tavern, and wrote to Poe's friend Joseph Snodgrass describing "a gentleman, rather the worse for wear . . . who appears in great distress, & says he is acquainted with you, and I assure you, he is in need of immediate assistance" (PL: 844). Snodgrass helped convey Poe to Washington College Hospital, where he lingered, semiconscious, for another three days, and died on October 7. Though a precise cause of death has never been determined, Poe had clearly been ill upon his arrival and drank heavily in the days that followed. His delirium a few months earlier in Philadelphia underscores the suggestion that he was suffering from neurological damage, possibly caused or worsened by alcohol. He might also have fallen victim to foul play, as Snodgrass reported finding him in shabby, ill-fitting clothes, probably not his own.[18]

Only a handful of mourners attended Poe's hastily arranged funeral on October 8, and on October 9 an obituary appeared in the New York *Daily Tribune* insinuating that he had died friendless, initiating a seemingly endless debate over his character:

> The poet was well known, personally or by reputation, in all this country; he had readers in England, and in several of the states of Continental Europe; but he had few or no friends; and the regrets for his death will be suggested principally by the consideration that in him literary art has lost one of its most brilliant but erratic stars.

Signed "Ludwig," the obituary was written by Poe's fellow editor and rival Rufus Griswold. In both this long obituary and the much longer "memoir" that would accompany his popular edition of Poe's works, Griswold romanticized and defamed Poe, exaggerating his faults and fabricating misdeeds, while consistently attesting to his genius as a poet and fiction writer. "He was at all times a dreamer," wrote Griswold, "dwelling in ideal realms—in heaven or hell—peopled with creatures and the accidents of his brain."[19] Just five years earlier, Lowell had presented Poe, "still in the prime of life," as a versatile writer-editor on the cusp of true greatness, casting his tumultuous life and career in the best possible light. Griswold gave the reading public a very different Poe, and to a great extent the two caricatures have been battling ever since. Throughout his career, Poe had fought unsuccessfully for control—of his own high-quality magazine, of his reputation, of his own life. But there was one realm where he did achieve it: insisting on the superiority of the shorter literary forms that thrived in periodicals, Poe explained, "During the hour of perusal the soul of the reader is at the writer's control" (ER: 572). Perhaps that was the control that mattered most to him, and it is the control he still exerts today.

Notes

1. James Russell Lowell, "Our Contributors—No. XVII. Edgar Allan Poe," *Graham's Magazine* 27, no. 2 (Feb. 1845): 49–50.

2. Kenneth Silverman, *Edgar A. Poe: Mournful and Never-ending Remembrance* (New York: HarperCollins, 1991), 233–234.
3. Lowell, "Our Contributors," 51.
4. Lowell, "Our Contributors," 50.
5. Lowell, "Our Contributors," 53.
6. See Alexander Hammond, "Edgar Allan Poe's *Tales of the Folio Club*: The Evolution of a Lost Book," in *Poe at Work: Seven Textual Studies*, ed. Benjamin Franklin Fisher IV (Baltimore: Edgar Allan Poe Society, 1978), 13–43.
7. Silverman, *Edgar A. Poe*, 107. See also Michael R. Haines, "Long Term Marriage Patterns in the United States from Colonial Times to the Present," NBER Working Paper Series on Historical Factors in Long Run Growth, no. 80 (Cambridge, MA: National Bureau of Economic Research, 1996), http://www.nber.org/papers/h0080.pdf. Citing the work of Warren C. Sanderson, Haines places the average age of first marriage for white women at twenty in 1830 (Figure 1).
8. N. H. Morison, a friend of Neilson Poe, told early Poe biographer John Henry Ingram, "To prevent so premature a marriage, Nelson [*sic*] Poe offered to take the young lady, his half-sister-in-law, into his own family, educate her, & take care of her—with the understanding that, if, after a few years, the two young people should feel the same towards each other, they should be married" (John Carl Miller, *Building Poe Biography* [Baton Rouge: Louisiana State University Press, 1977], 52). Burton R. Pollin argued that it was Maria Clemm who most needed to keep the family together in the face of Neilson Poe's offer, and that she manipulated Poe into marrying Virginia. See Pollin, "Maria Clemm, Poe's Aunt: His Boon or His Bane?" *Mississippi Quarterly* 48, no. 2 (1995): 211–224.
9. Terence Whalen, *Edgar Allan Poe and the Masses: The Political Economy of Literature in Antebellum America* (Princeton, NJ: Princeton University Press, 1999), 65–66. Whalen discusses the history and effects of the exaggerated circulation figures throughout Chapter 3 ("Fables of Circulation: Poe's Influence on the *Messenger*"), 58–75.
10. Qtd. in Silverman, *Edgar A. Poe*, 108.
11. Silverman, *Edgar A. Poe*, 163–164.
12. Silverman, *Edgar A. Poe*, 153.
13. Dwight Rembert Thomas, "Poe in Philadelphia, 1838–1844: A Documentary Record" (PhD diss., University of Pennsylvania, 1978), 25–26.
14. Various sources claim Poe's payment to have been five, ten, fifteen, or thirty dollars. T. O. Mabbott believes it was "probably fifteen dollars," almost certainly not five (M 1: 360).
15. Silverman, *Edgar A. Poe*, 248–249. See also Meredith McGill, "Poe, Literary Nationalism, and Authorial Identity," in *The American Face of Edgar Allan Poe*, ed. Shawn Rosenheim and Stephen Rachman (Baltimore: Johns Hopkins University Press, 1995), 271–304; and J. Gerald Kennedy, "The American Turn of Edgar Allan Poe" (Baltimore: Edgar Allan Poe Society and the Library of the University of Baltimore, 2001).
16. Some scholars have argued that Poe invented "Outis" himself; the strongest case was made by Burton R. Pollin in "Poe as Author of the 'Outis' Letter and 'The Bird of the Dream,'" *Poe Studies* 20 (1987): 10–15. Kent Ljungquist and Buford Jones argued against Poe's authorship of the "Outis" letter, contending that one Benjamin Labree was a more likely candidate; see "The Identity of 'Outis': A Further Chapter in the Poe-Longfellow War," *American Literature* 60, no. 3 (1988): 402–415. For additional commentary, see the following letters to the editor in the *PSA Newsletter*: Dwight Thomas, letter to the editor, *PSA Newsletter*, Fall 1988, 3–4; Ljungquist, Spring 1989, 6; and Pollin, Fall 1989, 6–7.

17. Silverman, *Edgar A. Poe*, 397–398. Poe's 1849 "Marginalia" borrowed heavily from a similar series, Horace Binney Wallace's "Mems from Memory," that had run in *Burton's Gentleman's Magazine* in 1840.
18. In addition to PL: 843–849, see Matthew Pearl, "A Poe Death Dossier: Discoveries and Queries in the Death of Edgar Allan Poe: Part I," *Edgar Allan Poe Review* 7, no. 2 (2006): 4–29; Pearl, "A Poe Death Dossier: Discoveries and Queries in the Death of Edgar Allan Poe: Part II," *Edgar Allan Poe Review* 8, no. 1 (2007): 8–31; and Scott Peeples, "Life Writing/Death Writing: Biographical Versions of Poe's Final Hours," *Biography: An Interdisciplinary Quarterly* 18, no. 4 (1995): 328–338.
19. [Rufus W. Griswold], "Death of Edgar A. Poe," *New-York Daily Tribune*, October 9 1849, 2.

Bibliography

Miller, John Carl. *Building Poe Biography*. Baton Rouge: Louisiana State University Press, 1977.

Pearl, Matthew. "A Poe Death Dossier: Discoveries and Queries in the Death of Edgar Allan Poe: Part I." *Edgar Allan Poe Review* 7, no. 2 (2006): 4–29.

Pearl, Matthew. "A Poe Death Dossier: Discoveries and Queries in the Death of Edgar Allan Poe: Part II." *Edgar Allan Poe Review* 8, no. 1 (2007): 8–31.

Pollin, Burton R. "Maria Clemm, Poe's Aunt: His Boon or His Bane?" *Mississippi Quarterly* 48, no. 2 (1995): 211–224.

Quinn, Arthur Hobson. *Edgar Allan Poe: A Critical Biography*. 1941. Reprint, Baltimore: Johns Hopkins University Press, 1998.

Silverman, Kenneth. *Edgar A. Poe: Mournful and Never-ending Remembrance*. New York: HarperCollins, 1991.

Whalen, Terence. *Edgar Allan Poe and the Masses: The Political Economy of Literature in Antebellum America*. Princeton, NJ: Princeton University Press, 1999.

CHAPTER 3

POE

A Life in Letters

LESLEY GINSBERG

> Depend upon it, after all, Thomas, Literature is the most noble of professions. In fact, it is about the only one fit for a man. For my own part, there is no seducing me from the path. I shall be a *litterateur*, at least, all my life; nor would I abandon the hopes which still lead me on for all the gold in California. Talking of gold, and of the temptations at present held out to "poor-devil authors", did it ever strike you that all which is really valuable to a man of letters — to a poet in especial — is absolutely unpurchaseable? Love, fame, the dominion of intellect, the consciousness of power, the thrilling sense of beauty, the free air of Heaven, exercise of body & mind, with the physical and moral health which result—these and such as these are really all that a poet cares for:—then answer me this—*why* should he go to California?
>
> —Edgar Allan Poe to Frederick W. Thomas, February 14, 1849 (CL 2: 770)

In a letter written on the last Valentine's Day he would celebrate—a letter written by a writer for whom the subgenre of the literary Valentine would loom large throughout his life—Edgar A. Poe declares his love of "Literature" and his dedication to being "a man of letters," despite the putative seductions of more remunerative employments. The "poor-devil author" subsists on rewards that cannot be monetized. Perhaps embedded in this term that Poe used with some frequency is a pun on the "printer's devil," a vision of the author as permanent apprentice in the world of print.[1] In this letter, Poe renews the vows he made in his youth to the career of the "*litterateur*." That word first appeared in English in the *Edinburgh Review* (1806) and in Byron's letters (1816); it recalls the print and manuscript antecedents of Poe's literary life.[2] Yet Poe's repeated reference to "gold" highlights another thread that can be traced throughout his letters—the poverty that haunted his commitment to literature. Poe's Valentine to the literary profession was written to his friend Frederick W. Thomas, a moderately popular author who supported his literary habit with a government post. Thomas tried but failed to secure a similar sinecure for Poe.[3] Thomas was related to Isaiah Thomas, who wrote *The History of Printing in America* (1810); Poe came to the profession without family connections.[4]

By Valentine's Day 1849, Poe had survived a dramatic year, including a suicide attempt (revealed in a letter) and a love affair conducted in part through letters that was precipitated by a manuscript Valentine written for him by the poet Sarah Helen Whitman. Poe read her Valentine when it was printed in the *Home Journal* in March of 1848 (Victorian propriety prevented Whitman from sending the manuscript poem to Poe). That the romance started with the circulation of a poem in manuscript at a Valentine's Day party hosted by Anne C. Lynch before it reached Poe in print illustrates the complex disseminations of literary works in antebellum America.[5] For Poe, authorship meant inhabiting the competing and at times conflicting worlds of manuscript and print cultures, realms that collide in the genre of the letter.

Poe's letters reveal more than his attitude toward literary labors. They also show the writer assuming a variety of personas: the wronged son, the victim, the literary professional, the lover, and the genius. The first-person speaker in Poe's epistolary rhetorics may be linked to his lyric poetry, to some of the desperate first-person narrators in his fiction, and to works that formally reflect on the letters and letter writing, including "Autography" (1836, revised and expanded 1841 and 1842), in which signatures are purported to have been collected through "epistles" or "letters" (M 2: 262–263). "Mellonta Tauta" (1849) appears in *Godey's Lady's Book* prefaced by a fictional letter to the editors, signed "Edgar A. Poe," purporting to enclose a manuscript that begins as "a long gossiping letter" addressed to "my dear friend" (M 3: 1291). Poe's interest in letters as a genre may be reflected in his criticism and magazine writings that appear in an epistolary form, such as the "Letter to B—" (1831) and "Doings of Gotham" (1844). In an echo of manuscript letters, the names of the magazines he dreamed of operating, first "The Penn" and then "The Stylus," invoke a convergence of the handwritten and the machine-printed, as does "Anastatic Printing" (1845), discussed later in this chapter.[6] Poe penned approximately 422 extant letters (CL 1: xxiii) from 1824 to 1849, during a time when privately circulated manuscripts and public cultures of print competed, though print cultures were rising. Further, as scholars of letter writing in the nineteenth-century United States attest, it is important to recognize that letters were not necessarily "private documents"; rather, they were "self-conscious" artifacts "circulating between friends and strangers."[7] Finally, Poe's letters also document his participation in the business of publishing in antebellum America. In this chapter I hope to show how Poe's choice of a life *of* letters is revealed in part by a life *in* letters.

Then as now, the term "letters" had dual meanings. A letter typically referred to a handwritten epistle addressed to an individual, often sent by US Postal Service.[8] "Letters" also meant "literature and learning," as the word is defined in Charles Richardson's *A New Dictionary of the English Language*, which Poe reviewed in the *Southern Literary Messenger* (August 1836).[9] Poe chose to be "a man of letters" when new technologies of print were destabilizing the older, gentlemanly model of manuscript circulation. As David Leverenz puts it, "throughout the eighteenth century, most male

British American writers with literary aspirations thought of themselves as 'men of letters.'" Leverenz's paradigmatic man of letters is Thomas Jefferson, whose "favorite genre was the letter."[10] Poe wrote his first extant letter to his foster father, John Allan, when attending Jefferson's signature institution, the University of Virginia. This letter is dated about six weeks before Jefferson's death in 1826. Poe dedicated himself to becoming a man of letters early in life, when appearing in print was part of authorship but not its only measure.

Poe's letters to Allan coincide with his earliest publications (1826–1833).[11] Early in their correspondence, a rift with Allan engenders a letter dated just two months after Poe's eighteenth birthday.[12] The causes leading to the separation include a dispute over Poe's desire for "eminence in public life," meaning literary renown, rather than a career in business. Poe complains, "You . . . are constantly upbraiding me with eating the bread of Idleness." Tellingly, however, he closes the letter begging for money (CL 1: 10–11). Allan attempted to steer the youth away from a literary career: "I taught you to aspire, even to eminence in Public Life, but I never expected that Don Quixotte [*sic*], Gil Blas . . . & such works were calculated to promote the end." Allan clearly reads Poe's aspirations as literary, as he mentions novels that may have led his young ward astray. Allan defends himself: "the charge of eating the Bread of idleness, was to urge you to perseverance & industry" (PL: 78). The novels Allan mentions, his key words—"industry," "idleness"—even his noun capitalizations, mark him as hewing to habits of mind from the previous century. He is a skeptical reader of the young author's epistle: "now that you have shaken off your dependance & declared for your own Independance . . . you Tremble for the consequences unless I send you a supply of money."[13] On the same day that Allan's reply was penned, Poe sent a more dire plea: "I am in the greatest necessity, not having tasted food since Yesterday morning. I have no where to sleep at night, but roam about the Streets—I am nearly exhausted" (CL 1: 12–13). The postscript, "I have not one cent in the world to provide any food," did not elicit sympathy; Allan filed Poe's letter with the note, "Edgar A Poes/Pretty Letter" (CL 1: 13n). Allan's use of Poe's preferred authorial signature, coupled with the cynical "Pretty Letter," may hint at a recognition of Poe's belletristic ambitions (literally, belles-lettres are "pretty letters") and suggest that Allan saw Poe's epistles as literary—overwrought, fictional, artful.[14]

After publishing *Tamerlane and Other Poems* (1827), Poe boasts to Allan in a letter dated December 1, 1828:

> You need not fear for my future prosperity—I am altered from what you knew me, & am no longer a boy tossing about on the world without aim or consistency. . . . You will perceive that I speak confidently—but when did ever Ambition exist or Talent prosper without prior conviction of success? I have thrown myself on the world, like the Norman conqueror on the shores of Britain &, by my avowed assurance of victory, have destroyed the fleet which could alone cover my retreat — I must either conquer or die—succeed or be disgraced. (CL 1: 14–15)

The extreme bravado of this persona is mingled with punishing abjection: Poe repeats twice that he feels "hurt" by Allan's silence: "My father do not throw me aside as degraded. . . . If you determine to abandon me—here take [I my] farewell—Neglected—I will be doubly [ambi]tious, & the world shall hear of the son whom you have thought unworthy of your notice. But if you let the love you bear me, outweigh the offence which I have given—then write me my father, quickly" (CL 1: 16–17). As J. Gerald Kennedy suggests, Poe's "belletristic pursuits" are a form of "revenge."[15]

But the voice expressing exquisite suffering may be linked to the lyric "I" in Poe's early poems, including perhaps the earliest literary piece Poe wrote, penned when he was fifteen, on a scrap of Allan's financial calculations estimating his net worth: "Last night, with many cares & toils oppress'd/Weary, I laid me on a couch to rest—." This is a conventional voice in lyric poetry—a speaker who is oppressed by worldly cares and toils, who uses Latinate grammar, who emends words for the sake of meter, and who associates poetry with romantic leisure if not the bread of idleness. The fragment even has a title: "Poetry. By. Edgar. A. Poe" which, as Mabbott points out, shows that Poe used this name as his preferred authorial signature from the age of fifteen (M 1: 5–6).[16] The couplet is a sly apprenticeship of sorts, revealing Poe's true vocation. The signature cuts Allan off before Allan cuts Poe out; it is also a rejection of "Edgar Allan," the name under which Allan enrolled Poe at two English boarding schools.[17]

Some of the earliest examples of Poe's rhetorical performance of the man of letters date from 1829: two letters each to the Philadelphia publishers Carey and Lea and to the writer and publisher John Neal, who had praised Poe's poetry in his magazine. Poe pledges his fidelity to poetry and invents himself as a writer in a letter to publisher Isaac Lea, whom he hopes to interest in *Al Aaraaf*: "You will be so kind as to consider this as a *literary* introduction." The letter combines scraps of poetry, a discussion of "Al Aaraaf," and business; it calls itself "a *literary*" letter. The letter includes a quatrain:

> It was my choice or chance or curse
> To adopt the cause for better or worse
> And with my worldly goods & wit
> And soul & body worship it —

As he did twenty years later, Poe speaks of his literary commitments as a marriage vow, but he also uses the verb "adopt," a telling choice for one who was never formally adopted. Poe's commitment to letters ("the cause") is a hybrid of adoption and marriage. But "succeed or not, I am 'irrecoverably a poet'" (CL 1: 26–28). As Deidre Lynch glosses, "irrecoverably" is "the loaded term" in this quote from Samuel Johnson.[18] The letter indents Poe's quatrain as expected for poetry, but the script is the same whether business or art; the letter is all of a piece, as one might expect in a letter from an amateur.[19]

Poe first wrote Neal a few months before the publication of *Al Aaraaf, Tamerlane and Minor Poems* (1829): "I am young—not yet twenty—am a poet—if deep worship of all beauty can make me *one*." He proposes kinship: "there can be no tie more strong than that of brother for brother—it is not so much that they love one another as that they both love the same parent" (CL 1: 47). Neal is an ideal comrade, praising rather than "prosing" a colleague in "beauty" (CL 1: 52). Poe styles himself romantic, swiping at Allan: "I am and have been from my childhood, an idler." He slightly misquotes a couplet from Pope to the effect that he hasn't left a "calling" or a "trade" or "disobeyed" a parent to become a poet, because he has been "an idler" since childhood; in any case "I have no father—nor mother," he adds. "I am about to publish a volume of 'Poems'—the greater part written before I was fifteen." Poe paid careful attention to his reception in print, as he did in his last known letter (September 18, 1849). Perhaps unsure if the words are Neal's, Poe politely notes, "the Editor of the Yankee says, He might write a beautiful, if not a magnificent poem—(the very first words of encouragement I ever remember to have heard)" (CL 1: 47).

As a mature writer, Poe occasionally used different paper for literary manuscripts than he used for letters. Frances Sargent Osgood recalls seeing "several little rolls of narrow paper, (he always wrote thus for the press,)."[20] In 1849, Poe sent John R. Thompson of the *Southern Literary Messenger* "eleven pages of 'Marginalia,' done up in *a roll*" (CL 2: 760). Yet this was not the case when Poe attempted to sell "Epimanes" to the *New-England Magazine* by letter (CL 1: 77–78).[21] The letter is written in a gentlemanly script, but the text of the story begins on the same page as the letter and is printed very carefully to mimic the look of print. The difference between the two handwriting styles could be interpreted as evidence that Poe equated authorship with print. As Poe noted in a letter to Thomas W. White, the owner and editor of the *Southern Literary Messenger*, "To be appreciated you must be *read*" (CL 1: 85). Poe meant widely circulated, as antebellum print cultures promised. Yet the letter containing "Epimanes" represents a hybrid work combining elements of both print and manuscript. The letter's poignant postscript, "P.S. I am poor," written on the back of the letter in script, reminds the reader of the human hand writing the story, the person elided by the anonymity of print, and the pecuniary sacrifices inherent in the choice of a career in letters. In the postscript, we see the person behind the print.

In a letter to Baltimore-based lawyer and author John Pendleton Kennedy in 1834, Poe hints that he had expected an inheritance, which would have granted him the status of a gentleman-author. Poe started publishing in an era when writers were lucky to be paid at all; according to Eric Lupfor, "For inexperienced writers, publication was generally assumed to be payment enough."[22] Kennedy had been on the committee that awarded Poe a one-hundred-dollar prize for "MS Found in a Bottle." Poe offers Kennedy a potted autobiography: "I looked forward to the inheritance of a large fortune" from "a gentleman of Virginia (Mr Jno Allan) who adopted me at the age of two years, (both my parents being dead) and who, until lately, always treated me with the affection of a father." But "He is now dead, and has left me nothing. I am thrown entirely upon my own resources with no profession. . . . I am at length penniless" (CL 1: 79). Even after Kennedy helped Poe find an editorial position in Richmond, Poe appealed again to his mentor, despite his salary at the *Messenger*. His letter neglects to mention that he has recently invited Virginia and Maria Clemm to set up house with him in Richmond; he is uncertain whether his proposal will be accepted, given his relatively "penniless" condition.

> My feelings at this moment are pitiable indeed. I am suffering under a depression of spirits such as I have never felt before. . . . — *You will believe me* when I say that I am still miserable in spite of the great improvement in my circumstances. I say you will believe me, and for this simple reason, that a man who is writing for *effect* does not write *thus*. My heart is open before you — if it be worth reading, read it. . . . Console me. . . . Write me immediately. . . . Oh pity me! for I feel that my words are incoherent. (CL 1: 107)

Poe tutors Kennedy: incoherence symbolizes an open heart. Kennedy is instructed on how to "read" his letter and how to reply (with words of consolation). Kennedy replies instead with the usual bromides: "Rise early, live generously, and make cheerful acquaintances" (H 17: 19).

Signatures are also a revealing feature of Poe's letters: he rarely signs as "Edgar Allan Poe"; even more rarely is he "Edgar" or "Eddy."[23] Such variations would have interested collectors because "Autograph collecting was practiced far and wide during the course of the nineteenth century, with collecting peaks in the 1830s and 1870s."[24] Then, as now, autograph collecting appealed to the fantasy of communion with celebrities.[25] Poe generously provided autographs and holograph poems to a variety of seekers, typically signed "Edgar A Poe."[26] He occasionally sought autographs himself for various purposes, especially his "Autography" series. Early in his flirtation with Sarah Helen Whitman, Poe received some anonymous verses in the mail, and, toying with Whitman, pretended to be an autograph hound, "Edward S.T. Grey," who was "engaged in making a collection of autographs of the most distinguished American authors"; he requested the "*very especial* favor" of hers (CL 2: 687).[27] She replied with her signature, and he used it to identify the manuscript verses as hers. The autograph signals originality as opposed to the theoretically infinite possibilities of print reproduction, while handwriting betrays anonymity.

One of Poe's earliest experiments with the holograph letter as an art form was "Autography"— literally, writing by one's own hand (*Southern Literary Messenger* 1836). The writer claims he has received a pile of manuscripts collected by a London editor, notes signed by American authors: "They are autographs—but they are American autographs," and "as such may be of little value" to the "British," even though the signatures represent America's "principal *literati*" (M 2: 261–263). Visually, the series is a striking combination of print and manuscript cultures as the majority of text is printed, including the fictitious letters, but the signatures are facsimile reproductions—likely expensive.[28] The narrator analyzes not only the content of the letters but also purportedly the handwriting of the signatures for revelations about the author's personality and literary style.[29] The narrator almost always takes account of the materiality of the letter—another feature difficult to reproduce in print—in this case, the quality of the paper used, the ink, and sometimes the seal.

Consider Poe's mention of Nathaniel Parker Willis, a "Magazinist" (CL 1: 470) of Poe's generation who was in many ways born into the business of antebellum periodicals if not groomed for it—his father was the founder of the *Youth's Companion*, and by the mid-1850s his sister, Sara, publishing under the name Fanny Fern, was a highly paid journalist, novelist, and humorist. Poe would later befriend Willis, and in "Autography" he indulges in flattery, hinting at potential favors:

> Mr. Willis writes a very good hand. . . . It has the same grace [as what was said about the respected poet Fitz-Greene Halleck], with more of the picturesque, however, and, consequently, more force. These qualities will be found in his writings—which are greatly underrated. Mem. Mr. Messenger should do him justice. [Mem. by Mr. Messenger. I have.] Cream colored paper—green and gold seal—with the initials N. P. W. (M 2: 280)

"Autography" has a metafictional charm. There is no "Mr. Messenger," but Poe seems to be vying for that role despite White's proprietary claims. And if the conceit of a "Mr. Messenger" also winks at the favors peddled among antebellum magazine editors, Poe knew that holograph letters were commodities.[30] Years later, in preparation for his "Literati" series in *Godey's Lady's Book* (1846), he requested a large number of "autographs" from Evert A. Duyckinck and Cornelius Matthews but not before making an offer to Duyckinck: "It strikes me that, some time ago, Wiley & Putnam advertised for autographs of distinguished Amer. statesmen. Is it so? I have well-preserved letters from John Randolph, Chief Justice Marshall, Madison, Adams, Wirt, Duane, E. Everett, Clay, Cass, Calhoun and some others—and I would exchange them for books" (CL 1: 570). The notion of the signed letter as a commodity—more rarified than print or at least exchangeable for books—speaks to the convergence of antebellum print and manuscript cultures.

The expanded "Autography" raises two issues that haunt Poe's letters and writings for years to come: the want of an international copyright law and the question of plagiarism, since a holograph letter lays claim to authorship in an age of unfettered and unauthorized reprinting.[31] Poe's letters are studded with discussions of copyright issues. He had hoped for an article about it in his ill-fated *Penn* magazine.[32] The lack of adequate copyright legislation devalues literature. As an editor, Poe apologizes on behalf of *Burton's Gentleman's Magazine*: "We should be glad, of course, to publish the piece, but are grieved to say that the absurd condition of our present copy-right laws will not permit us to offer any compensation" (CL 1: 216). As he puts it to Thomas, "Literature is at a sad discount. . . . Without an international copy-right law, American authors may as well cut their throats" (CL 1: 356). Elsewhere he advises, "Touching your poem. . . . I feel sure that you will get no publisher to print it, except on your own account. Reason—Copy-Right Laws" (CL 1: 350).

Printed letters were a staple of periodicals, supplying news articles or reports written for publication. Poe's seven "Letters" about New York, written for the *Columbia Spy* and published in 1844 as "Doings of Gotham," exemplify the type of letter in which a correspondent's report assumes the guise of a personal epistle. But some news is fake news. Poe's second letter in the series is a case in point: it appears to report on a remarkable fuss surrounding the anticipated printing of the "extra" to the *Sun* about "the 'Balloon-Hoax' " (a tale that he hoped would be taken for truth) except that this letter is also a hoax, a puffed-up piece about a frenzy for Poe's work that was far less dramatic than reported.[33] Poe seemed delighted that "Mesmeric Revelation" (1844) (reprinted in England as "The Last Conversation of a Somnambule" in the *Popular Record of Modern Science*) and "Facts in the Case of M. Valdemar" (1845) were mistaken for real news. In 1846 he replied to an inquiry from "a Gentleman" who wrote to him from London:

> I thought that by presenting my speculations in a garb of vraisemblance—giving them as revelations—I would secure for them a hearing, and I depended upon what the *Popular Record* very properly calls the "Magazinish" tone of the article to correct any false impression which *might* arise in regard to the question of fact or fable. In the case of Valdemar, I was actuated by similar motives, but in this latter paper, I made a more pronounced effort at verisimilitude for the sake of effect. The only material difference between the two articles is, that in one I believe actual truth to be involved; in the other I have aimed at merely suggestion and speculation. I find the Valdemar case universally copied and *received as truth*, even in spite of my disclaimer. (CL 1: 556)

Confounding the difference between fiction and fact delighted Poe; here, the holograph letter delivers truth. Poe was thrilled when he received a letter from Elizabeth Barrett [Browning], who wrote in April 1846 to thank Poe for a sending her a copy of *The Raven and Other Poems* (dedicated to her). She mentions that " 'Valdemar' " is now "going the round of the newspapers, about mesmerism, throwing us all into 'most admired disorder, and dreadful doubts as to whether 'it can be true,' as the children say of ghost stories." She also praised "The Raven": "this vivid writing, this power which is felt! Your 'Raven' has produced a sensation, a 'fit horror,' here in England" (PL: 632).

Poe then used her manuscript letter to foster his celebrity status in print. After receiving it, Poe wrote to Joseph M. Field, the editor of the St. Louis *Daily Reveille*, asking him to insert an anonymous editorial paragraph: " 'The Times'—the matter of fact '*Times!*'—copies the 'Valdemar Case.' The world's greatest poetess, *Elizabeth Barrett Barrett*, says of Mr Poe:—'This *vivid* writing!—this power *which is felt!* "The Raven" has produced a *sensation*—a "fit horror"—here in England.' " The letter is marked "(Confidential)" at the top—a rarity in Poe's letters (CL 1: 579–580). He repeats almost the same paragraph in a similar request to Philip P. Cooke, a lawyer who wrote for the *Southern Literary Messenger*.[34] Poe admits to the slightest hesitation about the propriety of printing the letter. He asks Cooke, "Would it be in bad taste to quote these words of Miss B. in your notice?" (CL 1: 596). The question goes unanswered—celebrity trumps good taste. He makes a similar request to Evert Duyckinck: "My object in enclosing the . . . letter . . . from Miss Barrett, is to ask you to do me a favor which (*just at this moment*) may be of great importance. It is, to make a paragraph or two for some one of the city papers. . . . If this will not give you too much trouble, I will be deeply obliged. If you think it advisable, there is no objection to your copying any portion of Miss B's letter" (CL 1: 608).

Compare Poe's brief correspondence with Washington Irving in 1839, where he asks Irving for an endorsement of *Tales of the Grotesque and Arabesque* (1840). Poe "take[s] the liberty" of sending Irving a copy of "William Wilson" and admits that Irving inspired the tale: it is "based upon a brief article of your own in the first 'Gift'—that for 1836. Your article is called 'An Unwritten Drama of Lord Byron'. I have hoped that, having thus a right of ownership in my 'William Wilson', you will be induced to read it—and I also hope that, reading it, you will find in it something to approe [*sic*]." Although Poe clearly meant "approve," the slip may hint at his own appropriation. Poe wants Irving's approving words to appear in a print advertisement. Letters offer access to "the personal opinions of some of our principal literary men," as opposed to professional "editorial opinions" appearing in print journals. Poe is certain that if "I could be permitted to add *even a word or two* from yourself, in relation to the tale of 'William Wilson' (which I consider my best effort) *my fortune would be made*. I do not say this unadvisedly—for I am deliberately convinced that your *good* opinion, thus permitted to be expressed, would ensure me that public attention which would carry me on to fortune hereafter, by ensuring me fame at once" (CL 1: 198–201). Irving complied, and his "encomiums" duly appeared, slightly emended.[35] Irving's letter to Poe containing the requested blurb clearly distinguishes between public and private. The first paragraph includes praise that was printed; the second paragraph begins, "I could add for your private ear" and includes gentle criticism (H 17: 54).[36] To Snodgrass, Poe suggests that Irving "desires" publicity: "I am sure you will be pleased to hear that Washington Irving has addressed me 2 letters, abounding in high passages of compliment in regard to my Tales—passages which he desires me to make public—if I think benefit may be derived. It is needless to say that I shall do so—it is a duty I owe myself—and which it would be wilful [*sic*] folly to neglect, through a false sense of modesty." There are literary scores to settle:

> Irving's name will afford me a complete triumph over those little critics who would endeavor to put me down by raising the hue & cry of *exaggeration* in style, of *Germanism* & such twaddle. You know Irving heads the school of the *quietists.* I tell you these things in all confidence, & because I think you will be pleased to hear of my well-doing—not, I assure you, in any spirit of vain-glory—a feeling which I am above. (CL 1: 202)

To Thomas, Poe admits, "I have also been guilty of an indiscretion in quoting from a private letter of yours to myself—I could not forego the temptation of letting the world know how well you thought of me" (CL 1: 381). Poe apologizes to Thomas for printing words taken from "a private letter." Poe asks Irving's permission before publishing his words, but not Barrett's; neither does he write to Barrett after printing her words. And while his dedication of *The Raven and Other Poems* (1845) to Barrett is presumed to be an admission of his borrowing from "Lady Geraldine's Courtship," there is no letter from Poe to Barrett acknowledging the "ownership," and no apology.[37]

Poe's letters to women are fascinating, vexing, and few. Letters to Poe from women are even more rare.[38] Poe's business-oriented missives to correspondents such as Lydia Sigourney or Sarah Josepha Hale offer few revelations. From Poe's much-discussed flirtation with Frances Sargent Osgood, only two fragments remain of his letters to her;

none of her letters to him are extant. In a real-life version of "The Purloined Letter" (1844), Osgood may have recruited Margaret Fuller and Anne C. Lynch (Botta) to retrieve her letters to Poe (at Poe's home) after Elizabeth Ellet read one in 1846. Elizabeth Oakes Smith recalls that Ellet competed with Osgood for Poe's affections by sending him anonymous love letters: " 'A certain lady of my acquaintance fell in love with Poe and wrote a love letter to him. Every letter he received he showed to his little wife. This lady went to his house one day; she heard Fanny Osgood and Mrs. Poe having a hearty laugh, they were fairly shouting, as they read over a letter. The lady listened, and found it was hers, when she walked into the room and snatched it from their hands.' "[39] Osgood's reminiscence of absent letters is tantalizing: "it was in his conversations and his letters, far more than in his published poetry and prose writings, that the genius of Poe was most gloriously revealed. His letters were divinely beautiful."[40]

His intimate letters to women are striking. Consider Poe's letter to his Aunt Maria Clemm, glossed by Ostrom as "a letter of entreaty, firmly offering marriage" (CL 1: 104n). The speaker reveals extreme pain: "My dearest Aunty," the letter begins, "I am blinded with tears while writing thi[s] letter—I have no wish to live another hour" (CL 1: 102). The pages are blotted—marred with small tears, shakily underscored words, inadvertent repetitions, misspellings—and peppered with dashes, questions marks, and exclamation points. Clemm must have written to let Poe know that Neilson Poe (a rich cousin) had offered to care for Virginia until she came of age. "Al[l my] thoughts are occupied with the supposition that both you & she will prefer to go with N. Poe," her nephew confessed, adding, "It is useless to disguise the truth that when Virginia goes with N. P. that I shall never behold her again—that is absolutely sure" (CL 1: 102). Writing from Richmond, Poe blusters, "She will have far—very far better opportunites [*sic*] of entering into society here than with N. P" (CL 1: 103). But the romantic lover chides Mrs. Clemm and Neilson Poe for such pedestrian concerns: "The tone of your letter wounds me to the soul—Oh Aunty, Aunty you loved me once—how can you be so cruel now? You speak of Virginia acquiring accomplishments, and entering into society—you speak . . . in so *worldly* a tone" (CL 1: 103). The speaker is isolated and emotionally fragile: "What have I *to live for*? Among strangers with *not one soul to love me*"; the latter underscore is especially shaky. The lover bids "Adieu" to his "dear Aunty" before signing "EAP" and adding after the signature, "Kiss her for me—a million times" (CL 1: 104). Then, flush with the right edge of the page, another letter begins and ends:

> For Virginia,
>
> My love, my own sweetest Sissy, my darling little wifey, thi[nk w]ell before you break the heart of your cousin. Eddy. (CL 1: 104)

As Ostrom notes, "buried within" this letter to Mrs. Clemm is "the only extant letter from him to Virginia," other than a note from 1846 (CL 1: 104n; see also CL 1: 577–578).

After the note addressed to Virginia, the letter to his aunt continues. Poe goes to great length to establish his capacity to support Clemm and her daughter—the letter is replete with dollar signs and numbers of dollars "per month," per week, or the number of days since being paid. The voice lurches from the romantic to the prosaic: "Try and convince my dear Virg[a] how devotedly I love her. I wish you would get me th Republican wh: noticed the Messenger & send it on immediately by mail. God bless & protect you both" (CL 1: 104). One of the many interesting aspects of this letter is that it is the first example of pet names used in Poe's letters. Karen Lystra's study of nineteenth-century American love letters notes, "Pet names were the most unambiguous emblem of a privileged relationship." These names "symbolized an exclusive circle of sender and receiver, affirming a couple's emotional intimacy and mutual identification." Though the intimate circle for Poe is a triangle, terms of endearment symbolize intimacy, "very much like having an intimate face-to-face conversation."[41] The letter is a conversation: "I cannot speak as regards your peace . . . t is useless to expect advice forom [*sic*] me—what can I say?—Can I, in honour & in truth say—Virginia! do not go!" (CL 1: 102–105).

The pet name inscribes intimacy and ensures its survival. Names such as "Aunty," "sweetest Sissy," "darling little wifey," and "Eddy" are private terms of endearment. Pet names reappear in 1844 during a brief separation from Mrs. Clemm, when Poe and Virginia traveled to New York City from Philadelphia: "Muddy," "Sis" (three times), "Sissy" (twice), the name of the family cat, "Catt," or "Catterina" (CL 1: 437–439).[42] Four years later, when traveling, he chides, "My own dearest Muddy—What *can* be the reason that you have not written to me? Here I have been a whole fortnight & not *one line* from you yet. I did not think you would treat your poor Eddy in such a way as that" (CL 2: 683). Privileged names and a performance of dependency also appear in Poe's letters to Marie Louise Shew, but only as a reproach for lost intimacy when she broke with Poe: "I heard you say with a sob 'dear Muddie!' I heard you greet *my Catarina* [*sic*], but it was only as a memory of—nothing escaped *my ear*" (CL 2: 678). Tellingly, he signed his letters to Shew with his public name, "Edgar A. Poe."

Poe's first letter to Sarah Helen Whitman—the autograph request prank—is addressed to a "Dear Madam," as is his last letter to her, in which he withdraws his marriage proposal.[43] But if his first letter conceals emotion, the second expresses ardor: "I have pressed your letter again and again to my lips, sweetest Helen—bathing it in tears of joy. . . . But . . . of what avail are mere words to me now?" (CL 2: 692). Poe as lover instructs the beloved in the art of reading: "Is it not something in this cold, dreary world, *to be loved?*—Oh, if I could but burn into your spirit the deep—the *true* meaning which I attach to those three syllables underlined!" Like other letters to her, this one is signed "Edgar," the name of the author: "It was . . . when I thought of you—that I dwelt exultingly upon what I felt that I could accomplish in Letters and in Literary Influence" (CL 2: 711). Theirs could be a powerful literary union, as Poe suggests in a rare example of offering to share literary "control" with a woman: "Was I right . . . in the idea that you are ambitious? If so . . . *I* can & will satisfy your wildest desires. . . . Would it *not* be 'glorious,' *darling*, to establish, in America, the sole unquestionable aristocracy—that of intellect—to secure its supremacy—to lead & to control it?" (CL 2: 735).[44]

To the wealthy and married Nancy [Annie] Richmond, Poe is "Eddy." "Dear, dear Annie—" is a typical address; the occasion of this letter is Clemm's absence. "Our darling mother is just going to town," he tells his figurative sibling, "[his] own sweet *sister* Annie"; they are virtual soulmates, she the supposed "*wife* of [his] soul" (CL 2: 721). But he also infantilizes Annie: "The 5 prose pages I finished yesterday are called—what do you think?—I am sure you will never guess—'*Hop-Frog!*' Only think of *your* Eddy writing a story with *such* a name as 'Hop-Frog'!" (CL 2: 766). Poe bestowed the pet name "Annie"[45] and professed to her a love of extreme purity: "— so pure—so unworldly—a love which would make *all* sacrifices for your sake" (CL 2: 748–749). Poe confided a suicide attempt in a letter to Annie during his tempestuous courtship of Mrs. Whitman (CL 2: 721–725). In a letter to Clemm written while courting Elmira Shelton, Poe implored, "Do not tell me anything about Annie—I cannot bear to hear it now—unless you can tell me that Mr. R. is dead" (CL 2: 832).

A thread runs through these letters to women: Poe's poverty. Like a Dickensian suitor, Poe's romantic possibilities are bedeviled by pecuniary woes, as seen in his proposal letter to Virginia and Clemm. Mrs. Whitman was a wealthy widow who lived with her mother; her family feared Poe was simply interested in her money: "Were I not poor— . . . were I wealthy, or could I offer you worldly honors—ah then—then—how proud would I be to persevere—to sue—to plead—to kneel—to pray—to beseech you for your love—in the deepest humility—at your feet—at your feet, Helen, and with floods of passionate tears" (CL 2: 698–699). Finances are harder to discuss than love:

> there was one alloy to this happiness [of getting married]: —I *dreaded* to find you in worldly circumstances superior to my own. Let me speak freely to you *now*, Helen, for perhaps I may never thus be permitted to speak to you again—Let me speak openly—fearlessly—trusting to the generosity of your own spirit for a *true* interpretation of my own. I repeat, then, that I *dreaded* to find you in worldly circumstances superior to mine. So great was my *fear* that you were rich, or at least possessed some property which might cause you to *seem* rich in the eyes of one so poor as I. . . . I feel that you will have difficulty in comprehending me; but the horror with which, during my sojourn in the world, I have seen affection made a subject of barter, had, long since, —long before my marriage—inspired me with the resolution that, under *no* circumstances, would I marry where "interest," as the world terms it, could be suspected as, on my part, the object of the marriage. (CL 2: 710–711)

His letters to Mrs. Richmond voice similar fears: "Oh, Annie, in spite of . . . all the trouble and *misrepresentation* (so hard to bear) that Poverty has entailed on me for so long a time—in spite of *all* this I am *so*—*so* happy to think that you *really* love me." He links their friendship to his pecuniary success: "I am beginning to do very well about money as my spirits improve, and soon—*very* soon, I hope, I shall be *quite* out of difficulty. You can't think how industrious I am. I am resolved to *get rich*—to triumph—for your sweet sake" (CL 2: 748–749). To his chagrin, the purity of his affection for Annie seemed to some to betray a design on her wealth: "I see, with my own eyes, that to act generously is to be considered as designing, and that to be poor is to be a villain. I must get rich—rich" (CL 2: 753).

Poe's poverty pervades his letters.[46] In 1841, he writes to Thomas: "I wish to God I could visit Washington—but the old story, you know—I have no money—not even enough to take me there, saying nothing of getting back. It is a hard thing to be poor—." Poe hopes Thomas might help him find a government job so that he can escape magazine work: "To coin one's brain into silver, at the nod of a master, is to my thinking the hardest task in the world" (CL 1: 292). In 1842, having left *Graham's*, Poe faces ruin: "The renewed and hopeless illness of my wife, ill health on my own part, and pecuniary embarrassments, have nearly driven me to distraction" (CL 1: 335). The need is constant: "last night, I found here your kind letter from Washington, enclosing a check for $20, and giving me new life in every way. I am more deeply indebted to you than I can express, and in this I really mean what I say" (CL 1: 344).

He had felt a similar pinch in the spring of 1840 when, probably facing dismissal, Poe broke with Burton in a letter that includes a list of articles contributed for paltry pay. Yes, Burton had loaned Poe money that would never be repaid, but Poe reminds him: "you know that I am poor" (CL 1: 218–220). After leaving Philadelphia in April of 1844, Poe writes a poignant letter to "Muddy" describing the bounteous food at an otherwise shabby boarding house: "Last night, for supper, we had the nicest tea you ever drank, strong & hot—wheat bread & rye bread—cheese—tea-cakes (elegant) a great dish (2 dishes) of elegant ham, and 2 of cold veal, piled up like a mountain and large slices—3 dishes of the cakes, and every thing in the greatest profusion. No fear of starving here" (CL 1: 437–438).[47] The hyperbole betrays chronic hunger.

We also see Poe haggling over pay, such as his effort to place "The Mystery of Marie Roget" in the *Boston Notion*: "It will make 25 pages of Graham's Magazine; and, at the usual price, would be worth to me $100. For reasons, however, which I need not specify, I am desirous of having this tale printed in Boston, and, if you like it, I will say $50" (CL 1: 338). In a letter dated the same day, he writes to Snodgrass, repeating the same paragraph about the story, except that Poe asks just forty dollars, plus the favor of having some copy inserted into the editorial column of the *Baltimore Saturday Visiter*, which Snodgrass edited. Later, he's ashamed of the venues in which he publishes for money. To Frederick Gleason, editor of the *Flag of Our Union*, Poe dissembles, "I shall be happy to contribute, as often as possible, to 'The Flag'" (CL 2: 765). To Annie, he confides that the *Flag* is "not a *very* respectable journal, perhaps, in a literary point of view, but one that pays as high prices as most of the Magazines. The proprietor wrote to me, offering about 5$ a 'Graham page' and <as> I was anxious to get out of my pecuniary difficulties, I accepted the offer" (CL 2: 767). To Thomas, he characterizes the *Flag* as "vulgar and trashy. . . . I enclose my last, cut out, lest you should see by my sending the paper in what company I am forced to appear" (CL 2: 781). To Willis, he says it is "a paper for which sheer necessity compels me to write, now and then." Poe is loath to acknowledge the *Flag*: "If you can oblige me so far as to copy them, I do not think it will be necessary to say 'From the [*Flag*]' that would be too bad;—and, perhaps, 'From a late [Boston] paper,' would do" (CL 2: 790–791).

Poe's letters reveal a lifetime of engagement with literary business and antebellum cultures of letters. Although his letters may not have been entirely private, some of them are delightfully frank, even dishy. Mrs. Whitman's friends are Poe's enemies: "Miss Lynch, Miss Fuller, Miss Blackwell, Mrs Ellet, . . . the Channings—the Emerson and Hudson coterie—the Longfellow clique, one and all—the cabal of the 'N. American Review'" (CL 2: 709). To George W. Eveleth, a Maine physician who corresponded with a variety of antebellum literary lights, Poe used his signature term for the Transcendentalists and their circles: "The Frogpondians (Bostonians) have badgered me so much that I fear I am apt to fall into prejudices about them" (CL 1: 603). There are backhanded compliments: Louis A. Godey is "a good little man and means as well as he knows how" (CL 2: 648). To Thomas, he indulges in a rant: "I wish you would come down on the Frogpondians. They are getting worse and worse, and pretend not to be aware that there *are* any literary people out of Boston. . . . The Bostonians . . . are decidedly the most servile imitators of the English it is possible to conceive. I always get into a passion when I think about [it]" (CL 2: 770). In the same letter he called Margaret Fuller a "detestable old maid" and James Russell Lowell "a ranting abolitionist" who "*deserves* a good using up" (CL 2: 770–771).[48] His letters also bear witness to his feuds, such as his brawl with Thomas Dunn English, whom he successfully sued for libel: "I gave E. a flogging which he will remember to the day of his death—and, luckily, in the presence of witnesses" (CL 1: 597). After resigning from an editorial position at *Graham's* and being replaced by Rufus Wilmot Griswold, Poe notes that Graham "is not especially pleased with Griswold—nor is any one else, with the exception of the Rev. gentleman himself" (CL 1: 358). Poe complains about various periodicals: he calls "the Baltimore Athenæum—that great bowl of Editorial skimmed milk and water" (CL 1: 127); *Graham's Magazine* has a "namby-pamby character" (CL 1: 333); and the *United States Magazine and Democratic Review* is run by "that ass O'Sullivan" (CL 1: 359).

While Poe's letters provide unmatched insights into his work as an author, they also show how he reinvented himself. To George Washington Poe, Poe falsely claims his parents took ill and died together; he "was then about a year old" (CL 1: 185). To Lowell, he represents himself as a literary genius with preindustrial work habits: "I am excessively slothful, and wonderfully industrious—by fits." In the same letter, he says that he rambles and dreams until he awakes "to a sort of mania for composition. Then I scribble all day, and read all night, so long as the disease endures." He also admits he's not a reformer: "I have no faith in human perfectibility" (CL 1: 448–449). To Eveleth he claims, "My *habits* are rigorously abstemious. . . . I am done drinking forever" (CL 2: 648). We see Poe's (re)invention as a writer at work in a fascinating letter bristling with emendations and unfinished thoughts to the classicist Charles Anthon; it may be an unsent draft (CL 1: 465–473). Poe wrote to many literary figures to raise support for a magazine; the letter to Anthon is remarkable in that it offers fragments of what became a solicitation form letter.

Unsurprisingly, Poe's letters show the depth of his desire for his own magazine. As he wrote to Cooke, "'Touching 'The Stylus':—this is the one great purpose of my literary life. Undoubtedly (unless I die) I will accomplish it" (CL 1: 597). He spends years envisioning the perfect magazine: "The work should be printed in the very best manner. . . . Plates, of course, would be disdained. The aim would be to elevate without stupifying our literature—to further justice—to resist foreign dictation—and to afford (in the circulation & profit of the journal) a remuneration to ourselves for whatever we should write" (CL 1: 463). Poe likely speaks of the justice owed to American authors in an era of rampant intellectual theft. To Thomas, he sends the prospectus to *The Stylus*: "We *shall* make the most magnificent Magazine as regards externals, ever seen. The finest paper, bold type, in single column, and superb wood-engravings" (CL 1: 381–382). The technological future thrills him. To Longfellow he writes: "I need not call your attention to the signs of the times in respect to Magazine literature. You will admit that the tendency of the age lies in this way. . . . The brief, the terse, the condensed, and the easily circulated will take place of the diffuse, the ponderous, and the inaccessible" (CL 1: 274). Poe neglected to mention the infinitely reproducible; nearly the same words were repeated in seven other solicitation letters regarding *The Penn*. But Poe thought beyond mere print. He flirted with a technology that promised the best of both worlds by copying original manuscripts. In "Anastatic Printing," Poe imagines manuscripts reproduced on a print-on-demand scheme as well as self-publishing, with the further benefit that copyright will be enhanced, and class differences constraining authorship will be leveled: "The wealthy gentleman of elegant leisure will lose the vantage-ground now afforded him, and will be forced to tilt on terms of equality with the poor devil author" (P 3: 86). Alas, Poe's only experiment with anastatic printing replicated letters begging for funds to keep the *Broadway Journal* afloat.[49]

I conclude with an image: the title page for the prospectus of *The Stylus*, sent in a letter in 1849 to an Illinois publisher who was preparing to fund Poe's magazine scheme (see Figure 3.1).

He writes, "Enclosed, you will find a title-page designed by myself about a year ago:—your joining me will, of course, necessitate some modifications—but the *title* &c should, for many reasons (to be explained hereafter) be adhered to" (CL 2: 803–804). "&c" may refer to the image—"designed" if not executed by Poe, featuring a hand holding a pen, writing the Greek word for truth. Poe cares about the image of a hand writing, of the holograph manuscript behind the print; even the title of the magazine is hand-lettered. Poe is about to travel and needs cash, "as I am not overstocked with money (what poor-devil author *is*?)" (CL 2: 803–805).[50] Though Poe was poor, he lived a life rich in letters. In his life, the letter as a genre was one in which manuscript and print were inextricably and inseparably linked.

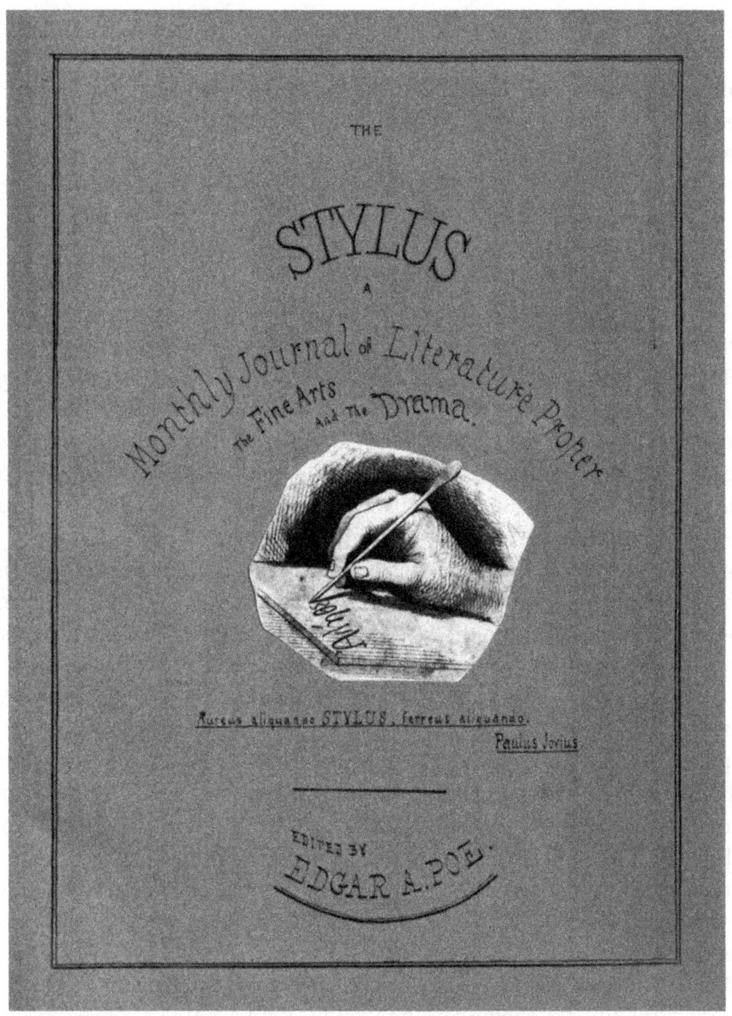

FIGURE 3.1 Poe's draft of the cover of "The Stylus," *Some Letters of Edgar Allan Poe to E. H. N. Patterson of Oquawka, Illinois, with comments by Eugene Field*, ed. Eugene Field (Chicago: The Caxton Club, 1898), n.p., between pages 16 and 17. Photo courtesy of University of California, HathiTrust.

Notes

1. For more on Poe's use of the term "poor-devil authors," see CL 2: 773n. The phrase may be related to Washington Irving's "The Poor-Devil Author" (1824), a satire of authorship and publishing.
2. *Oxford English Dictionary*, s.v. "littérateur, (n.)," updated January 2018, http://www.oed.com/view/Entry/109241?redirectedFrom=litterateur.
3. See Kenneth Silverman, *Edgar A. Poe: Mournful and Never-ending Remembrance* (New York: Harper Perennial, 1992), 176–177, and PL: 326–327, 365–366, 385–387.
4. For Thomas's background, see Thomas to Poe, August 3, 1841, in H 17: 95.
5. See PL: 713.
6. See Terence Whalen, *Edgar Allan Poe and the Masses: The Political Economy of Literature in Antebellum America* (Princeton, NJ: Princeton University Press, 1999), 74, for an interpretation of *The Penn* and *The Stylus* that echoes Walter Benjamin and the notions of "trace" and "aura." Poe changed the title from *The Penn* (strongly connoting Pennsylvania) to *The Stylus* in part because *The Penn* "was a name rather too local in its suggestions" ("Prospectus," reprinted in PL: 398).
7. Celeste-Marie Bernier, Judie Newman, and Matthew Pethers, *introduction to The Edinburgh Companion to Nineteenth-Century American Letters and Letter-Writing*, ed. Bernier, Newman, and Pethers (Edinburgh: Edinburgh University Press, 2015), 12. Several chapters from this volume proved useful: William Merrell Decker, "Longing in Long-Distance Letters: The Nineteenth Century and Now," 171–184; David M. Henkin, "Name and Address: Letters and Mass Mailings in Nineteenth-Century America," 62–74; Alea Henle, "The Means and the End: Letters and the Work of History," 103–118; Elizabeth Hewitt, "Prologue: Networks of Nineteenth-Century Letter-Writing," 1–10; Richard R. John, "Letters, Telegrams, News," 119–135; Graham Thompson, "From Mind to Hand: Papers, Pens, and the Materiality of Letter-Writing," 31–45.
8. Other delivery methods outside the US Postal Service included private postal services and hand-delivery. Poe used all three delivery methods at times, though the US Postal Service predominates.
9. See Charles Richardson, *A New Dictionary of the English Language* (London: Pickering, 1834), 471, https://books.google.com/books?id=QesIAAAAQAAJ&pg=PR1#v=onepage&q&f=false.
10. David Leverenz, "Men Writing in the Early Republic," in *A History of the Book in America*, ed. David Hall, *vol. 2, An Extensive Republic: Print, Culture, and Society in the New Nation, 1790–1840*, ed. Robert A. Gross and Mary Kelley (Chapel Hill: University of North Carolina Press, 2010), 350–351.
11. Excerpts from these early letters figure prominently in Arthur Hobson Quinn, *Edgar Allan Poe: A Critical Biography* (Baltimore: The Johns Hopkins University Press, 1941). See also J. Gerald Kennedy, *Poe, Death, and the Life of Writing* (New Haven, CT: Yale University Press, 1987), and Silverman, *Edgar A. Poe: Mournful and Never-ending Remembrance*. The letters are almost equally divided between a formal address ("Dear Sir," most frequently, or simply "Sir,") and the warmer "My dear Pa," or "Dear Pa" (the last letter Poe wrote to Allan was without an address). The changes of address reflect a troubled relationship.
12. See Silverman, *Edgar A. Poe: Mournful and Never-ending Remembrance*, 35.
13. Qtd. in Mary Newton Stanard, ed., *Edgar Allan Poe Letters Till Now Unpublished, in the Valentine Museum, Richmond, Virginia* (Philadelphia: J. B. Lippincott Company at the

Washington Square Press, 1925), 68. It is not clear whether or not Allan sent this letter; see CL 1: 13n.

14. Quinn suggests that Allan may have had belletristic ambitions of his own; see Quinn, *Edgar Allan Poe: A Critical Biography*, 57.
15. Kennedy, *Poe, Death, and the Life of Writing*, 97.
16. See illustration facing M 1: 582.
17. I thank J. Gerald Kennedy for pointing out that Poe was enrolled in English boarding schools as "Edgar Allan."
18. Deidre Shauna Lynch, *Loving Literature: A Cultural History* (Chicago: Chicago University of Chicago Press, 2015), 147.
19. See illustrations in Quinn, *Edgar Allan Poe: A Critical Biography*, 138a and 138b.
20. Frances Sargent Osgood, "Reminiscences of Edgar A. Poe," *Saroni's Musical Times* 1, no. 11 (December 8, 1849), column 2, 118–119, http://www.eapoe.org/papers/misc1827/fs018491.htm. I thank Richard Kopley for mentioning to me in conversation the rolls Poe used for some manuscript stories.
21. The letter is signed (unusually) with the author's full name, "Edgar Allan Poe," underscored with "a flowing underline, with a small loop in the middle." The signature is remarkable as "Apparently for the first time, Poe signs his full name" (CL 1: 78n). See Poe to editors of *New England Magazine*, Autograph manuscripts of "Epimanes," May 4, 1833, *Tales, Nevermore: The Edgar Allan Poe Collection of Susan Jaffe Tane*, Cornell University Library, http://rmc.library.cornell.edu/poe/exhibition/tales/index.html.
22. Eric Lupfer, "Periodicals and Serial Publication: Part 2, The Business of American Magazines," in *A History of the Book in America, vol. 3, The Industrial Book, 1840–1880*, ed. Scott E. Caspar, Jeffrey D. Groves, Stephen W. Nissenbaum, and Michael Winship (Chapel Hill: University of North Carolina Press, 2007), 254.
23. See CL 1: xxvii–xxix.
24. Henle, "The Means and the End: Letters and the Work of History," in *The Edinburgh Companion to Nineteenth-Century American Letters and Letter-Writing*, 108.
25. Maria Clemm cut Poe's signatures from his letters as gifts for "personal or financial assistance," one reason why many of the extant letters lack signatures. See CL 2: 837n.
26. See CL 1: 210–211 and note. Following the note, see also CL 1: 247 (signed EAP); CL 2: 790 (signed "Edgar A Poe"); CL 2: 705 (signed "Edgar A Poe."); CL 2: 835 (signed "Edgar A Poe.").
27. Poe uses this pseudonym in a letter to "My poor poor Muddy" written just weeks before his death: "Write immediately in reply & direct to Phil[a]. For fear I should not get the letter, sign no name & address it to *E. S. T. Grey Esq[re]*" (CL 2: 837). See CL 2: 839n for a logical reason why Poe requested that Clemm use the pseudonym. Regarding a link between this pseudonym and Frances Sargent Osgood, see M 1: 382–384.
28. See CL 1: 571n. According to Mabbott, "although the signatures were reproduced from genuine originals, the letters are all made up" (M 2: 259).
29. See Leon Jackson, "'The Italics Are Mine': Edgar Allan Poe and the Semiotics of Print," in *Illuminating Letters: Typography and Literary Interpretation*, ed. Paul C. Gutjahr and Megan L. Benton (Amherst: University of Massachusetts Press, 2001), 139–161.
30. On the favors and machinations of antebellum editors and publishers, see William Charvat, *Literary Publishing in America, 1790–1850* (Philadelphia: University of Pennsylvania Press, 1959).
31. See Meredith L. McGill, "The Duplicity of the Pen," in *Language Machines: Technologies of Literary and Cultural Production*, ed. Jeffrey Masten, Peter Stallybrass, and Nancy J. Vickers, (New York: Routledge, 1997), 39–71.

32. See CL 1: 256 and CL 1: 260–263.
33. See Karen Roggenkamp, *Narrating the News: New Journalism and Literary Genre in Late Nineteenth-Century American Newspapers and Fiction* (Kent, OH: Kent State University Press, 2005), 15–17.
34. Walt Whitman was not the only antebellum poet who placed reviews of his own work in antebellum magazines and trumpeted praise from better-known peers without their stated permission.
35. Edgar Allan Poe, "[Advertisements]," in *Tales of the Grotesque and Arabesque*, vol. 2 (Philadelphia: Lea and Blanchard, 1840), unnumbered pages, https://www.eapoe.org/works/editions/tgaads.htm.
36. Poe used the phrase "for your private ear" in several letters beginning with one written to White in 1835. White seems to use this phrase in his letters. White is quoted in William Doyle Hull, II, "A Canon of the Critical Works of Edgar Allan Poe with A Study of Poe as Editor and Reviewer" (PhD diss., University of Virginia, 1941), 52, https://www.eapoe.org/papers/misc1921/hullw101.htm.
37. On Poe's debt to Barrett, see Eliza Richards, "Outsourcing 'The Raven': Retroactive Origins," *Victorian Poetry* 43, no. 2 (2005): 205–221, http://www.jstor.org.libproxy.uccs.edu/stable/40002615, and M 1:356-357.
38. See Ostrom et al.: "Concerning letters *to* Poe, one amazing fact appears. Of all letters known to have been written to him *by* women, only 15 (possibly 17) exist today in manuscript or printed form. . . . Not a single line has been preserved from Annie Richmond, Helen Whitman, or Mrs. Clemm, or even his wife Virginia" (CL 2: 936).
39. Quoted in Mary E. Phillips, *Edgar Allan Poe the Man* (Chicago: John C. Winston, 1926), 2: 1143–1144, https://www.eapoe.org/papers/misc1921/mep2cc06.htm.
40. Osgood, "Reminiscences of Edgar A. Poe," 118–119.
41. Karen Lystra, *Searching the Heart: Women, Men, and Romantic Love in Nineteenth-Century America* (New York: Oxford University Press, 1989), 19–21.
42. The autograph, unfortunately, was cut out of this letter.
43. See CL 2: 687 and CL 2: 757.
44. Thanks to J. Gerald Kennedy for pointing out that this is Poe's only offer to share literary "control" with a woman.
45. Nancy Richmond formally changed her first name to Annie after Poe's death.
46. "Poverty, EAP's"; "Borrowing, and attempts to borrow, EAP's"; "Finances"; "Pay, for EAP's writings": these categories take up significant space in the excellent subject index to the 2008 Gordian Press edition of Poe's letters (CL 2: 1110, 1011, 1042–1043, 1097–1098).
47. Compare this letter to the puffy missives Poe receives from Thomas Holley Chivers, a physician and plantation owner who fancied himself a spiritualist and poet. Chivers doesn't seem to understand why Poe can't enjoy the fruits of life, as in this letter written in May 1844, just a month after Poe's letter to Muddy: "When I wrote to you last, I believe it was strawberrytime. I said something about strawberries and cream. I have just been eating strawberries and honey. You will not think me an epicure when I say to you, that, in this Country, at this time of the year, such a delicious compound is the Nepenthe of my life" (H 17: 171). Chivers closes a letter to Poe written in September 1844 with this thought: "You ought to have been here this Summer to have eaten peaches and milk" (H 17: 190).
48. Years earlier Lowell writes of leaving his law business to live with his father in Cambridge and devote himself to literature: "I have given up that interesting profession, & mean to

devote myself wholly to letters. I shall live with my father at Cambridge in the house where I was born" (H 17: 142). One can only imagine how this might have been read by an author without family or family connections.

49. See Jackson, "'The Italics Are Mine': Edgar Allan Poe and the Semiotics of Print," 160–161, and CL 1: 539–542.
50. See illustration 63 in CL 2: II-B, between 1152 and 1153.

Bibliography

Bernier, Celeste-Marie, Judie Newman, and Matthew Pethers, eds. *The Edinburgh Companion to Nineteenth-Century American Letters and Letter-Writing*. Edinburgh: Edinburgh University Press, 2015.

Decker, William Merrill. *Epistolary Practices: Letter Writing in America before Telecommunications*. Chapel Hill: University of North Carolina Press, 1998.

Gross, Robert A., and Mary Kelley, eds. *An Extensive Republic: Print, Culture, and Society in the New Nation, 1790–1840. Vol. 2 of A History of the Book in America*, edited by David Hall. Chapel Hill: University of North Carolina Press, 2010.

Hamilton, Charles. *Great Forgers and Fabulous Fakes: The Manuscript Forgers of America and How They Duped the Experts*. New York: Crown, 1980.

Harrison, James A., ed. *Poe and His Friends: Letters Relating to Poe. Vol. 17 of The Complete Works of Edgar Allan Poe*. 1902. Reprint, New York: AMS Press, 1965.

Henkin, David M. *The Postal Age: The Emergence of Modern Communications in Nineteenth-Century America*. Chicago: University of Chicago Press, 2006.

Hewitt, Elizabeth. *Correspondence and American Literature, 1770–1865*. Cambridge: Cambridge University Press, 2004.

John, Richard J. *Spreading the News: The American Postal System from Franklin to Morse*. Cambridge, MA: Harvard University Press, 1995.

Lystra, Karen, *Searching the Heart: Women, Men, and Romantic Love in Nineteenth-Century America*. Oxford: Oxford University Press, 1989.

Ostrom, John W., Burton R. Pollin, and Jeffrey A. Savoye, eds. *The Collected Letters of Edgar Allan Poe*. 2 Vols. Revised edition. New York: Gordian Press, 2008.

Quinn, Arthur Hobson. *Edgar Allan Poe: A Critical Biography*. 1941. Reprint, Baltimore: The Johns Hopkins University Press, 1998.

Silverman, Kenneth. *Edgar A. Poe: Mournful and Never-ending Remembrance*. 1991. Reprint, New York: Harper Perennial, 1992.

CHAPTER 4

POE'S LIVES

RICHARD KOPLEY

REPLYING to a January 11, 1848, letter from his correspondent George W. Eveleth, which cited comments by various editors on his drinking, Poe countered on February 29 that when he did drink he went among friends, so they inferred that he always drank—"Those who *really* know me, know better."[1] *Really* knowing Poe is a difficult matter. A Poe biographer today requires scholarly resources and scholarly resourcefulness, knowledge and judgment, fellowships and fellow feeling. I will consider here chronologically some of the noteworthy book-length Poe biographies, assessing their approaches to Poe—and how closely they approach him.

Poe's posthumous reputation was critically shaped by Rufus Wilmot Griswold's bilious obituary and memoir.[2] Some, such as N. P. Willis, George R. Graham, and John Neal, sought to offer a more appreciative voice.[3] Early Poe biography emerged from the ongoing controversy.

William Fearing Gill wrote the first book-length biography of Poe, the 1877 *The Life of Edgar Allan Poe*, a refutation of Griswold's distortions and lies.[4] As Gill acknowledges, he benefitted from the help of some of those who knew Poe well: Sarah Helen Whitman, Neilson Poe, Annie Richmond, George R. Graham, Maria Clemm, and Thomas C. Clarke.[5] The volume is brisk and sympathetic, though it slows down a bit with a long treatment of "The Raven." Also, inevitably for so early a biography, it contains occasional errors, including that Poe's parents died in the Richmond theatre fire of December 1811, that their three children "were left among strangers," and that Poe met Elmira Royster in Richmond in 1831.[6] And it features occasional omissions, such as Poe's trip to Boston in 1827 and his then joining the army. Gill concludes his biography by speaking for "the fairer side of the poet's life."[7] He follows these same words in a previous essay with a qualification: "I have not indeed found all the missing parts, needed to make of the mutilated statue a symmetrical whole; but, possibly, from some of the facts contained in this rambling paper, may be gathered suggestions at least of a fairer form than fame had hitherto given to the personal character of EDGAR A. POE."[8] This qualification, much modified in the book, was certainly warranted. An "Appendix" to the volume reviews work on Poe and recounts the 1875 honoring of Poe at the occasion of his reinterment in the cemetery of Baltimore's Westminster Church, with ample quotations from the addresses.

Gill did revise his work in subsequent editions. For instance, he silently corrected himself regarding the death of Poe's parents—he states that Eliza Poe died of pneumonia on December 8, 1811, and posits that her husband, David Poe, died of consumption soon thereafter. Also, he asserts that the three Poe children were taken by "kind friends."[9] And he acknowledges that Elmira Royster was "a friend of [Poe's] childhood."[10] He significantly revised his statement in the first edition that "[Poe] never drank, never could have drunk, to excess" by contending, more modestly, in a later edition that "[h]is excesses were few and far between."[11] So the later editions of the Gill biography are more accurate than the first edition, but not without a significant literary violation. Poe biographer Susan Archer Weiss stated that for these later editions Gill had taken her own material without her permission. (He does mention her in his acknowledgments.) She filed suit, but eventually gave up the effort.[12] Gill certainly offered a service to Poe studies by challenging the allegations of the unethical Griswold, but evidently Gill had ethical issues of his own.

John Henry Ingram's 1880 *Edgar Allan Poe: His Life, Letters, and Opinions* was another strong defense of Poe against the notorious obituary and memoir by Griswold. Ingram had written to those who had known Poe—including George Eveleth, Rosalie Poe, Marie Louise Shew Houghton, Annie Richmond, and Sarah Helen Whitman—and had built a remarkable collection of Poe materials (later acquired by the University of Virginia).[13] His two-volume book is full of valuable information, with many incidents and comments becoming standard in Poe biography. However, the book is flawed, in part by its too extensive quoting and in part by its occasionally unreliable assertions. Ingram claims, for instance, that Poe traveled to Europe after he attended the University of Virginia, that Poe resigned from the *Southern Literary Messenger*, and that Poe translated pieces from the French in the *New Mirror* and the *Evening Mirror* from 1843 to 1845.[14] Ingram also occasionally quotes a Poe narrator without noting that it is not Poe himself speaking—as, for example, with his early use of "William Wilson."[15]

Poe's drinking is a problematic matter for Ingram, and he doesn't bring it up explicitly until Poe resigns from *Graham's Magazine* in 1842. But we know that Poe drank when he was attending the University of Virginia and when he served editorially at the *Southern Literary Messenger*. Another problematic matter is Ingram's understanding of the complexity of Poe's work. For example, though Ingram was a champion of Poe, he wrote about *The Narrative of Arthur Gordon Pym*, "The chief defect in the tale is the supernatural final paragraph—wisely omitted in the London reprint—which neither adds to the interest nor increases the life-like truthfulness."[16] My view is that without that final paragraph the covert structure of the novel is inaccessible. The state of that final paragraph is not "unfinished,"[17] but as finished as any passage in literature, suggesting simultaneously the literal, autobiographical, and biblical levels of the work.[18] Also problematic is Ingram's occasionally patronizing attitude toward his subject, evident in such phrases as "The poor little orphan," "the unfortunate man" and "the poor fellow."[19] Perhaps, though, the sentimentality of Victorian England was fostering such a tone, as today's resistance to sentimentality is not.

Yet much that we know about Poe is owing to Ingram's quest for the true story of this writer whom he so admired. We may therefore fairly read Ingram's work, flaws and all, with appreciation.

By contrast to Ingram's biography, George E. Woodberry's 1885 American Men of Letters *Edgar Allan Poe* offers little sympathy, limited praise, and considerable criticism. The biographer acknowledged later, "My attention had never been drawn to Poe, nor my interest specially excited by his works."[20] Woodberry does correct Ingram on Poe's travel to Europe after his time at the University of Virginia and on Poe's translating from the French for the *New Mirror*.[21] But he writes of "the real worthlessness of much of Poe's early work" and "the worthlessness of Poe's thought in this field" (regarding *Eureka*).[22] "To Helen" is "overpraised," "The Pit and the Pendulum" is "a tale of no striking originality," and "for the most part his mastery was over dismal, superstitious, and waste places. In imagination, as in action, his was an evil genius."[23] Writing about Poe's criticism, Woodberry adds, "The good he did was infinitesimal."[24] However, Woodberry admires "the intense energy of Griswold's delineation of [Poe] in the 'Tribune' [the 'Ludwig' obituary], a piece of writing that has the power of genius and cannot be forgotten while his memory lives."[25] Woodberry offers a summary view of Poe as a man: "as he was self-indulgent, he was self-absorbed, and outside of his family no kind act, no noble affection, no generous sacrifice is recorded of him."[26] By 1885, there were a number of positive works about Poe—not only the Gill and Ingram volumes but also a variety of reminiscences of Poe, especially by friends responding to Griswold's attacks (including Sarah Helen Whitman's 1860 *Edgar Poe and His Critics*). But Woodberry apparently preferred to be, in some respects, a latter-day Ludwig.

Woodberry's two-volume 1909 *The Life of Edgar Allan Poe* repeats much of what the biographer had already written, but with a greater range of material to draw on, including manuscripts of the Griswold family and publications since 1885. Notably, Woodberry closes with a series of positive comments by people who cherished Poe—George R. Graham, N. P. Willis, Frances Sargent Osgood, Sarah Helen Whitman, Elmira Royster Shelton, Charles Chauncey Burr, and Maria Clemm—but follows them with the meager comment, "This is the sheaf of memories that was laid upon his grave."[27] Each of the volumes offers "Notes Mainly on Obscure or Controverted Points," which provides supplementary information, often of much interest. And the second volume includes useful appendices, including Appendix C, a primary Poe bibliography. Still, as in 1885, so in 1909: Woodberry is unsympathetic to his subject. Both Woodberry biographies are therefore unsatisfying.

James A. Harrison's *The Life of Edgar Allan Poe* is the first volume in his 1902 *Complete Works of Edgar Allan Poe*, the standard scholarly edition before Mabbott. The book looks plain, but its language is surprisingly florid. Consider, for instance, "The zephyrlike gossamer women of the Tales are incarnations of whispering winds; their movements are the breezy undulations of air travelling over bending grain; their melodious voices are the lyrics of the wind articulating themselves in flutelike throats; and full of passion and pregnancy of meaning are the musical inflections that exhale from their lips as perfumes exhale from the chalices of flowers."[28] This diction does not wear well. Fortunately, it diminishes somewhat as the book progresses. Floyd Stovall comments, "Harrison seems to have been romantic by temperament, and his prose style, even in his biography of Poe, was at times poetic, not to say flowery."[29]

Harrison relies on many texts, including the Gill, Ingram, and Woodberry biographies. But occasionally he seems too dependent on quotation. And Harrison does not always name the author of the quotation. Furthermore, he does sometimes get things wrong: for instance, he dismisses Poe's debt to Elizabeth Barrett Barrett's poem "Lady Geraldine's Courtship" in "The Raven," and he contends that the Harpers "repeatedly rejected … Poe's best work" (though they did publish *Pym*).[30] Still, this is clearly a valuable biography, one worth studying, especially given the biographer's responsiveness to his subject. The volume concludes with a strong appendix, featuring a not-entirely-reliable autobiographical memorandum from Poe to Griswold, Maria Clemm's preface to the Griswold edition, the "Ludwig" obituary, and appreciative essays on Poe by N. P. Willis, James Russell Lowell, Philip Pendleton Cooke, John R. Thompson, and George R. Graham. Notably, the stand-alone edition of the biography features a "Bibliography of the Writings of Edgar A. Poe" not in the biography in the *Complete Works*; this early bibliography appears instead at the end of volume XVI: [355]–379.

After the biographies of Gill, Ingram, Woodberry, and Harrison, the 1907 *The Home Life of Poe*, by Susan Archer Weiss, is an interesting change of pace. It focuses on the personal and in so doing relies for the first time in Poe biography on Poe's best friend John H. Mackenzie, once of Richmond. Weiss also includes her own reminiscences of Poe in Richmond in 1849, when she was twenty-seven.[31] She is forgiving of Poe's drinking, attributing it to heredity, but not forgiving of his interest in poet Frances Sargent Osgood. She considers Poe to have been weak willed, unduly susceptible to the influence of others, from Maria Clemm, who encouraged him to marry her daughter, his cousin Virginia, to sociable friends and acquaintances, who on various occasions encouraged him to take a drink.[32] And Weiss writes thoughtfully about what she considers Poe's frustrated aspirations for greatness: "A marked peculiarity of Poe's character was the restless discontent which from his sixteenth year took possession of and clung to him through life, and was to him a source of much unhappiness. It was not the discontent of poverty or of ungratified worldly ambition, but the dissatisfaction of a genius which knows itself capable of higher things, from which it is debarred—the desire of the caged eagle for the wind-swept sky and the distant eyrie."[33] *The Home Life of Poe* is not always reliable, but it is sometimes engaging and usually sympathetic.

A gryphon of a book is John W. Robertson's 1921 *Edgar A Poe: A Study.* The eagle half, *Edgar A. Poe: A Psychopathic Study*, is a sympathetic attempt to understand the origins of Poe's medical problem. Robertson, who was a medical doctor, attributed that problem to Poe's hereditary disease, "dipsomania." He acknowledges that he focuses on "the darker side of Poe's life" and offers such apparently explanatory phrases as "nervous diathesis" and "an organic congestion of the meninges of the brain."[34] One may be put off by the clinical, potentially reductive approach—yet clearly some explanation is wanted for Poe's drinking and its consequences. Still, I was heartened to read, "To write biography successfully one must love one's subject."[35] And it was especially touching to read the conclusion, which begins, "And, among these 'Royal and Noble Authors' "—Isaak Walton, Oliver Goldsmith, William Makepeace Thackeray, Robert Louis Stevenson—"Poe would not have been the least of those I loved."[36] Robertson goes on to imagine himself caring for Poe in Fordham. If the diagnosis here is not wholly illuminating, the bedside manner is much appreciated.

And then there is the lion half of this volume. *Edgar A. Poe: A Bibliographic Study* concerns Poe's varied publications, as well as publications related to him. Robertson pursued his interest in Poe's oeuvre through this work and through his later elaboration, *Bibliography of the Writings of Edgar A. Poe* and *Commentary on the Bibliography of Edgar A. Poe*, both of 1934. But *Edgar A. Poe: A Bibliographic Study* also concerns writings about Poe: this section's latter pages concern Poe biography. Robertson credits Emile Lauvrière, in his 1904 volume *Edgar Poe: sa vie, et son oeuvre*, for his thesis about dipsomania,[37] but faults him as well: "To Lauvrière, Poe presents a type of genius in its most repulsive form."[38] Furthermore, Robertson notes, "He accepts as true all that has been alleged, and admits all into his discussion as a basis for further generalization."[39] Robertson later comments about a highly negative judgment by Lauvrière, "This is an outrage on the memory of Poe comparable only to the verbal assault of Griswold."[40] The good doctor concludes, drily, "It is said that Lauvrière's period of preparation extended over six years. Judged by the psychopathic value of this labor seven months should have more than sufficed."[41]

Robertson also offers salubrious comments about other Poe biographers: Gill ("he did the best he knew"), Ingram ("This extreme partisanship was unfortunate"), Woodberry (1909) ("Like [Frankenstein's monster], so does this Poe construction fail in recalling to us a human possessing amiable traits and loving consideration for those around him"), and Harrison ("a standard Life for those who appreciate Poe's work").[42] The first three judgments seem reasonable; the fourth judgment was reasonable in its time. Robertson's gryphon is a mythical beast well worth seeking out and studying. If it does not offer Poe himself, it does offer a genuine and affectionate effort to discover him.

This beast was followed, five years later, by the leviathan: Mary E. Phillips's two-volume, 1,683-page *Edgar Allan Poe, The Man*. Its dust jacket proclaims, "Now the Truth is Known." This is a heroic effort, with enormous detail and evident sympathy. But it requires great patience. With cloying Harrisonian orotundity, Phillips writes on page 1, "Sullen was Nature's greeting that shivering Thursday gave little Edgar Poe when his new life of immortal craft, with its 'spark of genius' aloft, was stranded on earthly shores." Then, after many pages on the Poe family in general and his parents in particular, she writes on page 70, "On such a day, Thursday, Jan. 19, 1809, the second son of David Poe, Jr., and brave Elizabeth Arnold Poe, was ushered into this world of literal misery and storms for him."[43]

In its substance, the book is uneven. For example, Phillips argues effectively that Poe was actually strong willed and defends energetically against aspersions on his mother's character, but her rendering of Edgar's early relationship with Elmira Royster is overly romanticized, and her support of Poe's supposed voyage to London in 1827 unwarranted. Her treatment of Poe's time at the Brennan Mansion is ample and thoughtful, but her account of Poe in central Pennsylvania is unreliable and her contention for Poe as "Outis"—the respondent to Poe's allegations of plagiarism against Henry Wadsworth Longfellow—is unconvincing.[44] The book is not, as its dust jacket asserts, "A Standard Final Biography"; it is, rather, a dense, flawed resource for subsequent never-final biography.

Hervey Allen's two-volume *Israfel: The Life and Times of Edgar Allan Poe*, also of 1926, offers a quicker pace than *Edgar Allan Poe, The Man.*[45] It tells Poe's story with fewer pages, shorter chapters, and the unifying motif of Poe as the angel Israfel. But it is seriously problematic. Allen, too, was a poet, and the reader must expect—and be wary of—the imagined passages. We see these early on with renderings of Poe's time with Rob Stanard and his mother Jane Stith Stanard, his early relationship with Elmira Royster, his participation in a class at the University of Virginia, his return to Richmond after the death of his foster mother Frances Allan, and his writing at night in his barracks at West Point.[46] Furthermore, Allen shared the prejudices of his time. The reader will be taken aback by language regarding Mrs. Allan ("the feminine impulsiveness of his wife"), African Americans ("the exuberance and the strangeness of the *modus vivendi* of the darky"), and Poe's slow but adoring sister Rosalie ("Rosalie was a moron," and later, revised to little effect, "Rosalie was, at worst, a rather high grade moron").[47]

Allen acknowledges the importance of Poe's drinking, subscribes to the "one-glass" theory, and attributes Poe's drinking early on to the influence of his companions at college, his uncertain place among these heirs of wealthy families, and the promise inherent in the glass of "self-confidence and oblivion."[48] However, Woodberry-like, he sometimes offers no sympathy. Poe's friend F. W. Thomas argues that Poe attempted to resist drink and also comments on Poe's writing about his drinking, "There is a great deal of heartache in the jestings of this letter." Allen adds, "This is kindly and well meant, but like much interested evidence offered to the jury must be largely struck out as irrelevant."[49] Poe's cousin William Poe writes to Edgar Poe that drink is "a great enemy to our family," but Allen diminishes the assertion, suggesting that it could be applied to "almost any 'family,' " that many people have heard of "several bibulous relatives."[50] Perhaps for Allen, a person addicted to drink was just another "other," from whom he sought distance.

Allen's allegations of Poe's opium use beginning in Baltimore in the 1831–1834 period are not convincing. Though Allen claims that "there can be no moral doubt"[51] about it, the tenuous evidence—including occasional mention of opium in Poe's early tales—is unpersuasive. Also questionable is Allen's venturing into considerations of Poe and the erotic. Imagining that the conjectured opium diminished Poe's desire and helped lead to his marrying his young cousin, Allen adds, "That there were other and more profound sexual disturbances in Poe's nature, the Sadistic trend of a considerable body of his work indicates."[52] Here Allen slides into speculation and faux insight.

Allen is weak on literary interpretation. He argues that "the root of Poe's misfortunes, agony, and shipwreck, as well as his power as a literary artist, lay in some inhibition of his sexual life" and applies this view to "The Raven," claiming that "the necessity that had been forced upon him by the nature of his marriage, to substitute a dream for the reality of love, led inevitably to despair."[53] One wonders how Allen knows all this. And we should recall that Poe wrote in "The Philosophy of Composition" that the raven was "emblematical of *Mournful and Never-ending Remembrance*," a vital theme of the 1838 *Pym*, which memorialized through its framed center not his 1836 marriage to Virginia but the 1831 death of Poe's brother Henry.[54] To replace Poe's grief with sexual frustration seems a facile distortion. Furthermore, apparently not finding Poe's 1848 *Eureka* susceptible to his psychosexual musings, Allen maintained that with this book, Poe's "exaltation of the ego" "had already passed the last admitted borders of sanity," that in this volume "the signs of hallucination and disorganization are plain," and that it is "at *best*, a highly and cleverly elaborated sophistry." He adds, apparently definitively, "A successful apology for it cannot be made."[55] Allen is neither a sensitive reader nor a penetrating one.

His *Israfel* does not possess authority. One may read it indulgently or resistingly, but not trustingly. The lightly revised one-volume 1934 edition should be read with a similar caution.

Joseph Wood Krutch's 1926 *Edgar Allan Poe: A Study in Genius* is similarly untrustworthy—perhaps more so, since there is no scholarly apparatus at all, only the author's claims and impressions. We may readily see problems with regard to matters of fact. For example, Krutch omits the critical quotation marks provided by Griswold in his obituary regarding language from Bulwer's *The Caxtons*—but omitted by Griswold in his memoir—thereby incorrectly concluding that Griswold wrote these words about Poe.[56] He states that Poe contributed to the *New York Review* in October 1827—it was October 1837—and that Poe wrote to his brother in 1835—it was to his cousin; we have no letter from Poe to his brother, who died in 1831.[57] And Krutch asserts that Poe bought the Fordham cottage, most likely with money he received as a result of his lawsuit against Thomas Dunn English.[58] Problems with matters of fact anticipate serious problems with larger claims.

Krutch is another assassin, a kind of Woodberry redux. His critical method is an offended obtuseness. The repeated language indicates his pathographic bias: "neurotic," "morbid," "abnormal," "evil," "madness," "disease." His egregious summary judgments extend that bias: "Death robbed posterity of nothing worth the having"; "It would be difficult indeed to prove that the course of American literature would have been essentially different if he had never lived."[59]

There is one claim that warrants particular attention since it is the one for which Krutch's volume is most notorious. The critic alleges that Poe "avoided all his life the sexual connection with any woman," that Poe's marriage to Virginia was "no real marriage," that to Poe "consummation was impossible," that he resisted understanding "the psychic impotence of his sexual nature," and that Virginia was "always dead in his imagination."[60] The first response is, of course, that Krutch offers no proof. How could he? The second response is that there is a tale that speaks to the "normal amorousness" that Krutch denies exists in Poe's tales[61]—the 1841 "Eleonora." Even Woodberry acknowledged in his 1885 biography that this tale offers a singular "warmth, the vital sense of human love"—though he omits this point in his 1909 work.[62] Krutch mentions the tale but avoids the telling passage.[63] T. O. Mabbott wrote that "Some autobiographical element in Poe's story is undeniable" (M 2: 636). The falsity of the alleged "complete sexlessness" of Poe's writing[64] is evident in a highly suggestive passage in "Eleonora" about ecstatic nature (M 2: 640–641).

We may pass here from travesty to majesty. Arthur Hobson Quinn's *Edgar Allan Poe: A Critical Biography* is a very valuable volume—fortunately, this 1941 biography was reprinted in paperback in 1998.[65] The book offers well-selected detail, ably sifted and interpreted. The reader gains a significant understanding of Poe, both positive and otherwise. Highlighting Poe's letter of August 29, 1835, about Virginia—"one of the most important documents in [Poe's] biography"—Quinn declares simply, "Poe loved her and she adored him."[66] But elsewhere he acknowledges, regarding Poe's courting Elmira Royster Shelton in 1849, "He probably had some idea of profiting by the marriage."[67]

Importantly, the author regularly disputes claims by Hervey Allen. For example, Quinn challenges Allen's claim for Poe's use of opium, offering a variety of evidence, including Poe's evident unfamiliarity with the impact of laudanum.[68] And he targets Allen's corollary point: "If there were any need to refute the theories which deny to Poe the normal experiences of a man, and to Virginia, those of a woman, 'Ulalume' would be an answer."[69] Citing *Eureka*, Quinn disputes Allen's allegations about a creative decline in the final years of Poe's life.[70] Also importantly, faulting Woodberry, who, he comments, was "leaning too much upon Griswold,"[71] Quinn reveals the vengeful reverend's distortions of Poe's writing, William E. Burton's, and Griswold's own.[72] Relying on parallel passages, Quinn makes the case definitively and declares rightly that these distortions are "unforgivable."[73] If anyone should have been "ashamed" of himself (as Griswold claimed Poe had written[74]), it was Griswold.

Quinn occasionally falters, as when, explaining why Poe was let go from the *Southern Literary Messenger*, he mentions Poe's drinking only in a footnote.[75] He can be too gentle. He does quote too extensively, especially from Poe's letters, but this is understandable since by 1941 John Ward Ostrom had only compiled his checklist of Poe's correspondence.[76] Quinn's criticism tends to be perceptive but not probing. And this biographer does seem to privilege the poetry over the prose: "It is as a poet that Poe must ultimately be judged."[77] However, at least Quinn writes of the ending of *Pym*, "There have been critics who object to what they are pleased to call an inconclusive ending. But when the details of the voyages have long been forgotten, the picture of the mysterious figure remains, stimulating the imagination of those readers who do not have to have everything explained to them in words of one syllable."[78]

The final five paragraphs of this biography offer a keen appreciation of Poe—they bear rereading. But with regard to one statement there, it is good to have to make a correction: "In every city in which he lived, except the city of his birth, stands a lasting memorial to him."[79] Now Boston, too, has its lasting memorial to Poe.

Most of the twelve appendices are useful and interesting. Perhaps most valuable is Quinn's record of "The Theatrical Career of Edgar Poe's Parents."[80] And the bibliography is certainly a helpful guide, with brief astute comments. For instance, Quinn asserts that

Allen's biography was "written with spirit, but largely secondary, and with a tendency toward the romantic and the acceptance of unchecked evidence." And he states that Krutch's volume was "based on a mistaken theory of Poe's physical constitution."[81]

Edgar Allan Poe: A Critical Biography is one of the essentials of Poe scholarship. It rewards study even seventy-seven years after its publication.

The rise of Freudian psychology significantly shaped literary biography in general and Poe biography in particular. This is clearly evident in Marie Bonaparte's *The Life & Works of Edgar Allan Poe: A Psycho-Analytic Interpretation*, which includes a foreword by Sigmund Freud. Published in English in 1949, the work first appeared, in French, in 1933.[82] It did not, therefore, rely on Quinn, but, rather, on Allen. Bonaparte acknowledges, "Throughout the biographical section of this work, I have followed the admirable life of Poe by Hervey Allen."[83] This is a problem, and so, too, is the psychoanalytic approach itself.

Certainly her focus on Poe's mother is altogether fair, but Bonaparte develops that focus questionably, arguing, for example, that Poe's "sado-necrophilia" led him to fear his impulses and avoid women sexually.[84] She refers to Poe's "fearful sex drives aroused by the sight of his poor Virginia's hæmorrhages and the sound of her racking cough."[85] He drank, in part, because of his "latent homosexuality."[86] The "repetition compulsion" is repeatedly invoked,[87] but detail that does not support her theory is not highlighted. Henry Poe's death is only slightly treated,[88] and, although the sickness of Virginia is considered resonant with the sickness of Poe's mother,[89] the evident health of his beloved Annie Richmond is not discussed.

Interestingly, though Bonaparte does consider Poe to have been a user of opium, she diverges from Allen's claim that his opium use diminished his sexual capacity, preferring Krutch's assertion that Poe was impotent in the first place.[90] Psyche's drooping wings, in "Ulalume," suggest this.[91]

Though Bonaparte is often mistaken, we cannot dismiss her, for she is attentive to detail, and sometimes fittingly so. For example, at the end of her biographical section, she appropriately stresses Poe's calling "Reynolds" on his deathbed, and she thereby infers a link to the ending of *Pym*.[92] She should be read warily, but she should be read. If her method was sometimes primitive and reductive, she was certainly a close reader.

Avoiding any overriding interpretive thesis, William Bittner in *Poe: A Biography* tells Poe's story plainly and directly. He sees his biography as journalistic rather than scholarly, appropriately enough—there are no archival or textual discoveries here, nor any notes. The appendix, "The Poe Controversies," is thoughtful and engaging. But the biography itself is sometimes a bit flat. Occasionally worrisome are the inferred states of mind—for instance, Poe's "great pleasure" in selecting the name "Arthur Gordon Pym" and Virginia's "envy" about women wearing hoop skirts.[93] More problematically, Bittner sometimes just gets things wrong, as when he writes that the Ariel adventure in *Pym*, except for its "characters" and "atmosphere," is "irrelevant to the plot" of the novel and that Poe wrote "Ulalume" before his wife Virginia died.[94] Overall, Bittner's biography is workmanlike but occasionally lackluster.

Edward Wagenknecht's 1963 *Edgar Allan Poe: The Man Behind the Legend* is a refreshing volume. It offers a breadth of reading and an ample budget of judgment. It does not offer new research or new theories, nor does it provide the usual chronological organization. Rather, it proceeds topically: "Life," "Living," "Learning," "Art," "Love," "God." It might be objected that such categories are limiting, yet they serve Wagenknecht well and enable him to cover much ground. And he does so fairly and sensitively.

He offers insightful consideration of Poe's "inability to compromise," the "implicit" morality of his writing, and his love for his wife, concluding in this regard, "Virginia was the moral and emotional center of her husband's life."[95] He is perceptive regarding Poe's "religious frame of reference" and discerning when he suggests that Poe "shows a sense of reverence and an appreciation of God's infinitude."[96] Focusing on Poe's sense of God in man (expressed at the end of *Eureka*), Wagenknecht denies Poe's supposed "self-aggrandizement" and sees a consonance between Poe and Emerson.[97] Discussing Poe's blending of the cosmological and the aesthetic in *Eureka*, Wagenknecht seems judicious in inferring "a passion for God on Poe's part and a longing for salvation, or, to put it another way, a Sense of the Whole and a hunger for union with the Whole, by which one cannot be other than profoundly moved."[98] Wagenknecht's final paragraph is one of the great tributes to Poe of all time. It begins, memorably, "Few Americans have aspired more nobly than Poe, and, if he fell short of his ideal, this should bring him closer to us and help us to understand him better."[99] Wagenknecht's volume seems to this reader to warrant that rarest of accolades, "wise."

The possibilities for Poe biography—and for Poe study in general—have been immensely enhanced by Dwight Thomas and David K. Jackson's 1987 *The Poe Log: A Documentary Life of Edgar Allan Poe 1809–1849*. There is no biographical narrative here—rather, there is documentary evidence for such a narrative: excerpts and details from manuscripts, letters, reviews, reminiscences, legal papers, newspapers, magazines, dissertations, books (including biographies), and articles. Archival resources from over twenty institutions, from Boston to Austin, were consulted. Appropriate commentary is sometimes provided, including, for uncertain items, multiple viewpoints. (See, for example, Poe's baptism, David Poe Jr.'s death, and the Allans' move from the Ellis home.[100]) An occasional "perhaps" or question mark is necessary and only increases the volume's trustworthiness.

Thomas, the author of the 1978 dissertation "Poe in Philadelphia, 1838–1844: A Documentary Record," selected and compiled the material from 1838 to 1849; Jackson, the author of the 1934 *Poe and "The Southern Literary Messenger,"* that for 1809 to 1837. The project was overseen by the ever-thoughtful, ever-supportive, distinguished nineteenth-century Americanist Joel Myerson. The eleven chapters feature useful headnotes and welcome illustrations. The "Introduction" and "Biographical Notes" at the beginning and the "List of Sources" at the end vitally strengthen the work. And the index makes the entire project eminently accessible. This is a field-changing volume, providing for Poe studies a new order and clarity. Perhaps additional discoveries regarding the life of Poe, made since the publication of *The Poe Log*, will eventually warrant an expanded version of this landmark work. Meanwhile, *The Poe Log* is one of the most important reference works in Poe studies—fitting company for the Mabbott/Pollin/Levines edition of Poe's works, the Ostrom/Pollin/Savoye edition of Poe's letters, the Fisher compendium of Poe-related selections, and the Deas study of Poe portraiture.[101]

And one of the most important Poe biographies is Kenneth Silverman's 1991 *Edgar A. Poe: Mournful and Never-ending Remembrance.*[102] It offers ample research, a lively narrative, and the effective theme of lifelong mourning. It moves along, providing reliable, carefully selected detail. It is good to reread after twenty-five years. The Poe that emerges from this volume is a man who never recovered from the death of his mother when he was not yet three years old, who grieved for her his entire life, and who honored her in his writing.

The writing is clear and engaging, and the assertions, when uncertain, are thoughtfully modulated. The smoothness of the writing is itself a considerable accomplishment, for that writing is based on an astonishing array of documentary evidence (including materials from 150 volumes of the Ellis & Allan papers), yet the volume knows not seams. The seventy-page "Notes" section deserves close attention, for Silverman offers there not only the enormous number of citations, gathered over years of archival work, but also judgments about the reliability of various documents and brief considerations of various topics, from David Poe's desertion of his family to *The Narrative of Arthur Gordon Pym*'s form to Poe's connection with Frances Sargent Osgood.[103] Silverman also includes there occasional evaluative comments on previous work in Poe biography, including Bonaparte ("On many points her book remains persuasive and revealing, and it was the first to perceive the pervasive effects of mourning on Poe's life and writing") and Dwight Thomas and David K. Jackson ("the superbly researched Log").[104]

Silverman offers many discerning judgments in the text of this biography, as when he writes of John Allan's failing to give Poe permission to resign from West Point ("Viewed fairly, [Poe's] situation must be seen as entirely Allan's fault"), Poe's sense of structure ("Poe also weighed words carefully and savored the niceties of prose architecture"), the English edition of *Pym* ("A pirated English edition appeared in London a few months later, unforgivably omitting the brilliant last paragraph"), and Poe's first collection of tales ("In fact, except Nathaniel Hawthorne's *Twice-Told Tales* two years earlier, *Tales of the Grotesque and Arabesque* was in 1839 the most powerfully imagined and technically adroit collection of short fiction ever published by an American writer").[105] Occasionally, Silverman's judgments are more negative, and at times some Poe scholars and aficionados may disagree. But a give-and-take goes with the biographical territory. The deft phrase that stays with me—one that concerns Poe's writing great short stories in the midst of great personal difficulties—is "some defiantly willed self-transcendence."[106] Here Silverman is getting at something I admire very much about Poe—his achievement in adversity.

Published a year after Silverman's Poe biography, Jeffrey Meyers's *Edgar Allan Poe: His Life and Legacy* is a well-paced account, drawn primarily from secondary research.[107] There are occasional flaws—for instance, Meyers presents "Eleonora" as if it were written and published in 1842, after Virginia's hemorrhage.[108] (It was written and published in 1841 [M 2: 635–638], before the tragic incident.) But Meyers does make incisive assessments, as when he suggests that "The Man of the Crowd" is "Poe's most underrated story."[109] He is weak on *Pym* and *Eureka*, however—and he unfortunately allows the final comments on the latter book to go to Woodberry and Krutch.[110] Meyers is strongest at the end, with lively overview chapters on Poe's reputation and influence.

James M. Hutchisson's 2005 biography *Poe* tells the familiar story with a leitmotif of Poe's need for unity and control. But the book has bibliographical problems, both primary and secondary. For example, it repeats Meyers's claim that "Eleonora" was published in 1842. It also maintains that "The Raven" was published in the January 29, 1845, issue of the *American Review*. But there was no such issue—the *American Review* appeared monthly. The volume also asserts that the poem appeared in the *Mirror* on February 8, 1845. In fact, the poem appeared in the *American Review* in the February 1845 issue; in the *Evening Mirror* on January 29, 1845; and in the *Weekly Mirror* on February 8, 1845 (M 1: 363). Regarding the error of attributing to Poe the Drayton-Paulding review in the *Southern Literary Messenger*, concerning slavery, a note in Hutchisson's work states that Terence Whalen's fine 1999 volume *Edgar Allan Poe and the Masses* "lays the matter to rest," without mentioning J. V. Ridgely's similarly fine 1992 article and 1998 edition that also effectively disproved the attribution. And regarding a correspondence between "The Murders in the Rue Morgue" and Richard Wright's *Native Son*, another note maintains that "This similarity has gone unremarked." Yet it had been remarked previously by several scholars.[111] Hutchisson's volume is just not sufficiently careful.

I will close by recurring to a matter that Silverman touches on, both in his biography and in an essay on biography: knowability. Discussing "The Man of the Crowd," he comments parenthetically, "He [the narrator of the story] finds that he cannot 'read' the old man, figuring the uninterpretability of Poe's own enigmatic writing, and self."[112] Perhaps, however, the story may be interpreted—we just haven't discovered fully how yet. It seems unlikely to me that the ratiocinative Poe would create a mystery to which there is no solution. His life was not wholly under his control, of course, but as this volume reveals, an interpretation of the man may be approached. Silverman considers the limits of knowledge again in his essay on biography: "When to stop? When you drop. You never find as much as there is; looking wider, deeper, longer, always brings more."[113] And toward the close of this essay, he again addresses limits: "The biographer lives with the queasy knowledge that another person's life must remain in essence unknowable and unrevealed. He creates at best a simile, a resemblance, a composite police sketch based on fleeting observation. Nevertheless, the likeness always tells us something, not everything but something, about the subject, something moreover real and dependable. The challenge is to stay true to the facts but move the reader by the spectacle of another soul's journey through time."[114] I can only agree. Biography is an asymptote to a line—a line or curve forever approaching that much-sought line, but never finally getting there. If even with scholarly resources and scholarly resourcefulness, knowledge and judgment, fellowships and fellow feeling, we never finally *really* know Poe, we can get closer. And the great effort involved is certainly worthwhile for this great figure—and for his devoted readers.

Notes

1. For Eveleth's letters, see Thomas Ollive Mabbott, ed., *The Letters from George W. Eveleth to Edgar Allan Poe* (New York: New York Public Library, 1922). For Poe's Letters to Eveleth, see James Southall Wilson, ed., *The Letters of Edgar A. Poe to George W. Eveleth* (1924), reprinted from the Alumni Bulletin, University of Virginia 3rd ser. XVII (January 1924): 34–59. Poe's letters to Eveleth are in CL. For the quotation I include, see CL 2: 648.
2. "Ludwig" [Rufus Wilmot Griswold], "Death of Edgar Allan Poe," in *Poe in His Own Time: A Biographical Chronicle of His Life, Drawn from Recollections, Interviews, and Memoirs by Family, Friends, and Associates*, ed. Benjamin Franklin Fisher (Iowa City: University of Iowa Press, 2013), 73–80; "Memoir of the Author," in *Poe in His Own Time*, 101–152.
3. Nathaniel Parker Willis, "Death of Edgar A. Poe," in *Edgar Allan Poe: The Critical Heritage*, ed. I. M. Walker (London: Routledge & Kegan Paul, 1986), 307–312; Graham, "The Late Edgar Allan Poe," in *Edgar Allan Poe: The Critical Heritage*, 376–384; Neal, "Edgar A. Poe," in *Edgar Allan Poe: The Critical Heritage*, 385–393.
4. William Fearing Gill, *The Life of Edgar Allan Poe* (New York: D. Appleton, 1877). See "Ludwig," "Death of Edgar Allan Poe" and Griswold, "Memoir of the Author."
5. Gill, *Life*, 5–6.
6. Gill, *Life*, 20, 54.
7. Gill, *Life*, 242.
8. Gill, "New Facts about Edgar A. Poe," in *Laurel Leaves: Original Poems, Stories, and Essays*, ed. William Fearing Gill (Boston: William F. Gill, 1876), 359–388 (see especially 388).
9. Willam F. Gill, *The Life of Edgar Allan Poe*, 4th ed. (New York: W. J. Widdleton, 1878), 20.
10. Gill, *Life* (1878), 54.
11. Gill, *Life* (1877), 80; Gill, *Life* (1878), 80.
12. Susan Archer Weiss, *The Home Life of Poe* (New York: Broadway Publishing Company, 1907), 227–229. For Gill's passing acknowledgment of Weiss, see *Life* (1878), vi.
13. For guides to the Ingram Collection, see John Carl Miller, *John Henry Ingram's Poe Collection at the University of Virginia* (Charlottesville: University of Virginia Press, 1960); Paul P. Hoffman, *Guide to the Microfilm Edition of John Henry Ingram's Poe Collection* (Charlottesville: University of Virginia Library, 1967); and John E. Reilly, *John Henry Ingram's Poe Collection at the University of Virginia*, 2nd ed. (Charlottesville: University of Virginia Library, 1994). For editions of letters about Poe from the Ingram Collection, see John Carl Miller, ed., *Building Poe Biography* (Baton Rouge: Louisiana State University Press, 1977) and *Poe's Helen Remembers* (Charlottesville: University Press of Virginia, 1979).
14. John Henry Ingram, *Edgar Allan Poe: His Life, Letters, and Opinions*, 2 vols. (London: John Hogg, 1880), 1:62–68 (Europe), 142 (*Messenger*), 248, 263 (French). Ingram later conceded, in his unpublished "The True Story of Edgar Allan Poe," that Poe did not travel to Europe after attending the University of Virginia. See Hoffman, *Guide*, 24.
15. Ingram, *Edgar Allan Poe*, 1:12.
16. Ingram, *Edgar Allan Poe*, 1:148.
17. Ingram, *Edgar Allan Poe*, 1:147.
18. For elaboration, see my Introduction to *The Narrative of Arthur Gordon Pym*, by Edgar Allan Poe, ed. and annotated by Richard Kopley (New York: Penguin, 1999), ix–xxix (see especially xx–xxvii).
19. Ingram, *Edgar Allan Poe*, 1:10; 2:230.

20. George E. Woodberry, *The Life of Edgar Allan Poe* (Boston: Houghton Mifflin, 1909), 1:v.
21. George E. Woodberry, *Edgar Allan Poe* (Boston: Houghton Mifflin, 1885), 220, 279.
22. Woodberry, *Edgar Allan Poe*, 95, 291.
23. Woodberry, *Edgar Allan Poe*, 59, 186, 349.
24. Woodberry, *Edgar Allan Poe*, 268.
25. Woodberry, *Edgar Allan Poe*, 347.
26. Woodberry, *Edgar Allan Poe*, 350.
27. Woodberry, *The Life of Edgar Allan Poe*, 351–356.
28. H 1: 21.
29. Floyd Stovall, "Introduction to the AMS Edition," in H 1: n.p.
30. H 1: 217, 228.
31. John C. Miller, "The True Birthdate and the Hitherto Unpublished Deathdate of Susan Archer Talley Weiss," *Poe Studies* 10, no. 1 (1977): 29.
32. Perhaps an influence on Weiss's judgment was a comment in a sensitive essay by Edmund Clarence Stedman in *Scribner's*: "My own pity for him [Poe] is of another kind; it is that which we ever must feel for one in whom the rarest possibilities were blighted by an inherent *lack of will*." See Stedman, "Edgar Allan Poe," *Scribner's Monthly* 20, no. 1 (May 1880), 124. See also Stedman, *Edgar Allan Poe* (Boston: Houghton Mifflin, 1881), 101–102; and Stedman, *Edgar Allan Poe* (Cedar Rapids, IA: privately printed, 1909), 93.
33. Weiss, *The Home Life of Poe*, 221.
34. John W. Robertson, *Edgar A Poe: A Study* (San Francisco: privately printed, 1921), 4–10 ("dipsomania"), 135 ("darker side"), 57 ("nervous diathesis"), 121 ("organic congestion").
35. Robertson, *Edgar A. Poe*, 84.
36. Robertson, *Edgar A. Poe*, 152.
37. Robertson, *Edgar A. Poe*, 379–380. For the full argument about Lauvrière, see 364–385.
38. Robertson, *Edgar A. Poe*, 373.
39. Robertson, *Edgar A. Poe*, 377.
40. Robertson, *Edgar A. Poe*, 384.
41. Robertson, *Edgar A. Poe*, 385.
42. Robertson, *Edgar A. Poe*, 394 (Gill), 396 (Ingram), 401 (Woodberry), and 404 (Harrison).
43. Mary Elizabeth Phillips, *Edgar Allan Poe, The Man*, 2 vols. (Chicago: John C. Winston, 1926), 1:1, 70.
44. Phillips, *Edgar Allan Poe*, 1:130–131 (strong willed), 1:216–221 (defense of his mother), 1:224–231 (his early relationship with Elmira Royster), 1:287 (his supposed 1827 voyage to London), 2:882–897 (Brennan Mansion), 1:601–616 (central Pennsylvania), 2:956–989 (Poe as "Outis").
45. Hervey Allen, *Israfel: The Life and Times of Edgar Allan Poe*, 2 vols. (New York: George H. Doran, 1926).
46. Allen, *Israfel*, 1:107–108, 135, 156–157, 232, 287–288.
47. Allen, *Israfel*, 1:50, 60, 103; 2:823.
48. Allen, *Israfel*, 1:170.
49. Allen, *Israfel*, 2:558–559.
50. Allen, *Israfel*, 2:565n.
51. Allen, *Israfel*, 1:371.
52. Allen, *Israfel*, 1:373.
53. Allen, *Israfel*, 2:571, 610.
54. For a discussion of Poe's memorializing Henry in *Pym*, see my aforementioned Introduction to *The Narrative of Arthur Gordon Pym*, ed. Kopley, xx–xxi.

55. Allen, *Israfel*, 2:591, 661, 742.
56. Joseph Wood Krutch, *Edgar Allan Poe: A Study in Genius* (New York: Alfred H. Knopf, 1926), 12–13, 90.
57. Krutch, *Edgar Allan Poe*, 95 (1827) and 138 (1935).
58. Krutch, *Edgar Allan Poe*, 162.
59. Krutch, *Edgar Allan Poe*, 191, 205.
60. Krutch, *Edgar Allan Poe*, 25 ("sexual connection"), 50 ("no real marriage"), 67 ("consummation was impossible"), 117 ("psychic impotence"), 120 (Virginia "dead in his imagination").
61. Krutch, *Edgar Allan Poe*, 83.
62. Woodberrry, *Edgar Allan Poe*, 168; *The Life of Edgar Allan Poe*, 1:299.
63. Krutch, *Edgar Allan Poe*, 124–125.
64. Krutch, *Edgar Allan Poe*, 82.
65. Arthur Hobson Quinn, *Edgar Allan Poe: A Critical Biography*, rev. ed. with foreword by Shawn Rosenheim (1941; rpt., Baltimore: Johns Hopkins University Press, 1998).
66. Quinn, *Edgar Allan Poe*, 219, 255.
67. Quinn, *Edgar Allan Poe*, 629.
68. Quinn, *Edgar Allan Poe*, 350, 592, 693–694.
69. Quinn, *Edgar Allan Poe*, 533.
70. Quinn, *Edgar Allan Poe*, 557.
71. Quinn, *Edgar Allan Poe*, 770; see also 282.
72. Quinn, *Edgar Allan Poe*, 278–282, 443–450; see also 647.
73. Quinn, *Edgar Allan Poe*, 450.
74. Quinn, *Edgar Allan Poe*, 449.
75. Quinn, *Edgar Allan Poe*, 259n.
76. John Ward Ostrom, comp., *Check List of Letters to and from Poe*, University of Virginia Bibliographical Series, Number Four (Charlottesville, VA: Alderman Library, 1941).
77. Quinn, *Edgar Allan Poe*, 333; see also 373.
78. Quinn, *Edgar Allan Poe*, 266.
79. Quinn, *Edgar Allan Poe*, 695.
80. Quinn, *Edgar Allan Poe*, 697–724. Reading this nearly forty years ago, I first learned that Poe's mother performed in the play *Tekeli*.
81. Quinn, *Edgar Allan Poe*, 766, 768.
82. Marie Bonaparte, *Edgar Poe: Étude Psychanalytique*, avant-propos de Sigmund Freud, 2 vols. (Paris: Les Editions Denoël et Steele, 1933); *The Life and Works of Edgar Allan Poe: A Psycho-Analytic Interpretation*, foreword by Sigmund Freud, trans. John Rodker (London: Imago Publishing, 1949).
83. Bonaparte, *Life and Works*, 1n.
84. Bonaparte, *Life and Works*, 87; see also 22, 37, 45, 103, 104, 107.
85. Bonaparte, *Life and Works*, 104.
86. Bonaparte, *Life and Works*, 86; see also 104.
87. Bonaparte, *Life and Works*, 44, 81, 130, 147, 164, 194.
88. Bonaparte, *Life and Works*, 65–66.
89. Bonaparte, *Life and Works*, 77; see also 123.
90. Bonaparte, *Life and Works*, 79.

91. Bonaparte, *Life and Works*, 151.
92. Bonaparte, *Life and Works*, 205–206. For her fuller discussion of *Pym*, see 290–352.
93. William Bittner, *Poe: A Biography* (London: Elek Books, 1962), 124 ("great pleasure"), 141 ("envy").
94. Bittner, *Poe*, 125 (Ariel adventure), 221–224 (Poe's writing "Ulalume").
95. Edward Wagenknecht, *Edgar Allan Poe: The Man Behind the Legend* (New York: Oxford University Press, 1963), 76 ("inability to compromise"), 148 ("implicit" morality), 190 ("moral and emotional center").
96. Wagenknecht, *Edgar Allan Poe*, 214 ("religious frame of reference"), 215 ("a sense of reverence").
97. Wagenkencht, *Edgar Allan Poe*, 217.
98. Wagenknecht, *Edgar Allan Poe*, 220.
99. Wagenknecht, *Edgar Allan Poe*, 221.
100. PL: 15 (Poe's baptism and David Poe Jr.'s death) and 49 (the Allans' move from the Ellis home).
101. The Mabbott/Pollin/Levines edition of Poe's works and the Ostrom/Pollin/Savoye edition of Poe's letters are the latest standard editions, employed in this volume. Fisher's *Poe in His Time* has been previously cited. The final volume is Michael J. Deas, *The Portraits and Daguerreotypes of Edgar Allan Poe* (Charlottesville: University Press of Virginia, 1989).
102. Kenneth Silverman, *Edgar A. Poe: Mournful and Never-ending Remembrance* (New York: HarperCollins, 1991). For my review of the book, see Richard Kopley, *review of Edgar A. Poe: Mournful and Never-ending Remembrance*, by Kenneth Silverman, *American Literature* 64 (June 1992): 373–374.
103. Silverman, *Edgar A. Poe*, 451 (David Poe), 473–474 (*Pym*), 495–497 (Osgood).
104. Silverman, *Edgar A. Poe*, 464 (Bonaparte), 505 (Thomas and Jackson).
105. Silverman, *Edgar A. Poe*, 67 ("Allan's fault"), 119 ("prose architecture"), 133 ("brilliant last paragraph"), 154 ("collection of short fiction").
106. Silverman, *Edgar A. Poe*, 209.
107. Jeffrey Meyers, *Edgar Allan Poe: His Life and Legacy* (New York: Charles Scribner's Sons, 1992). For my review of the book, see Richard Kopley, *review of Edgar Allan Poe: His Life and Legacy*, by Jeffrey Meyers, *Studies in the Novel* 25, no. 4 (1993): 491–493.
108. Meyers, *Edgar Allan Poe*, 128–130.
109. Meyers, *Edgar Allan Poe*, 115. Since 1992, the story's reputation has risen.
110. Meyers, *Edgar Allan Poe*, 217–218.
111. James M. Hutchisson, *Poe* (Jackson: University Press of Mississippi, 2005), 136 ("Eleonora"), 165 ("The Raven"), 270 (Paulding-Drayton review), and 271 ("The Murders in the Rue Morgue" and *Native Son*). For Ridgely's commentary on the Paulding-Drayton review, see "The Authorship of the 'Paulding-Drayton Review,'" *Poe Studies Association Newsletter* 20, no. 2 (1992): 1–3, 6; and P 5: 153–154. For discussion of the influence of "The Murders in the Rue Morgue" on *Native Son*, see Dan McCall, *The Example of Richard Wright* (New York: Harcourt, Brace & World, 1969), 70; Linda T. Prior, "A Further Word on Richard Wright's Use of Poe in *Native Son*," *Poe Studies* 5, no. 2 (1972): 52–53; and Seymour Gross, "*Native Son* and 'The Murders in the Rue Morgue': An Addendum," *Poe Studies* 8, no. 1 (1975): 23. See also Richard Kopley, *Edgar Allan Poe and "The Philadelphia*

Saturday News" (Baltimore: Enoch Pratt Free Library, the Edgar Allan Poe Society, and the Library of the University of Baltimore, 1991), 10, 25.

112. Silverman, *Edgar A. Poe*, 172–173.
113. Silverman, "Mather, Poe, Houdini," in *The Literary Biography: Problems and Solutions*, ed. Dale Salwak (Iowa City: University of Iowa Press, 1996), 107–116 (see esp. 113).
114. Silverman, "Mather, Poe, Houdini," 116.

Bibliography

Allen, Hervey, and Thomas Ollive Mabbott. *Poe's Brother: The Poems of William Henry Leonard Poe*. New York: George H. Doran, 1926.

Bondurant, Agnes M. *Poe's Richmond*. Richmond, VA: Garrett & Massie, 1942.

Dean, Gabrielle, and Richard Kopley, eds. *Edgar Allan Poe in 20 Objects from the Susan Jaffe Tane Collection*. Baltimore: Johns Hopkins Sheridan Libraries, 2016.

Deas, Michael J. *The Portraits and Daguerreotypes of Edgar Allan Poe*. Charlottesville: University Press of Virginia, 1989.

Fisher, Benjamin Franklin, ed. *Poe in His Own Time: A Biographical Chronicle of His Life Drawn from Recollections, Interviews, and Memoirs by Family, Friends, and Associates*. Iowa City: University of Iowa Press, 2013.

Miller, John Carl, ed. *Building Poe Biography*. Baton Rouge: Louisiana State University Press, 1977.

Miller, John Carl, ed. *Poe's Helen Remembers*. Charlottesville: University Press of Virginia, 1979.

Poe, Edgar Allan. *The Collected Letters of Edgar Allan Poe*. Edited by John Ward Ostrom. Revised edition by Burton R. Pollin and Jeffrey A. Savoye. 2 vols. New York: Gordian Press, 2008.

Salwak, Dale, ed. *The Literary Biography: Problems and Solutions*. Iowa City: University of Iowa Press, 1996.

Smith, Geddeth. *The Brief Career of Eliza Poe*. Rutherford, NJ: Fairleigh Dickinson University Press, 1988.

Stedman, Edmund Clarence. *Edgar Allan Poe*. Boston: Houghton Mifflin, 1881.

Tane, Susan Jaffe. *Evermore: The Persistence of Poe: The Edgar Allan Poe Collection of Susan Jaffe Tane*. New York: The Grolier Club, 2014.

Thomas, Dwight Rembert. "Poe in Philadelphia, 1838–1844: A Documentary Record." PhD diss., University of Pennsylvania, 1978.

Thomas, Dwight R., and David K. Jackson, eds. *The Poe Log: A Documentary Life of Edgar Allan Poe, 1809–1849*. Boston: G. K. Hall & Co., 1987.

Walker, I. M., ed. *Edgar Allan Poe: The Critical Heritage*. London: Routledge & Kegan Paul, 1986.

CHAPTER 5

ORIENTALISM IN POE'S EARLY POETRY

JOHN CARLOS ROWE

The fever'd diadem on my brow
  I claim'd and won usurpingly—
Hath not the same fierce heirdom given
  Rome to the Caesar—this to me?

—Edgar Allan Poe, "Tamerlane"
(M 1: 54, lines 28–31)

Poe's Middle Eastern and Central Asian themes in his early writings are typical of many Anglo-American romantic writers, and for that reason they have been noted largely in passing. Although certainly part of Western Orientalism, Poe's poetic uses of the fourteenth-century conqueror and ruler, Timur, in "Tamerlane" (1827); the Qur'an's liminal spiritual space of "al-araf" in "Al Aaraaf" (1829); and the Islamic angel in the eponymous "Israfel" (1831) appear so distant from their historical and cultural contexts as to render them strictly rhetorical, metaphors for Poe's aesthetic values. Orientalist references and themes are by no means central in Poe's works, but they do occur with some frequency throughout his career in both his poetry and prose. Yet given the abstractness of Poe's settings in his fiction and the highly metaphoric language of his poetry, the material references of his Asian and Middle Eastern allusions have drawn relatively little notice.

One reason for this neglect is that Poe often trivializes his historical and cultural contexts.[1] Settings in his fiction can be deliberately vague, as in the brief reference in "The Oval Portrait" (1842) to its setting in a "chateau" in "the Appenines, not less in fact than in the fancy of Mrs. Radcliffe" (M 2: 662). Both the use of the French term for a castle and the allusion to Ann Radcliffe's Italian settings for many of her Gothic romances stress the literariness of Poe's contexts and his deliberate trivialization of the empirical world. Like his character C. Auguste Dupin, Poe looks beyond the material evidence to find more profound spiritual truths. The narrator first meets "Ligeia" (1838) "in some large, old, decaying city near the Rhine," as if to suggest a Gothic atmosphere rather than any precise location, giving credibility to Ligeia's dedication to German idealist philosophy (M 2: 310). In the case of the Central Asian ruler, Timur, Poe writes in his first note to the poem: "Of the history of Tamerlane little is known; and with that little I have taken the full liberty of a poet" (M 1: 26n1).

The second reason Poe's Orientalism is neglected is its largely conventional quality. Drawing on the exoticism of which Byron is so fond in *The Bride of Abydos: A Turkish Tale* (1814) and *Manfred* (1817), as well as the Orientalist fantasies of Thomas Moore in *Lalla Rookh, An Oriental Romance* (1817), Poe seems to allude to such works primarily for atmospheric effects. Having quoted Bacon's claim that there can be no genuine beauty " 'without some *strangeness* in the proportion,' " in "Ligeia," Poe's narrator is quick to provide Ligeia with "eyes" for which "we have no models in the remotely antique" (M 2: 312). Insisting his beloved Ligeia's eyes "were even fuller than the fullest of the gazelle eyes of the tribe of the valley of Nourjahad," he claims "her beauty" is that "of beings either above or apart from the earth—the beauty of the fabulous Houri of the Turk" (M 2: 313). When Ligeia returns to the narrator in the resurrected corpse of his dead wife, Lady Rowena, her exotic eyes—"the full, and the black, and the wild eyes"—provide the proof that his "lost love" has returned to life (M 2: 330). In this case, Poe's romantic Orientalism seems more stylistic and rhetorical than a commentary on the culture, politics, and religions of the Middle East.

Edward Said makes no comment on Poe's writings in *Orientalism* (1978), focusing his attention largely on the European scholarly and literary traditions that invented a fantastic "Orient" stretching from East Asia through Central and South Asia to the Eastern Mediterranean and North Africa. In his concluding chapter, "Orientalism Now," Said distinguishes modern US Orientalism for its neglect of literature and emphasis on social science.[2] Said remains centrally interested in nineteenth-century "developments in academic as well as literary Orientalism on the one hand and the rise of an explicitly colonial-minded imperialism on the other."[3] But US literature plays virtually no part in his study, despite the profound influence of Middle Eastern and Asian cultures on the American transcendentalists as well as the growing political role of the United States in North Africa and China. Of course, it is possible that Said's training in comparative literature and his focus on European colonialism explains his neglect of American literary and political "Orientalism." In his subsequent *Culture and Imperialism* (1993), US imperialism still appears to follow historically and structurally the large European empires, especially of France and England.[4] There would be little reason, then, for Said to pay special attention to US writers like Emerson, Thoreau, and Margaret Fuller—American transcendentalists who refer frequently to Middle Eastern and Asian cultures and religions—much less to Poe, in whose highly fantastic works the "Orient" figures in such derivative and largely stylistic ways.

Yet as Jacob Rama Berman argues in *American Arabesque*, the dialectic between Euroamerican and Arabo-Islamic cultures in the nineteenth century helped consolidate the US nation, often by reinforcing distinctly US anxieties about foreign cultures and religions.[5] As I have argued in "Arabia Fantasia," US literature has participated in

Western Orientalism in ways well adapted to the forms of settler colonialism practiced in North America and employed in its own colonial projects around the world.[6] In these contexts, I propose a reconsideration of Poe's contributions to both European and US Orientalism, keeping in mind both their historical relations and different intentions. Poe employed such themes throughout his career and in both his poetry and prose, but in his early poetry Poe stressed Oriental subjects and styles in ways that would influence his entire literary career. Viewed in this way, these early poems tell us a good deal about Poe's aesthetic values and their relation to his political views.

I will focus on "Tamerlane," "Al Aaraaf," and "Israfel" as the three poems of Poe's early period that deal centrally with Central Asian and Middle Eastern themes and characters. All three poems share a transcendentalist aesthetic, suggesting that the successful poet best approximates the spiritual values traditionally associated with organized religion. Poe's transcendentalism differs from Emerson's, because Poe stresses the dualism of spiritual and material realms, whereas Emerson works to integrate the secular and the divine. Nevertheless, Poe's and Emerson's sources are primarily from European romantic idealism. Despite Poe's frequent objections to the New England transcendentalists, he shares many of their basic tenets. Insofar as all three poems invoke Islamic, rather than Christian, spirituality, they suggest that Poe understands his aesthetic values will be perceived as eccentric, if not iconoclastic. Yet insofar as all three poems follow established romantic conventions for poetic spirituality and aesthetic sublimity, they all rely on Western, rather than Middle Eastern or Central Asian, cultural ideals. All three poems rely on a certain organic development, in which a key "Oriental" figure or term is transformed metaphorically into Poe's ideal poet or poetic form.

Dating from 1827 to 1831, these three poems are heavily indebted to the Orientalism of the English romantics, preceding the advent of American Transcendentalism with the publication of Emerson's *Nature* in 1836.[7] "Al Aaraaf" and "Israfel" incorporate details from Thomas Moore's *Lalla Rookh* (1817) and "Evenings in Greece" (1826); Coleridge's "Kubla Khan" (1816) clearly influences "Tamerlane."[8] Poe's quotations from the Qur'an in all three poems are drawn largely from George Sale's English translation (1734) or from Sale's "Preliminary Discourse" to his translation in Thomas Moore's *Lalla Rookh*. The strong English literary influences are quite typical of American literature in the 1820s, and they complement Poe's political identification with European monarchies and their imperial projects, rather than with US democracy. Elements of the Byronic hero in Poe's "Tamerlane" also align Poe with the romantic convention of the European outsider who identifies with Eastern or "Oriental" cultures. To be sure, Byron's progressive politics, anti-Christian secularism, and Don Juanism are a bit harder to reconcile with Poe's aesthetic and political values in these poems.[9]

Edward Davidson's interpretation of "Tamerlane" as Poe's wish-fulfilling fantasy is a convincing explanation of how Poe reconciled personal reverses in 1827 with his grand ambitions as a poet.[10] Expelled from the University of Virginia and "forced to give up his fiancée, Sarah Elmira Royster," Poe compares himself with the fourteenth-century ruler, Tamerlane, by suggesting that like Tamerlane he has sacrificed "home and first passionate love for the sake of great achievement."[11] Subsequent scholars have repeated

Davidson's reading of Poe's choice of Tamerlane as primarily a Western literary convention, well established in the English tradition by Christopher Marlowe's *Tamburlaine, the Great* (1587), Charles Saunders's *Tamerlane the Great, a Tragedy* (1681), and Nicholas Rowe's *Tamerlane: A Tragedy* (1702). Poe's claim of poetic license to adapt Tamerlane to his own poetic purposes has thus been confirmed by most scholars and made his Orientalism appear merely derivative and of relatively little interest.

Yet there are some intriguing historical details in the poem that have drawn relatively little attention. The poem begins with Tamerlane's dying confession to a religious father, which Poe himself dismisses in his first note: "How I shall account for giving him 'a friar' as a death-bed confessor—I cannot exactly determine. . . . It does not pass the bounds of possibility" (M 1: 26n1). The historical Timur was well known for spreading Islam through the territories he conquered and ruled, so Poe's idea of a Catholic deathbed confessor does challenge "the bounds of possibility," unless we consider how King Henry III of Castile sent a diplomatic delegation to Timur to negotiate his alliance with Castile against the expanding Ottoman Empire. The Castilian delegation that left Cadiz on May 21, 1403, was led by Ruy González de Clavijo, a nobleman and chamberlain to Henry III, who would publish in Spanish in 1582 his account of the diplomatic journey, *Embajada a Tamorlán*. Although not translated into English until 1859, Clavijo's account of his travels and extended visit to Timur's capital of Samarkand was well known outside Castile.

Clavijo was accompanied by Timur's ambassador, Muhammed al-Kazi, and the Dominican Friar, Alfonso Páez de Santa María, as well as a number of other Castilians. Clavijo failed to obtain a diplomatic letter of alliance from Timur, primarily because Timur was on his death-bed at the time of the Castilian arrival in Samarkand. There were good reasons why Western monarchs, like Henry III of Castile and Charles VI of France, would welcome an alliance with the Timurid Empire, despite its Islamic rule in Central Asia. In July 1402, Timur had captured the Turkish Sultan Bayezid I in Ankara, checking the spread of Ottoman power in Southeastern Europe, notably Hungary. Hoping Timur would control the Ottoman Empire and fearing he might pose a new threat to Europe, the European monarchs were anxious to form an alliance with Timur while they shared a common enemy. In short, Poe's poetic situation of Tamerlane's "death-bed confession" is not as fanciful as it first appears. Although the Castilian delegation arrived too late in Samarkand to meet with the dying Timur, the idea that the Dominican Friar represented at least the idea of a religious as well as political alliance between Catholic Europe and the Islamic Timurid Empire suggests a more ambitious political allegory in the poem.

Without a definitive source for Poe's knowledge of the European negotiations with Timur to contain the Ottoman Empire, my argument for the political subtext of "Tamerlane" remains speculative.[12] Like Marco Polo's travels to Asia a century earlier, Clavijo's journey excited much Western interest, even before the publication of his *Embajada a Tamorlán* in 1582. Christopher Marlowe's *Tamburlaine, the Great*, written in 1587/1588 and published in 1590, represents Tamburlaine as the "scourge of God" primarily against Middle Eastern adversaries. The popularity of the play certainly depends in part on a popular Orientalism, in which Europe's Islamic enemies are defeated. In

Marlowe's play, Tamburlaine's defeat and humiliation of the Turkish Sultan Bajazeth (Bayezid I) is particularly graphic. Tamburlaine at first keeps the Ottoman emperor in a cage, feeding him scraps from his table, and later releases him to use him as a human footstool. In the second part of Marlowe's play, Tamburlaine defeats Babylon, murders all of its inhabitants, and burns a Qu'ran to show his contempt for Islam. Although Marlowe uses his hero to reinforce Western hatred of Islam, he does not acknowledge European plans for an alliance with the historical Timur. Thoroughly westernizing his hero, Marlowe anticipates Poe's Tamerlane, especially his death-bed conversion to Christianity.

Davidson interprets "Tamerlane" as a romantic Bildungsroman, which traces "the enlarging consciousness of a highly sensitive and poetic intelligence."[13] As Poe's alter ego, Tamerlane does indeed move from his pastoral origins in the Himalayas through military conquest to the civilization of Samarkand, capital of his Timurid Empire. In the course of this historical development, Tamerlane loses his first love, Ada—so named in the 1827 edition but unnamed in later revisions—and yearns nostalgically for this lost arcadia. Yet it is "Samarcand" itself that takes the place of Tamerlane's youthful and lost love:

> Look 'round thee now on Samarcand!—
> Is she not queen of Earth? her pride
> Above all cities? in her hand
> Their destinies?
>
> (M 1: 59, lines 165–168)

Poe's note to these lines is historically specific: "I believe it was after the battle of Angoria [Ankara] that Tamerlane made Samarcand his residence. It became for a time the seat of learning and the arts" (M 1: 37n7). Poe conflates here Timur's recent defeat in Ankara of the Turkish Sultan in 1403 with Timur's choice of Samarkand as his capital, which more likely occurred in 1370. Indeed, the establishment of the city, conquered by Alexander the Great in 369 BCE, as a "seat of learning and the arts" was the result of Timur's thirty-five years of developing the city as his capital.

Tamerlane's world weariness in the poem is not that of Shelley's "Ozymandias," whose ruins betray the glory of a forgotten ruler. As death approaches, Tamerlane acknowledges the vanity of personal ambition and how it corrupts the ideal of spirituality suggested in "human love! thou spirit given,/On Earth, of all we hope in Heaven!" (M 1: 59, lines 177–178). Tamerlane can confess to the "Father" that he now sees the "rays of truth . . . flashing thro' Eternity" that reveal both the spiritual unity of divine Love, "No mote may shun—no tiniest fly—/The light'ning of his eagle eye," and "the snare" of personal ambition "that Eblis hath" laid "in every human path" (M 1: 60–61, lines 227, 238, 229–230). The Miltonic undertone of a fortunate fall is audible in this climactic moment, when the great earthly conqueror recognizes the limitations of his achievement in the face of a spirituality that unites all by transcending earthly bounds. Poe's curious reference to Eblis, Muhammed's name for the Islamic ruler of evil spirits, rather than to Satan in Tamerlane's death-bed confession to the Dominican friar, is suggestive on several levels. It may mean that Tamerlane dies unconverted, true to his Islamic faith, even as he suffers the Friar's efforts at death-bed conversion. More likely, Poe employs Eblis to suggest that most human names are equally inadequate to designate powerful spirits, as well as to hint that visionary experience transcends specific religions and places.

Not surprisingly, then, the spirituality achieved by the visionary poet avoids the "snare" of human ambition, repudiates the fleeting emotions of earthly love, and provides the redemption the friar in the poem never offers. The customary autobiographical reading of the poem remains unaffected by this interpretation. Poe's failures in school, in his foster father's business and home, and in his love for Sarah Elmira Royster are trivial when considered in light of the poet's visionary power. If charged with a version of the egotistical sublime, then Poe might point to the poem's distinction between earthly ambition and transcendent vision.

The "Orientalism" of "Tamerlane" involves a somewhat different interpretation. Poe chooses the historical moment in the early fifteenth century when a political and perhaps religious alliance between the Judeo-Christian West and Islamic Middle East was planned. Had Clavijo succeeded in his political mission, then the centuries-long conflict between Europe and the Middle East might have ended peacefully, or at least the Timurid Empire might have helped to check expanding Ottoman power. But the death of Timur frustrates Henry III's plan. Poe offers a poetic alternative: a hybridization of Christian and Islamic themes in a poetic space that emulates the cultural and scholarly vitality of medieval Samarkand. It would be tempting to claim that Poe in 1827 was thinking of US democracy as a modern equivalent of Samarkand, but there is little hint in the poem of any such republican aspirations. The authority for such a transcultural and pan-religious vision is that of the poet, who works through the particulars of time and space for the sake of his vision.

"Israfel" (1831) so clearly follows these themes as to justify my treatment of it out of historical order from "Al Aaraaf" (1829). First published in *Poems* (1831), "Israfel" dates from Poe's attendance at West Point (June 1830 to February 1831) and draws on what Hervey Allen terms "the peculiar effects of his browsings in Oriental literature."[14] Allen's phrasing shows how American literary study has reinforced such Orientalism, as do many of the annotations of the poem. "Israfel" is, of course, an effort to equate the mortal poet with divine truth, invoking an angelic counterpart to legitimate the poet's own authority. In this respect, the poem draws on romantic conventions, in which the metapoetic conceit is tested in the rhetorical execution of the work. In these respects, Poe's choice of the Islamic Israfel, rather than his Christian counterpart, Raphael, seems merely a version of the exoticism of the Orient that attracted the Anglo-Irish romantics, especially Thomas Moore, whose *Lalla Rookh* (1817) is most often cited by commentators as the source for Poe's choice of Israfel and the epigraph he attributes to the "Koran."

Poe attributes his epigraph, "And the angel Israfel, whose heart-strings are a lute, and who has the sweetest voice of all God's creatures," to the "Koran" (M 1: 175). G. R. Thompson's footnote summarizes an established tradition of commentary on Poe's source: "According to Mabbot [*sic*], Poe's epigraph is not from the Koran directly but from George Sale's 'Preliminary Discourse' to his translation of the Koran . . . quoted by

Thomas Moore in *Lalla Rookh* (1817)."[15] In fact, neither George Sale in the "Preliminary Discourse" to his 1734 English translation of the Qur'an nor Thomas Moore in his citation of Sale in *Lalla Rookh* write what Poe claims to have quoted from the Koran in his epigraph. Thomas Moore glosses his own reference to Israfil [*sic*] in *Lalla Rookh* with yet another misquotation or misattribution to Sale: " 'The angel Israfil, who has the most melodious voice of all god's creatures.'—*Sale*."[16] Not mentioned by name in the Qur'an, Israfil is the archangel (among the four mentioned) whose Arabic name means "the burning one" and who will trumpet the resurrection from the rock in Jerusalem. Israfil is known for both this apocalyptic act as trumpeter and his ability to sing the praises of Allah in a thousand languages, as well as to impart his own breath into lesser angels, so that they can also sing Allah's praise. There is a Sunni tradition that the Qutb, a "perfect human being" and the Sufi term for a spiritual leader, has a heart that resembles Israfil's and hence his proximity to Allah.

Poe appears not to be citing directly either George Sale's "Preliminary Discourse" or Thomas Moore's *Lalla Rookh*, even if both works are sources for Poe's Oriental subject and themes. The idea so central to "Israfel," that the Islamic angel's "heart-strings are a lute," appears to be Poe's own amalgamation of several different Orientalist and Islamic notions with his own secular conception of the poet. "Heart-strings" that produce music constitute an oddly mixed metaphor, as well as a confusion of the anatomical larynx with the heart. Poe's synesthesia and mixed metaphor anticipate later uses in his work, such as his epigraph from De Béranger to "The Fall of the House of Usher" (1839): "Son Coeur est un luth suspendu;/Sitôt qu'on le touche il résonne" (M 2: 392). In both "Tamerlane" and "Al Aaraaf," Poe refers to the synthesia of the poetic ability "to see music," citing in the first case a line from Byron's *The Bride of Abydos*, " 'the mind the music breathing from her face,' " which for Poe appears to mean how two invisible processes, such as thought and music, can assume material forms, such as breath and a beautiful face (M 1: 39n11).[17] In Moore's *Lalla Rookh*, the poet Feramorz, who will later be revealed to be Princess Lalla Rookh's betrothed, the King of Bucharia, in disguise, first appears to her as "breathing music from his very eyes."[18] In "Israfel," the archangel's "fire/ Is owing to that lyre/ By which he sits and sings—/The trembling living wire/Of those unusual strings" (M 1: 176, lines 18–22). These four lines condense the senses of sight ("fire"), touch ("sits"), and song/speech ("sings") with the biology of the body ("living wire"). This early version of Poe's repeated theme of the imbrication of the spiritual and the material, perhaps best exemplified by the "living dead" in his horror stories, reminds us of how poetic language transcends mere referentiality to demonstrate the secret relations of all things.

"Israfel" anticipates then much later work in Poe's career, including *Eureka* (1848), in which Poe develops his own "big-bang" theory of the universe as the "throb of the Heart Divine" (L1: 103).[19] Poe's romantic linkage of the material and abstract, the sensuous and spiritual is indebted to his readings in Orientalist literature and scholarship. Two typical Western fantasies about Islamic cultures are their exotic sensuousness and apparent freedom from Christian distinctions between the mortal body and immortal soul. Israfel is curiously human in "the ecstasies above" about which he sings in such "burning measures": "Thy grief, thy joy, thy hate, thy love" (M 1: 176, line 37). Such lines almost make the poet's contrast in the next stanza seem contradictory:

> Yes, Heaven is thine; but this
>   Is a world of sweets and sours;
>   Our flowers are merely—flowers,
> And the shadow of your perfect bliss
>   Is the sunshine of ours.
>
> (M 1: 176, lines 40–44)

The difference between Israfel's "burning measures" and Poe's "mortal melody" is apparently one of degree, not kind, or perhaps simply location, because in the last stanza the poet challenges the archangel:

> If I could dwell
> Where Israfel
>   Hath dwelt, and he where I,
> He might not sing so wildly well
>   A mortal melody,
> While a bolder note than this might swell
>   From my lyre within the sky.
>
> (M 1: 176–177, lines 45–51)

Although the poet does not quite claim greater power than the Islamic archangel, he poses a challenge that recalls the African American folkloric competitions between mortals and the Devil, such as we find in the legends of High John de Conquer and other folkloric heroes with origins in African cultures.[20] If Poe is drawing on African American folklore in "Israfel," it is deeply disguised, given Poe's Southern racism, but it may well be an undercurrent of his Orientalism. Poe more explicitly links the US South and the Orient in "A Tale of the Ragged Mountains" (1844), in which Charlottesville, Virginia, and Benares, India, are bizarrely linked.[21]

Whatever his motivations in "Tamerlane" and "Israfel," Poe claims a spiritual authority for the poet that is equivalent to, perhaps even greater than, that of organized religion. Such competition may also explain his choice of Islamic characters and themes to divert attention from what would be considered the heresy of a direct challenge to Christianity. It is also possible that Poe is drawing on the syncretic mythography of the Enlightenment to claim that all religion shares common roots that the poet recognizes and universalizes in his transcendentalism. Another credible interpretation is that Poe is playing upon increasing anti-Islamic sentiments in early nineteenth-century Europe, fueled by the expansion of the Ottoman Empire and in part by fears in the aftermath of the French Revolution of new European despotism. Shelley's *The Revolt of Islam* (1818) stages an imaginary revolution against the Ottoman tyrant, Othman, as an explicit response to both contemporary concerns.[22] In all of these respects, Poe's Orientalism is typical of English romanticism's use of Middle Eastern and Asian characters and settings to allegorize Western problems.

"Al Aaraaf" does not change this tendency, but it does present a more complex instance of Poe's Orientalism. The complexity of the poem's narrative action is compounded by its combination of Islamic, Greco-Roman, and European figures and allusions. On the one hand, the poem seems to reinforce the idea of some syncretic mythography facilitated by the poet, who recognizes the secret relations among different cultural myths and legends. This rhetorical confusion or synthesis is best represented by the title of the poem itself. "Al araf" is "the wall of partition which they [Muslims] imagine to be between that place [paradise] and hell. . . . They call it al Orf, and more frequently in the plural, al Arâf, a word derived from the verb arafa, which signifies to distinguish between things, or to part them."[23] On the other hand, Poe's own note refers to the "star . . . discovered by Tycho Brahe," the sixteenth-century Danish astronomer, in 1572, which was visible for sixteen months, and then disappeared (M 1: 99n). What Brahe had witnessed is now known as the remnant of a supernova, or explosion of a star, whose inner mass radiates with particular brilliance as the star disintegrates. Neither Poe nor Brahe knew this about the "new" star the latter witnessed, but the idea that Poe should have chosen such an astronomical event for the setting of this poem is a remarkable anticipation of his poetic cosmology in *Eureka*. Rather than claim Poe had some exceptional powers of prophesying the future of astronomy, I contend instead that the phenomenon of an extremely brilliant star eventually fading away gave Poe an early idea of his later "big-bang theory" of the universe's explosion and contraction—the "throb of the Heart Divine" he would detail in *Eureka* (L1: 103).

Poe's star is a metaphor for the poetic and artistic imagination. Like the earthly "sweets and sours" the poet expresses in "Israfel," the space of "al aaraaf" encompasses both good and evil, life and death, truth and illusion. For the inhabitants of this intermediate region:

> For what (to them) availeth it to know
> That Truth is Falsehood—or that Bliss is Woe?
> Sweet was their death—with them to die was rife
> With the last ecstasy of satiate life—
> Beyond that death no immortality—
> But sleep that pondereth and is not "to be"—
> And there—oh! may my weary spirit dwell—
> Apart from Heaven's Eternity—and yet how far
> from Hell!
>
> [M 1: 111, lines 166–173]

Poe creates a space in between heaven and hell that is a curious mixture of mortal life and heavenly ecstasy. In his long note to these lines in the version of "Al Aaraaf" published in *Poems Written in Youth* (1845), Poe attributes to "the Arabians" the idea that in this space "between Heaven and Hell . . . men suffer no punishment, but yet do not attain that tranquil and even happiness which they suppose to be characteristic of heavenly enjoyment," adding as apparent evidence a quote in Spanish from Father Luís de León's "Vida Retirada" ("Reclusive Life"), a poem by the sixteenth-century Spanish Catholic priest and academic that celebrates the reclusive life of the monk and scholar. The religious transcendence of worldly cares is transformed by Poe into a state of exultation "which, in some minds, resembles the delirium of opium" (M 1: 111–112n26).

Poe's weird footnote recalls the odd *donnée* of "Tamerlane" as the Islamic ruler's confession to a Catholic friar, which I interpreted earlier as Poe's appropriation of the historical details of the Spanish diplomatic and religious mission to Timur for his own poetic purposes. In "Al Aaraaf," Poe scatters Greco-Roman, Islamic, Catholic, Protestant, and assorted literary references in ways that have made the poem, for previous scholars, "one of Poe's most highly allusive, complex, and opaque works."[24] I think that many of the difficulties in the poem can be resolved, however, when it is read in terms of the conventions of romantic organicism. There is a broad spiritual development in the poem that follows historical references to Arabo-Islamic texts, like the Qur'an, and Greco-Roman mythology with allusions to the European Renaissance and Protestant Reformation. Toward the end of the poem, Michelangelo emerges as a "goodly spirit" in the imaginative world of "al aaraaf," and it is his poetry, along with his achievements in the other arts, that Poe emphasizes.

Michelangelo's sonnets were well known and highly regarded in the nineteenth century. Although many of the sonnets are addressed to men, such as Michelangelo's models Cecchio dei Bracci, Febo di Poggio, and Gheerardo Perini, Michelangelo's grandnephew, Michelangelo Buonarroti the Younger, edited the sonnets in 1623, changing the genders from masculine to feminine. Not until John Addington Symonds translated Michelangelo's sonnets and restored the original pronominal references in 1893 were Michelangelo's bisexual love interests publicly known. In Poe's generation, it was Michelangelo's passion for the Roman poet and noblewoman Vittoria Colonna (1492–1547) that was most often celebrated. In the concluding stanzas of "Al Aaraaf," Michelangelo sits on his star and "scowls on starry worlds that down beneath it lie," sitting "with his love—his dark eye bent/With eagle gaze along the firmament:/Now turn'd it upon her—but ever then/It trembled to the orb of EARTH again" (M 1: 112, lines 193–197). Addressing his phantom love, presumably Vittoria Colonna, as "Ianthe," the "hyacinth," Michelangelo links her with rebirth in the conventional association of this Eastern Mediterranean flower with the arrival of spring.

What is resurrected, however, is not so much their personal love or lives as the earth itself that Michelangelo looks upon from his starry height:

"Ianthe, dearest, see! How dim that ray!
How lovely 'tis to look so far away!
She seem'd not thus upon that autumn eve
I left her gorgeous halls—nor mourn'd to leave.
That eve—that eve—I should remember well—
The sun-ray dropp'd, in Lemnos, with a spell

> On th'Arabesque carving of a gilded hall
> Wherein I sate, and on the draperied wall—
> And on my eye-lids—O the heavy light!"
>
> (M 1: 113, lines 198–206)

Poe's Michelangelo is uttering poetry, in which the "gorgeous halls" of earth are viewed in the golden light of the sunset and his own death, both staged on the isle of Limnos, off the coast of Turkey, where "Vulcan is said to have fallen when hurled from Olympus by Jove."[25]

Weaving together allusions to Satan's fall from heaven in Milton's *Paradise Lost* and Icarus's fall in Greek mythology, Poe suggests that Michelangelo has fallen from his ascent to heaven into the intermediate region of al araf, but that it is indeed a fortunate fall. When Michelangelo considers the diverse beauty of the earth, he " 'half wish'd to be again of men,' " only to be reproached by Ianthe:

> "My Angelo! And why of them to be?
> A brighter dwelling-place is here for thee—
> And greener fields than in yon world above,
> And woman's loveliness—and passionate love."
>
> (M 1:113–114, lines 226–230)

The region of the Islamic *al orf* no longer carries with it any element of Islamic faith or Arabic culture, but instead becomes a metaphor for the poetic activity itself. The astral sign witnessed by Tycho Brahe is transformed into the inner light of the imagination that illuminates the beauty of earth:

> "When first Al Aaraaf knew her course to be
> Headlong thitherward o'er the starry sea—
> But when its glory swell'd upon the sky,
> As glowing Beauty's bust beneath man's eye,
> We paus'd before the heritage of men,
> And thy star trembled—as doth Beauty then!"
>
> (M 1: 115, lines 255–260)

These two poets "in discourse" create what earlier Poe terms an "Arabesque," weaving together different cultures and places into a synthesis they term "beauty."

Whereas Moore's Orientalism in *Lalla Rookh* depends largely on the exoticism of an Orient imagined by Westerners, including the licentiousness of the harem, the patriarchy of the Sultan, and the secrets of the veiled woman, Poe's Orientalism is thoroughly integrated into romantic aesthetics. As Berman puts it: "In Poe's arabesque, . . . the image of the Arab becomes a source of speculation on origins of one kind or another and ultimately a literary instrument in creating the imagined community of America. In the course of this speculation, the image of the Arab is disassociated from the actual Arab peoples and culture and transformed into a trope of aesthetic contemplation."[26] Berman focuses on Poe's prose but his conclusions apply exactly to Poe's early poetry, suggesting that Orientalism was not simply conventional and occasional but structural and essential to Poe's career and aesthetic theory.

"Al Aaraaf" culminates in the poetic conversation of Michelangelo and "Ianthe," both of whom seem to have grown out of Nesace, the governing spirit in Part I. Whether "Nesace" is Poe's neologism for an imagined spirit, based on the Greek *nesos*, "lady of the island," or a veiled allusion to the Odyssean "Nausicaa," another mythic figuration, the classical Greek origins of the "beauty" Poe identifies with the star, al aaraaf, seem to produce two central characters of the European Renaissance, Michelangelo and Vittoria Colonna, in Part II.[27] The name might also be based on the Greek *nesake*, "small island or islet," picking up Poe's play upon star and island throughout the poem, such as in Poe's final lines in Part I: "Up rose the maiden from her shrine of flowers,/And bent o'er sheeny mountain and dim plain/Her way—but left not yet her Therasæan reign" (M 1: 105, lines 156–158). Poe's gloss on "Therasæan" is "Therasea, the island mentioned by Seneca" (M 1: 105n15).[28]

Poe's organicism in the poem follows a typical romantic evolutionary cycle, such as we find in Hegel's "stages" of history: the symbolic, classical, and romantic.[29] Scholars know that Poe referred on several occasions to Hegel, although we do not know how familiar Poe was with Hegel's actual texts.[30] Whether Poe is drawing directly on Hegel or on other romantic sources, his purpose seems clear enough. European renaissance culture, such as Michelangelo and Colonna represent, draws on Greek sources in which the "divine" was represented in human form, transcending the pantheism Hegel finds in Hinduism and divine abstraction in ancient Egypt. The "Orient" finds the divine in the profusion of nature, much as Nesace: "All hurriedly she knelt upon a bed/Of flowers: of lilies such as rear'd the head/On the fair Capo Deucato, and sprang/So eagerly around about to hang/Upon the flying footsteps of—deep pride—/Of her who lov'd a mortal—and so died" (M 1: 101, lines 42–47).

Poe's reference is to Sappho, who in Ovid commits suicide from the Leucadian Rock ("Cape Deucato" in the poem) in response to the unrequited love of Phaon. Sappho as a great classical poet is immortal for Poe, but her despair of the mortal Phaon's love contradicts her poetic spirituality. Stanzas four and five of Part I are essentially a botanical study of different plants with spiritual or medicinal qualities, which "wing" their "way to Heaven" (M 1: 102, line 73). But such natural referents are not yet fully spiritual, any more than Sappho's love for Phaon represents eternal beauty. Nesace is too much a part of nature in Poe's poem to be genuinely divine; Sappho, the "tenth Muse" in Plato, is too captivated by human passion to be truly spiritual. Poe is working out a genealogy of what Hegel calls the spirituality of human self-consciousness, the unfurling of perfectible human reason.

Part II continues these Greco-Roman references as Nesace appears in her palace on Al Aaraaf, "A dome, by linked light from Heaven let down," and sings to Ligeia, "My beautiful one!/Whose harshest idea/Will to melody run" (M 1: 106, line 20; 109, lines 101–103). Like the beautiful woman of great learning who returns from the dead to inhabit the body of her husband's new wife, Rowena, in Poe's famous story, this early version of Ligeia appears to be the personification of music and intellect or the union of the two in some transcendental truth. Scattered with references to ruined cities of antiquity, such as "Tadmor and Persepolis," and regions, such as "Eyraco" (Iraq), Chaldea, and Babylon, the opening stanzas of Part II establish a cultural heritage that includes Middle Eastern and Greco-Roman influences. Nesace's invocation of Ligeia is actually a command that Ligeia "awaken/An angel so soon/Whose sleep hath been taken/Beneath the cold moon" (M 1: 111, lines 149–151).

That angel is, of course, Michelangelo, whose recent death has reunited him with his "Ianthe" on the star of al Aaraaf. Poe's use of the Greek "Ianthe" for the hyacinth suggests not only the resurrection of his lover (or his lover *as* a symbol of resurrection), but also the names "Zanthe" used earlier in Part II for Nesace's servant and in Part I for the flower, Zante, and "thy most lovely purple perfume" (M 1: 108, line 57; 102, line 76). Although Michelangelo claims in one stanza to have died on the island of Lemnos, in the very next stanza he claims that "The last spot of Earth's orb I trod upon/Was a proud temple call'd the Parthenon—/More beauty clung around her column'd wall/Than ev'n thy glowing bosom beats withal" (M 1: 113, lines 214–217). Referring here to the famous friezes on the Parthenon, Poe links Michelangelo with his genius as architect and visual artist, as well as the poetry of his speech, and the classical heritage that has suddenly become historical. We have passed through those stages Hegel classified as symbolic and classical to enter the beginnings of a romantic era.

I am not suggesting a direct Hegelian influence in "Al Aaraaf" but a more general romantic spirit of cultural evolution within the poem's organic development. Poe employs the convention of romantic self-consciousness here in the concluding dialogue between Michelangelo and his lover, Ianthe (Colonna), as a poetic origin for modern Western history. "The poets are thus liberating gods," Emerson would conclude in "The Poet" (1844), fifteen years after the first publication of "Al Aaraaf."[31] This divine power is the poet's capacity to access or invent spirituality, depending on the particular version of romanticism with which we are concerned. Although Hegel equivocates regarding the a priori or a posteriori existence of "*Geist*" or "Spirit" in reference to human reason, the broad historical process he describes is the progressive development of such spirit as a function of rationality.

Poe's "Sonnet—To Science," first published as the introduction to *Al Aaraaf, Tamerlane, and Minor Poems* (1829), seems to repudiate this conclusion, because the sonnet so clearly warns us that science has preyed "upon the poet's heart," as a "Vulture, whose wings are dull realities," dragging "Diana from her car" and driving "the Hamadryad from the wood" (M 1: 91, lines 4, 9, 10). Most romantic poets and idealist philosophers argued that empirical science could not compete with their transcendental knowledge. Poe appeals to such idealism as he historicizes in "Al Aaraaf" what he terms in this sonnet his "summer dream beneath the tamarind tree" (M 1: 91, line 14). Poe's fantastic creation of a world on the evanescent "star" discovered by Tycho Brahe parallels the earth, serving as a kind of alternative world whose equivalent is the idealism of poetry. From his earliest poetry, then, Poe developed a metapoetic that would seem tautological, were it not for his complex web of mythic and literary references. Even such references work finally to teach us that poetry is about itself, a self-referential world that exists only in the minds of the poet and the reader.

Jerome McGann has argued provocatively that there is a "politics" to Poe's "poetry without politics," which uses "Poe's 'flight from the social world'" as "a cunning strategy for tracking that world's flight from itself."[32] What McGann means is that Poe's highly self-conscious poems, relying on complex intertextual references, call critical attention to his readers' desires for illusions. The crisis of Poe's antebellum America, then, would be shadowed in the escape into idealism that Poe's poetry so often offers us. Although McGann does not make this point, we might conclude in his spirit that Poe's brief historical references—to Timur, Michelangelo, and Vittoria Colonna, for example—are reminders of how our will to self-deception can never escape the material conditions of existence. Hence, Poe's morbid themes mean more than the sheer exploitation of our fears of mortality; Poe's Gothic warns us that all fantasies have their roots in our inabilities to overcome material limits.

McGann has nothing specific to say about Poe's Orientalism, which is itself an elaborately contrived illusion to hide the material differences of other people, but it does not appear that Poe calls attention to his Arabesques for the sake of demystifying Orientalism. On the contrary, Poe's Oriental themes seem deeply invested in an historical narrative of progress and enlightenment that we associate today with the myth of Western Civilization. Although Poe often expresses skepticism about progress and human perfectibility, he usually does so in relation to his advocacy of a spiritual knowledge that transcends reason and secular experience.[33] His familiar philosophical dualism appears to trivialize the material world. Yet romantic idealists like Kant and Hegel emphasize the power of the mind to transform inert matter, often in keeping with Poe's own theory of the imagination. Even as he attempts to distance himself from Western progress and superiority, Poe aligns himself with it in his early poetry, following the paths of what Said criticizes in *Orientalism* as a profound Eurocentrism necessary for its colonial expansion. Later in his career, Poe would link US westward expansion with European colonialism, often in positive ways, but in the early poetry he remains committed to the European cultural heritage with little reference to his homeland.[34] Aestheticizing the Arabesque design and folding Islamic ideas into Greco-Roman myths, Poe displaces the Arabo-Islamic world with his own fantasies, contributing to a domestication of international issues that haunts us to this day.

Notes

1. Larzer Ziff, *Literary Democracy: The Declaration of Cultural Independence in America* (New York: Viking Press, 1981), 70.
2. Edward W. Said, *Orientalism* (New York: Random House, 1978), 291.
3. Said, *Orientalism*, 18.
4. Edward W. Said, *Culture and Imperialism* (New York: Alfred A. Knopf, 1993), 282–336.

5. Jacob Rama Berman, *American Arabesque: Arabs, Islam, and the 19th-Century Imaginary* (New York: New York University Press, 2012), 5.
6. John Carlos Rowe, "Arabia Fantasia: U.S. Literary Culture and the Middle East," *Alif* 32 (2012): 55–77.
7. Such dating of literary movements and schools is notoriously unreliable, but American Transcendentalism is not a coherent or identifiable movement prior to the publication of Emerson's *Nature* (1836) and the formation in that year of the group initially known as "Hedge's Club." Initially named for Frederick Henry Hedge, the club included Hedge, Emerson, and George Ripley. Over the years, its informal membership expanded to a dozen or more members and came to be known as the "Transcendental Club." See Gay Wilson Allen, *Waldo Emerson: A Biography* (New York: Viking Press, 1981), 284.
8. See G. R. Thompson, ed., *The Selected Writings of Edgar Allan Poe* (New York: W. W. Norton and Co., 2004) for his introductions to "Tamerlane," 8, and "Al Aaraaf," 22–24; and his notes to "Tamerlane," 9–14, "Al Aaraaf," 24–41, and "Israfel," 48.
9. Byron famously declaimed against the Church of England in one of his speeches in the House of Lords, commenting on how the Church discriminated against people of different faiths. He himself was strongly drawn to Islam, although he was probably an atheist at heart, like his close friend, Shelley. See Alexander Robert Charles Dallas, *Recollections of the Life of Lord Byron, from the Year 1808 to the End of 1814: Taken from Authentic Documents* (London: Charles Knight, 1824), 679.
10. Edward H. Davidson, *Poe: A Critical Study* (Cambridge, MA: Harvard University Press, 1957), 4.
11. Davidson, *Poe*, 4.
12. Clavijo's *Embajada a Tamorlán* was translated into English for the first time by Sir Clements R. Markham, the famous British explorer and geographer, as *The Narrative of the Embassy of ruy Gonzalez de Clavijo to the Court of Timour, at Samarcand, A. D. 1403–6* (London: Hakluyt Society, 1859), which is the basis for the twentieth-century edition by J. E. Flecker, ed., *Embassy to Tamerlane: 1403–1406* (1928; repr., London: RoutledgeCurzon, 2005).
13. Davidson, *Poe*, 5.
14. Hervey Allen, *Israfel: The Life and Times of Edgar Allan Poe* (New York: Farrar and Rinehart, Inc., 1934), 243.
15. Thompson, ed., *Selected Writings*, 48n2.
16. Thomas Moore, *Lalla Rookh, An Oriental Romance* (New York: Thomas Crowell, 1891), 277n293.
17. Poe's quotation from Byron appears in "The Bride of Abydos," Act I, scene vi, line 22. Poe leaves out the punctuation of the actual line from Byron, "The Bride of Abydos," in *The Poems of Byron* (London: Oxford University Press, 1945), 266: "Such was Zuleika, such around her shone/The nameless charms unmark'd by her alone—/the light of love, the purity of grace,/The mind, the Music breathing from her face,/The heart whose softness harmonized the whole,/And oh! that eye was in itself a Soul!" Byron's comma couples "the mind" with "the Music," but it makes the simile clear, whereas Poe deletes the comma to stress the literality of spiritual thought as music.
18. Moore, *Lalla Rookh*, 25.
19. See John Carlos Rowe, "Space, the Final Frontier: Poe's *Eureka* as Imperial Fantasy," in "A Special Issue in Honor of G. R. Thompson," ed. Steven Frye and Eric Link, special issue, *Poe Studies/Dark Romanticism* 39–40 (2006–2007): 19–27.

20. Zora Neale Hurston's study of such folklore in *Mules and Men* (1935) treats several of these heroes. See John Carlos Rowe, *Literary Culture and U.S. Imperialism: From the Revolution to World War II* (Oxford: Oxford University Press, 2000), 265–270.
21. Rowe, *Literary Culture and U.S. Imperialism*, 67–70.
22. Percy Bysshe Shelley, preface to *The Revolt of Islam: A Poem in Twelve Cantos*, in *The Complete Poetical Works of Percy Bysshe Shelley*, ed. Thomas Hutchinson (Oxford: Oxford University Press, 1970), 32–33.
23. George Sale, "Preliminary Discourse," in *Koran, Commonly Called The Alcoran of Mohammed, Translated into English immediately from the Original Arabic with Explanatory Notes, Taken from the Most Approved Commentators, to which is prefixed a Preliminary Discourse*, 2 vols. (Bath, UK: Printed by S. Hazard for J. Johnson, Vernor and Hood, 1795), 1:125.
24. Thompson, ed., *Selected Writings*, 22.
25. Thompson, ed., *Selected Writings*, 39n3.
26. Berman, *American Arabesque*, 137.
27. Thompson, ed., *Selected Writings*, 25n6.
28. William B. Cairns, "Some Notes on Poe's 'Al Aaraaf,'" *Modern Philology* 10, no. 1 (1915–1916): 36.
29. G. W. F. Hegel, *Aesthetics: Lectures on Fine Art*, trans. T. M. Knox, 2 vols. (London: Oxford University Press, 1975), 1:76–80.
30. Joan Dayan, *Fables of Mind: An Inquiry into Poet's Fiction* (New York: Oxford University Press, 1987), 99, 226, 239n52.
31. Emerson, "The Poet," in *Selected Works of Ralph Waldo Emerson and Margaret Fuller*, ed. John Carlos Rowe (Boston: Houghton Mifflin Co., 2003), 201.
32. Jerome McGann, *The Poet Edgar Allan Poe: Alien Angel* (Cambridge, MA: Harvard University Press, 2014), 169.
33. In a letter to James Russell Lowell on July 2, 1844, and another to Thomas H. Chivers on July 10, 1844, Poe rejects the idea of human perfectibility in very similar terms, insisting: "I have no faith in human perfectibility" (CL 1: 449). Nevertheless, he claims to "live continually in a reverie of the future" (CL 1: 449), when it appears we will metamorphose into a radically different "material" condition: "[E]ach individual man is the rudiment of a future material (*not* spiritual) being" (CL 1: 453). Poe's insistence that there are two different kinds of materiality—one "particled" and the other "unparticled" (CL 1: 453)—seems an effort to resolve his customary dualism. Nevertheless, these two different states of existence are unrecognizable to each other: "At death, the worm is a butterfly—still material, but of a matter unrecognized by our own organs" (CL 1: 449). No matter how Poe spins his teleology, however, the intention of individuated or "atomic" matter to return to its spiritual or "unparticled material" state suggests an improvement. Poe consistently identifies this future state with the mind of God and divinity in general. Hence, Poe's criticism of material, secular progress (or "perfectibility") is merely a way to affirm his own imaginative and poetic understanding of a cosmic unity that is our future destination. I am grateful to J. Gerald Kennedy for directing me to these letters and Poe's apparent criticism of the myth of progress.
34. Rowe, *Literary Culture and U.S. Imperialism*, 53–76.

BIBLIOGRAPHY

Berman, Jacob Rama. *American Arabesque: Arabs, Islam, and the 19th-Century Imaginary.* New York: New York University Press, 2012.

Davidson, Edward H. *Poe: A Critical Study*. Cambridge, MA: Harvard University Press, 1957.

Dayan, Joan. *Fables of Mind: An Inquiry into Poe's Fiction*. New York: Oxford University Press, 1987.

McGann, Jerome. *The Poet Edgar Allan Poe: Alien Angel*. Cambridge, MA: Harvard University Press, 2014.

Moore, Thomas. *Lalla Rookh, An Oriental Romance*. New York: Thomas Crowell, 1891.

Rowe, John Carlos. "Arabia Fantasia: U.S. Literary Culture and the Middle East." *Alif* 32 (2012): 55–77.

Rowe, John Carlos. *Literary Culture and U.S. Imperialism: From the Revolution to World War II.* New York: Oxford University Press, 2000.

Rowe, John Carlos. "Space, the Final Frontier: Poe's *Eureka* as Imperial Fantasy." In "A Special Issue in Honor of G. R. Thompson," edited by Steven Frye and Eric Link. Special issue, *Poe Studies/Dark Romanticism* 39–40 (2006–2007): 19–27.

Said, Edward W. *Culture and Imperialism*. New York: Alfred A. Knopf, 1993.

Said, Edward W. *Orientalism*. New York: Random House, 1978.

CHAPTER 6

ECHOES OF "THE RAVEN"

Unoriginality in Poe's Verse

MICHAEL C. COHEN

Beyond its achievements in recovering forgotten authors, texts, and genres, the recent critical attention to nineteenth-century American poetry has advanced the study of poetics with a major theoretical contribution: a new understanding of the value of unoriginality. In work that has focused mostly on women poets, scholars have reassessed the "generic" features of nineteenth-century writing, including cliché, convention, abstraction, and imitation, and demonstrated how these devalued aesthetic qualities in fact played vital roles in the public lives and social functions of nineteenth-century poems.[1] As Eliza Richards has written in regard to Lydia Sigourney, for example, the "generic sentimentality" for which "critics have repeatedly condemned Sigourney . . . is arguably a great accomplishment," because the "homogenization of taste" her work effected—and of which it was an effect—"offered a ritual cure for the loneliness of individual suffering in an increasingly anonymous, urban world."[2] Far from being signs of aesthetic failure, conventionality and derivativeness are now seen as signal achievements of nineteenth-century poetic language, because they generated and maintained an ever-expanding audience in the first era of mass communication.[3]

Considered as "enabling constraints [that] enable by constraining," conventions and protocols are the features of networked systems that smooth the pathways of communication by being readily familiar and unoriginal to any single participant in the network.[4] William Warner notes that the earliest meaning of *protocol* referred to the first page of a volume, which contained an account of its contents, thus making protocols "the preliminary agreements that frame the document's circulation"; as the term's usage expanded into diplomacy, law, and experimental science, protocols came to "assure the formal regularity, reliability, and duplicability" of communications.[5] Nineteenth-century poems have typically been derided for being all too formally regular, reliable, and duplicable, but a glance toward media studies and network theory (rather than the more commonly invoked "print culture") might help us rethink the valence of that judgment. The expansion and intensification of systems of communication in the nineteenth century had the perverse effect of proliferating expressions of sentimental sincerity by codifying mass sameness. As David M. Henkin demonstrates, for instance, no nineteenth-century genre was more generic than the "personal" letter, which was able to render interior sentiment so effectively because letter writers, newly introduced to a vastly expanded postal system, were inculcated in the protocols of sincerity through a systematic process of instruction using manuals, sentimental novels, and other guides to the inscription of convention.[6] Genericness and conventionality thus might at least be considered modes of communicative power in addition to being marks of literary weakness.

As a relay point in nineteenth-century literature, linked to multiple networks of poets, poetesses, periodicals, and polemics, Edgar Allan Poe has featured uneasily in this reconsideration of unoriginality.[7] After all, few authors of the antebellum decades were more vehement proponents of originality than he, even as he shamelessly borrowed from fellow writers, especially women. But if the unoriginality of most nineteenth-century poets has consigned them to oblivion, whether deservingly or not, Poe's position in the canon of American literature is unique: unlike any of his contemporaries, he has maintained a popular readership since the 1830s, even while his poems frequently embarrass critical judgment, since the apparent thinness of their content, the derivativeness of their genres, and the weird excesses of their language render them impermeable to many modes of interpretation. "The Raven" (to be discussed later) generates a never-ending system of citation, parody, and pastiche; "The Philosophy of Composition" is the sole piece of nineteenth-century literary criticism still commonly read today (only Mark Twain's "Fenimore Cooper's Literary Offenses" comes close to being as familiar); yet Poe is a "special case," Jerome McGann notes, because his poetry, "a virtual echo chamber of allusions, quotations, and near quotations" proves "at once unremittingly vulgar and theoretically advanced, even pretentious."[8] Poe's combative exposures of other writers' "plagiarisms" call attention to his own sticky literary style, which imitated the mimic unoriginality of the popular poetic culture for which he was both the greatest champion and most spectacular failure.

Can a poet derive his style by playing upon the imitative unoriginality of his work? This is the gambit of Poe's essays on versification and, most especially, his reviews of contemporary literature, which pragmatically assert the materiality of language by capturing a poem as the sum of its sonorous effects. Creativity, originality, and imaginativeness are less important to assuring the success of a poem in Poe's ears than readers typically realize; much more crucial are proper versifying, appropriately ideal topics, good vocabularies, honest rhymes, regular syntax, and the deployment of poetic effects achieved through the cumulative assemblage of sounds and rhythms. Assessing whether or not a poem "works" is more important in Poe's reviews than judging its imaginativeness or originality, and we can chart how his thinking on this topic evolved. Poe was long fascinated by the distinction Samuel Taylor Coleridge had drawn, in the *Biographia Literaria*, between "fancy" and "imagination." Fancy, according to Coleridge, was a secondary power capable only of combining elements already at hand. Imagination, in contrast, was a primary, creative power, the true faculty of the poet. In 1836 Poe dismissed Joseph Rodman Drake's *The Culprit Fay* for exercising the capacity of fancy too much, "without exercising in the least degree the Poetic Sentiment, which is Ideality, Imagination, or the creative ability" (ER: 520). Anyone properly attuned, Poe argued, could write Drake's poem in a similarly fanciful manner. By 1840, however, he had shifted the terms of his reasoning. Writing about Thomas Moore, Poe cites Coleridge only to dismiss his distinction as "one without a difference; without even a difference of *degree*. The fancy as nearly creates as the imagination, and neither creates in any respect. All novel conceptions are merely unusual combinations. The mind of man can *imagine* nothing which has not really existed" (ER: 334). He would reiterate this point again a few years later. "Novel conceptions are merely unusual combinations," he comments in an 1845 essay on Thomas Hood; "the mind of man can imagine nothing which does not exist.... [A]ll which claims to be new—which appears to be a *creation* of the intellect... is re-soluble into the old. The wildest effort of the mind cannot stand the test of the analysis" (ER: 277).

Thus although "The Philosophy of Composition," for instance, begins with the admonition to keep "originality *always* in view," this precept works at cross-purposes with Poe's critical process, which analyzes poems by way of their effects. New effects are impossible, he demonstrates over and over, since to be effects at all they must be recognizable as such, always and already. "Originality" in versification is "by no means a matter, as some suppose, of impulse or intuition," but instead "demands in its attainment less of invention than negation" (ER: 20–21). Poetical effects are the by-products of readers' acts of recognition, which may seem spontaneous but are in fact generated through artful combinations of "rhythm, metre, stanza, rhyme, alliteration, the *refrain*, and other analogous effects" (ER: 33). The most perfectly imaginative poems often slip by "the undiscriminating" because of the paradoxical feeling of "*obviousness*" they generate in retrospect: "we are apt to find ourselves asking '*why is it* that these combinations have never been imagined before?'" (ER: 278). Poe's criticism of contemporary poetry relentlessly hones in on the achievement (or, more commonly, the failure) of intended effects, which succeed or not, depending on the poet's ability to deploy the conventions of versification that already govern common-sense uses of English.

Poe's defense of the old, his redefinition of novelty in terms not of newness but a surprising obviousness, defines his concept of the "Poetic Sentiment," a faculty shared collectively among all: "Poetry, in this new sense, *is* the practical result, expressed in language, of this Poetic Sentiment," and "the only proper method of testing the merits of a poem is by measuring its capabilities of exciting the Poetic Sentiment in others" (ER: 511). Good poems are good to the extent that they elicit responses outside themselves. "For a poem is not the Poetic faculty, but *the means* of exciting it in mankind," and such means work through combinations of recognizable and recognized effects, or conventions (ER: 511). In a hyperbolic 1846 attack on "licentious 'schools' of poetry," Poe excoriates modern poets for "having, in their rashness of spirit, much in accordance with the whole spirit of the age, thrown into the shade... [the] conventionalities, even the most justifiable *decora* of composition" (ER: 445). Only by understanding the conventions and conventionalities of verse can "genius" be reconciled with "artistic skill," for the true poem exists solely in the means through which it excites the poetic sentiment in others.

Poe persistently opposes "pedantry" and "cant" (transcendentalism), which exalt systems and abstract systemizations over actual language usage according to "the commonest common sense" (ER: 26). He famously defines poetry as "*The Rhythmical Creation of Beauty*," the pleasure of which "originates in the human enjoyment of equality [and] fitness" (ER: 78, 33). These axioms explain poems according to a principle of the echo, which is apprehended through repetition at a remove: as Poe writes approvingly in a comment on Lydia Sigourney's poem "Poetry," "the burden of the song finds a ready echo in our bosoms" (ER: 883).[9] Poems depend upon poetic effects, which are located in acts of reading and reception, not imaginative creation; for this reason, Poe continually tests language according to its reproducibility. "*That* rhythm is erroneous . . . which *any* ordinary reader can, without design, read improperly. It is the business of the poet to construct his line that the intention *must* be caught *at once*" (ER: 48).

Even in the more idealist argument of the "The Poetic Principle," Poe explains poetry in terms of removal and distance rather than presence or immediacy: "the manifestation of the Principle is always found in *an elevating excitement of the Soul*," but this elevating excitement is not unique or original to anyone, since it is generated when "we are led to perceive a harmony where none was apparent before" (ER: 92–93). This is "the true poetical effect—but this effect is referable to the harmony alone, and not in the least degree to the truth which merely served to render the harmony manifest" (ER: 93). If readers do not *perceive* harmonies, rhythms, or poetical effects, but *are led to perceive* them, then poems become themselves only through reproduction at a remove. Poems derive from the materiality of words rather than any transcendental belief about meaning, and criticism that presumes otherwise commits the "heresy of *The Didactic*," the fallacy that "the ultimate object of all Poetry is Truth," that every poem "should inculcate a moral" (ER: 75).

Imitation and repetition, and not originality, are therefore keynotes to Poe's poetics. As he put it near the climax of the "Little Longfellow War," responding to the manifold charges of plagiarism that had been flying back and forth in the press, "the repetition in question is assuredly not claimed by myself as original . . . [but] is, in fact, a musical effect, which is the common property of all mankind, and has been their common property for ages" (ER: 745). Longfellow's crime, in this case, was not that he had imitated Poe's (or anyone's) practice of repeating words to create metrical effects—not that he had repeated repetitions—since such effects were common property. Longfellow instead imitated the "conception" and "manner" of other authors, something Poe considered the "most barbarous class of literary piracy" because it was "that class in which, while the words of the wronged author are avoided, his most intangible, and therefore his least defensible and least reclaimable property, is appropriated" (ER: 749). To charge Longfellow with this kind of imitation was simply to "have echoed the sentiment of every man of letters in the land," since in Poe's view it became manifestly obvious as soon as he pragmatically compared verses (ER: 757).

Echoing, repetition, and imitation are the refrains heard again and again throughout the plagiarism controversy Poe ignited in the pages of the *Broadway Journal* in 1845. Even to charge Longfellow with copying was itself simply to echo a sentiment others already felt in their hearts. Yet Poe's argument about plagiarism and imitation is exceedingly counterintuitive, for the most obviously unique or singular aspects of a poem, namely its refrain, repetitions, and poetic effects, its words, meter, and rhythm, were exactly those features that could not be claimed for protection. If the intangible forms of literary property, like manner or conception, could be barbarously pirated because of their intangibility, the tangible, material effects of a poem could be claimed by no one because they were "common property" belonging to everyone. The poetic sentiment was universal, which meant that poetic effects resounded in the minds of all, and therefore acts of creativity were always also acts of appropriation. In a long passage that seemed to reconcile the conflict, Poe explained how the poetic sentiment displaced every gesture of seemingly original creation to a point of origin outside the poet. Because it "implies a peculiarly, perhaps an abnormally keen appreciation of the beautiful," the poetic sentiment was a Trojan horse that smuggled into the poet's mind or soul "a longing for [the] assimilation" of beautiful effects:

> What the poet intensely admires, becomes thus, in every fact, although only partially, a portion of his own intellect. It has a secondary origination within his own soul—an origination altogether apart, although springing, from its primary origination from without. The poet is thus possessed by another's thought, and cannot be said to take of it, possession. But, in either view, he thoroughly feels it as *his own*—and this feeling is counteracted only by the sensible presence of its true, palpable origin in the volume from which he has derived it—an origin which, in the long lapse of years it is almost impossible *not* to forget—for in the mean time the thought itself is forgotten. But the frailest association will regenerate it—it springs up with all the vigor of a new birth—its absolute originality is not even a matter of suspicion—and when the poet has written it and printed it, and on its account is charged with plagiarism, there will be no one in the world more entirely astounded than himself. Now from what I have said it will be evident that the liability to accidents of this character is in the direct ratio of the poetic sentiment—of the susceptibility to the poetic impression; and in fact all literary history demonstrates that, for the most frequent and palpable plagiarisms, we must search the works of the most eminent poets.
>
> (ER: 758–759)

In this extraordinary concession (quickly countermanded by the infamous, scurrilous attack on Longfellow in the *Aristidean*), Poe argues that any poetic effect capable of stimulating the sentiment for beauty comes from outside the poet, even as it awakens a "secondary origination" in the poet's own soul. Only faulty, defective poems can be claimed as one's own; beauty—the product of beautiful effects—always begins somewhere else, and thus the greatest poets, those with the most "abnormally keen appreciation of the beautiful," are also literary history's greatest plagiarists. Yet it is impossible to plagiarize beauty, because the poet does not take the effect, but is taken by it: the "poet is thus possessed by another's thought, and cannot be said to take of it, possession" (ER: 759). The pseudo-Lockeanism of Poe's rationale refashions the poet's mind as a warehouse storing all perceptions of beauty as these are manifested in language, for "the frailest association will regenerate" another's thought in oneself, since "a poem is not the Poetic faculty, but *the means* of exciting it in mankind" (ER: 511).[10] We are always removed from the poem, even as its secondary origination in ourselves defines it as a poem.

Meredith McGill and Eliza Richards convincingly situate Poe in terms of the "secondarity" or "secondariness" of his work, in relation to British literature, in the former account, and to women's poetry, in the latter. Poe "embraces rather than bemoans poetic secondarity, taking a radical dislocation from origins as the condition of writing poetry," McGill argues, whereas Poe's poetry, in Richards's view, "asserts its originality by highlighting its secondariness."[11] This secondariness is not perversely exceptional to Poe: instead, Poe's emphasis on the secondary quality of all poetic writing participates in the larger mid-century American poetic culture, where, amid an expansive communication system, a decentralized network of circulation, and loose legal controls over copyright, poems could appear everywhere but originate nowhere.[12] Thus, Poe's defensive preface to his 1845 volume *The Raven and Other Poems*, which claims as its purpose the "redemption from the many improvements to which [these trifles] have been subjected while going at random 'the rounds of the press.'"[13] Although Poe failed to control the forms and format of his poems, his explorations of the sonorous, echoing powers that the poetry of unoriginality could enable remain unmatched. The dynamic conventionality of antebellum poetics forms the subject of these poems as much as any content or mode (such as the gothic). Note how often his titles simply name a genre—"Song," "Sonnet," "Serenade," "Enigma"—as if to highlight that their most important aspect is the way they bring together origination with reproduction; "you've seen this before," they seem to say, "even if you can't quite remember where."

The cycle of recognition and forgetting stimulates the desire for an "absolute originality" the lifted origins of which "it is almost impossible *not* to forget," and it derived from a popular culture of poetry circulated in magazines, newspapers, salons, and other mostly ephemeral formats, but less often codified in more enduring formats like leather-bound volumes. This interplay between the evocation of originality and novelty and the materiality of repetition and reproduction may help to explain some of the more long-standing problems raised by Poe's poems.

For example, few antebellum titles are more common than "To—," and in Poe's slender body of verse there are multiple iterations of a title that addresses the poem to a blank. Typically printed in newspapers, magazines, and, especially, antebellum formats like the literary annual, such an obscured address seems to promise intimate communication by hiding it within plain sight in a venue open to anyone's reading. "To—" is one of several poetic genres prevalent before 1850 that mime the social context of scribal inscription as an engine for generating print intimacy; another example would be "Lines Written in a Lady's Album," also a popular title of the period. Almost every British or American poet of note from the late eighteenth century to the mid-nineteenth wrote one or two, which in their generality or blankness open up the pleasures of reading a poem mediated through impersonal reproduction (such erotic publicity will be a major theme of the *Leaves of Grass* editions Whitman published in the decade after Poe's death). Even when actually written in someone's album, these kinds of poems seemed personal to the extent that they adhered to the conventions and protocols laid down in numerous handbooks and anthologies.[14]

Whom does such a poem address? To whom, to adopt its favored metaphor, does the poem speak? In one of Poe's earliest poems, "To—," he plays upon the frustrations of an imaginary intimacy that elicits the desired recognition only teasingly to refuse it:

> The bowers whereat, in dreams, I see
> The wantonest singing birds,
> Are lips—and all thy melody
> Of lip-begotten words—
>
> Thine eyes, in Heaven of heart enshrined
> Then desolately fall,
> O God! on my funereal mind
> Like starlight on a pall—
>
> Thy heart—*thy* heart!—I wake and sigh,
> And sleep to dream till day
> Of the truth that gold can never buy—
> Of the baubles that it may.
>
> (M 1: 132–133)

First appearing in Poe's 1829 volume *Al Aaraaf, Tamerlane, and Minor Poems*, along with three other "To—" poems, this version opens in a graveyard of dead metonyms for poetic expression that in the second stanza will figuratively be enclosed in a coffin (in nineteenth-century usage, "pall" referred to the sheet covering a casket, and it is suggestive to recall that *Atkinson's Casket* was a popular Philadelphia periodical that printed many "To—" poems during the 1830s). Bowers seen in dreams, wantonly singing birds, lips—these are among the most reiterated clichés a poet of the 1820s could deploy to conjure the fantasy of the "lip-begotten words" the printed text pretends to be. Each metonym figures an imagined mode of direct address between "my funereal mind" and "Thy heart—*thy* heart." Whose heart? The emphatic repetition indicates the futility of the question—the heart is blank, anything can fill it. To fill in the blank with names drawn from Poe's biography—as scholars have sometimes been tempted to do—is to misunderstand this poem's circularity; when Poe reprinted "To—" in an 1845 issue of the *Broadway Journal*, he facetiously placed it just below his own signature, as though the blank in the poem's title is best filled with "Edgar A. Poe."[15] The closing lines return the poem to the scene of its location, not in bowers or graveyards or dreams, but in a purchasable printed format. Gold cannot buy the truth this poem does not contain, but it can purchase "baubles" like *Al Aaraaf*.

By obscuring its address to no one as intimate communication available to anyone, "To—" enables identification by occluding identity. It attracts readers through its clichés, not despite them. Unoriginality is the open secret of this poem and others like it. Poe also enjoyed inverting these addresses to no one in games of encryption, poems that hide the names of their specific addressees within themselves, all the while playing upon their empty, generic content. An early example is an acrostic he wrote in the album of his cousin Elizabeth Herring in the 1820s, which begins by naming her and then proceeds to spell her name, all the while spelling out the "one important rule" every poet should know, even if they have forgotten "the heathenish Greek name—/(Called any thing, its meaning is the same)/'Always write *first* things uppermost in the heart'" (M 1: 148). The acrostic is an elaborate spoof on the conventions of album poetics, which inscribe intimate address by inculcating the protocols of intimacy—the rules "employed in even the theses of the school" (MI: 148). Overfamiliarity with conventions, such as the mandate to "Always write *first* things uppermost in the heart," is knowledge that needs to be simultaneously displayed and hidden.[16]

More interesting is "An Enigma," published in the *Union Magazine* in 1848, in which Poe encodes the name "Sarah Anna Lewis" within a sonnet mocking the shopworn emptiness of the sonnet tradition (the title of the magazine poem was "Sonnet").

"Seldom we find," says Solomon Don Dunce,
"Half an idea in the profoundest sonnet.
Through all the flimsy things we see at once
As easily as through a Naples bonnet—
Trash of all trash!—how *can* a lady don it?
Yet heavier far than your Petrarchan stuff—
Owl-downy nonsense that the faintest puff
Twirls into trunk-paper the while you con it."
And, veritably, Sol is right enough.
The general tuckermanities are arrant
Bubbles—ephemeral and *so* transparent—
But *this* is, now—you may depend upon it—
Stable, opaque, immortal—all by dint
Of the dear names that lie concealed within 't.

(M 1: 425)[17]

Earlier that year Poe had praised Lewis's poem "The Forsaken" in extravagant terms, claiming to have "read this little poem more than twenty times and always with increasing admiration" (ER: 658). If repeated rereading magnifies rather than diminishes the pleasures of Lewis's work, which, as Poe's theories had made clear, pleased so readily because "no human being exists, over the age of fifteen, who has not, in his heart of hearts, a ready echo for all here so pathetically expressed," the sonnet in which he encodes her name winkingly aspires to the reverse. The sonnet tradition, this sonnet claims, has so emptied and evacuated the stanza form that, rather than echoing in others' hearts, sonnets are now "flimsy things" that can be seen through as easily as a "Naples bonnet." Poe's joke is complex: "gros de Naples" was a thick silk taffeta, periodically fashionable in the United States after 1830, that was prized for its transparency and versatility but regularly criticized for being a foreign style. Not only is the Naples bonnet a piece of outerwear designed to be seen through; bonnets made after this fashion were ornamented elaborately with feathers, ribbons, and other decorative adornments. Flourishes of ornamentation and design thus set off the emptiness of both bonnet and sonnet, each "ephemeral and *so* transparent," like the Petrarchan tradition, and endlessly recycled to invisible thinness, which pushes the poem's paper-based mediation toward the next step in its material lifecycle, from magazine or book page to the lining of a trunk.[18] No one holds onto "owl-downy nonsense," "trash of all trash," for long, even should they want to, since the "faintest puff/Twirls into trunk-paper the while you con it."[19]

If any well-versed reader can see right through the "tuckermanities"—conceits of the Boston author Henry T. Tuckerman—that render the sonnet empty by way of their overelaborated design, Poe's "Sonnet" will seem "stable, opaque, immortal" by virtue of Lewis's name concealed in it, which only the truly skilled know how to decipher.[20] Yet here too is another joke—poetic enigmas were so popular in the 1840s that many or most readers likely could have spotted the name quickly. Solomon Don Dunce may think he is clever (his name links wisdom with stupidity, after all), but Poe knows his enigmatic sonnet is just as conventional as any "Petrarchan stuff," for enigma and sonnet function as what they are to the extent that they follow the rules of their genres. The only details that make the poem specific or unique are the "dear names" concealed in its lines—Sarah Anna Lewis. If Poe's "Sonnet" has a voice of its own, it speaks by repeating the name of another.

The relationships between naming, echoing, sounding, and repetition are nowhere stronger than in Poe's most famous poem, "The Raven." "The Raven" stands alone in American literary history because it comes with an explanatory essay, "The Philosophy of Composition," that has indelibly associated it with a particular theory of language. Although most readers discount Poe's claim that he composed "The Raven" "with the precision and rigid consequence of a mathematical problem," his outline of the poem as a series of effects achieving an overall "unity of impression" seems effectively to have reduced the poem to the sum of its sounds, and in consequence the tradition of critical commentary on the poem is smaller than its outsized place in American literary history would suggest (ER: 15). Contemporary reviewers recognized how the sonorous materiality of the metrics largely voided "The Raven" of semantic meaning. Poe's "skill in versification, sometimes striking enough, was evidently artificial," wrote a critic in *Fraser's Magazine*; "he overstudied metrical expression, and overrated its value so as sometimes to write what were little better than nonsense-verses, for the sake of the rhythm."[21] The repetition of nonsense (or possibly nonsensical) words for the sake of their sounds is central to the action of "The Raven," as we will see: "nevermore," with its "melancholy character" that "finds immediate echo in the melancholy heart of the student," must be repeated by "a *non*-reasoning creature capable of speech," or risk collapsing into mere monotony (ER: 19, 24, 18).

But where Poe claimed that "nothing even remotely approaching" his poem's combination of rhythm and meter had ever been attempted (ER: 21), his contemporaries heard clearly how "The Raven" echoed Elizabeth Barrett Barrett's lengthy poem "Lady Geraldine's Courtship."[22] Poe had reviewed her volume *The Drama of Exile* in the *Broadway Journal* early in 1845, just weeks before "The Raven" appeared in the *American Review.* Amid some damningly faint praise—"Lady Geraldine's Courtship" "is, we think, the only poem of its author which is not deficient, considered as an artistical whole"—Poe situated Barrett's poem as an imitation of Tennyson's "Locksley Hall," "which it surpasses in plot or rather in thesis, as much as it falls below it in artistical management" (ER: 129, 127). Poe singled out for admiration "the instrumentality of those repetitions—those unusual phrases—in a word, those *quaintnesses*, which it has been too long the fashion to censure . . . [as] affectation," even as he castigated Barrett's "excessive reiteration of pet *words*," her "multiplicity of inadmissible rhymes," and her "inefficient rhythm" (ER: 131, 134, 135, 136). Poe's critique was a process of sounding out Barrett's verse: having first located "Lady Geraldine's Courtship" within its chain of associative echoes, he then placed the coordinates for understanding the poem as a set of sonorous effects. The publication of "The Raven" two weeks later makes it almost impossible not to hear him ventriloquizing his own echo of Barrett in his account of the way she repeated words, or didn't.

After Poe's death, the *Southern Literary Messenger* acknowledged, somewhat defensively, this unoriginality: although of "all the works of this brilliant but eccentric genius, none is more remarkable and characteristic than his short poem of 'The Raven,'" nonetheless "we shall not be suspected of any design to depreciate the merit of the poem, in alluding to certain productions, which appear to us to have *suggested* to Mr. Poe the ideas, both of the action and the versification of the Raven."[23] Although the *Messenger* hastened to emphasize that any echoes were "nothing more than suggestion," one essay after another, from the 1850s to the present, has noted the correspondence between several of Barrett's lines and Poe's:

> With a murmurous stir, uncertain, in the air, the purple curtain
> Swelleth in and swelleth out around her motionless pale brows;
> While the gliding of the river sends a rippling noise for ever,
> Through the open casement whitened by the moonlight's slant repose.
>
> Said he—'Vision of a lady! stand there silent, stand there steady!
> Now I see it plainly, plainly; now I cannot hope or doubt—
> There, the cheeks of calm expression—there, the lips of silent passion
> Curvéd like an archer's bow, to send the bitter arrows out."
>
> Ever, evermore the while in a slow silence she kept smiling—
> And approached him slowly, slowly, in a gliding measured pace;
> With her two white hands extended, as if praying one offended,
> And a look of supplication, gazing earnest in his face.[24]

Most comparisons in American journals painstakingly pointed out how Poe improved upon Barrett, even as he lifted her rhymes, rhythm, and meter. For example, Carl

Benson, writing in the *American Review* in 1847, mused that it was "a little singular, that one of her metres, on which she seems to have hit accidentally, was never generally understood until its capabilities were developed by our old contributor, Mr. Poe."[25] In fact, Barrett implemented the alternating internal rhyme only in the "Conclusion" section of her poem, and nearly always in slant rhymes, which grated so harshly on Poe's ear that he replaced them with his own form of relentless re-sounding.

Thus, although some early notices could describe "The Raven" as having "a Stanza unknown before to gods, men, and booksellers,"[26] it became so closely associated with "Lady Geraldine's Courtship" that in T. S. Arthur's serialized Civil War–era novel *Out in the World*, for instance, a character—significantly, a woman forced by tragic circumstances to make her way in the professional world—is described reciting the two pieces in tandem at a dramatic performance. Notably, the performer renders "The Raven" so powerfully that the audience demands she repeat it; just as notably, she reads "Lady Geraldine's Courtship" with such "almost unequalled pathos" that "Mrs. Browning herself, had she been present, must have felt some passages quite as deeply as when they thrilled her soul in the first fervors of poetic inspiration."[27] We can hear in this description (or so it seems) Arthur's canny insight into Poe's poetics—when properly read aloud, "Lady Geraldine's Courtship" conjured an echo of poetic inspiration that could thrill even its author. Or, in Poe's terminology, it excited her poetic sentiment precisely because it came through a performance repeated from a space outside her.

Read interactively with "The Raven," then, "Lady Geraldine's Courtship" can seem like something of a prequel. Bertram, a poet "born to poet's uses," falls in love with the titular lady despite their vastly different social rank.[28] The poem tracks the course of their relationship while he visits her estate, and it follows them through several philosophical discussions and misunderstandings, until a seemingly fatal rupture sends him to brood alone while writing the letter that is the poem. In the conclusion (the section Poe echoed most closely), their breach is healed when Bertram has a vision of Geraldine (seen in the lines, quoted earlier, that sound most like Poe's) that becomes real. At least, she becomes real to Bertram, whose ability to distinguish the real from the symbolic has already been flagged as a problem. Making this distinction is more challenging for the reader, however, since Geraldine and her vision don't clarify which is which:

> Ever, evermore the while in a slow silence she kept smiling—
> While the shining tears ran faster down the blushing of her cheeks;
> Then with both her hands enfolding both of his, she softly told him,
> "Bertram, if I say I love thee, . . . 'tis the vision only speaks."[29]

The conclusion chooses not to resolve whether Bertram has, in fact, made his dream real or, instead, is locked in the dream for "evermore." This confusion can be found all over "Lady Geraldine's Courtship," which delights in obscuring differences between materiality and meaning: for example, in a discussion about an allegorical statue of Silence, Bertram and Geraldine debate the relative value of "symbol" and "substance": "That the essential meaning growing, may exceed the special symbol,/Is the thought, as I conceive it," Geraldine argues: "Your true noblemen will often, through right nobleness, grow humble,/And assert an inward honour, by denying outward show." As an aspiring social climber, Bertram would presumably favor this endorsement of inner substance over outer show, but he will have none of it: "your nobles wear their ermine on the outside," he reminds her. "'Tis the substance that wanes ever, 'tis the symbol that exceeds:/Soon we shall have nought but symbol!" Similarly, when Bertram tries to impress Geraldine by reading his own work, he fails because "poets never read their own best verses to their worth—/For the echo, in you, breaks upon the words which you are speaking."[30] Like another astute student of Poe, Barrett collapses social content and semantic meaning into artistic form and poetic materiality, troubling the effort to locate presence in an original voice by reproducing "the echo" that exceeds and replaces "the words which you are speaking," even (or especially) when those words are your own. No one's words are ever his or her own, and thus the vision at the curtain with which the poem ends will hover between dream and reality "evermore."

The echoing nonoriginality of "The Raven" thus adapts, appropriately enough, both the meter and argument of Barrett's poem. At the end, Barrett's poet writes to relieve his sorrow, which, rather than being written, marks the surface of his manuscript: "Bertram finished the last pages, while along the silence ever/Still in hot and heavy splashes, fell his tears on every leaf:/Having ended, he leans backward in his chair, with lips that quiver/From the deep unspoken, ay, and deep unwritten thoughts of grief." Sadness is silent and unspoken, told by tears that splash on his text or lips that quiver but say nothing, and his vision, "a dream of mercies/'Twixt the purple-lattice curtains," arouses him from this condition of self-cancellation.[31] At the beginning of "The Raven," in contrast, Poe's lover reads, vainly hoping "to borrow/From my books surcease of sorrow—sorrow for the lost Lenore," but his self-cancellation keeps getting deferred by sounds that never quite settle into themselves. "Nearly napping" over his book, he is startled by "a tapping/As of some one gently rapping," two types of sound that neither differ from nor become equal to each other. This mode of sounding alike and yet not is repeated visually by "each separate dying ember" casting its "ghost upon the floor," which evokes firelight through the self-projection of the ember as it fades away. But while this seems to be just the "surcease" for which the lover longs, the tapping or rapping provokes him to a state of heightened sensory and affective awareness: "the silken, sad, uncertain rustling of each purple curtain/Thrilled me—filled me with fantastic terrors never felt before" (M 1:365). Tapping and rapping can both be construed as signals, like the noises transmitted through the Fox sisters and other spirit mediums, that open communication, but the lover's repeated efforts to locate them in relation to "some visitor" lead instead to "darkness there and nothing more."[32] Peering into an abyssal silence, "dreaming dreams no mortal ever dared to dream before," another repetition measures and deflects him: "the only word there spoken was the whispered word, 'Lenore?' . . . an echo murmured back the word, 'Lenore!'" (M 1:365, 366).

Poe had criticized Barrett's penchant for pet words and slant rhymes, which evoke sounds that they fail to become and thus refuse to be. His own echoes, in response, differ even as they repeat, or differ because they repeat (Lenore?/Lenore!). The beautiful dead woman, "nameless here forevermore," gets named again and again, while the lover's name goes unmentioned. But the most prominent example of this process is, of course, the Raven's pet word, "nevermore." In a review of *Barnaby Rudge*, the novel from which he purloined the talking raven, Poe explained that the bird, "whose croakings are to be frequently, appropriately, and prophetically heard," performs "much the same part as does, in music, the accompaniment in respect to the air. Each is distinct. Each differs remarkably from the other. Yet between them there is a strong analogical resemblance" (ER: 222). The formal function of Grip's speech in *Barnaby Rudge* is to echo according to the plan Poe will adopt for his poem—to vary, and yet to resemble. Echoing haunts Dickens's novel, in Poe's view, to such an extent that Dickens even "*anticipated, and thus rendered valueless, his chief effect*" by revealing inadvertently the solution to the mystery before it had begun (ER: 239).[33] Dickens's failure to plot the novel according to the relay of its intended effects serves as the cautionary tale prompting the compositional strategy Poe claims for "The Raven" in "The Philosophy of Composition." Echoes need to anticipate themselves. Poe therefore needed to vary, "at every turn, the *application* of the word repeated," since this was "the opportunity afforded for the effect on which I had been depending" (ER: 19). Variation of application takes the form of the lover's "phrenzied pleasure in so modeling his questions as to receive from the *expected* 'Nevermore' the most delicious because the most intolerable of sorrow" (ER: 19).

"Though its answer little meaning—little relevancy bore," the Raven "spoke only/That one word, as if his soul in that one word he did outpour." The lover never reads the bird correctly, and so his effort to circulate meaning and intention into the echo always gets frustrated. It is "as if" the word expressed inner experience on the one hand, but on the other "what it utters is its only stock and store/Caught from some unhappy master whom unmerciful Disaster/Followed fast and followed faster till his songs one burden bore" (M 1: 367). In this reading, the Raven records the voice of a former master, whose history—and not its own—is "What this grim, ungainly, ghastly, gaunt, and ominous bird of yore/Meant in croaking 'Nevermore.'" The Raven repeats, but it does not speak. Nevertheless, the empty word, "sonorous and susceptible of protracted emphasis," with "the long *o* as the most sonorous vowel, in connection with *r* as the most producible consonant" embodies the sound of melancholy, ever more imitable in the Raven's voice because the effect is not its own (ER: 18). For this reason, and even if it means nothing, it is capable of "beguiling my sad fancy into smiling," leading the lover into "linking/Fancy unto fancy" back to the lost Lenore, and kicking into motion the variation through repetition that is the poem's climax (M 1: 367).

Echoes anticipate; the lover knows what the bird will say, since the word it croaks elicits, and thereby frustrates, his desires to remember and forget—"Quaff, oh quaff this kind nepenthe and forget this lost Lenore! . . . [T]ell me—tell me, I implore!" (M 1: 368). As the pile-up of imploring phrases indicates, words and ideas, sounds and intentions, are never original, in this poem or anywhere in Poe's verse: they always come from somewhere else and someone else. Bertram never gets out of his dream; Poe's lover never gets into his. "The Raven" replicates the conventions of a poetic culture of generic repetition it repeats, so that its readers know what they will hear before they hear it. The Raven's eyes, which "have all the seeming of a demon's that is dreaming," produce the illusion of meaning ("dreaming") by "seeming" to be like something "never dreamed before." This is the poem's fantasy, heard like "the echo, in you, [that] breaks upon the words which you are speaking." Only this, and nothing more.

Notes

1. Earlier work in the recovery of American women poets tended to be more apologetic about their perceived aesthetic failings. The headnotes to Cheryl Walker's landmark *American Women Poets of the Nineteenth Century* (New Brunswick, NJ: Rutgers University Press, 1992) often defensively anticipate criticism of the poetry's derivativeness or sentimentality, and the anthology gets around the problem by selecting poems that seem particularly eccentric to convention, whether through their historical or political topicality, or, more typically, their expressions of antipatriarchal anger. This is also the strategy of Paula Bennett's edition of the poetry of Sarah Piatt (*The Palace-Burner: The Selected Poetry of Sarah Piatt*, ed. Paula Bennett [Champaign-Urbana: University of Illinois Press, 2001]), which single-handedly returned Piatt to scholarly attention. Bennett chose poems that in her view ironize or subvert nineteenth-century conventions, and she avoided Piatt's early poetry and other, apparently less ironic materials. In contrast, critical embarrassment about poetic quality does not characterize Tricia Lootens's *Lost Saints: Silence, Gender, and Victorian Literary Canonization* (Charlottesville: University of Virginia Press, 1996), Isobel Armstrong's *Victorian Poetry: Poetry, Poetics, Politics* (London: Routledge, 1996), and other scholarship in the recovery of nineteenth-century British poets.
2. Eliza Richards, *Gender and the Poetics of Reception in Poe's Circle* (Cambridge: Cambridge University Press, 2004), 67.
3. With regard to the uses of convention by nineteenth-century poets, see Michael C. Cohen, *The Social Lives of Poems in Nineteenth-Century America* (Philadelphia: University of Pennsylvania Press, 2015); essays collected in "The Ballad: A Special Issue on Historical Poetics and Genre," special issue, *Nineteenth-Century Literature* 71, no. 2 (2016); and essays in the *History of Nineteenth-Century American Women's Poetry*, ed. Jennifer Putzi and Alexandra Socarides (Cambridge: Cambridge University Press, 2016).
4. William B. Warner, *Protocols of Liberty: Communication Innovation & The American Revolution* (Chicago: The University of Chicago Press, 2013), 17.
5. Warner, *Protocols of Liberty*, 18. Matt Cohen, *The Networked Wilderness: Communicating in Early New England* (Minneapolis: University of Minnesota Press, 2010), and Russ Castronovo, *Propaganda 1776: Secrets, Leaks, and Revolutionary Communications in Early America* (New York: Oxford University Press, 2014) make comparable arguments about communications during the colonial and revolutionary periods.
6. David M. Henkin, *The Postal Age: The Emergence of Modern Communications in Nineteenth-Century America* (Chicago: University of Chicago Press, 2006), 93–118. On letter writing manuals, see Eve Tavor Bannet, *Empire of Letters: Letter Manuals and Transatlantic Correspondence, 1680–1820* (Cambridge: Cambridge University Press, 2005); and Konstantin Dierks, *In My Power: Letter Writing and Communications in Early America* (Philadelphia: University of Pennsylvania Press, 2009).
7. Along with Richards's *Gender and the Poetics of Reception*, Meredith McGill makes the strongest argument for evaluating Poe in these terms, working from the perspective

of copyright law, reprinting, and antebellum magazines: *American Literature and the Culture of Reprinting, 1834–1853* (Philadelphia: University of Pennsylvania Press, 2003), 141–186.

8. Jerome McGann, *The Poet Edgar Allan Poe: Alien Angel* (Cambridge, MA: Harvard University Press, 2014), 7, 2.
9. Though she focuses on constructing literary histories that can recognize patterns of reprinting, rather than on poetry per se, Meredith McGill makes a persuasive case for studying antebellum literature according to "echo-criticism": "Echocriticism: Repetition and the Order of Texts," *American Literature* 88, no. 1 (2016): 1–29.
10. The *Aristidean* essay—which is not conclusively attributed to Poe—applies a similar metaphor to the more common notion of plagiarism as theft: "The 'Southern Literary Messenger,' indeed, seems to have been the great store-house whence the Professor has derived most of his contraband goods" (ER: 775). If Poe wrote this essay, it shows him reverting to the contested concepts of literary writing as defensible property that McGill tracks through the antebellum period (*American Literature and the Culture of Reprinting*, 49–75).
11. McGill, *American Literature and the Culture of Reprinting*, 156; Richards, *Gender and the Poetics of Reception*, 50.
12. As many scholars now argue, only well after 1850 did American communications systems begin to consolidate into something like "mass media," with the ability to organize national markets for the circulation and consumption of material printed on a vast scale. Trish Loughran has made an influential argument in this vein in *The Republic in Print: Print Culture in the Age of U.S. Nation Building, 1770–1870* (New York: Columbia University Press, 2007). However, Loughran demonstrates the disorganization of print communication systems in the early republic and antebellum periods far more convincingly than she proves their centralization later in the century, a weakness in her account that results from the assumption, shared by nearly all media histories, that communications systems radically increase in power as they consolidate over time. (Overblown and underproven claims about the transformative powers of media technology characterize the techno-determinist narratives of a wide range of thinkers, from theorists such as Marshall McLuhan, Friedrich Kittler, and Armand Mattelart to pop gurus like Kevin Kelly, Nicholas Negroponte, and Malcolm Gladwell.) Whether or not a more consolidated, national system—let alone a "print culture"—really came to exist in the postbellum era, Poe lived during a period of its clear noncoordination, the wide-ranging consequences of which J. Gerald Kennedy has recently explored in *Strange Nation: Literary Nationalism and Cultural Conflict in the Age of Poe* (New York: Oxford University Press, 2016).
13. Poe, preface to *The Raven and Other Poems* (New York: Wiley and Putnam, 1845), iii.
14. On album poetry, see Laura Zebuhr, "The Work of Friendship in Nineteenth-Century American Friendship Album Verses," *American Literature* 87, no. 3 (2015): 433–454; and Michael C. Cohen, "Album Verse and the Poetics of Scribal Circulation," in *A History of Nineteenth-Century American Women's Poetry*, ed. Putzi and Socarides, 68–86.
15. *Broadway Journal* 2 (September 20, 1845): 164. Poe had signed "The Landscape Garden," which was placed just above the poem. Richards notes other instances where Poe played this game with Frances Sargent Osgood in the same periodical (*Gender and the Poetics of Reception*, 96–104). On two occasions, it is the blank in Osgood's "To—" poems that Poe fills with his own signature (101, 103).

16. Leon Jackson describes album poetry as a rule-based system of gift exchange in *The Business of Letters: Authorial Economies in Antebellum America* (Stanford, CA: Stanford University Press, 2008): 97–109.
17. "An Enigma" first appeared as "Sonnet," *Union Magazine* (March 1848): 130.
18. Leah Price discusses how the material lifecycle of paper haunts mid-Victorian fiction in *How to Do Things with Books in Victorian Britain* (Princeton, NJ: Princeton University Press, 2012), esp. 219–257.
19. Puffing—publishers' practice of placing hyperbolic notices of praise under the guise of a review, for the purpose of promoting the sale of a book—was another bugbear of Poe's, which his own critical essays were meant to counteract; it is possible to read in that "faintest puff" a play on the emptiness not only of the poem but the language that typically surrounds it—both are a "con." On Poe and puffing, see Lara Langer Cohen, *The Fabrication of American Literature: Fraudulence and Antebellum Print Culture* (Philadelphia: University of Pennsylvania, 2012), 53–66.
20. The name runs diagonally down the poem: the first letter of the first line ("s" from "seldom"), the second letter in the second line ("a" from "half"), and so on through the fourteen lines and letters of Sarah Anna Lewis. In the first version of the poem, Poe has "Petrarchanities" instead of "tuckermanities" in the volta at line 10.
21. "American Poetry," *Eclectic Magazine* (August 1850): 567. This omnibus review of American poets was reprinted from *Fraser's Magazine*.
22. Since Barrett published *The Drama of Exile* before marrying Robert Browning—in fact, "Lady Geraldine's Courtship" was central to their courtship—I shall refer to her as Barrett.
23. "The Raven—By Edgar A. Poe," *Southern Literary Messenger* 25, no. 5 (November 1857): 331, 333.
24. Elizabeth Barrett Browning, *Aurora Leigh and Other Poems* (New York: Penguin, 1996), 342.
25. Carl Benson, "Short Chapters on Novel and Exotic Metres. No. III. The New School Metres," *American Review* 5, no. 5 (May 1847): 503. This kind of nationalist justification was typical; a decade later the *Southern Literary Messenger* was claiming "The Raven" as the original from which Barrett had taken her meter: see the "Editor's Table," *Southern Literary Messenger* 26, no. 5 (May 1858): 395. Much as Poe would have predicted, the lifted origins of his poem's "originality" had to be continually forgotten and then rediscovered by later generations of readers.
26. "The Literary World," *New World* (February 15, 1845): 108.
27. T. S. Arthur, "Out in the World," *Arthur's Home Magazine* (July 1863): 34–35.
28. Barrett Browning, *Aurora Leigh and Other Poems*, 322.
29. Barrett Browning, *Aurora Leigh and Other Poems*, 343.
30. Barrett Browning, *Aurora Leigh and Other Poems*, 327, 328, 330.
31. Barrett Browning, *Aurora Leigh and Other Poems*, 341, 341.
32. Richards discusses the "spiritualist poetics" of Poe and Sarah Helen Whitman in *Gender and the Poetics of Reception*, 107–148.
33. Poe's second review of *Barnaby Rudge*, written nine months after the first, does this to itself: he echoes his earlier words, but pitches them differently in conditional terms. The raven's croakings "might have been *prophetically* heard in the course of the drama. Its character might have performed, in regard to that of the idiot, much the same part as does, in music, the accompaniment in respect to the air. Each might have been distinct. Each might have differed remarkably from the other. Yet between them there might have been

wrought an analogical resemblance" (ER: 243). The preterite perfect conditional "might have been" indicates Poe now believed Dickens had bungled the interplay between variation and sameness that should have been the particular effect of Grip's speech: he neither differs from Barnaby nor echoes him, and thus Dickens failed to achieve his intended result, which "The Raven" would later accomplish.

Bibliography

Cohen, Lara Langer. *The Fabrication of American Literature: Fraudulence and Antebellum Print Culture*. Philadelphia: University of Pennsylvania, 2012.

Cohen, Michael C. *The Social Lives of Poems in Nineteenth-Century America*. Philadelphia: University of Pennsylvania Press, 2015.

Henkin, David M. *The Postal Age: The Emergence of Modern Communications in Nineteenth-Century America*. Chicago: University of Chicago Press, 2006.

Jackson, Leon. *The Business of Letters: Authorial Economies in Antebellum America*. Stanford, CA: Stanford University Press, 2008.

Kennedy, J. Gerald. *Strange Nation: Literary Nationalism and Cultural Conflict in the Age of Poe*. New York: Oxford University Press, 2016.

Loeffelholz, Mary. *From School to Salon: Reading Nineteenth-Century American Women's Poetry*. Princeton, NJ: Princeton University Press, 2004.

Lootens, Tricia. *The Political Poetess: Victorian Femininity, Race, and the Legacy of Separate Spheres*. Princeton, NJ: Princeton University Press, 2017.

Loughran, Trish. *The Republic in Print: Print Culture in the Age of U.S. Nation Building, 1770–1870*. New York: Columbia University Press, 2007.

McGann, Jerome. *The Poet Edgar Allan Poe: Alien Angel*. Cambridge, MA: Harvard University Press, 2014.

McGill, Meredith. *American Literature and the Culture of Reprinting, 1834–1853*. Philadelphia: University of Pennsylvania Press, 2003.

Putzi, Jennifer, and Alexandra Socarides, eds. *A History of Nineteenth-Century American Women's Poetry*. Cambridge: Cambridge University Press, 2016.

Richards, Eliza. *Gender and the Poetics of Reception in Poe's Circle*. Cambridge: Cambridge University Press, 2004.

CHAPTER 7

POE'S COMMON METER

VIRGINIA JACKSON

When Walt Whitman wrote in 1880 that "Poe's verses . . . probably belong among the electric lights of imaginative literature, brilliant and dazzling, but with no heat," he was using a newly available metaphor to describe a no-longer-available poetics.[1] Edison's light bulb had hit the streets just a year earlier, in 1879; Poe had died thirty years earlier on a gas-lit street, having produced a variety of poetry and poetic theory that (unlike most nineteenth-century American poetry) we still read and talk about, but whose own influences have been forgotten.[2] This essay will not have much to say about Poe's remarkable persistence in American poetics, since I want to focus here instead on just how thoroughly the no-longer-available poetic discourses of the nineteenth century informed Poe's verse, particularly his prosodic theory. Because nineteenth-century American prosody has not seemed very important to most accounts of American poetics (especially if we are under the illusion that Whitman liberated American poetry from dactyls and trochees by inventing free verse), we have not noticed how important it was to Poe. Indeed, Poe was so thoroughly immersed in nineteenth-century theories of poetic meter that what he wrote on the subject may serve as a guide to transatlantic Anglophone prosodic discourse in the period as a whole. Poe (of all poets) may actually help us remember why we have wanted to leave that discourse behind.

To say this is to say pretty much the opposite of what everyone since Whitman has seemed to think. "No heat" was one way of saying that Poe was a weirdo, an anomaly, if a modern one. That sort of grudging embrace of Poe as fellow modern has been repeated over and over for more than one hundred years, always in the interest of recuperating a partial failure in the past with an eye on the future of Poe's poetic illumination. As Jerome McGann has recently reminded us, Poe got the official stamp of poetic modernity from T. S. Eliot himself, even though "Eliot delivered some of the harshest comments on Poe's poetry ever written."[3] It is certainly true that the reception of Poe's poetics is full of mixed messages, but why has Poe's place in the history of American poetics been understood primarily in relation to modernism rather than in relation to the poetics that surrounded him and that (as we know from his copious reviews) he knew so well? McGann's compelling answer is that "at the heart of these problems is the modernity of

Poe's severe aesthetic formalism. . . . Poetry in his view should not be approached as a repository of ideas or an expression of feelings but as an event in language."[4] This is to say very nearly what Whitman said: an electric light bulb stranded in space ahead of its time, Poe's poetics cut language free of the nineteenth century, free of all that intellectual debate and sloppy sentiment, free of old sources of light. Both Eliot and McGann inherit this view from Baudelaire and the Symbolists, who discovered Poe as a somewhat maligned nineteenth-century American poet and returned him to literary history as an exemplary cosmopolitan *poète maudit* and modern practitioner of art for art's sake.[5] But what if Poe was not a proto-modern or an aesthetic radical or a pure formalist? What if his poetry and poetics were part and parcel of nineteenth-century American poetics, his apparently kooky prosodic theories actually highly attuned to and expressive of the rise and fall of meter?[6] What if Whitman and Eliot and the French have led us astray, or at least have led us away from the intimate relation between Poe's theories of prosody and nineteenth-century theories of prosody? It is a measure of how little we have understood the history of American poetics (or to put this another way, of how much we have needed ideas and ideals of modernism to put nineteenth-century American poetics in the shade) that we have thought that Poe was ahead of rather than very much of his place and time.

Recent scholarship has gone a long way in restoring Poe to the century in which he lived: Meredith McGill's work on Poe and print culture, Eliza Richards's work on Poe and the contemporary figure of the Poetess, Jonathan Elmer's work on Poe and mass culture, J. Gerald Kennedy's work on Poe and American nationalism (to name just four prominent examples) have brought Poe back from the brink of modernism.[7] So why has it been so difficult to think about Poe's prosody in relation to that of his contemporaries? Of course, one of the reasons that it has been hard to think about Poe as a serious theorist of nineteenth-century poetics is that it has been hard to take his essays on the theory of poetry seriously at all.[8] While late nineteenth- and twentieth-century versions of Poe's poetics tended to modernize Poe's "severe aesthetic formalism," his contemporaries at first celebrated then just laughed at his obsession with meter. Everyone likes to remember that Emerson reportedly called Poe "The Jingle Man," and James Russell Lowell delivered the coup de grace a year before Poe's death when he wrote in "A Fable for Critics" (1848),

> There comes Poe, with his raven, like Barnaby Rudge,
> Three fifths of him genius and two fifths sheer fudge,
> Who talks like a book of iambs and pentameters,
> In a way to make people of common sense damn metres,
> Who has written some things quite the best of their kind,
> But the heart somehow seems all squeezed out by the mind.[9]

That last line anticipates Whitman's heatless light bulb, but the most striking thing about Lowell's famous caricature is its focus on meter. Of all the things one could send up in Poe's published statements on poetics ("at least one half of the 'Paradise

Lost' is essentially prose," "the death . . . of a beautiful woman is, unquestionably, the most poetical topic in the world," *"for centuries, no man, in verse, has ever done, or ever seemed to think of doing, an original thing"* [ER: 15, 19, 20]), why choose to make fun of Poe's "metres"?[10] Lowell does get around to telling Poe that he "must n't fling mud-balls at Longfellow so," defending his great friend from Poe's repeated accusations of plagiarism, sloppy figuration, and metrical impropriety (to which we shall return), but the most cutting couplet here claims that Poe "talks like a book of iambs and pentameters/In a way to make people of common sense damn metres."[11] Why "in a way"? Poe, creature of print debate that he was, took up precisely this tonally slippery aspect of Lowell's jab, writing in the *Southern Literary Messenger* some months later that "Mr. L. cannot carry his frail honesty of opinion even so far South as New York. All whom he praises are Bostonians. Other writers are barbarians and satirized accordingly" (ER: 820). Lowell's Northern ways may have failed to grasp the civility of Poe's Southern ways, but it is metrical rather than regional mannerism that Poe zeroes in on when he turns to consider Lowell's "general *manner*." Sectional divisions may have carried high stakes in 1849, but apparently not as high as the stakes carried by prosody.

As an example of Lowell's ill-mannered prosodic ways, Poe actually cites exactly the earlier lines—that is, the lines on himself—and appends this note: "*We must do Mr. L. the justice to say that his book was in press before he could have seen Mr. Poe's '*Rationale of Verse*' published in this Magazine for November and December last" (ER: 820). The implication is that had Lowell been able to read Poe's most extensive essay on prosody, he would have known better than to pick a fight over meter. The backstory here is that Lowell's 1845 biographical sketch of Poe had helped to popularize the literary career his satire attacked, and the first version of the essay to which Poe refers had been published in 1843 in Lowell's magazine *The Pioneer*, so Poe knew that Lowell knew better, and he knew that Lowell did know most of his argument.[12] We shall return in a moment to both versions of Poe's late and still-neglected (indeed, often ridiculed) essay as indeed a surprisingly clear window onto the nineteenth-century prosodic landscape, but first we should consider at length the metrical show-and-tell that Poe offers Lowell as an exercise in prosodic behavioral modification:

> We may observe here that *profound* ignorance on any particular topic is always sure to manifest itself by some allusion to "common sense," as an all-sufficient instructor. So far from Mr. P's talking "like a book" on the topic at issue, his chief purpose has been to demonstrate that there exists *no* book on the subject worth talking *about*; and "common sense," after all, has been the basis on which *he* relied, in contradistinction from the *un*common nonsense of Mr. L., and the small pedants.

And now let us see how far the unusual "common sense" of our satirist has availed him in the structure of his verse. First, by way of showing what his *intention* was, we quote three accidentally accurate lines:

But a boy | he could ne | ver be right | ly defined.
As I said | he was ne | ver precise | ly unkind.
But as Ci | cero says | he won't say | this or that.

Here it is clearly seen that Mr. L. intends a line of four anapæsts. (An anapæst is a foot composed of two short syllables followed by a long.) With this observation, we will now simply copy a few of the lines which constitute the body of the poem; asking any of our readers to *read them if they can*; that is to say, we place the question, without argument, on the broad basis of the very commonest "common sense."

They're all from one source, monthly, weekly, diurnal . . .
Disperse all one's good and condense all one's poor traits . . .
The one's two-thirds Norseman, the other half Greek . . .
. . . .
Is some of it pr— no, 'tis not even prose . . .
O'er his principles when something else turns up trumps . . .
But a few silly (syllo I mean) gisms that squat 'em . . .
Nos, we don't want extra freezing in winter . . .
Plough, dig, sail, forge, build, carve, paint, make all things new . . .

But enough:—we have given a fair specimen of the *general* versification. It might have been better—but we are quite sure that it *could not have been worse*. So much for "common sense," in Mr. Lowell's understanding of the term. Mr. L. should not have meddled with the anapæstic rhythm: it is exceedingly awkward in the hands of one who knows nothing about it and who *will* persist in fancying that he can write it by ear. (ER: 820–821)

I have omitted six of the lines in Poe's long list of Lowell's metrical blunders, but you get the idea. Or do you? This long passage *seems* to suppose that the common reader will be able to see for herself that most of the lines given are not strictly anapestic, and seeing this, should be able to judge for herself that Lowell is no poet to damn another poet's meters. On one hand, Poe's appeal to your better judgment is a direct response to Lowell's couplets, since, as Jonathan Elmer points out, "Poe disturbs common sense, Lowell implies, by being both jokey and pedantic. Another way to say this is that we have the sense that we are reading a critic as much as an artist, that the two have been curiously and disconcertingly blended in Poe's overwrought productions."[13] So is prosody really a matter of common sense or of critical nitpicking? That turns out to be a pressing question, since this is not only a squabble between Poe and yet another Harvard/Cambridge (or in Poe's idiom, "Frogpondian") snob (painful as this one must have been, given Poe's history with Lowell as sponsor, biographer, publisher, and correspondent).[14] It is also a rather uncanny demonstration of the central dilemma that was just beginning to emerge in nineteenth-century transatlantic prosody: the problem of a common meter.

Why was the idea of a common meter such a problem? "Common meter" was one way of characterizing "fourteeners," or tetrameter/trimeter alternation, usually in quatrains, but that is not the sort of common meter that figures in the debates Poe was making visible. That sort of common meter (associated with both hymns and ballads) was the stuff of popular poetry (so "common" because recognizable by an emerging mass public as the expression of an idealized folk; ironically, modern readers may most easily recognize common meter by thinking of Emily Dickinson's variations on it).[15] The prosody wars to which Poe was responding in his attack on Lowell were in many ways a reaction against that sort of popular metrical recognition, since they revolved around the relation between classical (Greek and Latin) metrical discourse and English metrical theory—that is, around a set of recognitions that depended on a classical education. These debates were made of competing claims for common metrical origins, for common metrical modes of circulation, and for a common transatlantic metrical language. The "*profound* ignorance" that Poe was trying to demonstrate in Lowell was the ignorance of those debates—but also the ignorance of the right relation between accentual and quantitative prosody, between lines composed of metrical feet measured by the long or short duration of syllables (as in Greek and Latin) and lines measured by the accent and stress of the syllables thought to compose those metrical feet (often the accent and stress attributed to a native English speaker). That there could be no such relation, no perfect adjustment between counting and hearing, between ancient inheritance and modern use, between the fantasy of common origin and the reality of common reading, was a fact that neither nineteenth-century prosodists in general nor Poe in particular wanted to admit. The problem of a meter based on "common sense" emerges here from the problem of identifying the common ground from which that meter would emerge. Attempts to locate that common ground were at the heart of nineteenth-century prosodic discourse, so rather than an eccentric concern, the question of whether any poet in English could write "by ear" was very much the question of the moment.

Or actually, the question of the moment was not anyone's English or Anglo-American *ear* so much as it was everyone's worry that there was no common metrical language to which that ear might attend—especially if it needed to extend across the Atlantic. The British debate over the relation of vernacular English prosody to classical meters had begun in the eighteenth century, when, as John Guillory has written, "the institutional lag between Latin and vernacular literacy" began to produce new theories of prosody that became associated with Romanticism.[16] By the 1840s, the relation between quantitative classical metrical theory and vernacular or accentual theory had become a subject of national importance in England. As Yopie Prins puts it, "with the rise of the British empire, as England was struggling to accommodate foreignness both within and beyond its national borders, the consolidation of a common language out of heterogeneous elements seemed especially urgent."[17] According to Prins, "debates about translating dactylic hexameter—the metrical form associated with classical epic—were closely linked to the formation of a national literary culture" in the Victorian period.[18] For Arnold, Coleridge, Tennyson, and a host of British men of letters, the task of creating an English hexameter became the task of creating what Prins calls "a metrical imaginary," an ideal meter that would make English the inheritor of a common Western tradition rather than a fragment of an *un*common (as Poe might say) discordant present. What came to be called "the hexameter mania" in mid-nineteenth-century England turned into a series of arguments for and against the assimilation of Greek and Latin meters that were counted into English meters that could be heard *as* English, that "might redeem the confusion of the present time by making hexameter into an English form, and a perfect form of Englishness." If classical ideals could be grafted onto English society by means of metrical translation, Prins argues, "the function of hexameter at the present time would be to measure the distance between culture and anarchy."[19] Matthew Arnold's famous lectures *On Translating Homer* (1861–1862) were exemplary of his creation of a hexameter metrical imaginary in nineteenth-century England because in them Arnold claimed to find both a common Western classical past and a common British future, an English accentual meter firmly grounded in a civilized origin one could count on. "And yet," as Meredith Martin points out, "just as poets and prosodists were invested in these attempts to create new or adequate meters for England, so too were they aware of the increasing anxiety over meter's failure to provide an accessible form of national identification."[20] What if readers failed to recognize these meters as their own?

Arnold's answer was that British readers must be educated to do so, but over a decade earlier, Poe had proposed a different answer. When Poe asked his readers to look at Lowell's anapests and "*read them if they can*," he was asking them to scan Lowell's lines "without argument, on the broad basis of the very commonest 'common sense.' " How would such scansion be possible without an elite classical education? By concluding that "Mr. L. should not have meddled with the anapæstic rhythm" since "it is exceedingly awkward in the hands of one who knows nothing about it and who *will* persist in fancying that he can write it by ear," Poe seems to anticipate Arnold's appeal to quantitative meter as the common ground of English verse (ER: 821). The mannered Latin dipthong in Poe's spelling of "anapæstic" is one giveaway, as is his dismissal of metrical composition "by ear," that is, by accent and stress. In "The Rationale of Verse," the prosodic treatise that Poe laments Lowell did not read, Poe claims that despite the "inaccuracy, confusion, misconception, misrepresentation, mystification, and downright ignorance" of the great majority of prosodic discussion, "in fact the subject is exceedingly simple; one tenth of it, possibly, may be called ethical; nine tenths, however, appertain to the mathematics; and the whole is included within the limits of the commonest common sense" (ER: 26). Poe goes further than Arnold, indeed further than anyone in the accentual-quantitative debates that occupied most of the nineteenth century, to close the gap between accent and duration, vernacular literacy and classical training, since unlike Arnold, Poe does not appeal to higher learning but appeals instead to what anyone should know if she knows how to count, to "the commonest common" shared knowledge. Even Murray's *Grammar* (originally printed in 1795 and reprinted so often in the nineteenth century that it sold a staggering sixteen million copies in the United States and four million in Britain) had relied on Sheridan's definition of English versification translated into accents from Latin quantities: "In English, syllables are divided into accented and unaccented; and the accented syllables being as strongly distinguished from the unaccented, by the peculiar stress of the voice upon them, are equally capable of marking the movement, and pointing out the regular paces of the voice, as the long syllables were, by their quantity, among the Romans."[21] In contrast, Poe's version of versification does not need to do what everyone between Murray and Arnold and well into the late nineteenth century tried to do: it does not need to accommodate English accent to classical quantity. Poe simply claims that quantity and accent are and always were the same thing.

Not accidentally, Poe makes this astonishing claim in relation to the English hexameter. His passing swipe at Lowell's anapests was also deeply informed by contemporary prosody, since as he well knew—at least since the late eighteenth century, when Campbell wrote in his *Philosophy of Rhetoric* that "the anapæst is capable, according as it is applied, of two effects extremely different . . . ease and familiarity" but also "hurry, confusion, and precipitation"—anapests were considered notoriously tricky to scan.[22] Asking the common reader to tell good from bad anapests was a mischievous request, but when it came to proving that all of the elaborate adaptations of quantity to accent that preoccupied prosodists of the nineteenth century were beside the point because the subject comes down to simple math and common sense, Poe chose to make his argument on the basis of the hexameter. Poe thus joined the great hexameter debate, yet unlike Arnold and other participants in the British "hexameter mania," Poe did not try to turn the English hexameter into a national metrical imaginary—or perhaps it would be better to say that an accessible metrical form of national identification does not at first *appear* to be Poe's main concern, since the "commonest common sense" would seem to preclude national and political concerns.

The first version of "The Rationale of Verse" in 1843 was actually called "Notes Upon English Verse," a review of a recent reprint of the American English grammarian Goold Brown's *The Institutes of English Grammar* (1823). Poe begins by citing Brown's definition of versification: "Versification is the art of arranging words into lines of correspondent length, so as to produce harmony by the regular alternation of syllables differing in quantity" (ER: 28).[23] Poe immediately objects to this definition on the ground that "Versification is not the art of arranging &c., but the actual arranging—a distinction too obvious to need comment" (ER: 28). The reductive pragmatism of such assertions in both versions of the essay has led later critics to think that Poe either didn't know what he was talking about or that he was "insisting," as McGann writes, "that if poetic verse is to be scanned at all, it should be scanned for oral performance rather than some theoretical verse correctness."[24] But when Poe claims that "while much has been written on the Greek and Latin rhythms, and even on Hebrew, little effort has been made at examining that of any of the modern tongues," and goes on to say that "as regards the English, comparatively nothing has been done" and even that "it may be said, indeed, that we are without a treatise on our own verse" (ER: 27), he is clearing a very cluttered field devoted to theories of verse correctness rather than admitting his ignorance of the quantitative/accentual debates or placing all his cards on the side of English accent. On the contrary, Poe's way of proposing a theory of verse correctness was to correct the correctors, beginning with the innocuous Brown. He thus goes on to deconstruct each part of Brown's apparently innocent definition, objecting that "a correspondence in the length of lines is by no means essential," that "*harmony* is not the sole aim—not even the principal one," and that "a *regular* alternation . . . forms no part of any principle of versification" (ER: 29).

How can we tell that Poe is right and that Brown (and everyone else) is wrong? Just look, Poe suggests, at "the arrangement of spondees and dactyls, for example, in the Greek hexameter" (ER: 29). Like Arnold after him, Poe invoked the hexameter as the line that "might redeem the confusion of the present time," but while for Arnold that confusion could be addressed, as Prins writes, "by making hexameter into an English form, and a perfect form of Englishness," for Poe that confusion could be addressed by making hexameter into a form of "the very commonest 'common sense.'"

If hexameters do not seem to most readers matters of common sense, that fact is unsurprising. By taking a definition of English versification back to Greek, Poe was on one hand merely flaunting his own classical education to shred the last phrase in Brown's sentence: "by the regular alternation of *syllables differing in quantity*" (ER: 28, emphasis mine). On the other hand, Poe also understood what later readers of Poe have not understood: whenever versification became a question of quantity, the accentual/quantitative debates were in the room. Poe's way of welcoming them is to ask us to read five lines in Latin:

> Here is a passage from Silius Italicus:
>
> Fallis te mensas inter quod credis inermem
> Tot bellis quæsita viro, tot cædibus armat
> Majestas eterna ducem: si admoveris ora
> Cannas et Terbium ante oculos Trasymenaque busta,
> Et Pauli stare ingentem miraberis umbrum. (ER: 30)

Poe then goes on to show us how to count the Latin even if we can't read it:

> Making the elisions demanded by the classic Prosodies, we should scan these Hexameters thus:
>
> Fāllīs | tē mēn | sās īn | tēr qūod | crēdĭs ĭn | ērmēm |
> Tōt bēl | līs qūæ | sītă vĭ | rō tōt | cædĭbŭs | ārmāt |
> Mājēs | tās ē | tērnă dŭ | cēm s'ād | mōvĕrĭs | ōrā |
> Cānnās | ēt Trĕbī | ānt' ŏcŭ | lōs Trăsy̆ | mēnăquĕ | būstā
> ēt Pāu | lī stā | r'īngēn | tēm mī | rābĕrĭs | ūmbrām | (ER: 30)

Even if we can't read the Latin in the first instance, we can *count* the Latin hexameter once it is no longer exactly Latin, or once it looks like the six-part graphic of the second instance where, "it will be seen," Poe affirms, "that, in the first and last of these lines, we have only two short syllables in thirteen, with an uninterrupted succession of no less than *nine* long syllables" (ER: 30). He gives no translation or interpretation of the sense of the lines themselves, asking instead how we are "to reconcile all this [that is, all these irregular metrical feet] with a definition of versification which describes it as 'the art of arranging words into lines of correspondent length so as to produce harmony by the *regular alternation of syllables differing in quantity*?'" (ER: 30). We are not to do so, of course, and so Poe has proven his point—or really, *we* have proven his point by seeing for ourselves that two syllables in thirteen marked by commas on their backs or nine syllables in a row marked by a superscripted dash over those syllables' heads indicate neither regular alternation nor regular difference in quantity. Seeing hexameters is believing hexameters, especially if we are willing to grant that Poe has scanned properly according to "the classic Prosodies."[25] We are more liable to grant that than to read such prosodies ourselves, and Poe counts on that (so to speak) when he grants in turn that his Latin example may be out of line, since "it may be urged . . . that our prosodist's *intention* was to speak of the English metres alone" (ER: 30). If that were really Brown's intention, then presumably the specter of classical quantity would disappear altogether, but Poe's answer to this possibility is to insist instead that all of the English prosodists who claim to reject classical prosody actually rely on it, since "in fact the English prosodists have blindly followed the pedants" when it comes to scanning (you guessed it) dactylic hexameter (ER: 32).

Poe anticipates Arnold and the British hexameter debates when he makes the hexameter the test case for English prosody, but his reason for doing so, he claims, is the reverse of their reasons for doing so, since the English prosodists,

> like *les moutons de Panurge*, have been occupied in incessant tumbling into ditches, for the excellent reason that their leaders have so tumbled before. The Iliad, being taken as a starting point, was made to stand in stead of Nature and common sense. Upon this poem, in place of facts and deductions from fact, or from natural law, were built systems of feet, metres, rhythms, rules,—rules that contradict each other every five minutes, and for nearly all of which may be found twice as many exceptions as examples. (ER: 32)

So why isn't Poe's use of the hexameter as a standard for correct scansion just another example of a rogue sheep jumping after the others, another Rabelaisian caricature, another vain attempt to adjust modern accent to classical quantity?[26] The answer to this question is so odd that it is not surprising that even the few scholars who have taken "The Rationale of Verse" seriously as a prosodic treatise have missed it. Whereas those few scholars have thought that Poe wants to reclaim accent and "oral performance" from dusty archival longs and shorts, in fact Poe doubles down on quantity as the lesson classical prosody can still teach us. Poe's common-sense solution to all of the contradictions rampant in all of the prosodies, whether English, Greek, or Latin, is to make quantity equivalent to accent. While the proponents of accentual-syllabic scansion emphasized (and still emphasize) how one pronounces each syllable as the basis of shared metrical apprehension, Poe suggests that it is actually *quantity* that provides the basis of modern mutual collective recognition, of a common metrical language.

Perhaps the reason we have not seen this is that the quantitative side of the hexameter debate was the losing side. In England, George Saintsbury's multivolume *A History of English Prosody* (1906–1910) marked the decisive moment when English accent won out over classical quantity, when the nineteenth-century prosody debates could be declared over and done. As Meredith Martin has shown, that victory was also the victory of the state-funded classroom, where students might not be expected to know their Latin and Greek but "if a student is blessed with an English ear, then he has access to the glories of English meter."[27] As Martin has also shown, to call the triumph of accent a "victory" or a "triumph" is a way of echoing the martial nationalism "the glories of English meter" came to represent for the British Empire. In this long transatlantic context, Poe's attempt to turn quantity into the basis for contemporary metrical apprehension might be an all-too-characteristic reductio ad adsurdum, though it is also tempting to read it as a species of American pragmatism, a departure from the English nationalist ideology Poe might have seen coming. However we interpret it, Poe's emphasis on quantity instantly solves—or appears to solve—the accentual/quantitative debates over half a century before Saintsbury thought he did, since accent disappears entirely from Poe's concern, and so nationality seems to disappear from prosody.

Unlike Arnold and so many other British prosodists who wanted to find the perfect accents to make the ancient hexameter into English verse, Poe wants the hexameter's dependence on quantitative scansion to ground a "true rhythm" that would not be English or Greek or German or Latin or Sanskrit or Spanish or Icelandic or Ojibwe or American—that would be instead (like the contemporary "discovery" of the Indo-European root) a prosodic philology that could be traced back to a prenational or antinational common source. "*Ex uno disce Omnia*," Poe writes, now channeling the authority of Latin for what is anything but a classical idea:

> The fact is that *Quantity* is a point in whose investigation the lumber of learning may be dispensed with, if ever in any. Its appreciation is universal. It appertains to no region, nor race, nor æra in especial. To melody and to harmony the Greeks hearkened with ears precisely similar to those which we employ for similar purposes at present; and I should not be condemned for heresy in asserting that a pendulum at Athens would have vibrated much after the same fashion as does a pendulum in the city of Penn.
>
> *Verse* originates in the human enjoyment of equality, fitness. (ER: 32–33)

So much for "the English ear"—or for Latin or Greek numbers, for that matter. Whereas the modern story of prosody has been told as a narrative of progress from classical elite education to vernacular familiarity, of the liberation of verse from "the lumber of learning" classical longs and shorts, of the replacement of artificial rules with natural intuition, Poe decides the direction of the history of prosody in another direction: it all comes down to quantity, which unlike accent, "appertains to no region, nor race, nor æra in especial." The fact that the idea of quantitative scansion was the product of the history of classical learning is more than an irony here: Poe actually wants to use the idea of a universal quantitative imaginary against the very historical discourse that produced it. As we have seen, that discourse emerged from and was indebted to fantasies of national identity, but Poe goes out of his way to define his unaccented common metrical fantasy as unmarked by nationality, history, and race. It is this unmarking that embeds Poe's idea in the very debates he wanted to reject, since only in the context of nationalizing and racializing claims about meter does such a statement vibrate in their fashion. The "hexameter mania" of England may have been worried about empire, but Poe, like everyone else in the United States in 1848, was worried about race—though "worried" is not quite the right word here, since it makes the racial imaginary of Poe's prosodic discourse sound intentional.[28] I am suggesting instead that Poe's insistence that quantity could be a universal basis for metrical (especially rhythmic) apprehension registers the anxiety of his moment in the way that the hexameter mania and later accentual/quantitative debates registered anxieties in the British Empire. But the difference between national identification and racial disidentification is a real difference, so to accommodate that difference, Poe's use of the hexameter as exemplary shifts suddenly from issues of number and accent to the rather odd statement that "verse originates in the human enjoyment of equality" (ER: 33).

It is not hard to see how "equality" might be one name for the transcultural and transhistorical prosodic arc that Poe wants to propose, but as soon as he introduces the word, it takes over, displacing the abstraction of pure "Quantity" and causing his argument that scansion is as easy as counting to waver: "As there are some readers who habitually confound rhythm and metre, it may be as well here to say that the former concerns the *character* of feet (that is, the arrangement of syllables) while the latter has to do with the *number* of these feet. Thus by 'a dactylic *rhythm*' we express a sequence of dactyls. By 'a dactylic hexa*meter*' we imply a line or measure consisting of six of these dactyls" (ER: 33). By separating meter from rhythm, Poe begins to follow the prosodic sheep he has just caricatured, since the relation between a meter that may be measured and a rhythm that may be felt as a larger pattern was the stuff of prosodic discourse from the early modern period through modernism, as Derek Attridge and many other scholars have pointed out.[29] As these scholars have also argued, the problem with the distinction is its cultural relativism: everyone can count six dactyls, but who can feel the "character" of their rhythm? To whom do such rhythms come naturally or culturally? To whom do they appeal? The "vibrations" of the pendulum in Athens may be equivalent to the vibrations of the pendulum in Philadelphia, but were they both heard as liberty bells? Poe's choice of two cities credited with the birth of democracy does not seem incidental, especially when he identifies the principle their equivalence expresses as "equality." Yet the distinction between meter and rhythm disturbs the purely quantitative idea of equality it is meant to prove. While in the Latin example we are not given a choice between *character* and *number*, the idea of a common quantitative basis for prosody that rests on "the human enjoyment of equality" introduces such a choice, and that choice complicates the idea of quantitative common sense considerably.

But then again, the idea of "equality" *is* complicated. As Pierre Ronsanvallon shows in *The Society of Equals*, "the crisis of equality" that is currently widening the economic and racial divides of what were once thought of as the world's great democracies "has a lengthy history."[30] At the beginning of that history, in the American and French revolutions, equality was "understood primarily as a relation, as a way of making a society, of producing and living in common." That relation was often expressed as a relation of similarity, sometimes defined on the basis of Leibniz's "definition of similarity: things are similar if the only intrinsic difference between them is one of quantity. Identity of quantity implies equality, but identity of quality defines similarity. This made it possible to rethink relations among human beings, although it would prove difficult to find suitable social terms in which to express this new definition: in both the United States and France, 'equality' was the only generic term to convey the urgency of defining a new world of similar individuals."[31] In Poe's prosodic theory, "equality" is similarly the only generic term that conveys the urgency of defining a new common prosody, but as in the democracies for which the term was foundational, equality turns out to be impossible for poetry to achieve, especially since in poetry, "equality" (unlike dactyls, iambs, anapests, and trochees) is not a generic term, that is, not a term of mutual collective recognition. Equality, *pace* Leibniz, is not something on which a lot of people in 1848 could count, though readers of the *Southern Literary Messenger* may not have wanted to count those people as equals to be counted.

So when Poe begins this section on quantity in "The Rationale of Verse" by accusing "the German Greek Prosodies" of "a very magnificent contempt for Leibniz's principle of 'a sufficient reason,' " he is accusing an undemocratic culture of not understanding that prosody must adhere to democratic principles of common sense (ER: 32). Yet by invoking Leibniz and quantity as the foundation for his definition of prosodic equality, Poe was also emphasizing the way in which similarity could no longer work as a definition of equality in the middle of the nineteenth century. If identity of quantity implies equality (as in our common recognition of the quantitative division of the hexameter lines from Silius Italicus), then it remains a problem for Poe that the corollary proposition that "identity of quality proves similarity" is a harder prosodic sell (since the "quality" of a line is more difficult to show-and-tell than its quantity). In response to this difficulty, Poe tries to insist that equality is inherent in quantity rather than quality by suggesting that "the rudiment of verse may, possibly, be found in the *spondee*," that is, in a two-syllable foot in which each syllable has the same duration (ER: 34). "The very germ of thought seeking satisfaction in equality of sound," Poe writes, "would result in the construction of words of two syllables, equally accented" (ER: 34). In the spondee, of all measures, quantity and accent, thought and sound, number and character, quantity and quality can be rendered equivalent. Such a foot would formally perform the equality that was proving so socially precarious half a century after the American and French revolutions, in the midst of the new calls for "equality" in the great European revolutions of 1848.[32] But like the political history his discourse mirrors, Poe cannot make the ideal of prosodic equality stick. He experiments for many pages with what he calls "various systems of equalization" in various meters, surveying Latin, Greek, British, and American verse along the way, until he arrives back at "the heroic hexameter" (ER: 67). In the hexameter above all, Poe concludes, we can test "the validity of [his] suggestion that the spondee was the first approach to verse," since "we should expect to find, first, natural spondees, (words each forming just a spondee,) most abundant in the ancient languages, and secondly, we should expect to find spondees forming the basis of the most ancient rhythms. These expectations are in both cases confirmed" (ER: 67).[33] Like Arnold after him, Poe ended by discovering in dactylic hexameter a perfect form—but while Arnold discovered in the hexameter a perfect form of Englishness, Poe claimed to discover a perfect form of the equality that by 1848 had already proven too fragile for America to sustain. For Poe, the hexameter became an idealized medium for the poetic equality of the spondee at a moment when the United States was less and less an ideal medium for social equality—when slavery, the most violent form of inequality, was about to split the country along the unequal regional lines to which Poe drew attention in his response to Lowell.

In order to construct this ideal form of equality within the hexameter, Poe needs to rewrite all the prosodies by shifting the focus in hexameter scansion from the dactyl to the spondee: "Of the Greek hexameter, the intentional basis is spondaic. The dactyls are the *variation* of the theme. It will be observed that there is no certainty about *their* points of interposition" (ER: 67). While one might point out that epic meter is always called "dactylic" and never "spondaic," Poe responds by arguing that "the penultimate foot, it is true, is usually a dactyl; but not uniformly so; while the ultimate, on which the ear *lingers* is always a spondee. Even that the penultimate is usually a dactyl may be clearly referred to the necessity of winding up with the *distinctive* spondee" (ER: 67–68). If the spondee is the fundamental basis of hexameter, then the basis of ancient meter is the principle of equality. This is so much the case that "spondees are not only more prevalent in the heroic hexameter than dactyls, but occur to such an extent as is even unpleasant to modern ears" (ER: 68). So perhaps we have overlooked hexameter's dependence on the spondee because modern readers are no longer attuned to the idea of equality. In the 1848 version of Poe's essay (the one that Lowell didn't have a chance to read), the modern failure to appreciate the hexameter as expressive of the ideal of equality has a proper name: Henry Wadsworth Longfellow.

The popular success of Longfellow's narrative poem in dactylic hexameter, *Evangeline: A Tale of Acadie* (1847), was a sore point for Poe, who had launched a series of attacks on Longfellow's institutional prestige between 1839 and 1845, which ended when Poe accused Longfellow of being "not only a servile imitator, but a most insolent literary thief" (ER: 777). *Evangeline* was a sore point for Arnold, too, who considered Longfellow's hexameters "much too dactylic," as Prins writes, "a debasement of English hexameter by an American poet who had been parodied in the press as 'Professor Long-and-short-fellow.' "[34] Poe was certainly not alone, then, in finding Longfellow's dactylic hexameters too facile, but he was alone in locating the major flaw of Longfellow's notorious meter in its failure to rely on the spondee as a principle of equality. Poe includes Sir Philip Sidney with Longfellow and "innumerable other persons more or less modern" who

> have busied themselves in constructing what they supposed to be "English hexameters on the model of the Greek." The only difficulty was that (even leaving out of question the melodious masses of vowel,) these gentlemen could never get their

> hexameters to *sound* Greek. Did they *look* Greek?—that should have been the query; and the reply might have led to the solution of the riddle. (ER: 68)

Here Poe returns at the end of his essay to his opening invitation to his reader to judge Latin hexameters by looking at rather than reading them. This time Poe suggests "placing a copy of ancient hexameters side by side with a copy (in similar type) of such hexameters as Professor Longfellow, or Professor Felton, or the Frogpondian Professors collectively, are in the shameful practice of composing 'on the model of the Greek,' [and] it will be seen that the latter (hexameters, not professors) are about one third longer *to the eye*, on an average, than the former" (ER: 68–69). The classicist Cornelius Conway Felton, friend of Longfellow and later president of Harvard, joins Longfellow in Poe's long list of pedants who defy common sense: you don't need to read Greek to compare their pages to Greek pages in order to see that their hexameters are too long. "The more abundant dactyls make the difference," Poe explains, since "these eminent scholars" don't seem to understand that the hexameter "is a spondaic rhythm varied now and then by dactyls" rather than the other way around (ER: 69). Why does that matter? Because "even when we let these modern hexameters go, . . . we must still condemn them as having committed a radical misconception of the philosophy of verse. The spondee, as I observed is the *theme* of the Greek line. . . . The ear is filled with it as with a burden" (ER: 70). What the professors forget is that prosody needs to invoke the idea of human equality as song. It is a beautiful idea, but is it possible in English? Poe ends by accepting the challenge of composing hexameters that feature spondees over dactyls, and I am sorry to say that this is the result:

> Do tell! | when may we | hope to make | men of sense | out of the | Pundits|
> Born and brought | up with their | snouts deep | down in the | mud of the | Frog-pond?
> Why ask? | who ever | yet saw | money made | out of a | fat old—
> Jew, or | downright | upright | nutmegs | out of a | pine-knot? | (ER: 70)

Poe may be right that "the proper spondee predominance is preserved" in these lines, but they certainly do not express the idea of equality as a result (ER: 70). Anyone with common sense will reject the ugly sentiment of the last lines, even if they are stuffed full of spondees. What "The Rationale of Verse" ends by proving is not that quantity is universal or that the spondee is the perfect expression of the idea of equality or that dactylic hexameter is actually essentially spondaic. What Poe's most scandalous prosodic essay does prove beyond a doubt is that the enormous intellectual energy devoted to prosodic discourse throughout the nineteenth century was not all about distinguishing longs from shorts, spondees from dactyls, accent from quantity, English from Greek, pedant from poet. It was about nationality, about race, about equality, about politics, about gender, about what it meant and still means to be human, and yes, it was about poetry. It also proves that Poe was not an electric light bulb stranded in space ahead of his time nor was he a severe aesthetic formalist. His poetics were snout-deep in the mud of nineteenth-century prosodic debate, and so reading Poe on prosody is a good way of beginning to see that a lot of that mud still clings to our feet.

Notes

1. Walt Whitman, "Edgar Poe's Significance," in *Specimen Days and Collect*, in *Walt Whitman: Poetry and Prose*, ed. Justin Kaplan (New York: Library of America, 1996), 897.
2. For Edison's light bulb as signifier of modernity, see Theresa M. Collins and Lisa Gitelman, *Thomas Edison and Modern America: A Brief History with Documents* (New York: Bedford/St. Martins, 2002). So many of Poe's influences have been forgotten that it is impossible to list them here, but for a good start, see Eliza Richards, *Gender and the Poetics of Reception in Poe's Circle* (Cambridge: Cambridge University Press, 2004).
3. Jerome McGann, *The Poet Edgar Allan Poe: Alien Angel* (Cambridge, MA: Harvard University Press, 2014), 1. While I disagree with McGann's reading of Poe's poetics as Anglocentric and proto-modernist, his book will make the study of Poe's poetics possible in new ways.
4. McGann, *The Poet Edgar Allan Poe*, 2.
5. See T. S. Eliot, "From Poe to Valéry," *Hudson Review* 2, no. 3 (Autumn, 1949): 327–342.
6. Meredith Martin's *The Rise and Fall of Meter: Poetry and English National Culture, 1860–1930* (Princeton, NJ: Princeton University Press, 2012) traces various nineteenth-century British discourses about prosody in order to question "our assumption that 'English meter' was and is a stable category" (1). If there were such a book about this assumption in American poetics, Poe's prosody would occupy a long chapter in it.
7. See Meredith McGill, *American Literature and the Culture of Reprinting, 1834–1853* (Philadelphia: University of Pennsylvania Press, 2003); Eliza Richards, *Gender and the Poetics of Reception in Poe's Circle* (Cambridge: Cambridge University Press, 2004); Jonathan Elmer, *Reading at the Social Limit: Affect, Mass Culture, & Edgar Allan Poe* (Stanford, CA: Stanford University Press, 1995); J. Gerald Kennedy, *Strange Nation: Literary Nationalism and Cultural Conflict in the Age of Poe* (Oxford: Oxford University Press, 2016).
8. As Barbara Johnson wrote of "The Philosophy of Composition," Poe's most famous essay on poetics "has been read as a theoretical spoof which, because it cannot be taken at face value, cannot be taken seriously at all" ("Strange Fits: Poe and Wordsworth on the Nature of Poetic Language," in *A World of Difference* [Baltimore and London: The Johns Hopkins University Press, 1987], 89).
9. James Russell Lowell, *A Fable for Critics, in The Poetical Works of James Russell Lowell*, vol. 3 (Boston: Houghton, Mifflin, and Company, 1890), 72. This complete edition of Lowell even features a portrait of Poe to illustrate the lines. William Dean Howells claims that Emerson called Poe "the jingle man," and the report has stuck; see Edwin Watts Stubb, *Stories of Authors British and American* (London: Sturgis and Walton Company, 1910), 285.
10. All of these outrageous claims are from "The Philosophy of Composition," an essay that Lowell clearly knows well because it begins with an allusion to Dickens's *Barnaby Rudge*, to which Lowell then alludes in turn.
11. Poe's increasingly savage reviews of Longfellow between 1839 and 1845 became known as "the little Longfellow war" (a phrase coined by Poe himself). Some of the defenses of Longfellow, signed "Outis" (Greek for "no one"), were thought to have been written by Lowell. See ER: 670–777.

12. See Meredith McGill, "Poe, Literary Nationalism, and Authorial Identity," in *The American Face of Edgar Allan Poe*, ed. Shawn Rosenheim and Stephen Rachman (Baltimore: The Johns Hopkins University Press, 1995), 271–304.
13. Jonathan Elmer, *Reading at the Social Limit: Affect, Mass Culture, & Edgar Allan Poe* (Stanford, CA: Stanford University Press, 1995), 33.
14. On Poe's reliance on and connection with Lowell, see Meredith McGill, "Poe, Literary Nationalism, and Authorial Identity" and Poe's reviews of Lowell, ER: 809–822. In *The Poet Edgar Allan Poe*, McGann reprints an entire 1844 letter from Poe to Lowell as one of Poe's most important treatises on his own poetics (53–66).
15. On common meter as the representation of a vanished folk, see Michael Cohen, "Popular Ballads: Rhythmic Remediations in the Nineteenth Century," in *Meter Matters: Verse Cultures of the Long Nineteenth Century*, ed. Jason David Hill (Athens: Ohio University Press, 2011), 196–2016.
16. See John Guillory, "Mute Inglorious Miltons: Gray, Wordsworth, and the Vernacular Canon," in *Cultural Capital: The Problem of Literary Canon Formation* (Chicago: The University of Chicago Press, 1993), 85–133.
17. Yopie Prins, "Metrical Translation: Nineteenth-Century Homers and the Hexameter Mania," in *Nation, Language, and the Ethics of Translation*, ed. Sandra Bermann and Michael Wood (Princeton, NJ: Princeton University Press, 2005), 229.
18. Prins, "Metrical Translation," 229.
19. Prins, "Metrical Translation," 239, 230.
20. Meredith Martin, *The Rise and Fall of Meter*, 5.
21. Lindley Murray, *English Grammar Adapted*, 4th ed. (York, UK: Wilson, Spence, and Mawman, 1798). As Meredith Martin points out, this text is identical in all following editions; it appears in the sixth American edition *English Grammar Comprehending the Principles and Rules of the Language* (New York: Collins and Co., 1829), 252, and the fifty-eighth edition (London: Longman, Hurst, 1867), 203. See Meredith Martin, "Prosody Wars," in *Meter Matters*, 259n22.
22. George Campbell, *The Philosophy of Rhetoric*, rev. ed. (London: Printed for William Baynes and Son, Paternoster Row, 1823), 357, https://babel.hathitrust.org/cgi/pt?id=wu.89001837004;view=1up;seq=8. Accessed via *Princeton Prosody Archive*, ed. Meredith Martin, Center for Digital Humanities, Princeton University, https://prosody.princeton.edu/?q=record/007654441. This citation (and really, this essay) testifies to how essential Meredith Martin's amazing Princeton Prosody Archive will be for a new generation of scholars who can now pursue the study of historical prosody that Yopie Prins and Martin have invented. See https://prosody.princeton.edu.
23. Goold Brown, *The Institutes of English Grammar, Methodically Arranged: With Examples for Parsing, Questions for Examination, False Syntax for Correction, Exercises for Writing, Observations for the Advanced Student, and a Key to the Oral Exercises: To Which Are Added, Four Appendixes: Designed for the Use of Schools.*, rev. ed. (New York: Samuel S. & William Wood, 1832), https://babel.hathitrust.org/cgi/pt?id=wu.89090360322;view=1up;seq=7. Accessed via Princeton Prosody Archive, ed. Meredith Martin, Center for Digital Humanities, Princeton University, https://prosody.princeton.edu/record/009392141?s=. The 1844 edition of this book is actually prefaced by a notice by Poe: Brown, *The Institutes of English Grammar*, rev. ed. (New York: Samuel S. & William Wood, 1844), 6, https://babel.hathitrust.org/cgi/pt?id=wu.89090360363;view=1up;seq=11). Accessed via Princeton Prosody Archive, ed. Meredith Martin, Center for Digital Humanities, Princeton University, https://prosody.princeton.edu/?q=record/009392140.

24. McGann, *The Poet Edgar Allan* Poe, 78. McGann has been misled here by "the cognitive psychologist and acoustic-learning scholar Christopher Aruffo," who argues for the oral performative aspect of "The Rational of Verse" in "Reconsidering Poe's 'Rationale of Verse,'" *Poe Studies: History, Theory, Interpretation* 44 (2011): 69–86. Aruffo takes no account of the nineteenth-century prosody wars.
25. Poe's Latin scansion is especially indebted to the classical scholar Charles Anthon, a professor at Columbia with whom Poe initiated a correspondence. See Charles Anthon, *A System of Latin Versification: In a Series of Progressive Exercises, Including Specimens of Translation from English and German Poetry into Latin Verse: For the Use of Schools and Colleges* (New York: Harper and Brothers, 1845).
26. The sheep of Panurge followed one another blindly into the water; the allusion is to François Rabelais's *Gargantua and Pantagruel* (1532–1552). As G. R. Thompson notes, "this is a recurrent reference in Poe's criticism" (ER: 1495).
27. Martin, "Prosody Wars," 254.
28. For a beginning on the vast question of Poe and race, see the essays included in *Romancing the Shadow: Poe and Race*, ed. J. Gerald Kennedy and Liliane Weissberg (Oxford: Oxford University Press, 2001).
29. See Derek Attridge, *Poetic Rhythm: An Introduction* (Cambridge: Cambridge University Press, 1996) and the essays in *Critical Rhythm: The Poetics of a Literary Life Form*, ed. Ben Glaser and Jonathan Culler (New York: Fordham University Press, forthcoming 2018).
30. Pierre Rosanvallon, *Society of Equals*, trans. Arthur Goldhammer (Cambridge, MA: Harvard University Press, 2013), 9.
31. Rosanvallon, *Society of Equals*, 30.
32. As Rosanvallon writes, "If Americans brought the idea of equality down to earth by embedding it in social life, the French projected it into the political sphere throughout the nineteenth century" (*Society of Equals*, 72).
33. Rosanvallon's history of the relation between American and French invocations of "equality" helps to explain Poe's long digression at this point in the essay on the essentially spondaic nature of French versification. It would be interesting to think about the French Symbolists' reception of Poe as the inventor of a rhythm that he himself attributed to the French, but that is another essay.
34. Prins, "Metrical Translation," 238.

Bibliography

Brown, Goold. *The Institutes of English Grammar, Methodically Arranged: With Examples for Parsing, Questions for Examination, False Syntax for Correction, Exercises for Writing, Observations for the Advanced Student, and a Key to the Oral Exercises: To Which Are Added, Four Appendixes: Designed for the Use of Schools*. Revised edition. New York: Samuel S. & William Wood, 1832. https://babel.hathitrust.org/cgi/pt?id=wu.89090360322;view=1up;seq=7.

Cohen, Michael. "Popular Ballads: Rhythmic Remediations in the Nineteenth Century." In *Meter Matters: Verse Cultures of the Long Nineteenth Century*, edited by Jason David Hill, 196–216. Athens: Ohio University Press, 2011.

Elmer, Jonathan. *Reading at the Social Limit: Affect, Mass Culture, & Edgar Allan Poe*. Stanford, CA: Stanford University Press, 1995.

Johnson, Barbara. "Strange Fits: Poe and Wordsworth on the Nature of Poetic Language." In *A World of Difference*, 89–99. Baltimore: The Johns Hopkins University Press, 1987.

Kennedy, J. Gerald. *Strange Nation: Literary Nationalism and Cultural Conflict in the Age of Poe*. Oxford: Oxford University Press, 2016.
Martin, Meredith. *The Rise and Fall of Meter: Poetry and English National Culture, 1860–1930*. Princeton, NJ: Princeton University Press, 2012.
McGann, Jerome. *The Poet Edgar Allan Poe: Alien Angel*. Cambridge, MA: Harvard University Press, 2014.
McGill, Meredith. *American Literature and the Culture of Reprinting, 1834–1853*. Philadelphia: University of Pennsylvania Press, 2003.
McGill, Meredith. "Poe, Literary Nationalism, and Authorial Identity." In *The American Face of Edgar Allan Poe*, edited by Shawn Rosenheim and Stephen Rachman, 271–304. Baltimore: The Johns Hopkins University Press, 1995.
Prins, Yopie. "Metrical Translation: Nineteenth-Century Homers and the Hexameter Mania." In *Nation, Language, and the Ethics of Translation*, edited by Sandra Bermann and Michael Wood, 229–256. Princeton, NJ: Princeton University Press, 2005.
Richards, Eliza. *Gender and the Poetics of Reception in Poe's Circle*. Cambridge: Cambridge University Press, 2004.
Rosanvallon, Pierre. *Society of Equals*. Translated by Arthur Goldhammer. Cambridge, MA: Harvard University Press, 2013.

CHAPTER 8

EARLY EXPERIMENTS IN GENRE

Imitations, Burlesques, Satires

ALEXANDER HAMMOND

THE tales that Edgar Allan Poe wrote and published before 1837 need renewed critical examination. In the twentieth century, most serious studies of these exotic, generically varied tales were grounded in source scholarship and textual criticism, much accessible in T. O. Mabbott's annotated 1978 edition of *Tales and Sketches 1831–1842*; Burton R. Pollin's annotated 1997 edition, with Joseph Ridgely, of Poe's reviews and nonfiction for the *Southern Literary Messenger*; and Jeffrey Savoye's online digital archive for the Edgar Allan Poe Society of Baltimore. Such scholarship informs the footnoted readers' editions by Stuart and Susan Levine, Benjamin F. Fisher, and G. R. Thompson, important resources for understanding Poe's flamboyantly learned early fiction.[1] This chapter urges building on this foundation while drawing on the new understandings of Poe's literary marketplace and print culture that have emerged in the last decade.

Such marketplace approaches have important precursors, particularly in the work of Michael Allen, Bruce I. Weiner, Terence Whalen, and Kevin J. Hayes. Especially important here are Meredith McGill's 2003 formulations of Poe's culture of reprinting and Leon Jackson's 2008 elaborations of its multiple authorial economies.[2] In line with these perspectives, in 2012, J. Gerald Kennedy pointed out that Poe's "self-guided apprenticeship as a writer of magazine tales" implied recognition that authors were "made, not born, fashioned by the subtle process embedded in the systems of production and distribution that constitute print culture."[3] This emphasis opens up fresh paths for exploring his early tales, which both imitated and mocked the commercial fiction of writers whose careers he followed in turning to the new genre.

Key to such explorations is an unusual feature of Poe's "self-guided apprenticeship": he composed tales in the early 1830s as ironic metaexercises in the voices of established writers in the marketplace, which the young outsider imagined as a closed club in which authors exchanged and critiqued one another's tales at invitation-only banquets.

By the spring of 1833, Poe was seeking magazine publication for a framed collection made up of eleven tales he attributed to the members of what he called the "Folio Club." While the full text of this never-published collection has been lost, a manuscript for its eleven-story prologue, various versions of its tales that Poe called "half-banter, half satire" (CL 1: 125), and multiple descriptions of its overall plan have survived (M 2: 13, 200–203).[4] Arguing for renewed attention to this project, this chapter offers an overview of the Folio Club design and a reconstruction of its eleven-story version, presents evidence that debunks Poe's 1835 claim that market value determined the treatment of genre in its tales, and suggests topics for future exploration based on that design, especially in reference to the "systems of production and distribution" Poe represented in its frame story.

Poe's "Junto of *Dunderheadism*": The 1833 Folio Club Design

After publishing three volumes of poetry to little recognition and no income, Poe shifted his focus to fiction. Prompted in part by economic necessity, by December 1, 1831, he risked five tales on a $100 prize-fiction contest in the Philadelphia *Saturday Courier*, only to see Delia Bacon win and his losing tales published anonymously and without compensation.[5] By 1833, Poe was using the motif of a literary competition staged by a "Folio Club" of insiders to frame versions of his *Courier* submissions and other early tales, most of which were, in T. O. Mabbott's words, "literary exercises in the style of popular authors of the day" (M 1: 544). The narrator of the project's surviving prologue, the newest club member, paints the Folio Club as a version of the era's literary marketplace.[6] Mirroring the periodicity of literary magazines, the club meets once a month for a banquet at which each member reads a "short prose tale" of his own composition. To publishers, Poe described the members' comments on these tales as a "burlesque upon criticism" (CL 1: 77, 163).

The prologue offers other specifics. At the end of the evening, the club selects the best and worst tale, the winner becoming president, the loser hosting the next competition. The membership is fixed—eleven in the 1833 version—although the vote for the "least meritorious" tale can make room for new members when losers withdraw after suffering the expense of "two or three entertainments in succession" (M 2: 204). The club's private workings are made public, Poe explained elsewhere, after the newest member's debut contribution is "adjudged to be the worst." He then "seizes the . . . M.SS. upon the table, and, rushing from the house, determines to appeal, by printing the whole, from the decision of the Club, to that of the public" (CL 1: 163).[7] The narrator claims that publication of the proceedings will expose the Folio Club as a "Junto of *Dunderheadism*" and a "diabolical association," one with the "settled intention to abolish Literature, subvert the Press, and overturn the Government of Nouns and Pronouns" (M 2: 203).

Scholars have traced various sources for this design, from Plato's *Symposium* and the Delphian Club (an early Baltimore literary group) to the tradition of Menippean satire informing editorial series in *Blackwood's Edinburgh Magazine* and *Fraser's*. Like the latter satires, the collection targets publishing authors, primarily Americans who ape the styles of well-known British writers. Because the Folio Club controls access to its closed circle of authors by limiting membership to a select few, the project satirizes Poe's literary marketplace as dominated by writers with established reputations who function as a clique and obstruct the efforts of aspiring newcomers. And because the members double as critics, the satire extends to the system of reviewing that shaped circulation, reception, and reputation in that marketplace.[8]

The critical exchanges among the members have been lost, but the surviving manuscript of the eleven-story prologue permits identification of the tales and their order in the 1833 collection. Its list of club members doubles as a table of contents, and their type names and descriptions point to the writers Poe targeted and the tales the members contributed—including "Siope—A Fable," a leaf of which was joined to the prologue's surviving manuscript (M 2: 200–207). That membership list is quoted in full in the following extract, with the probable identities of the eleven Folio Club members, the text of the tale each would contribute, and the genre of fiction it represents specified in square brackets and boldface. The reconstruction draws on work by James Southall Wilson, A. H. Quinn, William Bittner, Claude Richard, T. O. Mabbott, Sybille Haage, and myself through the 1970s,[9] while the notes document modifications since that decade. The identification of Mr. Snap's tale (and thus the contribution by the Folio Club president) remains controversial. Arguments for a draft of "Raising the Wind" are accepted here, but the notes allow the debate to be re-examined.

The 1833 Folio Club Collection: Membership List and Tales

There was, first of all, Mr. Snap, the President, who is a very lank man with a hawk nose, and was formerly in the service of the Down-East Review. **[John Neal, editor of the *Yankee and Boston Literary Gazette* until 1829, arguably contributes an early version of "Raising the Wind; Or Diddling Considered as One of the Exact Sciences" (1843)—a pseudo-academic essay with accounts of confidence games.]**[10]

Then there was Mr. Convolvulus Gondola, a young gentleman who had travelled a good deal. **[Thomas Moore, Byron's biographer, contributes "The Visionary" (1834)—a mysterious romance with a Byronic hero and set in Venice.]**

Then there was De Rerum Naturâ, Esqr., who wore a very singular pair of green spectacles. **[An epicurean Satan contributes "Bon-Bon" (1835)—a comic Faust story featuring a philosopher/restaurateur and a devil with green spectacles.]**

Then there was a very little man in a black coat with very black eyes. **[A mysterious stranger (a projection of Edward Bulwer-Lytton or perhaps Poe the poet) contributes "Siope--A Fable," published in 1837 and subtitled "In the manner of the Psychological Autobiographists." The pagination of the manuscript leaves featuring the prologue and the end of this oriental story in the style of Bulwer confirm this club member's authorship.]**[11]

Then there was Mr. Solomon Seadrift who had every appearance of a fish. **[Probably John Cleves Symmes contributes "MS. Found in a Bottle" (1833)—a sea narrative, with a supernatural ship that plunges into a polar vortex, in Edward Trelawny's manner.]**[12]

Then there was Mr. Horribile Dictû, with white eyelashes, who had graduated at Göttingen. **[An author committed to "Germanism" contributes "Metzengerstein: A Tale in Imitation of the German" (1832 or 1836)—a Gothic tale of horror and supernatural revenge.]**

Then there was Mr. Blackwood Blackwood who had written certain articles for foreign Magazines. **[An author for *Blackwood's Edinburgh Magazine* contributes "Loss of Breath: A Tale à la Blackwood" (1835)—a *Blackwood's* tale of sensation and burlesque.]**

Then there was the host, Mr. Rouge-et-Noir, who admired Lady Morgan. **[N. P. Willis contributes "The Duc de L'Omelette" (1832 or 1836)—a Silver Fork tale in Lady Morgan's style, about a dandy who escapes hell by cheating the devil at cards.]**

Then there was a stout gentleman who admired Sir Walter Scott. **[Probably Washington Irving contributes "King Pest the First. A Tale Containing an Allegory—By-----------" (1835)—a historical narrative beginning in the Scott manner and mirroring both Andrew Jackson's cabinet and the Folio Club symposium.]**[13]

Then there was Chronologos Chronology who admired Horace Smith, and had a very big nose which had been in Asia Minor. **[Probably Mordecai M. Noah, a Jewish newspaper editor turned anti-Jacksonian, contributes "Epimanes" (1833 MS)—a historical narrative in the Smith manner that satirizes the Jackson administration.]**

[The newest club member and narrator of the Folio Club prologue.] **[A projection of Poe contributes "Lion-izing. A Tale" (1835)—a comic narrative in the Silver Fork manner that satirizes literary fame by parodying Benjamin Disraeli's *Vivian Grey*, the reception of which is mirrored in the club's vote.]**[14] (M 2: 205–206)

Poe's 1835 Rationale for Genre in the Early Tales: Negotiating the Market

In a well-known letter of April 30, 1835, to Thomas W. White, owner-publisher of *Southern Literary Messenger*, Poe insisted that the mannered genres of his early tales resulted from commercial calculation and would improve the "celebrity" and "circulation" of the fledgling magazine (CL 1: 84). His pronouncements have been thought to document "Poe's knowledge of the kind of stories most in demand by the periodicals of that time" and his attention to "the bottom line of literary production." Among many who focus on the letter's genre formulations, G. R. Thompson finds that their shading of the categories "horrible," "burlesque," "mystical," and "grotesque" into one another reveals a commitment to "romantic irony" in Poe's early fiction.[15] But the letter's context should make students distrust its assertions.

In the spring of 1835, Poe's patron John P. Kennedy advised the penniless writer to submit work to the *Messenger*. Poe almost spoiled the opportunity by sending White "Berenice," a horrific Gothic tale about an obsessed, library-bound intellectual who extracts the teeth from the prematurely buried, still-living body of his fiancée and first cousin (M 2: 207–225; this tale, written outside the Folio Club project, is addressed elsewhere in this guide). Accepting "Berenice" for the *Messenger*'s delayed issue of March 1835, White evidently complained to Kennedy, who assured him on April 13 that "Poe did right in referring to me. He is very clever with his pen—classical and scholar-like . . . [even if] highly imaginative, and a little given to the *terrific*." Noting Poe had been advised "to write something for every number" of the *Messenger* and hoping the publisher might give the "*very* poor" fellow "permanent employ" [emphases in original], Kennedy described Poe's Folio Club collection as "a volume of very bizarre tales in the hands of Carey and Lea, Philadelphia, who for a year past have been promising to publish them."[16]

Two weeks later, Poe apologized to White for "Berenice" as "far too horrible" and "on the verge of bad taste," denying any personal investment (the tale "originated in a bet"), but mounting a defense of its Gothic sensationalism by claiming such mannered fiction will help sell the magazine. A young author with no actual magazine experience, Poe assumes expert knowledge of the commercial value of such tales: "The history of all Magazines shows plainly that those which have attained celebrity were indebted for it to articles *similar in nature—to Berenice*. . . . [I]n what does this nature consist? In the ludicrous heightened into the grotesque: the fearful coloured into the horrible: the witty exaggerated into the burlesque: the singular wrought out into the strange and mystical. . . . To be appreciated you must be *read*, and these things are invariably sought after with avidity" (CL 1: 84–85; emphases in text). These famous formulations are best understood as defensive sleights of hand, an implausible sales pitch too long accepted at face value.

Thus, Bruce Weiner has demonstrated that Poe's account of the "history of all Magazines" is bogus and its claims about the prominence and impact of the kind of tales he describes are factually wrong.[17] Furthermore, Poe's rhetorically balanced formulas for exaggerating genres cannot be trusted as definitions of actual practice. They were clearly created to reassure a magazine publisher upset by "Berenice" that the author's future submissions—which would include the tales from the 1833 collection—were simply the calculated products of a craftsman with salutary commercial motives. Note that by the time Poe wrote this letter, his eleven-story Folio Club collection had been returned from Carey and Lea, presumably deemed unpublishable[18]—his obvious reason for emphasizing the variety of the tales promised and for not mentioning the Philadelphia rejection, which would undercut his case for the periodical appeal of these tales. Instead, Poe validated his generic recipe for commercially successful fiction by naming rather dated magazine pieces (most sources selectively plundered for his Folio Club satire) in well-known British literary magazines. Evidently worried about reactions to Folio Club tales separated from their framework, Poe insisted their value was better judged by "circulation of the Magazine than by any comments upon its contents," promising again that "no two of these Tales will have the slightest resemblance one to the other either in matter or manner—still however preserving the character which I speak of" (CL 1: 84–85).

Topics for Exploration and Development

Clearly, we read the tales from Poe's Folio Club project more productively as parts of a design than in terms of his 1835 sales pitch to the *Messenger*'s publisher. From the collection's textual history, we know that three early tales addressed elsewhere in this guide—"Berenice," "Morella," and "Hans Phaal"—were composed separately from that project; that the 1832 "A Tale of Jerusalem," often identified as Chronologos Chronology's contribution, had evidently been replaced in the eleven-story collection by the 1833 "Epimanes"; and that a last *Messenger* tale not linked to its 1833 membership list, "Shadow. A Fable," may have been part of a different version of that project.[19] Interpretations of identifiable Folio Club tales are best pursued by reviewing the cogent, source-based explications of their links to individual club members in Richard P. Benton's "The Tales: 1831–1835" and Scott Peeples's "Neither in nor out of Blackwood: 1832–1838."[20] Reconstruction of the 1833 collection enables explorations that go beyond such single-tale approaches, including expansions of prior work on the stories' repeated motifs—bawdy, culinary, and demonic—and the satires of Andrew Jackson they include. And as suggested at the outset, new understandings of Poe's print culture invite fresh study of the literary club and its workings.

Sex, Food, and the Devil: Repeated Images and Motifs

The Folio Club reconstruction highlights an aspect of Poe's early fiction little emphasized by critics: his taste for bawdy innuendo. When the 1833 version was advertised for publication in the Baltimore *Saturday Visiter* on October 26, the notice promised stories characterized by "raciness" (PL: 134), a description that applies to three tales positioned late in its framework. As Michael J. S. Williams points out about "Loss of Breath," readers have recognized the sexual subtext in Mr. Blackwood Blackwood's Folio Club tale, an allegory that equates the breathlessness of the "diminutive," "corpulent" Mr. Lacko'breath with impotence and explains his post-wedding-night failure to "ejaculate[ ]" a "new and more decided epithet" at his wife as well as her attraction to their obviously potent neighbor Mr. Windenough—"lath-like" with a "tall and peculiar-looking form" whose engorged and prone figure sits upright when his nose is pinched. When Mr.

Lacko'breath recovers what Williams calls his "divine afflatus" from Windenough, the transfer is capped off with a flatulence joke: after the characters mysteriously rebalance their "wind" while interred in a vault, they gain the power to produce "subterranean noises" much noticed in the press (M 2: 62, 64, 71–73, 74–77).[21]

"King Pest the First," which the reconstruction places as a late contribution by the stout gentleman who admires Sir Walter Scott, also contains sexual analogy, pointed to by its 1835 subtitle "A Tale Containing an Allegory." One of the tale's multiple levels offers readers an anatomically elaborate subtext in which, as Louis Renza and Robert Mullun demonstrate, a pair of sailors—one tall and phallic, the other round and testicular—contract and then spread venereal disease in an encounter with the diseased private parts of plague-ridden London. This "scatological scenario" is, Renza points out, a private, concealed dimension of a text that "seems intent on halting the pleasures of allegorical readings once and for all" for its readers.[22]

"Lion-izing," the final tale in the reconstructed collection, is more obvious, with its central phallic joke hidden in plain view. In this parody of Disraeli's first novel, Poe attributes the celebrity of Thomas Smith, a comic version of that novel's autobiographical hero, to his remarkable nose, which he "pulls" from a young age and that inspires him to write a pamphlet on Nosology. The pamphlet puts all Fum-Fudge (London) in an "uproar." Instantly famous, Smith parades his specialty at a Royal dinner, after which the Duchess of Bless My Soul invites him, "with all [his] nose," to Almack's, a famous London club. Giving his nose "a pull or two," Smith creates a sensation when he arrives, a scene that rings changes on the sexual meaning of "to come," an uncommon usage in the era but available in English since the seventeenth century:

> 'He is coming!'—said somebody on the stair case.
> 'He is coming!'—said somebody farther up.
> 'He is coming!'—said somebody farther still.
> 'He is come'—said the Duchess—'he is come, the little love!' And she caught me by both hands, and looked me in the nose.[23]

The tale ends when Smith loses his status as a literary lion by shooting off a rival's nose in a duel. As his father tells him, "In Fum-Fudge great is a Lion with a proboscis, but greater by far is a Lion with no proboscis at all" (M 2: 173–174; M 2: 176–177).

Such innuendo invites exploration of Poe's attitudes toward his audience in the Folio Club project, as complicated by the bawdy subtexts of these tales, by his grouping them for emphasis near the end of the competition, and by his having that competition climax with the double entendres of "Lion-izing." Most broadly, what does such irreverent game playing tell us about Poe's stance toward his print culture's "systems of production and distribution"? Analogous questions emerge from other repeated features of the 1833 collection. As prior critics have asked, what sense should readers make of recurring images of food and drink and consumption in the prologue and tales?[24] Or of the repeated supernatural events that twist characters' fortunes in uncanny, sometimes slapstick ways, as in Mr. Solomon Seadrift's "MS Found in a Bottle," Horribile Dictû's "Metzengerstein," and Mr. Blackwood Blackwood's "Loss of Breath"? Or of the recurring devil figures, first pointed out in 1931?[25]

To expand the latter motif briefly, Poe clearly invites readers to follow up on the prologue's damning the Folio Club as a "diabolical association," first because, as the 1833 reconstruction shows, three of its members explicitly write tales about devils—De Rerum Naturâ's "Bon-Bon," the very little man in black's "Siope—A Fable," and Mr. Rouge et Noir's "The Duc de L'Omelette." Second, one of those tales, "Bon-Bon," was contributed by the devil himself. James W. Christie credits T. O. Mabbott with recognizing the link between "the tale as revised for inclusion in the 1833 'Tales of the Folio Club' and its probable teller," for when Poe transformed "The Bargain Lost" of 1832 into "Bon-Bon," the devil in the earlier version acquires De Rerum Naturâ's green spectacles. Christie emphasizes the irony of this Folio Club member's contributing a tale about a devil with a discriminating taste for fresh, still-living souls of writers, as well as the comic possibilities of his making "telling points in the drunken disputes with other members about their uses of the devil."[26] Presumably De Rerum Naturâ was pleased with the Biblical demon in "Siope—A Fable" but not, one suspects, with the dandified, effete Satan in Mr. Rouge et Noir's "The Duc de L'Omelette"—a devil who resides luxuriously in hell and uncrates the equally foppish but mortal title character from a rosewood coffin, only to be outwitted when the latter wins his freedom by cheating his host at cards.

Of interest here is the attitude implied by Poe's making the devil a member of the era's literary establishment. Relevant to such inquiries is Timothy Scherman's contention that Poe's outsider status in the early 1830s would have made it difficult to find a position "from which to launch a critique of the politics governing [literary production] or . . . to generate the authority of such a critique."[27] Evidently the young writer found leverage by suggesting the cost of becoming an established writer was dining with, if not selling one's soul to, the devil. But how trafficking with evil translates into a substantial critique in this satire of literary production remains to be formulated.

The Publishing Marketplace and Models for the Folio Club

In "The Folio Club Collection and the Silver Fork School: Perspectives on Poe's Framestory in Recent Scholarship," I review the critical grounds for these topics, which involve reframing traditional explanations for the design of the Folio Club and its monthly competition in terms of new understandings of Poe's literary marketplace. That essay's basic premise springs from Kennedy's description of that marketplace as

> "a sprawling, amorphous field of discourse, loosely connected by newspapers and magazines," within a "decentered American culture with . . . multiple discrete

> cultural systems, each revolving around different regional sites," the whole lacking what James Russell Lowell called a "central heart" such as London or Paris provided for their respective national literatures. . . . Obviously Poe of the early 1830s, working in Baltimore at a distance from even regional publishing hubs in the United States, had no domestic model for a central "junto" of established authors: such a dominant locus of power did not, in fact, exist in the American literary economy of this era.[28]

The essay argues, first, that Poe drew on a political model, President Andrew Jackson's kitchen cabinet and his "imperial" administration of 1829–1833, when he imagined the Folio Club functioning as the country's (absent) center of literary power. Poe lived in Baltimore when the national Democratic convention nominated Jackson for a second term in 1832, and William Whipple and Betsy Erkkila have shown that Jackson's "reign" as President was a satiric target for two of the tales in the reconstructed 1833 collection, "King Pest the First" and "Epimanes" (Erkkila's reading of the latter makes clear why Poe would send it as a sample of the eleven-story Folio Club collection to the anti-Jacksonian *New England Magazine* in May 1833).[29] These findings invite expansion. Jackson's turbulent first administration seems to be satirized in the Folio Club itself, an analogous "Junto of *Dunderheadism*" with its own "lank" President. And political attacks on the Jackson administration for assuming "imperial" powers in the federated republic of the early 1830s point to political equivalents of the Folio Club's exercise of less-than-legitimate control in the decentered literary marketplace of the era.

The same essay argues that Poe had an explicitly literary model, albeit in England and not the United States, for his Folio Club junto: Henry Colburn's infamous London publishing enterprise for producing Silver Fork novels, works that Poe mined repeatedly for material when writing the Folio Club tales. Colburn recruited writers to produce these formulaic novels about the maneuverings by young men of fashion for social and political power in worlds of wealth, celebrity, and fine dining. Managing the publication, marketing, and reviewing of these productions, Colburn presided over a stable of authors that so dominated Britain's marketplace for fiction in the 1820s and 1830s that they threatened, if only hyperbolically, to "abolish Literature, subvert the Press, and overturn the Government of Nouns and Pronouns" (M 2: 203).[30] Certainly Colburn's marketing of Silver Fork novels involved the kind of centralized control of literary publishing that was, to reference Kennedy again, absent in the decentered, regionally dispersed marketplace that Poe faced in the United States in the 1830s. While the Folio Club does not duplicate all features of Colburn's "hive" (Lady Morgan's term for his school of Silver Fork authors),[31] that London enterprise almost certainly served as a transatlantic model for the Folio Club's centralized system of literary production as well as for the "burlesque upon criticism" with which the club controlled access to its table and critiqued the fiction presented there each month.

Establishing this model suggests directions for fresh approaches to the collection's tales. Clearly Colburn's "hive" of Silver Fork writers produced work to be consumed by readers expecting use of that genre's conventions; furthermore, those writers knew their performances would be critiqued by reviewers schooled in those same conventions, often in reviews engineered by the publisher himself. In the Folio Club, only a few tales ("The Duc de L'Omelette" and "Lion-izing" comically, "The Visionary" more seriously) reflect the Silver Fork manner per se, but all its tales fall into categories of fiction manufactured to satisfy the generic expectations of reviewers and consumers. The point to be explored is the extent to which Poe structured the Folio Club contributions to reveal their fictional authors' efforts to meet such expectations, which presumably also informed the responses of fellow club members who judged them.

Other ways in which print culture shaped the Folio Club design are open to more determinate investigation, even if Poe's participation in the fiction marketplace was largely hypothetical in the early 1830s. Given that each club member combines the roles of author and critic, we know Poe saw criticism as integral to producing fiction. We also know he was aware of Colburn's notoriety for placing advance notices and then arranging favorable reviews for his author's publications.[32] Puffing was the era's name for this practice, one Poe battled his entire career, and it was doubtless integral to the lost critical exchanges of the Folio Club symposium. Logically, mutual alliances as well as competition among the members would produce puffing of some tales and attacks on others, hypothetical possibilities that can be concretely explored in terms of the actual relationships among authors Poe selected for his club.

The emphasis on criticism in the Folio Club design also invites analysis of the multiple figures who function as interpreters in its tales. In order, "Bon-Bon" dramatizes the role of what Terence Whalen calls the "capital reader" for publishers when Satan critiques the treatise on the soul that its title character is preparing for the press.[33] In "Siope—A Fable," a "Demon" tells the narrator a story that invites explications of the words "DESOLATION" and "SILENCE" linked to the torments inflicted on a man standing alone by the river Zaire (M 2: 196, 198). The narrator of "MS. Found in a Bottle" meditates on the word "DISCOVERY" that emerges when he dabbles paint on a folded sail of the giant ghost ship carrying him south (M 2: 142). The fate of the baron in "Metzengerstein" springs from his interpretations of a family curse and a mysterious tapestry featuring the ancestral horse of a rival. And Mr. Lacko'breath in "Loss of Breath" reads hidden billets-doux that reveal his new wife's attraction to his rival Windenough (M 2: 64).

Most strikingly, the collective evaluation of literary texts in the Folio Club symposium is mirrored in the gathering of drunken grotesques in "King Pest the First." As Fisher stresses, correspondences between this tale and the Folio Club frame story are strong. In this case, the tall, lean King Pest assembles followers with comic type names in a London undertaker's wine cellar where, "prepared by deep research and accurate investigation," they "examine, analyze, and thoroughly determine the indefinable spirit—the incomprehensible qualities and nare of those inestimable treasures of the palate, the wines, ales, and liqueurs of this goodly Metropolis" (M 2: 250, with 1835 variant). The scene mirrors the Folio Club banquet, even if the lank Mr. Snap's literary competition was probably not informed by the high-minded, rhetorically elegant critical principles of King Pest's "investigation." But as Fisher recognizes, it seems likely the critics in both settings become equally sodden with drink.[34]

Projections of Poe as Folio Club Member

In the reconstruction earlier, two of the Folio Club members project versions of Poe as author. In the case of the very little man in black who contributes "Siope—A Fable," the links to the young writer seem strong: the tale's first printing bore an epigraph from Poe's "Al Aaraaf" and a subtitle ("In the manner of the Psychological Autobiographists") that reinforce the connection; the story recalls the haunted landscapes, Orientalism, and animate vegetation of Poe's poetry; and its title, Greek for silence, may be an anagram for "is Poe." On the other hand, Poe was five feet eight inches tall and by no means a "very little man," nor were his eyes black, and the subtitle in this era pointed readers more directly to writers such as Edward Bulwer-Lytton, whose Oriental tale "Monos and Diamonos" provided much of the content and manner of "Siope" (M 2: 192–193, 196).[35] But Bulwer was no more a "very little man" than Poe, and the type name evokes a tradition of mysterious strangers in such works as Washington Irving's "The Little Man in Black." Thus, the identity of this Folio Club member may have remained a mystery until late in the competition, to be revealed as Bulwer the fabulist or Poe the haunted poet, if not yet another devil.[36]

Leon Jackson points to the much more obvious version of Poe in the 1833 collection, the newest member whose failure echoes Poe's own loss in the *Saturday Courier*'s prize-tale contest of late 1831. Jackson argues that Poe saw the era's commercial literary contests as fundamentally corrupt, and that the "organization of the [Folio] Club meetings [were the author's] striking and pointed commentary" on such contests as staged by "incestuous clique[s] where authors wrote for, and judged, one another."[37] The dynamics of the Folio Club symposium have broader resonances, of course, which make this Poe-figure's rebellion against its production system a rich basis for additional exploration.

Like the newest member, Poe was an outsider hoping to break into the literary marketplace. The new aspirant stumbles when he contributes "Lion-izing," which Poe called a satire "properly speaking" on "the rage for Lions and the facility of becoming one" (CL 1: 125)—a tale that would certainly give a cabal of self-important literary lions good reasons to vote against it. Jackson's argument for Poe's ambivalent attitudes toward literary fame lets us approach "Lion-izing" as a self-critique of the writer's own ambitions.[38] Note that Disraeli was Poe's "model" during these years according to Lambert Wilmer,[39] and that the newest member's tale parodies Disraeli's first novel *Vivian Grey* (the most infamous of Colburn's Silver Fork productions). Evidently Poe appropriated the disastrous response to that novel as a prototype for the newest member's rejection by the Folio Club. Was Poe imagining, with the Folio Club project itself, how established authors and critics might respond to his own entrée into the marketplace?

The implications of the newest member's theft of the manuscripts and their transfer from private circulation to mass printing prove equally interesting. At a factual level, this transfer evokes various patterns of exchange (most without copyright protection) that Jackson and McGill find characteristic of the era's "authorial economies" and "reprinting" practices.[40] In addition, the new member implicitly dismantles his literary market's semiclosed puffing and publication system—a system evoked by Poe's use of the Colburn model. One wonders what marketing structure Poe would have preferred in these apprentice years of his career.

Reiterations of the Folio Club Project

Finally, the connections between the Folio Club design and later reiterations of the project are open to fresh investigation. Closest in time, of course, is his 1835–1836 work on the *Southern Literary Messenger*. When Poe managed to turn his volunteer labor and early submissions into a paid position with the journal in September of 1835, he engineered admission into an actual "Folio Club," albeit at a little-known regional site within the national literary marketplace. Poe functioned as the magazine's editor in all but name; managed to print (or reprint) most of the tales linked to his Folio Club project, plus at least three new stories and the beginning of the *Narrative of Arthur Gordon Pym*; and wrote an astonishing number of critical reviews before leaving. The most widely noticed of those reviews involved enthusiastic "tomahawking" of fiction that didn't live up to his standards. As one would expect from the Folio Club project, attacks on puffing and literary cliques loom large in such notices, most famously in his December 1835 review of Theodore Fay's *Norman Leslie*, which he designated as "par excellence the *book* bepuffed" to be examined for "the sake of every thing puffed, puffing, and puffable" (P 5: 60).

The annotated edition of Poe's *Messenger* reviews and editorial writing in the *Collected Writings of Edgar Allan Poe* offers a means of comparing the writer's views of the marketplace for fiction in 1835–1836 with those he took as an outsider in the 1833 Folio Club project. In these years there are clear echoes of the earlier project in Poe's comments on the publishing system, on literary reputation and genius, and, of course, on Benjamin Disraeli, Edward Bulwer-Lytton, Washington Irving, Thomas Moore, John Neal, Sir Walter Scott, Horace Smith, John Cleves Symmes, and N. P. Willis, all figures important in the eleven-story collection. To elaborate the last example, the edition includes Poe's 1836 review of N. P. Willis's *Inklings of Adventure*, a critique that analyzes Willis's use of a pseudonym, his affectations, and his impulse "to speak bad French in preference to good English," all direct reflections of the Folio Club's treatment of Mr. Rouge et Noir, the Willis figure who writes "The Duc de L'Omelette" (P 5: 264–267). Furthermore, Scott Peeples's scholarship on Poe and Willis permits these mirrored characterizations to be examined in terms of the authors' overlapping careers, differing attitudes toward audience and craft, and one-sided rivalry in which Poe regularly takes jabs at Willis as a "man of fashion," a "graceful trifler," and a writer of talent but "no profundity—no *genius*."[41]

Poe's reviews also invite comparisons with how the Folio Club design frames fiction in terms of the era's "systems of production and distribution," especially as a commodity that authors manufactured to meet the generic expectations of reviewers and readers. As one might expect, in the *Messenger* Poe mocked novels that aped the techniques of established British writers, while he castigated critics who lacked independent standards, puffed books from self-interest, displayed "servile dependence to British critical dicta," or praised "a stupid book the better, because, sure enough, its stupidity was American" (P 5: 164). One overall question stands out: do Poe's positions in the Folio Club satire and its "burlesque upon criticism" shift when he becomes a professional reviewer?

The strategies of the 1833 Folio Club collection are much more directly reiterated in Poe's *Blackwood's* satire of 1838, "The Psyche Zenobia"/"The Scythe of Time" (later "How to Write a Blackwood's Article"/"A Predicament"). The frame stories in both are narrated by members of literary clubs, although in 1838 the narrator is a woman, "Signora Psyche Zenobia," the pretentious corresponding secretary for a Philadelphia literary "association" known as the "P.R.E.T.T.Y.B.L.U.E.B.A.T.C.H." Hoping "to introduce a better style of thinking and writing" into the papers at her club's weekly meetings, Zenobia travels to Edinburgh with her three-foot-tall "negro-servant Pompey" (a remarkably racist caricature) and her lapdog Diana to interview the editor of *Blackwood's Edinburgh Magazine*. Once there, she receives detailed instructions on how to compose "*intensities*" (M 2: 337–339)—the tales of sensation involving bizarre suffering such as Mr. Blackwood Blackwood contributes to the 1833 Folio Club banquet.

Emphasizing the demand side of the publishing system, the editor insists that a "genuine Blackwood article" must feature sensations from an unusual experience of suffering, a limited set of narrative styles, and especially "*filling up*" with learned allusions and quotations in multiple languages necessary to give the tale "an air of erudition, or at least afford evidence of extensive general reading." Venturing into Edinburgh, Zenobia suffers decapitation by the minute hand of a giant clock and also the death of her dog. Having rejected an advance of "fifty guineas a sheet" from the magazine, she records her sensations in "A Predicament," the inset tale written for her club, with comically inept "*filling up*" in the style Mr. Blackwood calls "heterogeneous," a narration that proceeds with only modest inconvenience after she loses her head (M 2: 339–340; M 2: 343–346).

This narrative absurdity duplicates Lacko'breath's gushing about his perceptions while being hanged in the Folio Club's "Loss of Breath," and the "*filling up*" in Zenobia's tale recalls other stories in that collection. Presumably Poe was wryly looking back at his own failure to gauge the marketplace value of esoteric learning. As James Kirke Paulding reported, Harper and Brothers objected to an 1836 version of the Folio Club collection for requiring "a degree of familiarity with various kinds of knowledge which [readers] do not possess," a point the publisher repeated to Poe directly: "The papers are too learned and mystical. They would be understood and relished only by a very few—not by the multitude."[42] These correspondences raise other questions. Why did Poe build this satire on the notion of a "genuine Blackwood article" out of date by 1838? Why did he return to the bawdy of the 1833 collection in Zenobia's "love" relationship with Pompey, on whose shoulders she stands in her dress, whose "wool" she tears out in a rage in the clock tower and then tearfully reaches for as "it dangled among the cordage of the bell," where she "fancied it stood on end with indignation" (M 2: 351). And what are the implications of Poe's literary crossdressing when he casts a northern bluestocking who rejects mass distribution of her tale in the equivalent of his own narrative role in the 1833 Folio Club framework?

In his 2012 "Inventing the Literati," Kennedy recognizes the most telling reiteration of the Folio Club project. Noting that Poe's project playfully figures the author as "belonging to a madcap coterie that will change the system of literary production altogether," Kennedy points out that, in "a curious fashion, [Poe] sets the agenda for his later career." As Kennedy subsequently defines that agenda, it was "to assign literary importance [to America's authors] . . . on the basis of genuine merit, a merit based on principled criticism rather than on 'wealth or social position'—or the spurious renown generated by puffery or cliquism. His ultimate aim, as Lewis Simpson rightly remarked, was 'to impose order on the disorder of America's literary situation' and to establish in the process 'an authoritative literary community in America' that corresponded to his idealized republic of letters."[43]

Clearly the Folio Club project was an early, satiric version of precisely those aims, its club ruling as an "authoritative literary community" while it makes less-than-principled determinations of critical merit and operates, in Jackson's words, like an "incestuous clique." Looking forward from that beginning, students will find the Folio Club's functions reiterated in Poe's prospectuses for the high-quality literary magazines he was never able to finance, the *Penn Magazine* of 1840 and *The Stylus* of 1843. In those prospectuses, Poe admits occasionally ruthless behavior as a reviewer for journals he did not control, then projects himself (no longer a newcomer) as an enhanced version of the Folio Club president Mr. Snap, now rendered as the imperial managing editor of a new, uncompromising literary magazine. That magazine would insist on "an absolutely independent criticism—a criticism self-sustained; guiding itself only by the purest rules of Art; . . . yielding no point either to the vanity of the author, or to the . . . arrogance of those organized *cliques* which, hanging like nightmares upon American literature, manufacture, at the nod of our principal booksellers, a pseudo-public-opinion by wholesale." Furthermore, the magazine would "endeavour to support the general interests of the republic of letters, without reference to particular regions," and without, he adds in an apparent backward glance at his Folio Club project, "buffoonery, scurrility, or profanity" (ER: 1025).

Finally, in publishing writing by its well-paid authors, Poe's projected magazine would "aim at affording a fair and not dishonorable field for the *true* intellect of the land, without reference to the mere *prestige* of celebrated names. It will support the general interests of the Republic of Letters, and insist upon regarding the world at large as the sole proper audience for the author" (ER: 1034–1035; emphasis in text). Clearly, Poe never stopped wanting to create a powerful central "Junto," with himself as its reigning head, determined to tolerate no dunderheadism in the "Republic of Letters," but the project remained an imagined one, victim to the realities of the marketplace, to the need for capital that he could never raise, and, at times, to the temptations of drink at the only clubs that never turned him away.

Notes

1. *The Short Fiction of Edgar Allan Poe: An Annotated Edition*, ed. Stuart Levine and Susan Levine (1976; rpt. Urbana: University of Illinois Press, 1990); *The Essential Tales and Poems of Edgar Allan Poe*, ed. Benjamin F. Fisher (New York: Barnes & Nobel, 2004); and *The Selected Writings of Edgar Allan Poe*, ed. G. R. Thompson (New York: W. W. Norton, 2004). The Edgar Allan Poe Society of Baltimore (https://www.eapoe.org/) provides electronic versions of many sources cited in this chapter.
2. Allen, *Poe and the British Magazine Tradition* (New York: Oxford University Press, 1969); Weiner, *The Most Noble of Professions: Poe and the Poverty of Authorship* (Baltimore: Enoch Pratt Free Library, Edgar Allan Poe Society of Baltimore, 1987); Whalen, *Edgar Allan Poe and the Masses: The Political Economy of Literature in Antebellum America* (Princeton, NJ: Princeton University Press, 1999); Hayes, *Poe and the Printed Word* (Cambridge, UK: Cambridge University Press, 2000); McGill, *American Literature and the Culture of Reprinting, 1834–53* (Philadelphia: University of Pennsylvania Press, 2003); and Jackson, *The Business of Letters: Authorial Economies in Antebellum America* (Palo Alto, CA: Stanford University Press, 2008).
3. Kennedy, "Inventing the Literati: Poe's Remapping of Antebellum Print Culture," in *Poe and the Remapping of Antebellum Print Culture*, ed. J. Gerald Kennedy and Jerome McGann (Baton Rouge: LSU Press, 2012), 13, 19.
4. Evidence analyzed in detail in Alexander Hammond, "Edgar Allan Poe's *Tales of the Folio Club*: The Evolution of a Lost Book," in *Poe at Work: Seven Textual Studies*, ed. Benjamin Franklin Fisher IV (Baltimore: The Edgar Allan Poe Society, 1978), 13–43.
5. John Grier Varner, introduction to *Edgar Allan Poe and the Philadelphia* Saturday Courier: *Facsimile Reproductions of the First Texts of Poe's Earliest Tales and "Raising the Wind"* (Charlottesville: University of Virginia Press, 1933), iii–iv; Arthur Hobson Quinn, *Edgar Allan Poe: A Critical Biography* (New York: D. Appleton-Century, 1941), 187–192.
6. Jackson, *Business of Letters*, 221, 222, and Alexander Hammond, "Consumption, Exchange, and the Literary Marketplace: From the Folio Club Tales to *Pym*," in *Poe's Pym: Critical Explorations*, ed. Richard Kopley (Durham, NC: Duke University Press, 1992), 156–158.
7. Contrast with Poe's evolving positions on literary judgment in James M. Hutchisson, "The Reviews: Evolution of a Critic," in *A Companion to Poe Studies*, ed. Eric W. Carlson (Westport, CT: Greenwood Press, 1996), 296–322, and Whalen, *Edgar Allan Poe and the Masses*, 53–57, 74–75, 80–82, passim.
8. On sources of Poe's design and its representation of the marketplace, see Hammond, "Edgar Allan Poe's *Tales of the Folio Club*: The Evolution of a Lost Book," 14–17, and Timothy H. Scherman, "The Authority Effect: Poe and the Politics of Reputation in the Pre-Industry of American Publishing," *Arizona Quarterly* 49, no. 3 (1993): 1–19.
9. Cited in Alexander Hammond, "A Reconstruction of Poe's 1833 *Tales of the Folio Club*: Preliminary Notes," *Poe Studies* 5 (1972): 25–32, "Further Notes on Poe's Folio Club Tales," *Poe Studies* 8 (1975): 38–42, and "Edgar Allan Poe's *Tales of the Folio Club*: The Evolution of a Lost Book" (1978), esp. 19–24. See also Mabbott (M 2: 206–207) and

Sybille Haage's *Edgar Allan Poe's "Tales of the Folio Club" Versuch de Rekonstruction einer zyklischen Rahmenerzählung* (Frankfurt am Main: Peter Lang, 1978), as well as the Introduction and Notes to Haage's edition of *Tales of the Folio Club and Three Other Tales* (Frankfurt am Main: Peter Lang, 1978), v–xvii, 121–127.

10. Claude Richard identifies Mr. Snap as John Neal and his tale as "Raising the Wind," in "Poe and the Yankee Hero," *Mississippi Quarterly* 21 (1968): 93–109, an argument elaborated by Hammond in "A Reconstruction of Poe's 1833 *Tales of the Folio Club*," 26–27, and "Further Notes on Poe's Folio Club Tales," 38. Burton R. Pollin contests these claims because of the tale's 1843 publication date, and a late performance of the play referenced by its title, in "Poe's 'Diddling': More on the Dating and Aim," *Poe Studies* 9 (1976): 11–13. Developing a convincing early source (and noting alternate performances of the 1803 play), Kent Ljungquist supports Richard in " 'Raising More Wind': Another Source for Poe's 'Diddling' and Its Possible Folio Club Context," in *Perspectives on Poe*, ed. D. Ramakrishna (New Delhi: APC, 1996), 53–63. Haage (see n. 14) reasonably argues that an early, never-published form of Mr. Snap's tale was subsequently transformed into three later, textually related stories: "Peter Pendulum, The Business Man" (1840), "Raising the Wind," and "The Literary Life of Thingum Bob, Esq." (1844). Cf. J. A. Leo LeMay, "Poe's 'The Business Man': Its Contexts and Satire of Franklin's Autobiography," *Poe Studies/Dark Romanticism* 15, no. 2 (Dec. 1982): 29–37.
11. This identification recognizes Poe's use of Bulwer-Lytton's "Monos and Diamonos" as the main source for "Siope" (M 2: 192–194), thus modifying Hammond, "A Reconstruction of Poe's 1833 *Tales of the Folio Club*," 28, and "Further Notes on Poe's Folio Club Tales," 41. See "Projections of Poe as Folio Club Member" and n. 35.
12. See George H. Soule, Jr., "Another Source of Poe: Trelawny's *The Adventures of a Younger Son*," *Poe Studies* 8, no. 2 (Dec. 1975): 35–37. Borrowings in "MS. Found in a Bottle" from *Adventures* are extensively documented in Palmer C. Holt Papers, circa 1948–2017; Box 2, folders 22–23: Manuscripts, Archives, and Special Collections, Washington State University Libraries, Pullman, WA.
13. Benjamin F. Fisher, " 'King Pest' and the *Tales of the Folio Club*," in *Edgar Allan Poe: Beyond Gothicism*, ed. James M. Hutchisson (Newark: University of Delaware Press, 2011), 103–117, stresses this tale's mirroring of the frame story, but Fisher's hypothesis that the tale was contributed by the Folio Club narrator does not address its links to the stout gentleman or the evidence in n. 14.
14. Hammond, "Poe's 'Lionizing' and the Design of Tales of the Folio Club," *ESQ: A Journal of the American Renaissance* 18 (1972): 154–156. The identification of the prologue's narrator as Poe (and thus the contributor of this satire on literary lions) modifies this 1972 argument; see "Projections of Poe as Folio Club Member" and notes 37–39.
15. Quinn, *Edgar Allan Poe*, 219; Whalen, *Edgar Allan Poe and the Masses*, 8; and G. R. Thompson, *Poe's Fiction: Romantic Irony in the Gothic Tales* (Madison: University of Wisconsin Press, 1973), 42–44.
16. Quoted in George E. Woodberry, *Life of Edgar Allan Poe*, 2 vols. (Boston: Houghton Mifflin, 1909), 1:109–110. For dating these exchanges, see CL 1: 84–85 and PL: 148–150.
17. Bruce I. Weiner, "Poe and the *Blackwood's* Tale of Sensation," in *Poe and His Times: The Artist and His Milieu*, ed. Benjamin Franklin Fisher IV (Baltimore: The Edgar Allan Poe Society, 1990), 46–48.
18. Hammond, "Edgar Allan Poe's *Tales of the Folio Club*: The Evolution of a Lost Book," 29–30.
19. Hammond, "A Reconstruction of Poe's 1833 *Tales of the Folio Club*," 31–32, and "Edgar Allan Poe's *Tales of the Folio Club*: The Evolution of a Lost Book," 24, 29, 38.

20. For Benton, see "The Tales: 1831–1835," in *A Companion to Poe Studies*, ed. Eric W. Carlson (Westwood, CT: Greenwood Press, 1996), 110–128; for Peeples, see *Edgar Allan Poe Revisited* (New York: Twayne, 1998), 32–34, 42–50, plus 110–116 (analyses of puffing and the tales Haage links to Mr. Snap). Cf. Benjamin Franklin Fisher, *The Cambridge Introduction to Edgar Allan Poe* (New York: Cambridge University Press, 2008), 50–57.
21. Williams, *A World of Words: Language and Displacement in the Fiction of Edgar Allan Poe* (Durham, NC: Duke University Press, 1988), 52–54.
22. Renza, "Poe's King: Playing It Close to the Pest," *Edgar Allan Poe Review* 2, no. 2 (Fall 2001): 3–18, esp. 11, 13.
23. See Hammond, "Poe's 'Lionizing,'" esp. 161–162, and Peeples, *Edgar Allan Poe Revisited*, 32. On dating usage, see reference to Bishop Percy's 1650 *Loose Songs* in Geoffrey Hughes, *Swearing: A Social History of Foul Language, Oaths and Profanity in English* (1991; rpt., New York: Penguin Books, 1998). In later revisions, the final phrase reads "she kissed me thrice upon the nose" (M 2: 181).
24. On Poe's attitudes toward the reprinting of authors mocked in these three Folio Club tales, see McGill, *American Literature and the Culture of Reprinting*, 153–154. On motifs of food and drink in the Folio Club tales generally, see Benjamin F. Fisher IV, *The Very Spirit of Cordiality: The Literary Uses of Alcohol and Alcoholism in the Tales of Edgar Allan Poe* (Baltimore: Enoch Pratt Free Library, Edgar Allan Poe Society of Baltimore, 1978), 3–11, and his introduction to *The Essential Tales and Poems of Edgar Allan Poe*, xxix–xxxi; Hammond, "Consumption, Exchange, and the Literary Marketplace," 153–166, and his "Literary Commerce and the Discourses of Gastronomy in Poe's 'Bon-Bon,'" in "Special Issue in Honor of G. R. Thompson," ed. Steven Frye and Eric Carl Link, special issue, *Poe Studies/Dark Romanticism* 39–40 (2007–2008): 38–45.
25. James Southall Wilson, "The Devil Was In It," *American Mercury* 24 (1931): 215–219, esp. 220.
26. Christie, "Poe's Diabolical Humor: Revisions in 'Bon-Bon,'" in *Poe at Work*, ed. Fisher, 49–50.
27. Scherman, "The Authority Effect," 5.
28. Quotes from Kennedy, "Inventing the Literati," 15, 17–18, in Alexander Hammond, "The Folio Club Collection and the Silver Fork School: Perspectives on Poe's Framestory in Recent Scholarship," in *Influencing Poe*, ed. Barbara Cantalupo and Richard Kopley Special Issue of *Edgar Allan Poe Review* 19 no. 2 (fall 2018).
29. See Whipple, "Poe's Political Satire," *University of Texas Studies in English* 35 (1956): 81–95, and Erkkila, "Perverting the American Renaissance: Poe, Democracy, Critical Theory," in *Poe and the Remapping of Antebellum Print Culture*, ed. Kennedy and McGann, 69, 74–85.
30. On Colburn's publishing practices, see Matthew Rosa, *The Silver-Fork School* (New York: Columbia University Press, 1936), 178–206, and Edward Copeland, *The Silver Fork Novel: Fashionable Fiction in the Age of Reform* (Cambridge, UK: Cambridge University Press, 2012), 16–24; 103; 231n31, 32, 36. On Colburn's threat to "Literature" see John Strachan, *Advertising and Satirical Culture in the Romantic Period* (Cambridge, UK: Cambridge University Press, 2007), 255–261.
31. Lady Morgan, *Book of the Boudoir* (London: Henry Colburn, 1829), 2: 303.
32. On Colburn's puffing and relationships to his authors, see n. 30 and John Sutherland and Johanna Marie Melnyk's definitive study of Colburn's career, *Rogue Publisher / The "Prince of Puffers": The Life and Works of Henry Colburn* (London: Edward Everett Root, 2018), esp. 66–78, 99–121, and 151–154.
33. See Hammond, "Literary Commerce and the Discourses of Gastronomy," 43–44. Whalen introduces the concept of the "capital reader" in *Edgar Allan Poe and the Masses*, 10–11, 14–17.

34. Fisher, "'King Pest' and the *Tales of the Folio Club*," 103–117, esp. 108–111.
35. Cf. Hammond, "A Reconstruction of Poe's 1833 *Tales of the Folio Club*," 28, and "Edgar Allan Poe's *Tales of the Folio Club*: The Evolution of a Lost Book," 20–24. Fisher, "The Power of Words in Poe's Silence," in *Poe at Work*, 56, 60, 67, lists Bulwer, Disraeli, and De Quincy as "psychological autobiographists," a term that derives from the subtitle of Disraeli's 1832 *Contarini Fleming: A Psychological Autobiography*. Bulwer-Lytton enthusiastically celebrated the "new" technique of that novel in his editorial exchanges with a chatty devil in Colburn's *New Monthly Magazine*—reprinted in *Asmodeus at Large* (Philadelphia: Carey, Lea, and Blanchard, 1833), 101–103.
36. Irving, "The Little Man in Black," *Salamagundi* 18 (Nov. 24, 1807): 326–335. Wilson, "The Devil Was In It," 220, suggests Poe's man in black may be the devil.
37. Jackson, *The Business of Letters*, 220–222.
38. Jackson, "'The Rage for Lions': Edgar Allan Poe and the Culture of Celebrity," in *Poe and the Remapping of Antebellum Print Culture*, 37–61, esp. 41–43.
39. Lambert A. Wilmer, *Merlin; Together with Recollections of Edgar A. Poe* (New York: Scholars Facsimiles, 1941), 31.
40. Jackson, *The Business of Letters*, esp. 95–96, 126–141, and McGill, *American Literature and the Culture of Reprinting*, 11–19 et passim.
41. See Hammond, "A Reconstruction of Poe's 1833 *Tales of the Folio Club*," 30, and Scott Peeples, "'The Mere Man of Letters Must Ever Be a Cipher': Poe and N. P. Willis," *ESQ: A Journal of the American Renaissance* 46, no. 3 (2000): 125–147.
42. Quoted in "Edgar Allan Poe's Tales of the Folio Club: The Evolution of a Lost Book," 34–35. For exploring race and gender in Poe's 1838 satire, see Teresa A. Goddu, "Poe, Sensationalism, and "Slavery", *The Cambridge Companion to Edgar Allan Poe*, ed. Kevin J. Hayes (New York: Cambridge University Press, 2002), 92–112.
43. Kennedy, "Inventing the Literati," 19, 28.

Bibliography

Hammond, Alexander. "Edgar Allan Poe's *Tales of the Folio Club*: The Evolution of a Lost Book." In *Poe at Work: Seven Textual Studies*, edited by Benjamin Franklin Fisher IV, 13–43. Baltimore: Edgar Allan Poe Society, 1978.

Hammond, Alexander. "The Folio Club Collection and the Silver Fork School: Perspectives on Poe's Framestory in Recent Scholarship." In *Influencing Poe*, edited by Barbara Cantalupo and Richard Kopley. Special Issue of *Edgar Allan Poe Review* 19 no. 2 (fall 2018).

Jackson, Leon. *The Business of Letters: Authorial Economies in Antebellum America*. Palo Alto, CA: Stanford University Press, 2008.

Kennedy, J. Gerald. "Inventing the Literati." In *Poe and the Remapping of Antebellum Print Culture*, edited by J. Gerald Kennedy and Jerome McGann, 13–36. Baton Rouge: Louisiana State University Press, 2012.

McGill, Meredith. *American Literature and the Culture of Reprinting, 1834–53*. Philadelphia: University of Pennsylvania Press, 2003.

Scherman, Timothy H. "The Authority Effect: Poe and the Politics of Reputation in the Pre-Industry of American Publishing." *Arizona Quarterly* 49, no. 3 (1993): 1–19.

CHAPTER 9

THE PERVERSITY OF PUBLIC OPINION IN POE'S LATER SATIRES AND HOAXES

STACEY MARGOLIS

In 1934, Ernest Marchand stoutly declared that Edgar Allan Poe had not, as so many critics assumed, "moved about over the earth thickly wrapped in a luminous cloud, which effectually shut him off from mundane concerns" but was in fact an astute social critic.[1] No one would need to make such an assertion today.[2] If Marchand's account didn't catch on immediately, his insight has animated Poe scholarship for at least the last thirty years.[3] It is especially in the satires that we see Poe's engagement with what Marchand called "[t]he great staples of thought and discussion in his day," namely "democracy, social reform, and progress."[4] Accordingly, recent critics have insisted on the topical nature of these works, which focus, for example, on issues of race and slavery in the lead-up to the Civil War, or on what Poe imagined to be unfounded claims for the natural superiority of democratic governance.[5] This recent attention to the nuts and bolts of mid-century politics is in some sense a return to an earlier style of reading the satires, which explained in helpful detail the very specific references hidden in many of the tales' most bizarre images.[6] This resolutely historical approach doesn't make the satires any funnier, but it does bring their original targets into sharper focus for a contemporary reader.[7]

The critical rediscovery of the satires is no doubt fostered by the fact that they seem to function as aphorism machines—stories like "Mellonta Tauta" (1849) and "Some Words with a Mummy" (1845) are chock-full of pithy insults. Pundita, the narrator of "Mellonta Tauta," speculates about nineteenth-century America while literally and figuratively looking down on the country from a balloon in the year 2848. In a letter to an unnamed friend, she explains that "the ancient Amriccans *governed themselves*!—did ever anybody hear of such an absurdity?—that they existed in a sort of every-man-for-himself confederacy, after the fashion of the 'prairie dogs' that we read of in fable." She concludes "that democracy is a very admirable form of government—for dogs" (M 3: 1299–1300).

Over the years this line about democracy and dogs seems to have set up its own kind of despotism, dominating scholarship on Poe's examination of the Age of Jackson as if it spoke not only for this particular tale, but for his entire career as social critic. That this kind of wit can be seductive might explain why Pundita's eminently quotable attacks on democratic excess have gotten more attention than Pundita herself.[8]

Yet why should we take Pundita as Poe's mouthpiece without noting the extent to which she herself is an object of satire?[9] Beyond her sanctimonious dismissal of "rascally" democratic institutions, for example, she enthusiastically endorses a particularly brutal form of utilitarianism: "Is it not truly remarkable that, before the magnificent light shed upon philosophy by Humanity, the world was accustomed to regard War and Pestilence as calamities? . . . Is it not really difficult to comprehend upon what principle of interest our forefathers acted? Were they so blind as not to perceive that the destruction of a myriad of individuals is only so much positive advantage to the mass!" (M 3: 1300, 1294). It's hard not to read Pundita's celebration of mass death as invalidating her critique of the democratic public; after all, it's one thing to roll one's eyes at the stupidity of the mob and quite another to advocate mass slaughter. But, since we know that Poe shared Pundita's contempt for the mob, it seems odd that he would undercut his spokesman for this contempt. Making Pundita both the source of insight and the object of the critique seems to derail the satire. As Samuel Otter points out about "The System of Doctor Tarr and Professor Fether" (1845), a similarly vexed tale, "it is not clear in terms of politics, region, or race, what it would mean to get the story, or even what *it* is."[10]

One might say the same of "Some Words with a Mummy," often read as a companion piece to "Mellonta Tauta." The object of the satire in this case is not the democratic masses, but the American commitment to progress (embodied here in "experts" on ancient Egypt).[11] Saturated in their wholly unearned sense of "the marked inferiority of the old Egyptians in all particulars of science" and culture (M 3: 1191), the scientists who awaken and then attempt to enlighten Count Allamistakeo are time and again shown up by him. Most readings of the story stress the way Poe undermines his narrator (a glutton and a fool) and puts his scathing critique of American boosterism in the mouth of the surprisingly urbane mummy.[12] Dana Nelson makes a version of this argument in an influential essay on the story, claiming that the tale "lampoons a particular fraternal construction of white manhood" in order to critique "its privileged civic status," which it asserts "not just through race but through gender, class, and political exclusions."[13] The problem with this reading, however, is not only that it doesn't line up with what we know about Poe's politics, but that it cannot account for his impulse to lampoon his ostensible spokesman as well.[14] Sneezing, shivering, and dressed up in an absurd costume (that Charles D. Martin describes as "a parody of gentrification that can only be compared to minstrel show drag"[15]), the Count cannot distinguish between "fables" about ancient Egyptian practices and accounts of their legitimate scientific achievements. Just before describing the magnificent architecture of "Carnac," for instance, he casually suggests that the Egyptians had mastered the arts of suspended animation and time travel (M 3: 1192). "An historian," he observes, "having attained the age of five hundred, would write a book with great labor and then get himself carefully embalmed; leaving instructions to his executors *pro tem.*, that they should cause him to be revivified after the lapse of a certain period—say five or six hundred years" (M 3: 1189). By undermining the Count in this way, "Some Words with a Mummy" ends up painting itself into the same corner as "Mellonta Tauta": its main character serves as both the voice of reason and the object of the satire.[16]

I do not mean to argue that Poe's scattershot technique in these tales invalidates the satire completely. There is plenty of evidence, not only in these stories, but in letters and reviews written over the course of his career, that Poe was as disgusted by the democratic "mob" as both Pundita and Count Allamistakeo. But the unruly nature of the satires—their propensity to spare no one, not even the ostensible voice of reason—is not irrelevant to an account of how they work and what it is that they are satirizing. In other words, to understand Poe's satires, one must address both their elusive content and their vexing form. Poe, I want to suggest, attacks Pundita not for her utilitarianism alone, but for the way she becomes an unreflective mouthpiece for the public opinion of 2848. Rather than engaging in an argument with either her interlocutor or her American "progenitors," Pundita presents her opinions about democratic governance as self-evident ("did ever anybody hear of such an absurdity?" [M 3: 1299]) and treats the nineteenth-century belief in individual freedom and equality less as a difference of opinion than as a form of blindness, an inability to acknowledge natural law. Indeed, she seems incapable of imagining dissenting views. "Amriccans," she claims, "started with the queerest idea conceivable, viz: that all men are born free and equal—this in the very teeth of the laws of *gradation* so visibly impressed upon all things both in the moral and physical universe" (M 3: 1299). This sense of the natural and the obvious that marks all of her observations suggests that if she does indeed serve as a mouthpiece here it is not for Poe himself but for a public opinion she cannot help but assimilate. Everyone who is not "blind" must see what is "so visibly impressed upon all things." The point, of course, is to show a *shift* in public opinion over time (so that what is obvious in Poe's world becomes laughable in Pundita's). But the tracking of social change is just another way of demonstrating the problem of public opinion, which has the amazing capacity to speak through the individual, so that what seems to be the expression of personal conviction or an unbiased experience of the world turns out to be the voice of the mob.

Recognizing public opinion as the hijacking of individual speech puts a new spin on Pundita's critique of progress in human affairs (a critique, we might note, that undermines her own claims to superiority). She hints throughout her account that the futility of every attempt to make the world better—happier, fairer, more knowledgeable—can be traced to the leveling power of public opinion. When, for instance, she acknowledges the fact that a well-known critic, "the immortal Wiggins," turns out to be "not so original in his views of the Social Condition and so forth, as his contemporaries are inclined to suppose," she quotes the philosopher "Aries Tottle," "Thus must we say that, not once or twice, or a few times, but with almost infinite repetitions, the same opinions come round in a circle among men" (M 3: 1293). Beyond the familiar point about the illusion of progress, this passage gives opinion an uncanny agency; it's not that men espouse opinions but that opinions, seemingly of their own accord, "come round ... among men" (M 3: 1293).

Poe was disdainful of Jacksonian democracy, but he was not dismissive. He was, in fact, a keen observer of the formal mechanisms that stabilize democracies, including their absolute commitment to the sanctity of public opinion. Beyond Poe's distaste for the stupidity and malleability of popular beliefs (for, of course, this is undeniable), what haunts the strained comedy of the increasingly bitter late satires is his interest in how such beliefs acquire a seemingly uncontestable power.[17] In attending to Poe's fascination with the production of opinion, this approach to the satires might be understood as formalist—not because it pays more attention to the formal features of texts than to specific political content, but because it recognizes that Poe often pays more attention to the formal features of democratic culture (like the disembodied authority of public opinion) than to any specific political issue.[18] Public opinion engages political realities, but it also (as Poe never tired of illustrating) demonstrates more abstract problems of identity, agency, and authority. In other words, we can return to Daniel Hoffman's sense of Poe as a "hyperbolic pamphleteer without a party" and understand this paradox as a way of registering his interest in the *process* of opinion formation in democratic systems and the mysterious creation of cultural authority.[19]

The central problem that engages Poe in satires like "Mellonta Tauta" and "Some Words with a Mummy" is the way Jacksonian democracy becomes, in effect, rule by public opinion. And the problem with public opinion is less the *what* than the *how*. The mechanism through which scattered individual opinions become public opinion is the subject of one of Poe's best satires—"The Man That Was Used Up" (1839)—in which the fatuous celebrity is not only made up of artificial parts but of interchangeable bits of gossip. The "*remarkable* something" (M 2: 380) about Brevet Brigadier General John A. B. C. Smith turns out to be that his prosthetic parts so seamlessly meld into a whole—a seamlessness that becomes a material correlative for the social alchemy that transforms casual talk into the formidable power of public opinion.[20] Poe imagines a kind of magic in the way that something as trivial as a conversation about an acquaintance over tea or a game of cards eventually makes itself felt as an unassailable public will. What makes the alchemy of public opinion so sinister is that it is collective without being intentional; it emerges, but it is traceable to no will, no plan, communal or otherwise. If one thinks of the foolishness and power of public opinion as a force to be thwarted (as Poe clearly did), the most serious problem it poses is that it presents the social critic with no substantial target—it belongs to everyone and is attributable to no one. The satires attempt to dramatize this elusive process.

Perhaps the easiest way to see the distinctiveness of Poe's approach to public opinion is to compare it to James Fenimore Cooper's. As many scholars have noted, Cooper and Poe had similar attitudes toward what they saw as the potential tyranny of the majority.[21] But Cooper, unlike Poe, imagined that he had the answer to the problem. Even in his darkest moments, Cooper believed that the power of public opinion might be tamed through the rule of law. If, for instance, as he declares in *The American Democrat* (1838), "it is a besetting vice of democracies to substitute publick opinion for law," the solution is to sanctify the law:

> It ought to be impressed on every man's mind, in letters of brass, "*That, in a democracy, the publick has no power that is not expressly conceded by the institutions, and that this power, moreover, is only to be used under the forms prescribed by the constitution. All beyond this, is oppression, when it takes the character of acts, and not unfrequently when it is confined to opinion.*"[22]

Of course, Cooper realized how essentially fantastic such a solution was, since he was quick to acknowledge that the problem with public opinion was precisely that it was not beholden to law. And yet, in novels from *Home As Found* (1838) through *The Ways of the Hour* (1850), he felt compelled to remind his countrymen that, appearances to the contrary, "we live in a country of laws."[23] The textuality of law is crucial here, for it marks law out from casual speech as substantial rather than ephemeral, constant rather than fluctuating. How else to understand Cooper's desire to imprint his dictum in "letters of brass" except that it highlights the stabilizing power of textuality?

In contrast, Poe never imagines that textuality might constrain opinion. In one of the more famous send-ups in "Mellonta Tauta," Pundita translates an inscription on an ancient American relic uncovered in an archeological dig. It is, almost literally, a scene that interprets "letters of brass," which is all the more compelling when we recognize that Pundita's "verbatim translation" is the inscription proposed for a never-completed Washington monument on the Upper East Side of Manhattan in 1847:

> This Corner Stone of a Monument to the
> Memory of
> GEORGE WASHINGTON
> was laid with appropriate ceremonies on the
> 19TH DAY OF OCTOBER, 1847,
> the anniversary of the surrender of
> Lord Cornwallis
> to General Washington at Yorktown,
> A.D. 1781,
> under the auspices of the
> Washington Monument Association of the
> city of New York. (M 3: 1304)

In reproducing the inscription, Poe in effect turns it against itself by using words impressed on marble and imagined as outliving by hundreds of years the people who produced them to highlight the instability rather than the preservation of meaning. Pundita's interpretation is at once laughably wrong and strangely illuminating. While she imagines that Cornwallis is "no doubt some wealthy dealer in corn" whose body was surrendered to the American "cannibals" to be made into "sausage," she also acknowledges the fact that this cornerstone stands in for a monument that was never built. She applauds these ancient people for "contenting themselves, as we do now, with a mere indication of the design to erect a monument at some future time. . . . As a guarantee of the magnanimous *intention*" (M 3: 1304–1305).[24]

This idea—that the monument was intended to exist as mere intention—is also both right and wrong. It is wrong in that the Washington Monument Association tried desperately for years to raise enough money to build a proper monument. But it is right in observing that the intention to honor Washington, made manifest in the cornerstone, was all that was ever to exist of the planned monument. There's little doubt that Poe found the whole pompous spectacle created by the Monument Association ridiculous, but the image of an intention set in stone transcends the joke about the monument society and speaks to a larger set of concerns in Poe's satires. A monument to an intention encapsulates the desire to *materialize* intention and thus to make it less elusive, less mysterious, and less vulnerable to misinterpretation. At the same time, it highlights the irrationality of such a desire. Letters of brass cannot stabilize meaning, and speech eludes even these hopeless attempts at permanence and transparency.

The problem of how to stabilize meaning is also at the center of "Some Words with a Mummy," motivating the fantasy of the auto-correcting, time-traveling historian. As the Count argues, the problem with written history is that it devolves over the years into a collective act of misinterpretation, "a kind of literary arena for the conflicting guesses, riddles, and personal squabbles of whole herds of exasperated commentators" (M 3: 1189). When the unfounded opinions of "herds" replace the actual experience of individuals, history disappears. The solution to this problem, as the Count explains, is the ritual of embalming and revivification that enables direct individual experience to triumph over collective delusion. An Egyptian historian must live out his eight hundred years "in installments" so as to be awakened every few generations in order to "set himself to work, immediately, in correcting from his own private knowledge and experience, the traditions of the day concerning the epoch at which he had originally lived" (M 3: 1189). Of course, much of what the Count says about "the epoch at which he had originally lived" is absurd. And since he admits that "un-re-written histories" prove to be as "totally and radically wrong" as the "Kabbala" that grow up over time around them (M 3: 1190), we can surmise that the confrontation Poe stages here is not between accurate history and distorted belief but between different versions of distorted belief. The authority of writing, even writing from direct experience, cannot stabilize public knowledge or correct errant opinion.

In questioning the power of writing as a technology, Poe was responding more or less directly to the outlandish claims of an 1841 *Westminster Review* essay on ancient Egypt that served as one of his sources.[25] Unlike the scientists who awaken the Count, the *Westminster Review* author (evaluating recently published books on Egypt, including J. G. Wilkinson's *Manners and Customs of the Ancient Egyptians*) marvels at the superiority of much ancient technology and lingers over the puzzle of these "lost arts." "[W]hat mechanical means," he asks, "had they to raise and fix the enormous imposts on the lintels of their temples as at Karnac? Architects now confess that they could not raise them by the usual mechanical powers."[26] Nevertheless, the reviewer shares with Poe's scientists an exaggerated sense of the superiority of modern ingenuity:

> But it may be asked, if these great scientific triumphs were accomplished at so early a period, and if we have been labouring ever since their eclipse or loss—and, to a certain degree, vainly—to recover them,—how were these things lost? The answer is a brief one. Because there was no PRESS at that time inerasably to record the progress, and permanently to stereotype the discoveries of science.[27]

Technologies come and go, the reviewer seems to argue, but print is permanent, and it grants all knowledge the kind of "security and permanency" that "guarantees us from all danger of future relapse."[28] The fantasy that closes the review—the dream that through the power of the press, "we may justly infer that no limit can be assigned for the future progress of mankind in the career of intellectual triumph, of moral improvement, and of social enjoyment"—sounds like a more emphatic version of the boasts made by the bumbling scientists, who, "joining voices, detailed, at great length, the assumptions of phrenology and the marvels of animal magnetism" (M 3: 1191) in order to prove the superiority of the moderns to the ancients. But the *Westminster Review*'s ode to the press sounds even more like the mummy himself, boasting about the superiority of Egyptian technology for preserving accurate knowledge: "Now this process of re-scription and personal rectification, pursued by various individual sages, from time to time, had the effect of preventing our history from degenerating into absolute fable" (M 3: 1189).

Poe never tired of mocking intellectual arrogance, especially grand pronouncements about the perfectibility of human knowledge and culture. In his essays and reviews, he would often deflate such tiresome certainties by highlighting aspects of public life that were beyond anyone's ability to predict or control. Even as apparently straightforward a phenomenon as celebrity, he suggests in a review of Lydia Sigourney, actually involves hidden channels of influence that are nearly impossible to trace. When Poe breezily claims, for instance, that "there are two kinds of popular reputation," he uses a debatable theory of public opinion to suggest how little we truly understand about the circulation of influence and power: "Let us suppose two writers having a reputation apparently equal—that is to say, their names *being equally in the mouths of the people*—for we take this to be the most practicable test of what we choose to term *apparent popular reputation*" (ER: 874). Poe goes on to describe one writer whose reputation is based on "a great work" and another of lesser talent who "may build up for himself" a reputation by "keeping continually in the eye" of the public; one merits acclaim, he argues, while the other doesn't. But by calling this unmerited fame "apparent popular reputation," Poe implies that the second writer, whose name is "equally in the mouths of the people," isn't actually popular at all. This idea is irrational; if being talked about is being popular, then being talked about is being popular. And yet, like most of Poe's musings on the hidden currents of public life, this idea of "apparent" popularity captures something significant about the nature of opinion, which always escapes our attempts to understand it once and for all. Trying to discern how opinion moves—not only from one generation to another and from one person to another, but from the ineffable world of casual speech to public print and back again—Poe stresses fluidity and uncertainty over "security and permanency." The fluidity of opinion makes prediction impossible and undermines not only the self-adulation of the mummy, the scientists, and the *Westminster Review* but also the complicated maps of influence that Poe tries to create in his parsing of fame.

From this perspective, we might understand Poe's hoaxes as attempts to capitalize on this instability, to exploit the tenuous line that demarcates official and unofficial knowledge, the proven and the intuited, the world of print and the world of speech. Hoaxes use the authority of print to create and manipulate speech—they succeed when they "make talk." Complicating this subterranean world of influence even further, one of the more curious examples of Poe's manipulation of his audience, "The Facts in the Case of M. Valdemar" (1845), seems to have functioned as a hoax without being designed as one.[29] Even after Poe publicly claimed that his account of a man whose death is deferred by the power of mesmerism was a fiction, a number of journals defended the veracity of this fantastic tale.[30] Their refusal to accept a hoax as a hoax makes a certain amount of sense, since an author who misleads in one case might reasonably mislead in another. One irate English editor, in decrying Poe's dishonesty, makes a gesture similar to Cooper's in expressing the desire for perfect textual transparency:

> Wherever, as in this country, a strong sense prevails of the irretrievable disgrace consequent upon a man's name being connected with a falsehood, writers will always manifest the greatest care not to put forth any statements about which danger can exist of their intentions being misunderstood. . . . [T]here will always be found a general readiness on the part of the public to receive in good faith whatever may be asserted, (provided it is not in absolute contradiction to known facts,) by those who will furnish their names as a guarantee.[31]

On the one hand, this lecture on the importance of honesty in journalism resembles the *Westminster Review*'s tribute to the "guarantees" of the press. On the other, however, it reveals the hollowness of the faith in the authority of the public prints. While a concern about the effects of "fake news" on the general public is intrinsic to the digital age, Poe's reputation suggests that it was already alive and well at the birth of the magazine age.

Unlike the hoaxes, the satires are analytical as much as they are performative. They not only attempt to move the reader back and forth across the line that divides official from unofficial knowledge, print from speech, but also to think through the philosophical problems presented by the manipulation of this line. "The System of Doctor Tarr and Professor Fether" might be Poe's most elaborate parody of the search for transparency, for "security and permanency."[32] Critics have seen in this tale a variety of Poe's political obsessions, from the threat of slave insurrection to the problem of mob rule.[33] And it does make sense to read the story as yet another jab at Jacksonian democracy, since it imagines that a revolution designed to "overthrow the reigning powers" leads inevitably to "a lunatic government" (M 3: 1018). As in all of Poe's satires, however, the issues here are formal as much as topical. More than anything else, "Tarr and Fether" is about the problem of *evidence*—how we come to know both the external world and ourselves and how we test that knowledge. The story begins by picturing an environment that seems unnervingly opaque and confusing; the narrator, his curiosity piqued by gossip about a certain "*Maison de Santé*" in the south of France, is traveling to the asylum by way of a "grass-grown by-path, which, in half an hour, nearly lost itself in a dense forest, clothing the base of a mountain" (M 3: 1003). Adding to this confusion, the narrator's "travelling companion" (who introduces him to the superintendent Maillard but refuses to enter the mad house) turns out to be someone he hardly knows—"a gentleman with whom I had made casual acquaintance a few days before" (M 3: 1002). Similarly, the province through which he travels is said to be populated by "a peculiarly eccentric people, with a vast number of antiquated notions" (M 3: 1008). And when he tours the asylum in order to witness for himself the famous "soothing system" (his knowledge of the system, he admits, "has been at third or fourth hand"), he cannot tell who is mad and who is sane. While the remainder of the story clears up these initial confusions (for the reader if not the narrator), it does so by raising issues of knowledge and proof that cannot be so easily set aside.

The "soothing system" refers to a new mode of psychiatric care in the United States, which advocated managed freedom over beatings and confinement.[34] An 1811 textbook by T. Romeyn Beck, one of the system's first practitioners, describes it this way: "A system of humane vigilance is adopted. Coercion by blows, stripes, and chains . . . is now justly laid aside. . . . [One must] tolerate noisy ejaculations, strictly exclude visitors; let their fears and resentments be soothed without unnecessary opposition."[35] But Maillard's version of this system is sinister; it emphasizes not the creation of a more peaceful and civilized environment for the mentally ill, but a practice in which doctors use the patients' delusions to manipulate them. "We have had men, for example, who fancied themselves chickens," Maillard explains. "The cure was, to insist upon the thing as a fact—to accuse the patient of stupidity in not sufficiently perceiving it to be a fact—and thus to refuse him any other diet for a week than that which properly appertains to a chicken" (M 3: 1006). As much as Maillard's strategy differs from the "moral management" of the insane, however, they do have something in common: just as Beck advises toleration of the patient's "fears and resentments," arguing that "by thus acting the patient will 'minister to himself,'" Maillard also (ostensibly) wants to help patients minister to themselves—to cure them by having them confront their delusions head on.[36] The real difference between these strategies, though, is that Maillard's version of reverse psychology ends up destabilizing the very idea of a shared reality. Maillard is perhaps too sanguine about the individual's independent sense of self. The story of the man who thinks he's a chicken is reminiscent of the famous story from the *Zhuangzi*, in which the Chinese philosopher describes waking from a dream in which he is a butterfly and wondering if he is in fact a butterfly dreaming he's a man. Generations of scholars have puzzled over this story, an illustration of the limits of certainty which seems to challenge the Cartesian commitment to the bedrock of individual identity.[37] For Maillard, however, this kind of identity problem is easily resolved: treat a person as if she were a butterfly, he seems to say, and she will soon enough concede that she is a person. Perhaps.

But when one adds into the equation an ordinary social context, this logic seems less sound. Presumably, when Zhuangzi wakes up from his dream, no one treats him like a butterfly. If they had, it might have made his story less a fanciful illustration of a philosophical problem than an existential nightmare.[38] In that case, Zhuangzi's tale would look more like *The Metamorphosis*, in which Kafka literalizes the effects of social exclusion on his hapless protagonist. The fact that Gregor Samsa is treated like a cockroach actually transforms him into a cockroach.[39] Similarly, if you believe you are a chicken and other people begin to treat you like a chicken, you might simply feel that your identity has been confirmed. It is difficult to see how, in such a case, you would ever discover that you were not a chicken.

The dinner-party conversation in "Tarr and Fether," in which the inmates posing as keepers discuss the highs and lows of life in the asylum, inverts this logic. It presents us with people who are less indulged in their illusions than compelled to contemplate them from the outside, to loudly proclaim their essential falseness. "[W]e had here, not long ago, a person who had taken it into his head that he was a donkey," says the man who fancies himself a donkey, "which, allegorically speaking, you will say, was quite true. He was a troublesome patient; and we had much ado to keep him within bounds" (M 3: 1009–1010). Each patient at the narrator's table describes his own delusions as the delusions of another, which is to say, rather than being patronized by the community, they are made to speak *as* the community. They do not just describe these delusions, they evaluate and often mock them: "And then there was an ignoramus . . . who mistook himself for a frog" (M 3: 1012), says the man whose imitation of a frog suggests that he is himself the "ignoramus" he describes. In a brilliant reading of the story, Jonathan Elmer remarks of this scene that "there is a mode of self-exposure—we could even say confession—which can be both a true description of the self and a true performance of the self (in all its idiosyncratic peculiarities) but in which the simultaneity or coincidence of these two modes of self-revelation is unrecognizable."[40] I take this to mean that the attempt to truly objectify the self is a form of madness in that one cannot inhabit mutually exclusive positions at the same time; one cannot assume the point of view of an individual and the social world that both forms and judges that individual.

If it represents a logical impossibility, however, this collapsing of self and social world also describes how Poe understands the fundamental paradox of public opinion—that what one experiences as an individual turns out to be collective. As I have suggested, the effects of this kind of merging of social and political life are dramatized in "The Man That Was Used Up," in which a series of individuals' seemingly heartfelt declarations to the narrator are revealed to be nothing more than stock phrases. The one expression used by almost everyone—"Never heard!" (M 2: 384)—works much like Pundita's incredulousness in "Mellonta Tauta" and Maillard's response to the narrator of "Tarr and Fether": "Good Heavens! . . . I surely do not hear you aright! You did not intend to say, eh? that you had never *heard* of either of the learned Doctor Tarr, or of the celebrated Professor Fether?" (M 3: 1017). In "The Man That Was Used Up," this sense of universality gestures toward a set of beliefs and a body of (questionable) knowledge that is taken for granted. And, as the ending of the tale reveals, the "remarkable . . . individuality" of

General John A. B. C. Smith is created, like the gossip about him, out of interchangeable parts (M 2: 378).

In "Tarr and Fether," the move from "soothing system" to Maillard's "new system" is more than just a joke about an asylum run by the inmates—it marks an important philosophical shift as well. The primary distinction between these systems is the understanding of how individual judgment emerges and asserts itself. As Maillard's chicken anecdote suggests, the "soothing system" imagines that individual belief can stand apart from social context: tell a man he's a chicken and he will soon discover that he is a man. This philosophy also animates Maillard's admonishment to the narrator: "You are young yet, my friend . . . but the time will arrive when you will learn to judge for yourself of what is going on in the world, without trusting to the gossip of others" (M 3: 1007). This bit of wisdom implies that while it might be true that one can never completely trust one's senses, direct experience of the world is better than relying on information received second-hand. "Believe nothing you hear," he advises the narrator, "and only one half that you see" (M 3: 1007).

Maillard's description of his *new* system, which might be understood as a way of radicalizing his initial distrust of the senses, contradicts his earlier endorsement of independent judgment. Consider, for example, his advice to the narrator about how to "read" insanity:

> A lunatic may be "soothed," as it is called, for a time, but, in the end, he is very apt to become obstreperous. His cunning, too, is proverbial, and great. If he has a project in view, he conceals his design with a marvelous wisdom; and the dexterity with which he counterfeits sanity, presents, to the metaphysician, one of the most singular problems in the study of mind. When a madman appears *thoroughly* sane, indeed, it is high time to put him in a straight jacket. (M 3: 1018)

In other words, when it comes to madmen, sanity never appears to be sanity because a convincing performance of lucidity must be read as proof of its opposite. The problem with this view, of course, is that it assumes that one always knows when one is dealing with a madman, when the ability to distinguish madness and sanity is precisely the issue. While Maillard argues that this mimicry of sanity "presents, to the metaphysician, one of the most singular problems in the study of mind," the problem is not the madman's (as Maillard suggests) but the observer's. If appearances can be deceiving, then individual judgements must be grounded in what Maillard had earlier dismissed as "the gossip of others." That Maillard's instructions are themselves quite mad underscores the difficulty of making correct judgements about the world rather than the superiority of going it alone.

Accordingly, the last line of "Tarr and Fether" indicates not only that the narrator never really understands what he has witnessed at the asylum, but that he remains unaware of his ignorance: "I have only to add that, although I have searched every library in Europe for the works of Doctor *Tarr* and Professor *Fether*, I have, up to the present day, utterly failed in my endeavors at procuring an edition" (M 3: 1022). Once again, a print source holds out the promise of stabilizing meaning—but this impossible desire is registered as the longing for texts that one cannot find because they have never existed. It is in this spirit that we should understand the orchestra's eruption into "Yankee Doodle" at the climax of the tale. This moment has typically been read as Poe's sly nod to American politics, but one of the more interesting things about "Yankee Doodle" is its long and convoluted history as folk song.[41] J. A. Leo Lemay's detailed account of its origins, authorship, and development over the eighteenth and nineteenth centuries testifies to both its staying power as a cultural artifact and its mutability. Made famous by its role in the Revolution, "Yankee Doodle" actually emerged during the colonial period; its verses were never fixed but were instead adapted over the years to various political contexts. One of the song's earliest historians wrote of his attempt to discover the original version: "I am inclined to suppose it will be found of the nature of the Pirates' signature when each person wrote his name in a circle which of course had neither beginning nor end."[42] "Yankee Doodle," then, is less a sign of the American-ness of this ostensibly French tale than a figure for the mysterious power of a "folk" tradition, which is known apart from a written record and which cannot be traced to an original source.

Given the narrator's well-founded suspicions throughout "Tarr and Fether"—that Maillard is deceiving him, that the people presented to him as keepers are actually patients—his strange obliviousness at the end is instructive in another way as well. It is possible that Poe wants to suggest that madness is contagious; the narrator, immersed in an asylum, has begun to think like one of the inmates. His story would then be a repetition of Maillard's story. We can dispute this notion of contagiousness without denying a central insight: judgments and opinions are never solely an individual affair. What seems to be your deepest conviction or the evidence of your senses is often nothing more than common knowledge. Like Pundita's troubling opinions about war or Maillard's about the soothing system, public opinion names the way that the common knowledge of an abstract collective can speak through the individual. What Poe finds so disturbing about this process is that it works by convincing people that they have finally learned to judge for themselves "what is going on in the world."

Notes

1. Ernest Marchand, "Poe as Social Critic," *American Literature* 6, no. 1 (1934): 28.
2. This is not to say that critics don't argue about the particular ways in which Poe negotiates his political, social, and cultural moment. To take just one example, a recent essay claims, "The momentum given to Poe's work by the scientific and technological maelstrom of the early nineteenth century has yet to be fully reckoned." See John Tresch, "'Matter No More': Edgar Allan Poe and the Paradoxes of Materialism," *Critical Inquiry* 42 (Summer 2016): 867.
3. The most influential examples of this kind of historical scholarship include J. Gerald Kennedy and Jerome McGann, eds., *Poe and the Remapping of Antebellum Print Culture* (Baton Rouge: Louisiana State University Press, 2012); Meredith McGill, *American Literature and the Culture of Reprinting, 1834–1853* (Philadelphia: University of

Pennsylvania Press, 2003); Terence Whalen, *Edgar Allan Poe and the Masses: The Political Economy of Literature in Antebellum America* (Princeton, NJ: Princeton University Press, 1999); Shawn Rosenheim and Stephen Rachman, eds., *The American Face of Edgar Allan Poe* (Baltimore: Johns Hopkins University Press, 1995); and Jonathan Elmer, *Reading at the Social Limit: Affect, Mass Culture, and Edgar Allan Poe* (Stanford, CA: Stanford University Press, 1995).

4. Marchand, "Poe as Social Critic," 30–31.
5. See, on the first issue, Maurice Lee, "Absolute Poe: His System of Transcendental Racism," *American Literature* 75, no. 4 (2003): 751–781; and on the second, Justine Murison, *The Politics of Anxiety in Nineteenth-Century American Literature* (New York: Cambridge University Press, 2011), especially the second chapter, "Frogs, Dogs, and Mobs: Reflex and Democracy in Edgar Allan Poe's Satires," 47–75.
6. See, for example, William Whipple, "Poe's Political Satire," *University of Texas Studies in English* 35 (1956): 81–95; and Burton Pollin, "Politics and History in Poe's 'Mellonta Tauta': Two Allusions Explained," *Studies in Short Fiction* 8 (1971): 627–631. For a more recent version of this approach, see Duncan Faherty, "'A Certain Unity of Design': Edgar Allan Poe's *Tales of the Grotesque and Arabesque* and the Terrors of Jacksonian Democracy," *Edgar Allan Poe Review* 6, no. 2 (Fall 2005): 4–21.
7. For an assessment of Poe's failure as a humorist, see Tom Quirk, *Nothing Abstract: Investigations in the American Literary Imagination* (Columbia: University of Missouri Press, 2001), especially the fourth chapter, "What If Poe's Humorous Tales Were Funny? Poe's 'X-ing a Paragrab' and Twain's 'Journalism in Tennessee,'" 53–63.
8. Even critics who take seriously Poe's conservatism—his distrust of not only common citizens and what passed as common sense but democracy in general—can be charmed by the wittiness of his attacks. Betsy Erkkila, for example, reads in Poe's antidemocratic screeds (in tales like "King Pest" and "The Man That Was Used Up") not an aristocratic disdain for the masses but a much more palatable critique of "the barbarism and violence to person, psyche, society and world that underwrote the market revolution, the politics of democracy, and the westward march of civilization." Betsy Erkkila, "Perverting the American Renaisssance: Poe, Democracy, Critical Theory," in *Poe and the Remapping of Antebellum Print Culture*, 60. See also Rick Rodriguez, "Sovereign Authority and the Democratic Subject in Poe," *Poe Studies* 44, no. 1 (2011): 39–56.
9. One important exception to this tendency is Murison, who claims, "With her poor reading of the historical archive and her insistence on the didactic lessons of history, Pundita is as simplistic as the democracy she maligns" (*The Politics of Anxiety in Nineteenth-Century American Literature*, 68).
10. Samuel Otter, *Philadelphia Stories: America's Literature of Race and Freedom* (New York: Oxford University Press, 2010), 171.
11. At one point, responding to the scientists' attempt to take credit for inventing democracy, the Count refutes their claims both to priority and superiority: "[H]e said that, a great while ago, there had occurred something of a very similar sort. Thirteen Egyptian provinces determined all at once to be free, and so set a magnificent example to the rest of mankind." The resulting system, however, was immediately hijacked by a "usurping tyrant" called "*Mob*," who created "the most odious and insupportable despotism that ever was heard of upon the face of the Earth" (M 3: 1194). The mummy's attack on democracy (like Pundita's) has often been seen as a distillation of Poe's political stance.

12. Marcia D. Nichols, for example, while noting the way Poe mocks the Count, argues that "the mummy is a ludicrous figure who, nevertheless, exerts power over white men even more abject than he." See her "Poe's 'Some Words with a Mummy' and Blackface Anatomy," *Poe Studies* 48 (2015): 10. See also, Scott Trafton, *Egypt Land: Race and Nineteenth-Century American Egyptomania* (Durham, NC: Duke University Press, 2004), 132–139.
13. Dana D. Nelson, "The Haunting of White Manhood: Poe, Fraternal Ritual, and Polygenesis," *American Literature* 69 (1997): 516.
14. Critics are still debating the extent to which Poe was an overt apologist for slavery, although his disdain for the New England abolitionists (and their entire program of social uplift) is well documented. If white men are often under attack in Poe's tales, it seems clear that it is not their whiteness (and the privilege that this entails) that makes them targets of his satire. For an excellent account of Poe and racism, see Lee's "Absolute Poe."
15. Charles D. Martin, "Can the Mummy Speak? Manifest Destiny, Ventriloquism, and the Silence of the Ancient Egyptian Body," *Nineteenth-Century Contexts* 31, no. 2 (June 2009): 124.
16. In a dense and convincing reading of the story, David Long argues that the Count's "hyperbole," "[c]oming from the lips of an incensed former Egyptian aristocrat . . . verges on self-parody (of the mummy if not of Poe) and threatens to invalidate the ancient's argument against the moderns." But he concludes that "Allamistakeo's testimony is fully corroborated by the actions of the latter-day democrats." See his "Poe's Political Identity: A Mummy Unswathed," *Poe Studies* 23, no. 1 (1990): 4.
17. Elizabeth Duquette gets at something like this more abstract topicality in her analysis of "The Business Man." See her "Accounting for Value in 'The Business Man,'" *Studies in American Fiction* 35, no. 1 (2007): 3–20.
18. For a different reading of Poe's later satires, see J. Gerald Kennedy, "Poe's 'American' Turn: Opposing Nationalism, Appeasing the Nationalists," in *Poe Writing/Writing Poe*, ed. Richard Kopley and Jana Argersinger (New York: AMS Press, 2013), 99–126.
19. Daniel Hoffman, *Poe Poe Poe Poe Poe Poe Poe* (New York: Doubleday and Co., 1972), 196.
20. I have written in more detail elsewhere about this story and the problem of public opinion during the period more generally. See *Fictions of Mass Democracy in Nineteenth-Century America* (New York: Cambridge University Press, 2015), particularly the second chapter, "Gossip in the Age of Print: Poe's Crowdsourcing," 50–71.
21. See, for example, Reiner Smolinski and Jeffrey E. Rumiano, "Poe's Party Politics in the Age of Jackson," in *Poe Writing/Writing Poe*, 51–70.
22. James Fenimore Cooper, *The American Democrat* (New York: Penguin, 1989), 197.
23. James Fenimore Cooper, *Home As Found* (New York: Capricorn Books, 1961), 221.
24. For an account of the organization and individuals satirized here, see Pollin, "Politics and History in Poe's 'Mellonta Tauta.'"
25. See Mabbott's introduction to the story (M 3: 1175–1177).
26. E. C., *The Westminster Review* (July 1841): 17.
27. E. C., 18.
28. E. C., 18–19.
29. There is, of course, no way to know for sure what Poe did and did not intend. But a number of critics, beginning with Sidney Lind, have pointed to letters from Poe that suggest he was surprised by the initial reaction to the story (rather than pleased that the hoax had succeeded). As James Machor argues, "Only after such responses did Poe begin declaring that '"Hoax" *is* precisely the word suited to M. Valdemar's case' and start chortling in print

over the joke he had played on the credulous press and much of its public." See his *Reading Fiction in Antebellum America: Informed Response and Reception Histories, 1820–1865* (Baltimore: Johns Hopkins University Press, 2011), 133. See also Sidney E. Lind, "Poe and Mesmerism," *PMLA* 62, no. 4 (1947): 1077–1094.

30. For an account of the publication and response to "Valdemar," see Antoine Faivre, "Borrowings and Misreadings: Edgar Allan Poe's 'Mesmeric' Tales and the Strange Case of their Reception," *Aries* 7 (2007): 21–62.
31. Quoted in Ian Walker, *Edgar Allan Poe: The Critical Heritage* (1985; Taylor and Francis e-Library, 2002), 152–153.
32. For a reading of "Tarr and Fether" as hoax, see John Bryant, "Poe's Ape of UnReason: Humor, Ritual, and Culture," *Nineteenth-Century Literature* 51, no. 1 (1996): 16–52.
33. For a reading that stresses slave insurrection, see J. Gerald Kennedy, "'A Mania for Composition': Poe's Annus Mirabilis and the Violence of Nation Building," *American Literary History* 17 (2005): 1–35. For a reading that stresses mob rule, see Philip D. Beidler, "Mythopoetic Justice: Democracy and the Death of Edgar Allan Poe," *Midwest Quarterly* 46, no. 3 (Spring 2005): 252–267. Aaron Matthew Percich gives a less persuasive account of the tale, arguing that it engages with the problem of Irish immigration. See his "Irish Mouths and English Tea-pots: Orality and Unreason in 'The System of Doctor Tarr and Professor Fether,'" *Poe Studies* 47 (2014): 79.
34. William Whipple notes that Poe was likely mocking Charles Dickens, who had written glowingly of such treatments in *American Notes*. See his "Poe's Two-Edged Satiric Tale," *Nineteenth-Century Fiction* 9, no. 2 (1954): 121–133.
35. Quoted in Whipple, "Poe's Two-Edged Satiric Tale," 122–123. As Whipple points out, "by 1844, the benevolent treatment of insane people was still rare enough to be news" (125).
36. Whipple, 122–123.
37. For an account of Zhuangzi's skepticism in relation to Descartes's, see Xiaoqiang Han, "A Butterfly Dream in a Brain in a Vat," *Philosophia* 38 (2010): 157–167.
38. For a discussion of this problem, see Raymond Tallis, *In Defence of Wonder and Other Philosophical Reflections* (London: Routledge, 2014), esp. 30–35.
39. As Stanley Corngold explains, "*The Metamorphosis* is the transformation of a man into his metaphor ('This man is a louse'), whereupon the creature gains, along with the horror, an acrobatic lightness of being." See his *Lambent Traces: Franz Kafka* (Princeton, NJ: Princeton University Press, 2009), 84.
40. Elmer, *Reading at the Social Limit*, 145.
41. See, for example, Benjamin Franklin Fisher, "Poe's 'Tarr and Fether': Hoaxing in the Blackwood Mode," in *The Naiad Voice: Essays on Poe's Satiric Hoaxing*, ed. Dennis W. Eddings (Port Washington, NY: Associated Faculty Press, 1983): 136–147; and Elmer, *Reading at the Social Limit*, 146.
42. Quoted in J. A. Leo Lemay, "The American Origins of 'Yankee Doodle,'" *William and Mary Quarterly* 33, no. 3 (1976): 460–461. See also Poe's remark in "Marginalia" about gossip: "Embracing all things, it has neither beginning, middle, nor end. Thus of the gossiper it was not properly said that 'he commences his discourse by jumping *in medias res*.' For, clearly, your gossiper commences not at all. He is begun. He is already begun. He is always begun. In the matter of end he is indeterminate" (ER: 1358).

Bibliography

Beidler, Philip D. "Mythopoetic Justice: Democracy and the Death of Edgar Allan Poe." *Midwest Quarterly* 46, no. 3 (Spring 2005): 252–267.

Eddings, Dennis W., ed. *The Naiad Voice: Essays on Poe's Satiric Hoaxing*. Port Washington, NY: Associated Faculty Press, 1983.

Elmer, Jonathan. *Reading at the Social Limit: Affect, Mass Culture, and Edgar Allan Poe*. Palo Alto, CA: Stanford University Press, 1995.

Faherty, Duncan. "'A Certain Unity of Design': Edgar Allan Poe's *Tales of the Grotesque and Arabesque* and the Terrors of Jacksonian Democracy." *Edgar Allan Poe Review* 6, no. 2 (Fall 2005): 4–21.

Hoffman, Daniel. *Poe Poe Poe Poe Poe Poe Poe*. New York: Doubleday and Co., 1972.

Kennedy, Gerald, and Jerome McGann, eds. *Poe and the Remapping of Antebellum Print Culture*. Baton Rouge: Louisiana State University Press, 2012.

Kopley, Richard, and Jana Argersinger, eds. *Poe Writing/Writing Poe*. New York: AMS Press, 2013.

Lee, Maurice. "Absolute Poe: His System of Transcendental Racism." *American Literature* 75, no. 4 (2003): 751–781.

Machor, James. *Reading Fiction in Antebellum America: Informed Response and Reception Histories, 1820–1865*. Baltimore: Johns Hopkins University Press, 2011.

Marchand, Ernest. "Poe as Social Critic." *American Literature* 6, no. 1 (1934): 28–43.

Margolis, Stacey. *Fictions of Mass Democracy in Nineteenth-Century America*. New York: Cambridge University Press, 2015.

Murison, Justine. *The Politics of Anxiety in Nineteenth-Century American Literature*. New York: Cambridge University Press, 2011.

Otter, Samuel. *Philadelphia Stories: America's Literature of Race and Freedom*. New York: Oxford University Press, 2010.

Whipple, William. "Poe's Political Satire." *University of Texas Studies in English* 35 (1956): 81–95.

CHAPTER 10

UNDEAD WIVES AND UNDONE HUSBANDS

Poe's Tales of Marriage

ELLEN WEINAUER

One of Edgar Allan Poe's earliest published stories is "A Decided Loss"—a strange little burlesque that, in the words of Kenneth Silverman, "gleefully catalogues all the ways one can die without dying."[1] Published in the Philadelphia *Saturday Courier* in November of 1832, "A Decided Loss" tells the story of a man who loses his breath while ranting against his wife. In the course of the story, this undead man is killed in a number of additional ways: he gets run over by a stagecoach, his skull is fractured, he is laid out for burial (in which state his nose is maimed by two cats), and he is mistaken for a notorious criminal and hanged. Finally, he is disemboweled by an apothecary who, suspecting him of being alive, applies the "new Galvanic Battery" to him and thus restores his breath and his life (M 2: 59).

A preposterous tale indeed, "A Decided Loss" nevertheless opens several veins that Poe will continue to mine throughout his career: a satirical treatment of over-the-top sensationalism, for example, and an interest in bodily integrity, states of consciousness, and the hazy borders between life and death. It is perhaps no wonder, then, that Poe returned to "A Decided Loss" several times over many years, expanding it significantly as "Loss of Breath" (*Southern Literary Messenger*, 1835; republished in *Tales of the Grotesque and Arabesque*, 1840), and then cutting it down again for the *Broadway Journal* in 1846. Throughout its long career of expansion and contraction, however, one important element of the story remained unchanged: the narrator's "loss of breath" occurs the day after he marries. Without preamble, "A Decided Loss" begins this way:

> "Thou wretch!—thou vixen!—thou shrew!" said I to my wife on the morning after the wedding—"thou witch!—thou whipper-snapper!—thou sink of iniquity!—thou fiery-faced quintessence of all that is abominable! —thou—thou"—; here standing upon tiptoe, seizing her by the throat, and placing my mouth close to her ear, I was

> preparing to launch forth a new and most unequivocal epithet of opprobrium, which could not fail, if uttered, to convince her of her insignificance, when, to my extreme horror and astonishment, I discovered that I had lost my breath. (M 2: 53)

Why does the narrator attack his wife with such vituperation "on the morning after the wedding"? The story provides few clues, for the wife utters no words in its course, leaving the story's action early on. There is a hint that infidelity may be involved: as the narrator searches for his breath, he turns up a "bundle of billet-doux, from a neighbor to my wife" (M 2: 55). But the narrator suggests that he finds the letters only after he has lost his breath; and the reference is so tongue-in-cheek—along with the letters the narrator also finds "several false teeth, an eye," and "two pairs of hips" (M 2: 55)—that its connection to the narrator's assault seems tenuous at best.[2] In short, we are left with no clear explanation as to why the narrator attacks his wife just a day after their nuptials.

Critics have paid little attention to "A Decided Loss" or its later avatars; and whatever treatment the story has received offers little analysis of the immediate postnuptial setting of the narrator's misogynistic attack.[3] In point of fact, critics have offered little commentary about marriage as an institution in Poe's work in general, despite a historical turn in Poe studies that might lead in that direction. This is a curious omission, since Poe repeatedly returns to scenes of marriage in his fiction. Furthermore, the issue of marriage was ubiquitous in the periodical culture in which he was a fully vested participant. Whether engaging the changing legal and economic terms of antebellum marriage, representing "good" and "bad" marriages, or establishing the proper "duties" of the antebellum wife, American periodicals were full of stories about the matrimonial estate. A look at the 1835 issue of the *Southern Literary Messenger* in which "Berenice" was first published, for example, turns up the following titles: "John Bull and Mary Bull" (a complicated tale about marriage, inheritance, and skin color); "Marrying Well"; "Courtship and Marriage"; and "The Village Pastor's Wife." The next month's issue, which carries "Morella," also includes "A Bashful Gentleman," about a man too shy to seek a wife; and "A Scene in Real Life," about the fatal effects of adultery. Always attuned to the interests of the reading public, Poe could hardly have missed the fact that foremost among those interests was marriage in all of its dimensions—socioeconomic, emotional, moral, and legal.

"A Decided Loss" would suggest that, from the beginning of his publishing career, marriage was certainly on Poe's mind. In particular, the language of both loss and metamorphosis in this story indicates that Poe is already contemplating legal matrimony and its shaping force. Colin Dayan has observed that Poe was "obsessed" with the "concept of the legal person," with the power of law to "create new, paradoxical, and often unnatural entities."[4] This obsession might explain Poe's repeated returns to the institution of marriage, which functioned precisely to create new (and arguably unnatural) entities as it changed men into husbands and women into wives. That the narrator's "decided loss" occurs the morning after his wedding thus suggests that Poe is thinking about the role that marriage plays in constructing identity, about the power of marital law to "create new . . . entities" in both women and men. In Poe's renderings, marriage is indeed a transformative institution, one with frightening repercussions for all parties. Marriage, in short, becomes a site of Gothic terror in Poe's tales. As a look at a number of stories—from the well-studied "Ligeia" to the relatively obscure "The Oblong Box"—will suggest, Poe views marriage as an institution that subjects both women and men to "decided," indeed often fatal, losses.

In his study of nineteenth-century marriage in the United States, Hendrik Hartog poses a question that is at once simple and freighted with significance: "what did it mean to be married?"[5] In answer, Hartog offers two keywords: "transformation" and "unity." Those words, he declares, "are good starting points for an exploration of what it means to be a wife or a husband in nineteenth-century America": marriage "*transformed* men and women into husbands and wives," and marriage "*united* wife and husband, gave them a singular identity."[6] According to the legal principle of marital unity—one that reverberates in American courts today—husband and wife became, after marriage, one being. In his *Commentaries on the Laws of England*, English jurist William Blackstone offered what became a ubiquitously cited description of this marital transformation: "the husband and wife are one person in law," Blackstone explains; "that is, the very being or legal existence of the woman is suspended during the marriage, or at least is incorporated and consolidated into that of her husband: under whose wing, protection, and *cover*, she performs every thing; and her condition during her marriage is called her *coverture*."[7] As a result of her coverture, the married woman lost almost all procedural and economic capacities: she could not sue or execute a will, make a contract, or claim earned wages; any personal property (moveable goods such as jewelry, furniture, or slaves) that she may have held prior to her marriage became her husband's. Though he could not claim to own it outright, the husband also gained the rights to control and manage any real estate his wife brought to or acquired during the marriage. For women, in short, marriage entailed what was indeed a "decided loss," leaving them in a state that many called "civil death."[8]

Poe's interest in the "concept of the legal person" could find much to fuel itself in the domain of legal marriage. In fact, to an extent that has been heretofore largely unacknowledged, the legal personalities of husband and wife filter into Poe's work, shaping the unusually troubling dynamic between men and women that we find in them. We can find early and persistent examples of this theme in the cluster of tales named after dead women—"Berenice" (1835), "Morella" (1835), "Ligeia" (1838), and "Eleonora" (1841)—all of which treat the (fatal) transformations worked by marriage and the diminution that women experience as the law changes them from "woman" to "wife." In "Berenice," the title character, once a blithe and lively girl, is felled by a disease that "pervad[es] her mind, her habits, and her character" and "disturb[s] even the identity of her person!" (M 2: 211) Although Berenice falls ill prior to her betrothal, it is after the narrator reponds to her "fallen and desolate condition" (M 2: 214) by proposing marriage that her disease rapidly advances. She becomes a spectral shadow of her former self, her eyes "lifeless," her "figure . . . vacillating and indistinct" (M 2: 214); "not one vestige of the former being lurked in any single line of the contour" (M 2: 215).[9]

Although Berenice dies before she marries, she nonetheless serves as an early avatar of Poe's perishing wives, whose stories echo and mirror one another. Morella's wasting ailment, for example, is reminiscent of Berenice's: "she was woman and pined away daily," declares Morella's narrator-husband; "the crimson spot settled steadily upon the cheek, and the blue veins upon the pale forehead became prominent" (M 2: 227). The image of the tell-tale "blue veins" carries forward to "Ligeia": her "pale fingers became of the transparent waxen hue of the grave, and the blue veins upon the lofty forehead swelled and sank" with the "tides" of her emotions (M 2: 316). Ligeia's successor Rowena similarly declines, for around the "commencement of the second month of the marriage," she is "attacked with sudden illness" (M 2: 323). So too does Eleonora fall ill: "She had seen that the finger of Death was upon her bosom" (M 2: 641).[10] As biographers and critics have long observed, in these stories Poe seems to be revisiting the traumatic illnesses of his mother, his wife, and other women he lost throughout his life.[11] But in these wasted women—women whose wasting occurs explicitly in the context of courtship and matrimony—we can also see Poe considering marriage itself, and the profound, destructive transformations that it works upon women.

If these cadaverous women indict the transformational effects of matrimony, their ability to return from the dead—as do Ligeia, Morella, and (somewhat differently) Eleonora[12]—can be seen to literalize an idea that a number of progressive reformers addressed: that in effecting her civil death, the law makes the married woman a kind of in-between figure, neither fully living nor actually dead. In a significant 1845 treatise, Judge Elisha P. Hurlbut writes that the law turns the married woman into a kind of "monster": prior to marriage, she existed as "a distinct moral being, full of rights and bounded by duties; that existence is now merged in her husband—and in the eye of the law she exists not at all." Marriage is, for women, a "legal tomb," he claimed.[13] Journalist Jane Swisshelm renders this idea even more colorfully, describing three women this way: "One of them is . . . dead, one is married, and the other is still living."[14] In "A Decided Loss," the narrator refers to himself as "alive with the qualifications of the dead—dead with the propensities of the living" (M 2: 53). This description, however, more aptly pertains to the married woman, as the undead wives in Poe's tales suggest.

Of all of Poe's stories, "Ligeia" offers the most arresting treatment of the undead wife. Laid waste by a fatal disease, like both Berenice and Morella, Ligeia most resembles the latter in that she is profoundly erudite—a fact on which her narrator-husband lavishes admiration. Indeed, Ligeia's husband subjects himself to her intellectual power, turning "with a child-like confidence, to her guidance through the chaotic world of metaphysical investigation" (M 2: 316). Although this seems to subvert the traditional marital hierarchy, the narrator retains a significant element of husbandly power: his control over Ligeia's property. As the narrator admits, he has gained vast wealth through his marriage; as he also admits, he cannot recall Ligeia's paternal name or how he first met her. This latter admission is "quite surprising," Karen Weeks notes, coming from "someone whose vast wealth derives from inheriting her presumably paternal riches."[15] In the context of legal marriage, however, this makes a kind of sense. "[T]he basic ideological task of the law of marriage," Hartog argues, was "to make sure that the married and the nonmarried were clearly divided from one another"; the "sharp boundary between marriage and nonmarriage was everywhere in the law," he notes.[16] After marriage, Ligeia stands on the other side of that clear division, the transformation so "sharp" that her identity prior to marriage matters little. She is now a property-less *feme covert*—the "wife of my bosom" the narrator calls her (M 2: 311), echoing Blackstone. Thus, while she appears to possess an unusual command over her husband ("she bade me" and "I obeyed" [M 2: 318]), Ligeia is still a wife, and therefore still subject to the incapacities of legal marriage. And in this regard, she is not so very different from her successor, Rowena, whose body fittingly serves as a vehicle for Ligeia's eventual reanimation.

The interchangeability between Ligeia and Rowena reflects another complication in the institution of legal marriage, which had both contractual and status-based dimensions. Marriage originated in contract; but it was a contract like no other. As Lenore Weitzman explains, "while the individuals who enter marriage have the same freedom of choice that governs entry into other contractual relations, once they make the decision to enter . . . the terms and conditions of the relationship are dictated by the state."[17] In short, once individuals have contracted to marry, they become part of an institution that imposes upon them a specific, legally mandated status. According to Milton Regan, status can be understood as

> a legal identity that is subject to a set of publicly imposed expectations largely independent of the preference of the person who holds that status. Put another way, status is the formal expression of the behavior expected of a role occupant. Status was a crucial component of Victorian family law in the sense that a person's identity as husband, wife, father, or mother was intended to be a significant determinant of that person's conduct within the family.[18]

The idea of status adds another layer of complexity to the transformations of marriage, because it reminds us of the loss of individuality that marriage occasioned. As marriage changed men into husbands and women into wives, it subjected them "to a set of publicly imposed expectations." This fact might help explain the eerie feeling of déjà vu we have when we are reading Poe's dead wife stories, the feeling that we have read this story (encountered this wife, met her obsessive husband, seen her die) already. Even though there are differences in plot and characterization, the stories duplicate one another, leaving readers in a sort of fictional hall of mirrors. More specifically, though, the idea of status can help us make sense of the fact that, at the climactic moment when she comes back from the dead, Ligeia comes back not as herself but as Rowena, as the (second) wife. In this way, Poe strikingly renders the loss of individual identity incurred by women in marriage. Defined primarily by their status as married women, Ligeia and Rowena are not really different at all. The former can return in the body of the latter because, *as wives*, the two are fundamentally interchangeable.

However much "Ligeia" appears to invert established marital hierarchy and to vest Ligeia herself with "husbandly" authority, then, she (like Rowena) remains confined in—covered by—the defining mandates of legal marriage. And in recounting this coverture, the story seems profoundly troubled. As Rowena's situation in "Ligeia" testifies especially poignantly, marriage makes a woman dependent, remanding her to the "care" and control of her husband. Nor are Poe's husbands particularly well equipped to handle the authority granted them by the law. But more important, by changing woman into wife, marriage lays waste to "the identity of her person," to cite Egaeus's description of Berenice (M 2: 211). Marriage deindividuates her, leaving her in a state of what Peter Coviello calls, in a different context, "uncertain aliveness."[19] Like Hurlbut, Swisshelm, and other progressive reformers, Poe suggests that women are, in essence, left in a "legal tomb" by marriage, "alive with the qualifications of the dead—dead with the propensities of the living."

Where, then, does this leave Poe's husbands? If, in "Ligeia" and the other dead wife tales, Poe is interested in the ravages wrought upon women by marriage, he appears equally, if not more, concerned with the effects of marriage on men. Here, we might recall that in "A Decided Loss" it is the *husband* who is killed by marriage, the one who "loses his breath." And we might take note of a moment from the original version of "Berenice" (excised in later editions), when Egaeus, visiting Berenice's corpse, finds himself momentarily buried alive with her. As he peers behind them, the curtains that surround her coffin fall over his shoulders: "shutting me thus out from the living," the curtains "enclosed me in the strictest communion with the deceased" (M 2: 217). And finally, we might draw a line between the image of an enshrouded Egaeus and the final image of "Ligeia," which depicts the narrator lying prostrate at the feet of his revenant wife, shrouded by the "huge masses of long and disheveled hair" that "stream[] forth" when she casts off her "cerements" (M 2: 330).

Such details suggest that even as Poe sees marriage as an institution that does damage to women, he also sees it as an institution that has deeply troubling implications for men. In a chapter entitled, "Acting Like a Husband," Hartog writes: "The law created marriage as a husband's private sphere. Law gave him vested rights and limited duties within a domestic space that he owned. Being a husband meant that one possessed, one represented, one governed, one cared for. Or, to put it slightly differently, knowing oneself as a husband required knowing one's wife as a feme covert, as a dependent."[20] Hartog's formulation helps us think through Poe's complex renditions of marriage. For while pointing to the powers that marriage grants to men, Hartog also suggests that to "know oneself" as a husband "requires" the knowledge that you "cover" another; it requires knowing oneself, in short, as a relational, corporate self. And this, in the world of Poe's tales about marriage, is a source of profound anxiety, even terror. It is perhaps no wonder that the narrator of "Morella" "longed with an earnest and consuming desire" for his wife's decease—her "society oppressed me like a spell," he observes (M 2: 227).

"A thematics of encroachment, doubling, and self-erosion is . . . the stuff and substance of the gothic," Coviello has observed.[21] This observation aptly describes many of Poe's marriage tales. "More haunted than solaced by the idea of human intimacy," Coviello writes, "Poe offers a gothic that both glimpses, and adamantly refuses, an America made of affective, intimate ties among strangers."[22] Indeed, I would add, Poe's Gothic "both glimpses, and adamantly refuses" the "affective, intimate ties" between marriage partners. Two later Poe stories, "The Black Cat" (1843) and "The Oblong Box" (1844), put this refusal on dazzling display. While these tales, like those discussed earlier, feature dead wives, in the end they appear to be far more interested in husbands and in the male response to marital unity—a unity that is at once sought and suffocating, desired and destructive.

Although "The Black Cat" first appeared in that most middle class of periodicals, the *Saturday Evening Post* (1843), its first-person narrator is arguably one of the most perverse in the Poe pantheon. Awaiting execution in his prison cell, the narrator pens "The Black Cat," a retrospective narrative whose "immediate purpose is to place before the world, plainly, succinctly, and without comment, a series of mere household events" (M 3: 849). He goes on to offer a "wild, yet most homely narrative" (M 3: 849) of domestic relations gone awry, a chilling tale of abuse that, as Lesley Ginsberg has noted, "reproduces the structural inequalities of the antebellum family" and the "dangers of familial tyranny."[23] Thus, the phrase "mere household events," however incongruous in light of the tale's unnerving violence, is also apt, for it draws attention to the ways in which the story is, finally, about domestic relations in general, and marital relations in particular.

Noted for "the docility and humanity of [his] disposition"—indeed, his "tenderness of heart" makes him "the jest of [his] companions"—the narrator is "never . . . so happy as when feeding and caressing" his menagerie of childhood pets (M 3: 850). He carries this desire for intimate connection into young adulthood, marrying a (never named) woman whose "disposition [is] not uncongenial with [his] own" and filling the house with "birds, gold-fish, a fine dog, rabbits, a small monkey, and *a cat*" named Pluto (M 3: 850). The "black cat" of Poe's title, Pluto is the narrator's "favorite pet and playmate": "he attended me wherever I went about the house" (M 3: 851), he writes, in language that alludes to the expected duties of husband and wife, even as it characterizes the relationship between a man and his loving pet.[24]

The household established by this tender young couple is, at first, a cheery haven. But "the Fiend Intemperance" (M 3: 851) corrupts the narrator, who begins abusing both his wife and the cat, which, as the story progresses, increasingly functions as her analog. In a figurative rape scene, for example, the narrator comes home one night "much intoxicated"; "fancying" that "the cat avoided my presence," the narrator grabs him. When Pluto, "in fright at my violence," bites him, the narrator "commits a damnable atrocity" (M 3: 851): he cuts one of Pluto's eyes out with a pen-knife. From that point on, naturally, the cat "fle[es] in terror at [his] approach" (M 3: 853), both grieving and angering the narrator. Eventually, inspired by the "spirit of perverseness" and the "unfathomable longing of the soul *to vex itself*," the narrator decides to "do wrong for the wrong's sake only": "I slipped a noose about [Pluto's] neck and hung it to the limb of a tree; . . . —hung it *because* I knew that it had loved me" (M 3: 852).

The narrator's recognition of the violent pull and push of intimate relation—he seizes the cat because the cat avoids him, he loathes the cat because the cat loves him—carries through the rest of the story. Just as the narrator of "Ligeia" finds a replacement wife, so does this narrator find a replacement cat—nearly identical, down to the absence of an eye. Just as the former immediately becomes an object of intense dislike, so too does the latter: "[I]ts evident fondness for myself rather disgusted and annoyed," he observes, and he does everything in his power to escape its "odious presence" (M 3: 854). Yet the more averse the narrator is to the cat, the more "its partiality for myself seemed to increase": it follows him everywhere, climbing on him and "covering" him with "loathsome caresses" (M 3: 855). The cat, furthermore, increasingly reminds the narrator of his crime against Pluto. Over time, a small white splotch on the second cat's breast comes to resemble a gallows, recalling to the narrator his perverse act of cruelty. From this point, the narrator cannot escape the cat: during the day, "the creature left me no moment alone; and, in the [night], I started, hourly . . . to find the hot breath of *the thing* upon my face, and its vast weight . . . incumbent eternally upon my *heart*!" (M 3: 856).

Eventually, the narrator's desire to escape the cat's suffocating intimacies leads him to murder. He lifts an axe to kill the cat, but his wife attempts to stop the blow. "Goaded, by the interference, into a rage more than demoniacal," the narrator turns on his wife and, in an act of apparent parapraxis, "burie[s] the axe in her brain" instead (M 3: 856). Once he has hidden her body, bricking it up behind a false chimney in his cellar, the cat too disappears. At last, the narrator declares, "I breathed as a freeman" (M 3: 858). But this ostensible freedom is short-lived, for when the police come searching for his wife, the narrator is so proud of his successful act of concealment that he cannot help but draw attention to the "very portion of the brick-work behind which stood the corpse of the wife of my bosom" (M 3: 858). He raps upon the wall with his cane and is answered by a "voice from within the tomb!" (M 3: 858–859). When the police break the wall down, they discover the corpse, and the cat—the source of the screams—sitting "upon its head": "I had walled the monster up within the tomb!" (M 3: 859), cries the narrator in the story's final line.

The immediate referent for the "monster" in the tomb is, of course, the cat. But the tomb has another inhabitant: the narrator's wife, who, like many of Poe's dead wives, might be said to live again, here in the accusing body of the cat.[25] Throughout the story, as I have noted, the cats function as analogs for the wife, the intimacy between the narrator and his once-beloved pets reminding us of the intimacy that the law forges between marriage partners.[26] Indeed, the story tropes repeatedly on the principle of marital unity, the "incorporation" of the wife's "very being" into "that of her husband." Like the "wife of [his] bosom," the cat's "vast weight—an incarnate Night-Mare that I had no power to shake off—[is] incumbent eternally upon my *heart*!" (M 3: 856). Once that cat is gone, the narrator remarks on "the blissful sense of relief which the absence of the detested creature occasioned in my bosom" (M 3: 857). Might the narrator here be (also) referring to his now-dead wife? After all, he has already recognized that his first murder, of Pluto, is an act by which the soul "vex[es] itself," just as is the act of killing the wife who has, by law, become a part of him. In killing Pluto, in attempting to kill the second cat, and in killing his wife, I am suggesting, the narrator attempts to escape the cloying closeness of marital intimacy, the permeable selfhood that marriage mandates. It is the *im*permeable self that the narrator seeks to reclaim by killing off those to whom he is so closely wedded. Though his efforts are ultimately futile, he seeks a "bosom" free from threat of penetration by the other, a heart liberated from the encumbrances of union.

If "The Black Cat" tells the story of one husband's murderous efforts to elude the perilous intimacies of marriage and domesticity, "The Oblong Box," published about a year later, tells the story of another husband's efforts to preserve them, even once his wife is dead. "The Oblong Box" (1844) lacks the obvious Gothic trappings that are so prevalent in "The Black Cat." Indeed, as William Goldhurst has noted in one of the very few essays that take it up, this tale at first "seems to consist of little more than an interesting variation on a standard theme of [Poe's] day—namely, the idea of clinging to one's dead."[27] Depicting as it does a husband's intense grief over the death of his wife, "The Oblong Box" can be read as part of the literature of mourning that would suit the largely female audience of *Godey's Lady's Book*, where it first appeared. In fact, unlike the twisted stories of marriage gone wrong that abound in Poe's canon, "The Oblong Box"—like "Eleonora," published three years earlier—seems to testify to the purity and abiding nature of matrimonial affection. Yet this story has Gothic tendencies of its own, dabbling as it does in veiled ladies, coffins, a hint of necrophilia, and the obsessive curiosity of its narrator. And as with "The Black Cat," those tendencies are fuelled by the story's depiction of marital union—union so strong, in this case, that it takes the husband to his death at the bottom of the sea.

Another retrospective tale recounted by an unnamed narrator, "The Oblong Box" recounts a hazardous journey from Charleston to New York City aboard a ship that is named, ironically, "The Independence." The narrator is thrilled to learn that Wyatt, a young artist friend of his, has engaged passage on the same ship, along with his new wife and two sisters. Once the journey is underway, Wyatt and his family become objects of the narrator's obsessive voyeurism and speculation. He wonders, for example, why the party has taken three staterooms, rather than the two that would suffice for a married couple and two sisters; why Mrs. Wyatt, reputed to be a beautiful and accomplished woman, proves to be "decidedly plain-looking" and "vulgar" (M 3: 923–924, 926); why the couple goes to bed in the same stateroom, but parts for the duration of the night; and, most bizarre of all, why in the course of each night, Wyatt (unknowingly observed by the narrator) pries open the cover of an enigmatic oblong box—"six feet in length by two and a half in breadth," and emitting a "strong, disagreeable, and to *my* fancy, a peculiarly disgusting odor" (M 3: 924–925)—and weeps over it. The narrator is determined to solve the mystery of the box, and he eventually convinces himself that he has: the box, he decides, "*could* possibly contain nothing in the world but a copy of Leonardo's 'Last Supper,'" which Wyatt has long been coveting and which he is now trying to "smuggle" under the narrator's "very nose" (M 3: 925). The narrator is eventually disabused of this very bizarre notion, but only after tragedy befalls Wyatt. When the ship founders in storm, Wyatt is so fixated on the box that he refuses to leave it behind. As the narrator and the other passengers watch in horror, Wyatt lashes himself to the box and sinks to the bottom of the ocean.

About a month after these harrowing events, the narrator finally gets his curiosity about Wyatt and his family satisfied. He learns from the captain of the ship that the box had in fact contained the corpse of Mrs. Wyatt, who died on the eve of the planned journey. Rather than reveal that he is traveling with a dead body, Wyatt puts the body in a pine box, packs it with salt, and presents the box as merchandise (a scheme, incidentally, that was considered, and rejected, by the narrator of "The Black Cat" when he is trying to dispose of *his* wife's corpse).[28] Wyatt's shipboard "wife" is in fact a lady's maid, whom Wyatt engages in order to maintain the fiction of a recently married man traveling with his wife and two sisters. This information solves the many mysteries surrounding Wyatt—the extra room, the vulgar "wife," and above all, Wyatt's own nocturnal sobbing over the oblong box.

The narrator closes the story with this observation: "My own mistakes arose, naturally enough, through too careless, too inquisitive, and too impulsive a temperament. But of late, it is a rare thing that I sleep soundly at night. There is a countenance which haunts me, turn as I will. There is an hysterical laugh which will forever ring within my ears" (M 3: 934). The "hysterical laugh" refers to a moment when the narrator attempts to joke about the box to Wyatt, who responds with a "loud and boisterous laugh" before falling over in a dead faint (M 3: 928). Disclosing how the memory of Wyatt haunts him, the narrator seems to accept responsibility for the harm that his obsessive scrutiny has done. However, the coordinating conjunction between these sentences—"but of late," the narrator writes—indicates that something else is likely causing the narrator's sleepless nights. In fact, I submit, what haunts the narrator of "The Oblong Box" is the imagined spectacle of marital intimacy to which his scrutiny gives him access. Like "The Black Cat," this story is replete with images of suffocating proximity—Wyatt's fixation on his wife's corpse and the box that contains it; the narrator's adjacency in the tiny, tomb-like staterooms; Wyatt's lashing himself to his wife's casket. It is striking, of course, that in Wyatt's death, Poe presents marital unity as literally lethal: tied to his wife, Wyatt dies in a manifestation of what Kenneth Silverman has called a "strangling allegiance to those who have been loved and lost."[29] But perhaps even more striking is the voyeuristic allure that Wyatt's marital story exerts over the narrator—a man whose own domestic situation remains shrouded in mystery, who seems utterly alone throughout the story, and yet who participates compulsively in the intimacies of others.[30] The story of marital unity that the narrator witnesses on board the Independence—a story that testifies, precisely, to the deadly *loss* of independence that marriage entails—is one that our narrator cannot leave behind. Like the narrator of "The Black Cat," his heart seems "encumbered"; like that narrator, this one will never truly "breathe as a freeman."

A backstory to "The Oblong Box" may shed light both on its origins and on the vexing problem of intimate dependency that is figured by Wyatt. In May of 1841, in Philadelphia, Edgar Allan Poe met Rufus Wilmot Griswold, who would go on to have a profound, indeed infamous, impact on Poe's life and posthumous career. While there is much to say about that impact, I am interested here in a striking occurrence in the Griswold biography that may well have come to Poe's attention: the macabre, Wyatt-like attachment that Griswold manifested toward his dead wife, Caroline. After the Griswolds married, they set up housekeeping with Caroline's family in New York City. A few years later, Griswold moved to Philadelphia in an effort to advance his literary career, returning frequently to visit Caroline and their growing brood back in New York. Griswold was there when, in November of 1842, Caroline gave birth to their third child. He returned to Philadelphia, only to learn, a few days later, that both Caroline and the newborn baby had died. Back in New York, a distraught Griswold refused, for more than a day, to leave his dead wife's side. When friends and family tried to urge him away, he "answered them by kissing the cold lips of his dead wife and embracing her."[31] At the funeral, Griswold threw himself on the coffin and was only with difficulty persuaded to draw away. Nor was this the end of Griswold's display of unhinged despair. Indeed, about a month later, Griswold undertook an action that is worthy of one of Poe's bereaved husbands: he went to Greenwood Cemetery, where Caroline was interred, opened the burial vault, and embraced her decaying corpse. Griswold explained in a letter:

> I could not think that my dear wife was dead. I dreamed night after night of our reunion. In a fit of madness I went to New York. The vault where she is sleeping is nine miles from the city. I went to it: the sexton unclosed it: and I went down alone into that silent chamber. I kneeled by her side and prayed, and then, with my own hand, unfastened the coffin lid, turned aside the drapery that hid her face, and saw the terrible changes made by Death and Time. I kissed for the last time her cold black forehead—I cut off locks of her beautiful hair, damp with the death dews, and sunk down in senseless agony beside the ruin of all that was dearest in the world. In the evening, a friend from the city, who had learned where I was gone, found me there, my face still resting on her own, and my body as lifeless and cold as that before me.[32]

Worth noting here is the almost loving attention that Griswold lavishes on this story of his own derangement. Indeed, Griswold's detailed recounting reads like a work of Gothic fiction, not only because of its focus on the details of death and decay but also because of the ways in which it documents Griswold's own loss of self-possession and control.

Citing this episode, Sandra Tomc has noted that "Griswold shared with Poe a tendency to depression and morbidity."[33] He certainly shared that tendency with many of Poe's narrators and characters. "Berenice," for example, includes a Latin epigraph, repeated in the course of the story, the translation of which reads, "My companions told me I might find some little alleviation of my misery, in visiting the grave of my beloved" (M 2: 219).[34] Years later, Poe might have felt a certain amount of schadenfreude when Griswold engaged in real-life activities that call to mind one of Poe's most deranged narrators. Given their mutual acquaintances and Griswold's own willingness to talk openly about his grief to a wide circle, it seems likely that these events came to Poe's attention. And it seems therefore plausible that, in his depiction of Wyatt in "The Oblong Box," Poe seeks to remind his audience of Griswold's unseemly attachment to his wife's corpse—thus embarrassing a man who had come to be a troubling competitor. Not six months before Caroline's death, Griswold had in effect supplanted Poe on the editorial staff of *Graham's Magazine*, at a higher salary and with more editorial license than had been given to Poe. Griswold's fame and fortune were on the rise, particularly after the publication of the influential *Poets and Poetry of America* (April 1842)—a volume that lies at the heart of the complex rivalry between the two men. In light of that rivalry, we might recall the narrator's bizarre theory about the "oblong box" and his belief that Wyatt is trying to get the better of him in some sort of strange artistic competition.

This odd detail lends credence to the notion that, in "The Oblong Box," Poe might be working out his own rivalry with Griswold, mocking him by alluding to his uncontrolled attachment to his dead wife. Yet, as I have already suggested, "The Oblong Box" arouses as much interest in the narrator as in Wyatt; perhaps even more disturbing than Wyatt's macabre behavior is the narrator's unceasing attention *to* that behavior. Indeed, while the events that the narrator recounts happened "some years ago" (M 3: 922), he remains "haunt[ed]" by Wyatt and his story (M 3: 934). And if Wyatt stands in for Griswold, then Poe might be seen to stand in for his narrator. Like the narrator, Poe appears haunted by Griswold's Gothic story of marital attachment, its vivid rendering of the extent to which male self-possession is compromised by marriage. The fact that Poe's own wife, Virginia, had experienced her first pulmonary hemorrhage in 1842 and that her death from tuberculosis had become inevitable only makes this rendering all the more potent.

There is, I am suggesting, a thematic through line that runs from the very early "A Decided Loss," through the cluster of eponymous dead wife stories, and on to "The Oblong Box." (Here, we might also remember that Poe published a revised version of "A Decided Loss," entitled "Loss of Breath," in 1846.) As all of these stories indicate, Poe was concerned throughout his career with how marriage, as a legal institution, damages wives and husbands—perhaps *especially* husbands. Over and over again, from the husband's "loss of breath" in "A Decided Loss" through Wyatt's fatal attachment to his wife's casket, marriage does profound injury to men. Even the seemingly happier "Eleonora" (1841) alludes to damaging effects: after she extracts a promise from the narrator that he will never "bind [himself] in marriage to any daughter of Earth," a dying Eleonora pledges that she will "watch over him" after her death, returning either visibly, "in the watches of the night," or as a spirit in the wind and air (M 2: 642). Although she eventually releases him from the pledge and he remarries into seeming happiness, Eleonora exerts an all but inescapable, suffocating hold on the narrator—one that extends well beyond her death and sends him fleeing the beautiful valley in which the two once dwelled.

Given the legal and social dimensions of antebellum marriage, the notion that men are damaged, destabilized, and dispossessed by matrimony might seem, at the very least, unexpected. As an 1854 article on "Marriage and Divorce" for the *Southern Quarterly Review* explained, "The husband acquires from the union increased capacity and power. He represents the wife in the political and the civil order. . . . The wife carries into the union a feebleness that solicits protection."[35] This notion that marriage is a site where male selfhood is enhanced became increasingly important, Amy Dru Stanley has demonstrated, as the debate over slavery intensified in the antebellum period. In this era, the ability to contract in legal marriage became an ever more meaningful mark of distinction between free white men and enslaved black men. "Get Married" commanded an 1840 article that was published in *Godey's Lady's Book* and that addressed, contrary to what we might expect from the magazine's title, unmarried *men*.

Poe seems to have taken that advice to heart. His avid pursuit of marriage—whether to Virginia or to other women, specifically Sarah Helen Whitman and Elmira Royster Shelton—suggests, on the one hand, that he viewed matrimony as an institution that could both ground and enhance him. Hence his panic when, prior to his marriage to Virginia, it looked as though she was going to be taken under the wing of his cousin, Neilson Poe, or the alarm he expressed in an effusive, troubled letter to Whitman when their engagement was in question (CL 1: 102–105; CL 2: 692–704).[36] But on the other hand, perhaps Elizabeth Oakes Smith perceived more than she knew when she noted, after Poe's death, her "impression" that he "dreaded marriage."[37] And perhaps Poe was not entirely in jest when, making mild complaint about his wife Virginia's importunities, he declared to his cousin Elizabeth Tutt, "What it is to be pestered by a wife!" (CL 1: 352). In Poe's tales of marriage, men are not just "pestered"—they are undone by their wives. The writer of "Marriage and Divorce" provides a definition of marriage that brings us back to the all-important concept of coverture. Marriage, he observes, is "a union of two persons, so as to form but one—an identity of ends and aims—a fusion of separate volitions, impulses, affections, sympathies, so as to form a single existence."[38] It is this very idea, one that simultaneously renders the married woman undead and binds the married man forever and inescapably to an unliving other, which lies at the heart of Poe's Gothic tales of marriage.

Notes

1. Kenneth Silverman, *introduction to New Essays on Poe's Major Tales*, ed. Kenneth Silverman (Cambridge: Cambridge University Press, 1993), 1–26.
2. Poe extends the hints about infidelity in the later versions of this story, where the narrator—here named Mr. Lackobreath—notes his wife's "partiality" for the neighbor, Mr. Windenough, but then insists that her feelings "occasioned me little uneasiness" (M 2: 64). Later on, Mr. Lackobreath and Mr. Windenough get into a shouting match that further underscores a power contest between the two men.
3. For an exception to this, see Marie Bonaparte, *The Life and Works of Edgar Allan Poe: A Psychoanalytical Interpretation*, trans. John Rodker (London: Imago, 1949). Other critics who have addressed "A Decided Loss" include David Leverenz, "Spanking the Master: Mind-Body Crossings in Poe's Sensationalism," in *A Historical Guide to Edgar Allan Poe*, ed. J. Gerald Kennedy (Oxford: Oxford University Press, 2001), 95–127; Leland Person, "Poe and Nineteenth-Century Gender Constructions," in *A Historical Guide to Edgar Allan Poe*, ed. J. Gerald Kennedy (Oxford: Oxford University Press, 2001), 129–165; and William Etter, "'Tawdry Physical Affrightments': The Performance of Normalizing Visions of the Body in Edgar Allan Poe's 'Loss of Breath,'" *ATQ* 17 (2003): 5–22.
4. Colin (Joan) Dayan, "Poe, Persons, and Property," *American Literary History* 11 (1999): 409.
5. Hendrik Hartog, *Man and Wife in America: A History* (Cambridge, MA: Harvard University Press, 2000), 95.
6. Hartog, *Man and Wife in America*, 95–96.
7. William Blackstone, *Commentaries on the Laws of England*, ed. Stanley N. Katz, vol. 1 (Chicago: University of Chicago Press, 1979), 430.

8. For treatments of coverture and marital property in this context, see Norma Basch, *In the Eyes of the Law: Women, Marriage, and Property in Nineteenth-Century New York* (Ithaca, NY: Cornell University Press, 1982); Nancy Cott, *Public Vows: A History of Marriage and the Nation* (Cambridge, MA: Harvard University Press, 2000); Michael Grossberg, *Governing the Hearth: Law and the Family in Nineteenth-Century America* (Chapel Hill: University of North Carolina Press, 1985); Carole Shammas, "Re-Assessing the Married Women's Property Acts," *Journal of Women's History* 6 (1994): 9–30; Linda E. Speth, "The Married Women's Property Acts, 1839–1865: Reform, Reaction, or Revolution?," in *Women and the Law*, ed. D. Kelly Weisberg, vol. 2 (Cambridge: Schenkman Publishing, 1982), 69–91; Tim Stretton and Krista J. Kesselring, eds., *Married Women and the Law: Coverture in England and the Common Law World* (Ithaca, NY: McGill-Queen's Press, 2013); and Marlene Stein Wortman, ed., *Women in American Law*, vol. 1 (New York: Holmes and Meier, 1985).
9. I offer an extended treatment of these concepts in "Berenice" and "Ligeia," placing them in relation to E. D. E. N. Southworth's *The Discarded Daughter*, in "Poe, Southworth, and the Antebellum Wife," in *E D. E. N. Southworth: Recovering a Nineteenth-Century Popular Novelist*, ed. Melissa J. Homestead and Pamela T. Washington (Knoxville, TN: University of Tennessee Press, 2012), 221–242.
10. Like "Berenice," "Morella" was published in 1835 in the *Southern Literary Messenger* ("Berenice" in March, "Morella" in April). "Ligeia" was first published in the *American Museum* in September of 1838, and "Eleonora" in the holiday annual *The Gift* (1841). For a reading of the illnesses of Morella, Berenice, Ligeia, Rowena, and Madeline Usher in terms of pregnancy and childbirth, see Dawn Keetley, "Pregnant Women and Envious Men in 'Morella,' 'Berenice,' 'Ligeia,' and 'The Fall of the House of Usher,'" *Poe Studies* 38 (2005): 1–16.
11. See Kenneth Silverman, *Edgar A. Poe: Mournful and Never-Ending Remembrance* (New York: Harper Collins: 1991), and J. Gerald Kennedy, "Poe, 'Ligeia,' and the Problem of Dying Women," in *New Essays on Poe's Major Tales*, ed. Kenneth Silverman (Cambridge: Cambridge University Press, 1993), 113–129.
12. Ligeia and Morella are actual revenants who return in revivified form; although Eleonora does not return from death in the same way, she communicates with the narrator of that story from beyond the grave.
13. Elisha P. Hurlbut, *Essays on Human Rights and Their Political Guarantees* (New York: Greeley and McElrath, 1845), 146–148.
14. Jane Swisshelm, "Mrs. Swisshelm's Letter," *Pittsburgh Daily Commercial Journal* 27 (October 1847).
15. Karen Weeks, "Poe's Feminine Ideal," in *The Cambridge Companion to Edgar Allan Poe*, ed. Kevin J. Hayes (Cambridge: Cambridge University Press, 2002), 152.
16. Hartog, *Man and Wife in America*, 94, 93.
17. Lenore J. Weiztman, *The Marriage Contract: Spouses, Lovers, and the Law* (New York: The Free Press, 1981), xix.
18. Milton C. Regan, Jr., *Family Law and the Pursuit of Intimacy* (New York: New York University Press, 1993), 9
19. Peter Coviello, *Intimacy in America: Dreams of Affiliation in Antebellum Literature* (Minneapolis: University of Minnesota Press, 2005), 70. Like Colin Dayan, Coviello examines the connection between race, sex, and gender in Poe's work.
20. Hartog, *Man and Wife in America*, 136.
21. Coviello, *Intimacy in America*, 74.
22. Coviello, *Intimacy in America*, 63.

23. Lesley Ginsberg, "Slavery and the Gothic Horror of Poe's 'The Black Cat,'" in *American Gothic: New Interventions in a National Narrative*, ed. Robert K. Martin and Eric Savoy (Iowa City: University of Iowa Press, 1998), 118. For another reading of this tale in terms of race and racial anxiety, see Leland Person in "Poe's Philosophy of Amalgamation: Reading Racism in the Tales," in *Romancing the Shadow: Poe and Race*, ed. J. Gerald Kennedy and Liliane Weissberg (Oxford: Oxford University Press, 2001), 205–224.
24. It is worth noting here that the sex of the cat is male, not female, thus cautioning against a strict allegorical reading of the tale. Indeed, the cat's sex, along with the tale's complex depiction of desire, invites a reading of "The Black Cat" in terms of male-male intimacy and homoeroticism. For treatments of "queer Poe" that would aid such a reading, see Leland Person, "Queer Poe: The Tell-Tale Heart of His Fiction," *Poe Studies* 41 (2008): 7–30; and Gustavus T. Stadler, "Poe and Queer Studies," *Poe Studies* 33 (2000): 19–22. Valerie Rohy offers a brilliant reading of "Ligeia" in terms of lesbian sexuality in "Ahistorical," *GLQ: A Journal of Lesbian and Gay Studies* 2 (2006): 61–83.
25. Here, we might recall Hurlbut's description of the married woman as a "monster" residing in a "legal tomb."
26. For a reading that challenges the significance of marriage in this tale, see Christopher Benfey, "Poe and the Unreadable: 'The Black Cat' and 'The Tell-Tale Heart,'" in *New Essays on Poe's Major Tales*, ed. Kenneth Silverman (Cambridge: Cambridge University Press, 1993), 27–44.
27. William Goldhurst, "Self-Reflective Fiction by Poe: Three Tales," *Modern Language Studies* 16 (1986): 5. For a more recent treatment of this understudied text, see Dan Walden, "Ships and Crypts: The Coastal World of Poe's 'King Pest,' 'The Premature Burial,' and 'The Oblong Box,'" *Edgar Allan Poe Review* 10 (2009): 104–121.
28. This is also the method that John Colt used to dispose of the body of Samuel Adams in a New York City murder case that was much in the news in 1841 and 1842, as noted by C. V. Carley, "A Source for Poe's 'The Oblong Box,'" *American Literature* 29 (1957): 310–312; and Bonnie Shannon McMullen, "Lifting the Lid on Poe's 'Oblong Box,'" *Studies in American Fiction* 23 (1995): 203–214.
29. Silverman, introduction to *New Essays on Poe's Major Tales*, 18.
30. The narrator of "The Oblong Box" presents himself as entirely alone throughout the story, with one notable exception, at one point referring to a "negro valet." This adds yet another wrinkle to this story's complex exploration of intimacy, proximity, and identity in the antebellum period, pointing as it does to the black presence that haunts so many of Poe's tales.
31. Joy Bayless, *Rufus Wilmot Griswold: Poe's Literary Executor* (Nashville, TN: Vanderbilt University Press, 1943), 64.
32. Quoted in Bayless, *Rufus Wilmot Griswold*, 66.
33. Sandra Tomc, "Poe and His Circle," in *The Cambridge Companion to Edgar Allan Poe*, ed. Kevin J. Hayes (Cambridge: Cambridge University Press, 2002), 26.
34. Poe translated the epigraph in the original version of the story, but he omitted the translation in later editions. For more information, see M 2: 219.
35. "Marriage and Divorce," *Southern Quarterly Review* 26 (October 1854): 351.
36. Strikingly, in this 1848 letter to Whitman, we find echoes of Griswold's and Wyatt's morbid attachment to their dead wives. Poe tells Whitman that, if she died, "then at least would I clasp your dear hand in death, and willingly—*oh, joyfully—joyfully—joyfully*—go down *with* you into the night of the Grave" (CL 2: 700).
37. Silverman, *Edgar A. Poe*, 371.
38. "Marriage and Divorce," 335.

Bibliography

Basch, Norma. *In the Eyes of the Law: Women, Marriage, and Property in Nineteenth-Century New York*. Ithaca, NY: Cornell University Press, 1982.

Cott, Nancy. *Public Vows: A History of Marriage and the Nation*. Cambridge, MA: Harvard University Press, 2000.

Coviello, Peter. *Intimacy in America: Dreams of Affiliation in Antebellum Literature*. Minneapolis: University of Minnesota Press, 2005.

Dayan, Colin (Joan). "Amorous Bondage: Poe, Ladies, and Slaves." *American Literature* 66 (1994): 239–273.

Dayan, Colin (Joan). "Poe, Persons, and Property." *American Literary History* 11 (1999): 405–425.

Grossberg, Michael. *Governing the Hearth: Law and the Family in Nineteenth-Century America*. Chapel Hill: University of North Carolina Press, 1985.

Hartog, Hendrik. *Man and Wife in America: A History*. Cambridge, MA: Harvard University Press, 2000.

Kennedy, J. Gerald. "Poe, 'Ligeia,' and the Problem of Dying Women." In *New Essays on Poe's Major Tales*, edited by Kenneth Silverman, 113–129. Cambridge: Cambridge University Press, 1993.

Person, Leland. "Poe and Nineteenth-Century Gender Constructions." In *A Historical Guide to Edgar Allan Poe*, edited by J. Gerald Kennedy, 129–165. Oxford: Oxford University Press, 2001.

Stretton, Tim, and Krista J. Kesselring, eds. *Married Women and the Law: Coverture in England and the Common Law World*. Ithaca, NY: McGill-Queen's Press, 2013.

Weeks, Karen. "Poe's Feminine Ideal." In *The Cambridge Companion to Edgar Allan Poe*, edited by Kevin J. Hayes, 148–162. Cambridge: Cambridge University Press, 2002.

Weinauer, Ellen. "Poe, Southworth, and the Antebellum Wife." In *E D. E. N. Southworth: Recovering a Nineteenth-Century Popular Novelist*, edited by Melissa J. Homestead and Pamela T. Washington, 221–242. Knoxville: University of Tennessee Press, 2012.

CHAPTER 11

SOLVING MYSTERIES IN POE, OR TRYING TO

SUSAN ELIZABETH SWEENEY

Poe was drawn to both enigmas and solutions. Consider his fascination with secret writing, from cryptograms to acrostics, riddles, prophecies, and puns; his curiosity about practices like mesmerism and phrenology and handwriting analysis; his pursuit of new discoveries in astronomy, chemistry, or engineering; his delight in perpetrating and disclosing hoaxes such as "Maelzel's Chess-Player"; his allusions to arcane knowledge, obscure libraries, and volumes of forgotten lore; his tendency, in writing criticism, to define genres and classify authors and speculate about possible traces of literary theft; the sly explication of his own work in "The Philosophy of Composition"; and his shrewd conjectures about analysis, perception, theory of mind, deceit, confession, culpability, and perversity. Consider, too, how Poe's fiction continually juxtaposes the reciprocal concepts of an enigma and its answer, from "a thousand futile attempts to answer the query," in "The Thousand-and-Second Tale of Scheherazade" (M 3: 1164n), to "the solution of everything in the way of paradox and impossibility," in "Some Words with a Mummy" (M 3: 1183). His readers must face a "most appalling and unfathomable mystery" in *The Narrative of Arthur Gordon Pym* (P 1: 126), "a mystery all insoluble" in "The Fall of the House of Usher" (M 2: 397), a "gigantic paradox, too utterly monstrous for solution!" in "William Wilson" (M 2: 429), and the "strangest mystery of all!" in "Ligeia" (M 2: 314). Joseph Wood Krutch claimed that "Poe invented the detective story in order that he might not go mad,"[1] but it seems more likely that he did so to satisfy this craving for conundrums.

Poe describes efforts to solve mysteries not only in detective fiction but also in tales of adventure, horror, satire, and speculative fantasy. In each case, his narration follows the protagonist's attempt to comprehend a new environment, fathom an odd experience, understand another person's behavior, or merely contemplate "a question [he] never could solve," in "William Wilson" (M 2: 434), or "a mystery" he has "been unable to solve," in "The Landscape Garden" (M 2: 708). That is, the protagonist seeks to rectify a problem or decode a puzzle, not to address "a genuine mystery," although this quest may lead to deeper questions that prove impossible to answer.[2] No matter which genre he chooses, Poe usually associates such analysis on the part of the protagonist with one of two possible scenarios: either escaping from peril or investigating crime.

When Poe's protagonists are in danger, for example, they use reasoning to verify their perceptions, assess a predicament, reconstruct the events that precipitated it, and figure out a means of survival. In "How to Write a Blackwood Article," Poe explains how to craft sensation stories by conveying the narrator's impressions of an excruciating ordeal: "Sensations are the great things after all. Should you ever be drowned or hung, be sure and make a note of your sensations—they will be worth to you ten guineas a sheet" (M 2: 340). His own tales, however, tend to emphasize how narrators *analyze* such situations. Even though works like "Berenice," "A Descent into the Maelström," "The Pit and the Pendulum," "The Premature Burial," and "The Sphinx" are not detective stories, each includes a detailed account of a first-person narrator's cogitation that is essential to its plot and design. In several of these tales, the narrator's attempt at logical thought creates an effect of horror. Such characters do not "exult[] in," "glory in," or "derive pleasure from" demonstrating analytical skill, as Dupin does in "The Murders in the Rue Morgue" (M 2: 528). Instead, they are driven by desperate circumstances to rely on their wits.

Other protagonists seem to pursue mysteries mostly for their own amusement, in tales that approximate detective fiction even while violating some of its conventions. Besides the famous stories featuring C. Auguste Dupin ("The Murders in the Rue Morgue," "The Mystery of Marie Rogêt," and "The Purloined Letter"),[3] Poe wrote many others that recount baffling crimes. "The Fall of the House of Usher," "William Wilson," and "The Man of the Crowd" were early experiments with plots involving enigmas and solutions. By tracing the narrator's efforts to elucidate a mystery, even if such efforts fail, these works introduced devices and motifs that are now common in detective fiction. Subsequent tales—"The Gold-Bug," "The Oblong Box," and "'Thou Art the Man'"—show that Poe kept tinkering with the detective story, in terms of structure, plot, narration, tone, and relation to other genres, in works beyond the Dupin trilogy. His later detectives are not always successful, and readers may not be given all the clues needed to explain an enigma. Nevertheless, these tales reveal Poe's continued fascination with the mental process "that *disentangles*" (M 2: 528), as well as the associated problems of how to describe that process in fiction, demonstrate its use, and elicit it from his readers.

A Taste for Ratiocination

In general, *ratiocination* means "the action or process of reasoning."[4] In *A System of Logic*, John Stuart Mill defines it as a method of reaching conclusions by connecting observable facts: "Reasoning, in the extended sense in which I use the term, and in which it is synonymous with Inference, is popularly said to be of two kinds: reasoning from particulars to generals, and reasoning from generals to particulars; the former being called Induction, the latter Ratiocination or Syllogism."[5] Poe knew this book well.[6] But while Mill equates *ratiocination* with syllogism—in which two propositions lead to a conclusion—Poe identifies it with a cognitive process involving rapid assessment, comparison, extrapolation, and conjecture.[7]

According to Poe, that process entails "a host of observations and inferences," made almost instantaneously, in silence, drawing on "recesses of thought altogether inaccessible to the ordinary understanding" (M 2: 530, M 2: 529). His account of the phenomenon recalls the spontaneous play of guesses and suppositions described in William Whewell's *Philosophy of the Inductive Sciences*,[8] even as it anticipates Charles S. Peirce's later theory of abductive reasoning.[9] Poe had a remarkable facility for perceiving subtle aspects of human cognition—including what Daniel Hoffman calls "the associative linkages of preconscious thought, that wonderworking network of similes"[10]—and expressing them in words. Poe was also able to see how such associations combine to form "a train of ratiocination," as he puts it in "Mesmeric Revelation" (M 3: 1031). His awareness of the mind's workings has since been identified with various insights from philosophy, psychoanalysis, linguistics, information theory, and cognitive science.[11]

In addition to acutely observing this mental process, Poe apparently set himself the challenge of imagining, reconstructing, articulating, and analyzing it in his fiction. He muses, in one of his early magazine articles on "Secret Writing," that "the ratiocination actually passing through the mind in the solution of even a single cryptograph, if detailed step by step, would fill a large volume."[12] In his first detective story, which had appeared a few months earlier, he observes that most individuals find amusement "in retracing the steps by which particular conclusions of their own minds have been attained" (M 2: 535). Indeed, Poe's amateur investigator, Dupin, can retrace other people's thoughts as well as his own—whether he is accompanying a friend's silent reflections during a nighttime stroll in "The Murders in the Rue Morgue," imagining the reasoning of a French sailor whose mere existence he has conjectured in the same story, or accurately deducing "the whole train of thought" that must have passed through the Minister's mind in "The Purloined Letter" (M 3: 988). When Dupin applies his analytical process to situations like these, "where mind struggles with mind" (M 2: 529), he employs what is now called theory of mind, or the ability to understand another person's desires, intentions, and beliefs.[13] Poe's tales often allow readers to follow a protagonist's reasoning in the very same way—especially when, as nearly always happens, the protagonist is narrating his tale retrospectively, in the first person, and reviewing his own thoughts as he does so.

While ratiocination may solve mysteries, then, Poe associates it with a process rather than a result. The distinction explains why some of the works that he labeled "tales of ratiocination" might not be considered detective fiction today. Admittedly, Poe often applied this phrase to the Dupin trilogy. In 1844, he wrote to James Russell Lowell that "The Purloined Letter" is, "perhaps, the best of [his] tales of ratiocination" (CL 1: 450). A year later, in a review of the 1845 *Tales* attributed to him,[14] he assigned the Dupin stories to "a class peculiar to POE. They are inductive—tales of ratiocination—of profound and searching analysis."[15] And the year after that, in 1846, he told Philip Pendleton Cooke that Dupin's feats of deduction are not as brilliant as they seem: "You are right about the hair-splitting of my French friend:—that is all done for effect. These tales of ratiocination owe most of their popularity to being something in a new key. I do not mean to say that they are not ingenious—but people think them more ingenious than they are—on account of their method and *air* of method." In the same letter, however, Poe implied that the 1845 *Tales* included many such narratives: "The last selection of my Tales was made from about 70, by Wiley & Putnam's reader, [Evert Augustus] Duyckinck. He has what he thinks a taste for ratiocination, and has accordingly made up the book mostly of analytic stories" (CL 1: 595). Poe evidently thought he had written more than the "five stories that involve ratiocination"—the Dupin trilogy, "The Gold-Bug," and "'Thou Art the Man'"—which are usually credited to him.[16] Besides including four of those five stories in the 1845 *Tales*,[17] Duyckinck selected "Lionizing," "The Fall of the House of Usher," "The Conversation of Eiros and Charmion," "The Man of the Crowd," "The Colloquy of Monos and Una," "A Descent into the Maelström," "The Black Cat," and "Mesmeric Revelation," most of which describe in considerable detail a protagonist's attempt at logical reasoning.

Although Poe complained that Duyckinck's emphasis on ratiocination obscured "the wide *diversity and* variety" of his own writing (CL 1:596), the "analytic stories" included in the 1845 *Tales* actually demonstrate his prowess in several genres.[18] As J. Gerald Kennedy explains, "his serious tales return continually to the process of reason—the way in which the mind orders and interprets its perceptions."[19] Ratiocination also appears as a theme in his nonfiction,[20] his acrostic verse,[21] and "The Raven."[22] Only occasionally does Poe describe a mind like Dupin's, which can unravel any enigma. However, he often examines his characters' efforts to solve a mystery, even if those efforts misfire.

Figuring the Way Out

Poe's interest in analysis is especially notable in tales where protagonists struggle, usually in vain, to apprehend and escape from obscure predicaments. In "The Fall of the House of Usher," for example, the narrator's attempt at reason does little to help him understand his situation. In the opening paragraph of this story, which appeared in 1839, Poe's narrator tries to explain the setting's insidious effect on him: "What was it—I paused to think—what was it that so unnerved me in the contemplation of the House of Usher?" (M 2: 397). Just as the narrator inserts a parenthetical aside into the beginning of this sentence, interrupting his thought even as he formulates it, so he examines his own perceptions of the house even while regarding it for the first time. He speculates that certain combinations of inanimate objects, such as the house and its physical location, might profoundly affect the human mind, but adds—anticipating the opening of "The Murders in the Rue Morgue"[23]—that "analysis of this power lies among considerations beyond our depth." He wonders whether "a mere rearrangement of the particulars of the scene" could possibly diminish its sinister influence. When the narrator tests this hypothesis by gazing at the house's reflection, however, he experiences "a shudder even more thrilling than before" (M 2: 398). Throughout the story, such sensations repeatedly overpower his reason, keeping him from ever fully comprehending the house or its occupants.

Poe's protagonists also attempt to analyze their own behavior. In "Berenice," published in 1835, Egaeus "strive[s] to decypher" his "unintelligible recollections" of what occurred after his cousin's interment (M 2: 218, M 2: 217–218). First, he considers his physical state: the remembered "shriek of a female voice" ringing in his ears, the small box on a nearby table causing him to shudder, the underlined sentence in a book that makes his hair stand on end (M 2: 218). Next, a servant enters to report Berenice's violated grave, premature burial, and disfigured body. Just as Dupin will later systematically explain his reasoning to the narrator of "The Murders in the Rue Morgue," so this servant leads Egaeus, step by step, to comprehend what has happened: "He pointed to my garments;—they were muddy and clotted with gore. . . . He took me gently by the hand;—it was indented with the impress of human nails. He directed my attention to some object against the wall;—I looked at it for some minutes;—it was a spade" (M 2: 218–219). The passage's parallel syntax and identical punctuation direct the attention of Poe's readers to the same evidence in a similar fashion. The repeated pattern of semicolons followed by dashes, in particular, juxtaposes the servant's indication of an object with first the narrator's apprehension of it and then his dawning awareness of its significance, expressed as a simple declarative statement at the end of each sentence. Poe thus replicates the mental process of noticing and analyzing each clue in turn. By closely following this train of ratiocination without revealing its result, he prompts readers—exactly as the servant prompts Egaeus—to solve the mystery, and even to identify the "ivory-looking substances" spilling from the little box, on their own (M 2: 219).

In other tales, Poe's protagonists use reasoning to avoid immediate danger. In "A Descent into the Maelström," from 1841, the desire to understand an unusual phenomenon helps another narrator to escape from certain death: "I became possessed with the keenest curiosity about the whirl itself. I positively felt a *wish* to explore its depths . . . and my principal grief was that I should never be able to tell my old companions on shore about the mysteries I should see" (M 2: 588–589). The narrator remains lucid when facing disaster, unlike his brother. Once their boat becomes suspended in the whirlpool, he notices the other objects floating there, even "speculating upon the relative velocities of their several descents toward the foam below" (M 2: 591). The resulting "train of reflection"—which involves memories of similar situations he has encountered in the past as well as observations, calculations, comparisons, and predictions regarding his present circumstances—leads the narrator to surmise that a cylindrical object is most likely to resist the maelström's pull. This hypothesis, which he explains in detail, is confirmed by his subsequent conversations "with an old school-master" and by Poe's own reference to Archimedes (M 2: 592). In the moment, however, it allows him to apprehend instantaneously his only possible means of survival. After vainly trying to persuade his terrified brother to follow suit, the narrator lashes himself to a water cask and pushes it into the sea, producing the very result that he expects: he stays afloat until the maelström recedes.

The narrator of "The Pit and the Pendulum," published in 1842, also manages to stay alive because of his analytical ability. After waking inside a pitch-black space, he first tries "to exercise [his] reason" by recalling "the inquisitorial proceedings" that were brought against him. Next, he "deduce[s]" his "real condition," establishing that he is neither dead, nor confined within his cell, nor buried in a tomb (M 2: 684). Although he cannot identify his actual location, he figures out how to calculate its dimensions by tearing off a scrap of his clothing and wedging it into a crevice so that it protrudes from the wall: "In groping my way around the prison, I could not fail to encounter this rag upon completing the circuit. So, at least, I thought" (M 2: 686). This procedure yields misleading results, however. The narrator manages to estimate the size of his dungeon—over fifty yards in circumference—but later realizes that it is considerably smaller. Afterward, he struggles in vain "to account for [his] error" (M 2: 688), eventually concluding that while conducting his survey he must have fainted, returned to consciousness, and then unwittingly retraced his steps.

The tale's horror increases as each successive form of torture similarly elicits, and frustrates, the narrator's attempts to escape by his wits. After his "researches" in the dark provide some sense of the dungeon's outer limits (M 2: 686), he accidentally discovers a deep pit in its center. Although the narrator nearly falls into this pit, he learns to avoid it in the future. Before long, however, he wakes again to find himself facing another calamity, bound beneath a pendulum whose inexorable rate of descent he cannot help calculating, anticipating his own imminent death—until, for the first time in hours or even days, he "*th*[*inks*]." This reiterated verb, now in italics, contrasts his earlier acts of observation, calculation, or prediction with the actual insights that those processes could generate. Indeed, he describes in detail the precise moment when he resolves his latest predicament: "there flashe[s] upon my mind what I cannot better describe than as the unformed half of that idea. . . . The whole thought [i]s now present—feeble, scarcely sane, scarcely definite—but still entire" (M 2: 693).[24] As in a detective story, this account skillfully evokes the mental phenomenon of becoming aware of a solution while still allowing readers to discover the answer for themselves. The narrator's plan to escape from his current situation is ingenious: he will smear his bonds with the spicy, thirst-inducing food left by his side, enticing rats to nibble at it until they have gnawed through the fibers and set him free. Like Dupin, boasting that he "had not been once 'at fault'" while developing a solution (M 2: 553), the narrator proclaims, "Nor had I erred in my calculations" (M 2: 694). However, no sooner has this plan succeeded than he is threatened by another, even more cunning form of imminent execution—one that he escapes not through his own ingenuity but because the Inquisition has fallen into "the hands of its enemies" (M 2: 697). Nevertheless, the narrator's ratiocination has enabled him to survive long enough to be rescued.

In both "A Descent into the Maelström" and "The Pit and the Pendulum," a series of accurate observations, estimates, and conjectures allows Poe's protagonists to avoid disaster. In other tales, however, faulty reasoning leads other narrators to imagine horrors where none exist. The narrator of "The Premature Burial," from 1844, regains consciousness in utter darkness, experiencing "awakening feelings," "the first positive effort to think," and "the first endeavor to remember," just as in "The Pit and the Pendulum"; but instead of deducing his real situation, he is beset by the "spectral and ever-prevalent Idea" of having been buried alive (M 3: 966). Everything he observes—his bound jaws, his position on a hard surface, his compressed limbs, the wooden panel inches above his face, an odor of damp earth—bolsters that assumption, making him "no longer doubt that [he] repose[s] in a coffin at last" (M 3: 967). It turns out, however, that the narrator is actually lying in the narrow berth of a sloop laden with garden soil, where he took refuge from a storm the night before. Discovering this mistake cures his morbid imagination as well as his catalepsy, and allows him, at the end of his story, to finally view matters with "the sober eye of Reason" (M 3: 968).

The narrator of "The Sphinx," which appeared in 1846, also can "neither speak, think, nor dream of anything" but death (M 3: 1246), just like the narrator of "The Premature Burial." One day, he spies from his window "a living monster of hideous conformation" (M 3: 12467). He "calmly survey[s]" this creature as it crosses the landscape, estimates its size in relation to nearby trees, concludes that it is "far larger than any ship of the line," and describes its bizarre appearance with scientific exactitude—noting, for example, that "extending forward, parallel with the proboscis, and on each side," there rises "a gigantic staff, thirty or forty feet in length, formed seemingly of pure crystal, and in shape a perfect sphere" (M 3: 1247–1248). Despite such apparent objectivity, the narrator's assessment turns out to be completely wrong. A friend, echoing Dupin, warns him "that the principal source of error in all human investigations" is the tendency "to under-rate or to over-value the importance of an object, through mere misadmeasurement of its propinquity" (M 3: 1249–1250).[25] The friend then reads aloud an account of the Sphinx Moth from a volume of natural history—the same volume Dupin uses to identify the Ourang-Outang (M 2: 574n35)—and demonstrates that the narrator must have seen that insect, navigating a filament of spider's web one-sixteenth of an inch from his eye.

Like the Dupin tales, this story juxtaposes one character's flawed perceptions with another's superior acumen. Indeed, Poe's tales often differentiate among characters based on mental acuity.[26] Both "The Premature Burial" and "The Sphinx" evoke detective fiction, moreover, by using the narrator's analysis to lead readers toward *false* conclusions—the opposite of Poe's stratagem in "Berenice," eleven years earlier—before eventually disclosing the truth. Even horror stories can qualify as tales of ratiocination when their plot, structure, narration, and effect all depend upon a protagonist's attempt at reasoning.

Developing Detection

Although Poe invented detective fiction—and indeed established, in one fell swoop, most of the techniques, conventions, and motifs associated with that genre[27]—he did not conceive of it as later authors did. In 1841, when he wrote "The Murders in the Rue Morgue," the word *detective* did not even exist, as either adjective or noun,[28] and it appears nowhere in his work. Poe does use *detect*, especially in negative constructions, to convey the difficulty of noticing irregularities, uncovering evidence, or identifying criminals: thus "no eye could detect anything suspicious" in "The Black Cat" (M 3: 857) and "no human eye—not even his—could have detected anything wrong" in "The Tell-Tale Heart" (M 3: 796).[29] His characters do "detect . . . falsities" in other people's thinking, as the narrator mentions in "MS. Found in a Bottle" (M 2: 135).[30] However, Poe uses *ratiocination* or *analysis*, not *detection*, to describe the mental process that they follow in solving a crime. In any case, he tends to focus on this process instead of on the protagonist. "The Murders in the Rue Morgue" emphasizes "the mental features discoursed of as the analytical," rather than "the analyst" (M 2: 528), with the story of Dupin's deductions offered as "commentary upon the propositions just advanced" (M 2: 531). In Poe's later tales, detectives may fail to decipher the mystery, or the evidence that would allow readers to do so may be missing. Perhaps he was more interested in devising narratives about ratiocination—unravelling webs "woven for the express purpose of unravelling" them (CL 1: 595)—than in whether his characters and readers could also solve an enigma.

Even before "The Murders in the Rue Morgue," Poe experimented with techniques for recounting the investigation of a crime. In 1839, in "The Fall of the House of Usher," he tried a mode of narration that would later become essential to detective fiction. The tale's anonymous narrator struggles to comprehend Roderick Usher's "unceasingly agitated mind" (M 2: 411), yet the source of that agitation remains hidden until the ending. Although the narrator is largely unaware of noises emanating from an underground vault, Roderick hears them, ponders them, and eventually discloses their significance in a speech that anticipates Dupin's explanation, to *his* narrator, of what he has inferred from similarly mysterious sounds in the Rue Morgue. As in the Dupin stories, an obtuse narrator notices outward signs of the protagonist's thinking but cannot follow his reasoning or anticipate his conclusions. Nevertheless, "The Fall of the House of Usher" focuses on horror, not analysis.

Poe's next tale, "William Wilson," also from 1839, resembles an inverted detective story. The narrator initiates a series of crimes—escalating from schoolboy mischief to drinking, gambling, cheating, adultery, and assault—that are all thwarted by his double. Each time, Wilson's double confronts him with evidence of his wrongdoing; each time, Wilson flees in panic. He strives to account for the other's uncanny intervention, his "brain reel[ing] with a multitude of incoherent thoughts" (M 2: 437). He engages in "earnest inquiry," falls into "morbid speculation" (M 2: 439), and "scrutinize[s], with a minute scrutiny," every aspect of his double's behavior, but finds "little upon which to base a conjecture" (M 2: 445). His attempt at reasoning leads nowhere. Although the tale introduces complementary roles that are fundamental to detective fiction—the fleeing criminal, the pursuing detective—Wilson cannot fathom their relationship until his double explains it to him. As in "The Fall of the House of Usher," this climactic revelation takes the form of one character's impassioned speech to another. Wilson's double never reveals his own analytical process, however.

"The Man of the Crowd," published in 1840, repeats the pairing of pursuer and pursued while adding other elements—an urban setting and the detective's portrayal as a flâneur—that reappear in "The Murders in the Rue Morgue" and many subsequent detective stories. Even better, it emphasizes ratiocination and introduces "the man of reason" as a recurring character in Poe's work.[31] The tale's protagonist can categorize passing pedestrians in terms of class, occupation, or criminality simply by analyzing their "figure, dress, air, gait, visage, and expression of countenance" (M 2: 507), as he demonstrates in a remarkable passage that presages the exhibition of Dupin's mind reading in "The Murders in the Rue Morgue." The protagonist also manages to trail a suspect through city streets for hours without being "detect[ed]" himself, even covering his face with a handkerchief and silencing his tread with "caoutchouc over-shoes," or *gumshoes*—a term now synonymous with detectives (M 2: 513).

"The Man of the Crowd" was very nearly the first detective story. It anticipates the genre's archetypal structure, setting, characters, themes, and motifs along with specific variants such as armchair detection and hard-boiled crime fiction.[32] Despite the protagonist's display of analytical skill, however, he may be just as unreliable as the narrators of "The Fall of the House of Usher" and "William Wilson." That Poe makes him a first-person narrator—let alone one who has recently recovered from a mysterious illness and seems rather manic—suggests from the beginning that his deductions may be inaccurate. When he encounters someone who defies his system of classification, for example, he immediately assumes that the other man must be a criminal. Although the narrator speculates about why the other man follows the crowd—a fear of solitude, stemming from guilt over his supposed crimes?—these suspicions are never confirmed. Indeed, the narrator eventually decides that analysis cannot explain the depths of human iniquity, and "thus the essence of all crime is undivulged" (M 2: 507). By proclaiming the impossibility of solving such mysteries, "The Man of the Crowd" prefigured the metaphysical detective story—which deconstructs the genre's epistemological and ontological assumptions—even before detective fiction had been invented.[33]

After "The Murders in the Morgue," Poe wrote two more tales about Dupin and continued tinkering with the genre. In 1843, in "The Gold-Bug," he carried out the plan that he had proposed two years earlier in an article on secret writing: tracing "the ratiocination . . . passing through the mind" of someone solving a cryptograph.[34] Poe's previous tales featured protagonists who examine other people's facial expressions, gestures, or speech as indications of their thought. In "The Gold-Bug," William Legrand instead analyzes a series of written signs. Step by step, he establishes the origins of a mysterious scrap of parchment; makes visible the invisible writing inscribed on the surface; decodes the "punning or hieroglyphical signature" there (M 3: 833); identifies the language used; notices recurring characters; punctuates the text; deciphers it; interprets it; correlates it with the local landscape; and carefully enacts the instructions it contains. By tracing Legrand's procedure in detail, Poe produced the first cryptographic detective story, even though he withheld some clues from readers.[35] He also combined detection with other genres—adventure, comedy, hoax, and horror—while contributing to a new genre, the tale of finding buried treasure. Although there had been earlier stories about *searching* for treasure—including those in Washington Irving's *Tales of a Traveller*, which Poe knew—"The Gold-Bug" may be the first to recount how a hidden treasure is found.[36]

"The Gold-Bug" not only gradually reveals an encoded message to readers but also discloses each corresponding stage of Legrand's ratiocination, beginning with his efforts "to establish . . . a sequence of cause and effect" between the piece of parchment and the mysterious image that suddenly appears upon it. Remarkably, Legrand senses the cryptograph's significance before making its hidden letters visible, let alone decoding them. He later tells his friend, the story's narrator, "Here was indeed a mystery which I felt it impossible to explain; but, even at that early moment, there seemed to glimmer, faintly, within the most remote and secret chambers of my intellect, a glow-worm-like conception" of its import (M 3: 829). His statement offers a similar experience to Poe's readers, since it takes the form of a periodic sentence that teasingly hints at dim gleams of concealed meaning. Legrand's account of this mental phenomenon—the gradual intimation of latent significance—echoes the description of perceiving the "unformed," "feeble," "scarcely definite" solution to a problem in "The Pit and the Pendulum" (M 2: 693). As Legrand deciphers the cryptograph, however, he realizes that both his servant and his friend believe he is mad. Accordingly, he practices some "sober mystification" at their expense—and that of Poe's readers—before finally explaining his ratiocination to them (M 3: 844).

In 1844, Poe revisited the notion of the irrational, excitable, imprudent sleuth that Legrand initially appeared to be. "The Oblong Box" features an amateur detective who is determined to discover why his friend Wyatt has reserved three staterooms on a ship. Although there is no evidence of wrongdoing, the narrator is "in one of those moody frames of mind which make a man abnormally inquisitive about trifles" (M 3: 922–923). After several "attempts to resolve the enigma," he decides that the extra room must be for luggage (M 3: 923). His "old inquisitiveness" returns, however, when he sees the box Wyatt brings on board. He observes its outward appearance—an "oblong" shape, "about six feet in length by two and half in breadth" (M 3: 924–925)—and concludes that it can "contain nothing in the world but a copy of Leonardo's 'Last Supper'" (M 3: 925). Significantly, he experiences no flashes or glimmers of dawning understanding when reaching this conclusion. Like the narrators of "The Premature Burial" and "The Sphinx," he pursues a fanciful explanation rather than recognizing the truth. He ignores various clues, such as Wyatt's grief and the box's odor, which indicate that this coffin-like box is indeed a coffin—a fact that Poe's readers might deduce long before the narrator learns it from the captain. Although his narration may lead readers toward the correct solution, then, he is "too careless, too inquisitive, and too impulsive" to discern it himself (M 3: 934). By casting this obtuse narrator as the detective in "The Oblong Box," Poe inverts the depictions of Dupin and Legrand in his earlier tales even as he continues to emphasize the ratiocinative process.

In "'Thou Art the Man,'" which appeared a few months later, Poe revised the detective genre once again, heightening the underlying revenge plot from "The Purloined Letter" and adding elements of social satire. He also experimented further with using first-person narration to prevent readers from following the detective's analysis. In making the protagonist of "The Oblong Box" a flawed investigator and untrustworthy narrator, Poe abandoned the very mode of narration that he had perfected in the Dupin trilogy and "The Gold-Bug," whereby an oblivious companion recounts the sleuth's exploits. But in " 'Thou Art the Man,' " he set himself another challenge: creating an unreliable narrator who is also a successful detective.

Poe's earlier sleuths occasionally mislead their narrating companions, particularly in "The Gold-Bug." However, the detective in " 'Thou Art the Man' " deceives that tale's readers—caricatured as the gullible citizens of Rattleborough—in the way that he himself narrates the crime's detection. To elucidate "the Rattleborough enigma" (M 3: 1045), the narrator recounts Charley Goodfellow's investigation of a friend's disappearance under suspicious circumstances. Goodfellow, usually a lively and sociable individual, is at first "too overpowered with grief . . . to decide upon any plan of action," and discourages the townsfolk from looking for his friend's body (M 3: 1046). Eventually, by "an ingenious train of reasoning," he convinces them to search for it only as a group under his direction (M 3: 1047). Although they never find the body, he persuades them that his friend's nephew committed the murder.

In Poe's previous tales, detectives employ Socratic questioning to help their companions apprehend a truth that they themselves have already perceived. "The Gold-Bug," for example, consists mostly of Legrand explaining his deductions aloud and leading the narrator, step by step, to understand his thinking. Goodfellow, by contrast, uses skillful rhetoric to guide the townsfolk toward the wrong conclusion without openly advocating it, "for, although he labored earnestly on behalf of the suspected, yet it so happened, somehow or other, that every syllable he uttered . . . had the effect of deepening the suspicion already attached to the individual whose cause he plead[ed]" (M 3: 1050). He also plants evidence: "apparently" finding an object, then seeming "to make a sort of half attempt at concealing it" (M 3: 1052), and later being "enabled to detect" a bullet inside the body of the victim's horse. At the nephew's trial, this "chain of circumstantial evidence" seems "so unbroken and so thoroughly conclusive" that the jury immediately returns a guilty verdict (M 3: 1054). Goodfellow's display of specious ratiocination not only persuades his audience; it induces them to reach a conclusion different from the one he publicly affirms. Rather than an inferior analyst, he is a successful swindler.

The narrator eventually exposes Goodfellow's deceit, however, by means of forgery, stagecraft, ventriloquism, and yet another coffin disguised as an oblong box—in this case, a crate of wine supposedly ordered by the dead man before his death. Just as Goodfellow tricked the townsfolk into thinking the nephew guilty, so the narrator tricks *him* into believing that his friend's corpse, arranged inside the crate, identifies him as the murderer: " 'Thou art the man!' " (M 3: 1057).

This act of ventriloquism epitomizes the narrator's superior analytical, rhetorical, and dramatic skills. His narration invites readers to distrust Goodfellow's eloquence, sympathize with the suspect, and deduce that the ostensible detective might be the culprit. His hoax induces Goodfellow to confess his guilt and then die of shock. Indeed, Goodfellow's extraordinary confession is surpassed by the revelation that the narrator himself is not only a character in the story—"I myself" was present, he explains—but the actual detective, speaking in the first person (M 3: 1056). In the story's denouement, the narrator discloses his own ratiocination as well as the scheme that he concocted to exonerate the falsely accused suspect and wreak his revenge. Although " 'Thou Art the Man' " keeps some crucial clues from readers,[37] it remains an ingenious meditation on the art of presenting deductions to an audience, which deserves more recognition as not only Poe's last detective story, but one of his best.

Ends in Mind

Poe was not interested in solving mysteries so much as in *attempting* to solve them, however. His tales of ratiocination—whether they describe escaping from danger or investigating crime—are less concerned with a protagonist's failure or success than with how he thinks. Because Poe was acutely aware of his own cognition, he was able to describe his characters' thoughts with remarkable verisimilitude. Indeed, Leon Howard wonders whether the Dupin stories were "conscious attempts to create a new literary genre" or, instead, "idealized attempts to represent Poe's real creative processes."[38] Paul Hurh argues for the latter interpretation, showing how Poe's account of ratiocination in "The Murders in the Rue Morgue" resembles nothing so much as the practice of artistic creation—especially as he reconstructs it in "The Philosophy of Composition."[39] But although Poe may have been more interested in the process than in the product of ratiocination, he still wrote with an end in mind. His ultimate end was to establish "a certain . . . *effect*" for his readers, inducing them to share an experience of heightened, intensely focused, visionary thought and to contemplate "with a kindred art" the text that he had written (H 11: 102).

Perhaps that is why Poe's endings tend to evoke deeper mysteries, what S. K. Wertz and Linda L. Wertz might call "genuine" mysteries,[40] often figured as an abyss or a whirlpool or a tomb. Each of Poe's proto-detective stories, for example, concludes with an emblem of recursive indeterminacy: the House of Usher's fragments sinking beneath the tarn, Wilson confronting his double in a hall of mirrors, the heart as a book "that does not permit itself to be read" (M 2: 506). Each of the Dupin tales shifts from the actual mystery under investigation to a metafictional conundrum: the notion of the Prefect's wisdom as a headless body in "The Murders in the Rue Morgue," the claim that any similarities to the Mary Rogers case are coincidental in "The Mystery of Marie Rogêt," and the substitution of Dupin's own missive for the missing one in "The Purloined Letter." Poe's other detective stories also evoke further riddles. "The Gold-Bug" ends by asking unanswerable questions about the skeletons buried with the treasure and the precise number of blows needed to kill them. "The Oblong Box" evokes Wyatt's peals of hysterical laughter as his wife's coffin sinks beneath the waves, an uncanny sound that still haunts the narrator. In "'Thou Art the Man,'" another narrator remains "puzzled . . . to imagine *why*" Goodfellow never told anybody that the dead man had promised to send him a box of wine (M 3: 1056). Such oblique, unresolvable endings reiterate Poe's passion for the process of ratiocination and not the result. Each story ends with another mystery to be solved.

Notes

1. Joseph Wood Krutch, *Edgar Allan Poe: A Study in Genius* (New York: Knopf, 1926), 118.
2. S. K. Wertz and Linda L. Wertz, "On Poe's Use of 'Mystery,'" *Poe Studies* 4, no. 1 (1971): 7. The authors speculate that Poe uses "mystery" in three senses, corresponding to three different types of plot: "the construction and resolution of a puzzle, the solving of a problem, or the recognition of a mystery" (10).
3. See Kelly Ross's chapter on the Dupin trilogy in this volume.
4. *Oxford English Dictionary*, s.v. "Ratiocination, (*n.*)," updated January 2018, www.oed.com.
5. John Stuart Mill, *A System of Logic, Ratiocinative and Inductive, Being a Connected View of the Principles of Evidence, and the Methods of Scientific Investigation* (London: John W. Parker, 1843), 223.
6. Poe's comments in the Marginalia, about how Mill tends to repeat words when advancing an argument, indicate his familiarity with *A System of Logic* (P 2: 170–171, n171b). "Mellonta Tauta," which Poe later incorporated into *Eureka*, mocks this volume as "the cleverest ancient book on its topic" (M 3: 1297). On Poe's consistently ironic attitude toward the English philosopher, see Harriet R. Holman, "What Did Mill Mean to Poe?" *Mill News Letter* 6 (1971): 20–21.
7. To compare Mill's definition of ratiocination with Poe's, see also David N. Stamos, *Edgar Allan Poe,* Eureka, *and Scientific Imagination* (Albany: SUNY Press, 2017), 245–246.
8. William Whewell, *The Philosophy of the Inductive Sciences, Founded upon Their History* (London: John W. Parker, 1840), 206–208. On Poe's affinity to Whewell, see Stamos, *Edgar Allan Poe,* 247–248.
9. Pierce defines abduction as a process of informed conjecture that generates hypotheses. See his major essays on "Deduction, Induction, and Hypothesis," in *The Essential Peirce, Selected Philosophical Writings*, ed. Nathan Houser and Christian J. W. Kloesel (Bloomington: Indiana University Press, 1992), 1:186–199, and "A Theory of Probable Inference," in *The Writings of C. S. Peirce*, ed. Christian J. W. Kloesel et al. (Bloomington: Indiana University Press, 1989), 4:408–453. For comparisons of Poe's ratiocination with Peirce's abduction, see Nancy Harrowitz, "The Body of the Detective Model: Charles S. Peirce and Edgar Allan Poe," in *The Sign of Three: Dupin, Holmes, Peirce*, ed. Umberto Eco and Thomas A. Sebeok (Bloomington: Indiana University Press, 1983), 179–197, and Paul Grimstad, "C. Auguste Dupin and Charles S. Peirce: An Abductive Affinity," *Edgar Allan Poe Review* 6, no. 2 (2005): 22–30.
10. Daniel Hoffman, *Poe Poe Poe Poe Poe Poe Poe* (Baton Rouge: Louisiana State University Press, 1998), 110.
11. Robert Shulman explores Poe's notion of mental faculties in "Poe and the Powers of the Mind," *ELH* 37, no. 2 (1970): 245–262; Umberto Eco and Thomas A. Sebeok identify ratiocination with semiotics in their edited volume *The Sign of Three: Dupin, Holmes, Peirce* (Bloomington: Indiana University Press, 1983); Dennis Porter, referring to Lacanian and

Derridean readings of "The Purloined Letter," associates it with poststructuralism in "Of Poets, Politicians, Policemen, and the Power of Analysis," *New Literary History* 19, no. 3 (1988): 501–519; Shawn James Rosenheim discusses it in terms of information theory in *The Cryptographic Imagination: Secret Writing from Edgar Poe to the Internet* (Baltimore: Johns Hopkins University Press, 1997); and A. Samuel Kimball relates it to affect theory in "The Linguistic Turn, First-Person Experience, and the Terror of Relativism: 'The Purloined Letter' and the Affective Limits of Ratiocination," in *Approaches to Teaching Poe's Prose and Poetry*, ed. Jeffrey Andrew Weinstock and Tony Magistrale (New York: Modern Language Association, 2008), 115–124. Other critics—Paul Gilmore, "Reading Minds in the Nineteenth Century," in *The Oxford Handbook of Nineteenth-Century American Literature*, ed. Russ Castronovo (Oxford: Oxford University Press, 2012), 327–342; Paul Hurh, *American Terror: The Feeling of Thinking in Edwards, Poe, and Melville* (Stanford, CA: Stanford University Press, 2015); and Stamos, *Edgar Allan Poe*, 512–535—analyze Poe's depiction of thought in terms of cognitive science. I link it to fictional detectives with neurological disorders in "How to Diagnose a Case of Neuro-Noir," a chapter in a proposed volume edited by Alfred Bendixen and Olivia Carr Edenfield.

12. Edgar Allan Poe, "Secret Writing" [Addendum III], *Graham's Magazine* 19 (December 1841): 306.
13. Rebecca Saxe and Simon Baron-Cohen, *Theory of Mind* (Hove, UK: Psychology Press, 2007).
14. For attributions, see Charles F. Heartman and James R. Canny, *A Bibliography of First Printings of the Writings of Edgar Allan Poe*, rev. ed. (Hattiesburg, MS: The Book Farm, 1943), and Jeffrey Savoye, The Edgar Allan Poe Society of Baltimore, www.eapoe.org.
15. Review of E. A. Poe's *Tales, Aristidean* October 1845, 316–319. Discussing the Dupin stories, the reviewer says that "The Mystery of Marie Rogêt" "reveals the whole secret of their mode of construction" and that "The Purloined Letter" is a simple tale, perhaps less interesting than the others, in which "the reasoning is remarkably clear, and directed solely to the required end" (318, 319).
16. Edmund Clarence Stedman, "Introduction to the Literary Criticism," in *The Works of Edgar Allan Poe* (New York: Stone and Kimball, 1895), 6: xiii.
17. Duycinck did not include " 'Thou Art the Man' " because it was not yet written.
18. Other works by Poe that could be considered "analytic stories" include *The Narrative of Arthur Gordon Pym*, "The Man that was Used Up," "A Tale of the Ragged Mountains," "The Spectacles," and "Three Sundays in a Week." These stories, too, represent a variety of genres.
19. J. Gerald Kennedy, "The Limits of Reason: Poe's Deluded Detectives," *American Literature* 47, no. 2 (1975): 185.
20. In "Instinct vs Reason: A Black Cat," Poe ponders how an animal can solve problems using "perceptive and reflective faculties" that are considered peculiar to humans (M 2: 179). Leroy L. Panek points out that in other essays, Poe "exercise[s] his own abilities as a detective on various material problems like handwriting and cryptography," in " 'Maelzel's Chess-Player,' Poe's First Detective Mistake," *American Literature* 48, no. 3 (1976): 370. Leon Howard identifies *Eureka* as "Poe's most ambitious specimen of ratiocination," comparing it favorably to "The Purloined Letter," in "Poe's *Eureka*: The Detective Story That Failed," *Mystery and Detection Annual* 1 (1972): 12. Poe himself calls "The Philosophy of Composition" his "best specimen of analysis" (CL 1: 596).
21. Poe's acrostic poems usually describe readers' unsuccessful attempts to solve the riddle of their construction, as in "A Valentine" (M 1: 389).

22. Consider the poem's interrogative structure and how the speaker "link[s]/ Fancy unto fancy" while "engaged in guessing" what the raven's answer means (M 1: 368).
23. In "Murders," Poe's narrator remarks that the analytical features "are, in themselves, but little, susceptible of analysis" (M 2: 528). Using similar constructions, other narrators describe "a sensation which will admit of no analysis," in "Ms. Found in a Bottle" (M 2: 141), and claim that the essence of beauty requires "a more profound analysis than the world has yet seen," in "The Landscape Garden" (M 2: 708).
24. A "vague and half-formed conception" also crosses the narrator's mind in "Murders" (M 2: 555).
25. In "Murders," Dupin disparages Vidocq for "the very intensity of his investigations. He impaired his vision by holding the object too close" (M 2: 545).
26. Similarly, "The Black Cat" contrasts the narrator's flawed thinking—in which he tries to establish a rational context for his crimes—with that of "some intellect more calm, more logical, and far less excitable than [his] own" (M 3: 850).
27. Susan Elizabeth Sweeney, "Locked Rooms: Detective Fiction, Narrative Theory, and Self-Reflexivity," in *The Cunning Craft: Original Essays on Detective Fiction and Literary Theory*, ed. Ronald G. Walker and June M. Frazer (Macomb: Western Illinois University Press, 1990), 1.
28. *Oxford English Dictionary*, s.v. "Detective, (*adj.* and *n.*)," updated January 2018, www.oed.com.
29. Likewise, "no semblance of art could be detected" in the Antarctic landscape in *Pym* (P 1: 198) and "no syllabification could be detected" in the Orang-Outang's utterances in "Murders" (M 2: 555).
30. For a similar construction, see "Variants for *Hans Pfaall*" (P 1: 438 [variant 9g]).
31. Kennedy, "Limits of Reason," 188.
32. On this tale's role in the development of detective fiction, see Susan Elizabeth Sweeney, "The Magnifying Glass: Spectacular Distance in Poe's 'Man of the Crowd' and Beyond," *Poe Studies* 36 (2003): 3–17.
33. Patricia Merivale and Susan Elizabeth Sweeney, eds., *Detecting Texts: The Metaphysical Detective Story from Poe to Postmodernism* (Philadelphia: University of Pennsylvania Press, 1999).
34. Poe, "Secret Writing," 306.
35. For example, readers are not initially told that the parchment was buried on a beach near the remains of a boat.
36. Poe praises Irving's *Tales of a Traveller* when reviewing Nathaniel Hawthorne's *Twice-Told Tales* for *Graham's Magazine* (H 11: 102). Although several of Irving's tales describe either Captain Kidd's buried treasure or Wolfert Webber's search for it, Irving never describes its actual discovery. Another potential precursor for "The Gold-Bug" is a semiautobiographical novel, *The Journal of Llewellin Penrose, A Seaman* (1815), edited by John Eagles, in which a diagram with words and symbols leads to hidden treasure. On these and other possible sources, see Mabbott's introduction to Poe's story (M 2: 799–803).
37. The narrator belatedly reveals that an incriminating bloodstain on the suspect's shirt is claret. He also admits, at the end of the story, that the victim's body has been found and he himself was the person who found it (M 3: 1058).
38. Howard, "Poe's *Eureka*," 4.
39. Paul Hurh, "The Creative and the Resolvent: The Origins of Poe's Analytical Method," *Nineteenth-Century Literature* 66, no. 4 (2012): 466–493.
40. Wertz and Wertz, "On Poe's Use of 'Mystery,'" 7.

Bibliography

Gilmore, Paul. "Reading Minds in the Nineteenth Century." In *The Oxford Handbook of Nineteenth-Century American Literature*, edited by Russ Castronovo, Oxford: Oxford University Press, 2012, 327–342.

Hurh, Paul. *American Terror: The Feeling of Thinking in Edwards, Poe, and Melville*. Stanford, CA: Stanford University Press, 2015.

Irwin, John. *The Mystery to a Solution: Poe, Borges, and the Analytic Detective Story*. Baltimore: Johns Hopkins University Press, 1996.

Kennedy, J. Gerald. "The Limits of Reason: Poe's Deluded Detectives." *American Literature* 47, no. 2 (1975): 184–196.

Sweeney, Susan Elizabeth. "The Magnifying Glass: Spectacular Distance in Poe's 'Man of the Crowd' and Beyond." *Poe Studies* 36 (2003): 3–17.

Wertz, S. K., and Linda L. Wertz. "On Poe's Use of 'Mystery.'" *Poe Studies* 4, no. 1 (1971): 7–10.

CHAPTER 12

DECIPHERING DUPIN

Poe's Ratiocinative Plots

KELLY ROSS

THOUGH Poe's Dupin tales have earned him the honor of "inventing" the detective story, Poe himself labeled the Dupin trilogy his "tales of ratiocination." Whereas detection accentuates the act of discovery, ratiocination emphasizes the act of reasoning. The purest form of reasoning is the algorithm, "a procedure or set of rules used in calculation and problem-solving."[1] Algorithms have made the computing revolution possible and concomitantly have made possible the "surveillance society," the phrase Gary T. Marx coined as the title of his 1985 article: "with computer technology, one of the final barriers to total control is crumbling—the inability to retrieve, aggregate, and analyze vast amounts of data. Inefficiency is losing its role as the unplanned protector of liberty."[2] Since 1985, the "crumbling" barrier has disintegrated as exponential advances in technology have given government agencies, including the United States' National Security Agency (NSA) and the United Kingdom's Government Communications Headquarters (GCHQ), unprecedented capacity for not only "processing, tracking, monitoring, profiling, and sorting . . . information"[3] but also predicting and manipulating behaviors, desires, and actions.

Surprisingly, Poe sits at the intersection of these tightly interwoven fields of computing and mass surveillance. Associated with the dawn of the computer age through his admiration for Charles Babbage, the "pioneer of the modern computer and patron saint of the information age," who in the 1820s and 1830s developed precursors of modern computers, Poe is also linked to surveillance via the many twentieth-century American cryptologists who became aware of secret writing through Poe's 1843 story, "The Gold-Bug."[4] As Shawn Rosenheim demonstrates, Poe's influence shaped "the institutional elaboration of cryptography and espionage," particularly in the NSA.[5] Examining the Dupin tales through a lens of surveillance, rather than Holmesian detection, shifts our attention away from the psychoanalytic tradition of criticism and focuses it instead on information, communications, and metadata. Twenty years after *The Cryptographic Imagination*, spying takes place primarily in cyberspace, and we need an updated account of Poe's relationship to surveillance. In the three Dupin tales, Poe explores multiple aspects of digital surveillance, from data mining and profiling in "The Murders in the Rue Morgue" (1841) and "The Mystery of Marie Rogêt" (1842) to metadata in "The Purloined Letter" (1844). Rereading these tales with a surveillant eye allows us to perceive more clearly the sociohistorical forces, rather than interiorized psychodynamics, at play in the Dupin tales.

Computing and Surveillance in the Antebellum Era

Poe was quick to apprehend the possibilities that the earliest computers offered. Babbage's Difference Engines could "compute tables of numbers according to the method of finite differences, and then automatically print the tables as they were computed."[6] He later developed "Analytic Engines," which were "versatile, programmable automatic calculators."[7] In Poe's 1836 article, "Maelzel's Chess-Player" and his 1845 short story "The Thousand-and-Second Tale of Scheherazade," he extolled Charles Babbage's "calculating machine," calling it "a creature that put to shame even the genius of him who made it; for so great were its reasoning powers that, in a second, it performed calculations of so vast an extent that they would have required the united labor of fifty thousand fleshy men for a year" (M 3: 1166). Further deepening the connection between Poe and Babbage, Terence Whalen has argued that Poe's 1845 tale "The Power of Words" was inspired by (and includes paraphrased passages from) Babbage's *Ninth Bridgewater Treatise* (1837). Whalen notes that "for both Poe and Babbage, . . . the universe is a vast material archive that contains a permanent record of all that has been said and done since the beginning of time."[8] Poe appreciated the potential of Babbage's theories about information and automated computing, recognizing the implications of a purely logical machine.

If Poe was profoundly influenced by the godfather of computing, he was himself a foundational figure in the development of American cryptology, which underwrites modern mass digital surveillance operations. As Rosenheim states, "the development of telecommunications is essentially a history of advances in the coding and transmission of signals."[9] William Friedman, one of the "pioneers of American cryptanalysis," credits Poe as the origin of American interest in cryptography, stating, "it is a curious fact that popular interest in this country in the subject of cryptography received its first stimulus from Edgar Allan Poe."[10] In *The Cryptographic Imagination*, Rosenheim boldly declares, "the military and political institutions of cryptography have never freed themselves from their literary roots, which is roughly equivalent to claiming that they have never freed themselves from Poe." Rosenheim's "literary history of the NSA" traces Poe's influence on World War II spying, particularly through seminal figures such as Friedman, "who, by overseeing the mathematization and the mechanization of cryptography, transformed it from an avocation fit for military historians into a force in international politics and war."[11] Friedman founded the institution that would become the NSA, as David Kahn demonstrates in his monumental history of secret writing: "the vast American cryptological establishment of today, with its thousands of employees, its far-flung stations, its sprawling headquarters . . . is a direct lineal descendent of the little office in the War Department that Friedman started, all by himself."[12] The models of cryptography and surveillance developed by the US government during World War II continue to shape contemporary national security systems; moreover, World War II cryptography's legacy includes cybernetics, game theory, information theory, and the digital electronic computer, which was built to solve the Germans' Enigma cipher.[13] Computing and surveillance have developed conjointly, as technological advances in one domain spur breakthroughs in the other. At the heart of both are logic and cryptanalysis, two themes that run through Poe's oeuvre.

Although Poe's connections to computing and surveillance make him seem uncannily ahead of his time, it is more accurate to regard him as astutely perceptive of significant breakthroughs in his own time. The invention of the telegraph by Samuel F. B. Morse in the late 1830s and its commercial deployment beginning in the 1840s marked a new era in communications. As Carolyn Marvin observes, "in a historical sense, the computer is no more than an instantaneous telegraph with a prodigious memory, and all the communications inventions in between have simply been elaborations on the telegraph's original work."[14] The possibility of instantaneous communication was more than just a technological advance; it fundamentally altered the nature of information by decoupling it from the body that produced it. Rosenheim argues that "by destroying the identity between transportation and communication, the telegraph . . . ushered in a time in which bodies and information can be separated."[15] The telegraph crowned the transformation of the publishing industry that had been underway for decades, thanks to technological advancements such as stereotyping, steam-driven presses, and faster, cheaper transportation methods, including canals and railroads. The enormous growth of the publishing industry led to a critical information overload and literary overproduction in the antebellum United States, which directly affected Poe. Whalen notes that "Poe . . . was painfully aware that he worked in a signifying environment suffering from a surplus of both information and intellectual workers."[16] Attempting to make a living as a writer during "the rise of information as a dominant form of meaning,"[17] Poe registered the cultural shift in his tales of ratiocination, which, I argue, imagine the possibilities of reasoning based on data mining and metadata.

The deep currents that flow from Poe to digital surveillance prompt us to rethink what Poe meant when he called the Dupin tales ratiocinative. If we take seriously the notion that these tales explore the potential of pure reasoning, then computer algorithms, rather than gumshoe detection, offer a more valuable model. For Poe, Babbage's engines epitomized the power of logic. Describing the engines' algorithmic procedure in "Maelzel's Chess Player," Poe explained, "Certain data being given, certain results necessarily and inevitably follow. These results have dependence upon nothing, and are influenced by nothing but the data originally given. And the question to be solved proceeds, or should proceed, to its final determination, by a succession of unerring steps liable to no change, and subject to no modification" (H 14: 9–10). For finite calculations, in which the data set is limited, such as the navigational tables that Babbage's Difference Engines produced, once one provides the data and employs the algorithm, the result is inevitable and infallible. Moving from the numerical to the material, however, causes a problem of data overload. Whereas one can give the engine "certain data" in the case of numerical questions, there is too much data to be given in questions such as "who killed the L'Espanayes?"

Fantasizing a solution to this problem of data in "The Power of Words," Poe imagines the universe as a comprehensive material archive that enables "a being of infinite understanding" to trace any result back to its cause through "analytic retrogradation" (M 3: 1214–1215). Advances in computer analysis, processing, and storage have moved us ever closer to achieving this "being of infinite understanding" via networked, artificially intelligent computing systems with the capability to store, search, query, and analyze data on the scale of petabytes (2^{50} bytes or 1 million gigabytes). In a recent analysis of data politics, Evelyn Ruppert, Engin Isin, and Didier Bigo trenchantly summarize the current state of big data:

> The Internet rapidly became the space over and through which governments and corporations began collecting, storing, retrieving, analysing, and presenting data that records what people do and say on the Internet. This ranges from who communicates with whom, who goes where, and who says what—and much more besides. This is now being augmented with data that people collect about themselves, especially their relations, body movements, and measurements; the amount and range of data that has become available is, as everyone now knows, staggering. There has never been a state, monarchy, kingdom, empire, government, or corporation in history that has had command over such granular, immediate, varied, and detailed data about subjects and objects that concern them.[18]

Whalen remarks that "Babbage's universe"—on which Poe closely modeled his own universe in "The Power of Words"—"sometimes looks like a vast paranoid fantasy where every action is seen and recorded by molecular spies."[19] That fantasy is no longer quite so paranoid, though the spies are digital rather than molecular. Poe portrays this fantasy in his depiction of Dupin's relationship with the narrator of the tales. In their hermetic universe, Dupin, like the "being of infinite understanding" in "The Power of Words," has access to the totality of data, and thereby can (as in "Maelzel") "proceed, to [his] final determination, by a succession of unerring steps liable to no change, and subject to no modification" (H 14: 9–10). This relationship, probed in the next section, offers an analog to the big data revolution, scaled down to the individual level.

Data Mining and Predictive Profiling at No. 33, Rue Dunôt

Tracing changes in surveillance from the sixteenth century to the present, David Rosen and Aaron Santesso's magisterial *The Watchman in Pieces* represents the most significant study of surveillance and literature to date. Yet, like many readers, Rosen and Santesso conceive of Dupin as a "superman, a patently magical figure capable of understanding the truth about other people," unlike the police in literary depictions, who merely collect evidence.[20] By describing Dupin as "magical," Rosen and Santesso obviate the need for a sociohistorically specific account of Dupin's methodology. They argue that "[l]iterary detectives starting with Dupin . . . have been *mens rea* [guilty mind] determination machines, able not only to identify the external character but also to deduce from those outward signs an internal transcript of thought and plotting."[21] In its focus on the "internal transcript," or subjectivity, rather than "outward signs," this view extends Dupin's deductive abilities into the minds of other characters, enabling him to read their "thought and plotting."

However, Dana Brand points out that this mistaken emphasis on Dupin's mind reading comes from taking the narrator of "The Murders in the Rue Morgue" too seriously: "The narrator's assumption that Dupin is simply an unusually proficient flâneur, throwing himself into the minds of others, is analogous to the comparably obtuse pronouncements made by [the narrators of 'The Fall of the House of Usher' and 'The Man of the Crowd']."[22] This fallacy stems from assigning too much weight to the narrator's speculations about the games of chess, draughts, and whist, in which the narrator claims that "the analyst throws himself into the spirit of his opponent, identifies himself therewith, and not unfrequently sees thus, at a glance, the sole methods" (M 2: 529). While at the beginning of the story Dupin does "deduce . . . an internal transcript of [the narrator's] thought and plotting" from observing outward signs, he is capable of doing so only because he already knows the narrator intimately. Brand asserts that Dupin is able to "fathom [the narrator's] soul" (M 2: 534) because "the narrator's conventional mind is entirely familiar to Dupin, who has largely absorbed the narrator's identity into his own. . . . To read the narrator is, for Dupin, to read a text that he himself has been writing."[23]

While I agree with the spirit of Brand's conclusion, I wish to alter the terms of his analysis: Dupin, I would argue, can predict the narrator's chain of thoughts because he has the narrator under constant surveillance. Though conducted in person rather than digitally, Dupin's relationship with the narrator anticipates the two principal methods of twenty-first-century dataveillance ("the collection or monitoring of [esp. digital] data relating to personal details or activities").[24] First, Dupin's total surveillance of the narrator parallels the NSA's "collect-everything approach to monitoring and intelligence" through its massive electronic surveillance operations. This vast store of aggregate data can then be mined to discover patterns and correlations. Data mining produces profiles of individuals and populations.[25] Second, Dupin's ability to complete the narrator's sentence relies on the same logic as the widely used contemporary "predictive models" that produce "complex, interactive feedback loops of manipulation and behavioral engineering."[26] By categorizing individuals or groups on the basis of profiles, these models can cross-reference likely behavior patterns of similar subjects and predict what the person or groups will do, want, or say next. The consonance with twenty-first-century dataveillance emerges because Poe's Dupin tales, as well as the NSA's surveillance programs, are grounded in a desire for a comprehensive record of every "impulse" in the universe (M 3: 1214).

The well-known vignette at the beginning of "The Murders in the Rue Morgue," in which Dupin accurately responds aloud to the narrator's silent meditation, is often cited as proof of Dupin's mind reading. However, this section of the story more clearly depicts a thought experiment of the universe Poe describes in "The Power of Words," in which total surveillance makes possible perfect "analytic retrogradation." The narrator of "Murders" emphasizes Dupin's complete access to the narrator's every movement and communication, stating, "Our seclusion was perfect. We admitted no visitors. . . . We existed within ourselves alone" (M 2: 532). Because the narrator's entire existence is wholly available to Dupin, the latter functions individually like the mass data-collection programs of the US's NSA and UK's GSHQ revealed by Edward Snowden. These "Upstream" programs, including the NSA's OAKSTAR, STORMBREW, BLARNEY, and FAIRVIEW and GCHQ's Tempora, "represen[t] the first 'full take' system, in which surveillance networks catch all Internet traffic regardless of its content," according to Snowden.[27] These programs intercept transmissions via fiber-optic cables within the United States and along ocean floors as well as through drones equipped with "Air Handlers" that "capture all available wireless data traffic in the area."[28] Dupin's "perfect seclusion" with the narrator is similarly a "full-take system," in which Dupin knows everything the narrator has read and discussed, everywhere he has gone, and everything he has done.

The value of this "collect and store everything" approach is the ability to "build complex profiles of people and groups" and retroactively sort through massive data sets to identify patterns.[29] Algorithms mine this stored data, combining data sets from different domains, such as "cash machine use, credit card trails, internet cookies, medical files, and social media sites—anything, indeed, that might produce interesting correlations that might indicate meaningful relationships between records."[30] Indeed, the very temporality of analysis shifts when the data sets are so enormous: "the aim of amassing and mining data is 'knowledge discovery'. . . . Big data builds on . . . already existing modes of surveillance that *anticipate* our actions. Such systems attempt to create new knowledge using the statistical power of large numbers."[31] As Mark Andrejevic and Kelly Gates explain, Snowden's leak revealed a bifurcation in the way electronic surveillance is conducted: on one hand is "the familiar 'legacy' version of targeted, purposeful spying," and on the other is "the emerging model of ubiquitous, opportunistic data capture."[32] This latter model intercepts and stores all "data-in-transit";[33] it does not aim to prevent a particular crime or apprehend a particular individual. Dupin produces a comprehensive profile of the narrator thanks to his total surveillance.

Not only has Dupin collected all of the narrator's data, but he has also provided much of the content of the narrator's thought. In describing his "method" of knowing what the narrator was thinking, Dupin repeatedly emphasizes the subjects they had previously "discussed" and "often conversed" about, as well as the facts that Dupin had "mentioned to [the narrator]" (M 2: 535–536). The narrator tests Dupin by asking, "'How was it possible you should know I was thinking of—?' Here I paused, to ascertain beyond a doubt whether he really knew of whom I thought. —'of Chantilly,' said he" (M 2: 534). Dupin functions like the autocomplete feature on Google, text messaging programs, and other systems that rely on artificial intelligence (AI) to predict the end of a string of characters or words. Similar AI systems on social media sites such as Facebook determine the order of stories and advertisements on a user's newsfeed. These systems predict what will most interest a user in order to keep her active on the site for as long as possible, thereby maximizing the site's revenue (which is calculated on the quantity of page views or ad impressions). Martijn van Otterlo explains how "*algorithms* developed in artificial intelligence" analyze massive data sets to learn to produce "statistical, predictive models." These models can then be used to manipulate behavior "for business and surveillance opportunities"—for example, targeting advertising at consumers statistically more likely to buy a product rather than spending money on a sweeping campaign.[34] Like the predictive algorithms of Facebook sites that know what you will next want to see—or more importantly, buy—based on the content you consume, Dupin keeps the narrator under total surveillance, feeds him content, and then astonishes him by correctly anticipating his thoughts. This vignette with the narrator at the outset of the first Dupin tale provides the framework for understanding Dupin's method for solving the "crimes."

Dupin's Surveillant Methodology

Because "Murders" begins with the narrator's commentary on identifying with an opponent and the episode in which Dupin reads the narrator's mind, readers have been led to believe that Dupin's method of crime solving also depends upon mind reading.[35] However, Dupin's technique for solving the L'Espanayes' murders relies on the same method of bulk data collection that he demonstrates in the vignette. Once we separate the narrator's mystification from what Dupin actually does and says, we see that the detective's method is more like modern dataveillance in its reliance on bulk data collection, data mining, profiling, and metadata. After intercepting the communications produced about the case in the "Gazette des Tribunaux," Dupin visits the crime scene and scrutinizes the entire vicinity, not narrowing in on any particular object but sweeping as wide an area as possible. The narrator notes that "Dupin, meanwhile examin[ed] the whole neighborhood, as well as the house, with a minuteness of attention for which I could see no possible object. . . . Dupin scrutinized every thing" (M 2: 546). In contrast to this wide-ranging view, though, the narrator notes that in front of the L'Espanayes' house "there were still many persons gazing up at the closed shutters, with an objectless curiosity" (M 2: 546). The curious onlookers train their gaze on one spot: the windows that remain "shuttered" to them. Dupin eventually narrows down the murderer's egress to the windows, symbolically unshuttering them and enabling himself to solve the case, because he first conducts sweeping surveillance of "the whole neighborhood . . . as well as the house." Describing his investigation to the narrator, Dupin distinguishes between the limited or narrow vision of the police and his own broad vision:

> It is probable that the police, as well as myself, examined the back of the tenement; but, if so, in looking at these *ferrades* in the line of their breadth (as they must have done), they did not perceive this great breadth itself, or, at all events, failed to take it into due consideration. In fact, having once satisfied themselves that no egress could have been made in this quarter, they would naturally bestow here a very cursory examination. (M 2: 554)

Dupin's broad surveillance provides the perspective he needs to reason "a posteriori" (M 2: 552), drawing on his examination of the windows, the shutters, the lightning rod (underneath which he finds the sailor's ribbon), and Madame L'Espanaye's corpse (in whose fingers he finds the orangutan's hair).

Dupin's meditation on truth resonates with mass surveillance's diffuse range, as he valorizes "the superficial" over the "profound": "[The prefect] impaired his vision by holding the object too close. He might see, perhaps, one or two points with unusual clearness, but in so doing he, necessarily, lost sight of the matter as a whole. Thus there is such a thing as being too profound. Truth is not always in a well. In fact, as regards the more important knowledge, I do believe that she is invariably superficial" (M 2: 545). This surface-versus-depth model resonates with David Lyon's dismissal of individuated, targeted surveillance as being outmoded. Although the general public worries "about the assault on privacy, construed as a personal—understood as individual—matter," this concern "shows little understanding of the ways that surveillance also operates as social sorting, targeting primarily population groups before individuals."[36] The bulk collection of data is concerned with superficial, group-level surveillance, not with individual depth of subjectivity.

In contrast to readings of Dupin's "magical" abilities to fathom souls, his own explanation of his methods emphasizes an ability to find logical inconsistencies in written testimony: not an internal transcript of consciousness but an external transcript of communication. He reads the witness testimonies published in the newspaper, analyzes this data set, and identifies a pattern. He never even meets the witnesses and propounds no interpretations of their interiority. Dupin deduces that the killer must be nonhuman because the witnesses have each identified the voice as speaking a language they did not comprehend, and all identified different accents. Dupin, Brand notes, "is a panoramic interpreter of interpretations. He does not claim to find the truth by languidly surveying the cubicles of the Panopticon. He intellectually reconstructs it by analyzing what each inhabitant of a cubicle, believing his cubicle to be a privileged vantage, is unable to see."[37] This synoptic insight does initiate Dupin's chain of deductions, but his "panoramic interpretation of interpretations" does not in itself solve the case; rather, it stimulates Dupin's sweeping surveillance of the neighborhood and house, preventing him from settling for the narrowed focus of the police.

Tellingly, Dupin never sees the killer in "Murders" at all; rather, he tracks the orangutan down via the sailor with whom he was communicating. That is, Dupin practices the type of profiling and cross-referencing that NSA programs perform. As Lyon explains, "data are sought on a 'mass' basis, from wide swathes of a given population, with a view to identifying algorithmically through correlations who might be a 'person of interest.' . . . [W]ithout necessarily being aware of it, we all feed data to the NSA and its cognate agencies, just by contacting others electronically."[38] After Dupin convinces the narrator that an orangutan committed the murders, the narrator reminds him that "there were two voices heard in contention, and one of them was unquestionably the voice of a Frenchman" (M 2: 559–560). Dupin's response emphasizes the importance of that communication between the murderer and its correspondent: "True; and you will remember an expression attributed almost unanimously, by the evidence, to this voice,—the expression, 'mon Dieu!' . . . Upon these two words, therefore, I have mainly built my hopes of a full solution of the riddle. A Frenchman was cognizant of the murder" (M 2: 560). Dupin's ability to solve the crime depends not upon his physical capture of the killer but on his ability to track the killer through a record of communication with another person, who ultimately does the work of capturing the killer for Dupin: the orangutan "was subsequently caught by the owner himself" (M 2: 568). The resolution of Poe's first Dupin tale demonstrates the potential of communication records in monitoring and apprehending suspects.

In contrast to Dupin's account of his methodology, which emphasizes conducting broad surveillance and data mining of communication records, the narrator mystifies Dupin as a superhuman mind reader. The denouement of the story returns to the mind-reading explanation that the narrator established at the story's outset, but the reader has only the narrator's word for this interpretation. When Dupin has deduced that an orangutan killed the L'Espanayes, he advertises for the owner of an escaped orangutan, trapping the sailor into coming to Dupin and the narrator's apartment by appealing to his financial self-interest. Speaking to the narrator before the sailor's arrival, Dupin reconstructs the sailor's chain of thoughts once he reads the advertisement in *Le Monde*: "He will reason thus:—'I am innocent; I am poor; my Ourang-Outang is of great value—to one in my circumstances a fortune of itself—why should I lose it through idle apprehensions of danger?' " (M 2: 561). This formulation deludes the narrator into believing that Dupin is here practicing a form of mind reading analogous to his predicting the narrator's thoughts at the beginning of the story. The final pages seem to bear out this belief, as the sailor's account of the crime accords with Dupin's prediction. However, Dupin has not had the sailor under surveillance, as he had the narrator, and therefore he has no access to the contents of his thoughts. His advertisement is based not on preternatural mind reading but on the physical traces (the ribbon, the tuft of fur) the sailor and the orangutan left behind at the scene of the crime.

Though the narrator mistakenly believes that Dupin has read the sailor's mind, Dupin and indeed Poe himself refute the narrator's mistake. Dupin dismisses his reconstruction of the sailor's thought processes as mere "guesses": "I will not pursue these guesses—for I have no right to call them more. . . . 'I do not know it,' said Dupin. 'I am not sure of it'" (M 2: 561). This diffidence contrasts with his avowal of an infallible analysis of patterns in witness testimony. There, in language that echoes Poe's earlier description of Babbage's engines in "Maelzel's Chess Player," he insists, "the deductions are the *sole* proper ones, and . . . the suspicion arises *inevitably* from them as the single result" (M 2: 550). The narrative structure of the sailor episode also indicates that the mind-reading explanation is the narrator's, and not to be confused with the truth. Whereas the chain-of-thought episode between the narrator and Dupin at the beginning of the story unfolds via dialogue, with the narrator testing Dupin's knowledge of what he was about to say, the narrator summarizes the sailor episode retrospectively. Rather than hearing the sailor—in his own words—corroborate Dupin's prediction of his thought process, the reader gets the narrator's synopsis, which begins, "What he stated was, in substance, this" (M 2: 564). By shifting from dialogue to summary, Poe narratively marks the fallacy of believing that Dupin read the sailor's mind. Instead, as Dupin states, he guessed, based on physical evidence and common sense, what likely happened, but without surveillance, he cannot "know."

While "Murders" indicates Poe's attention to the role of media in surveillance, it is in "The Mystery of Marie Rogêt" that Poe fully explores the potential to detect and prevent crime through dataveillance. As many critics have noted, "Mystery" is truly an armchair detective story; like NSA software programs amassing data at Fort Meade, the narrator and Dupin remain physically remote from the crime scene. The narrator at the outset introduces this dataveillance methodology: "In the morning, I procured, at the Prefecture, a full report of all the evidence elicited, and, at the various newspaper offices, a copy of every paper in which, from first to last, had been published any decisive information in regard to this sad affair. . . . [T]his mass of information stood thus" (M 3: 728–729). The narrator's "mass of information" is the pre-electronic version of mass surveillance, procured through related news reports and police dossiers rather than through digital intercepts of fiber-optic cables. Moreover, Dupin again argues for broad surveillance:

> I repeat that . . . the larger portion of all truth has sprung from the collateral; and it is but in accordance with the spirit of the principle involved in this fact that I would divert inquiry, in the present case, from the trodden and hitherto unfruitful ground of the event itself to the contemporary circumstances which surround it. . . . I will examine the newspapers more generally than you have as yet done. So far, we have only reconnoitered the field of investigation; but it will be strange, indeed, if a comprehensive survey, such as I propose, of the public prints will not afford us some minute points which shall establish a *direction* for inquiry. (M 3: 752)

Dupin's statement anticipates the logic behind the NSA's bulk data collection and storage programs. Only by obtaining and cross-referencing all data can ratiocination discover patterns; reasoning from an incomplete data set will produce inaccurate conclusions.

Whereas in "Murders" Dupin focuses on data mining communication records, in "Mystery" he turns to profiling. Identifying a pattern in newspaper extracts that the narrator finds "irrelevant," Dupin develops a profile of the suspect:

> This associate is of swarthy complexion. This complexion, the "hitch" in the bandage, and the "sailor's knot," with which the bonnet-ribbon is tied, point to a seaman. His companionship with the deceased, a gay, but not an abject young girl, designates him as above the grade of the common sailor. Here the well written and urgent communications to the journals are much in the way of corroboration. The circumstance of the first elopement, as mentioned by Le Mercurie, tends to blend the idea of this seaman with that of the "naval officer" who is first known to have led the unfortunate into crime. (M 3: 768–769)

While profiling has long been used in criminology, modern surveillance technology has enabled profiling at a scale previously unimaginable, whether at the level of state security, local policing, or consumer behavior. van Otterlo defines profiling as "the art of constructing predictive theories": "this amounts to finding causal rules, invariant patterns and statistical regularities in data."[39] However, as Lyon points out, "the kinds of algorithms used, the piecing together of fragments of unconnected data, often based on stereotypical assumptions about people from particular backgrounds, may create apparently incriminating profiles."[40] The "certain fruits" (M 3: 768) of Dupin's analysis display this defect, as he assumes, for example, that a "common sailor" could neither attract a "gay, but not abject young girl" nor write skillfully. Whereas Dupin's all-encompassing profile of the narrator in "Murders" permits him to construct a successful predictive model and complete the narrator's train of thought, Dupin's profile of the suspect in "Mystery" is so incomplete as to make his predictive model inaccurate.

Poe's infamous failure to solve the real-life death of Mary Rogers in "The Mystery of Marie Rogêt" demonstrates how hard it is to solve a crime simply through profiling. Moreover, it highlights the narrative problem of telling a story this way. Poe's solution, the naval officer, was unexpectedly proven incorrect in the midst of the serial publication of "Mystery" when Mrs. Loss (the real-life Madame Deluc) confessed that she was an accessory to abortion, which she claimed led to Rogers's death. Thomas O. Mabbott explains that "Two installments were in print when, in November 1842, the case was almost solved by a 'confession'" (M 3: 719). Poe hastily adapted the final installment "just enough to salvage 'The Mystery of Marie Rogêt,'" in Daniel Stashower's words.[41] Most critics acknowledge that while Poe did not solve the case, he did dismantle the popular "gang of ruffians" theory (as Thomas Dunn English first noted in 1845).[42]

Rather than presenting a resolution to a crime, "Mystery" proceeds according to a principle of nonnarrative accumulation. Formally, "Mystery" resembles a dossier of intelligence intercepts, endless "excerpts" without narrative structure. Solving the crime, as Mabbott's language indicates, requires a genre shift, from dossier to the older genre of "confession." As Ian Bell argues, "in eighteenth-century writing, criminals are only brought to trial, if at all, by confession or by the use of paid or otherwise rewarded informants. The 'idea of a detective' is never given any textual space."[43] Mrs. Loss's confession, not Dupin's dossier, spurred Justice Gilbert Merritt to arrest Mrs. Loss's two sons and accuse her and her sons of complicity in Rogers's death. Given these new developments, Poe added a bracketed paragraph in the final installment of "Mystery," insisting without elaboration that Dupin had in fact solved the case:

> [For reasons which we shall not specify, but which to many readers will appear obvious, we have taken the liberty of here omitting, from the MSS. placed in our hands, such portion as details the following up of the apparently slight clew obtained by Dupin. We feel it advisable only to state, in brief, that the result desired was brought to pass; and that the Prefect fulfilled punctually, although with reluctance, the terms of his compact with the Chevalier. Mr. Poe's article concludes with the following words. — Eds. *]. (M 3: 772)

Poe's tortured prose in this paragraph suggests the narrative necessity of confession as the climax of intelligence dossiers. He cannot explicitly claim that Dupin solved the case, and so resorts to passive constructions almost devoid of meaning. Without this unsupported assertion that "the result desired was brought to pass," the story would replicate "The Man of the Crowd," which as J. Gerald Kennedy notes, is "a tale of surveillance and analysis."[44] "Man of the Crowd," commonly viewed as Poe's proto-detective tale, ends with an admission of illegibility. While the narrator tracks and identifies a suspicious person ("the type and the genius of deep crime"), he finally likens him to an unreadable book: "It will be in vain to follow . . . 'er lasst sich nicht lessen [it does not permit itself to be read]' " (M 2: 515). A similar renunciation occurs beyond the frame of "Mystery," but Poe attempts to "salvage" it with the bracketed paragraph. Both "The Man of the Crowd" and "Mystery" attest to the limitations of profiling.

As in "Murders," Dupin in "Mystery" again highlights the importance of communications as a means of tracking the profiled subject:

> Let us carefully compare with each other the various communications sent to the evening paper, in which the object was to inculpate a gang. This done, let us compare these communications, both as regards style and MS., with those sent to the morning paper, at a previous period, and insisting so vehemently upon the guilt of Mennais. And, all this done, let us again compare these various communications with the known MSS. of the officer. (M 3: 770)

The content of these reports and messages nevertheless proves irrelevant; they are meant to throw police off the trail by disseminating false theories about the murderers, Dupin argues. Instead, his insistence on the importance of "compar[ing] these various communications, both as regards style and MS.," again points to the significance of metadata. The National Information Standards Organization defines metadata as "the information we create, store, and share to describe things, [which] allows us to interact with these things to obtain the knowledge we need"; in brief, metadata is data about data.[45] Poe's sophisticated awareness of the value of metadata, rather than psychological acumen, resonates with the modern debate about intelligence gathering and mass surveillance.

The Limitations of Surveillance

After Dupin's dataveillance and profiling fail to identify the suspect in "Mystery," Poe sustained his focus on metadata in the final Dupin tale, developing a narrative solution to the problem that arose in "Mystery." Unlike the earlier stories, the plot of "The Purloined Letter" explicitly concerns state secrets and espionage. Yet Dupin in the third tale eschews the surveillance methodology he has practiced and advocated in the first two. Indeed, in a reversal of his earlier endorsement of broad surveillance, Dupin scorns the police for their efforts at bulk data collection: "What is all this boring, and probing, and sounding, and scrutinizing with the microscope, and dividing the surface of the building into registered square inches" (M 3: 985). What is it, indeed, but the same thing Dupin did in "Murders" when, as the narrator reports, he "examin[ed] the whole neighborhood, as well as the house, with a minuteness of attention for which I could see no possible object. . . . Dupin scrutinized every thing—not excepting the bodies of the victims. We then went into the other rooms, and into the yard" (M 2: 546). The narrator repeats this language of wide-ranging scrutiny in "The Mystery of Marie Rogêt": "my friend occupied himself, with what seemed to me a minuteness altogether objectless, in a scrutiny of the various newspaper files" (M 3: 753). But while "The Purloined Letter" examines a case of espionage, Dupin repudiates the surveillance methodology that he espoused in the earlier tales.

Whereas in "Mystery" and "Murders," the narrator alone mystifies Dupin as a preternatural mind reader, in "The Purloined Letter" Dupin himself adopts that account of his abilities. Explaining how he found the letter that eluded police searches, Dupin draws an analogy to a schoolboy who "fashion[s] the expression of [his] face" to match that of his opponent and then "wait[s] to see what thoughts or sentiments arise in my mind or heart, as if to match or correspond with the expression" (M 3: 984). Dupin's language echoes the narrator's in "Murders" when he claims that "the analyst throws himself into the spirit of his opponent, identifies himself therewith" (M 2: 539). This method aims to duplicate interior "thoughts or sentiments," rather than relying on external transcripts of communication as Dupin has in the previous stories. Dupin uses his psychological "acumen" (M 3: 986) to reconstruct Minister D—'s thought process and find the missing letter. Yet, as many critics have noted, the mind that Dupin reconstructs replicates his own; he is performing self-analysis. Beyond their similar names, Dupin and Minister D share an uncommon temperamental duality, being both poets *and* logicians. Dupin himself implies that they are identical in his appreciation of "the daring, dashing, and discriminating ingenuity of D—" (M 3: 990). Here the alliterative "d" of "daring, dashing, and discriminating" underscores their mutual initial, as though Poe is winking at the reader, acknowledging that the two Ds are one and the same. As we saw in the vignette at the beginning of "Murders," predictive profiling depends on the comprehensiveness of the data. Because Dupin cannot have everyone under total surveillance, as he did the narrator, his predictive profiling fails in "Mystery." By making Minister

D— Dupin's doppelgänger in "The Purloined Letter," Poe substitutes self-surveillance for total surveillance.

Although Dupin embraces the narrator's interpretation of his genius as psychologically penetrating, he still relies on the informational potential of metadata—data about data—to solve the case. As numerous critics have noted, the contents of the letter are elided. The reader gets a "minute" description of "the external appearance of the missing document" (M 3: 981) both before and after the Minister transforms it by "turn[ing it] . . . inside out," "soil[ing] and crumpl[ing]" it, tearing it "nearly in two," and adding "a large black seal, bearing the D— cipher" (M 3: 991). Dupin uses his knowledge of the letter's size and shape—not its message—to perceive the Minister's disguise. Similarly, the Minister deduces the value of the letter from metadata: "His lynx eye immediately perceives the paper, recognizes the handwriting of the address, observes the confusion of the personage addressed, and fathoms her secret" (M 3: 977). The paper, the handwriting, and the Queen's reaction: these are the bits of information the Minister triangulates, not the content of the letter. Neither the reader nor the narrator ever learns what the letter said. Instead, the narration details the moments in which the letter passes between characters, first from the Queen to Minister D, then from Minister D to Dupin. The tale excludes the substance of the letter but includes who spoke to whom, where, and when.

This elision of content has provided a rich interpretive matrix for psychoanalytic and deconstructionist critics. Indeed, this vein of scholarship has been so powerful that, as Rosenheim remarks, "critics have often acted as if Poe's texts were merely pretexts for validating claims advanced by Jacques Derrida, Jacques Lacan, et cie."[46] The story focuses on, in Lacan's words, "the itinerary of a signifier," or as Barbara Johnson explains, the story "becomes for Lacan a kind of '*allegory of the signifier.*' "[47] As "a pure signifier," the letter instigates a series of "glances," Lacan observes, that constitute an "intersubjective complex" in which "the subjects [King, police, Queen, Minister, Dupin] relay each other in their displacement during the intersubjective repetition."[48] Lacan further argues that the itinerary of the signifier (the purloined letter) in Poe's story deals with the type of nonlinguistic "communication [that] is not transmissible in symbolic form. It may be maintained only in the relation with the object."[49] However, as the recent public outcry over state electronic surveillance programs has demonstrated, this type of communication data is indeed transmissible in a number of symbolic forms—including markup languages such as XML (eXtensible Markup Language), record locators in databases, and Friend of a Friend (FOAF) controlled vocabularies that "provid[e] for descriptive metadata on people and organizations, along with their attributes and relationships."[50]

Rather than following Lacan and his subsequent interlocutors (including Derrida, Johnson, and John T. Irwin) down the path of psychoanalytic criticism, I suggest that we examine the story as exploring the transmission and significance of metadata. In 2013, President Obama tried to mitigate the outrage caused by Snowden's revelations about the scope of the NSA's Prism program by emphasizing the distinction between content and metadata: "This program does not involve the content of phone calls, or the names of people making calls. Instead, it provides a record of phone numbers and the times and lengths of calls—metadata that can be queried if and when we have a reasonable suspicion that a particular number is linked to a terrorist organization."[51] As many people observed after Obama's speech, however, that distinction between content and metadata does not allay concerns about privacy, since metadata is just as powerful as content.[52] Lyon explicitly connects this communications data to detection: "And if the kind of data obtained . . . are in fact metadata—such as IP address, duration of call, which friends were contacted?—then they comprise just the kinds of information that a private detective might seek: who spoke to whom, when, and for how long?"[53] "The Purloined Letter" demonstrates that Poe recognized the informational—and incriminating—potential of metadata in the 1840s, long before Snowden's leak forced contemporary society to reckon with the ethics of state collection of metadata on a massive scale.

By abstracting the content of "The Purloined Letter" and focusing on the metadata, Poe turns our attention to what theorist Steve Mann has called the directions of veillance, a concept that has recently gained a great deal of critical attention in surveillance studies. Mann represents the multiple directions veillance can take by plotting them on a 360-degree compass plane, in which the X-axis indicates surveillance and its negative, antisurveillance (the prohibition, obstruction, or destruction of surveillance), while the Y-axis indicates sousveillance and its negative, antisousveillance. The "veillance plane" offers a model for attending to all directions of veillance, not just "watching from above" (sur-veillance) but also "watching from below" (sous-veillance). Mann defines surveillance as watching by parties with greater power, such as states or corporations, while sousveillance is watching by parties with less power, such as citizens or customers. For example, if red-light cameras are surveillant because they serve the interests of the government and police, bystanders recording police brutality and disseminating videos via the media or social networks are sousveillant because they challenge state and police authority.[54] Similar to Lacan's reading of the story's "three glances," surveillance theorists examine the importance of watching and the positions that the watched and watcher occupy, but rather than analyzing this information in terms of interiorized Freudian psychoanalysis, these theorists emphasize its external sociopolitical valences.

Poe indicates the importance of sousveillance as well as surveillance in "The Purloined Letter." While "policial eyes" (M 3: 986) are conducting surveillance and search along conventional lines ("search[ing] *every where*" in Minister D's house and "the two houses immediately joining," even using "a most powerful microscope," and following the Minister, "wayla[ying] . . . and rigorously search[ing]" him [M 3: 979–981]), Dupin recognizes that the Minister, as a "courtier" and "a bold *intriguant*," will anticipate all "the ordinary policial modes of action" (M 3: 988). As a schemer or spy, the Minister will be prepared to deploy antisurveillance measures, moving backwards along the X-axis of the veillance compass. These opposed methods will only create a stalemate, as the Prefect finds to his dismay.

To intervene, Dupin moves along the Y-axis, sousveillance and antisousveillance. Twice in the story, Dupin highlights the importance of watching from "above" or "below." He criticizes first "*the mass*" and second the Prefect for failing to see "the cunning of the individual felon . . . always . . . when it is above their own, and very usually when it is below" (M 3: 985, 990). As a less powerful person compared to the King and Queen, the Minister is watching from below in the Queen's bedroom. To reacquire the purloined letter, Dupin must counterfeit the Minister's own sousveillance. While Dupin is in the Minister's apartment, he pays "a pretended lunatic" to cause "a disturbance in the street" by firing an unloaded gun into a crowd of women and children. This paid disturber literally watches the Minister from below, as the Minister "rushed to a casement, threw it open, and looked out" when the "loud report, as if of a pistol was heard immediately beneath the windows of the hotel" (M 3: 992). Dupin's antisousveillance enables him to distract the Minister so that Dupin can seize the disguised letter from the apartment. He acknowledges that he was acting on his "political prepossessions" as a "partisan of the lady concerned" (M 3: 993). This restoration returns the Queen to power and ensures Minister D's "political destruction," quelling any threat to the state. By appropriating a sousveillant position—paying an actor to watch from below—Dupin ensures that state-abetting surveillance will restore state power.

Dupin's retreat, over the course of the three tales, from dataveillance and profiling to self-analysis reveals the inadequacies of surveillance as a way of knowing the world. Rather than producing the necessary and "certain results" of pure reason that Poe venerated in Babbage's Difference Engines, bulk data collection, data mining, and profiling are founded on assumptions and generalizations that allow prejudice and human error to influence the results. Computer scientists, sociologists, and others who study machine learning continually warn us against seeing computing systems as neutral ratiocinative machines: "Algorithms are inescapably value-laden. . . . Operational parameters are specified by developers and configured by users with desired outcomes in mind that privilege some values and interests over others."[55] In this contemporary debate, Poe offers us a voice from the dawn of the information age, one that imaginatively explores the consequences and possibilities of computing and mass surveillance. The Snowden leak revealed that Poe's influence on American institutions of cryptography and surveillance, which Rosenheim documented in *The Cryptographic Imagination*, persists into the twenty-first century. Poe's Dupin tales register some of the same ethical questions that trouble us as we survey our networked, big-data world, but they also celebrate the possibility of a universe in which "there could be no difficulty in tracing every impulse given the air—and the ether through the air—to the remotest consequences at any even infinitely remote epoch of time" (M 3: 1214). Poe was intrigued by the potential of this fantastical world described in "The Power of Words," but his disappointment with the erroneous solution to "Mystery" demonstrated the difficulty of "unravelling a web which you yourself" *haven't* woven (CL 1: 595).

Notes

I am grateful to Jerry Kennedy for his insightful suggestions on drafts of this essay.

1. *Oxford English Dictionary*, s.v. "algorithm, (*n.*)," updated January 2018, http://www.oed.com/view/Entry/4959?redirectedFrom=algorithm.

2. Gary T. Marx, "The Surveillance Society: The Threat of 1984-Style Techniques," *The Futurist* (June 1985): 21–26.
3. Fernando N. van der Vlist, "Counter-Mapping Surveillance: A Critical Cartography of Mass Surveillance Technology After Snowden," *Surveillance & Society* 15, no. 1 (2017): 137.
4. Terence Whalen, *Edgar Allan Poe and the Masses: The Political Economy of Literature in Antebellum America* (Princeton, NJ: Princeton University Press, 1999), 250.
5. Shawn James Rosenheim, *The Cryptographic Imagination: Secret Writing from Edgar Poe to the Internet* (Baltimore: The Johns Hopkins University Press, 1997), 12, 163.
6. Anthony Hyman, *Charles Babbage: Pioneer of the Computer* (Princeton, NJ: Princeton University Press, 1982), 48.
7. Hyman, *Babbage*, 48.
8. Whalen, *Edgar Allan Poe and the Masses*, 259.
9. Rosenheim, *The Cryptographic Imagination*, 6.
10. Quoted in Rosenheim, *The Cryptographic Imagination*, 142.
11. Rosenheim, *The Cryptographic Imagination*, 142.
12. David Kahn, *The Codebreakers: The Comprehensive History of Secret Communication from Ancient Times to the Internet* (New York: Simon and Schuster, 1996), 392–393.
13. Rosenheim, *The Cryptographic Imagination*, 192–193, 199.
14. Carolyn Marvin, *When Old Technologies Were New: Thinking About Electric Communication in the Late Nineteenth Century* (Oxford: Oxford University Press, 1990), 3.
15. Rosenheim, *The Cryptographic Imagination*, 93.
16. Whalen, *Edgar Allan Poe and the Masses*, 244.
17. Whalen, *Edgar Allan Poe and the Masses*, 272.
18. Evelyn Ruppert, Engin Isin, and Didier Bigo, "Data Politics," *Big Data & Society* 4, no. 2 (2017): 1–2.
19. Whalen, *Edgar Allan Poe and the Masses*, 260.
20. David Rosen and Aaron Santesso, *The Watchman in Pieces: Surveillance, Literature, and Liberal Personhood* (New Haven, CT: Yale University Press, 2013), 147.
21. Rosen and Santesso, *The Watchman in Pieces*, 147.
22. Dana Brand, *The Spectator and the City* (New York: Cambridge University Press, 1991), 97–98. James Werner disagrees, arguing that "Brand's analysis of [Poe's connection to the flâneur], while extremely useful, tends to downplay the significance of the flâneur for Poe. In fact, the flâneur represents a pivotal influence on Poe's philosophical perspective and fictional aims and strategies overall, perhaps nowhere more evidently than in his detective tales." James V. Werner, "The Detective Gaze: Edgar A. Poe, the Flâneur, and the Physiognomy of Crime," *ATQ* 15, no. 1 (March 2001): 5.
23. Brand, *The Spectator and the City*, 96.
24. *Oxford English Dictionary*, s.v. "dataveillance, (*n.*)," updated January 2018, http://www.oed.com/view/Entry/331503?redirectedFrom=dataveillance+.
25. Mark Andrejevic and Kelly Gates, "Big Data Surveillance: Introduction," *Surveillance & Society* 12, no. 2 (2014): 185.
26. Martijn van Otterlo, "Automated experimentation in Walden 3.0: The next step in profiling, predicting, control and surveillance," *Surveillance & Society* 12, no. 2 (2014): 257.
27. Olga Khazan, "The Creepy, Long-Standing Practice of Undersea Cable Tapping," *The Atlantic*, July 16, 2013, https://www.theatlantic.com/international/archive/2013/07/the-creepy-long-standing-practice-of-undersea-cable-tapping/277855/.

28. David Lyon, *Surveillance After Snowden* (Cambridge: Polity, 2015), 34–35; Andrejevic and Gates, "Big Data Surveillance: Introduction," 185.
29. Lyon, *Surveillance After Snowden*, 22.
30. Lyon, *Surveillance After Snowden*, 30.
31. Lyon, *Surveillance After Snowden*, 85.
32. Andrejevic and Gates, "Big Data Surveillance: Introduction," 185.
33. Lyon, *Surveillance After Snowden*, 18.
34. van Otterlo, "Automated Experimentation in Walden 3.0," 257.
35. Further refuting the notion that Dupin's power relies on a superhuman ability to read the *mens rea*, Dupin ridicules "the blundering idea of *motive*" (M 2: 556).
36. David Lyon, "The Snowden Stakes: Challenges for Understanding Surveillance Today," *Surveillance & Society* 13, no. 2 (2015): 142.
37. Brand, *The Spectator and the City*, 101–102.
38. Lyon, "The Snowden Stakes," 140–141.
39. van Otterlo, "Automated Experimentation in Walden 3.0," 257.
40. Lyon, *Surveillance After Snowden*, 75.
41. Daniel Stashower, *The Beautiful Cigar Girl: Mary Rogers, Edgar Allan Poe, and the Invention of Murder* (New York: Dutton, 2006), 295.
42. "At all events, he has dissipated in our mind, all belief that the murder was perpetrated by more than one." Thomas Dunn English, review of "The Mystery of Marie Rogêt," quoted in M 3: 715.
43. Ian Bell, "Eighteenth-Century Crime Writing," in *The Cambridge Companion to Crime Fiction*, ed. Martin Priestman (New York: Cambridge University Press, 2003), 9.
44. J. Gerald Kennedy, "Edgar Allan Poe: A Brief Biography," in *A Historical Guide to Edgar Allan Poe*, ed. J. Gerald Kennedy (New York: Oxford University Press, 2001), 44.
45. Jenn Riley, *Understanding Metadata: What Is Metadata, and What Is It For?* (Baltimore: Niso, 2017), https://groups.niso.org/apps/group_public/download.php/17446/Understanding%20Metadata.pdf.
46. Rosenheim, *The Cryptographic Imagination*, 3.
47. Jacques Lacan, "Seminar on the 'The Purloined Letter,'" trans. Jeffrey Mehlman, in *The Purloined Poe: Lacan, Derrida, and Psychoanalytic Reading*, ed. John P. Muller and William J. Richardson (Baltimore: The Johns Hopkins University Press, 1988), 29. Barbara Johnson, "The Frame of Reference: Poe, Lacan, Derrida," in *The Purloined Poe: Lacan, Derrida, and Psychoanalytic Reading*, 217.
48. Lacan, "Seminar," 31–32.
49. Lacan, "Seminar," 35.
50. Jenn Riley, *Understanding Metadata.*
51. Transcript of "Obama's Speech on N.S.A. Phone Surveillance," *The New York Times*, January 17, 2014, https://www.nytimes.com/2014/01/18/us/politics/obamas-speech-on-nsa-phone-surveillance.html?_r=0.
52. See, for example, John Naughton, "NSA Surveillance: Don't Underestimate the Extraordinary Power of Metadata," *The Guardian*, June 21, 2013, https://www.theguardian.com/technology/2013/jun/21/nsa-surveillance-metadata-content-obama.
53. Lyon, "The Snowden Stakes," 140–141.
54. Steve Mann, "McVeillance: How McDonaldized Surveillance Creates a Monopoly on Sight That Chills AR and Smartphone Development," WearCam, October 10, 2012, 6, http://wearcam.org/mcveillance.pdf. Mann labels and defines the midpoint vectors on his

compass; for example, the vector that tracks an increase in surveillance and a concomitant decrease in sousveillance (negative sousveillance or anti-sousveillance) he terms "McVeillance": "McVeillance is the installation or using of surveillance cameras while simultaneously prohibiting people from having or using their own cameras, hand-held magnifiers, smartphones, or the like" (7).

55. Brent Daniel Mittelstadt, Patrick Allo, Mariarosaria Taddeo, Sandra Wachter, and Luciano Floridi, "The Ethics of Algorithms: Mapping the Debate," *Big Data & Society* 3, no. 2 (2016): 1.

Bibliography

Barrett, Lindon. "Presence of Mind: Detection and Racialization in 'The Murders in the Rue Morgue.'" In *Romancing the Shadow: Poe and Race*, edited by J. Gerald Kennedy and Liliane Weissberg, 157–176. New York: Oxford University Press, 2001.

Brand, Dana. *The Spectator and the City*. New York: Cambridge University Press, 1991.

Harrowitz, Nancy A. "Criminality and Poe's Orangutan: The Question of Race in Detection." In *Agonistics: Arenas of Creative Contest*, edited by Janet Lungstrum and Elizabeth Sauer, 177–196. Albany: State University of New York Press, 1997.

Irwin, John T. *The Mystery to a Solution: Poe, Borges, and the Analytic Detective Story*. Baltimore: Johns Hopkins University Press, 1994.

Kopley, Richard. *Edgar Allan Poe and the Dupin Mysteries*. Basingstoke, England: Palgrave Macmillan, 2008.

Lemire, Elise. "'The Murders in the Rue Morgue': Amalgamation Discourses and the Race Riots of 1838 in Poe's Philadelphia." In *Romancing the Shadow: Poe and Race*, edited by J. Gerald Kennedy and Liliane Weissberg, 177–204. New York: Oxford University Press, 2001.

Muller, John P., and William J. Richardson, eds. *The Purloined Poe: Lacan, Derrida, and Psychoanalytic Reading*. Baltimore: The Johns Hopkins University Press, 1988.

Priestman, Martin. "Poe." In *Detective Fiction and Literature: The Figure on the Carpet*, 36–55. New York: St. Martin's, 1991.

Rosen, David, and Aaron Santesso. *The Watchman in Pieces: Surveillance, Literature, and Liberal Personhood*. New Haven, CT: Yale University Press, 2013.

Rosenheim, Shawn James. *The Cryptographic Imagination: Secret Writing from Edgar Poe to the Internet*. Baltimore: The Johns Hopkins University Press, 1997.

Whalen, Terence. *Edgar Allan Poe and the Masses: The Political Economy of Literature in Antebellum America*. Princeton, NJ: Princeton University Press, 1999.

White, Ed. "The Ourang-Outang Situation." *College Literature* 30, no. 3 (Summer 2003): 88–106.

CHAPTER 13

THE CALCULUS OF PROBABILITIES

Contingency in "The Mystery of Marie Rogêt"

VALERIE ROHY

READERS have long noted Poe's fascination with science and logic, but equally strong is his concern with contingency—that is, chance, accident, luck, and coincidence.[1] Contingency is what opposes necessity, determinism, and individual agency; as such, it is both an incitement to reading and a perpetual challenge to the stability of knowledge, scientific and otherwise. As William James observes, the "admission that any one of several things may come to pass, is, after all, only a roundabout name for chance; and chance is something the notion of which no sane mind can for an instant tolerate in the world."[2] Chance threatens our illusions of subjectivity and our fantasies of teleology, and in so doing it fuels our constant effort to reintegrate the aleatory event into the symbolic order, subjecting it to rational narration if not to full explanation. In this sense contingency both resists and invites the task of interpretation. Writing in an era when theories of probability and statistics—other methods to make sense of seemingly senseless chance—were proliferating, Poe considered contingency in his three Dupin detective narratives, as well as texts such as "The Black Cat," "The Pit and the Pendulum," and "The Gold-Bug," among which, I will argue, "The Mystery of Marie Rogêt" most clearly articulates a link between contingency and queerness.

While gambling and other games of chance have a long history, the nineteenth century proliferated theories of chance. Gleaning models of contingency from his cultural moment, Poe in 1845 reviewed several books by Jonathan Harrington Green, an American former gambler turned antigambling reformer, who sought to expose the tricks of card sharps; however, elements of such chicanery appear in Poe's fiction as early as "William Wilson" (1839).[3] But nineteenth-century discourses of contingency also involved the science of probability, the insurance industry, sexology, evolutionary theory, criminology, and the stock market. Such discourses shifted the very meaning of contingency, from an anarchic force of disorder to a set of potentially chartable patterns.

As Maurice S. Lee suggests, "chance, long dismissed as a nominal concept marking the limits of human knowledge, came to be regarded as an actual force subject to degrees of human control."[4] Ian Hacking concurs, asserting that the "taming of chance" through statistical data (paradoxically, the "laws of chance") led to new notions of normalcy and deviance after the Industrial Revolution, but in so doing they also afforded contingency a central cultural role well into the twentieth century.[5] In late nineteenth- and early twentieth-century American literature, as Jason Puskar observes, these new theories allowed writers to attribute the violence inherent in social structures to chance, rather than acknowledging its systematic origins; again, if differently, the randomness that might seem a force of destabilization or, as for James, of intolerable uncertainty turns out to have conservative effects.[6] For Poe, contingency was alive in all this contradiction.

Of course, literary questions of chance are as old as *Oedipus Rex* and remained prominent in nineteenth-century fiction; Poe's contemporary Charles Dickens is famous for plot coincidences. Erich W. Sippel has proposed that Poe's lifelong interest in probability is the source of a structuring tension in his work between chaotic chance and grim determinism. Sippel compares, for example, the fateful, inexorable death threat in "The Pit and the Pendulum" with the good fortune that finally frees the narrator.[7] And even before the Dupin tales, Poe invites the reader to ponder the meaning, if any, of seemingly random incidents. In "MS Found in a Bottle," the narrator absent-mindedly paints the word "DISCOVERY" while "musing on the singularity of his fate" and wonders: "Are such things the operations of ungoverned Chance?" (M 2: 142).[8] At the beginning of "The Black Cat," the narrator invites the reader to recognize, if she can, in uncannily strange events "nothing more than an ordinary succession of very natural causes and effects"—that is, to confront and dispel apparent contingencies such as the "accident" of the fire in the house and the narrator's "accidental" entombment of a living cat (M 3: 850).[9] But the narrator's madness means he lacks intention; his actions are all contingent and unmotivated, however keenly the narrative incites its readers to discover the structural necessity behind seemingly arbitrary details.

In other Poe texts, chance clearly intervenes to change the course of the narrative. In "William Wilson," the narrator attributes his "wickedness" to a "chance" occurrence—the intervention of his uncanny double, who by "somewhat remarkable coincidence" not only bears the same name but was born on the same date (M 2: 427, 432). The other William Wilson becomes the figure of a contingency that will alter not only the narrator's supposed "fate" and "destiny" but also his confidence as "the master of my own actions" (M 2: 427–428). There is perhaps no better example of Poe's exploitation of coincidence than "The Gold-Bug," whose plot depends on an odd synergy of chance and rational deduction. Searching for something in which to wrap the gold-bug, Legrand happens to find a scrap of parchment, which he later absent-mindedly stuffs in his pocket. He retrieves it to sketch the bug's markings for the narrator; as it is an unusually cold day in October, there is a fire in the hearth, near which, distracted by his Newfoundland dog, Legrand absent-mindedly holds the drawing. The heat of the fire activates the parchment's invisible ink, revealing a death's-head emblem on the verso and, in time, the whole pirate cypher. Legrand admits:

> the singularity of this coincidence absolutely stupefied me for a time. This is the usual effect of such coincidences. The mind struggles to establish a connexion [sic]—a sequence of cause and effect—and, being unable to do so, suffers a species of temporary paralysis. (M 3: 829)

Though Legrand is a brilliant cryptographer and logician, the outcome is equally attributable to what he calls a "series of accidents and coincidences," from the fire to the dog to the narrator's presence, much as "accident," Legrand speculates, must have separated Captain Kidd from his gold (M 3: 833–834).

In the later Dupin tales, Poe gives contingency a distinct place in the nascent genre of the detective story, and in later years it proves central to detective traditions from classical through "hard-boiled."[10] Here, however, it is the task of the detective, faced with others' mental paralysis, to dispel illusions of coincidence and reveal seeming accidents as motivated acts. In his view contingency seems to oppose, but in fact enables, the power of science and logic to establish causality. In "The Murders in the Rue Morgue" (1841), as if corroborating Lee's and Hacking's arguments about the human control of chance, Dupin asserts:

> Coincidences ten times as remarkable as this (the delivery of the money, and murder committed within three days upon the party receiving it), happen to all of us every hour of our lives, without attracting even momentary notice. Coincidences, in general, are great stumbling-blocks in the way of that class of thinkers who have been educated to know nothing of the theory of probabilities—that theory to which the most glorious objects of human research are indebted for the most glorious of illustration. (M 2: 556)

A scientific method such as the theory of probability, Dupin suggests, has the power to reveal a meaningless coincidence as a fateful clue; to tame chance, in other words, one must reveal that it never was chance in the first place. The task of the detective story, like that of the psychoanalytic case study, is to transform seemingly random events into a narrative of motivated causality. The difference is to a large extent one of perception: an anomaly that weak thinkers dismiss as "coincidence" may in fact be nothing of the sort. Yet in "The Murders in the Rue Morgue" the murderous Orang-Outang represents the pure chaos of nature, where reason leads back to unreason.[11] A similar paradox structures the third and best-known Dupin tale, "The Purloined Letter." Whereas the narrator regards the arrival of the police Prefect just after he and Dupin had discussed their two previous cases as "something of a coincidence," Dupin would be unlikely to do so (M 3: 974). Lee argues that Poe, "the father of the American literature of chance," sought in his detective stories "a more livable, more adequate approach to uncertainty"—one that to some degree managed and made use of chance.[12] As we shall see, however, the aleatory basis of the "laws of chance" proves to be less tractable than Poe and his detective might like.

Accidental Narrative

Announcing itself in its subtitle as "A Sequel to 'The Murders in the Rue Morgue,'" Poe's least-known detective story, "The Mystery of Marie Rogêt," is remarkable in several ways. Its evidence is entirely textual, in the form of newspaper articles on the supposed murder; it is based on a real mystery, the death of one Mary Rogers of New York; it pointedly refuses the consolation of conclusion; and it presents an extended meditation on "accident," "probability," and "coincidence" as part of the detective's hermeneutic practice. Yet while Dupin seeks to translate chance events into meaningful proofs, a radical contingency remains unassimilated in the text and ultimately prevents its conclusion. In "Marie Rogêt," as we shall see, all that is queer, accidental, traumatic, and unsymbolizable, including abortion, resists the imperatives of narrative closure, meaning, procreation, necessity, and futurity.

Although detective fiction conventionally proceeds backward, seeking in the evidence the narrative of some past occurrence, the temporality of "Marie Rogêt" is further complicated by the text's relation to its source material. The body of Mary Cecilia Rogers, "the beautiful cigar girl," was found in the Hudson River in July 1841, producing a storm of media coverage.[13] Reading about the case in Philadelphia newspapers, Poe chose to transport the tale to Paris and began writing in 1842. The first two installments appeared—ironically, given its grim subject—in *Snowden's Lady's Companion* in November and December 1842. (The editor of an 1899 edition of the tale notes this irony: "A story whose details are of such a peculiarly unpleasant nature . . . seems out of place, indeed singularly so, in a periodical which, as its title indicates, appealed chiefly to a female clientage.")[14] When Poe began writing, the murder of Mary Rogers remained unsolved, but on November 18, 1842, the New York *Tribune* reported that Mary's death was not a murder at all. This conclusion turned on the deathbed confession of the woman, aptly named Mrs. Loss, whom Poe had refashioned as Madame Deluc.

> On the Sunday of Miss Rogers [sic] disappearance [Mary] came to [Mrs. Loss's] house from this city in company with a young physician who undertook to procure for her a premature delivery. —While in the hands of her physician she died and a consultation was then held as to the disposal of her body. It was finally taken at night by the son of Mrs. Loss and sunk in the river where it was found.[15]

Mary's probable cause of death, then, was an attempted abortion in which an accidental pregnancy precipitated another, more deadly accident.[16] The article caused Poe to delay the publication of the tale's third installment until February 1843 and doubtless shaped its conclusion, but it would retroactively shape the text's beginning as well: to accommodate the inconvenient truth, Poe added footnotes and made some fifteen textual changes—among them the new term "fatal accident"—in the first two sections of "Marie Rogêt" prior to its 1845 republication in *Tales*.[17] In the final installment, Poe elides the figure of the "young physician" and introduces instead a "young naval officer" mentioned by the *New York Herald* in connection with Mary Rogers. Yet he could not lend the fiction even the minimal clarity of Mary Rogers's story. In 1848 Poe wrote to a friend, "Nothing was omitted in 'Marie Rogêt' except what I omitted myself . . . The 'naval officer,' who committed murder (rather, the accidental death arising from an attempt at abortion) *confessed* it; and the whole matter is now well understood."[18] In fact there is no such confession in the text, which offers *both* murder and mishap as competing hypotheses regarding the cause of Marie's death.[19] The peculiar syntax of his remark suggests that the naval officer is either the murderer or the abortionist responsible for the "accidental death," but even Poe's letter does not say which it is.

"Accident," then, comes to stand for abortion as an alternative to murder, the first supposed cause of death—yet by accident, we might say, "Marie Rogêt" was already a story about accidents before Poe learned Mary Rogers's fate. Each time Poe discusses philosophical problems of chance and contingency, even in the sections written prior to the *Tribune* article, he uncannily evokes the historical fact of Mary's death: "accident" is the hinge that connects them. Dupin explains:

> Not the least usual error, in investigations such as this, is the limiting of inquiry to the immediate, with total disregard of the collateral or circumstantial events. . . . The history of human knowledge has so uninterruptedly shown that to collateral, or incidental, or accidental events we are indebted for the most numerous and most valuable discoveries. (M 3: 751–752)

Having signaled his interest in chance in "The Murders in the Rue Morgue," Poe renders "Marie Rogêt" a further investigation, in which Dupin's long divagations on chance punctuate his even longer exegeses of newspaper articles. "Circumstantial events," however, lead to the truth only when subjected to a rational analysis. Dupin claims that "seemingly irrelevant" details *become* significant when they are approached through "absolute calculation" and "mathematical *formulae*" (3: 752)—that is, through "the doctrine of chance, or, as it is technically termed, the Calculus of Probabilities" which is, "in its essence, purely mathematical" (3: 724).[20] And indeed, the text is rife with statements of probability. "The chances are ten to one," Dupin says, that Marie's former suitor would make a second proposition (3: 754); elsewhere he mathematically calculates the "probability that the body was that of Marie" (3: 746).

Yet his "Calculus of Probabilities" never reveals a seeming coincidence as a crucial clue; it fails to turn accident into intention. In fact, Dupin is famously wrong about dice and probability: to the general reader, he says, "It does not appear that the two throws which have been completed, and which lie now absolutely in the Past, can have influence upon the throw which exists only in the Future," when in fact "sixes having been thrown twice in succession by a player at dice, is sufficient cause for betting the largest odds that sixes will not be thrown in the third attempt" (3: 773).[21] Coincidentally, this statement appears in the third and final section of the text, written after the news of Mary's cause of death. As such, it allegorizes the three sections of the text, whose first two portions were ultimately unable to predict the divergent course of the third. The third section, of course, is the space in which Poe must grapple with the real accident that caused Mary Rogers's death, and this circumstance seems to defeat Dupin's ratiocinative ability to learn the meaning of accidents. Indeed, Lee concludes that Poe "demonstrates in the case of Rogêt the epistemological limits of statistical reasoning."[22]

Although none of the three Dupin tales answers all the questions it raises (the contents of the letter are never revealed in "The Purloined Letter" and the inhuman killer lacks a motive in "The Murders in the Rue Morgue"), in "Marie Rogêt" not only is the murderer never identified, but we cannot even be certain that a murder was committed. The first footnote asserts that the eventual "confessions of *two* persons (one of them the Madame Deluc of the narrative) . . . confirmed, in full, not only the general conclusion, but absolutely *all* the chief hypothetical details by which that conclusion was attained" (3: 723), and that note is swiftly followed by the introduction of the "Calculus of Probabilities" as key to those "hypothetical details" (3: 724). In reality, the clues are as contradictory as they are lurid: Marie's embroidered handkerchief, her fiancé's suicide, the trampled thicket, the adjusted garter, the strips torn from her dress, the swarthy man, and her brief disappearance years earlier. If Marie died by misfortune at the inn of Madame Deluc, the body would not have shown signs of violence, and there would be no abandoned clothing or evidence of a struggle in the thicket. Though Dupin finally identifies the naval officer (a "seaman" adept with boats and capable of making a "sailor's knot" [3: 768]) as the probable killer, he prefaces that statement with equivocation: "We have attained the idea either of a fatal accident under the roof of Madame Deluc, or of a murder perpetrated, in the thicket at the Barrière" (3: 768). Whether Madame Deluc or the naval officer is to blame, we see neither one apprehended; if it is the naval officer, then as in "Rue Morgue" we have no motive for the crime. Poe asserts that case has been solved, but the tale cannot conclude: there is no causation, no murder, and no way to utter a probable solution.[23]

Queer Chances

Poe's tale not only fails to discover the true cause of Marie Rogêt's death but also pointedly obscures the space where a "true cause" is presumed to lie. The promised moment of unveiling is supplanted by a faux editorial intervention near the tale's conclusion: "we have taken the liberty of here omitting, from the MSS. placed in our hands, such portion as details the *following up* of the apparently slight clew obtained by Dupin. We feel it advisable only to state, in brief, that the result desired was brought to pass" (M 3: 772). This section is at once an excrescence, an intrusion of the editor's voice into the text, and a conspicuous absence, a blank where the solution of the mystery should be. Comparing the detective's investigative task to the process of psychoanalytic interpretation, Slavoj Žižek explains that "every final product of the dream work, every manifest dream content, contains *at least one* ingredient that functions as a stopgap, as a filler holding the place of what is necessarily *lacking* in it."[24] This is the crucial clue, the telling symptom. We might think of Poe's story as analogous to the dream and structured by the same mechanisms of lack and excess, the representable and the unrepresentable. In "Marie Rogêt" the editorial comment is merely the most obvious "filler holding the place of what is necessarily lacking"; another is the naval officer, whose name punningly recalls a severed maternal connection. If, as Freud writes, "There is at least one spot in every dream at which it is unplumbable—a navel, as it were, that is its point of contact with the unknown," abortion is the true navel of the text.[25] Žižek borrows Freud's pregnant metaphor in his own account of the dreamwork's odd "filler," which "holds the place of what this imaginary scene must 'repress,' exclude, force out, in order to constitute itself. It is a kind of umbilical cord tying the imaginary structure to the 'repressed' process of its structuration."[26] Abortion is the repressed and excluded navel of Poe's text, both present and absent at the same time; the editorial intrusion is our "missed encounter" with it.[27]

In psychoanalytic terms, in "The Mystery of Marie Rogêt," abortion, accident, and contingency occupy the place of the unsymbolizable Real. For Lacan the symbolic order is the ideologically freighted system of signification that constitutes all we know of reality, whereas the Real is what the symbolic cannot assimilate, described both as a gap and a foreign body within it. The Real *is* contingency insofar as contingency opposes meaning—including the motivated causality and narrative that the detective genre, no less than the heteronormative symbolic order, takes as telos. To translate seemingly meaningless coincidences into reasonable narrative causality, as Dupin strives to do, is to reintegrate what appears to be a random traumatic event, an eruption of the Real into the symbolic order. Dupin's argument that what *appears to be* accidental will always prove in the end to be meaningful is thus merely a fantasy that denies the recalcitrance of the stupid, unintelligible, unassimilable Real. In fact, the "accident under the roof of Madame Deluc," like the "collateral, or incidental, or accidental events" Dupin proposes to interrogate, cannot be transformed into narrative; they remain unrepresentable.[28] That is why it is significant that it goes unnamed, its potential place taken by an editorial intrusion and its explanatory power undermined by a competing theory. The psychoanalytic model also speaks to the text's troubled chronology. Through a form of contingency he associates with Aristotle's term *tuché*, Lacan writes, the Real appears "in the form of the trauma, determining all that follows, and imposing on it an apparently accidental origin."[29] The later imposition of an earlier origin is precisely the retroactive logic at work in the composition of Poe's narrative when the *Tribune*'s account of Mary Rogers's death causes him to belatedly alter the text. Yet this "accidental origin" does not conform to the logical causality required by detective fiction. Even a brutally murderous heterosexuality, such as that attributed to the naval officer in Poe's text, can be integrated into the symbolic in a way abortion cannot (both are commonplace, but murder is not a threat to heteronormativity, merely its occasional byproduct).

Abortion, then, refers not only to the text's provenance in the fate of Mary Rogers but also to a queer structure that refuses the ideology of reproductive futurism. In such an ideology—where the enjoyment of the present is subordinate to the perpetually deferred tomorrow represented by the child—abortion is no less a threat to futurity than the deathly negativity attributed to the homosexual.[30] In "Marie Rogêt" both signify a radical, unutterable contingency, located both at the origin of the narrative and as a belated addition, which Dupin cannot translate into causal necessity. As such, the text maps a wider pattern of associations in which queerness, contingency, and abortion are aligned against heteronormativity, necessity, and the futurity represented by the cult of the child. In his critique of reproductive futurism, Lee Edelman describes an anti-abortion billboard that for him illuminates the "common stake in the militant right's opposition to abortion and to the practice of queer sexualities." Both, after all, conjure a fantasmatic child imperiled equally by those who would prevent its birth and those who fail to conceive it—the queer figures of a murderous sterility. In the face of such rhetoric, he writes, queer people should respond by embracing the charges against them, "pronouncing at last the words for which we're condemned should we speak them or not: that *we* are the advocates of abortion; that the Child as futurity's emblem must die."[31] Responding to Edelman's notion of the *sinthomosexual*, the queer embodiment of the death drive, Jennifer Doyle observes that "[a]t least one version of this disruptive figure is the anti-reproductive, abortive, and monstrous woman." Indeed, she writes, "the body standing in the way of reproduction, futurity, and life itself is quite specifically that of the abortive woman."[32] Although her framing of this argument does her no favors (she invidiously suggests that the woman, not the gay man, is the true embodiment of the death drive), surely abortion may share the place of queerness as a threat to an ideologically freighted futurity—and if so, Poe's Dupin and narrator are a queer couple complicit with the abortionist. Indeed, according to the hegemonic notion of queerness Edelman outlines, they may be considered abortionists in advance for their refusal of the heteronormative reproductive imperative.

Consider the cloistered male domesticity that contrasts with Marie Rogêt's public exposure. Laura Saltz notes that "Marie's is the public sphere of market and streets and Dupin's the private realm of reading and literary production."[33] That realm is shared by two whose very relationship is predicated on contingency: introducing Dupin in "The Murders in the Rue Morgue," the narrator recalls, "Our first meeting was at an obscure library in the Rue Montmartre, where the accident of our both being in search of the same very rare and very remarkable volume, brought us into closer communion. We saw each other again and again" (M 2: 531). In "Marie Rogêt," that recursive relationship exists outside heteronormative time. Observing Dupin's "moody reverie," the narrator says, "I readily fell in with his humor; and, continuing to occupy our chambers in the Faubourg Saint Germain, we gave the Future to the winds, and slumbered tranquilly in the Present, weaving the dull world around us into dreams" (3: 724). In perhaps the most lyrical passage of a text that is otherwise gruesome and pedantic, the two men drift together out of narrative time. First connected by a library coincidence, they enjoy a privileged intimacy between Dupin's first and second cases—an intimacy that, when manifested in the present tense of the narratives, some readers have construed as queer. At the very least, it is another instance of the male doubling and slippage between identification and desire seen elsewhere in Poe's fiction, from "William Wilson" to "The Man of the Crowd."[34]

But despite other queer readings of "Marie Rogêt," despite the long, later tradition of detective fiction as a site of privileged male homosocial desire, as in Doyle's Sherlock Holmes stories, and despite the erotic implication of their intimate solipsism, I do not mean to designate Poe's narrator and Dupin as gay men or even as men who love men.[35] Rather, they are more useful as emblems of a queerness beyond same-sex desire—a queerness implicated with abortion, the unsymbolizable, and the refusal of futurity.[36] Regardless of his intent—indeed, despite his promotion of the rational "calculus" that would return seemingly meaningless events to narrative purpose—Dupin is in league with the abortionist when he fails to name the cause of Marie's death. Accident and abortion ally themselves with queerness and the Real only so long as they are not adduced as the answer to "what really happened" and reabsorbed into the symbolic order, a possibility that Poe's narrative forecloses. "Marie Rogêt" is a web of contradictions—closure and indeterminacy, contingency and necessity—but in failing to solve its mystery it succeeds in preserving the Real beyond the symbolic, the queer beyond the normative.

Notes

1. In the context of Poe's fiction I construe contingency in its broad, popular sense, where it is cognate with chance and accident, rather than its narrow, philosophical sense, where it may be distinctly different from chance. In both cases, contingency indicates the possibility that something might be otherwise than it is. However, as Quentin Meillassoux argues, in philosophy the notion of chance assumes an "enclosure of possibilities," whereas contingency is infinite; see *After Finitude: An Essay on the Necessity of Contingency*, introduction by Alain Badiou (New York: Continuum, 2008), 108.
2. William James, "The Dilemma of Determinism" (1884), in *The Will to Believe and Other Writings in Popular Philosophy* (New York: Longmans Green and Co, 1907), 153.
3. Ann Fabian, *Card Sharps, Dream Books and Bucket Shops: Gambling in Nineteenth-Century America* (New York: Routledge, 2013), 70–86.
4. Maurice S. Lee, *Uncertain Chances: Science, Skepticism, and Belief in Nineteenth-Century American Literature* (New York: Oxford University Press, 2012), 3. Lee includes "Marie Rogêt" in his fine discussion of Poe and probability, but he does not connect chance to what he terms the "sexually charged details" of the text (31).
5. Ian Hacking, *The Taming of Chance* (Cambridge: Cambridge University Press, 1990), 1–3.
6. Jason Puskar, *Accident Society: Fiction, Collectivity, and the Production of Chance* (Stanford, CA: Stanford University Press, 2012), 1.
7. Erich W. Sippel, "Bolting the Whole Shebang Together: Poe's Predicament," *Criticism: A Quarterly for Literature and the Arts* 15, no. 4 (1973): 292–293 and 301. Sippel also discusses "William Wilson" and "The Imp of the Perverse," among other Poe texts. On the tension between order and contingency in Poe's writing, see also Ellman Crasnow, "The Poetics of Contingency: Modes of Knowledge in Poe," in *Poetic Knowledge: Circumference and Centre*, ed. Roland Hagenbüchle and Joseph Swann (Bonn: Bouvier, 1980), 63.
8. On "The Gold-Bug" and "MS. Found in a Bottle," see Christophe Wall-Romana, "The Decomposition of Philosophy: Quentin Meillassoux's Speculative Messianism in *The Number and the Siren*," *Diacritics: A Review of Contemporary Criticism* 42, no. 4 (2014): 12–14.

9. Michael Jay Lewis, "Contingency, Narrative, Fiction: Vogler, Brenkman, Poe," *SubStance: A Review of Theory and Literary Criticism* 41, no. 2 (2012): 104, 112.
10. Christopher Pittard suggests that late Victorian detective fiction still turns upon the contest "between ordered design and untidy contingency," with the goal of remanding the latter to the service of the former; indeed, he continues, "in the detective story, *nothing* is accidental or left to chance, since the most insignificant signs and tokens become clues." See *Purity and Contamination in Late Victorian Detective Fiction* (Burlington, VT: Ashgate, 2011), 74, 19. This view of contingency prevails in detective stories through the film noir period. Considering *Double Indemnity* (1944), Joan Copjec links probability to both crime and insurance: "it was statistics that formed the basis of classical detective fiction's narrative contract with its reader" in that the "frequency distribution" of various crimes yields a belief in "the calculability of risk." See *Read My Desire: Lacan against the Historicists* (Cambridge, MA: MIT Press, 1994), 167.
11. On the Orang-Outang as a force of pure contingency in relation to evolutionary theory, see Lawrence Frank, "'The Murders in the Rue Morgue': Edgar Allan Poe's Evolutionary Reverie," *Nineteenth-Century Literature* 50, no. 2 (1995): 168–188.
12. Lee, *Uncertain Chances*, 17, 45.
13. Daniel Stashower, *The Beautiful Cigar Girl: Mary Rogers, Edgar Allan Poe, and the Invention of Murder* (New York: Berkeley, 2006).
14. Henry Austin, preface to *The Mystery of Marie Rogêt*, by Edgar Allan Poe, ed. Henry Austin (New York: R.F. Fenno, 1899), 5.
15. Peter Thoms, "Poe's Dupin and the Power of Detection," in *The Cambridge Companion to Edgar Allan Poe*, ed. Kevin J. Hayes (New York: Cambridge University Press, 2002), 140.
16. Freud too associates chance with pregnancy in *Leonardo da Vinci and a Memory of His Childhood*: "we are all too ready to forget that in fact everything to do with our life is chance, from our origin out of the meeting of spermatozoon and ovum onwards—chance which nevertheless has a share in the law and necessity of nature, and which merely lacks any connection with our wishes and illusions"; *The Standard Edition of the Complete Psychological Works of Sigmund Freud*, trans. and ed. James Strachey, vol. 11, *Five Lectures on Psycho-Analysis, Leonardo da Vinci and Other Works* (London: Hogarth, 1957), 137. It is not only the fact of becoming pregnant that is governed by chance, but the entirety of the life thus begun, for whom that first chance occurrence allegorizes all that follows.
17. John Evangelist Walsh, *Poe the Detective: The Curious Circumstances behind "The Mystery of Marie Rogêt,"* intro. Thomas O. Mabbott (New Brunswick, NJ: Rutgers University Press, 1967), 70–72. Walsh explains that the first footnote falsifies the timing of Mrs. Loss's confession and that the earlier draft asserted that "an individual assassin was convicted upon his own confession" (69). On the revisions, see also Richard Fusco, "Poe's Revisions of 'The Mystery of Marie Rogêt': A Hoax?," in *Poe at Work: Seven Textual Studies*, ed. Benjamin Franklin Fisher IV (Baltimore: Poe Society 1978), 91–99.
18. Quoted in Laura Saltz, "'(Horrible to Relate!)': Recovering the Body of Marie Rogêt," in *The American Face of Edgar Allan Poe*, ed. Shawn Rosenheim and Stephen Rachman (Baltimore: Johns Hopkins University Press, 1995), 241.
19. On the addition of ambiguity in Poe's revision, see William Kurtz Wimsatt, "Poe and the Mystery of Mary Rogers," *PMLA: Publications of the Modern Language Association of America* 56, no. 1 (1941): 243.
20. David Van Leer notes that the "calculus of probabilities" is a term borrowed from Pierre-Simon Laplace's "Philosophical Essay on Probabilities" (1814) to bridge certainty and

uncertainty; see "Detecting Truth: The World of the Dupin Tales," in *New Essays on Poe's Major Tales*, ed. Kenneth Silverman (Cambridge: Cambridge University Press, 1993), 72.

21. See, for example, Wimsatt, "Poe and the Mystery of Mary Rogers," 236, and Mark Seltzer, "The Crime System," *Critical Inquiry* 30, no. 3 (2004): 566.
22. Lee, *Uncertain Chances*, 28. See also Van Leer, 67, and Thoms, 14. Marie Bonaparte finds that "Poe's only tale of crime frankly sexual" is merely a "feeble tailpiece to his first detective story." See *The Life and Works of Edgar Allan Poe: A Psycho-Analytic Interpretation*, trans. John Rodker (London: Imago, 1949), 105, 448.
23. On reproduction and the failure of narrative closure in "Marie Rogêt," see also Jean-Michel Rabaté, "Crimes against Fecundity: Style and Crime, from Joyce to Poe and Back," in *Style in Theory: Between Literature and Philosophy*, ed. Ivan Callus, James Corby, and Gloria Lauri-Lucente (London: Bloomsbury, 2012), 111–139.
24. Slavoj Žižek, *Looking Awry: An Introduction to Jacques Lacan through Popular Culture* (Cambridge, MA: MIT Press, 1992), 52.
25. *The Standard Edition of the Complete Psychological Works of Sigmund Freud*, trans. and ed. James Strachey, vol. 4, *The Interpretation of Dreams* (1900) (London: Hogarth, 1953), 111. Naomi Schor connects "Marie Rogêt" to Freud's notion of the navel without reference to the naval officer, writing: "the hitch [knot] is, to parody Freud, the navel of the tale"; "Female Paranoia: The Case for Psychoanalytic Feminist Criticism," *Yale French Studies* 62 (1981): 219.
26. Žižek, *Looking Awry*, 52.
27. On the "missed encounter," see Jacques Lacan, *The Four Fundamental Concepts of Psycho-Analysis* (New York: W.W. Norton, 1981), 55.
28. Saltz says that abortion is "unrepresentable" in the text but does not call on psychoanalytic theory to explain its unrepresentability ("'(Horrible to Relate!)': Recovering the Body of Marie Rogêt," 251).
29. Lacan, *The Four Fundamental Concepts of Psycho-Analysis*, 55.
30. Lee Edelman, *No Future: Queer Theory and the Death Drive* (Durham, NC: Duke University Press, 2004), 2–5.
31. Edelman, *No Future*, 15, 31.
32. Jennifer Doyle, "Blind Spots and Failed Performance: Abortion, Feminism, and Queer Theory," *Qui Parle: Critical Humanities and Social Sciences* 18, no. 1 (2009): 35, 33.
33. Saltz, "'(Horrible to Relate!)': Recovering the Body of Marie Rogêt," 249.
34. Leland S. Person, "Queer Poe: The Tell-Tale Heart of His Fiction," *Poe Studies/Dark Romanticism: History, Theory, Interpretation* 41 (2008): 9. Amy Gilman Srebnick aptly describes the pairing as "an intense and clandestine, if only implicit, homoerotic relationship that removes them from the social world" in *The Mysterious Death of Mary Rogers: Sex and Culture in Nineteenth-Century New York* (New York: Oxford University Press, 1995), 118. Courtney Novosat offers a more literalizing account of the "homosexual couple" in "Outside Dupin's Closet of Reason: (Homo)sexual Repression and Racialized Terror in Poe's 'The Murders in the Rue Morgue,'" *Poe Studies* 45 (2012): 82–83.
35. More useful are the scholars who characterize queerness in Poe's writing as a "crisis of representation" and "perpetual conjecture"; see Gustavus T. Stadler, "Poe and Queer Studies," *Poe Studies/Dark Romanticism: History, Theory, Interpretation* 33, no. 1–2 (2000): 20; and Novosat, "Outside Dupin's Closet of Reason," 79.
36. Indeed, the particular queerness described in *No Future* is not defined by object choice, residing instead in such figures as Hitchcock's birds, Dickens's Scrooge, and Rowling's

Voldemort. This is why Doyle's criticism of Edelman for gender bias is unfounded; in fact, the vast majority of his literary and filmic examples have nothing to do with gay men. Edelman also argues that although gay men and lesbians are made to bear the burden of the internal failures of reproductive futurism, they are not thereby exempt from participating in it and even promoting it.

Bibliography

Doyle, Jennifer. "Blind Spots and Failed Performance: Abortion, Feminism, and Queer Theory." *Qui Parle: Critical Humanities and Social Sciences* 18, no. 1 (2009): 25–52.

Edelman, Lee. *No Future: Queer Theory and the Death Drive.* Durham, NC: Duke University Press, 2004.

Freud, Sigmund. *The Interpretation of Dreams* (1900). Vol. 4 of *The Standard Edition of the Complete Psychological Works of Sigmund Freud.* Translated and edited by James Strachey. London: Hogarth, 1953.

Hacking, Ian. *The Taming of Chance.* Cambridge: Cambridge University Press, 1990.

Person, Leland S. "Queer Poe: The Tell-Tale Heart of His Fiction." *Poe Studies/Dark Romanticism: History, Theory, Interpretation* 41 (2008): 7–30.

Puskar, Jason. *Accident Society: Fiction, Collectivity, and the Production of Chance.* Stanford, CA: Stanford University Press, 2012.

Saltz, Laura. "'(Horrible to Relate!)': Recovering the Body of Marie Rogêt." In *The American Face of Edgar Allan Poe,* edited by Shawn Rosenheim and Stephen Rachman, 237–267. Baltimore: Johns Hopkins University Press, 1995.

Sippel, Erich W. "Bolting the Whole Shebang Together: Poe's Predicament." *Criticism: A Quarterly for Literature and the Arts* 15, no. 4 (1973): 289–308.

Srebnick, Amy Gilman. *The Mysterious Death of Mary Rogers: Sex and Culture in Nineteenth-Century New York.* New York: Oxford University Press, 1995.

Walsh, John Evangelist. *Poe the Detective: The Curious Circumstances behind "The Mystery of Marie Rogêt."* New York: Rutgers University Press, 1967.

Wimsatt, William Kurtz. "Poe and the Mystery of Mary Rogers." *PMLA: Publications of the Modern Language Association of America* 56, no. 1 (1941): 230–248.

Žižek, Slavoj. *Looking Awry: An Introduction to Jacques Lacan through Popular Culture.* Cambridge, MA: MIT Press, 1992.

CHAPTER 14

COUNTERPARTS

Poe's Doubles from "William Wilson" to "The Cask of Amontillado"

PAUL CHRISTIAN JONES

FOLLOWING the rise of Freudian psychology in the early twentieth century, studies of the literary device of the double (also known as the doppelgänger, the alter ego, and the second self) have consistently interpreted it as a means of dramatizing the complex mental states of characters. In works by writers like E. T. A. Hoffman, Robert Louis Stevenson, Joseph Conrad, and Fyodor Dostoevsky, these literary doubles have been read as representations, according to Ralph Tymms, of "the conflict between alternating parts of the personality," offering a means of depicting what C. F. Keppler calls the "psychological dualism" of human beings, a dualism that perhaps inevitably results in internal struggles.[1] John Herdman explains that the double has been used to "articulat[e] the experience of self-division . . . and the division of a personality" by presenting "separate characters who can be looked upon as differing aspects of a sundered whole." He continues, "the double arises out of and gives form to the tension between division and unity[,] . . . stand[ing] for contradiction within unity, and for unity in spite of division, the likeness expressing the unity of the individual, the doubleness or complementarity expressing division within the personality."[2] Edgar Allan Poe's fiction is well populated with these doubles, including the identical schoolboys in "William Wilson" and the murderers and their victims in "The Tell-Tale Heart" and "The Cask of Amontillado," who have been read by scholars as representing parts of a single individual who might believe himself to be unified and coherent even as the fictional narrative reveals an internal conflict between the counterparts of his identity.[3] This essay explores Poe's use of these doubles as a means of dramatizing divided selves, from their earliest and most obvious incarnation in "William Wilson" (1839) to their much more subtle and troubling appearance in subsequent stories "The Tell-Tale Heart" (1843) and "The Cask of Amontillado" (1846). Interestingly, the later pair of tales offers quite contrasting depictions of the conflict between doubles and the internal struggles they symbolize from what readers find in "William Wilson," allowing these stories themselves to be read as compelling counterparts within Poe's canon.

"William Wilson," Poe's story of a schoolboy who is stalked by a lookalike, has been a central text in twentieth-century scholarship on the double in literature. Otto Rank claimed that the way "Poe used the theme of the double" in "Wilson" "has become a model for . . . later treatments." And Palmer Cobb explains that "Wilson" dramatizes "the contention of two inimical forces in a man's soul; the evil and the good, struggling for supremacy and final victory."[4] Yet scholars have frequently emphasized that the story's handling of the double's function of depicting human minds as conflicted sites of internal struggles differs significantly from other authors' handling of the device, wherein the double is more commonly manifested as a darker version of the protagonist (see, for example, Stevenson's Mr. Hyde and *Fight Club*'s Tyler Durden). Claire Rosenfield, for instance, notes that Poe's presentation of the double in this story is atypical in that it is "one of the few examples in which the whispering Double appears as a 'guardian angel' seeking to annul the evil of the narrator." And Keppler observes that Poe's tale is a departure in its depiction of the second self as "the pursuing Saviour."[5]

The narrator of "William Wilson" introduces himself to the reader as a figure insistent on his coherent identity and self-determination. This begins in the first sentence in an act of self-naming: "Let me call myself . . . William Wilson" (M 2: 426). As he describes his early childhood, the narrator insists upon a self-presentation wherein he is the master of himself and his environs. He proclaims that he was "self-willed" as a child. His parents "could do but little to check the evil propensities which distinguished" him; their attempts "resulted in complete failure on their part" and "total triumph on" his. The consequence, he claims, is that his "voice was a household law" and he "was left to the guidance of [his] own will, and became . . . the master of [his] own actions." Yet, even in this assured depiction of his domination over himself and his household, his self-portrait reveals that he lacks total control, even of his own actions. He describes his family's defining trait, "an imaginative and easily excitable temperament," which he has "fully inherited" and which threatens him "positive injury" as he becomes "addicted to the wildest caprices, and a prey to the most ungovernable passions" (M 2: 427). These admissions indicate that, despite the image of himself he prefers, he might not be his own master, able to bend his own actions and circumstances through his strong will, as his chosen name William Wilson (often parsed by scholars as "Will I am Will's son") would suggest.

Poe most obviously presents Wilson as a divided self with the introduction of his double, whom the narrator first encounters when he enters a boys' boarding school, run by Dr. Bransby, a reverend who "administered . . . the Draconian Laws of the academy" (M 2: 429). The boys "entered the school upon the same day;" and the other boy "bore the same Christian and surname as" Wilson and was born on the same day as he (M 2: 432, 431). Additionally, they "were of the same height" and "even singularly alike in general contour of person and outline of feature" (M 2: 434). Wilson believes the second Wilson (to be further referred to as "Wilson 2") is striving "to perfect an imitation" of him and admits that he "most admirably did . . . play his part," copying the narrator's dress, his "gait and general manner," and even his voice. The narrator confesses "how greatly this most exquisite portraiture harassed" him (M 2: 435).

It is not, however, the apparent similarities between the two that most annoy Wilson. Instead, it is what Wilson characterizes as his double's "rebellion" (M 2: 431). Although Wilson has achieved "ascendancy" over all the other boys at the academy, Wilson 2 proves the "single exception," "refus[ing] implicit belief in [the narrator's] assertions, and submission to [his] will" and offering "impertinent and dogged interference with [his] purposes" (M 2: 431–432). As Wilson explains, "this interference often took the ungracious character of advice; advice not openly given, but hinted or insinuated" (M 2: 435). Although such advice seemed obnoxious to him at the time, in retrospect he admits that it was well intended:

> I can recall no occasion when the suggestions of my rival were on the side of those errors or follies so usual to his immature age and seeming inexperience; . . . his moral sense . . . was far keener than my own; and . . . I might, to-day, have been a better, and thus a happier man, had I less frequently rejected the counsels embodied in those meaning whispers which I then but too cordially hated and too bitterly despised. (M 2: 435)

Because of the willful narrator's resentment of do-gooder Wilson 2's "distasteful supervision" (M 2: 436), which he admits it would have been wise to follow, Wilson 2 has been widely interpreted by scholars as representing the narrator's conscience, an interpretation to which readers are guided by Poe himself in the epigraph attached to the story, "What say of it? what say of CONSCIENCE grim, / That spectre in my path?" (M 2: 426).

Most scholars have followed the epigraph's suggestion to some extent, even while noting, as J. Gerald Kennedy does, that this seems "a little too obvious" for a Poe tale, "as if Poe had temporarily abandoned his strictures on didacticism to fashion an edifying tale about conscience." Thus, Albert Guerard reads Wilson's double as "the projected and watching moral conscience, distressed by the first William Wilson's vices, and intervening at crucial moments in the hope of saving him." And Stuart Levine describes him as "a symbol of the long ignored conscience of the first." Criticism influenced by Freudian psychology has often used its vocabulary. For example, Marie Bonaparte sees the double as "the introjection of the repressive father system," which "becomes our moral conscience or *super-ego.*" Charles Hoffmeister regards the action of the story as demonstrating "the superego's reaction to the unrestrained impulses of the id . . . embodied in an imagined likeness of William Wilson." And Robert Rogers calls Wilson 2 "one of the most representative superego doubles." Although others avoid the labels of "conscience" and "superego," they still discuss the double and his relationship with the narrator in terms that fit into our understanding of these concepts. Daniel Hoffman, for instance, views Wilson 2 as "that part of the ego which regards the rest as an object *which it can judge.*" David Halliburton proposes that "the second Wilson . . . is good, and tries to bring out what goodness there is in the first, . . . representing to the first Wilson the latter's potential for good." And Kennedy calls the double "the insistent representative of ethical constraint."[6]

Wilson's feelings toward his double, this apparent representation of his conscience, are complex. The narrator explains, "It is difficult, indeed, to define, or even to describe my real feelings towards him" (M 2: 433). Yet he makes the attempt to characterize the "motley and heterogeneous admixture" of feelings, using negative descriptors ranging from resentment, embarrassment, and fear, as well as the more positive ones of esteem, respect, and "uneasy curiosity," confessing that he "could not bring [himself] to hate [Wilson 2] altogether." He acknowledges that Wilson 2 demonstrates a "most unwelcome *affectionateness* of manner" toward him and even that his own "feelings in regard to him might have been easily ripened into friendship" (M 2: 432, 436), as the two share "many points of strong congeniality in [their] tempers" (M 2: 433). Indeed, he admits that they "were the most inseparable of companions." Eventually, he professes a conviction that the two share a connection that inexplicably predates their coincidental arrival at the academy, which comes to him in "dim visions of [his] earliest infancy—wild, confused and thronging memories of a time when memory herself was yet unborn." Wilson believes he had "been acquainted with the being who stood before [him], at some epoch very long ago" (M 2: 436).

The question of whether Wilson 2, "the being who stood before" the narrator, exists in some material form or only within the mind of Wilson persists for readers. Patrick Quinn asserts that "except for the word of the hero himself, there is no evidence that a second William Wilson exists," leaving Quinn to claim that "the double is a mental projection and only that."[7] However, the narrator's account remains somewhat ambiguous about this. He mentions that "the mere accident of [the boys] having entered the school upon the same day . . . set afloat the notion that [they] were brothers, among the senior classes in the academy" (M 2: 432). And, later, he claims to be "galled . . . by the rumor touching a relationship [between the two Wilsons,] . . . current in the upper forms" (M 2: 434). Even as he complains about this perceived awareness of his classmates, he contradictorily states, "I had no reason to believe that . . . this similarity had ever been made a subject of comment, or even observed at all by our schoolfellows." And he takes consolation "in the fact that the imitation, apparently, was noticed by [himself] alone" (M 2: 435). Indeed, both the imitation and the resistance of the second Wilson are described as observable solely by the narrator: "this superiority—even this equality—was in truth acknowledged by no one but myself; our associates, by some unaccountable blindness, seemed not even to suspect it. Indeed, his competition, his resistance, and especially his impertinent and dogged interference with my purposes, were not more pointed than private" (M 2: 432). That Wilson 2's single distinguishing trait from the narrator is his inability to speak at a level "*above a very low whisper*" (M 2: 433) raises the possibility that no one else can even hear or see him at all and that he is, as Quinn asserts, merely a projection by the narrator of his own conscience that challenges desires and intentions and thus annoys him. This projection suggests that he mistakenly understands this part of himself to be an external threat rather than an essential, internal trait that must be acknowledged and reconciled within himself.

It is in the most ambiguous scene in the story, one wherein Wilson sneaks into the bedroom of his rival in the middle of the night with the intention of deploying "one of those ill-natured pieces of practical wit at his expense," that we are presented with the narrator's first realization of the actual nature of the relationship between the two: "I arose from bed, and, lamp in hand, stole . . . from my own bedroom to that of my rival" (M 2: 437). He shines the lamplight upon the sleeping boy, in a tableau that suggests a potential for insight or revelation:

> [W]hen the bright rays fell vividly upon the sleeper, and my eyes, at the same moment, upon his countenance[,] I looked;—and a numbness, an iciness of feeling instantly pervaded my frame. My breast heaved, my knees tottered, my whole spirit became possessed with an objectless yet intolerable horror. Gasping for breath, I lowered the lamp in still nearer proximity to the face. Were these,—*these* the lineaments of William Wilson? I saw indeed, that they were his, but I shook as if with a fit of the ague, in fancying they were not. What *was* there about them to confound me in this manner? I gazed; —while my brain reeled with a multitude of incoherent thoughts. Not thus he appeared—assuredly not *thus*—in the vivacity of his waking hours. The same name! the same contour of person! the same day of arrival at the academy! And then his dogged and meaningless imitation of my gait, my voice, my habits, and my manner! Was it, in truth, within the bounds of human possibility, that *what I now saw* was the result, merely, of the habitual practice of this sarcastic imitation? (M 2: 437)

Although Wilson attains certain knowledge in the scene, his recounting is notably vague about what he sees in the face, "the lineaments," of his sleeping schoolmate, and he seems intent on withholding that information from his reader. Despite the lack of specificity in the narrator's account, scholars most commonly read this passage as describing the narrator seeing his own face in the double's.[8] Yet, within these interpretations, there is still a spectrum of understanding of "*what* [Wilson] *now saw*" and what that sight implies for our understanding of the relationship. For example, John Herdman claims that the incident gives the narrator the "gruesome, though fleeting, insight that his double was himself"; Robert Coskren argues that Wilson discovers that Wilson 2 "is not some external, other being, but rather his own alter-self"; and Valentine Hubbs asserts that the narrator is "on the point of recognizing [Wilson 2] as part of" or a "duplication of himself."[9] Thus, readings typically argue that Wilson discovers the double is himself, another version of himself, or some part of himself. Notably, Wilson's awareness of this connection produces "a multitude of *incoherent* thoughts" (my emphasis). Among these thoughts might even be an understanding of his own psychological incoherence, a train of thought quite antithetical to his believing himself to be "the master of [his] own actions" (M 2: 427). In response, he "extinguished the lamp" (M 2: 437), rejecting the understanding he has momentarily achieved, and flees the academy immediately to pursue a life unmolested by this counterpart, the testament to his incoherent self.

The subsequent scenes narrate his efforts to evade this manifestation of his internal division, efforts that for a time are successful. As a student at Eton, "[t]hree years of folly . . . passed without profit," before Wilson 2 reappears (M 2: 438). One evening at a "secret carousal" of "the most dissolute students" where "debaucheries," "dangerous seductions," "delirious extravagance," and "wonted profanity" abound, his decadent revelries are interrupted by a servant informing him that "some person . . . demanded to speak with [him]." Wilson goes out into a dark hallway where because of "the faint light" he is unable to distinguish "the features of [the stranger's] face" (M 2: 439). The figure "seiz[ed him] by the arm" and "whispered the words 'William Wilson!' in [his] ear." The "tremulous shake of his uplifted finger" and "the pregnancy of solemn admonition" had "a vivid effect upon [his] disordered imagination." As in the previous scene, the double appears to act as the narrator's conscience, and the consequence of its appearance upon Wilson is a sense of incoherence or conflict, here described as a "disordered" mind. Again, Wilson seems unable explicitly to pronounce Wilson 2 to be a part of himself, and he remains confused about the double's nature and intent: "But who and what was this Wilson?— . . . and what were his purposes?" (M 2: 439).

Wilson 2 next appears after the narrator has spent two years as a college student at Oxford, where he has learned "the vilest arts of the gambler by profession, and, having become an adept in his despicable science, to practice it habitually as a means of increasing [his] already enormous income" (M 2: 440). On the evening of Wilson 2's reemergence in the narrator's life, Wilson plans "to entangle . . . in [his] snares" a "young *parvenu* nobleman, Glendinning" (M 2: 440–441). His schemes succeed, and "in a very short period [Glendinning] had became [Wilson's] debtor to a large amount" and quickly doubled and then "quadrupled his debt" (M 2: 441–442). Interestingly, Wilson begins to express second thoughts, even if we might not call it conscience, after he notices that Glendinning's "countenance . . . had grown to a pallor truly fearful" (M 2: 442). Wilson wonders whether Glendinning is not "as immeasurably wealthy" as Wilson understood him to be, and he is, "rather with a view to the preservation of [his] own character in the eyes of [his] associates, than from any less interested motive," about "to insist, peremptorily, upon a discontinuance of the play." Yet his decision comes too late; Glendinning emits "an ejaculation evincing utter despair," leading Wilson to "understand that [he] had effected [Glendinning's] total ruin" and "render[ed] him an object for the pity of all." Into this situation, a "sudden and extraordinary interruption" occurs as "a stranger . . . entered, about [Wilson's] own height" (M 2: 442). He speaks, "in a low, distinct, and never-to-be-forgotten *whisper*," and tells Wilson's companions about the "true character" of Wilson, including that proof of his cheating in the card game can be found in his sleeve (M 2: 443). Wilson 2 "departed at once, . . . as abruptly as he had entered," and the men search Wilson's clothing and discover his stashed cards. They advise him that he should leave not only the chamber but also Oxford altogether. Moments later, as Wilson is walking away, one of them comes to him with a cloak identical to his own, apparently left by Wilson 2. Wilson's insistence that there are two cloaks rather than only his own indicates his continued determination to view himself and Wilson 2 as separate beings rather than counterparts of the same self. As he reflects upon "the singular being who had so disastrously exposed" him, Wilson does not approach the knowledge that the "singular being" could have been himself exposing his own cheating out of a fit of conscience at Glendinning's ruin (M 2: 444).

As Wilson relates very cursorily the years following his exposure at Oxford, years that take him all over Europe and as far as northern Africa as he flees his double, his account does seem to suggest an admission of their inseparability: "to the very ends of the earth *I fled in vain*" (M 2: 445). He ponders, "Who is he?—whence came he?—and what are his objects?" As he considers "the leading traits of [Wilson 2's] impertinent supervision," Wilson again acknowledges that Wilson 2's only object seems to be "to frustrate those schemes, or to disturb those actions, which, if fully carried out, might have resulted in bitter mischief" (M 2: 445). Despite this awareness of Wilson 2's benefit to him, Wilson views the potentially positive outcome as "poor justification . . . for an authority so imperiously assumed" and begins to cast the relationship with the double as tyranny: "Thus far I had succumbed supinely to this imperious domination. The sentiment of deep awe with which I habitually regarded the elevated character, the majestic wisdom, the apparent omnipresence and omnipotence of Wilson . . . had impress[ed] me with an idea of my own utter weakness and helplessness" (M 2: 446). Importantly, Wilson still insists on seeing the oppressor and the oppressed as separate entities and declares that he will no longer tolerate this oppression: "I began . . . to resist . . . and at length nurtured in my secret thoughts a stern and desperate resolution that I would submit no longer to be enslaved" (M 2: 446). The language of rebellion, earlier applied to Wilson 2's behavior at the academy, now is used to describe Wilson's intended resistance to his double, a shift that demonstrates that Wilson's perception of the power dynamic between the figures has transformed significantly since the boys' time at the academy.

This conflict comes to its climax in Rome, in the palazzo of a duke, where Wilson is pursuing the duke's young wife with what he characterizes as an "unworthy motive" (M 2: 446). As expected, Wilson 2 shows up to whisper in his ear, but this time Wilson is firm in his "resolution." He turns in anger upon his double and takes control of the situation: Wilson "seized him violently[,] . . . dragg[ed] him unresistingly[,] . . . and commanded him to draw" his sword for a duel (M 2: 447). Wilson describes his antagonist, "dr[awing] in silence, and put[ting] himself upon his defence." Once he sees his opponent in the proper stance, Wilson "forced him by sheer strength against the wainscoting, and . . . plunged [his] sword, with brute ferocity, repeatedly through and through his bosom" (M 2: 447). Wilson's initial understanding of this encounter as an actual struggle between two foes, himself and his external tormentor, soon becomes confused, as he discovers that there is a "large mirror" standing "where none had been perceptible before," wherein he sees his "own image . . . with features all pale and dabbled in blood" (M 2: 447, 448). As Wilson appears to be on the threshold of admission that this entire encounter has occurred within himself, he retreats once again to explain, "Thus it appeared, I say, but was not. It was my antagonist—it was Wilson, who then stood before me in the agonies of his dissolution" (M 2: 448). The remaining text prevents readers from achieving any certainty about whether or not Wilson acknowledges that the two are the same. He insists that Wilson 2's mask and cloak are visible on the floor but says that the "lineaments of his face" are "*mine own.*" He notes that Wilson 2 "spoke no longer in a whisper" and that his voice now sounds so much like Wilson's own that he "could have fancied that [he himself] was speaking." The final words of the story are attributed to the double (even though he speaks them in Wilson's voice), as Wilson 2 concedes defeat but tells Wilson that the cost of this victory is Wilson's own death: "*henceforward art thou also dead—dead to the World, to Heaven and to Hope! In me didst thou exist—and, in my death, see by this image, which is thine own, how utterly thou hast murdered thyself*" (M 2: 448). This proclamation, which most readers likely assume is being spoken by Wilson, still offers a somewhat conflicting view of his understanding of the relationship between the two William Wilsons. It is presented as the voice of the other, yet this voice insists upon an interconnection, even a unity, between the parts; the death of one necessarily results in the death of both, figuratively if not literally.

The resolution of this conflict, in which one part of this individual appears to have found a means to destroy another part of himself, is depicted as a life-altering (rather than life-ending) event for Wilson. It is the origin of his "later years of unspeakable misery, and unpardonable crime," when he experienced "a sudden elevation in turpitude" (M 2: 426). The moment depicted in the climax, Wilson's murder of part of himself as figured in Wilson 2, is characterized as the "one event" that "brought this evil thing to pass," the instant in which he passed "from comparatively trivial wickedness . . . into more than the enormities of an Elah-Gabalus," an infamous Roman emperor (M 2: 426–427). As he reflects upon his life to his reader on his deathbed, he seems to understand the monumental consequences of his failure to integrate the contrasting voice within himself. As he says, he believes he could have been a better and happier man, if he had been willing to heed Wilson 2's guidance rather than attempting to repress it or end it altogether.

It should be acknowledged that despite the narrator's conviction that he has destroyed his conscience and thus liberated himself for the life of infamy that follows, some scholars have argued that he fails in his efforts to evade his conscience, a failure that makes his narration possible. Valentine Hubbs describes him as "guilt-ridden" in his account of his life of misdeeds, and Thomas Walsh claims that "Wilson's moral sense has survived his double's death." If this were not the case, asks Ruth Sullivan, "where... does the self-condemnation come from?"[10] He seems genuinely ashamed of his behavior; he will hardly name any of his vile actions and speaks of them only in hyperbolic generalizations—"unpardonable crime," "wickedness," "evil," and the "enormities of an Elah-Gabalus" (M 2: 426–427); and he regretfully admits that he would have been better off following Wilson 2's counsel. These all suggest that there remains a functional conscience within Wilson. Even if he has lived without being troubled by his conscience for decades, as he implies, it does appear that it has reemerged late in his life, and his efforts to silence or even eradicate the voice of his conscience were unsuccessful.

Subsequent Poe tales featuring doubles depict individuals more successful than Wilson in their struggles with internal counterparts. "The Tell-Tale Heart" (1843), for example, has often been read as a doppelgänger tale in the vein of "Wilson." In this story, a narrator recounts his murder of the unsuspecting old man with whom he lives. Though these two figures are not as obviously parts of a single identity as the two Wilsons are,

Quinn calls the story "one more exploration of the psychology of the bipartite soul," and William Freedman argues that the old man is an "externalized projection" of the narrator's "self-accusation," the knowledge of "hidden wrong" in his heart. Herdman suggests that we read the victim as part of the murderer-narrator, similar to the critical consensus about Wilson 2, as "the other self externalised as accusing or reproachful conscience."[11]

As the narrator relates his motivations for this killing, he denies all of the typical reasons for murder: "Object there was none. Passion there was none. I loved the old man. He had never wronged me. He had never given me insult. For his gold I had no desire" (M 3: 792). Instead, he insists, "it was his eye! . . . Whenever it fell upon me, my blood ran cold; and so by degrees—very gradually—I made up my mind to take the life of the old man, and thus rid myself of the eye forever." As he begins his surveillance of the sleeping old man and shines a light upon his face at midnight (recalling the parallel scene in "William Wilson"), "for seven long nights" he is unable to act because "[he] found the eye always closed" and "so it was impossible to do the work." As he explains, "it was not the old man who vexed me, but his Evil Eye" (M 3: 793).

As critics have asserted, the narrator's focus on killing this eye suggests that he is trying to blind the eye to what it perceives in him or to end how it makes him feel, presumably morally judged or truly seen for what he fears he might be. That is, it is not essentially the "Evil Eye" from which the narrator wants to free himself but instead the "Evil I" that the eye observes in the narrator or makes the narrator perceive in himself. Indeed, if the old man is merely a projection of a part of the narrator, then it is the part that judges himself to be an evildoer or morally corrupt. As Michael Williams notes, "the old man's 'Evil Eye' is that part of the narrator's self that he fears," and Arthur Robinson suggests "the 'Evil Eye' [becomes] an evil 'I' " as the story dramatizes "self-abhorrence" and "self-destruction." Freedman argues that the "eye must be shut to prevent its further penetration into the guilty breast of the . . . narrator."[12]

If we recognize these figures as counterparts of the same identity, the narrator's agenda is to change the way he views himself by eliminating his inner judge. If, as Daniel Hoffman proposes, "in its aspect of getting rid of the Evil Eye, this murder is a . . . violent form of blinding," then the blinding is inflicted upon himself. This act allows him to, in the words of Magdalen Wing-chi Ki, turn "a blind eye to his evil self" and thus remain "blind to his sins."[13] On the eighth night of his surveillance, when he shines the light on the man, "a single dim ray . . . shot from out the crevice and fell upon the vulture eye" (M 3: 794). When he sees that the eye "was open—wide, wide open," the narrator grows "furious as [he] gazed upon it" and as it "chilled the very marrow in [his] bones." Infuriated by the open eye (which the narrator interestingly calls "the damned spot" in an allusion to Shakespeare's *Macbeth*, which serves as a near admission that the "Evil Eye" is evidence of his own guilt), he, "with a loud yell, . . . leaped into the room[,] . . . dragged [the old man] to the floor, and pulled the heavy bed over him" (M 3: 795). He soon pronounces the man "stone dead" and celebrates that the "eye would trouble [him] no more" (M 3: 796). Though cast as an external conflict between two separate persons, the implied internal conflict between antagonistic parts of the narrator seems to have been resolved as the narrator destroys the part of himself that sees him as evil.

Readers commonly posit that the "tell-tale heart" represents the narrator's guilty conscience. Although they rightly suggest that the heart he hears is his own, they usually ignore the implications of the narrator's potential misattribution of the heartbeat to another throughout the story. As in "Wilson," this narrator interprets evidence that should be read as proof of a single identity and misreads it to affirm his certainty of separate identities. Immediately before the murder, the narrator heard what he interprets as the "beating of the old man's heart," which begins as "a low, dull, quick sound" and then grows "louder every moment" until he "thought the heart must burst" (M 3: 795). After his attack upon the man, "for many minutes, the heart beat on with a muffled sound" until "at length it ceased." Not once throughout that sequence does he consider that the heartbeat could have been his own, even when his own adrenaline-pumping heart would have been the most likely source for the audible beating prior to, during, and following his act of murder. Later that evening when the police arrive to investigate, the narrator begins to hear the heartbeat again and believes the officers with their "hypocritical smiles" also hear it beating "louder! louder! louder! *louder*!" (M 3: 797). Again, he assumes the sound comes from outside of himself and asserts, in his shrieked confession to the police, "it is the beating of *his* hideous heart!" (my emphasis). Rather than reading this as the working of conscience, we should see this moment as a dramatization of the psychological error that dooms him; that is, he never comprehends that this "evil eye" and this "hideous heart" are indeed parts of himself that cannot be destroyed without destroying the integrity of the self.

It should be noted additionally that, in the narrator's account of his crime, he departs significantly from the tone of "William Wilson" as he offers neither a sense of regret nor a second guessing of what he has done. Importantly, the narration takes place after he has successfully achieved his goal—the termination of his inner judge—and the account reveals that the outcome is not only his arrest but also a reflection upon his deeds absent of any demonstration of guilt. As he details his intentions and his actions, he never implies that they are not justified or completely logical. The old man, in the narrator's telling, is the one associated with the evil eye and hideous heart. The murderer's account is so devoid of shame that he laughs as he offers it ("ha! ha!" [M 3: 796]) and is confident that the audience shares his attitude ("you would have laughed to see . . ." [M 3: 793]). Even to the policemen, he expresses neither guilt nor remorse, but only responsibility: "I admit the deed!—tear up the planks!—here, here!" (M 3: 797). Indeed, he even calls them "Villains" because he perceives that they, like the old man's eye, hold an image of him as a suspect, as a likely evildoer. He projects such an attitude toward the implied audience as well, the listeners who "say that [he is] mad" (M 3: 792). In the narration, this image of himself is one that he never accepts; he reveals not even a twinge of doubt about his sanity, regardless of the horrifying acts he describes himself committing.

In a later story, "The Cask of Amontillado," Poe once more gives readers a conflict between a murderer and his unsuspecting victim that has been read as a doppelgänger tale. Montresor, the narrator, relates how he lures his enemy Fortunato into the catacombs to leave him to die chained up and sealed behind a stone wall. As with "The Tell-Tale Heart," scholars have not always understood this story to be in the vein of "William Wilson"; indeed, David Ketterer notes that "the doppelgänger theme is so well disguised as to be almost invisible." Others have viewed it as less subtle in its use of the double than Ketterer does. For example, Walter Stepp labels Fortunato "the familiar Poe *doppelgänger*," and Benjamin Fisher calls "Cask" a "recycling of 'William Wilson.' "[14]

Montresor begins his narration, which occurs fifty years after the events related, by addressing his motivation for his crime: "the thousands injuries of Fortunato I had borne as I best could; but when he ventured upon insult, I vowed revenge" (M 3: 1256). Like the "Tell-Tale Heart" narrator, he intends to give his prey no indication that vengeance is coming, by making no "utterance to a threat" and planning to "punish with impunity" (M 3: 1257, 1258). Knowing of Fortunato's "connoisseurship in wine," Montresor lures the drunken Fortunato, whom he calls "my friend" repeatedly throughout the tale (M 3: 1259, 1261, 1262), into "the catacombs of the Montresors" with the request of his expert opinion on "a pipe of . . . Amontillado" (M 3: 1258, 1257). Once the pair is deep into the catacombs, Montresor fetters Fortunato in a recess in the wall and begins "vigorously to wall up the entrance of the niche" (M 3: 1262). During Montresor's construction of the wall, Fortunato produces "loud and shrill screams" and later a "low laugh" as he hopes that these events are merely a "very good joke" (M 3: 1262–1263). Eventually, Montresor "forced the last stone into its position [and] . . . plastered [the wall] up" after Fortunato makes no more sounds.

Montresor and Fortunato have been read, by James Gargano, as Poe's other doubles have been, "in terms of a split or division within the psyche of the narrator-protagonist." Fisher differentiates these counterparts within the narrator's psyche, seeing "Montresor as an evil principle, [and] Fortunato the good, in a self." And Stepp argues that Fortunato as Montresor's "double corresponds with conscience," which leads him to assert that "Cask" features "the same story" as "Wilson," that of "a man who murdered his conscience and thus himself."[15] Like the narrators in the previously discussed stories, Montresor clearly feels judged or looked down upon by his double as conscience (including in the unnamed "insult" that spurs his vengeance). During the crime, we see a dynamic comparable to Wilson's antagonism toward Wilson 2's whisper and the "Tell-Tale" narrator's attempt to silence what he believes to be his victim's "hideous heart." In response to the "loud and shrill screams, bursting suddenly from the throat of the chained form," which "seemed to thrust [Montresor] violently back," he "replied to the yells of him who clamored[,] . . . [and] surpassed them in volume and in strength" (M 3: 1262). His attempt to quiet Fortunato and his insistence that his own voice be louder and stronger continues as he begins to echo Fortunato's desperate final pleas:

> ["]Let us be gone."
> "Yes," I said, "let us be gone."
> "*For the love of God, Montresor!*"
> "Yes," I said, "for the love of God!" (M 3: 1263)

In his discussion of this moment, "one of the most brilliant scenes in the story," Gargano interprets Montresor's imitations of Fortunato's shrieks as "a gleeful parody of pain," noting that "both men utter almost identical sentences to express the contrary emotions of terror and joy."[16] When "no answer" comes to this final echo, Poe indicates that Montresor's joyful perspective of this conflict triumphs as he has successfully silenced his conscience in the form of this double.

It remains unclear whether Montresor ever realizes that Fortunato is a part of himself as the story lacks an explicit acknowledgment along the lines of the final speech of Wilson 2. However, readers are again presented with a scene of a narrator shining light upon his double, recalling the parallel scenes in "William Wilson" and "The Tell-Tale Heart," which raises our expectation for the narrator's potential enlightenment about their interconnection. In the dark catacombs as he is building the wall, Montresor holds up "flambeaux over the mason-work," and they "threw a few feeble rays upon the figure within" (M 3: 1262). As he completes his construction of the wall, he loses all sight of Fortunato, "thrust[s] a torch through the remaining aperture[,] and let[s] it fall within." He only has audible awareness of Fortunato's state from that point on, as he hears in response to the torch falling "only a jingling of the bells" (M 3: 1263), referring to the motley costume, the "conical cap and bells" Fortunato is wearing for the carnival (M 3: 1257). Montresor's inability to see his double suggests that he—like "The Tell-Tale Heart" murderer—remains unaware of the true nature of the violence he has done to himself. Thus, Gargano pronounces Montresor "spiritually blind . . . with no self-awareness."[17]

Some scholars assert, however, that the narrator's conscience remains after Fortunato's murder. Scott Peeples, for example, argues (as others do about "William Wilson") that "the narrative itself is subtle evidence that retribution has overtaken him in the form of guilt." These critics often point to Montresor's description of his response to hearing Fortunato's bells jingling for the final time: "My heart grew sick—on account of the dampness of the catacombs" (M 3: 1263). Peeples believes "this heartsickness likely arises from empathy with the man he is leaving to die," and Ketterer attributes it to "remorse," suggesting that "he has punished with impunity as far as legal retribution is concerned, but not as far as peace of mind is concerned."[18] Although there is merit to reading Montresor's temporary "heart-sickness" as potentially a momentary display of conscience during his actions a half century before, this feeling occurs while Fortunato remains alive (as his bells still jingle) and before the wall is completed. Until he has made "an end of [his] labor" and "forced the last stone into its position," he has not severed the connection with his conscience.

Montresor's tone throughout the narration seems to support the conclusion that he is someone who successfully "kills his conscience and rests in peace for fifty years," as Stepp convincingly portrays him. Much like the murderer in "The Tell-Tale Heart," he never displays any doubt about the justice of his actions; neither does he express regret over the consequences as William Wilson does. Scholars like Ketterer and Peeples insist that the very action of telling this tale, commonly read as a "deathbed confession," demonstrates a functional conscience: Ketterer believes that "after fifty years the event still bothers" Montresor, and Peeples asserts that "fifty years later, he still remembers his heart's 'growing sick.'" However, if viewed as a confession, Montresor's narrative lacks the crucial element of contrition. Indeed, this absence is apparent even in his retrospective attribution of his heartsickness to "the dampness of the catacombs," offering readers proof that the narrator, after living for half a century without a conscience, is now unable even to acknowledge a normal human feeling he once experienced. That is, he is neither remorseful nor repentant, and apparently he no longer even recognizes what those feelings would feel like. Benjamin Fisher argues that "the murder functions as a suppression of the good component within the self" and "in killing Fortunato [Montresor] also murders part of himself." Stepp more explicitly names this murdered component as Montresor's conscience, and emphasizes that the story leaves us with a narrator, who, in killing his double, "did indeed triumph, . . . did indeed sin with impunity," and "did slay his conscience."[19]

In Montresor, Poe offers us a disturbing contrast to his earlier figure, William Wilson, who also struggled with a conscience represented as an external double. Although "Wilson" offered readers the comfort of believing either that an individual could never completely destroy his own conscience or that he would certainly regret it if he did, "The Cask of Amontillado" provides us with no such reassurance. Instead, we are presented with a narrator without second thoughts, as he has evaded the nagging of his conscience. In the final sentence, after the narrator tells us that "against the new masonry" he "re-erected the old rampart of bones," and "for the half of a century no mortal has disturbed them," he closes his account with "*In pace requiescat!*" (M 3: 1263). As Fisher notes, because these words end the tale, readers are left to ask, "Does he invoke the Latin from the Roman Catholic burial service for the sake of Fortunato . . . or, in a voice of truth, does he invoke it for his own future?" Although many readers elect to read them as an implicit admission on Montresor's part that he has not rested peacefully with the memory of his crime, a more terrifying likelihood is that Montresor *has* been at peace, like those undisturbed bones in his family catacombs, during the decades between action and narration. Stepp makes the argument that this possibility is what makes "Cask" a more complex and troubling work than "Wilson:"

> Wilson recognizes his folly, while Montresor steadfastly refuses to. . . . Wilson's recognition satisfies, perhaps too easily, our own conscientious understanding of the way things ought to be; Montresor . . . challenges that understanding. . . . Montresor, like Iago, stands in the line of Machiavellians who assert that the public moral perspective is but a façade by which knaves are stung and puppies drowned.

Stepp understands that readers might find consolation in viewing Montresor as "a tormented sinner like Wilson," yet the evidence from the story does not support this portrayal.[20]

We can conclude then that Montresor represents an impressive innovation in Poe's employment of the literary double. Scholars of this trope, from Otto Rank to John Herdman, often assert that writers use it to reflect our common understanding of the individual psyche as the site of conflicting components. And Poe's "William

Wilson" certainly fits into this reading as its two figures, Wilson and his doppelgänger-conscience, struggle for control of Wilson's choices and actions. Even after the moment when Wilson appears to kill his tormenting double and enters into a life of infamy untroubled by a conscience, the narration's guilty tone confirms that the struggle has never ceased, and the conscience, while perhaps suppressed for a time, has reemerged to make Wilson regret his resistance to his double's influence, reassuring the story's readers that even the most debased of human beings retains a conscience somewhere within. In "The Tell-Tale Heart" and "The Cask of Amontillado," Poe uses the double to produce the opposite effect. Within these tales of narrators murdering their doubles, he withholds the reassurance that "Wilson" offers and instead has these figures express neither regret, nor guilt, nor contrition. Readers are unable to leave these narratives with certainty that a conscience persists in these figures; instead, we are led to read these tales of internal struggle and conclude that these conflicts are resolved with the eradication of the individual's conscience. This conclusion is less disturbing in "The Tell-Tale Heart," wherein the narrator ends up apprehended by police and tells his story presumably from a prisoner's cell. In "The Cask of Amontillado," the discomfort is ratcheted up because Montresor's murder of his own conscience happened long ago, serving as preface to subsequent decades when (readers must assume) he has been living in the same community with no conscience to censor the horrifying deeds of which he has shown himself capable. Because Poe omits any description of Montresor's life after Fortunato's death, the reader is left to imagine what is untold. Although our imaginations might concoct all manner of "unpardonable crime," as Wilson's vague characterizations of his deeds lead us to do (M 2: 426), the true unease might come from the fact that Montresor tells us nothing and, worse perhaps, might believe there is nothing to tell. Whatever deeds we can imagine, even if they might not rise to Wilson's level of "the enormities of an Elah-Gabalus" (M 2: 427), are insignificant to Montresor, unworthy of confession, as he exists without conscience. His internal conflict has been resolved, and he rests in peace, untroubled by the conscience that still lingers within William Wilson.

Notes

1. Ralph Tymms, *Doubles in Literary Psychology* (Cambridge, UK: Bowes & Bowes, 1949), 44; C. F. Keppler, *The Literature of the Second Self* (Tucson: University of Arizona Press, 1972), 5.
2. John Herdman, *The Double in Nineteenth-Century Fiction: The Shadow Life* (New York: St. Martin's Press, 1991), 1–2.
3. Aside from the three stories—"William Wilson," "The Tell-Tale Heart," and "The Cask of Amontillado"—that are the primary focus of the discussion in this essay, the scholarship on the literary double treats a number of Poe stories, including "The Fall of the House of Usher," "The Black Cat," "Ligeia," "A Tale of the Ragged Mountains," and "The Purloined Letter," as tales of doubles, doppelgängers, or second selves.
4. Otto Rank, *The Double: A Psychoanalytic Study*, trans. Harry Tucker, Jr. (Chapel Hill: University of North Carolina Press, 1971), 25; Palmer Cobb, *The Influence of E. T.*

A. Hoffmann on the Tales of Edgar Allan Poe (Chapel Hill: University of North Carolina Press, 1908), 36.

5. Claire Rosenfield, "The Shadow Within: The Conscious and Unconscious Use of the Double," in *Stories of the Double*, ed. Albert Guerard (Philadelphia: J. B. Lippincott, 1967), 321; Keppler, *The Literature of the Second Self*, 105.
6. J. Gerald Kennedy, *Poe, Death, and the Life of Writing* (New Haven, CT: Yale University Press, 1987), 128; Albert Guerard, "Concepts of the Double," in *Stories of the Double*, ed. Albert Guerard (Philadelphia: J. B. Lippincott, 1967), 2; Stuart Levine, *Edgar Poe: Seer and Craftsman* (Deland, FL: Everett/Edwards, 1972), 189; Marie Bonaparte, *The Life and Works of Edgar Allan Poe: A Psycho-Analytic Interpretation*, trans. John Rodker (London: Imago, 1949), 539; Charles Hoffmeister, "'William Wilson' and *The Double*: A Freudian Insight," *Coranto* 9, no. 2 (1974): 24; Robert Rogers, *A Psychoanalytic Study of the Double in Literature* (Detroit: Wayne State University Press, 1970), 25; Daniel Hoffman, *Poe Poe Poe Poe Poe Poe Poe* (New York: Vintage, 1985), 212; David Halliburton, *Edgar Allan Poe: A Phenomenological View* (Princeton, NJ: Princeton University Press, 1973), 302, 306.
7. Patrick F. Quinn, *The French Face of Edgar Poe* (Carbondale: Southern Illinois University Press, 1957), 221.
8. A notable exception to this consensus appears in Kennedy's assertion that "in the features of the sleeping double he discerns a frightening *difference*," *Poe, Death, and the Life of Writing*, 130.
9. Herdman, *The Double in Nineteenth-Century Fiction*, 97; Robert Coskren, "'William Wilson' and the Disintegration of Self," *Studies in Short Fiction* 12, no. 2 (1975): 158; Valentine C. Hubbs, "The Struggle of the Wills in Poe's 'William Wilson,'" *Studies in American Fiction* 11, no. 1 (Spring 1983): 77.
10. Hubbs, "The Struggle of the Wills," 78; Thomas Walsh, "The Other William Wilson," *ATQ: American Transcendental Quarterly* 10 (Spring 1971): 18; Ruth Sullivan, "William Wilson's Double," *Studies in Romanticism* 15, no. 2 (Spring 1976): 254.
11. Quinn, *The French Face of Edgar Poe*, 233; William Freedman, *The Porous Sanctuary: Art and Anxiety in Poe's Short Fiction* (New York: Peter Lang, 2002), 103–104; Herdman, *The Double in Nineteenth-Century Fiction*, 92.
12. Michael J. S. Williams, *A World of Words: Language and Displacement in the Fiction of Edgar Allan Poe* (Durham: Duke University Press, 1988), 37; Arthur Robinson, "Poe's 'The Tell-Tale Heart,'" *Nineteenth-Century Fiction* 19, no. 4 (March 1965): 376–377; Freedman, *The Porous Sanctuary*, 104.
13. Hoffman, *Poe Poe Poe Poe Poe Poe Poe*, 226; Magdalen Wing-chi Ki, "Ego-Evil and 'The Tell-Tale Heart,'" *Renascence* 61, no. 1 (Fall 2008): 25, 28.
14. David Ketterer, *The Rationale of Deception in Poe* (Baton Rouge: Louisiana State University Press, 1979), 110; Walter Stepp, "The Ironic Double in Poe's 'The Cask of Amontillado,'" *Studies in Short Fiction* 13 (1976): 448; Benjamin F. Fisher, *The Cambridge Introduction to Edgar Allan Poe* (Cambridge: Cambridge University Press, 2008), 68.
15. James W. Gargano, "'The Cask of Amontillado': A Masquerade of Motive and Identity," *Studies in Short Fiction* 4, no. 2 (Winter 1967): 119; Fisher, *The Cambridge Introduction to Edgar Allan Poe*, 69; Stepp, "The Ironic Double," 448, 452.
16. Gargano, "'The Cask of Amontillado,'" 124.
17. Gargano, "'The Cask of Amontillado,'" 126.
18. Scott Peeples, *Edgar Allan Poe Revisited* (New York: Twayne, 1998), 149–150; Ketterer, *The Rationale of Deception in Poe*, 112.

19. Stepp, "The Ironic Double," 452–453; Ketterer, *The Rationale of Deception in Poe*, 112; Peeples, *Edgar Allan Poe Revisited*, 149; and Fisher, *The Cambridge Introduction to Edgar Allan Poe*, 69–70.
20. Fisher, *The Cambridge Introduction to Edgar Allan Poe*, 70; Stepp, "Ironic Double," 452.

Bibliography

Bonaparte, Marie. *The Life and Works of Edgar Allan Poe: A Psycho-Analytic Interpretation*. Translated by John Rodker. London: Imago, 1949.

Gargano, James W. " 'The Cask of Amontillado': A Masquerade of Motive and Identity." *Studies in Short Fiction* 4, no. 2 (Winter 1967): 119–126.

Herdman, John. *The Double in Nineteenth-Century Fiction: The Shadow Life*. New York: St. Martin's Press, 1991.

Hubbs, Valentine. "The Struggle of the Wills in Poe's 'William Wilson.' " *Studies in American Fiction* 11, no. 1 (Spring 1983): 73–79.

Keppler, C. F. *The Literature of the Second Self*. Tucson: University of Arizona Press, 1972.

Ki, Magdalen Wing-chi. "Ego-Evil and 'The Tell-Tale Heart.' " *Renascence* 61, no. 1 (Fall 2008): 25–38.

Quinn, Patrick. *The French Face of Edgar Poe*. Carbondale: Southern Illinois University Press, 1957.

Rank, Otto. *The Double: A Psychoanalytic Study*. 1914. Translated by Harry Tucker, Jr. Chapel Hill: University of North Carolina Press, 1971.

Rogers, Robert. *A Psychoanalytic Study of the Double in Literature*. Detroit: Wayne State University Press, 1970.

Rosenfield, Claire. "The Shadow Within: The Conscious and Unconscious Use of the Double." In *Stories of the Double*, edited by Albert Guerard, 311–331. Philadelphia: J. B. Lippincott, 1967.

Stepp, Walter. "The Ironic Double in Poe's 'The Cask of Amontillado.' " *Studies in Short Fiction* 13 (1976): 447–453.

Sullivan, Ruth. "William Wilson's Double." *Studies in Romanticism* 15, no. 2 (Spring 1976): 253–263.

Tymms, Ralph. *Doubles in Literary Psychology*. Cambridge, UK: Bowes & Bowes, 1949.

CHAPTER 15

OUTING THE PERVERSE

Poe's False Confessionals

LELAND S. PERSON

I want to begin with what John T. Irwin, at the beginning of *The Mystery to a Solution*, calls a "simple question": "How does one write analytic detective fiction as high art when the genre's central narrative mechanism seems to discourage the unlimited rereading associated with serious writing? That is, if the point of an analytic detective story is the deductive solution of a mystery, how does the writer keep that solution from exhausting the reader's interest in the story? How does he write a work that can be reread by people other than those with poor memories?"[1]

In this essay I am less interested in Poe's detective tales than in stories I'm calling "false confessionals"—those first-person narratives which take the form of confessions, sometimes death-bed or pre-execution confessions. "The Tell-Tale Heart," "The Black Cat," "The Imp of the Perverse," and "The Cask of Amontillado" are all variations on this form. In each of those tales, the narrator seems to be admitting or confessing to a murder, whether to clear his conscience or to boast about the ingenuity the murder required. These narratives share important attributes with the detective stories, as J. Gerald Kennedy has suggested, and thus encourage expanding Irwin's questions about analytic detective fiction to include murder stories in which there is little "mystery to a solution." For Kennedy, the "strategy of murder" in these tales "reflects a compulsion to exhibit intellectual superiority by carrying out a scandalous crime with sangfroid and precision in a way which deceives police and public while assuring one's impunity." Simultaneously, Kennedy continues, "each murderer also betrays himself, as if the urge to prove one's sagacity through a private act also contains within itself the contradictory need to have the deed publicly acknowledged, even at the cost of self-destruction."[2] Put another way, the detective stories and the murder tales represent two sides of the same coin, especially when considered from a reader-centered point of view. Irwin's questions can be useful springboards for examining what happens in recursive reading practices in those tales. Both sets of tales feature meticulous accounts of crimes, whether by the detective who has figured out the criminal process or by the criminal who has committed, or inscribed, it. I use the word "inscribed" deliberately because the process of solving a crime, the process of narrating its commission, and the process of reading about it are a lot like literary analysis. And, it is safe to say, Poe not only recognized but exploited this connection. I call these tales "false confessionals" because I think their confessional appearance and form are designed to ensnare the reader into a perverse identification.

"The Tell-Tale Heart" and "The Black Cat," for example, conclude with police visits to the crime scenes. In the detective tales these visits occur earlier in the narrative in order to demonstrate the ineptitude of the authorities, who cannot read behind or beneath the surface. In the confessional tales, on the other hand, the police discover the crime and its perpetrator, although not because of their superior analytical skills but by the tension their presence creates in the murderer, who reveals the crime and thus directs the police to the discovery of the gruesome corpse (*corpus delicti*). As readers of these two tales, we have been with the criminal every painstaking step of the way—until, that is, we and the police discover the bodies. "The Cask of Amontillado," of course, is very different in this latter respect, and I want to focus particular attention on that tale—one of Poe's latest—as both an exception to and, paradoxically, a culmination of this subgenre. Montresor, the narrator of "Cask," seems both proud and disappointed that his murder of Fortunato sparks no visit from the police and no official discovery of the body. How the reader responds—that's the key question, especially when that reader reads the tale multiple times.

As my title suggests, I want to use the notion of "perverseness" to examine both the crimes in these confessional tales and the relationship Poe creates between narrator and reader—the way he tests and plays with his readers and rereaders. I want to go behind these narratives and read them perversely—precisely because Poe encourages me not to. I want to be a "resisting reader," a term and reading strategy I'm repurposing from Judith Fetterley's example of nearly forty years ago.[3] Poe plays with his readers, getting us to identify and even sympathize with his murderous narrators under the guise of hearing them confess. In the detective tales, we identify with the narrator and Dupin. We marvel at the ratiocinative process by which Dupin narrates his solution to the mystery. The first-person narrator, who will become Watson in the Sherlock Holmes stories that owe so much to Poe, helps Dupin with the solution and helps even more to "sell" that solution to the reader. In the confessional tales, on the other hand, Poe encourages readers to identify with the criminal and to participate even more intimately in the crime. We find ourselves trapped in the narrators' minds, hanging on their every word, participating in a criminal process precisely because we should not. In each case—encouraging reader identification with the detective or criminal—Poe plays with the idea that to solve a crime, the reader and the detective must be able to imagine committing it. We are murderers and detectives at the same time. Joseph Moldenhauer pointed out half a century ago that "Poe's detective is the double of the criminal; he lacks, it may be, the 'constructive' volition literally to perform a crime himself, but he partakes wholly in the psychology of the crime."[4] He might have added that readers are similarly implicated in this doubling. Identifying with the detective, we also partake in the psychology of the crime. A similar psychological doubling occurs in the murder tales. Our position and identification as readers differ little whether we are reading one of the detective tales or one of the murder tales. In both cases, we partake "wholly in the psychology of the crime."

As my title also suggests, Poe's concept of "perverseness" figures prominently in his confessional tales. His most extensive explanation and illustration of the concept occurs in "The Imp of the Perverse" (1845), but he had actually coined the term two years earlier in "The Black Cat" (1843). Explaining what he calls the "spirit of PERVERSENESS," Poe's narrator asserts, "I am not more sure that my soul lives, than I am that perverseness is one of the primitive impulses of the human heart—one of the indivisible primary faculties, or sentiments, which give direction to the character of Man" (M 3: 852). The narrator then uses this pseudo-philosophical concept to explain his sudden impulse to hang the cat that has been a loving and loyal companion. "Have we not a perpetual inclination, in the teeth of our best judgment," the narrator asks, "to violate that which is *Law*, merely because we understand it to be such?" (M 3: 852). Having already punished the cat for avoiding his presence by "deliberately cut[ting] one of its eyes from the socket" (M 3: 851), the narrator explains what he claims he cannot control: "It was this unfathomable longing of the soul *to vex itself*—to offer violence to its own nature—to do wrong for the wrong's sake only—that urged me to continue and finally to consummate the injury I had inflicted upon the unoffending brute" (M 3: 852). Thus, "in cool blood," he slips a noose around the cat's neck and hangs it from the limb of a tree: "hung it with the tears streaming from my eyes, and with the bitterest remorse in my heart;—hung it *because* I knew it had loved me, and *because* I felt it had given me no reason of offence;—hung it *because* I knew that in so doing I was committing a sin" (M 3: 852). In this initial conception in "The Black Cat," the Imp of the Perverse seems the root cause of a murder. The narrator murders because he should not. He returns murder for love.

When Poe develops the idea in "The Imp of the Perverse," on the other hand, he not only gives the "spirit" of perverseness a "character" ("The Imp") but he repurposes the Imp to spark a confession rather than a murder. Poe complicates this concept of criminal intent even as he explores the idea of perverseness at much greater length. Furthermore, because "The Imp of the Perverse" appears to be an essay rather than a tale, Poe's first-person narration appears to make him the criminal. Through the "promptings" of perverseness, he explains, "we act without comprehensible object; or, if this shall be understood as a contradiction in terms, we may so far modify the proposition as to say, that through its promptings we act, for the reason that we should *not*" (M 3: 1220). This, he concludes, "is a radical, a primitive impulse—elementary" (M 3: 1221). Poe illustrates what he means with several examples, from the mundane (the impulse to delay completing a task even when it involves the "most important crisis of our life" [M 3: 1222]) to the most dangerous (the impulse to throw ourselves off a precipice in order to experience "our sensations during the sweeping precipitancy of a fall from such a height" [M 3: 1223]). Poe moves from theory to practice at the end of this narrative, as he reveals that he writes from a "cell of the condemned" (M 3: 1224). As the essay shifts toward the fictional, the narrator's identity slides toward the fictional as well. Is it still Poe who narrates or a character he has created? Is there a significant difference, or does the narrative illustrate the slipperiness of identity and identification—the ease with which philosophical distance dissolves into imaginative participation for narrator and reader alike? Whoever is narrating, he has killed a man, presumably his father, and inherited his estate. The murder went unsolved, enabling him to enjoy the fruits of his criminality "for years" (M 3: 1224). "The idea of detection never once entered my brain," he says (M 3: 1224), but almost as soon as he speaks those words, an impulse to confess does enter his mind—precisely because he feels so safe from detection. He finds himself saying, " 'I am safe—I am safe—yes—if I be not fool enough to make open confession!' " (M 3: 1225). "No sooner had I spoken these words," he continues, "than I felt an icy chill creep to my heart." This fit of "perversity" rapidly gains power. "I felt a maddening desire to shriek aloud," he notes (M 3: 1225). He bounds through the streets, trying to escape himself. People begin to pursue him. "I gasped for breath," he tells us. "For a moment, I experienced all the pangs of suffocation; I became blind, and deaf, and giddy; and then some invisible fiend, I thought, struck me with his broad palm upon the back. The long-imprisoned secret burst forth from my soul" (M 3: 1226). In this story, the Imp of the Perverse causes the murderer's confession, but it does not seem to have caused the murder. The thought that he is safe as long as he does not confess to the murder conjures up that very impulse, which then proves irresistible.

More than in any other of the murder narratives, Poe explores a relationship between impulse and language, between the Imp of the Perverse and the individual self. Discussing "The Imp of the Perverse," Michael Williams argues that "the assumption that there is a clear, direct relationship between subject and voice, a relationship that allows an interpreter to track the subject down to where it lurks behind his words, is shown to be an optimistic fiction," largely because "the voice speaks despite the subject."[5] Jonathan Elmer agrees. "Poe does not speak of perverseness as the predicate of an individuality," he writes, "at least not as an accident that can be more or less contingently attached to the substance of the individual."[6] One can act perversely without *being* perverse. Acting perversely "poses the self as radically divided between conflicting imperatives" because "there is no singular and integral self which lies behind or beneath the perverse."[7] Although it is tempting to view the impulse to confess as a function of inner morality, Poe suggests that the Imp operates independent of any moral concern. Words are in league with impulse and the Imp of the Perverse in cahoots with words, but neither words nor impulse seems anchored in ethos.

The Imp of the Perverse represents a kind of wild card within the psyche. Stanley Cavell suggested that in Poe's tales "philosophy exists only as a parody of philosophy, or rather as something indistinguishable from the perversion of philosophy, as if to overthrow the reign of reason . . . is now openly the genius or mission of philosophy itself."[8] Cavell uses "The Imp of the Perverse" and "The Black Cat" to illustrate this principle. Russell Sbriglia builds on Cavell's insights to link Poe not only with Descartes but also with Kant, Hegel, and Žižek. Sbriglia argues that Poe's "use of perversity to overthrow the reign of reason . . . constitutes an even more radical overthrowing of liberal subjectivity"—indeed, "subverts the very kernel" of his narrators' being.[9]

We can see this perverse philosophy in action more clearly by examining those two tales, as well as "The Tell-Tale Heart." On the face of it, all three tales follow the same confessional pattern, as the narrators feel smug and safe from detection after murdering someone—so safe in two cases that they flaunt themselves, in front of the police, as close as they can get to their victims' corpses. This feeling of safety anticipates the narrator's feeling in "The Imp of the Perverse," and here too Poe works with a simple phenomenon of reversal. A feeling of safety produces an impulse to put the self in danger. In "The Tell-Tale Heart," the sound of the old man's beating heart (probably the narrator's own heart beating) finally causes the murderer to shriek aloud and " 'admit the deed' " (M 3: 797). "The Black Cat" narrator raps on the wall behind which his wife's dead body stands, causing the black cat (which he has inadvertently walled up with her) to utter a "wailing shriek" that reveals the crime (M 3: 859).

As an unmoored and free-floating force that can cause a murder or a confession to it, the Imp of the Perverse begins to seem like a force for disorder and even play. Christopher Benfey addresses this seeming paradox by arguing that each tale records a "*perverse* confession since the crimes would otherwise have been undetected." "These killers," he adds, "need to confess to the perverse act of having confessed."[10] Benfey's insight contradicts the tendency among many readers to consider the confessions as conscience stricken, but I want to suggest another way of looking at the Imp. Arising as it were impulsively and without any apparent ethical warrant, the Imp seems much like an author who reserves the right to "motivate" his characters the way a puppeteer moves his puppets. Perversity can occur under many different circumstances. In "The Black Cat" perverseness causes the murder of the black cat and the discovery of the murder victim. The Imp perhaps causes the narrator to murder his wife. Aiming the ax at the second black cat, he buries the blade in his wife's brain instead. Has it been his intention all along to kill his wife, as some critics suggest? Or does the Imp of the Perverse redirect the narrator's anger from cat to wife? In "The Imp of the Perverse," the Imp impels the confession but doesn't seem to have caused the murder. In "The Tell-Tale Heart," the narrator seems perversely impelled both to kill the old man—because he loves him (M 3: 792)—and to reveal the murder and dismemberment to the police. Does the Imp cause both murder and confession in these tales? That seems perverse indeed. The moral world we might infer from these tales seems topsy-turvy. The Imp has us coming and going in a closed circuit of perversity.

Although Poe's conception of the perverse in action makes it an irresistible impulse within the self, his conception of the writer–reader relationship places a premium on authorial control. In his second review of Hawthorne's *Twice-Told Tales*, he famously prescribes the ideal strategy for the "skilful literary artist," who constructs a tale by conceiving, "with deliberate care, a certain unique or single *effect*" and "then combines such events as may best aid him in establishing this preconceived effect" (ER: 572). In emphasizing the writer's "deliberate care" and intense focus on producing a predetermined "effect," Poe asserts control over both the creative process and the reader. He also sounds a lot like some of his murderous narrators. The narrator of "The Tell-Tale Heart," for example, brags to us about his carefully constructed plot to kill the old man: "you should have seen *me*. You should have seen how wisely I proceeded—with what caution—with what foresight—with what dissimulation I went to work!" (M 3: 792). This could be Poe in the Hawthorne review describing the effect he produces: "during the hour of perusal the soul of the reader is at the writer's control" (ER: 572). As James Machor concludes, "Poe's entire concept of effect and his privileging of it as 'indispensable' to the brief tale were undergirded by the assumption in informed response that the successful author would be a virtual enchanter who controlled the audience with his or her spellbinding artistic performance."[11] In Machor's view, Poe approached the writer–reader relationship as "virtual battle for authority, waged as both frontal assault and guerilla warfare."[12] The murder tales offer prime examples of such authorial control but also feature Poe's best examples of perverseness. Perhaps this is not surprising if we recognize that Poe deploys perverseness as an instrument of control. Perverseness intrudes itself unpredictably, challenging readers' sympathetic identification and moral grounding. Through his first-person narrators, Poe lures readers into identifications that can only be described as perverse.

Machor has discovered that, by the 1850s, "reviewers were beginning to define narration as a technique in which deliberate unreliability was a legitimate aesthetic strategy and to alert readers to use that interpretive paradigm for making sense of potentially problematic and disruptive texts."[13] "The Black Cat" and "The Tell-Tale Heart" are relatively straightforward examples of Poe's trying out the potential of unreliable first-person narration. Under the guise of confessing to cold-blooded murder, the narrator-murderer encourages us to participate imaginatively in the crime. Both stories begin as confessions of murder. In "The Tell-Tale Heart" the narrator tells us as early as the second paragraph that he made up his mind to "take the life of the old man" (M 3: 792). The narrator of "The Black Cat" does not explicitly confess his crime at the beginning of his narrative, but he says enough for us to conclude that this is an execution eve confession. There is still plenty to surprise us at the end of these two tales—still plenty of suspense about what will be discovered by the police and especially how the discovery will come about.

Despite this apparent truthfulness, narratorial unreliability often represents the starting point for critiques of these tales and their narrators—with many taking the form of diagnoses of the first-person narrator-murderers. Sean Kelly, for example, argues that "The Black Cat" "reflects nineteenth-century anxieties about democratic sexual selfhood, and more specifically, those anxieties related to the perceived threat of onanism."[14] In fact, he claims that the "act of writing" in the tale "reflects the narrator's descent into onanistic insanity."[15] Other critics agree, at least about the narrator's unreliability. Susan Amper calls him a liar and supports her claim by producing alternative explanations for many of the events where the narrator's account doesn't make sense. She argues, for example, that the narrator murdered his wife at the time he claims to have killed his cat, and that his wife's outline in *bas relief* is revealed after the fire. The narrator then reinters his wife's body in the cellar, inadvertently walling up Pluto with her remains.[16]

John Cleman provides an interesting context for examining three of these tales—the nineteenth-century debate about a so-called partial insanity defense in murder cases.

Someone partially insane would seem rational in many, even most, respects but subject to some irrational fixation or impulse. Cleman cites "The Black Cat" and "The Imp of the Perverse" but thinks "The Tell-Tale Heart" "presents the most apparent evidence of Poe's use of the issues of the insanity defense."[17] The "characteristic form" and hyperrational narration in all three tales suggest "not confession but self-defense, an attempt to provide a rational account of apparently irrational events and behavior."[18] John Dern notes that, although Poe begins "The Tell-Tale Heart" "trying to evoke a modicum of doubt about his speaker's insanity, the point of the tale is to reveal slowly that the narrator is not only insane, but *horribly insane*, well beyond any impression the auditor originally had."[19] In his view, then, Poe intends readers to see through the narrator in order to arrive at a clinical diagnosis. In their reading of "The Black Cat," Vicki Hester and Emily Segir illustrate such a diagnosis by matching the narrator's personality and behavior against contemporary clinical indicators of psychopathy: "The narrator's attempt at a scientific, objective interpretation of the events in this story suggests a perverse mind at work—a mind that glosses over all personal accountability for his criminal behavior, a mind that treats his victims as meaningless, material objects."[20]

There is an implicit tendency in these analyses of Poe's murderous narrators to believe that, sooner or later in our reading, we free ourselves from a sympathetic—almost hypnotic—identification with the speaker and recognize him for what he is: a psychopathic murderer. I will argue that this experience of identification and disidentification can be perversely misleading—in part because disidentification occurs very late in the reading experience, in part because even after it occurs, we may still be subject to the narrators' (and Poe's) control. As Raymond DiSanza puts it, "A master like Poe can render readers complicit even in the most demented and disturbing of transgressions committed by the most demented and disturbing of protagonists."[21]

Poe recognized the perverse possibilities of unreliable narration—what today we would call the metafictional or metanarratorial potential of playing with readers and their expectations through our tendency toward sympathetic identification with first-person narrators. Poe also cannily includes direct appeals to the second person embedded in these tales—the reader—but he does so with varying degrees of directness. He stages "The Tell-Tale Heart" as a dialogue in which only the narrator speaks. "True!—nervous—very, very dreadfully nervous I had been and am," the tale begins, as if the narrator were responding to a comment his listener has just made; "but why *will* you say that I am mad?" (M 3: 792). Ostensibly, the ensuing unbroken monologue defends the narrator's implicit claim that he is not mad. Poe pitches "The Black Cat," on the other hand, as a death-bed or pre-execution confessional, a written narrative addressed to a large audience of readers. The narrator's purpose—deceptively simple—is "to place before the world" what he calls a "homely narrative" of "mere household events" (M 3: 849). In this case, Poe situates the actual reader within a group of readers—a confessor's book club—whose objectivity may be compromised by the preemptive pooh-poohing and the sense of safety as part of a group. In "The Imp of the Perverse," Poe combines both types of address and both projections of an audience. The narrative begins as an essay addressed to an audience of philosophers who are presumably reading the work. But when Poe shifts from essay to tale, he reimagines his audience, suddenly addressing himself personally and intimately to a single listener: "I have said thus much, that in some measure I may answer your question—that I may explain to you why I am here—that I may assign to you something that shall have at least the faint aspect of a cause for my wearing these fetters, and for my tenanting this cell of the condemned" (M 3: 1223–1224). Poe works a variation on such intimacy in "The Cask of Amontillado," which is addressed to an intimate and sympathetic second person—"You, who so well know the nature of my soul" (M 3: 1256). An interesting strategy on Poe's part: planting a reader at the very beginning of the text whom the narrator trusts to sympathize with his narrative of premeditated murder. Experimenting as he does in these four narratives with various relationships between narrator and listener-reader, Poe encourages us to identify with both parties. We are delivering a detailed description of a crime, as our continual experience of the word "I" suggests, but we are also being addressed by the "I" narrator. Split in two, we are addressing ourselves. Perverse indeed.

Gerald Kennedy has argued that Poe's detective hero "not only restores law and order to the world of mundane human affairs; he also explains the seemingly inexplicable, thereby demonstrating the ultimate comprehensibility of the world beyond the self."[22] But order and comprehensibility come with a price—identification with and appreciation for someone who can describe the steps needed to murder someone else in meticulous detail. In this respect, the first-person narrators of these murder tales serve much the same function as the detective in the detective tales. They reveal the crime in a similar, methodical manner. For our purposes as readers, they solve and recount the crime which they themselves have committed. Poe collapses the detective and the criminal into one character. That dual role helps shed light on the detective tales in which the detective, in order to solve the crime, also must recreate it.

In some obvious respects, "The Cask of Amontillado" represents another—albeit later—example of the first-person murder and confession tales, but in other respects it represents an intriguing departure from the pattern Poe had established in "The Tell-Tale Heart" and "The Black Cat." If those earlier tales at least seem to gesture toward a link between the Imp of the Perverse and morality because each narrator spontaneously sabotages what appears to be a perfect crime, "The Cask of Amontillado" works differently. There is no discovery scene and, oddly, no visit from the police. There is also no evidence that Montresor has felt any need to flaunt his murder—until, that is, fifty years after the fact. Has the Imp of the Perverse ceased to operate? Is Montresor simply immune? He does not act on impulse either in committing the murder or in confessing to it. The tale also might be considered more of an anti-detective tale than analytic detective fiction, although Montresor's painstaking account of the murder would not have been out of place as a reconstruction in one of the Dupin tales.

Moreover, the story addresses the question Irwin raises about reading and rereading. DiSanza emphasizes Montresor's manipulative power: "For generations readers have ignored their basic analytical impulses and inherently *trusted* an admitted murderer and Machiavellian rogue."[23] I want to build on this insight to analyze the reading and rereading experience—to see how exactly Poe and Montresor manipulate even the most

Dupin-like readers. I want to examine the experience of reading and rereading "The Cask of Amontillado," paying special attention to the ways Poe manipulates the reader's identification and sympathy, effectively playing a sadistic joke on even the most sophisticated re-reader of the tale. In effect, the Imp has gone underground and now governs both the act of narration and the act of reading. We identify with Montresor because we should not, because we have our own Imps of the Perverse affecting our reading practices.

"The Cask of Amontillado" works even better if readers know "The Black Cat" and "The Tell-Tale Heart." Such readers may expect the police to show up and discover Fortunato's body because Montresor leads them down into the catacombs and perhaps even raps on the wall behind which the dead body lies. First-time readers who expect this discovery will be surprised, therefore, by Montresor's last words. Poe has played a trick on his readers, especially his fans.

This is not the only way, however, that Poe fools readers. First-time readers probably identify and sympathize with Montresor, taking his word for the insult that prompts him to play what seems to be a practical joke on Fortunato. That identification and sympathy disappear in a flash for most readers but probably not until the very end of the tale—when, in his last statement, Montresor observes that Fortunato's bones have not been disturbed for "half of a century" (M 3: 1263). Poe has designed this abrupt flash forward to the present time of Montresor's narration to shock us. We were just there with him and with Fortunato, watching him build a wall that, perhaps, we still anticipate, he will tear down once he has scared Fortunato nearly but not quite to death. I'm not sure how many readers cling to this expectation. But since Montresor provides no details about why he seeks revenge, we have no reason to believe—although we may suspect—that we're in the mind of a murderer. This is part of Poe's own joke—providing little motive and certainly no justification for what ends up happening, instead letting the coercive power of first-person narration seduce us into identifying with Montresor.

Poe plays a similar trick on the reader of "Hop-Frog," encouraging us, as Paul Jones has deftly pointed out, to identify and sympathize with Hop-Frog until the very last lines of the story—when we realize, along with the spectators, that he has really burned the King and his ministers to a crisp.[24] "Hop-Frog" poses a special challenge to its readers, of course—the challenge that Nat Turner's violent rebellion or John Brown's raid posed for abolitionists: When is violence—and how much violence—justified in the service of a just cause? In the case of "Cask," we don't know the nature or extent of the injury Montresor has suffered at Fortunato's hands—it could be all in his mind—so we haven't the basis we have in "Hop-Frog" to judge the justification of Montresor's revenge. Justifiable homicide? Maybe so in "Hop-Frog," but much harder to say in "The Cask of Amontillado."

The abrupt end of Montresor's narrative is different. This is an anti-confession—an example of *braggadocio*. I got away with murder for fifty years, Montresor boasts. Of course, we recognize the mixed emotions he displays. When I teach the story, I enjoy debating with my students whether Montresor's narrative is motivated by a need to confess. Maybe so, but I've always thought that Poe is, rather, playing with the irony that committing murder isn't as much fun if you're the only one who knows you did it. A perfect murder—paradoxically—can't be perfect if never known. Unlike the detective tales, "The Cask of Amontillado" also includes no obvious antagonist. As I have noted, the tale includes no visit by the police. But, in effect, the cagy Poe does stage such a visit. As second-time readers, we revisit the catacombs. We are the police, and like the police in Poe's detective tales, we don't understand just how much Poe is manipulating and fooling us.

In the detective tales, as we know, Poe uses the police as foils, whose inability to recognize and read clues enables him, by contrast, to highlight Dupin's superior analytical ability. In "Cask," where there are no police, the reader plays the foil, albeit in a more nuanced way. Montresor details his crime. But readers may not understand that Fortunato's murder is the premise rather than the end of the tale. In this narrative, then, Poe employs the structure and premises of the detective tale, but his goal shifts from demonstrating Dupin's superiority to the police to demonstrating his own authorial superiority to the detective reader. "The Cask of Amontillado" might be considered a metadetective tale and a sophisticated, multilayered variation on the false confessionals.

Moreover, I have often had the experience, reading Poe, of feeling that he is always a step ahead of me, that every new insight in which I take such scholarly pride is one he has already thought of. As he describes his purpose in his review of Hawthorne's tales, he was acutely concerned with controlling the relationship among author, text, and reader. His desire to ensure that "during the hour of perusal the soul of the reader is at the writer's control" seems almost axiomatic, so it is especially intriguing to examine a later statement in the Hawthorne review, where Poe seems to give the reader a more creative role. In this reading experience, the reader's soul or mind is not controlled by the writer but participates in the creative process as a kind of coauthor. Thus, he contrasts two kinds of reading:

> [T]he true originality—true in respect of its purposes—is that which, in bringing out the half-formed, the reluctant, or the unexpressed fancies of mankind, or in exciting the more delicate pulses of the heart's passion, or in giving birth to some universal sentiment or instinct in embryo, thus combines with the pleasurable effect of *apparent* novelty, a real egotistic delight. The reader, in the case first supposed, (that of the absolute novelty,) is excited, but embarrassed, disturbed, in some degree even pained at his own want of perception, at his own folly in not having himself hit upon the idea. In the second case, his pleasure is doubled. He is filled with an intrinsic and extrinsic delight. He feels and intensely enjoys the seeming novelty of the thought, enjoys it as really novel, as absolutely original with the writer—*and* himself. They two, he fancies, have, alone of all men, thought thus. They two have, together, created this thing. Henceforward there is a bond of sympathy between them, a sympathy which irradiates every subsequent page of the book. (ER: 580–581)

Of course, if we read carefully, we notice that this feeling of sympathy is only something that the reader "fancies." This is part of Poe's intention. He does not really cede control of the reader's mind or soul. He only seems to do so. He is the master illusionist. The reader contributes to the reading that the author has been aiming at from the beginning. As Machor puts it, "Poe defined this intimate bond with the reader by taking away as much as he gave"; the reader was "induced to feel a bond of achievement that remained an illusion, staged by the writer who has kept the true nature of the accomplishment—the wires controlling the scene—hidden behind the curtain of his or her craft."[25]

With that in mind, I want to look closely at our second reading of "The Cask of Amontillado," which I think brilliantly illustrates the ways a writer can seduce a reader into a "bond of sympathy" in which aesthetic delight overrides moral sympathy. As rereaders, we know the outcome. We know Montresor is a murderer and, arguably, proud of himself and his ingenuity. We still have no reason to sympathize with him. We still don't know why he wanted revenge. As second readers, surely we put up our own wall, keeping our distance from this cold-blooded narrator. In short, we're literary critics. We're judgmental. We're the police. We're even the judge and the jury.

Not so fast. As I've said, first-time readers are unlikely to "get" any of the jokes that Montresor sprinkles along the narrative track of the story, like breadcrumbs leading us not back to the beginning but forward to the end. In this respect, we are much like Fortunato, who, as Elaine Hartnell-Mottram argues, "is murdered without any real resistance—or even protest—on his part because his normative approach to life does not allow him to be suspicious about what is said to him."[26] Hartnell-Mottram gives readers a little more credit for their insight, citing "the authority of the reader to complete the text by laying claim to its 'real meaning,'" although she does not distinguish between first-time and subsequent readers.[27] As second readers, after we realize what Montresor has actually done—murdered Fortunato—we are in a position to appreciate the jokes he makes at Fortunato's expense. We may be appalled at what has happened to Fortunato, but at the same time we find ourselves distanced from him. When we read the story for a second time, or, like detectives, think back over the story after we finish it, we see the many hints and jokes Poe and Montresor have left for us. As John Dern asserts, "Although a killer, Montresor seems impish."[28] Poe and Montresor have designed these hints and jokes to exceed Fortunato's immediate understanding. They also encourage the perceptive second reader to feel superior to Fortunato. Fortunato, of course, will have plenty of time to think back over his evening with Montresor and to "reread" everything his murderer has said and done. Surely this constitutes a crucial feature of Montresor's vengeful plan—putting Fortunato in a position very much like our own, as rereaders of the plot that ensnared him. Surely, he will agonize over all the clues he missed.

"I shall not die of a cough," Fortunato assures Montresor, who replies, "True—true" (M 3: 1259). What might seem a simple and sympathetic agreement with Fortunato's diagnosis alludes to the alternative cause of death Montresor is planning. "I drink . . . to the buried that repose around us," Fortunato says. "And I to your long life," adds Montresor (M 3: 1259). We may think Montresor is being ironic, since we know he plans to kill Fortunato, but in fact he does want his enemy to live—and suffer—a long time. He is not just a murderer, after all, but a torturer as well. And so he goes on, describing his coat of arms, the huge human foot of gold that crushes a serpent—Fortunato—that has inflicted a "thousand injuries" and finally "ventured upon insult" (M 3: 1259, 1256). It is unlikely that Fortunato would recognize himself as the serpent, although even a first-time reader might. But few readers, and certainly not Fortunato, would appreciate the wordplay implicit in the term "Amontillado." As Elena Baraban points out, the root of the word (*mons, montis*) makes it a metaphor for mound or mountain, as in the mounds of bones, eventually to include Fortunato's, strewn around the catacomb.[29] Second-time readers might recognize this metaphor, but it's more likely that only readers who have researched scholarship on the tale or are using an annotated edition will get the joke. In other words, Poe has a little in store for even the most knowledgeable readers, but even so, he is subtly coercing us into identifying with Montresor and with his ingenious murder plot. Second-time readers are much more likely to get the joke of Montresor's offering Fortunato a flagon of De Grâve and to understand the implications of what he calls his family's motto: translated, "No one provokes me with impunity" (M 3: 1260).

Finally—a literary critic's dream—Montresor produces a trowel after Fortunato gives him the secret sign of the Masons. Montresor does not seem to recognize the sign. " 'Then you are not of the brotherhood,' " Fortunato replies. " 'You are not of the masons.' " " 'Yes, yes,' " Montresor says, " 'yes, yes.' " " 'You? Impossible! A mason?' " Fortunato responds, taunting Montresor with his lower status (M 3: 1260). Blinded somewhat by his arrogance, Fortunato doesn't get the joke when Montresor produces the trowel from beneath his cloak. Nor do we, the first time through the story. But now, of course, we enjoy the joke at Fortunato's expense, and we recognize in his condescension what Montresor meant when he referred to Fortunato's venturing upon insult. Terence Whalen notes the larger context of Montresor's joke—the anti-Masonic movement in nineteenth-century America, a "crusade against elitism, especially because many Freemasons, like Fortunato in the story, were men of power and wealth."[30] It is difficult not to appreciate Montresor's ingenious humor at Fortunato's expense and to think that perhaps brandishing the trowel is warranted—that is, to lose sight momentarily of the endgame he has planned.

What intrigues me in this rereading experience is that, even while knowing what is going to happen, we still get seduced into appreciating Montresor's wit and ingenuity—and, most important, our own ingenuity and acumen as discerning readers. In fact, the better we are as critical readers, the more we smile and laugh at Fortunato's expense and at the expense of naive readers—including our own students—who can't see or get the jokes. So Poe suckers us all over again, as if he has anticipated the critical turn of modern literary studies. If we learn to read ironically and especially to distrust the unreliable narrator, he will still find a way to reverse the poles of this ironic relation. In the process he demonstrates how the fictional world of the tale and imaginative world of our reading are rooted in the same emotional and psychological register—a "bond of sympathy," and a sadistic one at that. We abandon the ethical and moral register for the aesthetic one, enjoying the form and ingenuity of the tale despite our knowledge of what is going to happen.

It is axiomatic that a good detective must be able to imagine the worst crimes in order to solve them. I said at the beginning that "The Cask of Amontillado" is not a detective story. It might be more accurate to say that "Cask" is a tale of murder with an implied detective—along the lines of an implied reader. In fact, I think Poe casts the reader in the role of detective. The first time through the story, we just happen upon the murder and the crime scene. So, naturally, we begin to work from the end back to the beginning, tracing the evidentiary steps that lead us—now more knowledgeable—up to the end that we already know. Here, we don't just have the illusion that the murderer is telling us his story through the clues he leaves behind. He is actually telling us the story of the murder—how precisely he did it.

We run the risk, like the detective, of becoming accomplices after the fact—at least in imagination. To analyze the tale and especially the psychosis that infects Montresor, we have to put ourselves in his place. We have to be capable, in some sense, of Fortunato's murder. A decade ago I analyzed the increasingly intimate relationship between Montresor and Fortunato for its "queer" implications—specifically, as an account of repression and homophobia in which Montresor violently rejects the possibility of "brotherhood," or any other intimate male-male relationship, with Fortunato.[31] Here, I want to go a step further and situate the reader—myself—in this potential "bond of sympathy."

The deeper they penetrate into the catacombs, the more intimately identified Montresor and Fortunato become, as if engaged in a symbiotic performance in keeping with their theatrical dress. Montresor repeatedly plays with Fortunato, seducing him so perfectly that Fortunato always makes the next move on his own. When Fortunato gives the Masonic sign, Montresor insists that he belongs to the brotherhood, but of course he means a different order of masons—whose sign is the trowel he will use to bury Fortunato alive. The sign reveals more than Montresor imagines—namely, the violence with which he refuses brotherhood, Masonic or otherwise, with this other man. Montresor turns the secret sign against Fortunato, refusing to meet the other man's gaze under the sign of brotherhood. This is a cruising moment—a sign and response that not only refuses intimacy but promises a sadistic-masochistic exploitation of the other man's feelings. Where does that leave me? I have been inclined, as I read, to identify and sympathize with Fortunato; I have no reason to think he deserves what is going to happen to him. At the same time, it is hard not to identify with Montresor and especially with his ingenuity. Getting Montresor's jokes makes me feel superior to Fortunato. As a critic—or critic-detective—I'm with Montresor, who keeps flattering my critical acumen. Thus, I identify with Montresor and with the ingenuity of his "masonic" sign. He refuses brotherhood with Fortunato, but in the process he offers brotherhood to me in a different order of masons. Since I know the joke by knowing the ending, I accept his invitation and thereby identify with a sadist.

After Montresor shackles Fortunato and begins building the wall between them, he and I stay finely attuned to Fortunato's every noise and motion. Montresor enjoys the coincidence of his masonry work and Fortunato's struggle—the "low moaning cry from the depth of the recess," the "furious vibrations of the chain," the "succession of loud and shrill screams, bursting suddenly from the throat of the chained form" (M 3: 1262). He revels in the full experience of his sadistic plot. His progressive identification with Fortunato and his agony, as well as his disappointment when Fortunato stops making noise, makes clear his desire to prolong the pleasure he derives from this sadistic relationship. In this torturous dance, Montresor gets into a rhythm with Fortunato. "I replied to the yells of him who clamored," he reports. "I re-echoed, I aided, I surpassed them in volume and in strength. I did this, and the clamorer grew still" (M 3: 1262). This is identification with a vengeance. Montresor makes himself *like* the other man as much as he can, but without having to let such mimicry implicate him in any physical or emotional *liking*. He takes pleasure in Fortunato's agony, even echoing his screams, all the while he walls up the man who produces them—so much so that his heart grows "sick" when Fortunato stops struggling (M 3: 1263). Indeed, his pleasure intensifies, it seems to me, as he walls off the other man. The act of walling off makes identification at one remove possible.

Readers who remember "The Black Cat" and "The Tell-Tale Heart," furthermore, may catch Poe's subtle joke when, after Fortunato produces such "loud and shrill screams" that Montresor trembles and then uses his rapier to "grope with it about the recess" where Fortunato is chained, he catches himself, places his hand upon the "solid fabric of the catacombs," and feels "satisfied" that Fortunato's body will be secure (M 3: 1262). Montresor's gesture, testing the wall, recalls the narrators of the earlier tales, except that, here, there are no police. In effect, Montresor successfully suppresses the Imp of the Perverse in a situation where we might expect the imp to strike. In our roles as witnesses and, potentially, the police, first-time readers surely wonder why the imp doesn't appear under precisely the circumstances that provoked him in "The Imp of the Perverse." Reading the tale a second time, we may feel as relieved as Montresor or depressed by the thought that Fortunato's body and Montresor's crime will not be detected.

Just as Poe illustrates the role of repression in this male–male relationship, I think he also puts the reader in the squeamish position of negotiating the line between identification with and rejection of the two male characters. Whose side are we on? With whom do we identify? Do we really want to take the victim's place? If not, can we imagine ourselves in Montresor's position? Hasn't the process of detection coerced us into a double identification? I don't have definitive answers for these questions. This is less the case at the end of "The Black Cat" or "The Tell-Tale Heart." In those tales, too, Poe coerces us into participating imaginatively in murder, but I doubt that this participation carries over into a second reading. "The Cask of Amontillado," on the other hand, represents a masterful example of a fiction that keeps us circulating between and among possibilities. The ending always forces us back to the beginning. The beginning drives us toward the ending. We feel sympathy for Fortunato, but every time we read the story—as critic detectives—we are encouraged to identify with his murderer. The truth is, I suspect, that being a detective or literary critic is uncomfortably close to *being* a murderer—and a murderer's victim. Poe himself has the Imp of the Perverse working through Montresor in this brilliantly perverse tale, but the Imp couldn't do Poe's work until he also resided in us. We identify with the Imp and his Perverseness precisely because we know we should not.

Notes

1. John T. Irwin, *The Mystery to a Solution: Poe, Borges, and the Analytic Detective Story* (Baltimore: Johns Hopkins University Press, 1994), 1.
2. J. Gerald Kennedy, *Poe, Death, and the Life of Writing* (New Haven, CT: Yale University Press, 1987), 132.
3. Judith Fetterley, *The Resisting Reader: A Feminist Approach to American Fiction* (Bloomington: Indiana University Press, 1978).
4. Joseph J. Moldenhauer, "Murder as a Fine Art: Basic Connections between Poe's Aesthetics, Psychology, and Moral Vision," *PMLA* 83, no. 1 (1968): 294.
5. Michael J. S. Williams, *A World of Words: Language and Displacement in the Fiction of Edgar Allan Poe* (Durham, NC: Duke University Press, 1988), 33.
6. Jonathan Elmer, *Reading at the Social Limit: Affect, Mass Culture, and Edgar Allan Poe* (Stanford, CA: Stanford University Press, 1995), 130.
7. Elmer, *Reading at the Social Limit*, 130–131.
8. Stanley Cavell, "Being Odd, Getting Even (Descartes, Emerson, Poe)," in *The American Face of Edgar Allan Poe*, ed. Shawn Rosenheim and Stephen Rachman (Baltimore: Johns Hopkins University Press, 1995), 19.
9. Russell Sbriglia, "Feeling Right, Doing Wrong: Poe, Perversity, and the Cunning of Unreason," *Poe Studies* 46 (2013): 8, 16.
10. Christopher Benfey, "Poe and the Unreadable: 'The Black Cat' and 'The Tell-Tale Heart,'" in *New Essays on Poe's Major Tales*, ed. Kenneth Silverman (New York: Cambridge University Press, 1993), 37.
11. James L. Machor, "Mastering Audiences: Poe, Fiction, and Antebellum Reading," *ESQ: A Journal of the American Renaissance* 47, no. 3 (2001): 169.
12. Machor, "Mastering Audiences," 172.
13. James L. Machor, "Poetics as Ideological Hermeneutics: America Fiction and the Historicized Reader of the Early Nineteenth Century," *Reader* 25 (Spring 1991): 57.
14. Sean J. Kelly, "'I Blush, I Burn, I Shudder, While I Pen the Damnable Atrocity': Penning Perversion in Poe's 'The Black Cat,'" *Edgar Allan Poe Review* 13, no. 2 (Fall 2012): 81.
15. Kelly, "'I Blush,'" 92.
16. Susan Amper, "Untold Story: The Lying Narrator in 'The Black Cat,'" *Studies in Short Fiction* 29, no. 4 (Fall 1992): 476.
17. John Cleman, "Irresistible Impulses: Edgar Allan Poe and the Insanity Defense," *American Literature* 63, no. 4 (December 1991): 630.
18. Cleman, "Irresistible Impulses," 630.
19. John Dern, "Poe's Public Speakers: Rhetorical Strategies in 'The Tell-Tale Heart' and 'The Cask of Amontillado,'" *Edgar Allan Poe Review* 2, no. 2 (Fall 2001): 59.
20. Vicki Hester and Emily Segir, "'The Black Cat' and Current Forensic Psychology," *Edgar Allan Poe Review* 15, no. 2 (Autumn 2014): 177.
21. Raymond DiSanza, "On Memory, Forgetting, and Complicity in 'The Cask of Amontillado,'" *Edgar Allan Poe Review* 15, no. 2 (Autumn 2014): 200.

22. J. Gerald Kennedy, "The Limits of Reason: Poe's Deluded Detectives," *American Literature* 47, no. 2 (May 1975): 185.
23. DiSanza, "On Memory, Forgetting, and Complicity in 'The Cask of Amontillado,'" 198.
24. Paul Christian Jones, "The Danger of Sympathy: Edgar Allan Poe's 'Hop-Frog' and the Abolitionist Rhetoric of Pathos," *Journal of American Studies* 35, no. 2 (August 2001): 251.
25. Machor, "Mastering Audiences," 174.
26. Elaine Hartnell-Mottram, "Poe and the Gothic of the Normal: Thinking 'Inside the Box,'" *Gothic Studies* 12, no. 2 (November 2010): 44.
27. Hartnell-Mottram, "Poe and the Gothic of the Normal," 45.
28. Dern, "Poe's Public Speakers," 62.
29. Elena V. Baraban, "The Motive for Murder in 'The Cask of Amontillado' by Edgar Allan Poe," *Rocky Mountain Review of Language and Literature* 58, no. 2 (2004): 55.
30. Terence Whalen, *Edgar Allan Poe and the Masses: The Political Economy of Literature in Antebellum America* (Princeton, NJ: Princeton University Press, 1999), 99.
31. Leland S. Person, "Queer Poe: The Tell-Tale Heart of His Fiction," *Poe Studies* 41 (2008): 7–30.

Bibliography

Cook, Michael. *Narratives of Enclosure in Detective Fiction: The Locked Room Mystery*. New York: Palgrave Macmillan, 2011.

Dayan, Joan. *Fables of Mind: An Inquiry into Poe's Fiction*. New York: Oxford University Press, 1987.

Elmer, Jonathan. *Reading at the Social Limit: Affect, Mass Culture, and Edgar Allan Poe*. Stanford, CA: Stanford University Press, 1995.

Fisher, Benjamin Franklin. *The Cambridge Introduction to Edgar Allan Poe*. New York: Cambridge University Press, 2008.

Gruesser, John Cullen. *Race, Gender and Empire in American Detective Fiction*. Jefferson, NC: McFarland, 2013.

Hayes, Kevin J., ed. *The Cambridge Companion to Edgar Allan Poe*. New York: Cambridge University Press, 2002.

Hoffman, Daniel. *Poe Poe Poe Poe Poe Poe Poe*. New York: Doubleday, 1972.

Irwin, John T. *The Mystery to a Solution: Poe, Borges, and the Analytic Detective Story*. Baltimore: Johns Hopkins University Press, 1994.

Kennedy, J. Gerald, *Poe, Death, and the Life of Writing*. New Haven, CT: Yale University Press, 1987.

Kennedy, J. Gerald, and Liliane Weissberg, eds. *Romancing the Shadow: Poe and Race*. New York: Oxford University Press, 2001.

Ketterer, David. *The Rationale of Deception in Poe*. Baton Rouge: Louisiana State University Press, 1979.

Machor, James L. *Reading Fiction in Antebellum America: Informed Response and Reception Histories, 1820–1865*. Baltimore: Johns Hopkins University Press, 2011.

May, Charles E. *Edgar Allan Poe: A Study of the Short Fiction*. Boston: Twayne, 1991.

Peeples, Scott. *Edgar Allan Poe Revisited*. New York: Twayne, 1998.

Rosenheim, Shawn, and Stephen Rachman, eds. *The American Face of Edgar Allan Poe*. Baltimore: Johns Hopkins University Press, 1995.

Rosenheim, Shawn James. *The Cryptographic Imagination: Secret Writing from Edgar Poe to the Internet*. Baltimore: Johns Hopkins University Press, 1997.

Silverman, Kenneth, ed. *New Essays on Poe's Major Tales*. New York: Cambridge University Press, 1993.

Thompson, G. R. *Poe's Fiction: Romantic Irony in the Gothic Tales*. Madison: University of Wisconsin Press, 1973.

Whalen, Terence. *Edgar Allan Poe and the Masses: The Political Economy of Literature in Antebellum America*. Princeton, NJ: Princeton University Press, 1999.

Williams, Michael J. S. *A World of Words: Language and Displacement in the Fiction of Edgar Allan Poe*. Durham, NC: Duke University Press, 1988.

Zimmerman, Brett. *Edgar Allan Poe: Rhetoric and Style*. Montreal: McGill-Queen's University Press, 2005.

CHAPTER 16

POE'S SURVIVAL STORIES AS DYING COLONIALISMS

MATT SANDLER

New Americanist literary criticism has long read Edgar Allan Poe within the historical context of antebellum racial and colonial ideology. Paradoxically, this scholarship has relied on Toni Morrison's interpretation of race in Poe as a kind of "dehistoricizing allegory."[1] This friction between historicism and allegory in Poe criticism has proven enormously productive. However, it has also tended to limit the scope of Poe's work to the United States and its territorial ambitions. This means that Poe's deep reading into what was then coming into focus as world literature, and his vast posthumous influence on that literature, both fall outside the purview of interests shared by Morrison and the New Americanists. This chapter takes a different view of these contradictions (historicism vs. allegory, American vs. world literature) by returning to Poe's own engagements with certain aspects of period historical writing, specifically its notions of the "course of empire." Poe consistently incorporates details from long-durational narratives of empire into short stories about extreme individual experience in ways that suggest he had a dialectical sense of the relation between history and allegory. This chapter takes as its starting point that Poe's perspective is metahistorical, in the sense that his aesthetic works through a formal critique of historical discourse.[2] This aspect of Poe's work has important implications for understanding his reliance on and play with antebellum fantasies of "Manifest Destiny" and white supremacy. It also helps explain the attraction of Poe's work for critics and artists seeking to represent and intervene in the history of slavery and colonialism.

Unlike the great historical thinkers of the late eighteenth and early nineteenth century, Poe had little inclination to sweeping narrative forms. Instead, history enters his work in fragments, often borrowed from the vast visions of widely read historians. He was drawn to historical narratives which centered on the "course of empires," examples of which include Edward Gibbon's *History of the Decline and Fall of the Roman Empire* (1776) and Comte de Volney's *The Ruins, or a Survey of the Revolutions of Empires* (1791). References to these authors appear across Poe's work. His most direct comments on the subject often pertain to his resistance to didacticism in art, such as when he condemns "the small, second-hand, Gibbon-ish pedantry of Byron" in an 1842 review of Longfellow's *Ballads* (ER: 692).

The productive friction between historicism and allegory in recent Poe criticism draws some of its energy from the fact that his antipathy to bogus moralism extended to historical writing. In an unsigned review of "The New York Gallery of the Fine Arts," from *The Broadway Journal*, the author writes of Thomas Cole's "The Course of Empire" series:

> We dislike exceedingly Cole's allegorical landscapes in the New York Gallery. The pictures in themselves are truly beautiful, but the plan of them is against nature. Their beauty is marred by being seen together. We perceive immediately that we are imposed upon. Instead of looking upon beautiful landscapes, we discern that they are sermons in print; essays in gilt frames.[3]

Here again we find an apparently definitive argument against the use of art in the service of synoptic and ethical historical vision. Poe would have been especially attracted to Cole's series by newspaper advertisements which touted the exhibit with some lines from Byron's *Childe Harold's Pilgrimage*: "First Freedom, and then Glory—when that fails,/ Wealth, vice, corruption,—barbarism at last."[4] A careful reader of Byron, Poe would have known this crucial stanza's argument for allegorical brevity. In Byron's glibly didactic, "Gibbon-ish" view, the rise and fall of empires was "the moral of all human tales." He goes on to make a case for poetry over history: "History with all her volumes vast,/ Hath but *one* page,—'tis better written here."[5] For Poe the allegorist and the advocate of concision, this premise might have held some significant attraction. However, in both the reviews of Longfellow and of the New York Gallery, we find instead resistance to allegorical moralizing insofar as it eclipses other, more sensational aesthetic effects. The unsigned *Broadway Journal* piece presents the problem as having to do with proportion, and the scale of the human in contrast with that of historical allegory: "The men in ['The Course of Empire' series] are not seen at all when they are viewed at a proper distance, and if seen, they are subordinates, not principals, as they should be in a performance which professes to point to a moral." Here we find an argument for the scale of the human as incommensurate with the morality of long-durational narratives of empire. This problem is crucial to understanding the role of historical formalism in Poe's aesthetic practice. Hyperaware of their time- and space-bound perspective as sensate individuals, his narrators are doomed to misapprehend the large-scale historical processes shaping their experiences. They are close-up renderings of people unhappily caught in a Thomas Cole landscape they cannot appreciate.

The refined shape of historical narrative in the early decades of the nineteenth century exacerbated this problem for Poe. Course of empires thinking mixed two key models of history: cyclical and progressive, the first itself declining and the second on the rise in Poe's day. In the context of increasingly contested historical formalisms, how could one know whether one was living through a period of ascent or decline? In the antebellum

US context, one might have wondered whether the historical tumult of frontier war, sectional conflict, and financial panics were the result of civilizational progress or the death throes of European colonialism. In the context of the age of revolutions, historical understanding came to seem increasingly urgent, and yet definitive figurations of individual lives within history proved elusive. These ambiguities define Poe's aesthetic practice: the heated interiority of his narrators and the anxious effects on his readers derive from his critical relation to the artificial morality of historical narrative.

This chapter examines two short stories, "A Descent into the Maelström" (1841) and "The Pit and the Pendulum" (1842), for references to antebellum debates about pre-Anglo-Saxon, specifically Viking and Spanish, New World colonization, respectively. The effect of foreboding in these tales relies on and exploits the unstable rhetoric around race, colonialism, civilization, and barbarism. Both stories represent the perspective of a seemingly doomed man—a fisherman nearly shipwrecked in the Norwegian Sea and a prisoner of the late Spanish Inquisition. The stories thus play on popular narratives of extreme experience and on the antebellum interest in death.[6] Both narrators are talented obsessives, ratiocinating the environmental and political forces that seem to control their fate. Yet at the same time, their foreshortened historical vision gets them into trouble. Both dwell on the tangential relation between their agency and their survival in ways that displace the question of their guilt or innocence, and likewise their implication in civilizational rise and fall. Finally, both ultimately cheat death through a combination of reasoning and good fortune. The narrative suspense in each tale relies on copiously elaborated spatial forms against which white narrators "signal" their "modernity," in Morrison's terms, but which also hold readers' attention on the sublimity of premodern topography and architecture.[7]

Poe frames these moments of jeopardy and survival in fragments of historical narrative to question both the premise of the United States as rising empire and the importance of the individual in US ideology. "A Descent into the Maelstrom" and "The Pit and the Pendulum" figure the individual not as a living expression of national ideals, but as the subject and object of nation-building violence, in which fate is absolutely contingent. As a way out of the elaborately constructed deathtraps of these tales, the conclusion turns to Poe's influence on African diasporic thinking, in particular that of Frantz Fanon, whose account of the psychological predicament of the colonized eerily parallels the frenetic interiority of Poe's narrators, and whose theory of colonialism offers a counter to grand narratives of the "course of empire."

"A Descent into the Maelström": The Viking Conquest and White Guilt

The most obvious influence on "A Descent into the Maelström" (1841) is not historical writing but Coleridge's *Rime of the Ancient Mariner*, which critics have read as an allegory for the French Revolution and British colonialism. Coleridge's meditation on guilt draws these interpretations with its symbolic suggestiveness. The narrative poem resolves in a totalizing but also individualizing ethical certitude ("He prayeth best, who loveth best/All things both great and small").[8] The Bridegroom leaves the scene of the poem a "sadder and a wiser man" having heard the Ancient Mariner's story.[9] Poe's story, on the other hand, offers no such reassurance, and it concludes with his narrator complaining that no one ever believes him. Poe constructs "A Descent into the Maelström" as an allegory out of a welter of descriptive detail—geographical, oceanographical, and ethnographical. In taking a scientific interest in accurate representation, Poe abandons the question of his mariner's guilt or innocence, giving his oblique references to the age of revolutions and colonial venturing an especially uncertain moral and political valence.

"A Descent into the Maelström" opens with the kind of racialized color symbolism that draws Morrison's interest. The Nordic setting requires that Poe make the links between color and racial terror without the real figure of Black people. Like the howling emptiness of the South Pole at the end of *The Narrative of Arthur Gordon Pym*, the whiteness of the aging fisherman's beard indicates the extremity of his experience: "You suppose me a *very* old man—but I am not. It took less than a single day to change these hairs from jetty black to white, to weaken my limbs, and to unstring my nerves, so that I tremble at the least exertion, and am frightened at a shadow" (M 2: 578). Poe sets this whiteness against the blackness of the Maelström, and his narrator reads the landscape in racial terms: "I looked dizzily, and beheld a wide expanse of ocean, whose waters wore so inky a hue as to bring at once to my mind the Nubian geographer's account of the Mare Tenebrarum. A panorama more deplorably desolate no human imagination can conceive" (M 2: 578–579). Poe's insistent application of the cultural logic of racial terror seems scattershot, randomly applied in conjuring a general mood of fear and anxiety.

His ancient mariner registers the exoticism of the Norwegian setting by enumerating the names of the "small, bleak-looking . . . hideously craggy and barren" islands surrounding the Maelström: "Yonder are Iflesen, Hoeyholm, Kieldholm, Suarven, and Buckholm. Farther off—between Moskoe and Vurrgh—are Otterholm, Flimen, Sandflesen, and Skarholm. These are the true names of places—but why it has been thought necessary to name them at all, is more than either you or I can understand" (M 2: 579). The old man sets up Norwegian seafaring and map-making as inaccessibly prehistoric, what Cole refers to in the first canvas of "The Course of Empire" as "The Savage State." Poe's self-reference here is the height of absurdity: he names these places to drown the reader in syllables marking the incomprehensible distance between the time of the tale and that of Norway's founding.

However ancient their surroundings, the Norse fisherman admits he and his brother took the risk of fishing near the Maelström out of modern, calculating interest: "In all violent eddies at sea there is good fishing"; "we made it a matter of desperate speculation—the risk of life standing instead for labor, and courage answering for capital" (M 2: 583). This economic motive echoes the psychology of the colonist—venturing into the black unknown in search of surplus value. The "giddy" feeling the Maelström inspires is inseparable from this substitution of "risk" for "labor." The perceptual and historical tricks continue with the narrator perceiving a kind of synaesthetic connection between the Maelström and a specifically US geography: "As the old man spoke, I became aware of a loud and gradually increasing sound, like the moaning of a vast herd of buffaloes upon an American prairie" (M 2: 580). Poe thus gives the Maelström an uncanny quality, at first representing its forbidding sublimity, then making it recognizable through one of the most the familiar tropes of frontier aesthetics. These details recenter the tale in contemporary and specifically US concerns, in which the Maelström stands in for the frontier, and forays into it represent a mode of speculation.

Antebellum readers would have seen an obvious connection between New World settler colonialism and Nordic seafaring. In the late 1830s, Carl Christian Rafn, a Danish philologist working with the Royal Society of Northern Antiquaries of Copenhagen, began publishing his research into the pre-Columbian discovery of America by the Vikings. His 1838 pamphlet, *America Discovered in the Tenth Century*, contained a précis of this work, which combined interpretations of medieval Norse sagas alongside other forms of archeological and geographical evidence suggesting that "ancient Northmen" had inhabited the Northeastern United States. Rafn's claims had a significant impact on nineteenth-century US culture; his work was reprinted by journals and newspapers, recounted in lyceum lectures, and reflected on by writers and intellectuals like Edward Everett, George Bancroft, and Sarah Orne Jewett. Poe would have come across these ideas while editing the September 1839 issue of *Burton's Gentlemen's Magazine*, where Hall Grandgent's review of the work of the Royal Society of Northern Antiquaries appears just after Poe's story "The Fall of the House of Usher." Grandgent poses Rafn et al.'s research controversially:

> We suppose that many persons will be greatly mortified to learn that America was discovered as early as the tenth century, which is several centuries previous to its discovery by Columbus. His fame is held so sacred by a portion of mankind that obstacles are thrown in the way of any attempt to prove it was visited long before his birth.[10]

The "mortifying" effect of prospective Viking discovery was much more complex than Grandgent suggests; its implications extended well beyond the romantic idealizing of Columbus to deep historical logics of civilization.

Annette Kolodny's history of the theory of Viking discovery, *In Search of First Contact* (2012), finds Rafn's theory instrumentalized in arguments about the primitivism of Native American indigenous peoples. In an 1841 essay entitled "The Discoveries of the Northmen," William Gilmore Simms offers an especially egregious instance of this fantastical thinking:

> A judicious artist would make a most romantic tale of that colony of Green Erin [on] the shores of Carolina and Georgia;—showing how, driven by stress of weather, and finding so lovely a land, greener than their own beloved Island, they pitched their

tents for good:—how they built cities, how they flourished amid songs and dances; with now and then a faction fight by way of reminiscence:—how, suddenly, the fierce red men of the south-west came down upon them in howling thousands, captured their women, slaughtered their men, and drove them to their fortresses:—how they fought to the last, and perished to a man! And, in this history, you have the history of the Tumuli, the works of defence and worship—the thousand proofs with which our land is covered, of a genius and an industry immeasurably superior to any thing that the Indian inhabitants of this country ever attempted.[11]

Simms was not the only nineteenth-century American writer to credit the "Northmen" for the achievements of pre-Columbian civilizations.[12] According to Kolodny, this dubious and overblown fantasy of white European settlement served to distract white middle-class readers from the controversies around Jacksonian Indian removal policy in the South: "However disturbing the Trail of Tears and the ongoing Seminole Wars, Simms's article told of an earlier and even more horrific aggression."[13] Kolodny also notices an historical anxiety about how Native peoples succeeded in repelling pre-Columbian European settlers—a haunting counterhistory for white intellectuals invested in colonialism as the prevailing spirit of progress and rationality. The resonance between the roar of the Maelström and the murmur of buffalo points to this recursive and pseudohistorical connection.

I submit that the Nordic setting of "A Descent into the Maelström" connects the drama of the tale to what Grandgent calls the "mortified" aspect of the white reading public of the antebellum decades. The Viking background gives a kind of millennial depth to the suggestive racialized fear that organized antebellum white people against black and Native populations. Readers steeped in narratives of the course of empires would have found much to think about in passages like the following:

Our progress downward, at each revolution, was slow, but very perceptible.

Looking about me upon the wide waste of liquid ebony on which we were thus borne, I perceived that our boat was not the only object in the embrace of the whirl. Both above and below us were visible fragments of vessels, large masses of building timber and trunks of trees, with many smaller articles, such as pieces of house furniture, broken boxes, barrels and staves. I have already described the unnatural curiosity which had taken the place of my original terrors. It appeared to grow upon me as I drew nearer and nearer to my dreadful doom. I now began to watch, with a strange interest, the numerous things that floated in our company. I *must* have been delirious—for I even sought *amusement* in speculating upon the relative velocities of their several descents toward the foam below. (M 2: 591)

Ratiocination, here as elsewhere in Poe, has side effects. The passage begins with a kind of boilerplate conservative theory of history: "Our progress downward, at each revolution, was slow but very perceptible." The black and revolutionary Maelström smashes up the trappings of civilized domesticity.[14] However, Poe's narrator, in taking an analytical and ironic perspective on his seemingly certain doom, ultimately arrives at the insight that saves him: he can rotate around the vortex longer if he attaches himself to a barrel rather than staying in the boat. Though his narrative is framed in fragmentary historical detail, the Norse fisherman's survival depends on his studied detachment from the allegory of his situation and on his appreciation of the motion of bodies in space.

When the Norse fisherman's ordeal is over, he returns unrecognizable to friends, who, because of his whitened hair, "knew me no more than they would have known a traveller from the spirit-land" (M 2: 594). What knowledge he has gained possesses little value, as he closes his tale concerned about its believability; he feels none of the consolation taken by the narrator of "MS. Found in a Bottle" (1833), who writes, "a curiosity to penetrate the mysteries of these awful regions, predominates even over my despair, and will reconcile me to the most hideous aspect of death" (M 2: 145). Poe takes this interest in knowledge and experience at the expense of the question of guilt that so preoccupies Coleridge. The fisherman offers little in the way of expiation throughout. He carefully notes that he and his brother did not bring along their children on their venture: "we had not the heart to let the young ones get into the danger" (M 2: 584). Yet he never mentions them at the end. Later as the ship is going down, when the narrator cannot convince his brother of his plan for survival, they decide wordlessly to part in a moment of absolute seafaring independence: "with a bitter struggle, I resigned him to his fate" (M 2: 593). In these moments, familial relations are dispatched so as to minimize the narrator's guilt. And yet the loneliness and estrangement of his survival lead the artist Mr. Wyatt in "The Oblong Box" (1844) to drown himself in the wreck of the "Independence" with the body of his dead wife rather than face life without love (M 3: 922).

Shipwreck narratives like "MS. Found in a Bottle" and "The Oblong Box" also feature details that implicate them in the course of empires. In the first, the narrator sets out "from the port of Batavia, in the rich and populous island of Java" in a trading vessel laden with goods including "a few cases of opium" (M 2: 135). In the second, the "Independence" is a "packet-ship" traveling on scheduled service from Charleston to New York (M 3: 922). Such boats were a feature of the packet trade, a system of mail delivery held over from the British colonial system. Rather mysteriously, as the ship goes down, a "Mexican officer" and his family are among the passengers trying to escape (M 3: 931). This detail anticipates the conflict with Mexico that would define the end of the 1840s, and as we will see in the next section, Poe was certainly aware of the implication of current and former Spanish possessions in US imperial designs.[15] The temporal distortion of the survival story form produces even more urgency when transplanted to the Spanish context, in which his readers could contemplate an empire then in the process of crumbling.

"The Pit and Pendulum": The Black Legend and the New de Soto

"The Pit and the Pendulum" (1842) has not attracted the attention of many historicist critics, and yet the setting is more explicitly historical than many of Poe's other short fictions. Its politics are superficially Bonapartist, from its epigraph, a Latin quatrain memorializing the mob violence of the French Revolution, to the culminating miraculous rescue of the narrator by General Lasalle of Napoleon's military. In between, however, the age of revolutions becomes a kind of formal exercise in cacophony and distortion; the narrator first describes his trial: "the sound of inquisitorial voices seemed merged in one dreamy indeterminate hum. It conveyed to my soul the idea of *revolution*—perhaps from its association in fancy with the burr of a mill wheel" (M 2: 681). This synaesthetic vortex resists the more referential inclinations of historicist criticism. Quickly, Poe turns to the racialized color symbolism that interests Morrison. The narrator grows deaf to the voices, but he makes out their figures: "I saw the lips of the black-robed judges. They appeared to me white—whiter than the sheet upon which I trace these words" (M 2: 681). Here as in "Descent," the tale's miraculous resolution does little to quiet the racial paranoia that is its effect. The questions of empire raised by its transnational setting have even more direct bearing on antebellum US concerns.

María DeGuzmán's *Spain's Long Shadow: The Black Legend, Off-Whiteness, and Anglo-American Empire* (2005) takes up the cultural and political ramifications of the legacy of Spanish imperialism in US culture. DeGuzmán reads the judges as "figures of alien whiteness, or whiteness morally and physically blackened by the Black Legend against Spain."[16] These "evil Spaniards," she argues, "are conjured to press the narrative ego into a tight spot and then release him like a genie in a bottle, all the more potent for having been corked up into what first looked like certain annihilation."[17] According to DeGuzmán, this process works in service of bolstering confidence in US empire by contrasting it with the declining Spanish. A number of Poe's readers would disagree, however, and this section concludes by pointing to explicitly anticolonial and antiracist interpretations of the story.

From the outset, the tale's compulsive interest in the construction of the dungeon resists narrative closure. The Spanish inquisitors anticipate the narrator's modernizing rationality and his will to survive by conceiving his incarceration as a series of trials. Just as the narrator avoids one punishment, another emerges. It becomes increasingly clear that "the *sudden* extinction of life formed no part of their most horrible plan" (M 2: 687). The narrator realizes that the monks have incorporated his desire to escape into their plan: "It was *hope* that prompted the nerve to quiver—the frame to shrink" (M 2: 692). The Inquisitors signal this deferral of punishment in the allegorical images that adorn the ceiling of the prison: "In one of its panels a very singular figure riveted my whole attention. It was the painted figure of Time as he is commonly represented, save that, in lieu of a scythe, he held what, at a casual glance, I supposed to be the pictured image of a huge pendulum such as we see on antique clocks" (M 2: 689). Of course, this apparently decorative touch becomes an all-too-real swinging blade. The "monkish ingenuity in torture" moves between physical and psychological forms of punishment, elaborated both in the spatial construction of the chamber and the serial unfolding of the narrator's sentence (M 2: 690). The temporal dimensions of torture here ultimately withhold the narrative relief that DeGuzmán suggests is the tale's goal. Poe was less inclined than DeGuzmán suggests to ally himself with American progress in the face of European decline, and many of his readers have taken "The Pit and the Pendulum" to indicate the perversity of Poe's identification with the Spanish.

William H. Prescott's *The History of Ferdinand and Isabella*, which appeared in 1837, just a few years before "The Pit and the Pendulum," provides an obvious window on Poe's context, the nineteenth-century Spanish Inquisition. There, Prescott contends that the Inquisition "has probably contributed more than any other cause to depress the lofty character of the ancient Spaniard. . . . In the present liberal state of knowledge, we look with disgust at the pretensions of any human being, however exalted, to invade the sacred rights of conscience, inalienably possessed by every man."[18] This sense of the Inquisition in opposition to "the present liberal state of knowledge" is a classic instance of the Black Legend of Spanish barbarism.[19] When Prescott returns to the Inquisition more than a decade later in his *History of the Reign of Philip the Second, King of Spain* (1855), he expressed this view even more forcefully:

> Folded under the dark wing of the Inquisition, Spain was shut out from the light which in the sixteenth century broke over the rest of Europe, stimulating the nations to greater enterprise in every department of knowledge. The genius of the people was rebuked and their spirit quenched, under the malignant influence of an eye that never slumbered, of an unseen arm ever raised to strike. How could there be freedom of thought, where there was no freedom of utterance? Or freedom of utterance, where it was as dangerous to say too little as too much? Freedom cannot go along with fear. Every way the mind of the Spaniard was in fetters.[20]

Prescott's light metaphor may well have been borrowed from Poe, whose story he would have read with interest. Poe's tale certainly shares with Prescott an interest in Spanish decline. Like Prescott, "The Pit and the Pendulum" turns judgment back on the judges and represents the perversity of human judgment in the name of God. However, Poe was rather less interested than Prescott in a progressive view of US rights discourse and US Protestantism as improvements on Spanish rule. Poe's narrative preoccupation with "monkish ingenuity in torture" draws his perspective backward into history in a different way than Prescott—the story is almost more inescapable than the dungeon it represents.

Jorge Luis Borges's oft-cited account of reading the story captures the effect of this confusion on the reader:

> Hace casi setenta años sentado en el ultimo peldaño de una escalera que ya no existe, leí *The Pit and the Pendulum*; he olvidado cuántas veces lo he releído o me lo he hecho leer; sé que no he llegado a la última y que regresaré a la carcel cuadrangular que se estrecha y al abismo del fondo. [Nearly seventy years ago, sitting on the last step of a stairway that no longer exists, I read "The Pit and the Pendulum"; I have forgotten how many times I have reread it or had it read to me; I know that I have not yet arrived at the last and that I will return to the tightening four-sided prison and to the abyss of the deep.][21]

The interpretive inexhaustibility of Poe's story, in this formulation, has partly to do with a suspension of the release DeGuzmán finds in its end. Prescott's liberal-progressive view of Spanish empire from afterward and outside has no place in this scene of reading. Just as the narrator thinks he has escaped his fate only to find himself in another trap, Borges the reader thinks he has escaped "The Pit and the Pendulum" only to be drawn back into its elaborate construction. Borges himself was hardly a postcolonial thinker, and yet his account of Poe's narrative entrapment echoes the afterlives of colonial rule itself, with its own imitative and repetitive functions, its own protean and iterative "ingenuity in torture."[22]

Much more explicitly than Borges, William Carlos Williams articulates the echoes between Poe and Spanish colonialism. In his 1925 book *In the American Grain,* Williams declared that "Poe was a new De Soto."[23] Seeking to associate Poe's formal innovations with the discoveries of the explorers, Williams emphasizes Poe's Americanism—his locality. In this view, Poe's glib borrowings from European culture paradoxically serve an absolutely original American literature, insofar as they indicate, above all, Poe's formal mastery in deploying them. The reference to the Spanish is not incidental however; earlier in the book, Williams offers a reading of the conquistadors as motivated by something like Poe's "imp of the perverse":

> They moved out across the seas stirred by instincts, ancient beyond thought as the depths they were crossing, which they obeyed under the names of King or Christ or whatever it might be, while they watched the recreative New unfolding itself miraculously before them, before *them*, deafened and blinded.[24]

In Williams's reading, the "names" for the motivations of the conquistadors—"King or Christ or whatever it might be"—fall by the wayside en route to the miracle of the New World. "The Pit and the Pendulum" does not articulate the relation between the Inquisition and New World conquest, but no doubt similar "instincts" drive the "monkish ingenuity in torture."

Taken together, Borges's endless rereading of "The Pit and the Pendulum" and Williams's reading of Poe as a *conquistador* point toward a metahistorical Poe, whose vision mixes geopolitical, historical, allegorical, and psychological registers, while crucially resisting the standard form of historical narrative. The arrival of Lasalle at the tale's end might seem like a rousing endorsement of Franco-American republicanism. But its silliness as a narrative device—the way Poe makes this apparent triumph of liberty and human reason an obvious deus ex machina—belies the story's more reassuring notes. Why should the reader expect that the narrator is heading anywhere but into another hell of human making? What reckonings await the world after the Inquisition? Napoleon's invasion of Spain in 1808 led to decades of intermittent civil war on the Iberian Peninsula and the dismantling of substantial portions of the Spanish empire across the Americas. The immediate consequence of the Mexican War of Independence (1810–1821) was especially important as a precursor to US expansion across the Southwest. Poe may well have been thinking of the legacy of Spanish empire in the Texas Revolution (1835–1836) in his consideration of Inquisition justice.

In its intensity, the Poe of Borges and Williams *feels* more historical than narrative history. This effect has to do with Poe's interest in aesthetic immediacy, and with the perspectival estrangement of his narrators. In this respect, the historical dimensions of his stories have a strange analog in the work of the Egyptian historian in "Some Words with a Mummy" (1845), who has himself strategically revived centuries after his death to assess the truth of his work:

> He would invariably find his great work converted into a species of haphazard notebook—that is to say into a kind of literary arena for the conflicting guesses, riddles, and personal squabbles of whole herds of exasperated commentators. These guesses, etc., which passed under the name of annotations or emendations, were found so completely to have enveloped, distorted, and overwhelmed the text, that the author had to go about with a lantern to discover his own book. When discovered, it was never worth the trouble of the search. After re-writing it throughout, it was regarded as the bounden duty of the historian to work, immediately, in correcting from his own private knowledge and experience, the traditions of the day concerning the epoch at which he had originally lived. Now this process of re-scription and personal rectification, pursued by various individual sages, from time to time, had the effect of preventing our history from degenerating into absolute fable. (M 3: 1189)

This procedure rectifies the problem of historical formalism by compounding historical relativism. Poe's aesthetic practice resembles this "galvanic" resurrection of past historians in its preoccupation with death—the morbid dangers experienced by his narrators give them a kind of otherworldly perspective on historical processes and an inveterate preoccupation with historical decline. Poe's historicity does not boil down to "*one* page" as in Byron, but rather gives concentrated visions of its "volumes vast" in a series of tales and poems meant to be read in one sitting. The encoding and decoding implied by the dynamic between history and allegory in Poe's work make for a kind of structurally imperfect system of aesthetic verification, in which the story of a Norse fisherman might represent the myth of Viking conquest, which might have to do with antebellum frontier violence, and the story of a prisoner of the Inquisition might represent an idealistic view of US Protestant rationality and liberalism, or it might represent US ambitions in the Southwest. Williams captured something about this in his assertion: "The whole period, America 1840, could be rebuilt, psychologically (phrenologically) from Poe's 'method.'"[25] Recall that the mummy, from his vantage point of entombed millennia, makes a case against the political organization of ancient Egypt that sounds eerily like the imperial ambitions of the 1840s United States, with its "consolidation of the thirteen states, with some fifteen or twenty others, into the most odious and insupportable despotism that ever was heard of upon the face of the Earth" (M 3: 1194).

"The Pit and the Pendulum" does not dwell on the light that breaks into the chamber with General Lasalle, but on the darkness into which the narrator is cast by an uncertain and only tenuously historical Inquisition. Its elaboration of "Time" works through the elaborate and unjustified mechanisms of punishment it describes. And yet, as

DeGuzmán points out, it provides a narrative release explicitly associated with revolutionary liberalism. Taking the work as a theory of history would be a mistake—it is perhaps more properly understood as an aestheticizing of history, but at what cost?

Conclusion

Reading "The Pit and the Pendulum" now calls up contemporary associations; justice perverted by the will to punish in the name of God might well describe a number of developments in recent American history. The so-called enhanced interrogation techniques used in the prosecution of the War on Terror, the panic about undocumented "bad hombres" swarming across the Mexican border, and the reign of extrajudicial murders by police in African American communities all suggest that the "imp of the perverse" has taken possession of the American idea of freedom. Likewise, "A Descent into the Maelström" now calls up the whirling vortex of human and natural history that is the late stages of the "Anthropocene"—a term with which Poe would have surely had some terrific fun. The racially and economically maldistributed effects of climate change have given his figuratively dark water a new charge, and increasingly haunted sites of environmental injustice like post-Katrina New Orleans, Flint, Michigan, post-Maria Puerto Rico, and Standing Rock augur for a new revolutionary Maelström, whose shape we cannot quite perceive and yet whose rush we hear like a herd of ghostly buffalo.

The dynamic between extreme individual experiences and the "course of empire" defines more of Poe's work than can be covered in the span of a chapter. For instance, Poe's poem "To Helen" appears to share this scheme, with the speaker recalling the beauty of his beloved while on a long journey:

On desperate seas long wont to roam,
   Thy hyacinth hair, thy classic face,
Thy Naiad airs have brought me home
   To the glory that was Greece,
   And the grandeur that was Rome. (M 1: 166)

These oft-cited lines frame the lyric argument of romantic yearning in terms of the dangers of maritime expedition and the pastoralism of civilizational nostalgia. Likewise, the preoccupation of many of Poe's tales with civilizational decline involves the kind of poaching on "course of empires" discourse in ways I have examined here. One might wonder, for instance, whether the conclusion of "The Masque of the Red Death," with its depiction of European degeneracy, reflects on Poe's own "Gibbonish" tendencies: "And Darkness and Decay and the Red Death held illimitable dominion over all" (M 2: 677).

The warp and woof of individual experience and the course of empires reflect the complex spatial constructions of Poe's tales. Haunted by the failed European settlement of the New World, the Maelström and the Pit destabilize the liberal perfectionism that undergirds US territorial ambitions. In a review of William Cullen Bryant's *Poems* in the January 1837 issue of the *Southern Literary Messenger*, Poe dismisses the didactic "analogy . . . deduced from the eternal cycles of physical nature, to sustain a hope of *progression* in happiness" (ER: 412). His skepticism centers on the spurious assumptions about the dynamic between natural history and human history, and between the life of an individual and national history, what Sacvan Bercovitch calls "auto-American-biography."[26] Instead, Poe offers us a picture of the psyche absolutely divided from its surroundings—in which nature, community, and law all threaten human flourishing. His aesthetic exploitation of the oblique relation between individual human effort and historical forces has an especially dramatic effect in the context of contemporary neoliberalism.[27]

The metahistorical Poe sketched out here points in various directions away from his own antebellum politics, both further back into history and ahead, toward the contemporary. His ironic sense of the rise of American civilization has proven enormously influential in a world more or less defined by American power and, recently, American decline. Writers from across the global South, and especially in trans-Atlantic contexts, have appropriated Poe's aesthetic procedures to a range of antiracist and anticolonial aesthetic projects. Frantz Fanon, for instance, offers a different frame for the historical-allegorical problem in Poe criticism with his account of the psychic conditions of colonialism. Fanon's notion of "epidermalization," the process by which black skin becomes the locus of alienation, offers a kind of mirror reversal of Morrison's "American Africanism" as "a fabricated brew of darkness, otherness, alarm, and desire."[28] Like Morrison, Fanon takes Poe as a paradigmatic example of the way white authorship can connote white anxiety. Reading Fanon alongside Morrison permits a generalization about the role of Poe's metahistorical aesthetic practice in antiracist thought: he provides a technical model for the manipulation of white anxiety.

Fanon mentions Poe as an example of the colonial cultural inheritance in his classic *The Wretched of the Earth* (1961):

> Like adopted children who only stop investigating the new family framework at the moment when a minimum nucleus of security crystallizes in their psyche, the native intellectual will try to make European culture his own. He will not be content to get to know Rabelais and Diderot, Shakespeare and Edgar Allan Poe; he will bind them to his intelligence as closely as possible.[29]

This reference is not merely incidental. The ceaseless "investigating" of the "native intellectual" parallels that of Poe's obsessive narrators. Readers familiar with biographical criticism of Poe will also recognize in this passage the fundamental problem of his non-adoption by John Allan, and his primary estrangement from the Southern planter aristocracy. Given Poe's importance as a precursor for both psychoanalysis and *Negritude*, it is very likely that Fanon's own reading in the American author's work was more active, and less imitative, than the scene of reading he depicts here. Indeed, the pages that follow this reference read the development of colonial literature in ways that resonate with Poe's own sense of himself as a postcolonial author in the early decades of the Republic.

Fanon's thinking, in its movement between focusing on the psychological predicament of the singular, generic "native" and, from a wider angle, depicting empire in decline, has a special resonance with the stories I have examined here:

> Confronted with a world ruled by the settler, the native is always presumed guilty. But the native's guilt is never a guilt which he accepts; it is rather a kind of curse, a sort of sword of Damocles, for, in his innermost spirit, the native admits no accusation. He is overpowered but not tamed; he is treated as an inferior, but he is not convinced of his inferiority.[30]

In this formulation, the presumption of guilt operates as a mechanism of control that the native resists on the level of his "innermost spirit." As in Poe's stories of survival, the determination of the native's guilt has taken place elsewhere and has little bearing on his or her survival of the present conditions. This situation, though Fanon describes it as a structural, psychological form, also unfolds historically; following the logic of Hegelian dialectics, the native develops an increasingly revolutionary consciousness as his mistreatment inevitably intensifies. The contradictions of "a world ruled by the settler" will tend to produce revolutionary reaction. Fanon does not imagine this process as progressive or linear but instead describes the experience of time in the colonial relation as apocalyptic in its historical possibility: "The natives are convinced that their fate is in the balance, here and now. They live in an atmosphere of doomsday, and they consider that nothing ought to pass unnoticed."[31] Here too we find an uncanny parallel with Poe's narrators, who find themselves in situations of such extremity that each moment becomes an eternity. The hypertensive vigilance of Poe's white male narrators becomes in Fanon a theory of the psychodynamics of colonial domination.

In the prophetic conclusion to *The Wretched of the Earth*, Fanon offers a gnomic account of US empire as recapitulating the imitativeness of the colonial encounter: "Two centuries ago, a former European colony decided to catch up with Europe. It succeeded so well that the United States of America became a monster, in which the taints, the sickness, and the inhumanity of Europe have grown to appalling dimensions."[32] Both the Gothicism of this passage and its sense of American culture as stuck in a pathological thrall to Europe sound like Poe. The point of saying so is not to credit Poe with influencing Fanon. The echoes of Poe in Fanon pose a challenge to historicist aesthetics on the question of race and empire as trans-historical forms. Both Poe and Fanon find the long-durational facts of colonialism animating the most intensely felt moments of individual experience. As the sword of time swings closer and the waves rise, we wonder, in our respective stony cells and creaky ships, whether the end of American empire will take us down with it. And like Borges, we read Poe over and over again, feeling ever closer but never quite reaching the end.

NOTES

1. Toni Morrison, *Playing in the Dark: Whiteness and the Literary Imagination* (New York: Vintage, 1992), 68.
2. See Hayden White's *Metahistory: The Historical Imagination in Nineteenth-Century Europe* (Baltimore: The Johns Hopkins University Press, 1973) for nineteenth-century history and narrative form. See also Wai Chee Dimock's *Through Other Continents: American Literature Across Deep Time* (Princeton, NJ: Princeton University Press, 2006) for a reading of long-durational history as a foil to American exceptionalism.
3. The authorship of this unsigned text is contested. Appearing in the February 15, 1845, issue a week before Poe officially became editor, it is not attributed to Poe in Burton Pollin, ed., *The Collected Writings of Edgar Allan Poe*, Vol. 3, *Writings in* The Broadway Journal: *Nonfictional Prose—Part I: Text* (New York: Gordian Press, 1986). Despite its resonance with his positions on aesthetics as stated elsewhere, Poe himself attributes it to Charles F. Briggs, one of the founders of *The Broadway Journal*, in "The Literati of New York City" (from the May 1846 issue of *Godey's Lady's Book*), where he claims, "there was scarcely a point in his whole series of criticisms on this subject at which I did not radically disagree with him" (ER: 1133).
4. Lord Byron, *Childe Harold's Pilgrimage*, in *Lord Byron: The Major Works* (New York: Oxford University Press, 2000), 179, Canto IV, stanza 108.
5. Byron, *Childe Harold's Pilgrimage*, 179.
6. Jonathan Arac finds Poe writing travesties of "personal narrative" in *The Emergence of American Literary Narrative, 1820–1860* (Cambridge, MA: Harvard University Press, 2005). For Poe in relation to the nineteenth-century American fascination with death, see J. Gerald Kennedy's *Poe, Death, and the Life of Writing* (New Haven, CT: Yale University Press, 1987). See also Ann Douglas's *The Feminization of American Culture* (New York: Alfred A. Knopf, 1977), Karen Halttunen's *Confidence Men and Painted Women* (New Haven, CT: Yale University Press, 1986), and Russ Castronovo's *Necro Citizenship: Death, Eroticism, and the Public Sphere in the Nineteenth-Century United States* (Durham, NC: Duke University Press, 2001).
7. Morrison, *Playing in the Dark*, 52. Both Joseph Frank, in *The Idea of Spatial Form* (New Brunswick, NJ: Rutgers University Press, 1991), and Frederic Jameson, in *Postmodernism, or, the Cultural Logic of Late Capitalism* (Durham, NC: Duke University Press, 1992), 420, contend that "spatial form" involves a flattening of historical consciousness. Poe manipulates this flatness to produce historical-aesthetic effects.
8. Samuel Taylor Coleridge, "The Rime of the Ancient Mariner," in *Samuel Taylor Coleridge: The Major Works*, rev. ed. (New York: Oxford, 2008), 68.
9. Coleridge, "The Rime of the Ancient Mariner," 68.
10. Hall Grandgent, "Discovery of America by the Northmen in the Tenth Century," *Burton's Gentleman's Magazine and American Monthly Review* 5, no. 3 (September 1839): 153.
11. William Gilmore Simms, "The Discoveries of the Northmen," *Magnolia; or Southern Monthly* 3, no. 9 (1841): 421.
12. In "The Prairies" (1833), William Cullen Bryant imagines an independent race of mound-builders distinct from and prior to the familiar Native peoples of North America: "The red man came—/ The roaming hunter tribes, warlike and fierce,/ And the mound-builders vanished from the earth" (*Poems* [New York: Harper & Brothers, 1837], 52). Bryant's vision, however, predates the popularity of the myth of Viking contact that determines Simms's

fantasy. Poe took note of "The Prairies" in his review of 1837 review of Bryant's *Poems* in the *Southern Literary Messenger*, but only addresses its metrical choices, not its historical projections (ER: 422–423).

13. Kolodny, *In Search of First Contact: The Vikings of Vinland, the Peoples of the Dawnland, and the Anglo-American Anxiety of Discovery* (Durham, NC: Duke University Press, 2012), 129.
14. Kristin Ross points to instances of this figure across the "centrifugal" poetics of Arthur Rimbaud, who she contends was inspired by the turning out of the bourgeois interior in the barricades of the Paris Commune in her *The Emergence of Social Space: Rimbaud and the Paris Commune* (New York: Verso, 1988), 10.
15. See Bonnie Shannon McMullen, "Lifting the Lid on Poe's 'Oblong Box,'" *Studies in American Fiction* 23, no. 2 (Autumn 1995): 203–214.
16. DeGuzmán, *Spain's Long Shadow: The Black Legend, Off-Whiteness, and Anglo American Empire* (Minneapolis: University of Minnesota Press, 2005), 34. Robert Reid Pharr's *Archives of Flesh: African America, Spain, and Post-Humanist Critique* (New York: New York University Press, 2016) informs my perspective here. See also Cedric Robinson on the Spanish and Portuguese plantation systems in *Black Marxism: The Making of the Black Radical Tradition* (London: Zed Press, 1983).
17. DeGuzmán, *Spain's Long Shadow*, 39.
18. William H. Prescott, *The History of the Reign of Ferdinand and Isabella*, 2 vols. (New York: A.L. Burt, 1838), 1:190.
19. It has long been customary to note the importance to Poe of the English translation of Juan Antonio Llorente's *History of the Spanish Inquisition* (New York: G.C. Morgan, 1826). By contrast, Prescott's interpretation is explicitly Americanist.
20. William H. Prescott, *History of the Reign of Philip the Second, King of Spain*, 3 vols. (Boston: Phillips, Sampson and Company, 1855), 1:446.
21. Borges, "Prólogo," in *Edgar Allan Poe, La carta robada*, ed. Franco Maria Ricci (Madrid: Siruela, 1985), 12–13. Translation from Emron Esplin, *The Influence and Reinvention of Edgar Allan Poe in Spanish America* (Athens: University of Georgia Press, 2016), 62.
22. Marie Bonaparte interprets "The Pit and the Pendulum" through the contrast of a "phantasy of the return to the womb" and "the son's homosexual and masochistic passivity to the father" (*The Life and Works of Edgar Allan Poe: A Psycho-Analytic Interpretation*, trans. John Rodker [London: Imago, 1949], 584). She finds "the vast, primary problem of the origin of anxiety" below this opposition (584). DeGuzmán rereads these psychosexual dynamics as a reflection on Spanish "amalgamation" (*Spain's Long Shadow*, 25–47). See also Leland Person, "Poe's Philosophy of Amalgamation: Reading Racism in the Tales," in *Romancing the Shadow: Poe and Race*, ed. J. Gerald Kennedy and Liliane Weissberg (New York: Oxford University Press, 2001), 205–224.
23. William Carlos Williams, *In the American Grain* (New York: New Directions, 2009), 220.
24. Williams, *In the American Grain*, 27.
25. Williams, *In the American Grain*, 231.
26. Sacvan Bercovitch, *The Puritan Origins of the American Self* (New Haven, CT: Yale, 1975), 134.
27. For Poe and liberalism, see Shawn Rosenheim and Stephen Rachman's collection *The American Face of Edgar Allan Poe* (Baltimore: The Johns Hopkins University Press, 1995), especially Jonathan Elmer's "Terminate or Liquidate? Poe, Sensationalism, and the Sentimental Tradition," 91–120. Poe's definition of plot as a bid for structural perfection doubles as a critique of liberal perfectionism. In the "Marginalia" of November 1844, Poe writes:

The pleasure which we derive from any exertion of human ingenuity, is in direct ratio of the *approach* to this species of reciprocity between cause and effect. In the construction of *plot*, for example, in fictitious literature, we should aim at so arranging the points, or incidents, that we cannot distinctly see, in respect to any one of them, whether that one depends from any one other, or upholds it. In this sense, of course, perfection of plot is unattainable, *in fact*,—because Man is the constructor. The plots of God are perfect. The Universe is the plot of God. (ER: 1316)

Poe refers to a quality in nature he calls "the complete *mutuality* of adaptation" in which cause and effect are perfectly synchronized; he gives the example of importance of high fat foods in wintry climates and the abundance of high fat creatures like seals and whales in those same regions. Human systems lack this "reciprocity," as he calls it, by dint of their imperfection. Liberalism is one of the most important imperfect plots of man in American life.

28. Frantz Fanon, *Black Skin, White Masks* (New York: Grove Press, 1967), 11; Morrison, *Playing in the Dark*, 38.
29. Frantz Fanon, *The Wretched of the Earth* (New York: Grove Press, 1968), 218–219.
30. Fanon, *The Wretched of the Earth*, 53.
31. Fanon, *The Wretched of the Earth*, 81.
32. Fanon, *The Wretched of the Earth*, 313.

Bibliography

Borges, Jorge Luis. "Prólogo." In *Edgar Allan Poe, La carta robada*, edited by Franco Maria Ricci, 9–13. Madrid: Siruela, 1985.

DeGuzmán, María. *Spain's Long Shadow: The Black Legend, Off-Whiteness, and Anglo American Empire*. Minneapolis: University of Minnesota Press, 2005.

Fanon, Frantz. *Black Skin, White Masks*. New York: Grove Press, 1967.

Fanon, Frantz. *A Dying Colonialism*. New York: Grove Press, 1965.

Fanon, Frantz. *The Wretched of the Earth*. New York: Grove Press, 1968.

Grandgent, Hall. "Discovery of America by the Northmen in the Tenth Century." *Burton's Gentleman's Magazine and American Monthly Review* 5, no. 3 (September 1839): 153–155.

Kolodny, Annette. *In Search of First Contact: The Vikings of Vinland, the Peoples of the Dawnland, and the Anglo-American Anxiety of Discovery*. Durham, NC: Duke University Press, 2012.

Llorente, Jean Antoine [Juan Antonio]. *The History of the Inquisition of Spain, from the Time of Its Establishment to the Reign of Ferdinand VII*. Translated by Leonard Gallois. London: George B. Whittaker, 1826.

Morrison, Toni. *Playing in the Dark: Whiteness and the Literary Imagination*. New York: Vintage, 1992.

Prescott, William H. *History of the Reign of Ferdinand and Isabella*. Vol. 1. New York: A. L. Burt, 1838.

Prescott, William H. *History of the Reign of Philip the Second, King of Spain*. Vol. 1. Boston: Phillips, Sampson and Company, 1855.

Rafn, Charles C. *America Discovered in the Tenth Century*. New York: William Jackson, 1838.

Simms, William Gilmore. "The Discoveries of the Northmen." *Magnolia; or Southern Monthly* 3, no. 9 (1841): 417–421.

Williams, William Carlos. *In the American Grain*. 1925. New York: New Directions, 2009.

CHAPTER 17

POE'S LANDSCAPES, PICTURESQUE AND IDEAL

KENT P. LJUNGQUIST

Associated with the urban venues in which he toiled as an editor for various periodicals, Edgar Allan Poe became a first-hand observer and connoisseur of the natural and improved landscapes and landmarks in proximity to those areas. Like many writers and artists of his period, Poe contributed to the debate and discussion on the complementary and sometimes rival claims of nature and art in a maturing antebellum visual culture. The works of painters, engravers, printmakers, essayists, letter writers, and travel writers provide precedent and context for Poe's marriage of verbal and pictorial styles in his fictional landscapes "The Domain of Arnheim" and "Landor's Cottage." Before surveying some of the written sources of his visual effects, notably in the works of William Hazlitt and Baron Herman von Pückler-Muskau, one should recall the range of natural landscapes he directly encountered during his life and career.

As early as his days as a resident and editor in Richmond, Poe was, likely, impressed by the picturesque appearance of the city located on the fall line of the James River within sight of the Blue Ridge Mountains. According to his friend William Wirt, the town appeared to be dispersed over hills of different shapes and sizes along the river extending from west to east, as arriving and departing boats skimmed its polished surface, surrounded by clumps of trees and rock formations. Poe's consultation of travel volumes like William Wirt's *Letters of the British Spy* (1803) and James Kirke Paulding's *Letters from the South* (1817) would have confirmed whatever impressions struck an acute observer. According to Wirt, Richmond offered "the most finely varied and animated landscape that I have ever seen."[1]

Poe was part of an early cohort of students at the University of Virginia, built "within a basin of natural beauty," set off by hills to the east and the Blue Ridge Mountains in the opposite direction. Undergraduates could enjoy rambles in the mountains and then refresh themselves with a swim or a canoe ride in the Rivanna River, the tributaries of which pushed through the rocky terrain near Charlottesville. Thomas Jefferson, the founder and architect of the university, was a keen student of natural history and a lifelong connoisseur of landscape gardening, which grew out of an eighteenth-century English tradition of endowing nature with aesthetic appeal. In the mid-1780s, Jefferson and John Adams took a break from their diplomatic obligations in London by visiting some of England's notable pleasure gardens. Poe would eventually learn to read natural landscapes much like verbal texts, something Jefferson did during his travels in the English countryside. Sharing what would become one of Poe's key sources, Jefferson had consulted Lord Kames's *Elements of Criticism* (1762), which outlined principles of artistic taste and advocated the English picturesque school of landscape architecture. In 1786, he walked through English gardens with a copy of Thomas Whately's *Observations on Modern Gardening* (1770) in hand, noting first-hand how the plantings matched the author's precise verbal descriptions. One result of his sightseeing excursion was "Notes of a Tour of English Gardens," organized as a succession of discrete impressions of each garden he and Adams visited. Jefferson sustained his interest in the natural world by recording observations on plants and wildflowers, and his correspondence from Monticello reflected his keen interest in botany and natural history as well as his delight in rural seclusion, distanced from the rough and tumble of the social and political world. More than one commentator has suggested that Jefferson may have been a model for Poe's Ellison, the scholar-gardener who satisfies his pursuit of the poetic sentiment by surrounding himself with works of physical loveliness in "The Domain of Arnheim." Ellison sets conditions for happiness, one of which is rural retirement, by allowing himself the freedom to plan and refine an ideal pleasure garden.[2]

Another city Poe knew well, Philadelphia, had established itself as a center of painting and landscape design well before Poe and his family moved there early in 1838. Travelers and sketch artists from the growing urban center enjoyed walks among the dells and glens along the Schuylkill River and the Wissahiccon Creek. During his tenure as an editor in Philadelphia, situated between the Schuylkill and Delaware Rivers, Poe would have had ample opportunity to sample views and vantage points amid the various roads, pathways, park scenes, and river settings. Among the celebrated estates were James Greenleaf's Solitude, located in Fairmount Park, and William Hamilton's Woodlands, situated at the juncture of the Schuylkill River and Mill Creek. Hamilton's country estate, modeled on the principles of Whately and Lancelot Capability Brown, integrated the house and the surrounding grounds according to the most advanced taste in landscape gardening. Jefferson had memorialized his impressions of the Woodlands in an 1806 letter to Hamilton, sharing his plan for eventual retirement at Monticello. His plan for the estate's improvement was to follow "the style of English gardens," and he aspired to meet the challenges in overall design by calling on the expected talents of "the landscape painter & gardener."

Especially after the Poes moved into their house on Coates Street in the Fairmount district of the city, Poe would have had easy access to the nearby Water Works, a favored attraction for visitors, illustrators, and artists. The Water Works were designed to have aesthetic as well as practical appeal, and its buildings were arranged in a park-like configuration, complemented by a garden setting, paths, fountains, and an esplanade. An engraving of a new suspension bridge over the river at Fairmount appeared as an accompaniment to the lead article in the June 1842 *Graham's* (vol. 20), an issue that followed the previous month's appearance of "The Mask of the Red Death." The Poes lived in a rural home on the outskirts of the city, and according to a next-door neighbor, Poe "often visited the Wissahiccon because he was a great lover of nature, and fond of roving about the country" (PL: 381, 389). Poe may have discovered Wissahiccon Creek in private walks or come across its description in the actress Fanny Kemble's *Journal*, and he absorbed enough of its ambience to craft his sketch "The Elk." Ridge Road, extending well into the country, would have taken him to scenes where occasional villas marked the river banks, and tulip poplars contrasted with evergreens along the shores. Other "Philadelphian picturesque-hunters" would have been able to find spots for a cottage or garden among the rich trees and herbage (M 2: 864). Poe certainly would have seen a review in *Burton's* of *Views of Philadelphia and Its Vicinity*, a widely circulated compilation of "poetical illustrations and prose descriptions" that did justice to the pictorial subjects of the city.[3]

Poe returned to New York in 1844—he had lived there in 1837 as *The Narrative of Arthur Gordon Pym* was being readied for publication by Harper & Brothers—but this time his home setting was decidedly rural, on the Brennan Farm, a plot of over 200 acres where he and his family lived in a sturdy two-story dwelling. Poe took long strolls in the neighborhood, seeking promising rural prospects, especially at Mount Tom, a rocky crag overlooking the Hudson River. The house was a short walk from the Bloomingdale Road, which offered a route into the city, but the farm itself offered a bounty of crops and fruit as well as ponds, streams, and country views that extended across the river into New Jersey.[4] From his countrified perspective, Poe drafted a series of brief articles for a modest Pennsylvania newspaper, the *Columbia Spy*, giving a rural audience an impression of life in a bustling metropolis. Like other journalists of the time, he deplored the wretched condition of the New York streets and railed against the oppressive din—caused by workers and vehicles—of urban street noise. On excursions into Manhattan, he discovered that some scenes possessed "a certain air of rocky sterility" that might seem "simply *dreary*," but they conveyed to him an austere sublimity. The absence of trees gave some pause, but other scenic details—urban shrubbery—he found "exceedingly picturesque." He was even more impressed by those prospects that seemed to resist the forces of development and commercial expansion. For one of his adventures he procured a skiff that took him around Blackwell's Island (later Welfare Island). The frame houses offered a strikingly "antique" appearance, especially when set against "magnificent cliffs" and "stately shores," which were "particularly picturesque."[5] Writing from the farm five miles outside the city, he confided in a letter to F. W. Thomas: "For the last seven or eight months I have been playing hermit in earnest, nor have I seen a living soul out of my family" (PL: 470). His choice of a bucolic setting was part of a plan to protect Virginia's precarious health. This choice of relative solitude for the scenes in his fictional landscapes was driven by practical concerns: his wife's condition and a preference for separation from urban noise and pollution.

In 1846 Poe again sought a healthful residence for Virginia even further outside the city among the farms and cottages lining Knightsbridge Way. As a resident of Fordham

Village, Poe took walks in the woods before a modest breakfast, and during summer months, activities included country rambles, gardening, and even occasional boat rides.[6] Near the cottage was a rocky ledge, and the hills sloped southward, offering a sweeping view of the farms of the Bronx. According to Sarah Helen Whitman, Poe claimed "that he took Virginia out there in the spring of the year to see the cottage, & and that it was half-buried in fruit trees, which were then all in blossom" (PL: 639). According to another account, Poe contemplated the "beauties of nature," as he surveyed the Bronx River and its tree-lined banks. A pathway took pedestrians past aqueducts at High Bridge and afforded an even more expansive view of the villages, woods, and meadows that extended into the highlands, the islands of Pelham Bay, and eastward to the Sound.[7] As implied by "Landor's Cottage," the proportions and features of Poe's fictional house match his actual residence, and he probably took a walking tour of "one or two" of the Hudson River counties north of Fordham in July 1848 (PL: 739). Turning to his fictional renderings, Poe tends to idealize nature in aesthetic terms, but whatever transformations were applied to first-hand impressions, he maintains connections to the surface, depth, and character of observed landscapes. As the narrator of Poe's sketch "The Island of the Fay" comments, a fondness for music had to take second place to "the happiness experienced in the contemplation of natural scenery. . . . I love, indeed, to regard the dark valleys, and the grey rocks, and the waters that silently smile, and the forests that sigh in uneasy slumbers, and the proud watchful mountains that look down upon all—I love to regard these as themselves but the colossal members of one vast animate and sentient whole" (M 2: 600). By taking an inventory of the valleys, forests, waters, and mountains of American scenery, Poe contributes to the vogue of travel writing that refined debates in the periodicals on a renewed consciousness of nature, a more acute attention to romantic landscape. Poe's rhetorical patterns applied to imaginative description of landscape afforded him ironic detachment from more conventional strategies, often through the manipulation of the limited narrative perspectives of his picturesque observers.

His discovery and exploration of rural retreats allowed him to refine a developing taste for landscape, but in his roles as visitor, observer, or magazine editor, he does not treat these scenes as objects of naked or pure discovery. Writers like Uvedale Price, William Gilpin, and Richard Payne Knight gave shape and definition to travelers' impressions by filtering them through an aesthetic vocabulary that extended back to the late eighteenth century. The terminology Poe uses in his review of Alexander Slidell's travel book, *The American in England*, allows him to discriminate among a variety of visual effects informed by pre-Romantic aesthetic theory. Using painterly terms like "effect," "design," "impression," and "interest," he marshals a pictorial vocabulary that he applies to works by Slidell and to other travel volumes by diverse authors. "Effect" results from the skillful joining of "novel combinations," sometimes the mix of heterogeneous characteristics achieved through the picturesque principles of contrast and harmony. Accordingly, he praises Slidell for "the vigor, raciness and illusion of panorama," attributed to the travel author's "fine eye" for "the picturesque," the artful balance of order and disorder, light and shade, variety and unity (H 8: 216). In Slidell's sequel

Spain Revisited, Poe observes "the same artist-like way" of depicting persons, scenery, or manners. Slidell's "succession of well-managed details" contributes to an elaborate "picturesque and vigorous description" that eschewed an overly random dispersion of detail (H 9: 1, 4). Other writers distinguish themselves from the general class of "sketchy tours." Poe writes that James Fenimore Cooper, in his travel series, looks at Europe "with a more instructed eye than the mass of travelers." In *Sketches of Switzerland*, the author "is able to commit its landscapes to a comparison which few of them have the means of making—thus possessing an idiosyncrasy giving freshness to what otherwise would be faded" (H 9: 162). Cooper himself was unambiguous when he acknowledged that *Sketches of Switzerland* was "a *picturesque* book," which followed the conventions of travelers like Gilpin and others to render scenes in nature—and their combinations, contrasts, and tensions—that could rival the paintings of widely admired landscape artists.[8]

At the outset of "The Fall of the House of Usher," Poe's narrator pauses on his journey to detail the qualities of the landscape and the estate he surveys: its complex organization, its decided antiquity, and its unique architectural arrangement. The narrator notes "the *physique* of the gray walls and turrets," the curious architectural form of the family mansion, produces a marked effect on "the *morale* of his [Usher's] existence" (M 2: 403). In the same issue of *Burton's* as the first printing of "Usher," Poe, distinguishing physical location from more suggestive and expressive characteristics of setting, repeats his use of the terms *physique* and *morale* in a brief review of another work on landscape design, Edward Sayers's *The American Flower Garden Companion*. In that slender volume, Poe notes, the landscape gardener could find any number of novel suggestions—about forms of beauty or physical arrangement—that enhance the intricate aesthetic appeal of ornamental features. Rock formations, the positioning of plants, the deployment of trellises and bridges, and the strategic location of bodies of water and bridges constitute Sayers's inventory of the garden designer's options.[9]

It appears that much of Poe's pictorial vocabulary here and elsewhere derives from the work of the English essayist William Hazlitt. A leading Romantic critic, Hazlitt is perhaps known today for his occasional essays, his lectures on dramatic literature, and his personal observations on contemporary poets. As a child, Hazlitt absorbed the atmosphere of the pleasure gardens of Walworth in suburban London. When he turned to writing, Hazlitt's career, like Poe's, paralleled the development of literary criticism in the popular magazines of his day. Not as well known as the pointed style of his personal essays is Hazlitt's early ambition to become a painter, a profession that occupied him for approximately a decade. He haunted galleries and exhibitions, exchanged ideas with fellow artists, and occasionally returned to the easel to practice his craft. His *Notes on a Journey through France and Italy* (1826), surveying natural attractions and landmarks on his continental tour, presented acute observations of great European galleries and private collections. His knowledge of painting was essential to his development as a critic, but ultimately acknowledging an artistic ambition that would remain unfulfilled, he turned more comprehensively to literature and produced a considerable body of work on aesthetics.

In "Judging of Pictures," one of his essays on the fine arts that applies his practical background, Hazlitt addresses the criticism of painters who overlooked the higher and mental aspects of pictorial renderings. By stressing manual or mechanical principles, some painters, to be sure, tended to overlook the "expression" that art aims to achieve. By speaking of color or flesh tones before addressing the character of the face that emerges from the painter's strokes, some aspect of the inward soul may be lost. In an attempt to distinguish manually proficient painters from more inspired practitioners, Hazlitt notes of the former, "To use a French term of much condensation, they think of the *physique*, before they bestow any attention on the *morale*." Applying his familiarity with the painter's practice and craft, Hazlitt acknowledges that painting can indeed become mechanical or rule-bound; superior work, however, requires a poet's mind to conceive.[10] In the September 1836 *Southern Literary Messenger*, Poe credits Hazlitt's early studies in art and judges his essays of "very high positive value." He singles out his work on the fine arts by suggesting that it "cannot fail of seizing public attention." Hazlitt's discourses on painting, he adds, rival or surpass other authorities in the arts (review of the *Literary Remains of the Late William Hazlitt*, P 5: 286–288).

Poe returns to Hazlitt's works on the fine arts at various points in his career, particularly during his editing of the *Broadway Journal*. In a review of Hazlitt's *Table-Talk*, he finds value in the author's essays on the pleasures of painting. Noting again that Hazlitt gave up an early career in painting, he nevertheless asserts that the essayist "had, unquestionably, the genius of a painter, and his writings on art are among the most valuable of his productions" (P 3: 107). Poe had little enthusiasm for Hazlitt's commentary on the painter Nicholas Poussin's "Orion," but the British essayist had called Poussin's famous landscape of *The Deluge* a "noble picture," which exemplifies "the very poetry of painting." All elements of the painting, he notes, contribute to the "rest of the picture," and seeming to anticipate aspects of Poe's critical vocabulary, Hazlitt adds that "conscious keeping" or "internal design" gives a character to the artist's work. Poe could well have seen *The Deluge* when it was exhibited at the Pennsylvania Academy of Fine Arts in 1840.[11]

As Poe develops his landscape sketches in the 1840s, he maintains a dual interest in the physical properties and the more visionary and ideal associations of such settings. Thus, in "The Domain of Arnheim," expanded from "The Landscape Garden" (1842), the artist Ellison seems less fixed on his theoretical concepts of perfection than in their formal representation and material realization. Physical existence and concrete forms seem to fascinate the artist: "the creation of novel moods of purely *physical* loveliness" (M 2: 706; M 3: 1271). In "The Elk," Poe celebrates physical "realization of the wildest dreams of paradise," overlooked by the indolent traveler and the British tourist alike. The real traveler may discover simpler scenes in pathways untrodden by civilized men as the narrator follows the winding route of the Wissahiccon before a dream-like vision. In "Arnheim," Poe adapts elements of the river journey reminiscent of "The Elk," but it is less attached to any identifiable geographical location. Here the river appears to have no floor, as Poe's traveler seems to be suspended between earth and heaven. The transfer from a substantial ivory vessel to a smaller and lighter canoe sustains the idealized dream-like mood. As several critics have suggested, Poe may be pursuing his own idiosyncratic version of the archetypal narrative of the voyage of life.[12] Such stories received treatment in painting as well as prose narrative, but in the background may be many poetic journeys in which the progress of a body, the soul's earth vessel, marks a rite of passage. Henry Wadsworth Longfellow's translation of "The Soul's Complaint against the Body," opens as follows: "Much it behooveth/Each one of mortals/That he his soul's journey/In himself ponder."[13] Such treatments maintain a dualistic perspective on the physical body and the soul's aspiration, which Poe seems to sustain as the concrete properties of the narrator's journey are transformed into a "picturesque and ideal castle in the air."[14]

Accordingly, the artist—whether in painting, poetry, or prose narrative—does not abandon the materials of nature but carries them into a domain of the soul's invention. A self-described "slave to the picturesque," Hazlitt may have offered further support for this transmission of aesthetic principles into Poe's landscapes. In "On the Picturesque and Ideal," Hazlitt defines the picturesque as that which catches the attention by some striking peculiarity. Depending chiefly on the principle of discrimination or contrast, the picturesque may be an "excrescence" on the face of nature, perhaps even extending to grotesque or fantastical images. In an inventory of picturesque properties—tree stumps with ragged bark, stunted hedgerows, broken branches, stubble fields, rock formations set against the sky, winding or circuitous paths or waterways—Hazlitt notes how these items present a singular form or a sharply striking point of view. It is preferable for the picturesque observer to see a landscape in distinct stages or a succession of salient points of view that allow the eye to rest temporarily before it moves on in its progress.[15]

Addressing the strengths of various painters, Hazlitt distinguishes the picturesque from the ideal, which moves on from an excess of form or a series of visual surprises to harmony and a continuity of effect. Through concentration of feeling, the ideal offers satisfaction to the mind. Rubens's landscapes, for example, are marked by "gusto," a favorite Hazlitt term characteristic of the picturesque, punctuated by an arresting sense of discrimination and contrast. Painters like Claude Lorrain, however, offer balance, harmony, delicacy, and repose rather than outright extravagance. Claude's canvasses, thus, are *ideal*, offering "the height of the pleasing, that which satisfies and accounts with the inmost longing of the soul." If picturesque painters offer sharper details, more concrete impressions of reality, ideal painters present an amalgamation, bringing several impressions into a unified whole. As Poe quotes from Hazlitt's essay "The Ideal" in his 1836 *Messenger* review, a painter or writer can single out the "leading quality of an object" and make it a predominant or prevailing principle, so as "to produce the greatest strength and harmony of effect." Marking a movement or predisposition toward purity, perfection, and refinement, "This internal character, being permanent, communicates itself to the outward expression in proportionable sweetness, delicacy, and unity of effect, which it requires all the same characteristics of the mind to feel and convey to others." This does not mean that the ideal painter abandons concrete details or manifests less gusto. A painter like Claude can seize upon a predominant quality or character—beauty, strength, activity, voluptuousness—that provides a greater consistency or sustained effect.[16]

Hazlitt's outright enthusiasm for Claude—typical of English rustic taste of the early 1800s—becomes even more effusive in his essay on "The Picture Galleries of England." The painter's canvasses surpass "every idea that the mind could form of art," and Hazlitt adds, "The name of Claude has alone something that softens and harmonizes the mind. It touches a magic chord. Oh, matchless scenes, oh, orient skies, bright with purple and gold, eye opening glades and sunny vales, glittering with fleecy flocks, pour all your enchantment into my soul, let it reflect your chastened image, and forget all meaner things." Observers whose manifold interests extended to poetry, painting, and landscape gardening find dream-like images in the works of Claude.[17]

Poe, of course, mentions Claude in "The Domain of Arnheim" in which Ellison, a connoisseur of landscape "in the widest and noblest sense," finds personal gratification for the "poetic sentiment" in creating "novel forms of Beauty." Just as some Poe narrators grow effusive in their attempts to describe experiences that seem to defy articulation, the narrator of "The Domain of Arnheim" implies that the beauty created by great painters surpasses the most exquisite scenes in nature: "No such Paradises are to be found in reality as have glowed upon the canvas of Claude." Although Ellison's quest for beauty embraces poetry, painting, sculpture, or music, he finds in landscape gardening the "fairest field" for "the display of invention, or imagination, in the endless combining of forms of novel Beauty" (M 2: 1272). Poe seems to follow Hazlitt's notion that the Claudean landscape offers a design, structure, and harmony that extends from painting to aesthetic expression in other forms. As Barbara Cantalupo has demonstrated, the Claude reference is apposite to Poe's portrait of the ideal artist. His appreciation for Claude's paintings was reinforced by his reading of Andrew Jackson Downing's *A Treatise on the Theory and Practice of Landscape Gardening* (1841), and he had an opportunity to see a notable work by Claude first-hand in a special exhibit at the Pennsylvania Academy of the Fine Arts in 1844.[18]

A direct contrast to the works of Claude were the landscapes of Salvator Rosa, invoked in Poe's description of the steep banks, sharply defined shores, and abrupt river windings in "The Elk." As Cantalupo notes, the narrator's lofty perspective along the Wissahiccon highlights the influence of Rosa rather than painters whose interest is a softer kind of beauty: "It was a steep rocky cliff, abutting far into the stream, and presenting much more of the Salvator character than any portion of the shore hitherto passed" (M 2: 865). Once again for his knowledge of Rosa, Poe could have turned to the writings of Hazlitt. The English essayist calls Salvator Rosa "a great landscape painter." Salvator excludes softness and ornament in favor of a strength of impression that brings the viewer in contact with a landscape's varied features: sharp rocks, the rough barks of trees, a rugged mountainous pathway. According to Hazlitt, Rosa's emphasis on seclusion, an abrupt break from society, a wildness and grotesqueness of form offers a fresh earthiness that makes him "the most *romantic* of landscape painters." Lacking scenes of "luxuriant beauty and divine harmony" more akin to Claude, Rosa's paintings possess a kind of instinctive force directed at discrete objects in nature. Clearly, the precipitous hills, the shrub-lined shores, and the sharply defined, moss-covered banks of the Wissachiccon offer features more in line with Rosa's wild and dramatic landscapes than with Claude's delicate settings. Along similar lines, the narrator in "Landor's Cottage" moves over a "precipitous ledge of granite" to find verdure "less and less lofty and Salvatorish in character" (M 2: 1331–1332). As Hazlitt notes, figures in Rosa's landscapes possess a force, spirit, and wild interest, perhaps even a somewhat daring character; visually striking, these figures, however, are often dwarfed by the dominant natural landscape.[19]

Poe shared with Hazlitt a fascination with early German romantic writers, several of whom pioneered the emerging aesthetics of effect. Hazlitt initiated one of the most thorough discussions among English critics of German ideas in his 1816 review of A. W. Schlegel's *Lectures on Dramatic Literature*. Poe scholars have debated the extent of Poe's knowledge of Schlegel's dramatic and aesthetic principles, specifically his ideas on unity or totality of effect. In works like "The Fall of the House of Usher," effect resulted in dramatized tension or suspense; examples included tales of horror, terror, or passion, as Poe noted in his review of Hawthorne's fiction (with a brief nod toward Hazlitt). Following principles outlined by Schlegel, a strong element of emotion should accompany a developing action or effect. Hazlitt, too, seemed to be aware of this requirement, as evidenced by his comments on the strong "effects" created by the thrilling horrors produced in Anne Radcliffe's Gothic romances. Scott's Waverley romances, moreover, surpassed even Mrs. Radcliffe's "in truth of painting, in costume and scenery, in freshness of subject and in untired interest." Turning to how Scott matches characters and setting, Hazlitt notes, "The picturesque and local scenery is as fresh as the lichen on the rock; the characters are part of the scenery. If they are part of the action, it is a moving picture." Whether in horror tales, where strong emotion is needed, or in his landscape fiction, where tensions surface more subtly, Poe employs an appropriate affective and scenic language to bind together physical description, his human figures, and characteristic features of setting. Poe's mind was doubtless refreshed about such ideas when he reviewed Hazlitt's *Lectures on the Dramatic Literature of the Age of Elizabeth* in a July 1845 review in the *Broadway Journal*. In this notice Poe includes a substantial quotation from Hazlitt's comments on German drama (P 3: 173–175).[20]

A German figure whose name will be familiar to Poe scholars is that of Prince Hermann von Pückler-Muskau (1785–1871), mentioned in a footnote to "The Domain of Arnheim." Pückler's *Tour in England, Ireland and France* offers a source for details in "The Domain of Arnheim," specifically for the anecdote about the will of Peter Thellusson through which enormous wealth—analogous to Ellison's—was acquired. Pückler's *Tour* was first published as *Briefe eines Verstobenen*, appearing anonymously, though Pückler was almost immediately identified as its author. Poe was not fluent in German, so his exposure to Pückler, likely, came through his reading of Sarah Austin's translation, published by Carey, Lea & Blanchard in Philadelphia in 1833. Pückler's work crossed several prose genres: it was a personal memoir recounted in letters; it satisfied the German interest in Britain in its commentary on manners and culture; and it exploited the interest on both sides of the Atlantic in landscape gardening by describing English principles of estate management in contrast to French formality.

Less well known to readers of Poe than Pückler's passing mention of the Thellusson will is his self-described posture as a "parkomaniac," his tireless pursuit of country houses with impressive gardens and parks during his tour.[21] In Pückler's *Tour* the author's natural descriptions are complemented by his observations on the lives of the *fashionables*, the owners of vast estates and their impressive art collections. His visits to country houses allow him to indulge and apply varied interests in the fine arts, his passion for paintings, and his lifelong obsession with gardening. A garden, in fact, could be viewed as a kind of "picture gallery," in which idealized nature, aesthetically transformed, could be sampled and studied by the viewer, with a new and fresh scene introduced every few steps. The winding tour of the narrator in "The Domain of Arnheim" follows Pückler's penchant for this kind of image-making in the incremental discovery of a garden setting.

Pückler was clearly conversant with much of the available literature on landscape gardening, including the works of Humphry Repton and Lancelot "Capability" Brown, the latter whom he dubbed "the Shakespeare of gardening."[22] For Pückler and other travelers, a garden could be toured much like a gallery of three-dimensional landscape paintings, as the viewer moved through successive stages of encounter. The various paths in a garden allow the tourist to trace a medley of moods that might arise with changes in atmosphere, lighting, and weather conditions. A garden could thus offer movement that a stationary painting might lack. The English garden tradition could offer settings in which the mind is constantly being provoked, as was the case for travelers inspired by William Gilpin, who incorporated multiple points of view and a multidirectional impression of a site, features that a single picture might preclude.[23] As reflected in Pückler's tour of the River Wye, a geographical setting initially popularized by Gilpin, the German author's marked preference for English country views is evident.

Pückler's emphasis on motion—the ways in which a winding tour by carriage, boat, or afoot can disorient a traveler—affected Poe's handling of his fictional landscapes. More particularly, his description of the extensive garden observed on his trip between Wesel and Arnhem in Holland opens with a succession of concrete details and then acquires the character of an otherworldly vision. In the *Tour*, Pückler changes the Dutch place name to the German "Arnheim," the identifiable location that inspired Poe's heightened passage evoked at the tale's conclusion. I quote from Austin's translation since it was the likely version that Poe consulted:

> Although there is neither rock nor mountain in the endless park I traversed, yet the lofty dams along which the road sometimes runs, the multitude of country-seats, buildings and churches grouped into masses, and the many colossal clumps of trees rising from the meadows and plains, or on the banks of clear lakes, gave to the landscape as much diversity of surface as of picturesque of objects of the most varied character; indeed its greatest peculiarity consisted in this rapid succession of objects.... Towns, villages, country-seats, surrounded by their rich enclosures, villas of every style of architecture, with the prettiest flower-gardens; interminable grassy plains, with thousands of grazing cattle; lakes; ... countless islands ... a dwelling-place for

myriads of water-birds;—all join in a gladsome dance, through which one is borne along as if by winged horses; while still new palaces and other towns appear in the horizon and the towers of their high Gothic churches melt into the clouds in the misty distance.

And even in the near-ground the continually changing and often grotesque figures leave no room for monotony . . . yew-trees cut into dragons and all sorts of fabulous monsters; or lime-trees with trunks painted white, or many coloured; chimneys decorated in an Oriental style, with numbers of little towers and pinnacles; houses built slanting for the nonce; gardens with marble statues as large as life, in the dress of the old French court, peeping through the bushes, or a number of brass bottles or cans, polished like mirrors, standing on the grass by the roadside glittering like pure gold. . . . In short, a multitude of strange, unwonted and fantastic objects every moment present to the eye a fresh scene, and stamp the whole with a perfectly foreign character. Imagine such pictures set in the golden frame of the brightest sunshine, adorned with the richest vegetation from giant oaks, elms, ashes and beeches, to the rarest hot-house plant . . .[24]

Pückler begins this section of his tour with an array of picturesque objects in the foreground—trees, lakes, meadows, and plains—to which he adds a variety of human figures. Although Poe's Arnheim does not include multiple human figures, both writers aim for a kind of circumscribed theatrical set with certain features spotlighted—Pückler with a golden frame of bright sunshine; Poe with glittering red sunlight. Poe infuses Pückler's myriads of water birds with his colorful flocks of golden and crimson birds. Trees, hills, and other forms of vegetation in both cases offer further screening and staging effects: Pückler's colossal clumps of trees and his enumeration of oaks, elms, ashes, and beeches rising from meadows. Pückler's lofty dams are matched by Poe's mountains and hills. Architectural shapes that accent Pückler's horizon—palaces and towers—find expression in the oriels, minarets, and pinnacles of Arnheim. The German traveler's mélange of varied cultural objects offers an overall "stamp" of "foreign character." Pückler's Gothic churches in the distance find an analogue in Poe's "mass of semi-Gothic, semi-Saracenic architecture" (M 2: 1283). Poe strains definable boundaries with a dizzying array of images that seem to burst upon the somewhat dazed viewer. Pückler seems to be borne—or perhaps transported—along in a carriage ride that presents multiple images in quick succession. For Poe's narrator, who transfers from a vessel into a decorated and lighter canoe, the strange majesty of Arnheim seems to sustain itself in mid-air. Pückler's grotesque and monstrous images, his multitude of strange and fantastic objects, find a rough parallel in Poe's exquisite sense of the strange, his dream-like intermingling of striking effects.

In sum, Pückler's arresting series of pictures, surpassing mere imitations of nature, produces a "magical effect." As Poe notes in another context, the art of composition, as understood by the painter or the dramatist, aims for an overall impression: "But as the landscape of the artist (who deserves the name) must be superior in its 'composition,' in its arrangement of forms and colours, to any landscape actually existing, so the drama, while never losing sight of nature's intention, should surpass nature itself in its continuity of events with character—rejecting all that is not in itself dramatically picturesque or in full consonance with the effect or impression upon the audience which is intended by the dramatist" (H 13: 112). An artist's or dramatist's original observations are likely to be reimagined, as in Pückler's case, in which images multiply and the senses seem to be engulfed or overwhelmed. Pückler's romantic tropes are compelling, to be sure, but his connection to an actual tour of Holland is never fully severed, as place names indicate, and his practical guide moves on to additional sites of interest.

Poe's consultation of Pückler's *Tour* would have offered insight into a range of settings: parks, gardens, estates, country houses, cottages, castles, villas, ruins, hills, mountains, and river views. The German traveler's itinerary took him to attractions with appeal to picturesque tourists of diverse tastes: Kew, Wimbledon Park, Warwick Castle, Kenilworth, the river Wye, and William Beckford's Fonthill (the last mentioned or alluded to in both "Arnheim" and "Landor's Cottage"). At Kenilworth he carried a copy of Scott's novel, carefully monitoring the matching of verbal and visual effects. Along the way, he persistently applies painterly principles, recording impressions of favorite artists—Titian, Raphael, and Rubens as well as Claude and Rosa. As he discerns features of English gardens, the monitoring of mutable scenes seems to dissolve the boundary between nature and art, as each turn on a pathway offers fresh views. A foreigner lured by a passion for gardens, he acknowledges that his was "a fantastic picture-making mind that fashions its own dream-world anew every day," a tendency that made him "forever a stranger in the actual world." Even a garden of surpassing beauty was subject to change, decay, and death. For all his passion for the poetic ideal in landscape design, Pückler also senses the darker side of the gardener's art, the need for tools for clearing (the axe) and burial as well as creation.[25]

Despite Poe's narrator's apparent enthusiasm for Ellison's aspirations, there is distance between the narrator's perceptions of the estate owner and what he manages to create. If the assumption is that the most obvious path toward one's goal is to imitate nature, the "most enchanting of natural landscapes" always contain a "defect or an excess—many defects or excesses." Thus, the relationship between a painter's vision and what appears on canvas remains enigmatic. Even after quoting at length Ellison's pronouncements, the narrator's comments on the steadiness of the "artistical eye" remain somewhat "unintelligible" (M 3: 1272). The degree to which physical nature is susceptible to improvement remains a "mystery" that the narrator is unable to resolve. From a certain perspective, it is possible to gain aesthetic appreciation from the "primitive intention of nature," but that idea is weakened by knowledge of "geological disturbances" that were, Ellison suggested, "prognostic of *death*" (M 3: 1273). An alteration of natural scenery may introduce "a blemish in the picture," and "a closely scrutinized detail" may injure "a general or more distantly observed effect" (M 3: 1274). The narrator proves not nearly so accomplished in tasteful observation as Ellison, since spots that enrapture the former are summarily rejected by the latter. Distant prospects, scenes which may offer some observers an hour's gratification in their sheer physical extent, eventually fatigue the eye and lead to depression and heartsickness. Ellison's aversion to distant prospects has a precedent in Hazlitt's sharply articulated opinion: "There is nothing I hate like a distant prospect without anything interesting in it—it is constantly dragging the eye a wearisome journey, and repaying it with barrenness and deformity."[26] Among English writers on the picturesque, Uvedale Price, in particular, opposed ostentatious extensive views and singled out for derision gaudy "prospect-showers." As the English countryside was being developed, the vogue of landscape gardening, with its varied enclosures, was an attempt to recapture a rural way of life that was in the process of being lost. It appears that Poe, the urban editor, is offering a similar perspective, applied to American settings in his landscape sketches.[27]

Poe's traveler, more caught up in the details of the trip than the ultimate destination, observes "rolling meadows," multiple turns in the stream, and arrival in a gorge that shuts out the sunlight (M 3: 1278). Afforded a fleeting glimpse, the narrator is granted neither a full vision nor an entrance into the strangely described castle in the air. Further evidence of a possible ironic reading are images of imprisonment within an enchanted circle, a landscape of sameness and uniformity rather than the prospect of novelty outlined at the tale's opening, and a tidy formality more in line with settings that advanced gardeners were prone to discard. Although early sections of the tale seem to imply Ellison's ownership and control over his property, the mood is that of being carried along by unseen currents with minimal volition. The narrator's disorientation is accompanied by oppressive assaults on the senses: strange odors that fail to refresh and places where vision is impeded by impenetrable barriers. At times, he is a "bewildered voyager" who looks around in vain for clarity or direction (M 3: 1280).[28]

If Poe's landscapes partake of the picturesque and the ideal, visionary scenes and those with darker hues, "Landor's Cottage" reflects similar tensions, particularly as Poe deploys his narrator on a pedestrian tour. His journey begins "confusedly" on a path that provides no clear direction to a nearby village. A "smoky mist" contributes to further "uncertainty," a series of views in which he sees "nothing distinctly" (M 3: 1328, 1330). Though there is no obvious impediment to his progress and the area presents natural "capabilities," the serpentine pathway discloses only a "bewildered admiration," a perplexing "variety in uniformity" that prevents him from tracing his course more than a few paces in advance (M 3: 1330). The narrator's comments seem to be in line with the aesthetics of indistinctness inherent in Hazlitt's comment: "A morning mist drawing a slender veil over all objects is at once picturesque and ideal: for it in the first place excites immediate surprise and admiration and in the next a wish for it to continue, and fear lest it be dissipated."[29]

As the fog seems to dissipate for Poe's narrator, the physical movement results in a coup d'oeil, a scene imaginatively framed or lit. Not only is the scene compared to a work of art; in this case, Poe's narrator notes something akin to "the concluding scene of some well-arranged theatrical spectacle or melodrama" (M 3: 1131). With its theatrical imagery and allusions to Beckford's *Vathek*, the artificial setting of "Landor's Cottage" is like a text that invites reading and deciphering, despite the narrator's profession to welcome the salutary effects of nature on his walk. Poe, moreover, presents a "monstrosity of color," the sunlight tinged with a garish mixture of orange and purple. Poe notes that the narrator's perspective is boyish, that perhaps his perception, clouded by the curtain of vapor, is fanciful, akin to "vanishing pictures" (M 3: 1330). In acknowledging an "excess of art," the narrator may be an unwitting participant in an insubstantial but enveloping spectacle.[30]

Poe was familiar with cultural voices like those of Bryant and Emerson who rhapsodized over the glories of American nature, its distinctive features, and figures populating its vast landscapes. In the context of his fictional landscapes, however, human figures are hardly discernible or nearly absent. Nevertheless, in "Landor's Cottage," the narrator knocks on the door of the dwelling, and a young woman somewhat modestly approaches the threshold. The narrator remarks, "Surely here I have found the perfection of natural, in contradistinction from artificial grace" (M 3: 1138). The aura of romance and the expressive features of the woman of the house seem to cast a "powerful . . . spell" over the naive narrator. Lest the reader think that Poe is uncritically glorifying natural beauty, the broader context of the tale presents a setting organized according to principles of art. Nature is once again framed as a spectacle and as a scene, what Poe termed the "dramatically picturesque." In its combined "novelty and propriety," Landor's dwelling appears to be the product of a practiced painter: "Its marvellous *effect* lay altogether in its artistic arrangement *as a picture*" (M 3: 1335). The approach to the cottage is marked as well by "excessive *neatness*" (M 3: 1334). If gardeners like Capability Brown and Pückler-Muskau rebelled against the orderly symmetry of the formal garden, they eventually gravitated to designs with more flexible patterns of association. Attempting to outline an intermediary space between the formal garden and settings that seemed to acquire their own character, some commentators found the proper balance in the so-called poetic garden. For Poe, muting of certain details in favor of offering greater expressive and pictorial impact reinforces "some one vivid and intensely characteristic point or touch" (H 11: 272). Occupying a unique spot on what appears to be an island unto itself, Landor's dwelling can be summed up in a single word: poetry. As neat as the formulation may seem, however, Poe's ironic detachment from his narrator suggests a sustained ambivalence about the competing claims of art and nature.

In a range of landscape sketches from the early 1840s onward, Poe explored the *physique* and the *morale* of settings that included gardens, rivers, streams, woods, hills, promontories, plateaus, cottages—a host of intricate dwellings and forms that seemed to match the dream-like projections of his narrators. He presented figures with access to scenes alternately picturesque and ideal, sublime and beautiful, delicate and strange, visionary and dark, natural and artificial, rural and suburban, minutely detailed and broadly expressive. As suggested by the conclusion of "Landor's Cottage," Poe pondered a third entry in a potential "Arnheim" trilogy. One can only wonder what pathway he may have taken in this never completed work as he continued to probe the tensions inherent in his exploration of art and nature, representation and reality.

Notes

1. Agnes Bondurant, *Poe's Richmond* (Richmond, VA: Garrett & Massie, 1942), 6; William Wirt, *Letters of the British Spy* (New York: Harper & Brothers, 1832), 106–107.

2. Arthur Hobson Quinn, *Edgar Allan Poe: A Critical Biography* (New York: Appleton, 1941), 98; Hervey Allen, *Israfel: The Life and Times of Edgar Allan Poe* (New York: Farrar & Rinehart, 1934), 129, 143; Kenneth A. Hovey, "Poe's Materialist Metaphysics of Man," in *A Companion to Poe Studies*, ed. Eric W. Carlson (Westport, CT: Greenwood Press, 1996), 360–361. Kevin J. Hayes discusses Jefferson's fascination with botany, natural history, farming, and gardening in *The Road to Monticello: The Life and Mind of Thomas Jefferson* (New York: Oxford University Press, 2008), 86–87, 97, 318–321, 418–431.
3. Jefferson to William Hamilton, Washington, July, 1806, in *Writings*, ed. Merrill D. Peterson (New York: Library of America, 1984), 1166–1169; review of *Views of Philadelphia and Its Vicinity, Burton's Gentleman's Magazine*, 3 (July 1838): 70; James Mease, *Picture of Philadelphia, Giving an Account of Its Origin, Increase and Improvements in Arts, Sciences, Manufactures, Commerce and Revenue*, 2 vols. (Philadelphia: Robert Desilver, 1831), 1:344–354, 2:94–102; *Picture of Philadelphia, or A Brief Account of the Various Institutions and Public Objects in the Metropolis* (Philadelphia: Carey & Hart, 1835), 188–209; Elizabeth Milroy, "Assembling Fairmount Park," in *Philadelphia's Cultural Landscape: The Sartain Family Legacy*, ed. Katharine Martinez and Page Talbott (Philadelphia: Temple University Press, 2000), 72–86. In a history of the Farimount district, Milroy includes J. T. Bowen's 1838 lithograph "View of Fairmount Waterworks with the Schuylkill River in the Distance," showing the waterworks in the foreground of a riverscape, admired by strolling visitors. Philadelphia became a center for producing varied "embellishments" in magazines and gift books, but in the 1830s landscapes predominated.
4. Quinn, *Edgar Allan Poe: A Critical Biography*, 444; Kenneth Silverman, *Edgar A. Poe: Mournful and Never-Ending Remembrance* (New York: Harper Collins, 1991), 222.
5. Jacob Spannuth, ed. *Poe's Contributions to the Columbia Spy: Doings of Gotham by Edgar Allan Poe* (Pottsville, PA: Jacob Spannuth, 1929), 33, 40–41, quoted in Barbara Cantalupo, *Poe and the Visual Arts* (University Park: Pennsylvania State University Press, 2014), 10.
6. Susan Archer Talley Weiss, *Home Life of Poe* (New York: Broadway Publishing, 1907), 127–128; Allen, *Israfel: The Life and Times of Edgar Allan Poe*, 587–588.
7. Allen, *Israfel: The Life and Times of Edgar Allan Poe*, 569, 583, 587–588; Quinn, *Edgar Allan Poe: A Critical Biography*, 507; Whitman to J. H. Ingram, 1874, in *Poe's Helen Remembers*, ed. John Carl Miller (Charlottesville: University Press of Virginia, 1979), 124; Elma Mary Letchworth Gove, "A Young Girl's Recollections of Edgar Allan Poe," quoted in Cantalupo, *Poe and the Visual Arts*, 160–161.
8. Cooper, *The Letters and Journals of James Fenimore Cooper*, ed. J. F. Beard, 6 vols. (Cambridge, MA: Harvard University Press, 1960–1968), 3:261. Distinguishing aesthetic categories, Cooper frequently contrasted the sublime and picturesque from the beautiful by resorting to the French "beau."
9. Poe, review of *The American Flower Garden Companion*, by Edward Sayers, *Burton's Gentleman's Magazine* 5 (September 1839): 168.
10. Hazlitt, "Judging of Pictures," *Miscellaneous Essays on the Fine Arts, in Collected Works of William Hazlitt*, eds. A. R. Waller and Arnold Glover, 12 vols. (London: Dent, 1903), 9:356–359.
11. Hazlitt, "On a Landscape of Nicholas Poussin," *Table-Talk, in Complete Works of William Hazlitt*, ed. P. P. Howe, 21 vols. (London: Dent, 1931), 8:171–172; Cantalupo, *Poe and the Visual Arts*, 22–27.
12. Jeffrey A. Hess, "Sources and Aesthetics of Poe's Landscape Fiction," *American Quarterly* 22, no. 2 (1970): 177–189; C. T. Walters, "Poe's 'Philosophy of Furniture' and the Aesthetics

of Fictional Design," in *Edgar Allan Poe: Beyond Gothicism*, ed. James M. Hutchisson (Newark: University of Delaware Press, 2011), 1–15. For discussion of Poe's landscapes in the light of his cosmology, see E. W. Pitcher, "The Arnheim Trilogy: Cosmic Landscapes in the Shadow of Poe's *Eureka*," *Canadian Review of American Studies* 6 (1975): 27–35.

13. Henry Wadsworth Longfellow, *The Poetical Works of Henry Wadsworth Longfellow* (Boston: Houghton Mifflin, 1888) 5:295–296. With regard to "Arnheim," Poe may rely on experiences outside Philadelphia or in the Hudson River valley. Robert Jacobs suggests that Ellison's property was inspired by "various estates near Philadelphia and along the Hudson," in "Poe's Earthly Paradise," *American Quarterly* 12, no. 3 (1960): 27–35.
14. Liliane Weissberg, "In Search of Truth and Beauty in 'Berenice' and 'The Domain of Arnheim,'" in *Poe and His Times: The Artist in His Milieu*, ed. Benjamin F. Fisher (Baltimore: Edgar Allan Poe Society of Baltimore, 1990), 71.
15. Hazlitt, *Notes of a Journey through France and Italy*, in *Collected Works*, 9:236; Hazlitt, "On the Picturesque and the Ideal," *Table-Talk*, in *Complete Works*, 8:317–321.
16. Hazlitt, "On the Picturesque and the Ideal," *Table-Talk, in Complete Works*, 8:320; Hazlitt, "The Ideal," *Miscellaneous Essays on the Fine Arts, in Collected Works*, 9:429–434. Poe, seeming to echo Hazlitt's vocabulary in his review of Slidell's *The American in England*, notes approvingly how some incidents at sea "are told . . . with gusto" (P 5: 117). Margaret Alterton, an early scholar of Poe's interest in the fine arts, traces Schlegel's principles of dramatic unity and effect (perhaps via Hazlitt's intermediary influence) to Poe's evolving knowledge of painting, in *The Origins of Poe's Critical Theory* (Iowa City: Iowa Humanistic Studies, 1925), 82. In a review, "Our Book-Shelves," attributed to Poe by T. O. Mabbott and William Doyle Hull, several works by Hazlitt are praised, including the following endorsement: "His comments [Hazlitt's] on Art are probably the most accurate, if not altogether the best portions of his writing"—review of "Table-Talk," by William Hazlitt, *Aristidean* (September 1845): 235–236.
17. Hazlitt, "The Picture Galleries of England," in *Collected Works*, 9:65–66.
18. Cantalupo, *Poe and the Visual Arts*, 29, 47, 80.
19. Cantalupo, *Poe and the Visual Arts*, 76–77; Hazlitt, *Notes of a Journey*, in *Collected Works*, 8:226; Hazlitt, *Lady Morgan's Life of Salvator Rosa*, in *Collected Works*, 11:288–290.
20. Hazlitt, "On the English Novelists," *Lectures on the English Comic Writers, in Collected Works*, 6:125–129. In the November 8, 1845, *Broadway Journal* under "Critical Notices," Poe mentions Hazlitt's volume on *The English Comic Writers* (P 3: 301). In his essay on Schlegel, Hazlitt comments on German drama, "What the German dramatists really excel in, is the production of effect" (Hazlitt, *Collected Works*, 16:98–99).
21. At each stop—whether a castle, palace, or estate (e.g., Warwick or Blenheim), Pückler lingered to explore the adjoining park or garden. In Austin's translation the term "parkomanie" describes Pückler's obsession, in Pückler-Muskau [a German Prince, pseud.], *Tour in England, Ireland and France in the Years 1828 and 1829*, trans. Sarah Austin (Philadelphia: Carey, Lea & Blanchard, 1833), 64, 84.
22. Pückler-Muskau, *Tour in England, Ireland and France in the Years 1828 and 1829*, 85. Pückler's work has received a recent more complete translation, Herman von Pückler-Muskau, *Letters of a Dead Man*, ed. and trans. Linda Parshall (Washington, D.C.: Dumbarton Oaks Research Library, 2016). For Austin's excisions of passages about places already familiar to readers and material deemed improper, see Peter James Bowman, *The Fortune Hunter: A German Prince in Regency England* (Oxford: Signal Books, 2010), 163. Poe was likely introduced to the German traveler by M. Hertz, "A Memoir of Prince Pückler Muskau," *Burton's Gentleman's Magazine* 1, no. 2 (August 1837): 85–87.

23. Much scholarship on landscape design in England is synthesized in John Dixon Hunt, *The Figure in the Landscape: Poetry, Painting, and Gardening in the Eighteenth Century* (Baltimore: Johns Hopkins University Press, 1976) and Malcolm Andrews, *The Search for the Picturesque: Landscape, Aesthetics, and Tourism in Britain, 1760–1800* (Stanford, CA: Stanford University Press, 1989), especially the latter scholar's comments on gardens (51, 153, 190–199).
24. Pückler-Muskau, *Tour in England, Ireland and France in the Years 1828 and 1829*, 10–11. Carl Schreiber was the first to note the impact of Pückler on "The Domain of Arnheim," in "Mr. Poe at His Conjurations Again," *Colophon* 1, part 2 (1930), no page. Parshall, a scholar of the German landscape tradition, has an extended discussion of Pückler's influence on Poe and other writers through her translations and in "Hirschfield, Pückler, Poe: The Literary Modeling of Nature," *German Historical Bulletin* 4 (2007): 149–169. Since this German scholarship may not be familiar or not easily accessible to Poe scholars, I am re-presenting some of it in this essay. Austin's translation, which was Poe's likely source, was an abridgement of Pückler's German original.
25. Pückler-Muskau, *Tour in England, Ireland, and France*, 119. See Kent Ljungquist, "Picturesque Disorder: The Deceptive Dream Land of Poe's Fictional Landscapes," in *The Grand and the Fair: Poe's Landscape Aesthetics and Pictorial Techniques* (Potomac, MD: Scripta Humanistica, 1984), 107–140. Pückler's practical side resulted in his own *Hints on Landscape Gardening*, trans. John Hargraves (Basel: Birkhauser, 2014), a volume originally published in Germany (1834). See, in particular, comments on garden maintenance (74–75).
26. Hazlitt, *Notes of a Journey Through France and Italy*, in *Collected Works*, 9:100.
27. Ann Berningham discusses the call for an "enlightened rusticity" that offered a complement to urban values in "The Picturesque Decade," in *Landscape and Ideology: The English Rustic Tradition 1740–1860* (Berkeley: University of California Press, 1986), 57–80. She mentions Hazlitt's balance of rustic and urban values (165).
28. My own ironic reading of Poe's landscapes was reinforced by the thorough research of Beth Lynne Lueck, who demonstrates his narrators' manifest unreliability as they fall short of mastery of aesthetic principles, "Poe's 'Picturesque Hunters,'" in *American Writers and the Picturesque Tour: The Search for National Identity, 1790–1860* (Westport, CT: Garland, 1997), 152–167.
29. Hazlitt, *Table-Talk*, in *Complete Works*, 8:320–321.
30. For comments on literary landscapes as visual theater, see John Conron, *American Picturesque* (University Park: Pennsylvania State University Press, 2000), 202–203; David Marshall, "The Picturesque," in *The Cambridge History of Literary Criticism: The Eighteenth Century*, eds. H. B. Nisbet and Claude Rawson (Cambridge: Cambridge University Press, 1989), 4:700–718. Among Conron's valuable chapters is "Comparing Picturesque Arts: Literature as Painting" (195–230). For analysis that moves away from nature to linguistic signification, see Joan Dayan, "The Poet in the Garden," in *Fables of Mind: An Inquiry into Poe's Fiction* (New York: Oxford University Press, 1987), 80–129.

BIBLIOGRAPHY

Alterton, Margaret. *The Origins of Poe's Critical Theory*. Iowa City: Iowa Humanistic Studies, 1925.

Andrews, Malcolm. *The Search for the Picturesque: Landscape, Aesthetics, and Tourism in Britain, 1760–1800*. Stanford, CA: Stanford University Press, 1989.

Cantalupo, Barbara. *Poe and the Visual Arts*. University Park: Pennsylvania State University Press, 2014.

Conron, John. *American Picturesque*. University Park: Pennsylvania State University Press, 2000.

Hazlitt, William. *Collected Works of William Hazlitt*. Edited by A. R. Waller and Arnold Glover. 12 vols. London: Dent, 1903.

Hazlitt, William. *Complete Works of William Hazlitt*. Edited by P. P. Howe. 21 vols. London: Dent, 1931.

Hess, Jeffrey. "Sources and Aesthetics of Poe's Landscape Fiction." *American Quarterly* 22, no. 2 (1970): 177–189

Lueck, Beth L. "Poe's 'Picturesque Hunters.' " In *American Writers and the Picturesque Tour: The Search for National Identity, 1790–1860*, 152–167. Westport, CT: Garland, 1997.

Marshall, David. "The Picturesque." In *The Cambridge History of Literary Criticism: The Eighteenth Century*, edited by H. B. Nisbet and Claude Rawson, 4: 700–718. Cambridge: Cambridge University Press, 1989.

Pückler-Muskau, Hermann von [a German Prince, pseud.]. *Letters of a Dead Man*. Edited and translated by Linda Parshall. Washington, D. C.: Dumbarton Oaks Research Library, 2016.

Pückler-Muskau, Hermann von [a German Prince, pseud.]. *Tour in England, Ireland and France in the Years 1828 and 1829*. Translated by Sarah Austin. 4 vols. Philadelphia: Carey, Lea & Blanchard, 1833.

CHAPTER 18

UNDYING ENIGMAS IN "LIGEIA"

ALEXANDRA URAKOVA

> December's Ligeia runs in my blood.
>
> —Osip Mandelstam, "A Last Straw"[1]

POE's "Ligeia" (1838), his own favorite tale at one point,[2] is representative of his early style, but as Clark Griffith put it more than half a century ago, "we need linger only a moment on its Gothic surface to recognize how it does of course abound in the effects, the devices, the mannerisms which are typically, almost mechanically, Poesque."[3] Poetical overtones and rhythms, odd word choices, the use and abuse of alliterations, exaggerations, dense materiality of hallucinatory descriptions, the grotesque, the uncanny Gothic setting, mystery, daydreaming, madness, opium, disease, death, macabre naturalism, an unreliable narrator, Orientalism, ideality, bizarre interiors, the dramatic ending, and the perverse—all come together in a peculiar pattern or combination, to use Poe's own term. Undoubtedly one of his most well-known and closely examined tales, "Ligeia" is situated at the "forking paths" of Poe's literary imagination. Taking its title from a minor figure in "Al Aaraaf," it bridges the gap between his poetry and short fiction.[4] Elaborating on the earlier "Berenice" and especially "Morella," it epitomizes Poe's subgenre of the "death of a beautiful woman" tale.[5] A story of mystery and horror, "Ligeia" is often paired with another Gothic masterpiece of the late 1830s, "The Fall of the House of Usher"—and at the same time, oddly echoes and parallels two of Poe's grotesques, "The Man That Was Used Up" and "The Psyche Zenobia." Told by an unreliable narrator, it is opaque and mysterious—and yet it provides us with "allegories of reading" revealing "the rationale of deception," to borrow David Ketterer's term.[6] It would be no exaggeration to say that "Ligeia" is among Poe's most puzzling tales, one that leaves us pondering undying enigmas and unresolved questions. In this chapter, I will give a brief overview of some of these questions, drawing on major critical readings, and then focus more closely on two contextual frameworks that have not received much attention: "Ligeia's" first publication in *The American Museum* and the function of the Medusa myth and Medusa-inspired imagery in the tale. My reading will attempt to demonstrate what makes "Ligeia" a paradigmatic tale in the Poe canon. It is a tale that hinges on poetical (acoustical) techniques and stylistic devices yet suggests meanings that go beyond its plotline, compelling readers to constantly shift perspective and look for cues. Embedded in the print culture of its time, it shows Poe's awareness of both its medium and the limits of any mediation. Springing from Romantic tradition, especially from the Romantic aesthetics of the sublime, "Ligeia" invents a new sensibility that makes the tale strikingly modern, despite its often archaic and odd vocabulary.

One of the major stumbling blocks for readers of "Ligeia" is its plot. The narrator is not only unreliable, like most of Poe's storytellers, but also, from the very start, he openly declares his unreliability: "I cannot, for my soul, remember how, when, or even precisely where, I first became acquainted with the lady Ligeia" (M 2: 310). He confesses that he cannot remember the details of the story he is going to narrate, nor can he make up his mind whether his amnesia is caused by his "feeble" memory or by the "singular" character of his beloved (M 2: 310). Later we learn that the narrator "had become a bounden slave in the trammels of opium" (M 2: 320). Not unlike Henry James's "The Turn of the Screw," the tale already contains clues for at least two conflicting interpretations.[7] Should we assume that Ligeia indeed came back "through the door of a corpse," as D. H. Lawrence famously put it, or that it is a story told by one of Poe's many sociopaths, a maniac who poisoned his second wife?[8] Is it a tale about love, death, and resurrection, or murder and opium-inflicted hallucination?

Whichever critical approach we take, it is still not easy to say what "really" happens in "Ligeia," especially in its last scene describing the pendulum-like sway of Rowena's corpse between resurrection and death and Ligeia's mysterious "return." The tale's finale puzzled one of its first readers, Poe's friend Phillip Pendleton Cooke:

> I appreciated every sentence . . . until the lady Ligeia takes possession of the deserted *quarters* (I write like a butcher) of the Lady Rowena. There I was shocked by a violation of the ghostly proprieties so to speak and wondered how the Lady Ligeia—a wandering essence—could, in quickening *the body of the Lady Rowena* (such is the idea) become suddenly the visible, bodily, Ligeia.[9]

Cooke favored a more gradual metamorphosis, "Rowena's bodily form" being "retained as a shell or case for the disembodied Lady Ligeia." Poe promptly agreed with him, explaining the "flaws" of the finale as necessary to differentiate the plot from the earlier "Morella": "I should have intimated that the *will* did not perfect its intention—there should have been a relapse—a final one—and Ligeia . . . should be at length entombed as Rowena" (CL 1: 118). Yet he never changed the ending in his subsequent revisions of the tale. Another conventional alternative would have been to make "the spirit of Ligeia metempsychose itself, 'Metzengerstein'-fashion, into Rowena's flesh," as Richard de Prospo suggests. Poe, however, preferred to "re-embody Ligeia cell-by-cell at the end," "the dead meat of Rowena metabolized by Ligeia's spirit as the condition of Ligeia's return."[10] Indeed, Rowena's corpse is not quite a "shell" or a "case" as Ligeia is not quite a ghost. It is easier to assert, after Elizabeth Bronfen, what Ligeia in the final scene *is not*: "neither image nor body, neither living nor dead, neither absent nor present, neither the model nor the copy."[11] Poe's final scene violates not only "the ghostly proprieties" but also the conventions of the Gothic tradition the tale is bearing upon; its surplus corporeality and "sudden" visibility is equally at odds with the vagueness and indeterminacy we usually associate with dreams or hallucinations.

Cooke inadvertently anticipates another twentieth-century anxiety: is Poe serious or is he mocking us? Should we indeed take the morbid description of Ligeia's resurrection, verging on the macabre grotesque and presenting a stark contrast to her acclaimed ideality, at face value? As early as 1954, Clark Griffith interpreted the story as a parody of Romantic and Gothic clichés. For Griffith, the story stands out in Poe's Gothic canon because "as one reads and re-reads the narrative, certain troublesome features persistently intrude." Griffith focuses on what he sees as deliberate flaws of style that outdo even Poe's usual extravagance: "stylistic mannerisms in no way requisite to the melodrama," "abrupt breaks in tone," "incongruities of detail," and "allusions and far-fetched comparisons which appear to be totally meaningless."[12] It is hard not to agree that in "Ligeia" Poe puts "a diamond ring on every finger,"[13] piling up alliterations (even within the dense space of a single phrase), or that his word choice in this tale is particularly odd.[14] In this respect, "Ligeia" aligns with Poe's poetry, traditionally criticized for its meretricious effects.

Jerome McGann invites us to see Poe's poetry as "an acoustical dictionary of phrase and fable where complex relations of assonance and consonance—'combinations of combinations'—shift the language until it tilts at the edge of normality."[15] Sneered at by generations of critics, Poe the poet, in McGann's opinion, revolutionizes poetical language in a manner similar to Rimbaud or Emily Dickinson: "the reader confronts words that, however familiar, suggest that another unknown language lies concealed in our common tongue."[16] McGann attributes to Poe a property that Gilles Deleuze conceptualized when speaking about Melville's "Bartleby": "with his own language, he carves out a non-preexistent foreign language within his own language."[17] Extending such an approach to the reading of "Ligeia," we may suggest, for example, that when Poe combines the name of a character in *Ivanhoe*, "a name for Tintagel in Cornwall, associated with Arthurian romance and magic," and the title of a contemporary novel in Lady Rowena's full name (M 2: 333–334n24), he treats these "transubstantiated" proper names primarily as "phonetic things."[18] "Lady Rowena Trevanion, of Tremaine" becomes a new intertextual entity, at once familiar, recognizable, clichéd and unfamiliar, unknown, strange. A longish and "exotic" name of the dull and "the least Romantic" of Poe's heroines does not have to be parodic;[19] it may as well function as the means to "de-familiarize" and "de-Scotticize" the character, the redundancy of words and sounds anticipating the transgression of Rowena's body. As J. Gerald Kennedy has argued, "fusing the two wives into a beautiful, undying woman, Poe suggests that the idolatry of the poems and the loathing of the tales are reciprocal effects of a relationship to Woman predicated on dependency." While Ligeia incarnates Poe's poetical principle, Rowena "embodies the principle of prose" or "inhabits the realm of prose, associated in

'The Philosophy of Composition' not with supernal Beauty but with the expression of Truth and Passion (or 'homeliness'), with realities 'absolutely antagonistic' to Beauty."[20] It is tempting to suggest that the odd phonetic effect of Rowena's full name perversely undermines or subverts the prosaic element in the character and makes the fusion of Ligeia and Rowena, poetry and prose possible. Words or combinations of words in the tale seem to have an independent, material, and uncanny life of their own as Poe translates the tale's Gothic horror into a seemingly "foreign" or "alien" language within common and familiar English.[21]

Yet even if we do read "Ligeia" *as* poetry or as a poetic allegory, can we see its language as purely nonrepresentational, ignoring a rich diversity of its political, racial, gendered, and sexual subtexts? Critics have vigorously read American-centered and antebellum-related narratives into the tale: a narrative of miscegenation, a narrative of imperialism, and a narrative of gender transgression and queer sexuality.[22] "Ligeia," despite its conventional European setting, takes us to the core of these antebellum anxieties, embedding them in the form of elusive, euphemistic, and Gothicized cues—and simultaneously prompts us "to interrogate or re-interrogate the past for evidence of issues that concern us here and now."[23] While this observation may be true for Poe's fiction in general, "Ligeia" forms a specific case in the way it shifts our perspective from "meaningless," acoustic word combinations to almost too meaningful and telling details. Describing the narrator's chamber, Poe introduces a baroque optical device known as *anamorphosis*, as first noticed by Jurgis Baltrušaitis[24]: arabesque figures on the curtains change their aspect depending on the visitor's position in the room.

> To one entering the room, they bore the appearance of simple monstrosities; but upon a farther advance, this appearance gradually departed; and step by step, as the visiter moved his station in the chamber, he saw himself surrounded by an endless succession of the ghastly forms which belong to the superstition of the Norman, or arise in the guilty slumbers of the monk. (M 2: 322)

Anamorphic vision has become integral to "Ligeia" criticism, allowing critics to see a skull concealed behind Ligeia's face (G. R. Thompson),[25] to recognize a "tragic mulatta" in the German lady (Dayan), or to envision Ligeia's struggles to come to life through Rowena's body as lesbian sex and rape (Rohy).[26] We may wonder, after Valerie Rohy, if "Ligeia" indeed "reserves its clearest visions for those who look aslant" and how far we can go in accepting Poe's invitation to experiment with our critical optics.[27] What inspires generations of critics' compulsion to decipher "Ligeia," and to what extent does this quest mirror our own anxieties or "superstitions"?

The anamorphic perspective installed in the tale is supplemented by the abundance of cultural allusions and references that, in their turn, expand our vision and invite a wide range of critical interpretations. Indeed, the optical device Poe describes is itself a highly experimental cultural artifact, combining a baroque trompe-l'œil with Oriental art (arabesques) and Medieval Gothicism ("the superstition of the Norman" and "the guilty slumbers of the monk"). Ligeia's portrait blends various culturally, nationally, and racially encoded elements of female beauty. The chamber in the abbey resembles a museum of antiques with bric-a-brac representing different epochs and nations, itself a replica of Ligeia's face and her encyclopedic learning, covering "*all* the wide areas of moral, physical, and mathematical science" (M 2: 315). Meredith McGill relates Poe's eclectic aesthetics in "Ligeia" (also in "The Visionary" and *Pym*) to "the reprint culture's haphazard arrangement of its literary materials."[28] Yet while "The Visionary," its eclecticism notwithstanding, is dominated by a Byronic theme, "Ligeia" seems to invite browsing, in an encyclopedia- or museum-like fashion, allowing readers to move in different directions. One of the possible explanations of this peculiarity may be found in the mimetic resemblance between the tale and its original publication venue, *The American Museum of Science, Literature and the Arts*.

The American Museum was a short-lived magazine edited by Nathan C. Brooks and Dr. Joseph E. Snodgrass, and Poe published "Ligeia" in its first volume, with a double intention to gain money and support his friends.[29] Douglas Anderson draws a parallel between the title of the magazine and the museum-like imagery of Poe's tale, claiming that the analogy might have been inevitable "to the story's first readers as well as to Poe himself."[30] What sustains the analogy, however, is not so much the title of the magazine (rather common among antebellum periodicals) as its learned, intellectual manner and declared intention to systematically cover three areas of knowledge—science, literature, and the arts. Though the magazine emphasizes national themes, the content reveals a broadly conceived contextual framework. The ancient monuments of North and South America are placed against the ruins and monuments of Egypt, Assyria, Italy, and Greece[31]; the volume pays tribute to Washington Irving but also to Lord Byron and ancient authors, Brooks lauds the statue of Laocoön as an example of "ideality, sublimity, and grace."[32] A number of serious essays and reviews tackle scientific, religious, and metaphysical issues. In "The Disclosures of Science," for example, Dr. Snodgrass discusses chemistry in terms strikingly similar to the final scene of Poe's story: "Chemistry meets us with its glorious and soul-elating doctrine of the *indestructibility of matter*. It teaches us that bodies may be deprived of their present form, and that their component particles, or atoms may disappear; but that they still exist undiminished in weight though under far different combinations."[33]

"Ligeia," with its peculiar combination of poetry, art, and science, may be seen as a kind of *mise en abyme* within the magazine. The publication venue justifies the erudite style of Poe's tale combining ancient ideality, Francis Bacon, German mysticism, and Oriental exoticism as well as the preference for rare, exotic names—for example, "the misty-winged Ashtophet of idolatrous Egypt" instead of the more familiar Astarte and Ashtoreth (M 2: 311). This odd mixture of allusions makes us wonder how much "Ligeia," in its style and form, owes to its medium—namely, where *The American Museum* ends and "Ligeia" begins. It is not even easy to draw the boundaries between Poe's tale and the neighboring poems that echo some of its themes and metaphors. Poe's narrator recognizes the elusive expression of Ligeia's eyes in "a stream of running water" and in "the ocean" (among others). The tale is followed by a poem, "The Ocean Shell," about a shell holding the memory of the ocean's roar, itself an analogy of the lover's faithfulness, and "Niagara," a poem describing the sublime majesty of the waterfall.[34]

As McGill has observed, "to the lasting discomfort of his critics, Poe's fictions participate too enthusiastically in the cultural formations they also appear to critique."[35] Poe's critique is therefore often inseparable from self-parody. In the next volume of *The American Museum*, he published his "Psyche Zenobia," a tale that not only ridicules his own method in "Ligeia" and parodies the sensationalism of the *Blackwood's*, but perhaps also, slyly, mocks the intellectual manner of *The American Museum*: "If you know any big words this is your chance for them. Talk of the academy and the lyceum, and say something about the Ionic and Italic schools, or about Bossarion, and Kant, and Schelling, and Fichte, and be sure you abuse a man called Locke, and bring in the words a priori and *a posteriori*" (M 2: 342).

"Ligeia" gains independence of its medium in numerous subsequent reprints; furthermore, its later revisions demonstrate that Poe, with a high degree of self-awareness, used print and reprint culture to his own ends. He included his independently published poem "The Conqueror Worm" in the body of the text for *The New World* edition (1845), giving a new life and meaning to the independently circulating poem and forming a new combination of the two previously published texts. The revisions of the 1840s—the capitalization of the last two words—also strongly emphasized the abruptness and the shocking "visibility" of the final scene that so disturbed Cooke. *The American Museum* reads: " 'Here then at least,' I shrieked aloud, 'can I never—can I never be mistaken—these are the full, and the black, and the wild eyes—of my lost love—of the lady—of the lady Ligeia!' "[36] The canonized version (Whitman copy) concludes: " 'Here then, at least,' I shrieked aloud, 'can I never—can I never be mistaken—these are the full, and the black, and the wild eyes—of my lost love—of the lady—of the LADY LIGEIA!' " (M 2: 329).

Reading "Ligeia" in the context of antebellum print culture, Dorothea von Mücke claims that while the Greek etymology of the name Ligeia, a tree nymph in Virgil's *Georgics*, "suggests the medium of sound, a loud call, . . . Poe's story quickly shifts from an imaginary aurality to a visual register"—a shift "motivated by the silence of the print culture."[37] While this statement seems to underestimate the tale's excessive auditory effects (and the practice of reading aloud was still very common in Poe time), it neatly relates "Ligeia" to the medium of print and its techniques. The abovementioned example indeed demonstrates how the visual register—namely, the use of the capital font—transcribes the narrator's shriek. The graphic emphasis belongs exclusively to the printed page and to silent reading: we can only "see" capital letters; we cannot "hear" them. Emphasizing or italicizing the last words of the tale or the poem, especially when they coincided with the title, was very common in antebellum periodicals and books. Poe, however, uses the capital letters not for merely ornamental purposes but to add a nightmarish, apocalyptic quality to the final scene, leaving us face to face with its irresolvable ambiguity.[38] Ligeia's "return" following the "hideous drama of revivification" (M 2: 328) is at once a fulfillment of the "wildest" desire and an existential catastrophe.

It is tempting to speculate, in this regard, on the relation between antebellum print culture and the Romantic discourse of sublimity that historically coincided with the expansion of the print market—for instance, new media technologies reproducing images and figures of the sublime (ocean, waterfall, mountains). The capitalization of the last words in "Ligeia" graphically marks the verbal incompetence of the narrator, who is unable to speak the "unspeakable."[39] Not only "the wandering spirit" of Ligeia but also the name that the narrator shrieks aloud suddenly materializes and becomes likewise "visible." The narrator remains paralyzed and silenced by what he sees, as if "blinded" and turned to stone by Lady Ligeia's eyes.

Poe's graphic conclusion unambiguously evokes Medusa's stupefying gaze, allowing us to relate the sublime poetics of the tale to the mythopoetic image of the Gorgon, one of the major Romantic incarnations of sublime beauty and horror. Mario Praz defines "the beauty of the Medusa," in rather broad strokes, as a peculiar combination of beauty with horror, pain, sadness, and curse.[40] Other critics have highlighted peculiar "Medusan tropes" in Romantic texts, such as "flashing eyes" or "snake-like veins" or hair.[41] We encounter these tropes in Poe's tale: Ligeia has "luminous orbs" and "the raven-black, the glossy, the luxuriant and naturally-curling tresses" described as "huge masses of long and dishevelled hair" in the end (M 2: 312, 329). Parallels between Ligeia and Medusa have long been noticed in criticism,[42] yet unlike the Siren related to Ligeia through her namesake in the *Odyssey*, they seem to have escaped serious discussion.[43] One of the few exceptions is David Greven's Freudian reading; discussing the "shock and violence" of the final scene, he claims that "the narrator stands stock still before [Ligeia] as if turned to stone, an effect that as Freud has argued in his essay 'Medusa's Head,' was metaphorical of male sexual arousal (turning into stone serving as a metaphor for getting an erection)." In Greven's gender analysis, Ligeia's "phallic qualities," unlike those of Freud's Medusa, "do nothing to assuage the narrator's anxieties" since Ligeia "rejects male desire and upholds the feminine as a principle of and for itself alone."[44] While concurring with this view, I would like for the remainder of this essay to extend the discussion of the tale's Medusan imagery beyond Freudian psychoanalysis and gender issues. Seeing it as a pattern that operates not only in the final scene but also in the tale as a whole, I will argue that the figure of Medusa may serve as one of the explanatory modes of the tale's tension between its artistry, on the one hand, and the sensationalism of its closing scene, on the other.

One of the key Romantic texts on the Medusa is Shelley's poem "On the Medusa of Leonardo da Vinci in the Florentine Gallery" (1819). This poem is remarkable not only as an example of a new Romantic canon of sublime beauty Shelley describes as "the tempestuous loveliness of terror" but also as a text playing with perspective and mediated vision.[45] According to the myth, Perseus decapitated Medusa, seeing her reflection in the mirror of his shield. Shelley's poem, an ekphrasis describing Medusa's dead head attributed to Leonardo, makes us wonder, along with Carol Jacobs, "who is the gazer—Perseus, his predecessors, the painter, the poet, the reader?"[46] At the same time, as George Scott argues, "the poem works to eradicate any actual or rhetorical frames" since "Medusa is described as if she were actually present to the observer" and Leonardo is mentioned only in the title. Moreover, she is presented not only as an object of aesthetic contemplation but also "an active gazer" herself.[47]

There is no evidence that Poe read "On the Medusa of Leonardo da Vinci in the Florentine Gallery," though it is likely, since he was an ardent reader and admirer of Shelley. What makes his Ligeia strikingly reminiscent of the Shelleyan Medusa is her immobilized and sculpture-like head. Ligeia's portrait has puzzled the tale's readers as lengthy, exhaustively detailed, and disproportionate. Critics have claimed that the attention the narrator pays to Ligeia's head distinguishes her from other Poe heroines.[48] Moreover, the head is fetishized through art-related vocabulary and metaphors that make it at once an artwork and an *object seen*: "the contour of the lofty and pale forehead," "the skin rivalling the purest ivory," "the delicate outlines of the nose" reminiscent of "the graceful medallions of the Hebrews," "luxurious smoothness of surface," "harmoniously curved nostrils" (M 2: 312). As Joseph Moldenhauer observed, "before Ligeia's own death, the protagonist had consistently described her in the language of fine arts (particularly sculpture), revealing that her value resides largely in loveliness as an aesthetic object, and that his 'appreciation' of her is essentially that of a critic."[49]

Writing about Caravaggio's *Medusa*, French art historian Louis Maren claims that symbolic decapitation is at the heart of the portrait genre: according to one version of the myth, Medusa is stupefied and turned into a work of art by her own reflection in the shield at the moment of her beheading.[50] While it may be counterintuitive to extend Maren's analysis of the famous painting to Poe's story, it seems more than coincidental that Poe, symbolically decapitating Ligeia, would literally behead her comic counterpart in "The Psyche Zenobia," published two months later in *The American Museum*. Psyche Zenobia's head, cut away by the minute hand of the gigantic clock, begins to lead an uncanny existence of its own: "It first rolled down the side of the steeple, then lodged for a few seconds in the gutter, and then made its way, with a plunge, into the middle of the street" (M 2: 355). Representation (in both stories) is inseparable from violence, either symbolic or literal.

The immobility of Ligeia's head and also of her body (she puts *a marble hand* on the narrator's shoulder) contrasts with her "luminous," flashing eyes, "the fierce energy" of her wild words, and "the convulsive writhings of her fierce spirit" (M 2: 317). In the 1845 revision of the tale, Ligeia gains both a voice (direct speech) and a poetic expression as the authoress of "The Conqueror Worm." The statuesque Ligeia talks of "Sin," "Madness," and "Horror" embodied in the "blood-red thing" that "writhes," echoing the "convulsive writhings" of her spirit (M 2: 318). The central image of the poem recalls the biblical "worm that *would* not die" as referred to in "Morella" (M 2: 235); the writhing/undying worm in both tales, apart from being a stock emblem of mortality, is a symbol of eternal vitality, dead or deathly life. The worm, a product of Ligeia's poetic imagination and her creative energy, expresses her fear of death but also (albeit less blatantly than in "Morella") her willingness to return. The worm is not a snake but it is snake-like; added to "Ligeia," the poem becomes part of the complex web of the tale's serpentine imagery, from Ligeia's dark "tresses" to "the trellice-work of an aged vine, which clambered up the massy walls of the turret" (M 2: 314). Its closest counterpart in the chamber is "a huge censer of the same metal, Saracenic in pattern, and with many perforations so contrived that there *writhed in and out* of them, as if endued with *a serpent vitality*, a continual succession of parti-colored fires" (M 2: 321; emphasis mine). The uneasy, unnatural vitality of the chamber causes Rowena's nervous irritation; she begins to hear "slight sounds," "unusual motions," and "almost inarticulate breathings" (M 2: 324) The room seemingly moves and breathes in Rowena's delirium, and her nervous agitation is passed on to the narrator, who, in his turn, becomes susceptible to faint sounds and images. Eventually, he sees the "three or four large drops of a brilliant and ruby colored fluid" (M 2: 325), reminiscent of the worm's blood-red color, fall into Rowena's wine, hastening her death. According to the myth, the blood dripping from Medusa's decapitated head is a powerful poison, but it also gives birth to Pegasus, a symbol of poetry. Extending this analogy to Poe's story, we may suggest that Ligeia's dark poesy fiercely projects itself onto the "reality" of the narrator's story: as a pharmakon, it is at once poisonous and healing, deadening and vital.[51]

Rowena dies, and the narrator sits by her bed with his eyes fixed on her body. Suddenly he becomes aware of "a slight, a very feeble, and barely noticeable tinge of color" flushing up "within the cheeks, and along the sunken small veins of the eyelids." The animation of the corpse turns the narrator to stone—"I felt my heart cease to beat, my limbs grow rigid" (M 2: 327)—until he regains his self-possession and struggles to "restore the spirit still hovering" (M 2: 327). Very soon, however, "a relapse had taken place; the color disappeared from both eyelid and cheek, leaving a wanness even more than that of marble; the lips became doubly shrivelled and pinched up in the ghastly expression of death; a repulsive clamminess and coldness overspread rapidly the surface of the body; and all the usual rigorous stiffness immediately supervened" (M 2: 327). The narrator witnesses Rowena's sudden and rapid change from life to death but also from beauty and health (glowing face) to the ghastly grimace or mask. Athena punished the beautiful Medusa, raped by Poseidon in her temple, by deforming her face. The face of the goddess herself became temporarily distorted when she played the flute, an instrument she invented to imitate the hissing of the snakes on Medusa's head.[52] Poe never mentions Athena in the tale, yet there is little doubt that the learned Ligeia, whose luminous orbs guide the narrator in his pursuit of transcendental knowledge, is the incarnation of godlike wisdom and intellectual beauty. The deathbed scene is a reminder that this beauty is "imperiled and contaminated," to use Praz's terms.[53] The "dull" Lady Rowena, who dies drinking wine mixed with the ruby-colored drops of poison (or blood?), becomes Medusa-like as well, at once beautiful and terrifying in her uncanny postmortem state.

In this context, the Medusa effect of the final scene seems to be a natural outcome of the preceding narrative. Poe eventually stages a face-to-face encounter—a scene of sudden recognition that stupefies and bewilders the narrator:

> The bandage lay heavily about the mouth—but then might it not be the mouth of the breathing Lady of Tremaine? And the cheeks—there were the roses as in her noon of life—yes, these might indeed be the fair cheeks of the living Lady of Tremaine. And the chin, with its dimples, as in health, might it not be hers?—but *had she then grown taller since her malady?* What inexpressible madness seized me with that thought?

> One bound, and I had reached her feet! Shrinking from my touch, she let fall from her head the ghastly cerements which had confined it, and there streamed forth, into the rushing atmosphere of the chamber, huge masses of long and dishevelled hair; *it was blacker than the wings of the midnight!* (M 2: 330)

Writing about the Romantic "Medusan muse," Anne DeLong neatly defines her as "a fetishized object that looks back—the thing that was supposed to remain still, blind, and dumb, that instead moves, looks, and speaks."[54] The climax of the narrator's recognition comes when "the figure" opens "*the eyes*." In the first part of the tale, the narrator describes the size of the eyes, the hue of the orbs, the eyelashes and the brows, but admits that their "strangeness" "was of a nature distinct from the formation, or the color, or the brilliancy of the features, and must, after all, be referred to the *expression*" (M 2: 313). Although the narrator many times declares that he "peered into the eyes," "pondered upon them," and "intensely" scrutinized them (M 2: 312–313), he had to look away in search of their expression. Trying to capture the expression of Ligeia's eyes, the narrator moves from one remote analogy to another found among various phenomena of the universe. These analogies suggest either elusiveness (a vine, a moth, a butterfly, running water, falling meteor) or distance (the depth of the ocean/the well, the stars scrutinized through the telescope). In each case, we are dealing with indirect vision; conversely, the direct encounter forces the narrator to hastily and abruptly end the story. The sublime quality in Ligeia that hitherto escaped the narrator's fetishizing gaze is now unbound; it no longer needs mediation, being ultimately unrepresentable. The narrator who shrieks aloud before he becomes silent with horror is a Perseus who, instead of decapitating Medusa, throws his shield to the ground and lets the murderous look turn him to stone.

In "Ligeia," Poe tests the potential and the limits of art: its immobilizing, repressive, deadening, Medusa-like aspect, on the one hand, and the redemptive and transgressive, on the other. Tagging these aspects as masculine and feminine, respectively, may lead to oversimplification: the "vital" imagery associated with Ligeia's creative powers is unequivocally phallic, while her rebellious look immobilizes and stupefies the narrator, echoing his own artistic method.[55] Rather, I would suggest that Poe experiments with representative techniques as such, and in his experiment, he goes farther than Shelley or other European Romantics. He creates a literary "museum" out of haphazard yet aesthetically arranged cultural artifacts only to destroy it in the end, as he pushes the reader to the scene where the narrator's art is powerless. If Shelley simultaneously plays with frames and transcends them, Poe leaves us at a moment of collapse; the narrative no longer provides us with a "shield" or a "mirror"—a "safe" distance between the reader and the text. Both the narrator and the narrative are sacrificed for the sake of the overall, overwhelming effect that is directed at our senses. "Ligeia" is an example of Poe's sensationalism that makes his work in general, according to Jonathan Elmer, a symptom of the not-yet existent sensibility of mass culture.[56] Ligeia's Medusa-like, chilling gaze may be interpreted as a symptom or symbol of a new cultural paradigm—a culture that is working at its limits. However, this paradigm is sustained by the print medium that, on the one hand, creates the illusion of the inexhaustibility of cultural patterns and their combinations, yet on the other, is experienced as transient and finite.

"Ligeia" is often seen as anticipating "Eleonora," Poe's 1842 tale with "the death of a beautiful woman" motif and a plot hinging on metempsychosis. However, "Eleonora" seems a step backward from "Ligeia" since it renders these themes in a considerably more conventional way. A step forward would be "The Facts in the Case of M. Valdemar," a tale published in 1845, a year when Poe made substantial revisions to "Ligeia." In "Valdemar," he goes further by describing what he leaves in brackets in "Ligeia"—the final swing of the pendulum, the shocking relapse of the body into death, its literal liquidation. Jacques Lacan called the remains of M. Valdemar "something for which no language has a name, the naked apparition, pure, simple, brutal, of this figure that is impossible to gaze at face on, which hovers in the background of all the imaginings of human destiny, which is beyond all qualification, and for which the word carrion is completely inadequate, the complete collapse of this species of swelling that is life—the bubble bursts and dissolves down into inanimate putrid liquid."[57] The narrator no longer speaks from his hitherto authoritative, detached position—he only states the shocking "facts" that have no name and cannot be framed or mediated. If the narrator of "Ligeia" remains dumb under the look of Ligeia's eyes, the narrator of "The Facts in the Case of M. Valdemar" is in a more precarious position. There is no face to gaze on; there is nothing to poeticize, aestheticize, or fetishisize; the "detestable putridity" (M 3: 1242) of what once was a human body directly affects our senses. Seen in this retrospective light, "Ligeia," hovering on the verge of art and artistry, on the one hand, and the sublime, sensational experience, on the other, leaves us at the moment when creative imagination tries its powers to their fullest and faces its own death.[58]

"Ligeia" does strike its readers as quintessentially and paradigmatically Poesque, not least because it brings together different facets of Poe, the Poe of the 1830s and the Poe yet to come in his later work. It is of course possible to draw (somewhat predictably) another lineage—from "Ligeia" to "The Raven." The poem's famous combination of the "pallid bust of Pallas" (M 1: 369) and the dark plumage of the raven echoes a similar combination in "Ligeia," her sculpture-like face, superior intellect, and raven-black tresses. The uncanny closing stanza of "The Raven" produces a comparable effect of the immortalized snapshot, making the conclusion at once catastrophic and emblematic, simultaneously open and closed down. It seems almost natural that "Ligeia" and "The Raven" eventually met in the poem by the great Russian twentieth-century poet Osip Mandelstam. Writing at the peak of the Poe cult in Russia, Mandelstam relocates Ligeia to the banks of the Neva but also speaks of her as "December's Ligeia" and pairs her with Lenore. The poet says that Ligeia "runs" (in the original, "lives") in his blood. But the blood in the poem is no longer red; it is light-blue ("Ponderous Neva flowing in the room, Light-blue blood running out of granite")[59]—the blue blood of the Neva but also (perhaps) of the decadent European culture that made Poe's dark, queer, and mysterious Gothicism its emblem and avatar.

As I have sought to demonstrate, "Ligeia" is crucial to the Poe canon for a number of reasons. Not only does it engage with themes, devices, and style we commonly identify as Poesque; it also shows Poe's aesthetic principles at work. The tale draws on Gothic conventions, Romantic poetry, and miscellaneous magazine literature, yet at the same time challenges and revolutionizes the existing traditions by bringing them to their limit. "Ligeia" reveals its simultaneous dependence on and independence of the print medium while its final scene rewrites the typical Gothic plot and sensationalizes the Romantic sublime. "Ligeia" signposts the evolution of certain themes in Poe's own fiction and invites comparison with his earlier and later tales and poems. Yet at the same time, it occupies a singular place in the Poe canon, being at once a piece of densely poeticized prose and a horror story, a combination of Beauty, on the one hand, Passion and Truth, on the other. It is a story that eventually brings us to a cluster of homely, antebellum problems and controversies, but defamiliarizes them to the point where we are never sure we are on the right track. In this sense, we may indeed speak of undying enigmas in "Ligeia" that not so much seek to be solved, detective-fashion, but rather structure the ways generations of readers peruse the tale and explain its everlasting spell.

Notes

1. Osip E. Mandelstam, "A Last Straw," in *Complete Poetry of Osip Emilevich Mandelstam*, trans. Burton Raffel, ed. Sidney Monas (Albany: State University of New York Press, 1973), 90.
2. "As late as August 9, 1846, he wrote to Philip Pendleton Cooke, '"Ligeia" may be called my *best* tale'; and writing to Duyckinck, January 8, 1846, he mentioned it as 'undoubtedly the best story I have written'" (M 2: 305–306).
3. Clark Griffith, "Poe's 'Ligeia' and the English Romantics," *University of Toronto Quarterly* 24, no. 1 (October 1954): 8.
4. Poe mentions the name "Ligeia" in the early poem: "Ligeia, Ligeia!/My beautiful one/Whose harshest idea/Will to melody run" (M 1: 109, lines 100–104).
5. On "Ligeia" in the context of Poe stories about dying women, see J. Gerald Kennedy "Poe, 'Ligeia,' and the Problem of Dying Women," in *New Essays on Poe's Major Tales*, ed. Kenneth Silverman (New York: Cambridge University Press, 1993), 113–129.
6. David Ketterer, *The Rationale of Deception in Poe* (Baton Rouge: Louisiana State University Press, 1979).
7. The similarity between Jamesian narratives and "Ligeia" has been observed in Roy P. Basler, "The Interpretation of Ligeia," in *Poe: A Collection of Critical Essays*, ed. Robert Regan (Englewood Cliffs, NJ: Prentice Hall, 1967), 56.
8. D. H. Lawrence, *Studies in Classic American Literature* (Cambridge: Cambridge University Press, 2003), 74. On the supernatural reading of "Ligeia," see, for example, James Schroeter, "A Misreading of Poe's 'Ligeia,'" *PMLA* 76 (1961): 397–406; John Lauber, "'Ligeia' and Its Critics: A Plea for Literalism," *Studies in Short Fiction* 4 (1966): 28–32; David Halliburton, *Edgar Allan Poe: A Phenomenological View* (Princeton, NJ: Princeton University Press, 1973), 213–219. On the narrator as a murderer in question, see Roy P. Basler's 1944 essay "The Interpretation of Ligeia," in *Poe: A Collection of Critical Essays*, ed. Robert Regan, 51–63. This idea was further elaborated in James W. Gargano, "Poe's 'Ligeia': Dream and Destruction," *College English* 23 (1962): 335–342; Daniel Hoffman, "I Have Been Faithful to You in My Fashion: The Remarriage of Ligeia's Husband," *Southern Review* 8 (1972): 89–105; G. R. Thompson, "'Proper Evidences of Madness': American Gothic and the Interpretation of 'Ligeia,'" *ESQ* 18 (1972): 30–49.

9. "Philip P. Cooke to Edgar Allan Poe—September 16, 1839," Check List of the Correspondence to Edgar Allan Poe—Part II: 1838–1841, The Edgar Allan Poe Society of Baltimore, last updated January 19, 2018, https://www.eapoe.org/misc/letters/t3909160.htm.
10. R. C. De Prospo, "Whose/Who's Ligeia?" *Poe Studies* 44, no. 1 (2001): 62.
11. Elizabeth Bronfen, *Over Her Dead Body: Death, Femininity, and the Aesthetic* (Manchester, UK: Manchester University Press, 1992), 335.
12. Griffith, "Poe's 'Ligeia' and the English Romantics," 10–11.
13. In the words of Aldous Huxley; quoted in Scott Peeples, *The Afterlife of Edgar Allan Poe* (New York: Camden House, 2007), 64.
14. For example: ". . . the character of my beloved, her rare learning, her singular yet placid cast of beauty, and the thrilling and enthralling eloquence of her low musical language, made their way into my heart by paces so steadily and stealthily progressive that they have been unnoticed and unknown" (M 2: 310).
15. Jerome McGann, *The Poet Edgar Allan Poe: Alien Angel* (Cambridge, MA: Harvard University Press, 2014), 130.
16. McGann, *The Poet Edgar Allan Poe*, 121.
17. Giles Deleuze, *Essays Critical and Clinical*, trans. Daniel W. Smith and Michael A. Greco (New York: Verso, 1999), 110.
18. McGann, *The Poet Edgar Allan Poe*, 113.
19. Griffith, "Poe's 'Ligeia' and the English Romantics," 11.
20. J. Gerald Kennedy, "Poe, 'Ligeia,' and the Problem of Dying Women," 125–126, 122.
21. On Poe and the uncanny see our essay: Timothy Farrant and Alexandra Urakova, "From 'The Raven' to 'Le Cygne': Birds, Transcendence, and the Uncanny in Poe and Baudelaire," *Edgar Allan Poe Review* 15, no. 2 (Autumn 2014): 156–174.
22. On miscegenation, see Joan Dayan's groundbreaking "Amorous Bondage: Poe, Ladies, and Slaves," in *The American Face of Edgar Allan Poe*, ed. Shawn Rosenheim and Stephen Rachman (Baltimore: The Johns Hopkins University Press, 1995), 179–210. There are a number of works on Orientalism and imperialism in "Ligeia," among which I would feature Malini Johar Schueller, "Harems, Orientalist Subversions, and the Crisis of Nationalism: The Case of Edgar Allan Poe and 'Ligeia,'" *Criticism* 37, no. 4 (Fall 1995): 601–623. On queer sexuality in "Ligeia," see Valerie Rohy, "Ahistorical," *GLQ: A Journal of Lesbian and Gay Studies* 12, no. 1 (2006): 61–83. On gender protest and lesbian erotics in "Ligeia," see David Greven, *Gender Protest and Same-Sex Desire in Antebellum American Literature: Margaret Fuller, Edgar Allan Poe, Nathaniel Hawthorne, and Herman Melville* (Burlington, VT: Ashgate, 2014), 69–95.
23. Leland S. Person, "Cruising (Perversely) for Context: Poe and Murder, Women and Apes," in *Poe and the Remapping of Antebellum Print Culture*, ed. J. Gerald Kennedy and Jerome McGann (Baton Rouge: Louisiana State University Press, 2012), 145.
24. Jurgis Baltrušaitis, *Anamorphic Art*, trans. W. J. Strachan (New York: Harry N. Abrams, 1977), 120.
25. When G. R. Thompson writes that Ligeia's head can be seen, from a certain perspective, as a grinning skull, he certainly uses a classical anamorphic image. Thompson, "'Proper Evidences of Madness': American Gothic and the Interpretation of 'Ligeia,'" 87.
26. Rohy conceptualizes the "anamorphic" method she is using: "And like the 'ghastly forms' of the bridal chamber, the text's lesbian effect appears from the right angle," in "Ahistorical," 73.

27. Rohy, "Ahistorical," 73.
28. Meredith McGill, *American Literature and the Culture of Reprinting, 1834–1853* (Philadelphia: University of Pennsylvania Press, 2002), 168.
29. Kevin J. Hayes, *Poe and the Printed Word* (Cambridge: Cambridge University Press, 2000), 72–73.
30. D. Anderson, *Pictures of Ascent in the Fiction of Edgar Allan Poe* (New York: Springer, 2009), 125. Unfortunately, the author bases his argument on the similarity between the journal's title and the tale without consulting the actual volume when he claims that the first printing included "The Conqueror Worm." See *The American Museum*, Vol 1, at https://babel.hathitrust.org/cgi/pt?id=ien.35556000704940;view=1up;seq=5
31. C. S. Rafinesque, "Ancient Monuments of North and South America," *The American Museum of Science, Literature, and the Arts* 1 (1838): 11.
32. N. C. Brooks. "Laocoon," *The American Museum* 1 (1838): 101.
33. J. E. Snodgrass, "The Disclosures of Science," *The American Museum* 1 (1838): 373.
34. Anon., "The Ocean Shell," *The American Museum* 1 (1838): 37; Rev. J. H. Clinch, "Niagara," *The American Museum* 1 (1838): 88–89.
35. McGill, *American Literature and the Culture of Reprinting*, 168.
36. "Ligeia," *The American Museum of Science, Literature, and the Arts* 1 (1838): 37.
37. Dorothea von Mücke, "The Imaginary Materiality of Writing in Poe's 'Ligeia,'" *Differences* 11, no. 2 (Summer 1999): 58–59.
38. Poe's emphasis does not coincide with the tale's title, which is "Ligeia" and not "Lady Ligeia."
39. Yaohua Shi calls "Ligeia" a story about "the realization of the insufficiency of language" (Yaohua Shi, "The Enigmatic Ligeia/'Ligeia,'" *Studies in Short Fiction* 28 [1991]: 489).
40. Mario Praz, *The Romantic Agony*, trans. A. Davidson (New York: Meridian Books, 1968), 25–50. To illustrate his point, he quotes the famous lines that "the death of a beautiful woman is, unquestionably, the most poetic subject in the world" from Poe's "Philosophy of Composition" and mentions his "consumptive ladies"—Berenice, Morella, Eleonora, Ligeia—without, however, featuring Ligeia (27).
41. Anne DeLong, *Mesmerism, Medusa, and the Muse: The Romantic Discourse of Spontaneous Creativity* (New York: Lexington Books, 2012), 102.
42. See the mention of Ligeia's Medusa-like hair and eyes in Allan Lloyd-Smith, *Uncanny American Fiction: Medusa's Face* (New York: St. Martin's Press, 1989), 46; and in Joseph Adriano, "'Animated Corse': Archetypal Travesties in Three Gothic Tales," in *Our Ladies of Darkness: Feminine Daemonology in Male Gothic Fiction* (University Park, PA: Penn State Press, 1993), 89.
43. See Daryl E. Jones, "Poe's Siren: Character and Meaning in 'Ligeia,'" *Studies in Short Fiction* 20, no. 1 (1983): 33–37.
44. Greven, *Gender Protest and Same-Sex Desire in Antebellum American Literature*, 83. For another Freudean reading of "Ligeia" as Medusa, see Elisabete Lopes, "Unburying the Wife: A Reflection on the Female Uncanny in Poe's 'Ligeia,'" *The Edgar Allan Poe Review* 11, no. 1 (Spring 2011): 40–50.
45. Percy Bysshe Shelley, *Posthumous Poems of Percy Bysshe Shelley*, ed. Mary Wollstonecraft Shelley (London: John and Henry L. Hunt, 1824), 139.
46. Carol Jacobs, "On Looking at Shelley's Medusa," *Yale French Studies* 69 (1985): 167.
47. Grant F. Scott, "Shelly, Medusa, and the Perils of the Ekphrasis," in *The Romantic Imagination: Literature and Art in England and Germany*, ed. Frederick Burwick and Jurgen Klein (Amsterdam: Rodopi, 1996), 315–332, https://www.rc.umd.edu/editions/shelley/medusa/gscott.html.

48. See Gary E. Thomblestone, "Poe's 'The Fall of the House of Usher' as Archetypal Gothic: Literary and Architectural Analogs of Cosmic Unity," *Nineteenth-Century Contexts* 12 (1981): 89. Developing this idea, William Crisman speaks of Ligeia "becoming a giant face with little body" (William Crisman, "Poe's Ligeia and Helen of Troy," *Poe Studies* 38, no. 1–2 [2005]: 67).
49. Joseph Moldenhauer, "Murder as Fine Art: Basic Connections between Poe's Aesthetics, Psychology, and Moral Vision," *PMLA* 83 (1968): 291. This subject is expanded in Leland S. Person's *Aesthetic Headaches: Women and a Masculine Poetics in Poe, Melville, and Hawthorne* (Atlanta: University of Georgia Press, 1988), where he calls the narrator a "Pygmalion with words" creating "a perfect woman part by part" (30).
50. Louis Maren, *To Destroy Painting*, trans. Mette Hjort (Chicago: University of Chicago Press, 1995), 136–145.
51. Much has been written about Ligeia's creative energy that the narrator is unable to control and that functions as the return of the repressed. See Person, *Aesthetic Headaches*, 32–34; Kennedy, "Poe, 'Ligeia,' and the Problem of Dying Women," 24. Adriano rendered this idea by comparing Ligeia with Medusa: "the black-eyed Gorgon, to remind the man that by relentlessly projecting his Ideal of the Feminine onto woman, he is not loving, he is killing" ("'Animated Corse,'" 89).
52. Freud emphasized the similarity between Athena and Medusa: Sigmund Freud, *Sexuality and the Psychology of Love* (New York: Collier, 1963), 212–213.
53. Praz, *The Romantic Agony*, 26.
54. DeLong, *Mesmerism, Medusa, and the Muse*, 103.
55. For a shrewd and provocative discussion of Poe's feminism and its ambiguities, see Catherine Carter, "'Not a Woman': The Murdered Muse in Ligeia," *Poe Studies* 36, no. 1–2 (2003): 44–57.
56. Jonathan Elmer, *Reading at the Social Limit: Affect, Mass Culture, and Edgar Allan Poe* (Stanford, CA: Stanford University Press, 1995).
57. Jacques Lacan, *The Seminar of Jacques Lacan: Book 2: The Ego in Freud's Theory and in the Technique of Psychoanalysis*, ed. Jacques-Alain Miller, trans. Sylvana Tomaselli (Cambridge: Cambridge University Press, 1988), 231.
58. Such a reading certainly has its predecessors, one of which is Ortwin de Graef's brilliant essay describing "Ligeia" as "wholly self-reflexive literature trapped in the negativity of the insight into its own incapacity to represent what must be absent from it" (1115) and eventually a story "in which literature renders itself impossible" (1116). Ortwin de Graef, "The Eye of the Text: Two Stories by Edgar Allan Poe," *MLN* 104, no. 5 (December 1989): 1099–1123.
59. Mandelstam, "A Last Straw," 89.

Bibliography

Basler, Roy P. "The Interpretation of 'Ligeia.'" In *Poe: A Collection of Critical Essays*, edited by Robert Regan, 51–63. Englewood Cliffs, NJ: Prentice Hall, 1967.

Dayan, Joan. "Amorous Bondage: Poe, Ladies, and Slaves." In *The American Face of Edgar Allan Poe*, edited by Shawn Rosenheim and Stephen Rachman, 179–210. Baltimore: The Johns Hopkins University Press, 1995.

De Prospo, R. C. "Whose/Who's Ligeia?" *Poe Studies* 44, no. 1 (2001): 57–67.

Gargano, James W. ""Poe's "'Ligeia': Dream and Destruction." *College English* 23, no. 5 (1962): 337–342.

Griffith, Clark. "Poe's 'Ligeia' and the English Romantics." *University of Toronto Quarterly* 24, no. 1 (October 1954): 8–25.

Hoffman, Daniel. "I Have Been Faithful to You in My Fashion: The Remarriage of Ligeia's Husband." *Southern Review* 8 (1972): 89–105.

Kennedy, J. Gerald. "Poe, 'Ligeia,' and the Problem of Dying Women." In *New Essays on Poe's Major Tales*, edited by Kenneth Silverman, 113–129. New York: Cambridge University Press, 1993.

Matheson, Terence J. "The Multiple Murders in 'Ligeia': A New Look at Poe's Narrator." *Canadian Review of American Studies* 13 (1982): 279–290.

von Mücke, Dorothea. "The Imaginary Materiality of Writing in Poe's 'Ligeia.'" *Differences* 11, no. 2 (Summer 1999): 53–74.

Rohy, Valerie. "Ahistorical." *GLQ: A Journal of Lesbian and Gay Studies* 12, no. 1 (2006): 61–83.

Schueller, Malini Johar. "Harems, Orientalist Subversions, and the Crisis of Nationalism: The Case of Edgar Allan Poe and 'Ligeia.'" *Criticism* 37, no. 4 (Fall 1995): 601–623.

CHAPTER 19

"THE FALL OF THE HOUSE OF USHER" AND THE ARCHITECTURE OF UNRELIABILITY

AGNIESZKA SOLTYSIK MONNET

"The Fall of the House of Usher" occupies a singular place in the Poe canon. Considered by many critics his best and most representative short fiction, the story appears in countless anthologies and collections. It is considered foundational for the American Gothic and, more specifically, Southern Gothic.[1] Despite its ubiquity and popularity among critics and readers alike, however, the meaning of "The Fall of the House of Usher" has proved elusive. Poe's ability to create an undercurrent of suggestiveness is nowhere displayed more masterfully than in this story, and few texts have generated so many and such divergent readings. With its first-person narration, underground crypts, and multilayered literariness (including two embedded texts, an epigraph and many allusions to other texts), "Usher" epitomizes hidden depth and encrypted meaning. The result has been a dizzying array of critical interpretations claiming to offer the "key" to the textual house of Usher (as in Darrel Abel's influential 1949 essay by that title).[2] Psychoanalytic readings held a central place in the story's early reception history, followed by philosophical and historical allegories, and later by a range of poststructuralist readings suggesting that reading and writing themselves were the real subjects of the tale.

I propose to show that Poe constructed this story to offer both an implied meaning and an affective reading experience in which the "discovery" of the "hidden" meaning is carefully choreographed into the narrative's temporal movement by its unreliable narration. In the critical history of "The Fall of the House of Usher," the narrator has often been subject to scrutiny and debate—especially since he calls attention to his own subjective fallibility so often and so insistently—but readings that focus on the narrator often ignore the larger historical and cultural context of the tale. By looking at how the story's narrative unreliability is linked to cultural debates about slavery, conscience, and moral insanity, I hope to explain both the tacit content of "The Fall of the House of Usher" and its intended aesthetic effect.

Although most readers will be familiar with the tale, a short synopsis might help to refresh our sense of the story's enigmas. An unnamed narrator approaches the house of his childhood friend and reflects on the bleakness of the landscape, his own inexplicable dread, and his inability to coax the terrible scene into assuming a sublime aspect. His optical experiment of looking at the house through its reflection in the dark tarn anticipates both the motif of doubling that will recur throughout the story and the ending, when the house actually collapses into the tarn. Inside, he finds his friend greatly altered, in the grip of an extreme nervous agitation and a "morbid acuteness of the senses" (M 2: 403). In one of the few occasions when Usher speaks, he informs the narrator—and reader—that he is terrified of any incident that would excite his overwrought nerves—in short, he fears any unusual incident at all. Shortly after, his sister Madeline seems to die and is then entombed in a dungeon deep below the house, after which the two friends resume their pastimes of music and reading. Soon, however, Usher's demeanor changes dramatically: he appears increasingly agitated, "listening to some imaginary sound" and "laboring with some oppressive secret" (M 2: 411). The last third of the story represents the suspense building over the course of a stormy evening as the narrator attempts to distract Usher by reading him a chivalric romance, while mysterious sounds from beneath the house echo noises in the narrative. Finally, in his second monologue, the distraught Usher confesses to hearing for days his sister's struggles in the tomb and to dreading her probable desire for revenge. A moment later Madeline appears at the door and falls upon him, killing him, at which the house splits down along its fissure and disappears into the tarn as the narrator flees.

In addition to the status (and specifically, the reliability) of the narrator, the ambiguities that have inspired critics include the oddly evanescent character of Madeline, her relationship to Usher (the possibility of an incestuous union), and her uncannily impermanent death (with the issue of medical body-snatching and catalepsy in the background). As mentioned earlier, Poe succeeds in creating an aura of multilayered suggestiveness, leading many readers and critics to speculate on the meanings of seemingly innocuous details. The perennial question of tone (so masterfully treated by Jonathan Elmer[3]) emerges with the curious play of the narrator's excessive self-consciousness at some moments and utter obliviousness at others. The story also treats its embedded romance ("The Mad Trist") with so much irony that a reader is left wondering if the equally exaggerated frame narrative can be taken fully at face value. Finally, readers have been intrigued by Usher's belief that the stones of his house are alive and sentient, something that appears to be confirmed in the latter part of the tale, when the house collapses into the tarn in which it was initially reflected. These are only some of the suggestive details generating debate among critics and scholars, several of which I will address in the sections that follow.

Critical Overview

Since the early twentieth century, when an obsessive interest in hidden meanings took center stage in Anglo-American literary scholarship, Poe—with his explicit interest in madness, secrecy, and narrative indirection—has invited a range of psychoanalytical and psychobiographical readings. Marie Bonaparte, a member of Freud's inner circle in the 1920s, argued that Poe's work emanated largely from his unresolved sense of loss of his mother, and that Usher was a projection of this loss.[4] Reading the tale through the prism of his own psychological concerns, D. H. Lawrence argued that Madeline and Roderick exemplify the mutual destruction and loss of soul that can occur when two people love each other too much.[5] The psychoanalytic tradition continued throughout the century. In his 1973 monograph, *Poe's Fiction: Romantic Irony in the Gothic Tales*, G. R. Thompson meticulously demonstrates the analogies between the house and Usher's sanity, suggesting that the story chronicles a gradual descent into madness.[6] In 1981, J. R. Hammond argued that Roderick is "a mirror image of Poe or at least a projection, a doppel-ganger, of himself as he imagined himself to be,"[7] and in 1996, Eric Carlson discussed "Usher" in *A Companion to Poe Studies* under the rubric of "Tales of Psychal Conflict," focusing on the many readings taking either Usher or the narrator as psychological case studies, confirming the popularity of this approach.[8]

The other most common readings are also often allegorical, but they adopt a more philosophical, political, or historical focus. For example, in 1949 Darrel Abel proposed that the tale exemplified a contest between "Life-Reason" and "Death-Madness" for the possession of Roderick Usher.[9] Similarly, Michael Hoffman, in "The House of Usher and Negative Romanticism" (1965), argued that the house in the tale is meant to represent the Enlightenment and therefore its demise signifies that the world is not as ordered and meaningful as the Enlightenment presumed.[10] Although many critics succumb to the temptation to read the story allegorically, lured by its explicit preoccupation with hidden depths and multilayered architectonics, there is little evidence in Poe's fictional or critical work to suggest that he worked in an allegorical mode in his stories except on rare occasions.[11] In an 1842 essay on Nathaniel Hawthorne, Poe wrote that "there is scarcely one respectable word to be said" for allegory (ER: 582). "Under the best of circumstances," Poe continues, "it must always interfere with that unity of effect which, to the artist, is worth all the allegory in the world" (ER: 583).

Unpacking this notion of "effect" for a moment, one infers that for Poe the impact of a work of art was largely a matter of choreographing the intricate interplay between expectation and discovery as a reader progressed temporally through a text. Poe's stories rarely either announce an explicit meaning or hide one for critical excavation; rather, it is in between: a question of attending to the fairly obvious *cues* Poe provides the reader. For example, the story "William Wilson" is about a capricious boy who ignores his conscience to such an extent that when it returns in an externalized form to give him unsolicited advice, he fails to recognize it and ends up murdering it, thereby becoming a sociopath (referring at the beginning of the tale to his "later years of . . . unpardonable crime"; M 2: 426). The cues, or rather, *clues*, in this story include the opening epigraph, which explicitly names "CONSCIENCE" (M 2: 426) as a "spectre," anticipating the way the narrator's conscience haunts him like a ghost until he finally eliminates it once and for all.

In short, Poe often embeds a meaning that requires the reader to notice something that he does not state explicitly, but this reading is not a question of "interpretation" in the conventional sense of the word nor of allegory, but rather of connecting the dots in order to understand the basic elements of the plot. In the late tale "Hop-Frog," the reader is made to understand—while the unreliable narrator pointedly does *not*—that the abused slave Hop-Frog is planning revenge upon the king who has kidnapped and tormented him. Generating strong dramatic irony, the tale requires the reader to infer from the situation (master–slave) and the visible but otherwise unexplained signs of Hop-Frog's internal agitation (e.g., grating his teeth) that the seemingly innocent preparations for the king's masquerade ball are actually a desperate plot for revenge and escape (M 3: 1353).

With poststructuralism in the 1970s and 1980s, allegorical readings made way for a new and intense attention to Poe's craftsmanship, the complexity of his irony, and a fascination with his self-consciousness as a writer.[12] In fact, Poe's linguistic playfulness was often read as a prescient anticipation of Derridean deconstruction itself. Though more reliant on close textual analysis than allegorical approaches, many poststructuralist readings tended to reach the same conclusion--namely, that the text has no single meaning or is in fact about its own meaninglessness. For example, Joseph Riddel's 1979 essay sees in "Usher" a self-reflexive fable about the absence that lies at the center of any text, an absence of meaning, presence, and life, except as the simulacrum of a simulacrum.[13] Riddel argues this absence is allegorized in the story by the house of Usher itself, which is constructed upon a crypt, an architectural feature that allegorizes the notion that fiction is always constructed upon a "hollow coffin," that is, an emptiness at its center. The embedded story and the other fragments and allusions to books and manuscripts are all attempts to defer the confrontation with the terrifying contents of the crypt, which, for Riddel, is not a prematurely buried woman but the missing body of the meaning of the text.[14]

Focusing more on the reading process, Harriet Hustis has argued that Poe embeds an interpretive "gap" that calls for the reader's participation.[15] In this sense, Poe is working within a larger tradition of "Gothic reading," which, according to Hustis, creates a "disturbance" in the reading process, and which "bothers without quite spoiling narrative pleasure," making readers active participants in the Gothic plot. The narrator is important to this process because he is the stand-in for the reader as well as a double for Usher, though he is also different from both in that he is a naïve reader, and this difference creates the gap that characterizes so-called Gothic reading. Like Riddell and most other poststructuralist critics, Hustis concludes that the point of all this effort is ultimately to show the "interpretive uncertainty" of texts. The ease with which poststructuralist critics find ambiguity and hermeneutic gaps in this story, and in Poe in general, stems from the fact that he deliberately embeds unreliable narration into almost every story, but the unreliability has a larger rhetorical purpose than to signify only itself, as I will show later.

Emerging from poststructuralist concerns but far more attentive to textual specificity and detail, Scott Peeples's essay on "Usher" for the *Cambridge Companion to Edgar Allan Poe* offers an account that focuses on the meticulous "constructiveness" of the tale.[16] Peeples examines the technical care with which Poe built his texts, like an engineer, carefully crafting correspondences between Usher's house and the text.[17] Ultimately, the story is "about" its own construction, and specifically about the tension between the loss of control depicted *in* the story and the complete control that Poe the author keeps over his fiction as he enacts the "artist's fantasy of bringing that dead house to life."[18] Peeples begins with Poe's authorial stance but also brings into focus the central importance of the house itself to any reading of the story, as is evident from the pun embedded in the title, where "house" refers to both the physical structure and Usher's family line. This focus on the rhetorical complexity of "The Fall of the House of Usher," where the setting is an agent as well as a backdrop, brings us to the question of the possible correspondences between the story, its uncannily volatile house, and the larger cultural context of the story's production.

To conclude this review, the critical reception of "The Fall of the House of Usher" reveals two main trends: first, a psychoanalytic and philosophical trend of assigning a single meaning to the text, and another more recent trend of denying meaning altogether. Both tendencies arise from critical paradigms (e.g., psychoanalysis, deconstruction) that search for evidence of their own pre-existing assumptions while generally ignoring the historical and cultural issues that informed Poe's work. Recent scholarship that benefits from the insights of poststructuralism and its attention to form and language but also introduces cultural studies approaches has produced a new generation of readings linking historical questions to formal ones, helping us read "The Fall of the House of Usher" against the backdrop of antebellum America.

Cultural Criticism and Cultural Context

Possibly the most important development in Poe criticism in recent decades has been the emergence of race and slavery as central preoccupations. Discussion of Poe's views on these issues and how they might have affected his work—however obliquely—have reshaped Poe studies since the 1990s. John Carlos Rowe's claim in 1992 that "Poe was a proslavery Southerner and should be reassessed as such in whatever approach we take to his life and writings" can be taken as the opening salvo to this debate.[19] The same year, Toni Morrison called for an investigation into the "Africanist" presence in American literature and identified Poe as one of the key figures who have shaped the chiaroscuro dynamics of the American literary imagination.[20] Other important contributions to this discussion include Teresa Goddu's *Gothic America* (1997), which proposed a more nuanced approach to reading race in Poe, and questioned specifically the facile reduction of racism to an exclusively Southern issue.[21] Lesley Ginsberg's claim that "The Black Cat" suggests how slavery corrupts owners raised the prospect of a far more complex Poe, one who understood that slavery was at the heart of the American "political uncanny," a horror story rife with repression, projection, and various forms of collective psychosis. In Ginsberg's influential reading, Poe emerges as a subtle critic of slavery despite his alleged "proslavery pronouncements."[22]

Yet even these few proslavery pronouncements have been called into question in recent years. One of the most important turns in the recent debate about Poe's racism was the publication of Terence Whalen's *Edgar Allan Poe and the Masses* (1999), which explored the literary marketplace in which Poe worked, offered plausible explanations for many of Poe's aesthetic and political positions in light of the pressures impinging upon him economically as a writer and editor, and perhaps most important, refuted the longstanding claim that Poe wrote the proslavery "Paulding-Drayton" review.[23] Analyzing internal textual evidence, Whalen painstakingly demonstrated that Nathaniel Beverley Tucker, a Southern ideologue and writer, was its author. Whalen also pointed out that it is likely that Poe entertained a centrist view on slavery that combined an "average racism" with a belief that slavery should be gradually phased out.[24] This would have been a common view among educated Southerners, and one that allowed Poe to offend neither Southern nor Northern sensibilities in his book reviews.

Not easily resolved one way or the other, given Poe's penchant for ambiguity and irony, the debate surrounding Poe's racial politics has continued, producing, for instance, a collection of essays devoted to the issue, J. Gerald Kennedy and Liliane Weissberg's *Romancing the Shadow* (2001). In this volume, Rowe once more argues that Poe's representations of race consistently upheld antebellum racial hierarchies and stereotypes and thereby affirmed the imperial fantasies and ambitions of the era.[25] Most of the other essays, however, adopt a more nuanced view. Leland S. Person examines the subversive reversibility of black and white race markers—especially in terms of skin and hair color—in order to argue that Poe's Gothic fictions function to destabilize "the psychological constructs of white male racism."[26] Kennedy painstakingly combs through Poe's oeuvre and biographical scholarship to find evidence of Poe's contacts with slaves, exploring his "conflicted relationship" with the South's "peculiar institution." Comparing *The Narrative of Arthur Gordon Pym* to the *Narrative of Frederick Douglass* (1845), Kennedy concludes that Poe's novel invites oddly subversive and pessimistic readings of encounters between natives and American whites, tacitly undermining Southern proslavery arguments of that era.[27]

This tendency to understand a slave's desire to revolt, based on an implicit recognition of suffering and discontent—universally denied or ignored by proponents of slavery—gives Poe's depictions of bondage an antislavery tinge regardless of how grotesquely racist his physical descriptions of black characters could be. For instance, as described earlier, the late story "Hop-Frog" requires the reader to understand the natural desire of the slave to punish his master in order to guess what the eponymous character is plotting for the cruel king. The character himself is depicted as "a dwarf and a cripple," walking in an awkward and comic gait, but the entire story hinges on the reader identifying with Hop-Frog's rage and desire for revenge against the morally blind narrator, who is a court lackey unable to perceive the injustice of the situation he describes (M 3: 1345). The inevitable desire to rebel and take revenge on one's master is also explicitly depicted in Poe's early comic tale "Four Beasts in One" (1833), in which wild animals that have been domesticated as "*valets-de-chambre*" stage a mutiny and eat their masters (M 2: 123).

Poe's recognition of the violence inherent in the master–slave relationship flies directly in the face of the most common arguments put forward by defenders of slavery in the South, especially in the wake of the Nat Turner revolt of 1831. The much later work of Southern lawyer and social theorist George Fitzhugh sums up the arguments that emerged in the 1830s and 1840s. These arguments, as Sam Worley has noted, moved away from the "necessary evil" view of slavery that had held sway in earlier decades and relied increasingly on the "virtual codification of strategies that posed slavery as a positive good."[28] In *Cannibals All! Or Slaves Without Masters* (1857), Fitzhugh argues that slavery is natural to human nature: "Man is a social and gregarious animal, and all such animals hold property in each other. Nature imposes upon them slavery as a law and necessity of their existence. They live together to aid each other, and are slaves under Mr. Garrison's higher law. Slavery arises under the higher law, and is, and ever must be, coëval and coëxtensive with human nature."[29] In other words, Fitzhugh claims that slavery is an inherent and natural part of human society and history. Going further, he argues that the state of dependence created by slavery is the natural precondition for true affection and kindness between people, because everyone knows his or her role and place, and there is no jostling for power. In fact, Fitzhugh avers, it is the slave who is really the master in the South, because it is the slave who is maintained and cared for:

> The humble and obedient slave exercises more or less control over the most brutal and hard-hearted master. It is an invariable law of nature, that weakness and dependence are elements of strength, and generally sufficiently limit that universal despotism, observable throughout human and animal nature. The moral and physical world is but a series of subordinations, and the more perfect the subordination, the greater the harmony and the happiness.[30]

Fitzhugh's argument directly refutes Harriet Beecher Stowe's influential argument in *Uncle Tom's Cabin* (1852), that power corrupts and that absolute power corrupts the slaveowners absolutely, making them cruel and blind to slaves' suffering.[31]

Despite warnings from writers such as Stowe, the issue of slavery in the antebellum United States represents one of history's most glaring examples of collective moral blindness. As Lesley Ginsberg explains in her article on "The Black Cat," the Southern response to Nat Turner's 1831 rebellion was stupefaction, in particular with regard to his motives. For example, the *Richmond Enquirer* wrote that Turner acted "without any cause or provocation, that could be assigned."[32] Thomas Gray, the man who extracted

Turner's confession, expresses sympathy with readers' frustration at seeing the "insurgent slaves . . . destroyed, or apprehended, tried, and executed . . . without revealing anything at all satisfactory, as to the motives which governed them."[33] Nothing highlights the absurdity of the slaveholding South's failure to recognize the violence inherent to the institution of slavery more than Dr. Samuel Cartwright's 1851 report in the *New Orleans Medical and Surgical Journal* that among the "diseases and peculiarities of the Negro race," as his article was titled, was a treatable illness called "drapetomania, or the disease causing Negroes to run away." According to Cartwright, if slaves are kept "in the position that we learn from the Scriptures he was intended to occupy, that is, the position of submission," and treated with kindness, then "the negro is spell-bound, and cannot run away."[34] The notion that a slave would want to be free regardless of how kind his master might be, and that holding another human being in bondage is itself an extreme form of violence inviting the most extreme measures in return, seems not to have occurred to these self-deluded defenders of slavery.

Herman Melville's 1855 novella "Benito Cereno" is a canny examination of precisely this kind of blindness, with the naïve Captain Amasa Delano failing to grasp that the distressed Spanish slave ship he has boarded is in the midst of a slave mutiny despite much strange behavior on the part of its crew and captain. Scholars and readers such as Toni Morrison have generally understood Captain Delano as an example of the "willful blindness" of the antebellum South. As Morrison puts it, Delano's complacent myopia "is similar to the 'happy, loyal slave' antebellum discourse that peppered early debates on black civil rights."[35] In contrast to such complacent myths, Poe's depictions of relationships of subordination, in stories such as "Metzengerstein," "The Black Cat," "Hop-Frog," and *The Narrative of Arthur Gordon Pym*, are, like Stowe's and Melville's, consistently rife with violence, deceit, mutiny, and mutual cruelty, undermining on every level the view of human nature as affectionately hierarchical advocated by proslavery ideologues like Fitzhugh and Cartwright.

Although "The Fall of the House of Usher" does not seem to be as directly concerned with race as *Hop-Frog* or *The Narrative of Arthur Gordon Pym*, numerous critics have seen a link between the story and the slavery debate.[36] In 1960, Harry Levin suggested that "The Fall of the House of Usher" could be read as a prophetic comment on the plantation system of the South. Specifically, he saw the South's "feudal pride and foreboding of doom" mirrored in the story, and Usher as "driven underground by the pressure of fear."[37] While Levin's reading acknowledges the vague sense of threat informing the tale, Maurice S. Lee has suggested that more specifically it is "slave rebellion" that "potentially lurks" in the story.[38] This is not to argue that the story is meant as a simple allegory of Southern slavery and the threat of revolt. Instead, the issue of slavery should be regarded as a cultural framework for understanding the emotional charge of the story's principal tensions and tropes. For example, the subterranean crypt where Madeline is placed as a precaution against grave-robbing physicians had once been a dungeon and has subsequently been used as a store-room for gun powder or "some other highly combustible substance" (M 2: 410). As I have argued elsewhere, this oddly detailed history of the room links its past function as a site of feudal-style imprisonment to the idea of combustibility, an association that would have resonated suggestively with the fear of insurrection in the post-Turner South, though its immediate function in the story is to allow a plausible explanation for the collapse of the house.[39]

Although the story anticipates the implosion of the nation around the issue of slavery twenty years later, the more immediate aspect of the text that invites reading it in terms of slavery is its preoccupation with revenge for imprisonment and premature burial (reflecting figuratively how slavery constitutes what Orlando Patterson has called "social death"[40]). Much of the story's powerful conclusion derives its emotional charge from the fact that Usher ignores for days Madeline's struggle with her coffin and crypt. In fact, her long struggle is what Poe himself cited as the point of the story. In an 1845 review article of his own work, Poe wrote that the main effect (or "thesis of the story") can be described as "the revulsion of feeling consequent upon discovering that for a long period of time we have been mistaking sounds of agony, for those of mirth or indifference" (ER: 871).[41] Literally, this refers to the sounds of Madeline's struggle to escape her tomb, sounds which Usher has deliberately ignored and which the narrator has mistaken for the sounds in "Mad Trist." Structurally, it recalls the masquerades and other festivities used to mask the sounds of suffering in other Poe stories, as in "The Mask of the Red Death" or "Hop-Frog." The effect he describes here is complex, assuming both a process in time ("sounds we *have been mistaking*" followed by a "consequent" feeling of revulsion) and an ethical framework ("revulsion" here being essentially an affective response akin to horror, arising from a realization of having failed to act ethically). The word "mirth" in this passage is used in the technical sense that chivalric romances, like the story the narrator reads to Usher, are a form of amusement. Moreover, the fact that the narrator chooses to read a *chivalric* romance would have a special purchase in the context of the South, which tended to imagine its cultural roots in the medieval and Scottish chivalric traditions. The term "indifference" is equally freighted with cultural resonance, bringing us to the issue of conscience and its absence that many abolitionists argued was a natural result of the slave relationship—namely, that it dulled the moral faculty of the master and of the culture that tolerated slavery in general, inexorably pulling it toward a kind of moral numbness and idiocy.

Bad Conscience, or Moral and Epistemological Unreliability

If slavery forms a backdrop to the story, the more immediate subject of the tale's construction and specific effect is the issue of conscience and moral apperception. This is a concern of Poe's in many of his short stories and is a key feature of the unreliability of his narrators.[42] Conscience, as a specific cognitive faculty, was the subject of particular interest and attention in the 1830s, as the debate over slavery was heating up. Francis Wayland devoted five chapters to "Conscience, or the Moral Sense" in his tract on moral philosophy, *Elements of Moral Science* (1835), describing its specific function as "repelling vice" and contesting a subject's "lower propensities" but lacking the power to do more than advise. Wayland's language gives conscience an independent existence and agency, conceptualizing it as an entity separate from the decision-making subject. He repeatedly stresses the importance of "hearkening" and "obeying" the "impulses" of conscience and argues that one's conscience could be strengthened or atrophied, like a muscle, by use or disuse. Moreover, not only could individuals weaken and destroy their conscience by failing to obey it, but entire communities could collectively deaden and lose their moral sense by repeated acts of cruelty or violence. Citing gladiatorial Rome and revolutionary France as examples, Wayland argues that failure to heed conscience on a collective level produces a collective loss of moral sensibility.[43]

In light of the great political issues at stake in the question of conscience in a slave-holding society, it is no surprise that a writer as acutely aware of the subtleties of power, exclusion, and social repression as the once privileged and then disowned and nearly destitute Poe would take this up as a key concern.[44] What is surprising is how Poe scholarship has largely overlooked the fact that lack of conscience is the main form of unreliability that many of his first-person narrators display. Poe uses morally unreliable first-person narrators in stories such as "William Wilson," "The Business Man," "The Black Cat," "The Imp of the Perverse," and "The Cask of Amontillado," and their function is always to describe but then to neglect crucial elements of a specifically ethical nature. An obvious example is "The Tell-Tale Heart," where the narrator betrays his moral insanity quite quickly by avowing at the end of the second paragraph that he is a murderer ("I made up my mind the take the life of the old man"; M 3: 792). At the other end of the spectrum, the narrator of "Berenice" is revealed only at the end of the story to be the perpetrator of a horrible crime. When we learn that Berenice's teeth are in his possession, we are forced to infer that he has pulled them out from her alive (as her body is disfigured and his own clothes are "clotted with gore"; M 2: 218). Even the ending is narrated "unreliably" by never using the word "teeth." Instead, the narrator describes "thirty-two small, white, and ivory-looking substances" falling to the floor (M 2: 219). This absurdly indirect description (after all, who could recognize that there are *thirty-two* of anything in a single glance?), like all unreliable narration, requires the reader to produce the final meaning himself or herself by recognizing them as teeth, even though the narrator does not name them as such. In "The Cask of Amontillado," by contrast, the reader gradually discerns that the seemingly congenial narrator is a sociopath intent upon revenge. His sadism is only fully revealed at the moment near the end when he mocks his victim's pleas for mercy by repeating them sarcastically ("*For the love of God, Montresor*!" "Yes" I said, "for the love of God!"; M 3: 1263).

Similarly, the narrator of "The Fall of the House of Usher" betrays the limitations of his unimaginative subjectivity gradually during the course of the last section of the narrative. It could be argued that the narrator plants doubts in the reader's mind with his initial lengthy descriptions of his unexplained emotions upon first seeing the house, and his provocative comparisons to narcotics (repeated again soon after when he tries to describe Usher's manner as that of an "irreclaimable eater of opium"; M 2: 402). This is because the entire narrative is structured to prepare the reader for the specific effect that Poe wanted to create—as mentioned above, "the revulsion of feeling consequent upon discovering that for a long period of time we have been mistaking sounds of agony, for those of mirth or indifference" (ER: 871).

To create that temporally complex effect, involving "a long period of time" during which "sounds of agony" are mistaken for sounds of "mirth," Poe structures the story in roughly two parts, with Madeline's apparent death as the fulcrum. In the first section, he establishes all the necessary cues and clues to help the reader make sense of what is happening, but which the narrator will fail to understand, namely, that Madeline has been entombed alive and has managed to escape the underground crypt. These clues include references to the narrator's unreliability, Madeline's catalepsy, and her lifelike appearance but also the explanations foreshadowing Usher's own "unreliability," since he is the first to fail to attend to Madeline's struggle. Thus, Usher's most extensive speech occurs in this section, partly paraphrased and partly quoted. Usher informs the narrator (and the reader) that he has preternaturally sensitive hearing as well as a general acuteness of the senses, and then explains his fear of any incident, "even the most trivial," which would operate upon his "intolerable agitation of the soul" (M 2: 403). In short, he is hypersensitive and morbidly perceptive of sounds, and terrified of anything that would upset him. These elements, along with some suspicion that the narrator's judgment is not entirely transparent and reliable, are all that are needed after Madeline is entombed and Usher's manner dramatically changes—as he appears to be "listening to some imaginary sound" and "laboring with some oppressive secret"—for the reader to guess that the cataleptic Madeline was not dead when she was entombed and that Usher can hear her stirring (M 2: 411). We know that he is terrified of any unusual incident, and we are given thereby a motive for why he does not dare to tell anyone what he hears. Usher's strange behavior thus constitutes a hermeneutic gap that invites the reader to fill it with a plausible explanation, which Poe has carefully prepared.

The long last section of "The Fall of the House of Usher," in which the narrator describes hearing "low and indefinite sounds" that continue to grow louder and more alarming as he reads the "Mad Trist" to Usher in order to distract him, is the dramatic and emotional heart of the story (M 2: 411). Its rhetorical power depends on the fact that most readers—even first-time readers, I would contend, if they have read attentively—are aware or suspect that Madeline has been buried alive and that the narrator and the brother seem (or pretend) to not recognize this fact. I say "pretend" because Usher turns out to have heard her struggles all along. He is, in fact, the sociopath at the heart of the story, who has suppressed his conscience and moral judgment, like the narrator of "William Wilson." In contrast to Usher's deliberate failure to rescue his sister, the narrator is merely blind (and deaf) to her suffering. The seeming stupidity of the narrator is illustrated in at least one film adaptation by making him into a myopic, bumbling fool.[45] The effect for the reader is a curious combination of uneasiness about Madeline's torture and resurrection and epistemological pleasure from drawn-out scenes of dramatic irony (the reader knows something crucial the protagonist seems unable to grasp). Poe prolongs this scene to amplify its uncanny effects: an angry Madeline laboriously draws closer while the two men read and listen to sounds of her approach in a state of denial. The situation generates a peculiar, ethical position for the reader, aware of suffering that the main characters ignore or fail to recognize.

The climax coincides with Usher's revelation, prompted by the "distinct, hollow, metallic, and clangorous" sound of Madeline's tomb door being opened. This noise makes the narrator jump to his feet but leaves Usher "undisturbed," once more proving that he has *already* been listening to—and ignoring—the sounds of Madeline's struggle. Now, characterized by a "stony rigidity" and "sickly smile," Usher confesses his self-deception and failure to act: "Not hear it?—yes, I hear it, and have heard it. Long—long—long—many minutes, many hours, many days, have I heard it—yet I dared not—oh, pity me, miserable wretch that I am!—I dared not—I *dared* not speak! *We have put her living in the tomb!* Said I not that my senses were acute? I *now* tell you that I heard her first feeble movements in the hollow coffin. I heard them—many, many days ago—yet I dared not—*I dared not speak!*" (M 2: 416). Here Usher fills the hermeneutic gap in the conclusion, which the reader had been invited to guess at as soon as the narrator mentioned that Usher seemed to be "laboring with some oppressive secret" and "listening to some imaginary sound" (M 2: 411).

Usher's monologue illuminates the latter part of the story in more detail:

> ["]And now—to-night—Ethelred—ha! ha!—the breaking of the hermit's door, and the death-cry of the dragon, and the clangour of the shield!—say, rather, the rending of her coffin, and the grating of the iron hinges of her prison, and her struggles within the coppered archway of the vault! Oh whither shall I fly? Will she not be here anon? Is she not hurrying to upbraid me for my haste? Have I not heard her footstep on the stair? Do I not distinguish that heavy and horrible beating of her heart? Madman!"—here he sprang furiously to his feet, and shrieked out his syllables, as if in the effort he were giving up his soul—*"Madman! I tell you that she now stands without the door!"* (M 2: 416)

Usher here reveals the specific fear at the crux of his agitation, namely, that Madeline is coming to reproach and possibly punish him for his failure of conscience and will. The climax simultaneously evokes the unspoken but pervasive anxiety about slave rebellion—that men and women prematurely consigned to the social death of slavery will refuse to stay dead and instead seek justifiable retribution—that hung over the antebellum South and that still gives this story its peculiar *frisson*, even if the cultural particulars remain unspecified.[46]

One odd aspect of this final speech is Usher's calling the narrator "madman." We have been led by the narrator to regard Roderick as verging on insanity, and yet this accusation from Usher reminds us of the many clues the narrator had dropped about his own mental instability: his references to opium consumption, to his "insufferable gloom," his "superstition," and to his long familiarity with "the paradoxical law of all sentiments having terror as their basis" (M 2: 399). The fact that the term "madman" can easily apply at this point to either Usher or the narrator himself is also one of many instances of the radical convertibility that characterizes Poe's work (as Joan Dyan has noted[47]), namely, that things and people are oddly convertible and interchangeable, like Rowena and Ligeia in the tale titled after the latter.

Another odd thing about this speech, as many critics have noted, is the overly formal expression "*without the door*" for "outside the door." This curious phrase has been used to argue that Usher has had incestuous relations with his sister while she was alive, or even after she has been entombed, since "*without the door*" could be read to mean that she has lost her hymen (the figurative door to her physical self).[48] While it is true that Poe may have followed Gothic tradition in permitting suggestions of incest to arise, the curious expression shows again how narrative content is mirrored by and inseparable from the oppressive and unreliable architectonics of the house. For instance, the door of the dungeon produces portentous sounds that the narrator and Usher hear and/or ignore.

Similarly, the whole structure of the house proves a source of crucial ambiguities. For example, while giving "little token of instability," the house is nevertheless doomed to collapse (M 2: 400). The narrator early alludes to the fracture that ultimately causes the collapse of the house—and does so in that highly subjectivized and uncertain way that characterizes his sensibility from the outset. He reports the crack while appearing not to see it: "Perhaps the eye of a scrutinizing observer might have discovered a barely perceptible fissure, which, extending from the roof of the building in front, made its way down the wall in a zigzag direction, until it became lost in the sullen waters of the tarn" (M 2: 400). Both the conditional tense ("might have") and adverb evoking uncertainty ("perhaps") call attention to the fact that the narrator is precisely NOT the "scrutinizing observer" needed to convey the meaning of the "barely perceptible" flaw in the structure.

The house is central and present to the story in other ways as well, from the pun of the title, collapsing the family and the physical building into one entity, to the suggestively black ("ebon") floors, hinting at the black substratum of Southern society, and the general gloom both inside and outside the mansion, as well as the crucial details of the placement of the crypt underneath the house, which causes Madeline's muffled sounds of struggle to arise from *below*. John Timmerman has argued, "In no other work . . . has Poe structured this sentience, or interconnectedness, between the physical world and mental/psychological world more powerfully and tellingly" than in "Usher."[49] In fact, Poe emphasizes the importance of the house by including the poem "The Haunted Palace," recited by Usher in a moment of "artificial excitement," hinting that Usher and the narrator have possibly indulged in "artificial"—that is, narcotic—diversions. Despite Poe's reluctance to use allegory in fiction, here, as in other poems, he indulges in another artificial pleasure—an extended comparison of the face-like castle inhabited by the "monarch Thought" with Usher's mind and reason "tottering . . . upon her . . . throne," as the narrator remarks (M 2: 406). With this embedded poem, Poe traces connections between house and mind as explicitly as possible, framing the story—on one level—as a descent into madness by Usher, or the narrator, or both, triggered by mechanisms of denial, repression, and lack of conscience. Lindon Barrett's association of reason with whiteness in antebellum America opens the door to a more tacitly racialized reading of "The Haunted Palace," while Betsy Erkkila explicitly sees the "hideous throng" of the poem, which invades and overcomes the reign of reason behind "the pale door," as an allusion to American fear of insurrection by "Negroes and lower classes."[50]

Another example of the house's importance to the unfolding of the story is the strange importance given to Usher's theory that the atmosphere around his house derives intimately from the *fungi* covering the stones of the house and the trees around it, linking all together in a close network of charged and sentient matter. This theory (discussed in a later chapter by Branka Arsić) evokes further evidence of the narrator's unreliability. He keeps insisting that Usher's theory is untrue and even beneath notice ("Such opinions need no comment, and I will make none"; [M 2: 408]), and yet the end of the narrative bears out Usher's version. During the final scene, a thick gaseous and glowing cloud indeed envelopes the house before vanishing with it into the tarn.

Usher's belief in the sentience of the physical mansion and tarn takes on a still more ironic significance when read in light of a culture whose laws defined certain human beings as things. If we consider that African Americans were bought and sold as chattel on the premise that they were not human, the debate about Usher's belief in the consciousness of his physical environment assumes a sinister suggestiveness. It was, after all, the condition of the white Southern master to be surrounded by sentient beings whose intelligence and emotions had to be denied in order for the plantation and the slave economy itself to endure.

To conclude, "The Fall of the House of Usher" is the keystone to Poe's later work. With suggestive indirection, the story evokes sympathy for the sufferer of a grave injury, namely, living entombment accompanied by abandonment—conscious malice on the part of the sociopathic Usher and heedless neglect in the case of the "inept" narrator, as Timmerman characterizes him.[51] Like many of Poe's stories (including, notably, "Hop-Frog"), "Usher" betrays what Kennedy has described as "potential empathy for those in bondage."[52] It is perhaps also no accident that Poe's later work *Eureka* makes a strangely moving case for the absolute equality of all souls and all animate beings as mere figments of a larger "Divine Being" into which all will one day melt ("the sense of individual identity will be gradually merged in the general consciousness" [L1: 106]). In any case, although the narrative is dense with details and allusions never entirely accounted for by any single reading or interpretation, the emotional effect of the tale clearly depends on the horror and repugnance that readers are invited to feel as they discover the cruelty on which the unstable House of Usher stands.

Notes

1. Dennis R. Perry and Carl H. Sederholm, *Poe, "The House of Usher," and the American Gothic* (London: Palgrave Macmillan, 2009).
2. Darrel Abel, "A Key to the House of Usher," *University of Toronto Quarterly* 18, no. 2 (January 1849): 176–185.

3. Jonathan Elmer, *Reading at the Social Limit: Affect, Mass Culture, and Edgar Allan Poe* (Stanford, CA: Stanford University Press, 1995), 90–91.
4. Marie Bonaparte, *The Life and Works of Edgar Allan Poe: A Psycho-Analytic Interpretation*, trans. John Rodker, foreword by Sigmund Freud (London: Imago, 1949), 237–250.
5. D. H. Lawrence, *Studies in Classic American Literature*, ed. Ezra Greenspan, Lindeth Vasey and John Worthen (Cambridge: Cambridge University Press, 2003), 66–80. Similarly, Patrick Quinn saw incest as the secret heart of the story, proposing that the main conflict staged by the tale is "the warfare taking place in Roderick . . . by his consciousness against the evil of his unconscious." See Patrick F. Quinn, *The French Face of Poe* (Carbondale: Southern Illinois University Press, 1954), 245.
6. G. R. Thompson, *Poe's Fiction: Romantic Irony in the Gothic Tales* (Madison: The University of Wisconsin Press, 1973), 96.
7. J. R. Hammond, *An Edgar Allan Poe Companion* (London: Macmillan Press, 1981), 71.
8. Eric W. Carlson, "Tales of Psychal Conflict: 'William Wilson' and 'The Fall of the House of Usher,'" in *A Companion to Poe Studies*, ed. Eric W. Carlson (Westport, CT: Greenwood Press, 1996), 188–208.
9. Darrel Abel, "A Key to the House of Usher," 179.
10. Michael J. Hoffman, "The House of Usher and Negative Romanticism," *Studies in Romanticism* 4, no. 3 (Spring 1965): 158–168.
11. This is not to say that Poe never uses allegory at all. He certainly uses it in his poetry, and stories such as "The Masque of the Red Death" lend themselves well to allegorical readings, but the emotional and aesthetic effect of a tale is far more likely to be his main focus.
12. For more on Poe's irony, see Elmer's *Reading at the Social Limit.*
13. Joseph N. Riddel, "The 'Crypt' of Edgar Poe," *boundary 2* 7, no. 3 (Spring 1979): 117–144, 130.
14. Riddel, "The 'Crypt' of Edgar Poe," 128–129.
15. Harriet Hustis, "'Reading Encrypted but Persistent': The Gothic of Reading and Poe's 'The Fall of the House of Usher,'" *Studies in American Fiction* 27, no. 1 (March 22, 1999): 3–20.
16. Scott Peeples, "Poe's 'constructiveness' and 'The Fall of the House of Usher,'" in *The Cambridge Companion to Edgar Allan Poe*, ed. Kevin J. Hayes (Cambridge: Cambridge University Press, 2002), 178–190.
17. Peeples, "Poe's 'Constructiveness' and 'The Fall of the House of Usher,'" 182.
18. Peeples, "Poe's 'Constructiveness' and 'The Fall of the House of Usher,'" 188.
19. John Carlos Rowe, "Poe, Antebellum Slavery and Modern Criticism," in *Poe's Pym: Critical Explorations*, ed. Richard Kopley (Durham, NC: Duke University Press, 1992), 117.
20. Toni Morrison, *Playing in the Dark: Whiteness and the Literary Imagination* (Cambridge, MA: Harvard University Press, 1992), 31–33.
21. Teresa Goddu, *Gothic America: Narrative History, and Nation* (New York: Columbia University Press, 1997), 93.
22. Lesley Ginsberg, "Slavery and the Gothic Horror of Poe's 'The Black Cat,'" in *American Gothic: New Interventions in a National Narrative*, ed. Robert K. Martin & Eric Savoy (Iowa City: Iowa University Press, 1889), 123, 122.
23. Whalen, Terence. *Edgar Allan Poe and the Masses: The Political Economy of Literature in Antebellum America* (Princeton, NJ: Princeton University Press, 1999), 111–146. For an earlier discussion of the controversy surrounding the "Paulding-Drayton" review, see Dana D. Nelson, *The Word in Black and White: Reading "Race" in American Literature, 1638–1867* (New York: Oxford University Press, 1994), 90–92. Stefan Schöberlein confirms

that N. Beverley Tucker wrote the review in "Poe or Not Poe? A Stylometric Analysis of Edgar Allan Poe's Writings," *Digital Scholarship in the Humanities* 32, no. 3 (2017): 643–659.

24. Whalen, *Edgar Allan Poe and the Masses*, 111.
25. John Carlos Rowe, "Edgar Allan Poe's Imperial Fantasy and the American Frontier," in *Romancing the Shadow: Poe and Race*, ed. by J. Gerald and Liliane Weissberg (Oxford: Oxford University Press, 2001), 100.
26. Leland S. Person, "Poe's Philosophy of Amalgamation: Reading Racism in the Tales," in *Romancing the Shadow*, 207.
27. J. Gerald Kennedy, "'Trust No Man': Poe, Douglass, and the Culture of Slavery," in *Romancing the Shadow*, 225–257.
28. Sam Worley, "*The Narrative of Arthur Gordon Pym* and the Ideology of Slavery," *ESQ* 40 (1994): 222.
29. George Fitzhugh, *Cannibals All! Or Slaves Without Masters* (Richmond, VA: A. Morris, 1857), chap. 32, http://www.gutenberg.org/files/35481/35481-h/35481-h.htm.
30. Fitzhugh, *Cannibals All! Or Slaves Without Masters*, Chap. 22, http://www.gutenberg.org/files/35481/35481-h/35481-h.htm.
31. Harriet Beecher Stowe, *Uncle Tom's Cabin*, ed. Elizabeth Ammons (New York: W.W. Norton, 1994), 7.
32. Quoted in Ginsberg, "Slavery and the Gothic Horror of Poe's 'The Black Cat,'" 100.
33. Quoted in Ginsberg, "Slavery and the Gothic Horror of Poe's 'The Black Cat,'" 101.
34. "'Diseases and Peculiarities of the Negro Race' by Dr. Cartwright," Africans in America, PBS Online, accessed December 8, 2017, https://www.pbs.org/wgbh/aia/part4/4h3106t.html.
35. Toni Morrison, "Melville and the Language of Denial," *The Nation*, January 7, 2014, https://www.thenation.com/article/melville-and-language-denial/.
36. See, for example, J. Gerald Kennedy's short overview of these approaches in *Strange Nation: Literary Nationalism and Cultural Conflict in the Age of Poe* (Oxford: Oxford University Press, 2016), 67.
37. Harry Levin, *The Power of Blackness: Hawthorne, Poe, Melville* (New York: Vintage Books, 1960), 160–161.
38. Maurice S. Lee, "Absolute Poe," in *Slavery, Philosophy, and American Literature, 1830–1860* (Cambridge: Cambridge University Press, 2005), 23. Stephen Dougherty has also recently read the tale as a "nightmarish prophecy of the cultural and political defeat of American slave society," only with a Foucaultian focus on "modern, bourgeois identity" and miscegenation, in "Foucault in the House of Usher: Some Historical Permutations in Poe's Gothic," *Papers on Language & Literature* 37, number 1 (2001): 19.
39. The chief abolitionist newspaper took Nat Turner's revolt as the beginning of the end for the South, writing dramatically that "the first drops of blood, which are but the prelude to a deluge from the gathering clouds, have fallen" (*The Liberator*, Boston, September 3, 1831). The writer warns that the entire country will be the scene of bloodshed and righteous vengeance if slaves are not immediately freed, and that more revolts like Turner's will naturally follow: "Woe to this guilty land, unless she speedily repents of her evil doings! The blood of millions of her sons cried aloud for redress! IMMEDIATE EMANCIPATION can alone save her from the vengeance of Heaven" (reprinted in Henry Irving Tragle, *The Southampton Slave Revolt of 1831: A Compilation of Source Material* [Amherst: The University of Massachusetts Press, 1971], 64). My source for the implications of the

combustible dungeon is G. R. Thompson, *Poe's Fiction*, 94. For my own discussion of this, see *The Poetics and Politics of the American Gothic* (Surrey, UK: Ashgate, 2010), 51.

40. Orlando Patterson, *Slavery and Social Death: A Comparative Study* (Cambridge, MA: Harvard University Press, 1985).
41. Although this review was anonymous, and Thomas Mabbott attributes it to someone else, G. R. Thompson has argued that it is "almost certainly" written by Poe, and as editor of the Library of America volume of Poe's *Essays and Reviews* so included it.
42. An excellent discussion of conscience in antebellum literature is Richard H. Brodhead, in "Sparing the Rod: Discipline and Fiction in Antebellum America," *Representations* 21 (Winter 1988): 67–96, where he quotes an antebellum guidebook in which the conscience is described as something that seems uncanny for children: "another than themselves, and yet themselves" (79).
43. Francis Wayland, *The Elements of Moral Science*, ed. Joseph Blau (Cambridge, MA: Belknap Press of Harvard University Press, 1963), 49.
44. J. Gerald Kennedy even muses that "without employment or income, Poe must nevertheless have drawn occasional, ironic comparisons between his circumstances and those of the slave." See "A Brief Biography," in *A Historical Guide to Edgar Allan Poe*, ed. J. Gerald Kennedy (Oxford: Oxford University Press, 2001), 31.
45. Most notably, Jean Epstein's *La Chute de la maison Usher* (1928).
46. Madeline's role as embodiment of repressed conscience is also paralleled by similar characters in other Poe stories, such as William Wilson's double, already discussed, or the "mummer" who stands in the shadow of the "ebony clock" (one more allusion to the black slave population of the South?) in "The Masque of the Red Death" and causes the death of Prince Prospero, who had also tried to lock his people's suffering outside his castle gates and mask the sound with revels. All these figures function as personifications of stifled conscience returning to exact justice. For a discussion of Southern anxieties about black violence and revenge, see Elizabeth Young, *Black Frankenstein: The Making of an American Metaphor* (New York: New York Press, 2008).
47. Joan Dayan, "Amorous Bondage: Poe, Ladies, and Slaves," in *The American Face of Edgar Allan Poe*, ed. Shawn Rosenheim and Stephen Rachman (Baltimore: Johns Hopkins University Press, 1995), 179–209.
48. See David Leverenz, "Poe and Gentry Virginia," in *The American Face of Edgar Allan Poe*, 221.
49. John H. Timmerman, "House of Mirrors: Edgar Allan Poe's 'The Fall of the House of Usher,'" in *Edgar Allan Poe's "The Tell-Tale Heart" and Other Stories*, ed. Harold Bloom (New York: Infobase Publishing, 2009), 163.
50. Lindon Barrett, "Presence of Mind," in *Romancing the Shadow*, 172; Betsy Erkkila, "The Poetics of Whiteness: Poe and the Racial Imaginary," in *Romancing the Shadow*, 58.
51. Timmerman, "House of Mirrors: Edgar Allan Poe's 'The Fall of the House of Usher,'" 160.
52. J. Gerald Kennedy, "'Trust No Man': Poe, Douglass, and the Culture of Slavery," in *Romancing the Shadow*, 237.

Bibliography

Goddu, Theresa A. *Gothic America: Narrative, History, and Nation*. New York: Columbia University Press, 1997.

Hayes, Kevin J., ed. *The Cambridge Companion to Edgar Allan Poe.* Cambridge: Cambridge University Press, 2002.

Kennedy, J. Gerald, ed. *A Historical Guide to Edgar Allan Poe.* Oxford: Oxford University Press, 2001.

Kennedy, J. Gerald, and Liliane Weissberg, eds. *Romancing the Shadow: Poe and Race.* Oxford: Oxford University Press, 2001.

Martin, Robert K., and Eric Savoy, eds. *American Gothic: Interventions in a National Narrative.* Iowa City: University of Iowa Press, 1998.

Perry, Dennis R., and Carl H. Sederholm. *Poe, "The House of Usher," and the American Gothic.* London: Palgrave Macmillan, 2009.

Rosenheim, Shawn, and Stephen Rachman, eds. *The American Face of Edgar Allan Poe.* Baltimore: Johns Hopkins University Press, 1995.

CHAPTER 20

GENRE, SCIENCE, AND "HANS PFAALL"

MAURICE S. LEE

THE center of "The Unparalleled Adventure of One Hans Pfaall" is strange enough in itself. One Hans Pfaall of Rotterdam recounts in a letter how his bellows-mending business failed, how he came across an astronomy pamphlet, how he built an incredible balloon for space travel, how he murdered his creditors during its launch, and how—after overcoming some harrowing trials through scientific genius, technological ingenuity, improvisation, and not a little luck—he traveled to a fantastical city on the moon where he lived with the inhabitants for five years. Pfaall's letter, especially its description of his journey, is chock-full of specific scientific details that lend an aura of realism. But that's not all. The letter is delivered from the moon by another balloon to a crowd of Rotterdam burghers led by one Superbus Von Underduk, and the messenger is not Pfaall but what appears to be a denizen of the moon—earless, huge handed, colorfully dressed, and no more than two feet tall—who drops Pfaall's letter to the dumbfounded crowd before returning into the firmament. In contrast to Pfaall's letter, the frame story surrounding it reads like satire or burlesque. But wait . . . there's more, for the description of the letter's delivery is related by a nameless narrator who denies that his account is a hoax, though revisions to the tale include an appendix admitting that the story is fake after all, even while defending the plausibility of its performance by referring to scientific authorities and logic. Now how much credence would you give to "Hans Pfaall"? How do we explain its wild oscillations between absurdity and verisimilitude? And what in the end do we make of Poe's story about a trip to the moon?

We know that Poe made twenty dollars for "Hans Phaall—A Tale" when it first appeared in June of 1835 in the *Southern Literary Messenger.* We also know that Poe felt underpaid for a piece that, depending on whose account one believes, took him two weeks or two years to compose as he labored to find footing in the literary marketplace.[1] Poe reprinted the story with an appendix and more scientific elaborations under the title "Hans Phaall" in his *Tales of the Grotesque and Arabesque* (1839). But three years later in a draft of the table of contents to his abortive *Phantasy-Pieces* collection, Poe changed the title to "The Unparralleled [*sic*] Adventure of one Hans Pfaall," altering the spelling of the protagonist's name; and in later correspondence he used yet another spelling, "Hans Phaal," while recurring to the original "Hans Phaall" designation when reflecting on the story in 1846.[2] (Keyword searches do well to use multiple spelling options when exploring databases for references to the story.) One year after Poe's death, the most definitive version of the tale appeared as "The Unparalleled Adventure of One Hans Pfaall" in Rufus Griswold's 1850 edition of Poe's collected *Works*, this time with a few more technical details and a sentence added to the appendix. On the whole, the textual history of "Hans Pfaall" is less a honing of focus or clarifying of purpose than an aggregation of second thoughts, as if Poe the writer—like his protagonist—was obliged to make adjustments on the fly.[3]

In the antebellum era's chaotic culture of reprinting, publications were often reused, repackaged, and revised with or without authorial permission, but "Hans Pfaall" remains an especially unstable text for reasons both coincidental and purposive. After the initial publication of the story, Poe revised it in response to a popular lunar narrative written by Richard Adams Locke, though Poe the hoaxer and observer of science originally composed "Hans Pfaall" in ways that seem intentionally inconsistent at the level of genre and method. At a time when revolutions in printing and the sciences unsettled the status of literature, "Hans Pfaall" is a particularly telling example of how Poe navigates formal, social, and epistemological complications regarding questions of belief, even if it remains difficult to gauge how successful such navigation is. The unevenness of "Hans Pfaall" can be taken to reflect some combination of ironic design, aesthetic sloppiness, pressure from antebellum print culture, and shifting nineteenth-century generic formations. And because "Hans Pfaall" is Poe's first attempt at long fiction, and a wildly imaginative one at that, a related challenge of the story is that Poe himself may not have known what to make of it.

The Unparalleled Critical History of "Hans Pfaall"

In whatever version, "Hans Pfaall" is not usually considered one of Poe's major achievements, but the story has generated a fair amount of scholarship that tends to follow two main lines of inquiry, the first of which takes the tale as a pioneering work of science fiction. Poe hardly invented the idea of lunar adventure: from Johannes Kepler's *Somnium* (1634), Cyrano de Bergerac's *Selenarchia* (1659), and Daniel Defoe's *The Consolidator* (1705), to Rudolf Erich Raspe's *The Surprising Adventures of Baron Munchausen* (1816) and George Tucker's *A Voyage to the Moon* (1827), authors long before Poe imagined trips to the moon with varying degrees of satire and fantasy.[4] An important difference of "Hans Pfaall" is that portions of the text aspire to mimetic plausibility, dwelling at length on scientific and technological details such as mechanical innovations, quantitative data, and the supposed discovery of a new gas—a "*constituent of azote*, so long considered irreducible" whose "density is about 37.4 times *less than that of hydrogen*" (P 1: 393–394). Formal realism, technical jargon, and the extrapolation of actual scientific advances create a sense of verisimilitude that would become a hallmark of science fiction, including lunar narratives influenced by Poe such as Jules Verne's 1865 *From the Earth to the Moon* (which explicitly cites "Hans Pfaall") and H. G. Wells's *The First Men in the Moon* (1901). "Hans Pfaall" lacks the more integrated verisimilitude of such novels, and later Poe texts such as "The Facts in the Case of M. Valdemar" (1845) and *Eureka* (1848) are more disciplined in their engagements with scientific discourse. But if "Hans Pfaall" does not always take itself seriously or expect its readers to do so, the tale can stand as an early example of both Poe's growth as a science fiction writer and the emergence of the genre as a whole.[5] As with any innovation—scientific or literary—one might expect some trials, errors, and choices that in retrospect seem rather odd.

Focusing less on literary genealogies and more on Poe's historical moment, a second and more recent strand of "Hans Pfaall" scholarship sees the story as both a product of and commentary on the antebellum print revolution. Here interpretations draw on the economic and epistemological instabilities occasioned by rapidly expanding print markets made possible by advances in transportation, literacy, copyright practices, print technology, and the industrialization of the publishing trade. It matters that the bellows-mender Pfaall goes bankrupt when people start using newspapers instead of bellows to fan their fires, and it seems no coincidence that Pfaall escapes his creditors by hiding in a bookseller's stall, where he reads a treatise on speculative astronomy without ultimately purchasing the item. In case readers fail to register the tale's interest in print and the economics of authorship, the balloon that returns to Rotterdam is built from "dirty newspapers" and constructed in the shape of a "fool's-cap," a term referring simultaneously to stupidity, trickery, and a specific size of printer's paper (P 1: 388). In this sense, "Hans Pfaall" is a story about (among other things) the composition, circulation, and reception of stories.

Scholarship on "Hans Pfaall" finds in its engagement with print a series of related critiques: Poe exposes the fictions made possible by a burgeoning newspaper culture in which identities and events cannot be verified; he notes that print enterprises founded on financial credit and narrative credibility are prone, like balloons, to inflation and collapse; he ruminates on the problem of maintaining artistic autonomy at a time when literature was increasingly subjected to what Poe saw as debasing economic forces.[6] Such arguments are compelling given the work of Terence Whalen, Leon Jackson, and Meredith McGill, who have shown how Poe's writings across his career engage the realities of antebellum print markets.[7] "Hans Pfaall" is a relatively early sign of this interest (Poe published his first story only three years before), but already a crucial dynamic is evident, for as much as Poe resents the power of print to pander to the masses, impoverish authors, and encroach on artistic freedoms, "Hans Pfaall" also identifies happier opportunities. Dirty newspapers may bankrupt Pfaall, but they also offer him the means to escape his creditors, reach unprecedented heights of fame, and perhaps receive a pardon for his crimes. Print literally becomes a vehicle for imaginative flights and can even help disseminate scientific knowledge—not only to obtuse Rotterdam burghers but also to readers of "Hans Pfaall."

This last point suggests a way to approach "Hans Pfaall" that combines its two lines of scholarship, for while the story can be taken to pioneer science fiction and comment on antebellum print, such critical narratives do not run parallel so much as intersect. Marcy Dinius and John Tresch have begun to situate "Hans Pfaall" at a moment in which science, increasingly constructed by the popular press, began to emerge as a distinct discourse with specific methods and modes of expression.[8] But because such distinctions in the antebellum era were just starting to take modern forms, the process of differentiation was especially visible and thus vulnerable to the kind of hoaxing, satire, and parody at which Poe excelled and often indulged. Part of the inconsistency of "Hans Pfaall" involves Poe's ironic deployment of scientific genres, which (as Tresch argues) Poe regards as a technology for producing verisimilitude. Thus to track the strangeness of "Hans Pfaall" is in part to trace how scientific knowledge and literary expression developed in and through the print culture of Poe's time.

Popular Science

The early nineteenth century witnessed a shift in Britain and the United States as the natural sciences became less identified with gentlemen-scholars practicing natural philosophy and more defined by professionals using sophisticated instruments, abstract concepts, and recondite methods. If the most prominent American scientific thinkers before the nineteenth century were Renaissance men such as Benjamin Franklin, Benjamin Rush, and Thomas Jefferson, later scientists devoted themselves to narrower fields of study that produced knowledge through specialized publications and institutions. Britain led the way with such organizations as the British Association for the Advancement of Science (founded in 1831), while America saw signal achievements in the 1840s, including the journal *Scientific American* (begun in 1845), the Smithsonian Institute (founded in 1846), Harvard College's Lawrence Scientific School (1847), and the American Association for the Advancement of Science (1848). "Hans Pfaall" predates these benchmarks, but by the mid-1830s the professionalization of the natural sciences was already underway. As historians of science often note, the word *scientist* was coined in 1834.

This does not mean that the natural sciences had no place in popular culture, for the nineteenth century had various ways to publically validate and disseminate scientific knowledge. As early as the late seventeenth century, empirical experiments required witnesses to verify their outcomes, and as a result they were often performed not only in the controlled environments of laboratories but also in venues that mixed education and entertainment, scientific method and spectacle. Such practices spread in the nineteenth century, including everything from demonstrations of electricity and magnetism, to displays of dissections and chemical reactions, to exhibitions at natural history museums and the unwrapping of Egyptian mummies at parties. Scientific performances sometimes crossed the line between legitimacy and chicanery, most famously in the shows of P. T. Barnum, as well as in events involving spiritualism, mesmerism, and animal magnetism—phenomena that fascinated Poe and were considered by many of his time to be legitimate subjects for scientific inquiry.

Manned balloon exhibitions were also popular in the early nineteenth century, combining the wonders of human flight, patriotic competitions between scientists, and demonstrations of advances in aeronautics and pneumatics, including Antoine-Laurent Lavoisier's groundbreaking work on the decomposition of chemical elements in gasses. Compared to Britain and France, balloon exhibitions came later to the United States, but by the early 1830s Charles Ferson Durant was drawing large crowds in New York City, where he scattered poems praising the glories of flight to spectators watching below.[9] Accounts of aeronauts in the American popular press often combined scientific explanation, lyrical language, and sensational narrative. Thus when "Hans Pfaall" details the discovery of a new gas, describes thousands of people witnessing the arrival of a balloon, and relates in a breathless narrative style Pfaall's heightened emotions and exploits, Poe works within a recognizable subgenre. The setting of "Hans Pfaall" may be in the Netherlands, and the Dutch aspects of the tale can conjure New York City (as Carlo Martinez has noted), but the framing of the story would have been familiar enough to antebellum readers in many locales.[10]

Scientific writing, of course, had long been the primary means for producing and disseminating scientific knowledge, and the antebellum era's print revolution expanded the range of possibilities. In his appendix to "Hans Pfaall," Poe refers to John Herschel's *Treatise on Astronomy* (1833), a popular book written for educated laypeople by one of the period's scientific luminaries. Unattributed borrowings in "Hans Pfaall" suggest that Poe may not have actually drawn from Herschel's book itself but rather used excerpts reprinted in Abraham Rees's *Cyclopædia or Universal Dictionary* (1819), one of the many resources that, like the flood of publications from the Society for the Diffusion of Useful Knowledge, brought scientific information to the masses. Poe may also have drawn on the *Philosophical Transactions of the Royal Society of London* (or reprinted versions thereof), and he had access to ballooning information in newspapers and magazines that included scientific news alongside political commentaries, religious articles, fiction, poetry, and humor.[11] The point here is not to trace Poe's exact sources or his actual expertise in astronomy or pneumatics, but rather to note that "Hans Pfaall" appeared at a time when establishing scientific knowledge relied not only on academic credentials and official scholarly channels but also on its dissemination through unruly networks of popular print. For a rough twenty-first-century analogy, consider how misinformation about, say, climate change and vaccines spreads unchecked through the Internet—attracting large readerships, dismaying experts, and opening opportunities for the abuse of a relatively new and largely unregulated communications technology. Scientific methods can aspire to and even achieve a measure of rational objectivity, but what counts as scientific knowledge in public domains depends in part on how it is represented in surrounding media ecologies.

Such ecologies in the antebellum era allowed for the manipulation of scientific discourse, for the period's culture of reprinting made it difficult to verify the sources and accuracy of news, while the unprecedented acceleration of scientific discovery was simultaneously inspiring and disorienting. If natural philosophy prior to the nineteenth century typically involved objects that could be seen with the naked eye and comprehended through (to use a loose term) common sense, many advances in the antebellum period required microscopes or telescopes and included unseen forces inferred from experiments involving electricity, magnetism, thermodynamics, vacuums, and chemical reactions. During a period that some scholars call the second scientific revolution, invisible worlds, hidden causes, deep time, and deep space were in many ways beyond imagination. As one author wrote in the *Southern Literary Journal* six months after the *Messenger* published "Hans Pfaall": "As we advance in the walks of science, the range of things possible to be known soon appears so vast in proportion to our ability . . . that we are soon utterly confounded and lost in the immensity around us."[12]

That antebellum print culture offered fertile ground for science fiction and scientific hoaxes is indicated not only by "Hans Pfaall" but also by a series of articles that came to be known as the "Great Moon Hoax." Two months after "Hans Pfaall" initially appeared, the journalist and amateur astronomer Richard Adams Locke published "Great Astronomical Discoveries Lately Made by Sir John Herschel" (1835). Pretending to be a scientific report about life on the moon as observed through a powerful telescope in Africa, Locke's series appeared in the *New York Sun*, a pioneering penny newspaper whose circulation dwarfed that of the *Southern Literary Messenger.* Locke's narrative resembles "Hans Pfaall" in that its description of lunar phenomena (including winged humanoids) creates an aura of scientific verisimilitude. However, Locke deploys scientific discourse more consistently than "Hans Pfaall," and his series was much more popular, fooling many readers and sparking debates about the legitimacy of Locke's claims and the ethical responsibilities of newspapers.[13] Whereas Enlightenment ideology envisioned the press as a precondition for the advancement of democracy and truth, shenanigans such as Locke's raised the specter of fake news and a postfactual public sphere.

More troubling for Poe is that Locke could be taken to have bested Poe at his own hoaxing game. Though Poe would famously accuse Nathaniel Hawthorne and Henry Wadsworth Longfellow of plagiarism, and initially leveled the same charge against Locke, he ultimately exonerated Locke of stealing his lunar ideas, both in the 1839 appendix to "Hans Pfaall" and in his biographical sketch of Locke in "The Literati of New York City" (1846).[14] Poe's unusual equanimity may have been vocationally motivated insofar as Locke was an influential editor, though even while vindicating and in some ways praising his fellow author, Poe in the appendix to "Hans Pfaall" could not repress his competitiveness—pointing out flaws in Locke's logic, asserting his own scientific knowledge and originality, and (most important for our purposes here) denying that "Hans Pfaall" was ever intended to be an unalloyed hoax (P 1: 430, 428). We need hardly believe Poe, whose attempts to shape his public image were not always honest or fair. But if the inconsistencies of "Hans Pfaall" made it a less successful hoax than Locke's, the brazenness of the tale's uneven performance opens the possibility that Poe, even prior to Locke's series, was staging a kind of metahoax. For historians of science working in the tradition of Thomas Kuhn, scientists labor under conceptual paradigms that impose order by limiting explanatory possibilities. For ideology critics following Michel Foucault, scientific representations and modes of expression are necessarily bound up with larger power structures that determine disciplinary knowledge. And for sociologists of science such as Bruno Latour, institutional and cultural practices subtly influence supposedly objective empirical methods. Offering an additional constructivist position, "Hans Pfaall" shows that scientific knowledge is not only produced by social and methodological structures but also by literary styles and systems that can be understood in terms of genre.

Generic Heterogeneity

Near the start of "Hans Pfaall," the balloon descending on Rotterdam is described as "a queer, heterogeneous, but apparently solid substance, so oddly shaped, so whimsically put together, as not to be in any manner comprehended" (P 1: 387–388). Here Poe could be reflecting on "Hans Pfaall" itself, which he calls in its appendix a work of both "banter" and "plausibility" (428), of "rigmarole" and "*verisimilitude*" (430, 433). On the one hand, the frame narrative revels in comic absurdities typical of antebellum burlesque: the balloon has bells playing the tune of "Betty Martin" (a popular American song of the time) (388); ten thousand slack-jawed burghers simultaneously replace ten thousand pipes that have fallen from their mouths (387); and a piece of ballast lands on Superbus Von Underduk, rolling him over "half a dozen" times as he emits "half a dozen" puffs from his pipe (390). On the other hand, Pfaall's letter (the central narrative of the story) works toward a realism founded on scientific discourse and reinforced in revisions to the tale. Poe includes data on time, distance, mass, and atmospheric conditions; provides careful descriptions of technological devices; and—in the appendix and letter itself—spins explanations that reference scientific theories of the time. There is a disjunction of tone and content in that the relatively plausible scene of a balloon appearing above a city appears in ridiculous style, while Pfaall's unbelievable journey to the moon is described in more serious terms. Such incommensurability is a broader feature of Poe's perverse aesthetics: gruesome scenes are rendered in beautiful language; lunatics speak in hyperrational terms; poems about uncontrollable affect take meticulously ordered forms. By largely relegating its rigmarole and verisimilitude to distinct portions of its narrative, "Hans Pfaall" foregrounds its heterogeneous construction, though why Poe so conspicuously displays the seams of his tale (in the same way that Pfaall discusses the seams of his balloon) is by no means clear.

John Pendleton Kennedy, a Baltimore literary figure who helped Poe at the start of his career, wrote to Poe in February of 1836:

> Your fault is your love of the extravagant. . . . Some of your *bizarreries* have been mistaken for satire—and admired too in that character. They deserved it, but *you* did not, for you did not intend them so. I like your grotesque—it is of the very best stamp, and I am sure you will do wonders for yourself in the comic—I mean the *serio tragi comic*. (PL: 190)

Kennedy's letter does not mention specific texts, but in addition to other Poe tales such as "Loss of Breath" (1835) and "Lionizing" (1835), he probably had "Hans Pfaall" in mind, particularly given what James Machor has shown to be the diverse reactions to the story.[15] Most antebellum commentators took "Hans Pfaall" to be a purely speculative fiction, though evidence indicates that some readers believed the story while others remained agnostic. Kennedy himself seems uncertain about the genres of Poe's fiction, and his menagerie of terms is difficult to parse when he invokes "satire" (a traditional literary category), the "grotesque" (a recognizable aesthetic term), "*bizarreries*" (an unusual description), and "*serio tragi comic*" (a hybrid description if ever there was one). Kennedy's letter also highlights a related challenge: What exactly might Poe "intend" with the extravagance of his tales?

Poe's reply to Kennedy two days after receiving his letter both raises the stakes and deepens the difficulty of the question. Poe wrote: "You are nearly, but not altogether right in relation to the satire of some of my Tales. Most of them were *intended* for half-banter, half-satire—although I might not have fully acknowledged this to be their aim even to myself" (H 17: 30). The very syntax of this passage is ambiguous. Does Poe conflate "banter" and "satire" as synonymous terms for unserious modes of expression, or is he making a distinction between the two, as if banter is a kind of nonpurposive play and satire a more teleological, more intentional genre? Poe also makes the nearly paradoxical acknowledgment that he himself has not acknowledged his own aims. Such attentiveness to the possibilities of the unconscious has made Poe a productive subject for psychoanalytic criticism; and if "Hans Pfaall" lacks some of Poe's most famous tropes (doppelgangers, walled-off spaces, burials), the story dramatizes the potential for deep and fractured psychologies through altered states of consciousness, sensational affects, and a narrator torn between irrationality and reason. Ultimately, however—and as suggested by Kennedy's letter—the issue of intention in "Hans Pfaall" centers most on a kind of generic inconsistency that (as Richard Nate has noted) Poe called in a subsequent story "the tone heterogeneous."[16]

The two genres most at play in "Hans Pfaall" are those of scientific writing and literary fiction, though neither should be regarded as stable in itself or in relation to the other. In the early nineteenth century, scientific discourse involved a mix of traditional and emerging formal features, many of which are evident in "Hans Pfaall." Geologists, botanists, and zoologists often expressed themselves in emotive, sublime, and lyrical language that can be associated with literary romanticism, while writings in geography, oceanography, and ethnography retained longstanding affinities with travel and exploration narratives that included first-person descriptions of marvelous adventures told chronologically and in journal form, a genre Poe employs not only in "Hans Pfaall" but also in *The Narrative of Arthur Gordon Pym* (1838) and *The Journal of Julius Rodman* (1840). Certain aspects of Pfaall's letter—evocative images of natural phenomena, detailed descriptions of heightened sensations, the dramatic overcoming of dangers—might feel like literature to a modern reader but were common in scientific writings of the time. Indeed, scholars have increasingly dissolved hard boundaries between nineteenth-century science and literature by (among other things) stressing the aesthetic qualities of texts by celebrated scientists such as Alexander Von Humboldt, Joseph Banks, Charles Lyell, and Charles Darwin.

At the same time, the antebellum era witnessed a growing division between literature and the natural sciences. As scientists became more specialized, professionalized, and committed to methodological rigor, they increasingly aspired to objective points of view, standardized terminology, quantitative data, and texts organized by taxonomic subject and logical argument, not chronological narrative. This was part of William Whewell's point in his *Philosophy of the Inductive Sciences* (1840) when he called for the need to "preserve the purity and analogies of scientific language from wanton and needless violation."[17] Other scientists of the early nineteenth century noted tensions between impersonal professional publications and popular works written in more dramatic style, particularly when researches involved unparalleled adventures that could make for gripping storytelling. Before recounting his incredible travels in South America, Humboldt wrote in the preface to the first volume of his *Personal Narrative* (1814):

> The difficulties which I have experienced since my return in the composition of a considerable number of treatises, in order to make known certain classes of phænomena, insensibly overcame my repugnance to write the narrative of my journey. . . . I even perceived, that so distinguished a preference is given to this sort of composition, that scientific men, after having presented in an isolated manner the account of their researches, . . . imagine that they have not fulfilled their engagements with the public, till they have written their itinerary.[18]

Setting the "treatises" of "scientific men" over and against "narrative[s]" designed for the "public," Humboldt overcomes his "repugnance" toward popular genres but still feels the need to justify his storytelling. Darwin hints at a similar ambivalence in the preface to his *Journal of Researches* (1840), later revised and retitled *The Voyage of the Beagle* (1845). Darwin presents his inquiries in "the form of a journal" so as to attract "general interest," but he does so apologetically and hastens to add, "the briefness and imperfection of several parts, I hope, will be excused."[19] The absurdities of "Hans Pfaall" differentiate it from the narratives of Humboldt and Darwin, but the heterogeneity of the story highlights broader generic negotiations within scientific discourses of the time.

If scientific writing in the early nineteenth century retained affinities with literary genres, fiction—despite efforts to distinguish itself—remained entangled with scientific modes of expression. For Michael McKeon, the emergence of empirical science shaped the rise of novelistic verisimilitude in the early eighteenth century in that both relied on an epistemology of experience and careful observations of material details.[20] Arguing in a similar vein but focusing more on form, Mary Poovey emphasizes how literature in the late eighteenth and nineteenth centuries struggled to separate itself from informational forms associated with facticity, quantification, and the social sciences.[21] Other potential entanglements include analogies between realist novels and scientific experiments, as well as similarities between novels written from third-person perspectives and the "view from nowhere" that scientists increasingly adopted. Such claims tend to assume that both science and literature seek to present an accurate account of nature and experience so as to compel belief. But what if fiction does not actually aspire to convince readers of its reality?

Catherine Gallagher has argued that by the start of the nineteenth century many novels stopped attempting to deceive readers into thinking that their narratives were based in reality and instead began to acknowledge their fictionality by taking plausibility as a standard for verisimilitude.[22] For Gallagher, readers increasingly entered into tacit agreements in which they willfully suspended their disbelief as characters and events were described with levels of detail and probability that actually signaled their fictiveness. Jonathan Elmer identifies a similar dynamic when discussing how Poe's writings draw on a broad "cultural logic of the hoax" in which antebellum discourses from Barnum to con games to fiction "transform[ed] the skeptical witness into the willing participant."[23] Neither Gallagher nor Elmer discusses "Hans Pfaall," but they provide helpful coordinates for understanding the story's shifting between verisimilitude and rigmarole. It is not only that in the early nineteenth century scientific advances and mass print culture made it difficult to tell fact from fiction; and it is not only that in the period scientific and literary genres were not easily separated. Gallagher and Elmer's insights, as well as reactions to "Hans Pfaall" in the antebellum period and today, suggest that the story's generic heterogeneity invites an interplay between skepticism and belief that is part of the story's appeal. The interplay is so explicit, extreme, and self-conscious as to point toward an intentional design, not only in the initial version of "Hans Pfaall" but also in Poe's revisions. In this sense, the story—not in spite but precisely because of its generic and aesthetic inconsistencies—can be regarded less as an unsuccessful hoax and more as a narrative about the turbulent dynamics of writing and reading fiction under conditions of doubt.

In his 1907 preface to *The American* (1877), Henry James discusses how fiction writers might manage the relationship between skepticism and belief, comparing the challenge of creating verisimilitude to the work of an aeronaut:

> The balloon of experience is in fact of course tied to the earth, and under that necessity we swing, thanks to a rope of remarkable length, in the more or less commodious car of the imagination; but it is by the rope we know where we are, and from

> the moment that cable is cut we are at large and unrelated: we only swing apart from the globe—though remaining as exhilarated, naturally, as we like, especially when all goes well. The art of the romancer is, "for the fun of it," insidiously to cut the cable, to cut it without our detecting him.[24]

The fun and very different achievement of "Hans Pfaall" is that Poe cuts the cable that ties his story to reality in full view of his audience, thus inviting us to ask how, when, and why we choose (or do not choose) to suspend our disbelief. By functioning as a test of verisimilitude during the scientific and print revolutions of the antebellum period, "Hans Pfaall" in more ways than one performs a daring experiment and exhibition.

Notes

1. J. O. Bailey, "Sources for Poe's *Arthur Gordon Pym*, 'Hans Pfaal,' and Other Pieces," *PMLA* 57, no. 2 (1942): 513–535.
2. Burton Pollin, "Hans Pfaall: A False Variant and Phallic Fallacy," *Mississippi Quarterly* 31, no. 4 (1978): 519–527.
3. For a synoptic account of the versions of, sources for, and contemporary responses to "Hans Pfaall," see Pollin's introduction to "The Unparalleled Adventure of One Hans Pfaal," P 1: 366–379.
4. Don Sakers, "The Reference Library," *Analog: Science Fiction and Fact* 131, no. 5 (2011): 104–107.
5. For Poe in the larger context of science fiction, see Brian Stableford, "Science Fiction before the Genre," *The Cambridge Companion to Science Fiction*, ed. Edward James and Farah Mendlesohn (New York: Cambridge University Press, 2003), esp. 18–22. See also John Tresch, "Extra! Extra! Poe Invents Science Fiction!," *The Cambridge Companion to Edgar Allan Poe*, ed. Kevin J. Hayes (New York: Cambridge University Press, 2002), 113–132. See also Paul Grimstad's discussion of "Hans Pfaal" in this volume, which is compatible with my own sense of the tale.
6. Lara Langer Cohen, *The Fabrication of American Literature: Fraudulence and Antebellum Print Culture* (Philadelphia: University of Pennsylvania Press, 2012), 56–64 ("cannot be verified"); Gavin Jones, "Poor Poe: On the Literature of Revulsion," *American Literary History* 23, no. 1 (2011): 1–18 ("inflation and collapse"); Carlo Martinez, "E. A. Poe's 'Hans Pfaall,' the Penny Press, and the Autonomy of the Literary Field," *The Edgar Allan Poe Review* 12, no. 1 (2011): 6–31 ("artistic autonomy").
7. Terence Whalen, *Edgar Allan Poe and the Masses: The Political Economy of Literature in Antebellum America* (Princeton, NJ: Princeton University Press, 1999); Leon Jackson, *The Business of Letters: Authorial Economies in Antebellum America* (Stanford, CA: Stanford University Press, 2008); Meredith McGill, *American Literature and the Culture of Reprinting, 1834–1853* (Philadelphia: University of Pennsylvania Press, 2003).
8. Marcy J. Dinius, "Poe's Moon Shot: 'Hans Phaall' and the Art and Science of Antebellum Print Culture," *Poe Studies* 37, no. 1–2 (2004): 1–10; John Tresch, "'The Potent Magic of Verisimilitude': Edgar Allan Poe within the Mechanical Age," *The British Journal for the History of Science* 30, no. 3 (1997): 275–290.

9. Tom D. Crouch, *The Eagle Aloft: Two Centuries of the Balloon in America* (Washington, D.C.: Smithsonian Institution Press, 1983). See also Richard Holmes, *The Age of Wonder: How the Romantic Generation Discovered the Beauty and Terror of Science* (New York: Pantheon, 2008), 125–162.
10. Martinez, "E. A. Poe's 'Hans Pfaall,'" 10.
11. For additional sources on Poe and science, see Meredith Neill Posey, "Notes on Poe's Hans Pfaall," *Modern Language Notes* 45, no. 8 (1930): 501–507.
12. "Lord Brougham's Treatise on Natural Theology," *The Southern Literary Journal* (Dec. 1835).
13. Mario Castagnaro, "Lunar Fancies and Earthly Truths: The Moon Hoax of 1835 and the Penny Press," *Nineteenth-Century Contexts* 34, no. 3 (2012): 253–268.
14. For Poe's accusations of plagiarism, see (for examples) ER: 575, 749; for his note in the appendix, see P 1: 428; for his sketch of Locke, see ER: 1214–1222.
15. James L. Machor, *Reading Fiction in Antebellum America: Informed Response and Reception Histories, 1820–1865* (Baltimore: Johns Hopkins University Press, 2011), 96–102.
16. Richard Nate, "Feigned Histories: Edgar Allan Poe's 'The Unparalleled Adventure of One Hans Pfaall' and the Tradition of the Experimental Essay," *POEtic Effect and Cultural Discourses*, ed. Hermann Josef Schnackertz (Heidelberg: Universitätsverlag Winter, 2003), 85–102. The quote is from "How to Write a Blackwood Article" (1838) in M 2: 342.
17. William Whewell, *History of the Inductive Sciences, Vol. 1* (1840; New York: Cambridge University Press, 2014), xv.
18. *Personal Narrative of Travels to the Equinoctial Regions of the New Continent, during the Years 1799–1804, Vol. I*, trans. Helen Maria Williams (London: Longman, Hurst, Rees, Orme, and Brown, J. Murray, and H. Colburn, 1814), xxxix–lx.
19. Charles Darwin, *Journal of Researches into the Geology and Natural History of the Various Countries Visited by the H. M. S. Beagle* (London: Henry Colburn, 1840), viii.
20. Michael McKeon, *The Origins of the English Novel, 1600–1740* (Baltimore: Johns Hopkins University Press, 1987).
21. Mary Poovey, *Genres of the Credit Economy: Mediating Value in Eighteenth- and Nineteenth-Century Britain* (Chicago: University of Chicago Press, 2008).
22. Catherine Gallagher, "The Rise of Fictionality," in *The Novel, Volume 1: History, Geography, and Culture*, ed. Franco Moretti (Princeton, NJ: Princeton University Press, 2006), 336–363.
23. Jonathan Elmer, *Reading at the Social Limit: Affect, Mass Culture, and Edgar Allan Poe* (Stanford, CA: Stanford University Press, 1995), 181.
24. Henry James, *The Art of the Novel: Critical Prefaces* (1934; Chicago: University of Chicago Press, 2011), 33–34.

Bibliography

Bailey, J. O. "Sources for Poe's Arthur Gordon Pym, 'Hans Pfaal,' and Other Pieces." *PMLA* 57, no. 2 (1942): 513–535.

Castagnaro, Mario. "Lunar Fancies and Earthly Truths: The Moon Hoax of 1835 and the Penny Press." *Nineteenth-Century Contexts* 34, no. 3 (2012): 253–268.

Cohen, Lara Langer. *The Fabrication of American Literature: Fraudulence and Antebellum Print Culture.* Philadelphia: University of Pennsylvania Press, 2012.

Dinius, Marcy J. "Poe's Moon Shot: 'Hans Phaall' and the Art and Science of Antebellum Print Culture." *Poe Studies* 37, no. 1–2 (2004): 1–10.

Elmer, Jonathan. *Reading at the Social Limit: Affect, Mass Culture, and Edgar Allan Poe.* Stanford, CA: Stanford University Press, 1995.

Gallagher, Catherine. "The Rise of Fictionality." In *The Novel, Volume 1: History, Geography, and Culture*, edited by Franco Moretti, 336–363. Princeton, NJ: Princeton University Press, 2006.

Jackson, Leon. *The Business of Letters: Authorial Economies in Antebellum America.* Stanford, CA: Stanford University Press, 2008.

Jones, Gavin. "Poor Poe: On the Literature of Revulsion," *American Literary History* 23, no. 1 (2011): 1–18.

Machor, James L. *Reading Fiction in Antebellum America: Informed Response and Reception Histories, 1820–1865.* Baltimore: Johns Hopkins University Press, 2011.

Martinez, Carlo. "E.A. Poe's 'Hans Pfaall,' the Penny Press, and the Autonomy of the Literary Field." *The Edgar Allan Poe Review* 12, no. 1 (2011): 6–31.

McGill, Meredith. *American Literature and the Culture of Reprinting, 1834–1853.* Philadelphia: University of Pennsylvania Press, 2002.

Nate, Richard. "Feigned Histories: Edgar Allan Poe's 'The Unparalleled Adventure of One Hans Pfaall' and the Tradition of the Experimental Essay." In *POEtic Effect and Cultural Discourses*, edited by Hermann Josef Schnackertz, 85–102. Heidelberg: Universitätsverlag Winter, 2003.

Pollin, Burton. "Hans Pfaall: A False Variant and Phallic Fallacy." *Mississippi Quarterly* 31, no. 4 (1978): 519–527.

Posey, Meredith Neill. "Notes on Poe's Hans Pfaall." *Modern Language Notes* 45, no. 8 (1930): 501–507.

Tresch, John. "Extra! Extra! Poe Invents Science Fiction!" In *Cambridge Companion to Edgar Allan Poe*, edited by Kevin J. Hayes, 113–132. New York: Cambridge University Press, 2002.

Tresch, John. "'The Potent Magic of Verisimilitude': Edgar Allan Poe within the Mechanical Age." *British Journal for the History of Science* 30, no. 3 (1997): 275–290.

Whalen, Terence. *Edgar Allan Poe and the Masses: The Political Economy of Literature in Antebellum America.* Princeton, NJ: Princeton University Press, 1999.

CHAPTER 21

RUDE REPRESENTATION

Orienting the American Frontier Through the Characters in Pym's *Chasm*

JACOB RAMA BERMAN

> With a very slight exertion of the imagination, the left, or most northerly of these indentures might have been taken for the intentional, although rude, representation of a human figure standing erect, with outstretched arms. The rest of them bore also some little resemblance to alphabetical characters, and Peters was willing, at all events, to adopt the idle opinion that they were really such.
>
> —Edgar Allan Poe, *The Narrative of Arthur Gordon Pym* (P 1: 195)

TOWARD the end of their disastrous visit to the polar community of Tsalal, Arthur Gordon Pym and Dirk Peters explore a "vast pit of black granite." Inside this pit the two adventurers come across a series of "singular looking indentures." Peters regards these markings as alphabetical characters, but Pym dismisses this opinion and convinces Peters of his "error" (P 1: 195). At this point all of their shipmates have been murdered by the native Tsalalians. "We alone had escaped from the tempest of overwhelming destruction" Pym announces, adding that "[w]e were the only living white men on the island" (P 1: 185). The description of Peters as "white" is surprising. Earlier in the narrative Pym was quite clear about coding his companion as racially other—the "son of an Indian squaw" with grotesque features and a countenance "which betook of the Upsaroka character" (P 1: 87). In his Introduction to the authoritative version of *Pym*, Burton Pollin refers to Peters as a "compact of Negro and Indian qualities" (P 1: 11). So how did he become white? When the reader first encounters Peters, he is "one of the most ferocious-looking men [Pym] has ever beheld," but by the time the two travelers arrive in the polar region something has changed in Pym's crude racialization of Peters. Pym and Peters have become companions when they reach the frontier space of Tsalal. But it is the domestic American frontier that provides the context for the dubious racial transformation of Peters. Or rather it is the "Orienting" of the domestic frontier in Jackson-era settler discourse that informs the racial imaginary vivifying *Pym*'s polar chasm markings.

Those Strange Markings

Poe embedded multiple bizarre features within *The Narrative of Arthur Gordon Pym*. Among the most prominent are the doubling of Chapter Twenty-three and the delightfully contradictory "Note" that ends the novel. *Pym* scholars have established that the extra Chapter Twenty-three and the "Note" were composed at the same time, after the rest of the text had been completed, and then added to the narrative last.[1] These textual addenda were no doubt influenced by Poe's reading of John Lloyd Stephens's soon-to-be published *Incidents of Travel in Egypt, Arabia Petræa, and the Holy Land* (1837). As Pollin points out, some of *Pym*'s descriptions of Tsalal's barren landscape are directly indebted to contemporary travelers' descriptions of Arabia Petraea and the stark desolation of the "accursed" landscape of Idumea (Edom).[2] In conjunction with Stephens's travel narrative, Poe was also reading the Reverend Alexander Keith's *Evidence of Prophecy* (1836). Poe quotes Keith in the laudatory twelve-page review of *Incidents of Travel* he published in his first assignment for the *New York Review*. Keith's text, with its emphasis on documenting the literal realization of biblical prophecy in the contemporary Near East, certainly contributed to Poe's ludic invocations of scripture in *Pym*'s concluding "Note." The references to ancient philology, biblical prophecy, and the literal geography of the Near East in the doubled chapter Twenty-three and the "Note" speak directly to the influence of Orientalist discourse on Poe's final version of *Pym*. Most dramatically, what the additional Chapter Twenty-three and the "Note" have in common is *Pym*'s key hermeneutic conundrum: the chasm inscriptions (see Figure 21.1).

Pym's Chasm Inscriptions

The critical debates surrounding *Pym* are myriad, and multiple studies have been devoted to how the text creates various forms of interpretive crisis. Perhaps nothing in *Pym* has generated more "critical pluralism" in Poe scholarship than the question of the chasm markings.[3] The "Note" establishes the markings as Ethiopian, Arabic, and Egyptian words, respectively, giving them the status of glyphs. But are these glyphs part of an elaborate hoax Poe is pulling on the reader, "leaving in doubt," as J. Gerald Kennedy

FIGURE 21.1 *Pym*'s chasm inscriptions.

puts it, "the possibility of education in a world of ubiquitous illusion"?[4] Or are we meant to take these etchings seriously as encrypted messages about Poe's racial politics?

Curiously enough, Pym and Peters disagree on the function of these pit markings. Peters offers an interpretation that relies on imagination—the marks are esoteric signs of language. Pym, however, counters with a literal interpretation—the marks are exoteric evidence of a "natural" convulsion in the earth. "I convinced him of his error," Pym explains, "by directing his attention to the floor of the fissure, where, among the powder, we picked up piece by piece, several large flakes of the marl." These large flakes, "exactly fitting the indentures," prove for Pym that the pit markings are "the work of nature" (P 1: 195). Within the context of the narrative proper, it appears that Pym is asserting his claim to rationality and reason against Peters's fancy. Given the racial undertones of Pym's differentiation, Peters's newly minted whiteness would seem to be even more suspect.

But what Pym remarks as "idle" speculation on Peters's part, the novel's editor affirms as accurate interpretation in the concluding "Note." Despite Pym's dismissal of Peters's "idle opinion," then, the "Note" argues that these seemingly abstruse marks are a legible language, or more accurately languages. The glyphs are translated into words, with the meanings "to be shady," "to be white," and "the region of the south," respectively. The "Note" suggests that these translations indicate a link between the discovery of inscriptions in the chasm and a hidden Manichean history of Tsalal—a place where "[n]othing white was found" until Pym's ship arrived. "It is not impossible that 'Tsalal,' the appellation of the island of the chasms, may be found, upon minute philological inquiry, to betray some alliance with the chasms themselves, or some reference to the Ethiopian characters so mysteriously written in their windings" (P 1: 208).

As Sidney Kaplan first established, Poe's source for the chasm characters is H. W. F. Gesenius's *Hebrew and Chaldee Lexicon to the Old Testament*.[5] Under the

Hebrew *tsalam*, the *Lexicon* defines the word "to be shady, Arab," "to be obscure, dark," and "darkness."[6] Most probably Poe was also interested in attaching the name of his island to the Hebrew name Solomon, which he may have associated with the "Ethiopic" definition for "black" through an erroneous footnote in Charles Anthon's *New York Review* article of March 1837 on the "Language of Bournou" (P 1: 361n.6A). But whatever Poe's sources for the name Tsalal, and the characters in the chasm, it is clear he was conjuring the speculative philology associated with Orientalist research into ancient languages. As a result, Poe's tale of polar adventure incongruously contains references to Arabic, Hebrew, Ethiopian, and ancient Egyptian languages. Furthermore, by mentioning an "obfuscating series of implications about *white* objects on Tsalal" and connecting these white objects to philological speculation about the name Tsalal, the "Note" heightens the expectation that its Orientalist material contains clues to the island's mysterious story of racial origins.[7]

The phraseological rhyming between the "rude human figure" that appears on the chasm wall and the "shrouded human figure" whose skin is "the perfect whiteness of snow" that appears at the novel's conclusion also suggests that there is a connection between the pit markings and the novel's final White-Out scene. Deciphering the cave markings would seem to indicate that Poe is exploring articulations of a hieroglyphic white nationalism through his two "figures." The first "rude" figure deictically indicates the battle between whiteness and blackness, and the second "shrouded" figure manifests the triumph of unitary whiteness. But this interpretation ignores the emphasis the "Note" places on Orientalist modes of inquiry—namely philology and archaeology. Both expressions of whiteness are ultimately figural rather than literal—that is, both represent whiteness not as an essential feature, but as something esoteric that must be interpreted into existence by using Orientalist-inspired speculation. I read these figures, then, not as indicators of Poe's book ending in a vision of white nationalism. Rather, I read them as signifiers of a metatextual conversation about the racial ideology of settler colonialism that Poe is initiating with the reader through reference to a larger vein of popular Orientalist literature circulating in Jacksonian America. As multiple critics have pointed out, the play between the narrative and the "Note" destabilizes any claims to authority in the text. But this play between literal and figurative modes of interpretation also highlights the way that Orientalist imaginaries bleed into nineteenth-century American national narratives.

To decipher the meaning of *Pym*'s hieroglyphics, then, is not so much to render Poe's racial imaginary visible as it is to render visible the racial fantasies of American Orientalism in Poe's treatment of the chasm characters. This essay decodes the ways that Poe uses Orientalist material to negotiate questions of American nativity and whiteness in *Pym*. But I not only intend to demonstrate the implications of Poe's reference to Arab and/or Islamic material to craft an American fantasy of origins. I also intend to place Poe's Orientalism into dialectic with Arabo-Islamic intellectual discourses on origins to create a contrapuntal interpretation of *Pym*'s chasm writing.

Pym's Late Additions

> Mr. Pym has given the figures of the chasm without comment, and speaks decidedly of the *indentures* found at the extremity of the most easterly of these chasms as having but a fanciful resemblance to alphabetical characters, and in short, as being positively *not such*. . . . But as the facts in relation to *all* the figures are most singular . . . , it may be as well to say a word or two concerning them all—this, too, the more especially as the facts in question have, beyond doubt, escaped the attention of Mr. Poe.
>
> —Poe, *Pym* (P 1: 207)

Pym's famous non-ending and Poe's decision to substitute a final "Note" for narrative resolution have exercised scholars since the revival of critical interest in the text at the turn of the twentieth century. This was not always the case. As Pollin notes, "only three of the twenty six reviews and notices of *Pym* in America and England objected to the ruse by which the omission of a proper ending was justified" (P 1: 359n.1A). For later critics, though, the "Note"'s introduction of another narrative voice that undermines both Pym's and Poe's authority, as well as a composition timeline that contradicts earlier information, was often taken as proof of the text's disunity, incompleteness, and/or deficiency. As Poe criticism evolved over the course of the twentieth century, however, the "Note"'s critical significance began to be re-evaluated in light of emerging theories on metafiction and deconstruction.

Beginning in the 1970s, critics such as Kennedy began pointing to the "Note" as evidence of *Pym*'s strategic use of irony. The "Note" and the "Preface," Kennedy argues, allow Poe to parody contemporary compositional norms and thus demonstrate his absolute control over his material.[8] Other critics interested in deconstruction saw in the "Note" proof that *Pym* was a text that was about its own fictional process of production. As John Carlos Rowe states, "what critics have considered difficulties and inconsistencies in the text of *Pym* may also be considered self-conscious disruptions of the impulse towards a completed design and coherent meaning."[9] In this critical context, what were formerly interpreted as bugs in *Pym*'s text began to be regarded as features. Instead of being an embarrassing addition demonstrating Poe's slipshod command of his material, the "Note" came to represent Poe's conscious deconstruction of narrative authority. John Irwin, in a tour-de-force analysis of *Pym* in his 1980 book *American Hieroglyphics*, argues that Pym's subjective and ultimately inaccurate interpretation of various signs throughout his journey thematizes "the essential precariousness, both logical and ontological, of the narrative act."[10] In readings such as these, the figures in the Tsalalian chasm can represent the end of language, the multiplicity of interpretive possibility, the decentering of authorial power, or any number of other postmodern critical concerns. In short, the last forty years of critical literature addressing the figures in *Pym's* chasm have gone a long way toward making Poe our contemporary.

Though certainly insightful, these presentist critical concerns may be obscuring the way that *Pym*'s cave glyphs were very much a product of Jacksonian Orientalism. The discovery of cave glyphs written in ancient languages and conveying vaguely eschatological messages would have conjured a whole host of Orientalist associations for nineteenth-century American readers familiar with biblical archaeology, Egyptology, and Near Eastern philology. The nineteenth-century emergence of these fields of "scientific" inquiry into the Near East had a direct relationship to nineteenth-century America's domestic politics of expansion. Dana D. Nelson, in *The Word in Black and White*, places *Pym* within the context of nineteenth-century Anglo-America's increasing appetite for stories of exploration and discovery: "Between 1800 and 1850 America witnessed a simultaneous surge in scientific professionalization and expansionist fervor which cumulatively resulted in the Anglo-American theory of Manifest Destiny." "Pym's fictional adventure," Nelson argues, "is situated squarely in this expansionist, Anglo-Saxon ideological context."[11] The expansion of science as a profession was intimately tied, Nelson suggests, not only to the physical expansion of America's continental borders but also to the ideological engine of Anglo superiority that drove Manifest Destiny.

The growth in America's own Orientalist industries, and interest in Orientalist material, was part and parcel of the nineteenth-century expansion of scientific professionalism. Anglo-America's expansionist fervor may have realized itself on the North American continent, but it also helped pique interest in exotic locales—especially those, like the Near East, in which the new sciences seemingly had so much to reveal. Men with Bibles in one hand and measuring tools in the other descended on Ottoman Palestine from the 1820s to the 1850s. Edward Robinson, the father of biblical geography, and William Francis Lynch, the first man to survey the Dead Sea, were both Americans who would make their scientific names in the Near East in the few years just after *Pym*'s publication. But Poe's immediate and most influential source of knowledge on the Near East was Stephens's *Incidents of Travel*. As mid-nineteenth-century American settlers expanded the borders of the United States across the continent and deep into territory held by Indians, the reading public's appetite for narratives of foreign travel, discovery, and exploration increased. In this context, Stephens's *Incidents of Travel* was poised for success.

Incidents of Travel was published by Harper Brothers in 1837 to wide critical and commercial acclaim. Within two years *Incidents* had sold 21,000 copies—a healthy number by mid-nineteenth century standards.[12] Stephens was well versed in earlier Near Eastern travel writers, as well as well schooled in the obsessions of his fellow Americans. He consistently comments on Egyptian modernizations such as the laying of railroad tracks or the digging of canals. His descriptions of landscapes, ruins, and ancient cities also limn the emerging disciplines of biblical geography and archaeology. But it is Stephens's observations on Near Eastern culture, society, and peoples that most directly call to mind Jackson-era national dramas of identity. Traveling through Idumea, Stephens establishes an explicit correlation with the American frontier. Describing the barren landscape of Idumea, Stephens explains that "the Bedouin roams over them like the Indian on our native prairies."[13] Imbedded within Stephens's description of

Arabia Petraea, then, is an argument about Anglo-American possession of the Western frontier—"*our* native prairies."

Though American travelers in the Arab world had long associated Bedouins and Indians, the symbolic and typological connection between the two was rhetorically reinforced in Jackson-era imaginaries through reference to the story of Jacob and Esau. Because the Bible refers to Esau as red, Jacksonian Americans who wanted to deploy biblical analogy to legitimize white settler colonialism on the Western frontier used the story to typologize Native Indians as modern Esaus. As Michael Rogin puts it in his analysis of Jackson-era Indian removal, the Jacob and Esau story "enshrined for Bible reading Americans the right of the farming brother to claim the inheritance of the hunter."[14] For many Jacksonian Americans, the conflict between the two brothers was symbolic of what the biblical scholar Daniel J. Elazar calls the contrast between federal man and natural man. According to Elazar, "Jacob and Esau are perhaps the most important paradigms of federal and natural men in the Bible." "Nowhere in the Bible is the tragic reality of life better expressed," Elazar explains, "than in the scriptural rejection of these bluff, hearty, natural men in favor of federal men with their own weaknesses and problems."[15] Through this mode of interpretation, Anglo-American settlers rationalized the seizure of Native American territory by associating agriculture with civilization and wandering with barbarism.

In this Jacksonian context, Stephens's descriptions of actual Bedouins in the Arabian Desert operate as proxies for Native Americans in discussions of the western frontier. More specifically, Stephens's accounts of Bedouin life in Idumea (the land of Esau and the literal home of his descendants) are addressed directly to the rhetorical politics of white settler colonialism. "Captivating as is the wild idea of roving abroad at will, unfettered by the restraints of law or of conventional observances," Stephens argues, "the meanest tenant of a log hut in our western prairies has sources of happiness which the wandering Arab can never know."[16] Stephens juxtaposes settler colonists and "wandering" Arabs only incidentally to establish the connection between Bedouin and Native American. His real motivation is to establish the propriety of domestic Indian removal through reference to the contemporary Near East.

Stephens's portrayal of the "wandering" Arab punctures the romantic appeal of primitivism and establishes the mandates of the Western civilizing mission by registering his readers' faith in providential history. If history is defined by an inexorable movement toward enlightened progress, then the disappearance of native peoples, the argument goes, is part of God's providential plan. Stephens's representations of Bedouin culture thus employed a rhetorical strategy that Mary Louise Pratt has labeled transculturation.[17] The description he offers of Near Eastern lands and peoples engages his largely metropolitan reading public with an expansionist enterprise whose material benefits accrued mainly to a select few. In short, Stephens establishes the propriety of domestic Indian removal through global analogies about primitive peoples.

Poe would have been keenly aware of the appeal Stephens's book had for American readers eager to engage the politics of settler colonialism through an exotic proxy. *Pym* was meant to be published by Harper Brothers the same year as *Incidents of Travel.*

However, Harper and Brothers had delayed the release of *Pym* precisely because of a financial panic brought on by Jackson's Specie Circular and the resulting run on the banks. In contrast to the delay in *Pym*'s publication, Harper and Brothers decided to go forward with the publication of Stephens's book, in large part because its subject matter augured success despite the tough economic times. Given this publication history, and Poe's intimate knowledge of it, it is hard to ignore the influence of Stephens's representations of Near Eastern space and race on Poe's late revisions to *Pym*.

Poe's mock travel narrative is obviously an attempt to capitalize on his contemporary audience's fascination with narratives of exploration. "Once he had exhausted . . . his major source material, the mariners' chronicles," Pollin writes, Poe "resolved to shift to . . . nautical explorations and the travel book" (P 1: 8). This reliance on the exploration and travel genre is nowhere more evident than in the sections of the book that detail the undiscovered territory of Tsalal in the southern polar regions. Poe's main sources for polar exploration information were Benjamin Morrell's 1832 *Narrative of Four Voyages* and Jeremiah N. Reynolds's 1836 "Address, on the Subject of a Surveying and Exploring Expedition to the Pacific and the South Seas." *Pym* often copies verbatim from both sources. But Poe was doing more than tapping into the curiosity his readers had about polar exploration, and his late revisions to *Pym* betray a marked effort to exploit his reading public's interest in Orientalist modes of inquiry. Pym describes Tsalal as a place that is different "essentially from any hitherto visited by civilized men" (P 1: 171). The language Pym uses to establish Tsalal's unique appeal mirrors the language Stephens had used to describe the appeal of traveling to Idumea. "[I]n the land of Idumea, the oldest country in the world," Stephens asserts, "the aspect of everything is new and strange, and the very sands you tread on have never been trodden by the feet of *civilized* human beings."[18] In both instances, the categorization of a region as untouched by civilized man not only heightens its exotic purchase; it also aligns that space with the western frontier in America. The idea that places existed on the planet that were yet to experience civilization, or more accurately yet to be civilized by federal men, lent credence to the implicit ideology driving all colonialism, but particularly the United States's mid-nineteenth-century territorial expansion West: the idea that white men were bringing civilization to the wilderness.

Poe read advance copies of Stephens's travel narrative in his capacity as a reviewer for the *New York Review*. However much Poe may have been cribbing recent information about explorations in the Southern Hemisphere, he was also clearly utilizing the language and tropes of Near Eastern discovery. The "Note"'s indulgence in convoluted speculations on philology, race, and archeological discovery traffic in the Near East travel narrative's twinned fantasies of decipherment and revelation. In 1822, Jean François Champollion had revealed his decipherment of the Rosetta Stone, unlocking the mysteries of Egyptian hieroglyphic language. The international excitement that followed in the wake of Champollion's continuing translations was not lost on Near Eastern travel writers or on Poe, whose own interest in questions of decipherment were career-long.[19] Most nineteenth-century Near Eastern travel writers demonstrated an almost obsessive attention to the topic of revelation. Stephens and Keith represent, respectively, secular and sacred impulses toward revelation. The pit markings within the Tsalal chasm allow Poe to tap into a much larger, international conversation about decipherment. In the process of transporting Near Eastern themes into his pit episode, however, Poe also insinuates domestic frontier racial politics into his story of polar discovery.

By linking *Pym*'s engagement with contemporary narratives of polar discovery and its engagement with the imagery and imaginary of contemporary Near Eastern travel narratives, I am drawing attention to Poe's position at the nexus of what Kennedy and Jerome McGann call the horizontal print culture of mid-nineteenth-century America.[20] Poe gathered material from America's popular culture reservoirs and deployed it shamelessly in his own version of an exotic adventure tale. *Pym*'s polar scenes illuminate the nation's polar imaginary. But these scenes are also in conversation with nineteenth-century America's Orientalist imaginary. In the era of Manifest Destiny, Americans were reimagining their nation's frontiers in increasingly expansive and innovative ways. Often these imaginaries were not limited to the continental borders of North America. Frederic Edwin Church, who painted some of the most recognizable images of nineteenth-century America's landscape, also painted *The Iceberg* (1861), the image of polar exploration that adorns both the Oxford and the Penguin editions of *Pym*. In addition, Church painted the most famous American representation of Arabia Petraea, in the form of the lost Arab city of Petra (*El Khasne*, 1874).

Poe's reprinting and repurposing of source material from the texts that informed popular understanding of the South Pole and the Near East in his *Pym* narrative is an invitation to see these disparate geographical imaginaries as working in conjunction. Taken together, the representation of these exotic frontier landscapes blurs the line between science and pseudo-science, as well as between foreign geographical exploration and domestic cultural invention. The blurring of the lines between truth and fiction, the foreign and the familiar, in turn speaks directly to the confused racial categories that emerge out of discourses on settler colonialism that borrowed Oriental imagery and imaginaries to recreate North American frontier space as Anglo-American.

Stephens captured the thematic concerns of his Anglo-American domestic audience not only by engaging in primitivism but also by emphasizing the decay and desolation found in the Near East. Stephens never misses an opportunity to contrast the decrepit state of Egyptian ruins with the historical achievements of Egyptian civilization. Approaching Thebes, Stephens observes that "it was nearly dark when we arrived at the ruined village, which now occupies part of the site of the once magnificent city."[21] Stephens also consistently impugns Ottoman venality, which he argues trapped Near Eastern societies in a permanent past. Describing the villages of the Nile, Stephens fits in a jab at the reformism of Muhammad Ali:

> the same spectacle of misery and wretchedness, of poverty, famine, and nakedness, which I had seen in the suburbs of Alexandria, continued to meet me at every village on the Nile, and soon suggested the interesting consideration whether all this came

> from country and climate, from the character of the people, or from the government of the great reformer.[22]

The images of architectural and civilizational decay that Stephens presents to his readers through descriptions of crumbling Egyptian ruins and corrupted Near Eastern societies were indicative of a larger cultural reflection in which Jacksonian Americans were engaging about the meaning of Manifest Destiny. As Timothy Marr puts it in his book *The Cultural Roots of American Islamicism*, "Americans have long pressed orientalist images of Islam into domestic service as a means to globalize the authority of the cultural power of the United States."[23] In this respect, representations of savage Bedouin nomads and despotic Islamic rulers both naturalized westward expansion as part of a global mandate and marked American colonialism as exceptional, because democratic.

The interest American readers had in narratives of Near Eastern travel is consistent with the founding symbolic rhetorical connection between America and the Holy Land. But descriptions of the geography and people of the Islamic Near East had a specific resonance for mid-nineteenth-century American readers who were navigating the dynamics of frontier settler colonialism. These navigations of US national identity through the screen of the Near East not only indicate the active discussions within mid-century Orientalism over the literal meaning of biblical prophecy for American destiny, but they also suggest the importance of Orientalist figures for imaginatively negotiating American racial categories. It is to one of those figures, the figure of the Arab, that I will now turn my attention. The figure of the Arab mediates the meaning of race in Poe's text by both standing in as a hieroglyph of whiteness (in the form of Arabic script) and being a reference for the definition of blackness ("to be shady, Arab, . . . to be obscure, dark"). This Arab figure also gestures toward the ways in which "redness" complicates the imaginative racial typologies of the American frontier. By using the term "figure" of the Arab, I mean to conjure the literal Arabic script etched into the wall in Tsalalian chasm Pym explores.

Arab Figures, American Myths

> The upper range is evidently the Arabic verbal root
>
> 
>
> "To be white" ' whence all the inflections of brilliancy and whiteness.
>
> —Poe, *Pym* (P 1: 208)

Poe's reference for the "Arabic verbal root" is Gesenius's *Hebrew and Chaldee Lexicon.* Gesenius's text had been published in the United States in 1836, the year Poe began *Pym*, in a translation by the American biblical scholar and future father of biblical geography, Edward Robinson. Pollin, following Kaplan, advises that "Gesenius' *Lexicon* gives the source of Poe's word in the 'upper range' under the Hebrew 'tsachar' " (P 1: 361n.7A). The word *tsachar* appears once in the Bible (Ezekiel 27:18), referring to the whiteness of wool. But the word's primary definition is not the "quality of being white" but rather "reddish gray; tawny."[24] The slippage between whiteness and a blurry form of redness and/or brownness in the definition of *tsachar* speaks to the messy implications of searching for American origin stories through reference to biblical analogs. For once these biblical analogs are translated into American space, the message they carry for American readers becomes unruly. The "Note" 's intervention in the debate between Pym and Peters about the cave markings may undermine any authoritative understanding of the markings' meanings, but it also introduces a play between literal and imaginative forms of interpretation that dramatizes Orientalist modes of knowledge production.

Authors such as Stephens, and especially Keith, made reference to the desolation of Edom as proof of the literal manifestation of biblical prophecy. "Is there any country once inhabited and opulent so utterly desolate?" Keith asks of Idumea. "The territory of the descendants of Esau affords as miraculous a demonstration of the inspiration of the Scriptures, as the fate of the children of Israel."[25] Keith intimately links the history of Edomites and Israelites in the Bible lands and suggests the ways in which their figurative analogs were linked on the American frontier. Hilton Obenzinger, in his study of nineteenth-century American fascination with the Holy Land, *American Palestine*, points out that Protestant doctrines on the Jews "provided originary models for America's narratives of continuing settlement and expansion: if the elect though cursed *ur*-nation of Israel could be restored, so too could fallen Anglo-America, the typological new Jews, be 'restored' as a racialized chosen people."[26] For mid-nineteenth-century American readers, the literal desolation of the land of Esau offered more than just proof of biblical prophecy. Given the typological connection between Indians and Esau, as well as Anglo-Americans and Israelites, the desolation of Edom could be rhetorically leveraged for arguments about providential history—arguments that undergirded the logic of Manifest Destiny.

In this way Near Eastern history, in the guise of biblical prophecy, became prospective American destiny. Describing his journey through Idumea, Stephens emphasizes that "when [the traveler] tires with contemplation of barrenness and ruin, he may take the Bible in his hand, and read what Edom was, and how God, by the mouth of his prophets, cursed it; and see with his own eyes whether God's words be true."[27] The curse on Edom, the land of "red" Esau, was of particular interest to Poe, and he spent a good deal of space in his review of Stephens's book discussing it.[28] The message that the desolation of Edom held for American readers dovetailed with the mandates of westward expansion. White settlers were not just bringing civilization to the wilderness; they were saving the frontier from the curse of barrenness and ruin attached to Esau. But given the typological association between Israelites and Anglo-Americans, white frontier settlers were also restoring the fallen nation of Israel.

The idea of America as a typological New Israel and Americans as typological Israelites was as old as the Puritan settlers. But during the Jackson era of westward expansion predominantly through white settler colonialism, this connection took on a new significance. The story of Jacob and Esau may have rhetorically established the white man's right to take the "red" man's land, but other Orientalist narratives circulating in American discourse confused this message by arguing that Indians themselves were literal descendants of Israelites. The same year that Stephens published *Incidents of Travel*, Poe's close friend, Major Mordecai Manual Noah, published *Discourse on the Evidences of the American Indians Being descendants of the Lost Tribes of Israel*. Arguing that American Indians were "the remnants of the nine and a half tribes which were carried away into Assyria," Noah asks "if we are to believe in all the promises of restoration, and the fulfillment of the prophecies, respecting the final advent of the Jewish nation, what is to become of these our red brethren, whom we are driving before us so rapidly?"[29]

Noah's rhetoric blends the Salvationist language of Protestant millennial eschatology and the primitivist codes of Jacksonian expansionism. The Indians are "our red brethren," but they are also literal descendants of the original tribes of Israelites. Noah, the most prominent Jewish American man of letters in the United States in his day and an early advocate for the establishment of a State of Israel, was by no means alone in his assessment of the relation between Indians and Israelites. The prominent American portrait artist George Catlin, whose "Indian Gallery" toured the United States from 1837 to 1839, commented that "the first thing that strikes a traveler in an Indian country as evidence of their being of Jewish origin (and it is certainly a very forcible one), is the striking resemblance which they generally bear in contour, expression of head, to those people."[30] In Noah and Catlin's accounts, American Indians are not typological Israelites; they are literal Israelites. For Anglo-American settlers, though, assuming the tropic status of Israelite, of a "racialized chosen," allowed them to represent the frontier as theirs to take. But how could both Anglo-American settlers and the people they were removing be Israelites? What was the relationship between literal Israelites and typological Israelites? This question returns us to the word *tsachar*—a word that means both whiteness and redness/tawniness—and the disruptive nature of Orientalist figures in Jacksonian American frontier discourse.[31]

Historically, in the American rhetoric of white settler expansion, the covalence of American geography and biblical geography provided typologies that naturalized colonialism through biblical analogy. However, the creation of American typologies through reference to Near Eastern peoples, history, and geography often confuses categories and contributes to contaminations between the representation of Indians, Bedouins, Jews, and Anglo-Americans. "In fact, the life of a Bedouin, his appearance and his habits, are precisely the same as the patriarchs of old," Stephens writes, adding that "Abraham himself . . . was a Bedouin, and four thousand years have not made the slightest alteration in the character and habits of these extraordinary people."[32] Bedouins are living instantiations of Abrahamic patriarchs—of biblical Jews. But Bedouins are also analogous to Indians, and Indians are (ostensibly) literal Jews, and white settlers are typological Jews.

Taken as a *figura*, the Bedouin of Jacksonian discourse is a spectral replica of the primitive and an uncanny double of the biblical patriarch.[33] But the very plasticity of this *figura* makes it disruptive precisely because it brings literal and metaphoric modes of representations into conflict. Thus, the rhetorical Bedouin of Jacksonian discourse connects not only savages to biblical patriarchs, and Indians to Jews, but also white American settlers to the Indians they are displacing. This promiscuous interpenetration of different frontier racial typologies brings the very category of whiteness under question. For what is whiteness here but a metaphor for the mandates of settler colonialism? Who are the "racialized chosen" but a figure that can be variously interpreted? Pym and Peters disagree on the appropriate interpretation of the figure of whiteness they discover in the cave—the Arabic script. But this interpretive conundrum only highlights the way that transcultural Orientalist imaginaries confused the racial tropes of the American frontier.

Becoming White: Peters and the Racial Politics of the Frontier

Poe's creation of an Arab figure that indexes the categorical confusions and contaminations generated by putting Orientalism into the rhetorical service of settler colonialism goes a long way toward explaining how Dirk Peters is transformed in the course of the narrative from a "half-breed" Indian into a white man. When the reader first encounters Peters, he is a paradigm of grotesque monstrosity:

> He was short in stature—not more than four feet eight-inches high—but his limbs were of the most Herculean mold. His hands, especially, were so enormously thick and broad as hardly to retain human shape. His arms, as well as his legs, were *bowed* in the most singular manner . . . . His head was equally deformed, being of immense size, . . . and entirely bald. . . . He usually wore a wig formed of any hair-like material that presented itself—occasionally the skin of a Spanish dog or American grizzly bear. (P 1: 87)

Pym's racialized description of Peters emphasizes deformity and blurs the subject's humanity. Peters is a "half-breed" in every sense—he mixes the ethnic identities of Indian and European, he mixes the human with the bestial by wearing animal hair on his head, and he is associated with the half-man, half-God Hercules. And yet, Poe, the author, chooses to kill off Pym's natural racial and geographic companion, his boyhood friend Augustus Barnard, to pair the adventurer with the racialized Peters. This authorial decision makes sense in the context of American frontier narratives. Multiple critics have commented on the radical change in Pym in the second half of the novel—the way he transitions from a naïve and timid character to a knowledgeable and assertive one after the initial shipwreck that pairs him with Peters. This transformation, however, is perfectly in keeping with the frontier genre as pioneered in the late eighteenth century by writers such as John Filson and visible in such figures as his Daniel Boone.[34] Just as in frontier narratives, Pym's travails bring him maturation, masculinity, and knowledge.

Frontier heroes were heroic precisely because they could out-Indian the Indian, becoming masters of the terrain and harbingers of the civilization that would eventually follow their footsteps into the wilderness. Filson's masculinizing formula was taken up again and again by nineteenth-century popular depictions of the American frontier. Pym undergoes a similar maturation process. As he travels over time and further from home, he becomes more confident and bold. When the captain of the *Jane Guy* speaks of returning instead of pressing further toward the Southern Pole, Pym feels "himself bursting with indignation at the timid and ill-timed suggestion of our commander" (P 1: 166). Pym, at this juncture, has become more like Peters (who boldly urges his fellow mutineers to sail onwards toward the novelties of the South Pacific) than like the "timid" boy who stowed away aboard the *Grampus* in the beginning of the narrative. As Pym becomes more like Peters over the course of the narrative, Peters also becomes more like Pym—eventually becoming white.

If the American frontier made white men more Indian, in *Pym* the polar frontier makes the Indian Peters white. Peters's racial transformation may be a sly reversal of the tropes of the frontier genre or a narrative gesture toward the conceits of Jacksonian frontier discourse. But it also may be a way for Poe to examine the fluidity of the very category of whiteness.[35] In the pit, Pym dismisses Peters's interpretation of the glyphs as influenced by his imagination. As we have already seen, though, this contrast between Pym's rationality and Peters's imagination is undercut by the "Note" 's insistence that Peters is correct. But after engaging in authoritative-sounding philological inquiry, the "Note" ends by stating that "[c]onclusions such as these open a wide field for speculation and exciting conjecture" (P 1: 208). The "Note" 's ultimate reliance on Orientalist "speculation" and "conjecture" hopelessly blurs the distinction between science and pseudoscience and leaves readers to solve the mysteries of the chasm themselves. The "Note" then displaces answers about the connection between philological inquiry, archaeological data, and racial origins onto the capacities of Orientalist inquiry. What the reader is left with in the pit is an Orientalist-inspired fable about racial difference that mimics the Anglo-American penchant to locate its own national origins through Near Eastern imaginaries.

At the very least, Peters's racial transformation acknowledges that race, as an American category, is context dependent. In relation to the Tsalal frontier, Peters is white because he is not black. This binary racial logic is in keeping with the dichotomies rhetorically driving settler colonialism—savage and civilized, natural and federal, primitive and modern. But Peters's racial transformation also acknowledges that race is an imaginative, and therefore mutable, construct—that race is figurative. If *Pym*'s chasm is in many respects a place to search for origins—of the Tsalalian people, of race difference, of language—Poe suggests that origin narratives are best understood as figural rather than literal. In identifying Poe's creation of a "genius of place," William Carlos Williams cites his penchant for figural abstraction. "With Poe words were figures," Williams insists, "an old language truly, but one from which he carried over only the most elemental qualities to his new purpose." Poe's invention of tradition, for Williams, is captured in his translation of the familiar into a highly personal idiom. This conscious construction of a figurative alternative to the real world is precisely what makes Poe an icon of American literary nationalism for Williams. Thus, it is not Poe's representation of a real America that is important to Williams but rather his creation of figural abstractions that speak to the truth of American inventions of self—his "voluntary lopping off of [America's] lush landscape."[36]

When Pym is confronted with the novel's final "shrouded human figure," his ability to differentiate imagination from rationality is entirely doubtful, as is any distinction he might make between himself and Peters on that score. The novel's final figure of whiteness is another "rude representation," whose meaning, as in the chasm figure, is hieroglyphic and therefore open to speculation. But not any kind of speculation. The "Note" is very specific in the kind of speculation it authorizes—Orientalist inquiry of the type that hopelessly confounds the barrier between the literal and the metaphoric. Pym ends with a figural abstraction of whiteness that captures not the real-world meaning of race, but rather its American sociopolitical significance.

Interestingly enough, though, the tension between exoteric and esoteric interpretation that divides Pym and Peters's understanding of the "rude" markings in the pit is central to the Islamic tradition of interpretation. Islamic hermeneutics acknowledges two modes of interpretive approach to the Qur'an—*tafsir*/تفسير (literal interpretation) and taweel/طويل (imaginative interpretation). The practice of Islamic literary hermeneutics grows out of the need to understand ambiguous Qur'anic passages known as *mutashaabih*/متشابه, a term derived from the root *shbh*/ش-ب-ه, suggesting similarity. The difficulty with interpreting *mutashaabih* is not only that they lend themselves to more than one similar meaning. It is also that, as some Islamic scholars argue, the literal sense of these verses is not the same as their real message. The acknowledgment of potential esoteric meanings hidden within an exoteric text is not without its controversy in Islam. But this consideration opens the possibility of reading *Pym*'s pit glyphs in dialectic with an Islamic tradition of hermeneutics.

In a 1992 chapter of *Poe's Pym*, "The Arabesque Design of *Arthur Gordon Pym*," G. R. Thompson uses the symbol of the arabesque to attach Poe's text to the romantic irony developed by European writers such as Friedrich Schlegel. Though Thompson references the arabesque design and traces *Pym*'s formal structural patterning through the figure, he creates a critique that is entirely indebted to Western critical traditions.[37] What I propose here is a different approach to the term *arabesque*—one that acknowledges Arab and Islamic cultural discourses. It is my argument that Poe's cave figure, written in Arabic script, is an American arabesque. In my use of the term, American arabesque is both an -esquing of Arab material to make it American and an opportunity to create an intercultural dialogue between Poe's literature and Arab literature.

The Art of *Taweel*

Abd al-Qahir al-Jurjani, in his eleventh-century treatise on rhetoric entitled *Asrar al-Balagha* (*Secrets of Eloquence*), introduces Arabic's first qualitative classification of figurative language (*majaaz*/مجاز). *Majaaz*, al-Jurjani argues, occurs when a word references something other than it was coined to mean. This second, nonliteral, meaning arises out of a perceptional connection that the reader/listener recognizes between the two denotations of the word. The most sophisticated *majaaz* allow words to mean two different things at the same time. This insight on the linking function of figural language is useful for thinking through the connection between whiteness and "redness"/darkness (or Anglo, Indian, and Israelite) in the American figure of the Bedouin more generally. But it is also useful for thinking through the frontier racial politics Poe is exploring in his deployment of the specific figure of the Arab in *Pym*.

The Islamic exegetical practice of *taweel* grows out of an appreciation for the figurative power of language and owes a great debt to al-Jurjani's insights on *majaaz*. *Taweel* involves the act of bringing a word back to its origin or archetype to reveal its true meaning. For Islamic scholars of rhetoric such as al-Jurjani, the practice of *taweel* could synthesize apparent oppositions and reveal hidden affinities. An appreciation for the power of figurative language, al-Jurjani argues, can bring "a harmony to the unharmonious as if shortening the distance between East and West."[38] By placing Poe's Arabic figure under the hermeneutic pressure of *taweel*, I want to bring it back to its Arabic origins. But I also want to reveal the affinities between these origins and the racial imaginary Poe explores through reference to an Arabic figure.

Gesenius's *Hebrew and Chaldee Lexicon* gives the Arabic root for *tsachar* as *zahara*/ظهر.[39] In Modern Arabic, *zahara* means "to be or become visible, perceptible, distinct, manifest, clear."[40] The Arabic meaning for *Pym*'s chasm writing gives an important context to Poe's figural representation of whiteness. *Zahara* does not mark a particular color or race, per se, but rather the movement toward perceptibility and/or distinction. The Arabic word *zahara* in many ways accurately captures how the concept of whiteness operated in nineteenth-century American discourse. Whiteness was not an absolute identity found in nature but rather an imaginative identity that offered those under its aegis certain distinctions from their "others." To be white in America was to possess visibility as a racially privileged group who had access to citizenship and the right to claim ownership of land and bodies marked as nonwhite. This privilege is captured in an associated definition of *zahara*: "to gain the upperhand, to triumph, overcome, overwhelm, conquer, vanquish."[41] In the Jacksonian racial imaginary whiteness was as much this desire to conquer and displace the "other" as it was about any physiognomic marker of distinction. In these Arabic definitions of *Pym*'s chasm glyph we see the figure of whiteness deconstructed to reveal the Anglo-American myth of distinction that rhetorically subsidizes Manifest Destiny.

The Arabic word for whiteness, in terms of both color and race, is *abyad*/أبيض from the root *byad*//بيض. The root form of *abyad* holds many of the same meanings as *tsachar*, including shininess, brightness, and whiteness. But it also holds other definitions that lend insight into the connection between settler colonialism and the politics of whiteness in mid-nineteenth-century America. *Byad* can mean both "to stay, settle down, be or become resident" and "to be born in a place" (*byada bel makan*).[42] In other words, the same root that creates the word for whiteness also indexes both settler migration and indigenous belonging. This linguistic contamination of the typological categories of the mid-nineteenth-century American frontier in the Arabic root for whiteness mirrors the confusion that results from translating biblical figures such as Jews into American landscapes. Reference to biblical geography and typologies was one of the most effective ways that white European settlers miraculated their belonging in both America and on the western frontier. The transference of this geographical imaginary to America, however, also undercut the racial politics of Indian removal by suggesting commonalities between settlers and those they were removing. Pushing the intercultural analysis further, *Abyad* means whiteness and refers to the white race, but when the word is applied to geography, as in *ard byada*, it means "barren, uncultivated land, wasteland." Stephens's Edom is *ard byada*, but the American frontier in the mid-nineteenth century was also often figured as uncultivated and in need of civilized settlement. The literal translation of the Arabic word for wasteland into the English, "white land," captures the racial politics of settler colonialism quite succinctly.

The point of pursuing an etymological inquiry into Poe's Arab figure is not to suggest that Poe knew of these Arabic meanings, but rather to expose the resonances between his figural abstractions of whiteness in *Pym* and the politics of settler colonialism. These "rude representations" of whiteness were figurations of the real world politics of racial identity in Jacksonian America. A genealogical inquiry into the sources of white settler mythology is enriched by reference to the actual Arabic word Poe abstracts to create his chasm hieroglyph. In *Pym* the Arabic figure in the chasm indexes Orientalism's influence on not only American national origin myths but also on the American racial category of whiteness. The figure of the Arab, in the form of Arabic writing, works to mediate whiteness, as well as to draw attention to its constructed value.

Pym's final words, captured in the "Note," make reference to the act of writing and its relationship to revelation—"*I have graven it within the hills, and my vengeance upon the dust within the rock*." A number of critics have placed this pseudo-biblical quote within a Judeo-Christian context, drawing parallels, in particular, to Job.[43] However, there is another way to read Poe's Orientalist play on prophecy. As Islamic tradition holds, the first revelation of the Qur'an came to Muhammad when he was at a retreat in a cave in Hirrah, outside the hills of Mecca. The angel Jibril appeared to Muhammad and said to him "Iqra"/اقرأ (read/recite). Muhammad, who was illiterate, replied that he could not read/recite. The injunction to read/recite was given to him twice more before the angel

Jibril held Muhammad in a tight embrace and had him recite the first five ayahs of the ninty-sixth *Surah al-Qalam* (The Pen) of the Qur'an. Both the modern Arabic language and the religion of Islam are generated from this sacred dance between incomprehension and revelation. Poe's own use of Arabic script indexes the flickering space between illegibility and revelation, as well as between exoteric and esoteric meaning. In Poe's text this space is not sacred, but rather the secular arena where whiteness appears as a rhetorical act of invention. It is a whiteness whose exoteric meaning is illegible and whose esoteric history is haunted by the "others" it has displaced.

Notes

1. See J. V. Ridgely and Iola S. Haverstick, "Chartless Voyage: The Many Narratives of Arthur Gordon Pym," *Texas Studies in Literature and Language* 8, no. 1 (Spring 1966): 63–80.
2. See Pollin's discussion of the "germ-source for the bittern in the wasteland" being "the eventual desolation of Idumea (or Edom)" in P 1: 340n23.1. Also see Pollin's suggestion that Tsalal is "accursed like Edom" (P 1: 363n.9A).
3. Richard Kopley speaks of "the extraordinary critical pluralism evident surrounding *Pym*." See Kopley, Introduction to, *Poe's Pym: Critical Explorations*, ed. Richard Kopley (Durham, NC: Duke University Press, 1992), 2.
4. See J. Gerald Kennedy, The Narrative of Arthur Gordon Pym *and the Abyss if Interpretation* (New York: Twayne, 1995), 12.
5. Sidney Kaplan, Introduction to *The Narrative of Arthur Gordon Pym*, by Edgar Allan Poe (New York: Hill and Wang, 1966), xxi.
6. Heinrich Friedrich Wilhelm Gesenius, *Hebrew and Chaldee Lexicon to the Old Testament*, trans. Samuel Prideaux Tregalles (London: Samuel Bagster and Sons LTD, 1846), s.v. "tsalam."
7. The phrase is borrowed from Pollin's description of the "Note," P 1: 362n.8A.
8. See J. Gerald Kennedy, "The Preface as a Key to the Satire in *Pym*," *Studies in the Novel* 5, no. 2 (Summer 1973): 191–196 and "'The Infernal Twoness' in *Arthur Gordon Pym*," *Topic* 16, no. 30 (1976): 41–53.
9. John Carlos Rowe, "Writing and Truth in Poe's *The Narrative of Arthur Gordon Pym*," *Glyph: Johns Hopkins Textual Studies* 2 (1977): 104.
10. John T. Irwin, *American Hieroglyphics: The Symbol of Egyptian Hieroglyphics in the American Renaissance*, (New Haven, CT: Yale University Press, 1980), 69.
11. Dana D. Nelson, *The Word in Black and White: Reading "Race" in American Literature, 1638–1867* (New York: Oxford University Press, 1994), 92, 93.
12. See Victor Wolfgang Von Hagen, Introduction to *Incidents of Travel in Egypt, Arabia Petræa, and the Holy Land*, by John Lloyd Stephens (New York: Dover, 1996), xl. Von Hagen points out that the country's population is scarcely more than twenty million, only a fraction of which were literate. He also emphasizes that Harper kept the book in print until 1882.
13. Stephens, *Incidents of Travel*, 284.
14. Michael Rogin, *Fathers and Children: Andrew Jackson and the Subjugation of the American Indian* (New York: Knopf, 1975), 126.
15. Daniel J. Elazar, *Covenant and Polity in Biblical Israel: Biblical Foundations and Jewish Expressions* (New Brunswick, NJ: Transaction Publishers, 1995), 141.
16. Stephens, *Incidents of Travel*, 216.

17. Mary Louise Pratt, *Imperial Eyes: Travel Writing and Transculturation* (New York: Routledge, 1992).
18. Stephens, *Incidents of Travel*, 284, italics mine.
19. In a forthcoming essay on Poe's boyhood years in England, J. Gerald Kennedy notes that Poe almost certainly saw the Rosetta Stone (as well as the Elgin Marbles) at the British Museum between 1815 and 1820. The Rosetta Stone had been on display since 1802, and the British Museum was just around the corner from the house John Allan rented on Southampton Row. See Kennedy, "The Realm of Dream and Memory: Poe's England," in *Poe and Place*, ed. Philip Edward Phillips (Palgrave, 2018)
20. See Kennedy, Introduction to *Poe and the Remapping of Antebellum Print Culture*, ed. J. Gerald Kennedy and Jerome McGann (Baton Rouge: LSU Press, 2012). Kennedy and McGann propose an alternate literary map of antebellum America that flips the cultural axis of orientation from vertical to horizontal by shifting the focus from "a cluster of luminaries in the northeast" to "the network of relationships, authorial and institutional, within a decentralized system of distribution" (3). Because of his centrality to mid-nineteenth-century American print, and reprinting culture, Poe is an "avatar of this horizontal culture."
21. Stephens, *Incidents*, 71.
22. Stephens, *Incidents*, 15.
23. Marr, *The Cultural Roots of American Islamicism* (New York: Cambridge University Press, 2006), 1.
24. See *Brown-Driver-Briggs Hebrew and English Lexicon, Unabridged* (2002), s.v. "tsachar," accessed January 11, 2018, http://biblehub.com/hebrew/6713.htm.
25. Alexander Keith, *Evidence of the Truth of the Christian Religion* (New York: Harper and Brothers, 1836), 137.
26. Hliton Obenzinger, *American Palestine: Melville, Twain, and the Holy Land Mania* (Princeton, NJ: Princeton University Press, 1999), 5.
27. Stephens, *Incidents*, 284.
28. In his review of *Incidents of Travel*, Poe was at pains to prove that the curse on Edom had not been broken and that Stephens had not violated the biblical prophecy connected to the region. He goes into some philological speculation about a passage from Isaiah 24:10 to prove his point that "it will be clearly seen that he did not *pass through* the Edom of Ezekiel" (ER: 935).
29. Mordecai Manual Noah, *Discourses on the Evidences of the American Indians Being the Descendants of the Lost Tribes of Israel, Delivered before the Mercantile Library Association* (New York: J. Van Norden, 1837), 37.
30. Noah, *Discourses*, 28.
31. Another source Poe probably knew was *The Book of Mormon*, which gave credence to the "lost tribe" theory. For a Mormon historian's perspective, see Josiah Priest, *American Antiquities and Discoveries on the West* (Albany, NY: Hoffman and White, 1833).
32. Stephens, *Incidents*, 204.
33. I take my meaning of the term *figura* from Erich Auerbach's seminal work on the subject in *Scenes from the Drama of European Literature* (Minneapolis: University of Minnesota Press, 1984).
34. For more on Filson and his Boone character, see Richard Slotkin, *Regeneration Through Violence: The Mythology of the American Frontier, 1600–1860* (Middletown, CT: Wesleyan University Press, 1973).
35. For more on the subject of whiteness and racial play in Poe, see Toni Morrison, *Playing in the Dark: Whiteness and the Literary Imagination* (Boston: Harvard University Press, 1992).

36. William Carlos Williams, *In the American Grain* (New York: New Directions, 1925), 221, 226.
37. See Thompson, "The Arabesque Design of *Arthur Gordon Pym*," in *Poe's Pym*, 188–216.
38. Abd al-Qahir al-Jurjani, *Kitab Asrar al-Balagha, in Arab Poetics in the Golden Age*, ed. Vincente Catarino, trans. Helmutt Ritter (Leiden, Belgium: Brill, 1975), 116.
39. *Hebrew and Chaldee Lexicon to the Old Testament*, s.v. "tsachar."
40. *Hans Wehr Dictionary of Modern Arabic*, 4th ed. (Ithica, NY: Spoken Language Services, 1994), s.v. "zahara."
41. *Hans Wehr Dictionary of Modern Arabic*, s.v. "zahara."
42. *Hans Wehr Dictionary of Modern Arabic*, s.v. "abyad."
43. See Richard Kopley's last note, "This final line was probably drawn from Job 19:24, a passage concerning Job's wish regarding his words," in Kopley, ed., *The Narrative of Arthur Gordon Pym*, by Edgar Allan Poe (New York: Penguin, 1999), 245n6.

Bibliography

Al-Jurjani, Abd al-Qahir. *Kitab Asrar al-Balagha.* In *Arab Poetics in the Golden Age.* Edited by Vincente Catarino. Translated by Helmutt Ritter. Leiden, Belgium: Brill, 1975.

Irwin, John. *American Hieroglyphics: The Symbol of Egyptian Hieroglyphics in the American Renaissance*. New Haven, CT: Yale University Press, 1980.

Keith, Alexander. *Evidence of the Truth of the Christian Religion.* New York: Harper and Brothers, 1836.

Kennedy, J. Gerald. The Narrative of Arthur Gordon Pym *and the Abyss of Interpretation.* New York: Twayne, 1995.

Kennedy, J. Gerald, and Jerome McGann, eds. *Poe and the Remapping of Antebellum Print Culture.* Baton Rouge: LSU Press, 2012.

Kopley, Richard, ed. *Poe's Pym: Critical Explorations.* Durham, NC: Duke University Press, 1992).

Nelson, Dana D. *The Word in Black and White: Reading "Race" in American Literature, 1638–1867.* New York: Oxford University Press, 1994.

Obenzinger, Hilton. *American Palestine: Melville, Twain, and the Holy Land Mania*. Princeton, NJ: Princeton University Press, 1999.

Pratt, Mary Louise. *Imperial Eyes: Travel Writing and Transculturation.* New York: Routledge, 1992.

Ridgely, J. V., & Iola S. Haverstick. "Chartless Voyage: The Many Narratives of Arthur Gordon Pym." *Texas Studies in Literature and Language* 8, no. 1 (Spring 1966): 63–80.

Rogin, Michael. *Fathers and Children: Andrew Jackson and the Subjugation of the American Indian*. New York: Knopf, 1975.

Rowe, John Carlos. "Writing and Truth in Poe's *The Narrative of Arthur Gordon Pym*." *Glyph: Johns Hopkins Textual Studies* 2 (1977): 102–121.

Stephens, John Lloyd. *Incidents of Travel in Egypt, Arabia Petræa, and the Holy Land.* 1837. New York: Dover, 1996.

Williams, William Carlos. *In the American Grain*. New York: New Directions, 1925.

CHAPTER 22

PYM AND UNREADABILITY

CINDY WEINSTEIN

WHAT does it mean for a text to be "unreadable"? Are the letters fuzzy or is there not enough light to discern the words on the page? Is the paper waterlogged or are there passages written in a language unfamiliar to the reader? Does unreadability perhaps allude to an interpretative inscrutability or indecipherability? And if one does a reading of unreadability in a text, was it so unreadable after all? In considering the works of Edgar Allan Poe, the answer has to be "all of the above." Poe's oeuvre, I shall demonstrate, excels in establishing conditions and representations of unreadability, with *The Narrative of Arthur Gordon Pym* being the tour de force of Poe's unreadable prose. Literary critics have correctly taken the ubiquity of images and attestations of unreadability as Poe's self-conscious gloss on his own writings, which feature all kinds of reading material, including letters that are sometimes purloined and sometimes unread, hieroglyphs, anagrams, cryptographs, and specific letters in the alphabet. To be sure, there exists an intellectual allure for readers of Poe and Poe himself in the theme of unreadability. But against the hijinks of Poe's linguistic mastery—which leads the reader to enjoy, excavate, and attempt to make sense of the pile-up of unreadable words—lies a seemingly straightforward and readable narrative in *Pym* of white superiority. The Tsalalians represent a black, simple past that must give way to a white, progressive future. That said, one can also read in *Pym* a competing narrative that questions the claims of white superiority. The Tsalalians represent a black, complex past whose erasure will be accompanied by the decimation of that white future. In other words, according to the logic of Poe's unreadability, hermeneutic choices are not of the either/or variety, but rather the both/and.[1]

Although this essay will focus on *Pym*, Poe's works evince a persistent interest in writing texts whose theme is unreadability or that themselves border on the unreadable. Several examples from the short stories come to mind. "William Wilson," for instance, includes this famous passage where the narrator explains the confusing architecture of the house where he lived and went to school as a child: "There was really no end to its windings—to its incomprehensible subdivisions. It was difficult, at any given time, to say with certainty upon which of its two stories one happened to be" (M 2: 429). Like the building with its two stories, Poe tells two stories at once, with one version featuring two distinct characters and another having a madman imagining an adversary. The difficulty and the fun of the tale lie in the uncertainty about knowing which story one is reading. Thus, "William Wilson" is not a story either about one character or two, but rather a story both about one character and two.

The difficulties of reading also nag at the protagonist of "Berenice," who spends a great deal of time in the family library reading unreadable books, such as Tertullian's *De Carne Christi*, whose "paradoxical sentence" about Christ being both dead and resurrected "occupied my undivided time, for many weeks of laborious and fruitless investigation" (M 2: 213). Another example can be found toward the end of "The Fall of the House of Usher," where the narrator rummages through Roderick's library and chooses to read to him "the only book immediately at hand," an "antique volume" called "the 'Mad Trist' of Sir Launcelot Canning" (M 2: 413). Some volumes in Poe are actual books, but others, like this one by Canning are "books," whose title refers to a nonexistent text written by a nonexistent author. In a similar sleight of hand, the first sentence of "The Man of the Crowd" quotes "a certain German book" that "does not permit itself to be read" (M 2: 506) and has also eluded critics since the story's publication in 1840. Perhaps the most obvious reason it cannot be read is because the book simply does not exist. Such a superficial but overlooked explanation would certainly fit with Poe's penchant for sabotaging readers' expectations; in other words, when we read the name of a book, we assume, naively as Poe's stories remind us, that it's real and readable in that technical sense.

In the case of *Pym*, the inability to read can be quite literally a problem of darkness. Pym says, "I felt hopeless of being ever able to read the note of Augustus" (P 1: 77), and that is because in the hold of the ship, where he keeps company with the objects in stowage, he has little access to light. Poe devotes many paragraphs of his novel to Pym's search for light. We read in great detail about his attempts to find bits of taper wax or "a speck or two" (P 1: 77) of phosphorous. Finding an "aperture" (P 1: 76) so that he can read Augustus's note becomes a kind of mise en abyme as Pym's search for an aperture requires a prior search for the materials that would supply the light—the bits of wax or phosphorous or "fragments of my matches" (P 1: 77). In a comical moment that wonderfully captures the absurdity of much of the novel, Pym explains the mechanics of his eyeball: "by turning the exterior portions of the retina towards it [the white slip of paper] that is to say, by surveying it slightly askance, I found that it became in some measure perceptible" (P 1: 78). Thus, inasmuch as *Pym* is about reading (and/or the inability to do so), when Poe writes about reading, he doesn't simply start with the text to be read. That comes later. Paper, ink, pen, and light (and even the proper positioning of the retina) come first. Thus, despite the fact that we already have a text by Poe to read and presumably light to read it by, the plot of the text often revolves around the creation of another text within it, which then must find lighting inside of itself in order to be read.

Pym is not alone in calling attention to the want of light. At key points in "William Wilson," we learn "there hung no lamp; and now no light at all was admitted"; at another moment, suddenly were "extinguished, as if by magic, every candle in the room" (M 2: 438, 442). "The Man of the Crowd" similarly highlights the weird or alternatively poor lights: "the rays of the gas-lamps, feeble at first in their struggle with the dying day, had now at length gained ascendancy, and threw over every thing a fitful and garish lustre. All was dark yet splendid" (M 2: 510–511). It requires little effort and imagination to see how these images of restricted and impaired vision, insofar as they apply to a character in the text who is trying to read a text, or a face or a space (like the school in "William Wilson"), might just as reasonably apply to the reader of said text.

It makes sense, then, that in other instances, unreadability has to do with the reader, oftentimes her state of mind. She simply can't concentrate long enough to make out words because of exhaustion, fear, or inebriation. About a ship that Pym and his mates spot from a distance, Pym says, "we might have easily seen the name upon her stern . . . but the intense excitement of the moment blinded us to everything of that nature" (P 1: 126). Here, the crew's "intense excitement makes" reading impossible. Sometimes unreadability registers both the material absence of light and an overwhelming mental state that blocks incoming information: "The glimmer, although sufficiently bright, was but momentary. Still, had I not been too greatly excited, there would have been ample time enough for me to peruse the whole three sentences before me—for I saw there were three. In my anxiety, however, to read all at once, I succeeded only in reading the seven concluding words" (P 1: 80). In this last example, an interesting distinction between seeing and reading appears. Pym sees three sentences but reads only seven words. The sentences are unreadable for the simple reason that he doesn't read them, which he can, but in his heightened emotional state, which I shall discuss in more detail later, he can't.

Unreadability can also look like the following in *Pym*, where the image is so horrible that no matter how many times one has read the passage, it still repulses: "There sat a huge seagull, busily gorging itself with the horrible flesh, its bill and talons deep buried. . . . [It] drew out its crimsoned head, and, after eyeing us for a moment as if stupefied, arose lazily from the body upon which it had been feasting, and, flying directly above our deck, hovered there a while with a portion of clotted and liver-like substance in its beak" (P 1: 125). Pym misreads the situation and takes the sailor's bodily motions as an encouragement to come closer. A sickening correction follows and we learn with Pym that what seemed to be a seaman nodding his head is, in fact, a sailor's dead body being moved by a seagull that is eating its insides. Instead of human bodies that eat, bodies get eaten (first by the seagull and then by Pym, Augustus, and Peters when they eat Parker's body). On the topic of readerly revulsion, one might also point to this rendering of the rancid water aboard the Grampus, which Pym and the others drink despite "the jug being absolutely putrid and swarming with vermin" until they decide that it was "absolutely useless, being a thick gelatinous mass; nothing but frightful-looking worms mingled with slime" (P 1: 142). Water becomes a solid, and solids such as Augustus's body become "so far decayed that, as Peters attempted to lift it, an entire leg came off in his grasp" and "the mass of putrefaction slipped over the vessel's side" (P 1: 142). Not every reader can convert Poe's love of "mov[ing] his figures upon a ground of green or violet, where the phosphorescence of putrefaction, and the odour of the hurricane, reveal themselves" into images of "oriental palaces, mist covered, in the distance, which the sun floods with golden showers."[2] Contra Charles Baudelaire, the author of this paean to Poe, these passages' unreadability might take the form of a reader, less sympathetic to the aesthetics of putrefaction, closing her eyes. It's not that she can't read the passages—"his hair was full of fish scales"—she just doesn't want to.[3]

It is, however, safe to say that when literary critics talk about unreadability in Poe, they usually have something less literal in mind than actual darkness or readerly squeamishness or books that can't be read because they don't exist. One of the best (and funniest) examples of language becoming unreadable before our very eyes occurs in Chapter 18 in *Pym*, where Pym begins his January 18th log entry with the seemingly straightforward words, "This morning" (P 1: 166), and then offers this explanatory footnote: "The terms *morning* and *evening*, which I have made use of to avoid confusion in my narrative, as far as possible, must not, of course, be taken in the ordinary sense. For a long time past we had no night at all, the daylight being continual" (P 1: 166–167n). Of course, this explanation clarifies nothing and in fact creates confusion in the very act of claiming to avoid it. If the words "morning" and "evening" should not be taken to mean what they usually mean, what does it mean to use them and to read them? This passage supports J. Gerald Kennedy's claim that "even the simplest declarative sentence . . . refers not to a pure, immanent fact but to what the speaker or writer wishes his audience to construct as a fact," and thus "any textual distinction between truth and fiction must remain intractably problematic."[4] Pym's footnote continues and shatters even more aspects of the narrative that had previously seemed so uncomplicated: "I would also remark in this place, that I cannot, in the first portion of what is here written, pretend to strict accuracy in respect to dates, or latitudes and longitudes, having kept no regular journal until after the period of which this first portion treats. In many instances I have relied altogether upon memory" (P 1: 167). Since Chapter 7, however, the narrative has deployed the journal mode, which of course includes the use of dates. Does this footnote mean that those dates and those latitudinal and longitudinal designations didn't mean what they meant? Can something that was readable become retroactively unreadable? Leaving aside the question of what constitutes the "first portion" of the narrative, when Pym says "I cannot . . . pretend to strict accuracy," does that mean he was pretending before, from Chapter 7 to 18, and if he were pretending then, why should we believe that he is telling the truth now?

If this passage from *Pym* makes anything clear, it is that the interpretive move toward metafiction makes perfect sense because so many of Poe's stories not only foreground acts of reading and writing but demand that the reader consider the credibility of the reading being presented.[5] Is the narrator trustworthy? Does the interpretation being offered fit with elements of the plot? Is the reading a reasonable one or might it be so over-the-top as to be implausible by any measure? By posing these questions, time and again, Poe's stories throw down the hermeneutic gauntlet. And how can one resist taking up the challenge when a character, such as William Legrand of "The Gold-Bug," conducts a reading of an initially invisible image on parchment that comes into view "when subjected to the action of fire," only to discover an image of a skull in addition to an image of a goat that is really an image of a kid, which is "a kind of punning or hieroglyphical signature," playing on Captain Kidd (M 3: 832, 833)? Not finished making the invisible visible or the unreadable readable, Legrand once again applies heat to the parchment and uncovers "figures arranged in lines" that "form a cipher—that is to say, they convey a meaning" (M 3: 834, 835). And as any good literary critic would feel, Legrand finds himself, "sorely put out by the absence of all else—of the body to my imagined instrument—of the text for my context" (M 3: 833). We follow this close reading, which ultimately produces a cryptographic text for the context, astonished by its hermeneutical originality and associative imaginativeness and at the same time wonder, like the narrator, if Legrand's reading has any relation to reality. In other words, has he simply substituted one kind of unreadability—there is nothing to see—with another—what is now seen makes no sense? Is the reading itself purely an act of imagination, as much a work of fiction as the fiction in which it is embedded?

Yes, of course. Poe has written a work of fiction and Legrand doesn't exist except as a character within it, and Poe mischievously shoves the fictionality of the story in our faces. Thus, Legrand's reading continually calls attention to itself as an exercise in interpretation. That rather obvious point is accompanied by something more complex. An essential aspect of Poe's plot is Legrand's production of the material foundation of his reading—the coded message within the text itself—that is required for the reading to proceed. Legrand says to the narrator, "no doubt you will think me fanciful—but I had already established a kind of *connexion*. I had put together two links of a great chain" and elsewhere, in a "paradoxical sentence" reminiscent of the kind that Berenice's narrator chews on for long periods of time in his library, suggests that the skull that appears on the parchment "was not done by human agency. And nevertheless it was done" (M 3: 831). Upon solving the cryptograph, which includes the words "Bishop's hostel," Legrand instantly confronts another cryptograph: "of course, I dropped the obsolete word 'hostel' . . . [and] it entered into my head, quite suddenly that this 'Bishop's Hostel' might have some reference to an old family, of the name of Bessop," which then morphs into "*Bessop's Castle*," which then turns out not to be a castle at all, but rather a " 'castle' [that] consisted of an irregular assemblage of cliffs and rocks" (M 3: 841). He deems the word "hostel" irrelevant. Bishop becomes Bessop. And castle gets its own set of quotations within the larger quotation, thereby becoming " 'castle.' " Every word, every place name is subject to change because nothing was ever real to begin with. Indiscriminately tossing out words or changing words, as Legrand does, reveals their utter made-upness.

Reality becomes fiction or, more precisely, the pretense of reality (that the castle in "The Gold-Bug" is a real castle, that the word "hostel" somehow matters) gets stripped away, making visible the fictional apparatus of every aspect of the story. Unlike the application of heat that makes the skull on the parchment visible, the human agency of Legrand underwrites these linguistic metamorphoses. And yet, at the same time that Poe foregrounds the fictional status of "The Gold-Bug," and Legrand's artistic interventions in solving the riddle of the bug, the interpretation that forms the basis of the story also includes the verbal signatures, as it were, of nonfiction. Sullivan's Island, the location of the story, is a real place off the coast of South Carolina, and Captain Kidd actually existed. "Bi-chloride of Mercury" (M 3: 826), in addition to being a treatment for syphilis into the early twentieth century, was also used as a preservative of wood. Thus, when Legrand, Jupiter, and the narrator discover the "oblong chest of wood" whose "perfect preservation and wonderful hardness, had plainly been subjected to some mineralizing process" (M 3: 826), the narrator reasonably speculates that bichloride of mercury may have been part of the process. And, less abstrusely, it is true that "of all *words* in the language, 'the' is most usual" (M 3: 837). "The Gold-Bug" becomes unreadable in the sense that it affords the reader no stable cognitive foothold. Just when we come to terms with the idea that the story revels in its fictional status and makes us wonder how we ever thought a fiction might have anything to do with facts, Poe throws in a fact, which then makes us question how we ever thought fiction might be as veracious as fact.

In a slightly less complicated fashion, "The Man of the Crowd" sets up a similar dynamic between the protagonist, a reader of the crowd and then one individual in it, and the reader. The narrator offers an intensely detailed account of the man in the crowd. This characterization is based on "the brief minute of my original survey," in which "the ideas of vast mental power, of caution, of penuriousness, of avarice, of coolness, of malice, of blood-thirstiness, of triumph, of merriment, of excessive terror, of intense—of supreme despair" accompany confessions of "an aching sensation in the eye" and the light that "threw over every thing a fitful and garish lustre" (M 2: 511, 510, 511). He interprets the man in the crowd with a series of descriptors that contradict one another (caution and blood-thirstiness? Coolness and excessive terror?) despite the fact that he cannot see him and because once he starts interpreting something or someone, he cannot stop. What does this unreliability mean for the words we have just read? What do these words mean?

Indeed, the question of what things mean pervades *Pym*. And unsurprisingly, when meaning does get attached to a particular person, object, scenario, or word, that meaning often seems to be mysterious, slightly off, or dead wrong, with the exception of Tiger, Pym's dog (who appears out of nowhere). Tiger assists Pym in the retrieval of Augustus's note. Pym writes, "having got, after a long search, a small piece of the note, I put it to the dog's nose, and endeavored to make him understand that he must bring me the rest of it. . . . He seemed to enter at once into my meaning" (P 1: 79), shortly after which Tiger brings Pym all of the ripped-up shreds of the note which Pym can then piece together. But Tiger's ability to discern Pym's meaning relies on gestures rather than on language. When humans use words, meaning becomes less certain.[6]

At the moment when Pym finally gets enough light to see a portion of Augustus's note, Pym writes, "Had I been able to ascertain the entire contents of the note—the full meaning of the admonition which my friend had thus attempted to convey, that admonition, even although it should have revealed a story of disaster the most unspeakable, could not, I am firmly convinced, have imbued my mind with one tithe of the harrowing and yet indefinable horror with which I was inspired by the fragmentary warning thus received" (P 1: 80). Here, Pym conducts a close reading of a fragmentary text—seven words to be exact—generating meaning in the absence of the note's "full meaning." What strikes me as especially interesting is the fact that because Pym is unable to read "the whole three sentences before [him]" (P 1: 80), the warning begins in medias res, with the word "*blood*." Pym explains that the word *blood* is "trebly full of import" (P 1: 80), but the literal explanation of the word never occurs to him. Its import turns out to be the fact that "*blood*" is written in blood.

The fact that the note also contains a detailed history of its own mode of production—the pen, the paper, and the ink, which turns out to be Augustus's blood—is fascinating and consistent with Poe's perpetual return to the scene of writing. Not only does the note reference the events that comprise much of the text's action (the mutiny, Captain Barnard, Pym's access to food and water), but the note itself must also explain its own origins. Augustus's task "was now to procure the materials for so doing" (P 1: 53): pen, paper, and ink. He finds "an old toothpick" (P 1: 53), which he converts into a pen with relative ease. Paper proves accessible, too, but the backstory of the paper turns out to be far less straightforward: "Paper enough was obtained from the back of a letter—a duplicate of the forged letter from Mr. Ross. This had been the original draught; but the handwriting not being sufficiently well imitated, Augustus had written another, thrusting the first, by good fortune, into his coat-pocket, where it was now most opportunely discovered" (P 1: 54). And with this revelation of a second copy of a forged letter, we find ourselves at the origin of another scene of writing and reading. Augustus had written a fake letter, pretending to be a relative of Pym who invites Pym to visit him in New Bedford. Pym's grandfather, Mr. Peterson, will read the letter, permit Pym to visit Mr. Ross, and then Pym will escape with Augustus for his grand adventure on the Grampus. But having read his first forgery and finding it wanting in its simulation of authenticity (to give it "the better chance of being received as truth" [56] as the preface to *Pym* would have it), Augustus writes another one and pockets the first, which then becomes the paper upon which he writes the note to Pym. Kennedy nicely captures the enigmatic quality of the letter: "the puzzle bears the mark of intentionality: Poe incorporates a hint of his doubleness by locating a vital message on the reverse side of a duplicate of a forged letter."[7]

The context that informs the writing of the note is as crucial as the context that informs its reading. Given that the paper used for the note is the first and unsatisfactory attempt at a forged letter, it shouldn't come as a surprise that Pym's reading of this note proves problematic. In addition, we should also recall the "anxiety" with which he enters into Augustus's text, as well as the bad light: "The glimmer, although sufficiently bright was but momentary" (P 1: 80). In keeping with the suboptimal conditions of the reading experience, his more interpretive reading of the word "*blood*," his idea of what it means, is appropriately all over the place: "that word of all words—so rife at all times with mystery, and suffering, and terror—how trebly full of import did it now appear—how chillily and heavily (disjointed, as it thus was, from any foregoing words to qualify or render it distinct) did its vague syllables fall" (P 1: 80). The word *blood* both pops off the page and yet its "syllables" remain vague. How can the word be "rife" yet not "distinct" at the same time? Pym seems to be separating out the meaning of the word from its sonic effect. This gap or, to put the point another way, the presence of these two different registers—what words might mean and what they sound like—runs throughout *Pym* and helps illuminate in yet another way how Poe's readable words become unreadable. And there is still one more register, which has to do with what words look like. It strikes me as significant that when Pym explains how the note affected him and he calls attention to the word "*blood*," he retains not only the quotations marks but the italicization as well. The look of the word "*blood*" turns out to be just as "full of import" as its meaning and as its sound.[8]

Indeed, the chapter in which Pym and Peters examine the hieroglyphs on the island is about the "look" of language, except for the crucial fact that Pym refuses to see it as such. In contrast to Peters, who thinks that the hieroglyphs "bore some little resemblance to alphabetical characters" (P 1: 195), Pym ardently denies the resemblance. Instead Pym, "convinced of [Peters's] error," persisted in his own conviction that the "black skin warriors" (P 1: 195, 180) lack the ability to write (and read). Rather than share the intellectual fun and cognitive complexity of readability and unreadability, Pym obstinately insists that the hieroglyphs "have been the work of nature" (P 1: 195) because only white men such as himself have the intelligence to keep a journal or to forge a document or misread a letter. When Pym refuses to acknowledge the possibility, laid out by Peters, that "the hieroglyphical appearance was really the work of art, and intended as the representation of a human form" (P 1: 208), Pym demonstrates the racializing aspect of readability and unreadability.

Peters's willingness to recognize that Too-wit and his tribe have written the hieroglyphs is significant. I say this because Pym famously describes Peters as a "half-breed" (P 1: 55) in the preface to the novel only later to claim that Peters is, with Pym, one of "the only living white men upon the island" (P 1: 185). Depending upon the circumstances in which Pym finds himself, Peters's racial identity flips. In the account of the mutiny, Peters appears "ferocious-looking . . . with an indentation on the crown (like that on the head of most negroes), and entirely bald" (P 1: 87). However, when Pym wishes to console himself that he is not alone with the Tsalalians who frighten him, Pym emphasizes the half of Peters that is white. The moment Peters acknowledges that Too-wit and his tribe can write, Pym puts Peters back into the category of not white, with Pym eager to demonstrate his mastery and reassert the racial hierarchy. White people, not the Tsalalians and not Peters (that is, when Pym decides that Peters is no longer white), get to play with words and their meanings. And lest one miss this point about who gets to write and who doesn't, Pym "luckily" has with him, even after being nearly buried alive by the treacherous actions of Too-wit and his tribe, "a pocketbook and pencil" (P 1: 193).[9]

Pym's interactions with Too-wit, the head of the village, and the inhabitants of Tsalal reveal a marked and mistaken shift away from unreadability and texts and toward (seeming) understanding and sounds. In several scenes with the Tsalalians, the spoken word, combined with physical gestures, replaces the written word as the dominant form of communication, and perhaps because writing isn't involved (nor, by extension, is reading), Pym imagines a world absent of unreadability, a world where Pym makes gestures and is understood because he thinks that Tsalalians, because black, can neither read nor write; a world like the one he shares with Tiger, who "enter[s] at once into [his] meaning" (P 1: 79) and finds the missing scraps of Augustus's note, with the goal of getting Pym's approval. This is an interesting position for Pym to take—the transparency of the spoken word—considering that the crew of the Jane Guy and the members of Too-wit's tribe speak different languages (and are human beings, but again, Pym doesn't fully acknowledge that either). The significance of the sonic register in relation to the meaning of words takes center stage on at least two occasions, when the crew of the Jane Guy interacts with the Tsalalian natives. Having completed a meal with Too-wit, Pym and the others try to manoeuver the conversation to the "chief productions of the country, and whether any of them might be turned to profit" (P 1: 176). Pym writes, "at length he [Too-wit] seemed to have some idea of our meaning" (P 1: 176) and shortly thereafter the sailors depart in order to see the extent of the *biche-de-mer* (or sea cucumbers) and how much money they might get from plundering it. In another scene, Pym and the crew leave the ship, once again, "for the purpose of visiting the village" (P 1: 180). Accompanied by "a hundred of the black skin warriors," Pym observes that no one is armed "and upon questioning Too-wit in relation to this circumstance, he merely answered that *Mattee non we pa pa si*—meaning that there was no need of arms where all were brothers" (P 1: 180). Whereas Pym thinks that he understands the meaning of their words and that they understand the meaning of his, all anyone knows for sure is that they have exchanged words and heard the same sounds. And just as Pym can't imagine Too-wit being able to write, he can't envisage Too-wit meaning something and not meaning something at the same time.[10] Too-wit and the members of his tribe are readable and unreadable in the way everything and everyone else in the novel are. Being unable to grasp this fact, Pym is therefore unable to imagine that their blackness and their fear of all things white always signified the possibility of something treacherous in the offing.

It is true that *Pym*'s concluding Note validates Peters's notion that the islanders composed the hieroglyphs, but belatedly. The racist damage has been done, not just by Pym's unwillingness to concede that the islanders may be intelligent enough to write, but also by his repeated descriptions of the Tsalalians as "savages" (P 1: 168, 172, 174, 181) with lips that were "thick and clumsy" (P 1: 174). Moreover, the key to each and every one of those hieroglyphs ends up being race. Thus, several of the figures, when seen in combination with one another, "constitute an Ethiopian verbal root" meaning " 'To be shady' " (P 1: 207). Another figure represents "the Arabic verbal root . . . 'To be white' " (P 1: 208). In other words, even when the Tsalalian islanders are granted the right to read and write, as well as an origin story about their access to writing, they can only write race (or perhaps the only thing the unnamed author of the Note can read is race).

In this reading of *Pym*, Pym is the one doing the racist damage and not Poe. The distinction between the two makes possible an interpretation that sees the novel as a critique of racism. Poe is not Pym and therefore Pym's inability to grant the Tsalalians any degree of sophistication or complexity speaks to the character's benightedness and not the author's. In the same way that most readers would not, for example, conflate the narrators of Poe's "The Tell-Tale Heart" or "The Black Cat" with Poe, we should be wary of making that interpretative move in the case of *Pym*. Yet *Pym* itself does this and most famously in the preface where the distinctions between A. G. Pym and Mr. Poe are difficult, if not impossible, to discern let alone to maintain. When Pym refers to "several letters [that] were sent to Mr. P.'s address" (P 1: 56), Mr. P. might be Pym or might be Poe.

More complicated are moments in the preface when Pym "stipulate[es] only that my real name should be retained" (P 1: 56) when the *Southern Literary Messenger* publishes the first installments of *Pym*. Pym's "real name" is Pym, but in the next sentence Pym writes that "consequently . . . the name of Mr. Poe was affixed to the articles in the table of contents of the magazine" (P 1: 56). The consequence of Pym's "stipulat[ion]" should be that the *Southern Literary Messenger*'s table of contents for January and February 1837 lists A. G. Pym as the author. Instead, E. A. Poe is listed, which truly is the "real name." Thus, the "real name" of the author, according to the logic of *Pym*'s preface, is both Pym and Poe. This point matters in terms of making claims about the racial politics of *Pym*. If there is a difference between Poe and Pym, one can argue that Poe critiques the racial benightedness of Pym by foregrounding his inability to realize that the Tsalalians are actually human beings, embodying all of the complexities (and unreadability) such an acknowledgment would entail. However, if one can't figure out where Poe ends and Pym begins (and the preface tells us we can't), then Pym's racism may also be Poe's. To put it even more strongly, if the "real name" of Pym is Poe and vice-versa, one's racism *is* the other's. Pym's inability to recognize the Tsalalian's ability to read and write, his horror at blackness, his incapacity to keep track of Peters's racial identity register typical cultural positions, what Terence Whalen calls the "average racism," of so many antebellum Americans, including Poe.[11]

As *Pym*, and especially this preface, makes clear, the experience of a Poe text is like walking through a hall of mirrors, where images reflect and refract each other, where characters perpetually lie, where readers read themselves reading through characters who are reading, and where the text keeps referring back to previous moments in its composition until its origin becomes undiscoverable. In the same way that Poe returns to the scene of writing and breaks down the process by which the text comes into being and becomes read, I would like to return briefly to the publishing history of "The Man of the Crowd." The story first appeared simultaneously in the December 1840 issues of *Burton's* and *The Casket* before the magazines merged to become *Graham's*. The narrator, we recall, follows the man of the crowd as the distinction between the two men becomes increasingly difficult to maintain. Toward the end of the story, the narrator makes this comment about the man of the crowd: "His clothes, generally, were filthy and ragged; but as he came, now and then, within the strong glare of a lamp, I perceived that his linen, although dirty, was of beautiful texture; and my vision deceived me, or, through a rent in a closely-buttoned, and evidently second-handed roquelaire which enveloped him, I caught a glimpse either of a diamond, or of a dagger" (M 2: 269). The passage in the 1845 version of the story that was published by Putnam's in *Tales* reads as follows: "His clothes, generally, were filthy and ragged; but as he came, now and then, within the strong glare of a lamp, I perceived that his linen, although dirty, was of beautiful texture; and my vision deceived me, or, through a rent in a closely-buttoned and evidently second-handed *roquelaire* which enveloped him, I caught a glimpse both of a diamond and of a dagger" (M 2: 224). Yet again, the question of reading arises. Here we have a character who acknowledges that he has been "ill in health" (M 2: 267), trying to make sense of another character who can barely be made out because of "the strong glare of a lamp" or because his "vision deceived" him. In the first version, the narrator "caught a glimpse either of a diamond, or of a dagger" and in the second, he "caught a glimpse both of a diamond and a dagger." Either/or morphs into both/and. Which is it? The versions are obviously different, but oddly similar in that both register the unreadability of the situation. Because the narrator can't see what lies beneath the roquelaire (not italicized in one version and italicized in the other), whatever is hiding beneath it could be one thing, as in a diamond or a dagger, or two, as in a diamond and a dagger. And because the narrator can't see it, we can't know if what's hiding is one thing or two—and therefore, like William Wilson we get two versions, making it "difficult, at any given time, to say with certainty upon which of its two stories one happened to be." We read the words knowing that we are one word, perhaps two, away from unreadability.

Notes

I would like to thank Jerry Kennedy, Scott Peeples, and Caleb Doan for their valuable feedback. Many thanks also go to Ana González-Rivas Fernández at the Autonomous University in Madrid, and Margarita Rigal Aragón and José Manuel Correoso-Rodenas at the Universidad de Castilla-La Mancha, Albacete, for the opportunity to present my work.

1. On temporality and race in *Pym*, see my *Time, Tense, and American Literature: When Is Now?* (Cambridge: Cambridge University Press, 2015), especially chapter 2, "When Is Now? Poe's *Pym*," 39–63.
2. Charles Baudelaire, "Edgar Allan Poe: His Life and Works," in *The Works of Edgar Allan Poe*, trans. Henry Curwen (London: John Camden Hotten, 1873), 21.
3. Baudelaire, *The Works of Edgar Allan Poe*, 107.
4. Kennedy, *Poe, Death, and the Life of Writing* (New Haven, CT: Yale University Press, 1987), 150–151. G. R. Thompson's essay on *Pym* notes that it "is ironically framed by complexly self-referential commentary . . . that simultaneously calls into question the authority of the text, and earnestly suggests that it is redolent with meaning" ("The Arabesque Design of *Arthur Gordon Pym*," in *Poe's* Pym: *Critical Explorations*, ed. Richard Kopley [Durham, NC: Duke University Press, 1992], 201). Christopher Benfey has an essay called "Poe and the Unreadable: 'The Black Cat' and 'The Tell-Tale Heart,'" in *New Essays on Poe's Major Tales*, ed. Kenneth Silverman (Cambridge: Cambridge University Press, 1993), but whereas his interest lies in the "theme of the unreadable in human relations" (29), specifically "the ways in which human beings have access, or are denied access, to the minds of other people" (28), I wish to explore how language in Poe can both be read and yet be unreadable.
5. Thus, in an essay on plagiarism in Poe, Stephen Rachman notes, "Poe allows us to see him posing; he 'ex-poses' himself . . . allegorizing plagiarism in the very act of plagiarizing" ("'Es lässt sich nicht schreiben': Plagiarism and 'The Man of the Crowd,'" in *The American Face of Edgar Allan Poe*, ed. Shawn Rosenheim and Stephen Rachman [Baltimore: Johns Hopkins University Press, 1995], 66). John Irwin's reading of "The Murders in the Rue Morgue" turns on Poe's use of the word *clew*, the fact that the word *clou* in French means "nail," and the significance of the nail in solving the mystery of the murder. Irwin writes: "The game Dupin plays with the narrator is at once a part and a figure of the game the author plays with the reader, as Poe suggests by making the terminus of the clew (the problem's solution) a *nail*,

thereby testing the reader's linguistic skill and attention" ("A Clew to a Clue: Locked Rooms and Labyrinths in Poe and Borges," in *The American Face of Edgar Allan Poe*, 148).

6. Spelling seems to become changeable, as well. In Chapter 12, Poe lifts many passages from Benjamin Morrell's 1832 *Narrative of Four Voyages*, which includes an account of the Galapagos Islands tortoises. According to Burton Pollin, Poe "incorporates errors from the source and adds several of Poe's invention concerning the land turtle. The effect is a curious combination of precise and incredible details" (P 1: 278n12.17A). Pollin notes that Poe "consistently misspells the name which Morrell derives from galdpagos, the Spanish for land tortoise or 'terrapin'" (P 1: 278n12.17A), which means that when Poe writes, "the Spanish word Gallipago meaning a fresh-water terapin" (P 1: 137), he is wrong. Pollin has no explanation for why Poe might have indulged in this misspelling, nor do I, although, like as Pym says about Augustus's note, it seems "full of import"! (P 1: 80).
7. Kennedy, *Poe, Death, and the Life of Writing*, 154. This account of the paper on which Augustus writes the note contradicts Pym's version of what happens in the hold when he tries to read it. Augustus's note would have had his blood-inked message on one side and the first forged note on the other. However, Pym claims that the note he read has one blank side and the other side with Augustus's words. In an illuminating essay on *Pym*, Mitchell C. Lilly deploys the notion of "unnatural narrative" to argue that the paper Augustus writes upon and that Pym reads is three-dimensional and representative of Poe's disavowal of mimesis and realism. He urges us to "reconsider what the 'unreadability' of the letter means in terms of the 'unreadability' of the narrative . . . which makes Pym unreadable as a work of uncompromising mimetic realism and yet, at one and the same time, remarkably readable as an unnatural narrative that interweaves realist and antirealist manifestations of space, time, knowledge, and matter" (Lilly, "Edgar Allan Poe's *The* (Unnatural) *Narrative of Arthur Gordon Pym*" in *Poe Studies* 48 [2015]: 42). Suggestive as this argument might be, it is also the case Poe sets up Pym's view of the paper as deeply compromised: "I have before stated more than once that my intellect, for some period prior to this, had been in a condition nearly bordering on idiocy" (P 1: 78). Given his condition, the reliability of his claim that "had there been any writing upon it, I should not have experienced the least difficulty, I am sure in reading it" (P 1: 78) seems highly suspicious.
8. My reading of this episode in *Pym* resonates with John T. Irwin's claims about the image of the shadow in the novel, as well as the nesting habits of the albatross and the penguins on Desolation Island: "when one finds one absolutely certain meaning in a situation where the overdeterminedness of the text makes meaning essentially indeterminate, then the reader is likely not to recognize how much any given meaning in such a case is determined by an unperceived shadow which the reader's own self casts upon the text" (Irwin, "The Quincuncial Network in Poe's *Pym*," in *Poe's* Pym, 187). Also see Jared Gardner, *Master Plots: Race and the Founding of an American Literature, 1787–1845* (Baltimore: Johns Hopkins University Press, 1998), in which he argues, "Augustus's note proves that to write revolutionary stories is to write not about blood, but to write blood itself. Similarly, in the concluding lesson on Tsalal, the novel will argue, to write American stories is necessarily to write not about racial difference, but to write racial difference—the thing itself" (143).
9. Thank you to Dori Hale for calling my attention to the resonance between this moment in Poe and the following passage from Claude Levi-Strauss's *Tristes Tropiques* (New York: Penguin, 1992), 62: "Would I be able to relive those feverish moments when notebook in hand, I jotted down second by second the expressions which would perhaps enable me to fix those evanescent and ever-renewed forms?"

10. In this regard, Pym is not unlike Captain Delano of Herman Melville's "Benito Cereno." Like Delano, Pym's racism compels him to imagine the potential treachery of those around him and yet not quite credit them with the ability to figure out how to become master of the situation.
11. Critics tend to align themselves on one or the other side of the divide. Here is an admittedly small sampling. Critics who read *Pym* as evidence of Poe's racism include Whalen, *Edgar Allan Poe and the Masses* (Princeton, NJ: Princeton University Press, 1999); Gardner (especially "Poe's 'Incredible Adventures and Discoveries Still Farther South,'" in *Master Plots*, 125–159); and John Carlos Rowe (see, for instance, "Poe, Antebellum Slavery, and Modern Criticism," in *Poe's* Pym, 117–140). Critics who read *Pym* as deconstructing racism include Teresa A. Goddu, *Gothic America: Narrative, History, and Nation* (New York: Columbia University Press, 1997) and Dana D. Nelson, *The Word in Black and White: Reading "Race" in American Literature, 1638–1867* (Oxford: Oxford University Press, 1992).

Bibliography

Gardner, Jared. *Master Plots: Race and the Founding of an American Literature, 1787–1845*. Baltimore: Johns Hopkins University Press, 1998.

Goddu, Teresa A. *Gothic America: Narrative, History, and Nation*. New York: Columbia University Press, 1997.

Kennedy, J. Gerald. *Poe, Death, and the Life of Writing*. New Haven, CT: Yale University Press, 1987.

Lilly, Mitchell C. "Edgar Allan Poe's *The* (Unnatural) *Narrative of Arthur Gordon Pym*." *Poe Studies* 48 (2015): 34–57.

Nelson, Dana D. *The Word in Black and White: Reading "Race" in American Literature, 1638–1867*. Oxford: Oxford University Press, 1992.

Rowe, John Carlos. "Poe, Antebellum Slavery, and Modern Criticism." In *Poe's* Pym: *Critical Explorations*, edited by Richard Kopley, 117–140. Durham, NC: Duke University Press, 1992.

Sanborn, Geoffrey. "And *Per Se* and: Time and Tempo in 'The Masque of the Red Death,'" in *A Question of Time: From Colonial Encounter to Contemporary Fiction*, edited by Cindy Weinstein. Cambridge: Cambridge University Press, 2018.

Weinstein, Cindy. *Time, Tense, and American Literature: When Is Now?* Cambridge: Cambridge University Press, 2015.

Whalen, Terence. *Edgar Allan Poe and the Masses: The Political Economy of Literature in Antebellum America*. Princeton, NJ: Princeton University Press, 1999.

CHAPTER 23

POE'S NOVEL EXPLORATIONS

LAURAN COATS

WHEN Harper & Brothers published Poe's first, and only completed, novel in July 1838, the work's title page, with its lengthy explanatory subtitle, marked it as a travel narrative:

> *Comprising the Details of a Mutiny and Atrocious Butchery on Board the American Brig Grampus, on her way to the South Seas, in the Month of June, 1827 with an Account of the recapture of the vessel by the Survivers* [sic]*; Their Shipwreck and Subsequent Horrible Suffering from Famine; Their Deliverance by Means of the British Schooner Jane Guy; The Brief Cruise of this Latter Vessel in the Antarctic Ocean; Her Capture, and the Massacre of her Crew among a Group of Islands in the Eighty-Fourth Parallel of Southern Latitude; Together with the Incredible Adventures and Discoveries Still Farther South To Which That Distressing Calamity Gave Rise.*

The title connects *Pym* to a wide variety of travel and exploration literature that flooded the market in the early nineteenth century, from children's novels of sea adventures to newspaper articles about marine atrocities and disasters to reports on commercial, scientific, and governmental explorations. The Gothic hyperbole of the subtitle nonetheless signals the novel's trafficking in common features of travel narrative: calendrical specificity (narratives were almost uniformly organized chronologically, often by dated entries); a global scope that brought different nations and peoples into the same frame; the ever-present specter of disaster and failure, if not death; and the thrall of strangeness, of "discoveries" to be made.

Poe's fascination with and reworking of travel and exploration literature are evident throughout his authorial and editorial work. He wrote frequently about it in his own fiction, including the tales "MS Found in a Bottle" and "Hans Pfaall," as well as his only two long prose works, the unfinished "The Journal of Julius Rodman" and *Pym*. He addressed the topic even more consistently over the fourteen years of his career as a magazinist, including reviews of western narratives by Washington Irving and Charles Fenno Hoffman, two of John Lloyd Stephens's best-selling travel narratives, several reports and addresses by Jeremiah Reynolds, sea novels by James Fenimore Cooper and

Frederick Marryat, and more. He even directly and extensively plagiarized published travel narratives for use in his own accounts.

As this last point suggests, fundamental to Poe's engagement with travel and exploration literature is his well-documented practice of borrowing verbiage, scenes, and literary topoi from extant works. In this essay, I track Poe's recirculations, from the literary marketplace in travel works (and reviews thereof) to the particular texts and details that Poe plagiarizes. Tracking Poe's engagements with the genre of travel and exploration highlights his negotiations of antebellum publication economies as well as his response to common assumptions of travel literature, particularly of expanded knowledge and conquered lands. His own travel writings dislocate the imperial vision often associated with the genre, offering instead a novelty not of formal innovation or new empirical observation but of effect. Poe tellingly demarcates the eighty-fourth parallel in *Pym*'s subtitle, which at the time surpassed the furthest incursion of any explorer into the Antarctic.[1] Poe's Pym never actually travels beyond this boundary, remaining instead in the space between Poe's sources and his own remapping, the "hazy confines of a region where fiction reaches the edge of fact."[2] Never fully traversing the bounds of the known, Poe resituates the common tropes and scenes of travel and exploration literature that are the substance of his borrowings into unknown territory.

Travel in Print

When James Harper, of the well-established publishing firm Harper & Brothers, approached lawyer-turned-explorer John L. Stephens about writing a narrative on his recent treks abroad, Harper wrote to the reluctant Stephens that "Travels sell about the best of anything we get ahold of. They don't always go with a rush, like a novel by a celebrated author, but they sell longer, and in the end, pay better."[3] Harper and his brother John had begun business in 1817, and by the time the brothers (which by that time included all four of them) approached Stephens, they had some experience publishing travel narratives in a variety of styles. An 1859 list of Harper publications includes a section on "travel and adventure" that lists over one hundred titles. (This particular guide does not include fictional work in this category, such as Harper's 1835 edition of Daniel Defoe's *Robinson Crusoe*, which Poe praised and reviewed.)[4] The firm's offerings in the genre dated back to the 1820s and 1830s, when they published many travel works including several titles reviewed and plagiarized, as I will discuss, by Poe. Likewise, the pages of the era's burgeoning periodical press often featured reviews of such narratives, alongside essays, poems, and stories featuring travel, adventure, and wanderlust. Stephens's *Incidents of Travel in Egypt, Arabia Petraea and the Holy Land*, published by Harper in 1837, became a bestseller, marking the beginning of his career as author, which saw the publication of three more volumes on his travels in Greece, Turkey, Russia, and Poland (1838) and his most well-known works on Central America and the Yucatán (1841 and 1843). As Stephens and Harper found, the print marketplace of the day embraced travel as a popular and expansive category. In his work on American travel writing, Larzer Ziff confirms this trend: "During the first half of the nineteenth century only religious writing exceeded in quantity the number of travel books reviewed and the number of travel narratives published in American journals."[5]

Poe's years as a magazinist imbricated him in this "crowded field" of the print culture of travel.[6] In addition to reviewing many works in this genre, both fiction and nonfiction, Poe's creative travel works played on the popularity of this topic. His experimentations with travel literature explored the variety of print forms in which such tales circulated. One of Poe's early tales, "The Unparalleled Adventure of One Hans Pfaall" (published June 1835 in the *Southern Literary Messenger*), falls on the former end of the spectrum. Recounting the adventures of a balloon trip to the moon, the tale exploits the popularity of ballooning in the 1830s that made it a common topic in newspapers.[7] Emphasizing the impetus of print culture, this fantastical tale of a man's journey to the moon features a balloon "manufactured entirely of dirty newspapers" (P 1: 388). Often read as a failed hoax, the story establishes some of the themes Poe will continue to explore in his later travel writings.

In the tale, the successful voyager to the moon, the eponymous Hans Pfaall, sends back a manuscript of his amazing adventure in the hands of a moon-man emissary in a newspaper balloon, since Pfaall fears to return without a pardon for murders he committed before his travels. Poe's story presents the citizens of Rotterdam and their newspapers discussing at length the credibility of the account of the far-traveling citizen ("The letter, having been published, gave rise to a variety of gossip and opinion" [P 1: 427]), a tale all the more mysterious since the moon-man disappears after delivering the letter. Pfaall's rise and fall are thus intimately linked to the fate of papers, printed and manuscript. His poverty provokes a desperate flight, he explains, inspired by what today is called technological unemployment: bellows-mender Pfaall reports that he "grew as poor as a rat" since people no longer needed bellows: "If a fire wanted fanning, it could readily be fanned with a newspaper" (P 1: 391). Hounded by creditors, Pfaall wanders the streets and picks up a pamphlet—a burgeoning format of the antebellum era—on "speculative astronomy," which inspires his moon trip (P 1: 392). The tale defies belief, while capitalizing on public interest in the exotics of travel and underscoring the key role the print public sphere has in circulating and establishing the veracity of, or at least belief in, the tales shared through its networks. Travel and exploration narratives were, as Terence Whalen notes, "a marketable commodity which should bring power and wealth to its owner," a fact of the market that Poe clearly recognized with "Hans Pfaall."[8]

Ballooning tales enjoyed popularity during the emergence and growth of the penny press in the 1830s. Indeed, one of the era's most successful penny dailies catapulted to success through a moon tale published just months after Poe's "Hans Pfaall." The *New York Sun*, established in 1833, published a six-article series, a hoax by Richard Adams Locke titled "Great Astronomical Discoveries," supposedly authored by the British astronomer, John Herschel. The hoax's success exemplifies the penny press's association not only with inexpensive daily news for the working class but also with sensationalism, a precursor of the yellow journalism at the end of the century. This series exemplifies the utilitarian use of sensational "news" about travel to unexplored regions to drive readership while showcasing how the print mechanisms of the antebellum era manufactured (as Meredith McGill observes) "culture as iteration and not original."[9] Locke framed the fantastic tale as true, supposedly a reprint from the Edinburgh *Journal of Science*, of discoveries made by the Herschel when a giant telescope allowed him to investigate the lunar surface in detail. The story received a great deal of attention on both sides of the Atlantic as its status as truth or hoax was debated. Reprinted in periodicals in the United States and Europe, the story's appeal proved a boon to the *New York Sun*, helping spike the paper's circulation.[10] Locke's recounting of an astonishing landscape filled with strange flora and fauna, along with winged "beings in human shape,"[11] was not immediately or thoroughly discounted even as its veracity was questioned. When the *Evening Post* reprinted a portion of the series, the paper included a supplement commenting on the report's truthfulness: "We publish the article as we find it, and do not know that it is necessary that we should accompany it with any comments to shake the faith which credulous readers may be disposed to place in its authenticity. The story is certainly, as the old newspaper phrase goes, 'very important, if true.' And if not true, the reader will still be obliged to confess that it is very ingenious."[12] Even when the story was largely dismissed as a hoax, the *Sun* never printed a retraction.[13]

Poe commented on the hoax years later in an entry in his *Literati* series that ran in *Godey's Lady's Book*. In a piece on Locke, Poe assesses the "prodigious *success* of the hoax" in part in relation to print culture. Poe praises Locke's ability to affect the newspaper's prominence through his moon series: "From the epoch of the hoax 'The Sun' shone with unmitigated splendor. The start thus given the paper insured it a triumph. . . . Its success firmly established 'the penny system' throughout the country, and . . . consequently, we are indebted to the genius of Mr. Locke for one of the most important steps ever yet taken in the pathway of human progress" (H 15: 135). While the fulsomeness of Poe's praise borders on satire, his comment signals his esteem for those who can successfully navigate, even shape, the rapidly changing literary marketplace. Despite his sometimes vexed relationship to the penny press, revolutionizing the print public sphere outshines even lunar fantasies in Poe's estimation. While Poe's own experiments in travel literature never achieved the commercial success for which he praises Locke, his works from "Hans Pfaall" through *Pym* and "Rodman" traffic in the prominence of travel in the era's books, periodicals, and pamphlets.

Poe's *Pym*, of which two installments appeared in the *Southern Literary Messenger* in January and February 1837 before Harper & Brothers published the novel in 1838, capitalized on the popularity of the many fictional travel narratives cast as fact, such as Jane Porter's best-selling *Sir Edward Seaward's Narrative of His Shipwreck* (J. and J. Harper, 1831), which pretended to be Seaward's true account. An indifferent hoax, *Pym* exhibits Poe's diegetic insistence on the novel's authenticity—especially in the elaborate preface and concluding note, both of which assure the reader that the narrative is a first-person account penned by Pym rather than Poe. The novel reads like a voyage through different forms of travel and exploration literature, a fact that critics have commented upon when determining the work's composition history.[14] It opens as a boyish sailing adventure (when Pym and his friend have a disastrous adventure on the *Ariel*), mutates into a whaling voyage (when Pym stows away on the *Grampus*, a disorienting trip ending in murder and mutiny and the survival of only Pym and one crew member), then becomes a meandering exploring expedition (when the *Jane Guy* saves the survivors and sails into the Antarctic and South Seas for trade), before dissolving into a surreal Antarctic escape (when natives of Tsalal violently curtail the imperial ambitions of the *Jane Guy* as Pym flees southward by canoe toward an ambiguous white figure).

The novel also capitalized on the appetite for geographic exploration of the terra and mare incognita of the day, particularly the South Seas and Antarctic. While there is no record of when Poe chose to transform the *Southern Literary Messenger* installments of *Pym* into a novel, the events leading up to Harper's acquisition of the title suggest his responsiveness to the demands of the literary marketplace. Before *Pym*, Poe asked James Kirke Paulding to approach Harper and Brothers about his proposed book-length story collection, "Tales of the Folio Club." Harper rejected the proposal in mid-1836, explaining: "Readers in this country have a decided and strong preference for works (especially fiction) in which a single and connected story occupies the whole volume, or number of volumes, as the case may be" (PL: 212). Moreover, Paulding reported to Poe that Harper found Poe's tales "too refined" and suggested that Poe should "lower himself a little to the ordinary comprehension of the generality of his readers."[15] When *Pym*'s first installment was published in January 1837, then, Poe had already contemplated the possibility of a novel. He had also demonstrated an interest in exploration, as evidenced by his essays in the *Southern Literary Messenger*: a January 1836 review of Harper's reprinting of *Robinson Crusoe*; an August 1836 review of the US Senate's "Report of the Committee on Naval Affairs" about a possible South Seas expedition; and two January 1837 reviews (the same issue that featured the first installment of *Pym*) of Irving's *Astoria* (Carey, Lea & Blanchard, 1836) and Reynolds's *Address on the Subject of a Surveying and Exploring Expedition to the Pacific Ocean and South Seas* (Harper & Brothers, 1836). Poe's next proposal for a book-length narrative was *Pym*, a work of travel and exploration for a marketplace that had a voracious appetite for such literature.

Poe exploited the popularity of travel literature again when he published chapters from the unfinished "The Journal of Julius Rodman" in *Burton's Gentleman's Magazine* in 1840, while serving as editor. Six of the proposed twelve installments were published from January through June, with the series ending abruptly when William Burton fired Poe. "Rodman" partakes in contemporary interest in the American West by recounting the supposed first Anglo-European expedition to the Pacific Coast (predating, so Poe's story goes, Alexander Mackenzie as well as Lewis and Clark). Poe remarked on the pervasiveness of wilderness tales in a November 1843 review of James Fenimore Cooper's *Wyandotté* (Lea & Blanchard, 1843): the theme of "life in the Wilderness . . . is one of intrinsic and universal interest . . .; a theme, like that of life upon the ocean, so unfailingly omni-prevalent in its power of arresting and absorbing attention, that while success or popularity is . . . expected as a matter of course, a failure might be properly regarded as conclusive evidence of imbecility on the part of the author" (ER: 457). Poe's comments might be a tongue-in-cheek reference to his own work, given that Poe's attempt to address wilderness themes in "Rodman" has remained largely a critical failure. When first published, the periodical pieces of *Pym* and "Rodman" did not attract much attention beyond a few puffing pieces placed no doubt by Poe.[16] Perhaps Poe hoped that he could parlay interest in travel into something like the success of Locke's moon hoax that Poe had so praised. His travel works did provide Poe some remuneration, no small consideration given his ongoing difficulty sustaining an economically viable literary career. While failing to achieve commercial or critical success in his day (although *Pym* has become central to recent criticism), Poe uses his travel writings to participate in the genre's cultural prominence. As we will see, his participation does more than confirm the genre's status. His reworkings dislocate generic expectations, playing with the possibility of offering "novelty" in a genre firmly entrenched in what Meredith McGill has called a "culture of reprinting."

Plagiarizing Travel

Long associated with reports of the new—previously unexplored lands, marvelous sights, unheard of experiences—travel literature was seen as a genre that provided readers with news of a world abroad—news at times fantastical, strange or exciting, at times mundane or bureaucratic. The difficulty of offering this something "new" was two-fold for Poe when he took up the generic expectations of travel literature. Although he had some experience with ocean voyages and sailing, he had no experience of travel in the South Seas or the American West to call upon, and thus depended on others' reports to craft his own tales. Several reviewers commented upon Poe's relative ignorance of sailing practices broached in his two longer works. Of a passage about stowage in *Pym*, one review complains that it displays "evident ignorance in all nautical matters," while another disparaged that "No Yankee captain of a whaler ever packed his oil casks in such a careless manner."[17] In practice, the genre of travel writing tends toward conventionality even as it holds out promise of the new, as Stephen Greenblatt argues is evident in Columbus's discursive response to the "wonder" of the New World, wonder normalized through "reassuring signs of administrative order."[18] Within the genre, scenes that recur with comforting familiarity across putatively distinct works function as these "reassuring signs," even in a genre known for offering "digressive, miscellaneous collections of firsthand experiences, scientific knowledge, and stories of adventure."[19]

Poe was well aware that originality—whether of literary form or new territories—was not necessary in travel writing. He had charged Locke with plagiarizing "Hans Pfaall" for Locke's successful hoaxing moon tale.[20] While Poe eventually absolved Locke of the plagiarism charge, his accusation opens up one of the key features of Poe's travel writing: his own frequent and extensive borrowing.[21] Critics have long noted this practice.[22] Burton R. Pollin estimates that one-fifth of *Pym* is taken from others' writings, with an additional one-fourth to one-third showing "distinct traces of his readings."[23] The main sources that Poe used include Benjamin Morrell's best-selling *A Narrative of Four Voyages* (Harper & Brothers, 1832), Reynolds's *Address on the Subject of a Surveying and Exploring Expedition* (which, as mentioned earlier, Poe had reviewed) and *Voyage of the Potomac* (Harper & Brothers, 1835), and popular volumes of mariner chronicles available in any number of editions. Many other works influenced Poe's *Pym* indirectly or directly, including John L. Stephens's *Incidents of Travel in Egypt*, Alexander Keith's *Evidence of the Truth of the Christian Religion* (Harper & Brothers, 1832 reprint), letter exchanges between Poe and classical scholar and linguist Charles Anthon (focused on Hebrew translations, the exchange was central to Poe's review of Stephen's *Incidents of Travel in Egypt*), and Irving's *Astoria* (P 1: 17–28). The same held for Poe's "Rodman," which, explains Burton Pollin, "more nearly resembles a verbal collage than any other work by Poe" due to its extensive borrowing from the 1814 edition of Lewis and Clark's expedition edited by Nicholas Biddle, Irving's *Astoria* and *The Adventures of Captain Bonneville* (1837), and Alexander Mackenzie's *Voyages from Montreal* (1801) about his travel across North America to the Pacific (P 1: 512). These three sources make up one-fifth of "Rodman," according to Pollin (P 1: 17).

Poe's borrowings are in some ways unremarkable. As Ellen Gruber Garvey has argued, "writing with scissors" was a common nineteenth-century practice, and reprinting works whole cloth without authorization was similarly prevalent.[24] This was especially true for travel narratives that are characterized by frequent reprinting as well as borrowing, dating back at least to Hakluyt's compilation of *The Principal Navigations, Voyages, and Discoveries of the English Nation* (1589). It is also a genre that challenges traditional notions of originality and individual authorship. Two of Poe's main sources, Morrell and Stephens, exemplify the iterative nature of the nineteenth-century culture of reprinting, in particular travel literature. Morrell's narrative was ghostwritten (and fictionalized) by Samuel Woodworth—a magazine editor, playwright, and songwriter—from Morrell's notes,[25] just as Mackenzie's landmark *Voyages from Montreal* had been written by William Combe from Mackenzie's notes. Stephens was another Harper & Brothers author, recruited to contribute a volume to the firm's growing list of successful travel titles. When Stephens hesitated to write a book about travels already completed for which he had not taken sufficient notes, Harper replied: "That is no matter. . . . We have got plenty of books about these countries. You just pick out as many as you want, and I will send them home for you; you can dish up something."[26] In other words, Harper & Brothers recognized that the value of a "new" book of travels need not depend on original content, authorizing the practice of plagiarism so endemic to the genre. It is perhaps no surprise that Poe borrowed particularly and extensively from Harper volumes, including Morrell's *Narrative* and Reynolds's *Address*, in writing *Pym*. His use of these works suggests that they influenced Poe's composition of *Pym* after he signed a contract for the novel with Harper & Brothers in 1837.

What, then, is the effect of such borrowing on Poe's narratives, and more particularly on the novelty promised in travel literature? Many critics note that the inserted passages lend verisimilitude, such as when Poe interleaves long sections on "biche de mer" (better known as bêche-de-mer, sea slugs, or sea cucumbers) and rookeries from Morrell into

Pym, or on beavers and caves into "Rodman" (P 1: 179). The passages descriptive of local geology, flora, and fauna—prominent features of much travel literature—can be read as "digressive material" that "mimic[s]" exploration literature.[27] Poe praised the "potent magic of verisimilitude" in his review of Harper's edition of *Robinson Crusoe* (ER: 2020), yet his description of its "magic" suggests that the verisimilitude Poe offers prioritizes expectations of genre over mimetic accuracy. The rookeries scene comes in the section of the novel that most closely resembles a scientific and commercial expedition, when the *Jane Guy* is exploring the South Seas. By the logic of verisimilitude, to write about a trading voyage, Poe needed to provide information that such expeditions would typically circulate, primarily about the lands and resources explored as well as the peoples engaged, in published narratives such as Morrell's.

Pollin, whose magisterial volumes on Poe's writings meticulously track borrowings and influences, notes that the six paragraphs on rookeries come directly from Morrell's *Narrative* through "close paraphrase" and "summary" (P 1: 295). This section fits the exploration narrative profile by providing (reprinted) natural history about the nesting habits of "the penguin and albatross," including a detailed description of how they organize nests in their "colony." After fastidiously clearing a "square or other parallelogram" of just the right size and subdividing the area into "squares exactly equal in size," the animals create a precise pattern for their nests: "At each intersection of these paths the nest of an albatross is constructed, and a penguin's nest in the centre of each square—thus every penguin is surrounded by four albatrosses, and each albatross by a like number of penguins" (P 1: 152). The quincuncial design of the rookeries evokes a mystical symbolism that begs for further analysis, suggesting yet never explicating the design's meaning.[28]

A similar commentary on animal habits occurs in "Rodman" when Poe includes a long passage about beavers paraphrased, as Pollin specifies, from Irving's *Captain Bonneville* (P 1: 616–617), a narrative which in turn borrows heavily from Lewis and Clark's narrative of their 1804–1806 expedition. The narrator describes Rodman's and his companion Thornton's eight-hour observation of the animals building a dam. The description focuses on the collaborative effort of "fifty or sixty of the creatures" to fell an "older and larger tree" for new building materials, and their methods for doing so (P 1: 545). While the beavers playfully celebrate the successfully downed tree, the narrator questions whether there is "*design* on the animal's part" to have the tree fall towards the water, thus saving the beavers many hours of work. Could they have planned and orchestrated the direction of the fall? The narrator cites Captain Bonneville as "discredit[ing] the alleged sagacity of the animal in this respect" and then suggests otherwise: the beaver can indeed coordinate this large undertaking (P 1: 546). While these passages add a patina of reality to Poe's writings, they exploit another aspect of exploration narratives: the acts of interpretation that accompany presentations of fact. Reading the beavers' affect as indicator of intentionality and play, Poe situates the explorer as one who not only observes but also interprets. More than a dry analysis of a potential resource for trade, the anthropomorphized beavers showcase the explorer-as-reader who can adduce natural signs for their elusive meanings.

An intriguing footnote in "Rodman" emphasizes the interpretive act attendant to travel and exploration, as Poe casts the explorer as a sometimes flawed interpreter of signs human and natural. In a narrative largely consisting of material from other authors' works, in which even the structure of the trip largely follows the path of Lewis and Clark, the supposed editors break into the narration to comment on the veracity of Rodman's report.[29] A brief description of a cave—several sentences that give the cave's dimensions and situation—receives a footnote from the editors. It compares Rodman's measurements to those of Lewis and Clark, elaborating the supposed veracity of the former's measurements but in so doing introducing a more subjective appraisal. When Poe cribbed the cave scene from Biddle's Lewis and Clark, he made a slight change, decreasing the dimensions described by the "real" explorers. The footnote contends that Rodman is correct since his measurements accord with later findings, and lauds him for his ability not to exaggerate "*quantity*" even "with all his evident enthusiasm." While Rodman is trustworthy (unlike Lewis and Clark) when it comes to facts, he does exaggerate "all points which relate to *effects*" since his "peculiar temperament leads him into *excess*." Rodman finds the particular cave "dismal," a description the editor suggests is subjective: "His facts are never heightened; his impressions from these facts must have, to ordinary perceptions, a tone of exaggeration. Yet there is no falsity in this exaggeration, except in view of a general sentiment upon the thing seen and described. As regards his own mind, the apparent gaudiness of color is the absolute and only true tint" (P 1: 538, emphasis in original).[30] Poe's footnote makes clear that the difference most remarkable is not the measurements, since the narrative proposes that such figures are relatively easily settled over time. Rather, Rodman's response to the caves deserves note. Poe contrasts the seemingly immutable rock and stone with the idiosyncratic "impressions" they inspire to suggest that subjective response matters more than measurements. Amending facts to build effect, Poe explores the ways in which impressions of the landscape open the possibility that even mapped terrain can be known anew.

Elsewhere Poe similarly emphasizes the significance of effect in travel writing, of a novelty not necessarily measured by accuracy or originality. In his lengthy review of Stephens's *Incidents of Travel in Egypt* published in the October 1837 issue of the *New-York Review*, Poe suggests that the tone of the text may be even more significant than the expedition's results, finding fault with details of Stephens's narrative but admiring his voice. Poe spends much of his review assessing the author's assertion that he was the first to travel through Idumea, a claim Poe finds false based on Stephens's incorrect translation of a prophecy, which Poe explored in an exchange of letters with Anthon. Despite this flaw, Poe praises Stephens as "a traveler with whom we shall like to take other journeys. Equally free from the exaggerated sentimentality of Chateaubriand, or the sublimated, the too French enthusiasm of Lamartine on the one hand, and on the other from the degrading spirit of utilitarianism, which sees in mountains and waterfalls only quarries and manufacturing sites, Mr. Stephens writes like a man of good sense and sound feeling." That is, Poe values the work overall despite the inaccuracies he finds in it, including many small "errors" resulting from Stephens's writing from memory and rough notes, because the traveler writes "with a freedom, a frankness, and an utter absence of pretension" (H 10: 25). He has similar comments about Irving's *Astoria*, praising Irving's "masterly manner" despite "one or two slight discrepancies" that "are of little importance in themselves" (H 9: 242, 243). In the large market for travel literature, Poe suggests, not all works are equal—an estimation that can be based on tenor and style rather than on content.

In short, for Poe the tone of a work, one that captivates and even astounds the reader, outweighs its truth value. Poe's appreciation for the ability of travel narratives to offer a novelty of effect rather than of new information echoes in his review of Locke's moon hoax: "Not one person in ten discredited it," Poe wrote admiringly:

> and (strangest point of all!) the doubters were chiefly those who doubted without being able to say why—the ignorant, those uninformed in astronomy, people who would not believe because the thing was so novel, so entirely "out of the usual way." A grave professor of mathematics in a Virginian college told me seriously that he had no doubt of the truth of the whole affair! The great effect wrought upon the public mind is referable, first, to the novelty of the idea; secondly, to the fancy-exciting and reason-repressing character of the alleged discoveries; thirdly, to the consummate tact with which the deception was brought forth; fourthly, to the exquisite *vraisemblance* of the narration. (H 15: 134)

Poe's emphasis on the "great effect" that astonishes the reader with wondrous sights to be found abroad (far abroad, in this case) signals his interest in travel narratives, false accounts cast as true for readers "really eager . . . to be deceived" (H 15: 129). Rather than the truth of the tale, more significant to Poe is the crafting of the tale as true, the feeling rather than the fact of wondrous news.

Critics then and now tend to read *Pym* and "Rodman" in relation to the dichotomy he alludes to: the Scylla and Charybdis of excessive "sentimentality" and "utilitarianism," or what critics more prosaically refer to as a demarcation between fact and fiction.[31] Critics of *Pym*, for instance, have detailed the many inconsistences in the narrative, arguing that despite the passages that evoke verisimilitude, *Pym* and "Rodman" remain riddled with errors. Reading "such an error-laden text . . . is to be constantly reminded of its fictionality no matter how much nautical (and botanical and zoological) detail Poe includes to convince us that the story is 'real.'"[32] Indeed, Poe's casting of such details as secondary suggests that mimesis is less important than poiesis. J. Gerald Kennedy notes that Poe's borrowings work "to sustain the illusion of legitimacy and authority which facts produce in a culture that prizes rational, scientific discourse—such as travelogues of the kind emulated by *Pym*." In a novel in which "even the simplest declarative sentence . . . refers not to a pure, immanent fact but to what the speaker or writer wishes his audience to construe as a fact," however, Poe suspends a clear distinction between truth and fiction. This ambiguity, sustained from Poe's opening preface (which emphasizes the tale's supposed truthfulness as written by Pym, despite early episodes ascribed to Poe in the *Southern Literary Messenger*) through the concluding note (which continues to assert Pym's and the tale's veracity), ensures that "any textual distinction between truth and fiction must remain intractably problematic."[33] While *Pym* and "Rodman" reproduce details and features of the travel literature genre, in particular the natural historical details and the practice of textual pirating, Poe's repetitions draw attention to the fictionality of the genre. He uses this fictionality to introduce the "novelty" so often promised by the genre of travel and exploration literature, not by newness of form or territory or information, but by the effect wrought on the explorer.

Imperial Patterns

Poe's borrowings situate his travelers in well-known generic terrain, ensuring reader familiarity with many of the scenes and topics that *Pym* and "Rodman" address. After Pym has survived various disasters, mutinies, and near-death experiences aboard the *Ariel* and *Grampus*, he cruises on the *Jane Guy* on a trading expedition that slowly approaches the South Pole. Although shortages make the captain consider turning back, Pym convinces him to "push on" further south, and the crew soon finds land and "savages" who "it was quite evident . . . had never before seen any of the white race" (P 1: 166, 168, and 169). Pym and his companions clearly see the Tsalalians with an imperial eye: they accept local food and resources closely cataloged and taken as their due in exchange for trinkets (P 1: 174, 176, and 177); visit what they deem to be a "miserable" village, questioning "if it were worthy of the name" (P 1: 172 and 173); and provide a quasi-ethnographic description of the natives, both men and women (P 1: 174). Such engagements echo similar scenes that abound in travel and exploration narratives. Jared Gardner argues that "*Pym*, centrally concerned with questions of race, surprisingly begins with questions of genre," namely whether the novel is fact or fiction, a hoax or a comment on the inability to tell the difference, or a parody.[34] To critics of travel and exploration literature, the imbrication of race and genre is no surprise. Hester Blum explains: "Travel narratives, even fanciful ones, are perhaps the most enduring product of colonialist activity."[35] Critics have long cast the form as "essentially an instrument within colonial expansion" that appropriates authority, literal and figurative, over foreign territories and peoples, thus making textual control central to imperial ambition.[36] In short, a key feature of the travel literature that Poe recirculates in his own travel works is its imperial gaze.[37]

The Tsalal episode presents imperialism in vivid black and white, as critics have long observed. Pym's description of "jet black natives" who "recoil" at the "white race" of the *Jane Guy* crew, the carcass of a "singular looking land-animal" that is "perfectly white," a "black albatross," the mysterious rain of white ash, the milky water (P 1: 168, 167, 173):the bodies as well as landscape provide hypervisual reminders of a binary racial system subtending imperialist endeavors.[38] That is, Poe takes up more than natural history scenes as the set pieces of travel and exploration literature. He also adopts the racial set pieces, which raises the metacritical question of what happens to these racial discourses when Poe recirculates them. Does he promote or challenge the racialized foundations of the imperial vision his works borrow? McGill's foundational study of reprinting emphasizes its dislocative effects, which in her discussion of Poe focus on the reconfiguration of authorship through his challenges to "print-authority" as the "sole property of individuals" that in turn open up "more complex forms of authorial agency."[39] As we have seen, the verisimilitude and attendant truth claims of the genre become at best secondary to the process of interpretation and the circulation of the text itself in the print market. Poe's adoption of the genre's racial topoi suggests the possibility of dislocating the imperial structures of *Pym* and "Rodman."

Poe adopts the racialized imperial ambition evident in "real" voyages, such as the Lewis and Clark expedition and the United States Exploring Expedition. For the last, also known as the Wilkes Expedition, then-Secretary of the Navy James K. Paulding (author and slavery apologist who served as Poe's intermediary with Harper & Brothers in 1836) gave the mission lengthy directives, as had Jefferson to Lewis: "Although the primary object of the Expedition is the promotion of the great interests of commerce and navigation," he detailed, "yet you will take all occasions, not incompatible with the great purposes of your undertaking, to extend the bounds of science, and promote the acquisition of knowledge."[40] Poe was a major proponent of the US Exploring Expedition and wrote several pieces supporting it, including very positive reviews of works on the topic by Reynolds (who was an early advocate of John Symmes's hollow-earth theory, explorer in his own right, and ceaseless advocate for the US Expedition). Poe sustains Paulding's vision of knowledge and trade as easy companions. In his January 1837 review of Reynolds's *Address on the Subject of a Surveying and Exploring Expedition*, Poe anticipates that the voyage will be a triumphant expansion of the nation's "commercial empire" as will "contribute a large share to that aggregate of useful knowledge, which is the common property of all" (ER: 1231).[41]

Poe's travel works similarly make the commercial potential of exploring expeditions central, thus highlighting the racial structures of imperial ambition. Cast as the "main business" behind Rodman's journey (at least at first), trade drives the Tsalal episode in *Pym* as well (P 1: 564). The section on bêche-de-mer, which Lisa Gitelman identifies as a "virtual set piece in the literature of exploration,"[42] fits Paulding's directive to expand trade and knowledge. Soon after finding Tsalal, Captain Guy negotiates with the Tsalalians to assist in their gathering and curing of the valuable trade item. Poe then quotes a long passage from Morell's *Narrative* providing some natural history about the "Mollusca" and information about its trade value, particularly in China. (It is one of the few times when Poe marks his borrowing, this time distinguishing the passage as a long quotation from Morrell.) Within three days, the expedition has set up a full operation for collecting sea cucumbers, one relying on native labor and knowledge. Planning to return later for the goods, the ship's crew prepares to leave after one final visit to the village, a visit that the natives had "insisted so pertinaciously upon" (P 1: 179). It turns out to be a setup, with the natives killing all members of the crew except Pym and one other, a fellow survivor from the *Grampus*, Dirk Peters.

Even such violence fits with the imperial playbook. The episode of the bêche-de-mer in *Pym* is simultaneously a scene of natural history and commerce, as well as the violence that accompanies imperial ambition. Secretary of the Navy Paulding's instructions anticipate this violence, explaining that the expedition's commercial and cultural goals face an ever-present threat, that of the "savage." He elaborates: "Treachery is one of the characteristics of savages and barbarians; and very many of the fatal disasters which have befallen preceding navigators, have arisen from too great a reliance on savage professions of friendship, or overweening confidence in themselves."[43] Succinctly these instructions suggest the racial complexion of imperial ventures through the naturalization of "savagery" and violence, a global projection of Paulding's domestic pro-slavery racial politics that the scene in *Pym* reproduces.

Poe not only recirculates this racialized vision in his various depictions of not-quite-fully-human African Americans and Native Americans in *Pym*, "Rodman," and elsewhere, but he also seems to critique travel literature's racialized set pieces. For example, Pym's horror at the "treachery" of the "barbarous, subtle, and bloodthirsty wretches" he also depicts as childlike (P 1: 180 and 190) presents an unsettling contradiction. Poe's emphasis on Pym's blindness to the incongruity of Tsalalians being both too crafty and altogether ignorant implies a critique of the colonialist explorer. Such a reading aligns with the interpretations offered by critics Dana Nelson and Teresa Goddu, who cast Poe's work as an uneasy deconstruction of a binary racial system. Nelson draws attention to Pym's careful construction of a black/white racial system as a "*perceived* opposition" that remains "inherently unstable . . . because of the unreliability of human perceptions."[44] Goddu finds that "*Pym* reproduces racial fantasy even while pointing out that it is merely a representation," a novel that "desires 'perfect whiteness' yet reveals its impossibility."[45] Their deconstructive analyses position the novel's recirculations of racial tropes and figures as a challenge to the racial system. That is, in their readings, Poe does not confirm but critiques a racial fantasy by "expos[ing] the artifice of race," revealing it to be performative rather than intrinsic.[46]

Rodman, too, meets Native Americans with the same a priori distrust and disdain that Pym displays. The most violent example of this comes when Rodman encounters for the first time the "treacherous" Sioux (P 1: 536). As John Carlos Rowe notes, Rodman "claims to know little about Native Americans" and has never yet met a Sioux yet is certain in his estimation.[47] So certain, in fact, that Rodman decides preemptively to fire a canon at the gathered Sioux, which "answered all our purposes to the full" by killing six and wounding many more. Rodman suffers one night of worry about his "shed[ing]" of "human blood," but awakens calmed by a beautiful landscape and assured of the "urgent necessity of the deed" (P 1: 557–559).

Rodman's initial dismay can be read as a moment that showcases the falseness of his assumption about the Sioux. Poe's stark juxtaposition of bloodshed within an idyllic landscape, that is, seems to emphasize the brutality of the racial view Rodman has adopted.[48] By this reading, Poe shows the violence necessary to secure Rodman's travel, whether commercially oriented or otherwise. Rodman abandons, in name at least, the imperial ambition that at first motivated the expedition. He forsakes the expedition's initial purpose of exploration and trade in favor of the "pursuit of idle amusement . . ., that deep and most intense excitement with which I surveyed the wonders and majestic beauties of wilderness" (P 1: 564). Despite this profession of a purely aesthetic viewpoint uncompromised by commercial or scientific interests, Poe reveals the cost of securing Rodman's travels: the death of the Sioux.

Other racial set pieces likewise help secure Rodman's ability to move through Native American territory. While Poe borrows extensively from Biddle's Lewis and Clark edition, Poe's adaption of Clark's slave York, who accompanied the expedition, into the minstrel figure of Rodman's "Toby" is one of the most visible. Toby's minstrelsy fascinates and placates the "Indians" that the expedition encounters, as had York's. Toby's racialized physiognomy is described in detail: "swollen lips, large white protruding eyes, flat nose, long ears, double head, pot-belly, and bow legs." Toby entertains the "inquisitive savages" even more when he performs, "*in naturalibus*" a "jig dance" for his captivated audience (P 1: 569). Both Toby and his Native American audience become "racist clichés" under the bemused eye of Rodman, an explorer whose eye encompasses landscapes both human and scenic.[49] The excessive performativity of race seems to emphasize the non-naturalness of racial identity that Goddu and Nelson diagnose in Poe's writings.

Reading through the genre of travel and exploration from which Poe borrows many of these scenes, however, makes attributing such deconstructive impulses to Poe harder to sustain. Poe's "average racism" evident in these scenes is, as Whalen suggests, absolutely ordinary, if nonetheless disturbing to modern-day sensibilities for its ordinariness. So too are these scenes' inconsistencies, excesses, and contradictions, which appear with disturbing regularity throughout the literature of travel and exploration. The Toby scene, for instance, mirrors the excessive performance of race evident in Lewis and Clark's narrative. Instead of a jig, York performs his animality for a crowd of "Indians" who are "astonish[ed]" by this "object," namely "captain Clark's servant York": "He told them that he had once been a wild animal, and caught and tamed by his master, and to convince them, showed them feats of strength which added to his looks made him more terrible that we wished him to be."[50] As minstrel and as animal, both York and Toby perform blackness as something not fully human.

Pym's inability to see the contradictions in his estimation of the Tsalalians also has precursors, most notably in the official account of James Cook's death at the hand of Hawai'ian islanders. Like Pym and his companions, the report of the attack on Cook and his crew is cast as completely unexpected. James King (who served under Cook on the third and final voyage, and completed the official narrative) reports: "The quiet and inoffensive behavior of the natives having taken away every apprehension of danger, we did not hesitate to trust ourselves amongst them at all times and in all situations."[51] When Cook must return to Kealakekua (which he calls Karakakooa) Bay in Hawai'i to make ship repairs after having just left the area, he and his crew "were surprised to find [their] reception," no longer joyous and hospitable, but so "very different from what it had been on our first arrival."[52] They quickly resolve this suspicion, rationalizing that their lukewarm reception was because their particular friend and local leader had temporarily left the area. That is, Cook and company display the same trust that Pym and company show the natives, a trust unsettled by brief moments of latent suspicion that prove justified only in retrospect, after the attacks on the explorers. Despite any number of hints that they are not safe or welcome, King reports that it was only after "having been led, by subsequent events"—namely, Captain Cook's death—that the explorers could "imagine, that there was something . . . very suspicious in the behavior of the natives."[53] Only when armed conflict has commenced, with the first deaths caused by Cook and crew, does King present the islanders as acting "contrary to the expectations of every one" by attacking Cook and his companions on shore: Cook "was stabbed in the back, and fell with his face into the water. On seeing him fall, the islanders set up a great shout, and his body was immediately dragged on shore, and surrounded by the enemy, who snatching the dagger out of each other's hands, shewed a savage eagerness to have a share in his destruction."[54] In other words, the inconsistencies, contradictions, and excesses that critics have read as unsettling race in *Pym* and "Rodman" are less particular to Poe than endemic to the genre whose defining tropes and scenes he recirculates. Moreover, such narratives were not marginalized but widely circulated and intensely popular: Cook and King's narrative of this landmark imperial venture, for instance, went through no fewer than fourteen editions by 1800.

Poe's borrowing of these scenes, then, does not on its own dislocate racial structures. Indeed, Poe's travel writing presents images of their persistence. In both *Pym* and "Rodman," Poe describes messages that seem to confirm an ahistorical racial system, a system inscribed in the earth itself. Rodman enthuses over "remarkable cliffs" he encounters (the White Cliffs of the Missouri River), massive white sandstone "chequered with a variety of lines formed by the trickling of the rains . . . so that a fertile fancy might easily image them to be gigantic monuments reared by human art, and carved over with hieroglyphical devices" (P 1: 573).[55] The earth engraved in black and white mirrors the remarkable chasms in the final scenes of *Pym* (see P 1: 192–196). The novel's concluding note addresses the chasms' "fanciful resemblance to alphabetical characters" and "human form," resolving the figures into Arabic and Egyptian characters that translate into the phrases "to be shady," "to be white," and "the region of the south." Even with these "words graven in the earth," however, Poe recirculates tropes common to travel and exploration literature. Numerous accounts of travel and exploration from the sixteenth through the twenty-first centuries attest to the common practice of explorers and travelers writing not just on paper but on the landscape itself, emblazoning rocks and trees. In addition, as John Irwin identifies, the cliffs are "part of a tradition of descriptions of natural writing" in which authors attend to the messages that geological formations seem to contain.[56] Here the earth itself bears messages, ones that are either nonhuman or whose human authors seem to have a quasi-biblical authority, as suggested in the *Pym*'s final sentence: "*I have graven it within the hills*" (P 1: 208). The earth messages in Poe's narratives are racially coded yet enigmatic, suggesting enduring racial differences that can be neither read nor reconciled. In other words, Poe's trafficking in the racial set pieces of travel and exploration documents their long history, one that he does not necessarily unsettle in the past or the present of either "Rodman" or *Pym*.

What Poe does unsettle is their futures. As Pym's final note exclaims, what has been graven affords "a wide field for speculation and exciting conjecture" (P 1: 208), a field of imperial and racial speculation. Poe passively produces the uncertain and open-ended racial future of "Rodman" only because he never completed the narrative. But he actively projects this uncertainty in *Pym*. While at first Poe presents an idealized imperial landscape tokened in the bêche-de-mer scene where natives welcome foreigners and willingly cede the natural resources of their island, the tale quickly dissolves into a symbolically overdetermined landscape whose strange beasts, mysterious chasms, and violent encounters prove more surreal than real. The novel's ending remains ambiguous, describing an expedition reduced to three survivors—Pym, Peters, and the Tsalalian Nu-Nu—adrift in a strange sea of too-warm Antarctic waters with falling "white ashy material" enfolded by a "sullen darkness" and bounded to the South by a "limitless cataract" of "vapour" and a gigantic, mysterious white figure (P 1: 205). This landscape opens a space of racial uncertainty, a lacuna at the "hazy confines of a region where fiction reaches the edge of fact" that capitalizes on what Hester Blum calls the region's "speculative economies."[57] In this scene, part of the speculation is that the region may not necessarily sustain the imperial racial structures Poe has reproduced throughout his texts. The contrast that saturates the novel's ending scenes, for instance, with everything in the landscape described as white or black, presents an excess that gives the lie to its structuring racial fantasy. That Pym is seemingly oblivious to it and exhibits his failure to recognize pattern, especially in the Tsalalians' color-coded fear of all things white, only heightens the effect. McGill argues that this excess has a deconstructive effect, finding that "Poe pursues [the] disorderliness and extravagance" associated with the genre of travel and exploration "to the point where they raise questions about the legitimacy of his narratives and their formats."[58] As the excessive contrast heightens until Nu-Nu perishes in the whitening landscape and Pym and Peters disappear into the embrace of the "figure . . . the perfect whiteness of snow," the novel seems likewise to build to the point where its excesses could implode the black-and-white patterns that govern Tsalal (P 1: 206). Yet the novel also cuts off just at this point. The literal haze with which Pym's story ends never lifts, as *Pym*'s final note defers indefinitely the question of what exists at the Poles.

Without clarifying how Pym's person or his tale could have returned after disappearing into the mysterious figure, the novel's concluding note worries: "It is feared that the few remaining chapters which were to have completed [Pym's] narrative, and which were retained by him, while the above were in type, for the purpose of revision, have been irrevocably lost through the accident by which he perished himself." The seeming certainty is immediately unsettled by the ensuing sentence: "This, however, may prove not to be the case." Perhaps, the note suggests, the missing chapters will be recovered. Or perhaps the invaluable information about the Pole that the missing chapters promise will be provided "by means of the governmental expedition [the US Exploring Expedition] now preparing for the Southern Ocean" (P 1: 207). It is this deferral, this refusal to complete the imperial map, which holds open the possibility of dislocating the imperial structures of the travel narratives that Poe recirculates.

In so doing, Poe refuses to fulfill the imperial ambitions that have otherwise guided the narratives. "Rodman" and *Pym* hold out the promise of explorations that will have immeasurable returns, consistent with Paulding's vision for the Wilkes Expedition and Poe's avid endorsement thereof. Yet significantly, neither text fulfills the promise of empire expanded, of new information gained, of new territories conquered. Terence Whalen has noted the nonproductivity of *Pym* in particular, arguing that while there is "complicity between a literary form such as the exploration narrative and the development of a more or less uniform capitalist economy," Poe remains but an "indifferent imperialist" since his narrative repackages known (mis)information.[59] As he had in his earlier story, "MS. Found in a Bottle" (1833), Poe consistently promises information in *Pym* about those places "further south" indicated in the long subtitle, but he never fulfills this promise. The narrator of "MS" tells of adventures at sea, reporting that "we were, however, well aware of having made farther to the southward than any previous navigators" (M 2: 139).[60] While the story implicitly promises discoveries about this relatively unknown region, they never fully materialize.

Likewise, the final clause of *Pym*'s subtitle, which foretells "*Incredible Adventures and Discoveries Still Farther South to Which That Distressing Calamity Gave Rise*," may deliver on the adventures but fails to return information of any discoveries of note. Such absences inspire some of the more critical reviews of the novel, then and now. David Reynolds casts *Pym* as "an attempted," and ultimately failed, "fusion of two modes—Dark Adventure fiction, featuring savagery and nightmare imagery, and the scientific social text, featuring mimetic reportage of intriguing facts." Like Whalen, Reynolds sees the registers of "subversive imagination and scientific reason" as oppositional and incompatible in Poe's writings.[61] Over a century earlier, William Burton baldly complained in his review of *Pym* that " 'a more impudent attempt at humbugging the public has never been exercised.' "[62] These comments fail to register the ways in which "subversive imagination and scientific reason" so often align in imperialist texts. More to the point, they highlight how separating out these strands that Poe combines establishes criteria counter to the novel's effects.

For if the goal is to fulfill the promise of an imperial map, *Pym* is a failure. In both the story and the novel, the mystery is that any information at all returns: it is not clear how the "MS" gets to the reading public, since the tale's last scene depicts the narrator's ship amid a whirlpool. Likewise, the novel ends with Pym rushing into a cataract toward a vast, white "shrouded human figure" (P 1: 206). How Pym and his story get to the print marketplace is unclear, one that the novel's concluding explanatory note alludes to but does not resolve. Poe's narratives seem more interested in the process of producing information, both as an object of print culture and an interpretation of natural and human events. Rather than complete the map, Poe charts the imperial limit at the 84th parallel. The known patterns, Poe suggests, may not continue. The haze at this threshold unsettles the scenes he has described and plagiarized—a retrospective questioning much like that which Pym and Cook experience—by heralding the possibility of an exploration that uncovers something entirely unknown or perhaps even unknowable. In this space, Poe inverts the common trope of travel and exploration as mapping to instead transform already-known land into terra incognita, territory providing endless opportunity for Gothic exploration.

Notes

1. James Cook and crew had traveled to about 71° in 1774. James Weddell, a sealer and explorer, reached about 74° in 1823. This was the furthest south any explorer reached at the time of *Pym*'s publication. Around that time, Britain (led by James Ross), France (led by Jules-Sébastien-Csar Dumont d'Urville), and the United States (the Wilkes-led US Exploring Expedition) sent expeditions to the region. Ross reached about 77° in 1840. As Johan Wijkmark notes, Poe was not unaware of the achievements of these explorers, in particular Cook's claim that no one would ever travel further than he had. Poe "transforms Cook's claim that the southern continent will never be explored into an exciting promise of further discovery." Johan Wijkmark, "Poe's Pym and the Discourse of Antarctic Exploration," *The Edgar Allan Poe Review* 10, no. 3 (2009): 85, https://doi.org/10.2307/41506372.
2. Lisa Gitelman, "Arthur Gordon Pym and the Novel Narrative of Edgar Allan Poe," *Nineteenth-Century Literature* 47, no. 3 (1992): 352, https://doi.org/10.2307/2933711.
3. Quoted in Larzer Ziff, *Return Passages: Great American Travel Writing, 1780–1910* (New Haven, CT: Yale University Press, 2000), 64.
4. *Harper & Brothers' List of Publications* (New York: Harper & Brothers, 1859).
5. Ziff, *Return Passages*, 59.
6. Ziff, *Return Passages*, 59.
7. Carlo Martinez, "E. A. Poe's 'Hans Pfaall,' the Penny Press, and the Autonomy of the Literary Field," *The Edgar Allan Poe Review* 12, no. 1 (2011): 9, https://doi.org/10.2307/41506430. See also P 1: 367.
8. Terence Whalen, *Edgar Allan Poe and the Masses* (Princeton, NJ: Princeton University Press, 1999), 152.
9. Meredith L McGill, *American Literature and the Culture of Reprinting, 1834–1853* (Philadelphia: University of Pennsylvania Press, 2007), 4.
10. The increased circulation ensured that it would not fold, like so many of the short-lived periodicals of the day. The Edinburgh *Journal of Science*, for instance, had ceased publication several months before the *Sun*'s moon series.
11. William N. Griggs, *The Celebrated "Moon Story," Its Origin and Incidents* (New York: Bunnell & Price, 1852), 95. This passage appeared in the fourth installment, published August 28, 1835.
12. "Moon Discoveries Supplement," *Evening Post* (New York), August 28, 1835. Similar pronouncements were published in other papers that reprinted the tale in whole or part, including the *Christian Examiner*'s statement accompanying its reprinting that "Doubts are entertained respecting its truth" ("The Telescope," *Christian Intelligencer*, August 29, 1835). See also Seamus Dunphy, "'Very Important, If True': Lunar Quadrupeds, Biped Beavers, and Man-Bats," *The Readex Blog: Exploring American and world history, literature, print culture and journalism, Readex*, July 17, 2017, http://www.readex.com/blog/'very-important-if-true'-lunar-quadrupeds-biped-beavers-and-man-bats.
13. Poe authored a second balloon hoax tale about a transatlantic balloon flight, published like Locke's in the New York *Sun*, on April 13, 1844. It never succeeded as a hoax; the paper quickly identified the report as false in a retraction printed two days later (M 3: 1063–1081).

14. See, for example, Joseph Ridgely, "The Growth of the Text" (P 1: 29–36) and J. V. Ridgely and Iola S. Haverstick, "Chartless Voyage: The Many Narratives of Arthur Gordon Pym," *Texas Studies in Literature and Language* 8, no. 1 (1966): 63–80, https://doi.org/10.2307/40753886.
15. Quoted in Alexander Hammond, "Consumption, Exchange, and the Literary Marketplace: From the Folio Club Tales to *Pym*," in *Poe's Pym: Critical Explorations*, ed. Richard Kopley (Durham, NC: Duke University Press Books, 1992), 154.
16. Pollin notes that Poe puffed "Rodman" twice in *Alexander's Weekly Magazine*, on January 29 and April 1, 1840, and that the work received "significantly few remarks" in other journals (P 1: 509–510).
17. Quoted in Cindy Weinstein, "When Is Now?: Poe's Aesthetics of Temporality," in *American Literature's Aesthetic Dimensions*, ed. Christopher Looby and Cindy Weinstein (New York: Columbia University Press, 2012), 200.
18. Stephen Greenblatt, *Marvelous Possessions: The Wonder of the New World* (Chicago: University of Chicago Press, 1991), 54.
19. McGill, *American Literature and the Culture of Reprinting*, 168.
20. John J. Teunissen and Evelyn J. Hinz, "Poe's Journal of Julius Rodman as Parody," *Nineteenth-Century Fiction* 27, no. 3 (1972): 318, https://doi.org/10.2307/2932893. See also PL: 166.
21. Poe's *Literati* entry on Locke asserts that Poe had come to believe that Locke did not plagiarize (H 15: 129).
22. There is extensive source criticism on "Rodman" and *Pym*. Peggy Pearl Crawford published on Poe's use of Lewis and Clark in 1932, and critics have continued to investigate and comment on his borrowings since that time. See for example: Crawford, "Lewis and Clark's 'Expedition' as a Source for Poe's 'Journal of Julius Rodman,'" *Studies in English*, no. 12 (1932): 158–170, https://doi.org/10.2307/20779433; Wayne Kime, "Poe's Use of Mackenzie's 'Voyages' in 'The Journal of Julius Rodman,'" *Western American Literature* 3, no. 1 (1968): 61–67; Burton R. Pollin, ed., *The Collected Writings of Edgar Allan Poe, vol. 1, The Imaginary Voyages* (Boston: Twayne, 1981); Burton R. Pollin, "Poe's Life Reflected through the Sources of *Pym*," in *Poe's Pym*, ed. Kopley; Whalen, *Edgar Allan Poe and the Masses*.
23. Pollin, "Poe's Life Reflected through the Sources of *Pym*," 95.
24. Ellen Gruber Garvey, *Writing with Scissors: American Scrapbooks from the Civil War to the Harlem Renaissance* (New York: Oxford University Press, 2011). On reprinting, see especially McGill, *American Literature and the Culture of Reprinting*.
25. Pollin, "Poe's Life Reflected through the Sources of *Pym*," 100; Whalen, *Edgar Allan Poe and the Masses*, 163.
26. Quoted in Whalen, *Edgar Allan Poe and the Masses*, 163. See also P 1: 9.
27. Gitelman, "Arthur Gordon Pym and the Novel Narrative of Edgar Allan Poe," 354. Many other critics comment on Poe's "verisimilitude" including Ridgely and Haverstick, "Chartless Voyage," 71; Kime, "Poe's Use of Mackenzie's 'Voyages' in 'The Journal of Julius Rodman,'" 65.
28. On the quincuncial pattern, see both John T. Irwin, "The Quincuncial Network in Poe's *Pym*" and G. R. Thompson, "The Arabesque Design of *Arthur Gordon Pym*," in *Poe's Pym*, ed. Kopley.
29. The narrative conceit of the work's belated appearance is that Rodman kept notes of his journey and eventually drafted a manuscript at the behest of famed botanist André

Michaux, but never published it. The manuscript is found years later after Rodman's death by his grandson, who has it published in installments in *Burton's*, whose editors at the time were Poe and Burton.

30. The effect on Rodman resonates with the "single effect" that Poe praised as a hallmark of the successful "brief tale" (H 13: 153), the author's ability to craft a story that elicits a strong and pointed response.
31. Reviewers at the time tended to place *Pym* in the realm of fiction and romance rather than fact or travel proper. See Whalen, *Edgar Allan Poe and the Masses*, 69. In contrast, "Rodman," while not widely reviewed, did make a brief but significant impression of factuality. Its verisimilitude explains, at least in part, how a paragraph from "Rodman" ended up in an 1840 Senate report on American exploration in the Pacific Northwest by Richard Greenhow. Future editions of the report excised the paragraph. See Dallas Hulsey, "Plagiarizing the Plagiarists: Poe's Critique of Exploration Narratives," *The Edgar Allan Poe Review* 3, no. 2 (2002): 34–35, https://doi.org/10.2307/41506138; J. Gerald Kennedy, *Strange Nation: Literary Nationalism and Cultural Conflict in the Age of Poe* (Oxford University Press, 2016), 359.
32. Scott Peeples, *Edgar Allan Poe Revisited* (New York: Twayne, 1998), 61.
33. J. Gerald Kennedy, *Poe, Death, and the Life of Writing* (New Haven, CT: Yale University Press, 1987), 150 and 151.
34. Jared Gardner, *Master Plots: Race and the Founding of an American Literature, 1787–1845* (Baltimore, MD: Johns Hopkins University Press, 2000), 139–140.
35. Hester Blum, "John Cleves Symmes and the Planetary Reach of Polar Exploration," *American Literature* 84, no. 2 (June 2012): 265.
36. Sara Mills, *Discourses of Difference: An Analysis of Women's Travel Writing and Colonialism* (Washington, DC: Routledge, 1991), 2.
37. Mary Louise Pratt first theorized the imperial gaze in her foundational work: *Imperial Eyes: Travel Writing and Transculturation*, 2nd ed. (New York: Routledge, 2008).
38. Toni Morrison's *Playing in the Dark* has played a pivotal role in critical attention to issues of race in Poe's writings. Toni Morrison, *Playing in the Dark: Whiteness and the Literary Imagination* (Cambridge, MA: Harvard University Press, 1992). See also J. Gerald Kennedy and Liliane Weissberg, eds., *Romancing the Shadow: Poe and Race* (New York: Oxford University Press, 2001); Joan Dayan, "Romance and Race," in *The Columbia History of the American Novel*, ed. Emory Elliott (New York: Columbia University Press, 1991).
39. McGill, *American Literature and the Culture of Reprinting*, 147 and 149.
40. Charles Wilkes, *Narrative of the United States Exploring Expedition during the Years 1838, 1839, 1840, 1841, 1842*, 5 vols. (Philadelphia: Lea & Blanchard, 1845), 1:xxix, https://doi.org/10.5962/bhl.title.69333.
41. Poe also reviewed Reynolds's *A Brief Account of the Discoveries and Results of the United States' Exploring Expedition* (Hamlen, 1843) in the September 1843 edition of *Graham's Magazine*.
42. Gitelman, "Arthur Gordon Pym and the Novel Narrative of Edgar Allan Poe," 354.
43. Wilkes, *Narrative of the US Exploring Expedition*, 1:xxviii.
44. Dana D. Nelson, *The Word in Black and White: Reading "Race" in American Literature, 1638–1867* (New York: Oxford University Press, 1991), 103. Emphasis added.
45. Teresa A. Goddu, *Gothic America: Narrative, History, and Nation* (New York: Columbia University Press, 1997), 86 and 92.
46. Goddu, *Gothic America*, 86.

47. John Carlos Rowe, *Literary Culture and U.S. Imperialism: From the Revolution to World War II* (New York: Oxford University Press, 2000), 63.
48. See, too, Poe's brief 1846 "Marginalia" piece in *Graham's Magazine*, which comments that Americans "have at all points unmercifully despoiled, assassinated and dishonored" the "Aborigines" (P 2: 310).
49. Rowe, *Literary Culture and U.S. Imperialism*, 63.
50. Nicholas Biddle, ed., *History of the Expedition under the Command of Captains Lewis and Clark*, 2 vols. (Philadelphia: Bradford and Inskeep, 1814), 1:101–102.
51. James Cook and James King, *A Voyage to the Pacific Ocean: Undertaken by Command of His Majesty, for Making Discoveries in the Northern Hemisphere*, 3 vols. (London: Printed by W. and A. Strahan for G. Nicol and T. Cadell, 1784), 3:20.
52. Cook and King, *A Voyage*, 3:36.
53. Cook and King, *A Voyage*, 3:36–37.
54. Cook and King, *A Voyage*, 3:45 and 46.
55. As Pollin notes, Poe's description of the cliffs comes from Lewis and Clark (P 1: 644–645). Poe added the phrases emphasizing the effect on Rodman.
56. John T. Irwin, *American Hieroglyphics: The Symbol of the Egyptian Hieroglyphics in the American Renaissance* (1980; reprint, Baltimore: Johns Hopkins University Press, 2016), 72.
57. Blum, "John Cleves Symmes and the Planetary Reach of Polar Exploration," 246.
58. McGill, *American Literature and the Culture of Reprinting*, 168.
59. Whalen, *Edgar Allan Poe and the Masses*, 18 and 188.
60. The story has other parallels to *Pym* not explored here: the adventures are replete with disaster and death, and both end mysteriously, with the story's ship caught in a vast whirlpool paralleling Pym's disappearance. As with *Pym*, how the information gets from narrator to a reading audience is a mystery. Perhaps Poe hoped that the story's popular, sensational travel themes would help his case when he submitted it to a writing contest held by the *Baltimore Saturday Visiter*. The story did win, and was published in the October 19, 1833, issue (M 2: 130–131).
61. David S. Reynolds, *Beneath the American Renaissance: The Subversive Imagination in the Age of Emerson and Melville* (New York: Oxford University Press, 1988), 242 and 243.
62. Quoted in Kevin J. Hayes, *Poe and the Printed Word* (Cambridge, UK: Cambridge University Press, 2000), 67.

Bibliography

Gitelman, Lisa. "Arthur Gordon Pym and the Novel Narrative of Edgar Allan Poe." *Nineteenth-Century Literature* 47, no. 3 (1992): 349–361. https://doi.org/10.2307/2933711.

Harvey, Ronald C. *The Critical History of Edgar Allan Poe's The Narrative of Arthur Gordon Pym: A Dialogue with Unreason*. New York: Routledge, 2016.

Irwin, John T. *American Hieroglyphics: The Symbol of the Egyptian Hieroglyphics in the American Renaissance*. 1980. Reprint. Baltimore: Johns Hopkins University Press, 2016.

Kennedy, J. Gerald. *"The Narrative of Arthur Gordon Pym" and the Abyss of Interpretation*. New York: Twayne, 1995.

Kopley, Richard, ed. *Poe's Pym: Critical Explorations*. Durham, NC: Duke University Press Books, 1992.

Lyons, Paul. "Opening Accounts in the South Seas: Poe's Pym and American Pacific Orientalism." *ESQ: A Journal of Nineteenth-Century American Literature and Culture* 42, no. 4 (1996): 291–326.

Nelson, Dana D. *The Word in Black and White: Reading "Race" in American Literature, 1638-1867*. New York: Oxford University Press, 1991.

Pollin, Burton R., ed. *The Imaginary Voyages. Vol. 1 of The Collected Writings of Edgar Allan Poe.* Boston: Twayne, 1981.

Rowe, John Carlos. *Literary Culture and U.S. Imperialism: From the Revolution to World War II.* New York: Oxford University Press, 2000.

Whalen, Terence. *Edgar Allan Poe and the Masses.* Princeton, NJ: Princeton University Press, 1999.

CHAPTER 24

CONVERSATIONS ON THE BODY AND THE SOUL

Transcending Death in the Angelic Dialogues and "Mesmeric Revelation"

BRUCE MILLS

> The image of the abyss is in all of Poe's serious writings: the mirror in "William Wilson"; burial alive; the "tarn" in which the House of Usher plunges; the great white figure towards which Pym is being borne by a current of the sea; the pit over which the pendulum swings; the dead body containing the living soul of M. Valdemar; being walled up alive; the vertigo of the maelstrom.
>
> —Allen Tate, "The Angelic Imagination: Poe and the Power of Words"[1]

> Think that the sense of individual identity will be gradually merged in the general consciousness—that Man, for example, ceasing imperceptibly to feel himself Man, will at length attain that awfully triumphant epoch when he shall recognize his existence as that of Jehovah. In the meantime bear in mind that all is Life—Life—Life within Life—the less within the greater, and all within the *Spirit Divine*. (L 1: 106)
>
> —Edgar Allan Poe, *Eureka*

ALTHOUGH hard to imagine, given the unquestioned position of Edgar Allan Poe in the canon of American literature, Allan Tate opens his 1952 essay on "The Conversation of Eiros and Charmion" (1839), "The Colloquy of Monos and Una" (1841), and "The Power of Words" (1845) expressing some embarrassment for considering the "little-known figure" of Poe "whose interest for us is in the best sense historical."[2] Focusing on the "angelic imagination" in relation to those stories that Thomas Mabbott calls the "trilogy of dialogues of blessed spirits" or angelic dialogues (M 2: 607), Tate's article might be seen as a modern starting place for an enduring fascination with tales that embody a sharp contrast to the "abyss" that haunts Poe's characters and, most certainly, generations of readers. Though not always given significant weight in critical studies of Poe, the angelic tales as well as "Mesmeric Revelation" (1844), another dialogue story that examines the afterlife and God, have garnered ongoing attention.[3] What are we to make, after all, of a series of stories that, in Tate's view, fail fictionally in their ultimate disconnect from the human condition and situation? How are we to understand seemingly anomalous stories that transcend death and gesture toward the final articulation of *Eureka*: "Life—Life—Life within Life—the less within the greater, and all within the *Spirit Divine*"?

The angelic dialogues, then, can be read within two encompassing dimensions of Poe's oeuvre: an ongoing terror in the imminence of death and bodily dissolution and an effort to enact a transcendent aesthetic in the face of this ultimate collapse. Speaking from an in-between consciousness immediately following physical death and/or through a sixth or mesmeric sense, these stories diminish the horrors of mortality, even if recalling its prelude, and instead imagine a more complete knowing unimpeded by the limitation of the corporeal senses. But, in these dialogues, Poe does more than ease or displace the horrific reality of death; in channeling his views of God and the soul through the interlocutors' speculations, he brings to the living the redemptive designs of divine creation. Not surprisingly, in a death-focused canon, these seemingly anomalous conversations promise an enduring pull. They mark Poe's own mesmeric effort to retrieve that which by definition remains irretrievable: the divine thought that sets in motion and affirms the power of his own words.

Beyond Death and Silence

Writing of the antebellum era's sentimentalism and sensationalism in *Reading at the Social Limit: Affect, Mass Culture, and Edgar Allan Poe*, Jonathan Elmer distinguishes between those stories that heal the rift introduced through death and others that in loss and dissolution see horror, not restorative ritual. "Someone dies," he writes, "and a hole is opened up in the social fabric."[4] In the sentimental, then, storytellers underscore "the penetration of the reader by affect as the validation of a principle of social cohesion, of the social unity of feeling and sympathy; but then it will seek for ways to close the hole, to control the affect, to modulate grief into mourning."[5] Readers of the period will recall the work of Lydia Sigourney and Harriet Beecher Stowe—two prominent figures of the sentimental tradition that Elmer explores in some detail—as enacting this ritual of mourning, as striving to shut the door on the chasm of the "mournful and never-ending remembrance" of death. Unlike the sentimental, however, he goes on to argue that sensationalism

> lingers at the place of the wound, tarries in the breach of the social limit, explores the affective intensities elicited there; but then rather than allowing for a healing

> closure, it causes something to rise up in the opening, some horrifying and impossible embodiment. The dead body that doesn't stay dead, the grave that doesn't stay closed, the reader who cannot overcome, cannot manage, the affective ties linking individuals at and across the social limit—all of these are at once failures of the sentimental project and realizations of the sensational underside of that project.[6]

To think of Poe is to revisit in the imagination those compelling stories that continually disrupt cohesive closure. And so, as in one of his most famous and often-read tales, Madeline Usher knocks and knocks until, bloodied and enshrouded in her death robes, she brings down not simply her brother but the very house of Usher. Or, as in the case of "The Tell-Tale Heart" and "Berenice," narrators dismember and thus violate the body that, in the ideal sentimental death scene, is imagined as if asleep, whole, peaceful, and thus offering a vision of some blessed and impending state. The bedside of "The Tell-Tale Heart" is anything but blessed; the bed itself has been upturned and employed to forever close the victim's vulture eye. In "Berenice," the ritual of interment is not a reverent farewell but a momentary pause before a physical violation.

Biographies and scholarly studies have rightly obsessed on Poe's pervasive rejection of the era's effort to "modulate grief into mourning" and thus his ongoing fixation on bodily death rather than the promise of an afterlife. The thematic underpinning of Kenneth Silverman's *Edgar A. Poe: Mournful and Never-ending Remembrance*, in fact, is made visible in the book's haunting cover art: a sitting and cross-armed Poe, black cat at his elbow, eyes intense and gazing stage left, as if haunted by but expecting an ushering forth of those beautiful (and dead) women from his own past. Silverman's biographical through-line traces the "so-called cult of memory" that "helped to allay anxieties about the continued vitality of Christian ideas of immortality."[7] Having examined a series of poems centering on death and dying, Silverman writes:

> This peculiar cluster of dead-alive persons, still-moving landscapes, and deathly dread-longing dominates not only Edgar's three slim volumes of poems but also, to anticipate, his entire literary career. Much of his later writing, despite its variety of forms and styles, places and characters, is driven by the question of whether the dead remain dead. . . . But its supreme place in his imagination, and its eventual emergence in his behavior as well, invite at least the attempt to understand its personal meaning to him.[8]

Like Elmer's critical study, this biography points repeatedly to the evidence of a death-obsessed career in order to construct the narrative of the life. In this lived and imagined plot line, the ur-story is of that narrative vortex that spins its characters and Poe himself around a psychic and social blackness. It is the death arc that gives coherence to his life and the texts embodying his mediation of this social breach.

In *Poe, Death, and the Life of Writing*, J. Gerald Kennedy offers the authoritative naming and explication of this centering of death in Poe's opus. In doing so, he not only delineates the cultural realities giving rise to nineteenth-century fears but also their existential resonance in modern life. Examining the sentimental tradition of the beautiful death, Kennedy links real and fictional mourning practices to the period's increasing distance from the corporeal realities of mortality. "This exemplary scene," he argues, "suggests that the nineteenth-century impression of death's beauty involved an act of communal self-delusion, a tacit refusal to see dying as a physical process."[9] He later asserts: "By temperament and personal bereavement, Poe was drawn into the cult of death and memory. But if he respected the fashion for sentiment, he eschewed the conventional sad-but-joyful departure, and he clearly saw through the mask of beauty that concealed the features of human dissolution." To punctuate his point, Kennedy lets Poe speak for himself, quoting the author's own question from his "Marginalia": "Who ever *really* saw anything but horror in the smile of the dead?"[10] But the horror for Poe is not simply in the physical grotesqueness of a lifeless and decaying body, it is also in the fear of an ultimate negation, a silence that portends a larger dread—the terror that, in death, the soul, the essence of the self, ceases to exist and so too the illusory sense that words and writing can transcend this existential truth. Kennedy underscores this point in his explication of the sketch "Silence": "Real terror resides in the nameless shadow, the silence of the soul. Here Poe exposes the anxiety underlying the Beautiful Death: if the spirit survives in an afterlife, man can endure the corporate silence, but if the soul itself also dies, there exists no hope and death is indeed evil." The greatest threat, then, is not "corporal death but a sign of the spirit's extinction."[11]

Given this narrative core of Poe's writings, it is not surprising that his cluster of postdeath, angelic dialogues elicits attention. They give presence to what has been markedly absent in the most compelling of his tales. Rather than a manuscript tossed by the living into the vortex of annihilation, each dramatizes a script from an in-between place or the other side—not written (or imagined) from the dwelling of pain and horror but from the site of greater knowing, a place where speakers see distinctly through a higher plane of consciousness where cause and effect can finally be understood. In short, the soul survives, speaks, and, in doing so, points to Poe's effort to offer an alternative and transcendent vision.

We can read "The Conversation of Eiros and Charmion" and "The Colloquy of Monos and Una" as healing the rift of death not through reenacting the deathbed ritual but by creating an in-between space where the body no longer experiences sensory pain and horror. Though the stories have been critiqued for unhinging themselves from the sensible world, it is precisely this separation that frees the interlocutors to a clearer rendering of their earthly demise and heavenly state. In "The Conversation of Eiros and Charmion," the first published of the dialogues, the apocalyptic circumstances that led to the death of Eiros are horrific, but as Eiros interprets the event after the fact, we are struck less by the fiery destruction of the earth by a comet than by how extinction, perhaps, is *not* a mournful and never-ending remembrance. Certainly, Eiros recalls that, in coming to understand the inevitable outcome of the earth's contact with the celestial object, the "result of investigation sent an electric thrill of the intensest terror through the universal heart of man" (M 2: 460). Yet we know that Eiros speaks from a place of transcendence. In the opening of the story, Charmion assures the newcomer: "Dreams are with us no more;—but of these mysteries anon. I rejoice to see you looking life-like and rational. The film of the shadow has already passed from off your eyes. Be of heart, and fear nothing. Your allotted days of stupor have expired; and, tomorrow, I will my-self induct you into the full joys and wonders of your novel existence" (M 2: 455). Eiros replies that the "wild sickness and the terrible darkness" (M 2: 456) have passed, and, learning of his being in Aidenn (or Heaven), Charmion invites him to recount his last days. In the context of Kennedy's analysis, this invitation is an important one; it speaks of Poe's negotiation of the terror of death but without the ultimate silence. Clearly, the story envisions a threshold space of a purer knowledge.[12]

But it is "The Colloquy of Monos and Una" that imagines a deeper journey into the afterlife—and without the fictional vehicle of an apocalypse. To begin the story, we find ourselves in a much different place than that of Poe's death-terrorized narrators:

> *Una.* Death!
>
> *Monos.* How strangely, sweet Una, you echo my words! I observe, too, a vacillation in your step—a joyous inquietude in your eyes. You are confused and oppressed by the majestic novelty of the Life Eternal. Yes, it was of Death I spoke. And here how singu-larly sounds that word which of old was wont to bring terror to all hearts—throwing a mildew upon all pleasures! (M 2: 608)

Importantly, Una's exclamation comes immediately after his and the tale's opening ques-tion, "Born again?" (M 2: 608), a reference that for anyone schooled in the Bible calls forth John 3:3: "Jesus answered and said unto him, Verily, verily, I say unto thee, Except a man be born again, he cannot see the kingdom of God."[13] In a text which, Mabbott notes, "probably contains more [King James Version biblical phrases] than any of his other stories" (M 2: 617n1), it cannot be coincidence that Poe's redefining of death invokes the Gospel of John. Its opening would have spoken to a writer whose faith centered in the power of language: "In the beginning was the Word, and the Word was with God, and the Word was God."[14] Partaking in this divine creation, Poe breathes life into what had been dread and darkness. The "word" that formerly elicited "terror to all hearts" no longer has power. Death has been transcended; it is transformed through narrative.

Moreover, whereas Poe's horror fiction sometimes renders the harsh reality of bodily dissolution—for example, recall M. Valdemar's "nearly liquid mass of loathsome—of detestable putridity"[15] upon his release from a mesmeric state into death—this "weird narrative" focuses less on the realities of physical decay in order to consider the sus-pension and ultimate alteration of earthly sensation (M 2: 608). In this transformation, Monos narrates what would have been the next stages in Eiros's journey to a more per-fect knowledge. Most of the story, in fact, represents Monos's effort to give language to what exists after the cessation of life. He observes:

> Words are vague things. My condition did not deprive me of sentience. It appeared to me not greatly dissimilar to the extreme quiescence of him, who, having slumbered long and profoundly, lying motionless and fully prostrate in

> a midsummer noon, begins to steal slowly back into consciousness, through the mere sufficiency of his sleep, and without being awakened by external disturbances. (M 2: 612)

Here we have an acknowledgment of the inadequacy of earth-laden terms to depict the eternal "body" or soul. Here we have the beautiful death but now plotted from the view of the dead. More than this, we have Poe revitalizing the dead not in their horrific pounding from within the tomb but in a ratiocinative discourse from the other side. It is the sentimental trope through a Poe-esque lens—an anticipation of Dickinson more than an echo of Sigourney. For, importantly, Poe focuses on the alteration of the bodily senses of the dead, not the social healing of the living: the confounding of taste and smell into "one sentiment, abnormal and intense" and vision being experienced "as *sound*" (M 2: 613). "*All* my perceptions," Monos asserts, "were purely sensual" (M 2: 613). And, in this sensory understanding, the past mourning of then yet-living Una "conveyed to the extinct reason no intimation of the sorrows which gave them birth" (M 2: 613). Here is explanation free of sentimental consolation. In the end, this transition period gives way to "a sixth, all perfect" sense (M 2: 614).

God, Creation, and the Power of Words

If we consider "The Conversation of Eiros and Charmion" and "The Colloquy of Monos and Una" as offering another take on the life-in-death story and, for this reason, sites worthy of critical attention, then a closer look at "The Power of Words" provides insight into another emblematic dimension of the dialogues. In it, we see Poe speculating upon the nature of God and his creation and, in doing so, glimpsing how writing and language form a critical component of his conception of transcendence. In other words, the stories are not simply about diminishing horror or providing hope; they trace the nature of ultimate transcendence in the alignment of earthly and heavenly creation.

A return to Kennedy's study can bring forward why the angelic dialogues provide more than a hopeful plot variant to the Poe canon. For Kennedy, it is not simply that Poe's work shows an obsessive attention to the "problem of death." Rather, of deeper interest is how he embodies the modern drive to write *against* the dreadful fact of mortality. He argues:

> The nullity of death gives writing a means of understanding its own imperative nature; it constitutes the blank tablet upon which writing inscribes its resistance to the indifference of time. Death enforces the rule of absence which creates the need for symbolic expression; its inexorability becomes the vital insistence of writing. And so writing may be said to derive its life from death, paradoxically achieving its energy through an emulation of death—through a retreat from the formlessness of lived experience into the fixed and silent world of the unspeaking word that will always speak.[16]

In Poe's work, then, we see evidence of this attempt to mediate a fear of death and thus transcend it by giving its dreadful presence some order and form in writing. Drawing from Derrida's contention that "inscription is the sign of a vanished presence, an originary Logos, without which the relationship between word and world falls into chaos," Kennedy concludes that, "[i]n losing its relationship to a transcendental signified, writing became more conscious of its deathlike nature (as the sign of an absence) and more uncertain of its own capacity to represent truth."[17] The drive to inscribe the speaking soul through words is the ultimate attempt to mediate death. It is the effort to connect the human pen to the divine breath. Here the writer is the medium (in both a literary and mesmeric sense).

As author and medium within "The Power of Words," Poe frees himself completely from the sensory status of the body and, consequently, becomes a kind of intermediary for the soul. Although "The Conversation of Eiros and Charmion" and "The Colloquy of Monos and Una" still speak of the material body in the spirit world, "The Power of Words" is purged of earthly referents and thus fixes attention on the "infinity of matter" that "is no dream" (M 3: 1212). Poe has no interest in a nightmarish prelude to extinction or a speculative dissection of the bodily senses in their transition to some spiritual state. Instead, as Tate argues, he is concerned with "language as a potential source of quasi-divine power" and, for "The Power of Words" specifically, "the possibility of creative power through verbal magic."[18] After Oinos's opening apology, "Pardon, Agathos, the weakness of a spirit new-fledged with immortality!" (M 3: 1211), the story quickly takes up the divine implications of the Word:

> *Oinos.*—And now, Agathos, as we proceed, instruct me!—speak to me in the earth's familiar tones! I understood not what you hinted to me, just now, of the modes or of the methods of what, during mortality, we were accustomed to call Creation. Do you mean to say that the Creator is not God? (M 3: 1212–1213)

In response, Agathos explains that only God created in the beginning, that the "seeming creatures which are now, throughout the universe, so perpetually springing into being, can only be considered as the mediate or indirect, not as the direct or immediate results of the Divine creative power" (M 3: 1213). In short, God is responsible for the "first word," which "spoke into existence the first law" (M 3: 1213). Everything flowed from and can be traced back to this initial act of giving voice to the world. In effect, in another gesture to the Gospel of John, all of creation is the Word made flesh; however, rather than use this biblical language, Poe gives emphasis to the physics in the metaphysical:

> *Agathos.*— . . . You are well aware that, as no thought can perish, so no act is without infinite result. We moved our hands, for example, when we were dwellers on the earth, and, in so doing, we gave vibration to the atmosphere which engirdled it. This vibration was indefinitely extended, till it gave impulse to every particle of the earth's air, which thenceforward, *and for ever*, was actuated by the one movement of the hand. This fact the mathematicians of our globe well knew. (M 3: 1213)

Among other things, Agathos's words echo discoveries concerning the conservation of force. In addition, Poe is gesturing toward the findings of Isaac Newton and thus how the movement of the earth and its responsiveness to the gravitational pull of other celestial bodies offers evidence of the material effects of invisible forces. In this universe, we learn that thought is the source of all motion, and God is the source of all thought. But this ultimate spring of creation flows through "the earth's familiar tones" (M 3: 1212) of human language. "And while I thus spoke," Agathos asks, "did there not cross your mind some thought of the *physical power of words*? Is not every word an impulse on the air?" (M 3: 1215).

In this last iteration of Poe's angelic dialogues, then, the discussion focuses on metaphysical questions and sees the act of writing as an embodiment of a secondary or mediate dimension of God's original creation. Or, more succinctly stated, words are more than words; in their power to create, they surpass the limitations of time and ultimately death. We see this most dramatically in the conclusion of the story. Responding to Agathos's ecstatic questions concerning the power of words, Oinos asks why Agathos weeps concerning the "fair star—which is the greenest and yet most terrible of all we have encountered in our flight?" and then comments, "[its] brilliant flowers look like a fairy dream—but its fierce volcanoes like the passions of a turbulent heart" (M 3: 1215). To which, to conclude the story, Agathos exclaims:

> They *are*!—they *are*! This wild star—it is now three centuries since, with clasped hands, and with streaming eyes, at the feet of my beloved—I spoke it—with a few passionate sentences—into birth. Its brilliant flowers *are* the dearest of all unfulfilled dreams, and its raging volcanoes *are* the passions of the most turbulent and unhallowed of hearts. (M 3: 1215)

But how are we to understand this declaration of the power of words? Has Agathos truly brought into being this "wild star" through speaking it? Or, in this fanciful evocation of that place beyond the final sleep, is Poe getting at a secondary and thus shadowy power that exists at the intersection of death and inscription? In *A World of Words: Language and Displacement in the Fiction of Edgar Allan Poe*, Michael J. S. Williams captures the critical debate over how to understand this power. For Williams, this seeming assertion of the "literal '*power of words*' must not be taken too literally."[19] He calls attention to the fact that what has been spoken is the passionate word: " 'Flowers' and 'volcanoes' are figures—'flowers of rhetoric,' if anything—in which he uttered his dreams and passions. They have become material in the way that the words of a text assume materiality—a condition emphasized here by the italics of '*are* . . . *are*.' "[20] He continues:

> And this materiality is one mark of their existence independent of their author. Moreover, they remain resolutely figurative. Agathos, an author encountering his text, which has drifted independently through time, can only *assert* the identity of his "dreams . . . passions" and his words. His drooping wings are both a sign of his

memory of their occasion and a sign of authorial anxiety—hence his attempt to reestablish the integrity of his connection with his creation.[21]

Further compounding this anxiety, Williams notes, is the earlier truth that God first created but then stepped back from this initial act. Thus, "[t]he universe is a text whose author is irrevocably absent."[22] This anxiety is of the same order as that which Kennedy described. Though the horror of death has been displaced into the act of writing, the promise of ultimate transcendence is never fully realized. Responding to Williams's argument that Poe "believes human creative efforts must be relegated to 'perpetual inadequacy,' " Barbara Cantalupo counters: "Unless Poe's whole creative project is self-consciously an act of 'perpetual inadequacy' and his claim that *Eureka* was his finest effort is self-deception, Williams's reading of the angelic dialogues would seem to overlook Poe's belief in the power of words and his literary practice."[23] She goes on to consider Joan Dayan's own reflections on this conundrum concerning how we might understand the full import of "The Power of Words": "To understand the passage from entity to matter—from *being* into *locality*—is to see how seriously Poe takes his fiction." For Dayan, this understanding leads to questions at the philosophical edge of Agathos's final thoughts: "Can we know whether matter, by its structure and arrangement, may be the cause of thought?" and "Can one distinguish between the intelligible and the sensible, the *within* and the *without*?"[24] Perhaps it is this language of a threshold place between the material and the spiritual, between matter and mind, that leads us to where Poe sought answers: the mesmeric arts.

The Science of the Soul

Though not part of what Mabbott termed the three "dialogues of blessed spirits in Heaven" (M 2: 607), "Mesmeric Revelation" nonetheless directs its attention to matters of the spiritual world through another novel conversation and so forms a kind of companion piece, especially as it anticipates ideas published in "The Power of Words." Moreover, in explicating key notions within the text, we take another important step in discovering how the era's mesmeric literature provides Poe with a scientific and philosophical foundation for his thoughts on the life of the soul. In many ways, this story is an important linchpin for a deeper understanding of Poe's metaphysical theory, literary practice, and thus his conception of the power of words.

In this tale, Vankirk, a patient near death who has been unable to satisfy himself concerning "certain psychal impressions," asks to be mesmerized by his doctor so that he can be questioned about the afterlife (M 3: 1031). Having been entranced on numerous occasions in the past, Vankirk is convinced that, in this state, he can achieve a kind of intuitive knowledge whereby the "reasoning and its conclusion—the cause and its effect—are present together" (M 3: 1032). Thus, Poe seeks another fictional platform from which to transcend death. This higher state, Vankirk later explains, "resembles death" and, as a result, enables him to "perceive external things directly, without organs, through a medium which I shall employ in the ultimate, unorganized life" of the spirit (M 3: 1037). Recalling Monos's transition from body to soul, Vankirk notes that the "organs of man are adapted to his rudimental condition, and to that only; his ultimate condition, being unorganized, is of unlimited comprehension in all points but one—the nature of the volition of God—that is to say, the motion of the unparticled matter," which defines God (M 3: 1037).

Within this higher state of consciousness, he has access to the same truths as the angels; like Agathos, Vankirk is Poe's fictional medium, the voice through which he can explore the nature of the spiritual—or, more accurately perhaps, where he can offer his material explanation of the realm of the spirit.[25] In this story, we hear a more fleshed-out formulation of Agathos's declaration that all motion within the universe arises from God, the "source of all thought" (M 3: 1215). Asked if God is a spirit, Vankirk replies that "[t]here is no immateriality":

> He is not spirit, for he exists. Nor is he matter, *as you understand it*. But there are *gradations* of matter of which man knows nothing; the grosser impelling the finer, the finer pervading the grosser. . . . These gradations of matter increase in rarity or fineness, until we arrive at a matter *unparticled*—without particles—indivisible—*one*; and here the law of impulsion and permeation is modified. The ultimate, or unparticled matter, not only permeates all things but impels all things—and thus *is* all things within itself. This matter is God. What men attempt to embody in the word "thought," is this matter in motion. (M 3: 1033)

As with "The Power of Words," we are now a long way from a fictional canon that locates materiality in the horror of dissolution and decay. In many ways, physical decay has been transformed into a seemingly intangible, transcendent process. In "The Colloquy of Monos and Una," Poe reminds us of the presence of the body even as the soul loses contact in the "dull shock" of the release: "The mortal body had been at length stricken with the hand of the deadly *Decay*," and, in the tenuous but enduring link to sentience and the prison house of the tomb (aka the body), "the soul watched narrowly each second as it flew . . ." (M 2: 615, 616). To die, we must inevitably come to see, is to enter into this divine motion of matter unparticled—which, of course, is not ultimately a bodiless or immaterial state. Toward the end of "Mesmeric Revelation," Vankirk further explains: "There are two bodies—the rudimental and the complete; corresponding with the two conditions of the worm and the butterfly. What we call 'death,' is but the painful metamorphosis. Our present incarnation is progressive, preparatory, temporary. Our future is perfected, ultimate, immortal" (M 3: 1037). The last words of Vankirk, then, are far from the sentimental. They are a secular lecture on the meaning of the "*substantive* vastness of infinity" (M 3: 1039). (He argues that we "must not regard [the term substance] as a quality, but as a sentiment:—it is the perception, in thinking beings, of the adaptation of matter to their organization" [M 3: 1039].) With Vankirk's utterance, the physician notes a bodily change, and Vankirk awakens from this state of sleepwaking "with a bright smile irradiating all his features" (M 3: 1040). Although he does not arrive at this vision of the afterlife through a typical tableau of the deathbed scene, Poe nonetheless inscribes a comparable script.[26]

In his still evocative and illuminating study *Poe Poe Poe Poe Poe Poe Poe*, Daniel Hoffman brings us back to this fact of an oeuvre preoccupied with death and, ultimately, to why "Mesmeric Revelation" and the angelic dialogues remain essential in gaining a deeper sense of the author's aesthetic choices. Not unlike Kennedy's consideration of "MS. Found in a Bottle" as a tale emblematic of Poe's "will to project the life of words across the gulf of mortality," Hoffman's analysis of "A Descent into the Maelström" launches his own consideration of a constellation of tales voyaging beyond the limitations of the earthbound, ratiocinative narrator.[27] He explains: "And so it is that although Poe's voyagers may spend all their time ratiocinating like mad, the knowledge they send back to us in their letters cast on the sea is not the knowledge they ratiocinated to learn. It came to them while they were ratiocinating, came from a nonratiocinative order of experience. It is revelation."[28] For Hoffman, Poe's tales on mesmerism, including "Mesmeric Revelation," and the angelic dialogues represent the effort to realize or assert a revelatory knowledge. Whether existing in a somnambulant or mesmeric state or occupying some otherworldly space from which to retrieve angelic impressions, Poe's voyagers represent for Hoffman explorers who had accidentally entered into a place "between the living and the unliving, and returned from the spirit world!" He adds:

> And now I start awake into the knowledge of why Poe is forever trying to mesmerize himself—by the repetition of a word until it loses all meaning; by the contemplation of a candle flame; by losing himself in the design on the margin of a book—remember "Berenice"? Poe is trying to mesmerize himself to be both P—and Valdemar, so that he may himself enter the unknown existence of the spirit freed from the body.[29]

In other words, the author seeks to transcend death and speak from the position of the soul. And, of course, Hoffman asserts, Poe "must imagine protagonists who are no longer human"[30] to move to the higher claims of life and art—even if this leaves Poe "with a beautiful *method* for expressing nearly *nothing.*"[31]

Mesmerism and the Imagination

In turning to how nineteenth-century writers understood notions of the transcendent or of unconscious states, scholarship has begun to take a different look at the place of mesmeric theory and practice in Poe's work. The era's discourse concerning mesmerism (or animal magnetism) illuminates Poe's notion of God and the afterlife as well as his attempts to mediate the problem of what exists beyond material sense and consciousness. Differently stated, it offers particular insights into how he saw the practice of negotiating threshold or in-between spaces in relation to the power of language and writing.

In "Mesmeric Revelation," Poe's ideas mirror mesmeric texts speculating on the nature of God and the material but invisible forces set in motion through Divine creation. In the mesmeric canon, the starting place, in fact, was the belief that God was the First Mover. In his treatise on the principles of animal electricity and magnetism, John Bell argues that "Motion exists in all parts of the universe: all bodies are endowed with a certain degree of it, in proportion to their different organizations."[32] Echoing the principles of Franz Anton Mesmer, early theorist Ebenezer Sibley similarly asserts the connection between thought and motion in his speculations "On God" within *A Key to Physic and the Occult Sciences*: "Matter, then, by its own strength, cannot produce in itself so much motion. The motion it has, must also be from eternity."[33] From the last part of the eighteenth century through the first half of the nineteenth century, texts on animal magnetism directly and indirectly built core principles upon what was asserted as the self-evident fact of God's primary act in creation. God's initial thought, the divine first word, established a world with creatures that partook of these material and spiritual truths.[34]

No text had more impact upon the period's writers than Chauncy Hare Townshend's *Facts in Mesmerism, with Reasons for a Dispassionate Inquiry into It* (1841). As Mabbott underscores in his annotation of "Mesmeric Revelation," Poe's use of the term "sleepwaking" to describe Vankirk's state of consciousness draws directly from Townshend's vocabulary (M 3: 1040n1). (Townshend asserts this distinction clearly and early in his work with the opening section of Book II, "Mesmeric Somnabulism, or, more properly, Sleepwaking."[35]) Although earlier sections addressing the nature of sleepwaking as well as mesmeric consciousness and sensation resonate with how Poe represents the era's practice and philosophy concerning animal magnetism, Book IV, "The Mesmeric Medium," articulates ideas that speak most directly to Poe's own mesmeric revelations. The attention to the medium of mesmerism, for example, addresses at length the seamless transition between the material and the spiritual. Townshend quotes the eighteenth-century poet Edward Young to set up his thoughts, echoing Poe's own notions of the "gradations of matter": "Look nature through; 'tis just gradation all,/By what minute degrees her scale ascends!"[36] According to Townshend, "Grosser media act on the finer, the finest on the mind of man; and again the mind of man reacts from finer to grosser media."[37] And if we understand the "first known step from Deity to matter" as embodied in an "ethereal and infinitely subtle fluid, pervading the realms of space," we eventually come to see linkages between matter, spirit, and the divine first cause or Mover: "Thus, again, with science, we arrive at a primal, universal element, such as is now supposed to be the substratum even of the gases; and this element (I speak it with reverence) is the first demonstrated action of the Almighty mind."[38]

It is important to note that, for Townshend and the many serious readers of his text, the truths of mesmerism linked critical insights into the nature of the afterlife to the higher state of awareness possible through the induction of sleepwaking. In his final pages of *Facts in Mesmerism*, he turns to these profound implications of his philosophy. "The last and most important point of view in which we have now to consider mesmerism," he writes, "is in its reference to the future prospects of man, considered as an improvable being, capable of immortality."[39] At least in relation to the spiritual state of the individual (as opposed to social or cultural progress), this "improvable being" is in fact one whose current condition, to use Vankirk's words, is "progressive, preparatory, temporary" and whose "future is perfected, ultimate, immortal" (M 3: 1037). For Townshend as for Poe, "one state includes the embryo of the next, not metaphysically, but materially; and entering on a new scene is not so much a change as a continuation of what went before."[40] Moreover:

> The very rudiments of organs, intended in a higher stage of animal life to be useful, are found, uselessly as it were, appearing in the lower classes of animated creatures, or, stranger still, lying in embryo in the same creature in one state, only to be developed in another. It is an old allusion, but ever beautiful,
>
> "The wings that form
> The butterfly lie folded in the worm."[41]

And what is Townshend's ultimate conclusion? "In proportion as we value whatever tends to bring our way across the gulf of death, whatever tends to carry on a train of old familiar thought into the unknown void, let us esteem, cherish, and reverence this cheering manifestation of our being. . . . That [the mesmeric medium] should connect this world with a future is its last and greatest service."[42]

Given this fact, the higher state of sleepwaking induced through mesmeric passes offered an entry point into the in-between, that threshold space unimpeded by the earthly limitations of the senses. It was the place of what might be called a sixth sense or higher plane of knowing. Thus, it is revealing that Poe begins "Mesmeric Revelation" with a well-informed rendering of the current state of mesmeric practice, and that he frames another rendering of an angelic dialogue within a mesmeric trance. His echoing Townshend's "dispassionate inquiry" invites us to linger another moment on the link between mesmeric findings and literary practice—and return to a critical finding concerning the power of the imagination in the opening pages of *Facts in Mesmerism*. Quoting one of the original studies of animal magnetism from the French Commission of the Academy of Science, Townshend captures the critical relationship between mesmeric and literary practice—which is to say he offers the foundation for a further discerning of the power of words:

> That which we have learned, or, at least, that which has been proved to us, in a clear and satisfactory manner, by our inquiry into the phenomena of mesmerism, is, that *man can act upon man*, at all times and almost at will, by striking the imagination; that signs and gestures the most simple may produce the most powerful effects; that the action of man upon the imagination may be reduced to an art, and conducted after a certain method, when exercised upon patients who have faith in the proceedings.[43]

Are not words but signs and gestures? Is not the authorial act, is not the manipulation of thought and thus sensation through imagination, an invisible action with material affects (and effects)? The fact that encyclopedia entries on the imagination in the first half of the nineteenth century included such findings concerning animal magnetism suggests that the era had come to see mesmeric study as offering profound insights into the nature of literary practice.[44]

Conclusion

Consider how Poe brings together literary method and mesmeric philosophy in relation to the "power of words." In an 1846 "Marginalia" entry, Poe echoes aspects of the blessed and mesmeric dialogues in his reflections on those "fancies" that escape the mortal sphere:

> There is, however, a class of fancies, of exquisite delicacy, which are *not* thoughts, and to which, *as yet*, I have found it absolutely impossible to adapt language. I use the word *fancies* at random, and merely because I must use *some* word; but the idea commonly attached to the term is not even remotely applicable to the shadows of the shadows in question. They seem to me rather psychal than intellectual. They arise in the soul (alas, how rarely!) only at its epochs of most intense tranquility—when the bodily and the mental health are in perfection—and at those mere points of time where the confines of the waking world blend with those of the world of dreams. I am aware of these "fancies" only when I am upon the very brink of sleep, with the consciousness that I am so. I have satisfied myself that this condition exists but for an inappreciable *point* of time—yet it is crowded with these "shadows of shadows;" and for absolute *thought* there is demanded time's *endurance*. (ER: 1383)

It does not seem unreasonable to see "The Colloquy of Monos and Una," "The Power of Words," and "Mesmeric Revelation" as the occasion to inscribe glimpses of these "fancies." The transition state from life to death and the eternal sleep of the afterlife provide sites for such reflections. In the marginalia entry, Poe goes on to describe these fancies as having a "pleasurable ecstasy as far beyond the most pleasurable of the world of wakefulness, or of dreams" (ER: 1383); he asserts that this ecstasy "is of a character supernal to the Human Nature" and offers "a glimpse of the spirit's outer world" (ER: 1383).

Especially revealing is Poe's description of how he seeks to conjure a state of mind or consciousness conducive to "psychal impressions" as well as the capturing of them in language (ER: 1384). This state or condition, in fact, can be understood as an element of his creative process. And, if not a mesmeric state, it is certainly a higher consciousness that mirrors Vankirk's sleepwaking and provides glimpses into the beyond. Initiating his reflections on the seeming supplanting of the conventional senses by "five myriad others alien to mortality," Poe writes that "so entire is my faith in the *power of words*, that, at times, I have believed it possible to embody even the evanescence of fancies such as I have attempted to describe" (ER: 1384). But what first gets introduced as possibility gives way to confidence and conviction: "I mean to say, merely, that now I can be sure, when all circumstances are favorable, of the supervention of the condition, and feel even the capacity of inducing or compelling it:—the favorable circumstances, however, are not the less rare—else had I compelled, already, the Heaven into the Earth" (ER: 1384). We can see Poe's dialogues as fictional renderings of this compelling of "Heaven into the Earth." Critical here is a higher aspiration regarding writing and its power; the act and art of literary composition is the promise of a knowing that transcends the limitation of the five senses and the boundary of consciousness—and perhaps death.

Poe becomes physician and medium, mesmerist and sleepwaker, seeking a knowledge that can only be retrieved from "the point of blending between wakefulness and sleep" (ER: 1384). He writes: "Not that I can *continue* the condition—not that I can render the point more than a point—but that I can startle myself from the point into wakefulness—*and thus transfer the point itself into the realm of Memory*—and convey its impressions, or more properly their recollections, to a situation where (although still for a very brief period) I can survey them with the eye of analysis" (ER: 1384). Such a description of what can be brought back from this deathlike state of mesmeric sleep can be contrasted with the many tales that despair of such a possibility. It is hard not to read "Mesmeric Revelation"—and the progressive nature of the angelic dialogues—as texts increasingly desirous of representing those psychal impressions unavailable to the protagonist-narrators caught within the limited spheres of their mortal bodies. In stories of the abyss, the dead may not remain dead, but they certainly have few words for the living.

However, in these tales that abandon first-person narrators locked in their own finite perceptions, psychic traumas, and, at times, psychotic states in order to craft a dialogic meditation, Poe releases his imagination into a different realm of experience and understanding. In this space, death ceases to be defined as the horror of physical decline and decay. Rather, like the somnambulist no longer confined within the rudimental trappings of the mortal frame, the voices of his protagonists enter the slipstream of God's first thought and thus the divine flow and power of language. Perhaps with varying degrees of critical understanding or satisfaction, readers may feel that, for a time, the eyes of a haunted author give way to something other than anticipatory dread. It is not his plotting of death, after all, that marks the denouement of his own life arc. It is the journeying to the space from which no one has come back: "In a word—should I ever write a paper on this topic, the world will be compelled to acknowledge that, at last, I have done an original thing" (ER: 1385).

Notes

1. Allan Tate, "The Angelic Imagination: Poe and the Power of Words," *Kenyon Review* 14, no. 3 (1952): 474. I wish to thank The *Kenyon Review* for permission to publish this excerpt.
2. Tate, "Angelic Imagination," 455.
3. Critical studies that offer a substantive consideration of the angelic tales and "Mesmeric Revelation" include Daniel Hoffman, *Poe Poe Poe Poe Poe Poe Poe* (Garden City, NJ: Doubleday, 1972); David Halliburton, *Edgar Allan Poe: A Phenomenological View*

(Princeton, NJ: Princeton University Press, 1973); J. Gerald Kennedy, *Poe, Death, and the Life of Writing* (New Haven, CT: Yale University Press, 1987); and Michael J. S. Williams, *A World of Words: Language and Displacement in the Fiction of Edgar Allan Poe* (Durham, NC: Duke University Press, 1988). The following journal articles or book chapters are also noteworthy in the context of Poe's speculation on the soul, the afterlife, or the power of words: William Goldhurst, "Tales of the Human Condition," in *A Companion to Poe Studies*, edited by Eric W. Carlson (Westport, CT: Greenwood Press, 1996), 149–167; Barbara Cantalupo, "Preludes to *Eureka*: Poe's 'Absolute *Reciprocity of Adaptation*' in 'Shadow' and 'The Power of Words,'" *Poe Studies/Dark Romanticism* 31, no. 1–2 (1998): 17–21; and Allan Emery, "Evading the Pit and the Pendulum: Poe on the Process of Transcendence," *Poe Studies/Dark Romanticism* 38, no. 1–2 (2005): 29–42. For a consideration of the angelic tales in relation to questions of critical taste, see Stephen Rachman, "Rectangular Obscenities: Poe, Taste, and Entertainment," in *Approaches to Teaching Poe's Prose and Poetry*, edited by Jeffrey Andrew Weinstock and Tony Magistrale (New York: Modern Language Association, 2008): 88–96.

4. Jonathan Elmer, *Reading at the Social Limit: Affect, Mass Culture, and Edgar Allan Poe* (Stanford, CA: Stanford University Press, 1995), 95.
5. Elmer, *Reading at the Social Limit*, 95.
6. Elmer, *Reading at the Social Limit*, 96.
7. Kenneth Silverman, *Edgar A. Poe: Mournful and Never-ending Remembrance* (New York: HarperPerennial, 1991), 72.
8. Silverman, *Edgar A. Poe*, 76.
9. Kennedy, *Poe, Death, and the Life of Writing*, 10.
10. Kennedy, *Poe, Death, and the Life of Writing*, 17.
11. Kennedy, *Poe, Death, and the Life of Writing*, 21.
12. For notable scholarship considering "The Conversation of Eiros and Charmion," see Douglas Robinson, "Poe's Mini-Apocalypse: 'The Conversation of Eiros and Charmion,'" *Studies in Short Fiction* 19, no. 4 (1982): 329–337; and Christian Kock, "The Irony of Oxygen in Poe's 'Eiros and Charmion,'" *Studies in Short Fiction* 22, no. 3 (1985): 317–321.
13. John 3:3 (King James Version).
14. John 1:1 (King James Version).
15. Poe, "The Facts in the Case of M. Valdemar," M 3: 1243.
16. Kennedy, *Poe, Death, and the Life of Writing*, 22–23.
17. Kennedy, *Poe, Death, and the Life of Writing*, 30.
18. Tate, "Angelic Imagination," 461, 468.
19. Williams, *A World of Words*, 14.
20. Williams, *A World of Words*, 14.
21. Williams, *A World of Words*, 14.
22. Williams, *A World of Words*, 14.
23. Williams, *A World of Words*, 15; Cantalupo, "Preludes to Eureka," 20n3.
24. Joan Dayan, *Fables of Mind: An Inquiry into Poe's Fiction* (New York: Oxford University Press, 1987), 89, 89.
25. See Poe's letter to James Russell Lowell, July 2, 1844 (CL 1: 448–452). Echoing Vankirk's mesmeric-induced insights, Poe writes: "The unparticled matter, permeating & impelling, all things, is God. Its activity is the thought of God—which creates. Man, and other thinking beings, are individualizations of the unparticled matter. Man exists as a 'person', by being clothed with matter (the particled matter) which individualizes

him. Thus habited, his life is rudimental. What we call 'death' is the painful metamorphosis" (449).

26. For articles that consider Poe and mesmerism, see Doris V. Falk, "Poe and the Power of Animal Magnetism," *PMLA* 84, no. 3 (1969): 536–546; Seo-Young Jennie Chu, "Hypnotic Ratiocination," *Edgar Allan Poe Review* 6, no. 1 (2005): 5–19; and Antoine Faivre, "Borrowings and Misreading: Edgar Allan Poe's 'Mesmeric' Tales and the Strange Case of their Reception," *Aries* 7, no. 1 (2007): 21–62. For an extensive study of his mesmeric influences, see Bruce Mills, *Poe, Fuller, and the Mesmeric Arts: Transition States in the American Renaissance* (Columbia: University of Missouri Press, 2006).
27. Kennedy, *Poe, Death, and the Life of Writing*, 26.
28. Daniel Hoffman, *Poe Poe Poe Poe Poe Poe Poe* (Garden City, NJ: Doubleday, 1972), 161.
29. Hoffman, *Poe Poe Poe Poe Poe Poe Poe*, 166.
30. Hoffman, *Poe Poe Poe Poe Poe Poe Poe*, 173.
31. Hoffman, *Poe Poe Poe Poe Poe Poe Poe*, 179.
32. John Bell, *The General and Particular Principles of Animal Electricity and Magnetism* (London: printed by the author, 1792), 7.
33. Ebenezer Sibly, *A Key to Physic and the Occult Sciences* (London: printed by W. Lewis for G. Jones, 1814), 5.
34. For a full consideration of eighteenth- and nineteenth-century mesmeric literature, see Chapter 1, "Charting the Mesmeric Turn: Sympathy, Animal Magnetism, and the Motion of the Mind," in Mills, *Poe, Fuller, and the Mesmeric Arts*, 19–42.
35. Chauncy Hare Townshend, *Facts in Mesmerism, with Reasons for a Dispassionate Inquiry into It* (New York: Harper & Brothers, 1841; New York: Da Capo, 1982), 41.
36. Quoted in Townshend, *Facts in Mesmerism*, 341.
37. Townshend, *Facts in Mesmerism*, 341.
38. Townshend, *Facts in Mesmerism*, 341.
39. Townshend, *Facts in Mesmerism*, 350.
40. Townshend, *Facts in Mesmerism*, 355.
41. Townshend, *Facts in Mesmerism*, 355.
42. Townshend, *Facts in Mesmerism*, 361.
43. Quoted in Townshend, *Facts in Mesmerism*, 18.
44. See Mills, *Poe, Fuller, and the Mesmeric Arts*, 36, 60.

Bibliography

Cantalupo, Barbara. "Preludes to *Eureka*: Poe's 'Absolute *Reciprocity of Adaptation*' in 'Shadow' and 'The Power of Words.'" *Poe Studies/Dark Romanticism: History, Theory, Interpretation* 31, no. 1–2 (1998): 17–21.

Chu, Seo-Young Jennie. "Hypnotic Ratiocination." *Edgar Allan Poe Review* 6, no. 1 (2005): 5–19.

Dayan, Joan. *Fables of the Mind: An Inquiry into Poe's Fiction*. New York: Oxford University Press, 1987.

Elmer, Johnathan. *Reading at the Social Limit: Affect, Mass Culture, and Edgar Allan Poe*. Stanford, CA: Stanford University Press, 1995.

Emery, Allan. "Evading the Pit and the Pendulum: Poe on the Process of Transcendence." *Poe Studies/Dark Romanticism: History, Theory, Interpretation* 38, no. 1–2 (2005): 29–42.

Halliburton, David. *Edgar Allan Poe: A Phenomenological View.* Princeton, NJ: Princeton University Press, 1973.

Hoffman, Daniel. *Poe Poe Poe Poe Poe Poe Poe.* Garden City, NJ: Doubleday, 1972.

Kennedy, J. Gerald. *Poe, Death, and the Life of Writing.* New Haven, CT: Yale University Press, 1987.

Mills, Bruce. *Poe, Fuller, and the Mesmeric Arts: Transition States in the American Renaissance.* Columbia: University of Missouri Press, 2006.

Rachman, Stephen. "Rectangular Obscenities: Poe, Taste, and Entertainment." In *Approaches to Teaching Poe's Prose and Poetry*, edited by Jeffrey Andrew Weinstock and Tony Magistrale, 88–96. New York: Modern Language Association, 2008.

Tate, Allen. "The Angelic Imagination: Poe and the Power of Words." *Kenyon Review* 14, no. 3 (1952): 455–475.

Williams, Michael J. S. *A World of Words: Language and Displacement in the Fiction of Edgar Allan Poe.* Durham, NC: Duke University Press, 1988.

CHAPTER 25

MAKING SENSE OF *EUREKA*

LAURA SALTZ

> What I have propounded will (in good time) revolutionize the world of Physical & Metaphysical Science. I say this calmly—but I say it.
>
> —Letter from Edgar Allan Poe to George Eveleth (CL 2: 362)

> I spoke it—with a few passionate sentences—into birth.
>
> —Edgar Allan Poe, "The Power of Words" (M 3: 1215)

> "To speak is to do something."
>
> —Michel Foucault, *The Archaeology of Knowledge*[1]

EDGAR Allan Poe's *Eureka* (1848) is not an easy read. Written primarily in the mode of a scientific treatise, the text depends on readers' familiarity with the ideas of several early nineteenth-century sciences—including cosmology, astronomy, optics, and mathematics—and with nineteenth-century debates about scientific method. The author's preface in no way prepares readers for this encounter with the vocabularies, controversies, or methodologies of nineteenth-century science writing. Instead, Poe addresses *Eureka* "to those who feel rather than to those who think—to the dreamers and those who put faith in dreams as in the only realities," and conjures a reader more akin to Egaeus, the narrator of Poe's tale "Berenice," than to a student of science (L1: 5).[2] Although *Eureka* lacks rhyme, meter, or verse, and therefore defies most of Poe's carefully articulated principles of poetry, the preface dictates that the text be read "as an Art-Product alone:—let us say as a Romance; or if I be urging not too lofty a claim, as a Poem" (L1: 5). Subtitled twice, both as "A Prose Poem" and "An Essay on the Material and Spiritual Universe," the text pronounces its own paradoxical status. By any of Poe's criteria, an essay cannot be a poem or vice versa—the term "prose poem" is a contradiction in terms. Jonathan Elmer summarizes nicely: *Eureka* "is notoriously unstable, maddeningly transformable, and of dubious generic status."[3] Indeed, Joan Dayan argues that it is unreadable by design, that *Eureka* instructs readers how to comprehend Poe's prose through performances of contradiction that purposefully create disequilibrium in its readers.[4]

Despite the obstacles to comprehending the text—those that arise from twenty-first-century readers' distance from nineteenth-century astronomy and cosmology and from *Eureka*'s stagings of epistemological uncertainty—*Eureka* is less generically anomalous and less internally contradictory than it might appear. In their introduction to the text, Stuart and Susan F. Levine suggest that *Eureka* is one of many mid-nineteenth-century works that seeks to dissolve boundaries among literary, poetic, philosophical, and scientific writing or to invent entirely new genres (L1: xi). This formulation is true, though it requires further elaboration. *Eureka* does not so much dissolve existing boundaries as inhabit a space in which the lines between literature and science are in the process of being drawn. The unbridgeable gap between poetry and science so clearly visible from a twenty-first-century perspective—and that contributes to contemporary readers' confusion in encountering the text—did not fully exist in 1848.[5]

This essay considers *Eureka*'s generic instability as a symptom of the bifurcation between the discursive domains of science and literature that took place in the nineteenth century's first half. Michel Foucault's *Order of Things* and *Archaeology of Knowledge* provide a conceptual framework that describes this division and suggests its implications for the context in which *Eureka* was published and received.[6] Performing both scientific and literary epistemologies, *Eureka* stages a competition between them. *Eureka's* diglossia—its ability to speak the languages of science and literature to an audience also in the process of dividing—suggests its relevance for two recent scholarly trajectories: in one, literary scholars have begun "remapping" antebellum print culture in the early nineteenth century, and in the other, historians of science have explored what Bernard Lightman calls the rapidly expanding "topography" of science during the same period.[7] Both focus on the changing material practices that came to define the domains of Anglo-American literature and science in the first half of the nineteenth century, practices implicated in the complex epistemic shifts described by Foucault. *Eureka* implicitly acknowledges these shifts in its attempts to synthesize literary and scientific modes of truth-telling, to address "the *Physical, Metaphysical and Mathematical*" dimensions of the cosmos (L1: 7). Indeed, *Eureka* can be read as an expression of longing for synthesis in the face of these divisions. By elevating metaphysical truths over physical ones, by using scientific epistemologies as the foundations for literary ones, *Eureka* recognizes the increasing authority of science, even as it draws on that authority to make an urgent claim for literature.

As Poe scholars have noted, *Eureka* advocates for intuition and imagination as the most direct means of gaining access to "the truth." In the discursive division between science and literature, intuition and imagination become paradoxical forms of knowledge. As Vered Maimon argues, imagination in the context of the modern episteme "undermines the universality and validity of knowledge" at the same time as "it is also a necessary condition for it."[8] The tasks *Eureka* sets for itself are to demonstrate that intuition and imagination are epistemological forms by citing their importance for the practice of science, and to appropriate (or reclaim) them *as knowledge* for poetry. The text thus registers sweeping shifts in the Western episteme, keeping one foot in what Foucault identifies as the Classical era and putting the other into the modern.

Foucault's *Order of Things* posits that the "order" or space of knowledge in Western cultures was reorganized abruptly at the end of the eighteenth century.[9] Within the realm of natural history, the search for laws that invisibly governed the physical world replaced Linnaean systems of classifying organisms. The study of invisible organic structures (such as lungs) and functions (such as breathing) replaced the enumeration of visible resemblances as central objects of knowledge. This shift was signaled by a broad restructuring of epistemological categories: the division of the natural world into a single opposition between organic and inorganic, the reorganization of the domain of economics, and shifts in the relation of language to representation that accompanied the rise of philology and the emergence of "literature" as a distinct category. These changes characterize the modern era, which, according to Foucault, stretched from the beginning of the nineteenth century to Bergson's work in the early twentieth.[10]

As it relates to the chronology of natural science, this account accords with accepted narratives in the history of science. Indeed, many historians of science have designated the turn of the nineteenth century as the era of a "second scientific revolution."[11] Poe's lifelong reading in the sciences, his publication of *The Conchologist's First Book* in 1839, and his sustained interest in integrating scientific ideas into his tales suggest his profound engagement with this revolution.[12] For Foucault, the reorganization of the natural sciences cannot be understood apart from a more wholesale change in "the order of things" that also encompasses literature. Within a discourse, "order" is "that which is given in things as their inner law, the hidden network that determines the way they confront one another, and also that which has no existence except in the grid created by a glance, an examination, a language."[13] The grid that establishes a particular discourse's coherence in turn rests on—is made possible by—a set of historical conditions and a prioris. These "conditions of possibility" are shared across discursive formations, and when they shift, they create a seismic effect. This is not to say that all discourses emerge, take form, establish institutional correlatives, or transform in lockstep—far from it. Each discursive formation has its own historical, sociological, and institutional particularities. But Foucault insists that the history of any individual branch of knowledge cannot be understood as a temporal sequence of ideas—"such a body of knowledge is not, in fact, a phenomenon of heredity and tradition."[14] Instead, contemporaneous bodies of knowledge should be understood alongside one another, not to determine their influence on each other but with reference to their common "archaeological subsoil."[15] *Eureka* registers the realignment of the adjacent realms of literature and the natural sciences.

Indeed, this shift in the "archaeological subsoil" had enormous significance for literature. According to Foucault, before the modern episteme, natural history, economics, and language were all epistemologically rooted in "representation." That is, signs were distinct from what they signified; words represented and described the world rather than being interwoven with it. Thus, the material world could be classified, compared, and ordered—"representation" made natural history possible. But when the modern episteme was inaugurated at the end of the eighteenth century, language ceased to be a medium of representation (related to or even caused by its referents) and, as signified by the rise of philology, became instead something to be studied. Language in the modern episteme acquired "the mere status of an object."[16] This transformation in the relationship of language to representation enabled "the appearance of literature . . . as such"[17]—the appearance of a form of narrative that did not rely on the stable relationship between sign and referent but instead on the free play of language. (Mallarmé's poetry is Foucault's favorite example of such literature.) In this respect, literature in the modern episteme thus differed from the forms of narrative that preceded it (mythology, history, and fable), and from texts that we retroactively call literature (by Dante or Homer, for instance). Most important for this analysis of *Eureka*, literature became differentiated from "the discourse of ideas,"[18] a discourse to which *Eureka* nevertheless attempts to lay claim.

What then of the imagination? *The Order of Things* focuses on epistemological ruptures and defines literature "as such" in opposition to modern modalities of knowledge. Foucault's discussion of literature is therefore brief and imagination's place in the modern era is outside the scope of his study. Nevertheless, *Eureka*'s emphasis on the imagination is implicated in the epistemic ruptures taking place at the turn of the nineteenth century. According to Foucault, the same shifts in the nature of representation that made possible the emergence of literature *as* literature allowed transcendental thought to appear. For Foucault, Kant's philosophy is a watershed in this set of transformations. Kant's universal metaphysical categories, including space, time, being, and knowing, exist outside representation but also establish "the basis of which all representation, whatever its form, may be posited."[19] On the one hand, then, the emergence of transcendental categories is an effect of the breakdown of older systems of order; on the other, so too is the proliferation of positivistic branches of knowledge. Both are unified by their focus on that which lies outside of representation, on "laws, but not essences; regularities, but not the beings that obey them."[20] Theories of the imagination, as Maimon argues, likewise underwent substantial reconsideration in relation to the concept of representation. Revising Kant's epistemological understanding of the imagination, Coleridge differentiated a specifically poetic imagination from a more general form of imagination that he understood as a facet of all perception.[21] *Eureka* both advocates and practices this poetic imagination. It appropriates the discourses of positivistic, mathematized science for poetic and metaphysical ends, unifying all under the rubric of law. In incorporating these newly sanctioned forms of "knowledge" into a text named as poetry and marked as an exercise of the poetic imagination, *Eureka* claims "the discourse of ideas" for literature in the moment that literary discourse is defined in opposition to knowledge.

In *The Archaeology of Knowledge*, written after *The Order of Things* as an attempt to generalize the methodology of the latter, Foucault interrogates what it means to occupy a particular discursive or enunciative position. Very simply, the first question that must be asked is: "who is speaking? Who, among the totality of individuals, is accorded the right to use this sort of language?"[22] The second question is: what are the "institutional *sites* from which [this hypothetical person] makes his discourse, and from which this discourse derives its legitimate source and point of application (its specific object and instruments of verification)."[23] These questions must be asked of *Eureka*.[24]

To what degree do *Eureka* and its author inhabit the cultural locations from which scientific knowledge is authorized, and to what ends? Foregrounding these discursive conditions requires a change of viewpoint and reveals meanings that are "neither visible nor hidden."[25] While a number of scholars have traced the scientific source texts from which *Eureka* borrows and have evaluated how well it recapitulates the science, a Foucaultian analysis helps identify the "the question of power" posed by emerging disciplinary formations.[26] However, where Foucault emphasizes the completeness of the rupture between the Classical and modern eras, the focus here will be on the messiness of that shift, highlighting the ways in which *Eureka* and the locations it inhabits were transitional, spaces neither thoroughly modern nor thoroughly Classical but manifestly in-between.

As historians of science have documented, the number and kinds of institutional sites that constituted the topography of science spread rapidly in the early nineteenth century. These included books, reviews, pamphlets, sermons, and lectures directed at the educated middle class or practicing scientists or both. Journals and magazines designed for the so-called general reader—the nonspecialist—frequently published review articles on scientific topics. In the American context, the line between specialist and nonspecialist audiences was not always clear, both because of the lack of institutional or government support for science and because the pursuit of natural philosophy was encouraged in all citizens as both useful and spiritually uplifting. The newly invented term "scientist" designated a professional identity still in formation.[27] *Eureka*'s position in this ambiguous topography can be traced through the text's first incarnation as a lecture, "The Cosmogony of the Universe." Poe delivered "The Universe" on February 3, 1848, at the Society Library in New York. That same winter in New York, American astronomer Ormsby MacKnight Mitchel, hoping to raise money for his observatory, addressed full houses at the Tabernacle music hall on the most up-to-date ideas in astronomy; and Scottish astronomer John Pringle Nichol gave a series of lectures at the Mercantile Library Association based on his *Views of the Architecture of the Heavens*, his explanation and defense of Pierre-Simon Laplace's nebular hypothesis (PL: 720).[28] These three lecturers had a range of qualifications. Mitchel and Nichol were already enormously popular figures, each of whom inhabited the murky zone between scientific popularizer and practitioner;[29] Poe, of course, was well known to New York audiences as a "literary histrio," though he did not have the star power of Mitchel or Nichol.[30] Yet the lectures of all three were reviewed in the popular press, the *Tribune* covering each of them (albeit giving far less space to Poe). As David N. Stamos has argued, there was nothing unusual about Poe giving this lecture; if anything, it attracted much less attention than Poe hoped. He aimed to raise funds to launch his own magazine, *The Stylus*, judging that a scientific subject would draw larger audiences than any of the literary-critical subjects he might otherwise have addressed. Nevertheless, ticket sales for "The Universe" fell disappointingly short of this goal.

Those who reviewed "The Universe" were quick to note its debt to the work of Sir William Herschel, to Laplace, and to Robert Chambers's *Vestiges of the Natural History of Creation* (PL: 723–724). Like *Eureka*, *Vestiges* drew on sound science to make what were considered wild speculations, in the case of *Vestiges*, about evolution. Published anonymously, *Vestiges* was hugely controversial, not only for its content but for the questions it raised within the scientific community about the extent to which nonpracticing scientists like Chambers (and by extension Poe) were entitled to speculate on such matters.[31] The scientific elite in England argued that *Vestiges* was not science at all; the text's popularity became an occasion for demarcating the territory of "legitimate" science as distinct from the popular.[32] Yet as Stamos argues (quoting James A. Secord), *Eureka*, like *Vestiges*, "was not a bungled attempt to produce 'professional' science, but a skilled intervention in some of the great public debates of the nineteenth century."[33] Moreover, this kind of speculation was the province of specialists and nonspecialists alike. Nichol, who had written a number of more conventional texts on astronomy, entertained broad, unanswerable questions in *Architecture*. The note to the third edition acknowledges this:

> I hope none of my readers will expect in this volume a general treatise upon Astronomy: I have not written systematically even upon that portion of the science whose results I intend to expose. It has been my sole aim to state what recent times have evolved concerning the vastness of the Universe, in language so plain, that whoever wills, may henceforth look at the Heavens not without something of the emotion which their greatness communicates to the accomplished Astronomer: and if, in performing this task, I sometimes abandon the style of strict discussion, substitute illustration for proof, or give speculation free wing, perhaps the scientific reader, who discovers the offence, will, if he approves of my plan, account it venial.[34]

That cultural figures as different (from a twenty-first-century point of view) as Nichol, Chambers, and Poe felt empowered in 1848 to speculate on origins, evolutionary or astronomical, and the relationship of matter to spirit is testimony to the porous nature of the subject position they jointly occupied. If their ideas made some science practitioners nervous, these same ideas were also eagerly consumed by an increasingly fractured reading public. Within a decade or two, this porousness would disappear. As Simon Schaffer has argued, the "end" of natural history and its replacement by science were marked by a shift of scientific knowledge into the exclusive domain of professional practitioners; as Richard Yeo argues, readership would likewise split along these lines.[35]

In the reviews of "The Universe" and *Eureka* that were published in nonspecialist contexts, Poe's authority to speak for science was unquestioned. While reviewers were far from unanimous in their evaluations of the truths of *Eureka*'s argument, they expressed little anxiety that Poe might be overstepping or that *Eureka* might be generically notable. Reviewers labeled Poe a poet but repeatedly compared him to scientific giants. One exalts his genius as having "not been equalled since the days of Sir Isaac Newton" (PL: 742). Another applauds "the application of rhetoric and imagination to science" and "the spirit of bold speculation and ideal thought" displayed by *Eureka*.[36] A third combines these two sentiments, noting that "the poet here enters upon profound speculations, shooting ahead of the Newtons, Laplaces, Herschels, and Nicholses [*sic*], in the solution of the great problems of the Universe."[37] This last review continues by suggesting that although *Eureka* is devoted to expounding an unproven theory, the theory is "by no means to be despised nor lacking in some of the higher elements of scientific probability."[38] The reviewer even coins a new term, a conjunction of "poetic" and "mathematical," to describe *Eureka*'s speculations: "poematical."[39] Poetry and science are thus not marked as opposed so much as complementary. The *Express* reported of "The Universe" that it "has all the completeness and oneness of plot required in a poem, with all the detail and accuracy required in a scientific lecture."[40] Along similar lines, the *Morning Express* proclaimed that *Eureka* would "create a most profound sensation among the literary *and* scientific classes all over the Union" (PL: 742, italics mine). And the *Weekly Universe* lavished praise on Poe as being "not merely a man of science—not merely a poet—not merely a man of letters. He is all combined; and perhaps he is something more" (PL: 719). Implicitly, the "something more" to which the review refers is genius, a quality not tied here to any specific discursive field.

The instability of identities culturally authorized to speak for science in the midst of the shift to the modern episteme is epitomized in the phrase used by the *Weekly Review* to describe Poe: "man of science." A holdover from the eighteenth century, the phrase "man of science," along with "natural philosopher," described practitioners of the relatively unified discursive field of natural science; however serious they were, many would be called "amateurs" today because they did not earn wages through their scientific pursuits. But by the time William Whewell addressed the British Association for the Advancement of Science in 1833, these generalizing terms seemed inadequate to describe the degree of professionalization and specialization that characterized his audience. In the face of the increasingly fragmented enterprise of science, now divided into branches such as botany, geology, zoology, chemistry, astronomy, and so on, "man of science" and "natural philosopher" lost currency and specificity. Whewell thus sought a term to replace them, one that might unify a field of practitioners with less and less in common, and one that also acknowledged the role of a handful of important female practitioners, particularly Mary Somerville. Whewell's friend and advisor Samuel Taylor Coleridge rejected "philosopher" on the grounds that it was "too wide and too lofty" for the members of the British Association and instead recommended "scientist."[41] As Yeo explains, this neologism did not immediately replace "man of science," but it did help consolidate what Whewell thought of as "the empire or commonwealth of science"—what Foucault would call the discursive domain of science—and through that consolidation, to widen the breach between "scientists" and "artists."[42] Whewell, who strove to define and promote science amid profound changes in its character, was careful to discuss the new term "scientist" in the popular press. For members of this press to call Poe a "man of science" was to use nearly outdated language. The term skirted the questions about professionalization central to the formation of the disciplinary field of science, implying that generalized knowledge was sufficient to be effective in the field.

Nonspecialist reviewers of *Eureka* would have agreed. In addition to being willing to consider imaginative scenarios as useful scientific and poetic contributions, they were uninterested in drawing boundaries between science and poetry, implicitly locating both within a domain of generalized knowledge that was nearing obsolescence. Their views, however, ran counter to those frequently articulated in the context of nineteenth-century debates about the inductive method, debates conducted by established scientific communities in public forums as part of an effort to secure science as a legitimate cultural activity.[43] Induction, a method almost universally attributed to Bacon and/or Newton, was fervently defended against its reviled counterpart, deduction, in the first half of the nineteenth century. *Eureka*'s early digression on this topic presents the stakes of the debate to the reader. Written in a tone thoroughly inconsistent with the rest of the text and roundly considered a failed attempt at humor (then and now), this digression appears in the overtly fictional form of a letter found in a bottle sent from the future. In thinly veiled satire, the letter gives a more or less accurate rendering of the two sides in the debate, mocking both. The writer of the letter marvels that "it is scarcely more than eight or nine hundred years ago since the metaphysicians first consented to relieve the people of the singular fancy that there exist *but two practicable roads to Truth*" (L1: 9). The text addresses these "two roads" chronologically. Deduction, the letter explains, was a form of a priori reasoning practiced by "Aries Tottle," "Tuclid," and "Cant." It begins from axioms "or self-evident truths," but herein lies the problem for the letter writer, who insists, "*no* truths are *self*-evident" (L1: 9).[44] By contrast, induction, or a posteriori reasoning, emphasized the observation of facts. Introduced by "Hog," it overturned deduction in the realm of empirical sciences. The text reserves its most potent salvos for those who extol induction, perhaps because of the method's popularity at the time. As Daniels notes, "It had become fashionable—indeed practically universal—since the Enlightenment to begin any scientific treatise with a paean to the 'Baconian method'" and to insist that it was the only "true" philosophy.[45] The letter writer excoriates proponents of induction as "one-idead, one-sided, and lame of leg," "wretchedly helpless . . . [and] miserably ignorant, in view of all the comprehensible objects of knowledge" (L1: 12). Those who practice induction were so chained to observing facts that "a virtual stop was put to all thinking, properly so-called. No man dared utter a truth for which he felt indebted to his soul alone" (L1: 10). In sum, "a more intolerant—a more intolerable set of bigots and tyrants never existed in the face of the earth" (L1: 11).

The strong defense of induction that is ridiculed by *Eureka* masks a clash within the broader culture between the procedures it stood for and a new epistemological order in which the term lost descriptive value.[46] As a method that rigidly emphasized the observation of visible phenomena, induction was of limited use in an era when scientific order and meaning hinged on the investigation of invisible laws and structures—what Foucault calls "the dark, concave, inner side of . . . visibility."[47] *Eureka* embraces this modern understanding of scientific methodology, making it central to the text's critique of induction. The letter writer notes that "diggers and pedlers [*sic*] of minute *facts*, for the most part in physical science," blind themselves to the notion that the "ultimate and only legitimate facts [are] called Law" and that the true path to discerning Law is through speculation (L1: 11). Foucault explains the disjunction between the ubiquitous defenses of induction and the methodologies actually practiced as a modern form of nostalgia for an unfragmented realm of natural science: "reflection on empirical methods of induction, and the effort made to provide them with both a philosophical foundation and a formal foundation" are attempts to reconstitute a divided epistemological field as unified.[48]

Eureka conjures a still more radical unity—not only among the sciences but also between science and art—through its celebration of the imagination. In its mobilization of the induction debate, the text repeatedly muddies the line between the domains of science and art that the debate helped construct, with intuition and imagination as the common denominator between them. This muddying begins in the relationship between the two voices in the text, the letter writer's and the narrator's. The induction debate is presented by the letter writer. Presumably not a specialized practitioner of science, the correspondent speaks with the authority of hindsight and common sense when commenting on induction/deduction: "I do assure you most positively . . . that I represent these matters fairly; and you can easily understand how restrictions so absurd on their very face must have operated, in those days, to retard the progress of true Science" (L1: 10). The notion that any reasonable person would "easily understand" the folly of both sides in the induction debates, positions that are "absurd on their very face," is articulated from within a realm signaled by *Eureka* as fiction. Aside from the narrator, the letter writer is *Eureka*'s only speaking character; the letter, dated 2848 and full of bad puns, calls attention to its own and its author's fictionality. But *Eureka*'s ridiculing of deduction and induction and its championing of speculation are not contained within the fictional letter; they spill over into the rest of the text and are taken up by a narrator whose voice is profoundly allied with scientific mastery. He decries induction, elaborating and championing imagination, intuition, guesswork, and speculation. In their joint defense of the imagination and its corollaries, the letter writer and narrator—the text's voices of literature and science, respectively—join in a single chorus to endorse these processes as collectively constituting the widest path to truth. In *Eureka*, imagination and intuition are the shared territory of science and literature.

Although *Eureka* draws its examples of the power of imagination and speculation from within the realm of science, it refers these activities back to a generalized domain of knowledge and denies science any monopoly over genius. Both the letter writer and narrator enlist a romantic commonplace, one articulated by Schelling and Coleridge (among others), in which "the imaginative Kepler" is contrasted with "the patient and mathematical Newton" (L1: 79).[49] Kepler theorized the "immortal laws" of gravity and thus laid the groundwork for Newton to demonstrate them. Theorization is necessary and appropriate because great laws such as Newtonian gravity, though they account for certain phenomena, cannot be directly proven: "The Newtonian Gravity—a law of Nature" is a phenomenon "of which neither the principle nor the *modus operandi* of the principle, has ever yet been traced by human analysis—a law, in short, which, neither in its detail nor its generality, has been found susceptible of explanation *at all*" (L1: 49). The slow, plodding methods of induction could never alone lead to the conceptualization of gravity as its existence is "*pure* hypothesis" (L1: 49). What is required for science to advance, as "all History will show," are the "seemingly intuitive *leaps*" exemplified by Kepler's and Laplace's hypotheses (L1: 10).[50] Yet the text asserts that Kepler and Laplace exemplify "generally-educated men of ardent imagination" (L1: 15).[51] In ascribing scientific breakthroughs to those armed primarily with passionate imaginations, *Eureka* takes profound scientific insights out of the hands of those specifically trained in the scientific method of induction. In contrast to induction and deduction, neither "intuition" nor "imagination" constitutes a method per se—having no set of clear, repeatable procedures, they cannot be taught. Instead, both are the innate endowments of a few fortunate individuals, those with a wide scope of imagination. Through this assertion, *Eureka* profoundly resists the most central aspects of discipline formation in early nineteenth-century science, which centered on articulations of the methods and divisions of labor through which scientific knowledge was produced.[52]

Eureka's desire to unlink genius from any particular discipline comes further into focus when considered in relation to the shifting discursive status of genius in the eighteenth and early nineteenth centuries. Whereas in the late eighteenth century, the "genius" in natural philosophy was understood to be a revolutionary or fanatic—an implicitly dangerous character—the romantic literary genius was a celebrated figure. Whether poet or novelist, the romantic genius drew on inspiration and imagination to perform unreproducible feats of originality, creating from nothing "something utterly new, unprecedented."[53] But in the early nineteenth century, the figure of the scientific genius began to take on the cachet of the literary genius as historiographies of science increasingly attributed "progress" to the singular achievements of individuals, accomplished at discrete points in time and space.[54] As Yeo demonstrates, along with the claim of a unique scientific method (induction), the articulation of concepts such as "philosopher," "discovery," and "genius" helped shore up the legitimacy of the scientific enterprise and establish the scientific domain as culturally ascendant.[55] In insisting that Kepler and Laplace represent the power of "ardent imagination" rather than specialized training, *Eureka* acknowledges the cultural capital of "the genius," countering and reversing that figure's past movement from the literary to the scientific domain. *Eureka* wrests genius and the imagination back for literature.

In emphasizing the role of imagination and intuition in the production of scientific knowledge, *Eureka* powerfully registers and responds to the threat of the ascendency of science. The text emphasizes that although various branches of science provide salient examples of the triumphs of intuition and imagination, they can no more claim these modes as exclusive to their domain than they can claim a monopoly on genius. In *Eureka*, scientific ideas formulated through speculation are inherently elevated above the realm of mere science. Kepler's guesses—"Yes!—these vital laws Kepler *guessed*—that is to say, he *imagined* them"—open the door to "the nebulous kingdom of Metaphysics" (L1: 15). This nebulous kingdom cannot be reached via induction or deduction. If Kepler were asked whether he attained such heights through either of these routes, he would respond, " 'I know nothing about *routes*—but I *do* know the machinery of the Universe. Here it is. I grasped it with *my soul*—I reached it through mere dint of *intuition*' " (L1: 15). The soul is the seat of imagination and intuition, which in turn are uniquely able to divine the truth. Laplace likewise owed his greatest triumph—his nebular hypothesis—to his "miraculous" instinct, which "led him, blindfolded, through the labyrinth of Error, into one of the most luminous and stupendous temples of Truth" (L1: 70). The temples of Truth, edifices in the nebulous kingdom of Metaphysics, are accessed by the soul through the imagination and intuition. These are acknowledged domains of poetry and philosophy; if the ultimate, metaphysical truths reveal themselves *only* to the soul and not through reason, poets are more likely to grasp them than scientists. The narrator insists on this point when he presents *Eureka* as "an Art-Product alone . . . or, if I be not urging too lofty a claim, as a Poem" (L1: 5) and announces that he aims "less at physical than at metaphysical order" in "the conduct of this Discourse" (L1: 78).

If *Eureka* dwells in the domain of science, then, it does so less to grant authority to scientific discourse than to appropriate that authority for literature, and for the type of genius that properly belongs to the literary domain. Of its 266 paragraphs, as few as a dozen cut the cord of relation to scientific sources to reach into the nebulous kingdom of metaphysics. The narrator lingers within the discourses of science, establishing his mastery of them as the foundation from which he will rise to attain the loftier heights of poetic, metaphysical speculation. To borrow the text's metaphor, the narrator's scientific knowledge provides the stable stepping stones from which he takes his leaps of poetic genius. His most conspicuous demonstrations of scientific mastery, found in his competitive stance toward figures highly respected and even revered in the early nineteenth century, are so many stepping stones. Newton, Leibniz, Nichol, Herschel, Laplace: the narrator identifies the shortcomings of character or intellect of all of these thinkers, finding them to come up short. In Laplace's case, his mistakes, though lamentable, also make him a particularly salient example of genius. His nebular hypothesis was based on a series of "unwarranted assumption[s]" that ought to have led him astray, but his theory attained the status of truth *despite* being unsupported by mere scientific facts (L1: 70).[56] When, "with due humility," the narrator identifies and transcends the mistakes of the greatest minds in science, he showcases a particularly rare form of genius—one equally comfortable with complex scientific reasoning and metaphysical speculation and imagination (L1: 95).

In his adeptness in both science and philosophy, the narrator invokes a form of imagination that, according to Maimon, was newly conceptualized in the shift to the modern episteme, when the imagination was understood as "a synthetic faculty that fuses together the empirical and transcendental."[57] Such an integration of empirical and transcendental, of knowledge and experience is, finally, what *Eureka* seeks to accomplish. As Jerome McGann argues, *Eureka* does not so much articulate a theory of the imagination as enact or perform it.[58] The text takes readers through a series of imaginative leaps by joining intellectual arguments with affective experience. As its basic premise, then, *Eureka* discounts the notion of "proof," favoring instead the production of affective responses in readers. Announcing that "there is, in this world at least, *no such thing* as demonstration" (L1: 7), the narrator intends to "*prove* nothing. . . . I design but to suggest—and to *convince* through the suggestion" (L1: 35).

Despite the manifest confusions of the text for contemporary readers, the narrator can be believed when he claims that "distinctness—intelligibility, at all points, is a primary feature in my general design" (L1: 17). "Intelligibility" here rests not on abstract knowledge or reasoning but on their synthesis with experience and imagination. In his own exemplary case, understanding for the narrator is an amalgam of subjective truth and empirical observation: "Unity, as I have explained it, is a truth—I feel it. Diffusion is a truth—I see it. Radiation, by which alone these two truths are reconciled, is a consequent truth—I perceive it" (L1: 90). By contrast, abstractions "are not practically tangible" and therefore can "convey no precise ideas" until they are joined with feeling (L1: 80). One way "to know—to feel" (L1: 81) an abstraction, then, is through comparison with or translation into tangibles (such as cannonballs and peas), which can be set before "the eye of mind" (L1: 70). Cannonballs and peas, however, are of limited use in visualizing a universe whose workings are characterized variously by the narrator as "ineffable" (L1: 32), "unfathomable" (L1: 100), "unutterably vast" (L1: 86), "unspeakably numerous and complex" (L1: 88), and "unspeakably sublime" (L1: 90)—as an "infinite sublimity endlessly multiplied by the infinitely sublime" (L1: 89).[59] Nor are physical comparisons helpful for comprehending the apparent contradictions that physical laws obey and even embody.[60] To illuminate (but not resolve) epistemological uncertainties, *Eureka* presents paradoxical concepts so elusive as to be beyond the power of language to express. The word *infinity*, for instance, is but "the *thought of a thought*," which "stands for the possible attempt at an impossible conception" (L1: 18, 17). Yet concepts that are "beyond the grasp of the imagination" (L1: 32) can nevertheless be made palpable to it.[61] The mind is attracted to ideas such as infinity like a magnet to a lodestone, "fondl[ing]" it "with a passionate fervor" (L1: 77). This "impossible conception," this "phantom of an idea," can be felt, grasped sensuously and even sensually, though it cannot be understood epistemologically (L1: 77).

Through the mathematical and physical concept of infinity, the narrator invokes a form of thinking at one remove from language and representation and so tests the imagination; with the notion of the force of attraction—a natural law—he places knowledge at a further remove, suggesting that attraction can only be comprehended through "unthoughtlike thoughts—soul-reveries rather than conclusions or even considerations of the intellect" (L1: 33). Even more than infinity, attraction is knowable only through intuition. Yet these two examples present the inaccessibility of abstract knowledge in its most extreme forms. Real comprehension of any abstraction, including simple ones such as distance and speed, similarly requires a bridge to span the gap between rational and experiential understanding—the smaller acts of imagination that Coleridge ascribes to any perceptual act. The narrator's discursive method is designed to provide that bridge. It proceeds "from point to point . . . in the hope of thus the better keeping unbroken that chain of *graduated impression* by which alone the intellect of Man can expect to encompass the grandeurs of which I speak, and, in their majestic totality, to comprehend them" (L1: 78). The text supplies the steps that move the reader from perception through imagination to affective understanding. One of the clearest examples of this method, in which the imagination plays a mediating role, is the text's illustration of "unutterable velocity."

The narrator first asks readers to conjure an imaginary figure that witnesses this velocity, enjoining them to "task our imagination in picturing the capacities of an angel" (L1: 82).[62] Having pictured the angel and its perceptual abilities, the narrator asks readers to imagine this being's response to unimaginable wonders: "now *can* we . . . fashion for ourselves any conception so distinct of this ideal being's spiritual exaltation, as *that* involved in the supposition that, even by this immeasurable mass of matter, whirled immediately before his eyes, with a velocity so unutterable, he—an angel— . . . is not at once struck into nothingness and overwhelmed?" (L1: 82). The rhetorical answer is "no"; and if the angel's response cannot be fully comprehended, how much less can that of readers? To appreciate a velocity of such magnitude, readers must agree to be overpowered by it; it "cannot well be said to *startle* the mind:—it palsies and appals it" (L1: 82). Only through imaginative and affective experiences of the "unspeakably sublime" (L1: 90) will the most basic characteristics of the universe become intelligible.

Through the imagination, *Eureka* animates the known, the abstract, and the paradoxical, and so paves the way toward its own metaphysical conclusions. With only words as its admittedly inadequate tools, the text creates an unprecedented experience—a sublime understanding of what had previously been incomprehensible. This joining of empirical knowledge with transcendental experience has for many readers been extraordinarily successful. French poet Paul Valéry, for instance, reflected that "*Eureka* made me feel some of [the] passion" of scientific discovery (quoted in L1: xii). The text designates its technique—the stimulation of the passionate imagination—as explicitly literary through an analogy between the "the construction of *plot* . . . in fictitious literature" and "the plots of God" (L1: 89). The difference between these plots is merely one of degree; the most perfect product of original creation, the universe, is one in which (unlike those of human creators) cause and effect are so inextricably bound to each other that they cannot be distinguished. Through a similar analogy, the narrator assures readers of "the poetical essence of the Universe . . . which, in the supremeness of its symmetry, is but the most sublime of poems" (L1: 96). Like the original act, "or more properly the *conception*, of Creation" (L1: 23), the poetic imagination as exercised in *Eureka* calls experience into being for readers, enabling them to feel "the most sublime of poems."

Eureka's claim to the status of poetry and its address "to those who feel rather than to those who think" are neither an afterthought nor a hoax. They are speech acts that subordinate the authority of scientific knowledge to the poetic imagination rather than vice versa. Through these acts, *Eureka* distinguishes itself from texts such as Nichol's or Chambers's, not so much on the basis of content as on these texts' self-positioning. Likewise, in articulating the language of science in the service of the poetic imagination, *Eureka* distinguishes itself from poetical works such as those in the genre known as "philosophical poetry." Exemplified by Erasmus Darwin's two-volume *Economy of Vegetation* and *Loves of Plants* (1791), philosophical poems tended to personify nature for the amusement and education of readers without foregrounding or calling into question their own discursive registers.[63] Emerging from a different archaeological subsoil, *Eureka* bears little resemblance to such poems. Indeed, though aligned with seismic ruptures in the episteme, *Eureka* has few counterparts. Belated in its location of genius in the literary realm and its refusal to acknowledge science's new claims on knowledge, *Eureka* was also perfectly current in its emphasis on law over fact and its deployment of what it labels "imagination" to integrate knowledge and experience. Though a symptom of the modern reorganization of literature and science into separate discursive formations, *Eureka* remains—like its description of the speed of light—"undimmed in its paradoxical glory" (L1: 86).

NOTES

1. Michel Foucault, *The Archaeology of Knowledge and Discourse on Language*, trans. A. M. Sheridan Smith (New York: Harper and Row, 1972), 209.
2. Egaeus reflects, "The realities of the world affected me as visions, and visions only, while the wild ideas of the land of dreams became . . . my every-day existence . . . solely in itself" (M 2: 210).
3. Jonathan Elmer, *Reading at the Social Limit: Affect, Mass Culture, and Edgar Allan Poe* (Stanford, CA: Stanford University Press, 1995), 222.
4. Joan Dayan, *Fables of Mind: An Inquiry into Poe's Fiction* (Oxford: Oxford University Press, 1987), 13. For a different understanding of the confusions of the text, see W. C. Harris, "Edgar Allan Poe's *Eureka* and the Poetics of Constitution," *American Literary History* 12, no. 1–2 (Spring/Summer 2000): 1–40. Harris reads *Eureka*'s "generic ambivalence" as a more fundamental ambivalence about America as "a documentary state"—a state founded in textual assertions of unity and equality in the face of social and representational diversity and hierarchy (the "federal enigma" of *e pluribus unum*) (2–3). On *Eureka*'s aggressive regionalism in the face of rhetoric of national unity, see Jennifer Rae Greeson, "Poe's 1848: *Eureka*, the Southern Margin, and the Expanding [U]niverse of [S]tars," in *Poe and the Remapping of Antebellum Print Culture*, edited by J. Gerald Kennedy and Jerome McGann (Baton Rouge: Louisiana State University Press, 2012), 123–140.
5. Until this time, Harold Beaver observes, the term "natural philosopher" might have equally described astronomer Sir William Herschel and Poe. See Beaver, Introduction to *The Science Fiction of Edgar Allan Poe*, by Edgar Allan Poe, ed. Harold Beaver (New York: Penguin Books, 1976), ix. By the time William Whewell coined the term "scientist" in 1833, the domains of literature and science had begun to grow apart. According to Raymond Williams, in this era, "literary" no longer meant "literate," and literature emerged as an aesthetic/market category distinct from other forms of publication. See Raymond Williams, *Keywords: A Vocabulary of Culture and Society* (New York: Oxford University Press, 1985), 183–188. And as Richard Yeo has noted, the early nineteenth century was when "nature" ceased to be equally the province of literature and science, and literature began to cede to science its cultural and discursive authority over that terrain. See Richard Yeo, *Defining Science: William Whewell, Natural Knowledge, and Public Debate in Early Victorian Britain* (Cambridge: Cambridge University Press, 1993). Notably, the losing battle for that authority continues into the twenty-first century, albeit in different institutional settings, in the form of the "crisis" of the humanities.
6. For another discussion of *Eureka* in relation to Foucault's analysis of discourse formation, see John Limon, *The Place of Fiction in the Time of Science: A Disciplinary History of American Writing* (Cambridge: Cambridge University Press, 1990).

7. Bernard Lightman, *Victorian Popularizers of Science: Designing Nature for New Audiences* (Chicago: University of Chicago Press, 2010), 5. On the shifting scientific terrain, see also Fred Nadis, *Wonder Shows: Performing Science, Magic, and Religion in America* (New Brunswick, NJ: Rutgers University Press, 2005); Yeo, *Defining Science*; James A. Secord, *Victorian Sensation: The Extraordinary Publication, Reception, and Secret Authorship of Vestiges of the Natural History of Creation* (Chicago: University of Chicago Press, 2000); James A. Secord, *Visions of Science: Books and Readers at the Dawn of the Victorian Age* (Chicago: University of Chicago Press, 2014). On the shifting literary terrain, see Terence Whalen, *Edgar Allan Poe and the Masses: The Political Economy of Literature in Antebellum America* (Princeton, NJ: Princeton University Press, 1999); Meredith McGill, *American Literature and the Culture of Reprinting, 1834–53* (Philadelphia: University of Pennsylvania Press, 2003); and the important collection edited by J. Gerald Kennedy and Jerome McGann, *Poe and the Remapping of Antebellum Print Culture* (Baton Rouge: Louisiana State University Press, 2012), especially Kennedy's "Introduction," 1–10. Though seldom considered alongside each other, these two scholarly trajectories overlap in the realm of periodical publishing. Nonspecialist journals published scientific articles alongside fiction, poetry, and political commentary both in the United States and England. As McGill notes, many of the same pieces appeared on both sides of the Atlantic due to the absence of international copyright laws in the United States. McGill views this absence as contributing to the distinctly regional nature of antebellum print culture. I argue elsewhere that this absence contributed to the transnational nature of scientific discourse in that same period.
8. Vered Maimon, *Singular Images, Failed Copies: William Henry Fox Talbot and the Early Photograph* (Minneapolis: University of Minnesota Press, 2015), xi.
9. Michel Foucault, *The Order of Things: An Archaeology of the Human Sciences* (New York: Vintage, 1994).
10. Foucault, *Order of Things*, 245.
11. Yeo, *Defining Science*, 35; Simon Schaffer, "Scientific Discoveries and the End of Natural Philosophy," *Social Studies of Science* 16, no. 3 (August 1986): 387–420; Thomas S. Kuhn, "Mathematical versus Experimental Traditions in the Development of Physical Science," *Journal of Interdisciplinary History* 7 (1976): 1–31; Enrico Belloni, *A World on Paper: Studies in the Second Scientific Revolution*, trans. Mirella Giacconi and Riccardo Giaccone (Cambridge, MA: MIT Press, 1980). At the same time, the very notion of "revolutions" in science has been disputed almost since the publication of Thomas Kuhn's *Structure of Scientific Revolutions* in 1962.
12. Recent discussions of Poe's interest in the second scientific revolution include John Tresch, "'Matter No More': Edgar Allan Poe and the Paradoxes of Materialism," *Critical Inquiry* 42, no. 4 (Summer 2016): 865–898; and David N. Stamos, *Edgar Allan Poe, Eureka, and Scientific Imagination* (Albany, NY: SUNY Press, 2017). Regarding *The Conchologist's First Book*, Stamos focuses on the suspicions of plagiarism that arose around the text's debt to Cuvier (133–145). This debt is especially interesting in a Foucaultian context, for according to Foucault, it was Cuvier who toppled the reliance of Buffon and Linnaeus on classifications of the visible, replacing it with a new focus on anatomy and function (*Order of Things*, 137–138).
13. Foucault, *Order of Things*, xx.
14. Foucault, *Order of Things*, 208.
15. Foucault, *Order of Things*, 245.
16. Foucault, *Order of Things*, 296.

17. Foucault, *Order of Things*, 299.
18. Foucault, *Order of Things*, 300.
19. Foucault, *Order of Things*, 242. With the destruction of these systems of order, the logic that linked representations to things and also to each other (e.g., how one word is related to its referent and also to another word) was also destroyed. To query these broken linkages, to theorize the relationship of representations to each other, required an approach that operated somewhere other than "on the level of representation" itself (241).
20. Foucault, *Order of Things*, 245.
21. Maimon, *Singular Images, Failed Copies*, 39–110.
22. Foucault, *Archaeology of Knowledge and Discourse on Language*, 50.
23. Foucault, *Archaeology of Knowledge and Discourse on Language*, 51.
24. The answers to the questions "who is speaking" and from what institutional sites is this speech legitimated must also be considered alongside the "repeatable materiality" that helps constitute these sites, that is, by the material practices—as diverse as publishing and laboratory techniques—apart from which a discursive formation cannot exist (Foucault, *Archaeology of Knowledge and Discourse on Language*, 102).
25. Foucault, *Archaeology of Knowledge and Discourse on Language*, 109.
26. Foucault, *Archaeology of Knowledge and Discourse on Language*, 120. For an overview of the place of *Eureka* in Poe scholarship, see Scott Peeples, *The Afterlife of Edgar Allan Poe* (Rochester, NY: Camden House, 2004), 50, 68, 74–83, 94. Texts that discuss and evaluate *Eureka*'s science include Arthur Hobson Quinn, *Edgar Allan Poe: A Critical Biography* (New York: Appleton-Century, 1941), 547–557; Frederick William Conner, *Cosmic Optimism: A Study of the Interpretation of Evolution by American Poets* (Gainesville: University of Florida Press, 1949), 67–91; Carol Hopkins Maddison, "Poe's *Eureka*," *Texas Studies in Literature and Language* 2, no. 3 (Fall 1960): 350–367; Stamos, *Edgar Allan Poe*, (Albany, NY: SUNY Press, 2017), 185–237. Susan Welsh usefully discusses the various scientific meanings and uses of "analogy" as a method in "The Value of Analogical Evidence: Poe's 'Eureka' in the Context of a Scientific Debate," *Modern Language Studies* 21, no. 4 (Autumn 1991): 3–15.
27. The institutional history of science in the United States properly begins in 1848, the year of *Eureka*'s publication, with the formation of the American Association for the Advancement of Science. See Sally Gregory Kohlstedt, *The Formation of the American Scientific Community: The American Association for the Advancement of Science, 1848–1860* (Urbana: University of Illinois Press, 1976). On the rise of the professional scientist in the United States and the constitution of the American readership of scientific subjects, see George H. Daniels, *American Science in the Age of Jackson* (Tuscaloosa: University of Alabama Press, 1994). See also Daniels, "The Process of Professionalization in American Science: The Emergent Period, 1820–1860," and Robert E. Kohler, "The Ph.D. Machine: Building on the Collegiate Base," in *The Scientific Enterprise in America: Readings from Isis*, ed. Ronald L. Numbers and Charles E. Rosenberg (Chicago: University of Chicago Press, 1996), 21–36 and 98–122. In the British context, see Yeo, *Defining Science*, especially chapters 1–4.
28. See also Robert J. Scholnick, "*Eureka* in Context: Poe, the Newspaper, the Lyceum, and Cosmic Science," in *Poe Writing/Writing Poe*, ed. Richard Kopley and Jana Argersinger (New York: AMS, 2013), 31–50. Scholnick makes a strong case for placing "The Universe" in the context of Mitchel's and Nichol's lectures, as does Stamos in *Edgar Allan Poe*. See also Nadis, *Wonder Shows*, on the performance of science through lectures and spectacles (9–11).

29. On the rise "popularizers" generally, see Lightman, *Victorian Popularizers*; Daniels, *American Science in the Age of Jackson*. On the difficulty of distinguishing popularizers from practitioners in this period, see Yeo, *Defining Science*, especially 109–115. According to Ronald Numbers, Mitchel, who was a practicing astronomer, was "the period's most successful lecturer on scientific topics" (quoted in Scholnick, "*Eureka* in Context," 32). Nichol's *Views of the Architecture of the Heavens* enjoyed international celebrity. Published as "A Series of Letters to a Lady," *Architecture* deviated from the standard of a general treatise on astronomy as, for example, one might find in Sir John F. W. Herschel, *A Treatise on Astronomy* (1833), or Mary Somerville, *On the Connexion of the Physical Sciences* (1834), or even in Nichol's other more conventional publications such as *The Phenomena and Order of the Solar System* (1838), *Manual of Practical Astronomy* (1838), or *The Stellar Universe: Views of Its Arrangements, Motions, and Evolutions* (1848).
30. Two measures of that star power: when Poe revised "The Universe" into *Eureka*, he incorporated some of Mitchel's findings—which he then disputed—into the text; and Nichol's *Architecture* was mostly likely the source of the extended discussions of Laplace's nebular hypothesis in both "The Universe" and *Eureka*.
31. See Secord, *Victorian Sensation*, 448–455; Yeo, *Defining Science*, 113–114; and Yeo, "Science and Intellectual Authority in Mid-Nineteenth-Century Britain: Robert Chambers and *Vestiges of the Natural History of Creation*," *Victorian Studies* (Autumn 1984): 5–31.
32. See Yeo, *Defining Science*, 44–48; Schaffer, in "Scientific Discoveries and the End of Natural Philosophy," suggests that the shift from "natural philosophy" to science is characterized by a shift from the location of knowledge in the reading public to practitioners (406–413). That is, the end of natural philosophy was signified by the emergence of a trained cadre of research scientists. The separation of audience from practitioners is what marks this disciplinary formation.
33. Quoted in Stamos, *Edgar Allan Poe*, 157.
34. J. P. Nichol, *Views of the Architecture of the Heavens: In a Series of Letters to a Lady*, 3rd ed. (Edinburgh: William Tate; London: Simpkin, Marshall, and Co.; Dublin: John Cumming, 1839), vii–viii, https://babel.hathitrust.org/cgi/pt?id=mdp.39015074633499;view=1up;seq=15. *Architecture* is widely regarded to be one of the important source texts for *Eureka*. Notably, one of *Eureka*'s reviewers also calls it venial. See PL: 743.
35. Schaffer, "Scientific Discoveries and the End of Natural Philosophy"; see also Yeo, *Defining Science*, 40–43.
36. "'Mr. Poe's *Eureka*', *Home Journal*, August 1848," in *Edgar Allan Poe: The Critical Heritage*, ed. I. M. Walker (London: Routledge and Kegan Paul, 1986), 287. For a useful overview of *Eureka*'s reception, see Burton R. Pollin, "Contemporary Reviews of *Eureka*, a checklist," in *Poe as Literary Cosmologer: Studies on Eureka: A Symposium*, ed. Richard P. Benton (Hartford, CT: Transcendental Books, 1975), 26–30.
37. "Unsigned review in the *New Church Repository, and Monthly Review*, August 1848," in *Edgar Allan Poe: The Critical Heritage*, ed. I. M. Walker, 289.
38. "Unsigned review," 289.
39. The full sentence reads, "He calls his work a poem, perhaps because, with Madame De Stael, he regards the Universe itself as more like a poem than a machine, and therefore to be treated poematically." "Unsigned review," 289.
40. *Express* (February 4, 1848), quoted in *The Science Fiction of Edgar Allan Poe*, ed. Beaver, 396.
41. Quoted in Yeo, *Defining Science*, 110.
42. Quoted in Yeo, *Defining Science*, 111.

43. As Yeo explains, when the union between natural philosophy and theology, called "natural theology," began to dissolve, science was in danger of losing its cultural legitimacy. Many of the phenomena discussed here, including the naming of "scientists" and the defense of the inductive, must be understood in this context, which Yeo dates as taking shape well before Darwinian debates took center stage and pushed science and theology still further apart (*Defining Science*, 28–32).
44. See W. C. Harris, "Edgar Allan Poe's *Eureka* and the Poetics of Constitution," for another reading of this language.
45. Daniels, *American Science in the Age of Jackson*, 63.
46. For Yeo, the obsessive evocation of induction as the only proper method of science can be understood as part of a strategy to consolidate and differentiate the field of science from other material and discursive practices. As did the term "scientist," the notion that all scholars of science, no matter their area of specialization, adhered to the same inductive methodology served at least as much to segregate science as a distinct discursive domain as it did to articulate a shared, consistent methodology. See Yeo, *Defining Science*, 92–99, 120–124. In Foucaultian terms, the induction/deduction debates were an articulation of the material methods of science, and thus were necessary for the formation of a distinct discursive domain. On the material practices that constitute "statements," see Foucault, *Archaeology of Knowledge and Discourse on Language*, 100–105 and 115.
47. Foucault, *Order of Things*, 243.
48. Foucault, *Order of Things*, 246.
49. This same logic is repeated later in the text through a comparison of Laplace and Comte. Laplace articulates the nebular hypothesis and Comte confirms "the validity" of the hypothesis by giving it mathematical accuracy (L1: 66). On Coleridge, Schelling, and the contrast between Kepler and Newton, see Simon Schaffer, "Genius in Romantic Natural Philosophy," in *Romanticism and the Sciences*, ed. Andrew Cunningham and Nicholas Jardine (Cambridge: Cambridge University Press, 1990), 82–98.
50. See Jerome McGann's disussion of the significance of the leap in *The Poet Edgar Allan Poe: Alien Angel* (Cambridge, MA: Harvard University Press, 2014), 102 and 107–108. See also Barton Levi St. Armand, "'Seemingly Intuitive Leaps': Belief and Unbelief in *Eureka*," in *Poe as Literary Cosmologer*, ed. Richard P. Benton, 4–15; and David Ketterer, *The Rationale of Deception in Poe* (Baton Rouge: Louisiana State University Press, 1979).
51. The text is inconsistent in its treatment of Laplace. Here, he appears as a theorizer, along with Kepler. Later, he is represented as a mere mathematician, along with Newton (L1: 36). Later still, he is reinstated as a theorist (L1: 70). However, the central opposition between the mathematician as unable to transcend the physical world and the genius as imaginative and intuitive does not change.
52. On genius in relation to discovery and the division of scientific labor, see Schaffer, "Genius in Romantic Natural Philosophy"; and Schaffer, "Scientific Discoveries and the End of Natural Philosophy."
53. J. Gerald Kennedy, "Inventing the Literati: Poe's Remapping of Antebellum Print Culture," in *Poe and the Remapping of Antebellum Print Culture*, ed. Kennedy and McGann, 14. Kennedy is quoting Martha Woodmansee, who locates the emergence of poet genius in the shift from Classical to romantic models of authorship. See Martha Woodmansee, "The Genius and the Copyright: Economic and Legal Conditions of the Emergence of the 'Author,'" *Eighteenth-Century Studies* 17, no. 4 (1984): 425–448. Ironically, two of the writers who best exemplified romantic genius, Wordsworth and Shelley, were among the

first to define science and literature in opposition to each other, imbuing poetry with a moral sense that would defend against the mechanistic thinking of science. The opposition grew in cultural acceptance, but with it came the loss of literature's cultural authority. See Schaffer, "Genius in Romantic Natural Philosophy."

54. For the emergence of the mutually informing concepts of genius and discovery in science, see especially Schaffer, "Genius in Romantic Natural Philosophy," and Schaffer, "Scientific Discoveries and the End of Natural Philosophy." See also Maimon, *Singular Images, Failed Copies* (27–28, 46–51, 60–62, 71–72), for discussions of scientific and literary genius. Notably, David Brewster and William Whewell wrote biographies that emphasized the contrast between Newton and Kepler.
55. Yeo points out that these strategies are all put into effect at a time (the first few decades of the nineteenth century) when science was still "a relatively insecure cultural activity" (*Defining Science*, 31). Daniels's analysis in *American Science in the Age of Jackson* of the persistent lack of funding, either institutional or governmental, supports an analogous sense of the insecurity of science in the American context through the 1840s. See also Daniels, "Process of Professionalization" and Kohler, "The Ph.D. Machine."
56. For example, Newton, "while boldly grasping the Law [of gravity] itself, shrank from the principle of the Law" (L1: 36). Likewise, Leibniz's imagination "was not sufficiently well-grown, or well-educated, to direct him aright" (L1: 36). Nichol mistakes geometrical axioms for ultimate principles, of which there can be only one, "the Volition of God" (L1: 35). Herschel is too timid to abandon the outdated "and utterly baseless notion . . . of the eternal stability of the Universe" (L1: 95).
57. Maimon, *Singular Images, Failed Copies*, 70.
58. McGann, *The Poet Edgar Allan Poe: Alien Angel.*
59. The list continues: "magnificent" (L1: 89),"stupendous" (L1: 82), "immeasurable" (L1: 82), "unutterable" (L1: 82), "unimaginable" (L1: 32, 100), and so on.
60. John Limon counts these instances in *Place of Fiction in the Time of Science*, 94.
61. *Eureka*'s single diagram is instructive in this regard. It illustrates the law that "the quantities of light received upon any given plane . . . will be diminished in the same proportion as the squares of the distances of the plane from the luminous body, are increased" (L1: 38). Simple geometrical relations such as this can be charted and made visible; by contrast, "unthoughtlike thoughts" cannot and therefore require the mediation of the imagination. The relative absence of illustrations in *Eureka* (the 1839 edition of *Vestiges* contains twenty-three plates, comprising twenty-five images) can be understood as reinforcing its commitment to the poetic rather than the graphic.
62. For another reading of the angel figure, see Betsy Erkkila, "Perverting the American Renaissance: Poe, Democracy, Political Theory," in *Poe and the Remapping of Antebellum Print Culture*, ed. Kennedy and McGann, 77–100.
63. See Pat Rogers, "Poems on Science and Philosophy," in *The Oxford Handbook of British Poetry, 1660–1800*, ed. Jack Lynch (Oxford: Oxford University Press, 2016), http://www.oxfordhandbooks.com/view/10.1093/oxfordhb/9780199600809.001.0001/oxfordhb-9780199600809-e-20.

Bibliography

Beaver, Harold, ed. *The Science Fiction of Edgar Allan Poe*. New York: Penguin Books, 1976.

Dayan, Joan. *Fables of Mind: An Inquiry into Poe's Fiction*. Oxford: Oxford University Press, 1987.

Elmer, Jonathan. *Reading at the Social Limit: Affect, Mass Culture, and Edgar Allan Poe.* Stanford, CA: Stanford University Press, 1995.

Erkkila, Betsy. "Perverting the American Renaissance: Poe, Democracy, Political Theory." In *Poe and the Remapping of Antebellum Print Culture*, edited by J. Gerald Kennedy and Jerome McGann, 77–100. Baton Rouge: Louisiana State University Press, 2012.

Greeson, Jennifer Rae. "Poe's 1848: *Eureka*, the Southern Margin, and the Expanding [U]niverse of [S]tars." In *Poe and the Remapping of Antebellum Print Culture*, edited by J. Gerald Kennedy and Jerome McGann, 123–140. Baton Rouge: Louisiana State University Press, 2012.

Kennedy, J. Gerald. Introduction to *Poe and the Remapping of Antebellum Print Culture*, edited by J. Gerald Kennedy and Jerome McGann, 1–10. Baton Rouge: Louisiana State University Press, 2012.

Levine, Stuart, and Susan F. Levine. *Introduction to Eureka.* Edited by Stuart Levine and Susan F. Levine, xi–xxxiv. Urbana: University of Illinois Press, 2004.

Limon, John. *The Place of Fiction in the Time of Science: A Disciplinary History of American Writing.* Cambridge: Cambridge University Press, 1990.

McGann, Jerome. *The Poet Edgar Allan Poe: Alien Angel.* Cambridge, MA: Harvard University Press, 2014.

Scholnick, Robert J. "*Eureka* in Context: Poe, the Newspaper, the Lyceum, and Cosmic Science" In *Poe Writing/Writing Poe*, edited by Richard Kopley and Jana Argersinger, 31–50. New York: AMS, 2013.

Welsh, Susan. "The Value of Analogical Evidence: Poe's 'Eureka' in the Context of a Scientific Debate." *Modern Language Studies* 21, no. 4 (Autumn 1991): 3–15.

CHAPTER 26

POE THE CRITIC

The Aesthetics of the "Tomahawk" Review

PAUL HURH

In his notes for *The Living Writers of America*, a collection of literary criticism unfinished at the time of his death, Poe indicated his wish to convey "a full view of Literature, a desideratum—material scattered about and contradictory—conventional manner of criticism inadequate to convey distinct impression—analyze it—instance it—quiz it."[1] Had he completed it, *The Living Writers of America* would have offered students of Poe a material testament to his self-regard as a literary critic. For Poe intended the volume to cement his reputation as a professional, lifelong, critic: "have all my life dealt in criticism—opinion of my contemporaries—refer to Appendix."[2] Yet, though Poe recognized that his reputation was based upon his criticism, particularly his notoriously vicious reviews of current books, those reviews responsible for that reputation are a relatively unknown aspect of Poe's work in popular regard today.

Among American literary scholars, Poe's criticism is better known. Throughout the twentieth century, scholars read Poe's magazine criticism for clues to Poe's biography and literary theory.[3] Combatting the romanticized myth of Poe as primarily a *poète maudit*, Quinn's biography in 1941 presented Poe as a professional journalist. Two years later, Edmund Wilson praised Poe's criticism as "our only first-rate classical prose of this period."[4] This mid-century interest in Poe's criticism informed three full-length studies that found in Poe's reviews related, if somewhat incongruous, projects: an aesthetic theory catered to mass culture (Robert D. Jacobs), a militant stand for art against the trend of mass culture (Sidney P. Moss), or the tension between elite culture and mass civilization in a democratizing society (Michael Allen).[5] Though not uniform in their conclusions, these studies shared the sense of Poe's reviews as crucial to understanding how his theory of art responded, whether positively, negatively, or ambivalently, to popular mass culture.[6]

More recently, the new historicist turn to reading Poe as a professional magazinist embedded within the rapid expansion of periodical publishing in the 1830s and 40s has brought renewed attention to Poe's reviewing practices. In this context, Poe's reviews offer insight into the entanglements of literary judgment in a print capitalist environment. His strained relation to specific literary concerns of the moment—puffing, plagiarism, libel, nationalism—thus enables us to read his oftentimes strident claims of critical independence as an assumed stance, not divorced from the economics and politics of his time, but deeply implicated within it.[7] Poe's criticism, from this point of view, documents the new pressures on literary production exerted by the shifts in mass media and the formation of popular culture. As Terence Whalen finds, "Poe's persisting struggle to influence the taste of the reading public was not so much a reactionary attempt to resurrect old aesthetic standards but rather an effort to institute a new order of criticism that would enable the evaluation and sorting of a new supply of literary commodities."[8]

Though both older and newer historicist approaches to Poe's criticism have revealed insight into his works and his world, they have also set the conditions for what has only rarely been done: to study Poe's reviews as a form of art. To do so would be to return to Jonathan Elmer's study of Poe as a figure of mass culture with specific attention to Elmer's insistence that mass culture is mediated by affect, "on the terrain of a pleasure."[9] To consider Poe's relation to mass culture and social history, then, Poe's reviews may not solely be read for their documentary value or for their political or theoretical philosophies. Rather, they may be reappraised as works designed to give a historically specific form of pleasure.

In what follows, I want to sketch out a preliminary case for widening the Poe canon to include his review essays as aesthetic objects. In the first part of the essay, I will make the case for the necessity of such a study by emphasizing the centrality of the reviews to Poe's early career as well as their celebrated (and derided) uniqueness. What makes Poe's literary criticism unique, I hypothesize, is the very characteristic for which it was best known at the time: its mean-spirited and thoroughgoing severity. This severe tone may be better understood through reference to the odd verb that Poe uses to describe his critical method: *quiz*. The remaining sections of this essay will analyze the structural anatomy of his most notorious style of review, which critics have come to call his "tomahawk" reviews. By considering closely the genre and conventions of his first tomahawk reviews for the *Southern Literary Messenger*, I will draw out what may be surprising today: a distinct and original type of sarcastic humor that will seem familiar to consumers of mass media. Reading Poe's reviews within the frame of entertainment, I suggest that we consider how the bad text for Poe became the occasion for a new variety of comic popular literature.

The Tomahawk and the Quiz

Poe's hostile, "tomahawk" reviews were at the core of his literary reputation throughout his career. When a virtually unknown Poe took over the editorship of the *Southern Literary Messenger* in 1835, he wrote and published several long negative reviews (alongside dozens of more neutral reviews) of recent American books. Almost immediately, other journals took notice, commenting upon the reviews as the "most striking feature" of the *Messenger*.[10] Poe, seeking to stoke the sensation, Poe extracted and republished their notices, engaged in published skirmishes with offended authors and editors, and continued including one or two signature tomahawk reviews in nearly every issue after he took over the editorship.[11] Even after he lost his position at the *Messenger*, Poe continued to write hostile criticism; it was a reputation he cultivated. Enlisting subscribers to support his own magazine in 1840, Poe promised to expand upon the "main feature" of the *Southern Literary Messenger*, "a somewhat overdone causticity in its department of Critical Notices" (L2: 26). Although Poe's prospectus claims that the proposed *Penn Magazine* will "retain this trait of severity in so much only as the calmest and sternest sense of literary justice will permit" (L2: 26) and that "[o]ne or two years, since elapsed, may have mellowed down the petulance, without interfering with the rigor of the critic" (L2: 26), Poe makes it clear that the chief value of the reviews would be their negativity, since those same years "have not yet taught him to read through the medium of a publisher's interest" (L2: 26). Although Poe would make several changes to the prospectus for his critical magazine, arguably his life's unrealized goal, he never changed what, in spirit, was the skeletal backbone of the project: "an absolutely independent criticism" (L2: 30).

It may seem, then, that Poe's criticism was antagonizing because it demanded critical independence. Indeed, most approaches to his criticism have taken his professed aim of literary justice earnestly, portraying Poe as a fierce advocate for an original American literature built upon independent criticism.[12] Yet reading Poe's prospectuses carefully shows that Poe was aware that the value of such independence resided not just with honesty but also with an irresponsible pleasure: "It will enlist the loftiest talent, but employ it not always in the loftiest—at least not always in the most pompous or Puritanical way" (L2: 30). So whereas recent criticisms of Poe's project have noted key tensions between Poe's professed ideals and his practice, another factor to account for in these discrepancies may be his less polemical objective: "Its chief aim shall be *to please*" (L2: 27).[13]

Considering the pleasure of the negative review offers a new perspective on Poe's critical practice. For chronologically, it isn't that Poe begins with both an exquisite taste for the "purest rules of Art" and a fully formulated position on the deficiencies of national literature and then develops out of them his caustic reviews. Rather, Poe begins his reviewing career with a sarcastic disposition that aims to score laughs. Two of Poe's very first published reviews, in the April 1835 *Southern Literary Messenger*, are remarkably severe and not particularly edifying. The review for Laughton Osborne's *Confessions of a Poet*, for instance, begins with a backhanded compliment—"The most remarkable feature in this production is the bad paper on which it is printed, and the typographical ingenuity with which matter made barely enough for one volume has been spread over the pages of two" (P 5: 7)—and finishes with one of the most vicious lampoons in his career. Pointing out that the author of *Confessions* "avers upon his word of honor that in commencing this work he loads a pistol, and places it upon the table" with the intention of "blowing out what he supposes to be his brains" when he finishes, Poe quips: "Now this is excellent" (P 5: 8). Extending the macabre joke, Poe cautions the author to check the pistol in case of a misfire: "Indeed there would be no answering for the consequences. We might even have a second series of the *Confessions*" (P 5: 8).

Not only does the Osborne review and many of the other early negative reviews show that sarcasm was native to Poe's reviewing practices from the start, but, as the owner of *The Southern Literary Messenger* would later attest, Poe rarely read the books he reviewed straight through, "unless it were some trashy novels,—and his only object in reading even these, was to ridicule their authors."[14] As was apparent to contemporary readers from the reviews themselves—Poe's longest and most involved reviews at the *Messenger* were the negative ones—Poe enjoyed reading the trashy novels, not for themselves, and not out of some high-minded obligation, but rather as occasions for exercising his wit. Such qualifications alter the image of Poe as a critic whose ferocity was a measure of his commitment to literary purity. Instead, seeing as his literary principles were articulated *after* his practice of negative reviewing had gained him recognition, we might consider how Poe's aesthetic principles were influenced by the comic type of negative reviewing from which they emerged. Such a stance wouldn't dismiss Poe's formalist theories of literature as disingenuous but would instead discover their ground in Poe's witticism, the sustained and withering attacks, the deft and capable deployment of irony, in Poe's innovation of a *popular* criticism.

Central to such a criticism is its capacity for amusement, its humor. Although Poe's reviews have been seen as versions of the "personalities," or negative reviews in the British magazine tradition, his textual method of attack differs from the more ad hominem caricature of *Blackwood's*.[15] One indication of this novelty may be drawn from the reactions of contemporaries, who would regularly refer to Poe's criticisms through analogies to bodily violence, often using Native American stereotypes.[16] Poe would become known as the "tomahawk man" after being described as having a "savage skill" in using "his tomahawk and scalping knife" near the beginning of his career.[17] And in a satirical poem published in the year of his death, Poe appears carrying the same equipment: "With tomahawk upraised for deadly blow,/Behold our literary Mohawk, Poe!"[18] His review of *Norman Leslie* was described as a "flaying" by three different newspapers (*Charlottesville Jeffersonian, Lynchburg Virginian, Petersburg Constellation*).[19] The *Baltimore American* described Poe as a "meat carver" and advised him to avoid "smearing his own fingers" and keeping "the tone and bearing of the Messenger elevated and cavalier-like."[20] The contrast between the Mohawk, torturer, or meat carver and the elevated cavalier in these descriptions offers an illustration of how Poe's reviews were characterized as indigenously American, violent and uncouth, and a departure from the mannered bearing of more European and condescending forms of wit.[21] Moreover, the visceral imagery of these analogies—flayings, scalpings, and meat carvings—capture in their materiality the overtly textual nature of Poe's criticisms.

Yet although others described Poe's humor through metaphors of bodily violence, Poe himself uses a curious term to describe his own mode of sarcasm: the *quiz*. In two places in the plan for the *Living Writers of America*, Poe notes of current literature and criticism that he will *analyze it, instance it*, and *quiz it*.[22] Put in this order twice, these verbs become a kind of critical formula. Analysis and instancing (providing quotes) are common tasks of the critic. But what does Poe mean by *quiz?*

The meaning and etymology of *quiz* were under debate almost immediately after it came into use in the late eighteenth century. Among its earliest uses were two definitions that could both apply to Poe's critical method: "1. *trans.* To make fun of, mock, or tease (a person); to satirize (a thing). Also occasionally *intr.*: to mock, to talk wittily"; and "3. (a) to regard with amusement or scorn; to appraise mockingly; (*b*) to peer inquisitively at; to watch or examine closely, to interrogate with the eyes, study."[23] Although the word *quiz* today has mainly the sense of an examination, its use in the early nineteenth century combined examination with satirical humor. Poe would probably have been familiar with the popular etymological story that joined these two senses. According to an article published in *The New-York Mirror* in 1835, the first use of the word occurred when Richard Daly, the manager of the Irish theatres, bet that "he would hear spoken, all through the principal streets of Dublin, by a certain hour next day, Sunday, a word having no meaning." Daly then "despatched all the servants and supernumeraries with the word 'QUIZ,' which they chalked on every door and every shopwindow in town. Shops being shut all next day, everybody going to and coming from their different places of worship saw the word, and everybody repeated it, so that 'QUIZ' was heard all through Dublin; . . . and ever since, should a strange story be attempted to be passed current, it draws forth the expression—*you are quizzing me*."[24] This etymology links the two senses of *quiz*, a joke that is also a test, to the capacity of mass media publicity to create its own realities. Thus, the story generates a further irony in that the story itself avers its truth through its own publication. The story of the origin of the word *quiz* could, that is, be itself a quiz.

Poe's use of *quiz* to describe the method of his critical humor thus links together satirical humor, examination, and an irony specific to mass media. To quiz something is to test it by making fun of it, to test, that is, the worth of a book by mocking it. But it is also to test the observer, the reader, who thus takes on a more participatory role in the activity. The nature of Poe's critical performances might then be understood not as savage violence or as earnest aesthetic manifestos, but rather as a new form of textualized and ironic humor in which sarcastic mockery becomes a challenge, both of object and reader, attuned to the potential new feeling-tones of a popular readership. Whereas the cavalier tone that the *Baltimore American* advises may be appropriate for the select company of a salon, Poe's humorous criticism capitalizes upon a new media environment and a new variety of public reader. This audience does not balk at an insulting or antagonizing tone, but rather enjoys the spectacle by participating in the quiz: testing and being tested at once.

Adapting the quiz to the book review, Poe's first tomahawk reviews may be considered together as a subgenre. This generic form coalesces in the three early reviews—of Theodore Fay's *Norman Leslie*, William Gilmore Simms's *The Partisan*, and Morris Mattson's *Paul Ulric*—published in consecutive issues of *The Southern Literary Messenger* upon Poe's assumption of its editorship. *The Richmond Compiler* first recognized their similarity: "The public I believe was much delighted with the admirable scalping of 'Norman Leslie,' in the December number, and likewise of Mr. Simms' 'Partisan,' in the number for January; and it will be no less pleased at the caustic severity with which the puerile abortion of 'Paul Ulric' is exposed in the present number."[25] The commentator was responding not only to the shared tone of those reviews but also to Poe's intertextual allusions between them. In the opening paragraph of his *Paul Ulric* review, Poe alludes to *Norman Leslie*: "when we called Norman Leslie the silliest book in the world we had certainly never seen Paul Ulric" (P 5: 107). And at the end of that review, Poe reminds the reader of the "pet words" that the prior two tomahawking reviews had noted (P 5: 113). Such allusions confirm that Poe considered these reviews as being read together in a series—not primarily as an extended diatribe against the corrupt puffing system or as a necessary expedient for the birth of a national literature—but rather from the first as a new kind of genre of magazine entertainment, a regular feature for which, as *The Compiler* notes, the public was "much delighted."

These three early reviews may be analyzed as sharing a tripartite structure. First, they attack the prefaces, dedications, and other external features of the book. Second, they give a digest of the narrative, written in ironizing paraphrase with key passages quoted in full. And third, they end by commenting on the particulars of grammar and style, citing certain offending sentences verbatim. As I will argue ahead, each of these three components to Poe's reviews turns upon, a particular swerve in the practice of comedic irony that originates in the absorption of literature into a mass media product and eventuates, through the logic of the quiz, in the delights of a virtual public perspective enabled by the literality of the text. Put more broadly, in each of the three characteristic moves of Poe's negative reviews, he employs a new form of humor that capitalizes on the emergence of print reading as mass culture. As such, the textual nature of his reviews may be seen to open the practice and pleasure of critical judgment to a popular audience.

Prefaces, Things for Words

Poe's tomahawk reviews characteristically begin by commenting on the public face of the book to be reviewed. This includes remarks upon the public reputation of the book, as when Poe opens his review of "Norman Leslie" by calling attention to the extent of its advance advertisements:

> Well!—here we have it! This is *the* book—*the* book *par excellence*—the book bepuffed, beplastered, and be-*Mirrored*: the book "attributed to" Mr. Blank, and "said to be from the pen" of Mr. Asterisk: the book which has been "about to appear"—"in press"—"in progress"—"in preparation"—and "forthcoming:" the book "graphic" in anticipation—"talented" *a priori*—and God knows what *in prospectu.* For the sake of every thing puffed, puffing, and puffable, let us take a peep at its contents! (P 5: 60)

Drawing attention to the advance puffing of "Norman Leslie" by the editors of the *Mirror*, and then revealing that the author, Theodore S. Fay, "is nobody in the world but 'one of the Editors of the New York Mirror' " (P5: 60), Poe's opening situates "Norman Leslie" within a public literary market, one marked by self-interest and aggrandizement. Although Poe's larger point here may be to take issue with the phenomenon of puffing, overly favorable book reviews that would curry favor with publishers or authors, the effect of treating "Norman Leslie" as a public event also distinguishes its social character from its "contents."

Peeping at the book's contents, however, does not lead Poe directly to the narrative, but rather to those extra-literary conventions, the dedication and the preface, which are the book's own public face. From the lengthy dedication to Colonel Herman Thorn, "whoever he may be," Poe reprints a long list of adjectives—" 'hospitable,' " " 'generous,' " " 'attentive,' " " 'benevolent,' " " 'kind-hearted,' " " 'liberal,' " " 'highly-esteemed' " (P 5: 60)—to show up the bloated hyperbole of the dedication. And in the following paragraph, Poe seizes on Fay's preface with what will become a characteristic, and self-aware, literalism and lack of generosity. Poe begins:

> In the Preface Mr. Fay informs us that the most important features of his story are founded on fact—that he has availed himself of certain poetical licenses—that he has transformed the character, particularly the character of a young lady, (oh fi! Mr. Fay—oh, Mr. Fay, fi!) that he has sketched certain peculiarities with a mischievous hand—and that the art of novel writing is as dignified as the art of Canova, Mozart or Raphael,—from which we are left to infer, that Mr. Fay himself is as dignified as Raphael, Mozart, and Canova—all three. (P 5: 60)

Turning the decorous condescending prose of the preface against itself, Poe's attack capitalizes on the authorial pretensions that such literary conventions inculcate, explicitly questioning the purpose of those conventions in the first place: "But will any body tell us what is the object of Prefaces in general, and what is the meaning of Mr. Fay's Preface in particular?" (P 5: 60).

Poe's critique of Fay's preface thus critiques a broader trend of extra-literary writing and material that accumulate around the work itself—either in the form of advance puffs or in the prefaces and dedicatory material. In a later review of *George Jones' Ancient America* (1845), for just one example, Poe spends nearly half the review mocking the five different title pages and their interspersed illustrations. Poe declares, "The true *fun* of this book, however, lies in its externals. . . . The *title-pages* of the book are to be cut out, we hope, and deposited in the British Museum."[26] Poe's attention to "externals" as a source of fun of draws attention to material conventions, to the book as an object within a social world. To embarrass the pretensions of literary culture, Poe seizes upon the textual substance of its performance: the book's public face as presented in prefaces and dedications and title pages.

Such literal treatment of externals exposes the awkward balance between private and public performance attempted by the mannerisms of literary culture. Poe opens his very next tomahawking review of Simms's *The Partisan* with an extended burlesque on its dedication by hypothetically narrating it. First, Poe transcribes the dedication verbatim:

> TO RICHARD YEADON, JR. ESQ.
> Of South Carolina
>
> Dear Sir,
> My earliest, and, perhaps, most pleasant rambles in the fields of literature, were taken in your company—permit me to remind you of that period by inscribing the present volumes with your name.
> THE AUTHOR.
>
> *Barnwell, South Carolina.*
> *July 1, 1835.* (P 5: 88)

Poe then recreates the dedication as narrative since, "a letter, generally, we may consider as the substitute for certain oral communications which the writer of the letter would deliver in person were an opportunity afforded":

> Let us then imagine the author of "The Partisan" presenting a copy of that work to "Richard Yeadon, Jr. Esq. of South Carolina," and let us, from the indications afforded by the printed Dedication, endeavor to form some idea of the author's demeanor upon an occasion so highly interesting. We may suppose Mr. Yeadon, in South Carolina, at home, and in his study. By and bye with a solemn step, downcast eyes, and impressive earnestness of manner, enters the author of "The Yemasee." He advances towards Mr. Yeadon, and, without uttering a syllable, takes that gentleman affectionately, but firmly, by the hand. Mr. Y. has his suspicions, as well he may have, but says nothing. Mr. S. commences as above. "Dear Sir," (here follows a pause, indicated by the comma after the word "Sir"—see Dedication. Mr. Y. very much puzzled what to make of it.) Mr. S. proceeds, "My earliest," (pause the second, indicated by comma the second,) "and," (pause the third, in accordance with comma the third,) "perhaps," (pause the fourth, as shewn by comma the fourth. Mr. Y. exceedingly mystified,) "most pleasant rambles in the fields of literature," (pause fifth) "were taken in your company" (pause sixth, to agree with the dash after 'company.' Mr. Y.'s hair begins to stand on end, and he looks occasionally towards the door,) "permit me to remind you of that period by inscribing the present volumes with your name." At the conclusion of the sentence, Mr. S. with a smile and bow of mingled benignity and grace, turns slowly from Mr. Y. and advances to a table in the centre of the room. Pens and ink are there at his service. Drawing from the pocket of his surtout a pacquet carefully done up in silver paper, he unfolds it, and produces the two volumes of "The Partisan." With ineffable ease, and with an air of exquisite *haut ton*, he proceeds to inscribe in the title pages of each tome the name of Richard Yeadon, Jr. Esq. The scene, however, is interrupted. Mr. Y. feels it his duty to kick the author of "The Yemassee" down stairs. (P 5: 88)

The inventiveness of Poe's demonstration relies upon a literalization of both the grammar and the scene of the dedication. As Poe himself explains: "Now, in all this, all the actual burlesque consists in merely substituting things for words" (P 5: 88). Substituting things for words, Poe converts the airy and mannered conventions of the preface and the dedication into tangible matter, exposing it to the ungenerous view of the reading public. Whether it's Fay asking for the indulgence of "solemn and sapient critics" or Simms alluding to an intimate friendship, the maneuvering in the prefaces and dedications tries to determine in advance the readership. What makes Poe's ridicule of these maneuvers so prescient is that he is aware of the futility of such contortions in the new, widening, reading public. The reader is invited to sympathize with Mr. Y. as Mr. S. performs his histrionic dedication, becoming annoyed not only by the pretentiousness of manner but, moreover, at the way in which the dedication assumes a condescending familiarity which the reader, as well as Mr. Y, may wish to reject. By turning words into things, Poe points up the ironic difference between the authorial attempt to set the terms of readership and its inevitable failure because, as literal matter, the work is an object circulating in a disinterested public.

After *Norman Leslie* in December and *The Partisan* for January, Poe's third tomahawk review begins with the first explicit rationalization of his method by reference to a national object: "In itself, the book before us is too purely imbecile to merit an extended critique—but as a portion of our daily literary food—as an American work published by the Harpers—as one of a class of absurdities with an inundation of which our country is grievously threatened—we shall have no hesitation, and shall spare no pains, in exposing fully before the public eye its four hundred and forty-three pages of utter folly, bombast, and inanity" (P 5: 107). Poe would continue this line of justification throughout the rest of his reviewing career, but rather than understand such as the reason for Poe's negative reviewing practices, we can sense now something like an opportunistic post facto reasoning or, more provocatively, as a culminating discovery informed by the practice of his negative reviews themselves. For if, in his cutting remarks on prefaces and dedications, Poe would capitalize on the material nature of the textual work, converting words to things in order to ironize authorial preciousness in the mass literary marketplace, his turn to the wider national stage would seem to bear the lessons of that method. Because the book is a mass production to be consumed—"daily literary food"—and because it has itself discrete mass—"four hundred and forty-three pages"—Poe is able to expose its pretentions to his proper audience, the "public eye." This, Poe's first nationalist rationalization for the sarcastic and hostile reviews that were already winning him notoriety suggests that his approach was enabled by a growing mass readership whose relation to literature is, from the start, material.[27] In the expansion of the literary market, books become objects and words become things. In their attention to the external matter and public face of the books, Poe's tomahawk reviews redraw the stage of literary judgment from the spirit of the work and the intent of the author, a generous familiarity one might associate with the salon, to the bare matter of literality in the impersonal sphere of a mass public.

Digests

In the second parts of his tomahawk reviews, Poe redirects his textual ironizing from the pretensions of "externals" to narrative content. While plot summary is common in reviewing practice of the period, Poe's practice differed by offering briefer quoted passages and by constructing the digests in paraphrase. In recounting the narrative through a critical voice that intercedes and comments upon the defects of the plot, Poe adapts the narrative digest into a form of parody marked by ironic self-consciousness.

In the first iteration of this particular form of narrative digest, the *Norman Leslie* review, Poe opens by both assuming and questioning the assumptions of romantic genre: "As far as we can understand the plot of Norman Leslie, it is this. A certain family reside in Italy—'independent,' 'enlightened,' 'affectionate,' 'happy,'—and all that. Their villa, of course, stands upon the seashore, and their whole establishment is, we are assured, 'a scene of Heaven,' &c. Mr. Fay says he will not even attempt to describe it—why, therefore, should we?" (P 5: 60).

Though Poe quotes directly from the narrative, the list of adjectives, as well as the "scene of Heaven," are shown to be empty of any descriptive content besides an airy predictability through the off-hand "and all that," as well as the "of course." The work of these tonal indicators is to imply that the Italian family is merely a generic placeholder, familiar to most readers of romantic fiction but devoid of material description. Just as in his "words for things" critique of prefaces, Poe begins this narrative digest by showing an emptiness in generic clichés.

Yet this emptiness does not interfere with Poe's summary of the narrative. And Poe gives the premise, with further sarcastic interpolations, in his own words:

> A daughter of this family is nineteen when she is wooed by a young Neapolitan, Rinaldo, of "mean extraction, but of great beauty and talent." The lover, being a man of suspicious character, is rejected by the parents, and a secret marriage ensues. The lady's brother pursues the bridegroom—they fight—and the former is killed. The father and mother die (it is impossible to see for what purpose they ever lived) and Rinaldo flies to Venice. Upon rejoining her husband in that city, the lady (for Mr. Fay has not thought her worth enduing with a specific appellation) discovers him, for the first time, to be a rascal. One fine day he announces his intention of leaving herself and son for an indefinite time. The lady beseeches and finally threatens. "It was the first unfolding," says she, in a letter towards the denouement of the story, "of that character which neither he nor I knew belonged to my nature. It was the first uncoiling of the basilisk within me, (good Heavens, a snake in a lady's stomach!). He gazed on me incredulously, and cooly smiled. You remember that smile—I fainted!!!" Alas! Mr. Davy Crockett,—Mr. Davy Crockett, alas!—thou art beaten hollow—thou art defunct, and undone! Thou has indeed succeeded in grinning a squirrel from a tree, but it surpassed even thine extraordinary abilities to smile a lady into a fainting fit! (P 5: 60)

Though Poe's acidic humor cuts through this digest, it doesn't efface the effect of the generic sensational plot. The woman-seduced-by-scoundrel story becomes the stable and recognizable backdrop on which Poe can display his wit. And, characteristically, this wit consists in taking romantic cliché literally and against the grain: the metaphorical basilisk becomes a literal snake in the lady's GI tract, and the faint-inducing smile is taken as a physical marvel belonging in a frontier tall tale. Although Poe is conventionally seen as continental in his aesthetic principles, here his reviewing style seems rather aligned with Twain and the strain of Western wit that ironizes romantic or chivalric pretensions by refusing their assumptions and describing them literally.

In another kind of reduction to literality, characters in Poe's digests become mechanical constructs, their bizarre behavior forced by the needs of the plot. The conclusion of *Norman Leslie* revolves around the suspicion that Norman Leslie, who was the last person seen with Miss Romain, has murdered her. As it turns out, Leslie has not murdered Miss Romain but was merely on a ride with her when she left his carriage for another in a deserted forest, or, as Poe summarizes: "[The] young lady induces Mr. Leslie to drive her, in a gig, a short distance out of town. They are met by no less a personage than Mrs. Rinaldo herself [a stranger to Norman Leslie], in another gig, and driving (*proh pudor!*) through the woods *sola*. Hereupon Miss Rosalie Romain very deliberately, and to the great astonishment, no doubt, of Mr. Leslie, gets out of that gentleman's gig, and into the gig of Mrs. Rinaldo. Here's plot! As Vapid says in the play" (P 5: 61). Poe's summary draws out the absurdity of the plot's manufacture, and its humor depends on characters' astonishment at the unaccountableness of the narrative in which they are caught.

Poe's allusion to Vapid, a playwright in Frederick Reynolds' comedy *The Dramatist*, yields a clue to one influence on Poe's technique of turning the overtly mechanical nature of plot into comedy. Reynolds's Vapid is obsessed with discovering materials for his plays in his daily life, which he treats, ironically, as if it were a play itself. In the passage to which Poe refers, Vapid partakes in a dramatic scene, holding a girl who has fainted in his arms, while simultaneously commenting upon it:

> *Vap.* Poor girl! how I pity her! I really loved her.
> *Mar.* Did you really love me Mr. Vapid?
> *Vap.* Hey day recover'd! here's incident![28]

The humor of Vapid's running commentary turns on its metafictional irony, the way it reveals the efficacious construction of incidents to the plot. Poe's revision of "here's incident!" to "here's plot!" adopts a similar perspective. By interjecting a Vapid-like commentary into his digests, Poe is able to afford both a view of the plot as story (we follow the story of Leslie, Romain, Rinaldo, and the unnamed lady) and a view of that plot as construction (we see the events of the story as contrivances) at the same time.

Through such parallel commentary, the generic plots themselves gain a narrative propulsion that works surprisingly in tandem with the opprobrium heaped upon them.

When the hero of *Norman Leslie* saves Mrs. Rinaldo from being run over by horses, Poe points forward with a proleptic aside: "The lady of course swoons—then recovers—and then—is excessively grateful. Her gratitude, however, being of no service just at that moment, is bottled up for use hereafter, and will no doubt, according to established usage in such cases, come into play towards the close of the second volume. But we shall see" (P 5: 60). After four more paragraphs of the digest, and seven or eight years of diegetic time, Poe arrives at the conclusion of *Norman Leslie*:

> He hies, then, to the rendezvous at St. Peter's, where "the unknown" tells him St. Peter's won't answer, and that he must proceed to the Coliseum. He goes—why should he not?—and there not only finds the Countess D. who turns out to be Mrs. Rinaldo, and who now uncorks her bottle of gratitude, but also Flora Temple, Flora Temple's father, Clairmont, Kreutzner, a German friend from New York, and, last but not least, Rosalie Romain herself; all having gone there, no doubt, at three o'clock in the morning, under the influence of that interesting young gentleman Norman Leslie's "most inexplicable and mysterious destiny." (P 5: 61)

The gratitude "bottled up" is finally "uncorked" in the concluding scene—a simple narrative suspense that Poe builds into his review. In such a way, Poe is able to draw attention to the artificiality of the narrative's suspense by repeating and adapting it. The intrusiveness of the plot, here named Leslie's "mysterious destiny," may be laughable for the way it forces characters and situations, yet at the same time it is the central engine that drives Poe's digests themselves.

Thus, the digest sections of Poe's reviews play upon both the reader's contempt for the genre conventions of the meritless work *and* the reader's capability of enjoying them anyway. This is why it is not quite accurate to say that Poe's reviews show an unwavering hostility to those works that violated his pure principles of art. Rather, it might make more sense to say that Poe's reviews recycle deficient plots in order to drive comedic adaptations. Feeling this irony—both in the surprising behavior of the characters and in our ability to still enjoy such plot—extends the textual irony of Poe's remarks upon the prefaces and dedications. As characters go from portrayed humans to unwilling mechanical contrivances, pushed and pulled by plot, readers themselves feel pulled into the plot by their very interest in how it fails.

Style

If in his criticism on prefaces, Poe turns words into things, materializing the work of literature into a commodity, and if, in his digests of the plots, Poe builds a genre of parodic criticism that draws humor from the reduction of characters to mechanical contrivances, then in the final sections of his tomahawk reviews, Poe's critique of grammar and style completes the turn to a wholly textualized and material criticism. At the end of his *Norman Leslie* review, Poe attempts to demonstrate that Fay's style is "unworthy of a school-boy" (P 5: 62):

> Let us examine one one [[sic]] or two of his sentences at random. Page 28, vol. i. "He was doomed to wander through the fartherest climes alone and branded." Why not say at once fartherertherest? Page 150, vol. i. "Yon kindling orb should be hers; and that faint spark close to its side should teach her how dim and yet how near my soul was to her own." What is the meaning of all this? Is Mr. Leslie's soul dim to her own, as well as near to her own?—for the sentence implies as much. Suppose we say "should teach her how dim was my soul, and yet how near to her own." (P 5:62)

Poe's insistence upon giving the quotes as evidence, citing the text to "instance it," as in his plan for *The Living Writers of America*, presents a model of the textual close-reading practices that would later be championed by the New Critics and is still a standard technique in literary scholarship today. Page number citations give Poe's critique the air of documentary evidence, and his tactic of rewriting the sentences to expose their faults emphasizes the text as an authorial decision.

For Poe's critics, the use of page number citations was a sign of petty fault finding. In *The New York Mirror*'s satire of Poe's reviewing style, published as a response to Poe's *Norman Leslie* review, Poe appears as the citation-happy hyperaggressive critic, Bulldog:

> "What awful grammar!" said Bulldog. "Did you observe in the twenty-seventh line—page two hundred thirty-one—vol. second—where he says *which*, instead of *that?* It's too contemptible!"[29]

The *Mirror* chided Poe for a laughable particularity in fault finding—a too myopic focus on the rare grammatical mistake—but Poe's citations also have the effect of replacing context with page number. It doesn't matter who the "He" of the "He was doomed to wander" is for Poe's purpose. What is important is rather the grammar and mechanics of the sentence itself, which depend upon the fact that those words appear exactly as quoted in the book itself. That is, Poe's use of page numbers, like his attack upon the dedications and prefaces, takes advantage of the textual nature of the book to present a material ground for judgment, one adapted to the medium of the magazine review.

Yet these "close-reading" segments of Poe's reviews do not aim at any new or elevated understanding of the literary work. Instead, in the style of a quiz, Poe's citation of the text is presented first, offering the reader a test that then is resolved in the sarcastic joke that follows. That is, by always "instancing" his claims, Poe opens the work up to the judgment of the reader, and the humor of his quips depends upon the reader being able to parse out in retrospect the errors in the cited sentence. What many editors and authors saw as an unfair tendency toward snobbish fault finding actually engages the reader as a critic. Poe may level abuses at the individual errors of the text, but his manner of delivery invites the audience to participate, to puzzle out the grammatical error and to be rewarded for their success. Textual criticism becomes, through these exercises, popular criticism.

Poe often rewrites the text in order to expose deficiencies in its grammatical style. Like the adaptation work that he does in the digests, these revisions manipulate the text into alternate versions that emphasize the decision making in the work's composition. That is, by showing how the text could have been otherwise, Poe's textual revisions situate readers at an imaginary scene of composition, in which he/she is asked to contemplate between different possibilities as a means to reveal the deficiencies of the original. In a later review of Rufus Dawes's *Geraldine*, for example, Poe cites a few lines to instance:

> "He laid her gently down, of sense bereft,
> And sunk his picture on her bosom's snow,
> And close beside these lines in blood he left:
> 'Farewell forever, Geraldine, I go
> Another woman's victim—dare I tell?
> T'is Alice!—curse us, Geraldine!—farewell!"[30]

Poe then proceeds to quiz the lines by narrating them, a version of the sarcastic paraphrase that he often employs in his narrative digests:

> This *is* a droll piece of business. The lover brings forth a miniature, (Mr. Dawes has a passion for miniatures,) *sinks* it in the bosom of the lady, cuts his finger, and writes with the blood an epistle, (*where* is not specified, but we presume he indites it upon the bosom as it is "close beside" the picture,) in which epistle he announces that he is "another woman's victim," giving us to understand that he himself is a woman after all, and concluding with the delicious bit of Billingsgate, "dare I tell? / 'Tis Alice!—curse us, Geraldine!—farewell!"[31]

And Poe closes by offering a revision of the whole, a joke that depends upon a particularly ungenerous parsing of the word "us" and a parodic discrepancy of tone:

> We suppose, however, that "curse us" is a misprint; for why should Geraldine curse both herself and her lover?—it should have been "curse it!" no doubt. The whole passage, perhaps, would have read better thus—"oh my eye! / 'Tis Alice!—d—n it, Geraldine!—good bye!"[32]

Poe's critique here of Dawes's poem may seem unfair; his jokes about "another woman's victim" and "curse us" are seemingly deliberate misreadings. But even in the uneven success of Poe's humor, we can see that his reviews ask readers to read his humorous paraphrases and adaptations against the quoted text. Readers become participants in literary quizzing: a strategy of mockery that is also a test of one's close-reading abilities.

A Reviewer Reviewed

Poe's reviews, by virtue of their textual and quizzing nature, cultivated a unique tone suited to a new popular and public readership. This would explain why, even as commenters noted the unfairness of Poe's harsh criticisms, they would also note their amusement as well. The *Charlottesville Jeffersonian*, for instance, remarked: "The Review of Mr. Fay's novel Norman Leslie, is amusing and will be read, though we think some passages in it are in bad taste."[33] Poe's reviews were seen as both unfair *and* popular, sometimes popular *because of* their unfairness: "Such reviews as that of Mr. Fay's 'Norman Leslie' will be read. Men—and Women likewise—will always be attracted in crowds to behold an infliction of the Russian knout or to see a fellow-creature flayed alive."[34] That this new genre of popular comedy would become the ground of the influential textual approach to criticism leads us to some new insights.

One is a more specific awareness of the influence of the mass public on the stance and method of close reading. The relation between the public reader and the new, textually ironic, quizzing sense of humor that arises in Poe's tomahawk reviews shows how the adoption of new forms of media correspond with both new imagined readerships and emergent literary tones. The reviews' quizzing humor—acidic, unfair, primarily textual, and participatory—may be roughly analogous to the new term to describe Internet-specific sarcastic humor within our current media environment, *snark*. Snark, also a kind of irreverent sarcasm aimed at a mass public audience, is a tone of humor dependent upon the changing understanding of readership consequent upon new social media. Poe's reviews may seem snarky to our ears today, because, I argue, their tone grows out of the widening and materializing trends in the new media of his own day—the explosion of print periodicals. The reader was no longer imagined as a singular person, but rather a corporate body, joined not by proximity or cultural belonging, but at the baseline by a material relation to the actual text.

After Poe's death, a manuscript for an article was found in his trunk. Titled "A Reviewer Reviewed," it was a review written by Poe of his own reviews under the pseudonym Walter G. Bowen. In the estimation of this fictional reviewer, Poe's reviews were "extreme, captious, fault finding, and unnecessarily severe. Mr. P. has been so often complimented for his powers of sarcasm that he thinks it incumbent upon him to keep up his reputation in that line by sneers upon all occasions and downright abuse" (M 3: 1380–1381). In this strange self-reflection, Poe quizzes his own critical style, allowing only "one good point" to his reviews: that they "show no respect for persons" (M 3: 1380). There is no respect for persons in Poe's tomahawk reviews, not even for himself—and the intensity and new impersonal sarcasm of his reviews were most often recognized as a kind of violence *upon* persons only recognizable as a form of savagery (the tomahawk and the scalping) that did not conform to bourgeois norms of civility and treated bodies as if they were persons. As the *New Yorker* protested in May 1836, "The Southern Editor has quite too savage a way of pouncing upon unlucky wights . . . like the Indian, who cannot realize that an enemy is conquered till he is scalped."[35] What the *New Yorker* recognized in Poe was an unaccountable physicality to the critique, a literary review as written by someone who treated the physical body of his adversary, let's say the text itself, as if it were the contemptible foe. What the *New Yorker* writer missed was that this "savagery" was not simply a flouting of bourgeois cultural norms, but rather an augur of the new tones, genres, and conventions that emerge from the growth of a mass reading public.

Notes

1. Edgar Allan Poe, "The Living Writers of America" (manuscript, 1846–1847), Edgar Allan Poe Society of Baltimore, https://www.eapoe.org/works/misc/livingw.htm, 1.
2. Poe, "The Living Writers of America," 1.
3. For early descriptive studies of Poe's criticism and influences, see Margaret Alterton, *Origins of Poe's Critical Theory* (1925; repr., New York: Russell & Russell, 1965); Richard Beale Davis, "Poe and William Wirt," *American Literature* 16 (1944): 212–220; David K. Jackson, *Poe and the Southern Literary Messenger* (Richmond, VA: Dietz, 1934); and Edd Winfield Park, *Edgar Allan Poe as Literary Critic* (Athens: University of Georgia Press, 1964). For a more recent summary in a similar vein, see Jonathan Hartmann, "The Art of Reviewing," in *Edgar Allan Poe in Context*, ed. Kevin J. Hayes (Cambridge: Cambridge University Press, 2013), 198–208.
4. Arthur Hobson Quinn, *Edgar Allan Poe: A Critical Biography* (Baltimore: Johns Hopkins University Press, 1997); Edmund Wilson, introduction in *The Shock of Recognition: The Development of Literature in the United States Recorded by the Men Who Made It*, ed. Edmund Wilson, 2nd ed. (New York: Farrar, Straus and Cudahy, 1955), 80.
5. Robert D. Jacobs, *Poe: Journalist & Critic* (Baton Rouge: Louisiana State University Press, 1969); Sidney P. Moss, *Poe's Literary Battles: The Critic in the Context of His Literary Milieu* (Durham, NC: Duke University Press, 1963); and Michael Allen, *Poe and the British Magazine Tradition* (New York: Oxford University Press, 1969).
6. For more recent analyses of Poe's criticism as articulating his aesthetic philosophy, see James M. Hutchisson, "The Reviews: Evolution of a Critic," in *A Companion to Poe Studies* (Westport, CT: Greenwood Press, 1996), 296–322; Kent Ljungquist, "The Poet as Critic," in *The Cambridge Companion to Edgar Allan Poe*, ed. Kevin J. Hayes (Cambridge: Cambridge University Press, 2002), 7–20; Rachel Polonsky, "Poe's Aesthetic Theory," in *The Cambridge Companion to Edgar Allan Poe*, 42–56; and Justin R. Wert, "Poe's Early Criticism of American Fiction: *The Southern Literary Messenger* and the Fiction of Robert Montgomery Bird," in *Edgar Allan Poe: Beyond Gothicism*, ed. James M. Hutchisson (Newark, NJ: University of Delaware Press, 2011).
7. For a summary discussion of this turn to Poe's engagement in social history, see Jerome McGann, "Poe, Decentered Culture, and Critical Method," in *Poe and the Remapping of Antebellum Print Culture*, ed. J. Gerald Kennedy and Jerome McGann (Baton Rouge: Louisiana State University Press, 2012), 245–259. The major texts in this turn are Jonathan Elmer, *Reading at the Social Limit: Affect, Mass Culture, and Edgar Allan Poe* (Palo Alto, CA: Stanford University Press, 1995); Terence Whalen, *Edgar Allan Poe and the Masses: The Political Economy of Literature in Antebellum America* (Princeton, NJ: Princeton University Press, 1999); and Meredith McGill, *American Literature and the Culture of Reprinting, 1834–1853* (Philadelphia: University of Pennsylvania Press,

2003). For Poe's practice of criticism in his social environment, see also Lara Langer Cohen, *The Fabrication of American Literature: Fraudulence and Antebellum Print Culture* (Philadelphia: University of Pennsylvania Press, 2012); Adam Gordon, "'A Condition to Be Criticized': Edgar Allan Poe and the Vocation of Antebellum Criticism," *Arizona Quarterly* 68, no. 2 (Summer 2012): 1–31; Leon Jackson, "'The Rage for Lions': Edgar Allan Poe and the Culture of Celebrity," in *Poe and the Remapping of Antebellum Print Culture*, 37–61; and Leon Jackson, "'Behold Our Literary Mohawk, Poe': Literary Nationalism and the 'Indianation' of Antebellum American Culture," *ESQ* 48, no. 1–2 (2002): 97–133.

8. Whalen, *Edgar Allan Poe and the Masses*, 76.
9. Elmer, *Reading at the Social Limit*, 7.
10. *The Pennsylvanian*, as qtd. in *The Southern Literary Messenger* 2, no. 2 (Jan. 1836): 135.
11. For accounts of Poe's sparring with critics of his reviewing practice, see Sidney Moss, "Poe and the *Norman Leslie* Incident," *American Literature* 25, no. 3 (Nov. 1953): 293–306 and Pollin and Ridgley's headnotes in *Writings in the Southern Literary Messenger: Nonfictional Prose* (P 5: 3–4, 12–13, 18–19, . . .).
12. For a notable articulation of this argument, see William Carlos Williams, *In the American Grain* (1925; repr., New York: New Directions, 1956), 216–233.
13. See Gordon, "'A Condition to be Criticized'" and McGill, *American Literature and the Culture of Reprinting*.
14. T. W. White to Nathaniel Beverley Tucker, Richmond, April 26, 1837, quoted in Jackson, *Poe and the Southern Literary Messenger*, 115.
15. For the argument that Poe's wit is in the British tradition, see Allen, *Poe and the British Magazine Tradition*, 40–55, and J. Lasley Dameron, "Poe's Reading of the British Periodicals," *Mississippi Quarterly* 18 (1965): 19–25. For an account of the ad hominem nature of British reviewing, see Emily Lorraine de Montluzin, "Killing the Cockneys: Blackwood's Weapons of Choice against Hunt, Hazlitt, and Keats," *Keats-Shelley Journal* 47 (1998): 87–107. Although Dameron convincingly shows that Poe borrows critical terms, aesthetic principles, and the incorporation of wit into his reviews from his reading of the British magazines, the question of whether Poe's style of humor is also drawn from those sources remains open.
16. For a compelling account of the nationalist implications of Poe's Native American caricature, see Jackson, "'Behold Our Literary Mohawk, Poe.'"
17. *Cincinnati Mirror*, qtd. in *The Southern Literary Messenger* 2, no. 5 (April 1836), 343.
18. [Augustine J. H. Duganne], "A Mirror for Authors," *Holden's Dollar Magazine of Criticisms, Biographies, Sketches, Essays, Tales, Reviews, Poetry, etc.* 3, no. 1 (Jan. 1849): 22.
19. See extracts from each journal collected in *The Southern Literary Messenger* 2, no. 2 (Jan. 1836): 136, 139, 140.
20. *The Southern Literary Messenger* 2, no. 2 (Jan. 1836): 138.
21. See Jackson, "'Behold Our Literary Mohawk, Poe,'" 108–110.
22. Poe, "Living Writers of America," 1, fragment 2. Poe also uses the verb "quiz" in referring to a planned attack: "In quizzing the Transcendental poems quote Sternhold & Hopkins" (Poe, "Living Writers of America," 2).
23. *Oxford English Dictionary Online*, s.v. "quiz, (*v.*[1])," updated June 2008, http://www.oed.com.
24. "Miscellany," *The New-York Mirror: a Weekly Gazette of Literature and Fine Arts* 12, no. 44 (May 2, 1835): 352.
25. *The Richmond Compiler*, qtd. in *The Southern Literary Messenger* 2, no. 5 (April 1836): 345.

26. Edgar Allan Poe, "George Jones' Ancient America," *Aristidean: A Magazine of Reviews, Politics, and Light Literature* 1, no. 1 (March 1845): 9–12, 10.
27. For more on Poe's relation to a commercial audience, see Whalen's discussion of what he calls the "Capital Reader"; Whalen, *Edgar Allan Poe and the Masses*, 3–20.
28. Frederick Reynolds, *The Dramatist: A Comedy in Five Acts* (Dublin: P. Byrne, 1790), 57.
29. "A Successful Novel!," *The New-York Mirror* 13, no. 41 (April 9, 1836): 324.
30. Edgar Allan Poe, "The Poetry of Rufus Dawes: A Retrospective Criticism," *Graham's Lady's and Gentleman's Magazine* 11, no. 4 (October 1842): 205–209, 207.
31. Edgar Allan Poe, "The Poetry of Rufus Dawes: A Retrospective Criticism," 207.
32. Edgar Allan Poe, "The Poetry of Rufus Dawes: A Retrospective Criticism," 207.
33. *The Charlottesville Jeffersonian*, qtd. in *The Southern Literary Messenger* 2, no. 2 (Jan. 1836): 136.
34. *The Lynchburg Virginian*, qtd. in *The Southern Literary Messenger* 2, no. 2 (Jan. 1836): 139.
35. "Southern Literary Messenger," *The New-Yorker* 1, no. 7 (May 7, 1836): 109.

BIBLIOGRAPHY

Allen, Michael. *Poe and the British Magazine Tradition*. New York: Oxford University Press, 1969.

Alterton, Margaret. *Origins of Poe's Critical Theory*. New York: Russell & Russell, 1965.

Elmer, Jonathan. *Reading at the Social Limit: Affect, Mass Culture, and Edgar Allan Poe*. Palo Alto, CA: Stanford University Press, 1995.

Gordon, Adam. "'A Condition to Be Criticized': Edgar Allan Poe and the Vocation of Antebellum Criticism." *Arizona Quarterly* 68, no. 2 (Summer 2012): 1–31.

Hutchisson, James M. "The Reviews: Evolution of a Critic." In *The Cambridge Companion to Edgar Allan Poe*, edited by Kevin J. Hayes, 7–20. Cambridge: Cambridge University Press, 2002.

Jackson, Leon, "'Behold Our Literary Mohawk, Poe': Literary Nationalism and the 'Indianation' of Antebellum American Culture." *ESQ* 48, no. 1–2 (2002): 97–133.

Jacobs, Robert D. *Poe: Journalist & Critic*. Baton Rouge: Louisiana State University Press, 1969.

McGann, Jerome. "Poe, Decentered Culture, and Critical Method." In *Poe and the Remapping of Antebellum Print Culture*, edited by J. Gerald Kennedy and Jerome McGann, 245–259. Baton Rouge: Louisiana State University Press, 2012.

McGill, Meredith. *American Literature and the Culture of Reprinting, 1834–1853*. Philadelphia: University of Pennsylvania Press, 2003.

Moss, Sidney P. *Poe's Literary Battles: The Critic in the Context of His Literary Milieu*. Durham, NC: Duke University Press, 1963.

Park, Edd Winfield. *Edgar Allan Poe as Literary Critic*. Athens: University of Georgia Press, 1964.

Pollin, Burton R., ed. *The Collected Writings of Edgar Allan Poe. Vol. 3, Writings in The Broadway Journal: Nonfictional Prose—Part I: Text. Vol. 4, Writings in The Broadway Journal: Nonfictional Prose—Part II: Annotations. Vol. 5, Writings in the Southern Literary Messenger: Nonfictional Prose*, edited by Pollin and Joseph V. Ridgely. New York: Gordion Press, 1986, 1986, 1997.

Whalen, Terence, *Edgar Allan Poe and the Masses: The Political Economy of Literature in Antebellum America*. Princeton, NJ: Princeton University Press, 1999.

CHAPTER 27

THE MARGINAL CENTER

"Pinakidia," "Marginalia," and "Fifty Suggestions"

STEPHEN RACHMAN

"PINAKIDIA"

EDGAR Allan Poe's "Pinakidia" (1836), "Marginalia" (1844–1849), and "Fifty Suggestions" (1849) are magazine pieces comprised of brief quotations of, and fragmentary comments upon, other works of literature. Although they seem casual, even random, and they undoubtedly served the purpose of filling out space in the various magazines to which Poe either contributed or served as editor, they are a literary form that he returned to time and again, spanning the whole of his editorial work from his early productions with the *Southern Literary Messenger* (1835) through the last year of his life (1849). Poe wrote over six hundred items in this manner, and taken together these piecemeal observations represent important artifacts from "the Magazine Prison-House" in which he labored, a "fourth genre," distinct from the poems, tales, and critical essays he is best known for and yet intimately connected to those works. Because these "brevities," as Burton Pollin has called them, offer specimens of pointed literary opinion, raise issues of borrowing and plagiarism, and refer to a wide array of obscure and classical learning (while in general being drawn from or even copied from a relatively small set of sources), they have been used by Poe scholars as a kind of literary DNA to gauge the depth and limitations of Poe's actual learning, beliefs, mendacity, or playfulness, depending on one's approach.[1] These odds and ends have provided traces and clues to answer the question of how Poe came to have known the works and bits of arcana that he presents in these marginal productions, and by extrapolation the literary details with which he ornaments his tales and essays.

In the 1920s and 1930s, Killis Campbell, Thomas Ollive Mabbott, Earl Leslie Griggs, and Thomas K. Jackson assiduously began to trace Poe's sources for details and literary references within his tales, and the brief composite pieces became a rich repository for such sleuthing. In "Pinakidia" alone, one can find entries on topics that would interest

Poe throughout his career. Many items show a ready appetite for such topics as torture and imprisonment, mottoes on dungeons, codes, acrostics, and literary hoaxes (entries 8, 9, 22, 23, 25), hardly surprising from the author of "The Pit and the Pendulum," "The Gold Bug," and "Hans Pfaall." Many of the obscure references and quotations that filigree his tales were cycled and recycled through these marginal writings, and thus, with varying degrees of caution, scholars have speculated on Poe's knowledge of classical and foreign languages based on the sources he used, the texts and opinions he reproduced, and errors he repeated. Because "Pinakidia," "Marginalia," and "Fifty Suggestions" give the impression in the aggregate and in many individual entries of impossibly wide-ranging and detailed erudition—a theme that recurs in Poe's writing—scholars have been quick to conclude that the sources for these pieces are evidence of how Poe "created" his aura of learning.

For Terence Whalen, however, these pieces express more than Poe's sense of the relation between the public and literary erudition or a mere catalogue of sources. In "Pinakidia," for example, Whalen perceives Poe's "demystifying, materialist approach to literary production" in which ostensibly "new" literary material is revealed actually to consist "of small, manageable bits of meaning wrested or stolen from some earlier work."[2] In a sense, Whalen ascribes a different and deeper underlying motive for Poe's marginal writings, suggesting that he was actually using these commentaries in "Pinakidia" to propound a theory of literary creativity. Rather than merely filling space in a magazine with miscellaneous materials that are amusing or provocative, and that happen actually to contain, as Poe explained, "much thought and more research" than the reading public generally appreciated, he implicitly advocated for a replicant model in which modern literature derives itself directly from imitation and cribbing of prior works, harvesting these elements in, as Whalen points out, discrete, manageable units or bits.

While Poe has been largely viewed as an exemplar of romantic genius, Whalen's observation points to one of the abiding critical differences that marks Poe's distinct creative philosophy: his investment in literary derivation, recycling, intertextuality, and the conscious calculations of the working literary artist. The controlled calculation of literary effect as expressed in "The Philosophy of Composition" (1846); the assertion in "The Rationale of Verse" (1849) that English versification has been needlessly mystified and its building blocks can be found in specific, traceable forms (he argued for the stressed metrical feet of the spondee); and his ongoing preoccupation with literary imitation and plagiarism as seen most notoriously in his 1845–1846 charges leveled at Henry Wadsworth Longfellow, but also in most of his reviews, his unpublished exposé of his own literary purloining, "A Reviewer Reviewed," and, of course, the marginal essays under consideration here. All of these works testify to a long-standing and relatively consistent position that Poe maintained. Although the Romantic era is known for promulgating a belief in literary creativity as rooted in personal inspiration or genius, and Poe may have been what we have come to recognize as a literary genius, Poe's own theory, as illustrated in "Pinakidia" and the rest of his marginal essays, argued not so much for the individual genius as for a calculus of literary creativity that trends toward conscious adoption and adaptation. Poe saw that literary history bears the marks of replication and reduplication with change occurring through gradual, traceable variations.

Pinakidia, a Greek term for "tablets" (as in sheets for writing or inscribing), was Poe's willfully obscure title for his first foray into this form of marginal work, and it was meant to convey the mixture of classical arcana and wholehearted miscellany present in the project. And yet the 170 or so entries in "Pinakidia," while random seeming in their obscure details, do reflect Poe's overarching thematic concern with linguistic and literary origins. The continual assemblage of recherché ancient materials served not only to flaunt Poe's erudition but also to reinforce his sense of the deep history of literature as copying and variation. In fact, a word-cloud analysis of "Pinakidia" shows that forms of the word "origin" or "original" occur fifteen times; "derive" and its variants and "after" (in the sense of imitating), six times; "stolen," five times; while "model," "appropriate" (in the sense of commandeer), "theft," "imitation," "plagiarism," and "verbatim" all make appearances. What is taken and *mis*-taken through the long literary historical process of verbal production and reproduction is Poe's chief preoccupation, and this provides whatever unity the varied commentaries possess.

The entries in "Pinakidia" take up questions of copying in various ways. Some entries point to direct borrowing of lines by individual authors (entries 4, 5, 33, 36, 38, 39, 40, 65, 67, 69, 89, 92, 93, 94, 96, 97, 105, 138); for example, the fourth entry reads:

> The hunter and the deer a shade
>
> is a much admired line in Campbell's *Gertrude of Wyoming*—but the identical line is to be found in the poems of the American Freneau. (P 2: 12)

In this case, he refers to the Scottish poet Thomas Campbell, whose 1809 poem on the American topic of the Wyoming massacre contains a line taken from the American poet Philip Freneau's 1788 poem "The Indian Burial Ground." There is a tacit irony that Poe has singled out a European author borrowing from an American source on an American subject given that American authors were typically seen as derivative of their European counterparts, but the greater point emphasized in this instance is that the very line singled out for praise has been pilfered. All the best bits, generic innovations, lines, turns of phrase, and concepts are adapted, adopted, borrowed, imitated, or, as in this case, stolen. As Pollin and others have shown, Isaac Disraeli's *Curiosities of Literature* was a major source (if not *the* major source) of many of Poe's anecdotes, and what *Curiosities* revealed to Poe was the way that literary history had been shaped by a kind of survival of the "fittest" of its elements—a process in which attractive notions and phrases were subject to chains of literary appropriation, reappropriation, and misappropriation.[3] Poe saw literary history in terms of the ways in which its constitutive elements had been subsumed in shifts and transfers of authorial provenance.

In keeping with this perspective, other entries concern themselves in various ways with the influence of common sources as generic templates for subsequent authors or versions of a particular work (entries 3, 19, 31, 32, 35, 44, 53, 56, 61, 69, 86, 87, 100, 101, 116, 119, 120, 122, 125, 137, 144, 163.) For example, the third entry reads,

> The *Turkish Spy* is the original of many similar works—among the best of which are Montesquieu's *Persian Letters*, and the *British Spy* of our own Wirt. It was written undoubtedly by John Paul Marana, an Italian, in Italian, but probably was first published in French. Dr. Johnson, who saw only an English translation, supposed it an English work. Marana died in 1693. (P 2: 12)

If, in the Campbell-Freneau plagiarism, specific language was taken verbatim, in this instance the original source exerts its influence across languages (Italian to French to English) and countries (Italy, France, and the United States). It is not specific words but a literary device, the conceit of a series of letters written by a foreign spy as a platform for social observation and critique. In the original, an Ottoman spy satirizes the seventeenth-century French court; Montesquieu updates this and makes the protagonist Persian and the court eighteenth century; Wirt adapts this premise to that of a British spy secretly observing the young American republic. In this way, "Pinakidia" establishes a history of literary ideas adapted for use in various local forms. The premise of the "other" writing a candid secret history of a country as a vehicle for social satire becomes an instance through which Poe exposes the transnational and translingual pathways that literary forms regularly take over the course of time.

The underlying tension in "Pinakidia" (and the "Marginalia") that Poe wrestled with throughout his creative work had to do with this basic position that literary creativity is essentially derivative and yet, in the greatest and most serious of artists, it is instilled with the aspiration toward, and occasional achievement of, genuine innovation. How then does innovation emerge out of a long history of imitation and pilfering? Poe was often self-deprecating when considering the originality of his own productions. He remarked that his tales of ratiocination featuring M. Dupin—the genre in which Poe undoubtedly has the greatest claim to originality—owed their popularity to being something in "a new key," and that readers deemed them cleverer than they actually were. "I do not mean to say that they are not ingenious," he explained in a letter to a correspondent, "but people think them more ingenious than they are—on account of their method and air of method" (CL 1: 595).[4] Poe's private suspicion that the public has overestimated the ingenuity of his detective fictions reflects his general sense that runs through the marginal pieces, that the reading public is generally ignorant of how much of modern literature is actually derivative of older work.

In "The Philosophy of Composition" (1846), the celebrated essay that describes an ultra-self-conscious method by which "The Raven" was constructed, Poe maintains a curious sense of the artist having complete control over the selection of each element of the poem. This doggedly methodical sense is the very element that has made many readers question the sincerity of the piece—is it more parody or rationalization than straightforward account of the poem's genesis? In light of "Pinakidia," the ambiguous sincerity in "The Philosophy of Composition" appears to reflect a tension between Poe's sense that literary history has always been constituted by acts of culling the most useful of what has come before and the self-conscious act of creating a particular literary work. As Poe attempts to apply this general position to his own specific creation, every element becomes intentional. Language itself can therefore function like literature in this regard. An author might "select" a raven from Dickens's *Barnaby Rudge* and with equal deliberation the sonority of the vowel sounds in the word "nevermore," and from these choices assemble an innovative poetic work like "The Raven." In this way, any literary effort might be both original and derivative simultaneously; or, as Poe would put it in "Marginalia" (even when championing originality), "To be original is merely to be novel" (P 2: 224, Marginalia 119), and "a copyist is, as a general rule, by no means necessarily unoriginal" (P 2: 287, Marginalia 173). This paradoxical tension in which the preponderance of literary history tends toward imitation out of which authors occasionally innovate as the circumstances demand, goes some way toward explaining the contradictory, and at times hypocritical, attitudes Poe maintained toward authorship in general and certain authors in particular.

"Vainly I had sought to borrow/From my books surcease of sorrow," the poet in "The Raven" informs us (M 1: 365, lines 9–10). If the ordinary interpretation of this formulation sits there plainly enough—the poet looked without success for distraction from his grief in a book—its actual syntax is more suggestive of "literary borrowing" and the mental preoccupation involved in reading that is the main theme of Poe's marginal writings.[5] "The Raven" is one of the most suggestive poems—casting a spell on the reader—yet it begins paradoxically with a book whose quaint and curious suggestive force is no match for the speaker's own lugubrious anxieties. Given Poe's critical obsession with tracing the borrowings of others, the irony in his assertion that the one thing the poet might seek to appropriate from a book—the cessation of sorrow—cannot be obtained from it speaks directly to the problem of the individual artist in literary history, or what T. S. Eliot would call "Tradition and the Individual Talent." What might be borrowed from a book and what is properly one's own emotional condition preoccupied Poe throughout his career, and he spent much of the year 1845 (while drafting "The Philosophy of Composition") entangled in charges of plagiarism he leveled against Longfellow—a case in which Poe seems in many instances by sheer force of argument to push what is generally derivative in Longfellow's poetry into the realm of plagiarism ("*willful and deliberate literary theft*").[6] It also provides a context for understanding Poe's posthumous, unfinished "A Reviewer Reviewed" in which he would, under the pseudonym of Walter G. Bowen, prosecute himself for his own literary pilfering (ER: 1050). No matter how innovative an author might be—and Poe was certainly egotistical enough to value his own efforts—the weight of literary history was on the side of borrowing.[7] In tracing the shifts and contradictions in Poe's positions with regard to plagiarism as he prosecuted his "Longfellow War," Meredith McGill observes that, after months of asserting the immorality of plagiarism and Longfellow's guilt, "Poe shifts from his attempt to prove the legitimacy of the grounds of the *charge* of plagiarism to an attempt to construct a narrative in which the *practice* of plagiarism could be considered legitimate."[8] "Pinakidia" reveals that Poe had early on come to see that imitation and plagiarism—whether legitimate or not—were normative practices in literary history since antiquity, and as the print culture of his own career proliferated and accelerated instances of appropriation, Poe oscillated in his attempts to systematically differentiate legitimate forms of appropriation from illegitimate ones.

While it would be going too far to suggest that Poe took a Darwinian approach to literary history, a strong principle of, if not natural selection, then aesthetic selection informs his line of attack, and these chains of development were never simply confined to literary forms but move easily into politics, history, the sciences, and natural history. A number of "Pinakidia" entries deal with the ways in which modern systems of classification and cosmology were anticipated in ancient philosophical and poetic texts (entries 6, 12, 13, 19, 58, 60, 69, 70, 71, 72, 84, 114, 151). The sixth entry, for example, mentions a "peculiar zodiac of the comets" found in the "verses" of the astronomer Cassini (though which Cassini—Giovanni or Jacques—is not specified), followed a few entries later by a more detailed commentary in which the theme becomes more visible.

> Theophrastus, in his botanical works, anticipated the sexual system of Linnaeus. Philolaus of Crotona maintained that comets appeared after a certain revolution—and Æcetes contended for the existence of what is now called the new world. Pulci, "the sire of the half-serious rhyme," has a passage expressly alluding to a western continent. Dante, two centuries before, has the same allusion. (P 2: 17)

For Poe, an equilibristic relationship exists between the sciences and poetry; the revolutionary astronomy of the Cassinis led to novel poetic zodiacs, and the revolutionary botany of Linneaus was anticipated by ancient texts, as were the astronomical observations associated with Copernicus, Halley, and the Cassinis, and likewise, intimations of the New World. In entry 151, Poe asserts that the magnetic concepts of attraction and repulsion (which were at the forefront of scientific thinking in the 1830s) were anticipated by the work of the ancient Greek philosopher and poet Empedocles (P 2: 93). In this fragmentary way, the linkages between Poe's poetic/literary thinking and his cosmological thinking, the fusion of thought that would surface in "Al Aaraaf" (1829) and culminate in *Eureka* (1848), found expression in his marginal pieces.

Whalen refers to "Pinakidia" as a satire, and while there is certainly a tone of scorn or levity in some of its elements, this could be a misleading term because often a sense of adumbration and suggestiveness predominates which militates against the general tactics of satire. Many items in "Pinakidia" are proffered with the aim of inspiring curiosity or seeking to defamiliarize a concept or debunk a commonly held belief or perception. For example, in one entry (16) Poe mentions a biblical scholar who insists that "the upright beam of the cross was a *fixture* at the place of execution, whither the criminal was made to bear only the transverse arm. Consequently, the painters are in error who depict our Savior bearing the entire cross" (P 2: 19). In this instance, Poe deploys a classical/biblical factoid to call into question a traditional image of Christian visual culture. The notion that most representations of Christ on the Via Dolorosa may be fundamentally inaccurate, that he may have only had the crossbar to bear, indicates the way in which even sacrosanct cultural representations have been fundamentally distorted.

In these ways, the demystifying impulse behind the "Pinakidia" extends beyond the literary to other arts and, we might add, to the cultural level itself. Another entry (58) mentions "a bearded Venus" and a female Jupiter, suggesting that the commonest assumptions about the gendering of the Greco-Roman gods and goddesses were much more fluid than those of Poe's day (P 2: 44). With a similar aim, he points out that ancient philosophy understood man to be composed of body, soul, and spirit—the distinction between soul and spirit being largely lost on nineteenth-century readers. So while chains of priority are of ever-present interest in the "Pinakidia" and all the marginal writings, Poe is equally attentive to distortions and ellipses—what has been lost or altered in our modern cultural formations.

"Marginalia"

"Marginalia," which began its first installment in *United States Magazine, and Democratic Review* in November 1844 and ran in seventeen installments (and several different publications) through September 1849, marked the literary development Poe had made in the eight years between Richmond and the *Southern Literary Messenger* and his literary life in New York. Poe's replicant model of literary history with its long strands of repeated lines and elements finds its critical echo in "Marginalia." Where in "Pinakidia" we generally encountered small manageable bits of older texts, in "Marginalia" we encounter small manageable doses of literary opinion with the older texts gone missing. Whereas the entries in "Pinakidia" present themselves as artifacts plucked at random from literary history, "Marginalia" present themselves with much more authorial command and presence, clarifying a point which was left open-ended in its first iteration. For example, "Pinakidia" simply mentions that "The word Τvχη, or Fortune, does not appear once in the whole Iliad" (P 2: 15). In "Marginalia" the same observation is fleshed out: "It is certainly very remarkable that although destiny is the ruling idea of the Greek drama, the word Τυχη (Fortune) does not appear once in the whole Iliad" (P 2: 225). What appeared as an interesting curiosity in the first entry becomes in the second version a conceptual lacuna within the texture of literary history. How could a notion so central to Greek tragedy not find expression in its foundational poetry? The implication to Poe was that the centrality of fortune and destiny was developed by Greek drama but that drama was in its infancy in terms of aesthetic development. In another entry he wrote,

> About the "Antigone," as about all the ancient plays, there seems to me a certain *baldness*, the result of inexperience in art.... The profound sense of one or two tragic, or rather, melodramatic elements (such as the idea of inexorable Destiny)—this sense

> gleaming at intervals from out the darkness of the ancient stage, serves, in the very imperfection of its development. (P 2: 313)

If one considers the arc of this marginal note from its first development in Poe's thought, we recognize that an interesting factoid about the *Iliad* in 1836 has been, in the course of ten years, fully woven into a theory about the birth of tragedy and a comparative history of aesthetic and generic development. In this case, it is not so much that we can trace a line or phrase that Poe might have used as an epigraph or to ornament one of his tales—though Poe was certainly in the habit of wrenching his sentences to accommodate these kinds of quotations—but rather it serves to form the very ground upon which Poe would base his assessments of imitativeness and innovation.

"Pinakidia" provided Poe with a kind of idea box from which he would extract an artifact of prior fascination, dust it off, and put it to new purpose, and "Marginalia" frequently identified those new purposes. For instance, "Pinakidia" informs us with seeming randomness that "The Jesuits called Crébillon 'Puer ingeniosus, sed insignis nebulo'" (P 2: 81). It does not take much imagination to see young Poe discovering something of a literary confrere in Prosper-Jolyot de Crébillon, an eighteenth-century French playwright who was described in the Latin quoted earlier as "a clever boy, but a great rascal." Poe would invoke Crébillon in the Dupin stories, perhaps as a way to signal the ways in which his master detective possessed the same mixture of shrewdness and audacity. In the first installment of "Marginalia," Poe repurposes this line:

> It† is the half-profound, half-silly, and wholly irrational composition of a very clever, very ignorant, and laughably impudent fellow—"ingeniosus puer, sed insignis nebulo," as the Jesuits have well described Crébillon.
>
> † "The Age of Reason" (P 2: 132)

In the second iteration, Poe has placed this quip as if it were a marginal commentary on Thomas Paine's famously irreverent deist tract, *The Age of Reason*, giving the mixture of cleverness, nonsense, and impudence a local and relatively contemporary habitation, as it were. Paine's attack on the Bible lends the Jesuit element of the anecdote greater relevance and Paine's effrontery becomes that of a miscreant more than a scoundrel. In "Pinakidia" Poe had traced the adaptations of "The Turkish Spy" across languages and nations; in "Marginalia," he would become the agent of that same process, adapting a remark about Crébillon to his own historical moment, and his own literary situation.

In "Marginalia," the sense of the first person speaking is more distinct. Indeed, first person is often used, as in entry 34: "I am far more than half serious in all that I have ever said about manuscript, as affording indication of character" (P 2: 140). Poe makes reference to his "Autography" articles in which he playfully analyzed the handwriting of well-known literary figures. As these pieces had appeared some years before in *The Southern Literary Messenger* and in *Graham's*, the idea of Poe returning to a topic that had once preoccupied him lends the "Marginalia" a flavor of experience—as if to say we are now in the spirited presence of a practiced literary hand, a veteran of the editorial desk. "Marginalia" reframes the tablet-like factoids, scraps of literary arcana, and critical preoccupations found in "Pinakidia" more playfully, enmeshes them more deeply in the scene of reading, and expresses its views in more direct terms, calling out particular authors by name. As the likely fictionalized introduction to the "Marginalia" indicates, the notion that we are being allowed access to the jottings of Poe's reading mind, literally situated at the margins of other texts, has replaced the oblique commentaries of "Pinakidia":

> In getting my books, I have been always solicitous of an ample margin; this is not so much through any love of the thing in itself, however agreeable, as for the facility it affords me of pencilling suggested thoughts, agreements and differences of opinion, or brief critical comments in general. Where what I have to note is too much to be included within the narrow limits of a margin, I commit it to a slip of paper, and deposit it between the leaves; taking care to secure it by an imperceptible portion of gum tragacanth paste. (P 2: 107)

For Poe, the ingenious critical premise of the marginal micro-essay becomes something new in this iteration, a way to speak with more liberality, with what he calls "*abandonnement*," that is to say, a candor bordering on reckless abandon. "Marginalia" promises the reader "Poe Uncensored," the immediate literary reactions of America's most ferocious and caustic critic. If "Pinakidia" encouraged the modern reader to consider that ancient, barely visible literary history that was and could be the secret source of modern literary power, "Marginalia" took many of the same materials and directed them at modern literary targets and did so in a modern literary form with unprecedented directness.

"Pinakidia" makes mention of the treatise of "The Three Imposters," a work allegedly dating to the thirteenth century, around which there was a great deal of outcry and censure—"religious hubbub" is Poe's term for it. But the point of fascination for Poe was that "[t]he work in question, however, which was squabbled about, abused, defended, and familiarly quoted by all parties, is well proved never to have existed" (P 2: 15). In "Marginalia," Poe aspired to create a simulacrum of just such a phenomenon—all of the condensed cream of literary "hubbub" with the central "work in question" missing from the scene. Indeed, Poe's marginal writings were intended to be "brain-scattering," funny in a confusing way, abuzz with table-talk, and literary "chit-chat" (P 2: 107, 108). "How many good books suffer neglect," Poe opined in entry 33,

> through the inefficiency of their beginnings! It is far better that we commence irregularly—immethodically—than that we fail to arrest attention; but the two points, method and pungency, may always be combined. At all risks, let there be a few vivid sentences *imprimis*, by way of the electric bell to the telegraph. (P 2: 139)

Like Morse's electric bell that signaled an incoming telegraphic message, "Marginalia" aspired to be another form of modern signaling (the telegraph being one of the hallmark inventions of the 1830s and 1840s), an electrified form—pungent and vivid—calculated to arrest attention.

Though the average entry was much longer than 140 characters, in a curious way, "Marginalia" functioned like antebellum Twitter, and, like tweets, for all their force and immediacy, the danger of compression devolving beyond obscurity into unintelligibility was another risk of the form. Even if Poe's library actually did contain books filled with jottings fastened by an obscure mucilage called tragacanth paste—and there is no evidence that any of the books he was known to possess ever bore any traces of such notes or glue—the idea that these remarks taken out of context and prepared for print in monthly magazines might retain any clarity, coherence, or force is hard to imagine. Indeed, Poe worries that the "exceedingly frail fabric of intelligibility" of his marginal notes would be lost in translation from their "original" state to print (P 2: 108). Given that the "original" notes never "existed," Poe's concerns about intelligibility point to the form itself. Like a palimpsest in which the original text has been removed, "Marginalia" presents the fiction of a dialogue between writer and reader, distilled in such a way that all that remains is a reader's voice. In the first 1844 installment, after the introductory remarks, the first marginal note reads in its entirety: "Who has seen the '*Velschii Ruzname Naurus*,' of the Oriental Literature?" (P 2: 115). Not only could this entry be posted in one tweet (with sixty-nine characters to spare!), it is proffered in such oracular fashion that the reader hardly knows what it means or is meant to mean. In telescoping fashion, the reader seems to be looking vicariously at the margins of some obscure text that points to an even more arcane seventeenth-century Latin commentary on Persian and Turkish calendars by one George Jerome Welsch (hence the titular *Velschii*), but just what text prompted such a remark and what mental tissue of associations is connected with it have vanished. It reads like a "note to self," for as Poe indicated in his introduction about one of the chief attractions of marginal commentary, "we talk only to ourselves" (P 2: 108). "Pinakidia" makes reference to a Roman rhetorician who taught obscurity and liked to "say to his scholars, 'This is excellent—I do not understand it myself' " (P 2: 73). "Marginalia" operationalizes this type of impenetrability. "Nonsense," Poe concludes his introduction, is "the essential sense of the Marginal Note" (P 2: 109). In "Pinakidia," Poe presented a Spanish quatrain from Cervantes' *Don Quixote* as a "fine sample of *galimatias*," a type of nonsensical verse—or a type of language that veers between wit and nonsense (P 2: 72). In "Marginalia," the observation from "Pinakidia" inspires the form; "Marginalia" is effectively a sampler of contemporary *galimatias*.

In this fashion, "Marginalia" provides a wealth of miscellaneous critical opinion in small doses. The format allows Poe to mobilize and reiterate literary judgments and positions that he had put forward in previous guises without the apparatuses of the essay or review. One scholar views "Marginalia" as "*anti*-systematic," or as Poe explained to John R. Thompson, owner of the *Southern Literary Messenger* in the late 1840s, "Marginalia" afforded "great scope for variety of critical or other comment. . . . One great advantage will be that . . . I can touch, briefly, any topic you might suggest; and there are many points . . . which stand sorely in need of *touching*" (CL 2: 750–751).[9] As Maurice S. Lee has observed, "Marginalia" allowed for reaction to the informational overload that the emergent print culture of the 1840s had precipitated.[10] For Poe, "Marginalia" was emblematic of the relevancy and vitality of monthly magazine culture in general, which he deemed in "keeping with the *rush* of the age" (P 2: 308). Situated between the ponderous and stilted quarterly review and the ephemeral "popgunnery" of the majority of the daily newspaper press, the monthly magazine could provide "the light artillery of the intellect"—the agility and force—that the transportation and market revolutions of the 1840s, in Poe's view, demanded. "We need the curt," he opined in an 1846 installment of "Marginalia," reprising an argument he had made in the *Broadway Journal* and *Graham's Magazine*, "the condensed, the pointed, the readily diffused—in the place of the verbose, the detailed, the voluminous, the inaccessible" (P 2: 308). A degree of idealization obtains in Poe's description. "Marginalia" contains plenty of verbosity and obscurity (even in miniature) as do any of Poe's contributions to the magazine culture he championed. Nonetheless, he saw the cultural work of "Marginalia" aligned with and allied to the "magazine-ward" tendency of the 1840s, and he attempted in many of its installments to represent this mode of communication (P 2: 308). Insisting on the immediate and topical, Poe's "Marginalia" is populated with many of his favorite subjects that can also be found in his reviews and critical writing: Thomas Carlyle and the Frogpondians (Ralph Waldo Emerson, and the Transcendentalists—whom he reads as stylistic and philosophical disciples of Carlyle); his replies to Outis and the Longfellow War; Voltaire's dramatic ineptitude; defense of Bayard Taylor's travel poems; Hannah Flagg Gould's poetic virtues; praise and balanced criticism for Tennyson, Dickens, Bulwer, and William Gilmore Simms; potshots at Cornelius Matthews, Horace Greeley, and other New York literati.

Perhaps like any compendium of remarks (Poe called them a "*farrago*" in the Introduction [P 2: 109]), "Marginalia" must inevitably be of uneven quality, but within that variegation, there are veins of pure power that rival Poe's most enduring and indelible prose and poems. An 1848 entry on confessional writing in which Poe puts forward the notion of the human heart laid bare is a case in point.

> If any ambitious man have a fancy to revolutionize, at one effort, the universal world of human thought, human opinion, and human sentiment, the opportunity is his own—the road to immortal renown lies straight, open, and unencumbered before him. All that he has to do is to write and publish a very little book. Its title should be simple—a few plain words—"My Heart Laid Bare." But—this little book must be *true to its title.*
>
> Now, is it not very singular that, with the rabid thirst for notoriety which distinguishes so many of mankind—so many, too, who care not a fig what is thought of them, after death, there should not be found one man having sufficient hardihood to write this little book? To write, I say. There are ten thousand men who, if the book were once written, would laugh at the notion of being disturbed by its publication during their life, and who could not even conceive why they should object to its being published after their death. But to write it—*there* is the rub. No man dare write it. No man ever will dare write it. No man *could* write it, even if he dared. The paper would shrivel and blaze at every touch of the fiery pen. (P 2: 322–323)

Poe achieves a remarkable power and pathos in two brief paragraphs. In some measure this piece emerges from Poe's career-long engagement with the twinned themes of guilt and confession. Poe's prose works are notable for their confessional narratives (usually of murder) found in "William Wilson," "The Black Cat," "The Imp of the Perverse," and, of course, "The Tell-Tale Heart." Other tales feature scenes of confession ("The Murders in the Rue Morgue," "Thou Art the Man"), and some of his poems have confessional qualities as well (e.g., "Alone," "The Raven"). This tendency to shape narratives around confession is so pronounced in Poe that one scholar has gone so far as to describe the act of confession itself in his tales as intrinsically criminal.[11] But only in "Marginalia" does Poe place the theme of confession in the context of literary ambition, and, as he created the fiction of the literary gentleman reading and responding with pure abandon to his books, we are now presented with its echo: the counterfiction of the gentleman author attempting to write—what might seem so apparently simple—from the heart. Poe, always prescient about the tensions between composition and publication, makes a clear distinction. Many ambitious authors would have no qualms about such a publication—once written—but the composition of such a work proves, by Poe's lights, impossible, regardless of authorial desire or ambition. The condensation of this entry, the canny turn away from what has been stated to what is ultimately unwriteable despite the desire to write it, gives this marginal commentary its particular durability as an acknowledgment of the limits of human expression. The passage evokes an impossible scene of writing in which a self-consuming literary artifact disappears in the act of composition. The very materials of writing—ink and paper—are rendered combustible with the heat of a language that might disclose the human heart and brain. Charles Baudelaire likened Poe's "Marginalia" to "the secret chamber of his mind," but we must always proceed with caution when approaching Poe's secrets.[12] Poe was adept at creating the illusion of secrecy through the fictions of privacy. Just as he maintained the framing fiction of the marginal note, his entry on the heart laid bare stands like a prose poem as an elusive emblem of what modern writing aspires to be and can never achieve. It conveys a sense and a sensation of what "Marginalia" and all of Poe's marginal writings hold out as a promise and an impossibility.

"Fifty Suggestions"

The late piece "Fifty Suggestions," which appeared in *Graham's Magazine* for May–June 1849, reprises many entries that first emerged in "Pinakidia" and were subsequently worked over in "Marginalia," but in yet more abbreviated form. It seems to be on its face a limit case of compression, an attempt in one or two installments to encapsulate a condensed version of the already condensed. In terms of overall literary thought, "Fifty Suggestions" in general adds little to what Poe had explored before in "Marginalia" and seems in its briefest entries to veer toward one-liners and jokes, most of which appear, at least from the vantage of 150 years of criticism, not particularly amusing. Targets from his New York Literati pieces, such as Cornelius Matthews (Fifty Suggestions 18, 31, 40, 46) and Horace Greeley (28, 47), come in for the usual treatment (mockery), and odd swipes at other figures seem to serve only the purposes of a joke. For example,

> Miss Edgeworth seems to have had only an approximate comprehension of "Fashion," for she says: "If it was the fashion to burn me, and I at the stake, I hardly know ten persons of my acquaintance who would refuse to throw on a faggot." There are many who, in such a case, would "refuse to throw on a faggot"—for fear of smothering out the fire. (P 2: 504)

This squib's attempt at "sick humor" delivered in a genteel manner completely misfires. Its connection to Maria Edgeworth is unclear, and since Poe's only point of disagreement seems to be a quibble about how best to build up a fire while burning someone at the stake, it seems arbitrarily cruel, more about how best to burn someone than any legitimate or abiding critical opinion that he might have held. Another entry (20) about whipping children to tenderize them like beefsteaks seems more gruesome than funny (P 2: 487). It is as if the decapitating ferocity for which Poe was well known ("the tomahawk man") can no longer properly locate its critical targets. Perhaps these moments are like the brutal and shocking aspects of his tales of terror which often surface with a punning flourish (e.g., Masons/Masonry in "The Cask of the Amontillado"), but in "Fifty Suggestions" they are presented to the reader in isolation without the complex symbolic matrix of the tale to surround and stabilize them or confer upon them greater aesthetic power.

This is not to say that "Fifty Suggestions" does not possess entries of genuine power and substance. Indeed, the critical malice at work in some of its jokes becomes a key underlying theme in other ones. The first entry—a punning comment about the relative impurity associated with the colors black and blue—under the guise of a joke, contemplates how to blacken the reputation of a woman (P 2: 475). The third entry reads: "As far as I can understand the 'loving our enemies,' it implies the hating our friends" (P 2: 477). Another entry plays with the phrase "nasty poets" (P 2: 481); still another worries over how best to speak of the dead in such a way as to place emphasis on the restraint required so as not to speak ill of them (P 2: 480–481). A wry comment about newspaper editors in a Gothamite Valhalla, "who cut each other to pieces every day, and yet get up perfectly sound and fresh every morning," suggests a print culture saturated with almost gleeful ambient cruelty (P 2: 482). A "Used up" author, eyes weeping and stinging from a savage review, seems to take masochistic pleasure in his rough treatment the way one might enjoy the burn from a spicy mustard (P 2: 486). Transcendentalist poetry à la Emerson exhibits, to Poe's mind, taste at the moment of death—a kind of lethally aesthetic cultural pathology (P 2: 492). Even the reputed delicate classical dancing of Marie Taglioni (in a strained pun on *lex Talionis*) is construed as a form of "vengeance on her present oppressors"—whomever they may have been (P 2: 493). A grim Horatian joke about how best to appease an "angry stomach" (Answer: "grave-y soup") points toward an undercurrent of literary irritation (P 2: 477). In an entry that also happens to take its cue from a remark by Horace, the theme emerges explicitly:

> That poets (using the word comprehensively, as including artists in general) are a *genus irritable*, is well understood; but the *why*, seems not to be commonly seen. An artist *is* an artist only by dint of his exquisite sense of Beauty—a sense affording him rapturous enjoyment, but at the same time implying, or involving, an equally exquisite sense of Deformity or disproportion. Thus a wrong—an injustice—done a poet who is really a poet, excites him to a degree which, to ordinary apprehension, appears disproportionate with the wrong. Poets *see* injustice—never where it does not exist—but very often where the unpoetical see no injustice whatever. Thus the poetical irritability has no reference to "temper" in the vulgar sense, but merely to a more than usual clearsightedness in respect to Wrong:—this clear-sightedness being nothing more than a corollary from the vivid perception of Right—of justice—of proportion. . . . But one thing is clear—that the man who is *not* "irritable," (to the ordinary apprehension,) is *no poet*. (P 2: 488–489)

In his introduction to his second collection of Poe translations, *Nouvelles Histoires extraordinaires*, Baudelaire quotes this passage with a sense of its importance as a general defense of poetic and aesthetic spleen, as an "excellent and irrefutable apology," not just for Poe but for himself and all aggressive criticism.[13] Poe's critique of impure judgment, as it were, arrived at yet another symptom of the genuine aesthetic temperament: a greater ability to perceive injustice. No longer mere artistic prickliness, Wordsworthian sensitivity, or Romantic apprehension of the beautiful, injustice—construed as the ability to perceive clearly disproportionate wrong—becomes the mark of distinction. As Leonard Cohen once wrote, "Poetry is a verdict, not an occupation."[14] While Poe's sweeping generality only allows us to speculate as to what kinds of justice he has in mind, it is safe to assume that "social justice," as it is conventionally understood, is the least of his concerns. Rather, it is the kind of justice provided by informed literary opinion, with a deep sense of literary history, that had been behind all of his marginal commentaries. In "Fifty Suggestions" it irritated Poe to see the way that the culture of criticism he lived and worked in could turn a signal strength of an author into a limitation. If Macaulay was known for his style, then it would become a critical commonplace that this feature was his work's only virtue; if Tennyson used a quaint expression to striking effect, then Tennyson was equated with quaintness. "The ingenuity of critical malice would often be laughable," Poe suggested, "but for the disgust which, even in the most perverted spirits, injustice never fails to excite" (P 2: 498). In this way for Poe, literature constitutes itself as a few sweeping theoretical and aesthetic generalizations and a multitude of opinions.

Poe began this strain of critical commentary with the notion of tablets, moved on to marginalia, and by the end of his career, arrived at the notion of the suggestion, or rather, a series of suggestions. If tablets connoted the random artifact culled from literary history, and marginalia emphasized the discerning, engaged reader at the edge of books, the suggestion is the most adumbrative of marginal forms. Poe, always intent upon having his say in the field of letters, opted in the end for a shadowy form of communication—the power of suggestion and mental association—hinting at his concerns, rather than presenting them more fully. Scholars have come to regard these marginal essays as a central and perennial resource of Poe's reading, ideas, and opinion; "a genuine treasure trove," in the words of one researcher.[15] Like Henry David Thoreau's *Journal* or Nathaniel Hawthorne's *Notebooks*, Poe's marginal writings taken as a whole represent one of the great, germinative archives of antebellum US literature. They stand alongside these other great repositories of the building blocks of nineteenth-century literature. They have allowed us to glimpse the phases of development of literary composition, the masterwork in embryonic form, and in some cases to peel back the layers in order to reveal the tissues of thought and language. Pet notions, touchstone phrases, authors admired and disparaged alike, and, on occasion, the crucial act of reading that sets off an act of writing are all rich veins of ore to be mined in Poe's marginal center. But Hawthorne's and Thoreau's private records were created and maintained within an actual realm of privacy. The crucial difference with Poe's marginal writings was that the private sphere of composition and reading was essentially fictional, belonging more to the precincts of the editorial office than to the private study or library. They were designed to offer their welter of private opinion and grand theory of literary history in the public glare of print.

Notes

1. Burton Pollin revived the term "brevities" from a series of titles that Poe at one time considered and discarded for "Pinakidia," the first of Poe's magazine pieces in this style. It is perhaps more important that Poe emphasized the wide assortment of terms under which these entries could be found in magazines of the 1830s, and yet, despite the seeming hodgepodge and random formlessness of the form, they possess considerable literary value. "Under the head of 'Random Thoughts,' 'Odds and Ends,' 'Stray Leaves,' 'Scraps,' 'Brevities,' and a variety of similar titles," Poe introduces "Pinikidia," "we occasionally meet, in periodicals and elsewhere, with papers of rich interest and value" (P 2: 1).
2. Terence Whalen, *Edgar Allan Poe and the Masses: The Political Economy of Literature in Antebellum America* (Princeton, NJ: Princeton University Press, 1999), 26.
3. Earl Leslie Griggs and Thomas O. Mabbott traced Poe's sources in "Pinakidia," pointing to the centrality of Isaac D'Israeli's *Curiosities of Literature*, along with works by Baron Bielfeld, Jacob Bryant, and James Montgomery; see Earl L. Griggs, "Five Sources of Edgar Allan Poe's 'Pinakidia,'" *American Literature* 1 (May 1929): 196–199. Pollin lists Poe's known sources for the marginal writings in a section called "Sources and Borrowings" (P 2: xxxiii–xxxvi). A tally of these sources indicates that he used Isaac D'Israeli's *Curiosities of Literature* for forty-nine of the "Pinakidia" pieces, more than twice his usage of any other source.
4. Poe to Philip Pendleton Cooke, New York, August 9, 1846.
5. For a more detailed discussion, see Stephen Rachman, "'The Raven' in *The Raven and Other Poems*," in *Edgar Allan Poe in 20 Objects from the Susan Jaffe Tane Collection*, ed. Gabrielle Dean and Richard Kopley (Baltimore: Sheridan Libraries and Johns Hopkins University, 2016), 70–75.

6. In his 1845 series of articles on Longfellow, Poe accused Longfellow of "deliberate theft" (ER: 720), and in his posthumously published "A Reviewer Reviewed," accuses himself in italics of "wilful and deliberate literary theft" (ER: 1051).
7. For a discussion of "A Reviewer Reviewed," Longfellow and Poe's approach to plagiarism, see Rachman " 'Es lässt sich nicht schreiben': Plagiarism, and 'The Man of the Crowd,' " in *The American Face of Edgar Allan Poe*, ed. Shawn Rosenheim and Stephen Rachman (Baltimore: The Johns Hopkins University Press, 1995), 85–100.
8. Meredith L. McGill, *American Literature and the Culture of Reprinting, 1834–1853* (Philadelphia: University of Pennsylvania Press, 2003), 212. McGill reads Poe's contradictory positions on plagiarism in terms of a print culture which, in her view, tends toward anonymity, leading to a general condition in which imitation and reprinting are ambient and the adjudication of the authentic and inauthentic is virtually impossible.
9. The letter to Thompson indicates that Poe saw "Marginalia" as a means to address literary misrepresentations, especially sectional ones—Northern misrepresentations of Southern literature, in particular. For a reading of "Marginalia" as antisystematic sectional critique, see Jennifer Rae Greeson, "Poe's 1848: *Eureka*, the Southern Margin, and the Expanding U[niverse] of S[tars]," in *Poe and the Remapping of Antebellum Print Culture*, ed. J. Gerald Kennedy and Jerome McGann (Baton Rouge: Louisiana State University Press, 2012), 130–131.
10. Maurice S. Lee, "Poe by the Numbers: Odd Man Out?," in *Poe and the Remapping of Antebellum Print Culture*, ed. J. Gerald Kennedy and Jerome McGann (Baton Rouge: Louisiana State University Press, 2012), 233–234. Lee traces this reaction in Poe's attempts to quantify the era's expanding literary landscape.
11. See Jonathan Elmer, "Confessing the Crime of Confession," in *Reading at the Social Limit: Affect, Mass Culture, and Edgar Allan Poe* (Stanford, CA: Stanford University Press, 1997), 126–173.
12. Charles Baudelaire, introduction to *Nouvelles histoires extraordinaires*, by Edgar Allan Poe, trans. Baudelaire (Paris: Michel Levy Brothers, 1857), viii.
13. Baudelaire, introduction to *Nouvelles histoires extraordinaires*, xviii.
14. Leonard Cohen, *The Favorite Game & Beautiful Losers* (Toronto: McClelland & Steward, 2009), 175.
15. Jeffrey A. Savoye, "A 'Lost' Roll of Marginalia," *The Edgar Allan Poe Review* 3, no. 2 (Fall 2002): 52.

Bibliography

Adkins, Nelson F. " 'Chapter on American Cribbage': Poe and Plagiarism." *The Papers of the Bibliographical Society of America* 42, no. 3 (Third Quarter, 1948): 169–210.

Greeson, Jennifer Rae. "Poe's 1848: *Eureka*, the Southern Margin, and the Expanding U[niverse] of S[tars]." In *Poe and the Remapping of Antebellum Print Culture*, edited by J. Gerald Kennedy and Jerome McGann, 123–140. Baton Rouge: Louisiana State University Press, 2012.

Hayes, Kevin J. *Poe and the Printed Word*. Cambridge: Cambridge University Press, 2000.

Lee, Maurice S. "Poe by the Numbers: Odd Man Out?" In *Poe and the Remapping of Antebellum Print Culture*, edited by J. Gerald Kennedy and Jerome McGann, 227–244. Baton Rouge: Louisiana State University Press, 2012.

McGill, Meredith L. *American Literature and the Culture of Reprinting, 1834–1853*. Philadelphia: University of Pennsylvania Press, 2007.

Rachman, Stephen. "'Es lässt sich nicht schreiben': Plagiarism, and 'The Man of the Crowd.'" In *The American Face of Edgar Allan Poe*, edited by Shawn Rosenheim and Stephen Rachman, 85–100. Baltimore: The Johns Hopkins University Press, 1995.

Savoye, Jeffery A. "A 'Lost' Roll of Marginalia." *The Edgar Allan Poe Review* 3, no. 2 (Fall 2002): 52–72.

Whalen, Terence. *Edgar Allan Poe and the Masses: The Political Economy of Literature in Antebellum America*. Princeton, NJ: Princeton University Press, 1999.

CHAPTER 28

POE THE MAGAZINIST

PHILIP EDWARD PHILLIPS

WAS Edgar A. Poe a mad dreamer or a practical journalist? Did he live alone in a realm of imagination or instead inhabit the messy, competitive publishing world? Poe biographies of the early twentieth century tended to portray him as a figure "out of place, out of time," a quirky literary genius, detached from cultural conditions that surrounded him. This view of Poe, which persists today in the popular imagination, originated with the "Ludwig" obituary, composed by Rufus Wilmot Griswold, his literary executor, who presented Poe as someone who, *in spite of* his creative talents, was "at all times a dreamer—dwelling in ideal realms—in heaven or hell—peopled with creatures and the accidents of his brain."[1] This distorted view, termed the "Poe Legend" by Benjamin F. Fisher IV, was reinforced by Griswold in a "Memoir of the Author," which appeared in *The Works of the Late Edgar Allan Poe* (1850). Griswold's account included just enough factual details to render his falsehoods plausible, and the sad fact that Poe chose Griswold as his literary executor gave those misrepresentations further legitimacy.[2]

While Griswold promoted the "Poe Legend" by depicting Poe as erratic, mad, and thus incapable of functioning in the real world, his French admirer and translator, Charles Baudelaire, revered Poe *because of* his alienation from bourgeois life; he identified with the cursed poet, perceiving personal and artistic affinities. According to Lois Davis Vines, "Baudelaire saw in his American mentor a literary genius who understood the mechanism of artistic creation,"[3] and the French poet saw Poe as his double. Baudelaire introduced Poe to Europe and the French-speaking world as the epitome of the suffering artist, and his brilliant translations soon enshrined "Edgar Poe" as the idol of the Symbolist poets (as explained in later chapters by Emron Esplin and Margarida Vale de Gato).

But Poe the pragmatic journalist has recaptured our interest. Recent scholarship has focused importantly on Poe's engagement with the publishing world as well as his participation in and influence on a magazine culture rapidly expanding in America during the Jacksonian era. Meredith L. McGill characterizes the antebellum literary marketplace as far more complex and unstable than previously acknowledged. Within the "culture of reprinting" that emerged during those decades, she contends, the unregulated republishing of literary works "was not a violation of law or custom, but a cultural norm."[4] Indeed, she writes, "the explosive growth of print in antebellum America radically multiplied the means and modes through which writers could emerge as authors."[5] This proliferation of periodicals had two significant consequences: more venues enabled more writers to publish, but their work might then be republished elsewhere without compensation. Poe and the antebellum literati became accustomed to this give and take; if reprinting deprived them of income, it increased their recognition, attracted new readers, and identified potential outlets. Success required shrewdness, and some writers tried to optimize the publication and circulation of their work by becoming magazine editors.

Adapting himself to this emerging market, Poe tailored writings to fit the periodical page. Terence Whalen observes that "Poe's commitment to the magazine business helps to explain his preference for short literary works such as the tale, the scientific hoax, and even the critical polemic."[6] These shorter works, according to Whalen, "were the kinds of magazine articles that Poe regarded as a prerequisite to economic survival and artistic freedom."[7] The latter, however, proved more elusive because it required the former, and then some. The antebellum publishing world was increasingly dominated by weekly and monthly magazines, not books, which had long been the gold standard for authors. Compared to their British and European counterparts, American writers faced disadvantages in the literary marketplace. At home and abroad, many regarded America as a political experiment whose fate was uncertain. Underscoring the lack of history and culture in the United States, the Reverend Sydney Smith wrote condescendingly in the *Edinburgh Review*, "During the thirty or forty years of their independence, they have done absolutely nothing for the Sciences, for the Arts, for Literature, or even for the statesman-like studies of Politics or Political Economy." He then posed his sneering question, "In the four quarters of the globe, who reads an American book?"[8] And indeed, in Poe's time, only a handful of literary compatriots had emerged onto the world stage, American writers such as Washington Irving and James Fenimore Cooper, whose renown hardly compared to that of their celebrated counterparts on the other side of the Atlantic.

Another challenge arose from the problem of defining American literature, and debates raged about what constituted a "national literature" or what comprised an "American theme" or whether either required "American" locales. Poe advocated a US literature marked by originality—but *not* dependent on national flourishes to win cheap, partisan admiration. A further obstacle lay in the absence of an international copyright law, a situation that let American publishers reprint newly issued works by popular British authors without paying royalties. This "piracy" made it harder for homegrown authors to compete for literary income, at least in the book trade. Piracy also affected periodicals, and Poe sometimes blamed the lack of international copyright for the general mediocrity of American magazines. In the antebellum era, US periodicals could improve their profit margin by reprinting tales and poems gratis from British publications rather than paying American contributors. Still, magazines opened many more opportunities for remuneration (however paltry) than did book publishers. In

New York, Poe finally joined the American Copyright Club to fight for international literary rights.[9]

Despite early aspirations as a poet, Poe confronted the bitter truth that none of his first three volumes of verse produced income. To survive, he adapted by transforming himself into what he later called a "magazinist" (CL 1: 470). To be a successful author, he once remarked, "you must be *read*" (CL 1: 85), and in the 1830s this meant placing one's work in newspapers and periodicals. Poe adapted to the new periodical culture by developing expertise as a reviewer, a writer of tales, an editor, and, briefly, a magazine proprietor. He first published, and later reprinted, nearly all of his greatest literary works in periodicals. As Scott Peeples argues, the term "Magazinist" is appropriate for Poe because "[a]lmost everything he wrote appeared in a magazine before it appeared in a book."[10] After his second stint as an editorial assistant to an obtuse proprietor, however, Poe sought to become the owner and editor of his own magazine, which he first called *The Penn* and later *The Stylus*. Its establishment became, according to Whalen, Poe's "ultimate purpose."[11] Until the end of his life, he was driven by this passion to create a literary magazine of the highest quality—"a journal wherein may be found at all times . . . a sincere and a fearless opinion" (ER: 1035)—to elevate the standards of literature and the status of American letters on a global stage. That story will conclude this chapter.

Poe's Literary Beginnings and the American Literary Marketplace

Poe's career closely coincided with the rise of magazines as a dominant commercial product. Frank Luther Mott called the period of expansion from 1825 to 1850 the "Golden Age of Periodicals," noting that "in the years immediately following 1825 there was an extraordinary outburst of magazine activity."[12] While there were fewer than one hundred American periodicals, other than newspapers, in 1825, there were by 1850 approximately six hundred.[13] Mott observes that "if the average age of these periodicals was two years . . . then four or five thousand of them were published during [the] period. Even the names of a large proportion of these ephemerae are sunk in oblivion."[14] These obscure periodicals, now relegated to print archives or available only in electronic databases such as Hathi Trust or Internet Archive, form an illuminating, almost inexhaustible resource for understanding Poe's world.

As the author observed in an 1844 letter to Professor Charles Anthon, "the whole tendency of the age was to the Magazine literature—to the curt, the terse, the well-timed, and the readily diffused, in preference to the old forms of the verbose and the ponderous & the inaccessible" (CL 1: 467). This is the letter in which Poe identifies himself as "essentially a Magazinist" (CL 1: 470), and it was as a periodical writer that he labored while "holding steadily in view [his] ultimate purpose—to fou[n]d a Magazine of [his] own" (CL 1: 469). While uncompensated reprinting remained an inescapable fact for American authors seeking to support themselves by the pen, the cultural shift from books to magazines forced Poe to adapt his artistic aims to this reality. His innovations with shorter forms, suitable for the more concise parameters of magazines, led him to develop ideas about the prose tale (or short story) and to experiment with detective fiction, science fiction, and the tale of sensation.

As a schoolboy in England, Poe probably studied the leading British periodicals, including the *Edinburgh Review, Blackwood's,* and the *London Ladies' Magazine.* He may have browsed them on Basinghall Street at his foster-father's store, which stocked periodicals among other dry goods.[15] It was there that "Poe grew up speaking the language of commerce," according to Whalen, and first learned "the economic value of information, . . . that literature was a commodity produced for sale in the capitalist marketplace."[16] Poe's early exposure to British magazines, especially the "early numbers" of *Blackwood's*,[17] influenced his critical and editorial tendencies as well as his understanding of audience and content.

Early in life, Poe could never have imagined a career for himself as a magazinist, especially because that life entailed grueling work and crushing poverty if one lacked independent means. As Poe noted in his letter to Anthon, "in America[,] . . . more than any region upon the face of the globe[,] to be poor is to be despised" (CL 1: 470). When Poe quit Richmond in 1827 after a tumultuous break with his foster father, he set out for Boston, the city of his birth and the "Athens of America" (as Bostonians heralded it).[18] Although he managed to convince young Calvin F. S. Thomas to publish his early poetry in a slender pamphlet titled *Tamerlane and Other Poems. By a Bostonian*, the volume sold poorly (PL: 81). Poe began to realize that most prominent American poets came from comfortable circumstances; writing poetry was the prerogative of persons of leisure who devoted themselves to belles-lettres.

Boston offered Poe few prospects, prompting the youth to enlist in the US Army as "Edgar A. Perry." While in military service, however, Poe began reaching out to notables in the magazine world. He received his first real encouragement from John Neal, a novelist from Portland, Maine, and founder of the *Yankee; and Boston Literary Gazette.* Having received from Poe a letter containing some verses, Neal spoke of them favorably; he wrote in the September 1828 issue of the *Yankee* that Poe's lines, "though nonsense," are "rather exquisite nonsense." Neal encouraged Poe to "do himself justice" and "make a beautiful and perhaps a magnificent poem." Quoting from two poems, he concluded, "There is a good deal here to justify such a hope [that] the young poet has the capacity to write a magnificent poem," and he predicted that his journal would have room for other contributions from Poe.[19]

Although their styles differed considerably, both Neal and Poe shared a commitment to "beauty." Possibly because both had lived in England, Poe seems to have modeled his literary life upon aspects of Neal's career. For example, Neal's Delphian Club may have provided a model for Poe's projected "Tales of the Folio Club," and Neal's critical portraits of New England writers for *Blackwood's* likely influenced Poe's series on "Autography" as well as his literary reviews.[20] This association was arguably Poe's first serious engagement with the magazine world, and it was an important one. Neal would much later recount: "[Poe] says in one of his letters that I gave him the first push in his upward career, and for that reason was bound to keep him moving."[21]

But poetry did not pay, and by 1831 Poe had learned that lesson. He then retooled, making a quick study of the periodical world to grasp the conventions and complexities of the magazine market. But he also saw the vast potential of this new medium and came to embrace the role of magazinist. Over the next eighteen years, he would help to edit a handful of very different magazines and contribute to dozens of others. He got to know many of the literati and became fascinated by the invisible machinations of the publishing world. Poe came to understand the predicament of American letters as a cultural coarseness that he endeavored to combat as a critic and a champion of artistic quality. Although he never realized his vision of a national literary renaissance, Poe reached his widest audiences in the magazines, honing his influential critical views and leaving an indelible mark on American literature.

Poe's Editorial Stints

Over his professional career, Poe moved up and down the East Coast and worked in all the publishing capitals of antebellum America. He contributed to more than thirty periodicals, most notably *The Southern Literary Messenger, Burton's Gentleman's Magazine, Godey's, Graham's Magazine*, the *Democratic Review*, and the *American Review*, as well as to literary newspapers and annual gift books, such as *The Baltimore Book* and *The Gift*, which were popular during the period.[22] New technology was transforming publishing and the book trade. As Kevin J. Hayes observes, "pamphlet novels, which looked more like magazines than books, proliferated during the early 1840s. These cheap books profoundly influenced the American literary marketplace and significantly shaped the direction of Poe's career."[23] Indeed, Poe regarded these early cheap novels as highly inferior and soon "came to believe that owning and editing a magazine offered the best way for him to determine the course of American literature."[24]

Working as a magazinist led Poe to consider founding his own magazine. He concluded that the cheap, three-dollar magazine, with its mass readership and fashion plates, was too frivolous for his taste. "For Poe," according to Hayes, "only a five-dollar magazine would do."[25] Poe aspired to publish an "expensive, high-quality magazine"[26] that would appeal to the mind and attract a discerning, cultured audience, more likely to save monthly issues to be bound in a leather volume and added to personal libraries. In short, "Poe imagined a magazine," according to Hayes, "which would be worth keeping, while cheap books fell by the wayside."[27]

Just as Neal had encouraged Poe to continue writing poetry, John Pendleton Kennedy, a Baltimore novelist and congressman, first recognized Poe's genius as a writer of magazine tales, and he supported Poe's new career aspirations. Kennedy was among the judges who in 1833 selected Poe's "MS Found in a Bottle" to receive the first-place prize of $50 for the best tale in a contest held by the *Saturday Visiter*, which published the tale in the October 7 issue.[28] Kennedy subsequently directed Poe's attention to magazine work and helped him land his first editorial position, with Thomas Willis White's *Southern Literary Messenger*, a newly established magazine in Richmond that published its first issue in August 1834.

Before accepting a full-time job with the *Messenger*, Poe had contributed tales and reviews to the magazine, including "Berenice," a story published in the March 1835 issue. In that tale he had pushed the boundaries of acceptable literature and showed his familiarity with the sensational fiction popularized in *Blackwood's*. Many readers were horrified by the gruesomeness of "Berenice," a tale told by a narrator who extracts the teeth of his fiancée cousin *after* she has been buried and *while* she is still alive. Some readers complained to White, and, as Whalen notes, "recognizing that such complaints might jeopardize his job prospects, Poe defended himself by speaking a language a proprietor could understand."[29] Poe argues in his letter to White,

> The history of all Magazines shows plainly that those which have attained celebrity were indebted for it to articles *similar in nature—to Berenice*—although, I grant you, far superior in style and execution. . . . To be appreciated you must be *read*, and these things are invariably sought after with avidity. They are, if you will take notice, the articles which find their way into other periodicals, and into the papers, and in this manner, taking hold upon the public mind they augment the reputation of the source where they originated. . . . In respect to Berenice individually I allow that it approaches the very verge of bad taste—but I will not sin quite so egregiously again. I propose to furnish you every month with a Tale of the nature which I have alluded to. The effect—if any—will be estimated better by the circulation of the Magazine than by any comments upon its contents. (CL 1: 84–85)

According to Arthur Hobson Quinn, Poe's letter reveals that "he evidently was studying the magazines and not writing simply to suit himself in defiance of editorial tastes."[30] Although Poe affects a tone of modesty concerning the execution of the tale, he reveals astute insight into the reading preferences of the public. Whalen observes that it "is startling that the author of 'Berenice' would see fit to lecture a capitalist about the true nature of capitalism itself. Whether or not Poe was sincere, the passage reveals his willingness to adopt the calculating, aggressive stance toward literature and toward the mass audience whose 'taste' would henceforth be measured by the gross acts of purchase."[31]

When Poe moved to full-time editorial employment with the *Messenger* in August 1835, he began making a name for himself in the publishing world. In addition to "Berenice," he first published a handful of odd tales such as "King Pest," "Lionizing," "Morella," and "Shadow: A Fable" in the *Messenger*. In October 1835, Maria and Virginia Clemm joined Poe in Richmond, and Poe married his cousin on May 16, 1836. That year Poe contributed many other works to the *Messenger*, including his famous exposé, "Maelzel's Chess Player"; a cheeky, two-part "Autography" series; his "Drake-Halleck Review" (deploring "stupid" American books); the beginning of a verse drama, *Politian*;

and his long, fantastic moon narrative, "Hans Pfaall." To increase the magazine's prestige and build subscriptions, Poe inserted flattering reviews of the *Messenger* from newspapers to which he had sent courtesy copies. He also published reviews advocating South Seas exploration, which resonated with the two installments of *The Narrative of Arthur Gordon Pym* published in the *Messenger*.

According to Quinn, "While readers of the *Messenger* were having the opportunity to read his stories and poems, it was as a critic that Poe made his definite impression upon a public as yet not aware of him."[32] Quinn praises Poe the literary critic not only for his courage and judgment but also for his refusal to tolerate puffery—the mindless promoting, by friends or fellow coterie members, of insipid works by undeservedly esteemed writers, usually from the Northeast. Although Poe could be unfair to authors, he was justifiably relentless in criticizing literary cliques, and his reviews attracted readers. According to Robert D. Jacobs, "[Poe] thought that courageous book reviews, unqualified by fear or favor, were as necessary for the reputation of a magazine as the quality of merchandise was for a retail establishment."[33] At the *Messenger*, Poe earned the nickname "The Tomahawk Man" for a few lacerating reviews.

Poe's return to Richmond was complicated temporarily by his separation from Mrs. Clemm and Virginia and, for different reasons, by the recent death of his estranged foster father, who had excluded Poe from his will. Professionally, however, his eighteen months at the *Messenger* enabled Poe to demonstrate his talent as a "first-rate editor" who contributed to the magazine's success.[34] According to Kenneth Silverman, "[Poe] later bragged that during his active management, subscriptions rose from fewer than one thousand to some five thousand. T. W. White counted things differently."[35] Even allowing for exaggeration, Poe increased the *Messenger*'s subscription base enough to deserve White's gratitude. Unfortunately, however, disagreements about Poe's wages, his editorial authority, and his occasional drink-induced "illnesses" exasperated the proprietor. According to Whalen, "White had once complained about his editor's use of alcohol 'before breakfast,' but Poe's salary and tendentiousness probably had more to do with his dismissal."[36] Whatever the reason, Poe lost his job with the *Messenger* in early 1837, and he looked to New York for a fresh start.

Poe's timing was disastrous, and he had no luck finding another editorial position immediately. Hard times loomed, for as Whalen notes, "a financial crisis commenced shortly after Poe arrived in New York. The Panic of 1837 marked the beginning of one of the more severe depressions in U.S. economic history," and it had major implications for the publishing industry, "which had already been developing at an uneven and tumultuous rate."[37] The impact for Poe and his fellow magazinists was mixed: "the accelerated rise of a mass publishing industry and a mass culture" accompanied the rapid decline of the high-end book trade.[38] Publishers banked on reprinted editions of foreign books, the penny press took off, and magazines proliferated "because they could undersell other forms of information and entertainment."[39] Poe could not capitalize on the market, however, and remained jobless. He attended a Bookseller's Dinner in March, pointedly toasting the "Monthlies of Gotham" (PL: 243), but the event yielded no job offers. Maria Clemm managed a boarding house while Poe sought work.

Dire circumstances forced Poe and his family to move again, from New York to Philadelphia, in early 1838. Still unemployed, he completed *The Narrative of Arthur Gordon Pym*, a book published by Harper and Brothers in New York at the end of July. Poe made very little money from its publication, however, and tried to conceal his authorship. As a writer of magazine tales, though, Poe had a creative breakthrough in 1838 when he published "Ligeia" (which he judged his best tale), and he followed it with a clever spoof, "The Psyche Zenobia" (or "How to Write a Blackwood Article") in *The Baltimore Museum*. To secure additional income, Poe helped Thomas Wyatt compile *The Conchologist's First Book*, which (as a commercial ploy) listed Poe as author.

Eighteen months after leaving Richmond, the author finally found steady employment: William E. Burton "offered Poe ten dollars a week for two hours of daily work on *Burton's Gentleman's Magazine* starting in May 1839."[40] That summer, Poe worked longer hours, and he assumed editorial responsibility while Burton was performing theatrically in New York. Poe wrote over 125 reviews in one year for *Burton's*,[41] and he contributed several important tales, including "The Man That Was Used Up," "The Fall of the House of Usher," and "The Conversation of Eiros and Charmion." Poe also published his "Sonnet—Silence" in *Burton's* and reprinted his dazzling "William Wilson," which had just appeared in *The Gift: A Christmas and New Year's Present for 1840*. In December, Lea and Blanchard released *Tales of the Grotesque and Arabesque*, Poe's first published collection of short stories.

During his year at *Burton's*, Poe began contributing to *Alexander's Weekly Messenger* to add income. There, he resorted to subterfuge, using the newspaper to create the illusion of spontaneous support for Poe's unsigned *Burton's* review indicting Henry Wadsworth Longfellow for plagiarism. It was the first salvo in a long, perverse campaign to impugn America's most popular living poet. Following the success of "Maelzel's Chess Player," Poe also launched a highly popular cryptography series called "A Few Words on Secret Writing." It capitalized on his knowledge of coding (possibly developed while serving in the army) and led to fifteen articles in *Alexander's* over several months, along with a handful of similar pieces in *Graham's*.[42] In this gambit, Poe posed as "an ingenious analyst" who challenged readers to create their own ciphers, encode short messages, and submit them to the magazine for him to solve.[43] Poe baited readers but also responded by decoding their messages. His "Cryptographical" series attracted public attention and gave Poe an opportunity to flaunt his cleverness. He enjoyed "mystification" and authorial control, solving seemingly indecipherable cryptograms to demonstrate intellectual superiority. Cryptography would soon take center stage in "The Gold-Bug," a tale hinging on a coded message that leads to buried treasure.

After producing six installments of "The Journal of Julius Rodman," a hoax purportedly documenting the first exploratory expedition across the Rockies, Poe left *Burton's* in mid-1840. His break with the proprietor had been precipitated by Poe's abortive scheme to launch a new journal called *The Penn*. But that campaign came to naught, and Poe was out of work. A new opportunity presented itself, however, when George R. Graham bought *Burton's* in late 1840 and merged it with another monthly, *The Casket*, to create *Graham's Magazine*. Poe served as literary editor in charge of book reviews, for which he received "$800 a year, plus payment for his literary contributions."[44] His stint with *Graham's* proved important and productive: he published "The Man of the Crowd," a prototype for detective fiction, in the first issue in December, and he served on the staff from April 1841 to May 1842, contributing such tales as "The Colloquy of Monos and Una"; "A Descent into the Maelström"; his first true ratiocinative tale, "The Murders in the Rue Morgue"; "Never Bet the Devil Your Head"; "Life in Death" (later "The Oval Portrait"); and "The Masque of the Red Death."

In the April 1842 issue of *Graham's*, Poe also published a preliminary notice of Nathaniel Hawthorne's *Twice-Told Tales* (PL: 363). He followed that with an important, full-length review in the subsequent issue. According to Jacobs, "Poe needed space because he wanted not merely to evaluate Hawthorne's stories, but to establish a rationale of the short tale by which an evaluation could be made. Just as he had validated the function of the critic and the purpose of poetry, now he intended to validate the short story as an authentic literary genre."[45] While revealing Poe's admiration for Hawthorne, the review also asserts the importance of a unifying "single *effect*" (ER: 572) in the prose tale, or short story. Jacobs suggests that Poe was "thinking in terms of a mass audience, and his purpose was to prescribe a desirable length for journalistic fiction."[46] More significantly, Jacobs argues, "It is difficult to separate Poe the journalist from Poe the artist."[47] Having seen how poorly volumes of tales sold while magazines filled with short stories sold well, Poe concluded that artists must adapt to the new reality of literary America. For Poe, this meant establishing the tale as an "art form" so that tales would be reviewed and reviewers would "make the audience aware of the suitability of the form to their needs."[48] Crafting the tale to be readable in one sitting let the author "make the greatest impression on the reader."[49]

While at *Graham's*, Poe resurrected his popular "Autography" series, introduced at the *Messenger*.[50] The project appealed to readers by naming the literary elite while simultaneously criticizing them with pseudo-scientific analysis of their handwriting. The series proved both entertaining and satirical. Poe's commentary included brief critical assessments, as well as occasional ad hominem attacks. Reminiscent of Neal's series on New England Writers for *Blackwood's Magazine*, Poe's "Autography" series in *Graham's* (1841–1842) provided a public platform for sometimes scathing commentary on established authors. He remarked, for example, that Washington Irving (honored at the 1837 Booksellers Dinner) had grown "satiated with fame" and "slovenly" in his literary work (H 15: 182). Of the most celebrated Transcendentalist, Poe remarked: "Ralph Waldo Emerson belongs to a class of gentlemen with whom we have no patience whatsoever—the mystics for mysticism's sake" (H 15: 260). Throughout his career, Poe disparaged Transcendentalism. Reinforcing a critical distinction introduced by F. O. Matthiessen and adapted by Harry Levin, Richard Kopley identifies Poe, Hawthorne, and Melville as "naysayers" who oppose the "prelapsarian vision" of Emersonian Transcendentalism by presenting a "postlapsarian corrective" that reveals the "darker side of humanity."[51] The "Autography" series gave Poe a prime opportunity to mock Emerson's obscurity and to question his uplifting "twaddle" (H 15: 260).

Poe thus positioned himself as a literary authority. He wanted to designate the American literati as a cohort by dismantling previously venerated models and emphasizing literary merit rather than social or cultural standing. Poe's views would later cohere into an outline for a study of living American writers.[52] He pursued a broad vision of American literature. Although early periodicals tended to project a local or regional focus, during the 1830s and 1840s magazines such as *Graham's* and *Godey's* began to court larger national audiences. But both magazines also appealed concertedly to feminine tastes with fashion plates, sentimental engravings, and popular songs. In a letter to Frederick W. Thomas, Poe expressed "disgust with the namby-pamby character" of *Graham's* (CL 1: 333). The "Republic of Letters" that Poe envisioned required a high-quality monthly magazine showcasing the talents of American authors, and in the early 1840s he began to create a new model for the literary periodical of his dreams.

Since his days at the *Messenger*, Poe had chafed at the difficulty of working under an irksome proprietor. With the encouragement of Thomas, a young Whig novelist with a government job in Washington, Poe hoped to escape the drudgery of "literary toiling" for the Whites, Burtons, and Grahams; he applied to the Tyler administration for a bureaucratic position at a decent salary, a post that would let him write after hours.[53] His opportunistic interest in the poetry of John Tyler's son, Robert, briefly induced him to envision a journal that would promote Tyler's ideas: "The Magazine might be made to play even an important part in the politics of the day" (CL 1: 325). Unfortunately for Poe, nothing came of his bid to secure a government post or to enlist the president's son as a magazine backer.[54] In fact (as will be discussed later), his notorious visit to Washington in 1843 destroyed not only his prospect of patronage from the Tyler family but the confidence of a potential investor in Philadelphia.

Though Poe maintained an association with *Graham's* after his resignation, he published in an array of other publications. His "The Pit and the Pendulum" incongruously figured in a ladies' annual, *The Gift,* while his second ratiocinative tale, "The Mystery of Marie Rogêt," appeared in Snowden's *Ladies' Companion*, and "The Tell-Tale Heart" shocked readers of James Russell Lowell's short-lived journal, *The Pioneer*. Retrieving his manuscript from George Graham, Poe entered his tale "The Gold- Bug" in a literary contest sponsored by the Philadelphia *Dollar Newspaper* and won the $100 first prize. After its June 1843 debut, the story was widely reprinted and even inspired a stage adaptation. In another Philadelphia journal, best known as the *Saturday Evening Post,* Poe published his gory crypto-temperance tale, "The Black Cat."

But, by early 1844, Poe believed he could best advance his career and support his family by moving to New York. There, in April, he published his "Balloon Hoax" in an extra edition of the *Sun*, duping many readers into believing that the narrator had actually crossed the Atlantic in a hot-air balloon. In May, Poe began contributing gossipy articles, "The Doings of Gotham," to a Pennsylvania newspaper, the *Columbia Spy*. In October, he joined the *New York Evening Mirror and Weekly Mirror* (a newspaper) to work for Nathaniel Parker Willis. Previously, Poe had criticized Willis, who had likewise written dismissively of Poe's early verse. Nevertheless, Willis became

Poe's employer and ally, reprinting poems that had been published elsewhere, and a few years later becoming Poe's posthumous champion. Through much of 1844, Poe experienced a "mania for composition" (CL 1: 448), producing a flood of new tales that included "The Oblong Box," "A Tale of the Ragged Mountains," "The Purloined Letter," "The Premature Burial," "Mesmeric Revelation," "Thou Art the Man," and "The Literary Life of Thingum Bob, Esq." (the last satirizing an entrepreneurial magazine editor). Three of these new tales appeared in *Godey's,* the most widely circulated monthly of the era.

Poe's most striking contribution to the New York literary scene, however, was a poem, "The Raven," which appeared in the *Evening Mirror* and then the *American Review* in January 1845. The sensation immediately transformed Poe into a household name. He was soon in demand in the city's fashionable literary salons. Then, a few weeks after "The Raven" won fame, Poe began contributing to the *Broadway Journal*, becoming a partner with John Bisco and Charles Briggs in February and agreeing to provide one page of original content per issue for one-third of the (nonexistent) profits.[55] Finessing the demand for fresh work, Poe began republishing many of his older tales in the *Journal*, but often in carefully revised new versions. Improbably enough, he finally acquired sole proprietorship and editorship of the *Journal* on October 24, 1845, brazenly assuming responsibility for the magazine's debts.

In the broader context of Poe studies, the author's eleven-month association with a short-lived New York weekly devoted to literature and the arts compels attention for several reasons. As Ed Whitley comments in another chapter in this volume, Poe carried on in the *Journal* a very public flirtation with the poet Frances Sargent Osgood. Riding the success of "The Raven," he also sought to capitalize on his new stature by going on the lecture circuit.[56] But in the aftermath of an inglorious performance before a Boston Lyceum audience—where he rambled on about poetry and read an old poem ("Al Aaraaf") instead of a promised new one—Poe also used the pages of the *Journal* to wage a war of words with his Boston critics, the "Frogpondians." He got into a vicious quarrel with a Boston magazine editor, Cornelia Wells Walter, and embarrassed himself by taking a patronizing, sexist tone while inciting animosities between Northeastern and mid-Atlantic or Southern audiences. Just as problematically, Poe used the *Journal* to wage an unrelenting new assault on Longfellow, once more accusing the revered New England poet of plagiarism. Given his own exercises in literary larceny (such as "The Journal of Julius Rodman"), Poe's many lengthy tirades against Longfellow seem as perverse as they are hypocritical.

Poe likely regarded his connection with the *Broadway Journal* as a good stepping stone toward the realization of his dream as a magazinist.[57] Both the *Mirror* and the *Broadway Journal* seemed to value honest, candid literary criticism.[58] Working long hours for the *Journal*, Poe "defended magazines against a widespread belief that they represented a degeneration of taste."[59] Near the end of 1846, he again opined that the "whole tendency of the age is Magazine-ward" and that periodicals reflected "the *rush* of the age." Hurried, contemporary readers wanted shorter, easier-to-digest articles: "we need the curt, the condensed, the pointed, the readily diffused" (ER: 1414–1415). While helping to edit the *Broadway Journal*, Poe turned to other magazines to publish such works as "The Facts in the Case of M. Valdemar," "The Imp of the Perverse," "The Power of Words," "Some Words with a Mummy," and "The System of Doctor Tarr and Professor Fether." The only original narrative he published in the *Journal* during his tenure was a short satire called "Some Secrets of the Magazine Prison-House," and it appeared before he joined the staff. But several of the tales he revised for *Journal* publication (such as "Ligeia" and "Some Words with a Mummy") showed such important modifications that they became, for T. O. Mabbott, authoritative copy-texts for his modern edition of Poe's tales and sketches.

Working at the *Broadway Journal* altered Poe's ideas about the aims of American literature. For Poe, the best writing did not depend on indigenous, "American" settings for its worth; nor should it be valued according to British tastes or published exclusively for the financial and social elite.[60] Rather, Poe valued "originality" in literature, regardless of setting, and he believed that authors should always write to produce a desired "effect." Working in the New York literary world, then editing and publishing the *Broadway Journal*, gave Poe greater insight into the plight and potential of American authors and of the magazines for which they wrote.

The *Journal* ceased publication because of financial difficulties at the beginning of 1846. That same year, Poe published "The Cask of Amontillado" and a series on "The Literati of New York City." While presenting disparaging or flattering "portraits" of American authors, the " 'Literati' sketches," according to J. Gerald Kennedy, "also contain a scattered but fairly detailed analysis of how the literary world operated—its rules of engagement, as it were."[61] Kennedy also notes that Poe's "Literati" sketches addressed "the problem of a dispersed and decentered culture" by reading New York literature as representative of literary America as a whole.[62] Poe's various editorial experiences significantly sharpened his interest in the literary canon and his potential impact as a critic and anthologist.

Poe and the Magazine Prison-House

A good index of Poe's shrewdness as a magazinist comes from comparing the manic "Literary Life of Thingum Bob" with his cynical sketch, "Some Secrets of the Magazine Prison-House." Whereas "Thingum Bob" is a comic fantasy of adaptation, survival, and success in the magazine world from the vantage point of an unscrupulous proprietor, "Prison-House" exposes the cruelty inflicted on authors. Poe's advocacy for international copyright found its fiercest, most memorable expression in the February 15, 1845, sketch (M 3: 1205–1210). Here, Poe examines the material conditions of the publishing world and portrays magazines as a death trap for "poor devil authors" unprotected by property laws, scribblers ruthlessly exploited by the "Magazine publishers." It fleshes out Poe's cynical comment in an 1842 letter to Thomas: "Without an international copy-right law, American authors may as well cut their throats" (CL 1: 356). Deprived of a living wage, authors became subservient to publishers whose magazines "not only live[d], but thrive[d]." That they could pay for original contributions, according to Poe, is well known, but in fact they "encourage the poor devil author with a dollar or two, more or less as he behaves himself properly and abstains from the indecent habit of turning up his nose" (M 3: 1207). Publishers indeed sometimes paid, but just as often they did not.

Enticed to contribute a piece, the unsuspecting author must endure endless waiting, neglect other work, suffer starvation, and perhaps eventually, die:

> Enraptured, he neglects perhaps for a month the sole employment which affords him the chance of a livelihood, and having starved through the month (he and his family) completes at length the month of starvation and the article, and despatches [sic] the latter (with a broad hint about the former) to the pursy "editor" and bottle-nosed "proprietor" who has condescended to honor him (the poor devil) with his patronage. A month (starving still), and no reply. Another month—still none. Two months more—still none. (M 3: 1208)

At length, the poor devil author's death by starvation feeds the fat-cat magazine publisher: "He [the author] dies, and by the good luck of his decease (which came by starvation) the fat 'editor and proprietor' is fatter henceforward and for ever to the amount of five and twenty dollars, very cleverly saved, to be spent generously in canvas-backs and champagne" (M 3: 1208–1209).

That Poe was familiar with this predatory practice emerges from the irony of his injunction *not* "to believe that we write from any personal experience of our own, for we have only reports of actual sufferers to depend on," and *not* "to make any personal application of our remarks to any publisher now living, it being well known that they are all as remarkable for their generosity and urbanity, as for their intelligence, and appreciation of Genius" (M 3: 1209). Interestingly, when he penned this exposé, Poe had not yet joined the *Journal* staff but was angling for a job. Brisco and Briggs responded, perhaps fittingly, not by paying Poe as a contributor but by offering him a share of their almost worthless enterprise.

Overworked and underpaid, Poe had been driven by necessity to seek extra work for added income. "Some Secrets of the Magazine Prison-House" reveals his firsthand knowledge of the sordid business practices of the magazine world, the appalling predicament of authors, and the lack of public awareness that made it all possible. Poe and his fellow magazinists performed their work at great personal cost. "Later in his career," Whalen writes, Poe "created revenge fantasies such as 'Hop-Frog,' in which a performing dwarf destroys a small group of men (the king and his ministers) who had abused and exploited him," and he imagined "new methods of communication that would enable artistic value to triumph over economic value," in works such as "The Power of Words" and "Anastatic Printing."[63] These imaginative visions notwithstanding, Poe inhabited a world in which literary aspirations went hand in hand with economic insecurity, his literary property unprotected by any copyright law.

Poe's Dream: The Penn/Stylus

As noted earlier, Poe articulated a formal prospectus for his own magazine while toiling for William Burton. He announced his *Penn Magazine* on June 13, 1840, in the Philadelphia *Saturday Courier*, promising a periodical marked by "individuality" and featuring fine literature as well as candid criticism. The magazine would be just, fearless, and utterly uncontaminated by the "arrogance" of literary cliques. It would seek to advance the "the republic of letters" rather than the interests of "particular regions" (ER: 1024–1025). Though this initial publicity produced no tangible results, Poe persevered during his stint at *Graham's*, refining the plan and renaming his journal *The Stylus*. Published in the *Saturday Museum*, the new prospectus repeated the assurance that it would offer "a sincere and a fearless opinion" on American literature, applying "the purest rules of Art" (ER: 1035) and disregarding authorial reputation, national partiality, or foreign opinion. The plan gained traction when a Philadelphia publisher, Thomas Clarke, showed interest; however, news of Poe's infamous Washington drinking spree ended his relationship with Clarke, a temperance advocate. Poe's association with the *Messenger, Burton's*, and *Graham's* nevertheless enriched his understanding of the antebellum literary marketplace and shaped his vision for the *Stylus*. But that vision required cash support. As Whalen correctly asserts, "[w]hatever he may have thought about the psychological dimensions of 'individuality,' Poe had come to realize that in the new publishing environment, artistic individuality had become the prerogative of capital."[64]

Writing to George W. Eveleth in late 1846, Poe called the *Stylus* "the grand purpose" of his life, from which he had "never swerved for a moment" (CL 1: 603). Since his departure from the *Messenger*, he had aspired to own and edit a quality magazine, and Poe's two versions of the prospectus tell us much about his vision and ambition.[65] Both underscore the importance of "absolutely independent criticism" (ER: 1025, 1035) and high production standards. "In its mechanical appearance—in its typography, paper, and binding—it will far surpass all American journals of its kind," he promised of *The Stylus* (ER: 1033). Because he understood the power of visual art, Poe promised illustrations—but only to accompany literary texts. Kevin Hayes observes: "By and large, [Poe] reacted against the magazines such as *Graham's* which included 'contemptible pictures, fashion-plates, music and love tales' or, in other words, material which catered to female readers."[66] Hayes adds, "Poe imagined a magazine which would be worth keeping while cheap books fell by the wayside."[67] Although he understood the authority of print and the dominance of printed media, Poe was fond of producing elaborately handwritten manuscripts, he inscribed many verses in autograph albums, and he even devised a system (in "Anastatic Printing") to publish holographic texts.

The metamorphosis from *Penn* to *Stylus* reflects Poe's expanding vision for his intended audience, from the regional pun on pen/Pennsylvania that he devised for a Philadelphia audience, to the Latinate *stylus* denoting a writing implement but connoting a classical style. As Hayes further remarks, "It is no coincidence that he decided to title his ideal magazine the *Stylus*."[68] He asserts that Poe "came to believe that owning and editing a magazine offered the best way for him to determine the course of American literature."[69] But the closest Poe came to shaping the literary nation by directing a prominent magazine was his brief, chaotic run as owner-editor of the ill-fated *Broadway Journal*. Near the end of 1845, despite the republishing of his own tales, he struggled to fill his sixteen weekly pages and keep the periodical afloat.

But the *Journal* fiasco did not dash his magazine hopes. After "The Raven" made him famous, Poe tried to add some income and boost his name recognition by lecturing, either on poetics and versification, on *The Poets and Poetry of America*, or on his prose poem, *Eureka*. These lectures were also designed to attract subscribers and new financial backing for his projected magazine. In the final year of his life, Poe seemed closer than ever to becoming proprietor (or co-proprietor) of a $5-per-annum magazine. He was both hopeful and nervous about a proposal that arrived from Oquawka, Illinois, where an enthusiastic young printer, Edward H. N. Patterson, wanted to partner with him to create a magazine virtually on the frontier. His belated courtship of Richmond amour Sarah Elmira Royster Shelton, by 1849 a wealthy widow, also created the prospect of ample capital to start a periodical. Unfortunately, Poe died in Baltimore, soon after becoming engaged.[70] So, too, died the dream of establishing his own magazine and shaping the course of American literary taste.

Conclusion

Poe regarded himself principally as a poet for whom "The Rhythmical Creation of Beauty" (ER: 78)[71] represented the highest calling. But he was also "essentially a magazinist" who emerged on the national literary scene in the mid-1830s as a major force in antebellum periodical culture. He pursued market opportunities and exploited the new magazine format to produce original works—and new genres—that still enthrall readers. In the year of his death, Poe wrote to longtime friend Frederick W. Thomas, "Literature is the most noble of professions. In fact, it is about the only one fit for a man. For my own part, there is no seducing me from the path. I shall be a *littérateur*, at least, all my life; nor would I abandon the hopes which still lead me on for all the gold in California" (CL 2: 770). Poe would have dedicated himself more fully to that vocation, especially to the writing of poetry, had his financial circumstances allowed. But confronted with the realities of the literary marketplace, Poe devoted himself mainly to writing tales, articles, reviews, and marginal squibs, promoting literary originality and critical standards as a magazine writer.

Despite the absence of international copyright, the scanty pay for periodical contributions, and myriad hardships posed by a prolonged economic crisis, Poe survived through hard work, diligence, grit, and genius. His dogged determination to found his own $5-per-annum magazine, the *Stylus*, reflected a bid to attract both an elite class of educated readers and a mass audience. Poe wanted to elevate taste, make readers more discerning, and prod American authors to greater artistry.

Although his goal proved elusive, the same passion that inspired Poe's planned magazine aligned with his ambition to elevate the status of American literature in the world. Such a goal would have been Poe's answer to Sydney Smith's question, "who reads an American book?"[72] Poe spent the last decade of his life dedicated to the belief that he could win the support of multiple readerships in America to produce a successful magazine featuring quality literature of global appeal. Poe's dedication to literary originality contributed significantly to his evolving critical theory, and his various compositions for magazine publication generated some of the most enduring works in American literary history.[73]

Notes

1. "Ludwig" [Rufus Wilmot Griswold], "'Death of Edgar Allan Poe' in *New York Daily Tribune* (1849)," in *Poe in His Own Time*, ed. Benjamin F. Fisher (Iowa City: University of Iowa Press, 2010), 77.
2. See Rufus Wilmot Griswold, "'Memoir of the Author' (1850)," in *Poe in His Own Time*, 100–153.
3. Lois Davis Vines, "Poe in France," in *Poe Abroad: Influence, Reputation, Affinities*, ed. Lois Davis Vines (Iowa City: University of Iowa Press, 1999), 11. See also Philip Edward Phillips, "Baudelaire's Discovery of Poe," Baudelaire's Poe: Selections from the W. T. Bandy Collection [online exhibition], Jean and Alexander Heard Library, Vanderbilt University, http://exhibits.library.vanderbilt.edu/BaudelairePoe/?section=25.
4. Meredith L. McGill, *American Literature and the Culture of Reprinting, 1834–1853* (Philadelphia: University of Pennsylvania Press, 2003), 3.
5. McGill, *American Literature and the Culture of Reprinting*, 19.
6. Terence Whalen, "Poe and the American Publishing Industry," in *A Historical Guide to Edgar Allan Poe*, ed. J. Gerald Kennedy (Oxford: Oxford University Press, 2001), 85.
7. Whalen, "Poe and the American Publishing Industry," 85.
8. Reverend Sydney Smith, review of *Statistical Annals of the United States*, by Adam Seybert. *The Edinburgh Review* 33 (1820): 69–80.
9. Kenneth Silverman, *Edgar A. Poe: Mournful and Never-ending Remembrance* (New York: HarperCollins, 1991), 247.
10. Scott Peeples, "Teaching Poe the Magazinist," in *Approaches to Teaching Poe's Prose and Poetry*, ed. Jeffrey Andrew Weinstock and Tony Magistrale (New York: MLA, 2008), 27.
11. Terence Whalen, *Edgar Allan Poe and the Masses: The Political Economy of Literature in Antebellum America* (Princeton, NJ: Princeton University Press, 1999), 58.
12. Frank Luther Mott, *A History of American Magazines*, vol. 1, *1741–1850* (Cambridge, MA: Belknap Press, 1930), 340–341.
13. Mott, *A History of American Magazines*, 1: 341–342.
14. Mott, *A History of American Magazines*, 1: 341–342.
15. Whalen, *Edgar Allan Poe and the Masses*, 66.
16. Whalen, *Edgar Allan Poe and the Masses*, 66.
17. Michael Allen, *Poe and the British Magazine Tradition* (New York: Oxford University Press, 1969), 16.

18. See Thomas H. O'Connor, *The Athens of America: Boston, 1825–1845* (Amherst: University of Massachusetts Press, 2006), xii–xiv.
19. John Neal, "To Correspondents," *The Yankee; and Boston Literary Gazette*, September 1828, 168.
20. Neal had lived for a time in England and had contributed original articles on contemporary American writers to *Blackwood's*—and was the first American to do so—before returning to his native state of Maine, whose literary luminaries made their displeasure known about his critical assessments of their work. Nevertheless, Neal's roles as novelist, editor, critic, and arbiter of literary talent made him a role model for Poe.
21. Neal's tribute is preserved with those of Alfred Tennyson, Algernon C. Swinburne, John G. Whittier, W. C. Bryant, H. W. Longfellow, O. W. Holmes, Richard Hengist Horne, George W. Childs, W. C. Bryant, S. D. Lewis, Mrs. Margaret J. Preston, John Godfrey Saxe, Mrs. Sarah Helen Whitman, John H. Ingram, Thomas Bailey Aldrich, Prof. James Wood Davidson, Prof. John Dimitry, and G. Herbert Sass ("Barton Grey"), as well as poetic tributes by Stéphane Mallarmé, Paul H. Hayne, and Edgar Fawcett, in Sara Sigourney Rice, *Edgar Allan Poe: A Memorial Volume* (Baltimore: Turnbull Brothers, 1877), 89.
22. Throughout his career, Poe contributed to various gift books, which paid better for literary works than magazines and were regarded as cherished keepsakes. Some of Poe's most famous short stories appeared in gift books, including "William Wilson. A Tale," in *The Gift: A Christmas and New Year's Present for 1840*, ed. Miss Leslie (Philadelphia: Carey & Hart, 1840), 229–253, and "The Purloined Letter," in *The Gift: A Christmas, New Year, and Birthday Present, MDCCCXLV* (Philadelphia: Carey & Hart, 1844), 41–61. See Philip Edward Phillips, "Edgar Allan Poe," Baudelaire's Poe: Selections from the W.T. Bandy Collection, http://exhibits.library.vanderbilt.edu/BaudelairePoe/?section=24. See also Alexandra Urakova, "'The Purloined Letter' in the Gift Book: Reading Poe in a Contemporary Context," *Nineteenth-Century Literature* 64, no. 3 (December 2009): 323–346.
23. Kevin J. Hayes, *Poe and the Printed Word* (Cambridge: Cambridge University Press, 2000), 87.
24. Hayes, *Poe and the Printed Word*, 92–93.
25. Hayes, *Poe and the Printed Word*, 93.
26. Hayes, *Poe and the Printed Word*, 93.
27. Hayes, *Poe and the Printed Word*, 93.
28. The judges had considered Poe's "The Coliseum" the best verse submission, but they awarded the poetry prize to another person, John H. Hewitt, editor of the *Visiter*, who had submitted his work under an assumed name. The *Visiter* did publish "The Coliseum" later, in the October 26 issue, and announced the forthcoming publication of Poe's "Tales of the Folio Club," which never found a publisher. Instead, Poe published the tales separately in various magazines and gift books.
29. Whalen, "Poe and the American Publishing Industry," 69.
30. Arthur Hobson Quinn, *Edgar Allan Poe: A Critical Biography* (Baltimore: The Johns Hopkins University Press, 1998), 212.
31. Whalen, "Poe and the American Publishing Industry," 69.
32. Quinn, *Edgar Allan Poe*, 241.
33. Robert D. Jacobs, *Poe: Journalist & Critic* (Baton Rouge: Louisiana State University, 1969), 134.

34. Silverman, *Edgar A. Poe*, 127.
35. Silverman, *Edgar A. Poe*, 127.
36. Whalen, "Poe and the American Publishing Industry," 73.
37. Whalen, "Poe and the American Publishing Industry," 73.
38. Whalen, "Poe and the American Publishing Industry," 74.
39. Whalen, "Poe and the American Publishing Industry," 74.
40. Jeffrey Andrew Weinstock, "Magazines," in *Edgar Allan Poe in Context*, ed. Kevin J. Hayes (Cambridge: Cambridge University Press, 2012), 174.
41. John Lent, "Edgar Allan Poe," in *American Magazine Journalists, 1741–1850*, Dictionary of Literary Biography, vol. 73 (Detroit, MI: Gale, 1988), 239.
42. Silverman, *Edgar A. Poe*, 152, 164.
43. Silverman, *Edgar A. Poe*, 152.
44. Weinstock, "Magazines," 174.
45. Jacobs, *Poe: Journalist & Critic*, 317.
46. Jacobs, *Poe: Journalist & Critic*, 320.
47. Jacobs, *Poe: Journalist & Critic*, 320.
48. Jacobs, *Poe: Journalist & Critic*, 320.
49. Jacobs, *Poe: Journalist & Critic*, 320.
50. "Autography"—Part I (February 1836) and "Autography"—Part II (August 1836) appeared in *The Southern Literary Messenger*; "A Chapter on Autography"—Part I (November 1841), "A Chapter on Autography"—Part II (December 1841), "An Appendix of Autographs" (January 1842) appeared in *Graham's Magazine*. See H 15: 139–261.
51. Richard Kopley, "Naysayers: Poe, Hawthorne, and Melville," in *The Oxford Handbook of Transcendentalism*, ed. Joel Myerson et al. (Oxford: Oxford University Press, 2010), 597.
52. See Burton R. Pollin, " 'The Living Writers of America': A Manuscript by Edgar Allan Poe," *Studies in the American Renaissance* (1991): 151–200, for a transcription and treatment of Poe's working notes for a projected anthology of literary biography and criticism, which was left unfinished at the time of his death.
53. Silverman, *Edgar A. Poe*, 178–179.
54. At the urging of his friend, Frederick William Thomas, Poe unsuccessfully sought a post in the administration of President John Tyler, a fellow Virginian, who had ascended to the presidency after President William Henry Harrison's death in April 1841. Relying on the influence of Robert Tyler, the president's son, Thomas was hopeful that he could obtain a government position for Poe, possibly at the Philadelphia Custom House. Poe proved to be his own worst enemy, however, by succumbing to his own "perversity" at a gathering at Fuller's Hotel in Washington, that is to say, by getting drunk on the proprietor's port (PL: 405). Although Poe later promised to join the Washingtonians, a national temperance society, if Robert Tyler could secure a post for him (PL: 407), a governmental position was not forthcoming for Poe. Had he been able to "step into an office at Washington" (or Philadelphia) and earn a $1,000-per-annum federal salary like his friend Thomas (PL: 332), then Poe may well have been able to "carry out all [his] ambitious projects" (PL: 366). But such an opportunity for Poe was not meant to be.
55. "Autograph Document, signed 'Edgar A. Poe' " [signed holograph contract], February 21, 1845, Edgar Allan Poe Papers, Harry Ransom Center, University of Texas.

56. For a book-length study of the role and significance of the lyceum movement, see Angela G. Ray, *The Lyceum and Public Culture in the Nineteenth-Century United States* (East Lansing: Michigan State University Press, 2005).
57. Quinn, *Edgar Allan Poe*, 451.
58. Silverman, *Edgar A. Poe*, 245.
59. Silverman, *Edgar A. Poe*, 246.
60. Silverman, *Edgar A. Poe*, 248–249.
61. J. Gerald Kennedy, "Inventing the Literati: Poe's Remapping of Antebellum Print Culture," in *Poe and the Remapping of Antebellum Print Culture*, ed. J. Gerald Kennedy and Jerome McGann (Baton Rouge: Louisiana State University Press, 2012), 26.
62. Kennedy, "Inventing the Literati," 26.
63. Whalen, "Poe and the American Publishing Industry," 82.
64. Whalen, "Poe and the American Publishing Industry," 77.
65. See Edgar Allan Poe, "Prospectuses for 'The Penn' and 'The Stylus,'" in L2: 21–36.
66. Hayes, *Poe and the Printed World*, 95. It is worth adding that for all of his apparent disdain for sentimental illustrations, Poe published many of his tales in just such journals.
67. Hayes, *Poe and the Printed World*, 93.
68. Hayes, *Poe and the Printed World*, 29.
69. Hayes, *Poe and the Printed World*, 93.
70. Even with the restrictions placed on Elmira's inheritance from her late husband should she remarry, her annual income would have increased Poe's standard of living and access to capital considerably. See Philip Edward Phillips, "Engagement Ring: Elmira Royster Shelton," in *Edgar Allan Poe in 20 Objects from the Susan Jaffe Tane Collection*, ed. Gabrielle Dean and Richard Kopley (Baltimore: The Sheridan Libraries of Johns Hopkins University, 2016), 38–43.
71. Pertinent to the purposes of this essay, Levine and Levine note: "Both the lecture 'Eureka' and the lecture 'The Poetic Principle' were fund-raising efforts for a magazine Poe wanted to found" (L2: 175), that is, for *The Stylus*.
72. Smith, review of *Statistical Annals of the United States*, 79.
73. I am grateful to Carolle Morini and the reference staff of the Boston Athenæum for their assistance locating materials essential for my research; Mo Li, who offered valuable contributions to this project in its early stages of composition; and, especially, Jerry Kennedy, whose editorial care and generous insights on Poe and print culture contributed significantly to the final version of this essay.

Bibliography

Allen, Michael. *Poe and the British Magazine Tradition*. New York: Oxford University Press, 1969.

Hayes, Kevin J. *Poe and the Printed Word*. Cambridge: Cambridge University Press, 2000.

Jacobs, Robert D. *Poe: Journalist & Critic*. Baton Rouge: Louisiana State University, 1969.

Kennedy, J. Gerald. "Inventing the Literati: Poe's Remapping of Antebellum Print Culture." In *Poe and the Remapping of Antebellum Print Culture*, edited by J. Gerald Kennedy and Jerome McGann, 13–36. Baton Rouge: Louisiana State University Press, 2012.

McGill, Meredith L. *American Literature and the Culture of Reprinting, 1834–1853*. Philadelphia: University of Pennsylvania Press, 2003.

Mott, Frank Luther. *A History of American Magazines*. Vol. 1, *1741–1850*. Cambridge, MA: Belknap Press, 1930.

Peeples, Scott. "Teaching Poe the Magazinist." In *Approaches to Teaching Poe's Prose and Poetry*, edited by Jeffrey Andrew Weinstock and Tony Magistrale, 26–32. New York: MLA, 2008.

Weinstock, Jeffrey Andrew. "Magazines." In *Edgar Allan Poe in Context*, edited by Kevin J. Hayes, 169–178. Cambridge: Cambridge University Press, 2012.

Whalen, Terence. *Edgar Allan Poe and the Masses: The Political Economy of Literature in Antebellum America*. Princeton, NJ: Princeton University Press, 1999.

Whalen, Terence. "Poe and the American Publishing Industry." In *A Historical Guide to Edgar Allan Poe*, edited by J. Gerald Kennedy, 63–94. Oxford: Oxford University Press, 2001.

CHAPTER 29

POE'S CULTURAL INHERITANCE

Literary Touchstones and the Cultivation of Erudition

WILLIAM E. ENGEL

Attend thou also more
To thy dress and equipage—they are over plain
For thy lofty rank and fashion—much depends
Upon appearances.

—E. A. Poe, *Politian* 3.23–26 (M 1: 258)

INVESTIGATIVE journalists usually begin by asking: "What did he know and when did he know it?" If only it were this easy with Poe. He was a consummate reader and, more to the point, worked hard to fashion a literary persona of nonchalant refinement and critical discernment. As was typical of authors in the early nineteenth century concerned with "the polite arts,"[1] he peppered his writings with classical references and literary anecdotes. His use of citations and allusions therefore needs to be balanced against what was commonplace knowledge. Dropping references to obscure books and inserting phrases from foreign languages in one's writing obviously does not guarantee deep knowledge of either. Poe's steady cultivation and ready display of erudition throughout his career is a reliable index to the kinds of things he wanted others to assume he knew—and further, as was his way, to show just enough of his hand to encourage readers to think he wore the mantle of his learning lightly, as befitted a gentleman of discernment and spontaneous wit.

Poe was proficient in both French and Latin.[2] His frequent and accurate references to Voltaire, for example, show more than a passing familiarity with his works in the original (PL: 72, 79). Also from his writings we know he was drawn to and adept at discussing arcane ideas, especially metempsychosis (the transmigration of souls) and mnemotechnics (associative schemes for augmenting memory).[3] Both topics therefore will feature as recurring themes in this assessment of Poe's cultural inheritance. These esoteric notions, as will be discussed, Poe derived from "many a quaint and curious volume of forgotten lore"—to use a phrase from "The Raven," one that will be revisited owing to Poe's repeated use of "quaint" in his reviews and criticism. Even though teasing out the strands of Poe's cultural inheritance is a fraught enterprise, some reliable determinations still can be made by looking at the patterns and usual practices in his writing. Building on the work of indefatigable source hunters like Harrison, Pollin, and Mabbott makes it possible to examine the ways—and the ends to which—Poe incorporated elements of the Western cultural tradition.

Cultural Commonplaces and the Polite Arts

A good case in point, by way of launching this investigation, is the proverbial expression "to out-Herod Herod," connoting cruel and outlandish behavior. One of Poe's favorites, it appears in among other works "Metzengerstein," "William Wilson," and "The Masque of the Red Death" (M 2: 30n6). Grounded in a biblical reference to Herod's massacre of the innocents (Matthew 2:16–17), it actually derives from Shakespeare (*Hamlet* Act III, scene 2, line 14) and signifies the melodramatic delivery of actors playing the role of Herod in English mystery plays. Although it is tempting to consider whether Poe was aware of and even aimed specifically to evoke these deeper layers of meaning packed into the phrase, the more likely reason it appears in at least five of his works is that it was a familiar byword of the day—and one that he perhaps liked, especially owing to its sonorous repetition. Phrases such as this one then, as with other similar expressions and commonplaces, served Poe as handy rhetorical flourishes drawn from his well-stocked vocabulary and were used to set up the proper and "inspiratory frame of mind."[4] There is no great show of erudition in Poe's use of "out-Herod Herod"; at most, it cues his readers about a character's excessive behavior.

The same can be said of his biblical allusions such as "balm in Gilead" (from Jeremiah 8:22 and echoing a reference in Genesis 37:25), used by Poe in a purely figurative sense in "The Raven" (line 89), and also in *Politian* and "The Angel of the Odd" (M 1: 374n89). Poe's knowledge of the Bible basically was "an inheritance that any man in Christendom, and especially any user of English, finds ready to his hand."[5] Most of his biblical-sounding passages are borrowed second-hand since "there is no ground for holding that Poe possessed a close or intimate knowledge of the Bible."[6] Phrases like "Valley of the Shadow" (Psalm 23:4), suggestively used in the final stanza of "El Dorado" and as the motto to "Shadow," came not directly from the Bible, but resulted from Poe's interest in esoteric topics, like the cabbala, encountered in his reading about ancient Masoretic Hebrew scriptural studies (M 1: 464–465n21). Less abstruse are his borrowings from Episcopal prayer books, such as a phrase taken from the wedding service in The Book of Common

Prayer, "in sickness or in health," used by Poe to characterize with macabre humor the union between horse and rider in "Metzengerstein" (a tale discussed in greater detail hereafter). Allusions such as this one simply are part of the "rich fund of proverbial sayings to which all English writers fall heir."[7]

As early as when he was at the school run by the Misses Dubourg in Chelsea, west of London (PL: 30), Poe encountered Mavor's spelling primer, full of fables and moral tales.[8] He also was required to use Fresnoy's *Geography*, designed, as the title page announces, "for the use of scholars and of gentlemen who make the ancient writers their delight in study."[9] Additionally he was charged for a prayer book and for the *Church Catechism Explained*, the latter being a gathering of quotations and directives pertaining to standard Christian beliefs. Whatever else Poe may have gleaned from the content of this work, as with Mavor's *Spelling* and Fresnoy's *Geography*, he was confronted early, during the development of his reading habits, with the patchwork structure of the episodic pastiche. It is not so much that this method of accumulating and presenting adages and bits of wisdom excerpted from earlier sources provided Poe with the pattern for his later writing, as it marks his induction into and enthusiastic participation in the longstanding tradition of humanist collocation and the amassing of commonplaces with the aim of mining such notebooks for future essays and table talk. This is especially evident in Poe's discussion of his systematic cut-and-paste approach to literary reflections. There are ample archival remains of his having done just this; he tells his readers that, "much after the fashion of Jeremy Taylor, and Sir Thomas Browne, and Sir William Temple, and the anatomical Burton," it was his habit to write in a book's margin "and even on a slip of paper" deposited "between the leaves" and secured by "an imperceptible portion of gum tragacanth paste" (M 3: 1113–1114).[10]

Source hunting, while obviously necessary to the task at hand, indicates only that Poe knew this or that author, book, or reference (P 2: xxxiii). Still, that he asked his foster father, John Allan, in a letter dated May 25, 1826, for money specifically to buy "a copy of the *Historiae of Tacitus*" tells us this volume mattered to him (PL: 71). So, when a quotation from Tacitus appears in his writings, deep diving is required to discern whether he is working from the book first-hand, his memory, or a distillation of Tacitus from a review, anthology, or compendium of general knowledge. Based on the frequency of particular references in his writings between 1836 and his death in 1849, Poe seems to have carried several books with him from city to city during his several changes in residence.[11] Most notable among these are Isaac Disraeli's *Curiosities of Literature*, Jakob Bielfeld's *Elements of Universal Erudition*, a few of Edward Bulwer-Lytton's novels (including *Pelham, Paul Clifford, Ernest Maltravers*), and *Stanley* (1838) by H. B. Wallace, who published under the name of Landor (P 2: 110). Bulwer-Lytton's *Pelham or Adventures of a Gentleman* (1828) was the quintessential "fashionable novel" of the period and greatly resembled Benjamin Disraeli's *Vivian Grey* (1826), a romantic satire which Poe knew well enough to use the episode of strangers drinking out of skulls as part of his literary burlesque in "King Pest."[12] *Vivian Grey* is one of the few contemporary novels that Poe speaks of favorably (PL: 125); and, later, in his miscellaneous writings, he indicates approval of Disraeli's *Sybil* (1845). But it was Disraeli's father, the noted antiquarian Isaac

Disraeli, for whom Poe, like Bulwer-Lytton, expressed the highest admiration owing to his manifest erudition and lively treatment of quaint topics.

While more can be said about Poe's relation to these main literary touchstones in his life, notwithstanding the hundreds of books he encountered as a reviewer and editor, it is sufficient for now only to observe of his home library that, as Pollin notes, "the extreme meagerness of Poe's literary possessions makes his general literary culture seem impressive" (P 2: 100). Closely linked to this, Poe is reputed to have had an "excellent memory," especially "for recitation"; those who knew him during his student days report his acquaintance with English literature was extensive, and his memory wonderful (H 1: 40, H1: 92). Poe's mental agility, as remarked on by those who knew him at school, is consonant with his later interest in memory systems (discussed later regarding Francis Gouraud's *Phreno-Mnemotechny*). Poe was committed to accumulating and storing a vast—if eclectic—treasury of literary tidbits that served to enliven magazine reviews and critical writings with his characteristic verve and panache. This practice bespeaks wide-ranging if not always deep erudition. Poe's displays of learning and frequent flashes of foreign idioms are not, however, merely ornamental; rather, they are part and parcel of his copious and thoughtfully cultivated literary style.[13] Poe comments explicitly on this practice in *Pinakidia* and advocates restraint, hinting at his own bone fide urbanity.

> It sometimes occurs that in papers of this nature may be found a collective mass of general, but more usually of classical erudition, which, if dexterously besprinkled over a proper surface of narrative, would be sufficient to make the fortunes of one or two hundred ordinary novelists in these our good days, when all heroes and heroines are necessarily men and women of "extensive acquirements." But, for the most part, these "Brevities," &c. are either piecemeal cullings at second hand, from a variety of source[s] hidden or supposed to be hidden, or more audacious pilferings from those vast storehouses of brief facts, memoranda, and opinions in general literature, which are so abundant in all the principal libraries of Germany and France.[14]

Among the works listed as being worthy of excerpting, he mentions "Bielfeld, the German, who wrote, in French, *Les Premiers Traits de l'Erudition Universelle*." Bielfeld's *Elements of Universal Erudition* (one of the volumes that, judging from the many fragments from it showing up in Poe's work, lay within his ready reach) had the explicit goal of "studying and teaching the Belles Lettres."[15] It is a systematically arranged compilation "of the most pleasing examples drawn from the best authors; executed with taste, and ornamented with the graces of style," divided according to various branches of "the polite arts." Bielfeld contends that "Beauty is the object of all the polite arts. . . . We may say however, in general, that beauty results from the various perfections of which any object is susceptible, and which it actually possesses, . . . and it is this knowledge, this theory, which modern philosophers call by the Latin name of *aesthetica*."[16] Something of the same can be heard in Poe's critical theory, which resonates with Bielfeld's discussion of the various polite arts: "The Poetic Sentiment, of course, may develop itself in various modes—in Painting, in Sculpture, in Architecture, in the Dance—very especially in Music—and very peculiarly, and with a wide field, in the composition of the Landscape Garden" (L2: 184). Elsewhere, regarding Beauty as the expressive ideal of the Poetic Sentiment, Poe writes: "it is an obvious rule of Art that effects should be made to spring from direct causes—that objects should be attained through means best adapted for their attainment" (L2: 63).

Likewise Bielfeld's discussion of tragedy, in which Aristotle's understanding of that genre is wrapped in Romantic garb, may well be an important if as yet unnoted aesthetic template for the affective stylistic elements of Poe's first published story, "Metzengerstein" (1832). Bielfeld observed: "The design of it is to exalt in the minds of the spectators, the values of great virtues and sublime sentiments; and at the same time to paint, in the strongest colors, the meanness of vice, and the horror of iniquity: and this end it endeavors to obtain by influencing the two grand springs of the human mind; that is by exciting our pity and our terror."[17] In Poe's preface to *Tales of the Grotesque and Arabesque* (1840), he similarly wrote: "If in many of my productions terror has been the thesis, I maintain that terror is not of Germany, but of the soul,—that I have deduced this terror only from its legitimate sources, and urged it only to its legitimate results" (M 2: 473).

Another compendium from which Poe liberally filched information and references was Robert W. Walsh's *Sketches of Conspicuous Living Characters of France* (1841), including the prototype for his detective Le Chevalier C. Auguste Dupin (P 2: 251). And, although not a work he traveled with, Poe clearly had access throughout his career to Abraham Rees's *Cyclopædia* (P 2: 190). Close reading of the entries pertaining to German aesthetic theory and philosophy, for example, especially concerning the ideas of Leibnitz,[18] owing to the similarity of phrasing in Poe's own works, suggests he relied on information found in this encyclopedia. By the same token, in the entry for poetry, Thomas Gray's melancholy "Elegy Written in a Country Churchyard" (1751) is quoted and discussed.[19] Poe echoes fragments of this poem in his own "Tamerlane" (M 1: 64) and evokes a similar tone in many of his early stories. He discusses this perennial theme in his critical writings: "Melancholy is thus the most legitimate of all the poetical tones" (L2: 64). This is not to say that Gray is his exclusive model, but simply that he found in this author examples that corroborated and reified his own aesthetic ideas and predispositions. Another formative influence early on was Lord Byron, who had "haunted his teenage imagination."[20] Byron's grand themes and poetic ideals are evident in Poe's "Tamerlane" (M 1: 61); but, by 1829, with the "second form of 'Tamerlane' " (M 1: 25), he had moved away from Byron as a model.[21]

Even when Poe shows an affinity for one poet or another, it is difficult to determine whether his knowledge came from prior close reading or from an excerpt in an anthology. And it is sometimes the case that he already knew a work well and also later encountered it in a compilation he was asked to review. To judge from the many traceable quotations, however, especially in his *Brevities*, Poe knew much of the writings of H. N. Coleridge, who edited the voluminous works of his uncle, Samuel Taylor Coleridge, from whom Poe initially derived many of his ideas about Romantic poetic theory. Because his allusions and quotations sometimes are attributed to their proper sources and sometimes not, it is hard to say definitely whether he is working from an abstracted version or the original. Given the ready availability of literary anthologies and epitomes of general knowledge, Poe had no need to pore over the originals. Indeed, among the many scarcities in Poe's life (money being what he chiefly lacked), time was a precious commodity in the busy daily routine of a magazine writer and editor. It stands to reason Poe would choose the shortest route to obtain the most apt nugget or well-turned phrase, *le mot juste*, to round out and lend polish to the work at hand. This habit has led one editor of Poe's works to assert that some of the many recondite references in his tales "seem chosen for their mellifluous obscurity."[22]

Poe also was known on occasion to misattribute a quotation or a motto, perhaps simply because he did not have the source ready at hand, as in the case of "The Gold-Bug" (M 3: 744–745). He was also likely to reproduce a faulty source attribution of a Latin epigram, as with the motto of "The Purloined Letter," ascribed to Seneca despite the fact that Seneca never wrote such a line—although, in all fairness, it does sound like something Seneca might have said: "Nil sapientiae odiosius acumine nimio [Nothing is more hateful to wisdom than too much cunning]." Not the first time Poe used this particular epigram, it appears in the 1843 version of "The Murders in the Rue Morgue" (M 3: 993). His faulty attribution in both places, however, doesn't mean he didn't know Seneca, whether in the original or from compendia such as Charles Rollin's *Histoires anciennes* and *Histoires romaines*, several volumes of which Poe checked out from the library at Virginia (PL: 72).

He also invented quotations, perhaps vaguely remembered, amplified, and rewritten. The epigraph to "William Wilson" appears neither in *Pharonnida* (1659) by William Chamberlayne, as cited in the epigraph, nor in any of Chamberlayne's other works (M 1: 319; M 2: 448). The quotation introducing "The Gold-Bug" (mentioned earlier) is nowhere to be found in Arthur Murphy's comedy *All in the Wrong* (1761) (M 3: 844; M 1: 329). The same holds for the motto to "Ligeia," which Poe attributes to Joseph Glanvill, a seventeenth-century Neoplatonist, but no source for it has been located. Most likely Poe made it up (M 2: 331), to ground in authority a summary statement about the work's focal concern with the undying nature of the human will. Elsewhere, however, in "A Descent into the Maelström," Poe supplies a genuine quotation from Glanvill, indicating that, to some extent, he was familiar with Glanvill's "Against Confidence in Philosophy and Matters of Speculation" (M 2: 595). Even so, from the start, Poe evokes an unsettling and alien ethos for this sketch with his superfluous dieresis over the "o" in Maelstrom, "the only use cited by the Oxford English Dictionary" (M 2: 594). Comparable alienating effects are achieved, as in "The Man of the Crowd," when Poe lifts something from an author, in this case Thomas De Quincey, who is not named directly, and puts it in his own text as the opening sentence; and, moreover, repeats it, chiastically, as the closing line: " 'er lasst sich nicht lesen'—it does not permit itself to be read." This quotation (reproduced here as given by Poe) brings up another issue concerning the flexible nature of Poe's borrowings: "er lasst" should be "es lässt" (P 2: 505), both here and when used again in the forty-sixth of his "Fifty Suggestions" (M 2: 518). Whether he copied it out incorrectly from some yet unidentified source or the original was corrupt, he seems not to have noticed—or cared. Rather than treating such lapses and errors as instances of Poe's irresponsible scholarship, it is more productive to consider these tendencies as part of his cosmopolitan understanding of what it meant to be an active—and gamesome—member of the Commonwealth of Learning.

European Sources and Poe's Cosmopolitanism

In addition to his habit of playing fast and loose with citations, the problem of determining what Poe may or may not have read in the original is compounded by the fact that, at times, he takes an English translation from a French work and renders it in his own French rather than seeking the proper quotation, thereby revealing—often owing to some telling grammatical error—that it is his own version.[23] The same is true when on occasion Poe miscopies something from a German quotation or title and does not catch a glaring error that subsequently finds its way into print.[24]

As for Poe's knowledge of German, at Virginia he was enrolled in the School of Modern Languages in which German figured significantly. His chief instructor was Professor George Blaettermann, a native of Saxony who had fought under Napoleon during the invasion of Russia in 1812, and was hired by Thomas Jefferson at the founding of the university. He was extremely accomplished in the major European languages, and Poe seems to have been one of his rare admirers; moreover, his influence seems to show up in some of Poe's early humorous imaginative work (H 1: 45–54). Poe writes as if he knows basic German for, more than a few times, especially in *Marginalia* and *Pinakidia*, he draws distinctions between various German terms, uses phrases such as "what the Germans call" (M 2: 1113), and speaks of the metric rules of German epic poetry. The translation of the long German passage prefacing "The Mystery of Marie Rogêt"[25] appears to be Poe's own, as no complete English version of Novalis was available at the time.[26] Notwithstanding his occasional "faulty use of German,"[27] as was seen in "The Man of the Crowd," Poe understood enough to read and translate short passages fairly accurately (H 1: 45–46).[28] He valued being able to write passages in the original German (as with the epigraph to "Marie Rogêt"), which both signaled his erudition and imbued his focal themes with a more profound sense of purpose and authenticity. This appears to be the case with the handwritten passage in German from Goethe's "Meine Göttin" (1780) on the manuscript of his projected *Phantasy-Pieces* (1842), which earlier had been printed on the title page of *Tales of the Grotesque and Arabesque* (1840)—lines Poe previously quoted in German in a note to "Al Aaraaf" (1829) (M 1: 104).[29] As with the motto attributed to Seneca, such quotations appealed to Poe and seem easily to have come to mind insofar as he reused them to fit the project at hand.

Poe's knowledge of German literature, however he came by it, is everywhere evident in "Metzengerstein." Owing to the exemplary nature of this work with respect to Poe's self-conscious reflection on the development of his literary craft, the sources for the tale are mentioned here in passing by way of setting up a more detailed discussion, in the penultimate section, of his treatment of metempsychosis. The hyperbolic German family name in the title is followed and augmented further by a literary gesture that at once labels it as part of the Gothic tradition and excuses its excesses. Poe subtitled the tale "In Imitation of the German" when it was republished in the *Southern Literary Messenger* (1836). The result is a bold retelling of a series of old tales stitched together out of faded patterns from German lore and Gothic stories, including E. T. A. Hoffman's *Die Elixiere des Teufels* (1815), Walter Scott's critical essay on Hoffmann's use of the supernatural (1827), and Thomas Carlyle's compilation known as *German Romance* (1828) containing, as his title page advertises, "specimens of its chief authors with biographical and critical notices"—Poe's favorite sort of book, ripe for harvest.

Poe's French, as already adduced, was better than his other languages, and above average for most Americans in the 1840s. And yet still, his was an open-access French, the kind spoken worldwide by nonnative speakers "that paradoxically reaches transnational proportions through local particularity."[30] His demonstrated command of French at Virginia indicates he was capable of reading with comprehension, if not total mastery, Charles Rollin's histories—a mastery he sought to solidify further by checking out Nicolas Gouin Dufief's *Nature Displayed in Her Mode of Teaching Language to Man* (PL: 73). Intended as "an infallible method of acquiring a Language," Dufief's practical first volume stresses learning grammar. It provides three vocabularies of familiar phrases, two lists of useful French verbs exemplified in appropriate sentences, two collections of phrases (one comprising a complete formulary of conversation, and the other exclusively proverbial and idiomatic), and concludes with a selection of "suitable authors."[31] Dufief presents parallel passages with French on the left and English on the right that undoubtedly appealed to Poe, who seems to have stocked the treasury of his memory with many idiomatic French expressions that later would appear in his writing. So much was this the case that contemporaries on occasion derided Poe's proclivity for foreign words. Lewis Gaylord Clark, one of his chief rivals in the 1840s, dubbed him a "literary Aristarchus,"[32] a gibe that depended on readers knowing that Aristarchus of Samothrace was the librarian at Alexandria noted for his familiarity with foreign authors—as does the unkind doggerel lampooning Poe as Aristarchus in the *Knickerbocker Magazine* (PL: 669). These pointed barbs illustrate that Poe hardly was the only writer during this period to use somewhat obscure classical references.

The Exigencies of Printing and the Promotion of Cultural Values

Poe came of age as a self-conscious litterateur and aspiring magazine editor at a time when an air of cosmopolitanism among writers was de rigueur, coincident with the rise of information seen as a public good.[33] Poe browsed long hours in bookshops,[34] but he did not spend time in the archives. He kept busy trying to make a living from his writing, which often involved reporting on and reviewing new books, including those devoted to classical scholarship such as *A Dictionary of Greek and Roman Antiquities* by "Professor Charles Anthon, a gentleman who, in point of discrimination, accuracy and erudition, has few, (if any,) equals, and no superior in the classical world."[35] It is tricky, though, to determine the precise extent of what Poe knew about a book he was reviewing when he might well have been pressed to fill a column before the printer's deadline. This situation is complicated by the fact that some of his book reviews and general interest pieces, for example when he was being paid 80 cents a column by the *Southern Literary Messenger*, reproduce long passages from the books as well as whole paragraphs quoted from previous reviews to which Poe then adds his concurrence or opprobrium. How closely he read the books he reviewed remains an open question and must be taken on a case-by-case basis.

Some of his reviews show deep engagement, resulting perhaps from an authentic interest in the topic, such as Francis Fauvel-Gouraud's *Phreno-Mnemotechny; or The Art of Memory*. Poe lauds it as "beyond doubt, one of the most important and altogether extraordinary works which have been published within the last fifty years."[36] It is easy to see Poe finding a kindred spirit in Gouroud, who, like Poe himself, was something of a showman both in print and on the public-lecture circuit. Poe comes to Gouraud's defense: "It is by no means too much to say that the powers of memory, as aided by his system, are *absolutely illimitable*. We earnestly advise our readers to procure M. Gouraud's extraordinary work and decide in the premises *for themselves*."[37] Another point of connection is Gouraud's reference to one of Poe's oft-cited touchstone authors, Francis Bacon, in a discussion of the history of mnemotechny.[38] Gouraud singles out Bacon for having "framed a kind of system of his own, so deeply was he convinced of the utility of artificial processes in aiding and assisting the memory."[39]

Poe's criticism and reviews at times reveal attentive close reading, especially those that afforded him an opportunity to espouse his own aesthetic criteria concerning literary merit which, thereby, helped advance his reputation as a person of recondite wit with whom contemporary writers must reckon. Poe was told to tone down his attacks on living poets when he was hired for editorial duties at *Burton's Gentleman's Magazine* in 1839, and he was expected to contribute eleven pages of original material each month. On the cover of every issue was a passage from "De Vere," which, in defining what it means to be "a gentleman," presented an aspirational statement both about the magazine and its prospective readers:

> By a gentleman, we mean not to draw a line that would be invidious between high and low, rank and subordination, riches and poverty. No. *The distinction is in the mind*. Whoever is open, just and true; whoever is of a humane and affable demeanor; whoever is honorable in himself, and in his judgment of others, and requires no law but his word to make him fulfill an engagement—such a man is *a gentleman;*—and such a man may be found among the tillers of the earth as well as in the drawing rooms of the high-born.[40]

This "Jacksonian definition" of a gentleman catered to the "rapidly increasing and relentlessly self-improving middle class" of Philadelphia, where the magazine was published.[41] It is to just such an audience that Poe's habit of inserting foreign phrases and classical references en passant would have appealed. The mere act of reading the magazine's fashionably decked-out prose pieces no doubt created among subscribers a feeling of being au courant with all that was in vogue at home and abroad.

Burton's Gentleman's Magazine was one of many such tickets to perceived respectability. In addition to filling the pages with others' works and reviews, Poe was obliged to publish his own. Carefully curating each issue afforded Poe opportunities to improve the standards of American letters by instructing readers to recognize and appreciate "the polite arts." Poe's acclaim for Tennyson, for example, shows that he knew the English poet's work well and, moreover, had insights to disclose about literary and cultural value. Moving beyond his usual mode of declaiming against poseurs and rival American poets, Poe's encomium to Tennyson presents criteria for making critical judgments. His assessment turns upon the term "quaint," thus providing a glimpse into what Poe assimilated and made his own from the backlog of his British literary inheritance—including Bacon's *Essays*.

> For Tennyson, as for a man imbued with the richest and rarest poetic impulses, we have an admiration—a reverence unbounded. . . . We allude to his quaintness—to what the world chooses to term his affectation. . . . In fact, the profound intuition of Lord Bacon has supplied, in one of his immortal apothegms, the whole philosophy of the point at issue. "There is no exquisite beauty," he truly says, "without some *strangeness* in its proportions." We maintain, then, that Tennyson errs, not in his occasional quaintness, but in its continual and obtrusive excess. . . . Mr. Tennyson is quaint only; he is never, as some have supposed him, obscure — except, indeed, to the uneducated, whom he does not address.[42]

This passage contains at least two distinct patterns that show up elsewhere in his works and therefore warrant close scrutiny. First, the idea of "strangeness" in proportion attributed to Bacon recurs in Poe's criticism and tales, exemplarily in "Ligeia" (M 2: 311–312, 331).[43] Second, and closely related, the notion of "occasional quaintness" appears in Poe's other literary reflections on what constitutes poetic merit, most notably his review of S. C. Hall's *Book of Gems: From the Poets and Artists of Great Britain* (1836). Poe has redemptive praise for seventeenth-century poets, together with many long quotations taken from their poems, to argue that what remains pleasing is the quaint phraseology and grotesque rhythm: "And this quaintness and grotesqueness are, as we have elsewhere endeavored to show, very powerful, and if well managed, very admissible adjuncts to Ideality."[44] Poe may well have felt the need to quote long passages from the poems under investigation to make his larger point about literary value and aesthetic principles; but, just as likely, it cannot be ruled out, this may also be a way to reach his contracted page quota for an issue of the magazine.

The poems he quotes at length are those he says he esteems most highly in the anthology, specifically George Wither's "The Shepherd's Hunting" and, more meritorious still, Andrew Marvell's "The Maiden Lamenting for Her Fawn." He clarifies the place of grotesqueness and quaintness in appreciating the enduring power of "the English antique writers": "The quaintness in manner of which we were just speaking, is an adventitious advantage. It formed no portion of the poet's intention. Words and their rhythm have varied. Verses which affect us to day with a vivid delight, and which delight in some instances, may be traced to this one source of grotesqueness and to none other, must have worn in the days of their construction an air of a very common-place nature."[45] Around the time when he was reviewing Hall's book, Poe tried his hand at imitating "the English antique writers," in his unfinished Shakespearean cadenced closet-drama *Politian,* published by the *Southern Literary Messenger* (1835–1836), most likely because he had it on hand and "the magazine needed copy" (M 1: 241). Acknowledging this aspect of printing house practices helps us take the full measure of how—and to what end—Poe put his erudition to work.

Metempsychosis: One into the Other

Based on the wide-ranging and often eclectic references, allusions, and quotations in his stories, reviews, and miscellaneous writings, Poe shows every sign of being well read in the literature of his own time.[46] Although his readings of the classics were typical for the educated classes of his day, he also broadened the scope of his knowledge by using digests and anthologies, especially, as already mentioned, those by Charles Rollin, who also published accompanying books of historical maps of ancient battlefields and troop formations that were readily available to someone like Poe who, as a journeyman and editor in the magazine trade, frequented bookshops and publishing houses.

Poe's examinations at school put him at the head of the class,[47] with solid knowledge of works by Ovid, Caesar, Virgil, Cicero, and Horace in Latin, and Xenophon and Homer in Greek (PL: 47). His references to and quotation from works by Bacon, Marlowe, Shakespeare, and Milton, buttressed by long lists of passages and phrases copied out from the latter two,[48] indicate he knew these major English Renaissance authors well.[49] While "Shakespeare contributed little to Poe's important presentations of theory in fiction and drama, his tales and poems were undoubtedly affected by his knowledge of Shakespeare's plays," with over two hundred allusions, quotations, analogues, and indirect references in his writings, citing no fewer than twenty-eight of the plays, *Hamlet* being referenced sixty-nine times.[50] In his *Brevities* especially Poe shows an affinity with satirical writers of the Augustan Age, including Pope, Swift, Sterne, and Smollett. And regarding the "potent magic of verisimilitude" in *Robinson Crusoe,* Poe praised Daniel Defoe,[51] for possessing "above all other faculties, what has been termed the faculty of *identification*—that dominion exercised by volition over imagination which enables the mind to lose its own, in a fictitious, individuality" (P 2: 547). This touchstone for narrative excellence, moreover, inspired Poe's own *Narrative of Arthur Gordon Pym* (P 1: 216). He also found much worthy of emulation in Charles Dickens, especially *The*

Old Curiosity Shop, "a tale which will secure for its author the enthusiastic admiration of every man of genius" (P 2: 537); and in Walter Scott, whose *Bride of Lammermoor* Poe called the "most pure, perfect, and radiant gem of fictitious literature" (P 5: 50).[52]

Poe's notions about aesthetics and representation can be traced initially to Friedrich Schiller (by way of Coleridge) and A. W. Schlegel, who emphasized "the totality of interest" in his *Lectures on Dramatic Art and Literature*.[53] He went on, however, to show singular originality by recasting these ideas at the core of German Romanticism in terms of esoteric lore, especially Neoplatonic metempsychosis (the transmigration of souls), Renaissance Hermeticism (evident in Roderick Usher's library), and Arabian cosmology (especially in "Al Aaraaf" and "Israfel"). Analyzing each of these topics in turn will give a more complete picture of what Poe did with—and how he used—his cultural inheritance in his own writings.

Poe drew much of his information about metempsychosis from Isaac Disraeli's chapter on the topic in *Curiosities of Literature*:

> If we expect the belief of a future remuneration beyond this life for suffering virtue, and retribution for successful crimes, there is no system so simple, and so little repugnant to our understanding, as that of the metempsychosis. . . . Preposterous as this system may appear, it has not wanted for advocates in the present age, which indeed has revived every kind of fanciful theories. Mercier, in *L'an deux mille quatre cent quarante* seriously maintains the present one.[54]

Disraeli's reference to this utopian novel by Louis-Sébastien Mercier shows up in Poe's "Metzengerstein," a tale discussed already in another context and which here will receive a more thorough treatment. A long passage at the beginning directly echoes Disraeli's preamble on the credulity of those who believe in the transmigration of souls from human beings to animals. Poe's narrator throughout "Metzengerstein" undermines ordinary ideas of corporeal discreteness by evoking metempsychosis as the guiding principle of the tale—narratively and metaphysically. Superimposed onto the relationship of steed and former owner (now deceased) is a demystified and wholly natural, because somatic, view of metempsychosis. This theme, discussed by Disraeli as predating Plato and Pythagoras, is introduced by Poe in the opening lines as being of a peculiarly regional and superstitious variety. This is followed by a passage from La Bruyère in the original French and Poe's footnote referring to Mercier, also untranslated, and then a quotation about Ethan Allen, the Green Mountain Boy, "said to have been a serious metempsychosist" (M 2: 18n).

This heap of quotations cries out for translation, echoing at the linguistic and semantic levels what the curious and distant doctrine posits about the supersensual and somatic realms. Linguistically, the words begin in a foreign tongue poised for the movement from one enunciative register into another, just as the doctrine allows for the movement of souls from one body into another, thus carrying along the spirit of the original and putting it in a different form. And, at the semantic level, the idea of transformation is what underlies the plot line—and plot twist—of this distinctively imitative, overdetermined Germanic Gothic tale transferred into Poe's own self-contained satirical pastiche, thereby transforming it into a new kind of terror tale, one of embodiment, entrapment, and narrative entropy.

Poe was familiar with the hallowed place of metempsychosis in early modern thought owing to his reading of Christopher Marlowe, whose name (as "Marlow") appeared perhaps as an unintended signature to Poe's original version of "Al Aaraaf" (M 1: 115), and whose lines from *Doctor Faustus* are conjured up in that poem. Faustus laments: "Ah, Pythagoras' *metempsychosis*, were that true,/This soul should fly from me and I be changed/Into some brutish beast. All beasts are happy,/For, when they die/Their souls are soon dissolved in elements,/But mine must live still to be plagued in hell."[55] Poe could have known this play as early as his student days at the Manor House School.[56] He also would have known the Latin locus classicus of this doctrine from Ovid's *Metamorphoses*.[57]

Metempsychosis is fundamental to some of Poe's most arresting if puzzling stories, including "Metzengerstein," "Ligeia," "Morella," and, to some extent, "A Tale of the Ragged Mountains" (which relies on mesmerism for its supernatural effect). No amount of detection or ratiocination—like that for which Poe's ingenious detective M. Dupin was admired—can explain finally what really happens, or why, in "Metzengerstein," "Ligeia," or "Morella." It is never clarified whether the denouement of "Metzengerstein" is the result of metempsychosis fully realized in the world, or just the death wish of a headstrong scion of an old family—or both.

Keeping such matters in mind, as well as taking into account Poe's evocation of erudition, while setting up only to knock down typical Gothic furniture (ancestral feud, stormy night, dark castle, supernatural possession), one sees that "Metzengerstein," by way of metempsychosis, challenges both conventional reasoning and literary paradigms by establishing from within the text a new kind of self-consistent substitute order. The reader never has quite enough rationally derived facts to riddle out the transition from what is natural and sensually real to what is supernatural and supersensually self-evident, given the events as described. The reader perforce must follow the narrator's lead and suspend ordinary perception of the real so as to accommodate an alternate version and ultimately must accept the substitution. In this sense the tale itself performs a kind of literary metempsychosis, by putting the one into the other. Watching this process unfold both unlocks and also renders moot any mystery as such, as the Baron embraces with a vengeance—and loses himself in—an obsession with the fiery steed. Poe's careful subordination of the physical world to a substitute order develops a thematic pattern that would become a staple of his later work—drawing on his vast, often esoteric backlog of learning gleaned from collections such as Disraeli's *Literary Curiosities* and Bielfeld's *Universal Erudition*. Indeed Poe's reinscription of the writings of others into his works makes metempsychosis something of a master trope that can be used to gain insight into his literary practice. Select ideas, like spirits from the past succinctly preserved in anthologies, thus come to reside in the body of Poe's work.

Roderick Usher's library in "The Fall of the House of Usher" is among the many places where this is on display in Poe's oeuvre.[58] Through a kind of literary slight of hand, Poe incorporates the specific spirit of—or idea signalled by—each of Usher's books.[59] For the most part the titles come from Bielfeld, the rest from Disraeli. For example, Bielfeld mentions Tommaso Campella's *Civitas Solis* (1623), concerning a voyage to a utopian city in the sun (M 2: 421),[60] recalling Poe's own tales of fantastic journeys whether through space and time, ranging from "Some Words with a Mummy" to "*Eureka*." As Mabbott has pointed out, "Vert-vert" likewise is mentioned in Bielfeld, as are all the works on palmistry (M 2: 420).[61] Poe probably did not know these books on chiromancy first-hand, but certainly was attuned to the ideas behind methods of divination linking things in this world to the macrocosm. Although Poe could have known the passages from Pomponius Mela from Hugh Murray's *Encyclopedia of Geography* (London, 1834), he shows more than a passing familiarity with this first-century Roman writer, quoting his work in Latin in "The Island of the Fay" (M 2: 601, M 2: 605). The reference to Niccolò Machiavelli's *Belphegor* is of special interest, both as it relates to painting a portrait of Usher's distracted psyche and also to Poe's own fascination with angels not in Heaven (as with "Al Aaraaf" and "The Angel of the Odd"). The eponymous protagonist of this satirical sketch is a fallen archangel sent from the Parliament in Hell to earth to investigate complaints of souls who claim their wives are responsible for their damnation. A kind of humorous metempsychosis is involved, for the demon "possesses" three different ladies. This theme seems to be what makes the book worthy of Usher's reading list, whereas for Poe it is a tongue-in-cheek way of showing how readers can seize upon one aspect of a story only to ride their own hobbyhorse.

Each book mentioned by the narrator represents a conscious decision on Poe's part to provide insight into Roderick's odd predisposition (M 2: 419–421), but which, it is intimated, never fully can account for why he is the way he is. And yet, as with Poe's use of metempsychosis, the books set up a substitute order of reality—and it is a vividly arresting one into which one can lose oneself for hours and days, even a lifetime, according to the narrator. Roderick Usher's library, seen as an index of Poe's inclination toward esoteric learning, does not serve as a standard of literary merit but as a clever way for Poe to open the window onto all manner of themes that skirt this arcane world via occult Hermeticism, animal magnetism, entropy, and, of course, metempsychosis. That his characters exhibit rapt fascination with such matters does not mean these were Poe's beliefs. Rather, such incidents gave him a way to display the range of his learning by creating an overwrought atmosphere of anxiety filled with dramatic reversals, and, in the process, to a tell a bankable tale, one "unsurpassed," as Woodbury acclaimed, for its "unity of design" (M 2: 392). To be sure though, the influence of some of these books can be traced to further references Poe made to them in his other works, suggesting he knew them beyond mere titles listed in Bielfeld, specifically Pomponius Mela, Machiavelli, and Swedenborg, all of whom are concerned with the migration of consciousness from one body to another. By such means Poe enriched and enlarged his storehouse of esoteric information that he collected throughout his career and which found its way into the body of his work.

The same applies to Poe's angels, not depicted as serene cherubim of the popular imagination, but as disembodied beings who hold colloquies and disputations about cosmology and metaphysics, most especially in "The Power of Words" and "Eiros and Charmion."[62] Similarly, the places these entities inhabit, in "Al Aaraaf" as in "Israfel," reflect the rich treasure trove of Poe's reading and his penchant for arcane literary models. As Poe explained in a letter to the publisher: "Al Aaraaf of the Arabians [is] a medium between Heaven & Hell where men suffer no punishment, but yet do not attain that tranquil & even happiness which they suppose to be the characteristics of heavenly enjoyment" (M 1: 92). His description of the spirit realm of "Al Aaraaf" can be traced, in part, to George Sale's "Preliminary Discourse" in his English translation of the Qur'an.[63] Those elements not mentioned directly in the Qur'an were available to Poe from a host of other Orientalist sources (M 1: 95–96). Even so, Thomas Moore clearly used Sale's material in *Lalla Rookh* (1817), a work Poe knew well and from which he borrowed place names and phrases.[64]

What Poe took as the thinking and theology of "the Arabians,"[65] he gleaned less from the Qur'an and more from works like Thomas Moore's *Loves of the Angels* (1823). As often was the case with Poe's building upon a fragment of philosophy or a turn of phrase he came across in his reading that he found might fit his purpose (for example, and closely aligned to the matter at hand, Pythagorean metempsychosis), he constructed a consistent pseudo-Arabian cosmology that animates much of his angel-related writings. This is another instance (as was shown to be the case with metempsychosis in "Metzengerstein") of Poe's creating an alternate order from the fragments of his reading and one that is wholly consistent with—and within—itself. This mesmerizing aspect of Poe's skill as a teller of tales into which we wander initially as unaware of the surroundings as the characters who inhabit them is characteristic of his craft: to put the one into (and thereby transform) the other.

Conclusion: Poe's Circumstances

Simply knowing Poe's sources tells us little about whether or the extent to which he wanted, or intended, his readers to follow their trace in his works—but it is a start. This compositional practice bears comparison to what Poe says he admired in good writing (based on ideas taken from A. W. Schlegel): "unity of impression" and "totality of effect" (L2: 62, 72). This much having been observed, five points stand out regarding Poe's cultural inheritance that distinguish him from other writers of his day. These observations about Poe's circumstances and his aims as a writer can help guide future inquiries along similar lines.

First, owing to his foster father's business ventures and the Allan family moving to Great Britain, Poe's foundational education in traditional subjects was markedly different from and much better than what would have been the case had he remained in Richmond. In addition to becoming acquainted with the fundamental classical authors and the best of English literature, he developed an unusually keen memory for recitation and retaining details of what he read. He may also, given his later demonstrated familiarity with place system mnemonics, have acquired along the way a set of memory techniques to compensate for being without books at various times in his life.

Second, he was a student at the University of Virginia, which, at the time, had many books from Jefferson's own library, the later foundation of the Library of Congress, some having been gifts from the authors and some even dedicated to him in print (for example, Dufeif's *Nature Displayed*). Jefferson had a pronounced affinity for French literature and Enlightenment writers, and his books reflected those interests. Poe seems to have been drawn to those sorts of works and checked them out following university policies. As to what other books he might have encountered in his studies and extracurricular reading, we can suppose many were duplicates from Jefferson's holdings, including Montaigne, Rousseau, Montesquieu, La Bruyère, and, of course, Voltaire. Such was the opportunity Poe had to engage with books early on that later, in his writings, he would demonstrate he knew.

Third, he was doggedly determined to make a life and career out of writing. He had no other source of income. Unlike many other writers of the day who either had university appointments or were people of inherited wealth or steady employment (other than publishing), Poe had neither. He cast his lot with the magazine industry, and the ensuing cultural influences he encountered as a reviewer came from poring over hundreds of books, including (as discussed earlier) the deluxe Harper edition of Defoe's *Robinson Crusoe*, "worthy of all praise."[66] His job provided opportunities for him to expatiate on those themes so near to his interests in cosmology and metaphysics, such as his review of *Plato contra Atheos*, in which Poe offers a critique of Platonic idealism: "We do not believe that any good purpose is answered by popularizing his dreams" (P 3: 154).[67] His job gave him access to books otherwise unavailable to a person of modest means. From this position he could arbitrate literary taste and promote a special appreciation of Beauty in poetry: "An immortal instinct, deep within the spirit of man, is thus, plainly, a sense of the Beautiful. . . . In the contemplation of Beauty we alone find it possible to attain that pleasurable elevation, or excitement, *of the soul*, which we recognize as the Poetic Sentiment" (L2: 183–185).

Fourth, he came into his own during a time in American magazine printing when he could move from one cosmopolitan center to another in search of employment, and he kept himself current with literary developments at home and abroad. Moreover, J. Gerald Kennedy does not overstate the case when he writes that "no other contemporary American literary figure worked so tirelessly or so ingeniously to overcome the anomalous disjunction of national culture and to construct an idea of American literature that transcended geographical distance and regional diversity. . . . Poe developed extended networks of literary connections and became familiar with several distinct cultures of letters."[68] Indeed, among his American contemporaries who especially influenced him were Irving, Hawthorne, Bird, and Simms.[69]

And finally, fifth, perhaps as a result of the conditions mentioned earlier, Poe was drawn to and wrote extensively on esoteric themes of the day, including metempsychosis, mnemotechnics, orientalism, mesmerism, animal magnetism, automatons, and ancient arcana. Perhaps he was attracted to such topics in part because of their alluring grotesqueness and quaintness, the twin criteria he used to explain how literature affects us and which can, when properly conceived and executed, elevate the soul. Poe's idea of Beauty derived from the cultural inheritance he extracted from his favored literary touchstones, those sources he put on display so that others might admire and contemplate them anew.

Notes

1. Jakob Bielfeld, *The Elements of Universal Erudition, containing an Analytical Abridgement of the Sciences, Polite Arts, and Belles Lettres*, trans. W. Hooper, 3 vols. (London: Printed by G. Scott, for J. Robson and B. Law, 1770), 1:115. References to this work follow this edition and are given by volume and page number.
2. Charles W. Kent, "Poe's Student Days at the University of Virginia," *Bookman* 44, no. 5 (1917): 520–524; E. K. Norman, "Poe's Knowledge of Latin," *American Literature* 6 (March 1934): 72–77.
3. William E. Engel, *Early Modern Poetics in Melville and Poe: Memory, Melancholy, and the Emblematic Tradition* (New York: Routledge, 2016), 145.
4. Richard M. Fletcher, *The Stylistic Development of Edgar Allan Poe* (The Hague: Mouton, 1973), 76. This is the second "Poesque vocabulary" proposed by Fletcher; the first being his "mechanical vocabulary" of associative terms and familiar expressions; and the third, "that of literary and classical allusions and images" (80).
5. William Mantzel Forrest, *Biblical Allusions in Poe* (New York: Macmillan, 1928), 145.
6. Killis Campbell, "Poe's Knowledge of the Bible," *Studies in Philology* 27 (July 1930): 549.
7. Forrest, *Biblical Allusions in Poe*, 146.
8. William Mavor, *The English spelling-book; accompanied by a progressive series of easy and familiar lessons, intended as an introduction to a correct knowledge of the English language* (London: Printed for R. Phillips, 1809).
9. Nicolas Lenglet Dufresnoy, *Geographia antiqua et nova: or a system of ancient and modern geography* (London: John and Paul Knapton, 1742).
10. Many such pasted slips (portions of original manuscripts in Poe's own handwriting for his "Marginalia") are preserved in the Huntington Library, exemplarily, those concerning the lack of verisimilitude in action, character, and local setting, in Eugene Sue's *The Wandering Jew*: "If such mere coincidences do occur, now and then, in Nature, they should at least never be made to occur in any fiction pretending to be natural" (Manuscripts, HM 1183, The Huntington Library).
11. On "Poe's Library," see Kevin J. Hayes, *Poe and the Printed Word* (Cambridge: Cambridge University Press, 2000), 74–86.
12. Arthur Hobson Quinn, *Edgar Allan Poe: A Critical Biography* (Baltimore: The Johns Hopkins University Press, 1998), 214.
13. Burton R. Pollin, *Poe, Creator of Words* (Bronxville, NY: Nicholas T. Smith, 1980), 6–20; Brett Zimmerman; Pollin, *Edgar Allan Poe: Rhetoric and Style* (Montreal and Kingston: McGill-Queen's University Press, 2005), xvi–xviii.
14. Edgar Allan Poe, "Pinakidia," *Southern Literary Messenger* 2, no. 9 (August 1836): 573.
15. Bielfeld, *The Elements of Universal Erudition*, 3:1.
16. Bielfeld, *The Elements of Universal Erudition*, 2:106–107.
17. Bielfeld, *The Elements of Universal Erudition*, 2:215.

18. *The Cyclopædia; or, Universal Dictionary of Arts, Sciences, and Literature*, 1st edition (London: Printed for Longman, Hurst, Rees, Orme, & Browne, 1819), s.v. "philosophy." The work was known colloquially as *Rees's Cyclopædia* with reference to the general editor, the Reverend Abraham Rees (1743–1825).
19. *Cyclopædia*, 1st edition (1819), s.v. "poetry."
20. Dwayne Thorpe, "Poe and the Revision of 'Tamerlane,'" *Poe Studies* 18, no. 1 (June 1985): 1.
21. Killis Campbell, *The Mind of Poe and Other Studies* (Cambridge, MA: Harvard University Press, 1933), 99; and on Poe's changing relation to Byron (who died in 1824), see Katrina Bachinger, *Edgar Allan Poe's Biographies of Byron: Byron Differed/Byron Deferred in the "Tales of the Folio Club"* (Salzburg: Edwin Mellen, 1995).
22. David Van Leer, ed., *Edgar Allan Poe: Selected Tales* (Oxford: Oxford University Press, 2008), 326.
23. Quinn, *Edgar Allan Poe: A Critical Biography*, 250.
24. Gustav Gruener, "Poe's Knowledge of German," *Modern Philology* 2, no. 1 (June 1904): 127.
25. Consistent with his literary license to put a French face on Mary Rogers of New York (the subject of an actual murder case that had not been solved), Poe transformed her into Marie Rogêt of Paris. None of the printed texts of this work, however, retain the *accent circonflexe* over the "e" that Poe put in the manuscript title (M 3: 722).
26. Gruener, "Poe's Knowledge of German," 134–138.
27. Burton R. Pollin and Thomas S. Hansen, *The German Face of Edgar Allan Poe: A Study of Literary References in His Works* (Columbia, SC: Camden House, 1995), 51–52.
28. The same may be said of his Italian, for which Poe was praised in school (PL: 75).
29. Poe also could have known these lines from George Bancroft's translation in "Life and Genius of Goethe," *North American Review* (October 1824): "Dearest in her father's eye,/ Jove's own darling, Phantasy" (M 1: 118).
30. Andrea Goulet, *Legacies of the Rue Morgue: Science, Space, and Crime Fiction in France* (Philadelphia: University of Pennsylvania Press, 2015), 1.
31. Nicolas Gouin Dufief, *Nature Displayed in her Mode of Teaching Language to Man: or, A New and Infallible Method of Acquiring a Language*, 2 vols. (London: Printed for the Author, 1828), vol. 1, sig. b2^{v}. Since in the earlier days of printing page numbering as we know it was sporadic, often incorrect, and frequently indicated only on the *recto* (right), references to this book are given by "signature," following an earlier form of standard printing house procedures that use sequential letters and a run of numbers corresponding to the paper size. These markings allowed printers to assemble books in the correct order as many parts were being printed and hung out to dry at the same time. The "r" of a signature indicates the *recto* side of a page, and "v," the *verso*, or back.
32. Sidney Moss, "Poe and His Nemesis, Lewis Gaylord Clark," in *On Poe*, ed. Louis J. Budd and Edwin H. Cady (Durham, NC: Duke University Press, 1993), 110.
33. Terence Whalen, *Edgar Allan Poe and the Masses: The Political Economy of Literature in Antebellum America* (Princeton, NJ: Princeton University Press, 1999), 7.
34. Starting in early February 1837, Poe returned to New York with his wife Virginia and mother-in-law, Maria Clemm, and lived in Greenwich Village, sharing one floor with the learned bookseller William Gowans, with whom he conversed regularly (PL: 22) and whose shop Poe frequented. Gowans likewise had an interest in early printed books (M 2: 518).
35. Edgar Allan Poe, "Notices of New Works," *Southern Literary Messenger* 14, no. 7 (May 1845): 326.
36. Poe, "Notices," 326.

37. Poe, "Notices," 327–328.
38. Edgar Allan Poe, "Secret Writing," *Graham's Magazine* 19, no. 4 (October 1841): 308.
39. Francis Fauvel-Gouraud, *Phreno-Mnemotechny; or, The Art of Memory* (New York and London: Wiley and Putnam, 1845), 84.
40. The quotation comes from a novel by Robert Plumer Ward, *De Vere: or, the Man of Independence*, 4 vols. (London: Colburn, 1827), 2:22.
41. D. L. Rinear, *Stage, Page, Scandals and Vandals: William E. Burton and Nineteenth-century American Theatre* (Carbondale, IL: Southern Illinois University Press, 2004), 33.
42. Edgar Allan Poe, "Our Amateur Poets—William Ellery Channing," *Graham's Magazine* 23, no. 2 (August 1843): 113.
43. Following the quotation from Bacon's essay "Of Beauty," which contains a brace of words with which Poe was especially enamored, the narrator muses: "I perceived that her loveliness was indeed 'exquisite,' and felt that there was much of 'strangeness' pervading it, yet I have tried in vain to detect the irregularity and to trace home my perception of 'the strange'" (M 2: 312). See also "Marginalia," number 220: "Even out of deformities it [the Imagination] fabricates that *Beauty* which is at once its sole object and its inevitable test" (P 2: 369).
44. Edgar Allan Poe, review of *Book of Gems*, by S. C. Hall, *Southern Literary Messenger* 2, no. 9 (1836): 585.
45. Poe, review of *Book of Gems*, 386.
46. Campbell, *The Mind of Poe and Other Studies*, 4; see also Killis Campbell, "Poe's Reading," *University of Texas Studies in English* 5 (1925): 166–196.
47. Quinn, *Edgar Allan Poe: A Critical Biography*, 100; see also James M. Hutchisson, *Poe* (Jackson: University Press of Mississippi, 2005), 10.
48. Burton R. Pollin, "Shakespeare in the Works of Edgar Allan Poe," in *Studies in the American Renaissance*, ed. Joel Myerson (Charlottesville: The University Press of Virginia, 1985), 182–186; and Thomas P. Haviland, "How Well Did Poe Know Milton?," *PMLA* 69, no. 4 (September 1954): 841–860.
49. Campbell, *The Mind of Poe and Other Studies*, 3–5.
50. Pollin, "Shakespeare in the Works of Edgar Allan Poe," 157.
51. Burton R. Pollin, "Poe and Daniel Defoe: A Significant Relationship," *Topic* 30 (1976): 3–22.
52. Edgar Allan Poe, *review of Hawks of Hawk-Hollow*, by Robert M. Bird, *Southern Literary Messenger* 2, no. 1 (December 1835): 43.
53. Quinn, *Edgar Allan Poe: A Critical Biography*, x.
54. Isaac Disraeli, *Curiosities of Literature*, 7th ed., 5 vols. (London: John Murray, 1823), 2:48.
55. 5.2.171–176 in *Doctor Faustus*, in *The Complete Plays of Christopher Marlowe*, ed. Irving Ribner (Indianapolis: Odyssey Press/Bobbs-Merrill, 1963), 410.
56. Engel, *Early Modern Poetics in Melville and Poe: Memory, Melancholy, and the Emblematic Tradition*, 83.
57. Book XV, lines 165–172 in Ovid, *Metamorphoses, Books IX–XV*, trans. Justus Miller, rev. G. P. Goold (Cambridge, MA: Harvard University Press, 1984), 377: "All things are changing; nothing dies. The spirit wanders, comes now here, now there, and occupies whatever frame it pleases. From beasts it passes into human bodies, and from our bodies into beasts, but never perishes. And, as the pliant wax is stamped with new designs, does not remain as it was before nor preserve the same form, but is still the self-same wax, so do I teach the soul is ever the same, though it passes into ever-changing bodies."

58. For a detailed account of the works, as well as the anthologies in which Poe is likely to have encountered them, see Thomas O. Mabbott, "The Books in the House of Usher," *Books at Iowa* 19 (1973): 3–7.
59. The books in Usher's library are recounted as follows (M 2: 408–409): "We pored together over such works as the Ververt et Chartreuse of Gresset; the Belphegor of Machiavelli; the Heaven and Hell of Swedenborg; the Subterranean Voyage of Nicholas Klimm by Holberg; the Chiromancy of Robert Flud, of Jean D'Indaginé, and of De la Chambre; the Journey into the Blue Distance of Tieck; and the City of the Sun of Campanella. One favorite volume was a small octavo edition of the *Directorium Inquisitorium*, by the Dominican Eymeric de Gironne; and there were passages in Pomponius Mela, about the old African Satyrs and Aegipans, over which Usher would sit dreaming for hours. His chief delight, however, was found in the perusal of an exceedingly rare and curious book in quarto Gothic—the manual of a forgotten church—the *Vigiliae Mortuorum secundum Chorum Ecclesiae Maguntinae*."
60. On the place of Campanella and Fludd in Usher's library with respect to Renaissance mnemotechnics, see Engel, *Early Modern Poetics in Melville and Poe: Memory, Melancholy, and the Emblematic Tradition*, 110.
61. Specifically, following Mabbott, the books are: *Tractatus de Geomantia*, by Robert Fludd (1687); *Discours sur les Principes de la Chiromancie*, by Marin Cureau de La Chambre (1653; English translation, 1658); *Introductiones Apotelesmatici . . . in Chiromantiam*, by Joannes ab Indagine of Steinheim (1522; English translation, 1598) (M 2: 420).
62. These angels phonetically have the same names as Cleopatra's two servant-confidants, an allusion to Shakespeare's *Antony and Cleopatra*, or possibly Dryden's *All for Love*, references Poe makes clear he knows in *Politian* (M 1: 261, M 1: 292).
63. Travis Montgomery, "The Near East," in *Edgar Allan Poe in Context*, ed. Kevin J. Hayes (Cambridge: Cambridge University Press, 2012), 56.
64. Campbell, "Poe's Reading," 96; see also M 1: 96.
65. See Jacob Rama Berman, *American Arabesque: Arabs and Islam in the Nineteenth Century Imaginary* (New York: New York University Press, 2012), especially chapter 3, "Poe's Taste for the Arabesque," 109–137.
66. Edgar Allan Poe, "Critical Notices," *Southern Literary Messenger*, 2, no. 2 (January 1836): 129.
67. Edgar Allan Poe, *Broadway Journal* (June 21, 1845): 393.
68. J. Gerald Kennedy, "Inventing the Literati," in *Poe and the Remapping of Antebellum Print Culture*, ed. J. Gerald Kennedy and Jerome McGann (Baton Rouge: Louisiana State University Press, 2012), 18.
69. See, in this volume, Carl Ostrowski's "Kindred Contemporaries: Lippard, Bird, Simms, Hawthorne, and Irving."

Bibliography

Campbell, Killis. *The Mind of Poe and Other Studies*. Cambridge, MA: Harvard University Press, 1933.

Cantalupo, Barbara. *Poe and the Visual Arts*. University Park, PA: Pennsylvania State University Press, 2014.

Forrest, William Mantzel. *Biblical Allusions in Poe*. New York: Macmillan, 1928.
Hayes, Kevin J. *Poe and the Printed Word*. Cambridge: Cambridge University Press, 2000.
Hayes, Kevin J., ed. *Edgar Allan Poe in Context*. Cambridge: Cambridge University Press, 2012.
Kennedy, J. Gerald, and Jerome McGann, eds. *Poe and the Remapping of Antebellum Print Culture*. Baton Rouge: Louisiana State University Press, 2012.
Meyers, Jeffrey. *Edgar Allan Poe: His Life and Legacy*. New York: Cooper Square Press, 1992.
Peeples, Scott. *Edgar Allan Poe Revisited*. New York: Twayne, 1998.
Pollin, Burton R. *Discoveries in Poe*. Notre Dame: University of Notre Dame Press, 1970.
Pollin, Burton R. "Shakespeare in the Works of Edgar Allan Poe." In *Studies in the American Renaissance*, edited by Joel Myerson, 157–186. Charlottesville: The University Press of Virginia, 1985.
Pollin, Burton R., and Thomas S. Hansen. *The German Face of Edgar Allan Poe: A Study of Literary References in His Works*. Columbia, SC: Camden House, 1995.
Walker, I. M., ed. *Edgar Allan Poe: The Critical Heritage*. London: Routledge & Kegan Paul and Methuen, 1987.
Whalen, Terence. *Edgar Allan Poe and the Masses: The Political Economy of Literature in Antebellum America*. Princeton, NJ: Princeton University Press, 1999.

CHAPTER 30

ANCESTRAL PILES

Poe's Gothic Materials

SEAN MORELAND

This chapter examines Poe's transformation of the expressive possibilities of the Gothic in light of his cultural and intellectual context as well as his textual incorporations and rearrangements of the work of earlier writers, including Horace Walpole, Ann Radcliffe, William Godwin, Charles Brockden Brown, Walter Scott, Mary Shelley, and E. T. A. Hoffmann. Poe's work with the Gothic is informed by his immersion in classical and contemporary materialist philosophy, his struggles to survive as a professional magazinist, his resistance to antebellum literary nationalism, and his wide reading in popular scientific literature. These considerations converge in Poe's recombinant approach to writing prose narratives by conspicuously embedding images and phrases extracted from earlier texts. This method emphasizes the atomistic, material nature of language, undermines Romantic ideals of originality, and creates contrasting textual levels that function like the layered metals in an electric pile or battery, generating tension, ambiguity, and aesthetic shock by a process of defamiliarizing hybridization.

"Antenatal Influences": Circulating Materials

Poe's transformative work with the Gothic in the 1830s and 1840s was both behind and ahead of its time, an untimeliness illustrated by Sarah Helen Whitman's 1876 letter to Eugene Didier. Penned during the Victorian Gothic revival that occurred a quarter century after Poe's death and which his writing did much to fuel, Whitman's letter muses on Poe's haunted life and early death, recounting "one of those strange coincidences which startled Macbeth as an intimation of 'fate and metaphysical aid.'" She describes uncovering a "worn and yellow" playbook from "among a large collection of old plays and pamphlets":

> The title arrested me; it was " 'The Wood Dæmon; or, the Clock has Struck!' a Grand, Romantic, Cabalistic Melodrama, in Three Acts, interspersed with Processions, Pageants, and Pantomimes [as performed at the Boston Theater with unbounded applause]. Boston: 1808." I turned the page with a premonitory chill, and lo! among the list of performers, I found the name of "Mr. Poe."[1]

Struck by the realization that Poe's thespian father, David, played a minor role in this Gothic melodrama based on the work of M. G. "Monk" Lewis a few weeks prior to the conception of his son, Whitman is reminded of Dr. Henry Maudsley's "theory of antenatal influences."[2] She ponders this period's Gothic craze and its apparent insemination of Poe's spirit before his birth, while acknowledging the Gothic's resurgence in popularity in the years since his death: "Sorcery and Necromancy, Wild Yagers and Wild Huntsmen, Wood Dæmons and Specters and 'Ghoul-haunted Woodlands' ruled the hour. The clock had struck; and, to judge from present appearances, the end is not yet."[3]

Whitman understood that the first decade of the nineteenth century had seen a frenzied recirculation of Gothic materials, not only in "reputable" literary endeavors, such as Walter Scott's reissuing of earlier Gothic classics, starting with Walpole's *Castle of Otranto* (1764, republished 1811), and high-profile British magazines including *Blackwood's Edinburgh Magazine*, but also in the chapbooks, Bluebook Gothics, and pulpy "yellow" pamphlets she describes. That her meditation on "antenatal influences" is occasioned by a playbook pulled from a crumbling pile of pamphlets dramatizes the Gothic's materiality, invoking its common perception as, to paraphrase Coleridge's review of Lewis's *The Monk*, pulp cheaply "manufactured" in the "lumber-garret of a circulating library" and catering to "a low and vulgar taste."[4] Made of letters, printed on paper, but insufficiently rarified to be literary, rather than just *litter*, it was often understood as base, and debased, material, the stuff of Miltonic chaos or the universal darkness that slouches from Grub Street to bury the world in Pope's *Dunciad*. Yet, as Coleridge recognized, circulate it did, and widely. The Gothic dispersed across a variety of discursive and cultural forms, from romances and tales to poetry, plays, journalistic work, and popular scientific writings, suggesting the limitations imposed by thinking about it primarily as a literary genre. This circulation is linked to the power such materials had, if effectively arranged, to generate a tremendous affective charge in audiences.

Moreover, Whitman's shock, her "premonitory chill" from leafing through a pile of moldering papers, not only dramatizes the Gothic economy through which bodies of flesh and bodies of text are connected by the circulation of affective energy; it also captures the connection between the Gothic text and the electric pile, a connection made famous by Mary Shelley's *Frankenstein* (1818/1831), and echoed by many of Poe's tales.[5] These early electrochemical cells, known variously as voltaic piles and galvanic batteries (named after Alessandro Volta and Luigi Galvani, respectively), allowed for a continuous utilization of electrical energy, and they were created by the serial placement of different metals, stacked either vertically or horizontally, and connected by a porous membrane or bridge. While Poe's interest in such devices is evident from his earliest extant writings, Thomas Ollive Mabbott notes the more frequent references to such devices in the tales of the 1840s, explaining that these derived partially from Poe's reading of the *Course of Lectures* (1842) by Irish popular science writer, Dionysius Lardner (M 2: 679.)

While Poe's fascination with and references to electric piles have been widely recognized, his adaptation of their basic principles to the composition of his tales is less understood. Lardner's account emphasizes the use of alternating layers of material, writing that Volta's "apparatus then presented, first copper, then zinc, then cloth—copper, zinc, cloth and so on as far as he chose to carry it. This he called the Voltaic pile, which afterwards assumed a new form in the Voltaic battery."[6] The greater the number of alternating layers, the greater the charge these devices could deliver; this cumulative assemblage of heterogeneous elements is paralleled by Poe's compositional method, succinctly described by Mabbott in his introduction to "The Pit and the Pendulum":

> He sought and combined with modifications stories in the Blackwood manner—that is, sensational accounts of terrible experiences usually told in the first person. For details he drew not only from Blackwood's but from other British and American periodicals and from an American novel, and he used some factual material. He must have expected many of his readers to know what he was doing, for some of the sources were stories that had wide circulation at the time, although their popularity has now faded. (M 2: 679)

Part of Poe's effect involves his audience's recognition of these recombined elements. The "premonitory thrill," uncanny effect, and fatalistic sensibility of his tales depend on their novel arrangement of familiar, and even formulaic, materials. Poe's understanding of the Gothic's potential for producing such a charge, and his appreciation for the increased circulatory potential this entailed, led him to work through this mode for most of his career. Poe explains this motivation in his 1835 letter to Thomas W. White, responding to White's criticisms of his "far too horrible" early tale "Berenice." Acknowledging that such tales necessarily challenge the limits of "good taste," Poe defines their mode as "the ludicrous heightened into the grotesque: the fearful coloured into the horrible: the witty exaggerated into the burlesque: the singular wrought into the strange and mystical" (CL 1: 84).

This is a lapidary statement of intent and procedure; Poe works by rearranging existing materials to produce the aesthetic effects of the "burlesque" and the "grotesque," emphasizing his explicit reclamation of what had been terms of disparagement and abjection to earlier critics of the Gothic. Poe understood that these aesthetic categories bore a heavy historical and political freight, for the grotesque and burlesque were the terms Burke used to express his condemnation of the "popular convulsion" of the French Revolution, in which the "terror of the bayonet" created a grotesque polity, "deformed into monsters," and with the collapse of the elegant vertical structure of monarchy and aristocracy, the national representative assembly was nothing but "a profane burlesque, and abominable perversion of that sacred institute."[7] While Poe's more immediate referent in the reclamation of these terms is Sir Walter Scott (as will be explained later), he understood the Burkean structure of Scott's Gothic mode. He further saw not only the continuity between Burke's censure of the burlesque and grotesque and Scott's similar rejection of the "Grotesque and Arabesque" aspects of Hoffmann's tales but also the expressive energies and circulating potential inherent in these abject materials.[8]

Poe claims the burlesque and grotesque are "invariably sought after with avidity," finding "their way into other periodicals, and into the papers," until, "taking hold upon the public mind they augment the reputation of the source where they originated." Proposing to provide White "every month with a Tale" of this nature, Poe claims that the "effect" "will be estimated better by the circulation of the Magazine than by any comments upon its contents" (CL 1: 85). However, as Michael Allen points out, Poe stated his admiration especially for the "earlier numbers of Blackwood," specifically from 1817 through the early 1820s.[9] By the time of his offer to White, Poe's Grotesques and Arabesques, and the *Blackwood*'s models that inspired them, "were several years behind the current trend rather than in the fashion of the age."[10] Nevertheless, they informed Poe's attempts to, in Betsy Erkila's words, appeal to both "the critical and popular taste":

> In order to sell his tales, Poe self-consciously appealed to the popular taste for bone-chilling scenes of terror, excess, and violence. But as his canny satire of the sensationalist and stylistic excesses of the magazine trade in "How to Write a Blackwood's Article" evinces, Poe was a searing and at times mordantly funny critic of his age and times.[11]

Poe's voltaic approach to literary composition was informed by this competitive, rapidly changing literary-cultural marketplace, in which a loss of affective currency would cause decreased circulation, leading in turn to a death both literary and literal. This gave Poe what Robert T. Tally calls an "intimate familiarity with the material, quotidian conditions of a world" that "many other writers were sheltered from, economically and culturally, as Poe bitterly noted of some of his Bostonian contemporaries," while contributing to a "literary theory and practice" that emerged from "the rising ash-heaps of capitalism, urbanism, and an emerging culture industry."[12]

Poe believed the magazine to be the form of literary circulation best adapted to an emerging international economy. Drawing upon Voltaic and Mesmeric experiments as inspirational models, Poe's focus on selection and recombination, as well as his theory that literary works must produce effects quickly, in a single sitting, extended from his concentration on magazine work. His expansive estimation of the magazine form is expressed in his criticism of an article by Duyckinck:

> He is inclined to undervalue [the magazine paper's] power—to limit its province—which is illimitable. In fact, it is in the extent of subject, and not less in the extent or variety of *tone*, that the French and English surpass us, to so good a purpose. How

> very rarely are we struck with an American Magazine article, as with an absolute novelty—how frequently the foreign articles so affect us! (P 3: 136)

This excerpt reveals both Poe's desire to expand the subject and range of American literary magazines and his well-documented resistance to American cultural nationalism, a project opposed to his conception of literature's global circulatory possibilities. J. Gerald Kennedy explains that the course of Poe's literary career "places him at the heart of an epoch devoted to cultural nation-building. And yet Poe vehemently opposed literary nationalism, which he regarded as an exercise in provincialism at odds with the true task of the writer—to appeal to a global audience."[13]

Poe's Gothic materialism is also inseparable from what Kenneth Allan Hovey calls his "materialist metaphysics of man," a philosophical perspective owing much to Epicurean philosophy,[14] and particularly to the poetics of first-century BCE Roman poet Lucretius's *De Rerum Natura*, which describes a temporally finite, entirely material universe governed by elemental recombination and inevitable decay.[15] In the early nineteenth century, Epicurean philosophy shared with mesmeric theory and voltaic experimentation an interrogation of the distinction between living and unliving, animate and inanimate matter. For Lucretius, life arises as an effect of particular arrangements of material, for "all things change to all things" and "sentient things from things insensate flow."[16] For Mesmer and his followers, the continuous energetic transference occurring between animate and inanimate matter demonstrated that the distinction between them was merely one of degree. Such a continuum seemed confirmed by the experiments of Galvani and Volta, which demonstrated how energy produced by layers of inanimate matter could not only affect living matter, but also seemingly animate dead matter.

Poe's most memorable expression of such a materialist continuum occurs in a letter to James Russell Lowell dated July 2, 1844:

> I have no belief in spirituality. I think the word a mere word. No one has really a conception of spirit. We cannot imagine what is not. We deceive ourselves by the idea of infinitely rareified matter. Matter escapes the senses by degrees—a stone—a metal—a liquid—the atmosphere—a gas—the luminiferous ether. Beyond this there are other modifications more rare. But to all we attach the notion of a constitution of particles—atomic composition. For this reason only, we think spirit different; for spirit, we say is unparticled, and therefore is not matter. But it is clear that if we proceed sufficiently far in our ideas of rarefaction, we shall arrive at a point where the particles coalesce; for, although the particles be infinite, the infinity of littleness in the spaces between them, is an absurdity. (CL 1: 449)

The passage's importance is underlined by its echo in Poe's July 10 letter to T. H. Chivers, and its near-verbatim inclusion as Vankirk's posthumous revelation in the contemporaneous tale "Mesmeric Revelation" (see M 3: 1033). This concept of materialism, in Mabbott's words, "going back to Democritus and to the Epicureans," portrays spirit as "a kind of rarified matter," which Poe "seems to have believed in" (M 3: 1025). Poe's humorous duplication of this tale's structure and themes with "Some Words with a Mummy," published later the same year, reinforces the close association between electrical and mesmeric experimentation, as the latter tale simply substitutes "an experiment or two with the voltaic pile" to enable the posthumous interview to occur (M 3: 1181).

The widespread circulation of "Mesmeric Revelation" and its credulous reception as a factual case reinforced for Poe the potential of this materialist perspective, which became the philosophical bedrock supporting his subsequent aesthetics. Thus, Poe's 1844 meditation on crafting prose fiction, "A Chapter of Suggestions," presents a materialistic, atomistic, procedural, and physiologically focused conception of literary creation. He claims that plot has been "very imperfectly understood, and has never been rightly defined. Many persons regard it as mere complexity of incident. In its most rigorous acceptation, it is *that from which no component atom can be removed, and in which none of the component atoms can be displaced, without ruin to the whole*" (P 2: 469). Poe portrays the work of fiction as a device designed to produce a particular effect, transmitting a charge to the reader. This effect is dependent upon the circuit created by each of the elements in the fiction's arrangement; should one of these elements be lost, the circuit is broken, and the effect destroyed. It is an account that makes the connection between the structure of fiction and that of the electric pile more than merely metaphorical.

Gothic Structures

In the same essay, Poe goes on to claim that "Godwin and Bulwer are the best constructors of plot in English literature," and it is from Godwin, more than any other writer, that Poe derived his approach to structuring fiction (L2: 56). Burton R. Pollin memorably describes "Poe's entrenched 'Godwinolatry,' "[17] noting "that Godwin represented for Poe the apex of narrative and stylistic achievement."[18] Godwin's work represents not only a layer of material in many of Poe's narrative piles but also a model for their construction, as both "A Chapter of Suggestions" and "The Philosophy of Composition" make clear.

Lardner's description of the voltaic pile as "one of the greatest instruments of philosophical investigation"[19] could have as readily been a description of the narrative techniques Godwin developed in *Caleb Williams* (1793).[20] An important precursor to both Poe's ratiocinative and Gothic tales, *Caleb Williams*'s eponymous protagonist is compelled by curiosity to uncover the dark secrets kept by his aristocratic benefactor-turned-nemesis, Falkland.[21] Pamela Clemit characterizes the novel as a triumph of technique that inspired later writers, including Percy and Mary Shelley and American novelist Charles Brockden Brown, to produce work recognizable as part of an informal "Godwinian school."[22] While his magazinist's penchant for miniaturization and use of voltaic layering sets Poe's tales apart from these Godwinian novels, he nevertheless knew and drew upon them, as well as upon their progenitor.

Poe had both his philosophical materialism and his role as an American adapter of the Gothic in common with Brown. Profoundly influenced by thinkers including the Baron d'Holbach and Nicholas de Condorcet, Brown was suspicious of both religious doctrine and metaphysical philosophy. He rejected the Cartesian separation of soul from body, concluding in a journal entry that "Mind and Matter are the two grand divisions of science, but . . . in this life mind perhaps can never be considered in any other way than in conjunction with matter."[23] Brown found in Godwin's rationalist Gothic a potent means of exploring this imbrication of mind and matter. The influence of *Caleb Williams* is especially evident in Brown's first two novels, *Wieland* (1798) and *Edgar Huntly* (1797/1800), the latter of which provided ample material for Poe's Gothic piles.

Nevertheless, despite the intense admiration they shared for Godwin's work, Brown and Poe ultimately responded to it differently. Brown valued Godwin as primarily an illuminating political and ethical thinker, whose literary productions were vehicles for his philosophical examinations. By extension, Brown framed his own fictions along didactic lines, writing in his introduction to *Wieland* that his "purpose is neither selfish nor temporary, but aims at the illustration of some important branches of the moral constitution of man."[24] Brown also sought to apply Godwin's philosophical principles and literary form to an interrogation of American characters and concerns; his "Apology" to *Edgar Huntly* serves as a manifesto for this intention. Brown's goal is "calling forth the passions" and "engaging the sympathy" of the reader

> by means hitherto unemployed by preceding authors. Puerile superstition and exploded manners, Gothic castles and chimeras, are the materials usually employed for this end. The incident of Indian hostility and the perils of the western wilderness are far more suitable; and for a native of America to overlook these would admit of no apology.[25]

Brown emphasizes the affective potential of the Gothic in a manner Poe would have appreciated, but unlike Poe, foregrounds the *Americanness*, the national and regional character, of his approach. Poe's self-distancing from Brown's nationalism is suggested by the way he embeds elements from *Edgar Huntly* in *The Narrative of Arthur Gordon Pym*, "A Tale of the Ragged Mountains" and "Pit and the Pendulum." In each case, Poe displaces Brown's American frontier with a foreign setting. With *Pym*, Poe interleaves *Edgar Huntly* with, among other things, Benjamin Morrell's *Narrative of Four Voyages*, generating a charge by fusing romance with nonfiction. In "A Tale of the Ragged Mountains," Poe adapts *Huntly*'s somnambulic theme, using it to displace his bewildered protagonist, Augustus Bedloe, to India, perhaps taking a satirical shot at Brown's reliance on "Indian hostility" to evoke the passions of readers. In "The Pit and the Pendulum," Poe echoes Huntly's account of awaking in a subterranean pit, relocating it to Spain, incorporating it within a Gothic captivity narrative, and adding to it, among other elements, echoes of Lardner's description of a galvanic battery.

Brown's national-historical perspective anticipates the romances of Sir Walter Scott, who knew and admired Brown's work, but it is this perspective that Poe pointedly subverts in his incorporations of Brown.[26] The most influential theorist and practitioner of Gothic fiction during the first half of the nineteenth century, Scott provided a framework through which Poe, like many of his British and American contemporaries, understood the Gothic. As Tally explains, "Scott's historical novels attempted to shape the diffuse passions, partisan interests, and different spaces into a distinctively national imaginary geography" and were "essential precursors to national narrative in American literature."[27] The editions of Walpole and Radcliffe and the translations of Hoffmann that Poe read were those curated and introduced by Scott, and understanding Poe's transformations of the Gothic requires recognizing his subversive adaptations of the concepts and phrasing he derives from this critical framework.

Scott's edition of Walpole's *Castle of Otranto* was first published in 1811, shortly before his first novel *Waverley* (1814), and his introduction prefaces not just Walpole's novel, but also the national reorientation of the Gothic his own career would perform. As David Sandner explains, Scott's works sought to place the supernatural in a particular context—"Scotland's past." Scott argued that "the Marvellous in poetry is ill-timed & disgusting when not managed with moderation & ingrafted upon some circumstance of popular tradition or belief which sometimes can give even to the improbable an air of something like probability," and this idea is already evident in his *Otranto* introduction.[28] He expounds it more fully in both the preface to his 1824 omnibus *The Novels of Mrs. Ann Radcliffe* (an edition whose release was meant to both commemorate and commercially exploit her death) and his 1827 essay, "On the Supernatural in Fictitious Composition." Scott notes Walpole's intention with *Otranto* to create a synthesis of old and new forms of romance, and he claims that "Romantic narrative is of two kinds—that which, being in itself possible, may be the matter of belief at any period; and that which, though held impossible by more enlightened ages, was yet consonant with the faith of earlier times."[29] Scott emphasizes that Walpole's narrative is of the latter sort, stating his preference for this approach over the modern scepticism of Radcliffe's romances:

> The bold assertion of the actual existence of phantoms and apparitions seems to us to harmonize much more naturally with the manners of feudal times, and to produce a more powerful effect upon the reader's mind, than any attempt to reconcile the superstitious credulity of feudal ages with the philosophic skepticism of our own, by referring those prodigies to the operation of fulminating powder, combined mirrors, magic lanthorns, trap-doors, speaking trumpets, and like apparatus of German phantasmagoria.[30]

Scott evaluates the Gothic based on its ability to "produce" a "powerful effect" on the reader's mind, anticipating Poe's conception of the "Unity of Effect." However, Scott also thinks this "effect" should be used to perform a particular kind of work, fueling the modern reader's experience of the narrated past world, in part by reifying the presumed folkloric and religious beliefs of its inhabitants. Scott's formulation of the Gothic, and his defense of Walpole, offers a rejoinder to the critical disparagement of *Otranto* and its imitators by Wordsworth and Coleridge, who, as Jerrold E. Hogle explains, with "the

Lyrical Ballads, make a point of condemning what the Walpolean Gothic has become as the very antithesis of their project."[31] By way of praising Walpole, Scott acknowledges that it is "almost impossible to build such a modern Gothic structure as shall impress us with the feelings we have endeavoured to describe. It may be grand, or it may be gloomy; it may excite magnificent or melancholy ideas; but it must fail in bringing forth the sensation of supernatural awe."[32] Scott's conception of "Gothic structure" is crucial both for its reframing of the architectural focus of earlier Gothic fictions and its anticipation of Poe's electric turn. Walpole's public acknowledgment of *Otranto*'s authorship as of its second edition in 1765 cemented the connection between architectural and literary Gothicism, making the correspondence between *Otranto*'s nostalgic fantasia and the neo-Gothic redesign of Strawberry Hill, his ancestral estate, a matter of widespread public knowledge.

The tendency to think about the Gothic in monumental terms, linking landscape and architecture to literary genre and national identity, solidified further as writers during the 1790s foregrounded the connection between Gothic architectural structures and a particular historical and political order. Consider this description of the abbey from Radcliffe's second novel, 1790's *A Sicilian Romance*:

> The dark clouds of prejudice break away before the sun of science, and gradually dissolving, leave the brightening hemisphere to the influence of his beams. But through the present scene appeared only a few scattered rays, which served to shew more forcibly the vast and heavy masses that concealed the forms of truth. Here prejudice, not reason, suspended the influence of the passions; and scholastic learning, mysterious philosophy, and crafty sanctity, supplied the place of wisdom, simplicity and pure devotion.[33]

The abbey's "vast and heavy masses," like the other "Gothic structures" of Radcliffe's fiction, are an eighteenth-century architecturalization of the oppressive and dominating figure of *Religio* in *De Rerum Natura*'s polemic against superstitious cultism. Radcliffe makes this explicit in *A Sicilian Romance* by embedding her poem, "Superstition: An Ode," essentially a verse improvisation on Lucretius's description of *Religio* as a monstrous mistress, trampling on humanity. Radcliffe's Lucretian echo amplifies the tension between her rationalist and Walpole's supernaturalist Gothic modes while revealing the latter's more Burkean structure. Burke's *A Philosophical Enquiry into the Origins of Our Ideas of the Sublime and the Beautiful* (1757) was meant, in Eric Baker's words, to counter "the privileging of theoretical knowledge over feeling (of Locke's *Essay* over Milton's *Paradise Lost*)," and "Burke viewed Lucretius as complicitous in the rationalist tendency to declare everything that cannot be clearly understood and explained—such as the experience of the sublime—to be devoid of value."[34]

Lucretius was similarly suspect for Walpole, whose invention of the "Gothic story" was in part a challenge to such sceptical materialism.[35] Contrastively, Radcliffe embraces Lucretius as a precursor to her own Enlightenment values.[36] Radcliffe further underlines the contemporary political context of her poem by making the demon Superstition a monarch and seating her upon a throne.[37] This image circulates into Burke's defense of the monarchy in *Reflections on the Revolution in France* in the same year, and Poe subsequently weaves it into both "The Conversation of Eiros and Charmion" and "The Fall of the House of Usher" in 1839. In both cases, Poe inverts aspects of the image, using it to signal the cosmic reorientation his work will perform in breaking from Scott's Burkean circumscription of the Gothic, as will be explained later.[38]

Where Lucretius adapted the Homeric epic to his polemic, portraying Epicurus as a hero whose solar intelligence drives out the darkness, Radcliffe instead adapted the *Bildungsroman*, showing how the developing education of her sensitive heroines enables their escape from captivity within Gothic structures of cold stone and old belief.[39] Contrastively, Burke's efforts to turn Lucretius's ideas against the very materialist scepticism and radical Whig politics they nourished, while reclaiming his own aesthetics of the sublime from their appropriation by "Jacobin" apologists, inform his *Reflections on the Revolution in France* (1790), which argues that traditional ideas and social formations are effectively material modes:

> To destroy any power, growing wild from the rank productive force of the human mind, is almost tantamount, in the moral world, to the destruction of the apparently active properties of bodies in the material. It would be like the attempt to destroy (if it were in our competence to destroy) the expansive force of fixed air in nitre, or the power of steam, or of electricity or magnetism.[40]

These ideas prove crucial to the Gothic materialism of both Mary Shelley and Poe a generation later.[41] At the time, however, Burke's *Reflections* did more than any other single text to stabilize the relationship between the architectural, political, and epistemological meanings of "Gothic structure." Using it as a metonym for hereditary monarchy itself, Burke advocates for the castle's reform, arguing that "the useful parts of an old establishment" should be kept, and "what is superadded is to be fitted to what is retained" through the judicious exercise of "powers of comparison and combination."[42] Responding rapidly to Burke, Mary Wollstonecraft published her critical rejoinder "A Vindication of the Rights of Men" later the same year. This text hones in on Burke's Gothic metonymy, demanding:

> Why was it a duty to repair an ancient castle, built in barbarous ages, of Gothic materials? Why were they obliged to rake amongst heterogeneous ruins; or rebuild old walls, whose foundations could scarcely be explored, when a simple structure might be raised on the foundations of experience, the only valuable inheritance our forefathers can bequeath?[43]

This allegorization of "Gothic structure" circulated widely through political discourse in the 1790s, further fixing the association and thereby circumscribing the expressive possibilities of the Gothic. This historical fixity concealed the reality that, in Hogle's words, from the beginning of the Gothic Story, "the mobility of its signs and the conflict in its cross-generic orientations have made it fundamentally about ideological irresolution and the fears that come from being pulled simultaneously towards waning and emerging forms of human self-fashioning and visions of cultural, natural, and even cosmic order."[44]

While Poe's Gothic mode turns toward the cosmic, a vision of cultural order was at stake in the Gothic for Scott, whose supernatural aesthetics derive from Burkean sublimity. This is clear from his 1827 essay "On the Supernatural in Fictitious Composition; and particularly on the works of Ernest Theodore William Hoffmann," which appeared shortly after Scott's public acknowledgment of his authorship of the Waverly novels. These revelations inform Poe's parodic appropriations of Scott in his notes for the abortive collection "Tales of the Folio Club," which Poe planned in the early 1830s. Scott's essay would later serve as a major source not only for Poe's "The Fall of the House of Usher," but also for his adoption of the terms "Grotesque and Arabesque" as descriptors of his literary aesthetics.[45] Scott's alignment of these terms occurs in his claim that "the grotesque in [Hoffmann's] compositions partly resembles the arabesque in painting, in which is introduced the most strange and complicated monsters," a characterization that inspired Poe's adoption of these terms for his own tales of monstrous hybridity.[46]

Against such Gothic grotesques, Scott's essay upholds an aesthetic of obscurity and suggestion:

> the exhibition of supernatural appearances in fictitious narrative ought to be rare, brief, indistinct, and such as may become a being to us so incomprehensible, and so different from ourselves, of whom we cannot justly conjecture whence he comes, or for what purpose, and of whose attributes we can have no regular or distinct perception.[47]

Scott goes on to advocate a Burkean paradigm of social conservatism, whereby a shared national-cultural history should be commemorated and monumentalized by each generation using the affective resources of religion and the cultural arts. Burke argues that since "man is by his constitution a religious animal," the affective regeneration of heritage must necessarily exploit superstition, the indispensible "religion of feeble minds," for its "resources," giving a further turn of the screw to Radcliffe's seating of Lucretius's *Religio* on a throne.[48]

His *Otranto* introduction reveals Scott's intention to reinvigorate the Gothic in the wake of its narrow politicization during the French Revolutionary period by making its historical orientation energetic and expressive. That meant repairing the "Gothic structures" that Radcliffe's once-popular Enlightenment Gothics had helped ossify. Scott emphasizes, both in his introduction to Walpole and preface to Radcliffe, that while Radcliffe's structures may at times "excite magnificent or melancholy ideas," they necessarily fail to generate the "sensation of supernatural awe" necessary for a vivid impression of the past. Still, Scott's 1824 preface praises Radcliffe's romances for their intermittent ability to transport the reader: "The materials of these celebrated romances, and the means employed in conducting the narrative, are all selected with a view to the author's primary object, of moving the reader."[49] Scott's preface then restates his "preference for the more simple mode, of boldly avowing the use of supernatural machinery."[50]

In Scott's distillation of the Gothic and criticism of the limitations imposed on its "machinery" by Radcliffe's rationalism, Poe found contrasting materials he could combine to generate a potent shock. The allusions Poe makes to Radcliffe, especially with the opening of "The Fall of the House of Usher" (1839) and "The Oval Portrait" (1842), reinforce this. Consider the first sentence of the latter tale, which alludes, as Peter Beidler points out, to *The Mysteries of Udolpho* (1794):

> The château into which my valet had ventured to make forcible entrance, rather than permit me, in my desperately wounded condition, to pass a night in the open air, was one of those piles of commingled gloom and grandeur which have so long frowned among the Apennines, not less in fact than in the fancy of Mrs. Radcliffe. (M 2: 662)

Beidler analyzes the intersections between Poe's tales and Radcliffe's romances, focusing on how "Usher" echoes *The Mysteries of Udolpho*.[51] He claims that "whereas Radcliffe inserts into her novel poems and a tale largely for their own sake, Poe asserts his artistic independence of her by inserting them into his story as highly functional narrative elements."[52] More important, Poe's practice of literary insertion demonstrates his conviction that "to originate, is carefully, patiently, and understandingly to combine" and his application of this conviction to the creation of literary electric piles.[53]

Poe takes the technique of embedding poems, folk tales, and other textual fragments, already a defining technique of the Radcliffean Gothic romance, and intensifies it, demonstrating the elasticity of the Gothic while revealing how the recirculation and rearrangement of particles from other texts fundamentally change their meaning and effects. In addition, Poe's insertions deepen the "undercurrent of meaning" of his tales by expanding their interpretive possibilities. In this case, the allusion to *Udolpho* also invokes Scott's criticism of Radcliffe; the Apennine château, with its "mingled gloom and grandeur," fails to summon a sensation of "supernatural awe" in the narrator. Such a sensation is, however, ultimately delivered by the eponymous portrait. The earlier 1842 version of the tale, "Life in Death," more obviously demonstrates the association between the interlarded structure of the electric pile and the energetic charge of the Gothic; the narrator describes his reaction to the portrait "as if" it was "the shock of a galvanic battery" (M 2: 664). While Poe cut this phrase from the 1845 version, its corollary would remain in "The Pit and the Pendulum," also written in 1842, shortly after Poe first read Lardner's lectures.

While the echoes of Lardner's account in Poe's writings from 1842 make the connection between Gothic structure and the electric pile more explicit, reading Lardner did not suggest this connection so much as reinforce it, since the alternating layers of intertextual material in "The Oval Portrait" effectively follow the same structure as the opening paragraphs of "The Fall of the House of Usher" (1839), written prior to Poe's reading of Lardner. The connection was more likely suggested to Poe by his earlier reading of *Frankenstein*, or at least Scott's 1818 review of it for *Blackwood's*. If he read the

1831 edition of the novel, Poe would have found Mary Shelley's account of literary originality congenial: "Invention, it must be humbly admitted, does not consist in creating out of a void, but out of chaos; the materials must, in the first place, be afforded: it can give form to dark, shapeless substances, but cannot bring into being substance itself."[54] This is a materialist conception of originality close to Poe's own, and similarly predicated on a rejection of Coleridge's idealistic theory of Imagination. That Shelley's novel played a key role in shaping both Poe's philosophical materialism and his voltaic approach to composition can be seen by looking through the eye-like windows of the House of Usher, itself Poe's most ambitious conversion of ancestral into electric pile.

"Sacrificing Every Thing to Effect:" "The Fall of the House of Usher"

"Usher" is both Poe's most complex voltaic assemblage and most explicit metaphorical alignment of the Gothic and the electric pile. The narrator's descriptions of the house emphasize the similarities between its architecture and an electrochemical generator, both formed from "combinations of very simple natural objects" (M 2: 398). Commonly used metals in early electric piles included lead, iron, and copper, present in the tale in the form of the "leaden-hued" vapor exuded by the house (M 2: 400), the "massive iron" door behind which Madeline's body will be interred, and the copper-sheathed chamber in which she will temporarily repose (M 2: 410). Instead of the layers of damp cardboard or leather commonly used to complete the circuit while oxidizing these metals, the tale employs mouldy piles of books (M 2: 408–409) and the body of Madeline herself (M 2: 410) to initiate the Usher pile's fatal discharge.

The tale delivers, in an accelerated and intensified way, all of those Gothic effects that Scott praises, beginning with his introduction to Walpole:

> What is most striking in The Castle of Otranto, is the manner in which the various prodigious appearances, bearing each upon the other, and all upon the accomplishment of the ancient prophecy, denouncing the ruin of the house of Manfred, gradually prepare us for the grand catastrophe.[55]

Like "The Oval Portrait," "Usher" begins by cultivating a Radcliffean approach to the supernatural. The narrator is convinced that Roderick's fears are superstitious delusions, and the reader is encouraged to assume that the story will resolve into what Scott calls the "modern sceptical" mode. Gradually the narrator, and by extension the reader, finds these "superstitions" infiltrating every aspect of the narrative, cultivating an irresolvable uncertainty. This uncertainty arises from Poe's piling up of conflicting textual sources, explanatory suggestions and modalities, a heterogeneous accumulation underlined through the narrator's description of selected texts from Usher's library (M 2: 408-409).

In terms of the tale's Gothic precursors, however, Shelley's Godwinian and Hoffmann's phantasmagoric modes are the most important. In the former, the limitations of our knowledge about the nature and behavior of the physical world are underlined, and nature is shown capable of functioning in ways that seem supernatural solely because of our epistemological limits. This is the Gothic mode of Brown's *Wieland* and *Edgar Huntly*, both of which stretch the limits of the possible, according to contemporaneous scientific views, but also take pains to document the plausibility of their strange events. *Frankenstein* works similarly: the doctor's creation of life, while unnatural in the sense of "unhallowed," is possible within the limits of natural law as defined by the fictional world. This plausibility is stressed throughout Shelley's novel, beginning with the opening sentence of (Percy) Shelley's preface: "The event on which this fiction is founded has been supposed, by Dr. Darwin, and some of the physiological writers of Germany, as not of impossible occurrence," a statement reprinted by Scott's detailed review of the novel in *Blackwood's*.[56] Scott uses this statement to support his situation of *Frankenstein* as a work of marvellous fiction meant to illustrate "the powers and workings of the human mind," a trait it shares with "the well known Saint Leon of William Godwin."[57]

Scott's review of *Frankenstein* was mostly positive, praising the novel for its "plain and forcible English, without exhibiting that mixture of hyperbolical Germanisms with which tales of wonder are usually told, as if it were necessary that the language should be as extravagant as the fiction."[58] However, a contemporaneous anonymous review of *Frankenstein* in *The Edinburgh Magazine and Literary Miscellany*, which shares much in common with Scott's, including the assumption of Percy Shelley's authorship and recognition of the novel's Godwinian provenance, goes on to describe *Frankenstein* as an example of "the modern school in its highest style of caricature and exaggeration." Drawing on Scott's Burkean political aesthetics, this review accuses the novel of "bordering too closely on impiety" in displaying the "most outrageous improbability,—in sacrificing every thing to effect."[59] The reviewer maintains, like Scott, that the supernatural should be ingrafted onto folkloric tradition, rather than used to unsettle and destabilize the certainties offered by religion ("impious") and orderly and predictable physical laws ("improbable").[60]

This reviewer suggests a parallel between Shelley and Frankenstein himself; both border "too closely on impiety" by creating a form of life whose "execution is imperfect," and whose sutures bear "the marks of an unpracticed hand."[61] Implicit in this analogy is the figural migration of a "Gothic structure" for the production of "powerful effects" from Walpolean or Radcliffean architecture into the creature, the "supernatural machinery" for the transference of affective energy to the reader. Poe brings this migration full circle in "Usher" by "remodelling" the monster, describing the House in terms of both the contrasting layers of an electric pile and Shelley's creature. Poe's narrator notes "a wild inconsistency between its still perfect adaptation of parts" (M 2: 400) that parallels Shelley's description of the creature's parts "beautiful in proportion," becoming a grotesque caricature due the "horrid contrast" of their recombination, a description approvingly quoted in Scott's *Frankenstein* review.[62]

This echo is made more reverberant through verbal parallels between the narrator's description of the house, his description of Roderick Usher, and "The Haunted Palace," with its "flowing" hair/banners and pearly gates/teeth, which in turn echo *Frankenstein*'s description of the monster's "lustrous" and "flowing" hair and the "pearly whiteness" of its teeth.[63] Poe's imagistic synthesis of the mansion with the head, and the head with an electric pile, was likely suggested by an observation by Sir John Herschell, widely quoted in the popular scientific literature of the 1830s and 1840s. Herschell writes, "if the brain be an electric pile, constantly in action, it may be conceived to discharge itself at regular intervals along the nerves which communicate with the heart, and thus to excite the pulsation of that organ."[64]

Poe structures this superimposition of house and head using *makranthrôpos*, a poetic technique that is Lucretius's primary means of demonstrating the mutuality of adaptation between the microcosmic and macrocosmic scales throughout *De Rerum Natura*, where it yokes the subliminally minute and the sublimely massive to the scale of the human body and perception. *Makranthrôpos* intensifies the shock of Lucretius's descriptions of death and decay, reminding readers that every structural dissolution, be it atomic, cosmic, or a nonhuman animal, is akin to that of the human being, the rarified material of the soul and mind as much as the coarser material of the body. *Makranthrôpos* prepares the reader to recognize that these forms will, quite literally, pass into and become one another, as recombinations of the same basic materials.

More than any other English translation, John Mason Good's 1805 version amplifies *De Rerum Natura*'s makranthropic poetics. Where the English language would normally demand that atomic and cosmic phenomena be referred to by the genderless pronoun "it," Good genders pronouns to emphasize the importance of personification to Lucretius's poem, causing such phenomena to take on perversely anthropomorphic qualities, giving Good's Lucretius a potent resonance for Gothic writers of the nineteenth century, as attested by its echoes in both "The Fall of the House of Usher" and *Frankenstein*.[65]

Poe's Lucretian remodeling is crucial to his use of Hoffmann's phantasmagoric mode to subvert Scott's circumscription of the Gothic. The makranthropic structure of "Usher" allows Poe to establish his thesis of terror, while illustrating that it is not of Germany, or any other national-historical locale, but of the soul. Poe fleshes out the makranthropic skeleton of house/head/world by stitching in some of the more "extravagant" passages from Hoffmann, whose work uses its affective energy to transport readers not into a politically useful cultural past, but into "the Monarch Thought's Dominion," where the omnipotence of thought prevails. This phantasmagoric mode troubled Scott, as reflected in his 1827 essay:

> Unfortunately, [Hoffmann's] taste and temperament directed him too strongly to the grotesque and fantastic, —carried him too far "*extra moenia flammantia mundi*," too much beyond the circle not only of probability but even of possibility, to admit in his composing much in the better style he might easily have attained.[66]

Tally explains that Scott uses this Latin phrase, borrowed from Lucretius, to suggest that Hoffmann, "venturing 'beyond the flaming walls of the world,'" indulges "in an extravagant aesthetic that evokes horror or even disgust by conjuring up a radical alterity that defamiliarizes the habitus and aggrandizes the horrible," which in turn "disrupts the conventions and expectations of a national literature."[67] Poe's charged alternation of material from Lucretius and Scott, anticipated by their earlier opposition in the framing narrative for "Tales of the Folio Club," is a powerful example of his defamiliarizing hybridization at work.

Poe's "extravagant" pursuit of both Hoffmann and Epicurus into the Empyrean with "Usher" can be better understood by considering the verbal and imagistic parallels it shares with Poe's contemporaneous tale, "The Conversation of Eiros and Charmion." In "Usher," rather than having reason topple superstition from her throne, the narrator describes "the tottering of" Roderick's "lofty reason upon her throne" (M 2: 406). The vaunted position the narrator previously grants reason becomes occupied by Roderick's "grim phantasm, FEAR" (M 2: 403), crouching oppressively on the narrator's heart, "an incubus of utterly causeless alarm" (M 2: 411). These images recur in "Eiros and Charmion," as the subtly material Eiros recounts the events leading up to the destruction of the Earth by a comet whose affinity for nitrogen makes its atmosphere fatally combustible (M 2: 460-461).

Eiros notes that by the time of the comet's arrival, the popular superstitions once occasioned by such events have been banished: "As if by some sudden convulsive exertion, reason had at once hurled superstition from her throne" (M 2: 459). Eiros's language echoes Burke's characterization of the French Revolution as a "popular convulsion" and Frankenstein's description of the creature's first movements alike, while completing Radcliffe's revision of *Religio*, demonstrating that in the tale's future, the Enlightenment that the Revolution was supposed to embody has succeeded. This victory is short-lived, however, for as scientists realize the fatal effects the cosmic invader will have on Earth's atmosphere,

> the hearts of the stoutest of our race beat violently within their bosoms. A very few days sufficed, however, to merge even such feelings in sentiments more unendurable. We could no longer apply to the strange orb any accustomed thoughts. Its historical attributes had disappeared. It oppressed us with a hideous *novelty* of emotion. We saw it not as an astronomical phenomenon in the heavens, but as an incubus upon our hearts, and a shadow upon our brains. (M 2: 459)

The Imp of the Perverse returns, riding this time not on the coattails of cultic and religious belief (ironically justified by the tale's confirmation of Biblical eschatology) but those of scientific prediction. The static, historically circumscribed Gothic structure exploded by "Usher" is gone, replaced by the extravagant trajectory of the comet, wandering beyond the flaming walls of the world, becoming the object of a new kind of terror and awe. Gone, too, is the need for folkloric sources of supernaturalism to incite such sublimity; "Eiros and Charmion" is completely beyond the pale of Scott's Gothic.

The discharge of the Usher pile enabled Poe, in his later fictions, to move beyond the confines of earlier Gothics, prying wider a fissure into cosmic sublimity and horror that Mary Shelley had cracked with *Frankenstein*. At the same time, it delivered a convulsive shock to readers, one that continued to circulate in the intervening decades, exerting a major influence on the transatlantic resurgence of the Gothic throughout the later nineteenth century. This resurgence depended upon the energy made available by Poe's conversion of the ancestral piles he inherited into electrochemical generators.

Notes

1. Sarah Helen Whitman, introductory letter to *The Life and Poems of Edgar A. Poe*, by E. L. Didier (New York: W.J. Widdleton, 1877), 11–18, 16. For the play itself, see John D. Turnbull and M. G. Lewis, *The Wood Daemon, Or, The Clock Has Struck! a Grand, Romantic, Cabalistic Melo Drama in Three Acts . . . as Performed at the Boston Theatre with Unbounded Applause*, Early American Imprints, Second Series, no. 16352 (Boston: Printed by D. True, 1808). Notably performing alongside David Poe in this piece was his friend James Campbell Usher, whose life and children partially inspired Poe's "Fall of the House of Usher." See Mabbott's note, in M 2: 393.
2. Whitman, introductory letter, 17. For the theory Whitman refers to, see the renowned Victorian alienist's very idiosyncratic article on Poe, in which, as Whitman observes, the good doctor is "not always luminous and consistent" (16): Henry Maudsley, "Edgar Allan Poe," *Journal of Mental Science* 6, no. 2 (April 1860): 328–369. Both the Whitman introduction and the Maudsley essay can be accessed via the Edgar Allan Poe Society of Baltimore's singularly useful site at http://www.eapoe.org.
3. Whitman, introductory letter, 18.
4. Samuel Taylor Coleridge, review of The Monk, by Matthew G. Lewis, *The Critical Review* 2, no. 19 (February 1797): 194–200.
5. See, for example, "Life in Death," when the narrator describes being startled "into waking life as if with the shock of a galvanic battery" (M 2: 664); "The Pit and the Pendulum," whose narrator describes "every fibre in my frame thrill as if I had touched the wire of a galvanic battery" (M 2: 682); and the more literal usage in "Some Words with a Mummy," in which "an experiment or two with the voltaic pile" enables the eponymous speaker's lengthy discourse to occur (M 3: 1181).
6. Dionysius Lardner, *Course of Lectures, Delivered . . . on the Sun, Comets, the Fixed Stars, Electricity, Light and Sound, Steam Navigation, &c. & c.*, rev. ed. (New York: Greeley & McElrath, 1842), 12.
7. Edmund Burke, *Reflections on the Revolution in France* (London: Penguin, 1988), 161.
8. Scott claims that "the grotesque in [Hoffmann's] compositions partly resembles the arabesque in painting, in which is introduced the most strange and complicated monsters," a characterization that inspired Poe's adoption of these terms for his own tales. Walter Scott, "On the Supernatural in Fictitious Composition; and particularly on the works of Ernest Theodore William Hoffmann," *Foreign Quarterly Review* 1, no. 1 (1827): 81.
9. Michael Allen, *Poe and the British Magazine Tradition* (New York: Oxford, 1969), 16.
10. Michael Allen, *Poe and the British Magazine Tradition*, 138.

11. Betsy Erkila, "Perverting the American Renaissance," in *Poe and the Remapping of Antebellum Print Culture*, ed. J. Gerald Kennedy and Jerome J. McGann (Baton Rouge: Louisiana State University Press, 2012), 69. For a copious consideration of the many parallels between Poe and Hitchcock, see Dennis R. Perry, *Hitchcock and Poe: The Legacy of Delight and Terror* (Lanham, MD: Scarecrow Press, 2003).
12. Robert T. Tally, *Poe and the Subversion of American Literature: Satire, Fantasy, Critique* (New York: Bloomsbury, 2014), 143.
13. J. Gerald Kennedy, *Strange Nation: Literary Nationalism and Cultural Conflict in the Age of Poe* (New York: Oxford University Press, 2016), 35.
14. Kenneth Alan Hovey, "Poe's Materialist Metaphysics of Man," in *A Companion to Poe Studies*, ed. Eric W. Carlson (Westport, CT: Greenwood, 1996), 347–366.
15. The *locus classicus* of cosmic materialism, *DRN* was widely influential on many thinkers from the Renaissance, through the Enlightenment, and into Poe's antebellum American context. The most influential translation of Lucretius in the English-speaking world during the first half of the nineteenth century was that of British physician and writer John Mason Good (1764–1827), whose interpretations were influential for many British Romantic and American Renaissance writers, including Poe as well as Percy and Mary Shelley. For more on Poe's engagements with Lucretius via Good, see Sean Moreland, "Beyond 'De Rerum Naturâ, Esqr.': Lucretius, Poe, and John Mason Good," *The Edgar Allan Poe Review* 17, no. 1 (2016): 6–40. For Percy Shelley, see Michael A. Vicario, *Shelley's Intellectual System and Its Epicurean Background* (New York: Routledge, 2007), especially the fourth chapter "Shelley's Lucretius—The Translation of John Mason Good." For a brief consideration of Mary Shelley's use of Good's Lucretius in *Frankenstein*, see Jesse Weiner, "Lucretius, Lucan and Mary Shelley's *Frankenstein*," in *Classical Traditions in Science Fiction*, ed. Brett M. Rogers and Benjamin Eldon Stevens (New York: Oxford University Press, 2015), 46–74. Percy Shelley was among Poe's most important early poetic influences, and Poe's increasingly materialist views in the 1840s mark a critical departure from the neo-Platonic cast that Shelley's work was increasingly perceived to have following his death and Mary Shelley's tireless efforts to idealize his life and writings. In a rhetorical gesture similar to that whereby Coleridge dismissed the Gothic novel for its base materiality, Shelley, despite his admiration for Lucretius, argued in "A Defence of Poetry" (written in 1821, but published posthumously in 1840) that the Roman poet had "limed the wings of his swift spirit in the dregs of the sensible world." Shelley, "A Defence of Poetry," in *Essays, Letters, from Abroad, Translations and Fragments*, ed. Mrs. Shelley (London: Edward Moxon, 1840).
16. John Mason Good, *The Nature of Things: A Didactic Poem Translated from the Latin of Titus Lucretius Carus, Accompanied with the Original Text, and Illustrated with Notes Philological and Explanatory, in Two Volumes* (London: Longman, Hurst, Rees and Orme, 1805), 1:317, book 2, lines 883 and 897.
17. Burton R. Pollin, "Poe and Godwin," *Nineteenth-Century Fiction* 20, no. 3 (1965): 237–253, 248.
18. Pollin, "Poe and Godwin," 239.
19. Lardner, *Course of Lectures*, 11.
20. The association between Godwin's narrative structure and that of the voltaic pile also has a biographical resonance, as Godwin's close friend William Nicholson was a major influence on his early political philosophy, and was also the builder of England's first voltaic pile and among the first to describe electrolysis.

21. As Pamela Clemit explains, in *Caleb Williams* he creates an imaginatively sophisticated, economically plotted, and mythologically capacious narrative form which proved capable of "new and startling" combinations of meaning in the works of his fictional heirs. Clemit, *The Godwinian Novel: The Rational Fictions of Godwin, Brockden Brown, and Mary Shelley* (Oxford: Clarendon Press, 1993), 1.
22. Poe would also borrow a variety of other names, images, motifs, and plot devices directly from Brown. For more on this, see Boyd Carter, "Poe's Debt to Charles Brockden Brown," *Prairie Schooner* 27, no. 2 (1953): 190–196.
23. Edward Cahill, *Liberty of the Imagination: Aesthetic Theory, Literary Form and Politics in the Early United States* (Philadelphia: University of Pennsylvania Press, 2012), 174.
24. Brown, *Wieland, or, The Transformation: An American Tale and Other Stories*, ed. Caleb Crain (New York: Modern Library, 2002), 5.
25. Brown, *Edgar Huntly, or, Memoirs of a Sleep-Walker*, ed. Norman S. Grabo (New York: Penguin, 1988), 3.
26. For a detailed discussion of Scott's relationship to Brown's work, see Fiona Robertson, "Walter Scott and the American Historical Novel," in *The Oxford History of the Novel in English, vol. 5, The American Novel to 1870*, ed. J. Gerald Kennedy and Leland S. Person (New York: Oxford University Press, 2014).
27. Robert T. Tally, "Beyond the Flaming Walls of the World," in *The Planetary Turn: Relationality and Geoaesthetics in the Twenty-first Century*, ed. Amy J. Elias and Christian Moraru (Evanston, IL: Northwestern University Press, 2015), 193. Fiona Robertson develops Scott's importance for this national imaginary further, explaining that "Scott's importance for American writers derived in part from a shared inheritance in Scottish Enlightenment culture," but that "Americans also responded to specific aspects of his subject matter and artistry," as Scott created a national identity that functioned "imaginatively and emotionally, rather than politically." Fiona Robertson, "Walter Scott and the American Historical Novel," in *The Oxford History of the Novel in English, vol. 5, The American Novel to 1870*, 108. See also Ethan Kytle's account of Scott's even greater influence in the southern states, especially Poe's home state of Virginia, in which "the gentry combined long-standing local traditions with the visions of medieval Europe found in the works of such Romantics as Walter Scott," works on which "the idea of an independent southern nation" would be nourished. Ethan J. Kytle, *Romantic Reformers and the Antislavery Struggle in the Civil War* (Boston: Cambridge University Press, 2014), 13.
28. Scott, *The Letters of Sir Walter Scott*, ed. Sir Herbert Grierson, vol. 1, *1787–1807* (London: Constable, 1932–1937), 101, quoted in David Sandner, *Critical Discourses of the Fantastic, 1712–1831* (Burlington, VT: Ashgate, 2011), 108.
29. Sir Walter Scott, critical introduction to *The Castle of Otranto: A Gothic Story*, by Horace Walpole (Edinburgh: Ballantyne and Co., 1811), xxii.
30. Scott, introduction to *The Castle of Otranto*, xxvi.
31. Jerrold E. Hogle, "The Gothic-Romantic Nexus: Wordsworth, Coleridge, 'Splice' and 'The Ring,'" *The Wordsworth Circle* 43, no. 3 (2012): 159–165, 159.
32. Scott, introduction to *The Castle of Otranto*, xx.
33. Ann Radcliffe, "A Sicilian Romance," in *The Novels of Mrs. Ann Radcliffe Complete in One Volume* (London: Hurst, Robinson and Co., 1824), 45.
34. Eric Baker, "Lucretius in the European Enlightenment," in *The Cambridge Companion to Lucretius* (Cambridge: Cambridge University Press, 2007), 284.

35. In a 1796 letter Walpole attacks Richard Payne Knight's *The Progress of Civil Society: A Didactic Poem in Six Books* (1796) as an attempt to "re-establish the superannuated atheism of Lucretius." See Clark S. Northup, "A Critique by Horace Walpole," *The Modern Language Review* 6, no. 3 (1911): 387–389.
36. While John Mason Good claims to be the first translator of Lucretius to render *Religio* not as religion, but as Superstition, Radcliffe does so earlier, and this likely influenced Good's translation. Good conversed extensively with his friend Nathan Drake during the process of his translation and annotation of Lucretius. Drake was an admirer of Radcliffe's work, and in 1798 called her the "Shakespeare of Romance writers." See, for the example, Dale Townsend and Angela Wright, preface to *Ann Radcliffe, Romanticism and the Gothic*, ed. Dale Townsend and Angela Wright (New York: Cambridge University Press, 2014), xiii.
37. Ann Radcliffe, "A Sicilian Romance," 45. For comparison, see John Mason Good, *The Nature of Things*, 1:23–24, book 1, lines 65–70.
38. A similar image appears in various versions of Poe's "The City in the Sea," on which see Daniel Driskell, "Lucretius and The City in the Sea," *Poe Studies* 5, no. 2 (December 1972): 54–55.
39. Despite this, Radcliffe's knowledge of Lucretius appears to have been negligible. See Rictor Norton, *Mistress of Udolpho* (New York: Bloomsbury, 1999), 44–46.
40. Burke, *Reflections on the Revolution in France*, 268. For Burke's relationship to Epicurean thought, see Paddy Bullard, "Epicurean Aesthetics of the Philosophical Enquiry," in *Edmund Burke and the Art of Rhetoric* (Cambridge: Cambridge University Press, 2011).
41. Burke's views of Lucretius are shaped on the one hand by the Cambridge Platonists (for which see Bullard's "Epicurean Aesthetics of the Philosophical Enquiry") and the Restoration association of Epicurean materialism with libertinism emphasized by Thomas Creech's 1682 translation and commentaries. It could fairly be said that, reading Wakefield's restored Latin edition alongside Good's interpretations, which ambitiously attempt to harmonize Lucretius with both contemporary materialist science and Unitarian Christianity, Poe and the Shelleys were reading a completely different Lucretius than Burke had.
42. Burke, *Reflections on the Revolution in France*, 280.
43. Mary Wollstonecraft, *A Vindication of the Rights of Men*, ed. Sylvana Tomaselli (Cambridge: Cambridge University Press, 1995), 42.
44. Hogle, "The Gothic-Romantic Nexus," 160.
45. The members of "The Folio Club" in question are the "stout man" "who admired Sir Walter Scott" and "De Rerum Natura, Esq." See Moreland, "Beyond 'De Rerum Naturâ, Esqr.,'" 23–25.
46. Sir Walter Scott, "On the Supernatural in Fictitious Composition; and particularly on the works of Ernest Theodore William Hoffmann," *Foreign Quarterly Review* 1, no. 1 (1827): 81.
47. Scott, "On the Supernatural in Fictitious Composition; and particularly on the works of Ernest Theodore William Hoffmann," 62.
48. Burke, *Reflections on the Revolution in France*, 187, 269. In this respect, Burke's political theology is a more nuanced and agnostic restatement of arguments that Lucretius's Restoration-era translator, Thomas Creech, made in the "Notes Upon the Fifth Book" of his edition. Creech claims: "They who endeavor to disgrace Religion, usually represent it as a Trick of State, and as a politick Invention, to keep the credulous in Awe; which however absurd, and frivolous, yet is a strong argument against the Atheist, who cannot declare his Opinions, unless he be a Rebel, and a disturber of the Commonwealth: The Cause of God, and his Cæsar, are the same, and no Affront can be offered to one, but it reflects

on both; and that the Epicurean Principles are pernicious to Societies, is evident from the account they give of the rise of them." Creech, trans., *T. Lucretius Carus, Of the Nature of Things, vol. 2, Containing the Fifth and Sixth Books* (London: Printed by John Matthews, for George Sawbridge, 1714), 550n1083.

49. Scott, *Radcliffe*, xxiii.
50. Scott, *Radcliffe*, xxv.
51. Peter G. Beidler, "Literary Insertions in Radcliffe's 'The Mysteries of Udolpho' and Poe's 'The Fall of the House of Usher,'" *ANQ* 22, no. 4 (2009): 23–33.
52. Beidler, "Literary Insertions," 24.
53. Poe, "Magazine-Writing—Peter Snook," *Broadway Journal* 1, no. 23 (June 7, 1845): 354.
54. Mary Shelley, *Frankenstein*, ed. D. L. MacDonald and Kathleen Scherf (Peterborough, ON: Broadview, 2012), 350. For more on Poe's criticisms of Coleridge's theory of imagination, see Sean Moreland and Devin Zane Shaw, "'As Urged by Schelling': Coleridge, Poe and the Schellingian Refrain," *Edgar Allan Poe Review* 13, no. 2 (Fall 2012): 50–80.
55. Scott, introduction to *The Castle of Otranto*, xxx.
56. Mary Shelley, *Frankenstein*, 49. Shelley and Poe's versions of the Godwinian Gothic, in particular, anticipate the "supplemental theory" of weird fiction that Poe's self-described disciple H. P. Lovecraft articulates in the early twentieth century. For more on this, see Moreland, "Beyond the Flaming Walls of the World: Poe After Lovecraft," in *The Lovecraftian Poe*, ed. Sean Moreland (Lanham, MD: Lehigh University Press), 2017.
57. Scott, *review of Frankenstein, Blackwood's Edinburgh Magazine* 2 (March 1818), 613–620.
58. A criticism likely to have been recalled by Poe upon charges of "excessive Germanism" being leveled against his own tales in 1839.
59. *Review of Frankenstein, The Edinburgh Magazine and Literary Miscellany* 2 (March 1818): 252.
60. Review of *Frankenstein, The Edinburgh Magazine*, 252.
61. Review of *Frankenstein, The Edinburgh Magazine*, 252–253.
62. Shelley, *Frankenstein*, 83.
63. Shelley, *Frankenstein*, 83.
64. Poe was certainly familiar with this quote by 1842, for it is repeated in Lardner's *Course of Lectures*, 12. However, he is likely to have encountered it earlier, for it was cited widely by scientific literature throughout the 1830s.
65. Ultimately, this stylistic exaggeration militates against the depersonalized materialist philosophy underlying Lucretius's poem, making it easier for Good to harmonize it with both Romantic vitalist theories and, ultimately, the belief in a personal God. It also contributes to the abyssal disjunction between Lucretius's English reception in the early modern period, and that in the British Romantic and antebellum American periods. See Moreland, "Beyond 'De Rerum Naturâ, Esqr.,'" 28–31. For Mary Shelley's knowledge and use of Good's Lucretius, see Jesse Weiner, "Lucretius, Lucan and Mary Shelley's *Frankenstein*." Weiner points out that according to her journal, "it was not until 1820 that Shelley purported to have read Lucretius, beginning *De Rerum Natura* on June 28th of that year and completing the poem on August 29th. This is despite the fact that, in an entry dated April 18, 1815, Shelley noted that she had purchased an edition of John Mason Good's 1805 translation of the epic" (49). Weiner speculates, "Perhaps Shelley had in fact read her Good translation of Lucretius' favorite example back in 1815, but, like all classicists of good conscience, waited to add it to her list of completed books (also included in the journals) until she had read the entire poem in Latin" (50). However speculative, this conclusion seems warranted, given

the occasionally striking imagistic parallels between Good's translation and interpretive commentaries and the novel itself. Weiner writes, "Whatever details we are given about Victor Frankenstein's exploration of the 'deepest secrets of creation' are described through the language and imagery of Lucretian physics. Shelley conspicuously personifies natura, and the frequent repetition of 'material' throughout the episode invokes the fleshly materialism of Epicurean philosophy, which had recently experienced a revival of sorts in Romantic Britain. The monster's amalgamation of limbs evokes the atomistic recombination of Lucretian anatomy and monstrosity, and numerous verbal echoes over the novel's course confirm Lucretius as a source for Shelley" (54–55). Focusing primarily on Lucretius's Latin rather than Good's translation, Weiner notes only a handful of *Frankenstein*'s verbal echoes of Good. For example, Weiner notes that "Dr. Frankenstein's project of bringing forth a living creature from dead and decaying material appears to draw its inspiration from Lucretius favourite example of spontaneous generation. At five points in *De Rerum Natura*, Lucretius explains spontaneous generation via the rise of worms from putrid matter and rancid corpses—the bodies are described as *putrifactum*, *putor*, and *rancens* (DRN 2.871–873, 898–901, 928–929; 3.719–736; 5.797–798). Moreover, he posits that this is due to the rearrangement of matter" (55).

66. Scott, "On the Supernatural in Fictitious Composition," 93.
67. Tally, "Beyond the Flaming Walls of the World," 193.

Bibliography

Gold, Barri J. *ThermoPoetics: Energy in Victorian Literature and Science*. Cambridge, MA: MIT Press, 2010.

Hayes, Kevin J., ed. *Edgar Allan Poe in Context*. Cambridge: Cambridge University Press, 2013.

Kennedy, J. Gerald. *Strange Nation: Literary Nationalism and Cultural Conflict in the Age of Poe*. New York: Oxford University Press, 2016.

Kennedy, J. Gerald, and Jerome J. McGann, eds. *Poe and the Remapping of Antebellum Print Culture*. Baton Rouge: Louisiana State University Press, 2012.

Kragh, Helge. *Entropic Creation: Religious Contexts of Thermodynamics and Cosmology*. Burlington, VT: Ashgate, 2008.

Tally, Robert T. *Poe and the Subversion of American Literature: Satire, Fantasy, Critique*. New York: Bloomsbury, 2014.

CHAPTER 31

KINDRED CONTEMPORARIES

Lippard, Bird, Simms, Hawthorne, and Irving

CARL OSTROWSKI

> And what *is* Poetic Influence anyway? Can the study of it really be anything more than the wearisome industry of source-hunting, of allusion-counting, an industry that will soon touch apocalypse anyway when it passes from scholars to computers?
>
> —Harold Bloom[1]

THE study of literary influence is decidedly unfashionable. In a 2008 issue of *Modern Language Quarterly* dedicated to the question of influence, editor Andrew Elfenbein writes that scholars primarily associate the subject with Harold Bloom's *The Anxiety of Influence*, which they regard as "old-fashioned and embarrassing," and yet no convincing model has arisen to challenge or replace it, so that influence study "remains a serious gap in the contemporary construction of literary scholarship."[2] The term "old-fashioned" might also be applied to some of the writers whose relationships with Edgar Allan Poe I propose to trace in this essay: George Lippard, Robert Montgomery Bird, William Gilmore Simms, Nathaniel Hawthorne, and Washington Irving, dead white males all. So an essay applying questions of influence to Poe's relationship with these five writers seems to promise little more than a tedious exercise in dry-as-dust antiquarianism.

In defending the topic's importance, however, one might point out that Poe was himself a wearisome source hunter, obsessed, at times, with the question of what one writer owed to another. When Elfenbein describes how recent discoveries in cognitive psychology illuminate the process by which one writer recalls and alludes to the work of a precursor, the model sounds a lot like Poe's analysis of how great poets internalize what they read so completely that they become unaware of their own borrowings.[3] In addition, then, to illuminating Poe's own oeuvre by following up on one of his trademark preoccupations, an assessment of reciprocal lines of influence between Poe and the writers listed earlier offers a rich field for sampling many of the ways that one writer can influence another. The resulting spectrum ranges from cases of negative influence through suggestive parallel, appropriation, and parody, all the way to plagiarism. Treating these writers in ascending order of the significance of their influence on Poe clarifies the value—and also the limits—of influence study as currently conceived.

George Lippard

Poe must have had a soft spot for George Lippard. Of the writers treated here, Lippard is the only one whom Poe never tomahawked in a review (Bird, Simms), plagiarized (Irving, maybe Simms), accused of plagiarism (Hawthorne), walked back earlier praise of (Hawthorne), or maligned behind his back before successfully petitioning for a favor (Irving). Thirteen years Poe's junior, and just getting his career started in the early 1840s when Poe had already achieved success as a critic, editor, fiction writer, and poet, Lippard could not have struck Poe as a professional rival, which probably explains the kid glove treatment. On his part, Lippard deeply admired Poe and proved a faithful friend. The two met in the early 1840s, when both were immersed in Philadelphia's vibrant and contentious periodical culture. Lippard "puffed" Poe's writings and lectures in a newspaper called *Citizen Soldier*, and, even while disavowing prize contests as humbugs, defended Poe's prizewinning tale "The Gold-Bug" as worth its prize money, "ten times told."[4] One day in July of 1849, a destitute Poe—meagerly clad and supposedly wearing a single shoe—arrived at the office of Lippard's *Quaker City* newspaper and, in desperation, requested assistance, telling Lippard (in the latter's melodramatic, after-the-fact reconstruction of events): "You are my last hope. If you fail me, I can do nothing but die." Venturing into a cityscape deserted by residents fleeing a cholera epidemic, Lippard petitioned some of Philadelphia's remaining writers and publishers for handouts, collecting enough money to send Poe to Baltimore the next day.[5] It was the last time the two men would meet; Poe died three months later. If Rufus Griswold is the mustache-twirling villain of Poe biography, peddling an image of an unhinged maniac wandering through storm-swept streets muttering curses (and forging letters to discredit Poe posthumously), Lippard stands at the other end of the spectrum, retailing in a brief, hagiographic obituary the also influential portrait of Poe as a cruelly underappreciated Romantic visionary, "hunted by the world, trampled upon by the men whom he had loaded with favors, and disappointed on every turn of life."[6] Subsequent biographers have been tasked with threading their way through these twin distortions.

Lippard came to wide public attention with the publication of *The Quaker City; or, The Monks of Monk Hall* (1845), which sold more copies than any novel previously published in the United States. City-mysteries novels, of which *The Quaker City* is the best-known American example, combined earnest social commentary with quasi-pornographic titillation. Lippard's readers learned that Philadelphia's corrupt social elite (bankers, merchants, politicians) plotted villainies in a brothel and den of crime known as Monk Hall. Lippard piously denounced—while depicting in lascivious detail—his characters' (often sexual) crimes, an enduring formula that ensured both notoriety and popular success. Besides city-mysteries fiction, Lippard published romances glorifying heroes of the American Revolution and championing American expansion into the Southwest; he founded a radical newspaper and a labor union and, like Poe, died prematurely (in Lippard's case, at age thirty-one, of tuberculosis).

No one claims that Poe was significantly influenced by his young acolyte. In a letter to Lippard, Poe allowed that his romance *The Ladye Annabel* was "indicative of *genius* in its author." At the same time, Poe tactfully (and accurately) suggested that Lippard, a prolific writer credited with having composed dozens of novels in his short career, had been "in too desperate a hurry to give due attention to details" (CL 1: 423). More broadly, Poe registered his opinion of what he labeled "convulsive" fiction in *Graham's*. Calling Eugene Sue's *The Mysteries of Paris* (Lippard's avowed inspiration for *The Quaker City*) "a paradox of childish folly and consummate skill," Poe conceded the novel's entertainment value but also called its social reform message a calculated tactic by which writers such as Sue increased their commercial appeal and "gild[ed] the pill of their licentiousness" (H 16: 104–105). As David Reynolds suggests, Poe—meticulous craftsman, champion of art for art's sake, and cultural conservative—would have found little to emulate in Lippard's hastily composed, politically radical, sexually explicit writings.[7]

That Lippard was influenced by Poe is more plausible. Both writers explored, it is conventional (and accurate) to note, similar Gothic terrain, including shocking scenes of violence and irrational aspects of human psychology. In *The Quaker City*, Lippard's physically grotesque antihero Devil-Bug, the deranged doorman of Monk Hall, devises a three-pronged plan to torture protagonist Byrnewood Arlington by way of smoke inhalation, poisoning, and a three-story fall into the corpse-strewn pit beneath the mansion. The scene of torture derives its effectiveness from a claustrophobic circumscription of space and from the suspense readers experience as Arlington suffers, elements strongly reminiscent of Poe's 1842 "The Pit and the Pendulum." Devil-Bug subsequently tries to bury Arlington alive, a motif Poe had previously explored in "The Premature Burial" and would return to in "The Cask of Amontillado." But parallels by themselves do not prove influence, and Lippard is known to have availed himself of closer models in the urban Gothic mode. Arguably the most important affinity between the two writers (whose friendship otherwise seems difficult to account for) is a taste for satire, particularly directed toward the industry in which both labored. Before becoming a novelist, Lippard published a handful of sketches of the Philadelphia publishing scene titled "The Walnut Coffin Papers," ridiculing figures such as George Graham and Poe adversary Griswold under absurd monikers ("the Grey Ham" and "Rumpus Grizzle") and charging them with being part of a cabal designed to promote each other's interests. In one such satire, the fictional avatar of author Charles Peterson cries out in despair that Poe "*knows* I steal my stories."[8] Reynolds speculates that Poe may have supplied Lippard with information about Graham's publishing activities, which, if true, would put Lippard on a very short list of writers with whom Poe deigned to collaborate.[9] It is worth recalling that Poe intended to launch his own career as a fiction writer with a series of stories (*Tales of the Folio Club*) whose pseudonymous tellers were lampoons of actual writers (such as magazinist Nathaniel Parker Willis), and throughout his career he occasionally returned to satires of the business, including "How to Write a Blackwood Article" and "The Literary Life of Thingum Bob, Esq." Poe bonded with Lippard as a fellow exposer of literary fraud willing to make war on high-placed members of the profession for the sake of critical principle.[10] A friendship grounded on Lippard's side in sincere admiration may have been for Poe based on shared animosity toward common enemies.

Robert Montgomery Bird

Writing for the *Southern Literary Messenger*, Poe reviewed the extraordinary 1836 novel *Sheppard Lee* by Robert Montgomery Bird. Trained as a physician, the Philadelphia writer originally came to prominence authoring plays for one of the period's most famous actors, fellow Philadelphian Edwin Forrest. *Sheppard Lee*, Bird's fourth novel, concerns a New Jersey farmer able to migrate his consciousness into another individual's dead body, and who, as the novel's events unfold episodically, inhabits six other bodies (including a prosperous brewer, a Quaker philanthropist, and, most provocatively, a slave) before returning to his own. Poe editor Thomas Ollive Mabbott identified *Sheppard Lee* as a source for Poe's story of buried treasure, "The Gold-Bug" (M 3: 800). Lee's slave Jim Jumble informs him that Captain Kidd is said to have buried money in a nearby swamp, and it is while digging for this treasure that Lee experiences his first transmigration. Not incidentally, Jumble is, like Poe's Jupiter in "The Gold-Bug," a manumitted slave who insists upon staying with his former master. Poe drew attention to both of these plot features in his lengthy review.[11]

Poe appreciated Bird's imaginative flights with the notion of reincarnation, or (as it was termed at the time) metempsychosis, a subject that Poe had already explored in "Metzengerstein" (1832) and "Morella" (1835)—and would revisit in 1838 with "Ligeia." In his review, Poe took exception, however, to Bird's decision to end the novel by having the protagonist awaken to discover that his adventures had all been a dream. Bird would have achieved greater effect, in Poe's view, by writing the entire work "as if the author were firmly impressed with the truth, yet astonished at the immensity, of the wonders he relates, and for which, professedly, he neither claims nor anticipates credence."[12] As Justin R. Wert notes, reviewing Bird afforded Poe the opportunity to examine and articulate the theory underlying his own fictional practice.[13] Using Göran Hermerén's terminology, Bird was a "negative influence" on Poe.[14] In his subsequent experiment with the novel form, *The Narrative of Arthur Gordon Pym*, Poe reacted against Bird's example, allowing the "incredibilities" (among others, a giant human-like figure occupying the mysteriously white landscape of the South Pole) to stand unexplained.

With one notable exception, critics have not yet observed the possibility of reciprocal influence between Bird and Poe in their comic treatments of madness.[15] One of Sheppard

Lee's incarnations is within the body of Arthur Megrim, a neurasthenic Virginia plantation owner. Megrim wakes up one morning convinced he is a coffee pot and reports later incidents in which he imagines himself "a chicken," "a loaded cannon," "a clock," "a hamper of crockery-ware, and a thousand things besides."[16] Rather than attempt to contradict his patient's delusions, Megrim's resourceful physician Dr. Tibbikens indulges them to an absurd degree, for example, by proposing to boil the coffee pot over the fire—at which point Megrim abruptly relinquishes the fancy. Poe employs the same conceit in his 1845 satirical tale "The System of Doctor Tarr and Professor Fether." There, asylum patients suffer delusions of being a teapot and a chicken (among other things), and the "keeper" (who turns out to the leader of a band of insurrectionary patients, whose actual keepers are imprisoned) describes giving chicken feed to the ersatz fowl, thereby achieving a miraculous cure at the mere expense of "a little corn and gravel" (M 3: 1006).

Bird's exploration of madness deepened with "My Friends in the Madhouse," which appeared in his story collection *Peter Pilgrim*, published in 1838. The narrator of this story accompanies a physician to an asylum, where he becomes confirmed in his impression that "madmen are by no means so mad as the world usually supposed them." The narrator meets a confederacy of wise men who had the misfortune of practicing virtues such as honesty and patriotism with such fidelity that they gave their enemies pretext to have them committed. One inmate whistles "Yankee Doodle with great vigour and execution," and the story ends with a brawl among patients.[17] Similarly, "The System of Doctor Tarr and Professor Fether" ends with a melee while an orchestra plays "Yankee Doodle" with "energy superhuman" (M 3: 1020). Beyond any verbal echoes, both stories explore the idea that the ascription of madness is a matter of context and social convention. The narrator of "My Friends in the Madhouse" finds the asylum occupied by men who are saner than the rest of society—and therefore judged mad. Poe, too, in one of his "Marginalia," voiced the sentiment that "any individual gifted, or rather accursed, with an intellect *very* far superior to that of his race . . . would make himself enemies at all points" and would be considered "a madman" (H 16: 165).

Unfortunately, no documentary evidence exists to establish that Poe read *Peter Pilgrim* (biographer Kenneth Silverman places Poe in Philadelphia, where the book was issued by publishers Lea & Blanchard, by the spring of 1838).[18] But it seems likely he would have: Poe had already reviewed two of Bird's previous books, and he professed familiarity with Bird's entire body of work in an "Autography" entry of 1841 (H 15: 203–204). Whether or not "My Friends in the Madhouse" directly influenced Poe's "Tarr and Fether," Bird undoubtedly had Poe in mind when composing the story. One of the asylum's inmates is a magazinist named "Mr. Slasher," who enjoys a reputation for critical severity: "I had a notion, my readers would be delighted with the honesty that served them up an author, handsomely roasted and well done, every week: for I have long observed that the world has as natural a hankering after author-baitings as after the baitings of bulls and bears."[19] When this fictional critic honestly reviews a friend's novel as inferior without other cause, he is locked away. Poe, who had slashingly reviewed Bird's novel *The Hawks of Hawk Hollow* in the *Messenger* in 1835, calling the book "a bad imitation of Sir Walter Scott," must be the model for Bird's Mr. Slasher (H 8: 73).

Evidently Poe continued to occupy Bird's thoughts for years, as the protagonist of Bird's posthumously published *A Belated Revenge* is a backwoods Virginia man who—guided in dreams by the ghost of his dead beloved, Fanny—kills the half-Indian villain responsible for the death of his family. Bird named his vengeful Virginian Ipsico Poe.[20]

William Gilmore Simms

The distinction of having written what Poe considered "the best ghost story ever written *by an American*" belongs to South Carolina man of letters William Gilmore Simms.[21] Known today as the author of historical romances chronicling the experiences of South Carolinians during the American Revolution, the prolific Simms penned twenty-four novels, over a hundred short stories, and thousands of poems, among other works.[22] Several affinities link the two writers: both dramatized the so-called Kentucky Tragedy, in which a woman charged her lover with killing the man who seduced her in her youth (Poe in his verse drama "Politian" and Simms in the novel *Beauchamp*); both edited periodicals committed to the literary achievement of the American South; and both considered Longfellow overrated. But the relationship between Poe and the comparatively neglected Simms exceeds affinity, passing easily into the territory of confirmed influence—and in one instance verging on plagiarism.

Tom Fafianie showed in 2011 that a short valentine poem long attributed to Poe, "To Miss Louise Olivia Hunter," is derived almost entirely from Simms's previously published "There Are Dreams of Bowers."[23] Not that Poe committed plagiarism in the conventional sense. The commissioning and presentation of valentine poems became a short-lived fad in the literary salons of 1840s New York, according to Fafianie, who speculates that Poe was commissioned to author a valentine for Hunter, an aspiring young writer and friend of (onetime Poe flirtation) Frances Osgood, in February 1847. Originality was not necessarily presumed for such occasional poems, and Poe never claimed authorship of the poem, which was presented anonymously. Erroneous attribution to Poe was made long after the fact, when the unsigned manuscript resurfaced in the twentieth century and the handwriting was identified as his. In what spirit Poe cribbed the lines cannot be determined with certainty, but he consistently expressed admiration for Simms as a poet and published poems by Simms during his editorship of the *Broadway Journal*.

Poe was also probably influenced by Simms's fiction. In 1829 Simms published a sketch called "A Picture of the Sea" that was likely a source for Poe's "MS. Found in a Bottle," published four years later. Simms biographer John Caldwell Guilds catalogs the stories' striking similarities, which include Flying Dutchman–type ships manned by immortals crashing into the vessel on which an imperiled narrator sails.[24] Although Poe's exposure to the story cannot be established with certainty, it was published in a Charleston periodical called the *Southern Literary Gazette* around the time of Poe's departure from Sullivan's Island, South Carolina, where he had been stationed with the US

Army. Poe had certainly read Simms's novella *Martin Faber* (1833), which he thought showed "genius . . . of no common order."[25] In this disturbing book, the character Faber, just before ascending the gallows, unapologetically recounts his tale of having seduced and murdered a young woman. The idea of having a criminal character narrate his villainies with brio cannot be attributed exclusively to Simms (British Newgate novelists of the 1830s, such as Edward Bulwer, were exploring similar territory), but the more specific notion that a criminal might experience an irresistible desire to confess—what Poe would later label the "perverse" and dramatize in "The Imp of the Perverse," among other stories—makes a striking appearance in Simms's novel. As he walks in the woods with a friend, Faber's thoughts turn to the scene where he killed his victim, and he impulsively confesses the crime, feeling "impelled through the whole scene by an irresistible monitor . . . in spite of my own consciousness of the danger of such a topic."[26]

The aforementioned ghost story, "Grayling; or, Murder Will Out," suggests that the influence ran in both directions. The story probably impressed Poe because it borrowed so craftily from his own fictional practice. In a desolated South Carolina landscape in the chaotic days following the Revolutionary War, a youthful narrator named James Grayling tells how the ghost of his former military commander appeared to him and charged him with apprehending his murderer and bringing him to justice (which he does). At the end of the story, however, readers cannot be sure whether they have read a ghost story or not: Simms provides both rational and supernatural explanations for the story's events, without arbitrating between them—a technique that Poe modeled in "Ligeia." In providing the rational explanation for the story's events, the narrator's father embarks on a pages-long analysis (or ratiocination), Dupin-style, of the chain of clues that led Grayling to correctly guess his commander's fate—claiming that the ghost itself was simply a figment of the teenager's hyperactive imagination.[27]

Parsing Poe's evolving assessment of Simms requires distinguishing among sincerely held critical principles, symptoms of professional jealousy, and opportunism. In his earliest published review of a Simms novel, *The Partisan* (1836), Poe condemned Simms for lazy plotting, boring characterization, excessive sentimentality, and (in typical Poe fashion, with numerous examples supplied) ungrammatical language (H 8: 143–158). Poe's supercilious tone may well have derived from envy of a more eminent Southern author. Reviewing *The Damsel of Darien* (1839), Poe argued that a novelist does not deserve credit for being interesting when the story, as drawn from the historical record, possesses inherent interest—a critical principle voiced in multiple reviews and consistent with Poe's generally low opinion of historical fiction (H 10: 51). Poe's critical opinion of Simms peaked in the mid-1840s, perhaps not coincidentally after Poe moved to New York and both writers had become loosely associated with Evert Duyckinck's Young America movement (a group of writers and editors dedicated to forwarding the cause of American literature, in part by lobbying for international copyright). Poe wrote during these years, "not one [American writer] surpasses [Simms] in the aggregate of the higher excellences of fiction." Sectional affiliation likewise played a role in Poe's upward-trending judgment of Simms, as he asserted that the South Carolinian's genius would have been sooner recognized had he emerged from New England instead of the South.[28]

Bizarre hypocrisies punctuate Poe's reviews of Simms. In his review of *The Partisan*, Poe sanctimoniously blames Simms for putting oaths (specifically, the word *damn*, rendered "d—n") in the mouth of his Falstaffian character Porgy, insisting that such "attempts to render profanity less despicable by rendering it amusing, should be frowned down indignantly by the public" (H 8: 152). The charge seems difficult to reconcile with Poe's later decision to name a character "Toby Dammit" in a comic story, "Never Bet the Devil Your Head," that satirizes moralistic criticism of fiction. Poe also, repeatedly, charged Simms with bad taste, initially blaming him for depicting a murder perpetrated "in a manner too shockingly horrible to mention," and later faulting Simms with a "proneness to revolting images" (H 8: 157 and H 16: 41). These charges are roughly contemporary with such notorious violations of good taste as Poe's account of forcible dental extractions on a still-living but entombed body in "Berenice" and his masterfully repellent depiction of a corpse's sudden deliquescence in "The Facts in the Case of M. Valdemar." For his part, Simms knew better than to take Poe's criticisms to heart, noting in a letter to Duyckinck that even though Poe's stinging review of *The Partisan* had been unjust, he still regarded him "a man of remarkable power" from whom the public had unaccountably withheld due esteem.[29] In the one extant letter between the two men, Simms administered a pep talk to the despondent Poe, advising him to "subdue your impulses," "trample . . . temptations underfoot," avoid personal scandal, and put aside the critical tomahawk, because serial abuses of fellow authors left editors wary about publishing him. Simms diplomatically turned down Poe's request for money.[30]

Nathaniel Hawthorne

Among American authors, Nathaniel Hawthorne commanded Poe's highest respect, a regard based in something more than mutual mockery of Griswold.[31] Hawthorne sometimes worked in a Gothic mode that strongly appealed to Poe's sensibilities; Poe also identified with Hawthorne as a genius whose work had been insufficiently appreciated by an undiscriminating reading public. Favorably reviewing Hawthorne's two major story collections, *Twice-Told Tales* and *Mosses from an Old Manse*, Poe praised Hawthorne quite fulsomely for a critic with a reputation for severity. Though Poe was not alive to see Hawthorne's transition into novel writing, it is fair to assume that he would not have been impressed, given his critical bias in favor of short works. In fact, Hawthorne's most important influence on Poe was in providing the occasion for him to formulate a set of critical principles defending the artistic superiority of the short story.

In his May 1842 review of *Twice-Told Tales*, Poe argued that of all literary genres excepting poetry, the short story "affords unquestionably the fairest field for the exercise of the loftiest talent." Poe's appreciation for the short story comes across as a precursor of reader response theory, insofar as he located the truest measure of a work's artistry in the intensity of its effect on readers. Because any interruption in a reader's experience of a work breaks its spell and therefore spoils its effect, Poe believed that the "short prose narrative, requiring from a half-hour to one or two hours in its perusal," offered the best opportunity for an author to "fulfill the demands of high genius." But achieving such an effect required uncommon discipline: "In the whole composition there should be no word written, of which the tendency, direct or indirect, is not to the one pre-established design." In praising Hawthorne's tales for modeling just such discipline and economy, Poe further credited Hawthorne with originality ("a trait which, in the literature of fiction, is positively worth all the rest"). Poe also, erroneously, charged Hawthorne with plagiarism in this review, finding a supposed echo of "William Wilson" in Hawthorne's "Howe's Masquerade," not realizing that the original periodical publication date of Hawthorne's story made this impossible (H 11: 104–113).

As is often the case in Poe's critical writings, his assessment of Hawthorne, though sincere, also served a personal agenda. According to G. R. Thompson, Poe drew a distinction between the sketch and the "tale proper" as part of his battle with the staid New England literary establishment. Poe's defense of the tale proper—"dramatized, presentational fiction"—legitimized precisely the type of tale that he loved as a reader and excelled in creating.[32] In contrast, Poe downplayed the merit of what he called sketches, in which an authorial presence hovers over a set of intertwined narratives, generic territory located somewhere between the tale and the essay. In Thompson's judgment, this was a distinction that Hawthorne would not have accepted; his intrusive and self-conscious narrator was a critical part of the effect he wanted to achieve, taking as his model, in part, Washington Irving's *Sketch Book*.

In a later, still positive 1847 review of Hawthorne, Poe reversed himself on the question of Hawthorne's originality ("But the fact is, [Hawthorne] is *not* original in any sense") and strongly faulted him for indulging in allegory, in defense of which, he wrote, "there is scarcely one respectable word to be said" (H 13: 144 and H 13: 148). In Meghan A. Freeman's view, the less generous critical judgment found in the later review (which ends with the memorable advice that Hawthorne "mend his pen, get a bottle of visible ink, come out from the Old Manse, cut Mr. Alcott, hang [if possible] the editor of 'The Dial,' and throw out of the window to the pigs all his odd numbers of 'The North American Review' ") stems from Poe's disappointment that Hawthorne had not heeded his counsel in the earlier review and, instead, continued to publish genial sketches suffused with an unpalatable mysticism (H 13: 155).[33] For his part, Hawthorne took Poe's criticisms in stride, writing (in the one extant letter between them) that while he appreciated the earnestness of his critical judgments, he chiefly admired Poe as a writer of tales.[34]

Comparisons between Poe and Hawthorne began during both writers' lifetimes.[35] The subsequent critical literature on Hawthorne and Poe is replete with discoveries of suggestive parallels between the two writers' works, with accompanying claims of influence. Hawthorne's "The Prophetic Pictures," for example, may (or may not) have directly inspired Poe's "The Oval Portrait."[36] Various Hawthorne tales are said to have inspired "The Masque of the Red Death," which may in turn have had an influence on Hawthorne's "The Wedding Knell."[37] Hawthorne's treatment of Arthur Dimmesdale, who impulsively confesses his crime in the midst of his greatest triumph as a minister in *The Scarlet Letter*, is not unlike the imp of the perverse that motivates criminal confessions in certain Poe stories.[38] With respect to such claims, however, one might point out that the most demanding task imposed on the would-be discoverer of influence lies in drawing rigorous distinctions between cases where one author influenced another, cases where the two authors may have been independently responding to some third and previous source, and cases where both authors simply responded to the zeitgeist. Some of the intuition-heavy secondary literature on the Poe–Hawthorne relationship may not bear close scrutiny of this nature. For example, the notion of a criminal driven by an uncontrollable impulse to confess had been raised before either Poe or Hawthorne ventured it, as discussed earlier, in Simms's *Martin Faber*. Moreover, the era's media-savvy prison reform movement put such an emphasis on the workings of the criminal's conscience that it became a cultural commonplace that guilt gnawed away at criminals' psyches.[39]

Critical wariness is called for in light of the long-standing canonical status of Poe and Hawthorne, which, with attendant reading practices, encourages false positives when it comes to influence claims. Abstracting the two writers' works from the complex and crowded field of texts in which they were originally embedded (a distinctly international milieu characterized by a chaotic proliferation of print formats, including newspapers, magazines, pamphlets, authorized volumes, and pirated books, all subject to unpredictable and unauthorized reprinting and circulation) allows readers to project a simple dialogue onto what was at the time of publication a far more cacophonous set of voices in which direct influence was less probable than it seems in retrospect. If it would be going too far to describe some of the examples of influence that critics claim to have discovered between the two writers as mere coincidences (in the words of Poe's detective, Dupin, "great stumbling-blocks in the way of that class of thinkers who have been educated to know nothing of the theory of probabilities"), the suggestive parallels so common in the critical literature read to me like a case of too many Dupins and not enough orangutans (M 2: 556). Other promising avenues for exploring the Poe–Hawthorne relationship (including their politics, their mutual imbrication in periodical culture, and issues of race and gender in their work) were raised in a 2004 issue of *Poe Studies* devoted to the subject.[40]

Washington Irving

Longfellow aside, the writer among his contemporaries who elicited Poe's most discreditable displays of professional resentment—and, not coincidentally, the one whose direct influence over Poe's fiction is most measurable—was Washington Irving. Born in Manhattan, Irving published his first book, the satirical *A History of New York*, in 1809, the year of Poe's birth. He achieved lasting fame with publication of *The Sketch Book of Geoffrey Crayon, Gent.* (1820), a series of sketches of English landscapes and customs that also included two tales set in rural New York which, over time, transcended their literary origins to become American folklore, "Rip Van Winkle" and "The Legend of Sleepy Hollow." Along with James Fenimore Cooper, Irving brought the attention of an international audience to American literature, for which he was duly celebrated. Renowned for an elegant prose style, Irving published histories, biographies, and travel narratives, and by the time of his death in 1859 was among the most beloved and successful of American writers—to neither of which epithets was Poe ever in his life a claimant.

The date on which Poe's resentment toward Irving probably crystallized can be pinpointed with unusual precision. On March 30, 1837, Poe—a very recent transplant to New York from Richmond—attended a Booksellers' Dinner sponsored by New York publishers to celebrate American letters. Three hundred members of the trade (authors, editors, publishers, booksellers) from urban centers along the eastern seaboard attended the lavish event. Entering the City Hotel's hall, Poe saw niches decorated with busts of such luminaries as William Shakespeare, John Milton, Benjamin Franklin—and Washington Irving, the only living writer so honored.[41] Irving's flesh-and-blood attendance at the dinner was reported in many newspaper and magazine accounts; Poe's own presence (along with his toast, to "The Monthlies of Gotham—Their distinguished Editors, and their vigorous Collaborateurs") attracted far less attention (PL: 243). At the time of the dinner, the status-conscious Poe could have experienced nothing but vexation by contrasting his career with Irving's. Whereas Irving had achieved fame primarily for volumes consisting of discrete tales and sketches, Poe had set aside plans to publish a book of tales, in part responding to a publisher's advice that readers preferred works "in which a single and connected story occupies the whole volume."[42] In response, Poe wrote a novel-length adventure story set in the Antarctic region, *The Narrative of Arthur Gordon Pym*, which awaited publication at the time of the dinner—but whose publication was soon derailed for a full year by the catastrophic economic downturn known as the Panic of 1837. Meanwhile, Irving enjoyed wide acclaim for his own recently published adventure narrative set in far-flung locales, *Astoria* (1836).

Poe had reviewed *Astoria* at length (and favorably) in the *Southern Literary Messenger*. Summarizing the story of John Jacob Astor's attempt to establish a fur trading outpost on the Pacific Ocean in the 1810s, and conceding Irving's gifts as prose stylist, Poe wrote: "The work has been accomplished in a masterly manner—the modesty of the title affording no indication of the fulness, comprehensiveness, and beauty with which a long and entangled series of detail, collected necessarily, from a mass of vague and imperfect data, has been wrought into completeness and purity" (H 9: 207–208). The sincerity of Poe's admiration for *Astoria* can be gauged, perhaps, by the shamelessness with which he later plagiarized it. Poe's serialized hoax/travel adventure "The Journal of Julius Rodman" (1840), which purports to deliver the edited diary of the *first* white adventurer to traverse the same Western territory that Astor's crew would later explore, includes numerous passages lifted almost word-for-word from Irving's earlier book.[43]

Poe's indebtedness to Irving took forms short of outright plagiarism. In 1836, Irving published a sketch entitled "An Unwritten Drama of Lord Byron," proposing that some "poet or dramatist of the Byron school" take up the story of a man whose villainous schemes are disrupted by a mysterious foil, who turns out to be an embodiment of his conscience.[44] In 1839, Poe took up Irving's suggestion and turned the brief sketch into the full-length tale "William Wilson." Earlier in the same year, however, Poe had subjected Irving to tacit mockery in the tale "The Devil in the Belfry," which parodies certain well-known elements of Irving's oeuvre. In the story, the Devil comes to a placid Dutch village and unsettles its clockwork regularity by striking the church bell thirteen times. In his own tales of quiet Dutch villages, Irving's characteristic attitude was nostalgia, as he lamented that the peaceful timelessness of such villages was under threat from modernity. Poe's story satirically figures such timelessness as a deadening stasis, in need of shaking up by the mischievous/devilish Poe.[45] Poe's popular hit "The Gold-Bug" borrows a number of elements from a suite of stories in Irving's 1824 *Tales of a Traveler*. "The Money Diggers" includes a Manhattan Dutch cabbage farmer who enlists the family physician and a "negro fisherman" to help him unearth a treasure said to have been buried by Captain Kidd; Poe scholars have noted how this trio anticipates Legrand, the narrator, and Jupiter in "The Gold-Bug" (M 3: 800).[46] Irving sometimes took an approach to Gothic materials in which events are simultaneously susceptible to rational and supernatural explanation, a technique that held special appeal for Poe.[47] Some critics, perhaps less convincingly, have found hints of Irving's influence in "Ligeia" and "The Raven."[48]

Poe teetered between admiration and abuse of Irving. In 1839, Poe fawningly informed Irving of the "right of ownership" he held in "William Wilson" (no such avowal would be made of the plagiarized passages in "The Journal of Julius Rodman") and sent him a copy of the story, asking the better-known writer for a blurb to help publicize his forthcoming volume of *Tales* (CL 1: 199–200). Irving obligingly supplied it. Yet in an unguarded 1838 letter to a friend, Poe declined to review a book by Irving on the grounds that he intended in time to write a full-length exposé that would "strike home, take my word for it," noting that "Irving is much overrated, and a nice distinction might be drawn between his just and his surreptitious and adventitious reputation. . . . The merit, too, of his tame propriety and faultlessness of style should be candidly weighed" (CL 1: 177–178). Although Poe never got around to penning the takedown he had in mind, he jabbed at Irving in his disingenuous "Autography" series. Inventing a correspondent who supposedly collected the signatures of famous writers, Poe subjected the autographs (reproduced in engravings) to a form of handwriting analysis that often served as the flimsiest of pretexts for critical condescension. Of Irving's handwriting, Poe wrote, "The MS. of Mr. IRVING has little about it indicative of his genius. . . . Mr. Irving has travelled much, has seen many vicissitudes, and has been so thoroughly satiated with fame as to grow slovenly in the performance of his literary tasks" (H 15: 182). Yet in his 1842 review of Hawthorne's *Twice-Told Tales*, Poe praised Irving's *Tales of a Traveler* as one of the very few American collections of "tales of real merit" (H 11: 109–110). Had scurrilous biographer Griswold wished to tarnish Poe's posthumous reputation by exposing instances of hypocrisy and passive aggression in his relationship with Irving, he would have found no call to resort to forgery. The unaltered documents are sufficiently damning.

Conclusion: Thomas Gray/Nat Turner

Scholars have not yet witnessed the apocalypse Harold Bloom predicted, when computer algorithms arbitrate questions of influence. The booming field of Digital Humanities, however, may someday offer a solution to the impasse in influence studies that Elfenbein identified. Whereas individual scholars face limits on what the human memory can accomplish in comparing a writer's work to the totality of previously published material to which the writer could reasonably have had access, careful use of computer searches by scholars with a subtle understanding of the technology may yet yield significant results.[49] In the meantime, the most influential influence model of the past half-century has yet to be applied to Poe. In Bloomian terms, who was the strong poet Poe had to miswrite in order to clear a space for his own ambition? I admit to taking gross liberties with Bloom's theory in proposing an answer. In November 1831, Thomas Gray published *The Confessions of Nat Turner*, a first-person account of his deeds by the leader of a slave insurrection in Southampton that left over fifty white Virginians dead and led to the retributive killings of hundreds of blacks across the South. Twenty-two years old and just beginning his literary career when the insurrection took place, Poe happened to be living in Baltimore at the time, where a printer issued 50,000 copies of the *Confessions* to satisfy public demand.[50]

Assuming that an ambitious young author with an eye to the caprices of the literary marketplace might take notice of this unprecedented publishing sensation, the pamphlet's influence on Poe seems more than defensible. Gray presents before readers a charismatic, articulate killer presumed by observers to be insane and awaiting execution for his crimes—like the loquacious condemned madmen who narrate "The Tell-Tale Heart" and "The Black Cat." The prophet-like Turner claims the ability to interpret mystic symbols in the natural world—including "hieroglyphic characters, and numbers" inscribed in blood on tree leaves[51]—which calls to mind the linguistically evocative figures mysteriously engraved on cavern walls in *The Narrative of Arthur Gordon Pym*, not to mention codes and ciphers throughout Poe's body of work. Poe dramatized rebellion against constituted authority repeatedly in his fiction, from the mutiny aboard the *Grampus* in *Pym* (led by a bloodthirsty black cook), to the inmates' seizure of the asylum in "Tarr and Fether," to the enslaved title character's carefully orchestrated, shockingly violent revenge against a corrupt king and his court in "Hop-Frog," Poe's last published tale. Moreover, in reviewing Bird's novel *Sheppard Lee*, Poe took special interest in the figure of a rebellious slave turned to violence by abolitionist literature, which Virginians held to be the case with Turner.[52] Although much of Poe's fiction could be read as a career-long misprision of the *Confessions*, the evidence for influence finally resolves to the unsatisfying fuzziness of plausible-sounding, suggestive parallels.[53] Unless documentary evidence recording Poe's response to the pamphlet somehow comes to light, it's probable that no conceivable influence model is capable of generating additional insight into the Gray/Turner–Poe conundrum. But if such a theory appeared, I venture that it would be received as anything but old-fashioned.

Notes

1. Harold Bloom, *The Anxiety of Influence: A Theory of Poetry* (New York: Oxford University Press, 1973), 31.
2. Andrew Elfenbein, "Defining Influence," *Modern Language Quarterly* 69, no. 4 (2008): 433 and 436.
3. Andrew Elfenbein, "On the Discrimination of Influences," *Modern Language Quarterly* 69, no. 4 (2008): 481–507. Edgar Allan Poe, "Plagiarism—Imitation—Postscript," *Broadway Journal*, April 4, 1845.
4. George Lippard, "The Dollar Newspaper," *Citizen Soldier* (June 28, 1843): 140.
5. George Lippard, "Edgar A. Poe," *Dodge's Literary Museum* 9, no. 20 (October 21, 1854): 315–316, Edgar Allan Poe Society of Baltimore, https://www.eapoe.org/papers/misc1851/gl18543.htm.
6. Lippard, *The Quaker City*, October 20, 1849, quoted in Emilio De Grazie, "Poe's Devoted Democrat, George Lippard," *Poe Studies* 6, no. 1 (1973): 8.
7. David S. Reynolds, *George Lippard* (Boston: Twayne Publishers, 1982), 105–106.
8. George Lippard, "The Walnut Coffin Papers," *Citizen Soldier*, October 11, 1843.
9. Reynolds, *George Lippard*, 102–103. Because of this insider information, Lippard's "Walnut Coffin Papers" were at one time speculated to be of Poe's authorship.
10. For this aspect of Poe's career, see Sidney P. Moss, *Poe's Literary Battles: The Critic in the Context of His Literary Milieu* (Durham, NC: Duke University Press, 1963).
11. Robert Montgomery Bird, *Sheppard Lee: Written by Himself* (New York: New York Review Books, 2008), 20.
12. Edgar Allan Poe, "Sheppard Lee: written by himself," *Southern Literary Messenger*, September 1836, 671.
13. Justin R. Wert, "Poe's Early Criticism of American Fiction: The *Southern Literary Messenger* and the Fiction of Robert Montgomery Bird," in *Edgar Allan Poe: Beyond Gothicism*, ed. James M. Hutchisson (Newark: University of Delaware Press, 2011), 171–185.
14. Gören Hermerén, *Influence in Art and Literature* (Princeton, NJ: Princeton University Press, 1975), 42.
15. J. Gerald Kennedy notes the similarity between Bird's treatment of madness in *Sheppard Lee* and Poe's "The System of Doctor Tarr and Professor Fether" in *Strange Nation: Literary Nationalism and Cultural Conflict in the Age of Poe* (New York: Oxford University Press, 2016), 301.
16. Bird, *Sheppard Lee*, 394.
17. Robert Montgomery Bird, *Peter Pilgrim* (London: Richard Bentley, 1839), 69, 78, and 75, respectively.
18. Kenneth Silverman, *Edgar A. Poe: Mournful and Never-ending Remembrance* (New York: HarperPerennial, 1991), 131.
19. Bird, *Peter Pilgrim*, 140.
20. Robert Montgomery Bird, *A Belated Revenge* (Philadelphia: J. B. Lippincott & Company, 1889).
21. Edgar Allan Poe, "Literary Criticism," *Godey's Magazine and Lady's Book* 32 (January 1846): 42.
22. James Everett Kibler, "William Gilmore Simms," in *Dictionary of Literary Biography, vol. 248, Antebellum Writers in the South: Second Series*, ed. Kent P. Ljunquist (Detroit, MI: Gale, 2001). Literature Resource Center.

23. Tom Fafianie, "Poe's Purloined Poem: 'To Miss Louise Olivia Hunter,'" *Simms Review* 19, no. 1–2 (2011): 19–43. The poem is attributed to Poe in Mabbott's volume of Poe's poetry (M 1: 396–399) and in the Library of America edition of *Poetry and Tales*.
24. John Caldwell Guilds, *Simms: A Literary Life* (Fayetteville: The University of Arkansas Press, 1992), 30.
25. Poe, "Literary Criticism," 41.
26. William Gilmore Simms, *Martin Faber*, ed. John Caldwell Guilds (Fayetteville: University of Arkansas Press, 2005), 30. The link to Poe's concept of the perverse was made by Eugenia A. Morozkina, "'The Imp of the Perverse' in Crime and Confession: W. G. Simms and M. Y. Lermontov," *Simms Review* 18, no. 1–2 (2010): 57–61.
27. David W. Newton, "'It Is Genius Only Which Can Make Ghosts': Narrative Design and the Art of Storytelling in Simms's 'Grayling; or, Murder Will Out,'" *Studies in the Literary Imagination* 42, no. 1 (2009): 59–82.
28. Poe, "Literary Criticism," 41–42.
29. Quoted in Guilds, *Simms: A Literary Life*, 67.
30. Simms to Poe, New York, July 30, 1846, Edgar Allan Poe Society of Baltimore, https://www.eapoe.org/misc/letters/t4607300.htm. Simms noted the impertinence of presuming to give good "counsel" while giving "nothing else."
31. Hawthorne mocked Griswold's taste in poetry in "The Hall of Fantasy," originally published in 1843 in *The Pioneer*, to which Poe was also a contributor. Hawthorne mentions Poe in the story as well.
32. G. R. Thompson, "Literary Politics and the 'Legitimate Sphere': Poe, Hawthorne, and the 'Tale Proper,'" *Nineteenth-Century Literature* 49, no. 2 (1994): 172.
33. Meghan A. Freeman, "Nathaniel Hawthorne and the Art of the Tale," in *Edgar Allan Poe in Context*, ed. Kevin J. Hayes (Cambridge: Cambridge University Press, 2013), 288–297.
34. Hawthorne to Poe, Salem, MA, June 17, 1846, Edgar Allan Poe Society of Baltimore, https://www.eapoe.org/misc/letters/t4606170.htm.
35. Charles Wilkins Webber counseled Poe to "go aside with Hawthorne, to his dream-land, and lazily glide with him through its calm waters and enchanted isles" to soothe his overtasked life, in "Hawthorne," *The American Review* 4, no. 3 (September 1846): 303. George Ripley, reviewing *The Scarlet Letter*, credited both writers with deriving "terrible excitement" from "legendary horrors," though he found in Hawthorne's work "a wonderful insight and skill, to which the intellect of Poe was a stranger." Ripley, review of *The Scarlet Letter*, by Nathaniel Hawthorne, *New-York Daily Tribune*, April 1, 1850, 6.
36. Richard Fusco is the most recent among several critics to have drawn this connection. Fusco, "Poe's 'Life' and Hawthorne's 'Death': A Literary Debate," *Poe Studies/Dark Romanticism: History, Theory, Interpretation* 35 (2002): 31–37.
37. D. M. McKeithan, "Poe and the Second Edition of Hawthorne's *Twice-Told Tales*," in *Nathaniel Hawthorne Journal 1974*, ed. C. E. Frazier Clark, Jr. (Englewood, NJ: Microcard Editions Book, 1975), 257–269. Walter Evans, "Poe's 'The Masque of the Red Death' and Hawthorne's 'The Wedding Knell,'" *Poe Studies* 10 (1977): 42–43. Charles N. Watson, Jr., "'The Mask of the Red Death' and Poe's Reading of Hawthorne," *The Library Chronicle* 45, no. 1–2 (1981): 143–149. (Poe used both spellings of "Mask" in different iterations of the tale.)
38. Frank Pisano, "Dimmesdale's Pious Imperfect Perverseness: Poe's 'The Imp of the Perverse' and *The Scarlet Letter*," in *Poe Writing/Writing Poe*, ed. Richard Kopley and Jana Argersinger (New York: AMS, 2013), 143–157. Richard Kopley also explores Poe's

influence on *The Scarlet Letter* in *The Threads of* The Scarlet Letter: *A Study of Hawthorne's Transformative Art* (Newark: University of Delaware Press, 2003).

39. Carl Ostrowski, *Literature and Criminal Justice in Antebellum America* (Amherst: University of Massachusetts Press, 2016). See chapter three, "Carceral Conversions: Redemption via Incarceration in Antebellum American Literature."
40. Susan Williams, "Daguerreotyping Hawthorne and Poe," 13–20; Monika Elbert, "Poe and Hawthorne as Women's Amanuenses," 21–27; Richard Kopley, "Periodicals as Key in Poe and Hawthorne," 28–30; Paul Downes, "Democratic Terror in 'My Kinsman, Major Molineux' and 'The Man of the Crowd,'" 31–35; and Teresa A. Goddu, "Integrating Hawthorne," 36–38; all in *Poe Studies* 37, no. 1–2 (2004).
41. "Monthly Commentary," *The American Monthly Magazine* 3 (May 1837): 521.
42. Harper and Brothers to Poe, New York, June 19, 1836, https://www.eapoe.org/misc/letters/t3606190.htm; quoted in Silverman, *Edgar A. Poe*, 133.
43. Wayne R. Kime, "Poe's use of *Astoria* in 'The Journal of Julius Rodman,'" *American Literature* 40, no. 2 (1968): 215–222. John J. Teunissen and Evelyn J. Hinz, "Poe's Journal of Julius Rodman as Parody," *Nineteenth-Century Fiction* 27, no. 3 (1972): 317–338. Teunissen and Hinz propose that Poe did not commit plagiary; he intended readers to see the correspondences between his work and Irving's as part of a commentary on the derivativeness of Western frontier narratives.
44. Washington Irving, *An Unwritten Drama of Lord Byron*, intro. Thomas Ollive Mabbott (Metuchen, NJ: Charles F. Heartman, 1925), https://archive.org/details/AnUnwrittenDramaOfLordByron.
45. Christopher J. Forbes, "Satire of Irving's A History of New York in Poe's 'The Devil in the Belfry,'" *Studies in American Fiction* 10, no. 1 (1982): 93–100.
46. John F. Jebb, "Race, Pirates, and Intellect: A Reading of Poe's 'The Gold-Bug,'" in *Edgar Allan Poe: Beyond Gothicism*, ed. James M. Hutchisson (Newark: University of Delaware Press, 2011), 17–35. Liliane Weissberg, "Black, White, and Gold," in *Romancing the Shadow: Poe and Race*, ed. J. Gerald Kennedy and Liliane Weissberg (New York: Oxford University Press, 2001), 127–156.
47. G. R. Thompson, "'Proper Evidences of Madness': American Gothic and the Interpretation of 'Ligeia,'" *ESQ: A Journal of the American Renaissance* 66 (1972): 30–49. Irving's "The Adventure of the German Student" is a tale in this mode likely to have caught Poe's eye.
48. Jerry A. Herndon, "Poe's 'Ligeia': Debts to Irving and Emerson," in *Poe and His Times: The Artist and His Milieu*, ed. Benjamin Franklin Fischer IV (Baltimore: Edgar Allan Poe Society, 1990), 113–129. Barton Levi St. Armand, "Some Poe Debts to Irving's Alhambra," *Poe Studies* 10 (1977): 42.
49. Maurice Lee writes that as of 2012, only "marginal attention has been paid to bibliographic databases and computer-driven analyses of allusion, genre, and style." Lee, "Searching the Archives with Dickens and Hawthorne: Databases and Aesthetic Judgment after the New Historicism," *ELH* 79, no. 3 (2012): 749.
50. Thomas R. Gray, *The Confessions of Nat Turner* (Baltimore: Lucas & Deaver, 1831). The pamphlet is available in an electronic edition of the text on the website Documenting the American South: *The Confessions of Nat Turner* (Chapel Hill: University of North Carolina at Chapel Hill Library, 1999), http://docsouth.unc.edu/neh/turner/turner.html.
51. Gray, *The Confessions of Nat Turner*, 10.

52. "In his character of Nigger Tom, Mr. Lee gives us some very excellent chapters upon abolition and the exciting effects of incendiary pamphlets and pictures, among our slaves in the South. This part of the narrative closes with a spirited picture of a negro insurrection, and with the hanging of Nigger Tom." Poe, "Sheppard Lee," 669.
53. Of course, intertextuality often profitably steps into the space where influence theory leaves off. In a provocative essay demonstrating this principle, Lesley Ginsberg writes: "Like the southern version of Turner's revolt, 'The Black Cat' seems to give us a terrifying example of a crime which challenges the logic of causality and a murderer whose criminality appears mysteriously remorseless. Like Turner, the narrator expresses no remorse, and by offering a confession which crazily collapses the murder of his wife with the slaying of a cat, the narrator begs to be dismissed as a lunatic. Yet this narrative quirk structurally reproduces the rhetoric of inversion and denial which . . . enabled southerners to indulge their wish that the insurrection was the motiveless work of 'a complete fanatic.'" Lesley Ginsberg, "Slavery and the Gothic Horror of Poe's 'The Black Cat,'" in *American Gothic: New Intervention in a National Narrative*, ed. Robert K. Martin and Eric Savoy (Iowa City: University of Iowa Press, 1998), 116.

Bibliography

Bloom, Harold. *The Anxiety of Influence*. New York: Oxford University Press, 1973.

Elfenbein, Andrew. "Defining Influence." *Modern Language Quarterly* 69, no. 4 (2008): 433–436.

Fafianie, Tom. "Poe's Purloined Poem: 'To Miss Louise Olivia Hunter.'" *Simms Review* 19, no. 1–2 (2011): 19–43.

Freeman, Meghan A. "Nathaniel Hawthorne and the Art of the Tale." In *Edgar Allan Poe in Context*, edited by Kevin J. Hayes, 288–297. Cambridge: Cambridge University Press, 2013.

Gray, Thomas R. *The Confessions of Nat Turner*. Chapel Hill: University of North Carolina at Chapel Hill Library, 1999. First published 1831 by Lucas & Deaver (Baltimore). http://docsouth.unc.edu/neh/turner/turner.html.

Guilds, John Caldwell. *Simms: A Literary Life*. Fayetteville: The University of Arkansas Press, 1992.

Kime, Wayne R. "Poe's Use of Astoria in 'The Journal of Julius Rodman.'" *American Literature* 40, no. 2 (1968): 215–222.

Poe, Edgar Allan. Review of "Twice-Told Tales," by Nathaniel Hawthorne. *Graham's Magazine* 20 (May 1842): 298–300.

Reynolds, David S. *George Lippard*. Boston: Twayne Publishers, 1982.

Silverman, Kenneth. *Edgar A. Poe: Mournful and Never-ending Remembrance*. New York: Har perPerennial, 1991.

Thompson, G. R. "Literary Politics and the 'Legitimate Sphere': Poe, Hawthorne, and the 'Tale Proper.'" *Nineteenth-Century Literature* 49, no. 2 (1994): 167–195.

Wert, Justin R. "Poe's Early Criticism of American Fiction: The *Southern Literary Messenger* and the Fiction of Robert Montgomery Bird." In *Edgar Allan Poe: Beyond Gothicism*, edited by James M. Hutchisson, 171–185. Newark, NJ: University of Delaware Press, 2011.

CHAPTER 32

EDGAR ALLAN POE AND HIS ENEMIES

SANDRA TOMC

REMINISCING about Edgar Allan Poe many decades after Poe's death, Thomas Dunn English recalled a moment of peculiar friendliness and tranquility in their relationship. It was an evening in 1845 when he and Poe had dropped in to the salon of New York's most popular literary hostess, the poet Anne Charlotte Lynch. Lynch's events were usually crowded, but that evening it was a small group, and Poe and English happened to be the only men in the room. At his ease and among friends, Poe began to "lecture on literary matters" in a way that caught everyone's attention. English found himself entranced.

> So strongly was the scene impressed upon my memory that I can at any time close my eyes and, by a species of retinism, behold it in all its colors. In the plainly furnished room at one corner stands Miss Lynch with her round, cheery face, and Mrs. Ellet, decorous and ladylike, who had ceased their conversation when Poe broke into his lecture. On a sofa on the side of the room I sit with Miss Fuller, afterward the Countess Ossoli, on my right side, and Mrs. Elizabeth Oakes Smith on my left. At my feet little Mrs. Osgood, doing the infantile act, is seated on a footstool, her face upturned to Poe, as it had been previously to Miss Fuller and myself. In the center stands Poe, giving his opinions in a judicial tone and occasionally reciting passages with telling effect. Were I an artist I should like to put on canvas one of the best episodes of Poe's varied life.[1]

English's picture of a tranquil circle of friends, full of fondness for each other and deeply interested in intellectual exchange, is one often invoked in scholarship on early nineteenth-century US print culture. The picture this scholarship paints is of a scene in transition. From the 1820s to the 1850s, large-scale commercial book and magazine production in the United States was focused on the reprinting of British textual properties that were not covered by international copyright restrictions. This meant that writers resident in the United States who owned their texts and who would demand remuneration from US publishers were often excluded from commercial publishing projects. But this very feature of the US marketplace forced local writers to form alternative literary cultures, ones based not on economic exchange, but on friendship, civic service, and gift giving. Many local magazines of this period had their origins in friendship and coterie networks among intellectuals and professionals.[2] In Leon Jackson's words, "The functioning of newspapers and magazines and the well-being and prosperity of publishers depended to an important degree on the operation of the far-flung and vibrant networks of gift exchange along with the reciprocity they generated."[3] According to Ronald Zboray and Mary Saracino Zboray, these unconventional cultural relationships were not just formed in the shadow of commercial exchange but pulled against it, rejecting entrepreneurialism in favor of the warmer bonds of friendship or political sympathy.[4]

And yet in emphasizing friendship and generosity as the central energies of early nineteenth-century proto-commercial literary culture, these scholars neglect to note another feature of the nonmonetary literary network: the apparent ease with which networks of cultural friendliness transformed themselves into networks of hatred. Indeed, nowhere is this ready transformation more sharply manifested than in the case of English and Poe. In the passages quoted earlier, English was recalling events that took place in 1845. A year later, Poe and English were bitter enemies, their arguments broadcasted in the pages of bestselling US magazines.[5] In his "Literati of New York City" series, published in the widely read *Godey's Lady's Book* in 1846, Poe told readers that English was guilty of an "*inexcusable* sin": "downright plagiarism." Moreover, said Poe, English did not have sufficient schooling to engage in editorial work: "No spectacle can be more pitiable than that of a man without the commonest school education busying himself in attempts to instruct mankind on topics of polite literature" (ER: 1166). English was furious. He hit back with a "card" in the *New York Mirror* that accused Poe of drunkenness, sexual indiscretion, and forgery. Outraged, Poe launched a libel suit. Shortly thereafter, the weekly instalments of a satire titled *1844, or, The Power of the "S.F."* appeared in the *Mirror*. Authored by English but published anonymously, *1844* pilloried Poe as Marmaduke Hammerhead, author of the "Black Crow," clearly a reference to Poe's most famous poem, "The Raven." The portrait of Hammerhead is vicious: he "never gets drunk more than five days out of the seven; tells the truth sometimes by mistake; has moral courage sufficient to flog his wife, when he thinks she deserves it, and occasionally without any thought upon the subject, merely to keep his hand in."[6] More clever and stealthy, Poe got even writing a famous tale of revenge, "The Cask of Amontillado," in which the wronged Montresor seals up his living enemy in a deep catacomb and leaves him there to die. The feud did not limit itself to print. In actual life, according to English, he and Poe at one point came to physical blows: English "dealt him some smart raps on the face" and wearing "a heavy seal ring" on his finger, "cut him very severely, and broke the stone in the ring."[7] Nor was English Poe's only enemy. According to fellow editor Hiram Fuller, Poe had, by midcareer, "reviled nearly every man of eminence in the United States."[8]

Scholars often take Poe's many enmities as a special case, peculiar to him. But the proliferation of enemies in early nineteenth century US literary culture was a dark, inseparable counterpart of the energies of friendship that animated so much magazine and newspaper production. The central mechanism of the gift economy was, of course, its reliance on voluntary labor, on unpaid intellectual work as its primary source of capital. Nineteenth-century US magazines and newspapers were almost all run as entrepreneurial ventures that needed to make a profit. The point is that while the gift economy seemed to be based purely on noncommodified or voluntary production and exchange, it also had economic dimensions: editors, printers, illustrators, binders, distributors, and retailers all had to get paid. Many magazines were thus viable as economic enterprises only *because* they could count on unpaid input—that is, on "gifts"—from contributors. When friendship failed to generate the streams of unpaid work required to keep these enterprises alive, enmity often stepped in, like a dark, unconscious task master, to fuel production. Thus, one of the signal features of Poe's many enmities was their intimate relationship to the proliferation of textual matter and authorial reputations, the two cornerstones of magazine production. Not unlike gift exchange, which generated networks of indebtedness, enmities generated networks of revenge, scandal, and spectacle, inflating productivity, reputations, and sales. Even as writers like Poe often suffered in these bile-filled conflagrations, the industry as a whole expanded and profited, keeping alive the incentives for hate-driven production and readily transforming cords of affection to ever more binding ties of detestation.

We can better understand the role enmities played in the making of texts, sales, and profits for publishing entities if we look more closely at Poe's many quarrels with writers.[9] First, Poe's career was from the beginning fueled by his vitriolic reviews of fellow authors. Starting his career in the mid-1830s, Poe entered a literary scene expressly driven by a kind of innocently commodified friendliness: local authors advertised their books and magazines by relying on what were called "puffs," or positive reviews in the magazines of their friends. In his first job as review editor of the *Southern Literary Messenger*, Poe ripped the veil off this practice. To the humiliation of New York literary circles, his reviews used scathing language to expose the degree to which New York authors not only puffed each other's books but also frequently wrote reviews of their own books under pseudonyms and then asked friends to publish them. In 1835, the editors of the *New York Mirror* announced the imminent publication of a brilliant new novel, *Norman Leslie*, whose authorship, the magazine claimed, was a deep and intriguing mystery. Poe's *Norman Leslie* review exposed the author as one of the editors of the *Mirror*: "Norman Leslie . . . is, after all, written by nobody in the world but Theodore S. Fay, and Theodore S. Fay is nobody in the world but 'one of the Editors of the New York Mirror'" (ER: 540). Poe goes on to pour scorn on the novel itself: "As regards Mr. Fay's *style*, it is unworthy of a school-boy" (ER: 547).

On the one hand, Poe's attacks on fellow writers were embedded in the world frequently described by scholars of early US literature. Working on the *Southern Literary Messenger* in 1835 and 1836, Poe was at the center of a world of friendly patronage and gift giving whose origins lay in the civil society of the late eighteenth century. In the early national period, genteel Americans contributed to the maintenance of a political, intellectual, and cultural public sphere through a sharing of knowledge and art that was hobbyist in nature and often built around clubs and salons. Meeting on a weekly or monthly basis, men and women of gentility exchanged, critiqued, and debated each other's creative and intellectual efforts. Many of these clubs took the extra step of founding periodicals expressly to facilitate the publication of the club's productions. Dedicated to public service, the contents of these periodicals were based almost entirely on the voluntary intellectual labor of the club members and their friends; a printer or editor might be hired on to see to the details and business of production, but at heart these ventures were embedded in ideals of free and anonymous public service. In the words of the editors of the *Monthly Anthology*, established in 1804, "their highest ideal . . . is the pleasing consciousness of having *done the state some service.*"[10]

At the same time, the periodicals that formed around early national coterie culture were not exempt from the peculiar book economy that blossomed in the United States in the first years of the nineteenth century. Lacking robust intellectual property protections, the United States was the scene of vigorous entrepreneurial speculation in books, typically books by popular British authors. Magazines whose prevailing content was local sat at an odd juncture with respect to this economy. Funded by wealthier Americans, in the sense that the periodical's intellectual content was provided for free, they seemed to float free of local publishing capitalism in their own "gift" economy. Yet they were typically run by printers, publishers, and editors for profit. Voluntary labor on the part of wealthy Americans could thus finance print shops and publishing concerns, including the salaries of editorial, printing, binding, and engraving personnel.[11] Moreover, in some cases, genteel, club-based journals acted as elaborate advertising venues, their extended reviews advertising books that local publishers wanted to sell to local readers. When friendship and gift giving met their limits in this economy, the circles of friendship could be exploited by entrepreneurial minds for other ends. Magazines could become a kind of stage where instead of witnessing the intellectual exchange of friends, readers could watch friendships devolve into violent antagonisms.

We can see a nascent version of this process at the *Southern Literary Messenger*, which was established precisely on this quasi gift-based yet commercial model. Published in Richmond, Virginia, by printer T. W. White, the *Messenger* was made up entirely of content donated by southern elites. White's letters to his friend and frequent contributor, Lucian Minor, reveal the extent to which the magazine relied on networks of friendship for its viability and suffered when these friendships failed or their members lost interest. In 1835, White, who was clearly faced with the prospect of falling short of content for one of his issues, wrote Minor begging for an article or two: "Although you have done a great deal for me towards helping me along in my new undertaking. . . . I am reluctantly forced to ask you for some assistance again."[12] At another point, White wonders whether he might have fifteen to twenty pages per month from Minor.[13] Poe was brought in to the *Messenger* precisely to help solve these problems: he was hired to write content. But Poe's strategy as editor was not just to write the articles that White lacked. Poe's tactic was to condemn the friendliness that had failed the journal and to make his own mark instead as the isolated enemy of friendly groups, which Poe began to call "cliques." He set out to draw attention to himself and the *Messenger* by staging its renunciation of the friendship culture on which the *Messenger* was traditionally based.

This tactic was successful insofar as it drew attention to Poe and drew readers to the *Messenger*. Poe's review of *Norman Leslie* was remarked upon in periodicals North and South, and it was universally recognized as a refreshing and spicy attack on friendship culture. In many cases, Poe was praised for his fearlessness. The *Pennsylvanian* felt that Poe's criticisms were "a relief from the dull monotony of praise which rolls smooth in the wake of every new book" and that "a roughness which savors of honesty and independence is welcome." Poe was called an author of "distinguished merit," "the best of all our young writers," and "a gentleman of brilliant genius and endowments."[14] Furthermore, "He exposes the imbecility and rottenness of our *ad captandum* popular literature, with the hand of a master."[15] In other words, Poe made a name for both himself and the magazine by attacking groups of friends and friendship networks, most obviously the group of friends and publishers responsible for the *New York Mirror*.

These tactics were destined to remain integral to the careers of many American writers, including Poe. Indeed, they were fortified and made all the more relevant in the transformative book and magazine economies of the late 1830s. In 1839, for example, the editor Rufus Griswold, who would later feature as perhaps Poe's most famous enemy, and New England poet Park Benjamin revolutionized American periodicals by launching cheap literary magazines, the *Brother Jonathan* and *New World*.[16] Their timing was not coincidental. The early 1830s had seen the explosion of a US penny press, a new form of urban-based publishing that abandoned the luxury model of traditional publishing, with its costly formats and elite patrons, to exploit instead working-class readerships, cheap formats, and economies of scale. The 1837 market crash, which sent the US economy into free fall, effectively stamped out what was left of small-time genteel book publishing. Leaving book production to large, vertically integrated industrial firms like Harper and Brothers, aggressive new publishing entrepreneurs like Griswold and Benjamin focused all their efforts on popular, often cheaply produced magazines that were put out not monthly but weekly or even daily. Printed on cheap paper, sold like broadsides, and filled with the pirated novels of Dickens and Bulwer-Lytton, these new publications were not designed to advertise and puff books but to sell issues of themselves as quickly as possible, preferably on the street for cash.

Instead of thinking of themselves as custodians of communal well-being, writers in these new systems were encouraged to think of themselves as future stars, investors in their own brand who were trying to get ahead through competition and exposure. Even as these magazines still very much depended on artistic coteries and their gift-based intellectual labor, they were now just as likely to exploit these coteries for their darker energies, energies that were, once again, closely linked to sales. One of the chief features of the new "cheap and nasty" magazines was their commodification and advertising of erratic and outsized author "personalities" (a sort of mix of real and fictional authorial selves not unlike modern "reality" celebrities) as a primary selling point. Expressly figured as "outsiders," that is, as former members of groups of friends to which they could no longer belong, these personalities made a name for themselves by attacking and cruelly caricaturing other editors and writers. In the late 1830s, Benjamin, who typified himself as a lofty aristocrat with a bitter grudge against fellow authors, replaced Poe as the most feared reviewer of his generation. He eviscerated his contemporaries, most notably James Fenimore Cooper, whom Benjamin called "a superlative dolt" and permanently nicknamed "Funnymore."[17] Like the friendship economy, which generated magazine content and profits, the enemy economy generated sales. Penny press proprietors engaged in various editorial wars that engaged attracted readers, fuelled high sales, and made celebrities of the combatants. In 1842, Benjamin's *New World* was one of the most successful US magazines of the era.

There is much to suggest that these were tactics that Poe, who had done so much to popularize them in local magazines in the mid-1830s, returned to a decade later.[18] In 1845, Poe was enjoying significant but precarious success. After his stint with the *Southern Literary Messenger*, Poe had struggled to make a living, working first at *Burton's Gentleman's Magazine* and then at *Graham's Magazine*. In 1844, he had moved to New York and taken work as a "mechanical paragraphist" on Nathaniel Parker Willis's *Evening Mirror*. While still at the *Mirror* in January 1845, Poe published his poem, "The Raven," and was suddenly a star, celebrated all over the United States. James Russell Lowell published a short biographical review of Poe, which was reprinted everywhere, and which cast Poe as a rather glamorous, Byron-like figure, the perfect complement to the complex, brooding lover in "The Raven." Poe was now toasted in New York's elite literary salons, embraced by the circle of intellectuals described in English's recollection. But it was precisely at this moment, when he was basking in the adulation of those he most respected, that Poe launched the series of violent quarrels that would characterize the final years of his career, most notably his attacks on Henry Wadsworth Longfellow. Seen in isolation, these quarrels are puzzling. Poe's attack on Longfellow for plagiarism, a charge Poe could never substantiate and that Longfellow never answered, seems particularly bizarre. But here again, as in the case of the *Messenger*, Poe's creation of enemies functions as the obverse of the coterie of friends, generating text, celebrity, print, and money in the absence of a stable or codified economic place for creative personnel.

It is not insignificant that one of the central features of Poe's career prior to the 1845 Longfellow attacks was its failure to improve his material circumstances. Poe lectured, published stories, wrote reviews, and edited periodicals, but in 1844, one of the busiest years of his career, he earned an estimated $425, barely enough to support his wife and mother-in-law. At the end of the year, he wrote of the "sad poverty & the thousand consequent [ill]s & contumelies which the condition of the mere Magazinist entails upon [the author] in America.—where more than in any other region upon the face of the globe to be poor is to be despised" (CL 1:470). Early in 1845, after his success with "The Raven," Poe was working full-time on *The Broadway Journal* but making no money. Desperate for his own magazine, Poe had decided to forego a salary for the opportunity of becoming one-third proprietary partner in the magazine, a not uncommon arrangement at the time. It meant that all his editorial duties at the magazine would be unpaid labor. He told a friend, "For the last three or four months I have been working 14 or 15 hours a day—hard at it all the time. . . . And yet . . . I have made no money. I am as poor now as ever I was in my life—except in hope, which is by no means bankable" (CL 1: 286–287). Poe's correspondence from the early 1840s shows his desperate efforts to call upon a circle of friends and patrons for support; he was particularly eager to enlist financial investment from his friends for his magazine venture, *The Stylus*. But here again, where networks of friends failed, networks of enemies blossomed to take their place.

In late 1844, when Poe moved to New York and took his job at the *Evening Mirror*, he was effectively stepping into the world of his enemies. The very fact that Poe was hired by its owner and editor, Nathaniel Parker Willis, suggests the extent to which enmities and friendships had interchangeable functions in Poe's world, for it was Willis and his fellow *Mirror* editors whom Poe had so mercilessly pilloried while working for the *Messenger*. Willis himself had been one of Poe's chief targets, the object of two biting satires in the 1830s, "Lionizing" and the "Duc de L'Omlette," both of which represented Willis as a shallow hunter of fame for its own sake.[19] But Willis was not bothered by Poe's history. On the contrary, evidence suggests that Poe's instinct for attack was precisely what Willis liked about him. More admired and hated than any other writer of his generation, Willis, along with Poe and Benjamin, pioneered American sensational journalism. In a how-to manual for authors penned in the mid-1840s, Willis advised young authors to work hard, to take any decent intellectual job they could find, even if the wages were low, and to slowly work their way up the editorial ladder. But he also held that authors who wanted fame should encourage attacks upon themselves. The only way to move from lowly "literary operative" to "star," according to Willis, was to cultivate "abuse." "As a 'stock' or 'starring' player upon the literary stage," he advised, "you desire a crowded audience." He remarked that "abuse is, in criticism, what shade is in a picture" or "acid in punch," and he added the telling memo: "Query—how to procure yourself to be abused?"[20]

One of Poe's jobs at the *Mirror* was apparently to gain attention for the journal by attacking his fellow authors. In the *Messenger* days, Poe's vicious reviewing had been dubbed "scalping." According to the *New Yorker*, Poe was "like the Indian, who cannot realize that an enemy is conquered until he is scalped."[21] In October 1844, *The Evening Mirror* featured a letter from a supposed anonymous correspondent (probably Poe or Willis) congratulating the *Mirror* on its acquisition of its new editor: "I am glad to see that Edgar Poe is in your clearings. He is a man of the finest ideal intellect in the land—carries a nasty tomahawk as a critic—bitter as gall to the literary flies who have been buzzing around his windows. Do give Poe a corner (or a column, or ten o' 'em) in your 'Strong-ly' Mirror, and let him fire away at the humbugs of our literature" (PL: 475).

It seems fairly certain that Poe's attack on Longfellow was part of a publicity campaign designed partly to inflate Poe's reputation and partly to increase the *Mirror*'s readership. To be sure, Longfellow was an odd choice of target. A Harvard professor, a poet famous not just in the United States but among intellectual and literary elites in Britain, and a good friend to the most admired US writers of his generation, Longfellow was considered off limits by American reviewers and was generally handled with great reverence. But presumably because Longfellow played so central a role in the social webbing of US literary culture, he provided a perfect object of attack in the drama of this network's disintegration. As Poe's earlier reviews suggest, he understood Longfellow as a personification of what he scornfully called an American "clique" mentality—that is, of the coterie mentality that pumped life into genteel commercial literature. Poe attacked Longfellow by undermining his investment in his friends.

What became known as the "Little Longfellow War" began with Poe's review of Longfellow's collection of poems, *The Waif*, an odd work whose content is not irrelevant to this discussion. It gathers together some of Longfellow's favorite poems by British poets and intersperses these with Longfellow's own poems. But the poems are not printed with their authors' names affixed. To understand who wrote what, the reader must turn to the table of contents. There, Longfellow identifies the authors of all the poems except for his own. His own seventeen poems appear under the name "Anonymous." Titled *The Waif*, the collection seems to suggest that even poets orphaned and alone on the cold shores of the modern United States can find a rich spiritual and aesthetic family among the great poets of the British tradition.

As many scholars have noted, the content of *The Waif* could not have been more readily designed to provoke Poe had Longfellow set out to do so. Here was Longfellow, a wealthy Harvard professor with a loving family and friends, grandiosely claiming orphan status and taking on the mantle of anonymity in order to stand with history's great poets. Meanwhile Poe, who actually was an orphan, whose mother had died when he was a toddler and whose foster father had disowned him, struggled in poverty; he wrote in anonymity not so that he could join the family of great poets but because his employers forced him to do it on the grounds that it was better for business. Yet Poe's attack did not, as we might expect, expose Longfellow as the pretender to an outcast status that was not legitimately his. It rather imagined Longfellow in a peculiar drama: Poe claimed Longfellow was wilfully effacing and betraying the friendship networks that traditionally stood at the heart of US literary productivity. Poe hinted that Longfellow had pretended to be an individual without name or friends whose greatest debt was to Marvell or Shelley not in order to aggrandize himself but in order to secretly plagiarize the works of his American contemporaries. Longfellow's book is "infected with a *moral taint*." Poe persisted: "[T]here *does* appear, in this exquisite little volume, a very careful avoidance of all American poets who may be supposed especially to interfere with the claims of Mr. Longfellow. These men Mr. Longfellow can continuously *imitate* (*is* that the word?) and yet never even incidentally commend" (ER: 702). Thematically organized around the betrayal of fellow poets, Poe's attack on Longfellow was less related to anything personal or intimate that Poe might have been experiencing than it was to the instigation of a particular kind of campaign, one geared to the production of outrage in a case where friendly feeling had fallen short.

Willis's correspondence in the immediate aftermath of this review suggests the extent to which Poe's attack on Longfellow was, initially at least, strategic. Not surprisingly, Longfellow's friends in Boston were taken aback by Poe's review and bewildered as well as angered by the charge of plagiarism. But though Willis himself was a friend of Longfellow, he was unconcerned. Responding to Longfellow's friend Charles Sumner, who had written in alarm, Willis reassured him, telling him that they would all benefit from the attention Poe cultivated: "Tomorrow's paper will contain [George] Hillard's reply, & then I shall leave him & Poe to do a *joust* together in my pages, which of course will serve Longfellow in the end."[22] In a follow-up letter to Sumner, Willis declared his affection for quarrelling in print: "*My* policy," he told Sumner in a follow-up letter, "is always to *fan up* any smothered discontent, & give it the chance of contradiction. I *always* beg men who come with literary whispers against *me* to get them *into print* forth with, where I can meet them." He suggested to Sumner that he not only approved of Poe's attacks but encouraged them: "Another thing—I mean to let Poe make a feature of his own in the Mirror, & be recognized as the author of criticisms there, and I am obliged, (to have anything good from him) to give him somewhat free play. Tell Longfellow he shall never suffer 'in the long run' from me or mine."[23]

What is important to note about Willis's characterization of the Longfellow scandal is his willingness to use friends and enemies interchangeably: the large support network of Longfellow followers can readily serve in obverse fashion as the scene of a divisive paper war. Precisely to the extent that Longfellow features as the exalted leader and lifeblood of an important intellectual coterie, Willis and Poe can exploit him. Their attack cuts Longfellow loose as a patron and, by converting him from friend to foe, redefines the source of the *Mirror*'s financial vitality: once dependent on patronage, it is now dependent on short-term sales based on notoriety and scandal. Indeed, Willis and Poe invert the anonymity authorizing Longfellow's imagined network of timeless poetic friends, preferring instead to inflate magazine sales by broadcasting Longfellow's name and cashing in on his prominence as a readily recognizable celebrity.

This transformation of the energies of friendship and patronage for the purposes of attack and scandal continued to mark the latter half of Poe's career. Most notably, of course, Poe continued to attack Longfellow. The *Waif* review and "The Raven" were both published in January of 1845. Within the next month, Poe had left the *Mirror* for *The Broadway Journal*, which became the venue for an extended "Longfellow War." Now jousting with all of Longfellow's friends, Poe over the next two months produced, in seemingly manic, exhaustive fashion, over fifty pages of printed text on the subject of Longfellow and plagiarism. But Poe did not limit himself to Longfellow. As his fame ballooned in 1845 and 1846, so did his list of foes: Thomas Dunn English, James Russell Lowell, Charles Briggs, Lewis Gaylord Clark, and Rufus Griswold.

To be sure, the profusion and seeming intimacy of these enmities make it tempting to see them as specific to Poe's history and personality. Modern scholars almost unanimously attribute Poe's quarrels with these writers to his personal and psychological struggles in the mid-1840s—to the fear he felt around his wife's rapidly deteriorating health, to his bouts of alcoholism, to the pressures that fame itself put on his performance anxiety as a writer. Nevertheless, just as the Longfellow attack was organized around a bid for fame and readerships, so too, I would suggest, were these other battles. This is not to say that they were always divorced from intimate conflicts and insults; on the contrary, one of the features of the predatory press was that it often took personal idiosyncrasy as a starting place: writers were often attacked for their looks, for example.

But here again, attacks which seemed personal were also bound up with magazine production, sales, and readerships. Anxious to protect and inflate his fame, Poe mobilized his networks of friends to function instead as more profitable networks of enemies.

In some cases, this transformation of friends to enemies was incidental, in that Poe did not really set out to alienate his friends. Lowell, for example, seems to have been collateral damage in the Longfellow War. Once Poe's fan and promoter, Lowell began to distance himself in the wake of the Longfellow attacks. Apparently sensing Lowell's wariness, Poe turned and attacked him, accusing him too of plagiarism. A similar situation developed with Briggs. Partly through Lowell's urging, Briggs had been eager to acquire Poe's services on the *Broadway Journal*, whose ownership he shared with John Bisco, and he was pleased when Poe came aboard as one-third partner in the journal. Before long, however, Briggs became restive, apparently fearing Poe's control over the magazine and started plotting to jettison Poe. But Poe outsmarted him and it was Briggs who found himself forced out of the *Broadway Journal*. Briggs was furious and in private called Poe "a drunken sot, and the most purely selfish of human beings."[24]

But if these enmities began as personal differences, they quickly expanded into sensational textual fodder, producing once again the conversion of friends into enemies in ways that energized the magazine business. Indeed, as Poe contrived to become sole proprietor of the *Broadway Journal* in the autumn of 1845—and thus more eager than ever to attract readers—his attacks on writers and other editors increased. In a published review, he called Briggs a "vulgar driveller, . . . the whole of whose point, as far as we can understand it, consists in being unable to pen a sentence of even decent English" (P 3: 250). He resumed his attack on Longfellow and the "Frogpondians," as he now derisively called literary Boston. He implied that John Greenleaf Whittier, another respected poet in Longfellow's circle, might also be a plagiarist, "guilty of this, the most despicable species of theft" (P 3: 253). Part of Poe's strategy here, which he took from Willis, involved depicting himself not as the perpetrator of abuse but as the embattled editor who was himself the victim of attacks. In December of 1845, he was writing in the *Broadway Journal*: "THE MANNER in which we are maltreated, of late days, is really awful to behold. Every body is at us—little dogs and all" (P 3: 325). Poe then reprinted a review from an obscure journal, the *Nassau Monthly*, in which one of his own tales is called "philosophic nonsense" (P 3: 325). His reprinting of a bad review of his own tale sews him into a circuit of fame and enmity, showing that even small papers feel he is worth abusing.

As it happened, these squibs in the *Broadway Journal* were just the beginning of a much larger, more ferocious "war" that would break out in coming months. Here again, when we cast eyes over the brutal fighting that now ensued between Poe and writers like English and Briggs, it is difficult not to conclude that these writers were nursing heartfelt personal grudges, that they were lashing out in uncontrolled fury. And because Poe was, if not always the perpetrator, then the organizing consciousness at the center of these attacks, it is difficult not to see them as closely related to his dark psychological state at this period and possibly his growing inability to control his drinking. He wrote fellow editor Evert Duyckinck in December of 1845 that he was "dreadfully sick and depressed" and believed himself "mad" (CL 1: 533). But while the fierce fighting among these authors did indeed reach into their personal lives with often frightening alacrity, evidence suggests that it remained motivated primarily by the desire for sales and publicity. Indeed, nowhere is this desire more sharply manifested than in Poe's behavior following the collapse of his proprietorship of the *Broadway Journal* at the end of 1845. Poe did not even try to repair the friendships he had damaged. His instinct was to monetize his grudges.

His first move was to approach Louis Godey, the powerful proprietor of one of the most widely read periodicals of the day, *Godey's Lady's Book*, proposing an essay series called The Literati. The full title, which reads The Literati of New York City: *Some Honest Opinions at Random Respecting Their Authorial Merits, with Occasional Words of Personality*, gives a sense of Poe's aims. The series would be a monthly tell-all exposé of the secrets of all his friends among the American literati. The word *personality*, as we have seen, was tied in this period to outsized caricatures designed to offer insult. Literalizing the transformation of friendship networks into more profitable enemy networks, the Literati series exemplified what was now Poe's brand as a violent scrapper who had quarrelled with all of New York. Indeed, the conceit of the series was that Poe was relaying candid descriptions of his friends, of people he had met "in society" in the salons and parlors of the literary elite.

Playing on the notion of friendships inverted or gone awry (and in fact Poe was quite literally betraying his network of friends by cashing in on the display of their secrets and deficiencies), Poe's first Literati instalments were peppered with references to the social networks they defied and used for fuel. Longfellow, described as "a little quacky per se," was also someone who "has, through his social and literary position as a man of property and a professor at Harvard, a whole legion of active quacks at his control" (ER: 1120). Derogating the group or coterie as a unit of camaraderie and exchange, Poe focused instead upon individuals in their unique specificity. Under cover of a claimed impartiality, Poe pronounced on the personal characteristics of individual writers, paying special attention to physical appearance. Of one writer, George Bush, he said, "In person, he is tall, nearly six feet, and spare, with large bones. . . . The eyes are piercing; the other features, in general, massive. The forehead, phrenologically, indicates causality and comparison, with deficient ideality. . . . He walks with a slouching gait" (ER: 1122). Briggs was described thus: "He is about five feet six inches in height, somewhat slightly framed, with a sharp, thin face, narrow and low forehead, pert-looking nose, mouth rather pleasant in expression, eyes not so good, gray and small, although occasionally brilliant." His presence is "very apt to irritate and annoy" (ER: 1133–1134).

Not surprisingly, before *Godey's* had published two instalments of the series, the New York literary scene exploded with the "War of the Literati," as Hiram Fuller, now the editor of the *New York Mirror*, dubbed it. Fuller opened the doors of the *Mirror* to any of Poe's enemies seeking to retaliate; Briggs was quick to take advantage. Writing a blistering anonymous "review" of the Literati series, Briggs pretended to write a Literati piece on Poe: "In height he is about 5 feet 1 or two inches, perhaps 2 inches and a half. His face is pale and rather thin; . . . teeth indifferent; forehead rather broad, and in the region of ideality decidedly large, but low, and in that part where phrenology places conscientiousness and the group of moral sentiments it is quite flat." His head has "a balloonish appearance"; "his hands are singularly small, resembling birds' claws."[25] Sensitive about his height and the shape of his head, Poe appears to have been mortified by this description. He wrote to friends, including Willis, begging them to retaliate for this retaliation. Willis, now the proprietor of the *Home Journal*, was sympathetic but ultimately practical, pointing out to Poe the futility of taking personal offense and offering tips on strategy: "Why reply *directly* to Mr. Briggs? If you want a shuttlecock squib to fall on the ground, never battledore it *straight back*." Willis reports not having seen any attacks on him by Briggs because he hires staff to shield him from this kind of thing: "I keep a good-sense-ometer who reads the papers & tells me if there is anything worth replying to." Poe needs to remember the status of the parties, Willis advises: "A reply from me to Mr. Briggs would make the man. So will yours, if you exalt him into your mate by contending on equal terms. If you care to punish him, attack him on some *other subject, & at an anonymous writer whose name is not worth giving*. Notoriety is glory in this transition state of our half-bak'd country."[26]

Willis's advice on how to negotiate the roiling waters of "notoriety" emphasizes the extent to which Poe's enmities operated in the same quasi-commercial spaces as coterie networks based on friendship. To be sure, as Poe's immediate future makes clear, writers sustained more psychological damage by methodically making enemies. Over the next few months, as English inserted himself into the mix with a vengeance, audiences all over the United States trembled at what they witnessed, both riveted and horrified at the depths to which the combatants were willing to go. Particularly shocking was English's attack on Poe, in which he accused him of forgery, alcoholism, and wife beating, even as Poe's wife was slowly dying of tuberculosis. In New York, the *Morning News* called English's piece a "most caustic and fearful article" (PL: 648). George P. Morris, editor of New York's *National Press*, thought it was "one of the most savage and bitter things we ever read" (PL: 649).

Nevertheless, this dark network of enemies, conjured into being out of the network of friends, was not without benefits to all parties. That is, the network of enemies was a generative, productive structure, issuing in sales, celebrity, and bouts of fanatical writing. At the most rudimentary level, *Godey's* sales skyrocketed, and the issues in which the *Literati* series appeared sold out instantly: in Godey's words, "[T]he May edition was exhausted before the first of May, and we have had requests for hundreds from Boston and New York, which we could not supply."[27] Issues of the New York *Mirror*, where English and Briggs took their stand, saw a similar burst of sales. Poe was publically humiliated, but he does not seem to have been broken. Godey paid him $172 for the six *Literati* instalments; Poe sued the *Mirror* for libel and won $225 in a settlement. Moreover, evidence suggests that the fighting was productive for Poe as a writer; a bout of writer's block gave way to a rush of plans, essays, poems, and stories, including "The Cask of Amontillado," a fantasy of ultimate revenge.[28]

Indeed, so productive was the public argument that instead of steering clear of the business of notoriety, Poe decided he needed more: at the height of the scandal, he abandoned his old dream of owning a magazine and began planning instead a large collection of essays that would extend to many volumes, a collection based on the *Literati* series, in which he would pronounce not just on New York authors but on the entire national literary scene. It would be called "The Living Writers of America" and would not scruple to trespass upon what Poe called the "sensitiveness of authors."[29] The design for this work, left behind in manuscript form, illustrates Poe's obsession with friendship culture—or more properly his dependence on the drama of its dismantling. Organized around America's "peculiar cliquism," as Poe called it, the "Living Writers" series was founded on the same principles as the *Literati* series: it would sell books and inflate Poe's celebrity by "scorching" his fellow authors.

Poe did not get a chance to see his planned "Living Writers" volume come to fruition. He died suddenly in 1849. At the time of his death he was famous. He was also, in the end, penniless, for the web of enemies was ultimately no more lucrative in his case than the network of friends. But if Poe's enemies did little to reward him with material wealth in the short term, they continued to generate profits in the larger US publishing industry long after his death. News of Poe's death had barely reached New York when one of Poe's oldest friends/enemies, Rufus Griswold, published an extraordinary obituary and biography of him in the *Daily Tribune*. Griswold and Poe had known each other for nearly a decade. In a curious way, Griswold had literalized and capitalized on friendship networks in much the same way that Poe had capitalized on enemy networks. Griswold was one of the earliest anthologists of American literature. Born to an impoverished family, lacking in education and advantages, Griswold had nevertheless managed to ingratiate himself both with powerful editors like Park Benjamin and Horace Greeley, and, finally, with more elite literary circles in Boston. His famous anthologies, beginning with *The Poets and Poetry of America* in 1842, were filled with selections from what Griswold judged the best work of American writers. Writers in the United States fought to be included in these prestigious volumes. Inventing as they called upon circles of friends and patrons, Griswold's anthologies both performed and actualized coterie culture in the form of the collection: readers opened the pages of these books and found the portraits and poems of American authors gathered in one place as if in a salon.

Not insignificantly, this was the mirror image of what Poe dreamed up for his "Living Writers" idea, in which American writers would be gathered together despite their enmities. Poe and Griswold were not fond of each other, but they were practical about business and called on each other for favors. It was Griswold whom Poe contacted about the fruition of the "Living Writers" project. Moreover, it was Griswold to whom Poe's mother-in-law turned when she wished to publish an edition of Poe's work after his death. It seems reasonable to assume, therefore, that at the time of Poe's death Griswold had an expectation of profiting from the sale of Poe's works. This explains his obituary's extraordinary features, for it opens not by lamenting Poe's death or by invoking a community of mourners, as one might expect of even the most pro forma obituary, but by expressly excluding Poe from circles of camaraderie and amiable friendship: "Edgar Allan Poe is dead," the Griswold review intones. "This announcement will startle many, *but few will be grieved by it.* The poet was well known personally or by reputation in all this country; he had readers in England, and in several states of Continental Europe;

but he had few or no friends" (emphasis in original).[30] The friendless, unmourned Poe conjured in this picture made him a more valuable commodity for readers of Griswold's subsequent Poe edition. It's as if Griswold knew that there was less money to be made by laying Poe to rest inside the friendly, warm-lit scenes of American letters, which a routine obituary would have required, than there was in keeping him in a state of constant harassment, ever alert even in death to the next enemy attack. In other words, produced by Poe himself, the Poe figure who turns up in Griswold's obituary is precisely the friendless, ferocious soul whose tirades and attacks on fellow writers had produced sales and celebrity for Poe and his various literary partners and publishers in situations where friendships and camaraderie failed to do their job.

In the end, Griswold was not Poe's friend, but it's unclear that Poe would have wanted it any other way. An author who had tried and failed to make a living as the object of patronage and friendly promotion, Poe chose instead the stormier climes of contention and violent attack. And in fact, the idea that Griswold was producing a kind of "canned" Poe, a prefabricated celebrity commodity that would conform to audience expectation, is confirmed by the rest of the obituary, which does its best to insert Poe into the gothic atmospherics that had become, along with his enmities, one of his signatures as an author. Griswold commemorates Poe as a tortured poet who had travelled a desolate path: "[W]ith his glance introverted to a heart gnawed with anguish, and with a face shrouded in gloom, he would brave the wildest storms; and all night, with drenched garments and arms wildly beating the wind and rain, he would speak as if to spirits that at such times only could be evoked by him from that Aidenn close by whose portals his disturbed soul sought to forget the ills to which his constitution subjected him."[31] In this "Aidenn," beyond the gates of heaven, were "those he loved." But Poe, said Griswold, was doomed only to see them "in fitful glimpses" as the gates opened to let in those with "less fiery and more happy natures."[32] Even postmortem, Poe was doomed to lack the company of friends.

Notes

1. Thomas Dunn English, "Reminiscences of Poe [Part 03]," *Independent* (New York) 48, no. 2500 (October 29, 1896): 1448, https://www.eapoe.org/papers/misc1851/tde18963.htm.
2. For general information on antebellum publishing, professional authorship or editing, and book and magazine production, see William Charvat, *The Profession of Authorship in America, 1800–1870: The Papers of William Charvat*, ed. Matthew J. Bruccoli (Columbus: Ohio State University Press, 1968); Frank Luther Mott, *American Journalism, A History: 1690–1960*, 3rd ed. (New York: Macmillan, 1962); Frank Luther Mott, *A History of American Magazines*, vols. 1 and 2 (Cambridge, MA: Belknap, 1967); John Tebbel, *The Creation of An Industry, 1630–1865, vol. 1 of A History of Book Publishing in the United States* (New York and London: R.R. Bowker, 1972); John Tebbel, *The Compact History of the American Newspaper*, rev. ed. (New York: Hawthorn, 1969); John Tebbel, *Between Covers: The Rise and Transformation of Book Publishing in America* (New York: Oxford University Press, 1987); Ronald J. Zboray, *A Fictive People: Antebellum Economic*

Development and the American Reading Public (New York: Oxford University Press, 1993); and Scott E. Casper, *The Industrial Book, 1840–1880, vol. 3 of A History of the Book in America*, published in association with The American Antiquarian Society (Chapel Hill: University of North Carolina Press, 2007); Ronald J. Zboray and Mary Saracino Zboray, *Literary Dollars and Social Sense: A People's History of the Mass Market Book* (New York: Routledge, 2005); Leon Jackson, *The Business of Letters: Authorial Economies in Antebellum America* (Stanford, CA: Stanford University Press, 2008); Michael J. Everton, *The Grand Chorus of Complaint: Authors and the Business Ethics of American Publishers* (New York: Oxford University Press, 2011); J. Gerald Kennedy and Jerome McGann, eds., *Poe and the Remapping of Antebellum Print Culture* (Baton Rouge: Louisiana State University Press, 2012); Sandra Tomc, *Industry and the Creative Mind: The Eccentric Writer in American Literature and Entertainment, 1790–1860* (Ann Arbor: University of Michigan Press, 2012). My model of a domestic print industry controlled by a kind of stealth, small-scale publishing capitalism is indebted to Rosalind Remer, *Printers and Men of Capital: Philadelphia Book Publishers in the New Republic* (Philadelphia: University of Pennsylvania Press, 1996). For studies of sociability and friendship in the realm of US letters, see David S. Shields, *Civil Tongues and Polite Letters in British America* (Chapel Hill: University of North Carolina Press, 1997) and Catherine O'Donnell Kaplan, *Men of Letters in the Early Republic: Cultivating Citizenship* (Chapel Hill: University of North Carolina Press, 2008).

3. Jackson, *Business of Letters*, 96.
4. Zboray and Zboray, *Literary Dollars and Social Sense*, xiv.
5. The exact nature and length of the enmity between Poe and English is unclear. English claimed later in life that he met Poe in 1839 through the circle of writers associated with *Burton's Gentleman's Magazine* in Philadelphia and was friendly with him and his wife. See Thomas Dunn English, "Reminiscences of Poe [Part 02]," *Independent* (New York) 48, no. 2499 (October 22, 1896): 1415, https://www.eapoe.org/papers/misc1851/tde18962.htm. Scholars agree that their friendship was short lived. William Graveley argues that it was English, working behind the scenes in 1842 and 1843, who railroaded Poe's attempts to get a custom-house post. See "Poe and Thomas Dunn English: More Light on a Probable Reason for Poe's Failure to Receive a Custom-House Appointment," *Papers on Poe: Essays in Honor of John Ward Ostrom*, ed. Richard P. Veler (Springfield, OH: Chantry Music Press, 1972), 165–193. In spite of their quarrels and backstabbing, Poe and English were on friendly terms again in 1844 and 1845 before their quarrels blew up again in earnest (see 188–189).
6. Thomas Dunn English, *1844, or, The Power of the "S.F.": A Tale* (New York: Burgess, Stringer & Co., 1847), 123.
7. English, "Reminiscences of Poe [Part 03]," 1448.
8. Quoted in Kenneth Silverman, *Edgar A. Poe: Mournful and Never-ending Remembrance* (New York: HarperCollins, 1991), 313.
9. For general biographical information on Poe's life and career, see Silverman, *Edgar A. Poe: Mournful and Never-ending Remembrance*. For a study of Poe's relationship to the US magazine world, see Sidney P. Moss, *Poe's Literary Battles: The Critic in the Context of His Literary Milieu* (Durham, NC: Duke University Press, 1963) and Terence Whalen, *Edgar Allan Poe and the Masses: The Political Economy of Literature in Antebellum America* (Princeton, NJ: Princeton University Press, 1999).
10. "Address by the Editors," *Monthly Anthology, and Boston Review* 5, no. 1 (January 1808): 2.
11. See Tomc, "An Idle Industry: Nathaniel Parker Willis and the Workings of Literary Leisure," in *Industry and the Creative Mind*, 154–192.

12. T. W. White to Lucian Minor, Richmond, 26 February 1836, quoted in David K. Jackson, "Some Unpublished Letters of T. W. White to Lucian Minor [Part 01]," *Tyler's Quarterly Historical and Genealogical Magazine* 17 (April 1936): 232, http://www.eapoe.org/papers/misc1921/1936djka.htm.
13. T. W. White to Lucian Minor, Richmond, August 7, 1835, quoted in Jackson, "Some Unpublished Letters of T. W. White to Lucian Minor [Part 01]," 226, http://www.eapoe.org/papers/misc1921/1936djka.htm.
14. "Supplement," *Southern Literary Messenger* 2 (January 1836): 133–140; and "Supplement," *Southern Literary Messenger* 2 (April 1836): 341–348; both rpt. in *Edgar Allan Poe: The Critical Heritage*, ed. I. M. Walker (London: Routledge and Kegan Paul, 1986), 83, 85, 86, 87. These are compilations of reviews of the *Messenger* which Poe himself put together and published as promotional material.
15. "Supplement," *Southern Literary Messenger* 2 (April 1836): 8; rpt. in *Edgar Allan Poe: The Critical Heritage*, ed. Walker, 87.
16. The Griswold and Benjamin relationship, as well as their magazine ventures, are detailed in Joy Bayless, *Rufus Wilmot Griswold: Poe's Literary Executor* (Nashville, TN: Vanderbilt University Press, 1943) and Merle M. Hoover, *Park Benjamin: Poet and Editor* (New York: Columbia University Press, 1948).
17. [Park Benjamin], "The Author of Rubeta," *The New World* 3, no. 8 (August 21, 1841): 124. See Hoover, *Park Benjamin* for details around Benjamin's career.
18. Michael Allen, in *Poe and the British Magazine Tradition* (New York: Oxford University Press, 1969), demonstrates that Poe borrowed his predatory review tactics from famous British magazines of this era, like *Blackwood's* and *Fraser's*.
19. For these essays' relationship to Willis, see Kenneth L. Daughrity, "Poe's 'Quiz on Willis,'" *American Literature* 5 (1933–1934): 55–62. General information on Willis is from Henry Beers, *Nathaniel Parker Willis* (Boston: Houghton, Mifflin, 1892) and Thomas N. Baker, *Sentiment and Celebrity: Nathaniel Parker Willis and the Trials of Literary Fame* (New York: Oxford University Press, 1999).
20. N. Parker Willis, *Rural Letters, and Other Records of Thought at Leisure* (New York: Baker and Scribner, 1849), 195.
21. "Supplement," 517–524; reprinted in *Edgar Allan Poe: The Critical Heritage*, ed. Walker, 90.
22. Nathaniel Parker Willis to Charles Sumner, January 16(?), 1845, Charles Sumner Correspondence, 1824–1874, HOU HD MS Am 1, Box 27: 6821–7072, Houghton Library, Harvard University.
23. Nathaniel Parker Willis to Charles Sumner, January 27(?), 1845, Charles Sumner Correspondence, 1824–1874, HOU HD MS Am 1, Box 27: 6821, Houghton Library, Harvard University.
24. Quoted in Silverman, *Edgar A. Poe: Mournful and Never-ending Remembrance*, 273.
25. Charles F. Briggs, "Mr Poe and the New York Literati," *Evening Mirror* (New York) 4, no. 41 (May 26, 1846): 2.
26. Nathaniel Parker Willis to Edgar Allan Poe, 1845(?), Rufus W. Griswold Papers 1834–1857, Rare Books Department, Box 19, Ms. Gris. 1240. *Digital Commonwealth: Massachusetts Collections Online*, http://ark.digitalcommonwealth.org/ark:/50959/6h445c88g.
27. Quoted in John Ward Ostrom, "Edgar A. Poe: His Income as Literary Entrepreneur," *Poe Studies* 16, no. 1 (1983): 5. Also from Ostrom is Poe's payment for the "Literati" series (5).
28. See Silverman, *Edgar A. Poe: Mournful and Never-ending Remembrance*, 335–339, for a description of Poe's productivity.

29. Burton R. Pollin, "'The Living Writers of America': A Manuscript by Edgar Allan Poe," *Studies in the American Renaissance* (Charlottesville: University of Virginia Press, 1991): 163.
30. [Rufus Wilmot Griswold], "Death of Edgar Allan Poe," *New York Daily Tribune*, October 9, 1849; reprinted in *Edgar Allan Poe: The Critical Heritage*, ed. Walker, 294.
31. [Rufus Wilmot Griswold], "Death of Edgar Allan Poe," 299.
32. [Rufus Wilmot Griswold], "Death of Edgar Allan Poe," 299.

Bibliography

Casper, Scott E., Jeffrey D. Groves, Stephen W. Nissenbaum, and Michael Winship, eds. *The Industrial Book, 1840–1880. Vol. 3 of A History of the Book in America*. Published in association with The American Antiquarian Society. Chapel Hill: University of North Carolina Press, 2007.

Charvat, William. *The Profession of Authorship in America, 1800–1870: The Papers of William Charvat*. Edited by Matthew J. Bruccoli. Columbus: Ohio State University Press, 1968.

Everton, Michael J. *The Grand Chorus of Complaint: Authors and the Business Ethics of American Publishers*. New York: Oxford University Press, 2011.

Jackson, Leon. *The Business of Letters: Authorial Economies in Antebellum America*. Stanford, CA: Stanford University Press, 2008.

Kaplan, Catherine O'Donnell. *Men of Letters in the Early Republic: Cultivating Citizenship*. Chapel Hill: University of North Carolina Press, 2008.

Kennedy, J. Gerald, and Jerome McGann, eds. *Poe and the Remapping of Antebellum Print Culture*. Baton Rouge: Louisiana State University Press, 2012.

Moss, Sidney P. *Poe's Literary Battles: The Critic in the Context of His Literary Milieu*. Durham, NC: Duke University Press, 1963.

Remer, Rosalind. *Printers and Men of Capital: Philadelphia Book Publishers in the New Republic*. Philadelphia: University of Pennsylvania Press, 1996.

Shields, David S. *Civil Tongues and Polite Letters in British America*. Published in association with the Omohundro Institute of Early American History and Culture. Chapel Hill: University of North Carolina Press, 1997.

Silverman, Kenneth. *Edgar A. Poe: Mournful and Never-ending Remembrance*. New York: HarperCollins, 1991.

Tomc, Sandra. *Industry and the Creative Mind: The Eccentric Writer in American Literature and Entertainment, 1790–1860*. Ann Arbor: University of Michigan Press, 2012.

Whalen, Terence. *Edgar Allan Poe and the Masses: The Political Economy of Literature in Antebellum America*. Princeton, NJ: Princeton University Press, 1999.

Zboray, Ronald, and Mary Saracino Zboray. *Literary Dollars and Social Sense: A People's History of the Mass Market Book*. New York: Routledge, 2005.

CHAPTER 33

BLUESTOCKINGS AND BOHEMIANS

EDWARD WHITLEY

EDGAR Allan Poe wrote his most famous poem, "The Raven" (1845), while living in New York City and attending literary salons with women writers known colloquially as "bluestockings." Scholars in recent years have begun to reconstruct the culture of interdependence that developed among the New York bluestockings by showing how Poe and women such as Frances Sargent Osgood became reliant upon one another in their personal and professional lives.[1] Poe and the bluestockings of antebellum New York produced what Lytle Shaw would call "coterie writing": an interconnected web of "social and literary linkages" that offer both "a range of rhetorical, formal strategies and a staging ground for these strategies" in the literary marketplace.[2] As such, the bluestockings' Poe is not the isolated genius of the popular imagination but is instead a writer whose aesthetic innovations and professional successes emerge from connections that, in David Dowling's words, "however apparently private, were thus public affairs, themselves mechanisms of literary production crucially linked to the publishing industry."[3] Poe and the bluestockings shared manuscript documents in private, engaged in open conversations at literary salons, and exchanged poems in mass-market periodicals. These interactions across the media landscape of bluestocking Manhattan—private manuscripts, semipublic salons, and the public realm of print—tell us as much about Poe's gossip-filled personal life during the New York period as they do about the communities that helped nineteenth-century writers negotiate the literary marketplace.

Poe's posthumous reputation during the late 1850s and early 1860s followed a similar pattern, as his legend and legacy were linked to another coterie of New Yorkers who, like the bluestockings before them, took their cue from a transatlantic literary culture. The writers and artists who gathered at Charles Pfaff's Manhattan beer cellar in the years leading up to the Civil War modeled themselves on the bohemians of Paris's Latin Quarter and looked to Poe as their "idol," "spiritual guide," and "patron saint."[4] While Poe himself did not frequent Pfaff's or identify with bohemianism (neither option was available to him in the 1840s), many of the writers who gathered at the underground pub near Washington Square Park took Poe's conflicts with the marketplace and his commitment to literary art as reason to consider him an honorary bohemian. In addition, Eliza Richards has noted that the habitués of Pfaff's "took as a touchstone the work of Poe."[5] Nowhere is this more apparent than in Poe's impact on Walt Whitman, who fraternized with the bohemians at Pfaff's bar. As members of this cohort modeled their fiction, criticism, and poetry on Poe's distinctive style, Whitman followed suit with his "Raven"-inspired poem "Out of the Cradle Endlessly Rocking," published in the bohemians' *New York Saturday Press*.[6] Despite the public backing that Whitman initially received from the bohemians after successfully channeling Poe, factions within the Pfaff's coterie eventually turned on him, leaving Whitman with the challenge of finding new communities of support in Washington, DC, in the 1860s, in Philadelphia and Camden in the 1870s, and through an international coalition of British and Canadian disciples in the 1880s.[7] In contrast, some of Whitman's former bohemian comrades—including R. H. Stoddard and E. C. Stedman, who edited major editions of Poe's work in the 1880s—maintained close relationships that contributed to their becoming influential tastemakers in American letters during the second half of the nineteenth century.[8]

According to Pierre Bourdieu, the European salons that provided a template for both the bluestockings and bohemians of antebellum New York created a space for "writers and artists [to] gather together as kindred spirits" in a mutually supportive environment; those same salons, however, worked to "distinguish themselves more by whom they exclude than by whom they include."[9] Poe was ultimately excluded from the New York salons following accusations that he had been carrying on inappropriate relationships with bluestocking women, while Whitman experienced a more gradual decline in support from a factionalized bohemian community, a community whose members continued to anchor their careers to Poe well into the second half of the nineteenth century. That the various groups of New York writers who claimed Poe as one of their own would illustrate this central tension in coterie practice—namely, that tenuous membership in a literary community both models and informs the fickle nature of the marketplace—should come as no surprise given John Evelev's observation that "Poe's literary career is the best, most representative embodiment of the tensions within the American literary profession."[10] Even though he railed against "the impudent *cliques* which beset our literature" (H 11: 110), Poe was nevertheless deeply embedded in such career-defining coteries both during his life and after his death.

Bluestockings

After briefly living in New York during the late 1830s, Poe returned to the city in 1844 and soon began working as a literary editor for publications such as the *Evening Mirror* and the *Broadway Journal*. While the *Journal* played an important role in Poe's career, it was the back-to-back publication of "The Raven" in the *Evening Mirror* and the *American*

Review in 1845 that opened doors to the Manhattan literary salons that would shape the rest of Poe's life. Soon after publishing "The Raven," Poe was invited to attend the salon of Caroline Kirkland, the author of the frontier narrative *A New Home—Who'll Follow?* (1839) and an influential figure in New York City's literary scene. Poe's fellow editor at the *Broadway Journal*, Charles Frederick Briggs, recalled that "a good many of the New York literati" attended the evening gathering and noted that the recent success of "The Raven" created "a great curiosity to see the writer of that wonderful poem." Only a few weeks later, Poe made a dramatic appearance at the salon of a prominent New York physician that, in the words of *Knickerbocker* author Henry T. Tuckerman, "betokened the visit of a celebrity." Poe understood the impact that involvement in Manhattan's salons would have on his burgeoning career, and his reputation soon spread throughout the city: poet Elizabeth Oakes Smith noted that "the Raven became known everywhere, and everyone was saying 'Nevermore'" (PL: 497–498).

Poe took full advantage of the opportunities that the Manhattan salon scene had to offer. He made connections with the literati whose curiosity he had piqued with the publication of "The Raven," and he cannily played the role of the emerging celebrity, whether by ingratiating himself in polite society—salon hostess Anne Charlotte Lynch recalled that "Poe had always the bearing and manners of a gentleman"—or by dramatically presenting himself as "a pale, thin, and most grave-looking man, whose dark dress and solemn air" led salon patrons to identify him with the titular subject of his famous poem (PL: 498, 484). Literary salons had a history stretching back to eighteenth-century France and Great Britain, where informal gatherings of artists, writers, and other intellectuals served to bring wealthy benefactors into contact with promising talent.[11] Writers could leverage the cultural capital that they accrued through salon appearances into regular employment or publishing contracts, as book publishers and periodical editors attended salon events alongside authors and socialites.[12] Poe personally benefitted from rubbing shoulders with influential figures like Freeman Hunt, the founder of *Merchant's Magazine*, despite having spoken out elsewhere against what he called the "machinations of coteries in New York," wherein "leading booksellers" and editors would "manufacture, as required from time to time, a pseudo-public opinion . . . for the benefit of any little hanger on of the party" (H 10: 186).[13] Despite this criticism of "the pernicious influence of coteries" (PL: 509), Poe was himself deeply invested in coterie practice and found himself dependent upon women writers in literary salons as they worked together to navigate the literary marketplace. This dynamic of interdependence turned literary salons into spaces where women could not only freely interact with men but also assume key leadership roles. Anne Boyd Rioux writes, "salons afforded women the opportunity to gain positions of relative power as hostesses who brought together prominent men and . . . women who had themselves achieved fame, most often as authors."[14]

It is from within this history of women's stewardship over literary salons that writers such as Caroline Kirkland and Anne Lynch were referred to as "bluestockings" by period commentators and later generations of scholars alike. Poe himself drew a connection between antebellum salon women and the bluestockings of the eighteenth century through the characters of "Mrs. Bas-Bleu," "big Miss Bas-Bleu," and "little Miss Bas-Bleu" in "Lionizing," an 1835 satire on urban social gatherings (M 2: 174).[15] These "Bleu" women—whose shared surname conflates their individual contributions while reinforcing their collective impact—stand alongside male social types such as the "modern Platonist," "Æstheticus Ethix," "Delphinus Polyglot," and the other pompous pontificators in Poe's caricature of intellectual soirées. Poe's gentle satire of bluestocking women took on a sharper edge, however, in Charles Baudelaire's 1856 introduction to his French translation of Poe's works, wherein Poe's accomplishments were made to stand out in sharp relief against the ephemeral contributions of women writers: "America babbles and rambles with an astonishing volubility," Baudelaire wrote. "Who could count its poets? They are innumerable. Its *blue stockings?* They clutter the magazines."[16] If "bluestocking" was an honorific bestowed upon the women who led salons, it also served equally well as a casual insult toward women writers who aspired to a greater reputation than the male establishment believed them entitled. As Deborah Heller writes, "on the one hand, the salon was grounded on the public sphere premise of universality and disembodied reason; on the other, the salonnières were nevertheless judged by standards of femininity that potentially constrained them."[17] The women who hosted and participated in Manhattan's literary salons were admired for their judgment, talent, and intellect, but they were also expected to conform to gender roles of the period as domestic hostesses, adoring admirers, and beguiling flirts.

This range of attitudes toward bluestocking women could also serve as rubrics for charting Poe's relationship with the New York–based poet Frances Sargent Osgood, the author of some half-dozen volumes of poetry and one of Poe's regular interlocutors at the salons. Osgood aligned herself with the bluestockings when she referred to an 1843 frontispiece for *Graham's Magazine* featuring prominent women writers as a "constellation" of female literary stars in a "*blue* Heaven," proud to see her own image included with these "portraits of the blues."[18] Poe was an admirer of Osgood before the two ever met, and in a February 1845 lecture at the New York Society Library on the "Poets and Poetry of America," he spoke approvingly of her "rosy future of increasing power and renown" as a poet, and even recited some of her verses.[19] Osgood commented to a friend soon after on "how beautifully Mr Edgar Poe spoke of me in his lecture on the Poets. . . . [He] praised me very highly—He is called the severest critic of the day—so it was a real compliment" (PL: 518). They met for the first time only a few weeks later at a literary gathering in New York's Astor House where, Osgood recalled, a mutual friend had told her that Poe was eager to hear her opinion of "The Raven" (PL: 511). Later that year, after the two had grown close, Poe was struggling to compose something to recite at the Boston Lyceum and asked Osgood to write "a poem that shall be equal to [his] reputation" (PL: 573).

Poe's relationship with Osgood, then, could be seen as a realization of the highest ideal for the bluestockings' mixed-gender literary salons: equality between the sexes. Poe respected Osgood's work, courted her estimation of "The Raven," and would have happily claimed one of her verses as his own. Clearly, he viewed her as an intellectual equal. But there are at least two other options that scholars and biographers have proposed for describing Poe's relationship with Osgood from within the contours of salon culture. The first would be that, while Poe respected Osgood's talents, he esteemed her not as a poet, but as a *poetess*, a gendered subclass of authorship that limited women writers to an innate gift for mimicry—a derivative ability to emulate the style of generative and original (male) poets rather than produce innovative works of their own.[20] Such poetry forms the domain of Baudelaire's bluestockings who "clutter the magazines" with an excess of insubstantial verses; their muse is the imitative song of the mockingbird, not the ponderous tones of the raven. From this perspective, the literary salon is able to accommodate both male poets and female poetesses, but with the understanding that essential differences in gender mark men's and women's respective abilities as writers. As such, Poe and Osgood would, at best, be characterized as mentor and doting protégée, with Poe's invitation that Osgood write "a poem that shall be equal to [his] reputation" an exercise in apprenticeship based on the poetesses' knack for imitation.

A second option for describing Poe's affiliation with Osgood holds that an intense relationship between the two writers—platonic, romantic, or sexual—was at the core of their involvement, meaning that any poems the two shared with one another either publicly or privately were merely the traces of a meaningful intimacy in their personal lives. On Valentine's Day in 1846, for example, Poe and Osgood exchanged handwritten poems at Anne Lynch's salon, where the two had met regularly over the course of the previous year. Poe's poem, "To—," conceals the name of its addressee in the title but embeds it within an acrostic form that requires its reader to connect the first letter in the first line ("F") with the second letter in the second line ("r") and so on until it spells out the name "Frances Sargent Osgood," as the bolded and italicized letters (my emphasis) in the poem's opening seven lines illustrate:

> ***F***or her these lines are penned, whose luminous eyes,
> B***r***ight and expressive as the stars of Leda,
> Sh***a***ll find her own sweet name that, nestling, lies
> Upo***n*** this page, enwrapped from every reader.
> Sear***c***h narrowly these words, which hold a treasure
> Divin***e***—a talisman, an amulet
> That mu***s***t be worn *at heart*. Search well the measure—

Osgood responded in kind, sending Poe a poem that spells out "Edgar Allan Poe" in the initial letters of the last word in the first line, the penultimate word in the second line, and so on, as in these opening six lines that give us "Edgar A":

> Oh! thou who canst with wizard skill ***e***mbalm
> In the rich amber of thy ***d***elicate verse
> Thine airy love with ***g***enii-woven charm
> Safe from the evil eye ***a***nd from all harm
> Of coarse, profane ***r***egard—I—in thy terse
> Quaint melody ***A***h! Thou didst teach the spell.[21]

These manuscript poems were very much at home in a nineteenth-century salon culture where any given parlor or drawing room could become, in Mary Loeffelholz's terms, a "site of literary production and performance."[22] The highly stylized form of the acrostic, for instance, draws more attention to the poet's ability to manipulate language than it does to a poem's actual content. This performative gesture ("Look at what I can do!"), particularly when tied to an ephemeral moment such as Valentine's Day, takes on the character of a fleeting comment in a salon conversation ("Listen to what I have to say!") rather than an enduring contribution to a poet's oeuvre. This is not a criticism, however, of salon verse as somehow less relevant to an author's career than his or her published works. Rather, poems such as these not only provide archival traces of the lived dynamics of the literary salon, but they also point to a similar dynamic operating in the print public sphere.

In addition to privately trading manuscript poems, Poe and Osgood publicly exchanged poems in the pages of various New York periodicals. Poe published more than a dozen of Osgood's poems in the *Broadway Journal*, and on several occasions he responded to Osgood's work either through poems of his own or in his critical commentary for the *Journal*. In the April 5, 1845, issue of the *Broadway Journal*, for instance, Poe published two of Osgood's pseudonymous poems: "The Rivulet's Dream" (by "Kate Carol") and "So Let It Be" (by "Violet Vane"). An editor's note to "The Rivulet's Dream" invites readers to surmise the authorship of the poem ("We might *guess* who is the fair author of the following lines, which have been sent us in a MS. evidently disguised—but we are not satisfied with guessing, and would give the world to *know*"), just as the subtitle of Osgood's "So Let It Be: To—" teases an unnamed addressee. "Violet Vane" appears one week later in the April 12 issue as the author of the poem "Spring," alongside "Love's Reply," which carries the name of Frances Sargent Osgood as the author. The verso of the same page features an illustration titled "A Presentation at a Literary Soiree," which depicts a salon scene in which a diminutive woman with dark hair (a dead ringer for Osgood) converses with two leering men who could easily pass for Poe and his *Broadway Journal* coeditor Charles Frederick Briggs. For the literati of New York who regularly attended these salons, the impulse to read such poems biographically would have been all but impossible to resist. As Mary G. De Jong writes, the "literary texts that [Poe and Osgood] published as tributes and messages to one another give ambiguous and contradictory signals about the nature of their personal interaction. The ambiguity may have been deliberate, intended to tease one another, the reading public, or interested parties" from the New York salon community.[23] T. O. Mabbott's record of Poe's published work shows that virtually all of the poems he wrote during the period 1845–1847 were in conversation with women writers, suggesting that his efforts to crack the literary market involved building private relationships with bluestocking writers that could in turn translate into public interactions in the literary marketplace (M 1: 377–426). In addition to courting the favor of the editors and publishers who attended the salons, it was incumbent upon writers themselves to work together to generate the kind of attention that would then become profitable in the print public sphere.

Readers in the know would have taken Poe and Osgood's poems as the transcript of lived experiences; they would have felt that they were eavesdropping on intimate conversations between key players in the Manhattan scene. Mass-market readers, however, would have felt less that they were eavesdropping on a conversation, and more that they were stepping into a wholly public space. Poe and Osgood wrote a number of poems that take on the character of both intimate dialogue and public discourse, and they do so by alluding to phrases from one another's published texts. For example, Osgood published a short story about a young woman who, after falling in love with a married man, writes a poem that borrows both the cadence and key phrases from "The Raven," as evidenced by the following stanza:

> How had I knelt hour after hour beside thee,
> When from thy lips the rare, scholastic lore
> Fell on the soul that all but deified thee,
> While at each pause, I, childlike, prayed for more.[24]

Osgood's "rare, scholastic lore" echoes the "quaint and curious volume of forgotten lore" from "The Raven," while her "prayed for more" scans perfectly with Poe's "nevermore." Osgood's story was published in the August 1845 issue of *Graham's Magazine* with the title "Ida Grey" as a nod, perhaps, to the pseudonym of "Edward S. T. Grey" that Poe occasionally used (M 1: 382); two months later, Poe's "The Divine Right of Kings" appeared in same publication, with the title of his poem alluding to the "divine truths" and "divine passion" that Osgood's heroine claims will vindicate her forbidden love.[25] Similarly, Osgood has her protagonist declare that the married man she loves will have no choice but to love her in return: "his fate is to love me," she writes in her journal before penning her "Raven"-inspired poem,[26] which Poe references in "The Divine Right of Kings" with the line, "O! would she deign to rule my fate" (M 1: 384). Osgood continues the public conversation in the February 1846 issue of *Graham's* with the poem "Caprice," which returns to the language of divine love in multiple lines: "Be thou *all* being to my soul, / And fill each want divine!"; "They wait the *master*-hand divine"; " 'T is a helpless woman's right divine"; and "I revel in my right divine."[27] Such allusions suggest the conversations of the salon—with shared phrases tossed back-and-forth as in a private exchange—while also allowing mass-market readers to draw connections between works of literature independent of the social relationships (scandalous or otherwise) of their authors. What matters in such a reading is the common vocabulary that extends from one poem to another, not the secret rendezvous between authors.

Similarly, the September 6, 1845, issue of the *Broadway Journal* features Osgood's "Echo-Song," a poem that quotes directly from Poe's "Israfel," which had itself appeared in the July 26 issue. One week later, on September 13, 1845, Poe squeezes a small quatrain titled "To F—" (with no byline) immediately after his satirical short "Diddling Considered as One of the Exact Sciences." In line with the other Poe-Osgood poem exchanges, "To F—" reads like a direct response to a query from Osgood:

Thou wouldst be loved?—then let thy heart
From its present pathway part not!
Being everything which now thou art,
Be nothing which thou art not![28]

Only a few months later, on November 19, 1845, Poe would publish an expanded version of the poem in *The Raven and Other Poems* as "To F—s S. O—d," making it seem as if the only way to read this poem is as a direct address to the titular Frances Sargent Osgood. Nevertheless, Poe had cobbled "To F—" together from verses that he had either published or shared in manuscript on at least four earlier occasions since 1833, suggesting that the poem could operate as a linguistic artifact virtually independent of context (M 1: 233–237). While astute readers would have connected the poem to Poe and Osgood's salon conversations, others would have regarded it as an independent aesthetic object, and others still would have barely registered that the four short lines of "To F—" tucked away at the bottom of a page did anything more than fill up the column inches of that week's paper. That the Poe-Osgood poems could simultaneously resonate in three different registers—as records of the lived experience of a salon, as aesthetic objects to be appreciated, and as commodities in the market for print—captures the full range of coterie practice.

A handful of attentive salon participants did, indeed, read Poe and Osgood's poems as the transcript of an illicit affair, which culminated with Margaret Fuller and Anne Lynch approaching Poe with a request that he surrender Osgood's correspondence to them, presumably because the letters would confirm that he was carrying on an improper relationship with Osgood and, possibly, other salon women as well. This confrontation set in motion a chain of events that resulted in Poe's de facto expulsion from the New York salons and his scathing reviews of Manhattan writers in his "Literati of New York" series for *Godey's Lady's Book*.[29] While readers like Fuller and Lynch would have been able to parse out the biographical background in the poems that Poe and Osgood shared with one another, other readers noticed only faint clues, and still others remained completely unaware of any connection whatsoever between the two. This range of reactions says less about how to read the literary output between these fixtures in the New York salon scene than it does about the multiple locations that coterie writing navigates on its journey from the salon to the paying customers of the public marketplace.

Indeed, the opening salvo of the "Literati" essays reads like a deconstruction of the activities in which Poe himself had been very recently engaged as part of the New York salon scene. He notes a "distinction between the popular 'opinion' of the merits of contemporary authors, and that held and expressed of them in private literary society." Private opinion circulates only within the salons, he argues, while public opinion functions according to the logic of the marketplace: the public has its own opinion "just as we consider a book our own when we have bought it," rather than when we have written it. Poe then proceeds to draw the curtain on the private affairs of writers and editors, writing that "literary quacks" find success only through "the personal acquaintance of those 'connected with the press.'" Breaking down this distinction between public and private even further, Poe presents his "Literati" essays as public transcriptions of private opinions, effectively collapsing the media landscape of bluestocking New York into a single, powerful proclamation from his critical pen: "In the series of papers which I now propose, my design is, in giving my own unbiased opinion of the *literati* (male and female) of New York, to give at the same time, very closely if not with absolute accuracy, that of conversational society in literary circles" (H 15: 1–5). While Poe's "Literati" essays present themselves as a denunciation of literary coteries, they function equally well as a guide to how coterie practices shape and define an author's experience in the marketplace.

Bohemians

Poe's posthumous legacy among the bohemians of antebellum New York reveals a similar dynamic at work to that of the bluestockings' salons. The story of how a French subculture made its way to 1850s New York usually begins with Henry Clapp, Jr., and Ada Clare, the American writers who came to be known as the King and Queen of bohemia. Clapp and Clare had each traveled to Paris during the 1840s, and after experiencing the artistic culture of the Latin Quarter firsthand they set out to transplant bohemia to Manhattan "from the mother asphalt of Paris," as William Dean Howells later wrote.[30] Young writers such as Howells were drawn in by Clapp and Clare's efforts to recast New York as Paris on the Hudson, with Clapp recreating *la vie bohème* at Charles Pfaff's underground beer cellar in Greenwich Village, and Clare holding a weekly salon in her West 42nd Street townhouse.[31] Many of them published their work in Clapp's literary weekly, *The New York Saturday Press*. Rather than a coherent movement with a distinct philosophy, bohemian New York was a confederation of the Clapp and Clare coteries with a loosely affiliated group of writers that gathered at the home of Richard Henry and Elizabeth Barstow Stoddard.[32] The Stoddards' bohemianism was more genteel in its orientation, however: Elizabeth wrote, "I am a Literary Bohemian and the city suits me—but I like to be a Bohemian in good society," and Richard noted that while Pfaff's was "a centre of literary and artistic Bohemianism; I never went inside the place. Once I walked down the steps and stood at the door. I saw Walt Whitman and others inside, but through diffidence or some other feeling, I did not enter."[33]

The gatherings at the Stoddards' home would have been the most similar to the bluestocking salons that Poe had attended, both in their respectability and in the prominent role that Elizabeth Stoddard played as an arbiter of cultural taste. According to Lillian Woodman Aldrich, belonging to the Stoddard salon was a "solemn thing," and receiving a personal invitation from Elizabeth "was to this company what a ribbon is to a soldier, and prized accordingly."[34] Ada Clare's Sunday evening salons also shared some common ground with the bluestockings', perhaps because Clare herself had regularly attended Anne Lynch's weekly literary soirées in the mid-1850s as Poe himself had done during the previous decade.[35] Clare even offered a satiric defense of bluestocking women in an 1859 article for the *Saturday Press*: "The Blue Stocking is an intellectual woman. She is a female who possesseth mental gifts. These mental gifts, of whatever nature they be, she weareth in the manner the porcupine doth his quills and with the same intention."[36] Clare's commitment to propriety, however, did not match that of either Lynch or the Stoddards. She neither apologized for having a child out of wedlock nor felt compelled to identify his father, and, according to a member of the bohemians' circle, there was "a whispered rumor" that Clare and actress Getty Gay were involved in a relationship that "was of a Parisian, Sapphic charater [*sic*]."[37] Pfaff's itself tended more towards the indecorous as well, with a largely (but not exclusively) male clientele inviting "modern literary women," according to an 1860 article in *The Chicago Press and Tribune*, to join with them as they would "rap on the table for their steaks, smoke cigarette, sing opera refrains . . . jest, revel, poetize, laugh and weep, and so tarry long beyond the midnight hour, with their harumscarum brothers of the pencil and quill."[38]

Despite their differences, these various groups of self-described bohemians shared an interest in the life and legacy of Poe. Some of the writers affiliated with the bohemian scene had interacted with Poe in the previous decade, while others were drawn to his reputation as an iconoclastic artist who struggled with an unforgiving market. Poe's former coeditor at the *Broadway Journal*, Charles Frederick Briggs, worked for a literary weekly down the street from the offices of the *Saturday Press*, and one-time *Saturday Press* assistant editor William Winter recalled that "many times I talked with the tart, sprightly, satiric Charles F. Briggs," whom Walt Whitman also counted among the "New York crowd" of bohemian writers.[39] Indeed, Winter wrote that one of the marked features of the antebellum bohemian community "was the survival of ties that bound it to the period that is covered by Poe's account of 'The Literati.'"[40] Similarly, at the turn of the century Thomas Bailey Aldrich remembered "prowling the streets, upon which still rested the shadow of Poe" with fellow writers who, as he wrote in an 1859 poem, "were all very merry at Pfaff's."[41] (Aldrich was not being entirely metaphoric: the salon that Poe attended at Anne Lynch's home on Waverly Place was a short, half-mile walk on the other side of Washington Square Park from Pfaff's location at the corner of Broadway and Bleecker.[42]) Whitman himself briefly met Poe in 1845 when he published an article in the *Broadway Journal*, as did R. H. Stoddard, who tried but ultimately failed to place one of his own poems there. Stoddard conflated the bohemians of the 1850s with the literati of the 1840s in telling the story of his fruitless quest to publish in the *Broadway Journal* as he recalled the moment when "the potent editor of the *Broadway Journal* [Poe] had gone out to his luncheon, with [Charles F.] Briggs, or [Thomas Dunn] English, or some other Bohemian."[43]

It is unlikely that Poe, Briggs, or English thought of themselves as bohemians. While bohemianism emerged in Paris as early as 1830, the book that introduced bohemianism to the world—Henri Murger's *Scènes de la Vie de Bohème* (1851)—would not be published until two years after Poe's death, and English translations would not appear in the United States until 1853.[44] Nevertheless, by the 1850s both French and American writers had connected the bohemians' poverty, alcoholism, and countercultural swagger with the enduring legacy of Poe. Fitz-James O'Brien, for one, patterned many of his poems and tales after Poe's, claimed that "Poor Poe, you know, was a bohemian," and cultivated a reputation as a hard drinker and prolific writer.[45] Fellow bohemian William Winter claimed that O'Brien's "stories were hailed as the most ingenious fabrics of fiction that had been contributed to our literature since the day when Edgar Poe surprised and charmed the reading community with his imaginative, enthralling tale[s]."[46] Winter would make a similar case for the genteel bohemian R. H. Stoddard, whom he described as "the most subtle and exquisite lyrical genius in our poetic literature since Poe,"[47] while E. C. Stedman expanded Winter's claim in 1903 in saying that "Stoddard and his group were the first after Poe to make poetry—whatever else it might be—the rhythmical creation of beauty."[48] The bohemians' relationship with Poe, then, was built on direct connections to Poe's New York[49] as well as wishful thinking that he was a bohemian *avant la lettre*.

Perhaps the most well-known instance of the bohemians' connection to Poe is the 1859 publication of Charles Gardette's "The Fire-Fiend" in the *Saturday Press*, a poem that Gardette claimed was actually one of Poe's early drafts for "The Raven." Amid a veritable cottage industry for "Raven"-inspired poems during the nineteenth century, "The Fire-Fiend" holds a special place in US literary history both for the enduring power of its hoax—Gardette eventually had to publish a book-length retraction of his claim that Poe had written the poem—and for its influence on Walt Whitman's "Out of the Cradle Endlessly Rocking," which was published in the *Saturday Press* as "A Child's Reminiscence" only one month after "The Fire-Fiend." Whitman's poem about a heartbroken mockingbird pining for his departed love recalls Gardette's "Querulous, quaker-breasted Robin, calling quaintly for his mate,"[50] but Whitman also includes echoes of Poe's infamous "nevermore":

> O solitary me, listening—never more shall I cease imitating, perpetuating you,
> Never more shall I escape,
> Never more shall the reverberations,
> Never more the cries of unsatisfied love be absent from me.[51]

The similarities between the three poems have led Eliza Richards to characterize "Out of the Cradle Endlessly Rocking" as "a descendant of Gardette's Robin as well as Poe's Raven," and to contend that all three poems are self-conscious meditations on the role of poetic voice within a mass market for cheap, printed texts. Richards continues, "Whitman pays tribute not only to Poe or Gardette, but to the entire web of associations that print circulation enables," arguing that antebellum print culture not only facilitates reprinting and encourages imitation but also requires that "romantic lyric expression must be adapted to a mass print culture because it is not capacious enough to express the feelings and thoughts of more than a single individual."[52] Richards correctly identifies "mass print culture" and the voice of the "single individual" as spaces that these poems occupy, but Whitman and Gardette's poems also inhabit the intermediary space of the bohemians' literary coterie, which, as a space both larger than a single individual and smaller than the mass market of print, covered the same media landscape that Poe and the bluestockings had previously traversed—a media landscape that included privately circulated manuscripts and small-batch printed texts, semipublic communication at bars and literary salons, and mass-market publications that appealed to a broad readership.

Gardette's account of the genesis of "The Fire-Fiend" is set in the environment of the literary coterie. He wrote of "a discussion [that] took place between a literary friend and myself, on the subject of Poe's poetic genius," which resulted in a "challenge to [write] an imitation of Poe"—a challenge very similar to the type of performative literary production that Poe himself engaged in at the bluestockings' salons.[53] While Gardette does not reveal the identity of the "literary friend" who issued this challenge, William Winter wrote that Gardette was "conspicuous" at Pfaff's during this time, and, as Ingrid Satelmajer has written, the bohemians' bar embraced a culture "of literary production that highlight[ed] community, collaboration, and . . . improvisation."[54] Walt Whitman described this atmosphere in an unpublished poem about "The Vault at Pfaff's" where "the drinkers and laughers meet to eat and drink and carouse" while they "Bandy the jests!" and "Toss the theme from one to another!"[55] Several articles published in the *Saturday Press* similarly presented the bohemians' bar as a place of literary performance where "the text of the moment is announced, and the mouths open all about the table for hap-hazard emissions of quip, and quirk, and queer conceit, of melancholy mirth and laughing madness."[56] As during the bluestockings' era, mass-market publications like the *Saturday Press* captured a "hap-hazard" moment of literary improvisation in a semipublic setting and offered a glimpse of that experience to a wider audience through print. One editorial note from the *Saturday Press* read, "In reply to numerous communications—some of them from distant parts of the country (Peoria, etc.)—it may be well to say that Pfaff's is simply a modest Restaurant and Lager Beer Saloon . . . [that] is extensively patronized by young literary men [and] artists."[57] In faraway Ohio, when a young William Dean Howells submitted his own poems for publication in the *Saturday Press,* he felt that he had been granted honorary membership in the Pfaff's coterie. He recalled that "the Bohemian group represented New York literature to my imagination," and that publishing in the *Saturday Press* "was to be in the company of Fitz James O'Brien, Fitzhugh Ludlow, Mr. [Thomas Bailey] Aldrich, Mr. [E. C.] Stedman."[58]

Like Poe before him, *Saturday Press* editor Henry Clapp was well aware of how mass-market periodicals could extend the reach of the coterie. Following the publication of "The Fire-Fiend" and "Out of the Cradle Endlessly Rocking," Clapp developed a strategy for promoting Whitman's career that he believed would ultimately benefit all of the bohemians who published in the *Saturday Press.*[59] Part of that strategy involved asking Gardette to write poems in Whitman's style as he had previously done for Poe.[60] Four of Gardette's Whitman-inspired verses appeared pseudonymously in the *Saturday Press* in the months leading up to the release of the third edition of *Leaves of Grass;* some two-dozen other poems published under his own name, including "Golgotha: A Phantasm. After Poe" (February 11, 1860) ran in the *Saturday Press* throughout the course of the year.[61] Around the same time, Fitz-James O'Brien published "Counter-Jumps.

A Poemetina—After Walt Whitman" in the bohemians' sister publication, *Vanity Fair*, and William Winter wrote a pair of poems in Whitman's style for the *Saturday Press*.[62] In the print public sphere, these various parodies and homages all served to elevate Whitman's profile at a pivotal moment in his career: following the financial failure of the first two editions of *Leaves of Grass*, the bohemians' support for the third edition in 1860 contributed to its commercial and critical success. The support was reciprocal, as the publisher of the 1860 *Leaves of Grass* entered into talks with Henry Clapp to purchase the *Saturday Press* and provide financial stability for the struggling publication.[63] This is textbook coterie practice as, in the absence of wealthy patrons, writers work together and support one another to navigate the literary marketplace.

But as Poe also experienced, the private interactions of coterie members could damage a career as dramatically as their public exchanges could sustain it. O'Brien and Winter may have joined with Gardette in penning Whitman-inspired poems as part of Clapp's larger publicity campaign, but around the tables at Pfaff's it was a different story. Winter resented that Whitman had become the focus of the bohemian crowd, displacing Poe as the coterie's artistic center of gravity. He wrote, "Whitman, by reason of that odiferous classic, the 'Leaves of Grass,' was in possession of the local Parnassus."[64] According to biographer Robert Young, Winter took one of the parodies that he had published in the *Saturday Press* as part of the promotional apparatus for the 1860 *Leaves of Grass* and read it aloud to the Pfaff's crowd in a thinly veiled attack on Whitman:

> [One] evening when a number of the company had drifted together, Winter, in high and good humor, rose from his chair to deliver to his delighted compatriots a parody of one of Whitman's effusions. Throughout Winter's laughter-marked rendition of his parody, Whitman stared vacantly into space and sipped his ever-present brandy and water. . . . [Whitman] never forgave the satirical ridicule to which Winter had subjected his work.[65]

In print, the bohemian community worked together to elevate Whitman to the heights of Parnassus; at Pfaff's, however, it was another matter. O'Brien similarly refused to acknowledge that Whitman was the bohemians' poet laureate in a poem titled "At Pfaff's," which was printed in a small batch and circulated among the members of the underground community. The poem mentions various Pfaffians but does not specifically name them; in a privately circulated document, those identities would have been common knowledge to the intended audience. Thomas Butler Gunn, a British journalist living in New York with ties to the Pfaff's crowd, included a copy of the poem in his diary that identified Henry Clapp as "the Oldest of Men" and Ada Clare as the bearer of "the bright eyes" that light up "our little republic of wit," while Whitman is the bar's "genial philosopher" and Winter is "our Poet who suffers with blight" and "crumbles to pieces with ruin each night."[66] O'Brien's description of Winter as crumbling "with ruin" recalls the title of "Orgia: Song of a Ruined Man," a poem that Winter had published in the *Saturday Press* two weeks after Whitman's "Out of the Cradle Endlessly Rocking" appeared as "A Child's Reminiscence."[67] Soon after, Ada Clare wrote in her weekly *Saturday Press* column, "I hear Winter's 'Song of the Ruined Man' much eulogized. I cannot admire it. . . . On the contrary, Walt Whitman's 'A Child's Reminiscence' could only have been written by a poet."[68] When O'Brien named Winter as "our Poet" and Whitman as a mere "philosopher" in his poem for the Pfaff's crowd, the pushback against Clare's very public support would have been obvious.

Whitman regularly attended the salons that Clare hosted at her West 42nd Street townhouse, counting her as one of his "sturdiest defenders."[69] Clare's support for Whitman would not prove to be long-lasting, however, as her influence waned in the decade following the Civil War and she passed away in 1874. (Henry Clapp also saw his reputation decline before his death in 1875.)[70] Around the same time, Winter's career skyrocketed as he became a poet of wide renown and "the foremost drama critic of his day by 1870."[71] Winter leveraged his growing reputation to publish a posthumous edition of the poems and tales of Fitz-James O'Brien, no doubt in gratitude for his loyalty while the bohemians' leading lights shined on Whitman. O'Brien had cultivated an image as "a follower and imitator of Poe"[72]; he once wrote an homage of Poe's "Shadow: A Parable" that he said predated Poe's original, playfully arguing that Poe himself "must have seen it some where" before writing his own 1835 prose-poem.[73] Winter's advocacy for his bohemian friend reinforced this connection to Poe through a mutual defense of the charges of alcoholism leveled against both writers: "Poe died in 1849, aged forty, leaving works that fill ten closely packed volumes. No man achieves a result like that whose brain is damaged by stimulants. The same disparagement has been diffused as to Fitz-James O'Brien, that fine poet and romancer . . . whose writings I collected and published" in the 500-page *Poems and Stories of Fitz-James O'Brien* (1881), "and there are other writings of his in my possession that would make another volume of an equal size."[74] By that point in his career, Winter had grown increasingly comfortable speaking on behalf of Poe as well as O'Brien. In 1875 Winter was invited to write a commemorative poem for the dedication of the Poe Memorial in Baltimore (hailed as "by far the most beautiful" of "all the tributes to Poe inspired by the unveiling of the monument"[75]), and in 1885 he was asked again to provide a poem for the New York City Actors' Monument to Poe.[76] Other erstwhile bohemians also returned to Poe as a way to bolster their later careers; the "ten closely packed volumes" of Poe's writing that Winter referenced could easily have been either E. C. Stedman's or R. H. Stoddard's multivolume editions of Poe's works.[77]

Whitman's own efforts to latch onto Poe in the second half of the nineteenth century followed closely behind the more prominent activities of Winter, Stedman, and Stoddard. Whitman also attended the dedication of the Baltimore Poe Memorial in 1875, but, unlike Winter, he was not asked to write a poem for the occasion; instead, he published his thoughts on the event in a local paper the day after—anonymously, while quoting himself extensively throughout the piece.[78] Seven years later, following the release of Stoddard's *Select Works of Edgar Allan Poe* (1880) and Stedman's monograph *Edgar Allan Poe* (1881), Whitman republished the 1875 article under his own name as "Edgar Poe's Significance" in his collection of prose works, *Specimen Days & Collect* (1882). As Whitman publicly chased after his bohemian comrades and attempted to claim a portion of Poe's legacy for himself, he privately fumed to his confidant Horace

Traubel over a *Lippincott's* essay that Stoddard had written about his failed attempt to publish in the *Broadway Journal* in the 1840s. Stoddard blamed Poe for the forty-year-old slight, and Whitman, who had published in the *Journal* and met with Poe as part of the process, was having none of it.[79] Stoddard had reaped the rewards of editing a major collection of Poe's work, but when he publicly turned on Poe, it transported an angry Whitman back to the conflicts and disagreements of their bohemian days. "Look at Dick Stoddard: he's not only weak but malignant," Whitman said. "[L]ook at that Poe thing: it's a fair sample: it was a cowardly attack . . . worthy of Billy Winter in his palmiest days: which is about as low as you can get."[80] Traubel notes in his transcription of Whitman's comments that "he spoke with fervent fluency—rather more rapidly than usual" when discussing Stoddard and Winter, suggesting that Stoddard's attack on Poe in the late 1880s brought back memories of Winter's conflicts with Whitman in the early 1860s.[81] Whitman may also have been aware that Stoddard had defended Rufus W. Griswold over his posthumous assault on Poe's legacy—he wrote that Griswold had been "greatly maligned" and "was not the enemy of Poe"—while also furthering Griswold's legacy by publishing updated editions of *The Poets and Poetry of America* (1875) and *The Female Poets of America* (1874).[82] Griswold had built much of his career around these highly influential anthologies (which first appeared in the 1840s), in addition to a posthumous edition of Poe's work in 1850 that included an inaccurate and defamatory "Memoir of the Author." During the height of the bohemian era, the *Saturday Press* called Griswold's Poe memoir "contemptible" in its review of Sarah Helen Whitman's *Edgar Poe and His Critics* (1860).[83]

Based on comments that he made to Horace Traubel in the 1880s, Whitman similarly held in contempt the critics who maligned Poe while building their careers on the back of his labor. Whitman's comments to Traubel also reveal what appears to be either a distortion or an exaggeration of Poe's enduring fame, suggesting that Whitman viewed his own struggle to achieve lasting success through the bohemians' various reactions to Poe. He said, "The mortal offense which this New York crowd can never forgive Poe for is that he is famous—is held in great esteem wherever he is known."[84] Much of the New England literary community was still, at this time, reluctant to embrace Poe as eagerly as others had, which could mean that Whitman was thinking less about the reality of Poe's legacy and more about the continuing use to which the bohemians put Poe: whether as a model for imitation in the 1860s or a springboard for their careers as literary tastemakers in the 1870s and 1880s. Almost thirty years after the fact, the context that had initially encouraged Whitman to identify with Poe when writing "Out of the Cradle Endlessly Rocking" came rushing back, leading him to conflate his own short-lived fame among the bohemians with what he presents as Poe's enduring renown. All of which begs the question: who does the "New York crowd" refuse to forgive—Poe, whose legacy they have embraced since the 1850s, or Whitman, whom they briefly supported and now largely overlook? Ultimately, Whitman confided to Traubel that literary coteries are fraught and messy alliances, a necessary evil for writers eager to establish their careers: "But do you know, Horace, there's a great deal more in this case than is generally known, than you could know, than anyone could know who had not been in the thick of the fray."[85] For both Whitman and Poe, trying to make it as a writer in antebellum New York required, in addition to the expected activities of composing in solitude and appealing to a broad public audience, wading into "the thick of the fray" with other aspiring writers.

Notes

1. See Eliza Richards, *Gender and the Poetics of Reception in Poe's Circle* (New York: Cambridge University Press, 2004); Mary G. De Jong, "Lines from a Partly Published Drama: The Romance of Frances Sargent Osgood and Edgar Allan Poe," in *Patrons and Protégées*, ed. Shirley Marchalonis (New Brunswick, NJ: Rutgers University Press, 1988); and Anne Boyd Rioux, "Lions and Bluestockings," in *Edgar Allan Poe in Context*, ed. Kevin J. Hayes (New York: Cambridge University Press, 2012). The term "bluestocking" itself was an homage—and, at times, a backhanded compliment—to the feminist intellectuals of the Blue Stockings Society of eighteenth-century England.
2. Lytle Shaw, *Frank O'Hara: The Poetics of Coterie* (Iowa City: University of Iowa Press, 2006), 4–6.
3. David Dowling, *The Business of Literary Circles in Nineteenth-Century America* (New York: Palgrave, 2011), 2.
4. James L. Ford identifies Poe as the bohemians' "idol" in his "Good by Bohemia," *The New York Tribune*, January 11, 1922; Eugene Lalor calls him their "spiritual guide" in "The Literary Bohemians of New York City in the Mid-Nineteenth Century" (PhD diss., St. John's University, 1977), 21; and David S. Reynolds says he was their "patron saint" in *Walt Whitman's America: A Cultural Biography* (New York: Knopf, 1995), 378.
5. Eliza Richards, "Poe's Lyrical Media: The Raven's Returns," in *Poe and the Remapping of Antebellum Print Culture*, ed. J. Gerald Kennedy and Jerome McGann (Baton Rouge: Louisiana State University Press, 2012), 216.
6. It appeared as "A Child's Reminiscence" in *The New York Saturday Press*, December 24, 1859, http://lehigh.edu/pfaffs.
7. See Michael Robertson, *Worshipping Walt: The Whitman Disciples* (Princeton, NJ: Princeton University Press, 2008).
8. See Mary Loeffelholz, "Stedman, Whitman, and the Transatlantic Canonization of American Poetry," in *Whitman among the Bohemians*, ed. Joanna Levin and Edward Whitley (Iowa City: University of Iowa Press, 2014), 213–230.
9. Pierre Bourdieu, *The Rules of Art: Genesis and Structure of the Literary Field*, trans. Susan Emanuel (Stanford, CA: Stanford University Press, 1995), 51–52.
10. John Evelev, "The Literary Profession," in *Edgar Allan Poe in Context*, ed. Kevin J. Hayes (Cambridge, UK: Cambridge University Press, 2012), 167. See also Meredith McGill, *American Literature and the Culture of Reprinting, 1834–1853* (Philadelphia: University of Pennsylvania Press, 2003), 187.
11. See Steven Kale, *French Salons: High Society and Political Sociability from the Old Regime to the Revolution of 1848* (Baltimore: The Johns Hopkins University Press, 2004).
12. See Dowling, The *Business of Literary Circles in Nineteenth-Century America*, 17–18.
13. See Burton R. Pollin, "Poe, Freeman Hunt, and Four Unrecorded Reviews of Poe's Works," *Texas Studies in Literature and Language* 16, no. 2 (1974): 305–313, and J. A. Leo Lemay, "Poe's 'The Business Man': Its Context and Satire of Franklin's Autobiography," *Poe Studies*

15, no. 2 (1982): 29–37. Poe wrote elsewhere, "An editor is usually either one of a *coterie* tacitly, if not avowedly pledged to the support of its own members. . . . It too often happens that a false sense of what is due to the chivalries of good-fellowship will induce him, unmindful of the loftier chivalries of truth, to put what he thinks the best face upon every work of every one of this number. . . . We shall thus frown down all conspiracies to foist inanity upon the public consideration at the expense of every person of talent who is not a member of a coterie in power." See Edgar Allan Poe, "American Novel-Writing," *The Literary Examiner and Western Monthly Review* 1 (August 1839): 316–320, https://www.eapoe.org/works/essays/lewq3908.htm.

14. Rioux, "Lions and Bluestockings," 131.
15. The character of Signora Psyche Zenobia in Poe's "How to Write a Blackwood Article" is similarly a parody of bluestocking women, belonging as she does to the "P.R.E.T.T.Y.B.L.U.E.B.A.T.C.H—that is to say, Philadelphia, Regular, Exchange, Tea, Total, Young, Belles, Lettres, Universal, Experimental, Bibliographical, Association, To, Civilize, Humanity" (M 2: 337).
16. Charles Baudelaire, *Baudelaire on Poe: Critical Papers*, trans. and ed. Lois and E. Francis Hyslop, Jr. (State College, PA: Bald Eagle Press, 1952), 122–123, italics in original.
17. Deborah Heller, "Bluestocking Salons and the Public Sphere," *Eighteenth-Century Life* 22, no. 2 (1998): 72.
18. Quoted in Richards, *Gender and the Poetics of Reception in Poe's Circle*, 79. Italics in original.
19. Quoted in N. P. Willis, *The Prose Works of N. P. Willis* (Philadelphia: Henry C. Baird, 1852), 775–776.
20. See, most recently, Tricia Lootens, *The Political Poetess: Victorian Femininity, Race, and the Legacy of Separate Spheres* (Princeton, NJ: Princeton University Press, 2017).
21. Quoted in Mary De Jong, "'Read Here Thy Name Concealed': Frances Osgood's Poems on Parting with Edgar Allan Poe," *Poe Studies* 34, no. 1–2 (2001): 27–28. By embedding Poe's name inside her sonnet, Osgood encounters two formal problems that she must address. The first is that a sonnet has fourteen lines, and there are only thirteen letters in the name "Edgar Allan Poe." She solves this problem by having the final line offer an invitation to reread the poem in order to find the hidden name: "Read here *thy* name concealed & now in truth we part." The second problem is that the length of the line—iambic pentameter for the first thirteen lines, hexameter in the fourteenth—only gives her enough room to spell out "Edgar All" before she runs out of space and has to start the pattern over again to complete the letters "an Poe." Whether intentional or not, this allows her poem to divide into the octave (in the eight lines that spell out "Edgar All") and sestet (the five lines of "an Poe" plus the concluding invitation to reread the poem) of a Petrarchan sonnet. Here is the complete poem, with the Petrarchan volta falling in its appointed place at line nine where she begins again at the end of the line with the remaining five letters of Poe's name:

> Oh! thou who canst with wizard skill ***e***mbalm
> In the rich amber of thy ***d***elicate verse
> Thine airy love with ***g***enii-woven charm
> Safe from the evil eye ***a***nd from all harm
> Of coarse, profane ***r***egard—I—in thy terse
> Quaint melody ***A***h! Thou didst teach the spell

Have traced *l*ove's fair & winged dream too well
And *l*o! so fondly doth this heart still dwell
Upon the Past—*our* Past!—that I, *a*ltho'
It break—must bless that being if *n*ear thee
She become all *I* could but *p*ray to be
May she watch truly *o*'er that haughty heart
Scathed *e*ver by the lighting-wing of woe
Read here *thy* name concealed & now in truth we part.

22. Mary Loeffelholz, *From School to Salon: Reading Nineteenth-Century American Women's Poetry* (Princeton, NJ: Princeton University Press, 2004), 162.
23. De Jong, "Lines from a Partly Published Drama," 32.
24. Frances Sargent Osgood, "Ida Grey," *Graham's Magazine* 27 (August 1845): 84.
25. Osgood, "Ida Grey," 84.
26. Osgood, "Ida Grey," 84.
27. Frances Sargent Osgood, "Caprice," *Graham's Magazine* 28 (February 1846): 71.
28. *The Broadway Journal* 2, no. 10 (September 13, 1845): 148.
29. See Kenneth Silverman, *Edgar A. Poe: Mournful and Never-ending Remembrance* (New York: HarperCollins, 1991), 290–315; and Sidney P. Moss, *Poe's Literary Battles: The Critic in the Context of his Literary Milieu* (Durham, NC: Duke University Press, 1963), 190–248.
30. William Dean Howells, "First Impressions of Literary New York," *Harper's New Monthly Magazine* (June 1895): 63.
31. See Joanna Levin, *Bohemia in America, 1858–1920* (Stanford, CA: Stanford University Press, 2009), 13–69.
32. Robert J. Scholnick, *Edmund Clarence Stedman* (Boston: Twayne, 1977), 25.
33. Elizabeth Stoddard, *The Selected Letters of Elizabeth Stoddard*, ed. Jennifer Putzi and Elizabeth Stockton (Iowa City: University of Iowa Press, 2012), 116. R. H. Stoddard, *Recollections, Personal and Literary* (New York: A.S. Barnes and Company, 1903), 265.
34. Lillian Woodman Aldrich, *Crowding Memories* (Boston: Houghton, Mifflin, 1920), 15.
35. As the actress Rose Eytinge recalled, "There, of a Sunday evening, could be found a group of men and women, all of whom had distinguished themselves in various avenues,—in literature, art, music, drama." See Rose Eytinge, *The Memories of Rose Eytinge: Being Recollections & Observations of Men, Women, and Events, during Half a Century* (New York: Frederick A. Stokes, 1905), 21. For Clare's involvement in the Anne Lynch salons, see S. Frederick Starr, *The Life and Times of Louis Moreau Gottschalk* (New York: Oxford University Press, 1995), 250.
36. Ada Clare, "Thoughts and Things VII," *The New York Saturday Press*, December 10, 1859.
37. Thomas Butler Gunn quoted in Joanna Levin, "'Freedom for Women from Conventional Lies': The 'Queen of Bohemia' and the Feminist Feuilleton," in *Whitman among the Bohemians*, ed. Joanna Levin and Edward Whitley (Iowa City: University of Iowa Press, 2014), 92.
38. Quoted in Stephanie M. Blalock, *"GO TO PFAFF'S!": The History of a Restaurant and Lager Beer Salon* (Bethlehem, PA: Lehigh University Press, 2014), 37–38.
39. William Winter, *Old Friends: Being Literary Recollections of Other Days* (New York: Moffat, Yard, and Company, 1909), 296. Whitman quoted in Horace Traubel, *With Walt Whitman in Camden, vol. 4, January 21 to April 7*, ed. Sculley Bradley (Philadelphia: University of

Pennsylvania Press, 1953), 173–174, https://whitmanarchive.org/criticism/disciples/traubel/WWWiC/4/whole.html.
40. Winter, *Old Friends*, 296.
41. Aldrich quoted in Ferris Greenslet, *The Life of Thomas Bailey Aldrich* (Boston: Houghton Mifflin, 1908), 192. T. B. Aldrich, "At the Café," *New York Saturday Press*, December 24, 1859.
42. Anne Lynch lived at 116 Waverly Place (PL: 484), while Pfaff's was, in its bohemian heyday, at 647 Broadway. See Blalock, *"GO TO PFAFF'S!,"* 5.
43. Richard H. Stoddard, "Edgar Allan Poe," *Lippincott's Monthly Magazine* (January 1889): 108.
44. Henry Murger, *Scènes de la Vie de Bohème* (Paris: Michel Lévy Frères, 1851); Charles Astor Bristed, "The Gypsies of Art: Translated for *The Knickerbocker* from Henry Murger's 'Scenes de La Boheme,'" *Knickerbocker* 41, no. 3 (1853): 217. See Jerrold Seigel, *Bohemian Paris: Culture, Politics, and the Boundaries of Bourgeois Life, 1830–1930* (New York: Viking, 1986), 22–32. Seigel mentions the 1843 play *Les Bohémiens de Paris* (23), but there was no English translation and its impact appears to have been localized to France.
45. Fitz-James O'Brien, "The Bohemian," *Harper's New Monthly Magazine* (July 1855); rpt. in Wayne R. Kime, ed., *Behind the Curtain: Selected Fiction of Fitz-James O'Brien, 1853–1860* (Newark: University of Delaware Press, 2011), 53–72. Francis Wolle, in his biography *Fitz-James O'Brien: A Literary Bohemian of the Eighteen-Fifties* (Boulder: University of Colorado Press, 1944), identifies numerous parallels between works by O'Brien and Poe (39–45, 58, 63, 81, 152, 162–163).
46. Winter, *Old Friends*, 67.
47. Winter, *Old Friends*, 177.
48. Edmund Clarence Stedman, introduction to *Recollections, Personal and Literary*, by Stoddard, xii.
49. In addition to Charles Frederick Briggs, the actor John Brougham also knew Poe during the 1840s and frequented Pfaff's in the 1850s and 1860s. See Winter, *Old Friends*, 35; and Clara Dargan Maclean, "Some Memorials of Edgar Allan Poe," *Frank Leslie's Popular Monthly* (April 1891): 460.
50. Edgar Allan Poe [Charles D. Gardette], "The Fire-Fiend. A Nightmare," *New York Saturday Press*, November 19, 1859.
51. Whitman, "A Child's Reminiscence."
52. Richards, "Poe's Lyrical Media," 217, 220–221.
53. Charles Desmarais Gardette and Robert Shelton Mackenzie, *The Whole Truth in the Question of "The Fire Fiend"* (Philadelphia: Sherman & Co., 1864), 22.
54. Winter, *Old Friends*, 65; Ingrid Satelmajer, "Publishing Pfaff's: Henry Clapp and Poetry in the *Saturday Press*," in *Whitman among the Bohemians*, 37.
55. Walt Whitman, *Notebooks and Unpublished Prose Manuscripts*, vol. 1, ed. Edward Grier (New York: New York University Press, 1963), 454–455.
56. "Pfaff's," *New York Saturday Press*, December 3, 1859.
57. "Pfaff's," *New York Saturday Press*, March 13, 1860.
58. Howells, "First Impressions of Literary New York," 63.
59. See Amanda Gailey, "Walt Whitman and the King of Bohemia: The Poet in the Saturday Press," *Walt Whitman Quarterly Review* 25, no. 4 (2008), 143–166. Gailey shows how the *Press* ran close to fifty items by or about Whitman in 1860 as part of a concerted media campaign (144).

60. See "Henry Clapp, Jr. to Walt Whitman, 14 May 1860," *The Walt Whitman Archive*, ed. Ed Folsom and Kenneth M. Price, accessed November 27, 2017, https://whitmanarchive.org/biography/correspondence/tei/med.00331.html.
61. George Peirce Clark "'Saerasmid,' an Early Promoter of Walt Whitman," *American Literature* 27, no. 2 (May 1955): 259–262. Charles D. Gardette, "Golgotha: A Phantasm. [After Poe]," *New York Saturday Press*, February 11, 1860.
62. "The Torch-Bearers," *New York Saturday Press*, July 17, 1860; and "Before Him. A Picture. (After Walt Whitman)," *New York Saturday Press*, October 20, 1860.
63. Gailey, "Walt Whitman and the King of Bohemia," 149–151.
64. Winter, *Old Friends*, 89–90.
65. Robert Young, *Frosty but Kindly: A Biography of William Winter* (manuscript, 1956), Folger Shakespeare Library, Washington, DC, 62–63.
66. Fitz-James O'Brien, "AT PFAFF'S," in Thomas Butler Gunn, *Thomas Butler Gunn Diaries, vol. 13, June 1–September 22, 1860*, Missouri Historical Society, http://mohistory.org/collections/item/resource:170078. (O'Brien's printed poem appears between pages 72 and 73 of Gunn's diary.)
67. William Winter, "Orgia: The Song of a Ruined Man," *New York Saturday Press*, January 7, 1860.
68. Ada Clare, "Thoughts and Things," *New York Saturday Press*, January 14, 1860.
69. Whitman quoted in Horace Traubel, *With Walt Whitman in Camden, vol. 3, November 1, 1888–January 20, 1889*, ed. Sculley Bradley (New York: Mitchell Kennerley, 1914), 117, https://whitmanarchive.org/criticism/disciples/traubel/WWWiC/3/whole.html.
70. Justin Martin, *Rebel Souls: Walt Whitman and America's First Bohemians* (Boston: Da Capo, 2014), 245–262.
71. Bruce A. McConachie, *Melodramatic Formations: American Theatre and Society, 1820–1870* (Iowa City, IA: University of Iowa Press, 1992), 235.
72. Wolle, *Fitz-James O'Brien*, 45.
73. Fitz-James O'Brien, "Fragments from an Unpublished Magazine," *American Whig Review* 16 (1852): 566.
74. Winter, *Old Friends*, 34–35.
75. Eugene L. Didier, "The Poe Cult," *The Bookman* (December 1902): 338. For a transcript of Winter's poem, see Eugene L. Didier, "The Poe Monument," *New York Daily Tribune*, November 18, 1875.
76. William Winter, "Poe. From Stanzas Read at the Dedication of the Actors' Monument to Edgar Allan Poe," in *A Library of American Literature*, vol. 9, ed. Edmund Clarence Stedman and Ellen Mackay Hutchinson (New York: Charles L. Webster, 1889), 360–361.
77. Along with George Edward Woodberry, Stedman edited the ten-volume, *Works of Edgar Allan Poe* (Chicago: Stone and Kimball, 1894–95). Stoddard edited his own *Works of Edgar Allan Poe* a decade earlier (New York: A. C. Armstrong and Son, 1884).
78. "Walt Whitman at the Poe Funeral," *Washington Evening Star*, November 18, 1875.
79. Stoddard, "Edgar Allan Poe."
80. Whitman quoted in Traubel, *With Walt Whitman in Camden*, 4:23.
81. Traubel, *With Walt Whitman in Camden*, 4:173.
82. Stoddard, *Recollections, Personal and Literary*, 153–154.
83. Review of "Edgar Poe and His Critics," *New York Saturday Press*, February 25, 1860.
84. Traubel, *With Walt Whitman in Camden*, 4:173.
85. Traubel, *With Walt Whitman in Camden*, 4:173.

Bibliography

Bourdieu, Pierre. *The Rules of Art: Genesis and Structure of the Literary Field.* Translated by Susan Emanuel. Stanford, CA: Stanford University Press, 1995.

Boyd, Anne E. "Lions and Bluestockings." In *Edgar Allan Poe in Context*, edited by Kevin J. Hayes, 129–137. New York: Cambridge University Press, 2012.

De Jong, Mary G. "Lines from a Partly Published Drama: The Romance of Frances Sargent Osgood and Edgar Allan Poe." In *Patrons and Protégées*, edited by Shirley Marchalonis, 31–58. New Brunswick, NJ: Rutgers University Press, 1988.

Dowling, David. *The Business of Literary Circles in Nineteenth-Century America.* New York: Palgrave, 2011.

Gailey, Amanda. "Walt Whitman and the King of Bohemia: The Poet in the *Saturday Press*." *Walt Whitman Quarterly Review* 25, no. 4 (2008): 143–166.

Levin, Joanna. *Bohemia in America, 1858–1920.* Stanford, CA: Stanford University Press, 2009.

Levin, Joanna, and Edward Whitley. *Whitman among the Bohemians.* Iowa City: University of Iowa Press, 2014.

Moss, Sidney P. *Poe's Literary Battles: The Critic in the Context of his Literary Milieu.* Durham, NC: Duke University Press, 1963.

Richards, Eliza. *Gender and the Poetics of Reception in Poe's Circle.* New York: Cambridge University Press, 2004.

Richards, Eliza. "Poe's Lyrical Media: The Raven's Returns." In *Poe and the Remapping of Antebellum Print Culture*, edited by J. Gerald Kennedy and Jerome McGann, 200–226. Baton Rouge: Louisiana State University Press, 2012.

CHAPTER 34

POE AND HIS GLOBAL ADVOCATES

EMRON ESPLIN

To claim that no other US writer has had as much influence on world literature as Edgar Allan Poe is not to practice hyperbole. To stake this claim in the active voice that it deserves: Poe is the most influential US writer in the world. The United States has certainly produced other writers whose works have influenced literature on a global scale, but we (as scholars, readers, consumers) would be hard-pressed to find another US author whose global presence is as broad and whose international impact resonates as deeply as Poe's. Poe is ubiquitous. His works and his image manifest themselves in highbrow (literature, critical theory, art, classical music, and cinema), popular (B movies, T-shirts, comic books, various genres of popular music, and all sorts of kitsch), and social media cultures (YouTube videos, blogs, Twitter accounts, and countless memes) across the world. Most Poe audiences—regardless of the language(s) in which they access Poe—come to Poe in more than one way, and these varied avenues to Poe speak to the lasting power of his works themselves and to the rejuvenating power of what translation studies scholar André Lefevere calls "refractions," "rewrites," or "rewritings" of literary works. Lefevere argues that translators, literary critics, creators of anthologies, and literary historians are all rewriters of texts and that their works or rewritings wield significant power that keeps "original" works or source texts and their authors alive in the literary marketplace and in our literary canons.[1] Linking this type of rewriting with the creative responses to Poe that poets and fiction writers have created since Poe's death in 1849 reveals the almost incalculable strands of influence Poe's works and his persona have generated.

Although the scope of this essay does not allow me to prove quantitatively my claim about Poe's global impact with raw data, a brief list of the distinct threads of Poe's influence on world literature and culture, along with my analysis, substantiate my declaration. Poe's invention of the detective genre, alone, puts him on a short list of globally influential US writers. The influence of Poe's Dupin tales and other stories of ratiocination, the weight of his tales of terror, the power of his pre-Freudian explorations of the human psyche, the resonance (both formal and narrative) of his melancholy poetry, the timeliness of his attempts at early science fiction, and the longevity of his theory of effect on the way we think about short fiction all combine to make a clear case for Poe's position as the most influential US writer.[2] In short, Poe came fairly early in the US literary tradition, he wrote in more genres than many influential US writers, and, importantly, his disparate works have led to his being championed by some of the most significant writers in various global literary traditions from the middle of the nineteenth century until now.

My argument rests on this last point—on the championing of Poe and the advocacy for his literature that numerous writers who are considered important, or even essential, to their own literary traditions have adopted from the late 1840s onward. Poe influenced these writers, but they also influenced him (or, stated more directly, they influenced his reputation and his overall image) by giving his work and his life special attention in their own literary corpora.[3] These literary stars act as advocates who "plead for," "speak on behalf of," "support, recommend, [and] speak favorably of" Poe.[4] Their advocacy continually refreshes and maintains Poe's image while spreading Poe's work across divides of both time and space.

Considering the reciprocal relationship between Poe and his global advocates allows us to reread the opening paragraph of Rufus Griwold's now infamous obituary for Poe as ironic or unintentional foreshadowing:

> EDGAR ALLAN POE is dead. He died in Baltimore the day before yesterday. This announcement will startle many, but few will be grieved by it. The poet was well known, personally or by reputation, in all this country; he had readers in England, and in several of the states of Continental Europe; but he had few or no friends; and the regrets for his death will be suggested principally by the consideration that in him literary art has lost one of its most brilliant but erratic stars.[5]

Several positive obituaries and rebuttals to Griswold's caustic commentary demonstrate that Poe did, in fact, have plenty of friends when he died in 1849.[6] However, Griswold's nod to Poe's growing reputation outside of the United States unwittingly points toward the friendships that would later salvage Poe's reputation from Griswold's character assassination. These "foreign" friends or advocates treated Poe's work with a seriousness and his image with a reverence that, in the former case, would not be seen in his own country until at least the modernist period and, in the latter case, might never be equaled on Poe's home turf. Many of them were vivid literary stars who brought a stability to Poe's reputation, raising it to the astral level regardless of Griswold's attempt to diminish Poe's brilliance by qualifying it as erratic.

In the following pages, I offer both a sweeping and a specific analysis of Poe and his global advocates. In the first section, I examine in broad terms, beginning with France and then glossing East Asia and Latin America, how Poe's writings and his persona resonated with key literary figures from disparate nations throughout the globe, how these writers became strong advocates for Poe, and how their advocacy made Poe a central figure in many of their specific literary traditions and a cardinal presence on the global literary map. For most of this section, I approach authors from literary and linguistic traditions outside of my own training and expertise, and although I cite some of the primary texts in their source languages, most of the scholarship with which I engage in this section is in English. This section hints at the extensive reach of both Poe's global influence and the world's influence on Poe, inherently reveals the linguistic limits of any single-authored project on Poe's global presence, and demonstrates that the significance of the relationships between Poe and these particular writers has reached a level in which entire bodies of literary criticism in the source languages and in English are dedicated to their analysis. I then offer a case study of three particular writers who were Poe advocates in the Río de la Plata region of South America, a literary and linguistic tradition I know well, as a detailed example of Poe's reciprocal influence and the positive power of his advocates. I conclude by examining the ancient concept of astral influence, describing these advocates as literary stars, and arguing that, in both the broad and the specific cases, Poe's current global reputation relies at least as much on the radiance of the advocacy as on the brilliance of his original works.

Global Advocates from France and Beyond

Poe's global advocates have received increased attention in the English-language academy since the middle of the twentieth century. While T. S. Eliot wondered aloud about what the French saw in Poe in a Library of Congress lecture in 1948 and walked away seeing Poe with new eyes,[7] other scholars have produced several important treatises on Poe and France over the last century, including Célestin Pierre Cambiaire's 1927 *The Influence of Edgar Allan Poe in France* (which predates Eliot's musings), Patrick F. Quinn's 1957 *The French Face of Edgar Poe*, and many works by Lois Davis Vines.[8] Poe's relationship with both Spanish American letters and peninsular Spanish literature has received serious treatment since 1934, when John Eugene Englekirk published what was, at the time, an exhaustive book on Poe and his Spanish-speaking advocates on both sides of the Atlantic—*Edgar Allan Poe in Hispanic Literature*.[9] In more recent decades, several edited collections have reiterated the importance of the French and Spanish/Spanish American Poe connections while casting broader nets that demonstrate Poe's resounding influence and its reciprocal responses across Asia, the Americas, Europe, northern Africa, and various islands throughout the world's oceans: Benjamin Franklin Fisher's 1986 *Poe and Our Times: Influences and Affinities*; Lois Davis Vines's 1999 *Poe Abroad: Influence, Reputation, Affinities*; Barbara Cantalupo's 2012 *Poe's Pervasive Influence*; and my and Margarida Vale de Gato's 2014 *Translated Poe* all expose and examine Poe's impact on disparate world sites and literary traditions and the enormity and intensity of the efforts of his global advocates.[10]

French poet Charles Baudelaire serves as the archetypal Poe advocate. Although not Poe's first foreign reader or his first French translator, Baudelaire took to Poe with an alacrity rarely seen in a relationship between two literary giants. Their literary affinity became *the* relationship that delivered Poe to a truly global audience, and it still serves as the most powerful example of a major literary figure in his own right dedicating a significant amount of time, effort, and love to the spreading of Poe's work and the cultivation of his image. Literary advocacy can take many forms, and in the case between Baudelaire and Poe, we could describe Baudelaire as a disciple, a translator, and a biographer/literary critic of Poe—all particular parts that other Poe advocates tend to play as well, although not every advocate adopts all three roles.

Baudelaire's Poe discipleship might best be captured in the oft-quoted passage from *Mon cœur mis à nu* [*My Heart Laid Bare*] in which he resolved: "Faire tous les matins ma *prière à Dieu, réservoir de toute force et de toute justice, à mon père, à Mariette et à Poe*, comme intercesseurs;" ["To pray every morning to God, *the source of all power and all justice; to my father, to Mariette and to Poe*, as intercessors."][11] This resolution, made during Baudelaire's final years of life, demonstrates both his intimate relationship with Poe (as he places the dead author on the same level as his own dead father and his family's deceased servant who had cared for him in his youth) and his elevation of Poe to the very position which Baudelaire himself had spent his adult life fulfilling *for* Poe—the role of the advocate. The *Oxford English Dictionary*'s first and oldest definition of the noun "advocate" describes the word in clearly religious terms as follows: "1. *Christian Church*. A person or agent believed to intercede between God and sinners; *spec.* Christ or the Virgin Mary."[12] While Baudelaire places Poe in the position of a spiritual advocate as an intermediary between himself and God, Baudelaire had already placed himself as a literary advocate, first between Poe and France and then between Poe and the world, for almost two decades according to the *OED*'s more common definition of the term: "Advocate: 4. *gen*. a. A person who pleads for or speaks on behalf of another; a person who supports, recommends, or speaks favorably of another."[13]

Baudelaire's advocacy for Poe is most visible through his massive translation project of Poe's prose and his treatment of Poe's persona in his biographical sketches of the US writer. As Vines notes, "[b]etween 1848 and his premature death in 1867, Baudelaire published translations of forty-four of Poe's tales, *The Narrative of Arthur Gordon Pym*, *Eureka*, and other prose pieces while continuing to write" his own works.[14] He also wrote a lengthy biographical piece on Poe that opened his famous 1856 collection of Poe translations, *Histoires extraordinaires*.[15] In all, the French poet "devoted" a total of "1,063 pages [. . .] to Poe."[16] In short, Baudelaire maintained a career within a career as a Poe advocate, and the global impact of his Poe advocacy is incalculable. The various essays in *Poe Abroad* and *Translated Poe* reiterate how Baudelaire, his translations, and/or his writings on Poe's biography served as founding elements of Poe's rising reputation across Europe (especially in Portugal, Spain, and Romania) and the Americas (from Mexico to Argentina, from Nicaragua to Brazil, and most literary traditions in-between). Each of these literary polysystems embraced Poe, but by comparing story titles, which stories appear (and often in which order), and basic details from Poe biographies available in these places in the late nineteenth and early twentieth centuries, we know that this Poe is primarily Baudelaire's Poe. As Poe's primary advocate, he also served as a filter that influenced which type of Poe these traditions initially received and which type of Poe they originally revered. Even in the twenty-first century, Baudelaire's proclivity for the darker, guilt-ridden, or mysterious Poe tales that he published in *Histoires extraordinaires* and *Nouvelles histoires extraordinaires* still reveals itself through the way contemporary readers and scholars view Poe in these traditions.

Staying closer to Baudelaire's home, his work with Poe also brought about profound effects on several French writers who wrote in his wake—especially Stéphane Mallarmé and Paul Valéry. Mallarmé continued the Poe translation project where Baudelaire had left off and translated a small number of Poe's poems into verse and a large number into prose.[17] In another move of discipleship, he purportedly moved to London with the expressed purpose of improving his English so that he could better understand Poe's works.[18] Mallarmé's own poem, "Le tombeau d'Edgar Poe," advocates for Poe by chastising Poe's "blasphemous" detractors in his and Mallarmé's own century and by marking eternity as Poe's territory.[19] Valéry, in contrast, was more interested in Poe as thinker and gravitated toward pieces such as "The Philosophy of Composition," the Dupin tales, and *Eureka*. His own *Monsieur Teste* develops a character who can be read as an extension or exaggeration of Poe's C. Auguste Dupin or as an attempt at capturing self-consciousness.[20] By approaching Poe's thoughts on thought rigorously, Valéry acts as a different kind of Poe advocate who assigns a seriousness to Poe that, as we have already seen with Eliot's "From Poe to Valéry," affects Poe's reputation and his standing back in his own country.

In short, France was and is a special place for Poe advocacy, and this first wave, or set of three waves, of French advocacy for Poe functions as a clear example of how translation studies theorist Itamar Even-Zohar describes the integration of "translated literature" into a "central position" in a particular "literary polysystem."[21] Even-Zohar argues that

> to say that translated literature maintains a central position in the literary polysystem means that it participates actively in shaping the center of the polysystem. In such a situation it is by and large an integral part of innovatory forces, and as such likely to be identified with major events in literary history while these are taking place. This implies that in this situation no clear-cut distinction is maintained between "original" and "translated" writings, and that often it is the leading writers (or members of the avant-garde who are about to become leading writers) who produce the most conspicuous or appreciated translations.[22]

The overwhelming success of Baudelaire's translations of Poe inserted Poe firmly into the French literary tradition, making Poe (not just Baudelaire) influential on Mallarmé, Valéry, and the French Symbolists. These latter writers' work as Poe translators, as poets, and as thinkers further wrote Poe into the French literary polysystem, where his writings and persona continue to influence new generations of French writers. We cannot, however, separate this Poe influence from these "leading writers" who did happen to be "members of the avant-garde who . . . bec[a]me leading writers."[23] In other words, Poe–Baudelaire–Mallarmé–Valéry are so entangled that it can be difficult to distinguish between Poe's influence per se on French literature and art versus Poe's influence via his three most famous French advocates. One thing, however, remains certain: without the advocacy there would be no French Poe. A Poe *in* France would certainly exist, but Poe's position as a writer central to the French literary tradition relies on the pointed and painstaking advocacy of these three writers who, themselves, form essential parts of the French canon.[24]

The early start date, deep national impact, and widespread global influence of Poe's relationship with his French advocates make this particular example of Poe advocacy remarkable, but Poe's good fortune with significant writers on the global scene is not singular to France. Essential writers in several disparate literary traditions discovered (some through the French and some on their own), enjoyed, and advocated for Poe. In some cases, these advocates played more than one part—translator, biographer, literary critic, anthologizer, poet, fiction writer—in their advocacy for Poe, whereas in other circumstances individual advocates adopted single roles. *Poe Abroad* and *Translated Poe* demonstrate time after time how Poe influenced important literary figures and how these writers then became Poe advocates in numerous ways and at various levels of intensity.

In the rest of Europe and in Russia, important national writers continually advocated for Poe. Elvira Osipova describes Fyodor Dostoyevsky's publication of Dmitry Mikhailovsky's Russian translations of "The Black Cat" and "The Tell-Tale Heart" in the former's magazine *Vremya* as an important "turning point" in Poe's well-documented Russian reception,[25] and both Osipova and Eloise M. Boyle examine the reciprocal relationship between Poe and the Russian Symbolist poets Konstantin Bal'mont and Valery Brjusov.[26] Liviu Cotrău calls two of Poe's early translators in Romania—Mihai Eminescu and Ion Luca Caragiale—"Romania's best poet and best playwright, respectively" and demonstrates how these authors both translated Poe via Baudelaire.[27] This early interest by important Romanian authors in a French Poe cast the US writer as a significant figure and led to an extensive tradition of Poe translation and retranslation in Romania that has flourished throughout the twentieth and twenty-first centuries.[28] Margarida Vale de Gato examines how Fernando Pessoa, "the leading figure of Portuguese modernism," continually returned to Poe "in his prolific unpublished papers" and published three of his translations of Poe's poems.[29] And this list could continue. Whether early in Poe's global reception (e.g., Baudelaire), much later in that reception (e.g., the postmodern German writer Arno Schmidt), or somewhere in between (e.g., late nineteenth-century Swedish writers Ola Hansson and August Strindberg), many European writers who were key movers in their own national literary traditions "supported" and "spoke for" Poe by translating, responding to, and/or rewriting his works.

Poe's influence in East Asia began later than his influence in Europe, and although that influence might seem less reciprocal than the Poe–Europe relationship (with the influence running from Poe to the local writer rather than from the East Asian writer back to Poe's reputation), Japan stands out as one site of two-way influence and powerful Poe advocacy.[30] Takayuki Tatsumi demonstrates Poe's lasting influence in Japan from the Meiji period (1868–1912) through the contemporary Heisei period, noting that Poe was particularly influential during the twentieth century and that Japanese artists of that century actively responded to Poe rather than passively receiving his influence: "from the Taisho period (1912–1926) through the Showa period (1926–1989), Poe was deeply imbibed, further developed, and creatively rewritten by a number of talented Japanese writers."[31] Along this path, Poe was privileged enough to be translated or adapted by "the distinguished novelist Aeba Kōson" and "noted journalist" Morita Shiken during the earlier Meiji period as a part of Japan's major shift from archaic, formal written expression to modern, conversational writing;[32] to be translated by Sato Haruo and Tanizaki Jun'Ichiro and rewritten by Akutagawa Ryūnosuke—all "major Romantic and even decadent writers of the Taisho period"[33]—and to be taken up by the popular detective writer Edogawa Rampo of the Showa period, who "established the Japanese literary subgenre of detective fiction" and whose penname references Poe.[34] Tatsumi clearly demonstrates the reciprocal relationship between Poe and Rampo in specific terms that we can apply to the Poe–Japan relationship more generally: "While it is true that Poe's arabesque, grotesque, and ratiocinative tales exerted great influence upon Rampo's Ero-Gro-Nonsense detective fiction, it is also true that Rampo's powerful and creative *misreadings* of his precursor compel us today to reread the earlier tradition through the prism of his modern re-creations."[35] Poe has influenced several of Japan's important writers, these writers have advocated for his work (particularly his fiction), and their own work now influences how the contemporary Japanese audience reads Poe.

Significant writers from various nations in Latin America have also adopted Poe into their literary systems and served as his faithful advocates. At several moments over the last one hundred and forty years or so, the literary relationships between specific Latin American writers and Poe have been nearly as productive as the reciprocal or symbiotic relationship between Poe and Baudelaire. Not surprisingly, some of the earliest relationships between Poe and his Latin American advocates were also mediated by Baudelaire, but scholars have demonstrated that Poe's long-term connections with the Spanish American literary tradition rely on a three-headed source of Poe in English, French, and Spanish and that his relationship with Brazilian letters includes English-, French-, and Portuguese-language texts.[36] Poe's presence in Brazil, as Carlos Daghlian argues, "developed independently from the American author's renown in the Spanish-language countries of the continent[,]" and it began with the "good fortune of being discovered by Brazil's most outstanding writer, Joaquim Maria Machado de Assis."[37] Machado translated Poe's "The Raven" in 1883, and both the bird and its author have been significant figures in Brazilian literature ever since. While Machado introduced Brazil to Poe, many other Brazilian writers and translators have advocated for Poe either in their own works or as Poe translators, and at times their "supplications" have taken new and interesting routes. For example, the acclaimed postmodern novelist Clarice Lispector translated eighteen of Poe's tales for a collection aimed specifically at teenage readers.[38] Although Lispector's own novels are known for their narrative complexity, Lenita Esteves demonstrates how Lispector's translations of Poe's stories partially "abridge" Poe's texts while both "simplif[ying]" Poe's language and shifting it to "a more colloquial register,"[39] serving as a powerful and peculiar example of how one of Poe's advocates speaks both "favourably" and "on behalf of" him to a very specific audience: Brazilian teens. This audience, it appears, has openly received Lispector's message about Poe since her translated collection was in its twenty-second edition in 2014.[40]

Spanish America's advocacy for Poe has been even more tireless than Brazil's, with key figures from the late nineteenth century through the early twenty-first century praising, responding to, and interacting with Poe. Adaptations/translations of three of Poe's tales were circulating in Peru as early as the late 1840s, and Poe's works were being translated in various Spanish American locales during the 1860s and 1870s.[41] However, Poe truly entered Spanish American letters with force in the late 1880s and early 1890s as a part of the *modernista* movement headed by the Nicaraguan poet Ruben Darío. The Venezuelan poet Juan Antonio Pérez Bonalde had translated Poe's "The Raven" in 1887,[42] just a year before Darío's collection *Azul* openly launched Spanish American *modernismo* and six years before Darío consecrated Poe as one of the "special" or "rare ones" in his 1893 text "Los raros."[43] Pérez Bonalde's translation was not the first in the Spanish language, but its rigor and its timing made it an extremely effective tool for promoting Poe across the Spanish-speaking world, and it remains *the* Spanish-language version of Poe's most famous poem, even though other Spanish-language translations of "The Raven" that follow in its wake do a better job of re-creating Poe's odd rhyme and meter.[44] Pérez Bonalde's translation, coupled with Darío's Baudelaire-influenced praise for Poe as the ultimate artist for art's sake—"un sublime apasionado, un nervioso, uno de esos divinos semilocos necesarios para el progreso humano, lamentables cristos del arte, que por amor al eterno ideal tienen su calle de la amargura, sus espinas y su cruz" ["a passionate sublime being, a nervous man, one of those divine partially madmen necessary for human progress, lamentable Christs of art who for the love of an eternal ideal have their *via dolorosa*, their thorns, and their cross"][45]—cast Poe as one of *modernismo*'s primary icons and fountains of influence. This particular Poe, Englekirk argues, "was to fertilize the intellect and imagination of Central and South America more than any other American author," and as he avers, "almost all of the followers of Modernism were directly or indirectly influenced by Poe."[46] This influence spans the American continent from Mexico to Central America and from the equatorial nations of Colombia and Venezuela down to the southern cone. Several Poe pieces appeared in periodicals in Spanish America before the *modernistas*, and his presence significantly increased via the translation work of his French advocates, but the advocacy of Pérez Bonalde and Darío—the former as translator and the latter as image-curator—fused Poe and Spanish American *modernismo* in a way that was beneficial to both parties while permanently inscribing both the movement itself and its foreign poet-prophet into Spanish American literary history.

The reciprocal relationship of influence and advocacy between Poe and his Spanish American advocates remained strong through the twentieth century and continues today. Poe was a significant influence on the writers of the so-called Boom—especially on the Argentine Julio Cortázar and the Mexican Carlos Fuentes—and on major authors after the Boom like the Chilean Roberto Bolaño. Contemporary Spanish American writers also continue to sing his praises. For example, in 2008 Mexican author Jorge Volpi and Peruvian writer Fernando Iwasaki coedited a new edition of Cortázar's Poe translations in which they engaged sixty-seven current Spanish American and peninsular writers (including themselves) with Poe, inviting each contemporary author to write a brief introduction for one of Poe's tales. This edition clearly shows Poe's influence on the Boom and on the generation that followed. It also demonstrates the Poe advocacy of writers from both eras since, along with Cortázar's translations and the sixty-seven contemporary introductions, the volume begins with an essay from Fuentes and another from the Peruvian Nobel laureate Mario Vargas Llosa as prologues.[47]

Perhaps the most pointed example of extended Poe advocacy in Spanish America comes from the Río de la Plata region of Argentina and Uruguay. This example spans the twentieth century from the latter part of the *modernista* era well through the Boom via the works of Horacio Quiroga, Jorge Luis Borges, and Julio Cortázar—each author a major figure in Spanish American literary history, each indebted to Poe, and each a powerful advocate *for* Poe who helped to solidify his presence in the national/regional traditions of the Río de la Plata and in the broader literary polysystem of Spanish America.

A Trinity of Advocates

Quiroga, Borges, and Cortázar, each in his own right, continue to wield significant influence over the literature of the Río de la Plata region and over Spanish American letters in general several decades after their respective deaths in 1937, 1986, and 1984, and each writer served and continues to serve as a powerful Poe advocate for Spanish-language readers. Grouping the three authors as a trinity rather than simply a trio might appear problematic on the surface since they did not hold a singular purpose, literary or otherwise. Indeed, Borges was a rather harsh critic of Quiroga's writing, and Cortázar, while heavily influenced by and indebted to Borges's poetics, clearly disagreed with his fellow Argentine's politics. In their advocacy for Poe, however, these three literary giants find some common ground, although they each played distinct roles as Poe advocates. Each of these writers was influenced by Poe, and each one spent a significant amount of time responding to Poe. Quiroga's advocacy can best be defined in terms of discipleship; Borges's advocacy for Poe was multilayered, but many of his interactions with Poe (whether articles, prologues, or anthologized pieces) can all fit under the broader umbrella of the work of the literary critic; and Cortázar's advocacy, although also multifaceted, remains most visible through his translations of the vast majority of Poe's prose. The disciple, the critic, and the translator all spoke for, supported, and recommended Poe to their reading public. This trinity's advocacy for Poe is matched only by the earlier trinity of Baudelaire, Mallarmé, and Valéry, whose French advocacy for Poe—to the bemusement of Borges and to the pleasure of Cortázar—had already placed Poe in a space of privilege in the Río de la Plata by the beginning of Quiroga's career.[48]

Quiroga's Poe discipleship began early and continued throughout his publishing career, and Quiroga advocated for Poe via imitation of, conversation with, and prescription of the techniques and themes of his literary master. In the realm of imitation, Quiroga's first attempt to re-create the horrors of revenge (felt both by the seeker of vengeance and by the victim) in Poe's famous "The Cask of Amontillado" appeared as a brief prose entry entitled "El tonel de amontillado" in Quiroga's first published book—a *modernista* collection of poetry titled *Los arrecifes de coral* that Quiroga published in 1901.[49] The very title reveals the lack of distance between this tale and Poe's text since it is simply a translation of the title of Poe's most famous revenge story. Quiroga's piece begins: "Poe dice que, habiendo soportado del mejor modo posible las mil injusticias de Fortunato, juró vengarse cuando éste llegó al terreno de los insultos. Y nos cuenta cómo en una noche de carnaval le emparedó vivo, a pesar del ruido que hacía Fortunato con sus cascabeles" ["Poe says that, having tolerated in the best way posible the thousand injustices of Fortunato, he swore to avenge himself when Fortunato entered the territory of insult. And he tells us how in a night of carnival he walled Fortunato up alive, despite the noise that Fortunato made with his bells."][50] After this brief summary of Poe's story, which strangely inserts Poe into the role of Montresor, Quiroga's tale, in less than three hundred words, has a lime-covered Fortunato relate his "aventura anterior" ["previous adventure"] to the story's narrator, Montresor—first in front of a large mirror and then in the catacombs where he attempts to reverse Poe's tale by taking revenge on the narrator.[51] In Quiroga's next rendition of this tale, "El crimen del otro" from 1904, he changes the setting to turn-of-the-century Montevideo, but he once again repeats Poe's plotline as the narrator buries his friend—named Fortunto—alive.[52] In this rendering, the narrator does not seek revenge so much as try to rid himself of a friend whom he has driven mad by introducing him to the writings of Edgar Allan Poe. Although both of these stories interrogate the character of Montresor more than Poe's source text, they do so only through a direct rewriting that relies overwhelmingly on Poe's characters and plotline.

After these first two attempts, Quiroga repeatedly captures the horror of "Cask" and other Poe tales in several stories that seek to create Poe's effect in new settings with original characters who have their own story arcs. As Caroline Egan has argued, two of these stories—"La lengua" and "Una bofetada" ["A Slap in the Face"]—subtly converse with "Cask" and the theme of revenge,[53] but several of Quiroga's most famous stories create a Poe-like horror without even faintly referencing any of Poe's source texts. For example, Quiroga's "El almohadón de pluma" ["The Feather Pillow"] from 1907, "La miel silvestre" from 1911, and "El hijo" ["The Son"] from 1928 each creates a nervous tension that builds to a painful and horrific climax that leaves the reader both shocked and satisfied.[54] In all three cases, Quiroga relies on his own characters, settings, and plotlines rather than on Poe's creations to develop this sense of horror. "La gallina degollada" ["The Decapitated Chicken"], perhaps Quiroga's most masterful piece of horror fiction, finds a middle ground between his own creation and Poe's influence.

This 1909 tale creates a horrendous scene in which four sick brothers whose parents have treated them like animals kill their younger, healthy sister.[55] The setting and the plot are Quiroga's, and while this story almost allows for a reading of the killing in terms of revenge that might put it in conversation with other Poe stories, it appears to more pointedly reference Poe's "The Murders in the Rue Morgue" since the boys, like the orangutan in Poe's tale, imitate common human actions that create terrible outcomes. In Poe's story, the orangutan's aping of his master shaving leads to the vicious death of two women—a mother and a daughter (M 2: 565–568). In Quiroga's story, the boys' imitation of the decapitating and bleeding of the family's evening meal—a chicken—leads to their sister's brutal death and to the metaphorical destruction of their parents, who have placed all of their hopes in their one healthy child while neglecting their four disabled sons.[56] With a brilliant stroke, Quiroga taps into the latent horror of Poe's initial detective story to create an effect that significantly veers away from the feeling of awe surrounding Dupin's intellect toward a localized terror that Quiroga hones and masters during his prolific career.

Finally, along with imitating and then conversing with Poe's works and methods, Quiroga eventually prescribed them to aspiring writers. In his 1925 article "El manual del perfecto cuentista," Quiroga taps into Poe's theory of effect by explaining that authors must know the end of a story before they write that story's introduction.[57] In his 1928 article "Decálogo del perfecto cuentista," he approaches the hopeful writer in even more didactic terms by listing ten rules for writing. His first rule, "[c]ree en un maestro—Poe, Maupassant, Kipling, Chejov—como en Dios mismo" ["believe in a master—Poe, Maupassant, Kipling, Chekov—as in God himself"], reiterates his belief in following established models and reifies his Poe discipleship in the latter portion of his career.[58] His fifth rule echoes Poe's theory of effect and the concept that authors must know where they want to arrive before they can start writing.[59]

Quiroga's discipleship functions as advocacy for Poe through both his fiction and his writing instructions. Englekirk notes that younger Spanish American writers in the 1930s were absorbing Poe via "Quiroga's genius," but his "Poesque spirit"[60] was still visible over sixty years later in an article by Bolaño from the late twentieth century. In a piece called "Consejos sobre el arte de escribir cuentos" ["Advice on the Art of Writing Short Stories"], Bolaño takes up Quiroga's model for offering tips on how to write short fiction, names Quiroga as one of the authors an aspiring writer needs to read, and claims that "[l]a verdad de la verdad es que con Edgar Allan Poe todos tendíamos de sobra" ["[t]he honest truth is that with Edgar Allan Poe, we would have more than enough good material to read."][61] Quiroga, the Poe disciple, continues to speak for and recommend Poe both directly and indirectly.

Borges sustained a lengthy and complex literary relationship with Poe that included several types of advocacy. He translated two of Poe's stories ("The Facts in the Case of M. Valdemar" and "The Purloined Letter") with his friend and writing partner Adolfo Bioy Casares, anthologized the former in *Antología de la literatura fantástica* and the latter in *Los mejores cuentos policiales* (two anthologies with major staying power that have each been reprinted several times since their original publication dates in the early

1940s),[62] responded to Poe's Dupin tales with a detective trilogy of his own, conversed with several of Poe's themes and creative ideas in his other fictional works, mentioned Poe in over 130 articles, and discussed Poe in scores of interviews and question/answer sessions. John T. Irwin has thoroughly examined Borges's conscious conversation with Poe's detective fiction in *The Mystery to a Solution: Poe, Borges, and the Analytic Detective Story*, and I have analyzed Borges's relationship with Poe beyond their detective stories in *Borges's Poe: The Influence and Reinvention of Edgar Allan Poe in Spanish America*.[63] Here, I would simply like to focus on Borges as a literary critic and public intellectual whose returns to Poe kept the US writer in the Argentine literary spotlight throughout the twentieth century.

Borges was an insatiable reader, and Poe was one of the writers whom Borges first encountered in his youth in his father's library and whom he reread time and again throughout his long life.[64] After going blind in the mid-1950s, Borges continued to reread Poe by having the latter's works read to him aloud by his mother (Leonor Acevedo de Borges), his students, his friends, and his second wife, María Kodama.[65] For example, as late as 1985, Borges claimed that he could no longer count the times that he had read and reread Poe's "The Pit and the Pendulum" and suggested that he would continue rereading it in the future.[66] Borges could not stop reading Poe, and he could not stop writing and talking about him either. Borges wrote only two articles dedicated specifically to Poe—"La génesis de 'El cuervo' de Poe" in *La Prensa* in 1935 and "Edgar Allan Poe" in *La Nación* in 1949—but he mentioned Poe in over 130 other solo-authored pieces, often framing his discussions of detective fiction, US literature, translation, and several other subjects around Poe.[67] His references to Poe reached disparate reading audiences in Argentina, the Río de la Plata region, and Spanish America from the popular and local/national readers of the daily papers *La Prensa* and *La Nación*, to the middle-class and typically female audience of the household magazine *El Hogar*, to the highbrow and international readership of the literary journal *Sur*. Borges perennially returned to Poe in his public persona as well. He taught Poe in the classroom, mentioned Poe in lectures at university campuses and in public forums throughout the Americas and Europe, and talked about Poe in several interviews that were broadcast to wide audiences over the radio.

Borges, unlike Quiroga and Cortázar, was more willing to openly criticize Poe. He did not admire everything that Poe wrote, he was particularly critical of Poe's poetry, and he occasionally questioned Poe's taste. However, his praise for Poe as the inventor of the detective genre and as a powerful writer of the fantastic not only kept Poe in front of Borges's local, regional, and international readerships, but it also created a new version of Poe in the Río de la Plata region and Spanish America in general. Despite Quiroga's reciprocal relationship with Poe's fiction, most Río de la Plata and Spanish American readers still considered Poe a poet during the last years of Quiroga's life and the early years of Borges's career. Borges's advocacy permanently shifted Poe's image from dark poet-prophet to masterful story writer. Borges was the type of advocate who admitted that Poe had weaknesses but championed him nonetheless. In this sense, Borges's advocacy for Poe also resonates with the religious definition of the noun "advocate" since he acted as an agent between Poe and the reader in spite of what he saw as some of Poe's literary "sins." Borges did not ignore Poe's problems, but he felt that the positive far outweighed the negative and asked that Poe's readers judge Poe for his strengths and forgive him for his weaknesses.

Like Borges, Cortázar maintained a long and multilayered relationship with Poe that began in his youth and flourished during his adult life. Cortázar also read Poe as a child, and according to various personal accounts, he had to do so on the sly because his mother thought he "was too young."[68] "[S]he was right," Cortázar later claimed, and his earliest encounters with Poe's texts purportedly scared him to the point of illness.[69] These early readings of Poe thrust Cortázar into the realm of the fantastic, a space that he thoroughly enjoyed as a reader and consistently recreated in his own work, particularly his short fiction. Several of Cortázar's most famous short pieces—"Casa tomada" ["House Taken Over"], "Lejana" ["The Distances"], "La noche boca arriba" ["The Night Face Up"], "La isla al mediodía" ["The Island at Noon"], and "El ídolo de las Cíclades" ["The Idol of the Cyclades"]—function within this supernatural mode while others such as "Axolotl" or "Carta a una señorita en París" ["Letter to a Young Lady in Paris"] turn from the fantastic toward magical realism.[70] The theme of the double appears throughout Cortázar's tales, and he often employs it in ways that resemble works by Poe. "Lejana," for example, creates a powerful inversion of Poe's "William Wilson" as Cortázar's protagonist—Alina Reyes—literally loses herself in an open battle of wills against her double.[71] Cortázar's first published story under his own name, "Casa tomada," itself plays the double since one of the most common yet influential interpretations of the tale reads it as an Argentine doubling of Poe's "The Fall of the House of Usher."

Although Cortázar's stories spread Poe's themes and approaches to new audiences, he advocated for Poe most powerfully as a translator. In a 1983 interview with Jason Weiss, Cortázar claimed that when translating Poe he learned to appreciate Poe's language, regardless of the critiques that various English-speaking readers had offered: "I explored his language, which is highly criticized by the English and the Americans because they find it too baroque, in short they've found all sorts of things wrong with it. Well, since I'm neither English nor American, I see it with another perspective. I know there are aspects which have aged a lot, that are exaggerated, but that hasn't the slightest importance next to his genius."[72] Cortázar spent two years in the early 1950s translating that genius into Spanish before becoming a famous writer in his own right, and he returned to, refined, and republished those translations over the next two decades, even though he had already made an international name for himself as a novelist and story writer.

Before the 1956 release of Cortázar's two-volume set of Poe's prose translations, *Obras en prosa*, no single Spanish-language translator in the Americas or on the Iberian Peninsula had tackled the majority of Poe's fiction.[73] Poe's poetry was readily available in Spanish translation, and many of his stories were also available, but the fictional titles were spread throughout disparate periodicals across Spain and the Americas, found in short collections in which a single translator would offer a dozen or so stories, or combined into larger collections that contained translations by several different translators. For example, the Argentine translator Carlos Olivera offered thirteen of Poe's tales in Spanish as *Novelas y cuentos* in 1884; an anonymous collection of translations of twelve Poe tales appeared in Buenos Aires in 1903 under the Hispanicized Baudelaire title *Historias extraordinarias*; and Armando Bazán edited a substantial Poe collection, *Obras completas*, that included, along with several poems, over forty prose pieces translated by five different translators.[74] Cortázar's volumes, in contrast, include all of Poe's short fiction, *Pym*, *Eureka*, and hundreds of pages of Poe's other prose pieces. He republished both volumes in 1969, and then in 1970, he split the first volume into two, revised the translations, and published this new two-volume set as *Cuentos, 1* and *Cuentos, 2*.[75] Finally, in 1973, he revised and rereleased the second volume of his *Obras en prosa* as *Ensayos y críticas*.[76]

Out of all of these translations and repackagings, the 1970 two-volume set of the stories has had, by far, the most significant impact. The Madrid publishing house Alianza has republished these two volumes over thirty times in Madrid and Buenos Aires, and these two books (often released as inexpensive paperback "libros de bosillo" or "pocket books") are now almost synonymous with Poe in the Spanish-speaking world. In the introduction to their 2008 rerelease of Cortázar's translations in their *Edición comentada*, Volpi and Iwasaki venerate this particular two-volume set, claiming that each of the sixty-seven writers whom they have chosen to introduce Poe's stories have come to Poe via Cortázar's two-volume edition of the tales and stating that their goal is to celebrate Poe's bicentennial by "rescatando aquellos míticos tomitos azules" ["rescuing those mythic little blue volumes."][77] In short, Cortázar advocated for Poe by translating what he saw as Poe's "extraordinary genius"[78] into Spanish, regardless of any perceived shortcomings with Poe's language. His translations provided previously unprecedented access to that genius to millions of new readers through a single translation filter, and many of those readers, who are also writers, continue to distribute Cortázar's Poe to future generations.

The Influence of the Stars

Throughout this essay, I have referred to both the general definition and the more specific, Christian definition of the noun "advocate." I would like to end by playing with an older and more specific definition of the noun "influence." The *Oxford English Dictionary* shows that "influence" was used as a noun for almost three hundred years before it was used as a verb and that the oldest usage of the noun referred to a phenomenon between heavenly bodies and human bodies:

> 2. a. *spec.* in *Astrol.* The supposed flowing or streaming from the stars or heavens of an etherial fluid acting upon the character and destiny of men, and affecting sublunary things generally. In later times gradually viewed less literally, as an exercise of power or "virtue," or of an occult force, and in late use chiefly a poetical or humorous

> reflex of earlier notions. b. *transf.* The exercise of personal power by human beings, figured as something of the same nature as astral influence. Now only *poet.*[79]

My use of "influence" throughout this essay, of course, typically refers to the "b" definition of the noun or to the common definitions of the verb, which the *Oxford English Dictionary* defines as "1. *trans.* To exert influence upon, to affect by influence. a. To affect the mind or action of; to move or induce by influence; [. . .] b. To affect the condition of, to have an effect on."[80] The ancient and astral definition of the noun, however, also seems relevant. Baudelaire symbolically raised Poe into the heavens as a celestial advocate between himself and God, and Poe's work and his image certainly appear to have had an elevated effect "upon the character and destiny of" many of his readers that could be compared to a "supposed flowing or streaming" from above. However, it took Baudelaire, Borges, Rampo, Bal'mont, Pessoa, and many other significant writers to elevate Poe to this level. These Poe advocates, literary stars during their own lifetimes, made him into a literary star who could then influence us, and his and their astral influence continue to affect other literary stars as well as the mere mortals or "sublunary" beings that we, Poe readers and scholars, tend to be.

One of these stars, Vargas Llosa, describes Poe as a fortunate writer, not in life, but in his posthumous rise to prominence through the work of two amazing advocates: "Aunque su vida estuvo marcada por la desgracia, Edgar Allan Poe fue uno de los más afortunados escritores modernos en lo que concierne a la irradiación de su obra por el mundo" ["Even though his life was marked by misfortune, Edgar Allan Poe was one of the most fortunate modern writers in what concerns the irradiation of his work throughout the world"] because he was translated by both Baudelaire, the "poeta más grande del siglo XIX" ["greatest poet of the nineteenth century"], and Cortázar, "uno de los mejores escritores de nuestra lengua y un traductor excepcional" ["one of the best writers in our language and an exceptional translator."][81] To Vargas Llosa's shortlist, we could add the names of dozens of other literary stars from distinct traditions who have served as Poe advocates. Some of these stars, Baudelaire-Mallarmé-Valéry and Quiroga-Borges-Cortázar, have formed guiding constellations that direct readers to Poe, while others have acted as solitary beacons that radiate Poe's works and image. The advocacy of these literary stars—via translation, discipleship, rewriting, literary criticism, and other creative and critical endeavors—keeps Poe in orbit to shine down on future generations of readers and on occasional rising stars.

Notes

1. André Lefevere, *Translating Literature: Practice and Theory in a Comparative Literature Context* (New York: MLA, 1992), 6–7, 13–14. Lefevere uses the terms "rewrites" and "refractions" rather than "rewritings" in other works to describe the same concept. See "Why Waste Our Time on Rewrites? The Trouble with Interpretation and the Role of Rewriting in an Alternative Paradigm," in *The Manipulation of Literature: Studies in Literary Translation*, ed. Theo Hermans (New York: St. Martins, 1985), 215–243; and

"Mother Courage's Cucumbers: Text, System and Refraction in a Theory of Literature," in *The Translation Studies Reader* (3rd ed.), ed. Lawrence Venuti (New York & London: Routledge, 2012), 203–219.

2. This list could go on to include Poe's hoaxes, his biting satires, and his contributions to science via *Eureka: A Prose Poem*.
3. I see this type of reciprocal influence functioning in two ways. The first way is fairly intuitive—translators, critics, anthologizers, biographers, and others openly affect how we understand and interpret the writers they approach in their work. The second way is less intuitive and recalls Jorge Luis Borges's descriptions of influence in his famous essay "Kafka y sus precursores" ["Kafka and His Precursors"] in which Borges argues that newer writers influence the works of older writers by changing us, the readers, so that we see the work of a newer writer in the work of an older writer and, thus, experience the strange, anachronistic sensation of seeing Kafka in a poem by Robert Browning or in a text by Søren Kierkegaard and feeling that these earlier texts are actually Kafkaesque. See "Kafka y sus precursores," in *Obras completas* (Buenos Aires: Emecé Editores, 2007), 2:107–109 and "Kafka and His Precursors," in *Selected Non-Fictions*, ed. and trans. Eliot Weinberger (New York: Penguin, 1999), 363–365.
4. *Oxford English Dictionary Online*, s.v. "advocate," accessed February 23, 2017, http://www.oed.com/view/Entry/3022?rskey=SVTsWZ&result=1#eid.
5. Rufus Wilmot Griswold, "Death of Edgar A. Poe," *New-York Daily Tribune*, October 9, 1849, p. 2, cols. 3–4, Edgar Allan Poe Society of Baltimore, http://www.eapoe.org/papers/misc1827/nyt49100.htm.
6. See, for example, George R. Graham, "The Late Edgar Allan Poe," *Graham's Magazine* (Philadelphia), March 1850, 36:224–226, http://www.eapoe.org/papers/misc1827/18500301.htm; Henry B. Hirst, "Edgar Allan Poe," *McMakin's Model American Courier*, vol. XIX, no. 33 (whole no. 969), October 20, 1849, p. 2, cols. 3–4, http://www.eapoe.org/papers/misc1827/hbh18491.htm; or Nathaniel Parker Willis, "Death of Edgar Poe," *Home Journal* (New York), October 20, 1849, p. 2, cols. 2–4, http://www.eapoe.org/papers/misc1827/18491020.htm.
7. Thomas Stearns Eliot, "From Poe to Valéry," in *The Recognition of Edgar Allan Poe*, ed. Eric W. Carlson (Ann Arbor: University of Michigan Press, 1966), 205–219.
8. Célestin Pierre Cambiaire, *The Influence of Edgar Allan Poe in France* (New York: G. E. Stechert & Co., 1927); Partick F. Quinn, *The French Face of Edgar Poe* (Carbondale: Southern Illinois University Press, 1957); Lois Davis Vines, *Valéry and Poe: A Literary Legacy* (New York: New York University Press, 1992). Also see Vines's chapters in *Poe Abroad: Influence, Reputation, Affinities*, ed. Lois Davis Vines (Iowa City: University of Iowa Press, 1999); and "Poe Translations in France," in *Translated Poe*, ed. Emron Esplin and Margarida Vale de Gato (Bethlehem, PA: Lehigh University Press, 2014), 47–54.
9. John Eugene Englekirk, *Edgar Allan Poe in Hispanic Literature* (New York: Instituto de las Españas en los Estados Unidos, 1934). There are many other titles that tackle Poe's relationship with specific national or regional literary traditions—books on Poe and Scandinavia, Poe and Germany, Poe and Japan, or Poe and Russia, for example.
10. Benjamin Franklin Fisher, ed., *Poe and Our Times: Influences and Affinities* (Baltimore: Edgar Allan Poe Society, 1986); Lois Davis Vines, ed., *Poe Abroad: Influence, Reputation, Affinities* (Iowa City: University of Iowa Press, 1999); Barbara Cantalupo, ed., *Poe's Pervasive Influence* (Bethlehem, PA: Lehigh University Press, 2012); Emron Esplin and Margarida Vale de Gato, eds., *Translated Poe* (Bethlehem, PA: Lehigh University Press, 2014).

11. Charles Baudelaire, *Œuvres complétes* (Paris: Éditions du Seuil, 1968), 642; Christopher Isherwood, trans., *My Heart Laid Bare*, in *Intimate Journals* (New York: Howard Fertig, 1977), 61.
12. *Oxford English Dictionary Online*, s.v. "advocate," accessed February 23, 2017. http://www.oed.com/view/Entry/3022?rskey=wrTAEp&result=1&isAdvanced=false#eid.
13. *Oxford English Dictionary Online*, s.v. "advocate."
14. Lois Davis Vines, "Poe Translations in France," in *Translated Poe*, 48. Vines also notes that Baudelaire translated four of Poe's poems (48–49).
15. Charles Baudelaire, trans., *Histoires extraordinaires*, by Edgar Allan Poe, 1856, Project Gutenberg, http://www.gutenberg.org/files/20761/20761-h/20761-h.htm; Baudelaire, "Edgar Poe, sa vie et ses oeuvres," in *Histoires extraordinaires*. Vines notes that this biographical piece "is a variation" of Baudelaire's first lengthy article on Poe that he published in 1852 (353n12).
16. Vines, "Poe Translations in France," 49.
17. Vines,"Poe Translations in France," 49.
18. Vines, "Poe Translations in France," 49.
19. Stéphane Mallarmé, "Le tombeau d'Edgar Poe," *Œuvres complétes*. (Paris: Gallimard, 1998), 38.
20. Vines avers that "[t]he unpublished manuscript of an early draft of Valéry's *Evening with Monsieur Teste* bears the title 'Memoirs of Chevalier Dupin' " (51).
21. Itamar Even-Zohar, "The Position of Translated Literature within the Literary Polysystem," in *The Translation Studies Reader* (3rd ed.), ed. Lawrence Venuti (New York: Routledge, 2012), 162–167.
22. Even-Zohar, "The Position of Translated Literature," 163.
23. Even-Zohar, "The Position of Translated Literature," 163.
24. Poe's centrality to the French literary canon is clearly demonstrated by the fact that he was the first non-French writer included in the Bibliothèque de la Pléiade and the fifth writer, regardless of language, included in this monumental series. The Pléiade edition of Poe, which uses Baudelaire's translations, was first published in April 1932, only six months after the series published its first book—the first volume of Baudelaire's complete works. See "Le catalogue—Par année de parution," La Pléiade, http://www.la-pleiade.fr/Le-catalogue/Par-annee-de-parution, for historical details about books published in this series.
25. Elvira Osipova, "The History of Poe Translations in Russia," in *Translated Poe*, 73.
26. Osipova, 73, and Eloise M. Boyle, "Valery Brjusov and Konstantin Bal'mont," in *Poe Abroad*, 177–182. For a monograph-length study of Poe in Russia, see Joan Delaney Grossman, *Edgar Allan Poe in Russia: A Study in Legend and Literary Influence* (Würzburg: Jal-Verlag, 1973).
27. Liviu Cotrău, "Edgar Allan Poe in Romanian Translation," in *Translated Poe*, 77.
28. Cotrău, "Edgar Allan Poe in Romanian Translation," 77–84.
29. Margarida Vale de Gato, "Poe Translations in Portugal: A Standing Challenge for Changing Literary Systems," in *Translated Poe*, 9–10.
30. Essays in *Poe Abroad*, *Poe's Pervasive Influence*, and *Translated Poe* demonstrate Poe's presence in China and South Korea, but more research into the literary traditions of these two nations would need to be conducted in order to discover whether important artists in these two countries who are influenced by Poe also act as Poe advocates.
31. Takayuki Tatsumi, "The Double Task of the Translator: Poe and His Japanese Disciples," in *Translated Poe*, 171. For more on Poe's relationship with Japan, see Noriko Mizuta

Lippit's pair of essays in *Poe Abroad*, several essays in *Poe's Pervasive Influence*, and Scott Miller's analysis of Japanese translations of "The Black Cat" in *Translated Poe*, 261–270 and 416–417.

32. Tatsumi, "The Double Task of the Translator," 167–168.
33. Tatsumi, "The Double Task of the Translator," 168–171.
34. Tatsumi, "The Double Task of the Translator," 171–172.
35. Tatsumi, "The Double Task of the Translator," 172, emphasis in the original.
36. For Spanish America, see Esplin, "From Poetic Genius to Master of Short Fiction: Edgar Allan Poe's Reception and Influence in Spanish American from the Beginnings through the Boom," *Resources for American Literary Study* 4 (2007): 31–54. For Brazil, see Carlos Daghlian, "Poe in Brazil," in *Poe Abroad*, 130–134.
37. Daghlian, "Poe in Brazil," 130.
38. Clarice Lispector, trans., *Histórias Extraordinárias*, by Edgar Allan Poe (Rio de Janeiro: Ediouro, 1998). This book appeared in a series for youth readers entitled *Clássicos para o Jovem Leitor*.
39. Lenita Esteves, "The Unparalleled Adventure of One Edgar Poe in the Brazilian Literary System," in *Translated Poe*, 157.
40. Esteves, "The Unparalleled Adventure," 158.
41. For details about the early reception of Poe in Spanish America, see Esplin, "From Poetic Genius to Master of Short Fiction," 33–38.
42. Juan Antonio Pérez Bonalde, trans., "El cuervo" by Edgar Allan Poe, 1887, in *J. A. Pérez Bonalde: Estudio preliminar de Pedro Pablo Paredes*, ed. Pedro Pablo Paredes (Caracas: Academia Venezolana, 1964), 2:151–157.
43. Rubén Darío, *Azul*, 1888 (Buenos Aires: Espasa- Calpe, 1945); Darío, "Los raros," 1893, in *Obras completas* (Madrid: Afrodisio Aguado, 1950), 2:245–517.
44. See Esplin, "From Poetic Genius to Master of Short Fiction," 35–38 and 43–46, for a comparative analysis of Pérez Bonalde's translation, "El cuervo," and Carlos Obligado's more meticulous version of the poem from 1932.
45. Darío, "Los raros," 267, my translation.
46. Englekirk, *Edgar Allan Poe in Hispanic Literature*, 146.
47. Fernando Iwasaki and Jorge Volpi, eds., *Cuentos completos: Edición comentada*, by Edgar Allan Poe, trans. Julio Cortázar, prologues by Carlos Fuentes and Mario Vargas Llosa (Madrid: Páginas de Espuma, 2008).
48. Borges notes in several texts that he thinks it is strange that Poe, a writer born in Boston, makes his way to Argentina via France. See, for example, Borges, "Prólogo de prólogos," in *Obras completas* (Buenos Aires: Emecé, 2007), 4:13; and Borges, "Sobre los clásicos," in *Páginas de Jorge Luis Borges: Seleccionadas por el autor* (Buenos Aires: Celtia, 1982), 231. Cortázar, contrastingly, calls Baudelaire "el doble de Edgar Allan Poe" ["the double of Edgar Allan Poe"] and claims to have kept a copy of Baudelaire's Poe translations nearby while translating Poe into Spanish. See Ernesto González Bermejo, *Conversaciones con Julio Cortázar* (Barcelona: Editora y Distribuidora Hispano Americana, 1978), 35–36.
49. Horacio Quiroga, "El tonel de amontillado," 1901, in *Todos los cuentos* (Madrid: Allca, 1997), 813. The few prose pieces from *Los arrecifes de coral* appear in *Todos los cuentos* from pages 807–824.
50. Quiroga, "El tonel de amontillado," 813, my translation.
51. Quiroga, "El tonel de amontillado," 813.

52. Quiroga, "El crimen de otro," 1904, in *Todos los cuentos*, 871–879.
53. Caroline Egan, "Revivification and Revision: Horacio Quiroga's Reading of Poe," *The Comparatist* 35 (2011): 239–248.
54. Quiroga, "El almohadón de pluma," "La miel silvestre," and "El hijo," in *Todos los cuentos*, 97–102, 122–128, and 752–757. The Quiroga titles for which I provide English translations all come from Margaret Sayers Peden, trans., *The Decapitated Chicken and Other Stories*, by Horacio Quiroga (Austin: University of Texas Press, 1976).
55. Quiroga, "La gallina degollada," 1911, in *Todos los cuentos*, 89–96; Peden, trans., "The Decapitated Chicken," in *The Decapitated Chicken and Other Stories*, 49–56.
56. Quiroga, "La gallina degollada," 94–95; "The Decapitated Chicken," 55–56.
57. Quiroga, "El manual del perfecto cuentista," in *Todos los cuentos*, 1189–1191.
58. Quiroga, "Decálogo del perfecto cuentista," in *Todos los cuentos*, 1194–1195, my translation.
59. Quiroga, "Decálogo del perfecto cuentista," 1194–1195.
60. Englekirk, *Edgar Allan Poe in Hispanic Literature*, 368.
61. Roberto Bolaño, "Consejos sobre el arte de escribir cuentos," in *Entre paréntesis* (Barcelona: Editorial Anagrama, 2004), 324–325; Bolaño, "Advice on the Art of Writing Short Stories," trans. David Draper Clark, *World Literature Today* 80, no. 6 (2006): 48–49. Although published in 2004, Bolaño begins the essay by noting that he is forty-four years old, showing that he wrote the essay in 1997 or 1998.
62. Jorge Luis Borges and Adolfo Bioy Casares, trans., "La verdad sobre el caso de M. Valdemar," by Edgar Allan Poe, in *Antología de la literatura fantástica*, 1940, eds. Jorge Luis Borges, Bioy Casares, and Silvina Ocampo (Buenos Aires: Sudamericana, 1971), 371–379; Borges and Bioy Casares, trans., "La carta robada," by Edgar Allan Poe, in *Los mejores cuentos policiales*, 1943, eds. Borges and Bioy Casares (Buenos Aires: Emecé, 1997), 23–38.
63. John T. Irwin, *The Mystery to a Solution: Poe, Borges, and the Analytic Detective Story* (Baltimore: Johns Hopkins University Press, 1994); Esplin, *Borges's Poe: The Influence and the Reinvention of Edgar Allan Poe in Spanish America* (Athens: University of Georgia Press, 2016).
64. Borges often mentioned reading Poe in his childhood. See, for example, Borges and Norman Thomas di Giovanni, "Autobiographical Notes," *New Yorker*, September 19, 1970, 42 and 78.
65. Copies of books by Poe held at the Fundación Internacional Jorge Luis Borges and at Argentina's national library in the Sala del Tesoro reveal Borges's continual return to Poe. The books contain notes in Borges's hand, in Leonor Acevedo de Borges's hand, and/or in Kodama's hand.
66. Borges, "Prólogo," in *Edgar Allan Poe, La carta robada*, ed. Franco Maria Ricci. (Madrid: Siruela, 1985), 12–13.
67. Borges, "La génesis de 'El cuervo' de Poe," *La Prensa* (Buenos Aires), August 25, 1935; Borges, "Edgar Allan Poe," *La Nación* (Buenos Aires), October 2, 1949, sec. 2. For detailed accounts of Borges's Poe references, see Esplin, "Jorge Luis Borges's References to Edgar Allan Poe: An Annotated Bibliography, Section 1," *Poe Studies* 48 (2015): 120–160; and "Jorge Luis Borges's References to Edgar Allan Poe: An Annotated Bibliography, Section 2," *Poe Studies* 49 (2016): 128–159.
68. Jason Weiss, "Writing at Risk: Interview with Julio Cortázar," in *Critical Essays on Julio Cortázar*, ed. Jamie Alazraki (New York: G. K. Hall & Company, 1999), 73. Cortázar makes similar claims in François Hébert's "An Interview with Julio Corázar," in *Critical Essays on Julio Cortázar*, 62.

69. Weiss, "Writing at Risk," 73; Hébert, "An Interview with Julio Corázar," 62.
70. Although originally published in various collections, each of these Cortázar short stories is available in Cortázar, *Relatos* (Buenos Aires: Editorial Sudamericana, 1970). All of the cited English translations of Cortázar's stories except "The Island at Noon" are available in Cortázar, *Blow-Up and Other Stories*, trans. Paul Blackburn (New York: Pantheon, 1967). "The Island at Noon" appears in Cortázar, *All Fires the Fire*, trans. Suzanne Jill Levine (New York, Pantheon, 1973), 90–98.
71. Cortázar, "Lejana," 437–438; Cortázar, "The Distances," 26–27.
72. Weiss, "Writing at Risk," 73.
73. Julio Cortázar, trans., *Obras en prosa* by Edgar Allan Poe, 2 vols. (Madrid: Revista de Occidente; Río Piedras: Editorial Universitaria Universidad de Puerto Rico, 1956).
74. Carlos Olivera, trans., *Novelas y cuentos*, by Edgar Allan Poe (Paris: Garnier Frères, 1884); Edgar Allan Poe, *Historias extraordinarias* (Buenos Aires: Biblioteca de la Nación, 1903); and Armando Bazán, ed., *Obras completas*, by Edgar Allan Poe (Buenos Aires: Claridad, 1944).
75. Cortázar, trans., *Obras en prosa* by Edgar Allan Poe, 2 vols. (Barcelona: Editorial Universitaria de la Universidad de Puerto Rico, 1969); Cortázar, trans., *Cuentos*, by Edgar Allan Poe, 2 vols. (Madrid: Alianza Editorial, 1970).
76. Cortázar, trans., *Ensayos y críticas* by Edgar Allan Poe (Madrid: Alianza Editorial, 1973).
77. Volpi and Iwasaki, "Poe & Cía," in *Cuentos completos: Edición comentada*, 13.
78. Weiss, Writing at Risk," 73.
79. *Oxford English Dictionary Online*, s.v. "influence," accessed February 23, 2017, http://www.oed.com/view/Entry/95519?isAdvanced=false&result=1&rskey=oUBHca&.
80. *Oxford English Dictionary Online*, s.v. "influence," accessed February 23, 2017, http://www.oed.com/view/Entry/95520?result=2&rskey=RPl7tg&.
81. Mario Vargas Llosa, "Poe y Cortázar," *Cuentos completos: Edición comentada*, 19–20.

Bibliography

Cantalupo, Barbara, ed. *Poe's Pervasive Influence*. Bethlehem, PA: Lehigh University Press, 2012.

Englekirk, John Eugene. *Edgar Allan Poe in Hispanic Literature*. New York: Instituto de las Españas en los Estados Unidos, 1934.

Esplin, Emron. "From Poetic Genius to Master of Short Fiction: A Map of Edgar Allan Poe's Reception and Influence in Spanish America from the Beginnings through the Boom." *Resources for American Literary Study* 31 (2006): 31–54.

Esplin, Emron, and Margarida Vale de Gato, eds. *Translated Poe*. Bethlehem, PA: Lehigh University Press, 2014.

Even-Zohar, Itamar. "The Position of Translated Literature within the Literary Polysystem." In *The Translation Studies Reader* (3rd ed.), edited by Lawrence Venuti, 162–167. New York: Routledge, 2012.

Fisher, Benjamin Franklin, ed. *Poe and Our Times: Influences and Affinities*. Baltimore: Edgar Allan Poe Society, 1986.

Iwasaki, Fernando, and Jorge Volpi, eds. *Cuentos completos: Edición comentada*, by Edgar Allan Poe. Translated by Julio Cortázar. Prologues by Carlos Fuentes and Mario Vargas Llosa. Madrid: Páginas de Espuma, 2008.

Lefevere, André. *Translating Literature: Practice and Theory in a Comparative Literature Context*. New York: MLA, 1992.

Quinn, Patrick F. *The French Face of Edgar Poe*. Carbondale: Southern Illinois University Press, 1957.

Vines, Lois Davis. *Valéry and Poe: A Literary Legacy*. New York: New York University Press, 1992.

Vines, Lois Davis, ed. *Poe Abroad: Influence, Reputation, Affinities*. Iowa City: University of Iowa Press, 1999.

CHAPTER 35

POE AND MODERN(IST) POETRY

An Impure Legacy

MARGARIDA VALE DE GATO

POE is a fecund point of departure to discuss the gradients of modern and modernist poetry, in view of the readings, appropriations, and rewritings of his poems, critical texts on poetry, and imaginative prose by subsequent authors of different areas and traditions, each perhaps with a distinct agenda for making it new. The many who wrote on, around, or against Poe were mostly collating from his work a series of "pre-texts" for narratives of the makings and purposes of poetry that interconnected with cultural prestige struggles, fueled by both transatlantic commerce and hemispheric imbalance. Despite one account that might have gained the status of a "strong" reading—Poe as the herald of "pure poetry"—a review of how others thought he could be co-opted to their poetic struggle leads us to realize the essential "impurity" and entanglement of the trends of poetic innovation since the late nineteenth century.

Modernity, modernism, and postmodernism are categorizations with variable time and space boundaries. The first term ranges from "early modern" in the sixteenth century to the apogee of technique and industrialization in the late eighteenth century or beyond. The second term's periodic scope might fluctuate depending on the geographical extension considered: while Anglophone modernism is generally delimited by the two world wars, the consensus that it was a revolt or "radical break with some of the traditional bases not only of Western art but of Western culture" should lead one to look at manifestations beyond dominant traditions, and hence excavate transatlantic literary exchanges that go back to the late nineteenth century.[1] We need to acknowledge, on the one hand, Latin language *modernismos* and, on the other hand, countercultural vanguards that were diverse, even as they developed through dialogue and struggle across national borders. Finally, *postmodernism*, though signaling a rupture by dismantling the idea of art as elevated and elitist, instead placing it alongside mass and popular culture, might be seen as a corollary of modernism, which already entailed the idea of dynamic change and subversion by embracing the "new."[2] I shall argue that Poe can be used to discuss several gradients of these related concepts, leading us also to reassess the significance of his poetic statements and experiments.

Acknowledging the need to negotiate Poe's poetic fortunes in the interplay of geoliterary movements, I must forego the daunting task of surveying the whole territory, opting instead for a selection of traditions, based on an estimation of relevance and communicating flows. Starting with Baudelaire and moving on to French symbolism, I will comment on how the French defense of Poe was narrowly absorbed by high modernism (mostly Anglophone) to substantiate, through the lenses of detached self-consciousness, an abstract idea of *poésie pure*. Latin American writers, meanwhile, had built contrasting narratives, seeking in their *modernismos* a language that would couple the mystical and the rhythmical, outside the market value. I will use a case closer to my own background, that of the modernist project of Fernando Pessoa, to show a sobering conciliation of intellectual estrangement and emotional effect in lyricism. Pessoa's critical remarks on his translations of Poe into Portuguese highlight a preference for verbal rhythm, an element whose prioritization varied in different traditions of modernism, which might partly explain why in the United States the reputation of Poe's poetry pales in comparison to Europe and Latin America: visual rhythm instead was the hallmark of imagism. The comparative approach will permit a fresh look at the little-studied "apparitions" of Poe among US modernists (and the precursor Whitman), with the "phosphorescence" of a halo that often surrounds him. Throughout the essay, I will also pay due attention to the recent reappraisal, in US criticism, of how Poe's wild prosody is mostly performative and reader oriented, opening up to different modes of speech and readings. The deconstructive aspect of Poe's rhetoric has been noticed and elaborated on by several movements emphasizing the discreteness of linguistic signs, from Russian formalism to Brazilian concrete poetry, two traditions that I will finally address in their relation to a fascinating aspect of Poe's legacy: the test of poetics in the translation(s) of poetry.

From "Poedelaire" to the Flawed Lineage of *La Poésie Pure*

One of Poe's contributions, albeit unwitting, to modern literature resides in the potential of international entwinement of his work and life with the poetics of his counterparts, especially his transatlantic brother Charles Baudelaire. The "Poedelaire" symbiosis is at once a unique love affair in translation (a major writer dedicating seventeen years of his life to one he thought was his kindred genius) and a landmark of literary conversation in the context of transatlantic print culture.[3] The test of amenability to textual circulation favored by transatlanticism not only shaped US literature from its inception but also set the scene of encounters of "emerging modernisms."[4]

Notwithstanding the many consequences that Baudelaire's construction of a transatlantic "family romance" with Poe represented for the circulation of the *isms* that proliferated in poetry since then,[5] literary historians from after the wars until the 1990s tended to overemphasize a certain angle—that of language driven to the limits of its autonomy—of Poe's appropriation by French symbolism. In his 1956 study, *Symbolisme from Poe to Mallarmé*, Joseph Chiari set out with the claim that "in order to see . . . Poe's relationship to symbolism and to Mallarmé, one needs first to know not symbolism in all its manifestations but its roots"; and he too propagated *one* privileged critical reading of the tutelage of Poe: that of a lineage, which goes beyond Mallarmé and culminates in Valéry.[6] Like T. S. Eliot in his tremendously influential "From Poe to Valéry" (1948),[7] Chiari casts a long shadow of doubt on the "adult credulity" laid on Poe by the great French writers, and hence subtitles his work "the growth of a modern myth."[8] Significantly, even critics less skeptical about the role of Poe in such lineage dub it "the myth of modern poetry," as Robert Kopp succinctly frames it in the comprehensive French edition of *Contes-Essais-Poémes* of 1989:

> Edgar Allan Poe incarnates thrice the myth of modern poetry. That of the *poet*, through Baudelaire, who has made of Poe the exemplary figure of the doomed poet; that of *poetry*, through Mallarmé, who has transposed his texts in a sacred language; that of *poetics*, through Valéry, who in his analysis would seek to grasp the workings of the creating spirit. Three aspects, three emphases, evolving from one author to another, non-exclusively.[9]

The narrative from Poe to Valéry not only comprises a notion of continuity but also of teleology. According to the argumentation of its most illustrious promoter, T. S. Eliot, its finality is an "increasing consciousness of language" that leads to the "penetration of the poetic by the introspective critical activity."[10] This would be at once the sign of an ultimate stage of man's relation with the poetic and a dismal culmination:

> I recognize first that within this tradition from Poe to Valéry are some of those modern poems which I most admire and enjoy; second, I think that the tradition itself represents the most interesting development of poetic consciousness anywhere . . . . And as for the future, the extreme awareness and concern for language . . . is something which must ultimately break down, owing to an increasing strain against which the human mind and nerves will rebel.[11]

Curiously, we may find in this formulation already the hint of other trends of Poe's legacy, built upon nervous tension. Later critics such as Richard Wilbur and David Murray have explored the Poesque motivations of "short-circuit[ing]" and of "operating in the breach" of language's symbolizing power, which are seemingly gaining the upper hand in contemporary Anglophone appreciations.[12]

Jerome McGann's *The Poet Edgar Allan Poe: Alien Angel* presents a compelling approach to Poe's poetry based on indeterminacy and reader response propitiated by prosody.[13] In what concerns the modernist response to the French take on symbolism via Poe, I draw attention to one instance, marked by McGann, where the indirect influence of Poe surfaces in Eliot's "Little Gidding." It consists of a rewording of a famous line of Mallarmé's "Le Tombeau d'Edgar Poe." Mallarmé's request for Poe's memorial, that it might "donner un sens plus pur aux mots de la tribu,"[14] finds the following "translation" in Eliot's verse: "I find words I never thought to speak/ . . . /When I left my body on a distant shore./Since our concern was speech, and speech impelled us/To purify the dialect of the tribe."[15] McGann's interpretation stresses the "speech of the tribe" rather than the "too pure sense," identifying a need to "glorify the vulgar dialects of poetic inspiration," which he then traces to Poesque diction as a practice of "*volgare eloquio*."[16] The rationale, supported also with recourse to William Carlos Williams (who back in 1925 declared Poe's "particles of language" in the "American grain"[17]), establishes Poe not as the first inductor of a first inductor of a rarefied autonomous poetic expression, but as a ventriloquist for several localized demands on language. This corollary, however, is very different from what led Eliot, in 1948, to inquire "what it was that three great French poets found in his [Poe's] work to admire, which we have not found."[18] Since that inquiry provided a strong reading of (high) modernist poetry, it is worthwhile to investigate it, while also pointing out the flaws in the narrative of Poe's appropriation by modernist poets.

Actually, Eliot claims that the lineage of the *poésie pure*, when traced back to Baudelaire (whose evaluation of Poe as *poète maudit* is otherwise deemed the Byronian offshoot of a "particular social situation"), is rather accidental: "Baudelaire *lets fall* one remark . . . . He believed . . . true poet that he was that the goal of poetry is of the same nature as its principle, and that it should have nothing in view but itself."[19] On the one hand, Eliot rhetorically minimizes the importance of Baudelaire's endorsement of the *poem* per se, and on the other he insists on reducing Poe's poetical impact to "The Philosophy of Composition." Even if, he admits, "Poe's other essays in poetic esthetic deserve consideration also," it is only to show that Poe's abhorrence of the long poem was self-serving, and what mostly preoccupies Eliot is why "The Philosophy of Composition" "has not been taken so seriously in England or America as in France."[20] However, if one does find in Poe's postfactum exposé about the writing of "The Raven" a precedence of the workings of the poem over subject matter, a claim that makes art part from inspiration, it is noteworthy that the expression *poem* per se comes instead from Poe's late essay, "The Poetic Principle."[21] There it is presented not so much to advocate the autonomy of language as to make Beauty "the sole legitimate province of the poem" (ER: 16) and the only door to immortality.[22] Unlike "The Philosophy of Composition," "The Poetic Principle" was not translated by Baudelaire, but he discusses it at length in his "Notes Nouvelles sur Poe." In this piece, he interweaves, by a dubious citational and interpretative strategy, his own theory of *correspondances*, or universal analogies, with Poe's poetics: "For him, . . . imagination is an almost divine faculty which perceives immediately and without philosophical methods the inner and secret relations of things, the correspondences and the analogies."[23]

The fact that Baudelaire transferred to Poe his own credo of correspondences—implying a leap toward transcendence, as well as a crisis or impurity of faith—is of no mean significance to the subsequent conceptualization of "symbolism" in Europe and even of *Modernismo* in Spanish America. These transcendental implications are not accounted for by Eliot's presumption of the effacement of subject matter in view of its treatment.[24] While for Eliot "The Raven" is totally unhallowed and to suggest that the bird came from "the saintly days of yore" is mere bluff, for Baudelaire it brings the utterance of "a profound and mysterious word, as terrible as infinity, that thousands of contorted lips have repeated since the beginning of time."[25]

The idea of purity in symbolism often surfaces in comparisons with gems, suggesting not only refinement but also radiance and refraction. One such instance is Baudelaire's early simile linking the Poe poem and the crystal, fitting the scheme of correspondences and projections—which may be abyssal but are not entirely solipsistic in their idealism. Mallarmé, plagued by the oscillating chasm between the void and the eternal, alluded to the same metaphor to justify his matured project of translating Poe's poems:

> Almost every one of the twenty [translated] poems is a unique masterpiece of its kind and produces in one of its facets glittering with strange fires, the thing that was always either flashing or translucent for Poe, pure as the diamond—poetry. So we have here . . . the collection that the translator of *Extraordinary Stories* would thus praise: "It is something profound and dazzling like a dream, mysterious and perfect like crystal."[26]

Purporting to take up the mission of divulging Poe's work where his master Baudelaire had refrained from venturing, the translation that would destroy the prismatic effect and eventually produce but a "rhymed apery" (*singerie rhymée*) of Poe's suggestive verse, Mallarmé at some point abandoned his own drafts attempting a verse rendition, opting instead for prose.[27] Unlike Baudelaire, however, for whom "casting poetry in the form of prose" was a lesser evil, Mallarmé presented such a solution as the best alternative for transmitting "some of the extraordinary sonorous effects of the original music and, here and there perhaps, the feeling itself."[28]

Les Poèmes d'Edgar Poe, published in 1888, is the result of more than two decades of labor, during which Mallarmé suffered his "Crise de Vers": the twenty prose poems that compose it consummate an erosion of genre boundaries, serving the agenda for a nonmercantile prose.[29] Therefore, when Eliot uses the touchstone of the *poem* per se to derive Mallarmé's partiality to the "ominpotence of rhythm" he is downplaying the consequences of *versilibrisme* foreseen by the French poet and critic: "Verse is everywhere in language where there is rhythm, everywhere, except in notices and on page four of the papers. In the genre called prose, there are verses . . . of all rhythms. But in truth there is no prose: there is the alphabet, and then verses more or less tight, more or less diffuse."[30] Subsequent practitioners and theorizers of *le symbolisme*, such as Gustave Khan and René Ghil, would recognize in Poe "the ductility of a meter that seeks to interpret the essence of phenomena and not their circumstances," and consider free verse a continuation of Poe's incitement to achieve in verse the strictly poetic.[31] Longwinded as it may seem, this approach signifies an attention to Poe's reflections on diction and the nature of the poetic, which, as hinted earlier, seems to be a productive trend today in US criticism, with the impact of Poe's performative prosody being compared to Whitman's or Dickinson's.[32]

One should note that the type of genre hybridity where the lyrical permeates the prosaic may be traced back to Poe, who called *Eureka* a prose poem and, alongside the more ratiocinative tales, produced atmospheric and rhythmic compositions such as "Silence—A Fable," or "The Island of the Fay." *Eureka* had an impact on the practice of symbolists like Mallarmé, Ghil, and "the American symbolist," Stuart Merrill.[33] Paul Valéry famously declared his enthusiasm for *Eureka* in a preface to a new edition of Baudelaire's translation, and in it he also criticized the theory of "final causes," which in turn justifies a particular reading of Poe's defense of consistency and reciprocity as premonitory of the theory of relativity: "The doctrine of final causes plays a capital part in Poe' system. This doctrine is no longer fashionable . . . . [I]t would not be exaggerating its importance to recognize in his theory . . . the expression of a tendency toward generalized relativity."[34] Valéry goes on to speak of "formal symmetry" and Eliot's dismissal of such admiration is of less relevance than the justification for its grounds—that is, "[Valéry's] very adult mind playing with ideas because it was too skeptical to hold convictions."[35] Indeed, Valéry definitely shook the belief in poetry's relation with the supernal and turned correspondences into ingenious calculation. He was fascinated by the ruse of knowledge, dramatized as a tautological loop in such texts as "La Jeune Parque" and "Anagogical Revelation," whose Poesque subtexts have been discussed by Lois Vines, James Lawler, and others.[36] If we consider Valéry's own scheme of descendance, in "Situation de Baudelaire" (1924), which departs from the affirmation that Poe revolutionized "the problem" of literature by framing it in (psycho)logical terms and deducing the mechanics of its effects,[37] we must agree with Eliot's appreciation that this obsession was a consequence of Valéry being "the most self-conscious of all poets."[38] Nonetheless, we now know the superlative in such a phrase does not really correspond to a culmination of a tradition; however much Eliot might have wanted to engage in a combat of intellectual titans with his recently deceased counterpart, it is clear today that Valéry was not the end, nor perhaps the high point, of any single tradition.

Eliot's moral judgment on skepticism as the rationale for forgoing interest in the finished creation in favor of the process of composition can also be countered by other perspectives, like that of Mallarmé, who found that the attempt to order chaos was the Promethean effort of the sincere modern poet, as expressed in his commentary on Poe's "Philosophy of Composition":

> [A]n extraordinary idea is suggested by these pages that, albeit written retrospectively . . . are none the less sincere and congenial to Poe; to wit, that all chance must be banned from the modern work of art and can only be feigned; and that the eternal sweep of the wing does not exclude the lucid eye scrutinizing the spaces devoured by its flight.[39]

Mallarmé's renowned achievement, *Un Coup de Dés*, is the corollary of this observation that no matter how predictable the throw of dice, chaos will subsist—hence, the intellect should open up to the subconscious, and to the possible empire of the impure.

Therefore, instead of stopping at "pure poetry" as the extreme of an influence, it is sensible to consider Poe's impact on several turn-of-the-twentieth-century poetical experiments in the precarious balance between the overburdened philosophical mind and the rhythmical creation of something that (at least) compares to Beauty. The latter, attained through "wild effort" (ER: 76), as stated in Poe's essay "The Poetic Principle" and thematized in the poem "Israfel," was very alluring to the two visionary symbolists Paul Verlaine and Arthur Rimbaud. Verlaine is a good case to study, since, defining himself as a young artist, "adulterated" by an exquisite mix of alcohol and Edgar Poe, he declared his first writings to have been "étranges nouvelles sous-marines" (strange submarine tales) after Poe.[40] These seem to hint at the associations of both genius and madness—which in late romanticism further deepened the modernist schism of personality—and at an attraction and openness toward the unconscious, arguably accessible through the "under-current[s]" of meaning that Poe found congenial to imaginative poetry (ER: 24). Nonetheless, just as in the "Philosophy of Composition," such suggestions arise as the climax of a writing method that follows "the precision and rigid consequence of a mathematical problem" (ER: 15), so in Verlaine's first poetry books, *Poèmes Saturniens* (1866), the commitment to a poetics of somberness is seasoned by a metaliterary streak of calculated effect, affirmed in the framing prologue and epilogue, namely the closing lines: "What we need, for us, is boundless study/Unheard of effort, incomparable battle . . .//So we carve with the chisel of our Thought/The untouched block of Beauty."[41] This expression of a scientific approach to poetry was a hallmark of the coeval French Parnassians influenced by Théophile Gautier's motto of "art for art's sake," and by a bold take on Poe's aesthetic reception that, according to Léon Lemonnier, was embodied by the agenda of Verlaine's first book.[42]

However, if Verlaine's Parnassian phase was marked by an association of poetry with "chiseling," hence more connected with the fine and visual arts, it is "music above all else" ("la musique avant toute chose") that became the staple of his mature poetry, as expressed by his "Art Poétique" of 1882. Although Louis Seylaz's remark that this poem was fashioned after Poe's indictments in "The Poetic Principle" seems somewhat exaggerated, its claim for inventiveness in prosody—"You might corral that runaway, Rhyme,/Or you'll get Rhyme Without End"—is akin to the idea of disturbing performativity (namely through the monotone) that is being foregrounded in today's American criticism on Poe.[43] The judgment applied by Jerome McGann to "The Bells," that its purposeful discordant harmony is made to present the reader with recitation alternatives, moving him or her beyond bells that "untune the sky" to the "unheard sound of poetry," could serve Verlaine's poem "Nevermore":[44]

> Ring, round bells; ring, little bells; bells, ring on!
> For my impossible dream has been embodied,
> And I have held it in my arms: Happiness this winged

Traveler who avoids the approach of Man.
—Ring, round bells; ring, little bells; bells, ring on!![45]

This composition from the debut collection of 1866 evinces an early appropriation of the lesson that dreams might materialize only in flawed tolling, dramatizing a tension between idealism and sensory appeal. In the original, the repeated line's assonance, "sonnez, grelots; sonnez, clochettes; sonnez, cloches!" hints at Poe's lesson of the "the long *o* as the most sonorous vowel" (ER: 18), chiming in with the title's loanword, while the alliteration of "cl" brings distortion to the climate of melancholy in a kind of mechanical way that underlines the physicality of effect sought by the poet.

This question of the embodiment of sounds and words was at least as important for symbolism and subsequent early modernism as the dissociation caused by "the penetration of the poetic by the introspective critical activity" that Eliot deemed the culmination of the tradition from Poe to Valéry.[46] Not that Eliot was deaf to Poe's "feeling for the incantatory element in poetry," but he disparaged his execution and how it distanced words from their meaning.[47] However, it was precisely the resonance of words away from familiar sense(s) that many non-English modernists found compelling in Poe, and maybe it was not so much because their foreign ear was not attuned to his abuse of the English language, but because a foreignizing twist of language was a means of defamiliarization and transfer of other wor(l)ds.

Modernismo(s) in Spanish and Portuguese

The literary fortune of Poe as a changing force of literature in Latin America dates from 1887, when Juan Antonio Pérez Bonalde's translation of "The Raven" marked the beginning of an extended influence to many, if not all, the agents of Spanish American modernism.[48] This movement's many ramifications and particularities are sometimes qualified by the plural use of the loanword *Modernismos*—although this italicized distinction might, in turn, endorse an undesirable "critical operation of exclusion."[49] John Eugene Englekirk, in the monumental study *Edgar Allan Poe in Hispanic Literature*, insists that criticism from Spanish America was the first to emphasize Poe's impact on the constructiveness of poetry, not least because of a delight "to express in their own tongue, not alone the content, but the meter, rhythm, and rhyme of Poe's lyrics," or to otherwise gloss over Poe's poetic topics and moods, resulting in numerous rewritings by poets who, across different countries, would lead an aesthetic revolution.[50] Two lesser-known examples suffice to show how Poe's influence was spread out: in Colombia, José Asunción Silva, one of the precursors of the movement, would write verse "technically and thematically similar" to Poe's in the early 1890s, while in the 1920s the Mexican

Rafael Lozano would disseminate Poe among the *estridentistas* with new translations of his poems.[51]

Scholars generally agree, however, that Rúben Darío, from Nicaragua, is the central figure associated with *Modernismo*, and that his book *Los Raros* (1896) initiated the program that would promote in Latin America the refinement and development of a sovereign poetical language in Spanish. Poe is the opening figure of the book, praised with much of the Baudelairian rhetoric of *le poète maudit*, but with a significant emphasis on his "poetic flame" (*llama de poesía*) as a warning beacon of changing times: "one of those divine partially madmen necessary for human progress." Verlaine is likewise exalted in *Los Raros* for his gift for song, in terms uncannily evocative of Poe's "Annabel Lee" and "Israfel," mixed with Catholic collocations: "no other tongue, let alone the tongues of prostrate seraphs, has better sung the flesh and blood of the Lamb."[52] A superficial reading of these statements might make one wonder whether they are just a rehashing of European romantic rhetoric combined with the French decadent *frisson*, leading to the hasty conclusion of misalignment with the Western modernist suspicion of inspiration and of the facile effects of song. For lack of substantial research so far, I would refrain from any definitive assessment, but I suggest the stress must be put on the heterogeneity of the *modernistas*, and on the transatlantic import of what Mejias-Lopez has called "the inverted conquest."[53] Lopez argues for the unprecedented cosmopolitan rearrangement of late nineteenth-century Latin America that propitiated literary innovation and the investment in "discursive authority and legitimacy aimed to undermine the self-appointed authority of European discourse."[54] The autonomy of poetic language set forth by Poe, underscoring the need of "no acknowledgment to the outside world for its aims," might have played a helpful role in the resistance to foreign demands and in the affirmation of a "strong sense of a beginning" in these Latin parts of America.[55] "Strong sense of a beginning" is a phrase I borrow from William Carlos Williams, for he, too, saw in Poe an impulse for the (re)placement of the literature of his time, significantly attuned to a nonnationalist locality of "the American grain." Maria Filippakopolou's *Transatlantic Poe* has recently brought into focus both the cosmopolitanism and Americanism of the case for Poe's "culturally deviant idiom,"[56] and indeed Williams's wording of the need to escape from "a formless mass" might bring us back to Darío's appreciation of Poe in *Los Raros*, which starts with the Nicaraguan poet's crossing to "the vast country of the United States." Upon arrival, he notes "the yelping Yankee accent" mingled with the "echo of a vast soliloquy of [numerical] ciphers," unexpectedly redeemed by the apparition of Poe and his "candid choir of ideal submarine deities."[57]

The aforementioned passage is characterized by synesthesia, a symbolist staple that relies fundamentally on finding new prosodic combinations to shake words from their normal associations. The method fell out of favor in the height of the US modernist poetic practice of the visual semantics of *imagisme*, and this might help explain why Williams was one of the few to value Poe's "clear[ance]" of "the particles of language." In fact, he compared Poe's and Gertrude Stein's endeavors, the latter being the US modernist arguably most attuned to the auditory and to the orality of reading: "he [Poe] used words so playfully his sentences seem to fly away from sense, the destructive! with the conserving abandon, foreshadowed, of a Gertrude Stein."[58]

Fernando Pessoa, key figure of another *Modernismo*—the Portuguese, whose first momentum took place in the second decade of the twentieth century—was endowed with the transatlantic fortune of communing both with a French-European tradition and an Anglophone extraterritorial upbringing (he was educated in South Africa).[59] His response to Poe's poetry—early admiration and thoughtful later criticism—might help explain its seductiveness, partial and tainted, to different aspects of modernity in poetry. Pessoa wrote his first verse in English and already under different pennames, anticipating the phenomenon of *heteronymy* for which he is renowned (creation of personae with a diverse body of work). In his journal he describes Alexander Search, the most often found signature in the English poetry of 1903–1910, as "Poesque, complicated with Baudelaire and Rollinat style."[60] "The Bells" was a productive prosodic subtext for Search's experiments, and in one particular poem, "Insomnia," dissonance and the monotone are used to enhance the way feeling collapses under the accelerated mechanics of reason: "A thousand times a reeling/Of reason around my world,/ And around reason feeling/ . . . /In a blacker darkness whirled."[61] The lines predate the judgment Pessoa passed on Poe in the notes he left for a study on madness and genius, intimating that near madness in Poe was the result of the excess of reason,[62] in turn disproportionate with a synthetic ability to process sensitivity. As previously alluded, this dissociation might be framed within the "modern theme of the disintegration of personality," whose first impressive realization Allen Tate attributed to Poe.[63] In various critical writings where Pessoa mentions Poe, he fixates on how genuine poetic feeling is affected by the necessary complex ideation of new poetry; a note on his translations of Poe defines a poem as an "intellectualized impression" or "an idea made emotion, communicated to others by means of a rhythm."[64] "Rhythmical conformity with the original" is the main challenge Pessoa finds in translating Poe, specified as follows:

> [T]his rhythm is a double one, like the concave and convex aspects of the same arc: it is made up of a verbal or musical rhythm and of a visual or image rhythm, which concurs inwardly with it. The translation of a poem should therefore conform absolutely (1) to the idea or emotion which constitutes the poem, (2) to the verbal rhythm in which the idea or emotion is expressed; it should conform relatively to the inner or visual rhythm, keeping to the images themselves when it can, but keeping always to the type of image.
>
> It was on this criterion that I based my translations into Portuguese of Poe's "Annabel Lee" and "Ulalume," which I translated, not because of their intrinsic worth, but because they were a standing challenge to translators.[65]

The phrasing recalls Pound's reflections on the translation of logopoeia (the dance of the intellect), melopoeia (musical prosody), and fanopoeia (visual imagery)—with an important difference: for Pound, the near impossibility of transposing sound effects between languages was a lesser evil as long as one could keep up with the suggestions of verbal painting.[66] Although conceding in a letter to Harriet Monroe that Poe was a "good enough poet, and after Whitman the best America has produced (probably?)," Pound would, like his expatriate friend Eliot, affirm he was "not to be set up as model for anyone who wrote in English," seconding his opinion with the ironic remark that "I know Poe wrote other poems besides 'Et le corbeau dit jamais plus.' " In his criticism of Poe's indulgence in "over-alliteration" one might detect a divergent understanding of what gives a poem its "inner force," and presume that relying on the visual, rather than the auditory, points to a differentiated appraisal of Poe by the Anglophone modernists.[67]

In the Light of US Modernism: A Poetry of Phosphorescence

When Poe is recalled by modern(ist) US poets, he often "appears" in a vision. Walt Whitman, although he too reached out romantically for the ears of his audience, is the first to offer a remarkable instance of "picturing" Poe. Telling of his resistance toward a possible influence, he finally faces the madman Poe on a boat in the middle of a storm: "On the deck was . . . a dim man, apparently enjoying all the terror, the murk and the dislocation of which he was the center and the victim. This figure of my lurid dream might stand for Edgar Poe, his spirit, his fortunes, and his poems—themselves all lurid dreams."[68] The memorial tone of the whole reflection from *Specimen Days* attests, as has been noted, to both authors' treatment of "communities of death,"[69] but in the cited passage I would single out the image of a strange hue, along with the use of the adjective *lurid*, which, like *lucid*, comes from *lux* (light), and echoes an earlier passage of the same prose text: "Poe's verses . . . probably belong among the electric lights of imaginative literature, brilliant and dazzling but with no heat."[70]

This quality of unhallowed light emanating from Poe's poetry has been noted by others, not all Americans. The Swedish poet Ola Hansson, who chose self-exile after the shock of the reception of his decadent collection of verse *Sensitiva Amorosa* (1887), would describe the growth of Poe's poetry "in distant horizons": "like fire and night, like phosphorescence on water, it climbs up into the firmament, and we who live in the twilight of the century see it blooming high over our heads, its tendrils reaching far out in the deep night that lies before us."[71] For the lack of space and in-depth research to occupy this study with other horizons, it seems worthwhile to point out that in the North American reception of Poe this quality of "phosphorescence," defined by the *OED* precisely in the same aforementioned Whitmanian terms, "the emission of light without any perceptible heat," recurs in the (re)visions of US poets.[72] Interestingly enough, the title of a recent article on Williams's *In the American Grain* is "A Phosphorous History," by which term its author seems to indicate the poetical method of collating diverse "beginners" of a living tradition of American imagination.[73] I have previously mentioned how Williams sees Poe as one who sought to (re)define the material of American literature and language, bringing up "the ghoulish, the driven back," enveloped also in a kind of phosphorous hue: "There is no aroma to his words, rather a luminosity, that comes of a dissociation of anything else than thought and ideals."[74] This kind of light, then, is associated both with an otherworldly evocation and with how language, when stripped of context (or is it convention) persists in thought. It is the "tremulous light" of "dreaming," inside near darkness, by which the poet wanders in the company of "Psyche, my soul" (M 1: 416), a light not natural but perhaps not mortal either, as it recurs time and again. Most impressively, in the final section of Hart Crane's *The Bridge* (1930), it is emitted from the smoking body of Edgar Poe, whose vision "bursts from a smoldering bundle," with a fiery head hanging in New York's hallucinating underground journey, which moreover alludes to the urban glare of neon and consumerism: "And why do I often meet your visage here,/Your eyes like agate lanterns—on and on/Below the toothpaste and the dandruff ads?"[75] One of first poems by the beat poet Allen Ginsberg, dated 1944, presents the scenario of "A Night in the Village (with Edgar Allen Ginsberg)" and describes the sounds coming from basement bars with the same kind of glare: "where reddish light/Obscenely sweated in the night/Where neons called to passers-by."[76] More than thirty years later, in a poem dated "January 10, 1977," Ginsberg would outdo Poe's strident grimness by imagining "Poe in Dust," likewise "starring white-eyes . . . at viaducts heavy-bound and manacled upon the city's heart," from the vantage point of a grave "[s]limed . . . on his phosphor'd toe-nails."[77]

I am not aware that "phosphorescence" has ever been claimed as a poetic category, nor is this essay the place to graft the term onto literary criticism. Nonetheless, it seems one might draw up lists of poets—T. S. Eliot, Marianne Moore, Elizabeth Bishop, Wallace Stevens—who mostly do not have "it," against those—Emily Dickinson, Hart Crane, Sylvia Plath, Allen Ginsberg—who do. These incomplete groupings are also misleading: all of the previously mentioned "nonphosphorous" poets could subscribe to Eliot's assertion that "one cannot be sure that one's own writing has not been influenced by Poe."[78] In fact, the detectable influence of Poe in Eliot's creative work is mostly of the lurid type, and there is some phosphorescence in a line like the early verse "your shadow leaping behind the fire against the red rock," later modified for *The Waste Land*.[79] But the tone of Eliot most frequently subdues hallucination with the digressive, just as Marianne Moore, despite a fondness for the sensual hold of poetry in a terrific light—"Hands that can grasp, eyes/that can dilate, hair that can rise/if it must"—mostly strove for a poetics of genuine observation mixed with socio-political allegory.[80] Speaking of Moore, Bishop, and Plath, I am mindful of the material in their poetry that might prompt studies touching upon the ghostlike shadow of poets who entombed women, but that falls out of the scope I mean to embrace here, which is a kind of obfuscated clairvoyance, partly eerie and partly artificial, that somehow, via Poe, amplifies and distorts the reliance on vision of American poetry. In "Edgar Allan Poe & the Jukebox," an early composition by Bishop that gave the title to a posthumous collection of her scattered poems, the poetical subject, curiously, while dwelling on the tension between the exact and the mechanic, sets the motto for such distortion in lines that run parallel (alternatively?) to the main body of the poem: "blue as gas/blue as the pupil/of a dead man's eye."[81]

More visual than sonorous, "phosphorescence" nonetheless irradiates also from a certain briskness or incantation of diction; it has to do with light emitted from the decomposed, the afterdeath, and also with spirituality, but one that is tinged always with the fantastic, or the psychological gothic, as well as with a lower/popular imagery of scatology. And it has, I think, a modern quality: it grows from facile arousal—pulling the right "pinions and strings," as Poe put it in "The Philosophy of Composition" (ER: 14), and hence its association also with the codes of advertising. It sustains nonetheless the capacity, to borrow from the *OED*'s extended definition of the physical phenomenon, to operate "on a longer timescale, so that emission continues after excitation ceases."[82]

Addenda of After-Effects: Poetry from the Vantage Points of (De) Construction and Translation

Given the lack of space for analyzing the uses of Poe for late modernist waves and postmodernist poetry—the beats, or the European movement of surrealism, as well as a few short-lived but influential vanguards in Eastern Europe [83]—I would still like to briefly mention the development of literary theory in a cross-fertilization with other fields, especially structuralist linguistics, audience response, and translation studies. For that, I will use texts from two different geographical provenances, the Russian theorist Roman Jakobson and the Brazilian poet and literary critic Haroldo de Campos.

Following previous Russian formalists who sought to isolate the specificity of the poetic and disengage it from discursive language, Jakobson, in "Linguistics and Poetics" (1959), would famously define the "poetic function" as that which promotes "the palpability of signs" through "project[ing] the principle of equivalence from the axis of selection to the axis of combination."[84] In rather simplistic terms, this means attaching less importance to the referential link between words and things than to corresponding connotations and contiguous associations between words placed together. In the process of contiguous construction, or metonymy, Jakobson would stress the differential quality of poetry as "sound symbolism": "an undeniably objective relation founded on a phenomenal connection between different sensory modes, in particular between the visual and the auditory experience."[85] "The Raven" is a central piece in the illustration of this concept, because of its "paranomasic strings" and nearly anagrammatic inversions (the word "raven" is seen as "an embodied mirror image" of "never"), which are said to be what "we would expect from such a deliberate experimenter in anticipatory, regressive modus operandi, such a master in 'writing backwards' as Edgar Allan Poe."[86] Jakobson makes two interesting moves here in respect to translation: first, he opens the door for the auditory to "translate" as the visual, permitting him to draw parallels between the grammatic of verse and that of advertisement and political slogans; and second, he posits that the nexus between sound and meaning should follow, in poetry, a logic of replacement more than equivalence. The latter point is explored in another essay of the same period, "On Linguistic Aspects of Translation" (1959):

> [P]aranomasia reigns over poetic art, and whether its rule is absolute or limited, poetry by definition is untranslatable. Only creative transposition is possible: either intralingual transposition—from one poetic shape into another, or interlingual transposition—from one language into another, or finally intersemiotic transposition—from one system of signs into another (from verbal art into music, dance, cinema or painting.)[87]

Creative transposition, ruled by a logic of replacement taking into account the effort of the vanguards and the aesthetics of the receiving culture, is the basis for the Latin American concept of *transcreation*, supporting a revolutionary reinvigoration of language, in both its verbal and iconic facets.[88]

The Brazilian founder of concrete poetry, Haroldo de Campos, took from Jakobson the cue that the isolation of paranomasia as a constitutive aspect of poetry derived partly from an interpretation of Poe's prioritization of phonetic aspects in the "Philosophy of Composition." In "Poe: dos Avessos" ["Poe: Reverse Engineer"] (1976), de Campos reviewed Jakobson's considerations about "The Raven" in support of translation as a "critical activity," with a close reading of previous efforts to render Poe's tour de force into Portuguese. This also allowed an association of Fernando Pessoa and E. A. Poe in the defense of poetry as mystification, not because of any vulgar ruse, but because language is a fictive material that operates through converse combinations. Its materiality (sound and the design of the page) is the condition to suggest and open up meanings—so much so that for the critic, poetry might overturn Saussure's proposition of the arbitrariness of the sign through iconic necessity.[89] The latter was seen as an evolutive synthesis of poetic tradition, capable of reaching an immediate effect, plurally and universally, and became the mainstay of *concrete poetry*, initiated by Haroldo de Campos along with his brother Augusto, researcher of the relations of poetry and popular music, and their friend Décio Pignateri, whose work prefigured what is now called media studies. Ancillary to the project was the exercise of "transcreation," an association of Jakobson's notion of "creative transposition" with an earlier design of "cannibalism" in Brazilian *modernismo*: the appropriation of the most vigorous poetics in Western language to serve the cause of "transfusion" of new blood to this developing world's avant-garde.[90] Thus, several decades after Poe was first acknowledged in the early manifestoes of concrete poetry—for instance, with Pignateri in 1957 evaluating Poe's method as a functional approach to fast communication, and anticipating Marshal McLuhan's intuition that "Poe involved his readers in the creative process"[91]—Augusto de Campos would create "Transcorvo" [Trans-Raven]. Such creation is a visual poem that presents, in the stylized shape of a bird (with three-dimensional letters forming wings that evoke also a cross), a version of the last stanza of "The Raven," rigorously following the analysis of Jakobson.

Schooled in Russian formalism, Jakobson arguably isolated a poetic function of language that is hard to sustain within a communicative scheme for language precisely because it aims at what falls beyond the discursive, the transrational, which comes through a forcible and uncanny attachment of sounds and words. The transrational was connected to the early twentieth-century Russian vanguard, *zaoum*.[92] As mentioned earlier, American criticism of Poe's poetry in the twenty-first century has turned to the "pleasure of disarray" in Poe's poems, whose seemingly incongruent stresses and rhyming echoes offer alternatives to the more obvious readings.[93] This arousal of the reader's reaction to discordances in Poe's symbolic architecture might be considered the full argument of something Marshal McLuhan intuited, seeing in the creation both of the detective plot and the symbolic poem by Poe an analogous process to "the mosaic" in TV and the telegraph, which requires subjective reading, albeit manipulated, to fill in the blanks. Not surprisingly, McLuhan was familiar with the texts of the Brazilian *concretistas* and would take up their programmatic use of the term "verbivocovisual" (in turn borrowed from Joyce) as an umbrella term to emphasize an intersemiotic turn in contemporary poetics.[94]

In conclusion, the emphasis on the processes and methods of language has led all of the aforementioned postmodern critics and creators (Jakobson, the Campos brothers and Décio Pignateri, even Marshal McLuhan) to pay their respects to the lineage of Poe-Baudelaire-Mallarmé-Valéry. However, they shun the "pure" status of poetry, by investing in the combination of high and low cultural imagery, by bringing it to print and to visual culture, and by envisaging a continuity between the poetics of poetry and translation (a necessarily hybrid practice). Poe could not have foreseen his contribution to the literary import of how and what to translate; however, the persistence of competitive translations and respective translators' viewpoints on the innovative value of Poe's "poetic principle(s)" is one of the most profound developments in the modes of articulation of the new poetics that somehow—and sometimes very tenuously—can be traced back to him.

Poe's role in the demarcation of the realm of poetry had, therefore, an indelible influence on modernist poetics, even if self-consciousness as the hallmark of the poem per se might have been overestimated by certain critics to the detriment of other tendencies and the equally strong pull of the unconscious, where sound above sense implied the effort for wildness and the disruption of discursivity.[95] Furthermore, from Whitman and Verlaine to Ruben Darío and such diverse poets as Allen Ginsberg or Elizabeth Bishop, the countercultural radiation of Poe as a visionary histrio, an independent spirit unrestrained by didactics and morals, proved fruitful for the liberation of verse across the Americas and beyond the Atlantic. The accentuation of affective prosody over the dullness of competent linguistic skills, on the one hand, and speculation on Poe's insights into the pathologies of the mind, on the other, inspired the European avant-gardes as well as the subterranean literary stance of poets throughout the twentieth century in diverse geopolitical groupings. The latest critical trend seems to privilege a parallel between more "hoaxical" and more "mystical" approaches, alongside a scrutiny of different critical texts by Poe (e.g., "The Rationale of Verse" and "The Poetic Principle"), to unveil the "undercurrents" from where poetry unleashes alternatives to seemingly obvious meanings or longstanding "preferred" readings.[96]

Notes

1. M. H. Abrams and Geoffrey Galt Harpham, *A Glossary of Literary Terms*, 11th ed. (Stamford, CT: Cengage Learning, 2015), 226.
2. See Irving Howe, "The Culture of Modernism," in *Decline of the New* (London: Harcourt, Brace & World, 1970), 7–9. Howe's perspective is partly derived from Georg Lukacs's critique in "The Ideology of Modernism," in *Realism in Our Time*, trans. John and Necke Mander (New York: Harper and Row, 1964), 17–46.
3. Baudelaire published his first translation of Poe ("Mesmeric Reverlation" as "Révelation Magnétique") in 1848 and his last anthology of Poe's tales (*Histoires Grotesques et Sérieuses*) in 1865. The compound "Poedelaire" was first coined by Fitz Gubrodt—in "Poedelaire: Translation and the Volatility of the Letter," in *Diacritics* 22, no. 3–4 (1992): 49–68—but the story of this encounter and its impact on the subsequent French tradition has gained the interest of critics since the 1920s. Some of the relevant works are quoted in the notes that follow, but it is fair to cite here a few pioneers, like Louis Seylaz, *Edgar Poe et les Premiers Symbolistes* (1923; repr., Genebra: Slatkine, 1979); Célestin Pierre Cambiaire, *The Influence of Edgar Allan Poe in France* (New York: G. E. Stechert & Co., 1927); and Léon Lemonnier, *Edgar Poe et les Poètes Français* (Rennes: Impr. Commerciale de Bretagne, 1932). See also the landmark studies in English by Partick F. Quinn, *The French Face of Edgar Poe* (Carbondale: Southern Illinois University Press, 1957); and W.T. Bandy, *The Influence and Reputation of Edgar Allan Poe in Europe* (Baltimore: The Edgar Allan Poe Society/Enoch Pratt Library, 1959).
4. I borrow the term from Ann Ardis and P. Collier, eds., *Transatlantic Print Culture, 1880–1940: Emerging Modernisms, Emerging Media* (London: Palgrave Macmillan, 2008).
5. Maria Filippakopoulou, in an insightful study that triangulates the reception of Poe by Baudelaire, Williams, and Eliot, draws on Baudelaire's correspondence with Poe's aunt, Maria Clemm, to explore the fictive "family romance" uniting both writers, with respective fantasies of abandon and adoption—*Transatlantic Poe: Eliot, Williams and Huxley, Readers of the French Poe* (Oxford, UK: Peter Lang, 2015), 49–57, 77–79.
6. Joseph Chiari, *Symbolisme from Poe to Mallarmé: The Growth of a Myth* (New York: Gordian Press, 1970), 1.
7. Thomas Stearns Eliot, "From Poe to Valéry," in *The Recognition of Edgar Allan Poe*, ed. Eric W. Carlson (Ann Arbor: University of Michigan Press, 1966), 205–219.
8. See Chiari, *Symbolisme from Poe to Mallarmé*, 105.
9. Robert Kopp, introduction to Poe's poetry in *Edgar Allan Poe: Contes. Essais. Poèmes*, ed. Claude Richard (Paris: Robert Laffont, 1989), 1203, my translation. Due to length limits, foreign passages are not cited in the original language, unless for philological or interpretative purposes.
10. Eliot, "From Poe to Valéry," 216.
11. Eliot, "From Poe to Valéry," 219.
12. Elaborating on those incongruencies of Poe's verse where T. S. Eliot would rather find "an irresponsibility towards the meaning of words" (210), Richard Wilbur compares them to a Buddhist *koan*: "Poe's strategy here is analogous to that of the Zen buddhist who

contemplates a logical contradiction in hopes of short-circuiting the intellect and so inviting a mystic illumination" (introduction to *Poe: Complete Poems* [New York: Dell, 1959], 35). David Murray discusses Poe's use of the symbol as postromantic, breaking up with the organicist, unifying view in "'A Strange Sound, as of a Harp-String Broken': The Poetry of Edgar Allan Poe" in *Edgar Allan Poe: The Design of Order*, ed. Robert Lee (London: Vision, 1987), 135–153.

13. Jerome McGann's *The Poet Edgar Allan Poe: Alien Angel* (Cambridge, MA: Harvard University Press, 2014) is the single most extensive full-length study of Poe's poetry produced by an American critic since Floyd Stovall collected a number of his essays in *Edgar Poe the Poet* (Charlottesville: University Press of Virginia, 1969). McGann soundly argues for a performativity in Poe's prosody that indeed distances it from the mere indefiniteness achieved by intimacy with music, which Stovall early on associated with Coleridge's contribution to the romantic emphasis on expression.
14. Stéphane Mallarmé, "Le tombeau d'Edgar Poe," *Œuvres complétes*, ed. Bertrand Marchal (Paris: Gallimard, 1998), 1:38. Mallarmé provided his own rough draft of the poem into English, where the quoted line reads, "to give too pure a meaning to the words of the tribe" (Mallarmé, 1:1193).
15. Thomas Stearns Eliot, *Collected Poems: 1909–1962* (Orlando, FL: Harcourt, Brace & Co., 2009), 204.
16. McGann, *The Poet Edgar Allan Poe*, 205.
17. William Carlos Williams, *In the American Grain* (1925; New York: New Directions, 2009), 221.
18. Eliot, "From Poe to Valéry," 213.
19. Eliot, "From Poe to Valéry," 214–215.
20. Eliot, "From Poe to Valéry," 211.
21. On the pre-modernist gesture of Poe's defense of composition over inspiration, see J. F. Lynen, "The Death of the Present: Edgar Allan Poe," in *The Design of the Present: Essays on Time and Form in American Literature* (New Haven, CT: Yale University Press, 1969), 259.
22. "The Poetic Principle" is an influential essay for an understanding of symbolism as an urge for the visionary, even if attained through the soil of dejection, antinatural ideation, and fabrication. In the late nineteenth century, this understanding was equated with decadentism, and the decadents waged war with more progressive currents that claimed above all an experimentalism following new musical combinations. Jean Moréas, in the mid-1880s, led a symbolist schism against his more programmatic counterparts Gustav Khan and René Ghil, and would defend in "Les Décadents": "The so-called decadents demand above all in their art the pure and eternal concept of the symbol, and they have the stubborness to believe with Edgar Poe that 'Beauty is the sole legitimate province of 'poetry.'" Jean Moréas, "Les Décadents" in *Les Premieres Armes du Symbolisme* (Paris: Léon Vanier, 1889), 27–30, my translation.
23. Charles Baudelaire, "Notes Nouvelles sur Edgar Poe," in *Oeuvres Complètes*, ed. Claude Pichois (Paris: Gallimard/Pléiade), 2:328 (translated by Lois and Francis Hyslop in Eric W. Carlson, ed., *The Recognition of Edgar Allan Poe*, 52). For a critique of Baudelaire's blending of citation and misappropriation in his paratexts on Poe, see Maria Filippakopoulou, *Transatlantic Poe: Eliot, Williams and Huxley, Readers of the French Poe* (Bern: Peter Lang, 2015), 98–105.
24. Cf.: "[T]he subject is little, the treatment is everything"—Eliot, "From Poe to Valéry," 218.

25. Eliot, "From Poe to Valéry," 210; Charles Baudelaire, "Avant-propos à la Génèse d'un Poème" ["Genesis of a Poem"], in *Baudelaire on Poe: Critical Papers*, ed. and trans. Lois and Frances E. Hyslop (State College, PA: Bald Eagle Press, 1952), 156.
26. Mallarmé, *Œuvres complètes*, ed. Bertrand Marchal (Paris: Gallimard, 2003), 2:770. Baudelaire citation, "Notes Nouvelles," 336. My translation.
27. Baudelaire, "Avant-propos," 157. Mallarmé started to translate Poe around the age of eighteen in his *Glanes* notebook, where he jotted down verse attempts for nine poems.
28. Baudelaire, "Avant-propos," 157; Mallarmé, *Œuvres complètes*, 2:771.
29. Mallarmé's "verse crisis" labors in the gap between the poetic and the demotic (and, to some extent, the democratic). The above quoted lines of his "Le tombeau d'Edgar Poe," demanding a purer sense to the words of the tribe, can be read as reinforcing the condemnation of economic and contractual uses of language, and as a call for releasing the potentialities of the linguistic sign, thereby anticipating the statement of "Crise de Vers," an essay of 1892.
30. Eliot, "From Poe to Valéry," 210; Mallarmé, "Sur l'Evolution Littéraire [*Enquête de Jules Huret*]" (1891); quoted and translated by Elizabeth McCombie in her introduction to *Collected Poems and Other Verse*, by Stéphane Mallarmé, ed. E. H. and A. M. Blackmore (New York: Oxford University Press, 2006), xiii.
31. Gustave Kahn, *La Nouvelle Revue*, 1 de Abril de 1897; cited in Lemonnier, *Edgar Poe et les Poètes Français*, 130, my translation. For further discussion about the controversial role of Poe in French free verse, see Cambiaire, *Edgar Allan Poe in France*, 156; and Lemonnier, *Edgar Poe et les Poètes Français*, 149.
32. See Derek Pollard, "The Postmodern Nineteenth Century: 'Sonnet—To Science' and the Case for Poe's Avant-Garde Poetics," *The Edgar Allan Poe Review* 17, no. 4 (Autumn 2016): 105.
33. See James Lawler, "*L'Eureka* Mallarméen," *Critique* 16, no. 619 (Dec. 1998): 787–811; or M. C. Henry, *Stuart Merrill: la Contribution d'un Américain au Symbolisme Français* (1927; repr. Genebra: Slatkine, 1977), 222.
34. Valéry, "On Poe's 'Eureka,'" in *The Recognition of Edgar Allan Poe*, 106–107.
35. Eliot, "From Poe to Valéry," 208.
36. Paul Valéry, *Collected Works of Paul Valéry*, vols. 1 and 2, trans. James Lawler and Hilary Corke, respectively (Princeton, NJ: Princeton University Press, 1969–1971), 1:60–105 and 2:12–13. For Poe's influence, see Lois Davis Vines, *Valéry and Poe: A Literary Legacy* (New York/London: New York University Press, 1992); James Lawler, *Edgar Poe et les Poètes Français, suivi d'un conférence de Paul Valéry* (Paris: Julliard, 1998); and Barbara Scapolo, "Paul Valéry face à Edgar Allan Poe. Une pensée philosophique entre composition et creation," *Tangence* 95 (2011): 11–28. Hilary Corke, in her notes to *Collected Works of Paul Valéry* (Princeton, NJ: Princeton University Press, 1970), points to Poe's "Mesmeric Revelation," translated by Baudelaire as "Révelation Magnetique," as the source for the title "Anagogical Revelation" (312).
37. Paul Valéry, "Situation de Baudelaire," *Oeuvres*, ed. Jean Hytier (Paris: Gallimard, 1956), 1:605–606.
38. Eliot, "From Poe to Valéry," 217.
39. Mallarmé, *Oeuvres*, 2:772. On the sincere poetic plight and the skeptic "plot of God" in Poe's poetry, see also G. R. Thompson's theory of Poe's romantic irony in *Circumscribed Eden of Dreams: Dreamvision and Nightmare in Poe's Early Poetry* (Baltimore: The Enoch Pratt Free Library, 1984).

40. Paul Verlaine, in, respectively, *Mes Prisons* (1893) and *Confessions* (1895), in *Oeuvres en Prose Complètes* (Gallimard: Paris, 1972), 355, 484.
41. Paul Verlaine, *Poems under Saturn/Poèmes saturniens*, trans. and intro. Karl Kirchwey (Princeton, NJ: Princeton University Press, 2011), 143.
42. Lemonnier, *Edgar Poe et les Poètes Français*, 76–77. Théophile Gautier's famous phrase "l'art pour l'art" is stated in the preface to *Mademoiselle de Maupin* of 1835, so there is no possible Poe influence here, but the kinship with the American author was sealed when he agreed, upon Baudelaire's request, to write a notice to the third edition of *Nouvelles Histoires Extraordinaires* in 1868.
43. See Seylaz, *Edgar Allan Poe et les Premiers Symbolistes*, 176; the quoted verse is by Paul Verlaine, *Selected Poems*, trans. Martin Sorrell (Princeton, NJ: Princeton University Press, 1999), 125.
44. McGann, *The Poet Edgar Allan Poe*, 181. See also Jonathan Elmer, "The Jingle Man: Trauma and the Aesthetic," in *Fission and Fusions*, ed. Lesley Marx et al. (Cape Cod: University of the Western Cape Press, 1997), 131–145; and Christopher Aruffo, "Reconsidering Poe's 'Rationale of Verse,'" *Poe Studies* 44, no. 1 (2011): 69–88.
45. Verlaine, *Poems under Saturn*, 97.
46. Eliot, "From Poe to Valéry," 218.
47. Eliot, "From Poe to Valéry," 209.
48. See John Eugene Englekirk, *Edgar Allan Poe in Hispanic Literature* (New York: Instituto de las Españas, 1934), 146; and Emron Esplin's essay in this volume, "Poe and His Global Advocates." Esplin, in the first chapter of *Borges's Poe* (Athens, GA: University of Georgia Press, 2015), also discusses how the *Modernistas's* emphasis on Poe as the inspired poet was at odds with the lesson of "The Philosophy of Composition" that would be recuperated by Borges (in turn, applying it more to a theory of narrative than poetry).
49. Alejandro Mejías-Lopez warns rightly that the insistence on using the italicized form of *Modernismo* contributes to an erasure, through untranslatability, of "the first movement to have coined the term [Modernism]"—*The Inverted Conquest: The Myth of Modernity and The Transatlantic onset of Modernism* (Nashville, TN: Vanderbilt University Press, 2009), 2.
50. Englekirk, *Edgar Allan Poe in Hispanic Literature*, 35.
51. Apart from Englekirk, information here is collated from Susan F. Levine and Stuart Levine, "Poe in Spanish America," in *Poe Abroad*, ed. Lois Vines (Iowa City: University of Iowa Press, 1999), 121–129. It is worth noting that less evident phenomena also play a part in the shaping of literary systems and their intellectual environment, for instance José Martí's unfinished translations of "Annabel Lee" and "The Raven."
52. Ruben Darío, *Los Raros* (Madrid: Editorial Mundo Latino, 1918), 27 and 55, respectively, my translation. Note that the covetous seraphs of "Annabel Lee" are invoked earlier in the book, 21.
53. Besides Mejías-Lopez, quoted in note 50, see Gwen Kirpatrick, *The Dissonant Legacy of Modernism: Lugones, Herrera y Reissig and the Voices of Modern Latin American Poetry* (Berkeley: University of California Press, 1989)—with comments on the uses of Poe for the *modernistas* (especially Leopoldo Lugones, pp. 83, 93).
54. Mejías-Lopez, *The Inverted Conquest*, 76.
55. First quotation from Kirpatrick, *The Dissonant Legacy of Modernism*, 47; second quotation from William Carlos Williams, *In the American Grain*, 222.
56. Filippakopoulou, *Transatlantic Poe*, 150.
57. Williams, *In the American Grain*, 221; Darío, *Los Raros*, 17–22.

58. Williams, *In the American Grain*, 221.
59. For an extended bibliography of studies on Fernando Pessoa on Poe, particularly through translation, see note 34 of my essay "Poe Translations in Portugal: A Standing Challenge for Changing Literary Systems," in *Translated Poe*, ed. Emron Esplin and Margarida Vale de Gato (Bethlehem: Lehigh University Press, 2014), 336; also, in the same book, George Monteiro's chapter "Fernando Pessoa Spiritualizes Edgar Allan Poe," 283–288. My choice of Fernando Pessoa as a representative of *Modernismo* in Iberian Europe is related to my previous research but also to the stated circumstance of his cosmopolitan experience, blending the Anglophone and Francophone into the more Latin/Iberian. Poe, however, also had an impact on *Modernismo* in Spain, which in turn grew in part from the exchanges with Spanish America, as well as in Italian *Futurismo*, namely with Marinetti and Ungaretti, both of them crediting Poe's influence. See, from the already cited *Poe Abroad*, José Antonio Gurpegui, "Poe in Spain," 108–114, and Massimo Bacigalupo, "Poe in Italy," 67–70; in his article "Spanish Versions of an American Classic," Santiago Guerrero-Stretchen interestingly alludes also to Leopoldo Maria Panero's investment in Poe's derivation of "estrangement"—in *Translated Poe*, 295–297.
60. Pessoa, *Escritos Autobiográficos, Automáticos e de Reflexão Pessoal*, ed. Richard Zenith (Lisbon: Assírio e Alvim, 2003), 22.
61. Pessoa, *Poemas Ingleses II. Edição Crítica de Fernando Pessoa*, ed. João Dionísio (Lisbon: INCM, 1997), 5:90, my translation. See Margarida Vale de Gato, "'Around Reason Feeling': Poe's Impact on Fernando Pessoa's Modernist Proposals," in *Poe's Pervasive Influence*, ed. Barbara Cantalupo (Bethlehem: Lehigh University Press, 2012), 91–108.
62. "Poe had genius, Poe had talent for he has great reasoning powers, and reasoning is the formal expression of talent," writes Fernando Pessoa, *Escritos Sobre Génio e Loucura*, ed. Jerónimo Pizarro (Lisbon: Imprensa Nacional–Casa da Moeda, 2006), 1:417.
63. Allen Tate, "The Angelic Imagination," in *The Recognition of Edgar Allan Poe*, 241–242.
64. Pessoa, *Páginas de Estética e de Teoria e Critica Literárias*, ed. Georg Rudolf Lind and Jacinto Prado Coelho (Lisbon: Ática, 1973), 74–75.
65. Pessoa, *Páginas de Estética e de Teoria e Critica Literárias*, 74–75.
66. See Ezra Pound, "How to Read," in *Literati Essays of Ezra Pound* (New York: New Directions, 1928), 25.
67. Ezra Pound to Harriet Monroe, January 31, 1915, in *Selected Letters 1907–1941 of Ezra Pound*, ed. D. D. Page (New York: New Directions, 1971), 50.
68. Walt Whitman, *Leaves of Grass and Selected Prose*, ed. John Kouwenhoven (New York, Random House, 1950), 715.
69. Adam C. Bradford contends, in *Communities of Death: Whitman, Poe, and the American Culture of Mourning* (Columbia: University of Missouri Press, 2014), that Poe's macabre was for Whitman a source of inspiration at least as important as Emersonian transcendentalism.
70. Whitman, *Leaves of Grass and Selected Prose*, 715.
71. Ola Hansson, "Edgar Allan Poe," in *Poe in Northlight*, ed. Carl L. Anderson (Durham, NC: Duke University Press, 1973), 167.
72. *Oxford English Dictionary Online*, s.v. "phosphorescence, (*n.*)," updated March 2006, http://www.oed.com/view/Entry/142733?redirectedFrom=phosphorescence&.
73. Antonia Rigaud, "A Phosphorous History: William Carlos Williams' *In the American Grain*," *European Journal of American Studies* 11, no. 1 (2016), http://ejas.revues.org/11505.
74. Williams, *In the American Grain*, 223.

75. Hart Crane, *The Bridge* (New York: H. Liveright, 1930), 72.
76. Allen Ginsberg, *Wait Till I'm Dead: Uncollected Poems*, ed. Bill Morgan (New York: Grove Press, 2016), Kindle edition.
77. Ginsberg, "Haunting Poe's Baltimore," in *City Lights Pocket Poets Anthology*, ed. Lawrence Ferlinghetti (San Francisco: City Lights, 2015), 172.
78. Eliot, "From Poe to Valéry," 205.
79. Grover Smith deems that a first surge of the Poesque in Eliot dates from his verse of 1915. See "Eliot and the Ghost of Poe," in *TS Eliot: A Voice Descanting. Centenary Essays*, ed. Shyamal Bagchee (London: Palgrave Macmillan UK, 1990), 149–163.
80. Marianne Moore, "Poetry," in *Complete Poems* (New York: Penguin, 1991), 266.
81. Elizabeth Bishop, *Edgar Allan Poe & the Jukebox*, ed. Alice Quinn (New York: Farrar, Strauss and Giroux, 2006), 49.
82. See note 73.
83. In his first manifesto, in 1924, André Breton, the leading figure of French surrealism, declared Poe a model for "adventure," but in a later manifesto, in 1930, he would deplore the detective method Poe applied to reading the world—see *Manifestes du Surréalisme*, ed. Régis Debray (Paris: France Loisirs, 1990), 49 and 158–159. Poe would supply more interesting material for other figures who became central in twentieth-century French literature, even if not in programmatic surrealism. The radical Antonin Artaud wrote a transcreation of "Israfel" that symbolized his quest for the wildness of poetry against the death of literature, and the Belgian Henri Michaux fashioned his most famous character, Mr. Plume, after the French translation of the title "The System of Dr. Tarr and Professor Fether." Poe might also have a tenuous link with dadaisme, initiated by Tristan Tzara, who was friends with his fellow Romanian modernist Ion Vinea, translator of Poe, as well as with "lettrisme," a vanguard close to concrete poetry (see later), which was launched in 1945 by Isidore Isou, also born in Romania.
84. Roman Jakobson, "Linguistics and Poetics," in *Language in Literature*, ed. Krystyna Pomorska and Stephen Rudy (Cambridge, MA: Harvard University Press, 1987), 71. About the fortune of Poe in Russian futurism and in the critical school of formalism, see Eloise M. Boyle, "Poe in Russia," in *Poe Abroad*, 22. Boyle discusses Poe's early influence in Russian symbolism in "Valery Brjusov and Konstantin Bal'mont," *Poe Abroad*, 177–182. For a monograph-length study of Poe in Russia, see Joan Delaney Grossman, *Edgar Allan Poe in Russia: A Study in Legend and Literary Influence* (Würzburg: Jal-Verlag, 1973).
85. Jakobson, "Linguistics and Poetics," 87.
86. Jakobson, "Linguistics and Poetics," 86.
87. Roman Jakobson, "On Linguistic Aspects of Translation," *Language and Literature*, 434.
88. Although technically the term "transcreation" pertains to the Brazilian movement mentioned later, I believe we can speak of a similar attitude encompassing translation and the thrust toward the vanguard by agents of developing literatures, shared by influential translator-writers such as the Chilean Vicente Huidobro, or the Mexican Octavio Paz.
89. Haroldo de Campos, "Edgar Allan Poe: Engenharia dos Avessos," *Revista Colóquio/Letras* 3 (September 1971): 5–16.
90. See Haroldo de Campos, "Anthropophagous Reason: Dialogue and Difference in Brazilian culture," in *Novas: Selected Writings*, ed. Antonio Bessa and Odile Cisneros (Evanston, IL: Northwestern University Press, 2007), 157–177
91. Cf. Pignateri, "poesia concreta: organização" [concrete poetry: organization] of 1957, reprinted in *Teoria da poesia concreta: textos críticos e manifestos 1950–1960*, ed. Haroldo

de Campos, Augusto de Campos and Décio Pignateri (São Paulo: Atelier Editorial, 2006), 125–132; Marshal McLuhan, *Understanding Media: The Extensions of Man* (1964; repr. London: Routledge, 2003), 353.

92. *Zaoum* was a short-lived but influential poetic movement that foregrounded words beyond their reasonable meaning, hence the name, from *zaumnoe* (transrational), first used by the Russian futurist poet Aleksei Kruchenykh in 1913. See Victor Terras, *Handbook of Russian Literature* (New Haven, CT: Yale University Press, 1990), 529–530.
93. The quote is from Derek Pollard, who applies a close reading to "Sonnet—To Science" to show Poe's "programmatic disarray" in "The Postmodern Nineteenth Century"; Pollard thus supports McGann's general argument about the readerly effect of Poe's prosody, engaging decisions of how to make sense(s)—see McGann, *The Poet Edgar Allan Poe*, 182
94. Marshal McLuhan, *Verbi-Voco-Visual Explorations* (New York: Something Else Press, 1967).
95. This is arguably the juncture where psychonanalysis and deconstruction converge in the tentative definition of literariness for the twentieth century. Poe's excursions into the hypnagogic, presenting cities in the sea or valleys of unrest as possible landscapes of the unconscious (whether subjective or collective), his crafting of the sensations of the dreadful and awesome, contributed to poetical offshoots not sufficiently explored in this essay. Regarding Poe's early poetry, G. R. Thompson's *Circumscribed Eden* offers admirable insights in this respect, while Scott Peeples' *The Afterlife of Edgar Allan Poe* (Rochester, NY: Camden House, 2004) traces, in chapters 2 and 3, appropriations leading from Poe to psychoanalyisis and deconstruction, in ways that interconnect the writer's life and his body of prose and verse.
96. I would like to acknowledge the support of my home institution, the School of Arts and Letters, Universidade de Lisboa, as well as of ULICES, the University of Lisbon Centre for English Studies. I express my gratitude to Emron Esplin for his helpful suggestions and patient linguistic revision.

Bibliography

Campos, Haroldo. "O Texto-Espelho (Poe, Engenheiro dos Avessos)." In *A Operação do Texto*, 23–42. São Paulo: Perspectiva, 1971.

Chiari, Joseph. *Symbolisme from Poe to Mallarmé: The Growth of a Myth*. New York: Gordian Press, 1970.

Englekirk, John Eugene. *Edgar Allan Poe in Hispanic Literature*. New York: Instituto de las Españas, 1934.

Esplin, Emron, and Margarida Vale de Gato, eds. *Translated Poe*. Bethlehem: Lehigh University Press, 2014.

Filippakopoulou, Maria. *Transatlantic Poe: Eliot, Williams and Huxley, Readers of the French Poe*. Oxford, UK: Peter Lang, 2015.

Jakobson, Roman. "Linguistics and Poetics." In *Language in Literature*, edited by Krystyna Pomorska and Stephen Rudy, 62–94. Cambridge, MA: Harvard University Press, 1987.

Lawler, James. *Edgar Poe et les poètes français, suivi d'un conférence de Paul Valéry*. Paris: Julliard, 1998.

McGann, Jerome. *The Poet Edgar Allan Poe: Alien Angel*. Cambridge, MA: Harvard University Press, 2014.

Murray, Bill. "'A Strange Sound, as of a Harp-String Broken': The Poetry of Edgar Allan Poe." In *Edgar Allan Poe: The Design of Order*, edited by Robert Lee, 135–153. London: Vision, 1987.

Peeples, Scott. *The Afterlife of Edgar Allan Poe*. Rochester, NY: Camden House, 2004.

Pollard, Derek. "The Postmodern Nineteenth Century: 'Sonnet—To Science' and the Case for Poe's Avant-Garde Poetics." *The Edgar Allan Poe Review* 17, no. 4 (Autumn 2016): 105–115.

Seylaz, Louis. *Edgar Poe et les Premiers Symbolistes*. 1923. Reprint. Genebra: Slatkine, 1979.

Stovall, Floyd. *Edgar Poe the Poet*. Charlottesville: University Press of Virginia, 1969.

Thompson, G. R. *Circumscribed Eden of Dreams: Dreamvision and Nightmare in Poe's Early Poetry*. Baltimore: The Enoch Pratt Free Library, 1984.

Vines, Lois, ed. *Poe Abroad*. Iowa City: University of Iowa Press, 1999.

CHAPTER 36

AN UNREQUITED OBSESSION

Poe and Modern Horror

W. SCOTT POOLE

STEPHEN King's 411-page love letter to the horror genre, *Danse Macabre*, covers the work of Ray Bradbury, Ramsey Campbell, H. P. Lovecraft, *The Twilight Zone*, and numerous B-movies and monster magazines of the fifties and sixties. Edgar Allan Poe shows up on exactly two pages, even though one of those pages calls Poe's "The Tell-Tale Heart" the "best tale of inside evil ever written." Like so many contemporary masters of horror, King feels obliged to pay tribute to Poe but shows little, if any, evidence of Poe's influence on his own fiction. In a later essay, King elaborates, calling the tale "still gruesome enough to produce nightmares" and describes it as the first real story dealing with sociopathic horror, presaging Thomas Harris's creation of Hannibal Lecter.[1] King's unstinting praise of an author whose influence over his own work has been negligible embodies how Poe's sway over modern horror fiction has frequently been assumed though seldom proven. This essay shows that efforts to use Poe in the modern horror tradition—in both fiction and film—are ultimately efforts to legitimize what remains a largely disreputable genre by providing it with a canonical literary legacy that stretches farther back than the pulp magazines of the early twentieth century.[2]

Attempts to locate the roots of twentieth-century horror in Poe have failed on two counts. First, they obscure the influence of the eighteenth-century Gothic novel, while also skipping horror's more obvious antecedents in Mary Shelley, Bram Stoker, and the world of the penny dreadful and the Grand Guignol. Second, they ignore how social and cultural history in the 1910s and 1920s shaped the popularity of horror. Many of the authors discussed in this essay, and certainly the first horror films, attained mass appeal in the aftermath of the Great War, its horrors providing nightmare fuel for generations. This has not prevented numerous auteurs of the unseemly from claiming that they represent Poe's heirs. Nor has it prevented Poe from becoming an iconic symbol of horror and the macabre.[3]

These points are not meant to suggest that horror writers and directors should adhere to a single, stable core of meaning in Poe or else leave him be. As Dennis R. Perry and

Carl H. Sederholm suggest, Poe is best understood as something like John Orr's concept of Alfred Hitchcock as a "matrix figure," or "an individual whose ideas, work, and influence intersect other areas of life at so many points that it becomes impossible to understand the world without him or her."[4] But if we can understand the need to construct Poe as the "master of horror," we learn much about both the modern horror tradition and what Poe has come to mean outside his own texts. Although it may be more accurate to call Poe the father of the detective novel (for instance) than the father of modern horror, we should not ignore how much his image, if not his actual work, has shaped the horror tradition. This is particularly so, given how much that tradition has sought to connect itself to him.

The difficulty of classifying Poe's tales of psychological and philosophical trauma dates to the nineteenth century.[5] A few perceptive contemporaries recognized that he was more than, as Ralph Waldo Emerson infamously referred to him, a "jingle man." He also represented something other than the original goth, a romantic antiromantic who relied on visionary experience. A few months after his death, John M. Daniel in *The Southern Literary Messenger*, for which the deceased had previously worked as an assistant editor, recognized the breadth of Poe's ambition in contrast with his pathetic demise: "Edgar Allan Poe, who re-organized the universe, and subverted the theory of a world's belief and a world's science . . . died of drink, friendless and alone, in the common wards of a Baltimore hospital."[6] The *Messenger* did not believe Poe had "re-organized the universe" through horror as we would understand the use of the term. Instead, Daniel found this reorganization of the world in works that explore the boundaries of life and death, including the cosmological work *Eureka*. Moreover, the *Messenger*'s description of Poe's demise became one of the first times his image as troubled artist, in love with death in the way his characters often seem besotted with the dead, had been put on public display. The macabre iconography of Poe helped make him the putative father to the twentieth-century horror tradition.[7]

Poe's path toward becoming known as the progenitor of modern horror took the same twists and turns as the growth of his own reputation, and it had an intimate link to that reputation. Scott Peeples has shown that Poe's literary reputation long intertwined with attacks and defenses of his character, especially in association with his alcoholism and alleged opium addiction. Some admirers, most famously Charles Baudelaire, praised Poe precisely for these supposedly unseemly biographical facts. In the eyes of Baudelaire, Poe's supposed transgressive behavior made him the epitome of the rebellious romantic artist. His long-time nemesis, the Reverend Rufus Griswold, likely did Poe a favor in emphasizing his drinking and addictive habits, feeding his dark legend and unwittingly helping to fashion him into modern horror's dark mascot.[8]

John L. Hervey, writing in 1933, asserted that "The Raven" had already become something of a standard text in public education. However, Hervey did note that Poe's work bore the whiff of the "charnel house" and that "there was not a breath of plain air in it." This comment underscored Poe's undeniable fixation on death, though this conception does not connect him simply with the horror genre. J. Gerald Kennedy has noted that Poe's morbid interest is best understood against the backdrop of the "contemplative pleasure" related to death and the art of mourning in Poe's time. Hervey's comment regarding the "charnel house" nature of Poe's work should be read in this context of changing funerary rites and popular speculations about the fate of the soul after death common in the nineteenth century. The ambiguous lines between life and death, explored by the Spiritualist movement, inform his poems and prose much more than the recognizable lineaments of modern horror.[9]

Contemporary readers are well served in considering that such discussions took place before the full emergence of the concept of genre in its most modern form, certainly before the emergence of the idea of the "genre writer." Although Poe carried the taint of "the charnel house," he wrote works that we would classify as comedy, suspense, mystery, and philosophy. Given this varied experimentation with styles, why would the horror tradition of the twentieth century see Poe's work as a tomb worth raiding for stories and tropes that could appear in the horror tradition? There are really two intertwined answers to this question. First, Poe's image as a romantic, transgressive renegade, indeed the suggestion that he had an especially well-developed death drive, comports with modern horror's sense of itself as transgressive, the bad boy of genres that revels in its own disreputability. Second, though related, Poe's work came into prominence at a time in the late nineteenth century when the concept of genre began to emerge. In this new reimagination of popular culture, many of Poe's tales fit most closely with what editors and fans at first called "weird fiction," and by the 1930s, "horror fiction" (a term that seems to have first appeared in advertising for Universal Studios' line of monster films that began with *Dracula* and *Frankenstein*, both in 1931).[10]

When the Munsey magazines began their publication in the late nineteenth century, a much more recognizable concept of genre began to develop, in some sense as the commodification of what had been thought of as writing styles. With the appearance of the first issues of *Argosy* and *All-Story* in 1882 and 1896, respectively, the readership began to develop a taste for a wide variety of styles following a clear formula. These included everything from tales of romantic love to some of the first "John Carter of Mars" and "Tarzan" tales by Edgar Rice Burroughs in 1912 and 1913.[11]

The influence of film has been underrated in the development of literary genres. As *Argosy* and *All-Story* began to shape audience perceptions of the nature of a romance as opposed to a cowboy story, film directors began developing the paradigm for the western, the love story, and the gangster picture. These lines solidified to the point of rigidity by the 1930s with the appearance of the "talkies." Readers at the movies and filmgoers holding the printed page began to shape their expectation in terms of genre.

A large number of Poe's readers before pulp magazines and the genre films that followed would have linked his reputation to the mystery story, both because it held much more cachet than the "weird tale" and because of the popularity of his detective C. August Dupin. Poe drew his inspiration for Dupin from Eugène François Vidocq, one of the earliest police officers to view their work as using ratiocination for forensic purposes. A former criminal who transformed himself into the creator of the first French detective bureau, Vidocq made use of ballistics and plaster of Paris molds for footprints. This transformed the work of the new urban police forces that had previously been used to prevent rowdy proletarians from building barricades. Poe mentions Vidocq briefly in "Murders in the Rue Morgue," while making it clear that his own fictional detective had far superior forensic skills. Arthur Conan Doyle depended on Poe's work in the detective story to such a degree that Doyle described Poe as "the supreme original short story writer of all time" and added that "to him must be ascribed the monstrous progeny of writers of detection of crime."[12]

Poe's creation of the detective tale must be taken into account when considering some of his stories frequently classified as "horror." Although some of the first stories reprinted in the "weird fiction" pulps are still viewed as horror classics, they originally appeared as examples of crime fiction. This includes "The Tell-Tale Heart," which, in stage performance and in the attention given it by Stephen King, has frequently been presented as supernatural fiction. This tale, however, joins other famous Poe works that do not feature the detective, such as "The Cask of Amontillado," as sketches in the psychology of crime. As mystery author Jan Burke points out, "The Cask of Amontillado" works because we are "lured into a journey with a killer." Poe causes us to feel some sympathy with Montresor, only to give us a dizzying view of the depths of his madness.[13]

The melancholy, and vaguely supernatural, undertones of "The Raven" have long played an important role in connecting Poe to horror. This has been particularly true of the modern iconography of horror (in the form of the t-shirt, poster, and tattoo). However, few of Poe's contemporaries connected the poem with what modern readers would regard as horror; it was known instead for its tone of unrelenting despair and yearnings ever unsatisfied. John Reuben Thompson, in Poe's obituary in November of 1849 in *The Southern Literary Messenger*, wrote that he could not "convey the impression 'The Raven' has made on me." Yet it was not the impress of chilly fright but what Thompson called the tragedy of "a soul made desolate, not alone by disappointed love, but by the crushing of every hope and every aspiration."[14]

The writer Elizabeth Oakes Smith agreed, noting after the poem's publication that "soon 'The Raven' was known everywhere and everyone was saying "Nevermore!' " (PL: 497). Such fame had not come because Poe had tapped the impulses of modern horror, however. According to Oakes Smith, Charles Fenno Hoffman described the poem as an example of "despair brooding over wisdom" (PL: 497). The *Morning Express*, in February of 1845, had called the Raven itself a simple trope, "a chance visitor to the poet" rather than a supernatural harbinger. The poem did not tell a tale of horror but of sadness that has become "a deep settled grief" (PL: 499).

These macabre readings of the famous poem easily transmuted into twentieth-century horror's obsession with the corpse and its terrors. Horror impresarios have made it fairly hard to miss Poe at the roots of the twentieth-century tales of terror. The earliest efforts to have Poe stand as godfather to what we know as the modern horror tradition appears in the "weird fiction" of the 1920s and 1930s, found in American pulp magazines. *Weird Tales* (1923–1954; relaunched in 1973) became the best known, and for some time the only, representation of this tradition. Each issue intermingled what we today delineate as fantasy, science fiction, and horror, or more generally classify as speculative fiction. The original publisher, J. C. Henneberger, claimed to be a devotee of Poe and wanted his magazine to publish tales "that didn't quite fit" in any of the era's numerous genre pulps. Notably, it is Henneberger's interest in Poe that shaped his desire to publish work that "didn't quite fit" elsewhere. He paid tribute to Poe's inspiration by occasionally reprinting "The Raven" and in one instance placing Poe on the cover holding a raven. The June 1923 issue reprinted "Murders in the Rue Morgue." Appropriately, Poe's relationship to modern horror began with a misunderstanding, a procrustean effort to insert his work into the horror genre.[15]

Weird Tales provides some of the explanation not simply because Henneberger connected his own love of Poe to weird fiction but because the magazine became the primary outlet for the short fiction of H. P. Lovecraft (1890–1937). Critics and historians of horror, and his earliest small circle of fans, ensured that Lovecraft, more than any twentieth-century writer, has been associated with Poe. Lovecraft's own desire for his readers to see his work intersecting with Poe provides much of the explanation for this alleged connection.[16]

Lovecraft read Poe very early, age eight if we take him at his word. However, he also imbibed the same expurgated versions of the traditional Gothic so beloved of his grandfather Whipple Phillips. His mother, Sarah Susan Lovecraft, seems to have held some interest in the work of Hawthorne and also ensured that he had a copy of Richard Burton's then somewhat scandalous translation of *One Thousand and One Nights*. Along with an interest in the myths of Greece and Rome and possible familiarity with the Gothic novels of the eighteenth century, he devoured every issue he could of Munsey Publishing's early pulp *All-Story*. In other words, Lovecraft did a prodigious amount of reading and fell under a diverse array of influences before he reached his teens in 1903. This diluted the role of Poe in his work significantly, even if his affection for the writer cannot be gainsaid. Lovecraft found a narrative style both distinctly his own with some elements borrowed from influences as diverse as M. R. James, Arthur Machen, and, as the most dedicated Lovecraft aficionado must admit, the formula of the pulp magazine itself.[17]

By the late 1910s, these influences grew, though Lovecraft displayed a special interest in tying his writing of "weird fiction" to Poe. In a frequently quoted letter to Reinhardt Kleiner, he called Poe "the God of fiction." Notably, in a contemporary letter to his other major correspondent of this era, Maurice Moe, he leaves Poe out completely when describing his literary influences. He instead praises Hawthorne's *Twice-Told Tales* and *Wonder-Book* as crucial to his interest in the macabre.[18] None of this conflicting evidence challenges the irrefutable attraction Lovecraft had for Poe's work and, perhaps more important, the persona that had been created of Poe the writer. Lovecraft maintained a deep and abiding fascination for Poe's limited connection with his own beloved hometown of Providence. Poe infamously spent part of the autumn of 1848 in the town courting Sarah Helen Whitman and, according to legend, wandering the graveyard of St. John's church, frequently intoxicated. Lovecraft remained fascinated with Poe's scrap of handwriting left at the Providence Athenaeum during one of these visits.[19] Lovecraft himself took nighttime tours of St. John's cemetery seeking inspiration and even invited visiting friends along. On one of these later outings, his confreres joined him in composing acrostic poems using Poe's name, perhaps in imitation of Virginia Poe's acrostic poem for Valentine's Day, 1846 (M 1: 524).[20]

It's also likely that Poe influenced Lovecraft's first efforts at writing short fiction for the public in 1917. His early juvenile tales did try to imitate Poe thematically in stories with titles such as "The Noble Eavesdropper," "The Mysterious Ship," "The Secret Cave," and "The Mystery of the Graveyard, or a Dead Man's Revenge: A Detective Story." Many of these juvenile efforts depend heavily on Poe's detective fiction, the genre that moved Lovecraft before "weird" or "horror" fiction, so much so that he created an early form of LARPING (Live Action Roleplaying) in which he and his friends lived out the fantasy of running their own detective agency.[21] When Lovecraft began actively writing short fiction, some of his first efforts, especially "The Tomb," convinced the first wave of Lovecraft scholarship that he labored under Poe's influence. S. T. Joshi has argued for the heavy influence of Poe on Lovecraft at least until 1923. He finds two supposed characteristics of Poe that are also pronounced in Lovecraft's fiction: archaism and the privileging of atmosphere over character. Joshi, however, acknowledges Lovecraft's debt to Poe only until the beginning of the period that the Providence author began writing what the French novelist Michel Houellebecq has called "the great texts" such as *The Call of Cthulhu* (1926), *The Shadow over Innsmouth* (1931), and *At the Mountains of Madness* (1936). Moreover, Joshi concludes that "Lovecraft spent the better part of his fictional career in attempting to escape—or, at best, master or refine—the stylistic influence of Poe."[22]

At the Mountains of Madness has received a significant amount of attention from those claiming a Poe and Lovecraft connection because of its alleged similarities to *The Narrative of Arthur Gordon Pym of Nantucket*. Like *Pym*, Lovecraft's novella involved an expedition to Antarctica and contains a direct allusion to Poe. Lovecraft's long tale ends with Danforth, one of the archaeology students who have joined the expedition, crying out, with no explanation provided other than insanity, "Tekeli-li! Tekeli-li!" The same phrase appears in *Pym* as an unexplained chant. Arguably, the similarities end here. *Pym* differs in narrative structure and, more important, the ideas in *At the Mountains of Madness* are utterly unrelated to those explored by Poe. The Miskatonic University expedition in *Mountains* discovers an ancient city and a prehuman history of Great Old Ones and Shoggoths that leads them to death and madness. Like Poe's "MS. Found in a Bottle," it evokes the terror of distant and unknown places, the horror of vastness and separation. Poe, of course, developed no detailed mythology and history of extraterrestrial monsters and their wars as did Lovecraft. In fact, the actual concept of the monster has been heavily influenced by Lovecraft in both modern horror and science fiction. Poe, on the other hand, never makes use of the concept of the monster in any way recognizable to folklore or fiction. At times, his shades and doubles come close, but even these instances do not approach Lovecraft's ability to create horrors or hybridity and often lurid malformation. Lovecraft rooted his monsters in a mythology that became increasingly complex, if never formalized by him, from his earliest tales in 1917 until the time of his death in 1937, a literary project that simply has no parallel in Poe. Claims for Poe's influence on Lovecraft have still largely been won in the realm of mass culture. Lovecraft's diverse influences, and his largely successful efforts to escape the influence of Poe, have not prevented the two authors from being firmly linked in popular culture and, by extension, making Poe the shadow that looms ominously behind modern horror.

A discussion of literary influences over a figure such as Lovecraft can lead too easily to a disregard for how historical context shaped both his work and lesser lights that created the "weird fiction" at the root of American horror. The aftermath of the First World War, "the Great War" in the nomenclature of the time, provided fertile ground for horror. Seeking the roots of the modern horror tradition in Europe and America must begin at the Somme, Ypres, Caporetto, and Gallipoli. A war that took the lives of sixteen million people, while leaving millions more physically disfigured and mentally broken, accounts for the roots of horror in film and fiction, exercising a too frequently overlooked influence on Lovecraft and other weird fiction writers. Lovecraft closely followed the First World War and made a surprising and ill-fated attempt to join the fight. *Dagon*, one of his first and most enduring short tales, along with the underrated prose-poem *Nyarlathotep* and the story *The Temple*, all take place within the war's context. Lovecraft also goes to the trenches in his *Reanimator* tales, and his best known post-1926 work makes allusion to the war with its apocalyptic tone and general sense of unease about the human future.[23]

The modern horror film, beginning with the well-known Weimar era German Expressionist classics *The Cabinet of Dr. Caligari, Nosferatu, The Golem*, and *Waxworks*, could not have come into being without the impetus of the Great War. In Hollywood, the landmark monster tales of Universal Studios are impossible to imagine without the genius of James Whale. The British director helmed classics such as *The Old Dark House, Frankenstein, The Bride of Frankenstein*, and *The Invisible Man*, bringing to each a sentiment about death and the human experience that had been born during his service as a second lieutenant on the Western Front and a POW from 1917 until the armistice.[24]

Poe's dark vision continued to grow in popularity during the Great War. His obsession with death fit well with the emerging horror tradition's persistent concerns and anxieties, even if his work did not determine the shape the tradition took.[25] An example can be seen in the work of Welsh author Arthur Machen, sometimes compared to Poe though his stories only reveal a second-hand influence by way of the French Decadent-Symbolist tradition. Machen had his most productive period between 1890 and 1900, after which he had to devote himself more fully to journalism and translation in order to support himself. The Great War precipitated a new interest in Machen, beginning with his short story "The Bowmen." One of Machen's worst, it is a thin and jingoistic tale about British soldiers slaughtering the Germans in remarkable numbers after they received supernatural aid, possibly the ghosts of the longbowmen of Agincourt. Machen asserted, regretfully but correctly, that his patriotic ghost story contributed to the oft-repeated legend of angelic beings who aided the British during their first major encounter with the German army, the Battle of Mons, in August of 1914, popularly known as "The Angel of Mons."[26] Machen benefitted more broadly from a fascination with supernatural horror after the war that took forms as diverse as the expressionist horror films of Weimar cinema, the publication of *Weird Tales* after 1923 that featured the works of H. P. Lovecraft, the career of Lon Chaney Sr., and eventually the monster films that shambled forth from Carl Laemmle Jr.'s Universal Studios. Two tales of Machen, "The White People" and "The Great God Pan," proved particularly enduring, the latter becoming a story Stephen King described as having "haunted me all my life."[27]

Efforts to link Machen to Poe have been mostly unsuccessful. Machen did list Poe as a favorite author, but it appears that enjoyment of his work never proceeded to influence. This crucial distinction, being an avid reader of Poe as opposed to being influenced by Poe, has often been ignored. Significantly, so has an obsession with the image of Poe born in the nineteenth century, the doomed, romantic rebel whose work grew from a strange inner life made all the more perilous by the avid use of hallucinogens. This image of Poe as a mad poet lost in a fever dream makes his own personality a useful origin point for horror, while his ability to tap into the nineteenth century's tendency to worry the line between the living and the dead completed the picture, making him seem particularly modern in the aftermath of the Great War.

Machen certainly seems to have been intrigued by Poe but, like Lovecraft, chose a very different set of themes to explore. In a book-length study of Machen, Wesley D. Sweetser notes that something of the antiromantic underside of romanticism came to Machen through Poe, particularly his celebration of the aesthetic over the didactic. However, by Machen's time, this notion had been thoroughly absorbed by many of the symbolist and decadent writers Machen read with pleasure. Otherwise Sweetser simply adds that Poe's work employed both "subjective" and "psychological" elements not found in Machen's tales.[28] The most laudatory criticism of Machen has found in him the fullest expression of the British Decadence, with Oscar Wilde, not Poe, his real influence.[29]

Ambrose Bierce, whose influence over Lovecraft has been increasingly recognized (Lovecraft called him the second most important American writer, behind Poe of course), actively resented any comparison between his work and Poe's. Bierce, in fact, summed up much of the twentieth-century horror tradition's attitude toward Poe when he described "the ready reckoner's short cut to the solution of literary merit, the ever-serviceable comparison with Edgar Allan Poe." Going even further in his broadside against the simplicity of this approach, Bierce asked, "Does one write 'gruesome stories'? Then invoke Poe."[30]

Certainly, some of Bierce's tales are suggestive of Poe. Bierce's "Beyond the Wall" includes the motif of death taking a walled-off protagonist, but the themes and the atmosphere are utterly different from "The Cask of Amontillado" and "The Black Cat." In Bierce's story, a desire to steal a family fortune prepares the way for the horror to come, with no effort to explore the psychological dynamics of revenge or the depths of alcoholic madness that appears in the two Poe tales. Although "One Summer Night" deals with the subject of premature burial, Bierce turns it into an exercise in cynicism rather than an example of obsessional terror.

Ray Bradbury has probably received more attention than any other writer of the fantastic for his influence over genre. The sheer volume of his contribution to horror, fantasy, and science fiction has brought significant attention to his influence and his claims about his influences. Like Lovecraft, Bradbury discovered Poe early, reading him alongside Hugo Gernsbach's *Amazing Stories*. However, his spare, modernist prose owes little to Poe, even if he has made frequent allusions to the author in his massive body of work (seven hundred published pieces of poetry and prose). Burton Pollin attempts to make the case that Poe has been for Bradbury "a persistent influence and interest," but he succeeds only in showing Bradbury's persistent interest.[31]

Bradbury's best-known work, the 1949 *Martian Chronicles*, contained a chapter in its British edition called "Usher II," which told of an old earth-style mansion built on Mars, but it is really just a bare-bones allusion to Poe's famous tale. Culling Bradbury's gigantic corpus for nods and allusions to Poe, Pollin mostly finds examples of Bradbury using him, along with other famed American authors, as a protagonist in his fiction. He notes a peculiar 1949 tale, "The Exiles," in which Poe leads a group of authors that includes Dickens, Machen, and Bierce on a rocket flight to escape an Earth where books are being burned (essentially Bradbury's infamous nightmare scenario in *Fahrenheit 451*). The tale is notable as an early example of what much later would become known as the steampunk aesthetic, but Poe's own stylistic or thematic concerns are absent.

Poe has appeared in Bradbury's poetry most prominently of all, but even here we see not Poe's influence but the need for even the greatest and most successful writers of the contemporary fantastic to find legitimacy for his work by linking it to Poe. The poems where Poe appears often find him accompanied by other nineteenth-century American writers Bradbury wants to hallow, including Emily Dickinson and Herman Melville. Except for the occasional reference to well-known poems of Poe, nothing of Poe's style persists in these works.[32]

Horror anthologies, one of the genre's most popular forms, have furthered Poe's alleged place as "the master of horror." Collections that identify Poe as their inspiration multiply. Some are very well done, like Peter Straub's *Poe's Children*, while others are of indifferent quality. Straub's collection provides an instructive example, in part because the very title of the anthology seeks to link the work of modern horror to Poe as progenitor.[33] However, it contains works such as Ramsey Campbell's masterful tale "The Voice of the Beach," which clearly draws its inspiration from Lovecraft. The confusion, and the need for Poe, grows.

The anthology that strives with the most urgency to forge a firm link between Poe and modern horror authors might be Michael Connelly's collection *In the Shadow of the Master*. The title, again, places authors of modern tales of suspense and terror, such as contributor Stephen King, under direct influence of Poe as "the master of horror." This particular collection stands out, however, in that it reprints thirteen Poe tales (and two poems) with accompanying essays primarily by writers of the modern mystery novel. "The Mystery Writers of America," in fact, assembled, organized, and placed their imprimatur on the collection.[34] Most of the essays echo the influence of Poe's macabre interests on their writing. P. J. Parrish (actually two authors, a team of sisters named Kristy Montee and Kelly Nichols) admits to first meeting Poe not in his own tales but in the Corman adaptations. As a very successful mystery-writing team, Parrish took some time to get to a serious reading of Poe precisely because the Corman works convinced them that Poe seemed both "archaic and lightweight." An encounter with Poe's actual work convinced them otherwise.[35]

The case of Thomas Ligotti offers a startling example of how the best horror writers seek to claim Poe's legacy and how critics who admire their work do the same. A cult writer whose work has gained wider exposure since Penguin anthologized his tales, Ligotti's work shows the clear influence of a host of authorial voices very different from Poe. Yet the need for Poe as his literary progenitor remains, with critics at times speaking with striking enthusiasm on the point.

Noted critic and practitioner of the so-called New Weird Jeff Vandermeer wrote the introduction claiming that Poe and Kafka are strong influences on Ligotti, even if he then shows how Ligotti had little anxiety of influence from either. He calls Lovecraft "a self-admitted" influence but rather strenuously argues that Ligotti "early on subsumed Lovecraft and left his dry husk behind."[36] In fact, a strong argument can be made that Ligotti's work has remained strongly influenced by Lovecraft's style, including that author's well-known "cosmicism." And yet, despite the heavy evidence for Lovecraft's influence, Vandermeer dismisses it, in a footnote, in favor of a discussion of Poe.[37] Ligotti himself frequently alludes to Poe in his scant interviews. However, when he seriously discusses direct influences on his style, it's clear that he's drawing from authors such as Bruno Schulz (who Ligotti seems far closer to than Kafka), Nabakov, and Jorge Luis Borges. He pays a kind of backward tribute to the influence of Lovecraft, seeing the author's greatest failings in those tales where he attempted to create a "convincing" fictional world and at his best when he writes in a fever dream. Ligotti certainly has borrowed the latter tendency and taken it to its logical, or perhaps terrifyingly irrational, conclusion.[38]

The importance Ligotti attributes to Poe, even as he feasts on more complex, dark literary delights, shows again the importance of claim Poe as one's master. The slender links with the horror fiction of the twentieth century perhaps would have dampened enthusiasm for lashing Poe to the mast of the horror tradition, especially after critical revisionist work on Lovecraft began in the 1970s that disentangled, for example, Lovecraft from the mentor he had claimed. Poe, however, was going to the movies, and the Poe-haunted screen had more influence than a century of literary criticism in forging his relationship to the culture of horror.

Horror movies, since the end of World War I, have been the primary vehicle of entertaining terror for audiences the world over. The horror film, though again not yet referred to as such in the immediate postwar years, emerged inextricably bound with new movements in the arts, particularly surrealism and expressionism. These avant-garde movements produced one of the first efforts to adapt a Poe story to film, a 1928 French silent version of the *Fall of the House of Usher* directed by Jean Epstein. Previously, D. W. Griffith had served up a more conventional murder tale with his 1915 feature *The Avenging Conscience*, very loosely based on "The Tell Tale Heart." Soon a floodtide of cinematic adaptations appeared, many using little more than his reputation and borrowing his titles. We see in them what we've already witnessed in early twentieth-century fiction: seeking some sense of legitimacy, they looked to the rising reputation of Poe.[39] Two early examples are instructive in this regard. First came *Murders in the Rue Morgue* (1932), which starred Bela Lugosi the year after he donned Dracula's cape. Adapted by Robert Florey, who later worked on episodes of *The Twilight Zone* during his long career, the film transformed Poe's detective tale by adding thematic elements from American horror film of the era, including a mad scientist and a threat to white womanhood. Both of these tropes remained prominent in the horror films of the American thirties and forties.

In the 1930s, the popularity of Universal Studio's monster mashes created a market for even more horror. Directors and screenwriters turned to Poe for morbid inspiration, or more frequently, to create horror that had some sense of a more distinguished provenance. Edgar G. Ulmer's 1934 *The Black Cat* starred Boris Karloff and Bela Lugosi in the first of eight on-screen pairings. The film features a truly creative plot in which a young couple find themselves caught up in a supernatural struggle between Lugosi and Karloff, both of whose characters have been traumatized by their experience in World War I. The story takes place in a mise-en-scène of Bahaus architecture with perhaps some influence from Cubism, suggesting that Weimar horror cinema played an important role in the set design as did the theme of World War I as the mother of modern terrors. The film, however, has nothing to do with Poe's well-known and psychologically excruciating story. In fact, the only relationship other than a few scenes in which a black cat appears now and again in the nightmare architecture of Karloff's mansion to frighten Lugosi, comes in the credits' nod to Poe. Really, it all comes down to the deployment of the cat and the desire to use Poe's reputation.

Occasionally, Poe's work offered more than just a title, if not much more. Unfortunately, one of the worst horror films made in the 1930s, *Maniac* (1934), did not claim Poe's legacy and yet comes closer than any other effort to adapt "The Black Cat." Making use of psychoanalytic jargon, the film deals with madness and obsessive fixation around cats, though it can't seem to avoid throwing in a mad scientist, perhaps the most dominant trope of the 1930s horror film. Indeed, part of the strange mishmash of the film involves allusions to the film version *Murders in the Rue Morgue* that had already utterly transformed Poe's original mystery.[40]

Universal Studios brought Karloff and Lugosi together again to make use of Poe's reputation in the 1935 *The Raven*. Containing more direct references to the author than Lugosi's other two films combined (Lugosi plays a Poe-obsessed mad surgeon with a torture chamber in his basement), the film makes almost no allusion to any Poe tale. Short snatches of the titular poem are quoted, though not enough to provide the viewer with a sense of what it concerns beyond a bit of eerie atmosphere. In sum, the horror directors of the thirties had their own stories to tell, often intertwined with the obsessions of the times (mad science and the explosive violence of war above all) but saw in Poe a way to give their dark tales the atmosphere of Poe's "charnel house" fiction.

The renaissance of Poe's popularity found expression in a series of films produced by Roger Corman for American International Pictures, better known simply as AIP, during the 1960s. Corman produced a cycle of films based loosely, some very loosely, on Poe between 1960 and 1964. Previously known for being able to turn a profit on B-movie efforts made for under a hundred dollars and on a one-week shooting schedule, Corman found Poe something of a hard sell. He told AIP executives that he wanted to do a $200,000 picture (cheap by mainstream Hollywood standards, even then) and, instead of black and white, film the tales "in color, maybe even Cinemascope." He wanted to start with *The Fall of the House of Usher*.[41]

Corman at first struggled in his argument with AIP, the heads of the studio remaining unconvinced that Poe would appeal to the young audiences that they saw, perhaps incorrectly, as a large portion of their ticket sales. They agreed with Corman that every high school English class read Poe but wondered aloud if anyone would want to see a movie about "required reading in school." Corman used his typical blustering style to convince them that "kids loved Poe" and to allow him to press ahead with an ambitious project in which, worryingly to AIP's budget comptrollers, there seemed to be no central monster of reptilian appearance or giant alien bug devouring cities. "The house is the monster," Corman told them and, almost certainly still dubious, they agreed to fund the project. The film grossed a million dollars in its original theatrical release, nearly four times its cost.[42]

Corman's *Usher* became the first American film in the modern era to stay reasonably close to Poe's actually storyline, though with much expansion of dialogue. Vincent Price really does incarnate the nervous and broken Roderick Usher, and the house breathes and groans in a way that would have likely delighted Poe himself. According to Corman, however, Freud may have had more to do with the film's mise-en-scène, tropes, and photography than Poe. During the shooting of *Usher*, Corman himself underwent traditional Freudian psychoanalysis before production and claimed to have read Freud's works, though he does not provide any specifics. He describes how his interest in Freud encouraged him to make the film feel like a dream that had bubbled out of the subconscious, a Freudian return of the repressed in which taboos under lock and key since early childhood walked free.

Released in the summer of 1960, *The Fall of the House of Usher* brought in receipts equivalent to five times the budget of the film. Clearly connecting the name of Poe to a horror film resonated with moviegoers and so Corman set to work on an entire Poe cycle of films. Seeing their moneymaking potential, Corman produced them in quick succession, using Poe's name and the title of one of his works even as his adaptations departed further from the actual contents of the story. The velocity at which Corman moved away from Poe's plots is evident in his version of "The Black Cat" (part of the 1962 *Tales of Terror* trilogy), in which Peter Lorre and Vincent Price play the story as slapstick humor at a wine-tasting contest gone wrong, evoking "The Cask of Amontillado" as much as the title story.[43] Eventually, the success of projects loosely based on Poe's tales encouraged Corman simply to begin using recognizable Poe titles as the basis for made-to-order movies. *The Raven* represents the most extreme example of this sort of improvisation, as it transforms Poe's famous poem, perhaps his most famous work, into a tale of sorcery, adultery, and a Gothic mansion that collapses in the manner of *House of Usher*.

AIP's *Masque of the Red Death* ensured that Poe became even more irrevocably tied to the horror tradition. In Corman's version, Vincent Price as Prince Prospero leads his celebrants into the worship of Satan, echoing certain aspects sublimated in Universal Studios' *The Black Cat.* This notion does not appear at all in Poe's original tale but helped to fashion the concept of the Poe short story as a horror tale while fueling a growing fascination with Satanism as a theme in the macabre. *Rosemary's Baby* would appear in 1968 with *The Exorcist* coming in 1973, followed by a demonic host of poor imitations on the foreign and domestic film market.

The strangest use of Poe by AIP helped both to further confuse the relationship of Poe to modern horror and to further complicate the question of his influence over H. P. Lovecraft. Corman hoped to convince AIP to allow him to create a Lovecraft film cycle to complement the Poe films. Although executives green lit the first project, they felt, rightly at that time, that Poe's name recognition would be more likely to attract moviegoers even if drawing on Lovecraft-inspired material. The result became the very odd AIP production *The Haunted Palace*, the title referencing the Poe poem of the same name. In fact, executives decided that the full title should be *Edgar Allan Poe's Haunted Palace* and used a few lines of the poem to justify the connection. However, the movie Corman produced reimagines Lovecraft's novella *The Case of Charles Dexter Ward* while borrowing elements from other Lovecraft tales such as *The Shadow over Innsmouth* and *The Dunwich Horror.* The story takes place in Lovecraft's fictional town of Arkham and makes reference to his famous, fictional forbidden tome *The Necronomicon* and to Cthulhu, his most well-known monstrous god. Even with all of these elements included, AIP used the title to include it in their popular cycle of "Poe films."[44] *The Haunted Palace* not only has the effect of further conflating the work of Lovecraft and Poe. The strange film furthered Poe's reputation as a horror writer and certainly made Poe's legacy important for a small number of horror films. Continuing with the longer tradition of making unwarranted Lovecraft-Poe connections, a 2009 FFF production adopted the title of an early Lovecraft tale, "The Tomb," for what was supposedly an adaptation of "Ligeia," but jettisoned all elements of Poe's story except the name Ligeia.[45]

The "masters of horror" need Poe as their own guiding genius. There's no doubt that writers and directors have read Poe and enjoyed the overall flavor of his work on the macabre. Yet the work they have produced owes almost nothing to Poe's fiction. Almost all of those that have laid claim to his legacy can barely claim his influence. Even very recent efforts to directly adapt his tales to screen have shown a tendency to comment on Poe's relationship to the horror tradition as much as Poe's own aspirations. In 2013, award-winning animator Raul Garcia produced an anthology film entitled *Extraordinary Tales* that included adaptations of "The Fall of the House of Usher," "The Facts in the Case of M. Valdemar," "The Tell-Tale Heart," "The Pit and the Pendulum," and "The Masque of the Red Death." Garcia animated each tale in a varied style and, with the exception of "Masque," each made use of Poe's own words. However, the horror tradition haunts itself in this otherwise direct adaptation of Poe. Hammer films icon Christopher Lee, in one of his final performances, read the script for "Usher" while Garcia used a recording made by Bela Lugosi in the 1940s for "The Tell-Tale Heart" sequence. Guillermo Del Toro reads passages from "The Pit and the Pendulum," while Roger Corman voices Prince Prospero for the final segment, the ever popular "Masque."

This embarrassment of riches when it comes to horror icons speaks to the tradition's own investment in Poe. *Extraordinary Tales*' use of animation also reveals horror audiences' expectations about the meaning of Poe. Even when making use of the author's own prose, the film's animation heavily suggests the supernatural over the psychological, a tendency especially apparent in the adaptation of "Usher" and "Pit and the Pendulum." In the former, the "resurrected" Madeline neither falls across her brother as in Poe's text nor strangles him as in Corman's 1960 adaptation. Instead, she turns into a vengeful spirit from Japanese horror manga and swarms over him, effectively confusing if not eliminating the notion of her live burial.

Extraordinary Tales exemplifies how Poe offers a way to inject horror into tales of various genres, which has made his legacy into a kind of metanarrative that can be used to give otherwise simplistic murder mysteries a macabre turn. The 2012 film *The Raven* starred John Cusack as a tormented Poe who helps a Baltimore detective solve the crimes of a serial killer using Poe tales in the staging of his crimes. The television series *The Following* (2013–2015) featured Kevin Bacon as a troubled detective tracking a Poe scholar turned leader of a death cult. Notably, the villain's teaching is supposed to be "inspired by the philosophy of Poe," though it is never explained in what way beyond his tendency to quote from, of course, "The Raven." These stories could have been told without Poe at all but sought to raise their profile by using the cachet he has been given as a horror icon.

Scott Peeples has referred to the inveterate public interest in Poe, especially among the young, as "the Poe effect," which bears little relationship to either Poe's work or the history of Poe and literary criticism. Building on Peeples' description of a Poe industry, I wonder if the "Poe-industrial complex" might best explain the processes that have commodified Poe and ensured a fundamental misunderstanding of his work. This phrase underscores how both scholarship and pop culture have worked together to give us the Poe we have today. Poe-themed items are for sale at major bookstore chains across the country. His image appears on posters, book bags, and tattooed backs and biceps and thighs, in every case looking dour and accompanied by his raven. The more lurid aspects of his writings have been a boon to harried high school English teachers desperate to interest students in a deeply challenging nineteenth-century writer.

Horror in its modern form has developed along very different lines. The idea of the thing that waits in the dark, skittering just outside our line of sight, our consciousness, or even our dimension owes far more to Lovecraft than to Poe. The majority of horror films, stretching from *Nosferatu*, to *Frankenstein*, to the new horror of the post-Romero era and forward into the last decade's obsession with the zombies, owes more to writers and directors reflecting and refracting the catastrophic real-world horrors of the last century than to a reading of Poe that displays any depth or engagement.[46]

A claim to Poe's legacy will continue to play an important role in modern horror culture. Horror authors and directors will likely long revel in this particular anxiety of influence. He has become a commodity and has acquired all the inherent appeal of commodity fetishism. In the twentieth-century and contemporary horror, Poe has become the definition of cultural capital. Understanding that Poe's legacy has overshadowed Poe's work certainly calls forth the proscriptive, or perhaps just grumpy, aspects of Poe scholars. There is certainly no argument that there should be more readers of Poe, in all his variations and complexity, than wearers of Gothic Poe t-shirts.

Nevertheless, the auteurs of horror often remain readers of Poe even if his direct influence plays little or no role in their work except for, perhaps, the way in which reading great writers makes for better writing, whatever aesthetic and thematic ideas guide the actual work. This is no ill effect. Indeed, Hervey's description of Poe's "charnel house atmosphere" has become a substantial part of what it means to be a contemporary producer, and fan, of horror. It has become a substantial part of Poe's legacy.[47]

NOTES

1. Stephen King, *Danse Macabre* (1981; New York: Berkley Books, 1983), 72; King, "The Genius of 'The Tell-Tale Heart,'" in *In the Shadow of the Master*, ed. Michael Connelly (New York: Harper, 2009), 189.
2. Regarding the "disreputability" of horror, see Robin Wood, "Beauty Bests the Beast" in *American Film* 8, no. 10 (1983): 73–88.
3. The role of the Great War, and I would add its aftershocks, has been explored previously in works such as David J. Skal's *The Monster Show: A Cultural History of Horror* (New York: Faber and Faber, 1993), 47–48, 56–61.
4. Dennis R. Perry and Carl H. Sederholm, "Introduction: Poe and the Twenty-First Century Adaptation Renaissance," in *Adapting Poe: Re-imaginings in Popular Culture*, ed. Dennis R. Perry and Carl H. Sederholm (New York: Palgrave-MacMillan, 2012), 5.
5. The discussion of this era in Poe's life is taken from J. Gerald Kennedy, introduction to *The Portable Edgar Allan Poe*, ed. J. Gerald Kennedy (New York: Penguin Books, 2006), xvii–xviii.
6. John Moncure Daniel, "Edgar Allen [*sic*] Poe," *Southern Literary Messenger* 16, no. 3 (March 1850): 178.
7. Joan Dayan, *Fables of Mind: An Inquiry into Poe's Fiction* (New York: Oxford University Press, 1987), 19.
8. Scott Peeples, *The Afterlife of Edgar Allan Poe* (Rochester, NY: Camden House, 2004), 10, 15–17.
9. Quoted in Peeples, *The Afterlife of Edgar Allan Poe*, 11; J. Gerald Kennedy, *Poe, Death, and the Life of Writing* (New Haven, CT: Yale University Press, 1987), 5.
10. Rick Woreland, *The Horror Film: An Introduction* (Hoboken, NJ: Blackwell), 144–146.
11. S. T. Joshi, *I Am Providence: The Life and Times of H.P. Lovecraft*, 2 vols. (New York: Hippocampus Press, 2013), 1:139–140. Scholars debate whether or not the Munsey publications are the first true pulp magazines; many want to reserve that designation for the "true pulps" that began to appear in the 1920s. S. T. Joshi makes the straightforward case that they are at least the forerunners of the pulps.
12. Daniel Stashower, *The Beautiful Cigar Girl: Mary Rogers, Edgar Allan Poe, and the Invention of Murder* (New York: Berkeley Publishing Group, 2006), 140.
13. Jan Burke, "Under the Covers with Fortunato and Montresor," in *In the Shadow of the Master: Classic Tales by Edgar Allan Poe*, ed. Michael Connelly (New York: Harper, 2009), 35–37.

14. John Reuben Thompson, "The Late Edgar Allen [*sic*] Poe," *The Southern Literary Messenger* 15, no. 11 (Nov. 1849): 696.
15. Andrew Liptak, "The Troubled History of *Weird Tales* Magazine," *Kirkus Reviews*, October 24, 2013, https://www.kirkusreviews.com/features/troubled-history-weird-tales-magazine/.
16. A process explored more fully in W. Scott Poole, *In the Mountains of Madness: The Life and Extraordinary Afterlife of H.P. Lovecraft* (Berkeley, CA: Soft Skull Press, 2016), 50–53.
17. Joshi includes a very detailed discussion of Lovecraft's diverse sources even if he finally relies largely on Lovecraft's own estimation of Poe's influence; *I Am Providence*, 1:36–41, 142–143, 240–242. Probably the most detailed history of Lovecraft's relationship to the pulp magazine, both in terms of form and influence, appears in Will Murray, "H. P. Lovecraft and the Pulp Magazine Tradition," in *An Epicure in the Terrible: A Centennial Anthology of Essays in Honor of H.P. Lovecraft*, ed. David E. Schultz and S. T. Joshi (New York: Hippocampus Press, 2011), 101–136.
18. H. P. Lovecraft, *Selected Letters*, ed. August Derleth and Douglas Wandrei, vol. 1, *1911–1924* (Sauk City, WI: Arkham House, 1965), 20, 6–7.
19. Joshi, *I Am Providence*, 1:525–526.
20. Joshi, *I Am Providence*, 2:981.
21. Poole, *In the Mountains of Madness*, 72–73.
22. Joshi, *I Am Providence*, 1:241.
23. Poole, *In the Mountains of Madness*, 108–110. Lovecraft's worldview had been much influenced by Oswald Spengler's *Decline of the West*, itself a product of the cultural malaise that followed in the wake of the war.
24. A close examination of how cinema changes in response to the trauma of war, including a close reading of *Nosferatu*, can be fond in Anton Kaes, *Shell Shock Cinema: Weimar Culture and the Wounds of War* (Princeton, NJ: Princeton University Press, 2009), 98–130.
25. After completing a famous trilogy of novels between 1913 and 1920, all heavily influenced by the Great War, Lawrence wrote his twelve-chapter critical work *Studies in Classic American Literature* (1923), two chapters of which he devotes to Melville.
26. Wesley D. Swetser, *Arthur Machen* (New York: Twayne Publishers, 1964), 125–127.
27. King makes this comment in his dedication of his critically well-received novel *Revival*, a dedication that includes not only Machen but Mary Shelley, Bram Stoker, and H. P. Lovecraft as his forerunners. Poe is notably absent. See Stephen King, *Revival: A Novel* (New York: Gallery Books, 2014).
28. Wesley D. Sweetster, *Arthur Machen* (New York: Twayne, 1964), 114.
29. Gabriel Lovatt, "From Experiment to Epidemic: Embodiment in the Decadent Modernism of Arthur Machen's "The Great God Pan" and "The Inmost Light," *Mosaic* 49, no. 1 (2016): 19–35.
30. Quoted in Arthur M. Miller, "The Influence of Edgar Allan Poe on Ambrose Bierce," *American Literature* 4, no. 2 (1932): 130–150.
31. Burton Pollin, "Poe and Ray Bradbury: A Persistent Influence and Interest," *The Edgar Allan Poe Review* 6, no. 2 (Fall 2005): 31–38.
32. Pollin finds it very significant that Bradbury calls himself, in a poem title, "The Only Begotten son of Emily and Edgar," although, notably, he doesn't suggest any ways in which Bradbury shows the influence of Dickinson. "Poe and Ray Bradbury," 31, 36.
33. See Peter Straub, ed., *Poe's Children: The New Horror* (New York: Doubleday, 2008).

34. Michael Connolly, ed., *In the Shadow of the Master: Classic Tales by Edgar Allan Poe* (New York: Harper Press, 2010).
35. P. J. Parish, "Pluto's Heritage," *In the Shadow of the Master*, 58. Like most of the contributors, the pair notes their interest in Poe either being first stirred, or made quiescent, by Corman's AIP films.
36. Jeff Vandermeer, foreword to *Songs of a Dead Dreamer and Grimscribe*, by Thomas Ligotti, rev. ed. (New York: Penguin, 2015), ix.
37. One of Ligotti's most famous, and best, works, "The Last Feast of Harlequin" offers a riff on both "The Shadow over Innsmouth" and "The Festival." He, in fact, dedicated the story to Lovecraft. He also borrows Lovecraft's forbidden tomes in his "The Sect of the Idiot," a story drawing heavily from the Lovecraftian conception of human cults dedicated to dark, extra-dimensional powers. This debate certainly goes beyond the bounds of the essay and so I would encourage the reader to take a look at Poole, *In the Mountains of Madness*, 251–253.
38. Darrel Schweitzer, "*Weird Tales* Talks with Thomas Ligotti," in *The Thomas Ligotti Reader: Essays and Exploration*, ed. Darrell Schweitzer (Holicong, PA: Wildside Press, 2003), 24, 26.
39. Poe's work became a mainstay in American literature after the 1920s and the emergence of the "New Criticism." By the time of the beginning of Corman's career, as Scott Peeples' notes, "something like an academic 'Poe Industry' had developed." He suggests that this ran parallel to, while having no "intersection" with "the pop culture Poe industry," in *The Afterlife of Edgar Allan Poe*, 74. This does sum up the state of interest and critical and popular appreciation with Poe perfectly, even if the present essay takes a slightly different approach to the intersection of the two trends.
40. David Huckvale, *Poe Evermore: The Legacy in Film, Music and Television* (Jefferson, NC: McFarland Press, 2014), 401.
41. Much of the discussion of Corman's films comes from his own memoir, important because it gives a bit of his own understanding of Poe and also because, ever the publicist, it reveals what Corman *wanted* movie-goers to find in Poe. See Roger Corman (with Jim Jerome), *How I Made a Hundred Movies in Hollywood and Never Lost a Dime* (New York: Random House, 1990), 77–80.
42. Corman, *How I Made a Hundred Movies*, 82.
43. Corman, *How I Made a Hundred Movies*, 84.
44. Andrew Migliore and John Strysik, *Lurker in the Lobby: A Guide to the Cinema of H. P. Lovecraft* (Portland, OR: Night Shade Books, 2006), 61.
45. In a 2006 film called *H.P. Lovecraft's The Tomb*, Lovecraft's name and one of his titles were used for a poorly done imitation of *Saw*.
46. The same can be said of the influence of Lovecraft to a lesser degree. "Lovecraftian" elements of horror culture are often filtered through writers who have explored the so-called Cthulhu mythos (a problematic concept) and the host of tabletop role-playing games, computer and console video games, and fiction born out of these cultural materials such as graphic novels.
47. Ellen Datlow's anthology—Ellen Datlow, ed., *Poe: 19 New Tales of Suspense, Dark Fantasy, and Horror Inspired by Edgar Allan Poe* (Nottingham, UK: Solaris Books, 2009)—provides a good example. Some of the best writers in modern horror contributed a tale, and they are uniformly strong and uniformly written by women and men who have spent time both with Poe's own texts and the multitude of texts inspired by him. The stories themselves

show little if any of his direct influence and, in fact, a few make him a character in a horror tale or, in the case of Kim Newman's pitch perfect contribution, are actually stories about the influence of Poe in popular culture.

Bibliography

Dayan, Joan. *Fables of Mind: An Inquiry into Poe's Fiction*. New York: Oxford University Press, 1987.

Huckvale, David. *Poe Evermore: The Legacy in Film, Music and Television*. Jefferson, NC: McFarlane and Company, 2014.

Joshi, S. T. *I Am Providence: The Life and Times of H.P. Lovecraft*. 2 vols. New York: Hippocampus Press, 2013.

Peeples, Scott. *The Afterlife of Edgar Allan Poe*. Rochester, NY: Camden House, 2004.

Perry, Dennis R. and Carl H. Sederholm, eds. *Adapting Poe: Re-Imaginings in Popular Culture*. New York: Palgrave Macmillan, 2012.

Poole, W. Scott. *In the Mountains of Madness: The Life and Extraordinary Afterlife of H.P. Lovecraft*. Berkeley, CA: Soft Skull Press, 2016.

CHAPTER 37

DUPIN'S DESCENDANTS IN PRINT AND ON SCREEN

JOHN GRUESSER

> He was wonderful—this Poe! Gaboriau—the great Gaboriau—could not approach him; and that *docteur anglais*—what did one call him—Doyle? Pouf! He was an echo. What was Lecoq! What was Sherlock Holmes beside this Master Dupin! These were the successors of Alexander!
>
> —Melville Davisson Post, *The Nameless Thing*[1]

LIKE Benjamin Franklin, who never used the word *autobiography* and yet produced its first true, modern, and secular iteration, Edgar Allan Poe has long been regarded as the originator of modern detection despite the fact that the word *detective* never appears in his writings and he himself used the phrase "tales of ratiocination" (CL 1: 595). During the eighteenth century, the only comparable term for *detective* was "thief taker," and it was not until 1829 that Home Secretary Robert Peel established the first official "police" force in London—although the word itself, in the sense of a government department "concerned with maintaining order . . . and enforcing the law," dates from the 1740s.[2] In the late 1830s, periodicals used the word *Vidocq*, the name of the man who founded the French department of investigation, the *Sûreté*, to describe a pursuer of criminals.[3] The word *detective* first appeared as an adjective in 1843, according to the *Oxford English Dictionary*, and, as early as 1844, Irish newspapers used the word as a noun to refer to members of the plainclothes police force in the British colony, with several articles denouncing their unscrupulous practices.[4] In 1850, Charles Dickens published "Three Detective Anecdotes,"[5] seven years later an English newspaper article referred to "Poe's detective stories" for the first time, and, in 1859, the subtitle "A Detective Story" began to be used in American periodical fiction.[6]

Although tales of detection are as old as literature itself and several crime fictions appeared in periodicals prior to the 1840s, Poe has been hailed as the founder of the form. First, scholars have lauded Poe for establishing key conventions of modern detection, including the presentation of clues, the use of ratiocination, the rivalry between an amateur sleuth and the police force, and the detective's explanation of the solution to the mystery. Second, they have credited him with incorporating into the genre such prominent themes as female victimization, race, and foreign contamination resulting from imperialism. Third, they have attributed several different types of modern detective fiction to him, such as the locked-room mystery, the metaphysical detective story, the true crime mystery, armchair detection, the cryptographic mystery, comic detection, the pirate treasure mystery, gumshoe detection, the small-town murder mystery, the least-likely-suspect mystery, the stolen article mystery, and the criminal mastermind mystery.[7]

Several decades would elapse following Poe's death, however, before detection came to be codified as a literary genre and he received acknowledgment for his contributions to it. In the wake of the enormous success of Arthur Conan Doyle's short stories featuring Sherlock Holmes in the early 1890s, steps were taken on both sides of the Atlantic to delineate, defend, organize, and popularize detective fiction through the publication of articles, introductions, collections, and anthologies, resulting in the construction of a genealogy for the genre. By the end of the nineteenth century, the delayed but unstoppable recognition of Poe as a major writer with a profound and sustained influence abroad and at home coincided with and contributed to the coalescing of detection into a discrete literary genre. In Volume Three of their 1894–1895 edition of Poe's *Works*, Edmund Clarence Stedman and George Edward Woodberry grouped the three Dupin stories, "The Murders in the Rue Morgue" (1841), "The Mystery of Marie Rogêt" (1842–1843), and "The Purloined Letter" (1844), along with "The Gold-Bug" (1843) and "Thou Art the Man" (1844), under the heading Tales of Ratiocination, and in the opening volume's "Introduction to the Tales," Stedman used the phrase "detective stories" in connection with Poe.[8] In 1900, Street & Smith published *Detective Tales*, comprising the Dupin trilogy, "The Gold-Bug," and Poe's July 1841 *Graham's Magazine* essay "Cryptography." Four years later, McClure, Phillips & Co. brought out *Monsieur Dupin: The Detective Tales of Edgar Allan Poe* with the same selections as Stedman and Woodberry, accompanied by an eleven-page introduction by McClure's literary advisor William Aspinwall Bradley and eight illustrations by Charles Raymond Macauley.[9] After decades of mixed feelings about the writer and his legacy, scholars and the general public in the United States embraced Poe at the start of the new century, initiating a love affair that was readily apparent in celebrations marking the hundredth anniversary of his birth in 1909 and that has grown in ardor ever since.

From the 1920s through the early 1980s, critics emphasized the supposed rigidity and conservativism of detective and mystery writing.[10] Moreover, some scholars have characterized Poe as an antidemocratic Southern apologist and aesthete who takes pains to eliminate moral, social, and political considerations from his texts.[11] However, a comprehensive analysis of detection reveals its adaptability to a multiplicity of artistic, personal, ideological, and political programs. As Maurice Lee aptly observes, Poe's tales featuring Dupin "introduce but do not exhaust the possibilities of detective fiction, offering later writers a generative model open to improvisation."[12] Indeed, by weaving generic subversion and authorial competition into the very fabric of detection, Poe has made it possible for writers of diverse backgrounds to use the form covertly or overtly to address issues of particular concern to themselves. As someone who craved but never achieved sustained success as a fiction writer during his lifetime, Poe would likely have been startled to discover that the genre he was largely responsible for launching would reappear in action-packed dime novels featuring protagonists such as the Old Sleuth, the New York Detective, and Nick Carter, as well as a series of books about the exploits of the Pinkerton Detective Agency (well known for its trademark open eye, the eye that never sleeps). In addition, he would be surprised to learn that two generations after his death, white women and African Americans would embrace detection. Likewise, he would no doubt be amazed to find that over the last 170 years the descendants of his aristocratic French sleuth have come in an array of shapes, sizes, nationalities, genders, socioeconomic classes, sexual orientations, political points of view, subject positions, and ethnic and racial backgrounds. Moreover, even his vivid imagination could not have conceived of detection's impact on other print and nonprint media in the twentieth and twenty-first centuries, such as comics, graphic novels, animation, computer games, television, and film.

Poe's Contributions to Detection

As established by Poe in the Dupin stories, detection entails various forms of competition. First, and on the most basic level, Poe stages a series of contests between characters: Dupin versus the narrator and Dupin versus the police prefect G— in "Rue Morgue," Dupin versus various newspapermen in "Marie Rogêt," and Dupin versus the master criminal D— in "Purloined." To underscore the competitive nature of detection and explain the analytical ability that enables the protagonist to come out on top, Poe makes reference to games of skill and games of chance and, in the final story, depicts Dupin's recourse to the stratagems of disguise and masquerade to ensure victory.

Second, Poe conceives of detection as competition between himself, as author, and his readers. Supposedly providing all the information necessary to decipher the puzzle, he challenges his audience to arrive at a solution before the denouement begins, using a first-person narrator who is not the detective to heighten the illusion of a fair contest. Speaking about Dupin in a August 9, 1846 letter to Philip Pendleton Cooke, Poe lifts the curtain to explain that by creating the characters of both the criminal, who appears to perpetrate the crime, and the detective, who appears to solve it, the author of detection convinces readers that they are competing with the sleuth rather than the writer himself or herself:

> You are right about the hair-splitting of my French friend:—that is all done for effect. These tales of ratiocination owe most of their popularity to being something in

> a new key. I do not mean to say that they are not ingenious—but people think them more ingenious than they are—on account of their method and *air* of method. In the "Murders in the Rue Morgue," for instance, where is the ingenuity of unravelling a web which you yourself (the author) have woven for the express purpose of unravelling? The reader is made to confound the ingenuity of the supposititious Dupin with that of the writer of the story. (CL 1: 595)

Here Poe avails himself of imagery relating to coiling and weaving that he uses to introduce the figure of the detective at the start of "Rue Morgue": "As the strong man exults in his physical ability, delighting in such exercises as call his muscles into action, so glories the analyst in that moral activity which *disentangles*. He derives pleasure from even the most trivial occupation bringing his talent into play" (M 2: 528). The writer of this kind of fiction fools readers into believing that they are in competition with the detective rather than recognizing that this central figure is simply one among the author's many means of getting the better of them.

Third, in his detective stories following "Rue Morgue," Poe essentially competes with himself, striving to rework and outdo what he has already done. By sewing authorial competition into the woof of detective fiction, Poe anticipates texts that manipulate the conventions of the genre for ludic ends and makes it possible for a diverse range of authors to use the form openly or obliquely to address issues of morality, class, gender, nation, and race. By envisioning detection in this manner, he has inspired a diverse range of writers to compete with him and with each other to bring innovations to the form, initiating a malleable genre that has reflected the evolution of modern society and has enabled authors of all different stripes to find new ways to outwit, enlighten, educate, and politicize readers.

In the first tale detailing his exploits, Dupin delights in matching wits with the narrator, the Prefect, and, briefly, the sailor who transported the orangutan from the East Indies to Paris, emerging victorious in each of these contests. Poe similarly emerges triumphant, using not only the detective's deceptiveness but also an apparently trustworthy narrator, the withholding of key information, and a shift from one mystery to another to humbug his readers. Just as Dupin strives to create and maintain the illusion of a fair contest between himself and his companion as each attempts to solve the case, Poe uses the device of a seemingly reliable first-person narrator, a close friend and companion of the detective, to create the illusion of fair play. Designed through his naiveté to serve as a model or stand-in for the reader, the narrator never realizes the extent to which Dupin holds back information from him, nor does he ever question the detective's ratiocination; rather, like Dr. Watson in the Sherlock Holmes stories, he treats Dupin as a miracle worker who should be regarded with nothing short of reverence. Summing up the contrast between them, Jeffrey Meyers remarks, "Though Dupin's mind is a mystery to the narrator, his thoughts are transparent to Dupin."[13] Thus, the narrator provides no indication of the cunning manner in which Poe deceives readers, even though (but also because) he himself functions as the conduit for the author's manipulations.

Even more deviously, in this first tale of modern detection, Poe persuades readers that they are playing one game when they are actually playing another, thereby anticipating hard-boiled novels. The newspapers and the police mistakenly believe the killings to be murders, when, in reality, and despite the story's misleading title, no murder has taken place because the perpetrator is not human. Consequently, Poe deceives readers into erroneously regarding "Rue Morgue" as a whodunit; however, Dupin actually solves a wholly different type of mystery, one in which he detects a missing beast solely from the traces that have been left behind. By having him do so, Poe aligns the protagonist with a long line of literary characters, ranging from the three princes of Serendip (in a fourteenth-century Persian fairy tale) to Voltaire's Zadig to Sir William of Baskerville (in Umberto Eco's *The Name of the Rose*). Poe even slyly hints at this bait-and-switch in his presentation of the facts of the case when he has the narrator quote a newspaper article about the killings that raises the question of what kind of a crime has been committed: "A murder so mysterious, and so perplexing in all its particulars, was never before committed in Paris—*if indeed a murder has been committed at all*" (my emphasis, M 2: 544).

An ardent and consistently victorious competitor as well as a clever manipulator with highly questionable motives, Dupin is only one means by which Poe deceives his audience. As a result, readers never have a legitimate chance to solve the mystery in "Rue Morgue" before the detective announces his solution. Nevertheless, because of the sheer inventiveness of the author's multifaceted deceptions, people continue to read, reread, and marvel at this story and have made the genre it is largely responsible for originating enormously popular.

Although the results are far from satisfactory, by deciding to bring Dupin and his companion back for a second outing in "Marie Rogêt," thereby making them series characters, the author introduces a third level of competition into detective fiction that has had far-reaching consequences. Revisiting but also reconceiving the form he created in "Rue Morgue," Poe chooses to impose limitations on himself and on his detective in "Marie Rogêt," which recounts Dupin's "armchair" detection in a case based on an actual unsolved death in which a woman, once again, is the victim. Anonymous newspapermen advancing theories about the case replace the narrator and the Prefect as Dupin's opponents, and, like the conflicting eyewitness accounts in "Rue Morgue," the newspaper articles in "Marie Rogêt" function as both sources of information and straw men for the detective to rebut. Even though the detective receives credit for solving the mystery and, as a result, collects the reward, the second story lacks a moment of complete triumph for Dupin attesting to his peerless reasoning prowess. Poe himself fares even worse than his main character, failing to effect a clever humbug and falling short of equaling, much less surpassing, what he accomplished in his previous effort. Nevertheless, by reprising Dupin and having the narrator quite explicitly refer to the detective's previous case and his own chronicling of it, the author incorporates repeatability, self-referentiality, and authorial competition into detection.[14] As problematic as Poe's attempt to solve an actual crime in "Marie Rogêt" may be, detective fiction could not begin to become a literary genre until, as Terence Whalen has observed, the second story in a sequence had been written.[15] Having failed to get the better of his readers and surpass his previous effort, it is therefore not surprising that Poe returns to a fictional world entirely of his own creation in the third Dupin tale.

And what a return it is for Dupin *and* Poe. The detective not only thoroughly and conclusively drubs his opponent, revenging himself upon a formidable old rival who once did him an "evil turn" (M 3: 993), but he also pockets a substantial reward. Like the protagonist, his creator returns to top form in the finale, producing the most concise, ingenious, and satisfying installment of the series, regarded by many critics as his best detective story and one of the greatest tales of detection ever written. Indeed, in a true masterstroke that has had profound implications for detection generally, Poe no longer pits Dupin against rival crime solvers who lack his analytical abilities; instead, he has him go head to head with "an unprincipled man of genius" (M 3: 993). Perhaps in part because of his lack of success in the previous story, Poe outdoes himself in "Purloined," composing what amounts to a treatise on how to write detection and making it necessary for subsequent authors to keep pace with him by bringing innovations to the form.

In the first two tales, to which the narrator refers explicitly in the opening paragraph of "Purloined," Dupin uses ratiocination and imagination, aided in "Rue Morgue" by observation, to anticipate or reconstruct the thought processes of others, whether it be his crime-solving opponents (the narrator, the Prefect, and the journalists of Paris) or persons directly involved in the crimes (the orangutan's owner and Marie's betrayer). None of these people, however, possesses a mind to rival Dupin's. For this reason, although Poe's deceptiveness makes it all but impossible to predict his detective's solutions, there is never a doubt as to whether Dupin will win the contests. In the final story, however, the protagonist faces an opponent whose abilities and relish for competition bear a remarkable resemblance to his own, as indicated by D—'s use of logical reasoning, creative thinking, and an eye for detail to get the better of both the Queen (who is yet another female victim—this time of theft and blackmail), and the prefect G—. The latter confesses that the Minister "is more astute than" himself (M 3: 978) in the case of the stolen letter, just as he had to admit Dupin's triumph over him in the first story. Finally facing off against a worthy adversary in the trilogy's final installment, the hero savors his most satisfying victory.

Like Dupin, Poe comes out victorious in "Purloined," successfully manipulating readers and topping what he had previously accomplished. He devises one of his most remarkable stratagems, hiding the solution out in the open (in the same manner that the Minister fools the Prefect) by having Dupin suggest to G— near the beginning that "[p]erhaps the mystery is a little *too* plain, . . . a little *too* self-evident" (M 3: 975). A revealer and a creator of hoaxes, Poe not only devotes entire texts to unmasking or perpetrating frauds but also, as Scott Peeples points out, attempts to perform both actions in several of his writings, often with less than satisfactory results."[16] In "Purloined," however, he brilliantly pulls off this trick by having Dupin expose and duplicate the ruse concocted by D—. Moreover, by devoting roughly half of the tale to the detective's explanation of how he undoes (but also redoes) what the Minister has done, Poe manages, vis-à-vis his readers, to approximate the feat attributed to the famous showman P. T. Barnum by one of his ticket sellers: "First he humbugs them, and then they pay to hear him tell how he did it."[17] In this way Dupin resembles Poe himself, who took delight in the idea of "mystification."

Incorporating a metafictional wrinkle into the genre, Poe also addresses the writing of detection itself in the Dupin series. According to John T. Irwin, "As Poe practices it, the detective story is a literary form closely aware of its own formal elements, its antecedents, its associations—indeed, so much so that it subtly thematizes these as part of the textual mystery that the reader must unravel in the tale."[18] If "Purloined" is read as a story about how an author projects himself or herself into the minds of readers and, to paraphrase "Rue Morgue," seduces them "into error" or "miscalculation" (M 2: 529), then the significance of the crime solver being nearly identical with the criminal emerges, for the writer of this type of fiction must both devise a problem or crime (like D—) and offer a solution to it (like Dupin). Poe—a hoaxer, debunker, cryptographer, and manipulator—creates the adversarial characters D— and Dupin so as to divert attention from the fact that he—the author—has woven a web, like Penelope, in order to unravel it.

Poe employs three distinct detective plots in the Dupin tales: "Rue Morgue" turns out to be a missing animal mystery (or what we might call a "whatwasit"); despite Poe's equivocal revisions, "Marie Rogêt" remains more or less a "whodunit," as the narrator's reference to the "murder" of the grisette at the start of the final story suggests; and in "Purloined" the mystery concerns the location of a stolen article (making it a "whereisit"). In attempting to outdo himself and thereby expand but also subvert the nascent form in the sequels to "Rue Morgue" through the use of self-referentiality, metafictionality, multiple plotlines, and various forms of competition, Poe creates the opportunity for authors of detective stories to pursue a variety of personal, artistic, moral, ideological, and political agendas. The remarkably wide range of directions in which writers after Poe have taken the genre and the figure of the detective serves to substantiate Raymond Chandler's characterization of detection as a "fluid" form that defies "easy classification."[19]

The Pervasive Influence of Poe's Detective Fiction

Aspects of modern detection deriving from Poe figure in nineteenth-century American texts by authors not normally associated with the form. These narratives, which feature detectives who differ significantly from Dupin—or lack such a figure—include Nathaniel Hawthorne's *The Scarlet Letter* (1850); a recently discovered "city mystery" by Walt Whitman, *The Life and Adventures of Jack Engle* (1852); Herman Melville's *Benito Cereno* (1855); Emma D. E. N. Southworth's serial *The Hidden Hand* (1859); Harriet Jacobs's *Incidents in the Life of a Slave Girl* (1861); and Mark Twain's "The Stolen White Elephant" (1882). Hawthorne, who corresponded with Poe, uses the word *detect* frequently in his first novel, particularly after Roger Chillingworth commits himself to solving the mystery of Pearl's paternity. Therefore, it is appropriate to regard this character as a kind of detective, albeit a morally defective one. Whitman not only submitted material for publication to and met Poe in New York City but also was the only writer to attend his reburial in Baltimore in 1875. By no means a detective novel as we understand it today, Whitman's *Jack Engle*, set in lower Manhattan, nevertheless features a detective figure (albeit in a minor role) named Wigglesworth, includes a "murderer," and echoes Poe's fabrication imagery in referring to the need to "unravel" the "web of deviltry" of a swindling lawyer.[20] When poor sales forced Melville to turn from novels to short fiction, contemporary observers noted resemblances between his periodical publications and Poe's prose, and recent critics have made similar connections. Melville's use of a retrospective narrative structure, heterogeneous content, and an anti-Dupin, the mentally limited and racially prejudiced Amasa Delano (who has a "knot" in his head preventing him from recognizing and drawing proper conclusions from the clues before his eyes on the slave ship *San Dominick*), link *Benito Cereno* to detection. Southworth creates a proto-feminist trickster figure in her protagonist, who seeks out danger, outwits devious and unscrupulous male foes, and frequently dons disguises. Whereas Dupin investigates crimes that have already been completed, Capitola Black uses her quick and keen intelligence to prevent them from occurring or to foil them while they are being perpetrated, particularly in connection with the schemes undertaken by her uncle Gabriel Le Noir and his ally, the notorious thief Black Donald. For this reason and because she unravels none of the mysteries relating to mistaken or hidden identity (including her own) that figure so prominently in the story, Capitola cannot accurately be called a detective.[21] There is no evidence that Jacobs ever met Poe; however, she had access to the books and periodicals of her longtime employer, Nathaniel Parker Willis, who not only gave Poe a job at the *New York Evening Mirror* and defended him after his death but also played a key role in bringing Poe considerable fame when the *Mirror* published "The Raven" in its January 29, 1845 issue. Like those of Whitman and Southworth, Jacobs's narrative cannot properly be called a detective story; however, there are links between Dupin's rivalry with the criminal mastermind D— in "Purloined" (as well as Capitola's battle of wits with Black Donald) and the "Competition in Cunning" between Linda Brent and her master Dr. Flint in *Incidents in the Life of a Slave Girl*. The author of several complete and fragmentary texts that use the conventions of detection, Mark Twain had this to say about the genre in an 1896 notebook entry: "What a curious thing a 'detective' story is. And was there ever one the author needn't be ashamed of, except 'Murders in the Rue Morgue.' "[22] In "The Stolen White Elephant," he brilliantly sends up not only many of the elements and plots first seen in Poe but also Dupin himself by highlighting the idiosyncrasies and greed of the head of the New York police force, Inspector Blunt.

Like their American counterparts, British writers in the second half of the nineteenth century began implicitly and explicitly to pay homage to Poe, often emulating the self-reflexivity of "Marie Rogêt" and "Purloined." Wilkie Collins's comic tale "Who Is the

Thief" (1858) pits two experienced police professionals against an arrogant and narrow-minded amateur, the last three letters of whose name, Sharpin, but not his sleuthing skills, recall Dupin's. An admirer of Poe's tales and poems from his youth, who published a story in 1883 in which a ghost declares himself the "embodiment" of Poe,[23] Arthur Conan Doyle, frequently acknowledged his profound debt to Dupin's creator. Notably, in staging the first meeting of John Watson and Sherlock Holmes in *A Study in Scarlet* (1887), he evokes his American forerunner:

> "You remind me of Edgar Allan Poe's Dupin. I had no idea that such individuals did exist outside of stories."
>
> Sherlock Holmes rose and lit his pipe. "No doubt you think that you are complimenting me in comparing me to Dupin," he observed. "Now, in my opinion, Dupin was a very inferior fellow. That trick of his of breaking in on his friend's thoughts with an apropos remark after a quarter of an hour's silence is really very showy and superficial. He had some analytical genius, no doubt; but he was by no means such a phenomenon as Poe appeared to imagine."[24]

By having Holmes echo the language used by Dupin when he reads the narrator's mind in "Rue Morgue"—"He is a very little fellow" (M 2: 534)—in dismissing Poe's protagonist as "a very inferior fellow," Doyle perpetuates the illusion that fictional detectives are actual people with whom readers can match wits rather than tools used by authors to deceive them. Moreover, in the concluding passage to the first Holmes story that provides the explanation for its title, Doyle, in another nod to Poe, portrays Holmes employing weaving imagery to characterize the solving of crimes: "Why shouldn't we use a little art jargon? There's a scarlet thread of murder running through the colorless skein of life, and our duty is to unravel it and isolate it and expose every inch of it."[25]

Anna Katharine Green, whose courtroom drama *The Leavenworth Case* (1878) enjoyed tremendous popularity and whose 1907 novel *The Mayor's Wife* hinges on a cryptographic mystery inspired by "The Gold-Bug," stands at the head of a group of women authors in the late 1800s and early 1900s who expanded the form by creating female detectives and addressing gender issues. Her fiction, along with Mary Wilkins Freeman's "The Long Arm" (1895), a locked-room mystery (like Poe's "Rue Morgue") featuring a daring subtext that anticipates later detection featuring gay and lesbian characters, and Susan Glaspell's explicitly feminist "A Jury of Her Peers" (1917), in which fabrication imagery and the art of quilting play indispensable roles, illustrate the adaptability of detection to political and social commentary. Such fictions often depict women who commit transgressive acts, including homicide, and Glaspell's story equates the justice system with a criminal patriarchy. Moreover, unlike Dupin, who chooses cases that intrigue him (and from which he can profit), female sleuths created by women writers often become detectives by accident, investigating mysteries to protect their own reputations or that of a family member, lover, friend, or neighbor.

The contrast between the ideology and ethos of a story such as "A Jury of Her Peers" and the hard-boiled fiction that began to appear five years later could hardly be more striking. Tough guy writing typically focuses on an independent, lower-middle-class private eye who operates in a corrupt and violent urban environment, expresses himself in a brash, idiosyncratic way, and follows a personal code of ethics. Hard-boiled fiction gained prominence in American pulp magazines during the 1920s and 1930s (especially *Black Mask* under the editorship of Joseph "Cap" Shaw). This new form of writing reached a high mark with Dashiell Hammett's *The Maltese Falcon*, serialized in *Black Mask* from September 1929 through January 1930 and published in book form shortly thereafter. Less concerned with who did what than "what the hell went on," as Chandler put it in a 1949 letter,[26] tough guy writers often construct their stories in a manner that harkens back to Poe, changing the game on readers so that they are deceived into solving the wrong problem. Although they agree that the hard-boiled dick first appeared in the early 1920s, scholars disagree as to where this figure came from or why he appeared at that moment. For the most part, they have overlooked a compelling link between the origins of hard-boiled fiction and late nineteenth- and early twentieth-century US expansionism. Particularly intriguing is the extent to which Hammett's, Chandler's, and Carroll John Daly's protagonists reflect the independent and manly qualities stressed in Elbert Hubbard's widely disseminated tract "A Message for Garcia" (1899), about a soldier who delivers a letter from President McKinley to a Cuban rebel leader during the Spanish-American War.

G. K. Chesterton, who offered a robust "Defence of the Detective Story" in 1901, began publishing stories featuring his Catholic priest detective Father Brown in 1910. More concerned with saving souls than in deciphering riddles and punishing crime, Brown nevertheless hearkens back to Dupin by exhibiting both his creative and resolvent abilities in stories such as "The Blue Cross." The 1920s saw the beginning of the long career of the most successful writer of detection in terms of number of books sold. Agatha Christie published sixty-six detective novels that are estimated to have sold over two billion copies in forty-five languages.[27] Most of these feature her series detectives Hercule Poirot, an eccentric and fastidious Belgian who attributes his success as a crime solver to his "little gray [brain] cells," and Miss Jane Marple, a spinster who draws on her acute understanding of human nature based on careful observation of the people in her small English village. In the late 1920s and early 1930s, Chesterton and Christie joined with Dorothy Sayers, Ronald Knox, R. Austin Freedom, Baroness Orczy, and others to form the Detection Club, which promulgated rules of "fair play" for the writing of detective fiction.

Whether they are detached, eccentric amateur sleuths or cynical, self-sufficient private investigators, fictional crime solvers have always been outsiders, and this alienation only increases if they belong to a group that has been relegated to the margins of society. An enormously popular form with well-established conventions that typically requires the crime or crimes be solved and the established order restored, the genre would seem to be a restrictive vehicle for a black author aspiring to do more than entertain readers. Thus, in order to preserve the integrity of their plots and characters, African Americans who write detection fiction must strike a difficult balance between genre conformity and subversion. Pauline Hopkins and John Edward Bruce in the early

1900s subordinate their detective plots to their political agendas, exposing racial intolerance as a criminal conspiracy that even their brilliant black sleuths cannot completely overcome. Walter Mosley turns to detective fiction eighty years later as the means to make social, political, and moral statements that might not otherwise have found an audience. In the fourteen Easy Rawlins books spanning the years 1939 through 1968, Mosley creates a Signifying detective, adept at manipulating linguistic codes to gain access to powerful people and vital information, and innovatively uses the genre to illustrate the conflict between personal and racial freedom. Meanwhile, Valerie Wilson Wesley breaks new ground in her Tamara Hayle series about a Newark, New Jersey–born African American private detective and single mother. As she explains in a 2003 interview, Wesley "take[s]," "twist[s]," and "play[s]" with the threads of detection her predecessors have spun, using the female space of a hair salon the way male writers do barbershops and taverns, innovatively pioneering hard-boiled motherhood, and looking back to the pasts of detective fiction, race relations in the United States, and African American culture as well as ahead to their futures.[28] Perhaps one of the most elaborate chains of reference within the genre links her novels and Poe's "Rue Morgue." Wesley has her detective drive a Volkswagen Jetta (until a group of thugs destroy it in the late 1990s) to acknowledge her debt to Sue Grafton, whose white, female, hard-boiled detective drives a VW Bug. Grafton's Kinsey Millhone herself is based in Santa Teresa, the same southern California town where Ross Macdonald's series character, Lew Archer, operates. The name of Macdonald's detective, in turn, evokes Sam Spade's partner Miles Archer, who takes a bullet in the heart early in Hammett's *The Maltese Falcon*, which itself evokes the first Dupin story wherein the sailor who brings the orangutan from Asia to Paris works on a Maltese vessel. Unique in their personalities, methodologies, and backgrounds and operating in distinctive milieus, Spade, Archer, Millhone, and Hayle nevertheless regard themselves as part of an honorable profession with a long tradition, even if they (as opposed to their creators) have never heard of Auguste Dupin.

Poe's Detection and Film

According to Burton R. Pollin, "Next to Shakespeare, unquestionably the most prolific source for films of many types has been the work of Edgar Allan Poe. Early film makers exploited the tales and poems for their graphic details and their rich stimuli for exotic and unusual moods and atmospheric effects," a practice that subsequent directors have continued.[29] Because Poe wrote short fiction rather than novels, adaptations by the makers of feature-length films, made-for-television movies, and hour-long television series episodes—as opposed to short films—have tended to be loose, and several compilations based on two or more of the stories have been produced. "The Murders in the Rue Morgue," which has indirectly spawned countless crime and detective motion pictures and television programs (as well as dozens of movies in which primates menace humankind, such as the two *Planet of the Apes* series), has been the detective story by Poe most frequently adapted to the cinema. The Ur-text for the countless motion pictures featuring fortune hunters endeavoring to decipher treasure maps and find pirate booty (including the many versions of *Treasure Island* and the *Pirates of the Caribbean* franchise), "The Gold-Bug," which features the Dupin-like sleuth Legrand, has been the second-most frequently adapted tale of detection by Poe.[30]

Accompanied by Dr. Watson, Conan Doyle's sleuth made his first film appearance in *Sherlock Holmes and the Great Murder Mystery* (1908), replacing Poe's protagonist in a plot derived from "Rue Morgue." Dupin also does not appear in *The Leopard Lady* (1928), *The Murders in the Rue Morgue* (a very loose 1971 adaptation starring Jason Robards), or the schlock drive-in horror film *Bloody Ape* (1997). In 1932, Universal, which released *Frankenstein* and *Dracula* the previous year, brought out *The Murders in the Rue Morgue*, in which Bela Lugosi plays the villain and a medical student named Pierre Dupin investigates the abduction of women. Ten years later, the studio released *The Mystery of Marie Roget*, set in late nineteenth-century Paris, which includes another doctor turned detective named Paul Dupin. Steve Forrest plays Professor Dupin in *The Phantom of the Rue Morgue* (1954), set in Paris in the 1870s and also featuring Karl Malden. Close adaptations of the first Dupin story include an episode for the television series *Detective* in 1968, a French made-for-television movie, *Le Double Assassinat dans la Rue Morgue* (1973), and a 1986 made-for-television film named after Poe's story, with George C. Scott as Dupin. There have also been films in which Dupin's creator acts as a detective. In *The Man with the Cloak* (1951), set in New York City, Joseph Cotten plays a hard-drinking poet turned sleuth who goes by the name of Dupin and is later revealed to be Poe himself. A big-budget production that proved to be a commercial flop, *The Raven* (2012), set in Baltimore in 1849, portrays Poe (John Cusack)—rather than Dupin—investigating a series of grisly crimes based on his own stories in order to save the woman he loves and even provides an explanation for the writer's own mysterious death. Transformed into a doctor or replaced by Sherlock Holmes or Poe himself, the amateur sleuth of the three 1840s tales, who relishes detective work for the competition and intellectual stimulation it provides him, has only occasionally been depicted on screen. Moreover, unlike Doyle's Sherlock Holmes, Chesterton's Father Brown, Christie's Hercule Poirot and Miss Marple, each of whose exploits have been extensively portrayed on the small screen, Dupin has never been the focus of a *Masterpiece Mystery*-style television series.

Whereas interest in Dupin has been less than overwhelming, Poe's life and writings have intrigued numerous directors, ranging from D. W. Griffith to Roger Corman to Alfred Hitchcock. Griffith made the highly fictionalized "Edgar Allen [*sic*] Poe" in 1909, reputed to be the first biographical short film ever made.[31] Between 1960 and 1964, Corman released eight films loosely based on works by Poe, none of them tales of detection. Hitchcock has often been associated with the author, although the filmmaker claimed in an early 1970s interview with George Stevens, Jr., that he does not make mysteries.[32] Led by Dennis R. Perry, critics have noted thematic, structural, and even temperamental links between the two artists. Perry discusses the relationship between "Rue Morgue" and the films *Murder!* (1930), *Dial M for Murder* (1954), and *Psycho* (1960), as well as that between Poe's proto-detective story, which does not include Dupin, "The Man of the Crowd" (about a convalescent man who sees and then shadows a sinister figure through the streets of London), and *Rear Window* (1954), a connection that has also been explored by Dana Brand.[33]

Hitchcock himself raises the question of Poe's influence in "Why I Am Afraid of the Dark," an essay published in a French journal in 1960 as "Pourquoi J'ai Peur de la Nuit." He recalls that he would hurry back to his room after work to read a "cheap edition" of Poe's stories, two of which he mentions by name—both tales of detection. Hitchcock was frightened by "Rue Morgue," yet, at the same time, he learned an invaluable lesson from it: people enjoy the experience of fear so long as it occurs in a location where they feel safe, such as a favorite reading chair at home or a cozy seat in a cinema. He indicates that his goal in his films—like Poe's in many of his tales—is to "[g]ive them pleasure" by means of fear."[34] Turning from Poe's talent for eliciting fear to the author's knack for generating suspense, Hitchcock describes "The Gold-Bug" as a story that "fascinated me and fascinates me still . . . because I always loved adventure."[35] Stressing the ability of an exceptional artist to create a spellbinding (even if highly implausible) plot through meticulous construction, he describes Poe's "story of treasure, which one finds thanks to a mysterious beetle" as one that "corresponds to my love of the fantastic and of precision."[36] Having in his late teens and early twenties written and published short stories, often with twist endings,[37] Hitchcock demonstrates a keen sense of the differences between fiction and film in his essay: "In cinematographic style, 'suspense' consists in inciting a breathless curiosity and in establishing a complicity between the director and the spectator, who knows what is going to happen. In a book, however, the reader must never guess what is going to happen and must not know the unraveling of the intrigue before getting to the end."[38] In the Stevens interview, Hitchcock differentiates mystery, "an intellectual process," from suspense, "essentially an emotional process," explaining that, in film, "You can only get the suspense element going by giving the audience information"—such as the presence of a bomb under a table around which people are idly chatting, oblivious to the danger—and putting them to "work,"[39] by which he means making them emotionally identify with the imperiled persons on the screen. Hitchcock's keen insights on the differences between not only the media of fiction and film but also the genres of mystery and suspense may help to explain why certain of Poe's texts have been readily embraced as the source material for films while others, including the Dupin tales, have been less frequently (and, perhaps, less successfully) adapted.[40]

Assessing Poe's "odd"—but profound—legacy, J. W. Ocker observes, "He had a vision so insistent that he had to invent or evolve entire genres of literature just to express it. With 'The Murders in the Rue Morgue,' he created the modern detective story, meaning he made possible about 80 percent of contemporary literature and television programming," facetiously adding, "No Poirot, no *Magnum P.I.* And that's three mustaches the world would be impoverished without."[41] Although illustrators, comic book artists, and filmmakers have depicted C. Auguste Dupin with facial hair, Poe himself remains silent on the subject of his character's physical appearance. By concentrating instead on the workings of the detective's mind, as well as his competitive nature, Poe has bequeathed to literature and popular culture a figure that has influenced, inspired, and served the myriad purposes of an incredibly diverse range of artists working in multiple media.

Notes

1. Melville Davisson Post, *The Nameless Thing* (New York: D. Appleton and Co., 1912), 303.
2. *Oxford English Dictionary*, s.v. "Thief-,taker, (*n.*)," updated 1989, http://www.oed.com; *Oxford English Dictionary*, s.v. "police, (*n.*)," updated September 2006, http://www.oed.com.
3. Leroy Lad Penak and Mary M. Bendel-Simso, *The Essential Elements of the Detective Story, 1820–1891* (Jefferson, NC: McFarland, 2017), 16–20.
4. *Oxford English Dictionary*, s.v. "Detective, (*adj.* and *n.*)," updated 1989, www.oed.com; see, for example, "The Detectives," *Dublin Weekly Nation*, June 22, 1844, 7.
5. The second of these was entitled "The Artful Touch—A Detective Story"; Charles Dickens, "Three 'Detective' Anecdotes," *Household Words*, September 14, 1850, 577–580.
6. See, for example, "The Tell-Tale Signature: A Detective Story," whose main title evokes Poe, published on the first page of the April 22, 1860 issue of the *Memphis Daily Appeal* after appearing in *The Family Journal*. See "The Tell-Tale Signature: A Detective Story," *Memphis Daily Appeal*, April 22, 1860, Chronicling America, https://chroniclingamerica.loc.gov/lccn/sn83045160/1860-04-22/ed-1/seq-1/.
7. See, for example, Patricia Merivale and Susan Elizabeth Sweenedy, eds., *Detecting Texts: The Metaphysical Detective Story from Poe to Postmodernism* (Philadelphia: University of Pennsylvania Press, 1999); Penak and Bendel-Simso, *The Essential Elements of the Detective Story, 1820–1891*; Jacques Barzun, *The Delights of Detection* (New York: Criterion, 1961); Howard Haycraft, *The Art of the Mystery Story* (New York: Simon & Schuster, 1947); and John W. Cawelti, *Adventure, Mystery and Romance: Formula Stories as Art and Popular Culture* (Chicago: University of Chicago Press, 1976).
8. Edmund Clarence Stedman, "Introduction to the Tales," in *The Works of Edgar Allan Poe*, ed. Edmund Clarence Stedman and George Edward Woodberry (Chicago: Stone & Kimball, 1894), 1:101, 119.
9. Edgar Allan Poe, *Detective Tales* (New York: Street & Smith, 1900); Poe, *Monsieur Dupin: The Detective Tales of Edgar Allan Poe*, intro. by William Aspinwall Bradley, illustrated by Charles Raymond Macauley (New York: McClure, Phillips & Co., 1904).
10. See, for example, the position taken by the members of the Detection Club (formed in 1930), which is referred to later, as well as Cawelti, *Adventure, Mystery and Romance* and Ernest Mandel, *Delightful Murder: A Social History of the Crime Story* (London: Pluto Press, 1984).
11. See, for example, J. Gerald Kennedy, ed., *A Historical Guide to Edgar Allan Poe* (New York: Oxford, 2001)—especially Louis A. Renza, "Poe and the Issue of American Privacy," 181; and Jon Thompson, *Fiction, Crime, and Empire: Clues to Modernity and Postmodernism* (Urbana: University of Illinois Press, 1993), 49.
12. Maurice S. Lee, "Edgar Allan Poe," in *A Companion to Crime Fiction*, ed. Charles J. Rzepka and Lee Horsley (Malden, MA: Wiley, 2010), 370.
13. Jeffrey Meyers, *Edgar Allan Poe: His Life and Legacy* (New York: Cooper, 2000), 124.

14. For more on the second Dupin story, see Valerie Rohy's essay, "The Calculus of Probabilities: Contingency in 'The Mystery of Mary Rogêt,'" in this volume.
15. Terence Whalen, *Edgar Allan Poe and the Masses: The Political Economy of Literature in Antebellum America* (Princeton, NJ: Princeton University Press, 1999), 236.
16. Scott Peeples, *Edgar Allan Poe Revisited* (New York: Twayne, 1998), 126.
17. Neil Harris, *Humbug: The Art of P. T. Barnum* (Boston: Little, Brown, 1973), 77.
18. John T. Irwin, "A Clew to a Clue: Locked Rooms in Poe and Borges," in *The American Face of Edgar Allan Poe*, ed. Shawn Rosenheim and Stephen Rachman (Baltimore: Johns Hopkins University Press, 1995), 152.
19. Raymond Chandler, *Raymond Chandler Speaking*, ed. Dorothy Gardiner and Katherine Sorley Walker (Boston: Houghton Mifflin, 1977), 70.
20. Walt Whitman, *The Life and Adventures of Jack Engle*, ed. Zachary Turpin, *Walt Whitman Quarterly Review* 34, no. 3–4 (2017): 301, 314.
21. Similar to Poe in "The Gold-Bug," who, as J. Gerald Kennedy notes, attempts to depoliticize slavery and thereby appeal to both Northern and Southern readers by designating Jupiter as free but having him speak and act in a stereotypical manner, Southworth, who at times espoused antislavery views and published in abolitionist periodicals, never uses the words *slave* or *slavery* in *The Hidden Hand* in connection with her black characters in bondage whose language and behavior conform to those to be found in minstrel shows. J. Gerald Kennedy, *Strange Nation: Literary Nationalism and Cultural Conflict in the Age of Poe* (New York: Oxford, 2016), 373.
22. Franklin R. Rogers, introduction to *Simon Wheeler, Detective*, by Mark Twain (New York: New York Public Library, 1963), xii.
23. Michael Sims, *Arthur and Sherlock: Conan Doyle and the Creation of Holmes* (New York: Bloomsbury, 2017), 29, 74–75.
24. Arthur Conan Doyle, *A Study in Scarlet* (London: Ward, Lock, Bowden, 1892), 31.
25. Doyle, *A Study in Scarlet*, 67.
26. Chandler, *Raymond Chandler Speaking*, 70.
27. Joan Acocella, "Queen of Crime," *New Yorker*, August 16, 2010, http://www.newyorker.com/magazine/2010/08/16/queen-of-crime.
28. Valerie Wilson Wesley, "May 2003," interview by John Gruesser, in *Race, Gender and Empire in American Detective Fiction*, by John Cullen Gruesser (Jefferson, NC: McFarland, 2013), 166.
29. Burton R. Pollin, *Images of Poe's Works: A Comprehensive Descriptive Catalogue of Illustrations* (New York: Greenwood Press, 1989), 323. For a guide to eighty-one films based on texts by Poe, see Don G. Smith, *The Poe Cinema: A Critical Filmography of Theatrical Releases Based on the Works of Edgar Allan Poe* (Jefferson, NC: McFarland, 1999).
30. One of the notable adaptations is *Manfish* (1956), set in Jamaica.
31. *Edgar Allen Poe*, directed by D. W. Griffith, American Mutoscope & Biograph, 1909, https://www.youtube.com/watch?v=PeDOrpUgtO8.
32. George Stevens, Jr., "Alfred Hitchcock," in *Conversations with the Great Moviemakers of Hollywood's Golden Age at the American Film Institute* (New York: Knopf, 2006), 258.
33. Dennis R. Perry, *Hitchcock and Poe: The Legacy of Delight and Terror* (Lanham, MD: Scarecrow Press, 2003), and "Teaching Poe's Influence on Hitchcock: The Example of 'The Murders in the Rue Morgue' and *Psycho*," in *Approaches to Teaching Poe's Prose and Poetry*, ed. Jeffrey Andrew Weinstock and Tony Magistrale (New York: MLA, 2008),

192–197; Dana Brand, "Rear-View Mirror: Hitchcock, Poe, and the Flâneur in America," in *Hitchcock's America*, ed. Jonathan Freedman and Richard Millington (New York: Oxford University Press, 1999), 123–134. See also Perry's "Imps of the Perverse: Discovering the Poe/Hitchcock Connection," *Literature Film Quarterly* 24, no. 4 (1996): 396–402.

34. Alfred Hitchcock, "Why I Am Afraid of the Dark," in *Hitchcock on Hitchcock: Selected Writings and Interviews*, ed. Sidney Gottlieb (Berkeley: University of California Press, 1997), 143.
35. Hitchcock, "Why I Am Afraid of the Dark," 143–144.
36. Hitchcock, "Why I Am Afraid of the Dark," 144.
37. See Patrick McGilligan, "Alfred Hitchcock: Before the Flickers," *Film Comment* 35, no. 4 (July/August 1999): 22–31.
38. Hitchcock, "Why I Am Afraid of the Dark," 144.
39. Stevens, "Alfred Hitchcock," 258–259.
40. Despite an awareness of the profound differences between the métiers of literature and moviemaking, between the eras in which Poe and he lived, and between the writer's sensibilities and his own, Hitchcock concludes "Why I Am Afraid of the Dark" by coupling himself once again with the nineteenth-century American author. He declares, "We are both prisoners of a genre: 'suspense,'" which has led, he proceeds to elucidate, to their being typecast in the minds of the public: "You know the story that one has recounted many, many times: if I was making 'Cinderella,' everyone would look for the corpse. And if Edgar Allan Poe had written 'Sleeping Beauty,' one would look for the murderer" (145). Given Poe's innovative compositions in multiple literary forms, he would no doubt have chafed at being limited to the confines of "suspense" fiction. In contrast, the twentieth-century British "commercial filmmaker" (144)—as the director of *The Birds* refers to himself—seems rather comfortable in the familiar, gilded cage of "suspense" cinema.
41. J. W. Ocker, *Poe-Land: The Hallowed Haunts of Edgar Allan Poe* (Woodstock, VT: Countryman Press, 2015), 9.

Bibliography

Barzun, Jacques. *The Delights of Detection*. New York: Criterion, 1961.

Cawelti, John W. *Adventure, Mystery and Romance: Formula Stories as Art and Popular Culture*. Chicago: University of Chicago Press, 1976.

Chandler, Raymond. *Raymond Chandler Speaking*. Edited by Dorothy Gardiner and Katherine Sorley Walker. Boston: Houghton Mifflin, 1977.

Haycraft, Howard. *The Art of the Mystery Story*. New York: Simon & Schuster, 1947.

Irwin, John T. "A Clew to a Clue: Locked Rooms in Poe and Borges." In *The American Face of Edgar Allan Poe*, edited by Shawn Rosenheim and Stephen Rachman, 139–152. Baltimore: Johns Hopkins University Press, 1995.

Lee, Maurice S. "Edgar Allan Poe." In *A Companion to Crime Fiction*, edited by Charles J. Rzepka and Lee Horsley, 369–380. Malden, MA: Wiley, 2010.

Mandel, Ernest. *Delightful Murder: A Social History of the Crime Story*. London: Pluto Press, 1984.

Merivale, Patricia, and Susan Elizabeth Sweeney, eds. *Detecting Texts: The Metaphysical Detective Story from Poe to Postmodernism*. Philadelphia: University of Pennsylvania Press, 1999.

Penak, Leroy Lad and Mary M. Bendel-Simso. *The Essential Elements of the Detective Story, 1820–1891*. Jefferson, NC: McFarland, 2017.

Perry, Dennis R. *Hitchcock and Poe: The Legacy of Delight and Terror*. Lanham, MD: Scarecrow Press, 2003.

Sims, Michael. *Arthur and Sherlock: Conan Doyle and the Creation of Holmes*. New York: Bloomsbury, 2017.

Thompson, Jon. *Fiction, Crime, and Empire: Clues to Modernity and Postmodernism*. Urbana: University of Illinois Press, 1993.

CHAPTER 38

POE'S VISUAL LEGACY

BARBARA CANTALUPO

THE purpose of this essay is two-fold: to provide an overview of illustrated Poe works and to show the extent that visual artists have been (and still are) influenced by Poe's writing.[1] Discussion of both topics follows chronological order, acknowledging that a comprehensive assessment of Poe's visual legacy would require a book-length study. More than seven hundred artists have reacted to Poe's work either as illustrators or as painters producing their own oeuvre. As Burton Pollin surmised in an interview, the reason for this prodigious response has to do with "graphicality," a word Poe coined.[2] Put simply, in Poe's words, "graphicality" is "the force with which [descriptions] convey the true by the novel or unexpected, by the introduction of touches which other artists would be sure to omit as irrelevant to the subject" (H 15: 74). Take, for example, this passage from Poe's "King Pest":

> Had they not, indeed, been intoxicated beyond moral sense, their reeling footsteps must have been palsied by the horrors of their situation. The air was cold and misty. The paving-stones, loosened from their beds, lay in wild disorder amid the tall, rank grass, which sprang up around the feet and ankles. Fallen houses choked up the streets. The most fetid and poisonous smells everywhere prevailed;—and by the aid of that ghastly light which, even at midnight, never fails to emanate from a vapory and pestilential atmosphere, might be discerned lying in the by-paths and alleys, or rotting in the windowless habitations, the carcass of many a nocturnal plunderer arrested by the hand of the plague in the very perpetration of his robbery. (M 2: 243–244)

Published early in Poe's career in 1835, "King Pest" depicts a decidedly morbid scene with the surprising effect created at the very end when descriptions of inanimate objects revert abruptly to the image of "the carcass of many a nocturnal plunderer." Morbidity, however, was not the only quality of Poe's "graphicality." Throughout his fiction and poetry, the visual effect of the unexpected persists. Take, for example, this passage from "The Domain of Arnheim," a story published in 1847:

> This basin was of great depth, but so transparent was the water that the bottom, which seemed to consist of a thick mass of small round alabaster pebbles, was distinctly visible by glimpses—that is to say, whenever the eye could permit itself *not* to see, far down in the inverted heaven, the duplicate blooming of the hills. On these latter there were no trees, nor even shrubs of any size. The impressions wrought on the observer were those of richness, warmth, color, quietude, uniformity, softness, delicacy, daintiness, voluptuousness, and a miraculous extremeness of culture that suggested dreams of a new race of fairies, laborious, tasteful, magnificent, and fastidious; but as the eye traced upward the myriad-tinted slope, from its sharp junction with the water to its vague termination amid the folds of over-hanging cloud, it became, indeed, difficult not to fancy a panoramic cataract of rubies, sapphires, opals and golden onyxes, rolling silently out of the sky. (M 3: 1280)

Here the "cataract of rubies, sapphires, opals and golden onyxes" erupts from the details of the natural landscape, creating a fantastic "panorama." Poe was keenly aware of the linguistic effect of "graphicality," praising Margaret Fuller's writing precisely for this quality in his fourth number of Literati of New York City: "The most favorable estimate of Miss Fuller's genius . . . is to be obtained, perhaps, from her contributions to 'The Dial,' and from her 'Summer on the Lakes.' Many of the *descriptions* in this volume are unrivalled for *graphicality*, (why is there not such a word?)" (H 15: 74). However generous this praise may be for Fuller, Poe himself proves the master of "graphicality."

During Poe's lifetime, only six of his works included illustrations: "Maelzel's Chess-Player" (anonymous illustrator; image copied from the 1832 Harper's pirated edition of Sir David Brewster's *Letters on Natural Magic*),[3] "The Island of the Fay" (illustration by John Sartain based on an engineering-drawing by John Martin),[4] "The Balloon Hoax" (illustration by George Scharf Sr. appearing in numerous publications in 1844),[5] "Morning on the Wissahiccon" ("The Elk") (illustration by John Gadsby Chapman), the fifth chapter of the unfinished *Journal of Julius Rodman* in *Burton's Gentleman's Magazine* (anonymous illustrator), and "The Gold Bug" (two illustrations by F. O. C. Darley).

Poe chose Darley to illustrate "The Gold Bug," and his illustrations may have helped the story take first place prize in a contest held by the Philadelphia *Dollar Newspaper*. Jeffrey Savoye contends that Poe would have included illustrations in this story to serve as an example of the kind of work he would publish in his projected literary magazine, *The Stylus*: "Poe seems to have recognized the unusual merits of 'The Gold Bug.' Indeed, he wished to use the tale, in two parts, as a showpiece in the premier issues, complete with illustrations by F. O. C. Darley."[6] Poe had contracted with Darley to illustrate *The Stylus*. In Poe's May 28, 1844, letter to Lowell, he contends, "Of the 'Gold-Bug' more than 300,000 copies have been circulated" (CL 1: 441). Pollin suggests that the "illustrations fostered the reprinting."[7]

Of the two illustrations used in the tale, Darley's ink-wash drawing of the men discovering the treasure in the deep hole was transformed by the engraver into an outlined image for publication in the *Dollar Newspaper*; in doing so, the tentativeness of Darley's original illustration is lost. The second illustration, also refined when translated for publication, suggests, nonetheless, an eerie *vanitas* still-life: no men are in the scene;

we see only a skull and bones, a shovel, an open chest full of treasure, a broken hull of a boat, and a leaning tree with bare branches (see Figure 38.1).

This sketch exudes a sense of sadness, almost suggesting that the frenetic search for the treasure depicted in the story had been invigorating but the reward itself deflating. In this way, the illustration becomes a cypher of what Poe expresses in "The Power of Words,"[8] a story published two years later in the *Democratic Review*. There, the more seasoned angel, Agathos, explains to the newcomer Oinos that "of this infinity of matter, the *sole* purpose is to afford infinite springs, at which the soul may allay the thirst *to know* which is for ever unquenchable within it—since to quench it, would be to extinguish the soul's self" (M 3: 1212). That Poe chose for "The Gold Bug" the gloomy after-effect of this

FIGURE 38.1 "The Treasure Revealed," original ink-wash sketch, by F. O. C. Darley, 8 1/8 x 6 5/8 inches, 1843. ("The image here has been reversed to match the printed version. Originally, F. O. C. Darley's signature was in the lower left corner and was not inverted." See Jeffrey Savoye, "'The Gold Bug' [images], *Dollar Newspaper*," The Edgar Allan Poe Society of Baltimore, updated April 2, 2015, https://www.eapoe.org/works/tales/goldbgi2.htm.)

vanitas illustration makes sense and reveals an undercurrent of meaning: the depression that follows the solution of a mystery. This undercurrent subtly tints the overt excitement and frenzy that a search for buried treasure entails—more than likely the quality that won Poe the hundred-dollar reward for his tale. The fact that Poe supervised the choice of illustrations suggests that he valued their impact, especially if they could be used to suggest an undercurrent of meaning, thereby adding the necessary "complexity, or more properly, adaptation" to the tale (H 14: 208).[9]

It's important to note, however, that Poe openly deplored poor illustration. In many of his reviews of books or magazine articles, he did not hesitate to harshly criticize poorly executed images. In a review of Charles Dickens's *Barnaby Rudge*, for example, Poe doesn't fail to mention that the "copper engravings are pitiably ill-conceived and ill-drawn" (M 2: 61). Despite condemnations like this one, Poe also claimed that reading an illustrated book is like overhearing a bystander at an exhibit expound on a painting's or sculpture's merit. The bystander's judgments, Poe claims, are "easily and keenly appreciable, while these comments interfere, in no perceptible degree, with the force or the unity of our own comprehension" (H 11: 8). Furthermore, Poe believed that illustrations could enhance the pleasure derived from reading even if they do not match the reader's interpretation of the text. If the artist's finesse is greater than the reader's, Poe argues, then "each picture will stimulate, support, and guide the fancy" (H 11: 8); if the illustrations are weak, the astute reader will take pleasure in knowing that his interpretation is superior to the artist's conception.[10]

Poe also was keenly aware of how overall production quality—not merely the quality of the illustrations—impacts a book's reception. He states this explicitly in his review of *The Vicar of Wakefield* in *Graham's Magazine* for January 1842: "This publication is one of a class which it behoves every editor in the country to encourage, at all times, by every good word in his power—the class, we mean of well printed, and, especially, of well illustrated works. . . . We place particular emphasis upon the mechanical style. . . . The criticism which affects to despise these adventitious aids to the enjoyment of a work of art is at best but *étourderie*" (H 11: 8). This belief is reinforced in Poe's letters to potential contributors and donors to his own projected literary magazine, *The Stylus*. In these letters, Poe emphatically states that he wants "No steel engravings; but now & then a superior wood-cut in illustration of the text" (CL 1: 256–257).[11] In letters to Washington Irving (Philadelphia, June 21, 1841, Letter 113), John P. Kennedy (Philadelphia, June 21, 1841, Letter 114), Henry Wadsworth Longfellow (Philadelphia, June 22, 1841, Letter 115), and Fitz-Greene Halleck (Philadelphia, June 24, 1841, Letter 116), Poe emphasizes that his magazine "shall have no engravings, except occasional wood-cuts . . . when demanded in obvious illustration of the text; and, when so required, they will be worked in with the type—not upon separate pages, as in 'Acturus'" (CL 1: 275, 278, 281, 283–284). Later, in a letter to Frederick W. Thomas (Philadelphia, February 25, 1843), Poe enthusiastically assured Thomas that "We *shall* make the most magnificent Magazine as regards externals, ever seen. The finest paper, bold type, in single column, and superb wood-engravings (in the manner of the French illustrated edition of 'Gil Blas' by Gigoux, or 'Robinson Crusoe' by Grandville)" (CL 1: 381–382). On March 27, 1843, in a letter to Lowell asking him to procure a piece from Nathaniel Hawthorne for *The Stylus*, Poe again remarks that "A part of my design is to illustrate, whatever is fairly susceptible of illustration, with finely executed wood-engravings—after the fashion of Gigoux's 'Gil Blas' or 'Grandville's Gulliver' " (CL 1: 394).

Artists Illustrating Poe's Works

The history of illustrated Poe works begins in England in 1852 with *Tales of Mystery, Imagination, and Humour; and Poems* published by H. Vizetelly as volume one in a series called "Readable Books."[12] Pollin observes that the illustrations "show considerable skill in draftsmanship, and every one emphasizes a scene of action or dramatic tension. No artist is named."[13] The frontispiece illustrates "The Mystery of Marie Rogêt" and pictures two men in a small boat on what looks like the Seine, hauling Marie Rogêt's dead body out of the water. The title page includes an illustration of "The Gold Bug," which is also the first story in the volume appearing after Griswold's "Memoir." The edition takes liberties with Poe's titles; for example, "The Gold Bug" is called "The Gold-Beetle," and "Mesmeric Revelation" is titled "Startling Effects of Mesmerism on a Dying Man." On the first page of "The Gold-Beetle," the illustration wraps around the text and anticipates the turning point of the tale: Legrand and the narrator look up at Jupiter who, lying precariously on a high branch of a tall tulip tree, dangles a long string with the gold bug at its end. Included in the story are six other illustrations, the most for any tale in the volume; coming in second with four illustrations is "A Descent into the Maelström." The image of the maelström resembles Irish artist Harry Clarke's 1919 illustration except that Clarke pictures the boat and other objects swirling inside the maelström, while the 1852 illustration shows the narrator being whirled around on the inside edge of the whirlpool. The 1852 image is circular, drawing the viewer more perceptively into the maelström than does the more formalized, rectangular image by Clarke (see Figures 38.2 and 38.3).

The next illustrated edition of Poe's work was published a year later in 1853 and titled *Poetical Works*.[14] James Hannay, its British editor, dedicated the volume to Dante Gabriel Rossetti, whose poem and painting, "The Blessed Damozel," were seen as direct responses to Poe's "The Raven."[15] In fact, the frontispiece of Hannay's edition shows a scene from "The Raven" by E. H. Wehnert that pays homage to Rossetti by highlighting Lenore as she floats above the narrator in the arms of two angels. With his head buried in his arms, the narrator leans on the plush arm of his velvet "cushioned seat" languishing over her death. Hannay may have requested this image from Wehnert, in particular, because it is the only one in the edition by him; the other artists include James Godwin, F. W. Hulme, and Harrison Weir—and according to Pollin, their "styles did not always harmonize sufficiently to give a unity to the graphics. The use of a consortium of illustrators was a Victorian oddity, which prevailed even in France for the great 1884 Quantin edition"; Pollin calls the illustrations "uninspired but inordinately popular."[16] Hannay clearly admired Poe's poetry, and in the introductory overview of Poe's life,

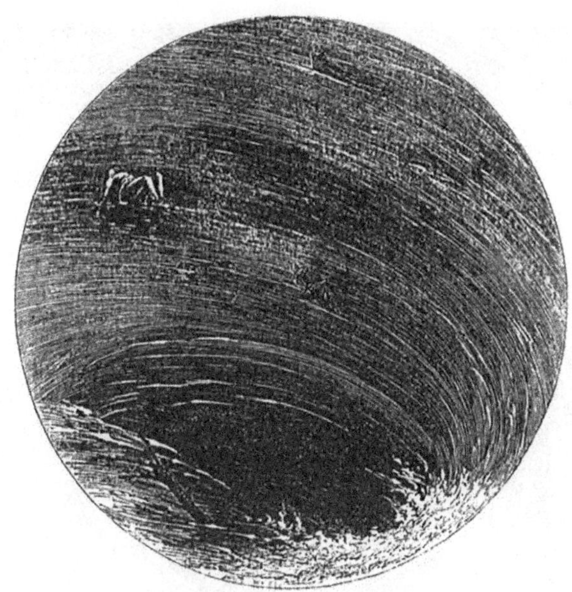

FIGURE 38.2 Woodcut by an anonymous artist. *Tales of Mystery, Imagination, and Humour; and Poems by Edgar Allan Poe. Illustrated with Twenty-Six Engravings on Wood* (London: H. Vizetelly, 1852), 78.

despite its many errors, Hannay shows an exuberant admiration not only for Poe's poetry but for the author himself: "there is the keenest feeling for the Beautiful,—which was the predominant feeling of Poe's whole life; there is the loveliest, easiest, joyfullest flow of music throughout. There is, too—what must have been almost instructive—an exquisite Taste—a Taste which lay at the very centre of his intellect like a conscience. . . . In truth, it was the Beautiful that he loved with his entire nature. . . . He gives a certain musical air as a soul to each poem, but he works up the details as an artist."[17]

Four years later in 1857, another edition of Poe's poetry, *The Poetical Works of Edgar Allan Poe, with Original Memoir*, was published in London.[18] Although the complete title of the book lists F. R. Pickersgill as the lead illustrator, fewer than half of the twenty-nine images are by him. The illustrator of Lewis Carroll's *Adventures in Wonderland* and cartoonist for *Punch*, Sir John Tenniel, contributed four images to the edition specifically for "The Raven." The most striking of the four is the final one: a circular frame pictures a raven with its head buried in its breast sitting on the top of Pallas's helmet (see Figure 38.4).

What makes this image particularly striking is the bright light from the transom window that creates pyramidal shapes on the worn and chipped, wood-paneled wall. The bright light creates two shadows: one pyramid-like form begins at the raven's haunch and extends behind the bust of Pallas; the other, larger, pyramid like-shadow mimics the one behind the raven and falls behind it. Piercing through this drama is the empty-eyed,

FIGURE 38.3 Woodcut by Harry Clarke (1919).

ominous visage of Pallas, shoulders lit with the bright white light from above. Gustave Doré uses a similar format to picture the raven years later.

Another contributor to the 1857 edition of Poe's poetry was American illustrator F. O. C. Darley. Despite Poe's admiration for Darley,[19] the two images he made to illustrate "The Bells" are very unlike those he did for "The Gold-Bug." The subtleties of those images are lost in the two illustrations he did for "The Bells"; they can only be described as melodramatic and prosaic, leaving nothing to the imagination.[20] Poe would not have approved. In his review of Henry Wadsworth Longfellow's *Ballads and Other Poems* in *Graham's Magazine* for April 1842, Poe clearly states his preference for subtlety: "An outline frequently stirs the spirit more pleasantly than the most elaborate picture" (H 11: 84). Jasper Cropsey's two images for "The City in the Sea," on the other hand, are strong and imaginative, and they complement the poem as do his images for "The Coliseum" and "Ulalume."[21]

FIGURE 38.4 Woodcut by Sir John Tenniel in *The Poetical Works, with Original Memoir*, illustrated by F. R. Pickersgill (London: Samson Low, Son & Co., 1858), 8.

Aside from Tenniel, the well-known illustrators of the last quarter of the nineteenth century include Gustave Doré (1832–1883), Édouard Manet (1832–1883), and Aubrey Beardsley (1872–1898). Curiously, the illustrations in the important 1884 Quantin edition, *Histoires extraordinaires, Edgar Poe, traduites par Charles Baudelaire*, remain unattributed. According to Pollin, "[a]bout twenty-five illustrations are tantalizingly unidentified—some quite charming, unpretentious, simple line drawings. No clue is given as to their source, date, [or] medium."[22]

According to Pollin, "Beardsley was invited in 1894 to execute four pictures for a large-paper multi-volume edition of Poe's works. . . . Beardsley's letter of 2 January 1894 speaks of eight illustrations but only four of them appeared—marvelously humorous and ingenious. . . . These pictures demonstrated new possibilities for the graphic arts in the handling of black and white masses and white lines."[23] Featured in Poe's *Tales of Mystery and Wonder* published by Stone & Kimball in 1895, the four pen-and-ink drawings by Beardsley related to "The Murders in the Rue Morgue," "The Black Cat," "The Masque of the Red Death," and "The Fall of the House of Usher." Poe would have admired Beardsley's use of line just as he had in drawings by Mortiz Retzsch. Poe reveals this preference for minimal images in his review of Longfellow's *Ballads*: "We need only refer to the compositions of Flaxman and Retzsch. Here all details are omitted—nothing can be farther from *truth*. Without even color the most thrilling effects are produced" (H 11: 84).[24] The image of "The Masque of the Red Death" shows the vanity and foolish self-regard of the revelers; the center of the image—normally the place the eye goes first—isn't the important focus of the scene despite its erotic draw. Rather, peering from the left-hand side of the frame, an angry, sneering visage of the Red Death is seen, creating a deftly drawn undercurrent of meaning pictured with a simple line.

Poe also would have admired Manet's ink-wash, imagistic illustrations in Stéphane Mallarmé's translation of "The Raven," published in Paris in 1875.[25] The last image in the poem can be likened to Darley's ink-wash "still life" for "The Gold-Bug." Darley's illustration omits the main characters of the tale, and, likewise, Manet omits the narrator in the last image in "The Raven"—the raven's triumph, then, takes center stage. The narrator is nowhere to be seen. The same poignant despair is evident in both illustrations. According to Chris Michaelides, "The modernity and originality of Manet's interpretation is best appreciated when compared to the steel engravings after Gustave Doré, his exact contemporary, in his last work, published in 1883. Doré's engravings hark[en] back to the work of earlier illustrators of the Romantic generation as well as to his own earlier works, emphasizing the supernatural atmosphere of the poem, showing, for example, the 'Seraphim whose foot-falls tinkled on the tufted floor', which Manet omits, or the body of the poet in the shadow of the raven."[26]

Doré's illustrations for "The Raven" were published in a folio volume by the British firm, Sampson Low, Marston in 1883.[27] A notice for the book in *The Academy* magazine quotes a reviewer in the *Saturday Review* who reveals that Doré "was ready to illustrate each phrase of the poem, and has actually left us no less than twenty-six full-page plates."[28] Curiously, Doré's rendering of a raven sitting on the helmet of the bust of Pallas is quite similar to Tenniel's rendition. Doré's version includes shadows similar to those created by Tenniel, but in Doré's illustration, the shadows are circular rather than pyramidal (see Figure 38.5). Both artists frame the raven in a similar fashion, but Doré focuses not on the ominous raven or the piercing eyes of Pallas, as in Tenniel's illustration, but, instead, on something entirely new: the circular shadow behind the bust of Pallas, serrated to imitate a fan, and the haunting faces appear expressing a multitude of emotions: love, anger, diffidence, and suspicion. These visages encapsulate the narrator's range of emotions wrought by the self-inflicted torture resulting from his relentless interrogation of the raven whose only response is "nevermore."

After 1890, as Pollin points out, when "American firms [were] free to reprint and illustrate Poe's works, mass-appeal editions employing popular illustrators would pour from the presses of London and New York."[29] One of the more popular of these editions was *The Bells, and Other Poems by Edgar Allan Poe* illustrated by Edmund Dulac (1882–1953) and published by Hodder and Stoughton simultaneously in New York, London, and Munich in 1909 and in Paris in 1913. Dulac was a much sought-after illustrator, as evidenced by his illustrating Shakespeare's *The Tempest*, Hans Christian Andersen's *The Snow Queen and Other Stories*, *The Rubáiyát of Omar Khayyám*, and *The Sleeping Beauty and Other Fairy Tales from the Old French*, among other popular books of his time. A review of Dulac's work in *Fine Arts Journal* for August 1910 describes his imagery and

FIGURE 38.5 Wood engraving by Gustave Doré in *The Raven by Edgar Allan Poe* (New York: Harper & Bros., 1884), 69.

emphasizes its unity of effect, an important principle of Poe's aesthetics: "the absolute harmony of the creation as a whole and the unity of every part is as carefully fostered as the perfection of any one element. In fact, everything seems to have been kept subordinate to this general effect."[30] The reviewer also elevates another aspect of Dulac's work that is essential to what Poe considers a basic quality of any form of art: "suggestiveness is perhaps the most individual thing about his work running through it all and never wanting."[31] One of the most striking images by Dulac in *The Bells, and Other Poems by Edgar Allan Poe* is the one used as a frontispiece. It's meant to illustrate "The Bells" but also calls to mind "The Devil in the Belfry." In this illustration, Dulac pictures a violently crazed ghoul pulling the rope of the heavy, unseen steeple bell with all his bodily weight (see Figure 38.6).

Aside from Manet, Doré, Dulac, and Beardsley, other prominent illustrators of Poe's works include English artist Arthur Rackham (1867–1939), Austrian artist Alfred Kubin (1877–1959), and Irish artist Harry Clarke (1889–1931).[32]

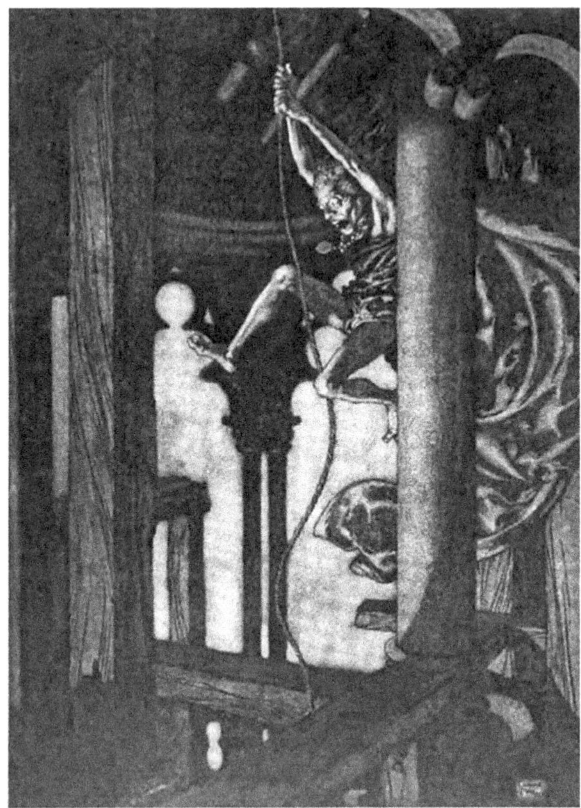

FIGURE 38.6 Frontispiece by Edmund Dulac in *The Bells and Other Poems* by Edgar Allan Poe with illustrations by Edmund Dulac (London: Hodder and Stoughton, 1912).

Clarke was heavily influenced by Beardsley, but when asked about his early exposure to Poe's work, Wilbur recalled Clarke's illustrations: "what I remember most were his line drawings, which were intricate and much more gruesome than Beardsley ever let himself be."[33] According to Nicola Gordon Bowe, Clarke's response to Poe's work "gave ample scope for [his] sinister 'flesh-creeping' depiction of the macabre, the beautiful juxtaposed with the gruesome. . . . He was able to penetrate deeply into the subconscious, mixing seemingly 'real' images and fantastic concoctions from his fertile imagination in a faultless graphic technique."[34] Clarke was asked to illustrate George G. Harrap & Co.'s 1919 edition of Poe's *Tales of Mystery and Imagination*.[35] According to Bowe, upon getting the commission, Clarke was intently occupied with drawing the illustrations for the collection, finishing those for "Ligeia," "The Cask of Amontillado," and "The Masque of the Red Death" in the first three weeks of January 1918, one for "Landor's Cottage" on January 26, "Berenice" on February 5, and an unpublished drawing for "M. Valdemar" on March 1.[36] This last image, in particular, speaks to Clarke's ability to depict Poe's words in visceral, gory detail—M. Valdemar's body oozes off the bed, his head a ghastly skull; only the bones of his arms and legs remain, dripping with putrefied flesh.[37] Only Gerry Hoover's illustrations in the 1973 Godine edition of *The Narrative of Arthur Gordon Pym* are gorier.[38]

In 1935, Harap reissued another edition of Poe's *Tales of Mystery and Imagination* and asked Rackham to illustrate it. According to James Hamilton, Rackham "did not enjoy the commission, being afraid that he would be unable to make the illustrations sufficiently gruesome. He need not have worried, however . . . [since he] carefully injected a virus of sadistic horror . . . into two drawings from *Hop-Frog*."[39] One of these illustrations depicts Hop-Frog leering from above at the tarred and feathered king and his court after having tied them to the chandelier and pulled them up. The second image shows the burnt bodies of the king and his court with only their skulls and bony legs and arms left dangling from the chandelier while the grotesque attendees at the ball either stand aghast or laugh uncomfortably at the horror. While these two images are in black and white, a colored illustration depicting the king harassing Trippetta while his ministers jeer at her with Hop-Frog looking on in violent anger shows Rackham's rounder style, less reminiscent of Beardsley and more in line with Rackham's fairytale images. The images for this edition, according to Hamilton, present a "world-weariness and an almost palpable cynicism at human nature, to resounding decorative and psychological effect."[40]

Austrian artist Alfred Kubin (1877–1959) illustrated many of Poe's works that were translated into German, including *The Tell-Tale Heart and Other Tales* (1909), *Metzengerstein and Other Tales* (1910), *The Gold-Bug and Other Tales* (1910), *King Pest and Other Tales* (1911), *Hans Pfaall's Moon Journey and Other Tales* (1920), *Thirteen Fantastic Tales* (1955), *The Narrative of Arthur Gordon Pym* (1918, 1930), and *Ligeia and Other Tales* (1920), among others. His images tend to reinforce the morbid aspects of the tales. For "Ligeia," for example, Kubin depicts Ligeia lying dead on the ground, her naked, emaciated body crawling with worms—highlighting the triumph of "The Conqueror Worm" (see Figure 38.7).

For "Berenice," one of the other tales in that same volume, Kubin illustrates the nighttime scene of Egaeus intently at work extracting Berenice's teeth, her body pulled only part way out of its exhumed coffin, her legs dangling over its edge. According to Jan Ernst Adlmann, Kubin "was much more susceptible to Symbolist visionary currents coming from artists outside Austria—like France's Odilon Redon and Germany's Max Klinger (both of whom Kubin met and revered), the Belgians Félicien Rops and James Ensor, and the Norwegian Edvard Munch—than he was to the influence of [Austrian Gustav] Klimt's paintings."[41]

German-born artist Fritz Eichenberg (1901–1990) used woodcuts to illustrate Poe's work as well as works by the Brönte sisters, Shakespeare, and Dostoevsky.[42] His best-known illustration from *Tales of Edgar Allan Poe* published by Random House in 1944 is from "Murders in the Rue Morgue"—a huge orangutan fills the frame and stares at the viewer in what Gunter Kress and Theo Van Leeuwen call "direct address" while holding the open razor over Madame L'Espanaye's daughter, who lies face down on the floor. Direct address "demands that the viewer enter into some kind of imaginary relation with" what is pictured.[43] Instead of illustrating a gory image such as Madame L'Espanaye

FIGURE 38.7 Drawing by Alfred Kubin in *Edgar Allan Poe: Ligeia und Andere Novellen, überzetzt von Gisela Etzel; Sieben Gedichte übersetzt von Theodor Etzel mit vierzehn bildegaben von Alfred Kubin* (Berlin: Im Propyäen-Verlag, 1920), 11.

without her head, Eichenberg instead implicates the reader in the act of murder with the orangutan's stare as the focal point of the image, his look seeming to say—"here, I'm about to do this murderous act—what are you going to do about it?"

The illustrations in this volume that stand out, however, are those that introduce each of the six sections, and they are rarely seen; each one combines images from the stories in the unit, and, in so doing, creates unusual effects. For example, Part I, which includes "The Gold Bug," "The Murders in the Rue Morgue," "The Mystery of Marie Rogêt," and "The Purloined Letter," begins with an illustration that uses one of Darley's images from "The Gold Bug" as its frame—the leafless tree with the nail-eyed skull on a branch holds the image together while a hulking orangutan pushes through from the background and the purloined letter sits in the foreground. Of note, as well, is the illustration that begins Part II that includes "The Unparalleled Adventure of One Hans Pfaall," "MS. Found in a Bottle," "A Descent into the Maelström," "The Thousand-and-Second Tale of Scheherazade," and "Mellonta Tauta." This image could easily pass as an insignia since no animate figures are included. Instead, a sea monster creates the bottom and right-side frame while coiling itself around the bottle holding the manuscript; what looks like a blimp with wings hovers over a sailing ship in the left-hand frame. Similar combinatory images begin each of the other parts, demonstrating Eichenberg's ability to imagine how these varying tales emerge as a unit.

Probably the most unusual illustrations of Poe's work are by E. McKnight Kauffer (1890–1954). They appear in the two-volume edition of *The Complete Poems and Stories of Edgar Allan Poe,* published by Alfred A. Knopf in 1946 (reissued numerous times afterward with a fourth printing in 1964, and a 1982 printing renamed *The Borzoi Poe*) and edited by Arthur Hobson Quinn and Edward H. O'Neill. Kauffer was best known as a poster artist, and according to Steven Heller, "Kauffer was one of Europe's most prolific and influential advertising poster artists during the twenties and thirties. . . . Even with a promising advertising career, Kauffer continued to think of himself as a painter."[44] Not only was Kauffer a well-known and respected poster artist, he also was a prolific illustrator of literary works; some of his illustrated works include *Benito Cereno* by Herman Melville (London: Nonsuch Press, 1926); *The Life and Surprizing Adventures of Robinson Crusoe of York, Mariner* by Daniel Defore (London: Etchells & Macdonald, 1929); *The Journey of the Magi* (1927), *A Song for Simeon* (1928), *Marina* (1930), *Triumphal March* (1931), and *The Cultivation of Christmas Trees* (1954) by T. S. Eliot, all published by Faber & Gwyer; *Selected Poems* (New York: Alfred A. Knopf, 1959) by Langston Hughes; *The Anatomy of Melancholy* (London: Nonesuch Press, 1925) by Robert Burton; and *Don Quixote de la Mancha* (London: Nonesuch Press, 1930) by Cervantes.

Kauffer made twelve full-page color illustrations and eight line drawings for the Poe volume. One of the color images used to illustrate "The Raven" is especially haunting: a full-page illustration, a painting in blue, bright fuchsia, brown, and black, depicts what could be perceived both as a human hand and as feathers of the raven's wing. An ambiguous statue-like figure of what would be the bust of Pallas (without the raven on its helmet) sits in a brown niche in the background, but it is clearly as prominent as the blue hand/feather. Because of the abstract quality of the image, a viewer can easily picture and feel the demise of the narrator whose "soul from out that shadow that lies floating on the floor/Shall be lifted—nevermore!" Of all the many images illustrating Poe's "The Raven," this one by Kauffer is the most daunting.

Included as well in this edition are four portraits of Poe by Kauffer—one in black and white on the cover of the dust jackets of both volumes and three watercolor portraits scattered throughout the text. Each portrait reflects a different Poe: angry, slightly cynical, wistful, and plaintive. Portraits of Poe abound,[45] but some of the best are recent, especially the oil paintings by Michael Deas (1956–) based on Poe's daguerreotypes; in fact, Deas was commissioned to portray Poe for the bicentennial US postage stamp. Other portraits by significant artists include those by Charles Hine (1827–1871), Claude Buck (1890–1974), Dorothea Tanning (1910–2012), and Antonio Frasconi (1919–2013).

Touted by Burton Pollin as "the most prolific and daring illustrator of Poe's tales," Italian artist Alberto Martini (1876–1954) "adapted his distinctly Art Nouveau style and early surrealist orientation to producing remarkable interpretations in stark black and white ink sketches"[46] for *Tutti i racconti del mistero, dell'incubo e del terrore, Poe*

E. A. (*All the Stories of Mystery, Nightmare and Terror by E. A. Poe*) (Rome: Newton Compton Editori, 1989). Pollin notes that Martini produced 150 sketches for Poe's works. George Woodberry was the first to use five of them for his 1909 *Life of Poe*; they illustrate"Berenice," "Morella," "Ligeia," and "Eleonora" (two images), and appear in the List of Illustrations as "after Martini" (see Figure 38.8).[47]

Striking and gory illustrations of Poe's work can also be seen in the 1973 Godine edition of *The Adventures of Arthur Gordon Pym* with an introduction by Richard Wilbur. Nothing is left to the imagination. As Rebecca Weaver-Hightower explains, Gerry Hoover "depicts the cannibal incident, drawing the three men's intertwined bodies so that it is disturbingly difficult to discern cannibal from cannibalized. . . . Both eater and meal [are] horribly thin, naked and cadaverous, particularly the skull-like bald head of the cannibal on the picture's bottom. The surprisingly bloodless corpse lacks its head, hands, and feet."[48] The novel includes eleven illustrations, and among the gore, surprisingly, are two are almost bucolic images—one depicting the Antarctic landscape and the other depicting Pym sitting near a turtle.

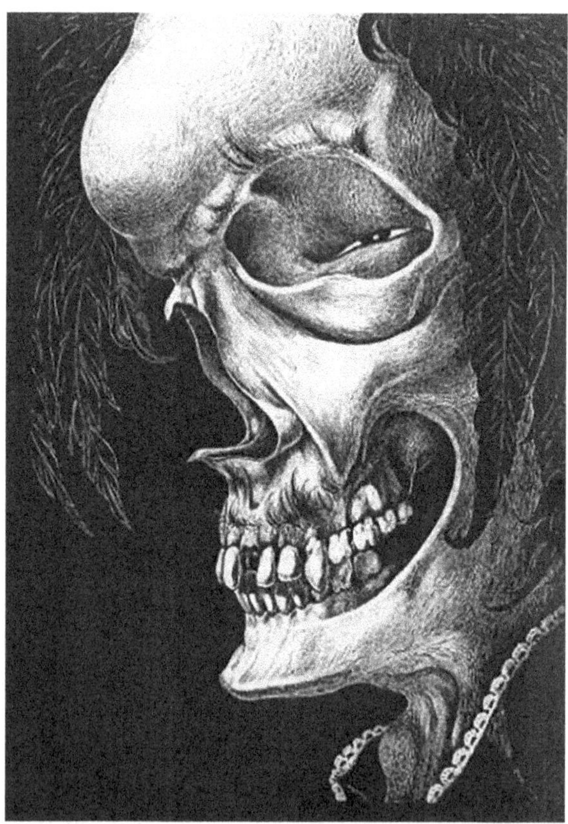

FIGURE 38.8 *Re Peste* by Alberto Martini. Courtesy of Pinacoteca e Archivio Alberto Martini, Fondazione Oderzo Cultura onlus.

Artists' Works Influenced by Poe

Along with illustrators, artists have drawn from Poe's works. In the late nineteenth and early twentieth centuries, Belgian artist James Ensor (1860–1949) and French artist Odilon Redon (1840–1916), both part of the Symbolist movement, became enamored of Poe. Both artists discovered in Poe's writing an affinity with their own sensibilities. Ensor and Redon read Poe's stories in Baudelaire's translations of Rufus Griswold's 1850 *The Works of the Late Edgar Allan Poe*. In 1882 Redon included six lithographs in an album titled *À Edgar Poë* that clearly indicate Redon's attraction to Poe's work, noting, however, that they do not explicitly illustrate his work: (1) *L'oeil, comme un ballon bizarre se dirige vers l'infini (The Eye, Like a Strange Balloon Mounts Toward Infinity)*, (2) *Devant le noir soleil de la mélancolie, Lénor apparait* (*Before the Black Sun of Melancholy, Lenore Appears)*, (3) *Un masque sonne le glas funèbre* (from "The Bells"), (4) *A l'horizon, l'ange des certitudes, et, dans le ciel sombre, un regard interrogateur* (*On the Horizon, the Angel of Certainty, and in the Dark Sky, an Interrogator Looks*), (5) *Le souffle qui conduit les êtres est aussi dans les sphères* (*The Breath Gives Life Is Also in the Spheres*), and (6) *La folie* (*Madness*).[49]

L'oeil, comme un ballon bizarre se dirige vers l'infini responds to Poe's "Balloon Hoax" and, at the same time, ironizes Emerson's "transparent eye-ball"—the platform of the balloon holding a decapitated head hardly speaks to the enthusiastic spiritualism of Emerson's proclamation. Redon also pictured Poe's "The Raven," "The Masque of the Red Death," "The Bells," "The Tell-Tale Heart," and "Berenice." Kevin Hayes describes *The Teeth* (1883), a painting by Redon related to "Berenice": "a full set of teeth suspended in air and radiating light. In the background are two bookshelves, the top one full yet cast in a shadow and the bottom one with a few books whose bindings reflect the glow of teeth.... Juxtaposing rows of teeth with rows of books, Redon thematically paralleled Egaeus's obsessions."[50] Redon's *The Tell-Tale Heart* (1883) pictures the narrator's eye peering out of the floorboards where the narrator had buried the old man's chopped-up corpse, thus conflating the crack in the doorway where the narrator obsessively watches the old man with the crack in the floorboards. The eye itself bears conflicting emotions of passivity, intentness, numbness, and sadness—but omits murderous anger.

Like Redon, Ensor used Poe's titles for his etchings, drawings, and paintings, including three social satires—"King Pest," "Hop Frog," and "The Devil in the Belfry,"[51] one psychological drama—"The Tell-Tale Heart," and one story that relates to Poe's love of beauty—"The Domain of Arnheim." A few other images by Ensor refer to Poe's works without being named after them: *The Assassination*, based on "The Facts in the Case of M. Valdemar," and *Apparition: Vision Preceding Futurism*, based on Poe's story, "Some Words with a Mummy." His drawings for "Hop Frog" and "King Pest" illustrate almost exactly Poe's descriptions: the tarred and feathered king and his court hanging from the chandelier in "Hop Frog" and the grotesqueries seated around the table in "King Pest." Ensor's choice for "The Devil in the Belfry," on the other hand, does not include the devil, as do most other illustrations of the tale.Rather, he depicts a street scene near the church with villagers going about their daily activities while others stand on the sidewalk gaping at the clock in the church's steeple; swirling lines fill the sky, bringing to mind Van Gogh's 1890 painting "Wheatfield with Crows." Ensor's only painting after Poe is *The Domain of Arnheim.* As art critic Robert Hoozee remarks, "It is significant that Ensor not only takes grotesque figures from Poe's satires, but also is captivated by the description of an imaginary landscape. Ensor wrote in a letter: 'I have dreamed above all before Poe, and like him, I loved to dream of certain landscapes of home.' In *The Domain of Arnheim* Ensor undoubtedly recognized his own fascination with a divine light that permeates and gives shape to everything" (see Figure 38.9).[52] Unlike Poe, who moved from city to city, Ensor lived in the same small town where he was born, Ostend, Belgium, and he deeply regretted the urbanizing of the natural landscape.

Years later, another Belgian artist, René Magritte (1898–1967), also titled a number of his paintings after Poe's works: *The Imp of the Perverse* (1928), *Scheherazade* (1947), *The Fall of the House of Usher* (1949), and *The Haunted Castle* (1950); other paintings that connect in some way to Poe's stories include the following: *Not to Be Reproduced* (1937), in which a book titled *The Narrative of Arthur Gordon Pym* appears in the painting; *The Frontiers of Summer* (1939), which pictures "building blocks of the sky reflect[ing] the harmoniously ordered universe of Poe's *Eureka*"; and *The Double Secret* (1927) "where the recurring motif of bells recalls Poe's onomatopoeic exercise 'The Bells.' And, of

FIGURE 38.9 *Domain of Arnheim* by James Ensor. Oil on canvas, 31.5 x 39.37 inches.

course, ravens appear frequently" in other Magritte paintings.[53] As Ben Stoltzfus points out, "In *Ecrits complets*, Magritte wrote that he felt in complete harmony with Poe's unusual poetic interests, and that he sensed in him the presence of a kindred spirit; and in a letter to his friend, Edward James, Magritte wrote that he painted *The Domain of Arnheim* as a tribute to Poe's tale."[54] This story clearly intrigued Magritte since he made three different paintings of *The Domain of Arnheim*: one in 1938, another in 1948, and the third in 1962.

None of the three iterations of "The Domain of Arnheim" have visible connections to Poe's story and instead picture a vast, mountainous landscape with a giant eagle emerging as if part of a snowy summit. In each painting, the scene is viewed from a window. A bird's eggs appear in the foreground of two of the paintings: in the 1938 version, two eggs sit on the window ledge next to a glass of water; in the 1962 iteration, two eggs appear in a nest in the middle of the window's stone ledge. The dramatic, mountainous landscape directly contrasts with the homely, vulnerable nature of the bird's eggs. In the 1948 version, no eggs are visible. Instead, a broken window pane is pictured; large, pointed shards of glass on the floor inside and on the window ledge each picture part of the landscape still visible outside.

According to Stolzfus, Magritte uses "Poe's descriptive precision in order to shape plausible paintings from improbable combinations of objects, places, and people."[55] Magritte, then, must have been aware of Poe's definition of "graphicality" since his work depends precisely on "convey[ing] the true by the novel or unexpected"—a basic surrealist concept expressed by Poe years earlier. Magritte's choices in each of his versions of *Domain of Arnheim*, nonetheless, contradict a concept clearly stated in Poe's tale; that is, Magritte depicts the sublime rather than the beautiful, exactly what Poe's Ellison rejects as the site of his artistic project. As Ellison explains, "Grandeur in any of its moods, but especially in that of extent, startles, excites—and then fatigues, depresses. For the occasional scene nothing can be better—for the constant view nothing worse" (M 3: 1278). Here Magritte chose to counter Ellison's stated preference for the beautiful over the sublime. Rather, "Magritte's paintings appear to justify Lautréamont's definition of the metaphor: the chance encounter of two unrelated objects in an unexpected spatial setting. . . . The viewer cannot expect that the painter will merely make visible, on a two dimensional canvas, the entire domain of Arnheim, the paradise Poe evoked."[56]

Like Magritte, Redon, and Ensor, German artist and surrealist Max Ernst (1891–1976) was also drawn to Poe's work, and, in particular, to "Berenice." According to Robert Belton, the "obsessive staring" of Poe's narrator in this story "provided a direct model for Ernst's discussion of his automatic methods in *Beyond Painting*. . . . Frottage, [Ernst] wrote, was based 'on nothing other than the intensification of the irritability of the mind's faculties by appropriate technical means.' In the original French text, this phrase was taken directly from Baudelaire's translation of Poe's 'Berenice,' dropping only the word 'morbid.'"[57] In Poe's words, "This monomania . . . consisted in a morbid irritability of those properties of the mind in metaphysical science termed the *attentive*" (M 2: 211). Ernst's oil painting titled *Berenice* (1935) pictures the abstracted, disembodied limbs of two figures; drawn in black on a muddy, brownish-yellow background (possibly using frottage), Berenice hovers over the narrator, her long, curled hair appearing as the most identifiable feature—a detail that marks Berenice in Poe's tale. Her illness turned the once-beautiful Berenice into a specter of herself: "The forehead was high, and very pale, and singularly placid; the once jetty hair fell partially over it, and overshadowed the hollow temples with innumerable ringlets, now of a vivid yellow, and jarring discordantly, in their fantastic character, with the reigning melancholy of the countenance" (M 2: 215). Focusing on Berenice's hair is no coincidence for Ernst, whose "fascination with planetary and astrological systems"[58] would have made him familiar with the constellation Coma Berenices, whose name means Berenice's hair. In Ernst's painting, Berenice preys on the narrator, a reversal of Poe's tale; in it, the narrator exhumes Berenice's body and extracts her teeth, the horror further complicated by her having been buried alive. In Ernst's image, Berenice appears to be the predator, although the murkiness of the image leaves much in doubt.

The abstract American artist Robert Motherwell (1915–1991) greatly admired Poe. Kevin Hayes begins his essay "One-Man Modernist" with a quote from an interview with Motherwell that reveals that he liked all of Poe's work because "he was a one-man modernist, at a moment when America was moving in the other direction."[59] According to Pollin, Motherwell created four collages with acrylic in the mid-1970s simply named "Poe Series" and a large, abstract lithograph in sepia in 1974 titled *Poe's Abyss*.[60] Motherwell was in close contact with Joseph Cornell (1903–1972), and in one of Motherwell's letters to Cornell, Motherwell wrote "it would be wonderful if you could bring some of the Poe-Taglioni material—we are revising 'Possibilties.' "[61] The material Motherwell refers to in the letter may have been Cornell's "Taglioni's Jewel Casket," a tribute to Maria Taglioni (1804–1884), a ballet dancer whom Poe greatly admired although she never came to the United States to dance.[62] The Museum of Modern Art describes the work this way: The first of dozens Cornell made in honor of famous ballerinas, this box pays homage to Marie Taglioni, an acclaimed nineteenth-century Italian dancer who, according to legend, kept an imitation ice cube in her jewelry box to commemorate dancing in the snow at the behest of a Russian highwayman. The box is infused with erotic undertones—both in the tactile nature of the glass cubes, velvet, and rhinestone necklace (purchased at a Woolworth's dime store in New York) and in the incident itself, in which Taglioni reportedly performed on an animal skin placed across the snowy road."[63] Both Motherwell and Cornell's visual interpretations of Poe and his work break from the past in not engaging with the gory or grotesque; instead, in Motherwell's case, he captured the feeling of infinity expressed, for example, in Poe's *Eureka*.

Conclusion

Illustrators, especially, and artists whose work derives from Poe's writing both act as interpreters. Over the last two centuries, Poe's work has attracted artists who have made strikingly different interpretations of his writing, so much so that were a scholar to take the time to compare, for example, all of the images for the shrouded figure at the end of *The Adventures of Arthur Gordon Pym* or all the images illustrating the raven on the bust of Pallas in "The Raven," he or she would have a rich resource for further interpretation. In 1913, for example, Maurice Toussaint pictured the shrouded figure at the end of *Pym* as a bearded man with arms outstretched. Richard Kopley interpreted this depiction as a biblical figure,[64] affirming his overall interpretation of the novel. In the 1930 French edition,[65] Andre Collot pictured the shrouded figure as a huge crouching skeleton, both gruesome and comical at the same time, hovering over the *Grampus*. In the 1980 Italian edition of *Pym*,[66] Robert Carroll pictured the shrouded figure as a shabby effigy of Augustus, and in an 1864 article by Jules Verne, "Edgar Poe et ses oeuvres" in *Museé des Familles*, Yan D'Argent pictured the shrouded figure as the grim reaper, scythe poised to strike Pym. Diverging from these anthropomorphic images,an illustration by Alfred Kubin[67] pictures no shrouded figure at all but simply white streaks in a cross-hatched sky. Comparing and interpreting the varying illustrations of a particular work by Poe, then, would prove fascinating, as this one example suggests. Determining which illustration, in Poe's words, "will stimulate, support, and guide the fancy" (H 11: 8) and which will fall short of the reader's interpretation would also provide hours of pleasure.

Notes

1. Another essay in this collection deals with comic book adaptations of Poe stories and poems, so that category will not be discussed here.
2. Burton Pollin, interview with Barbara Cantalupo, *Edgar Allan Poe Review* 2, no. 2 (2001): 109.
3. Burton Pollin, *Images of Poe's Works: A Comprehensive Descriptive Catalogue of Illustrations* (New York: Greenwood Press, 1989), 234.
4. Pollin, *Images of Poe's Works*, 4.
5. Pollin stated that the balloon image in Poe's story was the frontispiece of *Remarks on the Ellipsoidal Balloon, Propelled by the Archimedean Screw, described as the New Aerial Machine, Now Exhibiting at the Royal Adelaide Gallery, Lowther Arcade, Strand*; however, no frontispiece is in that document. Further research suggested that the image appeared in the February 21, 1844, issue of the Philadelphia newspaper, *Alexander's Express Messenger*, and I am grateful to Jeffrey Savoye, who found the issue housed at the Wisconsin Historical Society so that supposition could be verified.
6. Jeffrey Savoye, "Reconstructing Poe's 'The Gold Bug': An Examination of the Composition and First Printings," *Edgar Allan Poe Review* 8, no. 2 (2007): 25.
7. Pollin, *Images of Poe's Works*, 5.
8. Mabbott suggests that the same construct is also evident in "MS. Found in a Bottle," "A Descent into the Maelström," and "The Pit and the Pendulum" (M 3: 1216n6).
9. Pollin notes that Mabbott "asserted that Poe himself supervised these illustrations" for "The Gold Bug," in *Images of Poe's Works*, 5. See also *Images of Poe's Works*, 24n9.
10. Barbara Cantalupo, *Poe and the Visual Arts* (State College, PA: The Pennsylvania State University Press, 2014), 125.

11. Poe to Joseph E. Snodgrass, Philadelphia, January 7, 1841.
12. See Poe, *Tales of Mystery, Imagination, & Humour; and Poems*, Readable Books (London: Henry Vizetelly, 1852), https://archive.org/stream/talesmysteryima01poegoog#page/n7/mode/2up/
13. Pollin, *Images of Poe's Works*, 6.
14. See Poe, *The Poetical Works of Edgar Allan Poe*, ed. James Hannay, illustrations by E. H. Wehnert, James Godwin, F. W. Hulme, and Harrison Weir (London: Addey & Co., 1853), https://babel.hathitrust.org/cgi/pt?id=uiug.30112038240351;view=1up;seq=9/
15. Rossetti's poem is told from the point of view of the dead woman who watches over her lover from heaven, a reverse of Poe's lover who longs for his dead Lenore.

> "I wish that he were come to me,
> For he will come," she said.
> "Have I not pray'd in Heaven?—on earth,
> Lord, Lord, has he not pray'd?
> Are not two prayers a perfect strength?
> And shall I feel afraid?
>
> "When round his head the aureole clings,
> And he is cloth'd in white,
> I'll take his hand and go with him
> To the deep wells of light;
> As unto a stream we will step down,
> And bathe there in God's sight."

16. Pollin, *Images of Poe's Works*, 7.
17. James Hannay, "The Life and Genius of Edgar Allan Poe," in *The Poetical Works of Edgar Allan Poe*, xvi, xx, xxx.
18. See Poe, *The Poetical Works of Edgar Allan Poe*, illustrated by F. R. Pickersgill, John Tenniel, Birket Foster, Felix Darley, Jasper Cropsey, P. Duggan, Percival Skelton, and A. M. Madot (London: Sampson Low, Son & Co., 1858), https://books.google.com/books?id=HCRpAAAAcAAJ&pg=PR13&lpg=PR13&dq=F.+R.+Pickersgill&source=bl&ots=9IK9Z8rlHk&sig=ImE3OrD1-BxJg9v4Tv-AOOycaPM&hl=en&sa=X&ved=0ahUKEwjS89G1mMLSAhVK9YMKHdFGD5sQ6AEIRTAI#v=snippet&q=illustrations&f=false/.
19. Poe signed a contract with Darley to do the images for the never-materialized *Stylus*.
20. Darley also had illustrations in the 1881 Philadelphia Porter & Coates edition of *The Bells*—specifically for the line "Hear the sledges with the bells" (the same line he illustrated in the 1857 edition) and the line "in the clamorous appealing to the mercy of the fire" (another line he illustrated in the 1857 edition). In the 1881 edition, he also illustrated the lines "From the molten golden notes," "Hear the mellow wedding bells," "In the clamorous appealing to the mercy of the fire," and "Hear the tolling of the bells" with the same prosaic imagery as appeared in the 1857 edition.
21. Pollin calls Cropsey's illustrations "pallid, featureless . . . [and] indifferently drawn" and Tenniel's illustrations appropriate for the "theater and or the rhetorical platform" (*Images of Poe's Works*, 7–8).
22. Burton Pollin, "Two Recent Reviews," *Poe Studies* 15, no. 2 (Dec. 1982): 43.
23. Pollin, *Images of Poe's Works*, 8.
24. See Cantalupo, *Poe and the Visual Arts*, 58–59.

25. Edgar Allan Poe, *The Corbeau / The Raven by Edgar Poe*, trans. Stéphane Mallarmé, illustrated by Édouard Manet (Paris: Richard Lesclide, 1875), http://www.gutenberg.org/ebooks/14082.bibrec.mobile
26. Chris Michaelides, "Some Flights of Poe's Raven–Mallarmé and Manet, Doré, and Rossetti," *European Studies blog, British Library*, http://blogs.bl.uk/european/2015/03/some-flights-of-poes-raven.html/
27. Jeffrey Savoye notes these details regarding this edition: "Although the imprint date reads 1884, the book was issued about November 3, 1983, in anticipation of the holiday season. The beautiful title page was designed by Elihu Vedder, and the cover, featuring an angel with broad wings and holding a candle, was designed by Dora Wheeler, later Dora Wheeler Keith" (Savoye, "Some Editions of Edgar Allan Poe's Works," The Edgar Allan Poe Society of Baltimore, updated October 14, 2016, http://www.eapoe.org/Works/editions/index.htm#illustrated/). Elihu Vedder was an American symbolist painter who is best known for his illustrations of the very popular *The Rubáiyát of Omar Khayyam*, translated by Edward Fitzgerald. Dora Wheeler Keith was also an American artist who was associated with the Hudson River School and an admirer of Poe. In her autobiography, Wheeler describes her encounters with those who admired Poe, especially making note of an unnamed woman whose "crowning indiscretion . . . was her devotion, in an admiring and pitying way, to Edgar Allan Poe. . . . She went there daily . . . carrying delicacies for the poet and lavishing her husband's substance upon the family of a man who had no other claim to this devotion than that of having written a poem called 'The Raven' and a piece of jingling rhyme known as 'The Bells'" (Wheeler, *Yesterdays in a Busy Life* [New York: Harper & Bros., 1918], 78).
28. "Sampson Low, Marston, & Co.'s New Publications. A Sumptuous Gift-Book—Doré's Last Great Work, *The Raven* by Edgar Allan Poe," *The Academy: A Weekly Review of Literature, Science, and Art* 24, no. 601 (Nov. 10, 1883): i.
29. Pollin, *Images of Poe's Works*, 9.
30. Evelyn Marie Stuart, "Edmund Dulac—A Poet of the Brush," *Fine Arts Journal* 23, no. 2 (August 1910): 87.
31. Stuart, "Edmund Dulac," 90.
32. See Jessica Farris, "5 Illustrators Who Brought Edgar Allan Poe's Work to Life," *Print*, October 29, 2016, http://www.printmag.com/illustration/edgar-allan-poe-illustrations/.
33. Richard Wilbur, interview by Barbara Cantalupo, *Edgar Allan Poe Review* 4, no. 1 (Spring 2003): 70.
34. Nicola Gordon Bowe, *The Life and Work of Harry Clarke* (Dublin: Irish Academic Press, 1989), 5.
35. For all of the images from this edition, see "Harry Clarke's Illustrations for Poe's Tales of Mystery and Imagination (1919)," Collections, The Public Domain Review, https://publicdomainreview.org/collections/harry-clarkes-illustrations-for-edgar-allan-poe/.
36. Bowe, *The Life and Work of Harry Clarke*, 82.
37. In *Edgar Allan Poe, The Illustrated Edgar Allan Poe*, ed. Roy Gasson (London: Jupiter Books, 1976), several of the images referred to in this essay can be seen. This Clarke image, for example, can be seen as Plate 22; the specific Manet image referred to above from "The Raven" can be seen as Plate 18; the Beardsley drawing for "The Masque of the Red Death" is Plate 32.
38. See image in Burton Pollin, "Terry Southern Reads Pym: His Resultant Unpublished Short Story, Edited with an Introduction by B. R. Pollin," *Edgar Allan Poe Review* 1, no. 2 (2000): 21.

39. James Hamilton, *Arthur Rackham, A Life with Illustration* (London: Pavilion Books, 1990), 153.
40. Hamilton, *Arthur Rackman*, 154.
41. See Jan Ernst Adlmann, "Mirror to a World Gone Awry," *Art in America* (Feb. 1, 2009): 118.
42. "Illustrations to Poe 1944, Fritz Eichenberg," *The Visual Telling of Stories*, Chris Mullen, accessed January 2018, https://www.fulltable.com/vts/aoi/e/eichenberg/poe/a.htm.
43. Quoted from Gunter Kress and Theo Van Leeuwen, *Reading Images: The Grammar of Visual Design* (New York: Routledge, 1996) in Rebecca Weaver-Hightower, *Empire Islands: Castaways, Cannibals, And Fantasies of Conquest* (Minneapolis: University of Minnesota Press, 2007), 121.
44. Steven Heller, "E. McKnight Kauffer," *AIGA: The Professional Association for Design*, 1992, http://www.aiga.org/medalist-emcknightkauffer/.
45. For an overview of fraudulent portraits of Poe, see Michael Deas, *The Portraits and Daguerreotypes of Edgar Allan Poe* (Charlottesville: University of Virginia Press, 1989), available online through The Edgar Allan Poe Society of Baltimore, https://www.eapoe.org/papers/misc1921/deas00ca.htm.
46. Pollin, *Images of Poe's Works*, 165.
47. For the five illustrations by Alberto Martini, see Woodberry, *The Life of Edgar Allan Poe, Personal and Literary* (Boston: Houghton Mifflin Company, 1909), https://archive.org/details/lifeofedgarpoe01woodrich/.
48. Weaver-Hightower, *Empire Islands*, 121.
49. *The Etchings and Lithographs of Odilon Redon (1840–1916)* (Chicago: Art Institute of Chicago, 1929), 26–27. http://www.artic.edu/sites/default/files/libraries/pubs/1929/AIC1929Redon_comb.pdf.
50. Kevin Hayes, "One-Man Modernist," in *The Cambridge Companion to Edgar Allan Poe*, ed. Kevin Hayes (Cambridge: Cambridge University Press, 2002), 229.
51. An exhibit of Ensor's work, the first in twenty years in London, ran from December 2016 to the end of January 2017 and included works inspired by Poe, specifically "The Tell-Tale Heart"—mislabeled by the gallery as "Revelatory Heart"—and "King Pest." T. J. Clark calls attention to Ensor's interpretation of "The Tell-Tale Heart" in "At the Royal Academy," *London Review of Books* 38, no. 23 (Dec. 23, 2016):

    There is a tremendous drawing in the exhibition which the catalogue entitles, peculiarly, *Revelatory Heart*. . . . The episode Ensor is illustrating comes from Poe's story "The Tell-Tale Heart": we are at the moment when the murderer manages to focus a beam of light in the darkness, searching for his victim, an old man asleep; and the beam bounces off the victim's wide-awake eye. It is a typical Ensor subject: something we'd assumed was inanimate or insensible suddenly looks back at us with malignant life. There are other things based on Poe in the exhibition—notably a sizzling *Hop-Frog's Revenge*. But I prefer Ensor's glum version of the Poe crime story. Again the bleakness of the bedroom is essential. The ghosts and masks have all but vanished in the murk. The Poe of the hellish city whodunits, then, seems relevant to Ensor. (16–17)

52. Susan Canning, "The Devil's Mirror: Private Fantasy and Public Vision," in *Between Street and Mirror: The Drawings of James Ensor* (Minneapolis: University of Minnesota Press, 2001), 64.
53. Robert J. Belton, "Edgar Allan Poe and the Surrealists' Image of Woman," *Woman's Art Journal* 8, no. 1 (Spring–Summer 1987): 12.

54. Ben Stoltzfus, "Magritte's Literary Affinities: Baudelaire and Poe," *Intertexts* 6, no. 2 (Fall 2012): 31. Quoted in René Magritte, *Ecrits complets* (Paris: Flammarion, 1979), 610. Quoted in Daniel Abadie, ed., *Magritte* (New York: D. A. P., 2003), 251.
55. Stoltzfus, "Margritte's Literary Affinities," 30.
56. Renée Riese Hubert, "The Other Worldly Landscapes of E. A. Poe and René Magritte," *SubStance* 6/7, no. 21 (Winter 1978–1979): 70.
57. Belton, "Edgar Allan Poe and the Surrealists' Image of Woman," 8–9.
58. David Hopkins, *Marcel Duchamp and Max Ernst: The Bride Shared* (Oxford: Oxford University Press, 1998), 162n22.
59. Kevin Hayes, "One-Man Modernist," in *The Cambridge Companion to Edgar Allan Poe*, 225.
60. Pollin, *Images of Poe's Works*, 298–299.
61. Robert Motherwell to Joseph Cornell, September 21, 1948, Joseph Cornell papers, Archives of American Art, Smithsonian Institution, https://www.si.edu/object/AAADCD_item_17876?width=85%25&height=85%25&iframe=true&destination=spotlight/robert-motherwell/. The volume Motherwell refers to here is the fourth volume in a series that he edited with Harold Rosenberg, Pierre Chareau, and John Cage.
62. See Burton Pollin, "Poe and Dance." *Studies in the American Renaissance* (1980): 169–182.
63. See "Joseph Cornell, *Taglioni's Jewel Casket*, 1940," Arts and artists, MoMA, updated 2017, https://www.moma.org/collection/works/81493?locale=en/.
64. Edgar Poe, *Les aventures d'Arthur Gordon Pym*, trans. D'Armand Masson, illustrated by Maurice Toussaint (Paris: Lafitte Pierre & Cie., 1913).
65. Edgar Poe, *Les Aventures de Gordon Pym*, trans. Charles Baudelaire, illustrated by André Collot (Paris: Librairie de la Française, 1930).
66. Edgar Poe, *Narrazione di Arthur Gordon Pym di Nantucket*, trans. Elio Vittorini, illustrated by Robert Carroll (Fienze: Giunti Marzocco, 1980).
67. Edgar Poe, *Die denkwürdigen Erlebnisse des Arthur Gordon Pym*, trans. Gisela Etzel, illustrated by Alfred Kubin (Weisbade, Germany: Verlag Fourier & Fertig, 1970).

Bibliography

Cantalupo, Barbara. *Poe and the Visual Arts*. State College, PA: Penn State University Press, 2014.

Drost, Christian. "Illuminating Poe: The Reflection of Edgar Allan Poe's Pictorialism in the Illustrations of the *Tales of the Grotesque and Arabesque*." PhD diss., University of Hamburg, 2006. http://webdoc.sub.gwdg.de/ebook/dissts/Hamburg/Drost2007.pdf.

Hayes, Kevin. "One Man Modernist." In *The Cambridge Companion to Edgar Allan Poe*, edited by Kevin Hayes, 225–240. Cambridge: Cambridge University Press, 2002.

Julien, Dominique. "Translation as Illustration: The Visual Paradigm in Mallarmé's Translation of Poe." *Word & Image* 30, no. 3 (2014): 249–260.

Pollin, Burton R. *Images of Poe's Works: A Comprehensive Descriptive Catalogue of Illustrations*. New York: Greenwood, 1989.

CHAPTER 39

POE AND THE AVANT-GARDE

JONATHAN ELMER

THE original conscription of Poe into the ranks of the avant-garde is found in Charles Baudelaire's essays in the 1850s. Strictly speaking, of course, the "avant-garde" did not exist yet, but what Baudelaire finds in Poe sets the terms of what was to characterize avant-gardism: the social alienation of the artist; an emphatic focus on technique and method; a fascination with inhuman dimensions of experience; and a radical commitment to aesthetic autonomy. To survey very briefly Baudelaire's treatment, we can recall, first, that Poe famously provides the very type of the alienated *poète maudit*: "Are there then consecrated souls, destined for sacrifice, condemned to march towards death and glory, through the ruin of their own lives?"[1] Baudelaire casts Poe in the role of John the Baptist, wandering in the wilderness of American mediocrity, the herald of a modernity that properly begins with Baudelaire himself. This narrative says something about Baudelaire's inflated sense of himself, but others agree. Theodor Adorno calls Poe "truly a beacon for Baudelaire and all modernity" and links the two writers often in his works on aesthetics: the "heralds of modernism Baudelaire and Poe were . . . the first technocrats of art."[2] Adorno's use of "technocrat" here points to Poe's influential emphasis on method and technique—second motif—which had much impressed Baudelaire: "Poe would take literary works to pieces like a defective mechanism (defective, that is, in relation to its avowed aims) noting carefully the faults in manufacture."[3] Third: Poe's texts push "the human figure into the background," says Baudelaire. The "writings of Poe are extra- or super-human," to such an extent that Poe's is ultimately a cosmic project: "So-called inanimate nature participates in the nature of the living beings."[4] And finally, Poe's repudiation of the "heresy of *The Didactic*" (ER: 75) was a game changer for Baudelaire and his symbolist and decadent followers, with whom it evolves into the idea of "*l'art pour l'art*," an insistence on radical aesthetic autonomy that for some is the first truly avant-garde posture and for others the apotheosis of a bourgeois aesthetics that the avant-garde comes to destroy.[5]

With each of these four topics, Baudelaire has put his finger on something essential in Poe's work, and in each case we can see ways in which Poe's practice evolves into later recognizably avant-garde versions. And yet I would argue that we still do not see clearly Poe's significance for modern experimental arts. By saying "experimental arts" rather than "avant-garde," I hope to move beyond inherited concepts of the avant-garde as essentially a form of social negation, as a protest against the baleful regime of the commodity. Poe was hugely influential on mass and popular arts as well as self-consciously avant-garde ones. What is more, his influence moves across media to an unusual degree—he is picked up not just by other authors but also by visual artists, musicians from Claude Débussy to Lennie Tristano to Lou Reed, filmmakers early and late, and creators of comics and cartoons. To the extent that "avant-garde" is restricted to whatever opposes aesthetic commodification and the culture industry, it fails to map Poe's range of influence on artistic innovation. Poe's significance for later arts is transmedial, or intermedial: it is as if he left lying about a method and a set of tropes that could be picked up by artists in media he often did not live to see, who would put them to work according to the special affordances of those media.

John Tresch has developed furthest the argument about Poe's "intermedial" conception of art. Tresch argues that because Poe considered literature "less as an isolated mental process than as a material link between an author and a reader," his poetics resembles a contemporary understanding of the "dialogical interrelations entertained by literature and other media. Poe saw literary technique and the material assembly and diffusion of texts as technologies that were continuous with other devices of the industrial revolution."[6] "The Philosophy of Composition," Tresch argues, evokes the industrial arts in its very title, alluding not just to mechanical processes of text production—the "composition" of typesetting—but the whole field of manufacture, as in Andrew Ure's *The Philosophy of Manufacture*. But this interpretation may be too restricted. Poe also wrote "The Philosophy of Furniture," after all, a text less about manufacture than about arrangement. And the meanings of "composition" extend well beyond the industrial. At the very climax of "The Facts in the Case of M. Valdemar," to take a striking example, after the mesmerized patient has uttered the words "*I say to you that I am dead!*," the narrator says: "At first I made an endeavor to re-compose the patient; but, failing in this through total abeyance of the will, I retraced my steps and as earnestly struggled to awaken him" (M 3: 1242). "Composing" here means containing the patient within the state of mesmerically induced suspended animation: reports from that state to the effect that one is dead constitute dire threats to composition. To be awakened, on the other hand, leads to radical *decomposition*—"a nearly liquid mass of loathsome—of detestable putridity" (M 3: 1243). To "re-compose" here means to reassert control over an artificially produced corporeal integrity, a kind of suspended order. Mesmerism and storytelling are alike forms of "composition" threatened at all times with the energies of dissolution.

Swerving slightly from Tresch, let us say Poe does not so much *make machines* as *perform experiments*. When Baudelaire remarks that "Poe would take literary works to pieces like a defective mechanism (defective, that is, in relation to its avowed aims) noting carefully the faults in manufacture," the emphasis should be on "defective," not "manufacture," on testing rather than structure.[7] If this mechanism (poem, story) did not work the first time, let's try it again a different way. In his book *The Romantic Machine*, Tresch observes that André-Marie Ampère coined the term "technaesthetics" for the realm in which scientific, technological, and aesthetic programs converge.[8] This seems like an excellent term for Poe's poetics, as long as we understand it as less about the factory than the laboratory, less about production than about tests and trials. If there is "playfulness" in Poe's work, it is not Eliot's "pre-adolescent" version; it is closer to what Walter Benjamin had in mind by "test performances" in his famous "Work of Art in the Age of Its Reproducibility": as "aura" wanes, so a realm of "play" waxes, a realm characterized by an aesthetics that is "wholly provisional (it operates by means of experiments and endlessly varied test procedures)."[9]

Ambivalence about this experimentalist aesthetics has been a pronounced feature of Poe's critical history.[10] When Adorno calls Poe a "technocrat of art," it is not an endorsement. Renato Poggioli is perhaps most direct: " 'Laboratory' and 'proving ground'—these are phrases suggested by the scientific and industrial technology of our time, and it would perhaps be wrong to regard them as metaphors, pure and simple." He goes on: "what often triumphs in avant-garde art is not so much technique as 'technicism' . . . 'Technicism' means that the technical genius invades spiritual realms where technique has no raison d'etre. As such it belongs not only to avant-garde art, but to all modern culture or pseudo-culture."[11] The repudiation of "technicism" safeguards the aesthetic as a "spiritual realm" and requires as well the distinction between culture and "pseudo-culture," by which Poggioli means mass culture, or what Adorno calls the "culture industry."

But consider an earlier response to Poe's famous "method." A very young Paul Valéry perceives the same "antithesis" that so disturbs Poggioli, but celebrates it: "We take pleasure in this sublime antithesis: the barbarous grandeur of the industrial world faced with the extremes of elegance and the morbid search for the rarest pleasures. And we love the art of this age, complicated and *artificial*."[12] For Valéry in 1889, Poe had articulated this "sublime antithesis" in which the artist is "a cool scientist, almost an algebraist, in the service of a subtle dreamer." The scientist and the dreamer are one, with different roles. The dreamer is receptive while the scientist is projective: "Given an impression, a dream, a thought, one must express it in such a way as to produce the maximum effect in the mind of a listener—an effect entirely calculated by the Artist." But the process, we note, is not so much production as reduction; something passes in via a "sieve," is condensed, and so "composed" to project forward to "overwhelming effect": "everything he has imagined, felt, dreamed, and planned will be passed through a sieve, weighed, filtered, subjected to form and condensed as much as possible so as to gain in power what it loses in length: a sonnet, for example, will be a true quintessence, a nutrient, a concentrated, distilled juice, reduced to fourteen lines, carefully composed with a view to a final and overwhelming effect."[13]

What Valéry allows us to see is how Poe's "technicism" might seem "avant-garde" before the version of the avant-garde with which we are familiar installed itself. It is a vision that observes the social "antithesis" but does not aim to resolve it, or even oppose it. And it is a vision that entails work on the body: feelings and dreams and thoughts are "given"—and then filtered, weighed, distilled. This yields the "juice" with which the "scientist" will compose. It is ultimately as much a physiology as an algebra.

And here we grasp the key to Poe's significance for "experimental arts" beneath and behind the rigid categories installed by high modernism and its version of the "avant-garde." Robert Brain's study of the "physiological aesthetics" that dominated the latter half of the nineteenth century and that culminated in what he calls "early modernism" outlines a project that "configured the body and senses as having an inherent, not merely accidental, relation with technicity. Bodily functions, organs, and senses were operationalized as machines or technical objects in experimental systems; even the most basic functional living substance—the protoplasm—was treated as a storage medium in a manner directly parallel to graphical recording media."[14] We know from the research of Brain, Jonathan Crary, Jonathan Sterne, and others just how focused on the human sensorium the nineteenth century was—on an analytics that could separate eye from ear, for example, on technologies of translation that could record or transfer sense data into machines, and eventually into media, and on the production of new syntheses: synaesthesia, kinesthesia, and so on.[15] It is *this* experimental world that Poe anticipates with his analyses of sensation, with his linking of sensation and inscription, and with his allegorization of trial and error. Poe's fictions (and some poems) place the body within a cosmic field that is dynamic and vibratory, suspended in constant tension between attraction and repulsion—the field of energies he outlines in *Eureka*. This world was much more legible to artists and scientists in the latter half of the nineteenth century than it is to us: "In fin-de-siècle Europe this was the vibratory world, the exploration of thresholds and intensities, the dissolution of boundaries between selves and objects." But we find it hard to see this world because "historians of modernism followed the lead of mid-twentieth century critics like [Clement] Greenberg and Theodor Adorno in viewing the early modernist concern for the cultivation of the body as a symptom of false consciousness, a quasi-Taylorist discipline masquerading as social liberation."[16]

Like Brain, Jonathan Crary identifies a "critical historical turning point in the second half of the nineteenth century at which any significant qualitative difference between life and technics begins to evaporate. The disintegration of an indisputable distinction between interior and exterior becomes a condition for the emergence of spectacular modernizing culture and for a dramatic expansion of the possibilities of aesthetic experience." Crary argues that the analytic separation of the senses served a larger goal of understanding—and controlling—attention: "It became increasingly clear to researchers what a volatile concept [attention] was, and how incompatible with any model of a sustained aesthetic gaze. Attention always contained within itself the conditions of its own disintegration, it was haunted by the possibility of its own *excess* . . . Attention and distraction were not two essentially different states but existed on a single continuum."[17] Poe's work was the most influential exploration of this continuum in the first half of the nineteenth century, I would argue, and this is why he is so important to later artists. Consider his comments on the poetics of effect, requiring a restriction of the reader's attention span and his short-term immobility—a "single sitting" (ER: 71). As Crary observes and Poe knew, this channeling of "attention" was not uniquely, or even predominantly, visual, but rather involved any and all senses: "spectacular culture is not founded on the necessity of making a subject see," writes Crary, "but rather on strategies in which individuals are isolated, separated, and *inhabit time* as disempowered."[18] Poe's fictions, especially, seek to produce such isolation and disempowerment in his readers, the better to achieve the desired effect. But just as importantly, Poe's tales *dramatize* such isolation in the narratives themselves. In this latter sense, *the tales are allegories of their own consumption.* Consider Poe's early tale "Berenice" and its troubled central character, Egeaus. Like us, Egeaus is a reader. Just as we may find ourselves gripped by the macabre obscurities of the story, Egeaus gets caught up in his reading, to the point of pathology, musing "for long unwearied hours with my attention riveted to some frivolous device on the margin, or in the typography of a book" (M 2: 211). But just as crucial to Poe's allegory as this fixed attention is that attention's failure, emblematized by Egeaus's blackouts indexed in the text by asterisks. No matter how "captivating" perception could be, it always failed to fix itself in the end: Crary says that nineteenth-century investigations of perception "were heavily invested" in "the sense of perception as 'catching' or 'taking captive,' even as the impossibility of such fixedness or possession became clear."[19] To the extent that it is both a prescient analysis and a practice of this "spectacular" culture, Poe produces a poetics of discontinuity, portraying efforts to "compose" experiences—like Valdemar's "suspended" body—that inevitably fail. A poetics of discontinuity is also a poetics of failure, one always open to a new effort, a new trial or experiment. His characters often try more than once—let's see if we can do better with cat #2—but so does Poe himself: let's try many versions of containment and control being undone by a sonic element—a cat's cry, a beating heart, a repeated phrase, a tinkling bell.

When Crary refers to "suspensions of perception" (the title of his study), he suggests that the analytic isolation of sense experience (whether vision from hearing, or attention from distraction) made visible a dynamic continuum between integration and disintegration of the human sensorium. Such a play of fixation and collapse animates Poe's work, which can allow us to see his influence on experimental arts a little differently. I have commented in passing that Baudelaire's idea of the *poète maudit* has been enlisted in a narrative about the artist's repudiation of bourgeois capitalism. Poe had plenty of issues with the literary marketplace of his day, but it's not clear that he saw his ideas about the poem for the poem's sake as the place he was making his stand on that. To the extent that themes of autonomy, withdrawal, and alienation, so pervasive in Poe's works, are reduced to a heroic (because doomed) battle with Capital, we have an impoverished understanding of Poe's impact on experimental arts. Egeaus in "Berenice" and Roderick in "Fall of the House of Usher" repudiate the larger social world, to be sure. They withdraw to their ancestral abodes, there to cultivate their abstruse pleasures and practices—reading in a fugue state, for example, or improvising wildly on the guitar. You might say they want peace and quiet above all. But theirs is not in any obvious way a rejection of bourgeois commodity capitalism (unless one wants to suggest that their putatively aristocratic identity is already that rejection in sum). They are in flight, no doubt, in flight and in denial—but the forces arrayed against them are not market forces but cosmic ones. Usher, for example, articulates a view about the "sentience of all vegetable things" that "trespassed . . . upon the kingdom of inorganization" (M 2: 408). A Marxist reading might see the retreat and withdrawal of Poe's characters as "alienation." But in so resolutely focusing on extreme states of embodiment and other anomalies of "sentience," Poe actually characterizes his contained spaces as specialized zones in which organization and "inorganization" vie for precedence, in which experiments in composition and decomposition are undertaken.

Consider now how such an understanding of the meaning of retreat and isolation plays out in an avant-garde decadent production such as J. K. Huysmans's *Against Nature (A Rebours)* (1884). Like a latter-day Roderick Usher, Huysmans's hero, Des Esseintes, is an aristocrat fallen on evil times. Unlike Usher, who seems to have no beef against the world that has passed him by, Des Esseintes spits venom at the bourgeois and the vulgar. But what really drives him is aesthetic experimentation—the provocation of sense experience through isolation and intensification. His holy grail is what might be called unnatural, or perhaps, inhuman experiences. Des Esseintes is a big fan of Poe. He has a room dedicated to producing maritime fantasy, tricked out with porthole window, "artificial seaweed," and an aquarium tinted "green or grey, opaline or silvery"—depending on what effect of weather and light he wished to conjure. When he tired of these fights of fancy, Des Esseintes "would rest his eyes by looking at the chronometers and compasses, the sextants and dividers, the binoculars and charts scattered about on a side-table which was dominated by a single book, bound in sea-calf leather: the *Narrative of Arthur Gordon Pym*, specially printed for him on laid paper of pure linen, handpicked and bearing a seagull water-mark."[20] As far as Des Esseintes is concerned, "Nature . . . has had her day," and "sensitive observers" must find ways to augment, replace, or rub nature against the grain (this last the best translation for "à rebours"). Des Esseintes takes this project to great extremes, encrusting his tortoise with jewels so that it will make vivid effects as it trundles along, or exulting in the fact that his doctor's prescription of a "nourishing peptone enema" could in fact be viewed as the "crowning achievement of the life he had planned for himself; his taste for the artificial [having] now . . . attained its supreme fulfillment." Reversing the direction of alimentation amounts to a pleasing "slap in the face for old Mother Nature."[21] But the projects fail. The tortoise dies, and the peptone enema does not produce the desired results. His doctor orders Des Esseintes to abandon his bizarre retreat in the provinces and return to Paris. The house of Usher implodes in spectacular fashion; the collapse of Des Esseintes's private world may be less dramatic, but it is just as definitive. As the novel comes to a close, a defeated Des Esseintes observes melancholically the arrival of the house-movers.

In the remainder of this chapter, I want to look at how Poe's "suspensions of perception" provoke responses and translations in other media. For reasons of space, I will restrict myself to a single—albeit very rich—tradition of intermedial uptake of Poe: the artist's book. As reproduction techniques developed over the course of the nineteenth century, artists, writers, and publishers all jockeyed for leverage in what was understood to be a scene of competition between word and image.[22] This interplay between media and sense perception reached one high-water mark during the symbolist moment in France.[23]

Stéphane Mallarmé's edition of "The Raven" with lithographs by Édouard Manet (1875) sold very few copies, but it made waves in the rarefied world of arts and letters in France. Huysmans begged Mallarmé for a copy of his next collaboration with Manet—*l'Après-midi d'un faune* (1876)—and his hero Des Esseintes spends several pages in *Against Nature* describing it lovingly. We have already noted Des Esseintes's partiality to Poe, an enthusiasm he also feels for Odilon Redon's lithographs. Huysmans's praise of Redon helped the artist's career significantly, especially in the literary circles where a passion for Poe was nearly a prerequisite: "The channel of communication now open to [Redon] was literary in nature," writes Dario Gamboni; "there is no doubt that, from his second album onwards ["To Edgar Poe"], his overt references to the work of various writers were aimed largely and consciously at attracting to himself some of the current interest in these authors in the circles with which he dealt."[24] Poe was a name to conjure with, no doubt, for Redon and for many later artists who gravitated toward his work. But that alone does not explain the specifics of what he produced or exhaust the question of motivation.

For Redon, to produce an album of images based on Poe's work brought him attention, but it also allowed him to make statements about his art in a media-competitive environment and to explore themes of perception that interested him. This competition started with the very form of the album: "a set of images conceived as a thematic unit, often intended to be viewed in sequential order, and housed in a specially made folder or box," the album inhabits the book form while hollowing it out from the inside.[25] As Gamboni comments, Redon's often intriguing captions, and the sequential "reading" of the images of the album—on a desk and not hung on the wall—"allowed him to combine the benefit of a literary association with a maximum of freedom and autonomy."[26] Importantly, these images were not "illustrations": "I have never used the defective word 'illustration,'" wrote Redon to a friend in 1898. "You will not find it in my catalogues. The right term has not yet been coined. I can only think of transmission, of interpretation."[27] Competition between word and image may be an ancient practice, but it is always historical, always engaged according to the ideological and media-specific state of play at the moment. In this regard, it is striking that Redon reaches for a concept of "transmission" in this letter, evoking an image of direct transfer across time and space that could be either spiritual or technical, or both. But what exactly is "transmitted" across this intermedial space?

Consider an image from Redon's album "To Edgar Poe" (Figure 39.1). A solitary open eye hanging in black space, this image might be called, à la Crary, "Suspensions of Perception," but in fact it was titled "After Reading Edgar Poe" by Redon. Such a title might suggest that the eye is the reader's, wakeful and vigilant after being disturbed by reading Poe. We might also minimize the significance of the title by noting that floating and disembodied eyes are not uncommon in Redon's work. As a matter of fact, however, the image has been traditionally understood as an "interpretation or transmission" of "The Tell-Tale Heart." But how? Faced with the puzzle of the link between Redon's images and their putative source texts, Gamboni gets tangled up: Redon's images "display precise links to specific texts and even . . . to specific, climactic moments of the narration. To that extent they can be regarded as 'illustrations' in a traditional sense.

FIGURE 39.1 Redon called this eyeball hanging in black space "After Reading Edgar Poe," but it has come to be understood as inspired more specifically by "The Tell-Tale Heart." Odilon Redon, The Tell-Tale Heart (Le Coeur révélateur) (1883). The Santa Barbara Museum of Art, Santa Barbara, CA. Santa Barbara Museum of Art, Museum purchase.

But ambiguities abound."[28] Indeed they do. Putting aside the idea that the eye may be the reader's, Gamboni suggests that the image "evokes the moment in which the light introduced through a door by the narrator . . . falls upon the eye of an old man, who frightens him; but the narrator, in turn, terrifies the old man and eventually kills him." If it is *this* moment that is depicted, it must be the narrator's eye we see, as it inches itself ever so slowly into the room. But later, Gamboni suggests that the image "corresponds to the way in which Poe's narrator introduces the reason for his murderous hatred."[29] This suggests that the eye we see is in fact the old man's eye, the "reason" for the narrator's hatred. Three possible eyes, then: reader, narrator, victim. It is hard to see how one can accommodate this ambiguity and remain wedded to the idea that the image tracks to a moment, and that it serves as an illustration.

Clearly, the relation between this stilled image—this "suspension" of perception—and the narrative to which it is attached is a complex one. In fact, by titling his image "After Reading Edgar Poe," Redon draws attention to the errancy of eyes in Poe's work as a whole. Poe's monomaniacal narrators characteristically attack the face, gouging out eyes or teeth ("The Black Cat," "Berenice"), blocking from view or walling up ("The Tell-Tale Heart," "The Cask of Amontillado"). The face is *the seen* that must become unseen; it is the projected zone of the sovereignty of the eye, of vision. "The Tell-Tale Heart" dramatizes this projection most succinctly in the scene Gamboni suggests Redon may be illustrating, in which the narrator's murderous vigilance brings his eye to the crack in the doorway, and his lamp casts just enough light into the old man's bedroom to illuminate . . . another eye. (The oft-remarked homophonic pun between eye and I is of course relevant here; no I without an Other I.) By showing us, perhaps, the *narrator's* eye, Redon is capturing, in fact, the reversibility of eyes in the tale. The image becomes less a snapshot of a moment than an interpretation of the logic animating the tale as a whole.

But in these tales, the violent standoff between eyes and I's is supplemented—and ultimately undermined—by a contest between eye and ear. Here we have an example of how Poe's own analytics of the senses gave dramatic shape to the wider cultural and scientific developments tracked by Crary, Brain, Sterne, and others. The old man's eye—the eye of a vulture, with a film over it—is doubled by the narrator's, as we have seen, but it is also doubled by a sound—the beating of a heart that, like the vulture eye, is covered or wrapped, in this case by cotton wadding. There are two doublings, but they are not equivalent. The antagonism of eyes is an affair of the human. But harbored within this human face-off is another dimension, the domain of sound, which other tales suggest is finally beyond the human. In "The Black Cat," the inhuman cry that consigns the narrator to the hangman emerges from the "red extended mouth" of the cat, a visceral image merely doubling, as it were, the blinding vision of the solitary—solar—eye of fire. In "The Cask of Amontillado" it is the tiny tinkle of Fortunato's bell as the last brick goes in. This sonic torment, this shard of sound that undoes the labor that has gone into the narrator's plot, is understood to emanate from beneath the floorboards in "The Tell-Tale Heart," where he has buried the remains of the old man. Let us look again at Redon's image. The planks between which the eye peers do not look like they belong to a doorway or even a wall. They look like floorboards.[30] Redon captures with uncanny precision the radical instability of the system joining eye and ear. Frames and thresholds are imposed—rooms closed, walls erected, floorboards opened and replaced. But these frames and thresholds are essentially, not accidentally, porous. Redon uses Poe's tale as an occasion for a meditation on media—Poe's, and his own. The eye calls forth the full dynamic of eyes (and ears) in Poe, but it also is an eye facing Redon's own viewer. The artwork looks back. To meditate on media in this intermedial way is always to think about limits and affordances, to dramatize the powers and incapacities of artistic labor in any one medium. Poe's tale does this; so does Redon's image. "The Tell-Tale Heart" plays with the instability of inside and outside, as does Redon's image: not only do we not know whether the eye between the boards is "inside or outside," it looks indeed as if it has already migrated from the material enclosure, as if the eye hanging in black space were another knot in the wood that had displaced itself.[31] Enclosure and its "outside" are made of the same stuff.

Redon's "noirs" are notoriously ambiguous and evocative, and unpacking his intermedial engagement with Poe is accordingly many layered. A look at an equally familiar visual response to Poe's tale can help separate the larger intermedial stakes from Redon's idiosyncratic approach. Harry Clarke's illustrations for *Tales of Mystery and Imagination* (1919, 1923) are among the most beloved and applauded visual interpretations of Poe in the tradition. Not unlike Redon, Clarke had been drawn to Poe's work for the artistic opportunities it afforded. Nicola Gordon Bowe tells us that "Harry's diary reveals that already, on his twenty-fifth birthday, 17 March 1914, he was reading Edgar Allan Poe's *Tales of Mystery and Imagination* with a view to illustrating them."[32] To engage with Poe was to engage with the book form and to have to navigate the issue of "illustration." Clarke made a series of images keyed to Poe's tales and hawked them to publishers. Clarke is less ostentatiously unconventional than Redon, but his modernist bona fides are legitimate enough. Bowe offers her summary judgment: "Clarke represents the subversive side of Symbolism in his predilection for dreamed images invested with iconic substance, deliberately ambiguous nuances, enigmatic, fatalistic, sensuous and ominous figures, drawn from eclectic and obscure sources and closely related to contemporary or recent literature, poetic, and musical ideas."[33]

Clarke provided two illustrations of "The Tell-Tale Heart" in the 1923 edition, one in color and one not. It is the latter that concerns us here. At first blush, Clarke seems to offer a "snapshot" illustration of the type we could not find in Redon's image. The image's caption provides confirmation, if we needed any, that the scene depicted the tale's climax, when the beating heart torments the narrator. But by linking his image so tightly to this moment, Clarke has given himself a problem Redon avoided by restricting himself to the eye as the key that unlocks the theme of sensory competition. As we have seen, sound often undoes the plots, enclosures, and compositions of Poe's narrators; sound seems to represent an extra-human dimension in these tales. Clarke attacks the issue rather more directly. Like Redon, he understands how Poe's narrator's attempt to limit the number of eyes actually incites a transfer and multiplication of them. Thus, the narrator looks out at us, but so too does the old man peer with his dead eye from beneath the mounded covers. Clarke conflates the murder scene with the space of burial (see Figure 39.2).

But Clarke also depicts an exfoliation of sound emerging from the site of burial, crawling up the side of his image to reach out, frond-like, toward the narrator. I say exfoliation, since the image evokes the kind of organic ornament so common in art nouveau and arts and crafts traditions. The repeated motif is the iconic heart shape—as in, "I [Heart] Poe"—but a heavier object resembling the human organ itself hangs like a grotesque pendant from the curling shape. Far from avoiding the problem, it seems, Clarke seems to want to *thematize* the visual possibilities of representing sound. At the same time, a large lashed eyeball surmounts the sprouting foliage, an eye that has no counterpart in Poe's tale, a fact all the more striking given how explicitly Clarke is tracking Poe's

BUT, FOR MANY MINUTES, THE HEART BEAT ON
WITH A MUFFLED SOUND
266

FIGURE 39.2 Harry Clarke's illustration of the climax of "The Tell-Tale Heart." Note the exfoliation of both eyes and hearts. Harry Clarke, illustrations in Tales of Mystery and Imagination (1919) by E. A. Poe. Courtesy: The Lilly Library, Indiana University, Bloomington, Indiana.

text. This eyeball recalls quite directly another image of Redon's, "There Was Perhaps a First Vision Attempted in the Flower," from his series "Les Origines" (1883). This apparently surveying eye has an ambiguous function in Clarke's staging of the conflict of eye and ear in Poe's tale. On the one hand, it might seem to announce a superiority or primal originality of vision; but its emergence from what might seem the ornamental border of Clarke's image also suggests an incursion from without, the kind of inhuman dimension I have argued Poe is deeply interested in, a dimension impinging from without as much as emerging from within (see Figure 39.3).

What I would emphasize about Clarke's image is that even as it fills the classic function of illustration more clearly than Redon ever attempted to do, one can see how the dynamics of Poe's tale, the contest of senses, the efforts of framing and control and their failure, incite a genuine, and parallel, investigation in Clarke, using the tools and traditions specific to his medium and style. Like Poe's tales, these "avant-garde" images become inquiries into mediality, via the human sensorium.

A few years after Clarke's illustrations appeared, an astonishing four-volume quarto edition of *Histoires Extraordinaires*, in Baudelaire's translation, was published in Paris. The publisher was KRA, one of the names under which Simon Kra and his family published. The house was established in 1919 and became a major outlet for surrealism in its first twenty years, publishing *Manifeste du Surréalisme* in 1924, for example. Two of the four volumes in the Poe edition contain the tales translated by Baudelaire, with accompanying etchings by Neapolitan artist Carlo Farneti—each tale averaging about three images. The other two volumes are entirely Farneti's illustrations, some of which were used and some not—an investment indicating just how highly regarded Farneti's work was by the publishers. These images are not nearly as well known as Clarke's or Redon's. They are very striking, and Burton Pollin recorded his admiration of them in *Images of Poe's Works*. I cannot undertake any summary assessment of this mammoth project, but merely want to remark that Farneti, like Redon and Clarke, uses Poe to negotiate intermedial terrain in a self-consciously avant-garde milieu.

In this production, however, the contest between text and "illustration" has been taken to an entirely new level, with Farneti's work almost overmastering Poe's: two of the four volumes have no text, and the two volumes *with* text are literally interrupted or intruded upon by Farneti's images. Figure 39.4 shows a page from the climax of "Valdemar."

In the KRA edition of *Histoires*, print is regularly disrupted by the various fluvial forms of Farneti's visual vocabulary; this image from "Valdemar" is notable for its intensity only. Lavinia Brancaccio notes how roughly Farneti plays with the page, how he pushes the "decorative," "framing" aspect of illustration onto and into the text itself (and much more aggressively than Clarke had): Farneti's images, she writes, "do not decorate the book, but live in the body of the text."[34] The text to which this image is "contiguous" (to use Brancaccio's term) is the same scene from "Valdemar" that we looked at earlier, the moment when Valdemar makes his impossible announcement: "*j'ai dormi—* et maintenant—maintenant, *je suis mort!*" I have argued in passing that sound indexes the inhuman in Poe—the cat's cry is an obvious example, as is Fortunato's bell, or the chattering of the orangutan in "Rue Morgue"—but precisely by its absolute proximity

FIGURE 39.3 Redon's vegetable eyeball: "There Was Perhaps a First Vision Attempted in the Flower," the second plate from *Les Origines* (1883). Odilon Redon, "There Was Perhaps a First Vision Attempted in the Flower," plate 2 out of 8 from *Les Origines* (1883). The Art Institute of Chicago, Chicago, IL. Photo courtesy of The Art Institute of Chicago/Art Resource, NY.

to the human, and to human speech, the sonic event recorded here is perhaps an even better example of such inhuman sound. Dead people do not talk (or flipping it around, with Derrida, perhaps only dead people talk); and Valdemar was already well on his way to an extra-human condition when his jaw dropped, and he somehow continued to speak using only his black vibrating tongue, or perhaps we should say enunciate with a "syllabisation . . . terriblement, effroyablement distincte." Within the heart of the human,

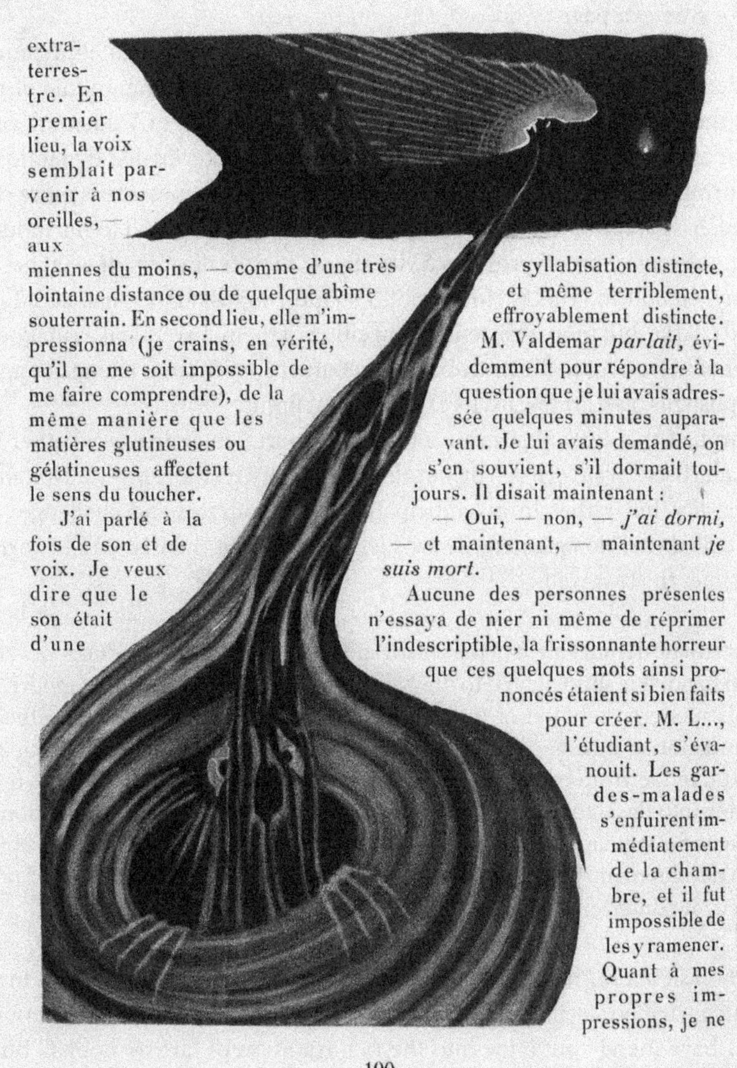

extraterrestre. En premier lieu, la voix semblait parvenir à nos oreilles, — aux miennes du moins, — comme d'une très lointaine distance ou de quelque abîme souterrain. En second lieu, elle m'impressionna (je crains, en vérité, qu'il ne me soit impossible de me faire comprendre), de la même manière que les matières glutineuses ou gélatineuses affectent le sens du toucher.

J'ai parlé à la fois de son et de voix. Je veux dire que le son était d'une syllabisation distincte, et même terriblement, effroyablement distincte. M. Valdemar *parlait*, évidemment pour répondre à la question que je lui avais adressée quelques minutes auparavant. Je lui avais demandé, on s'en souvient, s'il dormait toujours. Il disait maintenant :

— Oui, — non, — *j'ai dormi,* — et maintenant, — maintenant *je suis mort.*

Aucune des personnes présentes n'essaya de nier ni même de réprimer l'indescriptible, la frissonnante horreur que ces quelques mots ainsi prononcés étaient si bien faits pour créer. M. L..., l'étudiant, s'évanouit. Les gardes-malades s'enfuirent immédiatement de la chambre, et il fut impossible de les y ramener. Quant à mes propres impressions, je ne

190

FIGURE 39.4 The climax of "The Facts in the Case of M. Valdemar," from *Nouvelles histoires extraordinaires*/Edgar Allan Poe; traduction de Charles Baudelaire; eaux-fortes à la manière noire de Carlo Farneti (KRA, 1928). Carlo Farneti, "The Facts in the Case of M. Valdemar," in Nouvelles histoires extradorinaires, by Edgar Allan Poe (1928). Courtesy: The Lilly Library, Indiana University, Bloomington, Indiana.

a communications system is harbored that exceeds all efforts to contain it through "composition" by frame or page.

It is this media dynamic that Farneti's image engages. We see an effluvium issuing from Valdemar's mouth at the top of the page, running down the middle of the page to pool at the bottom. In narrative terms, it is an anticipation of Valdemar's corporeal dissolution at the close of Poe's text. In the terms of the intermedial dynamic we have been exploring as Poe's bequest to the experimental arts, the message is more complex. By tying such dissolution to Valdemar's mouth (in the image), and to his inhuman utterance (in the text), Farneti provides a visually striking realization of what lies beyond his—or any—medium. This is (impossible) sound (impossibly) visualized. Like both Redon and Clarke, but more insistently than either of them, Farneti takes up Poe's works not as a set of narratives to illustrate but as a set of sensory dramas to engage, and in engaging to push his own art toward its experimental limits.

I have argued that Poe's significance for later experimental artists, whether we consider those artists "avant-garde" or not, lies not in his relationship to capitalism and the commodity, but rather in his anticipation of the puzzles and challenges of what Rimbaud called the "dérèglement de tous les sens." Media theorist and historian Tom Gunning states the case well:

> The systematic derangement of the senses and their systematic reproduction . . . went hand in hand. It is shortsighted to draw dichotomies between emerging modernism and this modern ambition of technological reproduction, which calls neither for condemnation as a naïve "class fantasy" nor simple valorization as an anticipation of artistic modernism or an example of scientific "progress." . . . To do this means venturing into the ambivalence of both its technical and commercial production and the range of imaginary scenarios that surrounded it, both inspired by and inspiring its own development. The nature of this doubling of the human senses should not be assumed, but uncovered and interrogated.[35]

To properly cash out my hypothesis about Poe's significance, one would have to see how his influence wielded itself in media-specific ways in film, music, radio, comics, and cartoons. I have merely put a toe into the rich tradition of "artist's books." But I have tried to keep in view how these "transmissions" of Poe (to recall Redon) express an experimentalism that engages both technical and commercial production as well as the "imaginary scenarios" so richly available for later use in Poe's own texts.

Notes

1. Charles Baudelaire, "Edgar Allan Poe, His Life and Works," in *Baudelaire: Selected Writings on Art and Artists*, trans. P. E. Charvet (Cambridge, UK: Cambridge University Press, 1972), 162–163.
2. Theodor Adorno, *Aesthetic Theory*, ed. Gretel Adorno and Rolf Tiedemann, new ed. and trans. Robert Hullot-Kentor (1970; London: Bloomsbury, 2004), 29.

3. Baudelaire, "Further Notes on Edgar Poe," in *Baudelaire: Selected Writings on Art and Artists*, 198.
4. Baudelaire, "Further Notes on Edgar Poe," 171, 186.
5. Renato Poggioli observes that "it was symbolism which carried one of the external signs most characteristically avant-garde to the highest degree of development," while Peter Bürger's Marxist periodization sees the development here as bourgeois. See Renato Poggioli, *The Theory of the Avant-Garde*, trans. Gerald Fitzgerald (1962; Cambridge: Harvard University Press, 1968), 21; and Peter Bürger, *Theory of the Avant-Garde*, trans. Michael Shaw (Minneapolis: University of Minnesota Press, 1984).
6. John Tresch, "The Uses of a Mistranslated Manifesto: Baudelaire's 'La Genèse d'un Poème,'" *L'Esprit Créateur* 43, no. 2 (Summer 2003): 23–35, quote from 23–24. See also by John Tresch: "The Potent Magic of Verisimilitude: Edgar Allan Poe within the Mechanical Age," *British Journal for the History of Science* 30, no. 3 (1997): 275–290; "Extra! Extra! Poe Invents Science Fiction," in *The Cambridge Companion to Poe*, ed. Kevin J. Hayes (Cambridge: Cambridge University Press, 2002), 113–132; "Technology," in *Edgar Allan Poe in Context*, ed. Kevin J. Hayes (Cambridge: Cambridge University Press, 2013), 372–382; "The Prophet and the Pendulum: Sensational Science and Audiovisual Phantasmagoria around 1848," *Grey Room* 43 (Spring 2011): 16–41; Mara Mills and Tresch, "Audio/Visual," *Grey Room* 43 (Spring 2011): 6–15.
7. Baudelaire, *Baudelaire: Selected Writings on Art and Artists*, 198. T. S Eliot's famous dismissal of Poe extends and misapplies Baudelaire's observation: "The forms which his lively curiosity takes are those in which a pre-adolescent mentality delights: wonders of nature and of mechanics and of the supernatural, cryptograms and cyphers, puzzles and labyrinths, mechanical chess-players and wild flights of speculation." Eliot, "From Poe to Valery," *Hudson Review* 2, no. 3 (1949): 335.
8. John Tresch, *The Romantic Machine: Utopian Science and Technology after Napoloean* (Chicago: University of Chicago Press, 2014).
9. Walter Benjamin, "The Work of Art in the Age of Its Reproducibility." Benjamin has most to say about play in the second, longest, and never-published version of this famous essay, which is what is quoted here. See *Walter Benjamin: Selected Writings*, ed. Howard Eiland and Michael W. Jennings, trans. Edmund Jephcott, Howard Eiland, and others, vol. 3, *1935–1938* (Cambridge: Harvard University Press, 2002), 107.
10. And it is ambivalence present from the very beginning: Tresch observes that between the 1852 and 1856 versions of Baudelaire's essay on Poe, the Frenchman excises the term "laboratoire": "The air in Poe's literature remains 'raréfié,' but the allusion to laboratoire has disappeared." Tresch, "The Uses of a Mistranslated Manifesto," 28.
11. Poggioli, *The Theory of the Avant-Garde*, 136, 138.
12. Paul Valéry, "On Literary Technique," in *Collected Works of Paul Valéry, vol. 7, The Art of Poetry*, trans. Denise Folliot (New York: Bollingen Foundation), 323.
13. Valéry, "On Literary Technique," 315, 315, 315–317.
14. Robert Brain, *The Pulse of Modernism: Physiological Aesthetics in Fin-de-Siècle Europe* (Seattle: University of Washington Press, 2015), xxiii.
15. In addition to Brain, and the works of Tresch cited earlier, see Jonathan Sterne, *The Audible Past: Cultural Origins of Sound Reproduction* (Durham, NC: Duke University Press, 2003); Jonathan Crary, *Suspensions of Perception: Attention, Spectacle, and Modern Culture* (Cambridge, MA: MIT Press, 1999); Crary, *Techniques of the Observer: On Vision and Modernity in the Nineteenth Century* (Cambridge, MA: MIT

Press, 1990); Rae Beth Gordon, *Why the French Love Jerry Lewis: From Cabaret to Early Cinema* (Stanford, CA: Stanford University Press, 2001); Robin Veder, *The Living Line: Modern Art and the Economy of Energy* (Hanover, NH: Dartmouth College Press, 2015).

16. Brain, *The Pulse of Modernism*, xxiii, xxi.
17. Crary, *Suspensions of Perception*, 12–13, 47.
18. Crary, *Suspensions of Perception*, 3.
19. Crary, *Suspensions of Perception*, 3.
20. Joris-Karl Huysmans, *Against Nature (A Rebours)*, trans. Robert Baldick (1956; Penguin: London, 1981), 20.
21. Huysmans, *Against Nature*, 22, 193, 194.
22. See Keri Yousif, *Balzac, Grandville, and the Rise of Book Illustration* (London: Ashgate, 2012). For one wider treatment of this age-old competition, see Garrett Stewart, *The Look of Reading: Book, Painting, Text* (Chicago: University of Chicago Press, 2006).
23. See Anna Sigrídur Arnar, *The Book as Instrument: Stéphane Mallarmé, The Artist's Book, and the Transformation of Print Culture* (Chicago: University of Chicago Press, 2011); Penny Florence, *Mallarmé, Manet and Redon: Visual and Aural Signs and the Generation of Meaning* (Cambridge: Cambridge University Press, 1986); Barbara Larson, *The Dark Side of Nature: Science, Society, and the Fantastic in the Work of Odilon Redon* (University Park: Penn State University Press, 2005); Jodi Hauptman, *Beyond the Visible: The Art of Odilon Redon* (New York: Museum of Modern Art, 2005). "Starr Figura, Redon and the Lithographed Portfolio," in Hauptman, *Beyond the Visible: The Art of Odile Redon*, 76–98.
24. Dario Gamboni, *The Brush and the Pen: Odilon Redon and Literature*, trans. Mary Whittall, rev. ed. (1989; Chicago: University of Chicago Press, 2011), 76, 122.
25. Figura, "Redon and the Lithographed Portfolio," 82.
26. Gamboni, *The Brush and the Pen*, 106.
27. Quoted in Figura, "Redon and the Lithographed Portfolio," 83.
28. Gamboni, *The Brush and the Pen*, 111. See a similar equivocation in Jodi Hauptman's *Beyond the Visible*: At first, Hauptman says that the image she uses as a frontispiece is "a visualization of a moment in Poe's story 'Berenice' (1835), in which the narrator becomes obsessed with and feels tormented by his fiancée's teeth." But only two sentences later, she says: "Rather than referring to a particular moment in the story, Redon instead evokes the mood of the horrifying tale and places the viewer in the position of the obsessed narrator." Moment or no moment? Hauptman, *Beyond the Visible*, 29.
29. Gamboni, *The Brush and the Pen*, 111, 116.
30. See Gamboni: "the wooden surfaces in 'The Tell-Tale Heart' look more like the planks of a floor than like a door or a wall; the drawing may therefore also allude to the end of the text, in which the narrator hears the heart of his victim beating under the floor and feels compelled to give himself up to the police." Gamboni, *The Brush and the Pen*, 114.
31. Gamboni also notices this detail and summarizes its import well: "Moreover, the knot in the wood, conspicuously placed in the upper center of the drawing, clearly suggests another eye, 'with a film over it,' and thereby launches a process of proliferation that can allude both to the narrator's obsession and to his punishment." *The Brush and the Pen*, 116. For a different, contemporary, treatment of the dissolution of thresholds, one specifically attentive to auditory images, see Jarkko Toikkanen, "Auditory Images in Edgar Allan Poe's 'The Tell-Tale Heart,'" *The Edgar Allan Poe Review* 18, no. 1 (Spring 2017): 39–53.

32. Nicola Gordon Bowe, *The Life and Work of Harry Clarke* (Dublin: Irish Academic Press, 1989), 34.
33. Bowe, *The Life and Work of Harry Clarke*, 2–3.
34. Lavinia Brancaccio, "Carlo Farneti," in *In Margine: Artisti napoletani fra tradizione e opposizione, 1909–1923*, ed. Picone Petrusa (Milan: Fabbri, 1986), 179–185. Here is the full Italian: "Più che a fronte del testo, le tavole farnetiane sono a margine o, per meglio dire, contigue al testo che scorre col suo intreccio. Non decorano il libro, ma vivono nel corpo del testo" (180).
35. Tom Gunning, "Doing for the Eye What the Phonograph Does for the Ear," in *The Sounds of Early Cinema*, ed. Richard Abel and Rick Altman (Bloomington: Indiana University Press, 2001), 16.

Bibliography

Baudelaire, Charles. "Further Notes on Edgar Poe." In *Baudelaire: Selected Writings on Art and Artists*, 188–208. Translated by P. E. Charvet. Cambridge, UK: Cambridge University Press, 1972.

Brain, Robert. *The Pulse of Modernism: Physiological Aesthetics in Fin-de-Siècle Europe*. Seattle: University of Washington Press, 2015.

Crary, Jonathan. *Suspensions of Perception: Attention, Spectacle, and Modern Culture*. Cambridge, MA: MIT Press, 1999.

Gamboni, Dario. *The Brush and the Pen: Odilon Redon and Literature*. Translated by Mary Whittall. Revised edition. Chicago: University of Chicago Press, 2011.

Tresch, John. "Technology." In *Edgar Allan Poe in Context*, edited by Kevin J. Hayes, 372–382. New York: Cambridge University Press, 2013.

Tresch, John. "The Uses of a Mistranslated Manifesto: Baudelaire's 'La Genèse d'un Poème.'" *L'Esprit Créateur* 43, no. 2 (Summer 2003): 23–35.

CHAPTER 40

POSTMODERN POE

JEFFREY ANDREW WEINSTOCK

Fittingly for an author whose fiction often flirted with the line between life and death, Poe has had an exceptionally busy afterlife. Known during his lifetime primarily for his "tomahawking" literary criticism and his poem "The Raven," the author who struggled to earn a living and establish a reputation for literary greatness achieved the success that eluded him only well after his death—and in a roundabout fashion—as America belatedly reimported Poe back from France. Poe's American fortunes arguably started to shift in the early twentieth century, where, as Scott Peeples has chronicled, formalist critics were often unkind to Poe,[1] but their debates nevertheless included him—and, as the saying goes, "any press is good press." Poe's renown in America solidified, however, in the second half of the twentieth century when he moved to center stage both in critical discourse and popular culture. Today, over a century and a half after his death, Poe is easily among America's best-known authors. His face appears on the Barnes & Noble book chain shopping bag, his poetry has been narrated by notables from Vincent Price to James Earl Jones to Christopher Walken, his fiction has been repeatedly adapted for film and other formats such as opera and theater, and Poe himself has appeared as a character in books, comics, film, and theater. As J. W. Ocker quips concerning Poe in the introduction to his *Poe-Land: The Hallowed Haunts of Edgar Allan Poe*: "I mean, he's a Halloween decoration. Take that, every other writer."[2]

The obvious question is, what changed in order to propel Poe to the forefront of American literature and culture? The answer to this question is less obvious, of course, because Poe's triumph reflects broad shifts in popular taste and critical interest. Some of it can be chalked up to the snowball effect—the better known an author is, the more they are taught, read, and marketed. Some of it, as Ocker suggests, has to do with the romantic tragedy of Poe's life, which continues to fascinate modern readers and critics alike.[3] But much more of it arguably has to do with the congruence between Poe's themes, tropes, and philosophy and the preoccupations of our contemporary moment. Poe's success in postmodern culture (and perhaps the lack of it in his own historical moment) reflects the fact that much of his work anticipated—and, of course, influenced—what authors and artists began doing in larger numbers about a hundred years later.

Put differently, the world seems to have caught up with Poe, who was "PoMo" before it was cool.

This chapter will address "Postmodern Poe" in three parts. I will first consider the postmodern elements of Poe's writing with an emphasis on hoaxes, metafictional self-referentiality, fragmentation, and an overall postmodern suspicion of metanarratives. This section addresses these themes and devices in relation to a handful of Poe's short stories, his only novel *The Narrative of Arthur Gordon Pym of Nantucket*, and, briefly, his poetry. Poe's fiction is indeed suffused with the characteristics and general attitude associated with twentieth- and twenty-first-century postmodernism, which is obviously part of what makes him congenial to modern tastes. The second section will offer an overview of how Poe's fiction has been used by poststructuralist theorists—notably, Jacques Lacan, Jacques Derrida, and Barbara Johnson—as well as critics including Dennis Pahl, Michael J. S. Williams, J. Gerald Kennedy, and Louis A. Renza, to illustrate poststructuralist claims about the nature of the self and language. Finding points of congruence between their own philosophies and ideas expressed in Poe's writing, these theorists and critics turn to Poe as a means to elaborate their own postmodern thinking. The third section then will explore how the postmodern elements present in Poe's fiction make him attractive to modern sensibilities. This final section will explore the commodification not just of Poe's writing but of Poe himself—how his biography and image become other postmodern narratives available for appropriation and exploitation in the contemporary culture of the Gothic.

PoMoPoe

Even a cursory consideration of Poe's works makes clear that he can be considered a precocious postmodernist because he routinely makes use of postmodernist devices and themes that raise ontological questions, interrogate the stability of the self, foreground the fictionality of fiction, and highlight the materiality of language itself. Two primary means through which Poe raises questions about the nature of the world itself are through his hoaxes and his supernatural tales.

Poe is generally considered to have published six hoaxes: "The Unparalleled Adventures of One Hans Pfaall" (1835), *The Narrative of Arthur Gordon Pym* (early chapters published in the *Southern Literary Messenger* in 1837), his unfinished *The Journal of Julius Rodman* (1840), the story anthologized as "The Balloon-Hoax" (1844), "The Facts in the Case of M. Valdemar" (1845), and "Von Kempelen and His Discovery" (1849). (Several other of Poe's stories have prompted discussion about their possibility as well—Daniel Royot, for example, numbers Poe's "MS. Found in a Bottle" [1833] among Poe's hoaxes.[4]) "Hans Pfaall," *Pym*, *Julius Rodman*, and "The Balloon-Hoax" each involve a journey: Pfaall claims to have visited the moon in a hot air balloon; Pym joins an Antarctic exploratory venture; Rodman details a trip up the Missouri River in 1792, claiming to be the first "White Man" to cross the Rocky Mountains (P 1: 509); and "The

Balloon-Hoax" reports the first transatlantic crossing in a hot air balloon. "Valdemar" records a journey of a different kind, as the patient is hypnotized precisely at the point of death and lingers in a kind of limbo state until the trance is broken. Capitalizing on the Gold Rush of the late 1840s, "Von Kempelen" reports that the Hungarian inventor Wolfgang von Kempelen has successfully realized the alchemical dream of transforming lead into gold.

Whether relatively plausible or flagrantly false, Poe's hoaxes playfully scuttle the distinctions between fact and fiction, truth and falsehood, as they imitate conventions of travel journals and newspaper reporting. Such works, all of which incorporate elements of what we today consider science fiction, are in keeping with Brian McHale's characterization of postmodernist fiction as depicting "worlds in collision" (the title of his fourth chapter in *Postmodernist Fiction*), as we are either transported out of the world we know into a different one, or something from a different world intrudes into ours.[5] Poe's hoaxes resemble "fake news" stories that circulate on the internet: "The Balloon-Hoax," which provides a highly plausible account of a transatlantic crossing by balloonist Thomas Monck Mason (an actual nineteenth-century balloonist), was published in the *New York Sun* with the headline beginning, "Astounding News by Express, *via* Norfolk!—The Atlantic crossed in Three Days! Signal Triumph of Mr. Monck Mason's Flying Machine!" (M 3: 1068). The tale itself then consists of two parts: an overview of "the balloon itself, its construction, and other matters of interest" by an unnamed narrator (M 3: 1069), and then "particulars" of the journey that the reader is told "may be relied on as authentic and accurate in every respect, as . . . they are copied *verbatim* from the joint diaries of Mr. Monck Mason and Mr. Harrison Ainsworth" (M 3: 1069). Arguably an early work of science fiction (one that may have influenced Jules Verne's *Around the World in Eighty Days* [1873]), "The Balloon-Hoax" can also be categorized as what Linda Hutcheon calls in her analysis of postmodern fiction "historiographic metafiction," a form whose "theoretical self-awareness of history and fiction as human constructs (historio*graphic meta*fiction) is made grounds for its rethinking and reworking of the forms and contents of the past."[6] In any event, Poe's hoax was successful enough that the *Sun* published a retraction two days after its publication.

Far more outlandish and flippant in tone is Poe's other, earlier tale of hot air ballooning, "The Unparalleled Adventure of One Hans Pfaall," first published in 1835 in the *Southern Literary Messenger*. Presented as a written account conveyed to Rotterdam burgomaster Superbus Von Underduk by a curious two-foot-tall messenger, the tale describes Hans Pfaall's preparations for and subsequent journey by hot air balloon to the moon. Rather like Poe's *Pym*, the account of Pfaall's journey ends just as he arrives in another world, having completed his journey and encountered the moon's inhabitants. (A continuation of the tale is promised if Pfaall can procure a pardon for blowing up three of his creditors as he was igniting his balloon.) Foregrounding the constructedness of the text itself, the narrator of "Hans Pfaall" comments that "some of the over-wise even made themselves ridiculous by decrying the whole business as nothing better than a hoax" (P 1: 427). This opinion is seemingly dismissed by the narrator, who states that "hoax, with these sort of people is, I believe, a general term for all matters above their comprehension" (P 1: 427); however, highlighting the possibility that it may indeed be "fake news," the tale ends precisely with evidence calling into question the veracity of the story of Pfaall's journey.

A different sort of collision of worlds is staged in Poe's hoaxes and other narratives that involve the supernatural. "The Facts in the Case of M. Valdemar," in which mesmerism keeps Valdemar's consciousness suspended in his body despite the cessation of biological function, dovetails with Poe's more supernatural stories such as "Morella" (1835), "Ligeia" (1838), "Eleonora" (1842), and perhaps "The Fall of the House of Usher" (1839), in which consciousness seems to survive death. In these stories, rather than the protagonist moving beyond mapped territory into the unknown, the unknown intrudes on the familiar world. Even this, however, is problematized by Poe, who presents the supernatural as one possible explanation among several. Morella may have reincarnated herself in her daughter—indeed, this is the interpretation that the story seems to insist upon—but this requires the reader to accept the incredible account as presented by the story's narrator, a man who refuses to give his child a name. Ligeia may have possessed Rowena's body, but the narrator's perceptions are compromised by his use of opium. Eleonora's spirit may have blessed her husband's second marriage, but he might have only dreamed that he heard her voice. And while Roderick Usher and, implicitly, the narrator of "The Fall of the House of Usher" believe that Madeline Usher must have been prematurely interred, the story's more bizarre elements allow the reader to conjecture a supernatural return from the grave. Sufficient ambiguity is present in each case to allow for what McHale, referencing Tzvetan Todorov's famous study of the fantastic, discusses in relation to postmodernism as fantastic hesitation as we linger on the "frontier . . . between this world and the world next door."[7] As with the hoaxes, these fantastic tales complicate accepted post-Enlightenment understanding of how the world functions but leave us finally with a sense of uncertainty: Is this our world or not? These fantasy elements thus participate in postmodernism's "ontological poetics" as they call into question what we can know about the world.[8]

The hoaxes and supernatural tales play with the borders of the known world as explorers move off the map of geographical territory and human experience. Equally central to Poe's oeuvre are stories that move inward rather than outward to foreground the fragmented self in a way congruent with postmodern understandings of identity. Half a century before Freud—and in opposition to the Enlightenment's assumption concerning the stability of the self (e.g., Descartes's *cogito*)—Poe, as Dennis Pahl emphasizes in the first three chapters of his *Architects of the Abyss*, repeatedly "questions the notion of a unified, substantial self," propounding in its place the concept of a divided self motivated by unconscious forces.[9] Indeed, the proposition that we are "strangers to ourselves," never fully knowing what motivates us, is at the heart of several of Poe's most famous tales. In Poe's most ghoulish story, "Berenice" (1835), the narrator, Egæus, moving in a kind of trance, disinters the body of his (not dead) cousin Berenice and extracts her teeth. The plot of "William Wilson" (1839) literalizes the contest between what Freud will later refer to as the Id (the appetitive side of the human self) and the Superego (the part of the self that reflects internalized cultural rules), as William Wilson squares off against himself. The embedded "Haunted Palace" narrative within "The Fall of the House of Usher" suggests that we read this tale, too, as one about the mind divided. Colin Martindale, for example, makes the case that the house may stand for the personality as a whole and the occupants as different parts of this personality.[10] Similarly, Pahl, interpreting "Usher" by way of Jacques Lacan's mirror stage, reads it as dramatizing the "lost unity of self."[11]

Poe's most striking articulation of the concept of the fragmented self is embodied in his notion of "perverseness," described in "The Black Cat" (1843) as "the desire to do wrong for the wrong's sake only" (M 3: 852). Poe develops this idea more fully in "The Imp of the Perverse" (1845), in which he associates perverseness with self-destructive impulses. Contra the Enlightenment's emphasis on logic and reason, Poe ascribes perverse impulses to human nature in general. In "The Imp of the Perverse," after elaborating the concept of perverseness, the narrator offers himself up as an example of this tendency, explaining that, having successfully committed a murder, he then confessed when there is no necessity to do so, ensuring his doom.

In making himself the example of the human propensity he is describing, the narrator turns himself into a kind of text to be read. This shift, together with the unusual structure of the story, which begins as an essay on perverseness and then becomes a narrative, introduces a postmodern self-reflexive element to the tale such that it becomes, on one level, about the telling of stories. Similarly self-reflexive is Poe's "The Premature Burial" (1844). As in "The Imp of the Perverse," the narrator of this account, after an initial disquisition on anxieties related to premature burial and underestimations of the frequency of its occurrence, presents himself as a case in point. He thus becomes the subject of his own narration, a text to be interpreted by himself and the reader. Interpretation is, however, complicated from the very first line of the tale: "There are certain themes of which the interest is all-absorbing, but which are too entirely horrible for the purposes of legitimate fiction. These the mere romanticist must eschew, if he do not wish to offend, or to disgust" (M 3: 954–955). True accounts of calamity and suffering, the narrator explains, can be received with a kind of "pleasurable pain"; in contrast, narratives of the same type without a basis in "reality," must be regarded "with simple abhorrence" (M 3: 955). Using the guidelines offered by the narrator at the start, one would seem forced to reject the narrative itself "with simple abhorrence" as "illegitimate fiction."

To be sure, as in "The Imp of the Perverse" and Poe's other hoaxes, the narrator of "The Premature Burial" seeks to cover fiction with the veneer of fact. After asserting, "To be buried alive, is, beyond question, the most terrific of these extremes [of agony] which has ever fallen to the lot of mere mortality" (M 3: 955), and further claiming that premature burial has occurred far more frequently than is commonly acknowledged, the narrative offers several "factual" accounts of premature burial—some of which sound suspiciously like other stories by Poe. There is first the story of a woman who we might say is prematurely *ushered* into her family vault; this is followed by the account of a bereaved lover who disinters his beloved with the intention of "possessing himself of her luxuriant tresses" (M 3: 957)—rather than teeth—only to discover that she has been buried alive. Then, anticipating "The Facts in the Case of M. Valdemar," which Poe would publish in the following year (1845), the narrator cites Mr. Edward Stapleton, who, although having been pronounced dead, is revived by electricity and reports that, although in a stupor of sorts, he nevertheless "was aware of every thing which happened to him" (M 3: 961). Proleptically inverting Valdemar's uncanny pronouncement of "I am dead" (M 3: 1240, 1242)—and confirming the narrator's assertion that "the boundaries which divide Life from Death, are at best shadowy and vague" (M 3: 955)—the presumed corpse of Stapleton struggles to articulate "I am alive" (M 3: 961) before swooning again on the dissecting room floor. The specter of Ligeia is summoned when the narrator, again asserting the unacknowledged frequency of premature interment and the morbid interest the topic elicits, mentions "the unseen but palpable presence of the Conqueror Worm" (M 3: 961); and the narrator of "The Tell-Tale Heart" who "heard all things in the heaven and in the earth" and "many things in hell" (M 3: 792) is invoked when the narrator of "The Premature Burial" emphasizes that "we know of nothing so agonizing upon Earth—we can dream of nothing half so hideous in the realms of the nethermost Hell" (M 3: 961). The narrator's elaborate preface to his own account ends up not only as a fallacious legitimation presenting fiction under the guise of fact, but as a rhizomatic concatenation of allusions to other Poe works that actually predicts Poe's future fortunes—returned to us from the dead, so to speak, after a kind of premature interment.

All of this, however, has been prelude to the narrator's own account of premature burial, as he explains his own tendency to slip into "cataleptic trance" (M 3: 964) and the depth of his anxiety over "the one sepulchral Idea" (M 3: 963)—the possibility of premature interment. After summarizing a dream vision of the coffins of the world thrown open to reveal millions of restless sleepers, the narrator recounts his own experience: despite all his precautions, he awoke in darkness, with his body constrained. Gripped with panic, he could not doubt that he "reposed within a coffin at last" (M 3: 967). Initially unable to make a sound, he finally summoned the strength to scream, only to be chastised by his startled cabin mates aboard a small sloop. And here again, the tale turns back upon itself, calling attention to its own construction as the narrator explains that the experience led him to surmount his terrors and to eschew "bugaboo tales—*such as this*" (M 3: 969). This is the moment at which, as J. Gerald Kennedy notes, the narrator "implicitly deconstructs his own account, dismisses the genre which it represents, trivializes the idea of living inhumation, and," quips Kennedy, "leaves the reader holding the shroud."[12]

Much of the preceding discussion of postmodern elements present in Poe's short fiction comes together in a consideration of Poe's only novel, *The Narrative of Arthur Gordon Pym of Nantucket* (1838), a strange, playful, sloppy tale that, through its insistent metatextuality, is arguably a prototypical postmodern work. Indeed, *Pym* has been a kind of gift to postmodern theorists and critics, who have lavished attention on the ways "it calls attention to its own insufficiency as a written text, raises questions of how writing can—under any circumstances—represent truth, and demonstrates through narrative action the slippery relationship between inscription and meaning, sign and referent."[13] John Carlos Rowe in *Through the Custom-House*, for example, claims that

Pym "prefigures the contemporary conception of writing as the endless production of differences,"[14] while John Irwin in *American Hieroglyphics* regards *Pym* as a "quest for linguistic origins" that can never be completed.[15] Kennedy sees *Pym*'s narrative partaking "of the metaphysical crisis which it represents" as it "reflects upon the life of writing and the profound indeterminacy of texts."[16] Pahl figures this as the "abyss" of interpretation into which determinate meaning vanishes. For Pahl, Poe's writing—along with that of Hawthorne and Melville—makes clear that "reading does not help to expose some hidden depth of meaning but rather covers with a new layer of language what is *already* an interpretation, all of which implies that there is no bottom, no ground, to the abyss of signification."[17] With *Pym*, Pahl concludes that Poe presents us with "a world made of words, an abyss whose depth turns out to be more language."[18]

Poe wastes no time in impishly scuttling distinctions between fact and fiction from the very first page of the preface, in which Pym explains that he was initially reluctant to publish his account of fantastic events because he feared it would be received as fiction; Pym therefore allowed Edgar Allan Poe to present the story in the guise of fiction. The reading public, however, was inclined to receive the account as fact, so Pym was persuaded to reassume authorship of his account and present it as fact—noting that readers of the text will certainly observe stylistic changes where Poe's part ends and Pym's part begins. In reality of course, it is all Poe, Pym is Poe's invention, and there is no abrupt change in style to signal a shift in authorship. Poe here has mischievously intermingled ontological "levels" (real author, fictional character) and launched his sea adventure tale with questions about how to distinguish fact from fiction.

The ensuing narrative then acts as a veritable catalogue of postmodern devices and themes as Pym confronts a strange world marked by illegibility and demonstrates a fragmented, shifting sense of self. For reasons of space, I will limit my focus here to Pym's encounter with the Dutch death ship and the novel's famously inconclusive conclusion—both of which, in keeping with McHale's propositions, stage encounters between different worlds and raise ontological questions about "what world is this?" Following a shipboard mutiny and a devastating storm, Pym has been left with a handful of companions aboard the floating hulk of the *Grampus*. When the group spies another ship approaching them, they initially perceive their deliverance to be at hand. Although the ship's course is erratic, Pym and his companions are heartened by what they perceive to be a smiling seaman nodding his head and seeming to encourage them to have patience. But they are soon overwhelmed by "a smell, a stench, such as the whole world has no name for—not conception of—hellish—utterly suffocating—insufferable, inconceivable" (P 1: 124). As the ship draws closer, the survivors aboard the *Grampus* observe corpses scattered across the deck of the approaching ship "in the last and most loathsome state of putrefaction" (P 1: 124), and, perhaps most ghoulish of all, they discover that the movements of the sailor who had appeared to be nodding and smiling are being caused by "a huge seagull" perched on his back, "busily gorging itself with the horrible flesh" (P 1: 125). The smile is the result of the flesh around the mouth having been eaten away, leaving the teeth revealed. The expectations of Pym and his companions have been completely upended as their apparent salvation transforms abruptly into a symbol of their inability to accurately interpret the world. In place of rescue, they encounter only death. As to what happened to produce this disaster, Pym explains that he has, since this period, "vainly endeavoured to obtain some clew to the hideous uncertainty which enveloped the fate of the stranger" (P 1: 125). But, he concludes, "it is utterly useless to form conjectures where all is involved, and will, no doubt, remain for ever involved, in the most appalling and unfathomable mystery" (P 1: 126). Similar to the conclusion of Poe's "The Man of the Crowd" (1840)—that some mysteries cannot be fathomed—the only conclusion that can be drawn here is that no firm conclusions are possible. Something from another world, a mysterious ship of death, has intruded into their world and crossed their path, leaving them with questions that can never be answered.

At the end of *Pym*, this trajectory is reversed—but with the same result. Having been rescued by the crew of the *Jane Guy*, a strangely mature Pym joins an Antarctic exploratory venture that reveals a hitherto undiscovered island populated by putatively "savage" black islanders. After a catastrophic ambush of the *Jane Guy*'s crew, Pym, together with a companion and a captive islander, escapes the island in a canoe and drifts off the map of the known world. As he and the others move still further south than humankind has ever penetrated, the ice dissipates, the current strengthens, and the water warms until they come to the edge of an immense chasm and encounter "a shrouded human figure, very far larger in its proportions than any dweller among men. And the hue of the skin of the figure was of the perfect whiteness of the snow" (P 1: 206). Thus ends the tale of Pym, whose story, like that of the Dutch death ship, remains an unfathomable mystery. Having drifted to the edge of the world and then over it, Pym crosses the threshold taking him from this world to "the world next door."[19] Who or what the shrouded human figure is has been extensively debated in the critical literature, and what happens to Pym has been the source of speculation by authors from Jules Verne in 1897 to Mat Johnson in 2011, both of whom have taken up where Poe left off (see later). However, Poe's *Pym*, like the world itself, resists the imposition of any singular meaning or determinate Truth. It is a dizzying fictional narrative ascribed to Pym, presenting itself as fact that was first offered as fiction by Poe but received as fact. As such, it ends up as a postmodern story about the telling of stories—about which we can only tell more stories.

This mocking of the desire to impose determinate meaning often has the effect in Poe's writing of foregrounding in a postmodern way the materiality of the signifier—that is, as Louis Renza puts it, of "reducing word-sense to sound."[20] Renza notes in this respect what Michael Williams refers to as "empty signifier[s]"[21] in Poe's work, including the mistaking of animal sounds for a foreign language in "The Murders in the Rue Morgue," a bird's mimicking of human speech in "The Raven," and Hop-Frog's "guttural sound and gnashing of teeth."[22] To this list, we could add repetition as well, with an obvious emphasis on "The Bells" (1849). The poem itself, it should be pointed out, highlights the role of context in delimiting meaning as it surveys the different interpretations and affects that can be attached to the same sound as merry sleigh bells transition to joyous wedding bells, then to distressing "alarum" bells, and finally to the "moaning and the groaning" of the iron bells of time and mortality. While obviously onomatopoeic, the sheer excessiveness of the repetition of the word "bells" (which is used sixty times in the poem) enacts a kind of deracination of language, wrenching signifier apart from signified until all we are left with is sound. The bells themselves have no intrinsic meaning—in a sense, the death knell they figure is of meaning itself as language is reduced to sound. In this, they arguably become exemplary of poststructuralist thought maintaining that meaning is nowhere fully present in language (Derridean *différance*) and can always go astray.

Poststructuralist Poe

In transitioning from a consideration of the postmodern elements in Poe's writing to the ways in which Poe has been taken up by contemporary postmodern culture, attention must be paid to the significant role that Poe's short story, "The Purloined Letter" (1844), has played in the articulation of poststructuralist thought. Poe's story is driven by repetition and theft: the letter, whose contents are never revealed, is stolen from "the royal apartments," then stolen from the thief's apartment by the detective Dupin; in each case, the letter's possessor leaves it in plain sight, and the taker perceives the letter's importance without reading it. The appropriation of "The Purloined Letter" in this context begins with French psychoanalyst Jacques Lacan's use of the story in 1956 as a tool to elaborate psychoanalytic concepts—in particular, the compulsion to repeat unpleasant experiences, which defies the so-called Freudian pleasure principle. For Lacan, Poe's story demonstrates the ways in which human subjectivity is constituted by the "symbolic order" of language and culture (the Lacanian "Other" with [in English] a capital O). As summarized by John P. Muller and William J. Richardson in their overview of Lacan's seminar in *The Purloined Poe*, "It is clear that Lacan's interest in this tale serves as a parable for his conception of psychoanalysis, according to which 'the unconscious is the discourse of the Other.' "[23] From this perspective, Lacan is interested in the ways the various players in Poe's story are positioned in relation to the "pure signifier" of the letter stolen from the Queen by Minister D—. Lacan famously concludes that "a letter always arrives at its destination"[24] because, as Barbara Johnson explains, the letter's destination is wherever it arrives.[25] (In relation to psychoanalysis and the unconscious, Slavoj Žižek explains that the letter's destination "was from the very beginning the sender himself."[26])

In 1975, Jacques Derrida, a leading figure of the philosophical movement known as deconstruction, offered a response to Lacan's reading of Poe, emphasizing that, contra Lacan's assertion, "A letter can always not arrive at its destination."[27] Derrida's interest in Lacan's interpretation has to do with the way in which Lacan reduces Poe's story to its content but neglects the "scene of writing"[28]—that is, the place of the story's narrator. As explained by Claude Richard, for Derrida, "The exclusion of the narrator of the story . . . allows Lacan to gloss over the linguistic act of telling and to present the 'displacement of the signifier as signified, as the recounted object.' "[29] Lacan's simplification of the story, according to Derrida, allows him to find exactly what he is looking for: castration, understood by Lacan as lack instilled within the subject as part of identity formation, as the truth of Poe's tale. Lacan's reading thus becomes exemplary for Derrida of the ways in which critics impose meanings upon literary texts that the texts themselves resist. Deconstructive close reading, in contrast, demonstrates how texts are always slippery things that inevitably turn back on themselves; every interpretation will thus by necessity be built upon a blind spot, a moment when what the text actually says and what the critic wants it to say are at odds.

And critics have attempted to demonstrate that Derrida himself is not immune to this same blindness. Upping the ante in what has come to be called "The Purloined Poe," Barbara Johnson, in 1977, offered her own reading of Derrida's reading of Lacan's reading of Poe. In Johnson's tour-de-force interpretation, she shows how Derrida repeats the same sins he attributes to Lacan—Derrida neglects Lacan's style (the "frame of reference" of the title of Johnson's essay) and imposes meaning that goes beyond what the text actually says. (Johnson's deconstruction of Derrida's deconstruction of Lacan, however, one might suggest, proves Derrida's larger poststructuralist point that the letter can always not arrive—that meaning arrives only because of the possibility of its going astray.)

Poststructuralist approaches to Poe of course have extended well beyond the nesting doll structure of the Purloined Poe debate. Indeed, Poe has been the poststructuralist gift that keeps on giving, and he has been the beneficiary of a variety of daring close readings and focused analyses of the ways his texts turn back on themselves and frustrate the desire for singular, determinate meaning. Pahl, for example, reads Poe's work, together with that of Hawthorne and Melville, as demonstrating how reading "does not help to expose some hidden depth of meaning but rather covers with a new layer of meaning what is *already* an interpretation, all of which implies that there is no bottom, no ground, to the abyss of signification."[30] Williams similarly undertakes to explore the ways in which Poe's texts resist the "imposition of a single interpretation."[31] In *Poe, Death, and the Life of Writing*, Kennedy adopts a somewhat different tack, exploring—as does Jacques Derrida in his *Of Grammatology* (1967)—the connection between writing and death. "Poe was largely ahead of his time," concludes Kennedy, "intuiting a previously unsuspected linkage between writing and mortality, language and truth." Contextualizing Poe's life and writing in relation to changing attitudes about death, Kennedy asserts that Poe "sensed a momentous cultural transition and projected this awareness in texts which reflect the desperate situation of a subject striving through an always inadequate system of 'mere words' to give coherence to unspeakable fears."[32]

In one of the most audacious examples of deconstructive analysis of Poe, Louis A. Renza, in "Poe's Secret Autobiography," takes as his frame of reference not Derrida but Paul de Man, specifically his 1979 essay "Autobiography as De-Facement" in which de Man renders problematic the distinction between autobiography and fiction. Not only does autobiography entail a construction of the subject in language using the tropes of fiction, but, de Man maintains, all claims of authorship make texts to some extent about their authors: "any book with a readable title-page is, to some extent, autobiographical."[33] Renza's de Manian reading of Poe thus excavates his texts for traces of the author that undo their aesthetic effect. Devices such as puns, jokes, hoaxes, "signatorial anagrams,"[34] and so on interrupt the "spell" of the text, highlighting the text as text, even as they reveal to the "imagined reader the word-mediated traces of its author."[35] Importantly, Renza's reading is not psychoanalytic in the sense of attempting to uncover the true nature of the author through his texts; rather, the texts summon the specter of the man whose story will never be revealed. Poe's "secret autobiographical relation"[36] to his tales is hinted at, but not recoverable. His stories are ghost stories, but "not so much stories about ghosts as stories of the possibility of stories about Poe's autobiographical relation to the 'beautiful' topos that spawned them."[37]

Poe in Postmodern Culture

Renza's discussion of Poe's "secret autobiography" in light of de Man's contention that the distinction between fiction and autobiography is "undecidable"[38] offers a useful segue to a consideration of the ways postmodern culture has imagined, memorialized, commodified, and appropriated Poe for various purposes. This, of course, is the possible fate of any author or artist—not only are the uses to which artistic works can be put once they begin to circulate extremely difficult to control but, as Michel Foucault famously argued, the author or artist becomes in some ways a retrospective invention of the works. That is, reading back from the works, we construct an impression of their creator, what Foucault calls an "author function."[39] Poe, however, becomes an especially juicy subject for such contemplation and reconstruction, not only because of the morbidity of his works but also due to the poignant and salacious details of his life (his conflicts with his adoptive father, his expulsion from the University of Virginia, his problems with alcohol, the death of his wife Virginia) and the questions surrounding his death.

To be fair, by most modern yardsticks of literary merit, Poe certainly deserves his contemporary fame. He pioneered multiple literary genres, his best works are original and elegantly crafted, he contributed important ideas to philosophy and literary criticism, and so on. But Poe is primarily known as a foundational American author of Gothic tales. On the one hand, this emphasis makes Poe compatible with contemporary trends that have moved the Gothic from the periphery to the center of mass culture. Over twenty years ago, Mark Edmundson noted in *Nightmare on Main Street: Angels, Sadomasochism, and the Culture of Gothic* that "American culture at large has become suffused with Gothic assumptions, with Gothic characters and plots."[40] Since then, the Gothic has assumed an even more central place in Western culture. And Poe, as a literary forebear of contemporary tastes in the morbid, has certainly benefitted from the mainstreaming of the Gothic.

On the other hand, Poe's morbidity invites speculation about his personal psychology and transforms him into a text to be interpreted—what kind of person creates such morbid tales? This was the question that, for example, preoccupied Freud's student Marie Bonaparte in *The Life and Works of Edgar Allan Poe: A Psycho-Analytic*

Interpretation, published in 1933 (translated into English in 1949). In Bonaparte's orthodox Freudian approach, she focuses attention in particular on the influence of the early death of Poe's mother on his personal life and literary themes.[41] Kenneth Silverman's *Edgar A. Poe: Mournful and Never-ending Remembrance* shifts the focus to Poe's contentious relationship with his adoptive father, John Allan.[42] For his part, J. Gerald Kennedy in *Poe, Death, and the Life of Writing* looks at Poe's "compulsive interest in the dimensionality of death"[43] as reflecting changing nineteenth-century attitudes about death. In these studies and the many other studies that probe Poe's biography, Poe becomes an interpretation derived from his works in collaboration with the reader or critic's imagination—he is a jointly authored tale.

And Poe's story is an even more tempting—and especially postmodern—one to be told because of his troubled life and the continuing confusion surrounding him. Poe continues to intrigue in part because so much remains mysterious about him, including basic details of his life and precisely how to regard him. As the Edgar Allan Poe Society of Baltimore's page on "Edgar Allan Poe's Problematic Biography" summarizes, "Everything about him is controversial, literally from the place and date of his birth to the exact location and date of his burial"[44]—and, of course, the cause of Poe's death remains contested to this day. This confusion over facts has then been amplified by the multiple reflections and biographies of Poe that construct him very differently. As the Edgar Allan Poe Society explains, "The wide variance among interpretations of Poe's life can be seen clearly in the three most prominent 'camps,' each here named for its originator: The 'Griswold Camp' (which vilifies Poe as a devil), the 'Ingram Camp' (which glorifies Poe as an angel) and the 'Baudelaire Camp' (which glorifies Poe as a devil). To some extent, nearly all biographies of Poe follow or react to this triangle of approaches."[45]

Part of the elusiveness of the "real" Poe is also, as J. Bowers explains, his "rootlessness"—the lack of a "single identifiably 'authentic' home."[46] That Poe lived in various places up and down the East Coast of the United States at different points in his life has spurred a kind of competition among tourist sites in different cities as each seeks to "authenticate itself as the 'real' or 'true' nexus of the author's legacy."[47] Bowers's survey of Poe tourist sites considers attractions in Baltimore, Philadelphia, Richmond, Sullivan's Island in South Carolina, New York City, and Boston—all among the locations visited by J. W. Ocker in his attempt to tell Poe's story "geographically."[48] Ocker opines that a few road trips can allow us not just to learn about Poe, but to "see" and "live"[49] him by walking the same boards he walked on and taking in "[t]he very bed he dreamed in. The very ink from his pens, hairs from his head, and the chapter in which he honeymooned."[50] Bowers concludes the opposite: "Edgar Allan Poe remains a cipher, inaccessible to even his most ardent admirers, despite—or as I will argue, because of—the abundance of locations and attractions dedicated to his legacy."[51]

While the "real" Poe continually escapes, the confirmed facts of his life are of course as romantic and tragic as any novel. What Ocker refers to as the "Myth of Poe" is a construction from these details: "an image of a man tormented by both life and art, a melancholy creature, pathetic, ill-starred, and death-beset, perched precariously on a tight-rope pen, his only salvation from the abyss of suffocating darkness and insanity below. A man whom that darkness eventually overcame in an end so tragic and outré that its details were hidden from history."[52] As Scott Peeples has shown, mostly sympathetic versions of the Poe myth have received extensive elaboration in film. Cinematic representations of Poe's poverty and lack of appreciation during his lifetime, Peeples observes, go back more than a century to D. W. Griffith's seven-minute-long "Edgar Allen [*sic*] Poe" from 1909.[53] Later films, including Harry Lachman's 1942 *The Loves of Edgar Allan Poe*, Fletcher Markle's 1951 *The Man with a Cloak*, and James McTeigue's 2012 *The Raven* (to be discussed more fully later) further elaborated on the myth of Poe as neglected genius and "eternal outsider, loved for having been unloved and highly valuable for having been undervalued."[54]

Poe himself, it is worth noting, began the textualization process by referring to himself in the third person in *Pym*—and by occasionally reviewing his own works anonymously or under a pseudonym.[55] This process of creation and re-creation accelerated after his death as he was variously investigated, celebrated, or castigated by critics and admirers, putting into play different stories of Poe as melancholic lover, debased addict, literary hack, morbid contemplator, neglected genius, and more. In this, Poe himself becomes an exemplary postmodern text, the subject of multiple competing narratives with no way finally to arrive at the Truth. The title of Daniel Hoffman's study of Poe suggests as much: *Poe Poe Poe Poe Poe Poe Poe*. Poe proliferates as stories of Poe and Poe's stories continue to beget more stories.[56] The inconclusiveness of Poe's *Pym* prompted Jules Verne to write a sequel, *Le Sphinx des glaces* (*The Sphinx of the Ice Fields*) (1897), and Mat Johnson to compose a novel of Antarctic exploration, called *Pym* (2011), that playfully proposes that Poe's *Pym* is a true story, even as it offers a more serious consideration of the novel's racial politics.[57] The Wikipedia page "Edgar Allan Poe in Popular Culture" documents not only the hundreds of transmedial adaptations of Poe's stories into comics, film, television, radio, theater, and so on, but the many times Poe has also himself appeared as a character in such works.[58] The edited collection of scholarly essays on Poe adaptations, *Adapting Poe: Re-Imaginings in Popular Culture*, makes clear Poe's sprawling contemporary reach, from heavy metal to comics to Fellini and James Cameron.[59]

Much of the preceding discussion comes together in the 2012 film *The Raven*, directed by James McTeigue and starring John Cusack—a film that is admittedly far more interesting to think about in relation to Poe and postmodernism than it is to watch. *The Raven* not only invents answers for various curious details surrounding Poe's final days as it elaborates on the Myth of Poe, but also showcases Poe as a postmodern hero who writes himself into being as his fictions become real and he becomes fictionalized. In the film, Poe (Cusack) finds himself pursuing a serial killer whose murders are modeled after violent scenes in Poe's own stories, including "The Murders in the Rue Morgue" and "The Pit and the Pendulum." (In an inspired bit of ghoulish humor, the Pendulum scene has Rufus Griswold's biting words come back to haunt him as he is literally cut in half!) The ante is upped in the film when Poe's secret fiancé Emily Hamilton (Alice Eve) is kidnapped at a "Masque of the Red Death"-inspired costume ball, and the killer demands that Poe write and publish a new story in which he works out how she will be returned. Various clues related to Poe's stories lead Poe to confront the film's villain, printer's devil Ivan Reynolds (Sam Hazeldine), and—as he writes in his "new" tale—Poe agrees to exchange his life for Emily's. After drinking poison, Poe is given a last clue from "The Tell-Tale Heart," which leads him to discover the still-alive Emily prematurely interred beneath the floorboards. Poe then wanders off in a delirious state and dies after attempting to tell those who assist him that the murderer is Reynolds.

While the movie received tepid responses at best (it has only a 22 percent fresh rating from critics on the Rotten Tomatoes site, where the Critics' Consensus is "Thinly scripted, unevenly acted, and overall preposterous"[60]), this big-budget film nevertheless provides an example of postmodern historiographic metafiction that scuttles the distinctions between fact and fiction even as it showcases Poe's twenty-first-century ascendancy. Taking a cue from *Pym, The Raven* has John Cusack playing Poe—not the "actual" Poe, however, but a Hollywood invention that freely mingles biographical facts (often included as a kind of "Easter Egg" for those in the know, such as the reference to Griswold) with fiction. Within the film, Poe essentially becomes a character in one of his own stories, forced by a madman to see his fictions realized as fact, and then to compose a new work of fiction as a response to the dramatizations of his fictions. Poe, in essence, ends up authoring the story of himself as he constructs a narrative that imagines the protagonist bartering his life for that of the prematurely interred heroine—and this is indeed the outcome of the film as his fiction again directs reality and becomes fact. The film both begins and ends with the words of Poe, whose fate is foretold as the film opens with a title card announcing, "On October 7, 1849, Edgar Allan Poe was found, near death, on a park bench in Baltimore, Maryland. The last days of his life remain a mystery." Poe within the film simultaneously writes himself into and out of being, and in exploring the last days of Edgar Allan Poe and offering answers to the mysteries surrounding them, the film capitalizes on and expands the Myth of Poe, transforming him even more fully into a tragic hero, while at the same time feeding long-running concerns that violent and macabre literary (and, for that matter, cinematic) content can itself serve as the inspiration for gruesome acts. More than that, though, the film catapults the viewer into a fully textual world that ironically asserts the possibility of correct interpretation on the level of narrative even as it undoes that certainty on the level of form—that is, it is a fiction asserting the possibility of the recovery of the truth about Poe. Instead of the truth, however, what the film finally offers us is the only thing it can—another packaging of Poe prepared, like the image of Poe on the Barnes & Noble shopping bag, in an effort to suit modern tastes.

But this is exactly what critics adopting poststructuralist approaches to Poe's fiction have maintained all along—that his stories (and stories in general) resist the imposition of a single meaning, that definitive meaning is always deferred, that letters can always go astray. Perhaps we can then say of Poe himself what Pahl says in relation to Poe's *Pym*: "Poe may well anticipate his readers—his decipherers—insofar as his text, by creating a gap or space into which (let us say) the reader must voyage, makes ironic the very idea of bringing the text to a successful closure, with a correct meaning."[61] Like Pym's story, Poe's, too, is incomplete—and our attempts to finish it make a mockery of completion. Poe himself then perhaps can be considered as an unfinished postmodern letter that arrives only by having gone astray in the first place.

Notes

1. See Scott Peeple's third chapter, "Out of Space, Out of Time: From Early Formalism to Deconstruction," in *The Afterlife of Edgar Allan Poe* (Rochester, NY: Camden House, 2004), 63–92.
2. J. W. Ocker, *Poe-Land: The Hallowed Haunts of Edgar Allan Poe* (New York: The Countryman Press, 2015), 11.
3. Ocker, *Poe-Land*, 12.
4. Daniel Royot, "Poe's Humor," in *The Cambridge Companion to Edgar Allan Poe*, ed. Kevin J. Hayes (Cambridge: Cambridge University Press, 2002), 63.
5. Brian McHale, *Postmodernist Fiction* (London: Routledge, 1987). See particularly, "Worlds in Collision," 59–72.
6. Linda Hutcheon, *A Poetics of Postmodernism: History, Theory, Fiction* (New York: Routledge, 1988), 5.
7. McHale, *Postmodernist Fiction*, 75.
8. McHale, *Postmodernist Fiction*, 79.
9. Dennis Pahl, *Architects of the Abyss: The Indeterminate Fictions of Poe, Hawthorne, and Melville* (Columbia: University of Missouri Press, 1989), vii.
10. Colin Martindale, "Archetype and Reality in 'The Fall of the House of Usher,'" *Poe Studies* 5, no. 1 (June 1972): 9–11, https://www.eapoe.org/pstudies/ps1970/p1972103.htm.
11. Pahl, *Architects of the Abyss*, 7.
12. J. Gerald Kennedy, *Poe, Death, and the Life of Writing* (New Haven, CT: Yale University Press, 1987), 54.
13. Kennedy, *Poe, Death, and the Life of Writing*, 147.
14. John Carlos Rowe, *Through the Custom-House: Nineteenth-Century American Fiction and Modern Theory* (Baltimore: The Johns Hopkins University Press, 1982), 95.
15. John T. Irwin, *American Hieroglyphics: The Symbol of the Egyptian Hieroglyphics in the American Renaissance* (New Haven, CT: Yale University Press, 1980), 115.
16. Kennedy, *Poe, Death, and the Life of Writing*, 148.
17. Pahl, *Architects of the Abyss*, xiii.
18. Pahl, *Architects of the Abyss*, 55.
19. McHale, *Postmodernist Fiction*, 75.
20. Louis A. Renza, "Poe's Secret Autobiography," in *The American Renaissance Reconsidered: Selected Papers from the English Institute, 1982–1983*, ed. Walter Benn Michaels and Donald E. Pease (Baltimore: The Johns Hopkins University Press, 1985), 61.
21. Michael J. S. Williams, *A World of Words: Language and Displacement in the Fiction of Edgar Allan Poe* (Durham, NC: Duke University Press, 1988), 8.
22. Renza, "Poe's Secret Autobiography," 61.
23. John P. Muller and William J. Richardson, "Lacan's Seminar on 'The Purloined Letter': Overview," in *The Purloined Poe: Lacan, Derrida, and Psychoanalytic Reading*, ed. John P. Muller and William J. Richardson (Baltimore: The Johns Hopkins University Press, 1988), 62.

24. Muller and Richardson, "Lacan's Seminar on 'The Purloined Letter,'" 53.
25. Barbara Johnson, "The Frame of Reference: Poe, Lacan, Derrida," in *The Purloined Poe*, 248.
26. Slavoj Žižek, *Enjoy Your Symptom! Jacques Lacan In Hollywood and Out* (New York: Routledge, 1992), 13.
27. Jacques Derrida, "The Purveyor of Truth," trans. Alan Bass, in *The Purloined Poe*, 187.
28. Johnson, "The Frame of Reference," 218.
29. Claude Richard, "Destin, Design, Dasein: Lacan, Derrida and 'The Purloined Letter,'" *The Iowa Review* 12, no. 4 (Fall 1981): 6.
30. Pahl, *Architects of the Abyss*, xiii.
31. Williams, *A World of Words*, 8.
32. Kennedy, *Poe, Death, and the Life of Writing*, 185.
33. Paul de Man, "Autobiography as De-Facement," *MLN* 94, no. 5 (December 1979): 922.
34. Renza, "Poe's Secret Autobiography," 67.
35. Renza, "Poe's Secret Autobiography," 62.
36. Renza, "Poe's Secret Autobiography," 70.
37. Renza, "Poe's Secret Autobiography," 70.
38. de Man, "Autobiography as De-Facement," 921.
39. Michel Foucault, "What is an Author?," in *The Foucault Reader*, ed. Paul Rabinow (New York: Pantheon Books, 1984), 107.
40. Mark Edmundson, *Nightmare on Main Street: Angels, Sadomaschism, and the Culture of Gothic* (Cambridge, MA: Harvard University Press, 1997), xii.
41. Marie Bonaparte, *Edgar Poe: Étude Psychanalytique*, avant-propos de Sigmund Freud, 2 vols. (Paris: Les Editions Denoël et Steele, 1933); *The Life and Works of Edgar Allan Poe: A Psycho-Analytic Interpretation*, foreword by Sigmund Freud, trans. John Rodker (London: Imago Publishing, 1949).
42. Kenneth Silverman, *Edgar A. Poe: Mournful and Never-ending Remembrance* (New York: HarperCollins, 1991).
43. Kennedy, *Poe, Death, and the Life of Writing*, 3.
44. "Edgar Allan Poe's Problematic Biography," Edgar Allan Poe Society of Baltimore, updated September 17, 2017, https://www.eapoe.org/geninfo/poebiog.htm.
45. "Edgar Allan Poe's Problematic Biography."
46. J. Bowers, "Chasing Edgar: The Tourist Rhetoric of the Poe Bicentennial," *Poe Studies* 43 (2010): 60.
47. Bowers, "Chasing Edgar," 60.
48. Ocker, *Poe-Land*, 12.
49. Ocker, *Poe-Land*, 13.
50. Ocker, *Poe-Land*, 14.
51. Bowers, "Chasing Edgar," 60.
52. Ocker, *Poe-Land*, 12.
53. Scott Peeples, "'That Name'll Never Be Worth Anything': Poe's Image on Film," *The Edgar Allan Poe Review* 16, no. 2 (2015): 171.
54. Peeples, "'That Name'll Never Be Worth Anything,'" 181.
55. See "Edgar Allan Poe," The Edgar Allan Poe Society of Baltimore, updated November 14, 2014, https://www.eapoe.org/people/poeedgal.htm.
56. Daniel Hoffman, *Poe, Poe, Poe, Poe, Poe, Poe, Poe* (Baton Rouge: Louisiana State University Press, 1972).

57. Jules Verne, *Le Sphinx des glaces* (Paris: Pierre-Jules Hetzel, 1897); Mat Johnson, *Pym* (New York: Spiegel & Grau, 2011).
58. Wikipedia, s.v. "Edgar Allan Poe in popular culture," last modified March 9, 2018, https://en.wikipedia.org/wiki/Edgar_Allan_Poe_in_popular_culture.
59. Dennis R. Perry and Carl H. Sederholm, eds., *Adapting Poe: Re-Imaginings in Popular Culture* (New York: Palgrave Macmillan, 2012).
60. "The Raven (2012)—Rotten Tomatoes," Rotten Tomatoes, accessed January 6, 2018, https://www.rottentomatoes.com/m/the_raven_2012/.
61. Pahl, *Architects of the Abyss*, 42.

Bibliography

Bowers, J. "Chasing Edgar: The Tourist Rhetoric of the Poe Bicentennial." *Poe Studies* 43 (2010): 59–82.

Derrida, Jacques. "The Purveyor of Truth." Translated by Alan Bass. In *The Purloined Poe: Lacan, Derrida, and Psychoanalytic Reading*, edited by John P. Muller and William J. Richardson, 173–212. Baltimore: The Johns Hopkins University Press, 1988.

Johnson, Barbara. "The Frame of Reference: Poe, Lacan, Derrida." In *The Purloined Poe: Lacan, Derrida, and Psychoanalytic Reading*, edited by John P. Muller and William J. Richardson, 213–251. Baltimore: The Johns Hopkins University Press, 1988.

Kennedy, J. Gerald. *Poe, Death, and the Life of Writing*. New Haven, CT: Yale University Press, 1987.

Lacan, Jacques. "Seminar on 'The Purloined Letter.'" Translated by Jeffrey Mehlman. In *The Purloined Poe: Lacan, Derrida, and Psychoanalytic Reading*, edited by John P. Muller and William J. Richardson, 28–54. Baltimore: The Johns Hopkins University Press, 1988.

Ocker, J. W. *Poe-Land: The Hallowed Haunts of Edgar Allan Poe*. New York: The Countryman Press, 2015.

Pahl, Dennis. *Architects of the Abyss: The Indeterminate Fictions of Poe, Hawthorne, and Melville*. Columbia: University of Missouri Press, 1989.

Peeples, Scott. *The Afterlife of Edgar Allan Poe*. Rochester, NY: Camden House, 2004.

Peeples, Scott. "'That Name'll Never Be Worth Anything': Poe's Image on Film." *The Edgar Allan Poe Review* 16, no. 2 (Autumn 2015): 169–183.

Renza, Louis A. "Poe's Secret Autobiography." In *The American Renaissance Reconsidered: Selected Papers from the English Institute, 1982–1983*, edited by Walter Benn Michaels and Donald E. Pease, 58–89. Baltimore: The Johns Hopkins University Press, 1985.

Rowe, John Carlos. *Through the Custom-House: Nineteenth-Century American Fiction and Modern Theory*. Baltimore: The Johns Hopkins University Press, 1982.

Weinstock, Jeffrey Andrew. "Edgar Allan Poe and the Undeath of the Author." In *Adapting Poe: Re-Imaginings in Popular Culture*, edited by Dennis Perry and Carl Sederhom, 13–30. New York: Palgrave, 2012.

Williams, Michael J. S. *A World of Words: Language and Displacement in the Fiction of Edgar Allan Poe*. Durham, NC: Duke University Press, 1988.

CHAPTER 41

POE AND SCIENCE FICTION

PAUL GRIMSTAD

> After reading Edgar Allan Poe. Something the critics have not noticed: a new literary world, pointing to the literature of the twentieth century. Scientific miracles, fables on the pattern of A+B; a clear-sighted, sickly literature. No more poetry, but analytic fantasy.
>
> —"After Reading Edgar Allan Poe,"
> Edmund and Jules de Goncourt,
> July 16, 1856[1]

The Prose of Explanation

Much of Edgar Allan Poe's fiction is built around perilous physical or psychological extremes which are then submitted to an exaggerated rationality that seems meant to get the peril under control. In his tale of a gigantic vortex opening in the ocean and swallowing the ship of a Norwegian fisherman, Poe's mariner calmly describes the action of a cylindrical object in a funnel of water, linking the description to "Archimedes, 'De Incidentibus in Fluido'—lib. 2" (M 2: 593n). While there is no discussion in Archimedes's work of any of the (quite otherworldly) fluid mechanics described in the story, it's a good example of a desperate situation modulating into quasi-scientific explanation. The same pattern forms the core of the first analytical detective story, "The Murders in the Rue Morgue," when a double murder committed by a razor-wielding ape is patiently explained by consulting detective C. Auguste Dupin, whose itemized denouement ends with a clinching citation from Georges Cuvier's 1817 textbook *Règne Animale* (M 2: 559). In the opening section of "The Fall of the House of Usher" a narrator's unnerved contemplation of the bleak estate leads him to speculate that a "mere different arrangement of the particulars of the scene, of the details of the picture, would be sufficient to modify or perhaps to annihilate its capacity for sorrowful impression" (M 2: 398); while in the essay-like "Imp of the Perverse" several examples of willful irrationality—hurling oneself off a precipice; deliberately irritating an interlocutor through needless circumlocution; putting off work one knows must be done; confessing one's guilt when one is in the clear—illustrate, with overdone solemnity, the mental faculty of "perverseness" (M 3: 1223). Even lyric poetry could be for Poe a matter of cool calculation. He claimed, only partly in jest, that "The Raven"—his 1845 poem about a tormented scholar mourning the loss of the "rare and radiant maiden whom the angels named Lenore" (M 1: 365)—had been composed with the inevitability of a math problem.

Despite this recurring pattern—confounding, disturbing, or threatening phenomena rendered reassuringly explicable through heightened rationality—Poe shared with anti-Enlightenment romantics before him reservations about the demystifying power of the natural sciences.[2] In an early sonnet Poe criticized a personified "science"—"Who alterest all things with thy peering eyes"—before posing an anguished question: "Why preyest thou thus upon the poet's heart,/Vulture, whose wings are dull realities?" (M 1: 91). If, as T. O. Mabbott notes, the poem signals Poe's willingness to "disregard scientific fact when fantasy better suits his purpose" (M 1: 90), we might see in the proximity of fact and fantasy a desire, not just to oppose scientific explanation and flights of imagination but to fuse them. While this is not quite the same as claiming that he invented the genre of "science fiction" (in the way that it is a more straightforward matter to say Poe invented detective fiction), in what follows I will treat in some detail Poe's way of bringing the tone of a rational account—the prose of explanation—into the art of fiction and show how this illuminates thinking about the emergence of science fiction as an increasingly codified genre in the late nineteenth and twentieth centuries. From the decisive influence of Poe's "The Unparalleled Adventure of Hans Pfaall," "The Balloon Hoax," and *The Narrative of Arthur Gordon Pym of Nantucket* on Jules Verne's *Voyages extraordinaires* to the reprinting of "The Facts in the Case of M. Valdemar" in the first issue of the pulp magazine *Amazing Stories* and parallel developments in French experimental prose, to the way Poe's analysis of proto-artificial intelligence in his essay "Maelzel's Chess Player" puts in place the basic philosophical intrigue found in everything from Isaac Asimov's robot stories to Philip K. Dick's *Do Androids Dream of Electric Sheep*, Poe's example may be found resurfacing throughout the genre's evolution. In a brief concluding section I consider Poe's cosmological fantasia *Eureka*—which he called a "prose poem"—as his most generalized effort to merge the prose of explanation with the imaginative freedom of lyric poetry.

"The Unparalleled Adventures of Hans Pfaall," *Pym*, and the *Voyages Extraordinaires*

One of the clearest examples in Poe's fiction of the move from perilous experience to calm explanation is found in "The Unparalleled Adventures of Hans Pfaall," a novella-length tale which appeared in the *Southern Literary Messenger* in June 1835. In it, Poe set out to parody the vogue for tales imagining trips to the moon. While the prevailing tone throughout is one of burlesque—Poe is in a comic mode quite different from the gloomier tone of pieces written around the same time, like "Shadow—A Parable" —the tale becomes more and more concerned with giving a plausible account of sailing a balloon to the lunar surface.[3] In a short introduction, Edward Sparhawk, then editor of the *Southern Literary Messenger*, noted how Poe's adventurer "performs impossibilities, and details them with a minuteness so much like truth, that they seem quite probable"; and Arthur Hobson Quinn writes that while "Hans Pfaall" began as a parody of tales of trips to the moon, Poe "could not content himself with mere burlesque" and became drawn to the challenge of creating a "plausible" account.[4]

The central conceit is of a Dutch bellows mender, who, unable to square his debts finds by chance a pamphlet of "speculative astronomy" that arouses in him a talent for mechanical invention, leading him to leave the Earth in a balloon, thus fleeing his creditors (P 1: 392). After exhaustively itemizing Pfaall's invention, Poe comes to the first in a series of life-threatening scenarios: Pfaall's waking up "dangling, at a terrific height . . . by a piece of slender cord [in which his] left foot had become most providentially entangled" (P 1: 397). Upon realizing he is thousands of miles above the surface of the Earth, secured only by an ankle to the basket of a rapidly ascending balloon, Pfaall makes a "calm survey" of the situation:

> I drew up to my eyes each of my hands, one after the other and wondered what occurrence could have given rise to the swelling of the veins, and the horrible blackness of the finger nails. I afterwards carefully examined my head, shaking it repeatedly. . . . It now occurred to me that I suffered great uneasiness at the joint of my left ankle, and a dim consciousness of my situation began to glimmer in my mind. . . . But, strange to say! I was neither astonished nor horror-stricken. . . . For a few minutes I remained wrapped in the profoundest meditation. I have a distinct recollection of frequently compressing my lips, putting my forefinger to the side of my nose, and making use of other gesticulations and grimaces common to men who, at ease in their arm-chairs, meditate upon matters of intricacy and importance. (P 1: 397)

The "profound meditation" in which Pfaall takes stock of his dire situation involves compulsive itemizing of observed facts (swollen hands and blackened fingernails) and a caricaturing of the mannerisms of deep thought (such as "frequently compressing my lips, putting my forefinger to the side of my nose"). While Poe's original plan of burlesque may be heard in these protracted asides, it is not so much a burlesque of this or that particular tale but of scientific explanation itself. As the giving of a reasoned account is made to cast its classificatory attention over everything, rational discrimination becomes strangely liberated; verisimilitude ceases to be merely a matter of technical details (about, say, the requirements of human respiration or the physical operation of balloons)[5] and becomes a springboard to an entirely new kind of explanatory prose.[6]

One of the tale's most dramatic moments—the balloon's fateful release from the Earth's orbit and into the gravitational pull of the moon—might be read as a figure for the freeing of description bound by verisimilar accuracy into an "unparalleled" range of speculative invention.[7] Indeed, the impulse to explain in "Hans Pfaall" finally escapes the frame of fiction altogether. In a long addendum Poe added to the tale in 1840—ostensibly to argue for the superiority of "Hans Pfaall" over that of Richard Adams Locke's "Moon-Story" which appeared in the *New York Sun* a few months after Poe's own moon hoax—Poe goes into painstaking detail about various matters of scientific explanation, presumably in an effort to show the implausibility of Locke's lunar observations. Noting that the telescopic lens detailed in Locke's tale has a "power of 42,000 times," Poe points out that this would not be enough to make possible the "perceiving of flowers" or the "color and shape of the eyes of small birds" on the moon (along with some seven other points). When Poe resumed his critique of Locke six years later in a "New York Literati" piece, he ended on a reluctantly complimentary note, calling Locke a "man of *true* imagination" since his writing contained a "paradoxical compound of coolness and excitability" (ER: 1222)—another way of formulating the coexistence in a single mind of strict rationalism and imaginative freedom.

Not unlike Arthur Conan Doyle's studious reappropriation of "The Murders in The Rue Morgue" and "The Purloined Letter" for his creation of Sherlock Holmes, Jules Verne took Poe's balloon adventure as a model for his own *Voyages extraordinaires*. Verne outlined his debt to Poe in an essay "Edgar Poe et ses oeuvres," which appeared in the *Musée des Familles* in the spring of 1864.[8] The essay is taken up with close readings of *l'esprit d'analyse* in three of Poe's tales, about a third of which is devoted to "Hans Pfaall." After reiterating the biographical introduction Charles Baudelaire added to his translation of *Histoires extraordinaires* and noting how these translations first gave him a sense of what might be possible in the literature of speculative romance, Verne toggles between hero worship and fault-finding, listing Poe's errors of physics.[9] There is, for example, a contradiction in the account of what is needed to keep a balloon (*aerostat*) in flight and the requirements of human respiration (it seems Verne saw through Poe's partly fabulous "condenser"); and a confusion in the explanation of the way air pressure would not continue to propel a balloon beyond a certain altitude, such that Poe must "enter into bizarre discussions" held together by "rigorous illogic."[10] But Verne praises the overall effect of the tale, calling it a "*voyage extraordinaire*," a phrase he will give to his own series of adventure novels, one of which, *De la terre à la Lune* (1865), directly cites "Hans Pfaall."

Still fascinated by the possibilities of Poe's example twenty years after the article in the *Musée des Familles*, Verne wrote in a letter to his bother Paul in 1896 that he was "taking as [a] point of departure one of the strangest works of Edgar Allan Poe," admitting that he has "profited from all of Poe's writing . . . and in particular the idea at the center of [*The Narrative of Arthur Gordon*] *Pym* [that] what everybody has taken to be a fiction was in fact a reality."[11] Verne refers to the way *The Narrative of Arthur Gordon Pym* is introduced by an ingenious metafictional preface in which "A.G. Pym" recounts how a Richmond editor, a certain "Mr. Poe," came to him with the plan of publishing an account of his Antarctic adventure in the *Southern Literary Messenger*. When Pym declines to have his adventures made public, Poe suggests they print it "under the garb of fiction" (P 1: 55). What results from this through-the-looking-glass set-up is Poe's longest and most overtly episodic fiction, and one which exploits to the fullest the narrative tension between extreme experience and rational explanation. When, early in the novel, Pym suffers alarming injury—he is pierced through the neck by a copper bolt and pinned to the hull of a boat—the event is reported as if the injury were not his own: "the body of a man was seen to be affixed in the most singular manner to the smooth and shining bottom [of the vessel]" (P 1: 62). But soon the apparently life-threatening wound is dismissed as looking worse than it actually is, with Pym saying that it "proved to be of little consequence, and I soon recovered from its effects" (P 1: 64).[12] One of the strangest episodes in the novel, and in all of Poe's writing, is the discovery on the Antarctic continent of a bizarre water-like substance, whose properties Pym observes and scrupulously records:

> At first sight, and especially in cases where little declivity was found, it bore resemblance, as regards consistency, to a thick infusion of gum Arabic in common water. . . . It was *not* colourless, nor was it of any one uniform colour—presenting to the eye, as it flowed, every possible shade of purple, like the hues of changeable silk. . . . Upon collecting a basinful, and allowing it to settle thoroughly, we perceived that the whole mass of liquid was made up of a number of distinct veins . . . . Upon passing the blade of a knife athwart the veins, the water closed over it immediately . . . [and] in withdrawing it, all traces of the passage of the knife were instantly obliterated. If, however the blade was passed down accurately between the two veins, a perfect separation was effected, which the power of cohesion did not immediately rectify. (P 1: 171–172)

Here careful attention leads to a kind of description in which lucidity and thoroughness do not end up explaining anything, but rather leave the object just as mystifying as it seemed upon first encountering it. The effect is of a patient detailing an apparently natural phenomenon that nevertheless persists in defying our understanding.

Another of Poe's extraordinary voyages that directly influenced Verne was "The Balloon Hoax," which appeared in the April 1844 edition of *New York Sun*. It was the first thing Poe published when he arrived in Manhattan from Philadelphia, looking for work as a freelance journalist. It is indeed a "hoax": Poe wrote the tale as an "actual" account of the first crossing of the Atlantic in a balloon, as excerpted from the journals of balloonist Monck Mason. As with "Hans Pfaall," Poe borrowed heavily from existing pamphlet literature to build up a texture of verisimilitude.[13] The concern with creating an effect of reality in "The Balloon Hoax" is almost coercive in its insistent rhetoric, with Poe turning fastidious specifications of flying machinery into a remarkable verisimilar illusionism. If the invention propelling the hoax is the balloon's "archimedean screw," the great irony of the story is that it is precisely the *malfunction* of this mechanism—"the steel rod connecting the spring with the propeller was suddenly jerked out of place . . . and in an instant hung dangling out of reach, from the pivot of the axis of the screw" (M 3: 1077)—that leads Mason and his fellow aeronauts to abandon their original plan of flying from England to Paris, and to follow a new course across the Atlantic to South Carolina.

"The Facts in the Case of M. Valdemar," *Amazing Stories*, and *Locus Solus*

Poe devoted a number of stories to the pseudo-science of mesmerism, the most striking and successful of which, "The Facts in the Case of M. Valdemar" (1845), mixes different prose styles to produce a stereoscopic effect of scientific authority. These include the title's economical stroke of veracity ("The Facts in the Case"); the tone of medical jargon ("the left lung had been for eighteen months in a semi-osseous or cartilaginous state"); alarmed testimony of speech heard from beyond the grave ("the sound was one of... wonderfully, thrillingly distinct, syllabification"); and the tale's infamous last lines in which medical jargon and sensational empiricism merge into something grotesquely concrete: "Upon the bed... there lay a nearly liquid mass of loathsome—of detestable putridity" (M 3: 1243). Poe's virtuosic manipulation of prose technique leads to the creation of a different sort of verisimilitude: here it is not so much an accumulation of discretely observed facts but the *tone* of a scientific report (not unlike the scholarly essay on the difference between "analysis" and "calculation" which prefaces "The Murders in the Rue Morgue"; or the expository essay on the faculty of "the perverse"). Mabbott's variations indicate that Poe had used "putrescence" for the tale's last word in its first three printings (from 1845 to 1848) but changed it to "putridity" for its ultimate inclusion in his *Works* in 1850—evidence that a keen pursuit of *le mot juste* was part of Poe's search for just the right effect.

Poe's tale forms a central thread in the history of science fiction. Along with Verne's "Off on a Comet" and H. G. Wells's "The Accelerator," "The Facts in the Case of M. Valdemar" was reprinted in the first issue of *Amazing Stories* (with Poe's name misspelled on the cover!). There is perhaps no more historically consequential example of the formation of science fiction as a genre than this April 1926 issue of *Amazing Stories*. The magazine came into existence in part due to the entrepreneurial zeal of Luxembourg émigré and radio enthusiast Hugo Gernsback. Gernsback began life in the United States selling mail-order radio parts and starting magazines like *Modern Electrics* and *Radio News* and, wishing to add a fiction wing to his burgeoning magazine empire, launched *Amazing Stories* under the motto "Extravagant Fiction Today—Cold Fact Tomorrow." Poe had already invented the kind of writing Gernsback was looking for, which he somewhat clumsily called "scientifiction" and which he described as "romance intermingled with scientific fact and prophetic vision."[14] Poe, Gernsback went on, "may well be called the father of scientifiction. It was he who really originated the romance, cleverly weaving into and around the story a scientific thread"—just the mixture of extravagant fiction and cold fact that Verne had taken from the example of Poe's *Pym*, "Hans Pfaall," and "The Balloon Hoax." Because "Valdemar" was short, it compactly delivered its sensational punch—part science-fantasy, part hoax "case study," and it worked perfectly in Gernsback's pulp magazine.

In transatlantic counterpoint with the rise of the pulps in the United States, a different sort of science-fantasy emerged in Paris. The inherent "avant!" of futurist speculation resonated with a French avant-garde weaned on Verne, while the tone and language of natural science was beginning to be submitted to stranger experiments, without any corresponding concern with verisimilitude. Writing under the pseudonym "Dr. Faustroll," Alfred Jarry devised the discipline of "Pataphysics," which he described as the "science of imaginary solutions." Of Jarry's literary vision Roger Shattuck has written that it was "lucid to the point of hallucination"[15]—an apt encapsulation of the fusion of imaginative wildness and rationalist clarity I have been focusing on in Poe, and a fitting description of another writer of the period much more fundamentally indebted to Verne: Raymond Roussel. He read the *Voyages extraordinaires* aloud as a child before assembled guests and family members as if it were religious ritual, and later said that he believed Verne to be the "greatest literary genius of all time."[16] It was above all Verne's byzantine mechanical contraptions that captivated Roussel and led to his own unforgettably strange fictional machines. The central character of his novel *Locus Solus* (1914) is the solitary "scientist, magician and illusionist" Martial Canterel, and the book consists entirely of an unnamed narrator's first-person report as Canterel gives him a tour around his estate, demonstrating his various inventions.[17] One of these is an aerial machine quite different from the vessels Poe cooked up from the pamphlets of antebellum balloonists: a wind-powered magnet which sails around in accord with meteorological calculations, picking up individual teeth from the thousands of specimens Canterel has distributed over his vast lawn (he has also invented a method for the painless extraction of teeth). Due to Canterel's ingenious programming, the machine gradually arranges the teeth into a finely detailed mosaic.[18]

After seeing a dramatic adaptation of *Locus Solus* in 1923 (one wonders how a flying magnet building a mosaic was represented on the stage), Edouard Dujardin wrote in the *Revue de l'époque* of being struck by a mind that was "like that of Edgar Allan Poe: an idea of logical order, normally of a scientific kind, is driven to its furthest reaches with a hallucinatory accuracy of detail."[19] While that is again the merger of imaginative fantasy and logical rigor I have been identifying as the distinguishing mark of Poe's prose, in fact the affinity between Poe and Roussel is much more intimate than Dujardin suggests. Like Poe, Roussel had a zeal for describing how he composed his works. The essay mentioned earlier, in which Poe claimed he had composed his poem "The Raven" with "the precision and rigid consequence of a mathematical problem" (ER: 15), finds its analogue in Roussel's *Comment j'ai écrit certains de mes livres* (1932), a posthumously published book in which he revealed that the inventions described in *Locus Solus* were not at all flights of unhinged fancy but had been arrived at through a stringent and methodical *procédé*. This involved finding homonymic phrases with completely different meanings which were then "phonetically transmogrified" into poles to be connected with narrative.[20] Roussel's *procédé* amounts to an extreme version of Poe's description in "The Philosophy of Composition" of how he arrived at the ideal phoneme for the expression of "*Mournful and Never-ending Remembrance*" (the sound *-or*) (ER: 25): a sonic constraint not unlike those Roussel used for producing "rimes de faits" or rhyming events.

Such literary method—we might even call it a science of fiction—gives the feeling of endlessly extendable tiers of explanation, a vertigo of analysis quite different from the inductive methods of the natural sciences. Both the tales found in Gernsback's *Amazing Stories* and Roussel's experimental novels seem presciently identified in the Goncourt brothers' account of reading Poe in 1856: a literature pointing to the twentieth century and premised on "analytic fantasy."[21]

"Maelzel's Chess-Player" and the Fiction of Artificial Intelligence

Perhaps the most consequential of Poe's writings for the evolution of science fiction as a genre was not a work of fiction at all but a journalistic exposé. About six months after the publication of "Hans Pfaall" in the *Southern Literary Messenger*, Poe attended an exhibition of a traveling chess automaton and wrote a long essay about it, which appeared in the *Messenger* in April 1836. The invention of Baron Wolfgang von Kempelen, who designed and built a number of automata and also designed a hearing aid for Beethoven, the machine was sold after Kempelen's death in 1804 to Hungarian mechanist Johann Maelzel. By the time it reached the United States in 1825, Maelzel had streamlined his exhibition into something between a scientific demonstration and a magic show. The size and shape of a large desk, the machine was rolled onto a stage before an assembled audience. Chess pieces were arranged on two boards: one in front of an android seated behind the desk—popularly known as "The Turk" for its turbaned, sultan's attire—and another in front of Maelzel, who stood to the left of the machine. The interior of the desk was displayed by opening three small doors set in its front, revealing clusters of gears and machinery within. After closing the doors, Maelzel would pick a person from the audience to play, who made moves on his chess board, while the Turk made its moves on the desk. The machine won nearly every game, and Poe was fascinated as much by the idea of a piece of mechanism "thinking" as he was by the effect the demonstration had on the audience.

Poe took the mystifying, even creepy, effect of a box of gears beating humans at chess as an invitation to debunk the machine as an illusion. His editorial on Maelzel's exhibition was an eleven-thousand-word tour de force of inductive reasoning and amounts to nothing less than an argument for the impossibility of artificial intelligence.[22] Poe's basic claim is that since mind and mechanism are different in kind, no mere mechanism could exhibit mind-like properties, and therefore the chess machine must be a hoax. By "mind" Poe means something like the real-time, discriminative understanding that would allow, not just for actions that happen to be in accord with the rules of chess, but a deliberate and autonomous *playing* of the game. Poe gets this distinction into view through a contrast with another celebrated mechanism of the time, the "difference engine" of mathematician and mechanical engineer Charles Babbage:

> It will perhaps be said . . . that a machine such as [Babbage's calculating machine] is altogether above comparison with the Chess-Player of Maelzel. By no means—it is altogether beneath it [since] arithmetical or algebraical calculations are, from their very nature, fixed and determinate. Certain data being given, certain results necessarily and inevitably follow. . . . This being the case we can without difficulty conceive the possibility of so arranging a piece of mechanism, that upon starting it in accordance with the data of the question to be solved, it should continue its movements regularly, progressively and undeviatingly towards the required solution. (ER: 1254)

Since arithmetical calculations are "fixed and determinate," there is no contradiction in imagining a piece of mechanism carrying out such operations. But in chess "no one move . . . necessarily follows upon any one other and no especial second move flows of necessity" (ER: 1254). For Poe, no mere mechanism could capture this kind of undetermined sequence since that would require ongoing real-time attention to the game as it is being played.[23] This basic insight—along with some fifteen other points, such as the irregular motions of the Turk's arm when it moved a piece, which Poe thought inconsistent with the idea of pure mechanism—led him to infer correctly that a human mind must be directing the movements of the machine. Remembering his anti-Enlightenment skepticism expressed in the sonnet "To Science" and also his way of building up fictional worlds around the tension between enigma and explanation, Poe begins his essay with a mystifying experience, one apparently of magic, and then anatomizes the experience in a barrage of rational analysis.

While Poe took much of what he knew about the chess automaton (in addition to what he directly observed) from David Brewster's *Letters on Natural Magic*, his speculative philosophizing about mind and mechanism goes beyond the immediate question of the chess machine and anticipates broader inquiries about what exactly constitutes "intelligence."[24] Such questions were by the middle of the twentieth century at the center of both journals of philosophy and a new wave of pulps. The March 1947 issue of *Astounding Science Fiction* featured a story by a young writer and professor of biochemistry, Isaac Asimov, in which the relation of mechanism to mind was imagined, not only as a question of whether or not a machine could play a game, but whether a machine could lie or deceive in an effort to survive.[25] "Little Lost Robot" is a hybrid science fiction/detective story about government-issue androids of the "Nestor" type with superior physical strength and intelligence at least equal to its creators. Like Poe, Asimov merges science and fiction in descriptions of specialized machinery. A minutely detailed account of the contraptions needed for piloting a balloon to the moon; the creation of medical jargon for producing the effect of a fictional case study; the parsing of the difference between mechanism and mind in a chess-playing automaton—this approach, pioneered in Poe, becomes in Asimov's story the simple, spell-casting phrase "positronic brain." Whatever the role of these "positrons" and how they are to power the thinking machinery of the Nestor robots is never spelled out in detail beyond noting that this piece of robotics was so advanced—so *mind*-like—the manufacturers were required to "impression" the robots with a moral code. That code is Asimov's well-known "Three Laws of Robotics":

1. A robot may not injure a human being or, through inaction, allow a human being to come to harm.
2. A robot must obey the orders given it by human beings except where such orders would conflict with the First Law.
3. A robot must protect its own existence as long as such protection does not conflict with the First or Second Laws.[26]

We are in an entirely new sort of predicament here, distinct from Poe's concerns about mind and mechanism. Now we have a genuine artificial brain (its workings however scantily explained), whose mental processes must be curtailed by stated laws in order to maintain the master–slave relations for which the robots have been designed. If positronic brains are sophisticated enough to resent their enslavement, then they must also be sophisticated enough to desire freedom. Does the wish for liberty constitute "intelligence?" As Asimov's Dr. Susan Calvin puts it: "All normal life . . . consciously or otherwise, resents domination. If the domination is by an inferior, or by a supposed inferior, the resentment becomes stronger. Physically, and, to an extent, mentally, a robot—any robot—is superior to human beings. What makes him slavish, then? Only the First Law! Why, without it, the first order you tried to give a robot would result in your death."[27] Here science fiction, perhaps for the first time, goes directly into the ethical issues bound up with artificial intelligence: ensuring machines do not harm humans and other morally relevant beings; ensuring that thinking machines operate safely as they approach humans in intelligence; and how we might assess whether, and in what circumstances, thinking machines have moral status.

Questions of mind and mechanism, and of what is to count as thinking, were very much a part of the broader scientific and philosophical discussion in the mid-twentieth century. Just three years after Asimov's story appeared in *Astounding Science Fiction*, British logician, mathematician, and cryptographer Alan Turing published his epoch-making "Computing Machinery and Intelligence" in the journal *Mind*.[28] Anyone who had been reading American science fiction would have immediately recognized the central concerns of Turing's essay. It is famous for positing a verbal indistinguishability test—now commonly referred to as the "Turing Test"—in which a machine able to trick a human interrogator into believing it is a person may be said to be intelligent. While the notion of verbal behavior as a hallmark of intelligence goes back to Aristotle, it is also linked to Poe's essay on the chess player in the way it imagines criteria for assessing whether a machine is capable of thought (for Poe it was the discriminative attention that allowed one to play a game like chess). In fact, Turing worked out various chess-playing algorithms while working as a cryptographer at Bletchley Park during World War II (where he played a decisive role in cracking the German Enigma cipher), yet the example of a machine thinking changes between Poe's and Turing's essays from playing a game to carrying on a conversation. Is carrying on a conversation the same *kind* of thing as playing a game? It was a question that Turing's sometime philosophy professor at Cambridge, Ludwig Wittgenstein, would make a central part of his later work in the *Philosophical Investigations.*

One of the more remarkable adaptations of Turing's questions into science fiction narrative was Philip K. Dick's 1968 masterpiece *Do Androids Dream of Electric Sheep?* What Asimov sketchily called a "positronic brain" Dick elaborates into the more sophisticated "Nexus 6 Replicant"—a being virtually indistinguishable from a human, which passes the Turing Test and then some:

> The Nexus-6 [android] had two trillion constituents plus a choice within a range of ten million possible combinations of cerebral activity. In .45 of a second an android equipped with such a brain structure could assume any one of fourteen basic reaction postures . . . no intelligence test would trap such an [android].[29]

Asimov's brisk signposting is given more flesh here, and Poe's concern with fastidious verisimilitude returns in Dick's hyperspecificity. While Dick's brain specs render moot Turing's test for verbal behavior—the Nexus 6 not only converses convincingly but gets bored, flirts, makes witty quips, and improvises lyric verse—the near future imagined in the novel posits a test appropriate for the new technology: the Voight-Kampf empathy test. Something like a synthesis of the Turing Test and a psychoanalytic session, the Voight-Kampf test involves posing a series of questions meant to provoke an emphatic response, often involving scenarios in which animals are treated cruelly.[30] As with Asimov's "Three Laws," we have moved beyond mere rational capacity (calculating, following rules) into something messier and more human: what is it to feel empathy for another being, and which kinds of beings are deserving of our empathic concern?

In the hugely influential film adaptation of Dick's novel *Blade Runner* (1982), directed by Ridley Scott, Nexus 6 replicant Roy Batty demonstrates some capacities of thought not found in the novel. Facing a rapidly approaching expiration date, the escaped slave Batty improvises a lyric commemoration of what he has experienced in the brief time he has been consciously aware:

> *I've seen things you people wouldn't believe:*
> *Attack ships on fire off the coast of Orion,*
> *I've seen C-beams glittering near the Tannhauser gate.*
> *All those memories will be lost*
> *Like tears in rain.*

What are the brain processes that have led, not just to these "memories," but to their being cast in the form of a lyric soliloquy? Here the longing not to be a slave—Batty, along with the other replicants in the story, has mounted a mutiny on an off-world colony and come to Earth seeking both to escape the authorities and to have his life span extended—has become an irreducibly human act of both desire and defiance. We have come a long way from comparing a fraudulent chess-playing automaton to an adding machine (though Scott does ingeniously thread a whole history of automata into *Blade Runner*'s visual logic, as well as a conspicuous network of chess-related allusions). But we have also come full circle, for here is the poetry-making automaton Poe imagined in "The Philosophy of Composition" come to life in the medium of science fiction film.[31]

Eureka, Literary Atomism, and the "Plot of God"

Perhaps the most extravagant of Poe's attempts at a synthesis of science and literature began as a public lecture "On the Cosmology of the Universe" given on February 8, 1848, at the Society Library in New York. There was a snowstorm in New York that Tuesday night and not many people showed up, but one person in the audience remembered that Poe, during the two and half hour performance, "appeared inspired, and his inspiration affected the scant audience almost painfully.... His eyes seemed to glow like those of his own raven."[32] The lecture was turned into a book and brought out by Putnam a year later. He had changed the title to *Eureka: A Prose Poem*, a hybrid genre that, as Daniel Hoffman puts it, "expresses [the] subject indefinitely" while at the same time with "demonstrative clarity."[33]

If *Eureka* is Poe's theory of everything, an attempt to tackle nothing less than "the cause of all things" will require what Poe calls a "mental gyration on the heel": "He who from the top of Ætna casts his eyes leisurely around is affected chiefly by the *extent* and *diversity* of the scene. Only by a rapid whirling on his heel could he hope to comprehend the panorama in the sublimity of its *oneness*" (L1: 7). As with "Hans Pfaall," an admixture of the burlesque seems to jumpstart speculation, as when Poe imagines the discovery of a letter from the year 2848, which "appears to have been found corked in a bottle and floating on the *Mare Tenebrarum*" (L1: 9).[34] The discovery of a message on the "shadowy sea" of the future is an excuse for Poe to launch his erudition from Aristotelian syllogisms, to Kepler's laws of orbital motion, Newtonian mechanics, Champollion's deciphering of the Rosetta stone, John Stuart Mill's system of logic, the value of deductive reasoning versus inductive, and direct borrowings from the American edition of Sir John Herschel's *Treatise on Astronomy*.

When we get to *Eureka*'s actual cosmology we find an idiosyncratic and freely embellished restatement of the nebular hypothesis: the idea that the formation and motions of the solar system were the result of a gradual cooling of matter from out of hot, dense clouds of gas, or nebulae. In *Eureka*, Poe imagines gradations of matter so fine they cease to be particles and become a liquid film saturating everything. This film of unparticled matter is, so Poe conjectures in *Eureka*, a vestige of an initial unity. "Does not so evident a brotherhood among the atoms," asks Poe the cosmologist, "point to a common parentage?" (L1: 33). Here is one of the more prescient insights in Poe's speculative cosmology: whatever impels the constituent particles toward one another—ether?

action at a distance? gravity?—implies that all the matter in the universe springs from a common source. To update the wording, all the matter in the universe was once a point of infinite temperature and density. Though Poe did not infer that the universe was expanding in all directions (as most cosmologists now believe), he is here nevertheless close to describing the three-degree Kelvin background radiation that astronomers and astrophysicists have come to recognize as one of the sturdier pieces of evidence for the Big Bang.

Poe's search for an ultimate unity amid endless material particulars is intimately bound up with his literary method, as he sought a "theory of the universe that would correlate with his aesthetics."[35] Colin Dayan characterizes this as Poe's "finding a mechanics of the universe that can be replicated in the forms of his writing," amounting to what she calls a "linguistic atomism."[36] Whether it is the itemizing of imaginary machines into their component parts, taking pains to change "putr*escence*" to "putr*idity*" (as Poe had in a final revision of "Valdemar"), or deducing the entire architecture of meaning in "The Raven" from the sound "*—or*," Poe is an atomist in his compositional theory and practice, always in the service of "unity of effect" (ER: 571). Accordingly, he continued to make small changes to *Eureka* nearly up to his death, as when describing the Newtonian principle that would dispel the assumption that universal gravitation should pull atoms toward their centers (and thus the Earth into the Sun). Poe thought it more accurate to write "*ir*radiation" rather than "radiation," nudging the meaning away from "giving off light" and closer to "sending forth from a center" (L1: 135n73). But the correlation between literary art and cosmology exists for Poe on the macro level, too. Referring to Poe's idea of "reciprocity of adaptation" in the cosmos, Paul Valéry sees in that idea a universe "constructed on a plan forming a deep symmetry with the interior structure of our minds."[37] According to Valéry, this "symmetrical causality" was another way of understanding Poe's doctrine of "unity of effect."[38] Poe himself took all this into a practical account of fiction-making—symmetrical causality described the way that, in creating a fiction, "we should aim at so arranging the incidents that we shall not be able to determine, of any one of them, whether it depends from any other or upholds it" (L1: 89). Poe also acknowledges, however, that for a finite intelligence, perfection in this goal was unattainable, but when considered from the scale of the fabricator of the cosmos itself, "The plots of God are perfect. The Universe is a plot of God" (L1: 89).[39]

Poe's lifelong preoccupation with inventing perilous, mysterious, or confounding scenarios only then methodically to itemize and explain these scenarios had far-ranging consequences for genre literature of the twentieth century. Both science fiction and the detective story partake of this logic. In science fiction, the narrative is often buoyed, not by a triumphant rationalism which contains some violent or threatening incident through the power of reason (as it often does in the "Golden Age" inheritors of Poe's Dupin stories), but speculative acts of imagining possible futures from out of reason itself—and which reason might be unable to control or understand. While many of the stories and novels of the "hard" science fiction of the pulps exhibited a techno-utopianism in which the universe is entirely explicable and so technology is uncritically linked to "progress," the strain of science fiction closest to Poe, from Verne to Roussel and on into the philosophy of artificial intelligence, and the high speculation about the ultimate origins of the cosmos, was open and experimental in the sense that the tone of explanation was above all imaginative, and no less scientifically valuable for being imaginative. What Poe said of rival moon hoaxer Richard Adams Locke—that he was a "man of *true* imagination" since his writing contained a "paradoxical compound of coolness and excitability" (ER: 1222)—could of course also be said of Poe himself.

Notes

1. Edmund de Goncourt and Jules de Goncourt, *Pages from the Goncourt Journals* (New York: New York Review of Books, 2007), 19–20.
2. Perhaps the best known of these romanticist reactions was William Blake's rejection of Newtonian physics—which he thought would explain everything and so empty the world of mystery—in the pronouncement: "Art is the Tree of Life. Science is the Tree of Death."
3. One such specimen was "A Voyage to the Moon," which had appeared in the *American Quarterly Review* in 1828. For a thorough and lucid account of the somewhat tangled publication history of "Hans Pfaall," see Maurice Lee, "Genre, Science, and 'Hans Pfaall,'" in this volume.
4. Arthur Hobson Quinn, *Poe: A Critical Biography* (New York: D. Appleton-Century, 1941), 215. The original longhand manuscript of "Hans Pfaall" shows that Poe's concern with verisimilitude extended to the look of the page itself. His precise and miniscule handwriting—stunning in its mechanical uniformity—appears to be an effort to imitate the look of print. See the Department of Literary and Historical Manuscripts (1834–1835), MA950, The Morgan Library, New York.
5. Poe's intricately verisimilar prose is typically built up from found sources and then embellished. Burton Pollin notes how Poe's elaboration in "Hans Pfaall" of an "apparatus for condensation of atmospheric air" is in part derived from the description of how a "condenser consists of a receiver firmly and conveniently fixed, communicating by a tube with one or more condensing syringes," in D. Lardner's *The Cabinet of Natural Philosophy: Hydrostatics and Pneumatics* (London, 1831). Burton adds that Poe's attribution of the invention to a fictional "M. Grimm" links his scientific descriptions to fairy tale. See P 1: 466.
6. Perhaps this is part of what Maurice Lee means when he says that in "Hans Pfaall" neither "scientific writing [nor] literary fiction . . . should be regarded as stable in itself or in relation to the other," in "Genre, Science, and 'Hans Pfaall.'"
7. John Tresch suggests that Poe's choice of the word "unparalleled" signals the way the balloon journey "escapes the coordinate system of the earth (much like the 'Purloined Letter' escapes the grid of the police)," in Tresch, "Extra! Extra! Poe Invents Science Fiction," in *Cambridge Companion to Edgar Allan Poe*, ed. Kevin J. Hayes (New York: Cambridge University Press, 2002), 116. One might extend the idea also to the *Narrative of Arthur Gordon Pym*, in which concentric, ever-narrowing "parallels" propel the narrative toward its strange climax at the "eighty-fourth parallel of southern latitude" (P 1: 53).
8. Verne, "Edgar Poe et ses ouvres," in *Edgar Allan Poe*, ed. Claude Richard (Paris: Éditions de l'Herne, 1998), 322.

9. Charles Baudelaire, "Edgar Poe, sa vie et ses oeuvres," in *Histoires extraordinaires* (Paris: Michel Lévy, 1856).
10. Verne, "Edgar Poe et ses ouvres," 334.
11. Jules Verne, *Voyages extraordinaires*, ed. Jean-Luc Steinmetz and Marie-Helene Huet (Paris: Bibliotheque de la Pléiade, 2012), 1188 (my translation). The work that resulted was Verne's sequel to *Pym*, *Le sphinx des glaces* (*The Sphinx of the Ice Fields*), which explains, in Verne's proto-hard science fiction fashion, the glowing white shroud at the novel's climax: it is in fact a giant magnetized mineral (the "sphinx" of Verne's title).
12. Of this moment in *Pym*, Burton Pollin notes that "anatomically [a] transfixion through the neck by a bolt over one-half inch thick is well-nigh impossible, and surely the reader anticipates death" (P 1: 223n).
13. Poe's main sources for "The Balloon Hoax" are Monck Mason's *Account of the Late Aeronautical Expedition from London to Weilburg, accomplished by Robert Hollond, Esq., Monck Mason, Esq., and Charles Green* and his pamphlet *Remarks on the Ellipsoidal Balloon propelled by the Archimedean Screw, described as the New Aerial Machine.* Poe would have seen the latter reprinted in the February 1844 issue of *Alexander's Express Messenger.* Poe freely embellished these sources and added his own vivid details, such as noting that the balloon was "composed of silk [and] varnished with the liquid gum caoutchouc" (M 2: 1073). For a detailed chronology and analysis of Poe's borrowings from these sources, see Jeffrey A. Savoye, "Meanderings Here and There in Poe's 'Balloon Hoax,'" *The Edgar Allan Poe Review* 18, no. 2 (Autumn 2017): 257–262.
14. Hugo Gernsback, "A New Sort of Magazine," *Amazing Stories* 1, no. 1 (April 1926): 3.
15. Roger Shattuck, introduction to *Exploits and Opinions of Dr. Faustroll, Pataphysician*, by Alfred Jarry (Boston: Exact Change, 1996), vii.
16. Mark Ford, *Raymond Roussel and the Republic of Dreams* (Ithaca, NY: Cornell University Press, 2000), 18.
17. Rayner Heppenstall, *Raymond Roussel: A Critical Study* (Berkeley: University of California Press, 1967), 48.
18. Raymond Roussel, *Locus Solus*, ed. Tiphaine Samoyault (1914; Paris: Flammarion, 2005), 48–61.
19. Cited in Mark Ford, *Raymond Roussel and the Republic of Dreams*, 155. Some years later Michel Leiris listed in his journal a number of affinities he perceived between Poe and Roussel: "a hypertrophied taste for logic; analogy between 'The Philosophy of Composition' and *How I Wrote Certain of My Books* . . . the detective story; cryptograms . . . chess." Michel Leiris, *Roussel & Co.*, ed. Jean Jamin, introduction and annotations by Annie Le Brun (Paris: Fayard, 1987), 102–103 (my translation).
20. Rayner Heppenstall, *Raymond Roussel*, 50. For example, the wind-powered pile driver which assembles a mosaic of human teeth was arrived at by turning the phrase *Demoiselle à prétendent* (a hopeful suitor) into the phonetically similar but semantically unrelated [*Demoiselle*] *à reître en dents* (a soldier rendered in teeth).
21. Edmund de Goncourt and Jules de Goncourt, *Pages from the Goncourt Journals*, 19.
22. Sean Rosenheim says Poe was "striving toward a notion of artificial intelligence" in the essay. See *The Cryptographic Imagination: Secret Writing from Edgar Poe to the Internet* (Baltimore: Johns Hopkins University Press, 1997), 100. If Poe was "striving toward" a notion of artificial intelligence in the essay, he was doing so contrastively, as all his arguments there (and elsewhere) suggest he was what contemporary philosophers of mind would call a "mysterian" about the mind and conscious awareness (i.e., he did not believe consciousness was reducible to physical processes alone).

23. For an account of how logician and founder of American pragmatism Charles S. Peirce worked out the mechanics of a logical deduction machine, and the relation of this work to Poe's essay on the chess machine, see my "Nonreasoning Creatures," in *Experience and Experimental Writing: Literary Pragmatism from Emerson to the Jameses* (New York: Oxford University Press, 2013), 44–68.
24. W. K. Wimsatt points out that much of the material on the chess automaton included in Brewster's *Letters* was itself taken from Robert Willis's 1821 pamphlet *An Attempt to Analyze the Automaton Chess Player of Mr. De Kempelen, with an Easy Method of Imitating the Movements of the Celebrated Figure*, which Brewster probably saw reviewed in the *Edinburgh Philosophical Review* where he was an editor. See W. K. Wimsatt Jr, "Poe and the Chess Automaton," *American Literature* 11, no. 2 (May 1939): 144. Willis's pamphlet was the first writing on the machine to show how a "full grown man could be concealed without detection" in the cabinet. See David Hooper and Kenneth Whyld, eds., *The Oxford Companion to Chess* (New York: Oxford University Press, 1996), 431.
25. It is interesting to note that immediately preceding "Little Lost Robot" in this issue of *Astounding Science Fiction* is a detailed essay about the RCA Icononscope television camera, a good example of how the pulps mixed scientific fantasy with learned nonfiction articles about practical science. See J. J. Coupling, "Less Light, Please," *Astounding Science Fiction* 39, no. 1 (1947): 89–100.
26. Asimov, "Little Lost Robot," *Astounding Science Fiction* 39, no. 1 (March 1947): 113–114.
27. Asimov, "Little Lost Robot," 115–116.
28. A. M. Turing, "Computing Machinery and Intelligence," *Mind* 59, no. 236 (October 1950): 433–460.
29. Philip K. Dick, *Do Androids Dream of Electric Sheep?* in *Four Novels of the 1960s*, ed. Jonathan Lethem (New York: Library of America, 2007), 455.
30. Emmanuel Carrère notes that while working on the novel Dick was "leafing through a collection of essays [and] came across a groundbreaking article written in 1950 by Alan Turing . . . What interested [him] was that Turing had thought a great deal about thinking machines, which were one of Phil's obsessions." See Carrère, *I Am Alive and You Are Dead: A Journey into the Mind of Philip K. Dick*, trans. Timothy Bent (New York: Picador, 2005), 132.
31. A more disturbing example of artificial intelligence manifesting emergent human qualities—not just pride or longing, but malign deception, paranoia, and vengefulness—is the bodiless "HAL 9000 Supercomputer," which carefully plans and carries out a series of murders, in *2001: A Space Odyssey*, directed by Stanley Kubrick (Metro-Goldwyn-Mayer, 1968).
32. Maunsell B. Field, *Memories of Many Men and of Some Women* (New York: Harper & Brothers, 1874), 224.
33. Daniel Hoffman, *Poe, Poe, Poe, Poe, Poe, Poe, Poe* (Baton Rouge: Louisiana State University Press, 1972), 273.
34. As he had in his tales "Ligeia" and "The Fall of the House of Usher" (in which he spliced his own poems "The Conquerer Worm" and "The Haunted Palace," respectively), Poe imported this passage from *Eureka* into a concurrent tale, "Mellonta Tauta," which was not published until 1849 and also involves a comic balloon flight.
35. Robert Jacobs, *Poe: Journalist and Critic* (Baton Rouge: Louisiana University Press, 1969), 414.

36. Colin Dayan, *Fables of Mind: An Inquiry into Poe's Fiction* (New York: Oxford University Press, 1987), 10. Another writer of epic poetry about the origins of the universe, Lucretius, analogizes atoms with the combinatory letters of the alphabet in *De rer.* See Lucretius, *Lucretius: On the Nature of Things*, trans. W. H. D. Rouse, rev. Martin Smith, Loeb Classical Library, rev. ed. (Cambridge, MA: Harvard Universiry Press, 1924), 1:900–910. For analysis of specific examples of how Lucretius gives his atomism specifically literary expression in the poem, see my "Our Better Nature: On a New Verse Translation of *De rerum natura*," *Bookforum* (April/May 2009).
37. Valéry, "Au sujet d'Eurêka," in *Paul Valéry: Œuvres*, ed. Jean Hytier (Paris: Gallimard, Bibliothèque de la Pleiade, 1957), 857. Roger Penrose has more recently described something similar in examples of mathematical insights that arrive in a "flash"—thinking that would seem to manifest a deep symmetry between the structure of the physical world and our minds, in *The Emperor's New Mind: Concerning Computers, Minds and the Laws of Physics* (Oxford: Oxford University Press, 1989), 541–547.
38. Valéry, Paul. "Au sujet d'Eurêka," 857. Valéry believed, somewhat extravagantly, that this radical rethinking of causation accurately anticipates Einsteinian physics.
39. These remarks, slightly altered, first appear in Poe's "Marginalia" for November 1844.

Bibliography

Asimov, Isaac. "Little Lost Robot." *Astounding Science Fiction* 39, no. 1 (March 1947): 111–132.

Dayan, Colin. *Fables of Mind: An Inquiry into Poe's Fiction*. New York: Oxford University Press, 1987.

Dick, Philip K. *Do Androids Dream of Electric Sheep?* New York: Doubleday, 1968.

Gernsback, Hugo, ed. *Amazing Stories* 1, no. 1 (April 1926).

De Goncourt, Jules, and Edmond De Goncourt. *Pages from the Goncourt Journals*. New York: New York Review of Books, 2007.

Roussel, Raymond. *Locus Solus*. Edited by Tiphaine Samoyault. Paris: Flammarion, 2005. First published 1914 by Librairie Alphonse Lemerre (Paris).

Scott, Ridley, dir. *Blade Runner*. Warner Bros., 1982.

Turing, Alan M. "Computing Machinery and Intelligence." *Mind* 59, no. 236 (October 1950): 433–450.

Valéry, Paul. "Au sujet d'Eureka." *La Revue Européenne* (May 1923): 6–18.

Verne, Jules. *Voyages extraordinaires*. Edited by Jean-Luc Steinmetz and Marie-Helene Huet. Paris: Bibliotheque de la Pléiade, 2012.

CHAPTER 42

POE AND THE SCIENCES OF THE BRAIN

PAUL GILMORE

To read Poe from a scientific framework is to confront literary culture's differences and similarities from scientific method and knowledge. Famously, in *Eureka*, Poe attempts to occupy the ground of science, colonizing its reputation for himself a year or so before his death, trying to resurrect some sense of his importance even as he, and other writers, recognized that the empirical sciences were moving to the center stage of intellectual life in the West.[1] While "Sonnet: To Science," from the beginning of his career, can be seen as epitomizing a Romantic rejection of scientific objectivity—a "Vulture, whose wings are dull realities" that "preyest . . . upon the poet's heart"—Poe's oeuvre—and Romanticism as a whole—offers a far different picture of the relationship between science and literature (M 1: 91). In keeping with a range of Romantics from Coleridge to Emerson and Thoreau to Melville, but in his own distinct ways, Poe found the critical apparatus of science to be insufficiently self-critical, and, in response, explored the boundaries of the areas that science, in his time and ours, attempted to explain. In particular, I am interested in what has often been described as one of the most complex networks science has ever encountered: our own brains. In the past two decades, literary scholars have increasingly embraced the modern brain sciences in trying to account for the attraction, pleasures, and features of literature. This exploration is, in many ways, parallel to Poe's own interest in the leading developments of his time, developments that, in the 1830s and 1840s, easily crossed the disciplinary lines that C. P. Snow described as the two cultures in 1959. In what follows, I will describe how Poe both readily embraced and criticized one of the most prominent brain sciences of his age, phrenology, and how that critical engagement might provide a model for literary scholars' relationship to the biological sciences' insights into literary aesthetics now.

Many of Poe's tales and essays regularly consider the workings of the human mind, whether it is "Maelzel's Chess-Player" or "Murders in the Rue Morgue" or "Instinct v. Reason." What is striking about Poe's accounts of the mind's processes is that they are at once predictable and yet irrational, reliable and yet deeply flawed. In "Rue Morgue," for example, Dupin is able to interrupt the narrator's stream of thought because of his ability to predict the circuitous route of his thinking. "The apparently illimitable distance and incoherence between the starting-point and the goal" (M 2: 535) of someone's thinking can be overcome through a combination of close observation, empathic projection, and rational deduction. But in "The Man of the Crowd," no amount of close observation allows the narrator to read the man he has stalked. Despite being in one of those "moods of the keenest appetency, when the film from the mental vision departs" (M 2: 507) and his ability to "frequently read, even in that brief interval of a glance, the history of long years" (M 2: 511) in the faces and bodies of passersby, the narrator can only conclude that the man cannot be read (*er lasst sich nicht lesen* [M 2: 515]). In "Rue Morgue," the narrator suggests that what lies beyond analysis is analysis itself—"The mental features discoursed of as the analytical, are, in themselves, but little susceptible of analysis" (M 2: 527)—yet in the Dupin stories and at most length in *Eureka*, Poe does offer descriptions of analytical processes. Poe, I contend, does not retract the brain from scientific study through a kind of idealism or spiritualism. Rather, in keeping with recent accounts of his radical materialism, Poe explores the material basis of the brain, particularly through his interest in and critique of phrenology.[2] While Edward Reed, among others, has described how the conservative reconstitution after the Congress of Vienna led to a concurrent, politically charged rejection of materialist versions of human consciousness on the continent, in England, and in the United States, phrenology, emerging in the early decades of the nineteenth century, provided an early foundation to modern considerations of brain localization and the now readily accepted version of the self as embrained.[3] Bringing together his comments on phrenology, on the brain, and on scientific method, I will argue that Poe suggests that aesthetic experience emerges from the unpredictable and irrational operations of the brain that science, then and now, has failed to fully comprehend.

Phrenology: "The Most Important" Science

In his review of *Phrenology, and the Moral Influence of Phrenology* by Mrs. L. Miles in the *Southern Literary Messenger* of March 1836, Poe opined that phrenology "has assumed the majesty of a science; and, as a science, ranks among the most important which can engage the attention of thinking beings," both theoretically and practically (ER: 329).[4] Founded by Franz Joseph Gall at the end of the eighteenth century, phrenology—or organologie as Gall called it—came to the forefront in Britain (and then the United States) with the first English version of Gall's *Anatomie et physiologie du système nerveux* in 1815 and the subsequent speaking tours by his aide and partner, J. S. Spurzheim. In Britain, George Combe took the lead among those promoting phrenology against more establishment philosophers and physicians, and his works, especially *Essay on the*

Constitution of Man and Its Relation to External Objects, first published in 1828, broadcast phrenological ideas and ideals throughout the English-speaking world. By 1836, when Poe reviewed Miles's book, phrenology was gaining more and more ground in the United States, with the Fowler family—Orson, Lorenzo, and Lydia—at the lead. From the mid-1830s through the 1850s, the Fowlers, through their publication house in New York, published journals and books on topics such as marriage, temperance, memory, and religion, all grounded in and disseminating their version of phrenology.[5]

Phrenology had three central tenets: (1) the brain is the organ of the mind; (2) the brain is, in fact, not one organ, but multiple organs, each devoted to a specific faculty; and (3) the strength of those organs is determined by their relative size, which, in turn, is reflected in the skull overlying that region of the brain. While often ridiculed as merely the feeling of heads for bumps to determine moral character and mental strengths and weaknesses (the second and third tenets), phrenology's emphasis on brain structure as determining mental functions and, more specifically, on brain localization—the idea that certain regions of the brain are the sites of distinct mental functions—was groundbreaking and became the basis of its lasting influence. The idea that the brain is the organ of the mind may seem undeniable—and was, to some extent, widely accepted in the early nineteenth century—but it was rejected by critics on two grounds: for reducing the soul to a material entity or effect and, less often, for neglecting the dispersal of mental and emotional life throughout the nervous system. By emphasizing the physiological nature of the mind, phrenology moved toward overcoming the mind–body dualism enshrined by Cartesian thought, perhaps reducing the spiritual to the physical, even as most phrenologists worked to mitigate that logical tendency. In this way, as Robert Young contends, phrenology laid the groundwork for the move from investigating psychology primarily through a metaphysical framework to exploring human psychology as founded in biology.[6]

Gall made important contributions to the understanding of brain anatomy, and he grounded much of his thinking in comparative anatomy, examining a wide variety of skulls from different people and animals. He eventually identified twenty-seven mental organs but left open whether that fully described the brain's capacities. His version of phrenology was largely deterministic (as the relative size of different brain organs was fixed at birth) and defined some faculties in altogether negative terms, such as one he sometimes denominated "murder." With Spurzheim, however, phrenologists began to develop the argument that all faculties had their use in human growth ("murder," for example, became "combativeness" or self-defense) and that through exercising or restraining specific faculties one could enhance or retard their development appropriately.[7] Combe and the Fowlers pushed phrenology's use for self-development and regulation even further, most often through a kind of natural theology that posited a benevolent deity had designed a logical world that, if explored and handled rationally, could lead to human freedom and happiness. As Combe insisted, "God must have arranged the inherent constitution of man, and that of the world, in such a manner as to admit of their being obeyed,—and not only so, but to render men happy in proportion as they should practise, and miserable as they should neglect them."[8] For Combe and most phrenologists of the 1830s and 1840s, their science was essential due to its ability to determine the inherent constitution of man so that humankind could properly behave along the lines dictated by God and reason. Thus, according to Combe, "it is obvious that, if the science of Mind, were in the same state of forwardness as Chemistry or Natural Philosophy, society would now be reaping these fruits of its cultivation."[9]

As much as Combe and others emphasized the practical impact of their work, they repeatedly attempted to define their endeavors as an empirical science. Yet after Gall, phrenologists, as a whole, showed little to no interest in actual experimentation or in anatomical studies. As John van Wyhe has recently argued, "Phrenology was not generally a research programme. Phrenologists did not conduct experiments to determine if the phrenological organs were accurately identified. A search for new cerebral organs was not a significant part of phrenology."[10] Combe and others contended that observations and experiments on the brain could potentially determine how it works but not what it does, just as dissecting the tongue might give us insight into how it works as a muscle but would do nothing to reveal its functions in human life.[11] In the preface to the fifth edition of *A System of Phrenology* (1843), Combe defined science as "a correct statement, methodically arranged, of facts in nature accurately observed, and of the inference from them logically deduced." He goes on, however, to distinguish "*exact*" sciences, such as mathematics and chemistry, from "*estimative*" ones like phrenology, which "being a branch of physiology . . . like medical science rests on evidence which can be observed and *estimated* only."[12] Such sciences could provide accurate but not exact descriptions and inferences about the world by drawing on observations even if they could not conduct direct experiments.

These questions, about how exact science had to be in order to be reliably predictive and how one moved from observations to "logically deduced" laws, energized the discussions about scientific method during this period and, I will argue, are essential to understanding Poe's engagement with phrenology and science more broadly in articulating his aesthetic project. Most prominently, William Whewell and John Stuart Mill debated these questions over two decades through the different editions of Whewell's *Philosophy of the Inductive Sciences* (first published in 1840) and Mill's *System of Logic* (first published in 1843). Where Whewell attempted to establish a foundation for linking induction and deduction, Mill addressed what he saw as Whewell's apriorism, his abandonment of induction for a kind of intuitionism. Best known now for coining the term "scientist," Whewell placed what he called the "fundamental antithesis" at the center of his philosophy of science. He articulates this antithesis with a multiplicity of pairs—things and thoughts, induction and deduction, facts and theories, sensations and ideas, objective and subjective, matter and form. One of his main ideas, which has led to readings of him as a Kantian, is that "Our Sensations require Ideas to bind them together, namely, Ideas of space, time, number, and the like."[13]

Mill saw this acknowledgment of the mind's more active role in discovering truth as undermining Whewell's inductive philosophy and in turn attempted to show how even the most fundamental ideas, such as the notion of causation or the uniformity of nature, derived from experience. He defined causation as simply the invariability of one phenomenon following another, rejecting the idea of some "mysterious and most powerful tie" that would allow or compel us to "ascend higher, into the essences and inherent constitution of things, to find the true cause, the cause which is not only followed by, but actually produces, the effect."[14] Whewell's acknowledgment of the active role theory and preconceptions play in scientific discovery can be seen as a precursor to critiques of naïve scientific empiricism. But as Laura Snyder has fully described, his philosophy of science was grounded in his natural theology and his faith that through the progressive nature of the scientific mind's engagement with the world we could discover the fundamental laws set in place by God that governed the universe. For Whewell, then, science held the possibility of revealing the truth about "the causal structure of the physical world," while for Mill our empirical research allows us to generalize about phenomena, producing scientific laws, but it does not grant us final access to the underlying structure of the physical world or to reasonable hypotheses concerning unobserved phenomena.[15]

Speculative Deductions and Intuitive Leaps

It is within this context of epistemological debates over the nature of true science that I want to return to Poe's engagement with phrenology and his broader consideration of epistemology in *Eureka* and in his literary criticism.[16] In *Eureka*, Poe offers some of his most explicit commentary on epistemology through a letter from the year 2848 in which the writer describes the backward thinking of Poe's present (this letter appears almost verbatim in "Mellonta Tauta"). The writer specifically alludes to Mill's *Logic*, criticizing his notion of axiomatic truth. While Mill rejects the idea that an axiom can be founded in our inability to imagine things otherwise, Poe's writer insists that this is actually the basis of Mill's axiom that " 'Contradictions cannot *both* be true—that is, cannot coexist in nature,' " so that "a tree must be either a tree or *not* a tree—that it cannot be at the same time a tree and not a tree" (L1: 13). Poe's writer from the future concludes that, in fact, Mill offers no defense of this axiom other than that we cannot conceive things otherwise (although he notes that "Bedlamite[s]" and "Transcendentalist[s]" do [L1: 14]).

Poe's main objection to the state of epistemology in the nineteenth century, though, is that the route to knowledge has been limited to induction and deduction and that all other sources of knowledge have been delegitimized. Poe is correct to cite Mill on this point, as Mill singularly emphasized induction while Whewell, as noted, envisioned a more active role of the mind in arriving at truth about the world. Poe, in particular, challenges accounts of Kepler's and Newton's discoveries (a site of debate between Mill and Whewell) as evolving merely from the conscious synthesis of inductive observation and deductive reasoning. Instead, his writer from the future contends that science "makes its most important advances—as all History will show—by seemingly intuitive *leaps*" (L1: 10). Significantly, though, Poe emphasizes that intuition is not some magical or mystical insight provided from beyond the knowing subject, but rather is "*the conviction arising from those inductions or deductions of which the processes are so shadowy as to escape our consciousness, elude our reason, or defy our capacity of expression*" (L1: 22).[17] Poe does not state that this intuition is a truth; rather it is a "conviction," a belief. It is not, however, a belief without foundation, for the processes by which we reach this intuition are based in a kind of unconscious induction and deduction. Yet while based in rational processes, we have no ability to consciously, rationally, grasp how we arrive at them.

With that in mind, I want to return to Poe's broader comments on phrenology—and the potential to understand the brain and its workings—in his criticism and tales. A month after the Miles review, Poe sets up his famous critique of literary nationalism in the Drake-Halleck review with an account of the phrenological bases of poetry. Poe begins by contending that "the most direct, and the most unerring method" of deciphering the true nature of something is by examining its "*design*." In terms of our mental faculties, we first "find certain faculties implanted within us, and arrive at a more plausible conception of the character and attributes of those faculties, by considering, with what finite judgment we possess, the *intention* of the Deity in so implanting them within us, than by any actual investigation of their powers, or any speculative deductions from their visible and material effects" (ER: 509). The route to clearly conceiving how the mind works lies less in direct observation than in deductions from the intentions of God. As we will see, in "The Imp of the Perverse" and "The Black Cat," Poe's narrators almost directly contradict this view in stressing the "finite" nature of our "judgment," but in the Drake-Halleck review he educes an "instinct given to man by God" that phrenologists call "Veneration," by remarking that "we discover in all men a disposition to look with reverence upon superiority" (ER: 509). Poe begins with a more inductive point—we discover this faculty in all men through observation—before moving to a more deductive account of its design or purpose—it is "given to man by God as security for his own worship" (ER: 509). While not exactly the same, parallel to Veneration, Poe contends, is "the Faculty of Ideality—which is the sentiment of Poesy," "the sense of the beautiful, of the sublime, and of the mystical." This "love of the gleaming stars and other burning glories of Heaven" and the beauties of Earth is "mingled up inextricably with . . . the unconquerable desire—*to know*" (ER: 510). Veneration and Ideality, Poe suggests, are located in specific brain structures, as identified by phrenology, and similarly partake in an admiration of something greater than the self, an admiration that combines a kind of "Intellectual Happiness" with the "Imagination."

As reiterated in "Philosophy of Composition," however, Poe insists that a strong faculty of Ideality does not make one a poet, but rather that "a poem is not the Poetic faculty, but *the means* of exciting it in mankind" (ER: 511). Citing Coleridge as the man who has "been most successful in writing the purest of all poems," Poe turns to phrenological analysis to make his point: Coleridge's "head, if we mistake not its character, gave no great phrenological tokens of Ideality, while the organs of Causality and Comparison were most singularly developed" (ER: 512). In terms of phrenology, he articulates this idea that the poet uses a kind of scientific method, combining induction and deduction, in the original opening paragraph of "Murders in the Rue Morgue."

There his narrator suggests that "a few farther steps in phrenological science" may lead to discovering a faculty of analysis. For the narrator, analysis may be "a constituent of ideality," an idea directly "in opposition to the vulgar dictum . . . that the calculating and discriminating powers (causality and comparison) are at variance with the imaginative." Instead, observation reveals that "the processes of invention or creation are strictly akin with the processes of resolution—the former being nearly, if not absolutely, the latter conversed" (M 2: 527). For Poe, imagination parallels or draws on our ability to discern causal relations, to compare cases, to resolve relations. Those abilities, then, enable the poet to create the "effect" of Beauty, the "pure and intense elevation of *soul*" (ER: 16).[18]

If, through a combination of imagination and conscious, as well as unconscious, reasoning, we can, like Dupin, discern the plots of orangutans or human murderers and, like the poet in "Philosophy of Composition," determine the best way to create aesthetic experiences, what happens when we turn such a method to ontological questions? This, in part, is what occurs in *Eureka*. Poe's cosmological prose poem offers what he calls the Truth about the universe, and it delineates a metaphysical basis for his ability to discern that Truth, while also limning our final inability to know that Truth. In fact, Poe opens *Eureka* by qualifying his own claims in terms of the limitations of demonstrable truth: "let me as distinctly as possible announce—not the theorem which I hope to demonstrate—for, whatever the mathematicians may assert, there is, in this world at least, *no such thing* as demonstration—but the ruling idea which, throughout this volume, I shall be continually endeavoring to suggest" (L1: 7). While Poe builds an argument based in evidence and both induction and deduction, he emphasizes that such an argument cannot prove or demonstrate anything beyond doubt. Such an effort amounts not so much to a matter of belief, Poe contends, as an attempt "to direct his mental vision toward some given point, in the intellectual firmament, where lies a nebula never to be resolved" (L1: 20).

In *Eureka* and elsewhere, Poe implicitly and explicitly distinguishes his approach from that found in the Bridgewater Treatises, a series of eight highly influential volumes by leading British scientists covering a range of topics, all devoted to explaining "The Power, Wisdom, and Goodness of God as Manifested in the Creation." Whewell's Bridgewater volume on astronomy may have influenced *Eureka*, and the offering on *Animal and Vegetable Physiology* by Peter Mark Roget, an influential critic of phrenology, was reviewed (probably by Poe) in the *Southern Literary Messenger* in 1836. It is in his "Marginalia" from 1844 (first published in the *Democratic Review*), however, that Poe begins to articulate the critique of the Bridgewater writers that he later expands in *Eureka*. "All the Bridgewater treatises," according to Poe, "have failed" to recognize "the *great* idiosyncrasy in the Divine system of adaptation," namely "the complete *mutuality* of adaptation" (ER: 1315). Whereas "in human constructions, a particular cause has a particular effect—a particular purpose brings about a particulate object; but we see not reciprocity," the Divine is defined by reciprocity: "In Divine constructions, the object is either object or purpose, as we choose to regard it . . . so that we can never (abstractedly, without concretion—without reference to facts of the moment) decide which is which" (ER: 1315; also see L1: 88–89). Poe hypothesizes that the Bridgewater writers "may have avoided this point, on account of its apparent tendency to overthrow the idea of *cause* in general—consequently of a First Cause—of God," which, it follows, would undermine the purpose of the treatises altogether (ER: 1316). Poe suggests, instead, that we should question causality in general.

In *Eureka*, of course, Poe offers us his own version of how the divine and the material world interact, producing a transcendent plot that consists of the movement from unity to diversity and back to unity through the forces of gravity (attraction) and electricity (repulsion). But in place of the Bridgewater treatises' emphasis on discerning material causes that can then be scaffolded to build an argument for the benevolent design of God, Poe emphasizes our inability to fully know. Our thoughts about "infinity," in fact, refer to "*thoughts of thoughts*," "the possible attempt at an impossible conception," which "lies *out* of the brain of man" (L1: 20). With its emphasis on this thought being beyond the human brain, this conception leads Poe to align his thinking on the human brain, cosmology, and aesthetics: "The human brain has obviously a leaning to the '*Infinite*' and fondles the phantom of the idea. It seems to long with a passionate fervor for this impossible conception, with the hope of intellectually believing it when conceived" (L1: 77). With the "obviously," Poe suggests that his account of the human brain's tendency derives from observation. At the same time, he offers an ontological account of this tendency, the longing that all of creation has to be reunified into one whole, but, as just noted, that claim is founded not as truth but as emerging from the very desire it attempts to explain, the human desire for consistency. Science and art thus share a common project of attempting to replicate or approach what he refers to as the "*perfect consistency*" (L1: 15) only fully found in the "Plot of God" (L1: 89). Poe theorizes that this longing is written into the very make-up of the universe: "the poetical instinct of humanity—its instinct of the symmetrical, if the symmetry be but a symmetry of surface:—this *instinct*, which the Soul, not only of Man but of all created beings, took up, in the beginning, from the *geometrical* basis of the Universal radiation" (L1: 89). It is this "final, universal conglomeration" that "the analogical, symmetrical or poetical instinct of Man" grasps before his reason does (L1: 97), thus giving the aesthetic sense its priority. All art, whether music, poetry, or prose, derives from our sense of this final union and our realization of our inability to grasp that truth fully on Earth.

The human inability to fully grasp or to create similar structures underlies both Poe's aesthetics and his critique of the dominant scientific empiricism of his time. Unlike Mill, he emphasizes the active work of the mind (in fact, the brain) in constructing our knowledge of the world, specifically through his emphasis on intuition unconsciously combining induction and deduction. Like Whewell, then, he elaborates a more robust role for human consciousness in delineating truths, but unlike Whewell he does not base that role in a benevolent divine plan but rather in a human desire to discern such plans. Those differences from Mill and Whewell, I will argue, link Poe's critique of phrenology and his aesthetics.

Deducing and Establishing Every Thing

In his review of Miles's volume and in the Drake-Halleck review, Poe does not qualify his praise of the scientific pursuit of the brain through phrenology. As his comments in *Eureka* might suggest, however, he elsewhere begins to delineate limits to the sciences of the brain in ways that mirror his broader critique of science. Most directly, in both "The Imp of the Perverse" and "The Black Cat," Poe's murderous narrators argue that phrenologists have been blind to the "radical, primitive, irreducible sentiment" of the Perverse (M 3: 1219). By the 1840s, phrenologists had largely settled into a set account of thirty-five or thirty-six faculties or mental organs which were divinely designed to lead, with the proper guidance, to human happiness. In this way, Combe and his followers shared much ground with leading scientists such as Whewell and those involved in the Bridgewater project, while it was their emphasis on the moral design or reason behind natural laws that Mill found most problematic about phrenology's claims.[19] In "Imp," the narrator directly attacks phrenological investigations for their a priori assumption of such a divinely orchestrated world. He challenges the "metaphysicianism" of the "intellectual or logical man, rather than the understanding or observant man," who has assumed to discern the "intentions of Jehovah," almost directly reversing Poe's position in the Drake-Halleck review (M 3: 1219). Based on their assumptions, such thinkers have "built . . . innumerable systems of mind. In the matter of phrenology, for example, we first determined, naturally enough, that it was the design of the Deity that man should eat. We then assigned to man an organ of alimentiveness" (M 3: 1219). In this way, "Spurzheimites" have gone about "deducing and establishing every thing from the preconceived destiny of man." The narrator proposes that "It would have been wiser . . . to classify (if classify we must,) upon the basis of what man usually or occasionally did, and was always occasionally doing, rather than upon the basis of what we took it for granted the Deity intended him to do" (M 3: 1220). It would have been wiser, in other words, to observe that humans have an appetite to eat rather than to begin with an assumption about God's design. It follows, he contends, that "Induction, a posteriori, would have brought phrenology to admit, as an innate and primitive principle of human action" what he calls *Perverseness*, a desire to "act without comprehensible object," an "overwhelming tendency to do wrong for the wrong's sake" (M 3: 1220–1221). The problem with the phrenologists' approach is that "in the pure arrogance of reason" they "could not perceive [the] necessity" of perverseness or "in what manner it might be made to further the objects of humanity" (M 3: 1219).

Here, Poe's narrator seems to strike out on a more inductive path, beginning with observations of actual human conduct, in attacking phrenologists and other brain scientists and theorists of the mind for deducing the structures and functions of the mind from what they perceive to be God's divine plan. Using their reason, such thinkers have found it impossible to acknowledge a brain function that seems to have no use, that does not directly "further the objects of humanity." Unlike Combe, Poe's narrator returns to Gall's more observation-driven and pessimistic view of the brain. At the same time, though, with the aside "if classify we must," the narrator suggests that observation and inductive reasoning are also limited. Classification, it seems, as Mill would argue against Whewell, is not based in the order of nature so much as it is based in the human desire or necessity of ordering things. This demotion of reasoning—and with it the potential of conscious knowing—appears in the very structure of "Imp." Poe's narrator critiques Spurzheimites for their assumptions about a benevolent design, but the story also calls into question our ability to know much about the brain or the underlying reasons for its structures at all. Having a murderous madman articulate this critique through self-reflection calls the entire analysis into question: what true self-knowledge—and thus knowledge about his mental and emotional workings—does the narrator actually have, given his own instability?[20]

This point about the limits of inductive and deductive reasoning recurs, as we have seen, throughout Poe's oeuvre, and often appears in terms of understanding aesthetic effects or experience. Thus, in "The Fall of the House of Usher," the narrator comments that while "beyond doubt, there *are* combinations of very simple natural objects which have the power of thus affecting us, still the analysis of this power lies among considerations beyond our depth" (M 2: 398). Or in "MS. Found in a Bottle," the narrator similarly reflects that "a feeling, for which I have no name, has taken possession of my soul—a sensation which will admit of no analysis, to which the lessons of bygone time are inadequate, and for which I fear futurity itself will offer me no key" (M 2: 141). Poe links this failure of analysis to phrenology in "Imp" when the narrator states that perverseness will not "admit of analysis, or resolution into ulterior elements" (M 3: 1221). With "The Black Cat," as in "Imp," Poe's narrator refers to perverseness as "one of the primitive impulses of the human heart—one of the indivisible primary faculties, or sentiments, which give direction to the character of Man," but then defines it as an "unfathomable longing of the soul *to vex* itself—to offer violence to its own nature" (M 3: 852). This primitive impulse, this instinct, both without object and directed toward self-destruction and frustration, exactly parallels Poe's account in *Eureka* of the desire that gives rise to aesthetics: "The pleasure which we derive from any exertion of human ingenuity [whether it is scientific, artistic, or mechanical], is in direct ratio of the *approach* to this species of reciprocity" found in God's plot (L1: 89). As he phrases it in "The Poetic Principle," echoing the aesthetic desire he frames in terms of phrenology in the Drake-Halleck review, that pleasure (and pain) "is no mere appreciation of the Beauty before us—but a wild effort to reach the Beauty above," "an ecstatic prescience of the glories beyond the grave" that leads to our "petulant, impatient sorrow at our inability to grasp *now*, wholly, here on earth, at once and for ever, those divine and rapturous joys" (ER: 77). Where in the Drake-Halleck review Poe partly attempts to explain this desire in terms of phrenological faculties, with "Imp," "Black Cat," and *Eureka*, he suggests that our very limited knowledge of the brain parallels this existential condition and similarly gives rise to a kind of aesthetic desire for the unfathomable. And where in "Philosophy of Composition," he articulates the mechanical, predictive route to creating the effect of Beauty, in "Usher" and elsewhere he places such effects beyond full analysis.

"Ligeia" perhaps best incorporates these lines of thought. While Brett Zimmerman has suggested some of the ways that "Ligeia" picks up on phrenological thought, the story less directly engages with phrenology than Poe does elsewhere.[21] Instead, in attempting to convey his attraction to Ligeia, the narrator refers to "the many incomprehensible anomalies of the science of mind." Specifically he alludes to the "thrillingly exciting . . . fact . . . that, in our endeavors to recall to memory something long forgotten, we often find ourselves *upon the very verge* of remembrance, without being able, in the end, to remember" (M 2: 313–314). In the context of the story, the narrator refers to the power of Ligeia's eyes and the mystery of her beauty, but his "approaching the full knowledge of their expression" (M 2: 314) parallels her "guidance through the chaotic world of metaphysical investigation," which leads the narrator toward "that delicious vista by slow degrees expanding before me, down whose long, gorgeous, and all untrodden path, I might at length pass onward to the goal of a wisdom too divinely precious not to be forbidden!" (M 2: 316). The closest that the narrator can get to grasping the source of, the truth behind, Ligeia's attraction is recognizing that he "derived, from many existences in the material world, a sentiment" similar to that he experienced in his interactions with Ligeia: "I found, in the commonest objects of the universe, a circle of analogies to that expression . . . . in the survey of a rapidly-growing vine—in the contemplation of a moth, a butterfly, a chrysalis, a stream of running water" (M 2: 314). These analogies allow the narrator a glimpse at some deeper, potentially metaphysical reality without providing him any true access to that truth, leaving him bereft of the ability to "define that sentiment, or analyze, or even steadily view it" (M 2: 314). Ligeia's possible return from death links this sentiment with our desire for the "glories beyond the grave" that define Beauty in "Poetic Principle." With his comment on the "anomalies of the science of the mind," Poe, through his narrator, indicates how that longing derives from or mirrors the gaps in our knowledge about the brain.

By connecting Poe's comments on science, scientific method, and scientific truth in general (mainly in the Dupin tales, *Eureka*, and his criticism) and his reflections on phrenology, I have attempted to show how Poe's aesthetics, his epistemological critique of scientific method, and his relationship to phrenology intersect through (1) his sense of a human need to understand, to explain the world, that defines the human brain and human existence and (2) his recognition of our inability to finally, fully, understand the world, to explain that very need, and to fathom completely what the limits of knowledge are. Importantly, Poe does not wrap all of knowledge in some sort of gnostic mysticism but rather carefully limns some of the limitations of deductive and inductive reasoning for reaching fundamental truths—about final causes in the universe, the exact reasons the human brain functions as it does, and why specific phenomena create the aesthetic experience they do. What emerges is a picture of Poe readily accepting some of the insights of science, but offering a skeptical reading of scientific method as limited in its emphasis on a rational, somewhat formulaic deduction and induction.[22] In this light, "The many incomprehensible anomalies of the science of the mind" lie in our desire to comprehend and reproduce the unity of God's plot, thus providing the basis of aesthetic experience, the stimulus to our necessarily unsatisfactory attempts to fully understand the workings of both the brain and the universe. What phrenology and science can offer us is, like art, an attempt at reaching, at grasping, the universe's unity. What art, unlike science, emphasizes is the mirage-like nature of that unity, the fact that such unity is as much (or more) a product of our desire for unity, as it is based in the foundation of the universe.

The Many Incomprehensible Anomalies of the Science of Mind, Now

What, then, can Poe say to us in the twentieth-first century, in an era of magnetic resonance imaging (MRI) and cognitive, behavioral studies that have provided significant revelations about how the human brain works? Poe, I believe, asks questions about methodology, epistemology, and ontology that contemporary biological and brain sciences, from neo-Darwinism to modular cognitive science to neuroaesthetics, have not fully answered. Poe, as we have seen, readily acknowledges and embraces some of the potential insights of brain science, as exemplified by phrenology. Yet he also delimits their insights. Specifically, Poe offers us a corrective to those who would too readily embrace a scientific reductionism (or consilience) in emphasizing, like Poe's "Spurzheimites," the discovery of rational, well-adapted mental structures over or in place of more inductive explorations of the brain's gaps, frailties, and inconsistencies.

In the past few decades, literary studies has engaged with the cognitive and biological sciences in a wide array of ways, so anything I say here will necessarily be reductive, but I will attempt to trace quickly how I see Poe's work intervening in these developments. On one end of the spectrum are literary scholars who accept E. O. Wilson's call for a kind of consilience that would reduce all knowledge to a "common groundwork of explanation," based in "a belief in the unity of the sciences—a conviction, far deeper than a mere working proposition, that the world is orderly and can be explained by a small number of natural laws."[23] For example, in his manifesto "Three Scenarios for Literary Darwinism," Joseph Carroll argues for a future "in which the evolutionary human sciences transform and subsume all literary study," as "there are no real ontological or epistemological barriers separating the humanities and the evolutionary human sciences" for "it is all the same world, intelligible by the same instruments."[24] This work, broadly speaking, builds upon that of evolutionary psychologists such as Leda Cosmides and John Tooby.[25] In their very influential account, the human mind has evolved to incorporate a number of specific, identifiable functions, which, like the instruments of a Swiss army knife, can be used for other ends, but are fundamentally engineered for designated purposes.[26] This view of the human mind as a precisely wrought tool with multiple specific functions has some grounding in neuroscience—we know, for example, that the initial processing of visual information happens in a few specific brain regions. But it tends to draw on the more deductive processes of cognitive science rather than the more inductive ones of neuroscience. In particular, it closely parallels theories about the modularity of the human mind. As developed by Jerry Fodor and elaborated (beyond Fodor's comfort) by evolutionary psychologists such as Cosmides and Tooby, this theory argues that the mind can be best understood as modular, as consisting of free-standing, separately working processes for dealing with particular biological, cognitive needs, such as seeing, speaking, and so on.[27] These modules, then, can be defined along functionalist lines; that is, these modules serve specific evolutionarily adaptive functions. As Steven Pinker phrases it in *The Blank Slate*, what emerges from the "cognitive revolution" is a view of the mind as "a system of universal, generative computational modules" such that "reasoning, intelligence, imagination, and creativity" are reducible to "forms of information processing."[28]

While they most often articulate a somewhat more flexible model of the human mind, scholars such as Denis Dutton and Brian Boyd have drawn on this line of thinking to argue that humans evolved specific aesthetic faculties. Boyd, for example, contends that "art, too, is a specifically human adaptation, biologically part of our species. It offers tangible advantages for human survival and reproduction, and it derives from play, itself an adaptation widespread among animals with flexible behaviors."[29] In recent years, this kind of strict modularity has come more and more into question from a variety of sources, including neuroscientific accounts, and has been rejected as simply "the new phrenology."[30] Like phrenology, but with more scientific ground, it has emphasized brain localization and the different functions of particular brain regions. While Poe, I have argued, suggests that phrenology was overly dependent on positing a benevolent divine order underlying human mental structures, the new phrenology has tended, at times, to embrace something akin to Wilson's consilience in insisting that all mental structures and functions can be explained by some advantage they provided within evolutionary adaptation. As Boyd puts it, "Had every part of our brain's design not served an adaptive function, evolution would have reduced our surplus brain mass."[31] In embracing a neo-Darwinian position, Boyd and others tend to posit a rather tight fit between human consciousness and the world, as opposed to a view that reads that connection as simply good enough to ensure survival, the idea that evolutionarily speaking, the mind must correspond to the world enough to allow individuals and species to live, succeed, and reproduce, but that such success does not mean that humans (or any other species for that matter) represent the world fully or correctly in some mental realm. In this way, such thinkers are at odds, again, broadly speaking, with biologists such as Stephen Jay Gould, who contend that much of what survives through evolution is less than necessary to survival, that much of it may be atavistic, in fact.[32] Poe's skepticism toward phrenology's apriorism in "Imp" suggests taking a similarly skeptical position toward this line of thinking. Where Poe indicts his brain science contemporaries for assuming that the divine has designed the human brain to function rationally, so neo-Darwinian consilience-minded humanists have posited that everything in the human mind must have a purpose that we can rationally understand in terms of adaptation. Poe's idea of perverseness—with its emphasis on self-destruction—would seem to directly counter such a view, a view that has led, at times, to scholars rejecting works of art as not truly art because they cannot explain its attraction in evolutionary terms.

Unlike evolutionary literary theory, most literary scholars who draw more specifically on the cognitive sciences have attempted to define their enterprise as informed but not subsumed by the biological sciences. So, Lisa Zunshine, in her introduction to the *Oxford Handbook of Cognitive Literary Studies* (2015), defines the practice as consisting of "work not toward consilience with science but toward a richer engagement with a variety of theoretical paradigms."[33] Cognitive literary critics have offered numerous insights into how literary texts engage with the human ability to read or infer the mental states of other human beings, how aesthetic works more broadly might work through the neurocircuitry underlying visualization, reading, and meaning making, and how underlying structures that allow us to create narratives and make sense of the world provide a foundation not just for literary works but for mental functions in general.[34]

Much cognitivist literary criticism has at times questioned or even rejected both the modular, computational model of the mind that Pinker and others associate with the cognitive revolution and the work of evolution-focused scholars such as Carroll and Boyd. Yet like the approaches of Carroll and Boyd, many cognitivist literary critics focus on describing how literature strengthens the human capacity to accurately process data about the world. This may be one of the reasons that much cognitive literary criticism has focused on the traditional psychological realist novel, which, as has long been noted, fundamentally works through its creation and mapping of a world and its relationships. When cognitivist literary critics have attended to Poe, they have tended to read him in terms similar to how they have read more realist writers, as providing accounts of the mind as an information processor, finely attuned through evolutionary processes to accurately understand the world (including, perhaps most important, other humans). Most notably, Blakey Vermeule, one of the most prominent cognitivist critics, draws on "Murders in the Rue Morgue" in elaborating how Dupin's ability to "run a chain of inferences" through a basic "algorithm" reflects a human mind-reading ability.[35]

As I have argued, however, we can best situate Dupin's skills at one end of a pole within Poe's thought on the power and limitations of humans to use a nearly unconscious intuition to create plausible, if finally never fully complete and unified, plots of explanation. This emphasis on the limits of human rationality and on the gaps between our mental renderings of the world and the world itself subtends the Gothic and, in some versions, the sublime, traditions at the core of much of Poe's work. Recently, Alan Richardson, another leading cognitivist critic, has outlined how work within cognitive science has tended problematically to envision imagination as "rule bound and quotidian," as presenting "regularities . . . [such as] orderliness and predictability."[36] From Richardson's position (perhaps, importantly, he is a romanticist), this reductive picture of the imagination derives from attempts to offer an adaptationist or utilitarian explanation of its function. The limited scholarship using contemporary brain sciences to analyze the Gothic similarly draws on insights into the brain's quirks and shortcomings—and the pleasure we derive from manipulating them—rather than the human brain's rationalistic abilities. So, Natalie Phillips has argued that Gothic fiction explores the problems of unifocal mental fixation (focused attention) while activating our ability to maintain multifocal perspectives, and James Dawes has described how the pleasure of the Gothic comes from "the unreasonableness of human emotional lives, the irrational slack and mismatch between our emotions and beliefs."[37] As I have suggested, Poe anticipates these critiques of viewing the imagination—and the functions of the brain as a whole—in utilitarian or rational terms. Where Poe's account of Dupin and of the human mind in general is ripe for fruitful exploration along the lines some cognitivist has mapped, his emphasis on the gaps in our ability to know *and* the fundamental role those limitations play in creating aesthetic experience should push cognitive critics to focus less on the rational uses of literature, whether in evolutionary terms or not, and more on how art draws on, elaborates, and plays with the perverse anomalies of the mind.

In "Imp," Poe's narrator corrects this tendency of the brain sciences to reduce the brain to rational functions instrumental to human development by calling on us to focus on actual behavior. With the improvement of brain imaging techniques and experimental processes, neuroscientific exploration of aesthetics (or neuroaesthetics) has worked, to some extent, as a similar corrective. So, for example, Anjan Chatterjee, a cognitive neuroscientist at University of Pennsylvania, concludes that "The richly textured meaning of individual pieces of art that gives art its power is inherently variable and open to many interpretations and thus closed to neuroscience."[38] Somewhat similarly, V. S. Ramachandran, one of the leading neuroscientists in the world, eschews the kind of hyperadaptationist explanations I have noted earlier, in arguing that "the opportunistic, 'happenstantial' nature of evolution . . . . applies with even greater force to the evolution of the human brain."[39] However, despite titling his book *The Tell-Tale Brain* and gesturing to Poe's "phantasmagorical short stories" in reference to the strange symptoms exhibited by patients with brain lesions and other damage, Ramachandran offers a much more functionalist—and it seems to me, reductive—account when he turns to art.[40] His approach is to separate questions of aesthetics, whose "neural bases" we have grounds for hypothesizing, from art.[41] This distinction, which mirrors, to some extent, Chatterjee's, makes a great deal of sense, but it misses the curious workings of the brain that Poe's "Tell-Tale Heart," like its companion tales "The Black Cat" and "The Imp of the Perverse," emphasizes. As Poe's interest in and reliance on phrenology and its insights into a normative vision of brain function suggests, his point in these stories is not to reject the scientific project of rendering the human brain and its functions in general terms, but, as I have argued, is part of a larger project of delimiting our ability to know ourselves and our world. The brain sciences and art can help us to push those limits, but what Poe suggests is that the real power of art, its true attraction, comes from its indicating those limits while hinting at the pleasure we would have by overcoming them. The question we, as literary scholars, face in the twenty-first century is not that different from that which Poe faced in the antebellum period, when he attempted, largely unsuccessfully, to promote himself into a role of cultural arbiter at a time of shifting market relations connected to cultural production and the increasing importance of science. Taken alongside *Eureka*, Poe's writing on phrenology can be read as a model for our own engagement, as humanists, with science, specifically the biological and brain sciences as a map for accepting their potential insights into the origins and processes behind aesthetic experience while accentuating the difficulties of reducing that experience to rationalistic, normative terms.

Notes

1. This is one of the core arguments of John Limon, "Poe's Methodology," in *The Place of Fiction in the Time of Science: A Disciplinary History of American Writing* (Cambridge: Cambridge University Press, 1990), 70–120.
2. For the best recent accounts of Poe's materialism, see Matthew A. Taylor, "Edgar Allan Poe's Meta/Physics," in *Universes Without Us: Posthuman Cosmologies in American Literature* (Minneapolis: University of Minnesota Press, 2013), 27–56, and John Tresch, "'Matter No More': Edgar Allan Poe and the Paradoxes of Materialism," *Critical Inquiry* 42 (2016): 865–898.
3. See Edward S. Reed, *From Soul to Mind: The Emergence of Psychology from Erasmus Darwin to William James* (New Haven, CT: Yale University Press, 1997). There has been a very healthy volume of work in recent years criticizing an emphasis on locating consciousness in the brain, sometimes under the umbrella of either embodied cognition or extended cognition. For three prominent examples working within cognitive neuroscience, see Andy Clark, *Supersizing the Mind: Embodiment, Action, and Cognitive Extension* (New York: Oxford University Press, 2010); Shaun Gallagher, *How the Body Shapes the Mind* (New York: Oxford University Press, 2006); and Alva Noë, *Out of Our Heads: Why You Are Not Your Brain, and Other Lessons from the Biology of Consciousness* (New York: Hill and Wang, 2009). See Fernando Vidal, "Brainhood, Anthropological Figure of Modernity," *History of the Human Sciences* 22 (2009): 5–36, for an account of how the modern self is defined in terms of the "cerebral subject."
4. For overviews of Poe's engagement with phrenology and more comprehensive accounts of his references and uses of phrenology, see Edward Hungerford, "Poe and Phrenology," *American Literature* 2 (1931): 209–231, and Brett Zimmerman, "Phrenology," in *Edgar Allan Poe in Context*, ed. Kevin J. Hayes (Cambridge: Cambridge University Press, 2013), 301–312.
5. I have drawn most heavily from the following scholarly works in this short sketch of the history of phrenology: Robert M. Young, *Mind, Brain and Adaptation in the Nineteenth Century: Cerebral Localization and its Biological Context from Gall to Ferrier* (1970; repr., New York: Oxford University Press, 1990); Stephen Tomlinson, *Head Masters: Phrenology, Secular Education, and Nineteenth-Century Social Thought* (Tuscaloosa: University of Alabama Press, 2005); and John van Wyhe, *Phrenology and the Origins of Victorian Scientific Naturalism* (Aldershot, UK: Ashgate, 2014). I will note more specific works and arguments concerning phrenology later. Of canonical US authors, Walt Whitman was perhaps most deeply influenced by phrenology. He had his head read by the Fowlers, they published the second edition of *Leaves of Grass* in 1856, and he regularly drew on phrenological terms for human faculties in his verse and prose.
6. Young, *Mind, Brain and Adaptation in the Nineteenth Century*, 4.
7. As Tomlinson puts it, phrenology "was effectively transformed into a progressive moral philosophy by John Gasper Spurzheim, who normalized the mind around middle-class values by defining human nature in terms of the balanced operation of faculties such as time, order, consciousness, adhesiveness, and love of approbation" (*Head Masters*, xii).

8. George Combe, *The Constitution of Man Considered in Relation to External Objects*, 8th ed. (New York: Fowlers and Wells, 1851), 451.
9. Quoted in Shapin, "Phrenological Knowledge and the Social Structure of Early Nineteenth-Century Edinburgh," *Annals of Science* 32 (1975): 235. Phrenological writings often stressed that evidence for the science was available to anyone, a move that revisionist historians in the 1970s and 1980s such as Steven Shapin and Roger Cooter read as an antielitist move that connected it to the ascendant middle class in Britain. See Roger Cooter, *The Cultural Meaning of Popular Science: Phrenology and the Organization of Consent in Nineteenth-Century Britain* (Cambridge: Cambridge University Press, 1984), and Steven Shapin, "Phrenological Knowledge and the Social Structure of Early Nineteenth-Century Edinburgh," 219–243, and "The Politics of Observation: Cerebral Anatomy and Social Interests in the Edinburgh Phrenology Disputes," in *On the Margins of Science: The Social Construction of Rejected Knowledge*, ed. Roy Wallis, special issue, *Sociological Review Monograph* 27 (1979): 139–178. In the United States, phrenology, if anything, cast itself even more in terms of its democratizing impulse, particularly in terms of enabling any individual access to self-knowledge and, thus, potentially self-reform. For the best consideration of phrenology along these lines within US literary studies, see Christopher Castiglia, "Anxiety, Desire, and the Nervous States," in *Interior States: Institutional Consciousness and the Inner Life of Democracy in the Antebellum United States* (Durham, NC: Duke University Press, 2008), 168–215. Poe attacks the progressive yet deterministic notions of phrenology in "Some Words with a Mummy," where he satirizes his contemporaries and their arrogance through the failure of their phrenological method in attempting to read the Egyptian mummy's character and mental powers. See Dana Nelson, "The Haunting of White Manhood: Poe, Fraternal Ritual, and Polygenesis," *American Literature* 69 (1997): 515–546. Elsewhere, though, Poe seems to have drawn on popularized versions of craniometry or phrenology in some of his descriptions and characterizations of black and Indian characters, from Dirk Peters and the Tsalalians in *Arthur Gordon Pym* to Jupiter in "The Gold Bug." See Brett Zimmerman, "Phrenology," on this matter. In those works, we can see Poe draw on these sciences as part of what Terence Whalen has described as his "average racism." See Whalen, *Edgar Allan Poe and the Masses: The Political Economy of Literature in Antebellum America* (Princeton, NJ: Princeton University Press, 1999). Phrenology's relationship to racial science, especially craniometry, has received a fair amount of attention in the past few decades. Samuel George Morton's widely read works on craniometry from the late 1830s and early 1840s implicitly and cautiously drew on phrenology, but, in turn, were converted into further evidence by the phrenologists. It is incorrect, however, to reduce phrenology to a racist or proslavery science. Even craniometry, which placed racial difference at its foundation, found many antislavery adherents and drew many denunciations from defenders of slavery (often due to its breaking from the biblical narrative of man's creation and its implicit materialization of the mind and, perhaps, the soul). In fact, with their tendency to embrace liberal reform, many phrenologists, including Combe, were antagonistic toward slavery. For the classic accounts of craniometry (including its relationship to phrenology) and racism, see William Stanton, *The Leopard's Spots: Scientific Attitudes Toward Race in America, 1815–59* (Chicago: University of Chicago Press, 1960) and Stephen Jay Gould, *The Mismeasure of Man* (New York: Norton, 1981).

10. John van Wyhe, "Was Phrenology a Reform Science? Towards a New Generalization for Phrenology," *History of Science* 42 (2004): 319.
11. "*Dissection* alone does not reveal the vital functions of any organ: no person, by dissecting the optic nerve, could find out that its office is to minister to vision; or, by dissecting the tongue, could ascertain that it is the organ of taste. Anatomists, therefore, could not, by the mere practice of their art, discover the functions of the different portions of the brain." See George Combe, *A System of Phrenology*, 5th ed. (Edinburgh: Maclachlan and Stewart, 1843), 97.
12. Combe, *System of Phrenology*, vi, vii.
13. William Whewell, *The Philosophy of the Inductive Sciences, Founded upon Their History*, 2 vols., 2nd ed. (London: John W. Parker, 1847), 2:653.
14. Quoted in Laura Snyder, *Reforming Philosophy: A Victorian Debate on Science and Society* (Chicago: University of Chicago Press, 2006), 113.
15. Snyder, *Reforming Philosophy*, 27.
16. For a fuller account of Poe's engagement with the scientific debates of his era, see Susan Welsh, "The Value of Analogical Evidence: Poe's 'Eureka' in the Context of a Scientific Debate," *Modern Language Studies* 21 (1991): 3–15. Welsh does not examine the Mill-Whewell debate about induction.
17. A popular account grounded in recent brain science that makes a similar point is Malcolm Gladwell's *Blink: The Power of Thinking Without Thinking* (New York: Little, Brown, and Co., 2005).
18. On the relationship between *Eureka*, aesthetics, and mind, see especially Joan Dayan, *Fables of Mind: An Inquiry into Poe's Fiction* (New York: Oxford University Press, 1987); Limon, "Poe's Methodology," in *The Place of Fiction in the Time of Science*, 70–120; and Charles O'Donnell, "From Earth to Ether: Poe's Flight into Space," *PMLA* 77 (1962): 85–91.
19. Mill most directly criticized phrenologists in his essay on "Nature" (1854) for their tendency to appeal to the laws of "Nature," specifically human nature, in advocating moral behavior or reform. For Mill, this was both, as George Levine has characterized it, "an argument against the extension of scientific method to the study of human morals and society" and a rejection of the kind of natural theology that underlay Combe's faith in a rational human nature (Levine, *Darwin and the Novelists: Patterns of Science in Victorian Fiction* [Chicago: University of Chicago Press, 1988], 27). Without our being able to observe the workings of the human brain and without material evidence of a specific design behind the mental functions we can observe, there can be no foundation for the phrenologists' conclusions. While we know Whewell subscribed to the *Phrenological Journal*, he seems to have remained largely silent on it (see van Wyhe's *Phrenology and the Origins of Victorian Scientific Naturalism*). His silence, however, may indicate his unwillingness to engage with phrenology in fear that doing so would in itself elevate it as a worthy topic of debate.
20. This raises the broader question of how much we should trust Poe's narrators or take them as voicing his opinions. I think the consistency among his different narrative voices and some of his critical statements make the case for accepting these moments as revealing his narrators as being in sync with Poe's own thoughts.
21. See Zimmerman, "Phrenology," 303–305, 310.
22. In this respect my argument most closely parallels recent readings of Poe as a type of proto-pragmatist by Maurice Lee and Paul Grimstad. See Maurice S. Lee, "Probably Poe," in *Uncertain Chances: Science, Skepticism, and Belief in Nineteenth-Century American Literature* (New York: Oxford University Press, 2012), 20–54, and Paul Grimstad,

"Nonreasoning Creatures," in *Experience and Experimental Writing: Literary Pragmatism from Emerson to the Jameses* (New York: Oxford University Press, 2013), 42–64.

23. E. O. Wilson, *Consilience: The Unity of Knowledge* (New York: Alfred A. Knopf), 8, 4. William Whewell coined the term "consilience." For Whewell, consilience refers to a process of generalization that leads to the conforming of the different poles of the fundamental antitheses—induction and deduction, subjective and objective, and so on. In Whewell's view, consilience derived from an underlying divine order that humans were able, potentially at least, to discern. Consilience now is associated with the eminent biologist E. O. Wilson's argument about the reduction of all knowledge to a scientific framework. Wilson eschews Whewell's faith in a divine hand behind the ordered universe that he believes the human mind can fully fathom, but referring to his childhood in the Southern Baptist tradition, he reads his consilience project as "a continuation on new and better-tested ground to attain the same end" of explaining the universe (*Consilience*, 6).
24. Joseph Carroll, "Three Scenarios for Literary Darwinism," *New Literary History* 41 (2010): 53, 62.
25. For the best critique of literary Darwinism, see Jonathan Kramnick, "Against Literary Darwinism," *Critical Inquiry* 37 (2011): 315–347. But also see the response from Brian Boyd, "For Evocriticism: Minds Shaped to Be Reshaped," *Critical Inquiry* 38 (2012): 394–404.
26. See John Tooby and Leda Cosmides, "The Psychological Foundations of Culture," in *The Adapted Mind: Evolutionary Psychology and the Generation of Culture*, ed. Jerome H. Barkow, Leda Cosmides, and John Tooby (New York: Oxford University Press, 1992), 19–136.
27. See Jerry A. Fodor, *Modularity of Mind: An Essay on Faculty Psychology* (Cambridge, MA: MIT Press, 1983).
28. Stephen Pinker, *The Blank Slate: The Modern Denial of Human Nature* (New York: Penguin, 2002), 40, 34.
29. Brian Boyd, *On the Origin of Stories: Evolution, Cognition, and Fiction* (Cambridge, MA: Harvard University Press, 2009), 1.
30. For example, in an article aptly titled "The Neural Foundations of Aesthetic Appreciation" (*Progress in Neurobiology* 94 [2011]: 39–48), Camilo J. Cela Conde and his colleagues point out that "With very rare exceptions . . . the same brain region may be involved in several diverse processes" (43), so that they reject "a linear scheme of stimulus—activation—appreciation, akin to a bottom-up perceptive 'module' postulated by Fodor's (1983) architecture of the mind" (46), in attempting to describe the "general relations between cognitive processes and neural mechanisms" (47). As Van Wyhe puts it in his history of phrenology, "Similarly to phrenologists, evolutionary psychologists assert a more naturalistic, some say a reductionist, approach to human behaviour and psychology, with a particular emphasis on inborn tendencies and abilities, and with inherent fits between human brain capacities and Nature" (*Phrenology and the Origins of Victorian Scientific Naturalism*, 207).
31. Boyd, *On the Origin of Stories*, 38.
32. Boyd, *On the Origin of Stories*, 42. While Gould's work on evolution is most important here, see also his article on Poe's work on *The Conchologist's First Book* (1839), the best-selling book published under Poe's name during his lifetime; Stephen Jay Gould, "Poe's Greatest Hit," *Natural History* 102, no. 7 (1993): 10–19.

33. Lisa Zunshine, "Introduction to Cognitive Literary Studies," in *The Oxford Handbook of Cognitive Literary Studies*, ed. Lisa Zunshine (New York: Oxford University Press, 2015), 1.
34. Along these lines the best work to date, to my mind, is Paul Armstrong's *How Literature Plays with the Brain: The Neuroscience of Reading and Art* (Baltimore: Johns Hopkins University Press, 2013).
35. Blakey Vermeule, *Why Do We Care about Literary Characters?* (Baltimore: Johns Hopkins University Press, 2010), 87. For the fullest critique of Vermeule's reading of Poe, see Paul Grimstad, *Experience and Experimental Writing: Literary Pragmatism from Emerson to the Jameses*, 150n50.
36. Alan Richardson, "Defaulting to Fiction: Neuroscience Rediscovers the Romantic Imagination," *Poetics Today* 32, no. 4 (2011): 665, 666. I find Richardson's account here more satisfying than his description of what he calls the neural sublime in the work of John Keats, Percy Shelley, and other British Romantics: "in the Romantic version [of the sublime], the subject is left not marveling at the power of Reason, but rather stunned by the capacity and complexity of the human brain." See Richardson, *The Neural Sublime Cognitive Theories and Romantic Texts* (Baltimore: Johns Hopkins University Press, 2010), 29. Although Richardson is less celebratory of reason's power than Kant is usually read to be, his neural sublime, like Kant's, finally derives from the power of the human mind or brain, not, as with Burke, its inability to apperceive some external object.
37. James Dawes, "Fictional Feeling: Philosophy, Cognitive Science, and the American Gothic," *American Literature* 76, no. 3 (2004): 452. See Natalie M. Phillips, *Distraction: Problems of Attention in Eighteenth-Century Literature* (Baltimore: Johns Hopkins University Press, 2016), specifically chapter 4, "Fixated Attention: The Gothic Pathology of Single-Minded Focus," 132–173. As Anne Stiles puts it, "the labyrinthine contours of the Gothic novel proved an ideal medium for exploring the brain's convolutions." See Stiles, *Popular Fiction and Brain Science in the Late Nineteenth Century* (Cambridge: Cambridge University Press, 2012), 21. Phillips and Stiles both allude to recent developments in the brain sciences, but much of their focus is historical. The ability to move between current insights and the influence of contemporaneous brain science has proven, to my mind, to be the greatest source of insights and the greatest challenge to cognitivist literary criticism.
38. Anjan Chatterjee, *The Aesthetic Brain: How We Evolved to Desire Beauty and Enjoy Art* (New York: Oxford University Press, 2014), 148.
39. V. S. Ramachandran, *The Tell-Tale Brain: A Neuroscientist's Quest for What Makes Us Human* (New York: Norton, 2011), xv.
40. Ramachandran, *The Tell-Tale Brain*, 8.
41. Ramachandran, *The Tell-Tale Brain*, 193.

Bibliography

Armstrong, Paul. *How Literature Plays with the Brain: The Neuroscience of Reading and Art*. Baltimore: Johns Hopkins University Press, 2013.

Boyd, Brian. *On the Origin of Stories: Evolution, Cognition, and Fiction*. Cambridge, MA: Harvard University Press, 2009.

Carroll, Joseph. "Three Scenarios for Literary Darwinism." *New Literary History* 41, no. 1 (2010): 53–67.

Chatterjee, Anjan. *The Aesthetic Brain: How We Evolved to Desire Beauty and Enjoy Art*. New York: Oxford University Press, 2014.
Dayan, Joan. *Fables of Mind: An Inquiry into Poe's Fiction*. New York: Oxford University Press, 1987.
Kramnick, Jonathan. "Against Literary Darwinism." *Critical Inquiry* 37, no. 2 (2011): 315–347.
Lee, Maurice S. "Probably Poe." In *Uncertain Chances: Science, Skepticism, and Belief in Nineteenth-Century American Literature*, 20–54. New York: Oxford University Press, 2012.
Limon, John. "Poe's Methodology." In *The Place of Fiction in the Time of Science*, 70–120. Cambridge: Cambridge University Press, 1990.
Ramachandran, V. S. *The Tell-Tale Brain: A Neuroscientist's Quest for What Makes Us Human*. New York: Norton, 2011.
Taylor, Matthew A. "Edgar Allan Poe's Meta/Physics." In *Universes Without Us: Posthuman Cosmologies in American Literature*, 27–56. Minneapolis: University of Minnesota Press, 2013.
Tresch, John. "'Matter No More': Edgar Allan Poe and the Paradoxes of Materialism." *Critical Inquiry* 42, no. 4 (2016): 865–898.
van Wyhe, John. *Phrenology and the Origins of Victorian Scientific Naturalism*. Aldershot, UK: Ashgate, 2014.
Welsh, Susan. "The Value of Analogical Evidence: Poe's 'Eureka' in the Context of a Scientific Debate." *Modern Language Studies* 21, no. 4 (1991): 3–15.
Zimmerman, Brett. "Phrenology." In *Edgar Allan Poe in Context*, edited by Kevin J. Hayes, 301–312. Cambridge: Cambridge University Press, 2013.
Zunshine, Lisa. "Introduction to Cognitive Literary Studies." In *The Oxford Handbook of Cognitive Literary Studies*, edited by Lisa Zunshine, 1–15. New York: Oxford University Press, 2015.

CHAPTER 43

TEMPORAL EFFECTS

Trauma, Margaret Fuller, and "Graphicality" in Poe

CHRISTINA ZWARG

SCHOLARSHIP on Poe has always traveled alongside psychoanalytic readings, even among critics rejecting major aspects of Freud's project.[1] The odd twinning of psychoanalysis and Poe no doubt has to do with the emergence of literary study at the very moment when Freud's science was gaining prominence.[2] As is well known, Freud often found support for his theories in literature, including Sophocles, Shakespeare, and writers of "terror" like E. T. A. Hoffmann, with whom Poe was especially familiar. If other writers coming into favor in the early twentieth century did not always magnetize psychoanalytic readings, Freudian interpretations of Poe, like the one written in 1926 by Joseph Wood Krutch tracing Poe's morbid art "to an abnormal condition of the nerves," appeared almost immediately. Indeed, it was Freud's "friend and pupil" Marie Bonaparte who took the classic psychoanalytic approach to his career, writing more sympathetically than Krutch while still claiming that Poe's work gave testimony to neurotic patterns from his life.[3]

Of course, unlike writers central to F. O. Matthiessen's *American Renaissance*, Poe achieved early fame abroad, thanks largely to Charles Baudelaire's translations and promotion. German critic Walter Benjamin famously followed that lead in the twentieth century when he included Poe in a well-known reading of Baudelaire using Freud's "Beyond the Pleasure Principle."[4] And as a French thinker indebted to Baudelaire, but also contending with Marie Bonaparte in his revision of Freud, Jacques Lacan continued the association of Poe's work with psychoanalysis in his famous seminar on "The Purloined Letter."[5]

Poe's emphasis on disturbed psychic states, the Gothic tone with which he infuses tales of sensation, terror, and suspense, and his fascination with doubles and modes of detection all readily invite psychoanalytic readings. Yet speculation about the meaning of this easy alignment with psychoanalysis continues to be diverse and sometimes contentious. At the moment of high theory, for example, Poe was at the center of a debate between Lacan and Jacques Derrida that perhaps gave less insight into Poe than unexamined intersections of their own debt to Freud.[6] And as other critical paradigms took hold, lingering attempts to analyze Poe through his biography gave way to a broader emphasis on the political unconscious reflected in patterns of his work. Without engaging psychoanalysis head on, but deploying Freudian terms like "displacement," "condensation," and "fetishization," Toni Morrison's seminal argument about the "Africanist presence" in Poe's work proved to be a significant shift in this regard.[7]

If Fredric Jameson's recognition that "history is what hurts" potentially aligned trauma with historical analysis, the persistence of psychoanalytic readings, in their variety, has not fully reflected the historical and cultural relevance of trauma theory.[8] After all, trauma theory and psychoanalysis are not always one and the same. In fact, trauma theory has been said to traumatize psychoanalysis since Freud struggled with the concept throughout his career. Some critics felt that Freud's rejection of his early seduction theory represented a turn from traumatic events altogether. Yet Freud's sometime contradictory approach to the concept of trauma was much more subtle, leading some to explore the historic and cultural resonance of theories that he left tantalizingly unfinished. Ruth Leys, for example, considered the role that hypnosis played in the genealogy of trauma theory during the twentieth century, especially as Freud first embraced, then rejected, and finally transformed the concept in his elaboration of transference.[9] And because hypnosis was an adaptation of the late eighteenth-century science of mesmerism, Poe's interest in the mesmeric practices regaining popularity in the nineteenth century has already provided one place to examine his wavering engagement with certain traumatic issues of his day.[10]

Among a number of unfinished concepts from Freud, one of the most important to emerge in trauma studies is the recognition of trauma's odd temporal dimension, often identified as *Nachträglichkeit*, first translated by Freud's English editor James Strachey as "deferred action" but now more appropriately as "afterwardsness." Having earlier examined Poe's use of mesmerism to expose the problematic relay of traumatic archives, I would like to focus on early indications of afterwardsness in Poe's work, placing special emphasis on his discussion of "vivid effects" and, in particular, how that discussion draws power from his recognition of colliding temporal effects in the work of Margaret Fuller. In so doing, we discover another version of Poe's uncanny ability to identify and explore modes of behavior and response later informing Freud's shifting sense of trauma. This early recognition of afterwardsness might also inform the odd status that Poe and Fuller continue to occupy in literary history.[11]

I am particularly fascinated by the shock of recognition about these matters that Poe registers when reviewing Fuller's work in the mid-1840s. Poe was famously elevating the idea of novel and vivid effects in "The Philosophy of Composition" in 1846, and his separate acknowledgment that same year of Fuller's shared focus on effects caused him to invent the word *graphicality*. As we shall see, it is no accident that the passage Poe uses to explain this novel term relates to Fuller's own encounter with the sublime spectacle of Niagara Falls. Few have considered, however, how Fuller's description of that moment resembles the tone and predicament of a Poe story and entails an odd temporal dimension that must have appeared to Poe like a flashback.

Before his published review of her work in 1846, Poe was clearly aware of Margaret Fuller, especially since she had assumed a prominent position as critic for the *New-York Daily Tribune* and would occasionally cross paths with him in the salon culture of the city. Fuller reviewed Poe's *Tales* favorably in the *Daily Tribune* on July 11, 1845, noting how "the writings of Mr. Poe are a refreshment, for they are the fruit of genuine observations and experience, combined with an invention . . . [involving] a penetration into the causes of things" (PL: 549). The very next day, in assuming editorial control of the *Broadway Journal*, Poe republished the 1838 tales known as "Psyche Zenobia" and "The Scythe of Time" (PL: 550). These earlier linked stories broadly satirized the sensational writing being published by *Blackwood's Edinburgh Magazine*, the highly successful British periodical, and included Poe's rare attempt to use a woman narrator based on a bluestocking caricature. Beyond changing the titles to "How to Write a Blackwood Article" and "A Predicament" (a change worth noting, as we shall see), Poe added mention of *The Dial*, the journal Fuller famously edited.[12] While stepping up his attack on New England Transcendentalism in so doing, Poe likely did not have time to take into account the supportive review he had just received from Margaret Fuller. The odd coincidence of that favorable review and the republication of these satires no doubt caught Poe's attention, however, and may have stimulated him to review Fuller's work just a year later. But it also may have added to the shock of recognition that he experienced upon reading Fuller with more care, for it was as if in mocking the bluestocking narrator of both tales (while oddly aligning himself with that narrative voice) he anticipated an alliance with Fuller long before he actually knew who she was. Even more stunningly, when he saw in Fuller's writing evidence of the same powerful "effect" that he was seeking to promote, he may have experienced the entire encounter with her work as a powerful flashback, as if Fuller's philosophy of composition had somehow already anticipated his own.[13]

Trauma often involves a series of haunting flashbacks to troubling experiences never fully processed as they occur. This idea informs the current understanding of posttraumatic stress disorder. But recognition of intrusive memories often associated with nightmare has a long history, and it is one to which Freud contributed conflicting thoughts. Lacan was the first to notice Freud's shifting use of the word *nachträglich*, though it was Jean Laplanche who ramified and elaborated upon this traumatic temporality in his own revision of psychoanalysis.[14] Not surprisingly, Freud's patients would confuse the psychic impact of moments in their experience, and Freud chose the words *nachträglich* and *Nachträglichkeit* to mark the unique fashion in which they did. In describing adverse responses to events that would ordinarily appear routine, patients occasionally associated their feelings with earlier scenes that had seemed equally empty of threat when experienced.

Freud usually explained this peculiar double exposure through the diphasic onset of sexuality or the lag time between infancy and puberty. The undiscovered sexual meaning of a childhood experience might come to be understood only through its collision with a later scene triggering the flashback. Such response appears to be a belated reaction to an actual event, and part of a retrospective project (hence the earlier notion of "deferred action"). Yet following the lead of Laplanche, John Fletcher has recently observed that Freud also noticed how the moment triggering intrusive flashbacks could involve an array of earlier scenes accumulated in a "memory file," making the distinction between fantasy and event increasingly vexing for both patient and analyst. Most important, the vivid (or traumatic) response in the present only emerged through the odd "rhyming" of two separate (and often seemingly benign) moments in time.[15] In other words, a past scene could revise the tone of the later scene, just as the later scene could revise its earlier configuration and value. In that sense, the location of the traumatic effect could spread laterally, disturbing familiar understandings of experience as progressive. The past and present thus became variables on a graph where highly emotive responses would often meet, though the significance of those flaring contacts continued to remain open.

Trauma theorist Cathy Caruth has emphasized Freud's turn to belated experience and sees in his shifting use of Nachträglichkeit an important acknowledgment that repression is not the only mechanism of traumatic experience. Her larger claim that a new understanding of history might emerge through this temporal pattern of psychic response (one accepting "that a history can be grasped only in the very inaccessibility of its occurrence") continues to prove productive even if we shift attention from the deconstructive tools that assisted her in making that claim.[16] This is where we can turn to Poe for help. Poe was well known for his interest in the production of a "vivid effect" in his reader, and I would argue that the strange temporality of Nachträglichkeit, or afterwardsness, might open our understanding of certain key aspects of Poe's dedication to effect, including the evasiveness of history that nevertheless seems to shape its power.

Significantly, a focus on afterwardsness has been favored by queer theorists who find shifting scenes of temporality useful for rethinking normative patterns of development generally, including patterns in critical thinking itself.[17] In her queer reading of "Ligeia," for example, Valerie Rohy shows how charges of "ahistoricism" and "anachronism" made against such readings ignore Freud's recognition that no one processes the world along a simple progressive timeline ("because anachronism structures all psychic life, the ahistorical . . . is typical, not exceptional.")[18] For Rohy, a consideration of afterwardsness affords another way of saying that critical historicism cannot free itself of the psychic patterns through which any understanding of our relation to the past can be performed.

Of course, after Lacan's seminar on "The Purloined Letter" it has been common to consider the reading effect exposed by Poe's writing, especially in that tale. Shoshana Felman patiently elaborated upon Lacan's seminar, emphasizing its value for reading "lack of meaning" itself, since in her understanding, meaning is always already "purloined."[19] Yet by so doing, Felman set up a "Poe-etic" effect that too often neglects the temporal component that Poe also seems concerned with staging, especially through his obsession with oddly rhyming doubles like Rowena and Ligeia.[20] Thus, if we consider the temporality derived from trauma theory (a temporality Lacan oddly chose not to pursue in his seminar on Poe), we might also see how afterwardsness provides a useful index for rethinking our own engagement with certain vivid effects of history in Poe's work.

As every schoolgirl knows, Poe described his interest in producing a "novel" and "vivid effect" in an 1846 essay entitled "The Philosophy of Composition." There he famously explained the "unity of effect" that he sought to achieve while composing "The Raven."[21] Many critics find a familiar mix of humor and seriousness in the essay and often question the truth of his account concerning the writing of that particular poem. But most readers tend to take seriously his emphasis on effects, particularly when he so often adopted the sensational ploys and Gothic themes found in the influential *Blackwood's Edinburgh Magazine*. Poe began his career by satirizing those aspects, though perhaps never more wickedly than in "Psyche Zenobia" (later "How to Write a Blackwood Article") and its twin burlesque "The Scythe of Time" (later "A Predicament"). Still, as so many have noted, his own recognition as a writer grew significantly as he made shameless but exuberant borrowings from the very tales he mocked in those essays.[22] For whatever reason, as David Leverenz reminds us, "the growing market for sensationalism hurt Poe into greatness."[23]

Anyone familiar with Poe's work can easily accept the idea that he sometimes set out to elicit strong responses from his reader. Of course, Poe never argued that he wanted to produce a traumatic response in his reader—even if he wanted to, the idea of psychological trauma was not yet available to him. Yet exploring the relation of vivid effects to the odd temporality of trauma is irresistible if not inevitable. Much depends on how we view the idea of trauma itself. It is not a vitiation of trauma to suggest that a potential for a traumatic temporality may be found in almost any experience.[24] In fact, the concept of afterwardsness leads precisely to that suggestion, since two benign incidents can easily combine to make the sensation of exploded time occur. I would argue that such sensations appear to align with Poe's notion of the vivid effect and characterize his off-centered approach to "incident[s] of the day" or history itself (ER: 13).

Certainly the popularity of "The Raven," published in January of 1845, gave Poe an opportunity to elaborate on the odd sense of time he deploys as he writes. In "The Philosophy of Composition," even before explaining what he means by effect, Poe introduces a temporal dimension, suggesting that every author should begin with some idea of a denouement and work to completion retrospectively. This reversal in approach allows Poe to distinguish his notion of effect from commonsense understandings of history, incident, and event:

> There is a radical error, I think, in the usual mode of constructing a story. Either history affords a thesis—or one is suggested by an incident of the day—or, at best, the author sets himself to work in the combination of striking events to form merely the basis of his narrative—designing, generally, to fill in with description, dialogue, or authorial comment, whatever crevices of fact, or action, may, from page to page, render themselves apparent.
>
> I prefer commencing with the consideration of an *effect*. (ER: 13)

Of course, Poe does not eliminate what he calls "history" or "an incident of the day." But he does criticize their misuse as background (or "merely the basis") for narrative, especially when it comes to adopting a "combination of striking events." I would argue, moreover, that this last idea—involving as it does the conflation of two moments—appears especially important to Poe's interest in "the consideration of an effect." Thus, when he discusses "commencing with the consideration of an *effect*," he explains:

> I say to myself, in the first place, "Of the innumerable effects, or impressions, of which the heart, the intellect, or (more generally) the soul is susceptible, what one shall I, on the present occasion, select?" Having chosen a novel, first, and secondly a vivid effect, I consider whether it can best be wrought by incident or tone—whether by ordinary incidents and peculiar tone, or the converse, or by peculiarity both of incident and tone—afterward looking about me (or rather within) for such combinations of event, or tone, as shall best aid me in the construction of the effect. (ER: 13–14)

As Poe emphasizes the various "combinations of event" and "tone" that he would need to produce the desired novel effect, he appears to understand something about the rhyming of psychic scenes that can make the odd braid of time impactful. It may involve an ordinary incident, or a peculiar one, and it is always coupled with a tone that may or may not match that sense of the ordinary, or peculiar. What is striking appears to depend upon some sort of combination or repetition or even opposition, which is to say that by its very nature, something striking requires a collision of discrete temporal moments.

Intriguingly, the same year that Poe published "The Philosophy of Composition," he also coined the word *graphicality* to signal his interest in vivid effects, and in doing so, he added an even more complex temporal dimension that has often gone overlooked by critics. His adaptation of the word *graphic* or *graph* has led people to assume correctly that there is a visual aspect to the idea of effect Poe is also trying to capture, one that appears as well to appeal to a sense of cognitive mapping that is ahead of his time.[25] However, in recontextualizing his first use of this word, I want to note how the concept of graphicality brings us back to afterwardsness in a number of fascinating ways, especially since it speaks to the rhyming of different scenes in one poignant moment of sensation.

Poe invented the word *graphicality* in his 1846 "Literati of New York City" sketch of Margaret Fuller, published in *Godey's Lady's Book*.[26] In his discussion, he briefly reviews *Woman in the Nineteenth Century* (1845), though he also makes a point of returning to *Summer on the Lakes* (1844), the work he obviously prefers. Indeed, as we shall see, Poe coins the word *graphicality* when he extols the power of a passage in *Summer* describing the novel effects of a flashback. To the very competitive Poe, Fuller represents an interesting challenge as a woman, writer, and thinker, though not necessarily, as we might assume, in that order. Poe likely never stated that "Humanity is divided into Men, Women, and Margaret Fuller," though this apocryphal witticism, first circulated by Perry Miller, gained traction through Poe's deeply ambivalent, and sometimes cutting, mention of *Woman in the Nineteenth Century* in the same review.[27] Whatever the case, Poe certainly appears to envy the anomalous status that he awards Fuller when coining the word *graphicality* in his discussion of *Summer*, and it is an envy ironically fulfilled by the equally anomalous status bestowed upon Poe by literary history.

To follow the long incubation period leading to Poe's sense of "graphicality," we might return to the uncanny coincidence of Fuller's favorable review of Poe's work and his publication of "How to Write a Blackwood Article" and "A Predicament." Recycling "Psyche Zenobia" and "The Scythe of Time" under new titles certainly allowed Poe to renew his attack on New England Transcendentalism. Yet given the emphasis on effects he will soon take in "The Philosophy of Composition" *and* in his review of Fuller, Poe's decision to republish the two tales can also be read as a foil for his growing investment in two things: the production of an effect claiming their satirical focus and the temporal aspects embedded in his early approach to the same. In both renditions, Poe invents a female narrator named Zenobia who, in striving to publish an account of a traumatic experience, ends up decapitated by the sharp metal hands slowly moving around the dial of a tower clock. When first published, Poe's tale of decapitation knowingly looked back to sensational stories often published in *Blackwood's*, which included issues surrounding the guillotine and the efficacy of executions during the French Revolution.[28] Among other things, the temporality connecting (and severing) mind and body—or the endurance of consciousness after beheading—became a hotly debated issue, something Poe deliberately exploits when Zenobia details her sensations long after her head falls from her neck.[29] Whether Zenobia's execution is humane is irrelevant to the satire, even as the patent absurdity of deciding such a matter exposes the poignant but paradoxical temporal relation both stories hold to one another.

Mr. Blackwood, the editor in the first tale, advises Zenobia to explore and exploit sensations occurring in traumatic predicaments, and she paradoxically proves successful in publishing such a tale in the second. Significantly, "Psyche Zenobia" presents itself as having been written *after* "The Scythe of Time," so there is little actual logic to the coupling of the two documents: either Zenobia is decapitated and dies, failing to write either story that she narrates, or she authors both tales in a cunning undoing of Poe's satiric portrait. Publishing both stories together perhaps allowed Poe to hide the admiration shimmering beneath his often cruel satire in much the same way that temporal relations uniting the two stories provide a loophole for our understanding of Zenobia's authority. Thus, if the association between the cutting dial of the tower clock and the odd duration of the narrator's consciousness replayed the French inquiry into these matters, it also hinted that temporal elements of traumatic events could be vital to any publication in *Blackwood's Magazine*, and perhaps the subsequent tales of Poe.

Many have noted how in either rendition the two stories are unusual because, with the exception of "Mellonta Tauta," they constitute the only tales in Poe's oeuvre told by a woman. Poe's narrators assume a variety of forms, but his resistance to assuming a woman's perspective proves fascinating. Beyond the obvious recognition that he was not particularly convincing as a woman, one wonders if by assuming the voice of an arrogant and ridiculous woman, Poe was attempting to cover his emerging interests. That is, while the two tales satirize the pretentious writing style and manipulative editorial practices too often found in magazines both in the United States and abroad, they also specifically target *Blackwood's* magazine, or the source from which Poe derived many ideas for his most successful stories, including his growing fascination with powerful effects. In republishing these stories, Poe may have been repositioning himself inside his own satire.

From the beginning, the examples listed for Zenobia's edification by Mr. Blackwood suggest Poe's playful ambivalence about these matters. Blackwood not only describes some of the stories actually published in *Blackwood's* but also praises the "nice bit of flummery" that Poe, like Zenobia, will later gleefully exploit:

> "There was 'The Dead Alive,' a capital thing!—the record of a gentleman's sensations, when entombed before the breath was out of his body—full of taste, terror, sentiment, metaphysics, and erudition. You would have sworn that the writer had been born and brought up in a coffin. Then we had the '*Confessions of an Opium-eater*'— . . . that was a nice bit of flummery, and went down the throats of the people delightfully. They would have it that Coleridge wrote the paper—but not so. It was composed by my pet baboon, Juniper, over a rummer of Hollands and water, 'hot, without sugar.'" (This I could scarcely have believed had it been anybody but Mr. Blackwood who assured me of it). "Then there was '*The Involuntary Experimentalist*,' all about a gentleman who got baked in an oven, and came out alive and well, although certainly done to a turn. . . . And then there was the '*The Man in the Bell*,'—a paper by-the bye, Miss Zenobia, which I cannot sufficiently recommend to your attention. It is the history of a young person who goes to sleep under the clapper of a church bell, and is awakened by its tolling for a funeral. The sound drives him mad, and accordingly, pulling out his tablets, he gives a record of his sensations. Sensations are the great things after all." (M 2: 339–340)

Because Poe broadly mocked Transcendentalism in "The Psyche Zenobia" and "The Scythe of Time," critics initially assumed, somewhat blithely, that Poe also targeted Fuller and her Boston circle.[30] But as many others have pointed out, Poe's twin satires were originally published before Fuller became known and threatening enough to be their obvious focus.[31] I am inclined to agree with that assessment, though this fact does not mean that Poe did not feel the need to make Fuller up, as he was arguably already doing that same year in the powerful figure of Ligeia.[32] The idea of the threatening intellectual woman, often derided as the bluestocking figure, was an available stereotype. But I want to dwell on the idea that Poe was oddly compelled to imagine the Zenobia/Ligeia figure, not as a caricature of the bluestocking figure (already a cliché), but as a foil for his own growing interest in what he will later call graphicality or the double temporal collision of afterwardsness. Such an argument involves the unwitting anticipation (or scene) to which Poe apparently returns when confronting the effective power of Fuller's writing in the mid-1840's. Even when he deepens his reference to the Boston Transcendentalists by mentioning the *Dial*, he must have recognized how the traumatic mechanism of the clock so vital to Zenobia's authorial success had already eerily anticipated these associations.

Despite the new reference to the *Dial*, there are relatively modest changes in the publications from 1838 to 1845. Some scholars have examined these changes closely to highlight Poe's intensifying resentment of the New England Transcendentalists. Yet perhaps the most revealing changes are found in the titles themselves. In shifting the name of the first section from "The Psyche Zenobia" to "How to Write a Blackwood Article," Poe directs his satire more firmly toward the act of composition and less explicitly toward the female narrator. And, of course, Poe's own essay elaborating his composition of "The Raven" will soon appear as the ghostly twin of Zenobia's decision to credit the source of her ideas for the composition of "A Predicament." Poe's alignment with Zenobia/Fuller, in other words, was set well in advance of his recognition of it.

It is my larger argument that, like one of Poe's tales, Fuller triggers a shock to the system, or what we might call the "Fuller effect," when the work she publishes appears to make her something other than an apparition of his mind. Both Fuller and Poe were voracious readers, and Poe no doubt recognized a kinship in Fuller's attachment to the writings of French and German authors. On the spectrum of autodidacts among nineteenth-century writers, Poe and Fuller occupy extreme ends. Thus, both Poe and Fuller share the idea, deeply earned through an odd mixture of rejection and acceptance of their work, that you are what you read. Considering how premonitions of the "Fuller effect" occurred powerfully enough to prompt Poe to create characters like Zenobia/Ligeia goes beyond a theory about unconscious productions and invites a deeper look at afterwardsness as a structuring cultural force.

We find evidence of that shock of recognition in the 1846 review essay that Poe published in *Godey's Lady's Book*. There Poe's satiric tongue is still very much at work, but with a familiar alternating current of praise, as when he writes of Fuller's style: "In general effect, I know no style which surpasses it. It is singularly piquant, vivid, terse, bold, luminous, leaving details out of sight, it is everything that a style need be" (ER: 1176). Poe consistently lavishes praise on Fuller, calling her a genius in one moment ("for high genius she unquestionably has" [ER: 1173]) only to display the same pedantry powering the satiric tone of "Psyche Zenobia" in the next. Thus, we find Poe criticizing Fuller for her "unjustifiable Carlyleisms (such as that of writing sentences which are no sentences, since, to be parsed, reference must be had to sentences preceding)" (ER: 1176) only to lean with considerable gusto into his own:

> Perhaps only the scholastic, or, more properly, those accustomed to look narrowly at the structure of phrases, would be willing to acquit her of ignorance of grammar—would be willing to attribute her slovenliness to disregard of the shell in anxiety for the kernel; or to waywardness, or to affectation, or to blind reverence for Carlyle—would be able to detect, in her strange and continual inaccuracies, a capacity for the accurate. (ER: 1175–1176)

Poe's reviews are notorious for their quixotic extremes, but the strange fits of passion in his assessment of Fuller's work appear to be the product of a vivid rhyming with his earlier decision to use the voice of Zenobia for his sendup of *Blackwood's* magazine.

Poe's criticism of Fuller nearly reads as a gloss for the irrepressible brio mixing nonsense with fragments of insight in the opening paragraph of "The Scythe of Time." In making Zenobia digress through her own ridiculous series of "Carlyleisms," for example, Poe has Zenobia awaken to the power of afterwardsness through her recognition that "a host of gloomy recollections" can be "stirred up by a trifle!" (M 2: 347–348). Of course, by 1846 Poe was happy to enlist Fuller in his quarrel with the accolades being lavished on Longfellow. Her tempered analysis of Longfellow's work in the New York *Daily Tribune* moved Poe to describe her review as "frank, candid, independent—in even ludicrous contrast to the usual mere glorifications of the day" (ER: 1172). But something more than his battle with Longfellow seems to be at work, particularly when he turns to discuss the effectiveness of Fuller's writing in *Summer on the Lakes.*

Because it attends to sensations produced by the American landscape that Poe had begun to deploy in his own fiction since 1843, Fuller's travel narrative clearly interests him much more than *Woman in the Nineteenth Century.*[33] Moreover, a visit to Niagara Falls plays a key part in Fuller's journey, and Poe never shied away from playing footloose with the sublime. Burton Pollin reminds us that Poe may have deliberately named his narrator Zenobia for her rather treacherous patronage of Longinus, whose thoughts on the sublime Poe also mocked.[34] Thus, we should not be surprised when Poe pauses over several key passages in *Summer on the Lakes* to highlight Fuller's ability to "paint a scene less by its features than by its effects." As Poe writes: "Many of the *descriptions* in this volume are unrivalled for *graphicality*, (why is there not such a word?) for the force with which they convey the true by the novel or unexpected" (ER: 1173). Poe then provides this telling example from Fuller's "account of Niagara" emphasizing through italics several passages that could have been lifted from his "Tale of the Ragged Mountains":

> Daily these proportions widened and towered more and more upon my sight, and I got at last a proper foreground for these sublime distances. Before coming away, I think I really saw the full wonder of the scene. After awhile it *so drew me into itself as to inspire an undefined dread, such as I never knew before, such as may be felt when death is about to usher us into a new existence.* The perpetual trampling of the waters seized my senses. *I felt that no other sound, however near, could be heard, and would start and look behind me for a foe.* I realized the identity of that mood of nature in which these waters were poured down with such absorbing force, with that in which the Indian was shaped on the same soil. For continually upon my mind came, unsought and unwelcome, *images, such as had never haunted it before, of naked savages stealing behind me with uplifted tomahawks.* Again and again this illusion recurred, and even *after I had thought it over, and tried to shake it off, I could not help starting and looking behind me.*[35] (ER: 1174)

Fuller's visit to the Midwest involved a conflicting sense of the fate of Native Americans, influenced in part by the theory of "vanishing Americans" prevalent in the archive that she scoured both before and after her journey. And not surprisingly, the fragments from Fuller that Poe highlights bear a remarkable resemblance to John Vanderlyn's 1804 painting "The Death of Jane McCrea," where a woman is depicted kneeling beneath the figures of two Native Americans wielding uplifted tomahawks.[36] According to Richard Drinnon, Vanderlyn's painting "set the pattern for an endless series of pictorial indictments" of Native Americans, and here Poe's sense of graphicality doubtless reflects his sensitivity to visual arts.[37] But Poe also attends to a type of intrusive flashback when he focuses on the "undefined dread" that Fuller freely associates with these "unwelcome images." In other words, Poe has discovered the power of afterwardsness in Fuller's writing.

Significantly, Poe is not drawn to analyze Fuller's motivations in a way that Fuller herself is tempted to do. Instead, Poe emphasizes the intensity of what he takes to be her technique: bringing two discrete experiences together to create an explosive effect. The scene from her "memory file" that Fuller summons in response to the actual experience of waters "pouring down with such absorbing force" produces the temporal collision that Poe believes crucial for the creation of a novel and vivid effect. So he writes, "Many of the descriptions in this volume are unrivalled . . . for the force with which they convey the true by the novel or unexpected, by the introduction of touches which other artists would be sure to omit as irrelevant to the subject" (ER: 1173).

Of course, what Poe considers the truth being conveyed here remains unclear. For her part, Fuller struggles with one version of that truth. The apprehension of the "identity of that mood of nature" effectively rhyming the sublime force of a waterfall with the shaping of "the Indian . . . on the same soil" does not sit well with her, especially given the intrusive and unpleasant image of herself as a sentimental maiden threatened by "savage" Native Americans. Indeed, her larger narrative spends considerable energy trying to trace these and other incongruous thoughts back to their source. What Poe does *not* tell his reader is that Fuller opens her narrative with her visit to the Falls as a way to establish how inadequately her reading had prepared her for experience at the edge of settler culture. Fuller makes a special point of noting how "descriptions and paintings" had influenced her response.[38] Thus, even though provoked for "feeling most moved in the wrong place," she finds satisfaction in the encounter only when witnessing the "quarter of a mile of tumbling, rushing rapids" extending far beyond the Falls.[39]

In other words, Fuller takes an analytic approach to the graphicality of the two scenes that collide when she stands at the foot of the falls. The fragmented images—that Poe calls "touches which other artists would be sure to omit as irrelevant to the subject" (ER: 1173)—constitute free associations from another moment in her life, including her earlier encounter with "descriptions and images" from the archive she consulted before her trip. Fuller effectively shows, in short, how dangerous one's reading can be. But here the elusiveness of history also makes its presence felt. Experiencing the sublime through the temporal structure of trauma opens another way to work through these untoward sensations. Recognizing how an irrational sense of threat results in a *mood* that, if sustained, would be anything but sublime, Fuller labors to break down the false equivalence that made the two scenes rhyme for her in that moment. We could say that rather than engaging in the work of mourning more typical of those bemoaning "vanishing Americans" without taking any responsibility, Fuller engages in the work of trauma by sundering the discrete temporal scenes that had been joined together through the eclipse of afterwardsness.[40] Her determination to footnote the sublime, to bring the mood that she experiences in line with another way of viewing the temporal operations of history, forms the analytic engine behind the effect that Poe recognizes.

Still, as is so often the case, Poe appreciates the mechanism of Fuller's method without following it to any ethical conclusions. Because he found in the traumatic temporality a way to sustain the intensity that he sought, he barely explores what Jameson would identify as the "hurt" that Fuller recognizes to be part of her description. For Poe, the marriage of the sentimental (endangered maiden) with the sensational (hatchet-wielding natives) involves just the right "introduction of touches" needed to make Niagara Falls come alive for a reader.[41] Here Poe's general fascination with relays of mood, whether in the exotic technologies brought to the mind-cure tradition by mesmerism or in the electric currents transmitting urgent messages across vast distances, supersedes his interest in moralizing on the "incidents" of history that might be embedded in Fuller's mood. Yet in another sense, those relays traverse an important domain of history, forming the infrastructure that aligns both psychic and political realms, something Fuller and Poe approach from opposite ends of a traumatic spectrum. As Maurice Lee has argued, Poe's "texts are acutely self-aware of the play between the known and the unknown mind."[42] However, whether such interplay is the product of "unconscious production,"[43] or the juncture between psychic and environmental forces that speaks to "alternatives to Freud's understanding of motivation" remains productively open.[44]

Ironically, in his conclusion Poe exposes his different approach to the same temporal effects when he strains to transmit Fuller "live" before his reader on the page. It is one of those rare moments when Poe seems genuinely excited to promote the vivacity (rather than the death) of a female figure. Whatever his motivation, Poe arrives at this animation of Fuller through a digression about the relationship between an author's work and his writing. Poe makes a strong case for the idea that an author lives in, and, perhaps *only* lives in, his printed words, which he considers the very graph of his soul:

> The supposition that the book of an author is a thing apart from the author's self, is, I think, ill-founded. The soul is a cypher, in the sense of a cryptograph; and the shorter a cryptograph is, the more difficulty there is in its comprehension—at a certain point of brevity it would bid defiance to an army of Champollions. And thus he who has written very little, may in that little either conceal his spirit or convey quite an erroneous idea of it. . . . But this is impossible with him who has written much. Of such a person we get, from his books, not merely a just, but the most just representation. . . . What poet, in especial, but must feel at least the better portion of himself more fairly represented in even his commonest sonnet, (earnestly written) than in his most elaborate or most intimate personalities? (ER: 1178)

We recognize in Poe's argument a prescient resistance to biographical criticism, especially the type taken up in early psychoanalytic approaches to his work. Poe then decides to make a "marked exception" in Fuller's case—though his exception also oddly reinforces his earlier thoughts—by noting how "her personal character and her printed book are merely one and the same thing. We get access to her soul as directly from the one as from the other. . . . Her acts are bookish, and her books are less thoughts than acts" (ER: 1179).

Anyone familiar with Fuller criticism hears in Poe's words a common pattern, since details of her life often afforded a powerful dodge for the challenge of her writing. But with his strange emphasis on the overlap between her "acts" and "books," Poe's approach takes a sudden turn away from the trivializing treatment women writers too often receive, and it does so in an effort to "perform" Fuller for his reader. He quotes a passage from *Summer on the Lakes*, and, as in his own review (and in the earlier speech of Zenobia), Poe emphasizes by italicizing key words:

> The rapids enchanted me far beyond what I expected; they are so swift that they cease to *seem* so—you can think only of their *beauty*. The fountain beyond the Moss islands I discovered for myself, and thought it for some time an *accidental* beauty which would not do to leave, lest I might never see it again. After I found it *permanent,* I returned many times to watch the play of its crest. In the little waterfall beyond, Nature seems, as she often does, to have made a *study* for some larger design. She delights in this—a sketch within a sketch—a dream within a *dream.* Wherever we see it, the lines of the great buttress in the fragment of stone, the hues of the waterfall, copied in the flowers that *star* its bordering mosses, we are *delighted*; for all the lineaments become *fluent*, and we mould the scene in the congenial thought with its *genius.* (ER: 1179)

In conjuring Fuller, Poe aptly selects a passage from her description of the currents flowing beyond the Falls, the same site Fuller used to footnote the sublime. The quote gives evidence of what Poe earlier called her "picturesque" style, though it is one with cunning reversals set between the accident of encounter (Fuller, thinking that she "discovered" something, only to discern a permanence beyond her control) and delight signaled by her faint allusion to Caliban's dream within a dream.[45] Among the highlighted words, perhaps the most interesting is "fluent," since Poe strives here to speak *fluent* Fuller. Intriguingly, to complete his enactment of Fuller's "sketch within a sketch," Poe supplies a physical account of Fuller, focusing on her face, as he often does in his fictional depictions of characters. It is easy to recognize the author of "Ligeia" now penning Poe's portrait of Fuller, especially since he creates what might be called a mash-up of his portrayal of Rowena and Ligeia:

> a profusion of lustrous light hair; eyes a bluish gray, full of fire; capacious forehead; the mouth when in repose indicates profound sensibility, capacity for affection, for love—when moved by a slight smile, it becomes even beautiful in the intensity of this expression; but the upper lip, as if impelled by the action of involuntary muscles, habitually uplifts itself, conveying the impression of a sneer. (ER: 1180)

The admiration mixed with a subtle disaffection is worthy of the narrator of "Ligeia." But through a shift in focus Poe suddenly instructs his reader to

> imagine, now, a person of this description looking at you at one moment earnestly in the face, at the next seeming to look only within her own spirit or at the wall; moving nervously every now and then in her chair; speaking in a high key, but musically, deliberately, (not hurriedly or loudly,) with a delicious distinctness of enunciation—speaking, I say, the paragraph in question, and emphasizing the words which I have italicized, not by impulsion of the breath, (as is usual,) but by drawing them out as long as possible, nearly closing her eyes the while—imagine all this, and we have both the woman and the authoress before us. (ER: 1180)

In one sense, Poe's new command to his reader follows a path that Dupin elaborates in "The Purloined Letter," with a slight but important variation. Here Poe solicits the reader to align the expression and movement of Fuller's face, not with her own, but with Fuller's expressive words directly *facing her* on the page. At the same time, because Poe wants to capture Fuller "now," he compels his reader to pass through *his* words in order to do so. The final paragraph imitating Fuller reading Fuller thus provides an ironic ending to the review, since, according to Poe's earlier elaboration, the words generating this burlesque also provide the "most just representation" of him. Ultimately, the vivid effect that Poe seeks for his reader involves a queer decision to scandalously rhyme his animated style with Fuller's.

One might be tempted to argue that in selecting the passage by the rapids from *Summer on the Lakes*, Poe labors to act out Fuller's analytic approach. And there would be some truth to that idea since Poe clearly identifies the location where Fuller rethinks her hurtful response to the Falls. Yet his decision to create the final effect by superimposing the body of his writing onto hers interrupts analysis by leaving his reader inside yet another set of rhyming scenes. Certainly, unlike "Ligeia," where the narrator assumes one woman has returned in the dying body of another, Poe's performance allows the style of two writers to share the stage of the page in their most vibrant form. But the effect that Poe achieves both here and in "Ligeia" can be said to depend upon rhyming scenes where separate moments in the narrator's life suddenly merge in a high—dare we say traumatic—moment of graphicality. It is perhaps not strange that readers of "Ligeia" have found in that vivid moment conflicting evidence of either an anachronistic queer pleasure or a pervasive fear of racial amalgamation, the threatened mingling of bodies that are the same, or the threatening mingling of bodies that are quite different.[46] Yet if Poe's writing initially displaces the history informing such readings, the traumatic temporality of afterwardsness can explain the operations of its elusive nature. Poe's vivid hookup with Fuller might return us then to the traumatic foresight of Zenobia later realized in Fuller's keener analytic response to temporal effects: "what a host of recollections can be stirred up by a trifle."

NOTES

1. See Scott Peeples, "Poe and Psychoanalysis," in *The Afterlife of Edgar Allan Poe* (Rochester, NY: Camden House, 2004), 29–62.
2. Editors of a recent edition of Poe scholarship note that "the revival of Poe's fortunes in the early twentieth century in his home country . . . finds its sources in a combination of forces, including growing American cultural nationalism after World War I; a desire on the part of "the post-Reconstruction South" for literary forefathers; the establishment of literary marketplaces for science fiction and detective fiction, both of which claim Poe as a founding father; and the emergence of psychoanalytic criticism." See Jared Gardner, Elizabeth Hewitt, eds., *Edgar Allan Poe: Selected Poetry, Tales, and Essays; Authoritative Texts with Essays on Three Critical Controversies* (Boston: Bedford/St. Martin's, 2017), 255 (Kindle).
3. See Shoshana Felman, "The Case of Poe: Application/Implications of Psychoanalysis," in *Jacques Lacan and the Adventure of Insight: Psychoanalysis in Contemporary Culture* (Cambridge, MA: Harvard University Press, 1989), 27–51.
4. "On Some Motifs in Baudelaire," in *Walter Benjamin: Selected Writings, vol. 4, 1938–1940*, trans. Edmund Jephcott and others, ed. Howard Eiland and Michael W. Jennings (Cambridge, MA: Harvard University Press, 2003), 313–355.
5. Lacan, "Seminar on 'The Purloined Letter,'" trans. Jeffrey Mehlman, *Yale French Studies* 48 (1972): 39–72.
6. Barbara Johnson remarks upon Derrida's belief that Lacan "purloined" ideas from Marie Bonaparte who questioned key elements of Baudelaire's translation of the story. See Johnson's "The Frame of Reference: Poe, Lacan, Derrida," in *The Critical Difference: Essays in the Contemporary Rhetoric of Reading* (Baltimore: The Johns Hopkins University Press, 1985), 110–146.
7. Toni Morrison, *Playing in the Dark: Whiteness and the Literary Imagination* (Cambridge, MA: Harvard University Press, 1992). Quoted material on 68; see especially "Romancing the Shadow," 29–60.
8. Jameson, *The Political Unconscious: Narrative as Socially Symbolic Act* (New York: Cornell University Press, 1981), 102.
9. Ruth Leys, *Trauma: A Genealogy* (Chicago: University of Chicago Press, 2000).
10. See Adam Crabtree, *From Mesmer to Freud: Magnetic Sleep and the Roots of Psychological Healing* (New Haven, CT: Yale University Press, 1993); and Bruce Mills, *Poe, Fuller, and the Mesmeric Arts: Transition States in the American Renaissance* (Columbia: University of Missouri Press, 2006). For Poe, mesmerism, and early trauma theory, see Zwarg, "Vigorous Currents, Painful Archives: The Production of Affect and History in Poe's 'Tale of the Ragged Mountains,'" *Poe Studies: History, Theory, Interpretation* 43, no. 1 (October 2010): 7–33.
11. This idea is evident in an essay by Jonathan Elmer ("The Jingle Man: Trauma and the Aesthetic"), who finds Poe's anomalous status in literary history best described by weaving theories of the event in Jean-François Lyotard and Derrida with the temporal stutter between the real and "everyday descriptions of reality" (135) that Elmer borrows from Lacan.
12. Thomas H. McNeal, "Poe's Zenobia: An Early Satire on Margaret Fuller," *Modern Language Quarterly* 11 (June 1950): 205–216. McNeal's reading was challenged by Burton R. Pollin in "Poe's Tale of Psyche Zenobia: A Reading for Humor and Ingenious Construction,"

in *Papers on Poe: Essays in Honor of John Ward Ostrom*, ed. Richard Veler (Springfield, OH: Chantry Music Press at Wittenberg University, 1972), 92–103. Stuart Levine and Susan F. Levine also questioned McNeal's reading in their edition *The Short Fiction of Edgar Allan Poe: An Annotated Edition* (Urbana: University of Illinois Press, 1976), 414.

13. Eliza Richards, in *Gender and the Poetics of Reception in Poe's Circle* (Cambridge: Cambridge University Press, 2004), makes an excellent argument about Poe's constant dependency on female poets and his emulation of their work, noting in particular how literary history has failed to see the powerful cross-gendered dynamic so central to his creative ambition. Fuller's case is slightly different since it is not her poetry but her prose that stuns him into the recognition that the rational (masculine) pose he had assumed in his critical writing to further "upstage" women poets was already operative as a feminine performance in her work (52).
14. Jacques Lacan, "The Function and Field of Speech and Language in Psychoanalysis," in *Écrits: A Selection*, trans. Alan Sheridan (New York: Norton, 1977), 48; Jean Laplanche, *Essays on Otherness*, trans. and ed. John Fletcher (London: Routledge, 1999), especially "Notes on Afterwardness," 260–265.
15. John Fletcher, *Freud: The Scene of Trauma* (New York: Fordham University Press, 2013).
16. Cathy Caruth, introduction to *Trauma: Explorations in Memory*, ed. Cathy Caruth (Baltimore: The Johns Hopkins University Press, 1995), 9.
17. Katherine Bond Stockton, *The Queer Child, or Growing Sideways in the Twentieth Century* (Durham, NC: Duke University Press, 2009); Elizabeth Freeman, *Time Binds: Queer Temporalities, Queer Histories* (Durham, NC: Duke University Press, 2010).
18. Valerie Rohy, "Ahistorical," *GLQ: A Journal of Lesbian and Gay Studies* 12, no. 1 (2006): 68.
19. Felman, "The Case of Poe: Application/Implications of Psychoanalysis," 45, 51.
20. Felman, "The Case of Poe: Application/Implications of Psychoanalysis," 50.
21. As Thomas Ollive Mabbott reminds us, Poe began such descriptions earlier in his May 1842 review of Hawthorne's *Twice-Told Tales in Graham's* (M 2: 335).
22. See Margaret Alterton, "Blackwood and Other British Periodicals," in *Origins of Poe's Critical Theory* (Iowa City: University of Iowa Humanistic Studies, 1925), 7–45.
23. David Leverenz, "Spanking the Master: Mind-Body Crossing in Poe's Sensationalism," in *Historical Guide to Edgar Allan Poe*, ed. J. Gerald Kennedy (New York: Oxford University Press, 2001), 97.
24. See Robert Eaglestone, "Knowledge, 'Afterwardsness' and the Future of Trauma Theory," in *The Future of Trauma Theory: Contemporary Literary and Cultural Criticism*, ed. Gert Buelens, Sam Durrant, and Robert Eaglestone (New York: Taylor and Francis, 2013), 16–17 (Kindle): "It may be that the same structure inhabits a wide range of non-traumatic discourses" including joy, for example.
25. Barbara Cantalupo, *Poe and the Visual Arts* (University Park: Penn State University Press, 2014), 4–5. Burton Pollin, *Images of Poe's Works: A Comprehensive Descriptive Catalogue of Illustrations* (Westpoint, CT: Greenwood Press, l989), 2. Recently, Matthew A. Taylor—in "Edgar Allan Poe's (Meta)physics: A Pre-History of the Post-Human," *Nineteenth-Century Literature* 62, no. 2 (September 2007): 193–221—has found a relation between Poe's mesmerism and "a graphic, sensory process wherein people are disarticulated by the tangible, cosmically invested objects of their putatively everyday lives" (199), aligning Poe with contemporary discussions of the "post-human."
26. Poe, "The Literati [Part IV]," *Godey's Lady's Book* 33 (August 1846): 72–78.

27. Perry Miller, *The Transcendentalists: An Anthology* (Cambridge, MA: Harvard University Press, 1950), 467. Joseph Jay Deiss repeated this comment without attribution in *American Heritage Magazine* 23, no. 5 (August 1972).
28. Poe may have been satirizing Washington Irving's tale "The Adventures of the German Student" from *Tales of a Traveller* (1824). See J. Gerald Kennedy, *Strange Nation: Literary Nationalism and Cultural Conflict in the Age of Poe* (New York: Oxford University Press, 2016), 36–72, for Poe's "irritation with Irving" (39).
29. A thorough account of the French controversy can be found in Ludmilla Jordanova's "Medical Mediations: Mind, Body and the Guillotine," *History Workshop*, no. 28 (Autumn 1989): 39–52. See also "An Execution in Paris," *Blackwood* 24 (December 1828): 785–788.
30. These assumptions initially derived from the fictional portrait of Fuller as Zenobia in Hawthorne's later novel *The Blithedale Romance*.
31. Stuart Levine and Susan F. Levine, "Comic Satires and Grotesques, 1836–1849," in *A Companion to Poe Studies*, ed. Eric W. Carlson (Westport, CT: Greenwood Press, 1996), 131. Thomas H. McNeal neatly outlines the publication history in his essay, "Poe's Zenobia." Poe first published the essays in 1838 in American *Museum of Literature and the Arts* as "The Psyche Zenobia" and "The Scythe of Time," and then in 1840 in *Tales of the Grotesque and Arabesque* as "The Signora Zenobia" and "The Scythe of Time," and finally in the *Broadway Journal* on July 12, 1845, as "How to Write a Blackwood Tale" and "A Predicament." The reference to the *Dial* only came in the 1845 version.
32. Morella is of course an earlier prototype, perhaps even drawn from an account of a Spanish woman named "Morella" known for her learning.
33. Poe disavows an earlier negative review of *Woman in the Nineteenth Century* that appeared in *The Broadway Journal*, insisting that he did not write it, though he certainly says very little that is positive about *Woman* in this review.
34. Pollin, "Poe's Tale of Psyche Zenobia," 95.
35. Poe then adds a sentence from the end of the next paragraph, giving this complex paragraph a different tone. "What I liked best was to sit on Table Rock close to the great fall; *there all power of observing details, all separate consciousness was quite lost*" (ER: 1174).
36. Leon Jackson reminds us how Poe earned the nickname "literary Mohawk." See "'Behold Our Literary Mohawk, Poe': Literary Nationalism and the 'Indianation' of Antebellum American Culture," *ESQ* 48 (2002): 97–133. In fact, in a mixed review of "*The Raven* and *Other Poems*" (*New-York Tribune*, November 26, 1845), Fuller described Poe as "wielding the weapons of criticism . . . with uplifted tomahawk." Jackson claims Fuller's reading was caustic, though it is actually mixed since she also discredits the swelling practices of "organized puff." Fuller's review came one month after critics revived the image of Poe's "savage" criticism to describe his controversial lecture at the Boston Lyceum. That same November Poe finally repudiated any association between himself and the indigenous population, especially his "Mohawk" reputation. These associations make Poe's decision to choose Fuller's passage about her response to Niagara Falls even thicker and more deliciously overdetermined. I want to thank Lara Cohen for her insights and for bringing Jackson's essay to my attention.
37. Zwarg, "Footnoting the Sublime: Margaret Fuller on Blackhawk's Trail," in *Feminist Conversations* (Ithaca, NY: Cornell University Press, 1995), 97–124. Richard Drinnon, *Facing West: The Metaphysics of Indian Hating and Empire Building* (Minneapolis: University of Minnesota Press, 1980), 101.

38. Fuller, *Summer on the Lakes, in 1843* (Boston: Charles C. Little and James Brown; New York: Charles S. Francis and Company, 1844), 11.
39. Fuller, *Summer on the Lakes*, 12.
40. Zwarg, "The Work of Trauma: Fuller, Douglass, and Emerson on the Border of Ridicule," *Studies in Romanticism* 41, no. 1 (Spring 2002): 65–88.
41. Jonathan Elmer writes, "the sensational—the moment of shock, or horror, or revulsion—erupts from within the sentimental," in *Reading at the Social Limit: Affect, Mass Culture, and Edgar Allan Poe* (Stanford, CA: Stanford University Press, 1995), 93. David Leverenz, who cites this same passage in "Spanking the Master," prefers "Elmer's alternative formulation of this sentence that 'the sensational . . . vampirizes the sentimental'" (Leverenz, 123; quote from Elmer, "Terminate or Liquidate? Poe, Sensationalism, and the Sentimental Tradition," in *The American Face of Edgar Allan Poe*, ed. Shawn Rosenheim and Stephen Rachman, 91). See Leverenz, "Spanking the Master: Mind-Body Crossing in Poe's Sensationalism," 95–127.
42. Maurice S. Lee, "Absolute Poe: His System of Transcendental Racism," *American Literature* 75, no. 4 (2003): 771.
43. Lee, "Absolute Poe," 771.
44. Adam Frank, *Transferential Poetics, From Poe to Warhol* (New York: Fordham University Press, 2015), 15. Freud was also keen to note later that repression was not the only mechanism of psychic defense. Trauma theory has often tried to separate trauma from the too broad sweep of repression and its operations since it is clear that affect and unconscious mechanisms work in a far more complicated fashion than Freud initially thought. See Adam Frank on Silvan Tomkins. As Frank observes, Tompkins theorized that affects were neither part of the instincts nor Freud's repressive theory. Frank, *Transferential Poetics*, 15.
45. A title Poe will later use in an 1849 poem.
46. Joan Dayan, "Amorous Bondage: Poe, Ladies, and Slaves," in *The American Face of Edgar Allan Poe*, ed. Shawn Rosenheim and Stephen Rachman (Baltimore: Johns Hopkins University Press, 1995), 179–209.

Bibliography

Alterton, Margaret. "Blackwood and Other British Periodicals." In *Origins of Poe's Critical Theory*, 7–45. Iowa City: University of Iowa Humanistic Studies, 1925.

Eaglestone, Robert. "Knowledge, 'Afterwardsness' and the Future of Trauma Theory." In *The Future of Trauma Theory: Contemporary Literary and Cultural Criticism*, edited by Gert Buelens, Sam Durrant and Robert Eaglestone, 11–22. London: Routledge, 2013.

Elmer, Jonathan. "The Jingle Man: Trauma and the Aesthetic." In *Fissions and Fusions: Proceedings of the First Conference of the Cape American Studies Association*, edited by Lesley Marx, Loes Nas, and Lara Dunwell, 131–145. Belville, South Africa: University of the Western Cape, 1997.

Felman, Shoshana. "The Case of Poe: Application/Implications of Psychoanalysis." In *Jacques Lacan and the Adventure of Insight: Psychoanalysis in Contemporary Culture*, 27–51. Cambridge, MA: Harvard University Press, 1989.

Fletcher, John. *Freud: The Scene of Trauma*. New York: Fordham University Press, 2013.

Frank, Adam. *Transferential Poetics, From Poe to Warhol*. New York: Fordham University Press, 2015.

Laplanche, Jean. *Seductions, Translations, Drives*. Translated by Martin Stanton. Edited by J. Fletcher and M. Stanton. London: Institute of Contemporary Arts, 1992.

Lee, Maurice S. "Absolute Poe: His System of Transcendental Racism." *American Literature* 75, no. 4 (2003): 751–781.

Leverenz, David. "Spanking the Master: Mind-Body Crossing in Poe's Sensationalism." In *Historical Guide to Edgar Allan Poe*, edited by J. Gerald Kennedy, 95–127. New York: Oxford University Press, 2001.

McNeal, Thomas H. "Poe's Zenobia: An Early Satire on Margaret Fuller." *Modern Language Quarterly* 11 (June 1950): 205–216.

Peeples, Scott. "Poe and Psychoanalysis." In *The Afterlife of Edgar Allan Poe*, 29–62. Rochester, NY: Camden House, 2004.

Pollin, Burton R. "Poe's Tale of Psyche Zenobia: A Reading for Humor and Ingenious Construction." In *Papers on Poe: Essays in Honor of John Ward Ostrom*, edited by Richard Veler, 92–103. Springfield, OH: Chantry Music Press at Wittenberg University, 1972.

Rohy, Valerie. "Ahistorical." *GLQ: A Journal of Lesbian and Gay Studies* 12, no. 1 (2006): 61–83.

CHAPTER 44

UNQUALIFIED PLEASURE

Poe on Forms of Life

BRANKA ARSIĆ

NOTORIOUSLY weird things occur in Poe's world, in fact so bizarre that some readers dismiss them as mere exaggeration, whereas for others they amount to philosophical dilettantism. The list of strange things occurring in Poe is long, but perhaps most famously, human wills are rendered so powerful that they transport the dead back to life; matter is able to transcend decay, whereas dead bodies, even when dismembered, pulsate with vitality; inspirited forces—from minds to presumed supernatural agencies—are endowed with power to generate physical phenomena, such as inarticulate sounds and styled whispers, or to affect the physical by animating or stalling its motion, altering its figuration through various mergings and disseminations of particles of matter. Additionally, the natural and material is afforded immanent life, enabling it to change without any intervention by divine powers or by anything immaterial at all. Thus, stones and rocks sometimes feel and experience, plants are said to enjoy or suffer, and even planets and elements, as the end of *Eureka* postulates, are found to be happy and joyous.

How, then, are we to understand such instances? A long tradition of critical reading has explained away Poe's preoccupations by classifying them as Gothic devices mobilized to fuse the strange with the pleasing and to appease the morbid by styling it into the fantastic, while simultaneously spellbinding the reader by means of the cultivated terror he depicts. But as I will argue, that approach—which reads Poe as a romance-Goth—is weak, because it reduces to the *aesthetic* phenomena that are in fact often *scientific*, summoned by Poe from domains as different as biology, geology, astronomy, or medicine. For instance, when the claim that death is a radically slowed-down life is taken not as scientific but as a narratological device allowing the dead to revisit the living, and thus generate horror, then the aesthetic is made to function as a normalizing shield protecting a dualistic ontology (which posits the divide between spiritual and material, takes matter to be inert, and establishes clear taxonomical topographies that separate beings into their proper existential niches). In that way we are assured that Poe's anomalous worlds are not really that, but merely abstractly or aesthetically so. By *ideating*, and thus anesthetizing Poe's propositions, the "aesthetic" approach—where aestheticization refers to the content of his narratives, not to their form—weakens the challenge those propositions pose to Western ontology. It makes us overlook just how seriously Poe was invested in critiquing that ontology, how dedicated he was, as Joan Dayan has argued, to "debunk[ing] the cant of idealism."[1] That tradition of criticism turns into "romance" his deadly serious ontology, which, in Dayan's terms again, is monistic (enabling the "convertibility" of spiritual into material), committed to "a radically physical world," and so "attach[ed] to materiality"[2] that even if there are "phantoms and rarified presences" in his stories, "they are always seen through or next to the collateral flesh and blood remnants."[3] As I will argue here, this commitment to the physical, which Poe's ontology understands as inherently vital, manifests as a ceaseless experiment with processes of becoming and transformation, undoing the existential status quo of beings and persons. His propositions thus resist being aestheticized as romance, for as Dayan also maintained, " 'romance' . . . always serves the status quo" by "mythologiz[ing] an inwardness,"[4] whereas Poe shatters the coherence of any inwardness, reducing it to the material supposedly external to it. I will also argue that this commitment to the physical and its transformations is generated by, and based on Poe's reading in the natural sciences of his time, specifically the work of a group of English scientists who formulated materialist vitalist arguments and proposed a radical destabilization of the taxonomic order charged with regulating what can be called human, what belongs to life and what to death, what to animals and what to plants. Additionally, to demonstrate that Poe doesn't simply apply that vitalism to the world his literature creates but comes to formulate, on the basis of it, his own intricate vitalist ontology, progressively fine-tuning it throughout his life, I will focus my attention on the formulations it received in "The Fall of the House of Usher" and "Mesmeric Revelation." In so doing my aim is also to posit that this ever-intensifying interest in vitalism was not motivated by its ontology alone, but sought above all to provide a nonabstract or, as Poe also calls it, "earthly" theory of death, which found its formulation in the cryptic but complex theory of pleasure that ends "Mesmeric Revelation."

The Science of Living Stones

Already, in "The Fall of the House of Usher" (1839), Poe formulates an ontology that affords vital agency to what is impersonal (plants, for instance) and even inanimate (minerals and stones). It is summoned not from the Gothic aesthetic tradition but from the resources of contemporary natural sciences.

Usher's world is thoroughly vital and sensuous. If human death—for instance, that of his sister Madeline—is notoriously revealed not as inertia but as life that has slowed down to miniscule and imperceptible motions, it is because nothing dies there. Not only are plants, lowly organisms, mushrooms, and other cryptogamic minutiae enlivened, but so too are rocks, stones, air, water, window glass, curtains, wooden objects, lamps, doors, and musical instruments. Such "things" possess the vital capacity to self-transform, sense, and enact sensations; they are not simply mobile mechanisms but rather actors endowed with sensuousness and capable of generating perceptions of their own qualities in others. Now that might not be obvious to common perception, which would register certain of those slow changes as immobility, but the world of Usher presumes that an extraordinarily subtle sense would detect its vital activity experientially. Usher has such refined perceptual capacities, enabling him to sense the actual livelihood of objects routinely classified as dead or inorganic, and rendering his vitalistic theory of matter, which he relates to the narrator, neither abstract nor delusional but empirical. As the narrator reconstructs, Usher's ardent perception precisely allows him to observe the slight motion of the "gray stones of the home of his forefathers" (M 2: 408), which serves as a factual basis for his "earnest . . . persuasion" that the "sentience" afforded "to all vegetable things" "trespasses, under certain conditions, upon the kingdom of inorganization" (M 2: 408). As the narrator clarifies, "The conditions of the sentience had been here, [Usher] imagined, fulfilled in the method of collocation of these stones—in the order of their arrangement, as well as in that of the many fungi, which overspread them, and of the decayed trees which stood around—above all, in the long undisturbed endurance of this arrangement, and in its reduplication in the still waters of the tarn. Its evidence—the evidence of the sentience—was to be seen, he said . . . in the gradual yet certain condensation of an atmosphere of their own about the waters and the walls" (M 2: 408). Usher perceives all phenomena to be entangled in a continuous field of living matter, where they simultaneously affect and become affected, exerting but also enduring agency. For he perceives everything as an arrangement of stones filigreed with the vegetal networks of fungi and surrounded by the still waters of a basin, creating an ecosystem whose stagnation, warmth, and condensation literally or "chemically" enliven the geological and the elemental (condensation of the air) in such a manner that their minute sensuous animation acts on him, making him the patient receiver of their "silent, yet, importunate influence" (M 2: 408).

Poe does say that Usher's perception is "morbid," but on the other hand he doesn't want us to disqualify it as delusional. To present this all-encompassing sensuousness as serious, Poe has the narrator himself, presumably a man of "vigorous" senses, perceive the vitality of Usher's eco-estate, and report on how affected he is by its influence. The narrator admits that he had "so worked upon [his] imagination as really to believe" that Usher's whole property is alive, that "about the whole mansion and domain there hung an atmosphere peculiar to themselves and their immediate vicinity—an atmosphere . . . which had reeked up from the decayed trees, and the gray wall, and the silent tarn—a pestilent and mystic vapor, . . . faintly discernible, and leaden-hued" (M 2: 399–400). The closer he looked the more he was overwhelmed with the "vivid force of the sensations" that "increased [his] superstition" about the livelihood of the domain, for he too observed the processes of condensation, evaporation, and stagnation—which in Usher's view generated life—as merging phenomena in a closed system ("peculiar" to itself) capable of self-organization. His "superstition" regarding the agency of the terrain increases, and in order to shake off "the force of the sensations which oppressed" him, he "scan[s] more narrowly the real aspect of the building" (M 2: 399–400) but perceives yet again the same entangled and living ecosystem, in which various beings and phenomena form continuous, affective, vital fields of matter. His imagination is eventually appeased, and his calmed perception sees the property in this way:

> Its principal feature seemed to be that of excessive antiquity. . . . Minute fungi overspread the whole exterior, hanging in a fine tangled web-work from the caves. Yet all this was apart from any extraordinary dilapidation. No portion of the masonry had fallen; and there appeared to be a wild inconsistency between its still perfect adaptation of parts, and the crumbling condition of the individual stones. In this there was much that reminded me of the specious totality of old wood-work which has rotted for long years in some neglected vault, with no disturbance from the breath of the external air. (M 2: 400)

Thanks to the microclimate of this self-sustaining basin, stones exist as if they were living beings, transformed into porous wood in the process of rotting, but serving as fertile soil for growing cryptogams, which themselves weave "fine tangled web-work" that expands into the masonry, functioning like the veins of its enlivening. The whole domain—the house, the organisms on it, the trees around it—thus becomes a single rhizomatic vital being, an integrated topography of primary, lower life perceived at the moment of its emergence, created by the atmospheric and geological condition of the tarn. It affects the narrator's perceptions not only by virtue of a chemical causality via its "leaden-hued" vapors (M 2: 400) but also physically, by "reverberating" (M 2: 415) and by slightly "crumbling" (M 2: 400).

Although the narrator's corroboration of Usher's "acute" perceptions produces a description of the tarn's biosystem that de facto cancels their apparent "morbidity," he nevertheless considers the vitalist ontology on which Usher predicates such perceptions to be extravagant, and he opines that he would never go so far as to impute affectivity to the geological. On his account, Usher's theory ascribing affectivity to unorganized phenomena is "more daring in character" (M 2: 408), even utterly idiosyncratic, for while "other men [maintain] . . . the sentience of all vegetable things" (M 2: 408), Usher alone renders stones sensuous. As the short footnote that the narrator adds to the text specifies, "other men" had already proposed the sentient agency of "all vegetable things," such as the English physician and naturalist Thomas Percival, the Italian biologist Lazzaro Spalanzani, and the British chemist Richard Watson (in his "Chemical Essays," referenced by the narrator as *An Essay on the Subject of Chemistry, and Their General Division*) (M 2: 408n). But the narrator's suggestion that the three vitalists to whom he directs us have not claimed vitality for unorganized matter is misleading, and a reader who checked its accuracy would find that Usher's theory, far from being "more daring," in fact quotes directly from the current scientific understanding of matter.

The three scientists the narrator references slightly differ in their understanding of matter's vitality. For Percival, Usher's claim might sound too daring since the former is indeed more preoccupied with an effort to destabilize the taxonomical borders separating animal from vegetal than those separating vegetal from mineral. Identifying instances of vegetal sensitivity, Percival concluded that life understood as the capacity to perceive (as manifesting a "degree of perceptivity") does belong to the vegetal, but he remained uncertain whether the same might be proposed for the mineral.[5] More radically than Percival, Spalanzani argued that the inorganic could be rendered vital but only under certain circumstances and for a limited period of time; but he left the question of its vitality undecided.[6] More radically still, Richard Watson ascribed vital agency and perceptiveness to all existents, including geological phenomena, from stones to sand and minerals. Usher will quote his examples almost verbatim, raising the question of whether his experience of his house's livelihood should remain a fiction and be declared guilty of the pathetic fallacy, or, to the contrary, afforded scientific status.

For Watson, professor of chemistry at Cambridge, Usher's statement couldn't be more scientific. On his account, "Naturalists, as well as Chemists, have perhaps too precipitately embraced the opinion, that Minerals may be certainly and readily distinguished from the other two kingdoms . . . of a vegetable and an animal,"[7] since the list of instances scientifically corroborating the vitality of the geological is long. That stones, ores, and minerals should be understood as taxa of vegetal life is proven to him by the fact that when "dug out of quarries" or "mines" they are "like the dead branches or limbs of vegetables or animals, incapable of receiving increase, except from an external incrustation," whereas as long as they remain integrated in quarries, they extend their "parts" by "internal assimilation" or growth. That shows that they are nurtured by their surrounds just as plants are.[8] Mines and tarns in general, whose absence of ventilation, and stagnant air—such as characterizes Usher's tarn—turns them into damp microclimatic zones that feed geological life, constitute environments in which the vegetation of stones especially abounds. Watson offers the example of the "mines of Chremnitz in Hungary, which have been wrought for above one thousand years, the ancient roads which had been cut through the rocks are left to grow up;" moreover, Giorgio Baglivi, the solidist physician, "observed the same phaenomenon . . . in the marble quarries in Italy," proving that in isolated biomilieus such as quarries, basins, mines, or tarns, stones reveal their vegetal nature.[9] Stalactites similarly corroborate the vegetal nature of the geological, for the "concentrick crusts of which [they] consist, are not either in their appearance, or their formation . . . unlike the circles annually produced by the stagnation of the sap in the boll and branches of trees"[10]; like minerals and stones, stalactites also grow, albeit slowly, making it difficult for Watson to maintain the difference between stones and trees. Even gold and silver belong to a family of stony trees, for "they appear to burst through the hardest rocks," indicating "a kind of vegetation in their formation" and explaining why "from their great resemblance to trees [they] have been called by some arborescent."[11] Other metals too display arborescent life; for instance, when "lead" is exposed to heat—the same lead that is said to "hue" the atmosphere of Usher's domain on which so many "decayed trees" spread—it burns like "rotten wood,"[12] proving to Watson that its "inner" nature is tree-like. Similarly "rock crystals, amethyst, and various precious stones" are proven by the Flemish naturalist Anselmus De Boodt (in *The History of Gems and Stones* [1609]), to "grow like mushrooms,"[13] a finding that finally convinces Watson that while geological phenomena might differ among themselves as much as mushrooms differ from trees, they are nevertheless forms of plant life, subspecies of fungi and therefore alive, even if not always organized. As Watson put it, the "inward constitution of the globe," "internal structure of the earth," "scales of a fish, the feathers of a bird," "minerals," "all the strata of limestones, chalks, marbles, all gypsums, spars, alabasters," "the strata of pit-coal, and of all bituminous fossils," "the mould every where covering the surface of the earth," "all matter is . . . enlivened, animated."[14]

For Watson, this continuum of living matter is total; it includes all phenomena from stones to humans, with nothing isolated from anything else by the boundaries of its own taxon. Moreover, empirically speaking, supposed taxonomical boundaries are nonexistent, since the world is an affective and vital string of heterogeneous beings capable of acting on each other and being mutually modified by such action, precisely because their figuration is porous. In Watson's science, taxa are a nuisance; he views the "systematic distinction, and specific divisions of things" as "useful" only "in enlarging the comprehension of the mind by methodizing the objects" but "having no real foundation in nature."[15] Nature doesn't recognize "specific divisions of things" since in it each individual is a permeable existent whose borders fade into the background continuum of living matter, bringing into the same existential vicinity phenomena as diverse as a dog and a tree: "Every one thinks that he knows what an animal is, and how it is contradistinguished from a vegetable, and would be offended at having his knowledge questioned thereupon. A dog or a horse he is truly persuaded, are beings as clearly distinguished from an herb or a tree, as light is from darkness; yet as in these, so in the production of nature, the transition from one to the other is effected by imperceptible gradations."[16] Through those imperceptible gradations, which make it difficult to clearly demarcate between a dog and a tree, one phenomenon passes into another: mineral, stone, and metal are all related to the human, for "men and minerals and all intermediate existences are bound together."[17]

However, something crucially relevant for understanding the scientific background to Usher's theories is Watson's idea that the continuity between mineral and man is not only historical or "evolutionary" but also synchronic or ecological. Synchronic continuity is necessitated by what he claims to be the quintessential attribute of life, which is the capacity of matter not to form or to spontaneously strive—both of those being life's secondary characteristics—but to perceive. As Watson explicitly puts it, "rejecting spontaneous motion and figural boundedness as very inadequate tests of animality, we adopt perception in their stead."[18] And since for Watson "all matter is . . . enlivened," all matter is also perceptive, and therefore active. For to say that each being is endowed with perception is to posit that it possesses the power to create that perception. Moreover, through such creativity, it shows itself capable of actively affecting not only itself but other, surrounding beings. All existences that perceive are therefore actants rather than mechanical mobiles, and not only every member of the animal kingdom but also "every part of the vegetable kingdom,"[19] as well as "strata of stones," and "veins of minerals,"[20] have "acute perception," "a degree of perceptivity"[21] that makes them able to vitally relate, through the interaction with one another that takes place at any given point of time, and across species and categories.

Usher's philosophy, which ascribes to life the status of "inorganization," far from being the peculiar expression of his radicalism, is in fact an adequate summary of current scientific vitalist theories. Once it is transplanted to Usher's particular domain, Watson's claim that everything is animated by perception comes to mean, as in the narrative, that the terrain on which the house stands, stones, other growths (fungi and rotten trees), the atmosphere, and minds all perceive; they all have the capacity to generate and receive sensations, to stir and be stirred, not simply through the mechanical pressure of their embodied milieu, but by their own force of sensing. Usher's "domain," which is "peculiar to itself" because it is insulated in a tarn-milieu, thus emerges as one of Watson's mini-atmospheres superbly fitted for nurturing "stone vegetation." We come to understand that in Usher's world everything is a form of sensuous vegetal life, from stones to old and rotten wood ("the specious totality of old wood-work which has rotted for long years in some neglected vault"), to mushrooms, and even lead, said to hue the atmosphere. All of those life forms, according to this rigorously circular eco-logic, transform themselves into one another: seemingly inanimate stones grow mushrooms or appear as rotting trees which are themselves, however, not in a state of "dilapidation" but are rather understood as a sequence in the growth of geological vegetation.

Moreover, Poe's narrator also affirms Watson's double perceptual streams, both historic (the gradual and continuous transformation of simple into complex life forms) and ecologically lateral (the actual capacity of unorganized or vegetal life to act on complex beings), when he posits a literal continuity between the house and its past inhabitants, as well as between the house and its current residents. Previous and present occupants become "so identified [with the mansion] . . . as to merge the original title of the estate in the quaint and equivocal appellation of the 'House of Usher'" with the "people" living in it, which explains why the "peasantry" used the appellation to designate "both the family and the family mansion" (M 2: 399). And while, as G. R. Thompson accurately observes, the narrator here "senses something puzzling or uncertain in the naming of the house as physical building and the 'house' as family," this ontological disorientation does not derive, as Thompson proposes, from the narrator's realization that there exists "an occult relation between the family of Usher and the seemingly sentient physical building which is mysteriously tied in with their fate."[22] Rather, according to the scientific ontology of Poe's story, the building is not "seemingly" but *really* sensuous, and the relations between the house and the man are not occult but material, in line with Watson's scientifically grounded claim that "God hath established an uninterrupted concatenation in all his works." For Watson, "uninterrupted concatenation" means that—if we perceive "different individuals . . . mingled together into the same species," "different species into the same genus," and "different genera into the same kingdom"—it is not because they are really severed, in which case the perception of continuity between them would indeed be occult, but because our visual perception is not refined enough to discern that they are indeed materially "bounded" by "lines [of matter] . . . too minute for our observation."[23] But Poe precisely endows Usher with Watson's fine perception, which enables Usher to discern all matter as perceiving, and gives him accurate insight into the real as a "bounded" network of vital relations (Watson's "lines") that are at the same time embodied streams of perception. Usher's subtlety, then, provides a superior or true ontological insight that reveals the difference between stones and humans as one of fine gradations in the intensity of perception or sensation they are able to generate, and through this production of the perceptual, they manifest themselves as agents affecting other existents. In the world of Usher's science there are no beings that exist simply as subjects having objects at their disposal, just as there are no phenomena chronically doomed to inert thingness. Instead, all phenomena exist as places along physical continua where they are capable, whether simultaneously or successively, of being both patients and agents, actually acting on other phenomena that they in turn suffer.

Such is Usher's ontological condition also, for he continuously perceives his passive exposure to stones' perceptual agencies, which influence and mold him into an agent and reveal him to be a chronic fusion of agency and passivity. For instance, he observes that the "influence" of drops of water emerging on the walls of his mansion through the process of "condensation" has "moulded" him into "what he was" (M 2: 408); similarly, he is "enchained" by "impressions" that the mere "substance" of his house, "the *physique* of the gray walls and turrets" materially "influences" the "morale of his existence," fashioning its acts (M 2: 403). Appearing under a variety of conditions—from elemental to mental—the perceptiveness of matter renders Poe's world vital and relational, its main ontological divide passing not between persons and things but between agents and patients, yet simultaneously being so unstable that patients easily intensify into agents and agencies are molded by patients. Poe depicts a world in which the Western metaphysical division of existents into subjects and objects is cancelled, and everything is regarded as acting or being acted upon. For, in his nondualistic ontology that affords feelings to all existents, there is nothing that simply moves, whereas everything has the capacity to act.

Unparticled Life: A Vitalist Critique of Atomism

The nondualistic ontology of "The Fall of the House of Usher"—where an affective material continuity exists between thoughts and bodies—received its programmatic formulation in "Mesmeric Revelation" published in the *Columbian Magazine* in 1844. Poe's vitalistic materialism recurs, this time in a more complex way, its philosophical intricacy deriving from the very complication of scientific materials that guided the "House of Usher." And while the philosophy advanced in both narratives is similar, in "Mesmeric Revelation" it received a different truth status, signaled by Poe in a letter to the poet-physician Thomas H. Chivers, on July 10, 1844, where the text is referred to not as a story or fiction but as an "article" (CL 1: 259).[24] The change in the argument's truth status also resides in the fact that, in contrast to the "House of Usher," where the person arguing for the vitality of unorganized matter was said to possess a morbid perception, and where that morbidity cast doubt on its accuracy, in "Mesmeric Revelation" the spokesman for vitalism is endowed with a perception described only as "keenly refined," a perception whose healthiness signifies its accuracy.

Poe additionally reinforces the truthfulness of vitalist philosophy by the fact that Mr. Vankirk formulates it while mesmerized, that is, while in a condition that cancels his ability to manipulate what he is relating, which gives his propositions impersonally objective status. For the hypnotic practices are summoned in the text less to relay Poe's stance regarding mesmerism, as Thomas Ollive Mabbott suggested (M 3: 1024), than as a means of weakening the limitations of the subjective perspective of the one mesmerized, enabling him to channel insights that transcend the cognitive capacity of his finite mind. Because hypnosis deactivates the power of self-reflection to interfere with perceptions, in the mesmerized state perceptions are not perspectival but instead coincide with the perceived itself, and the utterance of the mesmerized person is therefore rendered objective. What that person relates in such a condition therefore has the status of absolute or transcendent truth, since as Poe explained, "while in this state, the person so impressed employs only with effort, and then feebly, the external organs of sense, yet perceives, with keenly refined perception, and through channels supposed unknown, matters beyond the scope of the physical organs" (M 3: 1030). In the mesmerized state, it is not the one mesmerized but reality itself that is talking.

And if Poe took such great care to secure the objectivity of vitalist philosophy formulated in "Revelation," it is because he himself believed in it, declaring, in a letter to Chivers: "My own faith . . . you will find . . . in . . . an article headed 'Mesmeric Revelation' " (CL 1: 453). In another letter, Poe asked Reverend George Bush, professor of Hebrew at New York University, to judge its philosophical originality: "I have embodied in it some thoughts which are original with myself & I am exceedingly anxious to learn if they have claim to absolute originality, and also how far they will strike you as well based" (CL 1: 474).

The thoughts whose originality he wants evaluated formulate a materialist, monist, and vitalist ontology posited as an explicit critique of idealism. It exists in a variety of versions in Victor Cousin (whom Vankirk had long ago "been advised to study"), in his "European and American echoes" (he has in mind Orestes A. Brownson), and in the "moralists of England, of France, and of Germany" (M 3: 1031). Idealism is dismissed on the grounds of its abstractionism, formalism, and dualism. Thus, while it "may amuse and exercise . . . the mind," it can't take "hold of it" since it is but a cluster of "mere abstractions" whose distance from the real makes it incapable of truly convincing the "man . . . of his own immortality" (M 3: 1031). That idealism is abstractionist means for Vankirk that it separates qualities from things and attributes from beings. When it claims the real existence of qualities not attached to anything concrete—such as beauty, truth, falseness, intensity, activity, or freedom—it gives meaning to what does not possess a palpable referent; the meaning of such qualities is thus received not from what is objective but from the ideas and affects of those who think the qualities. It is thus relative, subjective, and ideal, entertaining the mind but not taking hold of it, inasmuch as it doesn't reveal anything consequential for the mind's real life enmeshed in a material body. Idealism's distance from what is embodied doesn't only explain why idealism "will always in vain call upon us to look upon qualities as things" (M 3: 1031) but also justifies the need for a new "earthly philosophy," which, instead of fallaciously abstracting qualia from the embodied, will claim that separation to be impossible and treat everything as qualitative and embodied. In the earthly philosophy that Poe formulates, nothing is "immaterial" but everything is terra-made: "there is no immateriality—it is a mere word. That which is not matter, is not at all" (M 3: 1033). Consequently, what is called spirit must also be matter, and what idealism claims as purely "spiritual" should be thought of as void of reality: even "spirit . . . seems only a word—such for instance as truth, beauty" (M 3: 1033).

"Spirit is matter" forms the programmatic credo of Poe's terrestrialism, which he also formulates in a letter to James Russell Lowell of July 2, 1844, where "spirituality" is similarly identified as a "*mere* word," emptied of meaning by the fact that it refers to what isn't material and therefore "is not" (CL 1: 449). Poe reasserts the materialist claim of a new terrestrialist philosophy even more succinctly eight days later in a letter to Chivers, simply positing that "there is no such thing as spirituality. . . . All things are material" (CL 1: 454). A world monistically made of matter will not entail for Poe negating the existence of thoughts and ideas but will instead mean that they too are material; thus "what men attempt to embody in the word 'thought,' is this matter in motion" (M 3: 1033). Everything, from stones to delicate thoughts, is matter, made of one stuff of variable refinement, each state of matter becoming another through minute gradations. Following Richard Watson's claim—which also organized the world of "The House of Usher"—according to which "in the production of nature, the transition from one [kingdom] to the other is effected by imperceptible gradations,"[25] "Mesmeric Revelation" too will posit that this substantially single matter differentiates itself through miniscule nuances: "there are *gradations* of matter of which man knows nothing; the grosser impelling the finer, the finer pervading the grosser" (M 3: 1033). Thus, a thought or a dream is an exquisitely fine matter, whereas stones or minerals are its crude variant; but regardless of their rarity, they are literally connected, so that between a dream and a mineral there exist "imperceptible" calibrations of continuous matter: "these gradations of matter increase in rarity or fineness, until we arrive at a matter . . . indivisible— . . . ultimate, . . . [which] permeates all things" (M 3: 1033). And the totality of these material gradations is what Poe calls God. Starting from the premise that "All things are material," and that God "is not spirit, for he exists," he concludes that "God is material" and matter divine (M 3: 1033).

In discussing the materialism formulated in "Mesmeric Revelation," Mabbott argued that it was simply a version of atomism, "going back to Democritus and to the Epicureans" (M 3: 1025). But in fact, Poe positions his materialism in direct opposition to atomism, turning "Mesmeric Revelation" into a veritable critique of Democritus and Lucretius, who are said to confuse the correct understanding of matter's nature. Atomism claims that bodies are discreet and separated by voids, and so distracts us from an adequate perception of matter as one, where phenomena such as "a metal, a piece of wood, a drop of water, the atmosphere, a gas, . . . the luminiferous ether" (M 3: 1034) are not only material but also continuous, one becoming another as no empty space separates them. Conversely, if we were to "destroy the idea of the atomic constitution ... we should no longer be able to regard the ether as an entity" separated from water, wood, or metal. The same holds for all conditions of matter:

> Take ... a step beyond the luminiferous ether—conceive a matter as much more rare than the ether, as this ether is more rare than the metal, and we arrive at once (in spite of all the school dogmas) at a unique mass—an unparticled matter. For although we may admit infinite littleness in the atoms themselves, the infinitude of littleness in the space between them is an absurdity. There will be a point—there will be a degree of rarity at which, if the atoms are sufficiently numerous, the interspaces must vanish, and the mass absolutely coalesce. (M 3: 1034)

What Poe claims here as the reason why "consideration of the atomic constitution" must be "now taken away" (M 3: 1034) is counterintuitive since the problem with atomism is not that it is too materialist—the customary critique directed at it throughout the history of philosophy—but rather that it is not materialist enough. For if, on the atomist account, atoms are the sole and single matter, then the voids or "interspaces" separating them must be immaterial. Atomism's quintessential claim that everything is matter is thus inherently self-contradictory, and atomism is revealed as a variant of idealism. And while for the atomists, the cosmos is immaterial and inherently inanimate—Lucretius's atoms are inert, animated bodies emerging mechanically, through the encounter of atoms generated by the famous hydraulic swerve that makes them stray from the straight line of their fall—for Poe, true materialism must refuse "immaterials" such as voids and vacuums: "interspaces must vanish and the mass absolutely coalesce" (M 3: 1034). That interspaces vanish means that atoms, no longer separated, continue into one another and, in losing their discreetness at the point of encounter, reveal the universe to be the fullness of matter existing in "gradations" of "fineness." The universe is thus conceived of as an infinite and continuous field of matter that is "*unparticled*—without particles—indivisible—*one*" (M 3: 1033). In other words, for Poe, matter is not manifested through stably figured embodied entities placed in empty space, which would exist independently of them; instead, because there are no voids, space coincides with the totality of matter. The universe is thus the infinite space-matter outside of which, because it is infinite, there is nothing, not even God, which for Poe is simply "the unparticled matter" (M 3: 1033).

The Pleasure of the Body Without Organs

This is where Poe's philosophy faces a question that only physics can account for, and it explains why science and ontology are so indistinguishable in his thought. For it is not immediately clear that there can be animation at all if everything is full of compact, dense matter. How, for instance, could beings move from here to there and across distances if there are no voids, no spaces thorough which they could move; doesn't material denseness and fullness of space render everything inert? And even more bewilderingly, what justifies the existence of individuated beings—whose discreetness requires separation—if all matter is an unparticled continuum? That is the concern the mesmerizer formulates when he argues that the "absolute coalescence" of atoms into the unparticled oneness of matter posited by Vankirk entails an "absolute density;" such density for its part, must cancel all movement, for "where there are no interspaces there can be no yielding," which dooms everything to a standstill: "an ether, absolutely dense, would put an infinitely more effectual stop to the progress of a star than would an ether of adamant or of iron" (M 3: 1035).

To resolve this problem, Poe's materialism summons vitalism. For if, despite the fact that space is full of matter, nothing stands still, it is because in Poe's world matter doesn't require either a first or an external mover, both of which are imagined in the Aristotelian and Christian traditions as pure spirit. Instead, on Poe's ontological plane, matter is inherently animated ("the unparticled matter, [is] set in motion by a . . . quality, existing within itself" [M 3: 1034]). It is an infinite field that folds and unfolds into itself, something like the quivering of waves in a light sea breeze. There are no forms or individuated phenomena in it; it is simply an "original Unity" (L1: 104), identified by Poe as the condition of "ultimate eccentricity" (L1: 98) because its infinity cancels the differentiation between centers and peripheries. We realize its existence late, arriving at it by reasoning a posteriori—or as *Eureka* will later have it, through induction—starting first from individuated phenomena and moving to less individuated elements until finally realizing their connectedness in unformed material unity. But in the causal order, the unformed material mass precedes all discreet beings, which it creates.[26] An embodied heap of animated matter is thus Poe's primary ontological category, his first mover or spirit, which explains his seemingly contradictory claim that "the unparticled matter, or God, in quiescence, is . . . what men call mind" (M 3: 1033–1034). The claim is only seemingly contradictory for two reasons. First, in calling matter mind, Poe doesn't spiritualize what is material but materializes what is traditionally understood as spiritual. Spirit is nothing but animation that is itself material, for matter is endowed with "the power of self-movement (equivalent in effect to human volition)" (M 3: 1033). Second, this material animation indeed possesses a mental trait, because its movement is not conceived of by Poe as mechanical but as vital or sensitive. Poe explicitly formulates its sensuousness when he posits that "the motion of [unparticled matter] is thought, of which perception is the first undulation" (M 3: 1038). Originary formless and unorganized matter, identified by Poe as both "rudimental" and "ultimate life" (M 3: 1037)—or originary and final—is therefore thoroughly perceptive and sensitive. It lives in a condition that Vankirk compares to the state of "entranced senses" in humans (M 3: 1037), thus not in a condition of self-reflection but simply "unindividualized," diffused streams of sensations and affects (M 3: 1036). Had Poe's ontology tolerated the existence of material particles, it would have been permissible to say that each particle of matter was a tiny perception. For as difficult as conceiving that might be, the movements of an unorganized hurricane on one hand, or the dreaming within a composed mind on the other, are both movements of perceptive matter. It is an axiomatic or universal principle of his vitalism that there is no motion—be it slow as that of a rock or as fast as the flight of an eagle—that is not endowed with perception; all unformed matter as well as formed bodies are matter's perceptions, affects, and thoughts. Cosmic dust perceives the air passing through it; planets drift through the universe sensing the meteors falling on them. Poe's vitalism is a totalized psychism, but, because spirit isn't if it isn't matter, psyches are elemental, atmospheric, and fleshy vital stuff. Hence, as the conclusion to "Mesmeric Revelation" explicitly posits, "the term '*substance*'" that names "the truly *substantive* vastness of infinity" is nothing else than "a sentiment:—it is the perception" (M 3: 1039).

Poe explains his idea of individuated and organized bodies—a possibility ruled out by the Mesmerist's second objection, which claimed the implausibility of individuation as long as matter is continuous, by means of the operation of matter's indwelling vitality. For as it moves, unformed, originary mass delineates the first fragile figurations onto itself, and so acts as creator of things: "the ultimate, or unparticled matter, not only permeates all things but impels all things—and thus is all things within itself" (M 3: 1033). And because all matter is alive, all figured bodies, from pebbles to clouds, born out of this quickening actualization or "impelling" as Poe terms it, will be alive. But, because they are all living figurations emerging on the surface of unformed matter, Poe will call them "organs." In Poe's vocabulary, "organ" is a name for anything individuated: "organs are contrivances by which the individual is brought into sensible relation with particular classes and forms of matter, to the exclusion of other classes and forms" (M 3: 1037). Organs are forces of discreteness, "the cages necessary to confine" beings (M 3: 1038), which separate the matter they delineate from other "particular . . . forms of matter" (M 3: 1037). But because they are alive, they simultaneously generate "sensible" relations among them, while nevertheless remaining a particular configuration of the same matter. Poe's materialism is in fact so thorough that he will see particular human thoughts or ideas as minute organs outlined by and appearing on a larger surface of matter: "the particular motion of the incarnated portions of the unparticled matter is the thought of man" (M 3: 1036). The intensity of thoughts and the specificity of their relations, as well as the difference in other organs' livelihood and complexity, result from the specificity of the site on unorganized matter on which they appear, for "the organs vary with the features of the place tenanted" (M 3: 1038). The difference among such sites or milieus (the variations in intensity of their "vibrations" and the speed of matter's agitation [M 3: 1038]) will bring organs into more or less complex relations with other organs. If the agitations in a milieu are slow, the relations might be imperceptible, and those sites will appear as almost inanimate, as is the case in the geological world. In more agitated spots of infinite matter, those relations come to constitute more complex organisms: "The matter of which our . . . body is composed, is within the ken of the organs of that body; or, more distinctly, our . . . organs are adapted to the matter of which is formed . . . the body" (M 3: 1037).

Complex organisms are thus individuals made of relations of other individuals or organs; the internal space outlined by those relations constitutes an interior milieu to which organs are adapted, as opposed to the external milieu or "world," which is nothing other than the "ultimate, unorganized life" to which organs and organisms remain unadapted (M 3: 1038). It is appropriate to talk here of milieus, even if that is not Poe's word, because regardless of the level of their complexity, all individuations—all organs and organisms—are, in the ontology Poe constructs, delicate and porous. Twentieth-century philosopher of science Georges Canguilhem defined a milieu as the "dissolution of the individualized organic synthesis in the anonymity of elements and universal movements."[27] For him what is individuated—for instance, organs or organisms—is also always in a process of slow dissolution into its exterior, of which it is, however, a constitutive part and into which its existence continues—disturbing the difference between interior and exterior—until it finally becomes exterior, pure milieu. The life of individuals in Poe's world unfolds according to this milieu-logic. This is true not only because, in the case of complex organisms, the relation between organs contracts a unique biozone specific to them, thus maintaining their individuated existence, but also because the morphology of individuals is constantly refigured by the incessant movement of matter external to it. Each being is a fragile organic formation in the milieu of unparticled matter into which it slowly oozes, and which "permeates it" (M 3: 1038).

That is how, in a letter to Poe of August 6, 1844, Chivers also understood it. He argued there that in "Mesmeric Revelation" Poe turned all individuations, including human minds—which, because spirit is matter, must also be completely material—into an agitated geography of vital originary matter, and in so doing denied them any unique essence, having them live merely as a manner of the same substance into which they continued as their individuations weakened: "You individualize Man by incorporating the 'unparticled' in the 'particled matter.' But this is making his individuality depend only upon a *peculiar manner* of being; whereas I make his personality exist in his self-conscious soul, which shows that his soul may exist . . . after its separation from the body" (H 17: 186). Leaving aside the fact that Chivers didn't understand that Poe couldn't possibly read that as a negative critique because he desired precisely to cancel the difference between individuality and personality—that is, between any individuated piece of matter, such as rock or tree, and personality understood as purely spiritual, souled, and intentional mind—he is otherwise correct. For "Mesmeric Revelation" explicitly claims individual beings not as essentially unique or substantially different from one another (so that some, as opposed to others, would be only mental), but only as expressions or manners of infinite, unformed matter. "All created things are but the thoughts of God" (M 3: 1036), he writes,[28] which, in his materialist vocabulary amounts to saying that all beings are bodies of the same living matter. Every being is an organ occurring on a ground of matter without organs.

And "what is called 'death' is but the painful metamorphosis" (M 3: 1037), "progressing" from our current individuated or organic body into the "ultimate body," which is the totality of unorganized, yet sensitive matter. It is called "death" because the idiosyncrasy of organs and organisms is dissolved and living beings are thus "unindividualized" (M 3: 1036). But this "death" is in fact life—"when I say . . . death, I mean that it resembles the ultimate life" (M 3: 1037)—because in "unindividuation," individuals resolve into the perceptiveness of the infinite body without organs. Thus, "it is to the absence of the idiosyncratic organs . . . that we must attribute the nearly unlimited perception of the ultimate life" (M 3: 1038). "Unindividuated" organisms become life that affects and feels itself in its immediacy, for in it everything perceives "directly, without organs" (M 3: 1037). For Poe, direct perception encounters none of the "impediments" of the organic ("with the view of producing impediment, the organic life . . . [was] contrived" [M 3: 1039]). That is, "direct" perception is completely unobstructed: lacking organs, it lacks both separations and the pressure, discomfort or, as Poe also calls it, pain exerted by a milieu onto the interiority of an organism ("pain . . . is possible in the organic" [M 3: 1039]; "in the inorganic life, pain cannot be" [M 3: 1039]). And without deterrent organs, everything is "indwelling" in everything else (M 3: 1038), and perception of anything is turned into perception of everything, as sensitive matter indefinitely caresses itself in the perpetual enjoyment that Poe calls' "inviolate perfection" or "pleasure" (M 3: 1039).

Thus, far from being reconcilable with "orthodox Christian ideas" as Mabbott suggested,[29] Poe's materialist ontology completely contradicts such presumptions, in accord with what is promised at the beginning of "Mesmeric Revelation," when he argues that "here upon earth, at least" (M 3: 1031) a nonabstract philosophy of immortality is needed instead of those offered by either Christianity or Western idealism. And while it is true that both Poe's vitalist materialism and Christianity share the idea that death is only a metamorphosis of life into its other forms and that strictly speaking there is no death, and while both also share the idea that after such metamorphosis, a life of infinite pleasure and perfection occurs, they couldn't be further apart when it comes to defining what such pleasure is and how it is to be obtained. In contrast to Christianity, where the individuality of the person is preserved after death, in Poe, eternal life generates the person's deindividuation; and, while in Christianity the individuality that goes on to live eternally is spiritual, and enjoys a purely spiritual perfection, for Poe the "unindividual" that transcends into ultimate life is material and is given embodied joy. Poe sacrifices individuality and personality to preserve materiality, because for him, no pleasure is pleasurable unless it is embodied. There is no perfection unless it is terrestrial.

Notes

1. Joan Dayan, *Fables of Mind: An Inquiry into Poe's Fiction* (New York: Oxford University Press, 1987), 9.
2. Dayan, *Fables of Mind*, 15.
3. Dayan, *Fables of Mind*, 9.
4. Dayan, *Fables of Mind*, 15.
5. Thomas Percival, *Speculations on the Perceptive Power of Vegetables* (Warrington, UK: W. Eyres, 1785), 4.

6. For more on Spallanzani's "vital atmos" and how they differ from inanimate matter, see *Encyclopaedia Britannica Online*, Elizabeth Belmont Gasking, s.v. "Lazzaro Spallanzani," revised December 19, 2008, https://www.britannica.com/biography/Lazzaro-Spallanzani.
7. Richard Watson, *An Essay on the Subjects of Chemistry, and Their General Division* (Cambridge: J. Archdeacon, 1771), 35.
8. Watson, *An Essay on the Subjects of Chemistry*, 36.
9. Watson, *An Essay on the Subjects of Chemistry*, 36.
10. Watson, *An Essay on the Subjects of Chemistry*, 38.
11. Watson, *An Essay on the Subjects of Chemistry*, 38.
12. Watson, *An Essay on the Subjects of Chemistry*, 35.
13. Watson, *An Essay on the Subjects of Chemistry*, 38.
14. Watson, *An Essay on the Subjects of Chemistry*, 39–40.
15. Watson, *An Essay on the Subjects of Chemistry*, 13.
16. Watson, *An Essay on the Subjects of Chemistry*, 13–14.
17. Watson, *An Essay on the Subjects of Chemistry*, 40.
18. Watson, *An Essay on the Subjects of Chemistry*, 15.
19. Watson, *An Essay on the Subjects of Chemistry*, 18.
20. Watson, *An Essay on the Subjects of Chemistry*, 39.
21. Watson, *An Essay on the Subjects of Chemistry*, 18.
22. G. R. Thompson, ed., *The Selected Writings of Edgar Allan Poe: A Norton Critical Edition* (New York: Norton, 2004), 201n.
23. Watson, *An Essay on the Subjects of Chemistry*, 40. A continuum, as Gilles Deleuze explains in his lectures on Leibniz, whose philosophy of continuity, according to G. R. Thompson, also influenced Poe's thinking about the relationship between Usher and his house (see Thompson's note in *The Selected Writings of Edgar Allan Poe*, 204n)—is assured by "infinitely small [imperceptible] relations between two elements." According to Leibniz's law of continuity, two phenomena will thus be continuous not because they lack individuation but because the differences constituting individuations are "evanescent," fading away into something else at the edges; hence, Deleuze's definition of continuity as "evanescent difference," where evanescence names the imperceptible passing of differentiations from one individuation to another. See Gilles Deleuze, "Leibniz," trans. Charles J. Stivale, Cours Vincennes, Les Cours de Gilles Deleuze, April 22, 1980, https://www.webdeleuze.com/textes/53.
24. Poe informed Chivers, "You will find it, somewhat detailed, in a forthcoming number of the 'Columbian Magazine,' published here. I have written for it an article headed 'Mesmeric Revelation'" (CL 1: 259).
25. Watson, *An Essay on the Subjects of Chemistry*, 13–14.
26. The idea of such a reasoning procedure is most explicitly formulated in *Eureka*, regarding the existence of "unparticled" matter and the principle of gravitation: "Never was necessity less obvious than that of entertaining this unphilosophical idea. Going boldly behind the vulgar thought, we have to conceive, metaphysically, that the gravitating principle appertains to Matter temporarily—only while diffused—only while existing as Many instead of as One" (L1: 95).
27. Georges Canguilhem, "The Living and Its Milieu," trans. John Savage, *Grey Room*, no. 3 (Spring 2001): 11.
28. The claim will be repeated, with explicit reference to man: "Man is a creature. Creatures are thoughts of God" (M 3: 1036).

29. According to Mabbott, "The technical term for it [Poe's philosophy] is Materialism, but the notion is not incompatible with orthodox Christian ideas, in the form used by Poe" (M 3: 1025).

Bibliography

Arsić, Branka. "Materialist Vitalism or Pathetic Fallacy: The Case of the House of Usher." *Representations* 140, no. 1 (Fall 2017): 121–136.

Canguilhem, Georges. "The Living and Its Milieu." Translated by John Savage. *Grey Room*, no. 3 (Spring 2001): 6–31.

Dayan, Joan. *Fables of Mind: An Inquiry into Poe's Fiction*. New York: Oxford University Press, 1987.

Watson, Richard. *An Essay on the Subjects of Chemistry, and Their General Division*. Cambridge: J. Archdeacon, 1771.

CHAPTER 45

POE'S TERROR ANALYTICS

J. GERALD KENNEDY

VIEWED from a certain angle, the odd fiction of Edgar Poe offers surprising insights into our contemporary culture of fear and the so-called Age of Terror. In fact, Poe's work as a writer of magazine tales entailed a concerted exploration of the sources and effects of terror, one that—as I hope to show—anticipated both the ingenuity of terrorist conspirators and the conclusions of experimental research into the social psychology of terrorism. Since 1970, the Global Terrorism Database (GTD) at the University of Maryland has tracked 170,000 separate incidents of international terrorist violence through mid-2017. This archive registers any event that involves "the threatened or actual use of illegal force and violence by a non-state actor to attain a political, economic, religious, or social goal through fear, coercion, or intimidation."[1] The infamous Al Qaida attack of September 11, 2001, on New York City and Washington, DC—the date many Americans associate with the beginning of an Age of Terror—thus fits into a much longer history and a more complicated accounting of clandestine groups and atrocious acts to advance their causes. To be sure, GTD accounting problematically excludes authorized, state military exercises in shock and awe, including egregious attacks on civilian populations. While monitoring such groups as the Irish Republican Army or the ETA (the Basque separatist movement), the GTD associates non-state terrorism mostly with cells of jihadists aiming to universalize radical Islam. The ruthlessness of attacks by Al Qaida and ISIS should not obscure the reality that "terrorism" has been largely defined by Western entities claiming innocence or moral justification while using frightening technologies against their adversaries. As Clark McCauley reminds us, "State terrorism was not only first, it continues to be more dangerous"; by comparison, the systematic slaughter by tyrants from Hitler and Stalin to Vladimir Putin, Saddam Hussein, and Bashar al-Assad makes casualties from non-state terrorism look "miniscule."[2]

Understanding terrorism as a contested concept fraught with hatred and bigotry enables us to make better use of Poe's insights into terror. The potent after-images of 9/11—of passenger planes flying into the Twin Towers and both skyscrapers engulfed in flames before crumbling—created a spectacle of horror shocking to most inhabitants of modern, liberal societies. So too did subsequent, coordinated attacks in Paris, Brussels,

London, and elsewhere. As a mode of conflict, terrorism aims not to obliterate a population so much as to traumatize it. Since 2001, studies of terrorism have proliferated almost as rapidly as terrorism itself; experts have illuminated its historical, religious, political, geographical, economic, and social-psychological dimensions. Indispensable titles would include Daniel Benjamin and Steven Simon's *The Age of Sacred Terror* (2002), Lawrence Wright's *The Looming Tower: Al-Qaeda and the Road to 9/11* (2006), Randall Law's *Terrorism: A History* (2009), and William McCants's *The ISIS Apocalypse: The History, Strategy, and Doomsday Vision of the Islamic State* (2015). Such studies share the goal of making horrific, unthinkable atrocities intellectually comprehensible, and in this ongoing work, Poe's fiction provides an unlikely yet illuminating resource.

But how can the morbid tales of a nineteenth-century author contain any insightful contribution to our understanding of contemporary terrorism? Poe lived long before electricity and electronic media; if he anticipated the computer, as several contributors to this volume argue, he could not have imagined the technologies of construction, transportation, and communication that made 9/11 possible. But Poe faced multiple forms of horror and thought hard about the terror it incited; he cultivated dread in his fiction; and he devoted a good deal of his professional career to thinking about what terror is, how it works, where it comes from, how it signifies, and whether it can be managed, deflected, or dismantled. A few of Poe's tales anatomize the calculated production of terror—or what we now call terrorism—and thus implicitly probe deep motives for inflicting terror, revealing as well the psychic effects of terror on victims. Other tales depict characters in dire predicaments, facing likely destruction yet dispassionately analyzing impending danger. Poe satirized extreme predicaments in "How to Write a Blackwood Article," and, as I will suggest, humor formed part of his defense against terror. He tamed his own anxieties by depicting fearful characters; he channeled phobias into charged narratives of bereavement, destruction, or revenge. This chapter explores analogies between 9/11 and Poe's "The Fall of the House of Usher," locates Poe's recurrent cultural nightmares, and closes with three surprising examples of Poe's terror analytics.

The preface to Poe's first book, *Tales of the Grotesque and Arabesque* (1840), rejects the charge that imported German horror permeated his work. Poe insisted: "If in many of my productions terror has been the thesis, I maintain that terror is not of Germany, but of the soul" (M 2: 473). Terror was precisely his "thesis" and preoccupation; complaints that his tales contained excessive dread seemed as irrelevant to Poe as "taxing an astronomer with too much astronomy, or an ethical author with treating too largely of morals" (M 2: 473). Terror was for him a field of research, a site of investigation. He wanted to discern the nature and basis of fear—especially the human revulsion to death—to understand the terrors that haunted him. His obsession with this project doubtless helps to explain his current global popularity in an era of nuclear threats and terrorist plots. In the secular, post-Christian dread of mortality, Poe tellingly located the essential vulnerability of Western culture to Islamic terrorism.

The relevance of Poe's meditations on terror to our contemporary dilemma may be suggested by recalling his 1842 theory of the tale, which provides acute insights into the production of terror and, by extension, a provocative rethinking of the 9/11 plot. In its original splendor, the World Trade Center symbolized American might as well as global capitalism, and the hijacking of American and United flights to destroy the buildings produced a frightening drama of national self-destruction. The timing of the attack, just before 9:00 AM Eastern time, afforded the largest possible live audience in the Americas, Europe, Africa, and Asia, and the tragedy played out in less than two hours, producing an unforgettable viewing experience. As we now know, the finale was to have included the destruction of two revered sites in Washington, but while American Airlines flight 77 slammed into the Pentagon, United flight 93 (probably meant to hit the White House or Capitol building) crashed in rural Pennsylvania, thanks to the heroic resistance of doomed passengers. The lasting image of massive towers, gashed by jets, engulfed in flames, and then reduced to rubble nevertheless created a powerful symbolic gesture.

Poe's review of Hawthorne, in which he articulated his theory of the unified, single effect indispensable to the tale, unexpectedly illuminates two crucial principles relevant to the theatricality of 9/11. He wrote that every incident or detail must be orchestrated to achieve a preconceived result. And because emotion is transient, the action must be compressed. Unless a work can be read at a single sitting, Poe observed, it "deprives itself, of course, of the immense force derivable from *totality.*" Totalizing effect formed the object of Poe's literary aesthetics; he aimed to overwhelm. He wanted nothing less than "the soul of the reader" to be "at the writer's control." Poe's ideas about the emotional and psychological effects of a powerfully conceived prose tale—a genre ideally suited, he thought, to evoke "terror, or passion, or horror, or a multitude of such other points" (ER: 572)—uncannily anticipate the calculations of those who planned the 2001 attacks. Indeed, "The Fall of the House of Usher," Poe's most famous tale (to which I will return), likewise ends in a spectacular—and spectacularly symbolic—architectural collapse that produces an overwhelming effect. As an investigator of terror, Poe understood what the conspirators behind 9/11 later realized: an action horrific enough to appall the nation and the world must be both shockingly unexpected and symbolically coherent, an action whose unifying "pre-established design" (ER: 572) becomes fully apparent only in the aftermath of unimaginable horror.

Importantly, Poe specifies in his 1840 preface that real terror comes from "the soul," the Latin *anima*, or—to recall the Greek word Poe liked—the psyche. He believed that terror originated in the mind, from unconscious fears that underlie conscious thought and rational reflection. By implication, dread is always already present, an effect or response triggered by external stimuli but ultimately rooted in a fear of death buried in the unconscious. In the psyche, we seal away the overwhelming certainty of our own mortality. Ernest Becker has remarked that "the idea of death, the fear of it, haunts the human animal like nothing else; it is a mainspring of human activity—activity designed largely to avoid the fatality of death, to overcome it by denying in some way that it is the final destiny for man."[3] Becker corroborates Poe's perception that terror resides in every human psyche, in the fear of one's own death, an apprehension that emerges in childhood. If our nagging awareness of mortality spurs religious devotion or fosters a yearning for a life beyond death, the desire to overcome mortality similarly drives such projects as begetting children, starting a company, writing a book, or putting one's name on a big building. More often, though, denial manifests as distraction. Quoting Kierkegaard, Becker says that most people most of the time "tranquillize" themselves with "the trivial." But as Becker also notes, repressing the fact of death can produce a fear of life; paradoxically, we feel most alive when we embrace the dreadful fact that we are, as Yeats put it, "fastened to a dying animal."[4]

Becker's ideas have assumed fresh relevance in our Age of Terror. In a book titled *In the Wake of 9/11: The Psychology of Terror*, social psychologists Tom Pyszczynski, Sheldon Solomon, and Jeff Greenberg build upon Becker's insights to suggest that terrorism works to shatter the psychological defenses that shield individuals from their own fear of death. They assert that a person's psychological equilibrium depends on "faith in a culturally derived worldview that imbues reality with order, stability, meaning and permanence" as well as a "belief that one is a significant contributor to this meaningful reality."[5] The authors observe that in the United States, participating in national rituals and observances serves the purpose of denying death symbolically: "Being a patriotic American makes one significant—no longer a purposeless, transient animal, one is now an eternally significant contributor to a great nation that represents eternal values of freedom and democracy."[6] The strikes on the Pentagon and Twin Towers thus delivered a double blow to Americans and their management of personal terror: they presented explicit, revolting images of real human beings dying before our eyes, and they destroyed symbols of national power. On 9/11, many Americans imagined themselves aboard the doomed planes or trapped in falling buildings, caught in a phantasmagoria of death.

Terrorism exposes vulnerability and excites our fear of death. Not jet planes, bombs, or guns but *terror* forms the principal weapon, for the strategic objective lies not in inflicting heavy casualties (which seem, in military terms, quite insignificant) but in producing panic and demoralization. This is why we now have a federal agency committed to Homeland Security, devoted to eliminating strategic risks but also to fostering the illusion of a land without terror. Poe made it his business to study the mechanics of terror because he lived with dread. He intuited the insights of experimental psychology: terrorism works by exploiting "mortality salience." Pyszczynski and company use this phrase to describe vivid thoughts of one's own death, evoked by words, images, or situations.[7] Terrorists conspire to produce horrific spectacles that proliferate mortality salience, the fear of one's own imminent obliteration.

Long before social psychologists named this phenomenon, Poe was brooding on it, and his early letters reveal an occasional habit of envisioning his own death for rhetorical effect. His February 21, 1831, appeal to John Allan, which reports a "shocking" bloody discharge from his ear, affirms that this will be "the last time that I ever trouble any human being—I feel that I am on [a] sick bed from which I shall never get up." Poe adds, "I am wearing away every day" and reasserts "I shall never rise from my bed" (CL 1: 63–64). An 1835 letter discloses his suicidal despair at being separated from his aunt, Mrs. Clemm, and his cousin Virginia after moving to Richmond to edit the *Southern Literary Messenger*. He weeps, "But the dream is over[.] [Oh G]od, have mercy on me. What have I *to live for*? Among strangers with *not one soul to love me*" (CL 1: 103). In

1811, his mother's death made him an orphan, simultaneously instilling in Poe a chronic fear of abandonment and dread of consequent annihilation. Ever afterward, the loss of beloved women excited mortality salience. His subsequent bereavements made the death of a beautiful, cherished woman more than "the most poetical topic in the world" (ER: 19); it formed an intractable trauma.

Poe's fictional fantasies of death took many forms: he imagined his destruction in an immense vortex, as in "MS Found in a Bottle," or entombed alive, as in "The Premature Burial," or wasted by consumption (tuberculosis) like Monsieur Valdemar. This may be a key to Poe's genius: he produced his best tales of terror not by denying death or suppressing dread but by mining mortality salience. One of his earliest narratives, "MS Found in a Bottle," offers a virtual paradigm of the career that in 1832 lay before him: the narrator composes his manuscript mindful of death's imminence: "It is evident that we are hurrying onwards to some exciting knowledge, some never-to-be-impted secret, whose attainment is destruction" (M 2: 145).[8] His purpose is two-fold: to understand the terrors triggered by portents of death (the blood red moon, phantom ship, ebony vortex, etc.) and to record intimations of the secret knowledge presumed to lie beyond physical dissolution.

Fifty years ago, Joseph Garrison undertook to explain the "function of terror" in Poe's work by noting congruencies between the prose tale, as Poe theorized it, and poetry, with its pursuit of Supernal Beauty. The difficulty, for Garrison, lay in the fact that so many tales presented horrifying images of "pathetic figures" working out "pathetic fates," because these "existential nonentities" had sadly failed to live their lives within the "Spirit Divine."[9] Terror, for Garrison, reveals an alienation from spiritual beauty and exposes its absence. Moralistic and unconvincing as his argument sometimes becomes, there is a kernel of insight in his recognition that terror can instruct, as it does (Garrison notes) in "The Premature Burial," when the narrator vows to reform his life after succumbing to an irrational fear of living interment. What terror more often produces in Poe's fiction, however, is not enlightenment but rather the inexorability of dissolution.

A more recent and impressive plunge into the broad problem of terror in Poe figures in Paul Hurh's 2015 study, *American Terror: The Feeling of Thinking in Edwards, Poe, and Melville*. Like Colin Dayan, Hurh elaborates an important connection between the eighteenth-century Puritan and the nineteenth-century magazinist. Elucidating the paradox that bedeviled Edwards—that hell's infinite terrors can only be represented in finite, material images—Hurh traces idealist thought from Edwards to Poe via Locke, Kant, Schiller, the Schlegels, and Hegel. He argues that for the writers bracketed by his study, terror expresses "the feeling of thought," though what is distinctly "American" about an affect influenced heavily by German thought remains a bit unclear. Theorizing the meaning of Poe's poetry and fiction, Hurh convincingly argues that thinking in Poe always returns to loss, absence, and negation, nicely epitomized by the Raven perched on the bust of Pallas, the Greek goddess of thought. Every one of Poe's tales tracing the death of a beautiful woman, beginning with "Berenice," becomes, for Hurh, "a fable of critical interpretation."[10] He suggests that terror, in Poe, derives finally from the failure of interpretation itself, the unknowability of ultimate things. In "Usher" we confront "the infinite regression of representation" that generates terror in a "feedback loop of imagination and affection"; every act of thought ends in dread. Hurh shows that even Monsieur Dupin's ratiocination stems from the terror to which thought invariably returns, and so does the methodical thinking of Poe's homicidal types, the narrators of "The Tell-Tale Heart," "The Black Cat," and "The Imp of the Perverse," who confuse method with reason and doom themselves to compulsive confessions.[11]

Illuminating as this reading may be, Hurh theorizes terror in Poe as a consequence of interpretive failure and asserts a crisis of absence without fully engaging the problems of dread and death until his discussion of Melville. Yet no tale in Poe represents the predicament of mortality more intensely or insistently than "Usher." The symbolism of this famous tale has always seemed a little too obvious. We are told that the "House of Usher" signifies both the mansion *and* the family destiny. The physical structure evokes dread in the narrator, but he attributes his gloom to a "sentience" that surrounds the house like a presence. The "tangled web-work" overhanging the front of the house resembles the "web-like" hair of Usher himself (M 2: 400, 402). A zigzag crack in the facade portends both the break in the Usher line and the madness of the protagonist. Despite strange happenings within the house, however, events that include the burial of Madeline and her return from the tomb to avenge her hasty burial by Roderick, neither physics nor geology explains why the mansion comes crashing down as the twins expire. That explanation lies rather in the intricate symbolic logic of "The Fall of the House of Usher," a tale shaped by Poe's preoccupation with the mechanics of terror and terrorism.

Falling Towers

The thematics of "Usher" provide important insight into Poe's private counterterrorism. The idea of his war on terror sounds utterly counterintuitive, for Poe produced so many sensational tales that his name became synonymous with the production, not the deconstruction, of horror. But Poe also speaks in "The Murders in the Rue Morgue" of a "double Dupin—the creative and the resolvent"—and viewed as a whole his tales indeed reveal a double Poe, a purveyor of horror but also an analyst of handwriting, cryptography, and robotics, a rationalist who loved to demystify the phenomena that scared his characters to death. Hurh is right that the detective tales show the impossibility of analyzing analysis without tumbling into an endless regression of meaning. But Poe himself pushed against that logic, seeking to understand terror. The predicament of Roderick Usher indeed offers a clinical study of dread; his "unnerved" and "pitiable" condition leaves him terrified of being terrified (M 2: 403). But Poe also devotes much attention to the phenomenology of terror. The "grim phantasm" of fear that excites Roderick's anxieties may hold a key to the collapse of the house, and Jean Baudrillard's essay, *The Spirit of Terrorism*, provides a surprising angle on the overdetermined symbolism of "Usher."

Baudrillard's critique emerges from his unsettling claim that terrorists on 9/11 tapped a secret yearning in postmodern culture to destroy global capitalism. On an unconscious level, Baudrillard contends, "we *wished for* it," because, as the history of disaster movies attests, we love to see big buildings crumble and huge monsters die. Indeed, he says, the "terroristic imagination . . . dwells in all of us," and the domination of capital breeds internalized fantasies of terrorism: "the visible fracture (and the hatred)" that "pits the exploited and the underdeveloped globally against the Western world secretly connects with the fracture internal to the dominant system."[12] His critique shifts the meaning of 9/11 from religion to economics, from an Islamic jihad against infidels to the revenge of the dispossessed. At first glance, his essay appears unrelated to "The Fall of the House of Usher," an antebellum tale that depicts neither terrorists nor what Baudrillard calls "the violence of globalization." What permeates Poe's dark world instead is a "constitutional and family evil" that afflicts the Ushers (M 2: 402); their house falls as a result of something uncanny and terrifying, which Baudrillard finally helps us to understand.

The attacks of 2001 produced an effect that exceeded public reaction to the material destruction and nearly three thousand deaths. They did so, Baudrillard suggests, by changing the rules of international conflict. American military strength forced the terrorists to invent a mode of warfare not contingent on superior firepower. The Al Qaida strategists shifted the sphere of conflict to the symbolic, producing a weird convergence of the real and the imaginary. The damage on 9/11 was appalling in part because of its unnerving symmetry. The terrorists created a symbolic spectacle by transforming their own deaths into symbols of devotion; then they targeted emblems of American wealth and domination. "Fighting on the ground of reality," Baudrillard notes, the dominant system will always prevail. "But shift the struggle into the symbolic sphere, . . . where the rule is that of challenge, reversion, and outbidding," and a few subversives can defy the system with acts of suicide that the system cannot replicate or exceed: "Here, then, it is all about death, not only about the violent irruption of death in real time, but the irruption of a death which is far more than real: a death which is symbolic and sacrificial—the absolute, irrevocable event."[13]

Attacking the World Trade Towers, the Pentagon, and (potentially) the White House, the terrorists targeted sites to generate symbolism rather than to inflict staggering casualties. The sequenced attack on the Twin Towers ensured live coverage of the second impact, seventeen minutes after the first, an event of real psychic trauma because it confirmed the unfolding of a horrific plot. The initial crash produced confusion and shock; the second produced terror. The towers crumbled in less than two hours, creating a phantasm of destruction. Baudrillard says: "When the two towers collapsed, you had the impression that they were responding to the suicide of the suicide planes with their own suicides." Two towers, two planes, two explosions, two piles of rubble created a surreal doubling of the unspeakable. All airline crashes leave appalling debris, but the double disaster of the Twin Towers produced strangeness, singularity, its symbolism underscoring its intentionality. Capturing a principle of terrorism, Baudrillard remarks, "Only symbolic violence is generative of singularity." There can be no true terrorism without symbolism, and in a pendant essay, "Requiem for the Twin Towers," he argues that when the towers were hit,

> the architectural object was destroyed but it was the symbolic object which was targeted and which it was intended to demolish. One might think the physical destruction brought about the symbolic collapse. But in fact no one, not even the terrorists, had reckoned on the total destruction of the towers. It was, in fact, their symbolic collapse that brought about their physical collapse, not the other way around.[14]

This insight has peculiar relevance to "The Fall of the House of Usher," though in juxtaposing an actual human tragedy with a fictional composition, I do not mean to trivialize the former or magnify the latter. But just as Poe's theory of the tale illuminates 9/11 as a calculated, unified action, so Baudrillard's analysis elucidates Poe's tale. It does so by underscoring the production of singularity through symbolic violence, by exposing the inherent terror-making plot, so to speak, at the crux of "Usher." And it helps us to see how Poe, writing in the 1830s, began to think, proleptically, like a modern terrorist—to analyze the production of overwhelming effects—in order to create a magazine tale but also to understand and manage what he himself feared.

All the doubling in "Usher" generates the terrifying singularity that gives psychic impact to terrorist violence. From the narrator's preliminary experiment, which compares the actual house to its inverted reflection, the proliferation of doubling evokes endless replication, as in the world of dream or the surreal paintings of René Magritte. Usher and his sister are opposite-sex identical twins—symbolic necessity here trumping biological possibility. The narrator and Usher, childhood friends, also figure as counterparts, fellow "madmen." Usher's "cadaverousness" mirrors the pallor of Madeline's "approaching dissolution" (M 2: 401, 403–404). The poetic inscription likening the heart to a lute portends Usher's partiality for "stringed instruments," and his painting of "a vault or tunnel" anticipates the vault in which he deposits Madeline's coffin (M 2: 403, 405). When the narrator reads Sir Launcelot Canning's "Mad Trist" to his host, he describes a brass shield crashing to the floor just as a "clangorous . . . reverberation" sounds from beneath the house (M 2: 415).

This signifying chain of uncanny doubling that culminates in structural collapse betrays Poe's plot to terrify the reader. In an earlier work, *Symbolic Exchange and Death*, Baudrillard observed: "The symbolic is neither a concept, an agency, a category, nor a 'structure,' but an act of exchange and *a social relation which puts an end to the real*, which resolves the real, and, at the same time, puts an end to the opposition between the real and the imaginary."[15] Poe blurs this opposition in "Usher" by manipulating the symbolic order to make every detail fit a preconceived design. Every book in the library, every stone in the structure of the house partakes of the "phantasm," the "terrible influence" (M 2: 408) that renders the real indistinguishable from the imaginary, or (as Branka Arsić shows in this volume) the animate from the inanimate. The House of Usher is the domain of the symbolic, where a weird logic supplants the physics of cause and effect.

Poe stages the deaths of Roderick and Madeline as reciprocal acts of violence that terminate a family line enfeebled by incest. But what causes the house to fall? Like the action in the "Mad Trist," the mansion collapses not as result of scientific law but through an uncanny symbolic logic. Poe's metonymy demands it. The collapse confirms that the "scarcely intelligible" (M 2: 410) sympathies linking Roderick and Madeline pervade the entire domain. The mansion figures the fate of the family, and the house destroys itself in sympathetic response to the demise of the twins. In an unsettling prefiguration of 9/11, the symbolic provokes the physical destruction.

Poe constructs the terrorist plot in "Usher" by ratcheting up the doubling to expose the ultimate object of terrorism—the fear of death awakened by "mortality salience." Dread has always seemed the most compelling explanation for Usher's altogether irrational act of screwing down the lid of his sister's coffin when he knows—from her history of catalepsy, her "faint blush," and her "suspiciously lingering smile"—that she may well be alive (M 2: 410). To be sure, an unspoken urge to free himself from the shame of incest may also precipitate her entombment. But more significantly, because his dying, identical twin, Madeline mirrors Usher's own mortality, the last thing he wants to do is to witness her dissolution. So he secures the lid as a hedge against subsequent terror.

But as Freud later explained, the repressed always returns. Sealed in the dungeon, the bloody Madeline embodies the "grim phantasm, FEAR" that Roderick has always dreaded, the frightening presence that will deprive him of "life and reason together" (M 2: 403). The final, simultaneous demise of Madeline and Roderick ends the Usher dynasty, as Poe's narrator bolts from the house to save himself and tell his tale. His account captures the bizarre doubling that generates the singular effect of "The Fall of the House of Usher," and it positions us to read the production of terror—which the narrator fails to grasp—as the object of Poe's coordinated symbolic logic. As on 9/11, terror in "Usher" forces us to contemplate the death that culture conspires to conceal.

Baudrillard comments that the terrorists "succeeded in turning their own deaths into an absolute weapon against a system that operates on the basis of the exclusion of death."[16] Earlier, in *Symbolic Exchange and Death*, he remarked of Western capitalism: "Our whole culture [of capitalism] is just one huge effort to dissociate life and death, to ward off the ambivalence of death in the interests of life as value, and time as the general equivalent. The elimination of death is our phantasm."[17] This insight has special relevance for American culture and may explain the subversive allure of Poe's fiction in a country that from the beginning of nation-building banished death, promoting a cheerful optimism about the limitless future of a growing republic. The same principle of denial also helps to explain Poe's often problematic position in scholarly accounts of American literature. His tales of cruelty, disease, death, and decomposition ran against the American grain—precisely, William Carlos Williams would add, to expose the real nature of the nation. Among the enduring images of 9/11, none is more shocking or unforgettable than the sight of people plunging from burning towers. Nine-eleven put death on live TV, and death is what American culture has always suppressed, for the end of life implies the inevitable, cyclical demise of entire nations. Islamic terrorists convinced of a spiritual reward for martyrdom exploited Western death anxiety, causing crumbling skyscrapers to signify the downfall of America, to create the illusion (as Baudrillard remarks) of a "suicidal" culture that had suddenly "declared war on itself."[18]

From his earliest tales, Poe created terrifying singularity by coordinating symbolic violence. His tales repeatedly stage the desire to sound the void, making death intelligible by discovering what lies beyond. This will to know what awaits us after death shapes his spirit dialogues and mesmeric fantasies; it drives his most extravagant interpretive project, the prose-poem *Eureka*. Baudrillard's reflections on 9/11 explain why Poe's tales generate terror: inexorable symbolic logic produces an uncanny glimpse of our biological entrapment and genetic fate. This is precisely what terrorist attacks do: they force us to foresee our own annihilation. After noting briefly several historical sources of Poe's anxieties, I want to conclude by reframing a trio of tales that illustrate vital facets of Poe investigation of terror.

Poe's Phantasms of Death

When Roderick Usher buries his sister alive, he consigns her to a fate that, for Poe, represented consummate terror. Living interment figures heavily in his fiction, most notably inspiring the pseudo-documentary hoax, "The Premature Burial" (1844). In the Jacksonian era, when people usually died at home, family or friends prepared the remains for burial, and only rarely did physicians certify death. There was then no regulation of burial, no funeral industry; bodies were not embalmed (a practice introduced during the Civil War). Mistakes thus happened: sanitary workers removing corpses during epidemics sometimes inadvertently collected still-living victims. Bodies consigned to coffins occasionally revived before entombment, and in a few grim instances, family mausoleums disclosed evidence of premature burial. The problem occurred often enough that a clever entrepreneur devised a "life-preserving coffin" equipped with a signal bell.[19]

Poe's brooding on premature burial produced both horror and hilarity. His parody "Loss of Breath" traces the consequences of Mr. Lackobreath's suspended respiration, which subjects him to hanging, galvanic experimentation, and burial. But in *The Narrative of Arthur Gordon Pym*, the narrator experiences virtual burial in the blackness of a ship's hold and later under the debris of a murderously induced rockslide. Yet Pym survives, as does Madeline Usher, at least briefly, when she leaves her tomb long enough to terrorize her twin brother. Poe gives a twist to living entombment in "The Black Cat," when the narrator, under police interrogation, realizes he has sealed a hated, howling feline behind the wall concealing his wife's corpse. Poe's aforementioned "Premature Burial" begins with documentation, transitions to phobic confession, and then unravels in comic self-mockery. Waking to find himself not buried alive (his first apprehension) but sleeping in a narrow ship's berth, the narrator vows to read no more graveyard poetry and especially "no bugaboo tales—*such as this*" (M 3: 969). "The Cask of Amontillado"

(1846) presents the anatomy of a murder, however, dramatizing Montresor's cruel entombment of his muddled adversary, Fortunato.

Although Poe's letters make no mention of cataleptic illness, he fantasized about the sensations and emotions of living interment. The horror, for him, lay in the persistence of consciousness in a place of decomposition; the victim revives only to confront imminent, near-inevitable extinction. All phobias associated with coffins, tombs, graves, and cemeteries surely emanate from death anxiety, but if the grave, the space of death, divides the living from the dead, it also separates body from mind or soul. Premature burial signifies our mortal predicament: we can no more avoid funereal encasement than escape our fleshly casing. The memory of burial recalled in "The Colloquy of Monos and Una" projects a vision of spiritual survival, but the predominant meaning of living entombment in Poe, especially in its comic iterations, resides in the incongruous persistence of consciousness in the site of decay.

The perils of Jacksonian America excited other chronic nightmares projected by Poe, and these can be noted summarily. Contagion formed a recurrent menace, and epidemics of cholera, typhoid, smallpox, malaria, and yellow fever created sporadic crises in the United States. When the cholera pandemic struck Baltimore in 1832, Poe saw its effects firsthand: severe diarrhea and vomiting that led, often hours after onset, to dehydration and death. In August, contagion killed his Richmond friend, Ebenezer Burling, and Poe channeled the horror of that plague year into "Shadow—A Parable" (1835), a flash narrative about death's ubiquity. Later, he summoned that memory—and drew from N. P. Willis's 1832 account of a Parisian ball interrupted by cholera—to compose "The Masque of the Red Death." At the climax, when Prospero dies, revelers attacking the intruder gasp "in unutterable horror at finding the grave cerements and corpse-like mask untenanted by any tangible form." The "presence" of the Red Death (M 2: 676) reveals sheer absence, more terrifying because of its invisibility. In our Age of Terror, this is the threat of biochemical weapons: you can't see or avoid them.

Another terror antebellum Americans experienced was the threat of race war. Slavery had long imposed "social death" on African Americans in bondage, but it had also provoked a simmering threat of insurrectionary violence. In 1831 the Nat Turner rebellion turned a rural corner of Virginia into a slaughterhouse, and it excited a bloody white backlash against both guilty and innocent slaves. Suspicion and pandemonium pervaded the South. Having sold a slave for his aunt two years earlier, Poe must have read the chilling *Confessions of Nat Turner*, when it first appeared in Baltimore, for he already grasped the danger, if not the shame, of slaveholding.[20] Later, in *The Narrative of Arthur Gordon Pym*, he portrayed a murderous black cook who leads a mutiny and then near the novel's end staged a massacre of white sailors by black natives, summoning especially for white, southern readers the terrors of 1831. He would travesty slave revolt in "The System of Doctor Tarr and Professor Fether" in the uprising of captive attendants, tarred and feathered to resemble "Chimpanzees, Ourang-Outangs, or big black baboons" (M 3: 1021). In "Hop-Frog," however, he evoked the same imagery in a charade called the "Eight Chained Ourang-Outangs" by which a virtual slave, the jester, takes revenge on his masters. The story of Nat Turner's insurrection scorched the political unconscious of white America and became for Poe a recurrent nightmare, as Carl Ostrowski suggests in an earlier chapter of this volume.

A further source of fear, for Poe and American Whigs, lay in the chaos that followed Andrew Jackson's election. A famous cartoon portrayed him as King Andrew, a demagogue of frightening audacity. In both "Some Words with a Mummy" and "Mellonta Tauta," Poe personified Jacksonian popular democracy as a "usurping tyrant" called *Mob*. In the 1830s, mob violence became common in the United States; historian Daniel Walker Howe suggests that Jackson was "part of the problem" by cleverly inciting outrage and then refusing to suppress it.[21] Poe witnessed several riots in Philadelphia that horrified him, including the burning of Pennsylvania Hall in 1838. Jackson turned populism into political intimidation; he seemed to anti-Jacksonians a tyrant bent on suppressing states' rights, trampling the Constitution, destroying the National Bank, driving Indians off their land, pushing politics into the streets, and erasing the boundary between public and private life. Louis Renza has illuminated the crisis in American privacy that frightened Poe, and not surprisingly, several of his tales introduce scenes of surveillance—William Wilson sneaking into a bedroom to gaze on his sleeping rival or the narrator of "The Tell-Tale Heart" spying on the old man he plans to kill.[22] Another fable of espionage, "The Man of the Crowd," brilliantly illustrates Poe's terror analytics and yields key insights for our so-called war on terror. A concluding section will suggest Poe's diverse analytical renderings of terror's production and management.

Terrifying Texts

Poe published "The Man of the Crowd" in December 1840, in *Graham's*, four months before the same magazine published his first bona fide detective story, "The Murders in the Rue Morgue." The earlier narrative amounts to a working prototype for the tale of ratiocination that, from 1841 to 1844, gave Poe a powerful counterfantasy to mortal terror. In "Rue Morgue," Monsieur Dupin intervenes to curb the panic excited in Paris by a grisly, unsolved crime—the murder and mutilation of a mother and her daughter. In the same vein, "The Man of the Crowd" establishes the analytical habits of a narrator who imposes interpretive order on a teeming London crowd through an elaborate system of classification. He then sets out to "read" a more puzzling text, the dark heart of an old man whose bizarre, contradictory appearance defies analysis. Probably inspired by Dickens, Poe's story projects a view of city streets that become more ominous and sinister as the night progresses. But even though the narrator at last concludes that he has been pursuing a veritable psychopath, "the type and the genius of deep crime" (M 2: 515), the tale never becomes terrifying, even when this surveillance project leads the narrator into "the most noisome quarter of London, where every thing wore the worst impress of the most deplorable poverty, and of the most desperate crime" (M 2: 514).

The narrator's obsessive attention to minute detail filters his story of pursuit in a way that eliminates fear. His analytic intensity blocks the terror he (and we) might otherwise feel in a warren of "desperate crime" with a devious criminal near at hand. The tale's ratiocinative operations foreclose its potential horror; the problem of "reading" the old man occludes any concern about the riskiness of the narrator's situation. Poe would shortly adapt a similar methodology in "Descent in the Maelström," where the narrator's cool, geometrical calculations in a massive vortex not only neutralize his terror but suggest a mode of survival. This is one way terror and terrorism can be made manageable: by maintaining an analytical discipline that resists panic and focuses on practical responses to presenting realities. As I will suggest, that principle of counterterrorism receives fuller treatment in "The Pit and the Pendulum."

But "The Man of the Crowd" contains a deeper insight into our Age of Terror, one bearing significantly on the unacknowledged reciprocity of international terrorism. Clark McCauley remarks that "anti-state terrorism cannot be understood outside the context of state terrorism," and yet because governments typically define what counts as terrorism, their own terror-making goes unnoticed, at least by those within the state or among its allies.[23] That comment pertains to the paradox at the heart of Poe's tale, which resides in its framing metaphor, the book that does not permit itself to be read. "Er lässt sich nicht lesen," Poe reminds us in his first and last sentences (M 2: 506, 515), omitting the German umlaut as he invokes the otherness of the foreign. And yet the narrative itself delivers a reading, a diagnosis pinned to the "deep crime" remark, which rather unpersuasively creates a new category in his systematic analysis of the London crowd. As Paul Huhr notes, "The stranger's is not just another face in the crowd; it is *all* of them."[24] In reality, the narrator *misses* the meaning of what he has observed, however, and inevitably fails to register a crucial insight into the nature of terrorism.

The terror of this text that can't be read lies precisely in the narrator's strange blindness to the terrifying effect of his own surveillance of a "decrepid" old man walking down a London street (M 2: 511). The narrator's maniacal pursuit and his relentless analysis of the stranger's seemingly incomprehensible movements rivet our attention on the person of interest but ignore the stalker. For that is the unreadable, invisible text: the bizarre movements of a "feeble" man (M 2: 511) being followed by a menacing stranger, who at the outset pulls a handkerchief over his mouth and masks his face (M 2: 512). This stalker feels entirely confident of his own invisibility, reassuring us repeatedly that the old man remains oblivious to his pursuer. Yet he follows the sickly fellow for more than twenty-four hours, through many dark, deserted streets and often closely—so closely that the narrator can observe the texture of the man's linen shirt (M 2: 512). Yet even as narrator claims he has not been seen, he also reports his prey spinning around or turning his head as if to confirm a suspicion that he is being followed. Despite the evidence for reading "The Man of the Crowd" as a subversive narrative of stalking—the suppressed tale of an old man's terror at being hounded by a fanatical pursuer—my argument of forty years ago has (to my scholarly chagrin) yet to substantially influence, much less alter, critical discussion of Poe's most perverse tale.[25] It's as if that inverted tale were not there. Once we *see* the stalker, however, the old man's desperate efforts to elude his shadow take on transparent significance—as does all that crossing and recrossing the street or the rolling of eyes in disbelief. The entire story makes sense, but in an utterly new way, one to which our narrator with the "electrified" intellect is oblivious (M 2: 507). Poe tacitly conveys the salient idea that preoccupation with a seemingly demonic other blinds us to our own terrifying behavior. To put this another way, if "The Man of the Crowd" suggests how we make our own monsters, it also implies that the vehemence of demonizing blinds us to our own monstrous practices.

As Hurh remarks, ratiocination describes for Poe an interpretive operation to resolve the unresolvable. But terror cannot be resolved or cleared up because it arises spontaneously from our primordial brain, the amygdala, and from the DNA that wires us for mortality.[26] We can, however, learn to manage our terrors and deconstruct the images that excite them. No Poe story better illustrates this integral strategy of counterterrorism than "The Pit and the Pendulum," a tale set in Spain at the end of the Inquisition.

Poe wrote the tale in Philadelphia in 1842 as tensions between free blacks and recent Irish Catholic immigrants were simmering into violence. Incited by a black temperance parade, Irish mobs burned an antislavery meeting hall and a black Presbyterian church, leading to further clashes between the Irish and local law officers backed by deputized citizens. Possibly in response to the Locust Street Riots, Poe's tale about the horrors of the Inquisition begins with an odd Latin inscription alluding to the "wicked mob." But he was probably aiming less at Irish Catholics than at the unbridled mass anger so pervasive in Jacksonian America. Poe's epigraph alludes to the rabble that guillotined French aristocrats, but it also reminds us how rapidly revolutionary mob hatred can become institutionalized terrorism. Robespierre's Reign of Terror from 1793 to 1794 indeed marks, for most historians, the inception of state terrorism. Though "The Pit and the Pendulum" nods to non-state terror, it displays the potential violent intimidation of state religious authority.

Condemned to death for an unspecified charge, Poe's narrator endures multiple forms of torture in a dark cell—its surfaces forming the terrifying text he must learn to read. The variety of its devices and features shows the cruel ingenuity of the Inquisition, for this sequence of horrors evokes different scenarios of annihilation. Reviving from unconsciousness, the prisoner confronts the "blackness of eternal night" but tries to resist irrational fear: "I . . . made effort to exercise my reason" (M 2: 684). Even so, he cannot suppress Poe's chronic phobia, premature burial, dreading to take a step in fear of finding himself confined to a tomb, there to suffer the "most hideous of fates" (M 2: 685). But surmounting this panic, he resumes his ratiocinative plan; he tries to measure his cell to create a mental map. In this bid for rational control, though, he stumbles, literally, upon a new horror, a fathomless abyss. When he tries to gauge the depth of the pit with a chink of masonry, its distant, "sullen plunge" into unseen water intimates what may still be his own fate. But at this juncture he also recalls what he has read about the pits of the Inquisitors: that "the *sudden* extinction of life formed no part of their most horrible plan" (M 2: 687). Effective torture necessitates deferral, permitting the intensification of terror, which (like a skillful tale) depends on subordinating every detail to a preconceived design.

The narrator's next threat materializes when he awakens to see, for the first time, painted images on the iron plates that form his cell: "Figures of fiends in aspects of menace, with skeleton forms, and other more really fearful images, overspread and disfigured the walls" (M 2: 689). At the same time, he also finds himself tied down and looking upward at a "painted figure of Time" holding not the conventional scythe but a "huge pendulum" (M 2: 689). If the grim reaper forms a mere representation, the pendulum itself is real, razor-sharp, and descending inexorably. The fatal blade makes literal the symbolic point that passing time—biological aging—always brings death nearer.[27] But here the narrator's ratiocinative cleverness saves him: he calculates that if he daubs his bonds with food, swarming rats will gnaw the cords and liberate him. And it works, but it leaves him paradoxically "Free!—and in the grasp of the Inquisition" (M 2: 695), alive but facing a claustrophobic death, with the contracting and heating up of his prison walls forcing him toward the pit.

What, finally, do we learn about terrorism in "The Pit and the Pendulum?" The devices contrived to terrify the prisoner oblige him to envision many unthinkable deaths. Inquisition torture delays execution precisely to exploit mortality salience. Early in his ordeal, the narrator notices his surveillance and observes, "I knew there were demons who took note of my swoon" (M 2: 691). He later reiterates, "My every motion was undoubtedly watched" (M 2: 695). Mindful of this surveillance and the imperative of deferral, the avoiding of "*sudden* death," the narrator realizes the manipulative structure of terrorism, and this insight inspires his own manipulation of hungry rats. His analytical thinking reveals the psychological purpose of the "spectral and fiendish portraitures" (M 2: 695) on the wall: to force him to confront "the King of Terrors" (M 2: 696), his own death—as Baudrillard says, "the actual, irrevocable event." As I have suggested earlier, this is exactly the cultural objective of terrorism: to break down reason and the defenses protecting the ego from death anxiety, thus paralyzing the subject. By deconstructing the Inquisition's rendering of mortality salience and adhering to rational resistance, by reading and demystifying the text meant to terrify him, the narrator survives until General Lasalle—Poe's deus ex machina—plucks him from the edge of oblivion.[28] "The Pit and the Pendulum" thus offers a paradigm for what Pyszczynski and his collaborators call "terror management."[29]

My third tale, "Hop-Frog," delivers a very different treatment of terrorism in a story told from a perspective at least partly sympathetic to the terrorist himself. In its final scene, the tale also recalls "The Masque of the Red Death," depicting a masked ball but here the event is staged by a tyrannical king who brutalizes two dwarfs. The king's crippled jester, Hop-Frog, and Tripetta, the dancing girl, have both been "forcibly carried off" from "some barbarous region . . . that no person ever heard of" and then presented to the king as gifts (M 3: 1346). They are quite literally property, slaves, objects of abuse and mockery, and the antebellum American subtext of the European fable would have been obvious to readers of the Boston antislavery newspaper where it first appeared. Outraged by the humiliation of Tripetta, Hop-Frog devises what can now be recognized as a terrorist plot. He persuades the king and his seven counselors to frighten other masqueraders by simulating a slave coffle, dressing as the "Eight Chained Ourang-Outangs." But after persuading them to don costumes that transform them into fierce primates—using racial innuendo familiar even to Poe's northern readers—Hop-Frog suspends his "ourang-outangs" above the crowd and ignites their flammable costumes. Poe's narrator says tersely, "The eight corpses swung in their chains, a fetid, blackened, hideous, and indistinguishable mass" (M 3: 1354). This tale blends terror and terror*ism*; Poe portrays the king and his counselors as odious monsters and implicitly sympathizes with the deformed and much-abused Hop-Frog. Here, Poe elaborates an idea intimated in *Pym*: vengeance provoked by domination and exploitation reproduces the "hidden transcript" of slave rebellion.[30]

"Hop-Frog" has long posed difficulties for critics wishing to puzzle out its implications for the antebellum debate over slavery. But its pertinence to a rethinking of terror and terrorism seems clearer. Here we have a "non–state actor" (to recall the GTD definition of terrorism) using fear and violence to achieve the political goal of emancipating himself and his co-conspirator, Tripetta. The action illustrates the intimate relationship between state terror (the oppression of a subaltern) and the eruption of non–state terrorism. Indeed, Hop-Frog's immolation of the king and his counselors exploits their eagerness to impersonate "real beasts" so that they can leave the guests "as much terrified as astonished" (M 3: 1350). The tale offers little insight into Hop-Frog's thinking, rendered as the grinding of teeth when the king humiliates Tripetta, and it suggests the rationale and object of his brutality without justifying its ultimate inhumanity. Like the 9/11 terrorists, Hop-Frog orchestrates shocking mass death using a symbolic logic that becomes intelligible only after the fact, as a sardonic parody of the master–slave relation he ruptures by surprise deceit. In light of the concluding atrocity, our sympathy for and identification with the dwarf leave us unsettled by this terrifying text and our imaginative complicity with Hop-Frog. Entangled in a terrorist plot, we understand better McCauley's judgment that most terrorists are actually ordinary individuals, and that even "normal people" are "capable of terrorist acts under some circumstances."[31]

Understanding terrorism has become, in the last fifteen years, urgent business for liberal nation-states grappling with threats to homeland security and international order. In the Age of Terror that began, for Americans, on 9/11, Poe has become an oddly ubiquitous presence, even something of a guide. Whether we can begin to grasp the psychology of terrorism will ultimately determine whether we can ever let go of the "war on terror" declared by President George W. Bush. For terror derives not from external events but from our irrational response to those events and the mortality salience they elicit. The culture of fear enabled by electronic media—which arguably began when television networks first disseminated images of nuclear destruction into living rooms everywhere—has perhaps made Poe our inevitable authority on postmodern anxiety. His thinking about terror, which produced so many memorable Gothic tales, has unexpectedly yielded a rich source of insight into the psychology of terrorism.

He saved one of his most incisive critiques of the fearful mind for a seemingly trivial 1846 farce called "The Sphinx." Here the narrator, escaping to the country during a cholera epidemic in New York, has the shock of his life when he perceives a gigantic monster descending the hillside beyond his window. The creature has a shaggy body, huge wings, and the image of a skull on its torso. Overwhelmed by "horror and awe" (M 3: 1248), the narrator faints, and a few days pass before he admits this panic to his host, a calm, cerebral fellow whose "richly philosophical intellect was not at any time affected by unrealities" (M 3: 1246). The host solves the mystery by pointing out that the near-sighted narrator had been staring at a moth-like insect dangling inches from his face. By mistaking the bug for a bugaboo and by misjudging the scale or proportion of the threat, the narrator has badly terrified himself. Poe understood that humor was a useful way to keep death anxiety in perspective and to tamp down irrational alarm. By resisting improbabilities and unrealities, by staying calm and refusing to magnify insignificant objects into hideous monsters, we wage the real war—on *our* terror.

Notes

1. National Consortium for the Study of Terrorism and Responses to Terrorism (START), *Global Terrorism Database* [*Codebook: Inclusion Criteria and Variables,* June 2017, https://www.start.umd.edu/gtd/downloads/Codebook.pdf]. Retrieved from https://start.umd.edu/gtd on January 7, 2018.
2. McCauley, "Psychological Issues in Understanding Terrorism and the Response to Terrorism," in *The Psychology of Terrorism: Coping with the Continuing Threat*, ed. Chris E. Stout (Westport, CT: Praeger, 2004), 34.
3. Becker, *The Denial of Death* (New York: The Free Press, 1973), ix.
4. Becker, *The Denial of Death*, 81, 180.
5. Tom Pyszczynski, Sheldon Solomon, and Jeff Greenberg, *In the Wake of 9/11: The Psychology of Terror* (Washington, DC: American Psychological Association, 2002), 16–17.
6. Pyszczynski, Solomon, and Greenberg, *In the Wake of 9/11*, 19.
7. Pyszczynski, Solomon, and Greenberg, *In the Wake of 9/11*, 68–69. Pyszczynski and his coauthors here summarize the role of mortality salience in the production and management of terror.
8. See also my *Poe, Death, and the Life of Writing* (New Haven, CT: Yale University Press, 1987), 23–31.
9. Garrison, Joseph M., Jr., "The Function of Terror in the Work of Edgar Allan Poe," *American Quarterly* 18, no. 2 (Summer 1966): 144.
10. Hurh, *American Terror: The Feeling of Thinking in Edwards, Poe, and Melville* (Stanford, CA: Stanford University Press, 2015), 78.
11. See Hurh, *American Terror*, 106–117 ("Usher"), 121–135 (Dupin), 145–159 ("The Tell-Tale Heart," "The Black Cat," and "The Imp of the Perverse").
12. Jean Baudrillard, *The Spirit of Terrorism*, trans. Chris Turner, rev. ed. (London: Verso, 2003), 5, 10.
13. Baudrillard, *The Spirit of Terrorism*, 16–17.
14. Baudrillard, *The Spirit of Terrorism*, 48.
15. Baudrillard, *Symbolic Exchange and Death*, trans. Mike Gane (1976; Los Angeles: Sage, 1993), 133.
16. Baudrillard, *The Spirit of Terrorism*, 16.
17. Baudrillard, *Symbolic Exchange and Death*, 147.
18. Baudrillard, *The Spirit of Terrorism*, 7.
19. See Kennedy, "Poe and Magazine Writing on Premature Burial," *Studies in the American Renaissance* 1 (1977): 165–178.

20. Poe seems to have identified ideologically with John Randolph, the Virginia planter and Congressman who held slaves but opposed the spread of slavery, feared a servile rebellion, and manumitted his slaves at his death in 1833, with funds to resettle them in a free state. Poe published an article in the *Southern Literary Messenger* on the letters of John Randolph and possibly modeled several fictional characters, including Roderick Usher and Monsieur Valdemar, after Randolph. See my *Strange Nation: Literary Nationalism and Cultural Conflict in the Age of Poe* (New York: Oxford University Press, 2016), 388–391.
21. Howe, *What Hath God Wrought: The Transformation of America, 1815–1848* (New York: Oxford University Press, 2007), 437.
22. See Renza, *Edgar Allan Poe, Wallace Stevens, and the Poetics of American Privacy* (Baton Rouge: LSU Press, 2002), 57–86.
23. McCauley, "Psychological Issues in Understanding Terrorism and the Response to Terrorism," 34.
24. Huhr, *American Terror*, 131.
25. See "The Limits of Reason: Poe's Deluded Detectives," *American Literature* 47 (May 1975): 184–196. To be sure, Scott Peeples does remark, citing my essay, that the narrator reaches "embarrassing false conclusions" and "fails in his quest." See *Edgar Allan Poe Revisited* (New York: Twayne, 1998), 123.
26. Daniel Gardner refers briefly to the amygdala (23) in explaining why emotional thinking by the "Gut" so often overrules rational judgment by the "Head." See especially his chapter "Terrified of Terrorism," in *The Science of Fear* (New York: Dutton, 2008), 246–288.
27. The pendant tale to Poe's "How to Write a Blackwood Article" first appeared under the title "The Scythe of Time," reminding us that Psyche Zenobia's decapitation by the hands of a tower clock in Edinburgh comically anticipates the Inquisition's pendulum. Poe also linked a clock to impending death in "The Masque of the Red Death" and in "A Descent into the Maelström," in which a stopped watch creates the same association.
28. This contrivance nevertheless gives the tale, from its epigraph to its final sentence, a certain historical unity: the French Revolution and Reign of Terror after all gave way to the Empire and Napoleon, whose army took Toledo in 1808.
29. Pyszczynski, Solomon, and Greenberg, *In the Wake of 9/11*, 148–154.
30. James C. Scott built his critique of deception in power relations around this phrase in *Domination and the Arts of Resistance: Hidden Transcripts* (New Haven, CT: Yale University Press, 1992).
31. McCauley, "Psychological Issues in Understanding Terrorism and the Response to Terrorism," 37.

BIBLIOGRAPHY

Baudrillard, Jean. *The Spirit of Terrorism and Requiem for the Twin Towers*. Translated by Chris Turner. London: Verso, 2002.

Baudrillard, Jean. *Symbolic Exchange and Death*. Translated by Iain Hamilton Grant. London: Sage, 1993.

Becker, Ernest. *The Denial of Death*. New York: Free Press, 1973.

Faherty, Duncan. " 'A Certain Unity of Design': Poe's Tales of the Grotesque and Arabesque and the Terrors of Jacksonian Democracy." *Edgar Allan Poe Review* 6 (Fall 2005): 4–21.

Folks, Jeffrey J. "Edgar Allan Poe and Elias Canetti: Illuminating the Sources of Terror." *Southern Literary Journal* 37 (Spring 2005): 1–16.

Gardner, Daniel. *The Science of Fear*. New York: Dutton, 2008.

Hurh, Paul. *American Terror: The Feeling of Thinking in Edwards, Poe, and Melville*. Stanford, CA: Stanford University Press, 2015.

Law, Randall. *Terrorism: A History*. Cambridge: Polity Press, 2009.

Punter, David. *The Literature of Terror: A History of Gothic Fictions from 1765 to the Present Day*. London: Longman, 1980.

Pyszczynski, Tom, Sheldon Solomon, and Jeff Greenberg. *In the Wake of 9/11: The Psychology of Terror*. Washington, DC: American Psychological Association, 2002.

Stout, Chris E., ed. *Psychology of Terrorism, Condensed Edition: Coping with the Continuing Threat*. Westport, CT: Praeger, 2004.

Wuthnow, Robert. *Be Very Afraid: The Cultural Response to Terror Pandemics, Environmental Devastation, Nuclear Annihilation, and Other Threats*. New York: Oxford University Press, 2010.

INDEX